Central Asia

THIS EDITION WRITTEN AND RESEARCHED BY

Bradley Mayhew,
Mark Elliott, Tom Masters, John Noble

PLAN YOUR TRIP

ON THE ROAD

JANE SWEENEY / GETTY IMAGES ©
BAYTEREK MONUMENT, ASTANA, KAZAKHSTAN P98

WWW.SETBOUN.COM / GETTY IMAGES ©
BAZAAR, BUKHARA, UZBEKISTAN P187

MARTIN MOOS / GETTY IMAGES ©

Contents

KUHNA ARK & KALTA MINOR MINARET, KHIVA, UZBEKISTAN P203

ON THE ROAD

MARTIN MOOS / GETTY IMAGES ©

WAKHAN VALLEY, TAJIKISTAN P348

JAMIE MARSHALL / GETTY IMAGES ©

URGUT BAZAAR, UZBEKISTAN P181

Contents

ZENKOV CATHEDRAL, ALMATY, KAZAKHSTAN P56

BJORN HOLLAND / GETTY IMAGES ©

PAMIR HIGHWAY, TAJIKISTAN P351

UNDERSTAND

SURVIVAL GUIDE

SPECIAL FEATURES

Welcome to Central Asia

With its medieval blue-domed cities, kinetic bazaars and remote yurtstays, Central Asia encapsulates the romance of the Silk Road like nowhere else.

Footprints of History

From Alexander the Great to Chinggis (Genghis) Khan to Timur (Tamerlane), Central Asia's page-turning history litters the land at every turn. Viewed from the right angle, the storied oasis caravan stops of Samarkand and Bukhara, with their exotic skylines of minarets and medressas, really do seem to be lifted directly from the heyday of Marco Polo. Share a round of kebabs with an Uzbek trader or wander an ancient caravanserai, and historical romantics will find the past and present begin to blur into one.

Mountains & Yurts

East of the desert and steppe settlements rise the snowcapped Pamir and Tian Shan ranges of Kyrgyzstan and Tajikistan, home to traditional herding communities and some truly epic mountain scenery. Here community-based tourism projects can bring you face to face with nomadic Kyrgyz herders, meeting them in their yurts and on their terms. Ride out to remote lakes on horseback, hike from one village homestay to another, or take a 4WD out to remote archaeological sites. The scope for adventure and exploration here is almost limitless.

Travel off the Map

For decades – centuries even – much of the world has regarded Central Asia as little more than a blank on the map, synonymous with the middle of nowhere, rather than the heartland of Asia. For a certain type of traveller, this is all part of the attraction of a land that has been largely off-limits to travellers for the past 2000 years. Head even a little bit off the beaten track and you'll likely have the place to yourself. Authentic cultural interactions can be found across Central Asia. The region's little-visited oddities, namely Turkmenistan and most of Kazakhstan, are even further removed from the modern world and offer an addictive interest all of their own.

A Warm Welcome

Whether you want to explore the architectural gems of Bukhara or take a horse trek across the high Pamirs, everywhere in Central Asia you'll be greeted with instinctive local hospitality and offered a shared meal, a helping hand or a place to stay. Add to this the intrinsic fascination of a forgotten region fast emerging as a geopolitical pivot point and you have one of Asia's most absorbing hidden corners.

Why I Love Central Asia

By Bradley Mayhew, author

Each republic in Central Asia has its own joy for me. In Tajikistan I love the unrivalled mountain scenery and the incredible tradition of hospitality among the local Wakhi and Kyrgyz. In Uzbekistan it's the glorious weight of history and the sense of travelling in the sandprints of some of history's greatest travellers and invaders. There's also something unique and even slightly weird about Central Asia, as if the normal rules of tourist engagement don't quite apply. For me it's a completely addictive place; I'm a total shashlyk-phile.

For more about our authors, see page 520.

Above: Yurts, Tian Shan mountains, Kyrgyzstan

Central Asia

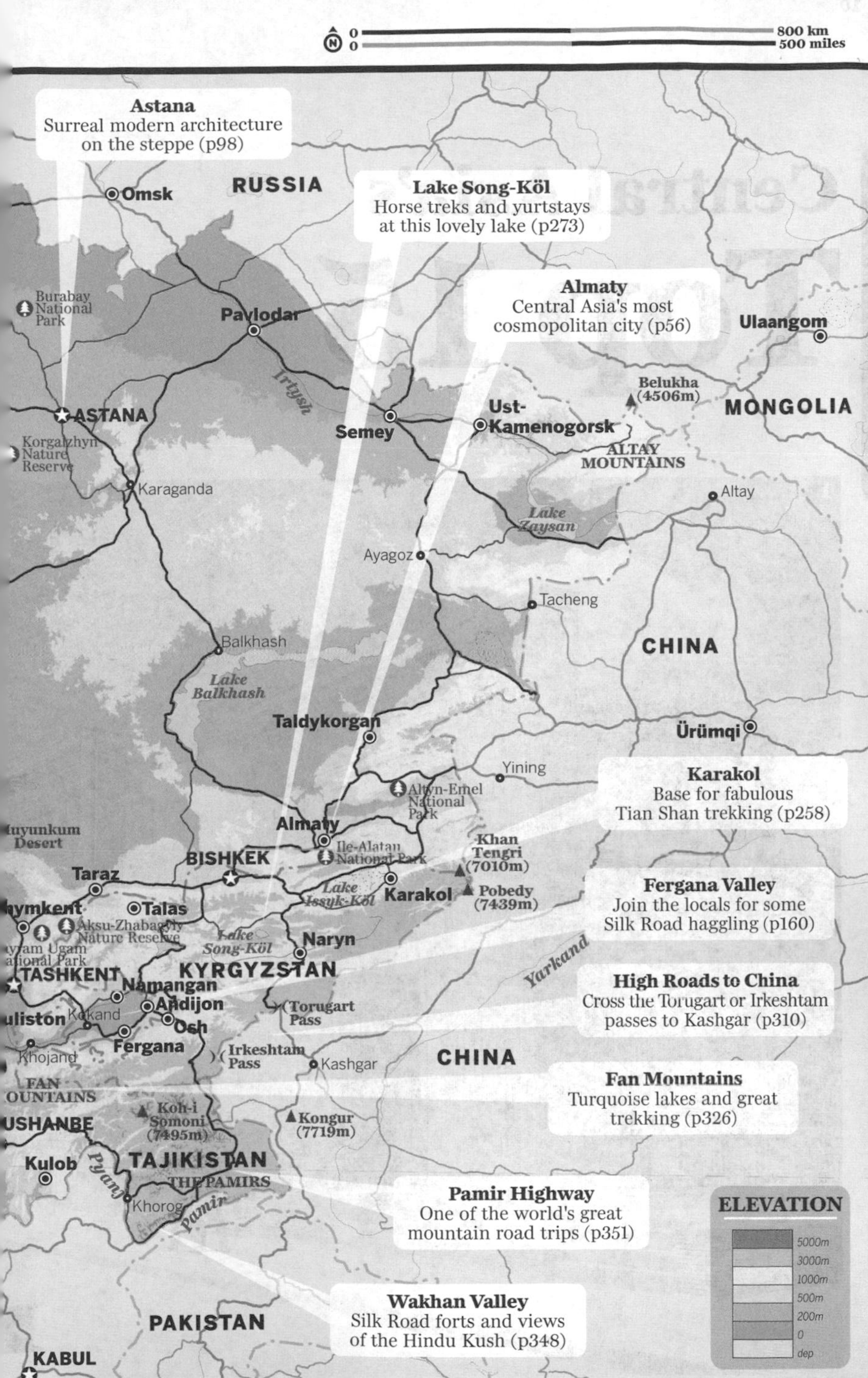

0
0
800 km
500 miles
Astana
Surreal modern architecture on the steppe (p98)
Lake Song-Köl
Horse treks and yurtstays at this lovely lake (p273)
Almaty
Central Asia's most cosmopolitan city (p56)
Karakol
Base for fabulous Tian Shan trekking (p258)
Fergana Valley
Join the locals for some Silk Road haggling (p160)
High Roads to China
Cross the Torugart or Irkeshtam passes to Kashgar (p310)
Fan Mountains
Turquoise lakes and great trekking (p326)
Pamir Highway
One of the world's great mountain road trips (p351)
Wakhan Valley
Silk Road forts and views of the Hindu Kush (p348)
RUSSIA
Omsk
Burabay National Park
Pavlodar
Irtysh
ASTANA
Korgalzhyn Nature Reserve
Karaganda
Semey
Ust-Kamenogorsk
Belukha (4506m)
MONGOLIA
Ulaangom
ALTAY MOUNTAINS
Altay
Lake Zaysan
Ayagoz
Tacheng
CHINA
Balkhash
Lake Balkhash
Taldykorgan
Ürümqi
Yining
Altyn-Emel National Park
Almaty
Ile-Alatau National Park
Khan Tengri (7010m)
Pobedy (7439m)
BISHKEK
Taraz
Karakol
Lake Issyk-Köl
Talas
Aksu-Zhabagly Nature Reserve
Lake Song-Köl
Naryn
KYRGYZSTAN
Yarkand
TASHKENT
Namangan
Andijon
Kokand
Osh
Fergana
Torugart Pass
Irkeshtam Pass
Kashgar
CHINA
Khojand
Koh-i Somoni (7495m)
Kongur (7719m)
Kulob
Pyanj
TAJIKISTAN
THE PAMIRS
Khorog
Pamir
PAKISTAN
KABUL
ELEVATION
5000m
3000m
1000m
500m
200m
0
dep

Central Asia's Top 15

1

Samarkand

1 Although already an important oasis town, it was Timur (Tamerlane) who turned Samarkand (p169) into one of the most beautiful cities in Asia. Visit Timur's own mausoleum, the Gur-E-Amir, followed by the spectacular street of tombs of his Timurid relatives. For epic and audacious architecture it's hard to beat the crumbling remains of the epic Bibi Khanum Mosque, built for Timur's wife. Then throw in the breathtaking Registan Square (one of the Islamic world's greatest architectural ensembles), some great bazaars and the 2000-year-old remains of Afrosiab, the original Silk Road trading town. Shah-i-Zinda (p173)

Bukhara

2 Central Asia's most interesting town, Bukhara (p187) is the one urban space that best rewards some serious exploring. Visit the medieval Ark from where Emirs ruled with a cruel, vicelike grip; sip green tea beside the Lyabi-Hauz pool; and then start at the towering Kalon Minaret for a stroll through the surrounding network of bazaars, bathhouses and trade halls. Best of all are the labyrinthine backstreets, home to hidden synagogues, Sufi shrines and half-forgotten medressas. Bukhara also boasts the region's most stylish B&Bs, many in converted merchants' houses. Kalon Minaret (p192)

SEUX PAULE / GETTY IMAGES ©

2

TRAVEL INK / GETTY IMAGES ©

Astana's Architecture

3 Kazakhstan's custom-built capital (p98) rises from the steppe like a mirage to reveal some of Asia's most audacious and cutting-edge modern architecture. From the Norman Foster designs of the world's largest tent and the glass-pyramid design of the Palace of Peace and Accord, Astana is the symbolic brainchild of President Nazarbaev and the face of post-Borat Kazakhstan. The constantly evolving city will get an additional boost from hosting the 2017 World Expo. Khan Shatyr (p98)

Khiva

4 The former khanate of Khiva (p203) is an entire walled city of traditional mud-baked architecture, frozen in time in the desert wastes of Khorezm. It may lack the lived-in backstreet life of Bukhara but in return you get the best preserved medieval city in Central Asia, if not the Islamic world. You can wander city walls, former slave markets and extensive royal palaces, where khaki walls burst with green and blue tilework. Wall and ceiling decoration

4

Wakhan Valley

5 The Tajik side of the Wakhan Valley (p348) feels like a hidden Shangri-la. Bordered by the Hindu Kush and a finger of remotest Afghanistan, the valley is dotted with Silk Road forts, Ismaili shrines and village homestays run by welcoming Wakhi Tajik families. It's an essential add-on to a Pamir Highway trip and a potential springboard into Afghanistan. Even Marco Polo was impressed when he passed through. To get the most out of the valley, hire transport or hike the valley. Tajik family

Trekking

6 Central Asia has some of the world's most beautiful mountain scenery. Karakol, Kyrgyzstan, is the most popular base for treks to the lush alpine meadows of Tian Shan, while the high-altitude Pamir valleys also offers top trekking. You can hike from homestay to homestay in the Jizeu (Geisev) Valley (p342), or go with an agency on a supported trek to the stunning amphitheatre of Khan Tengri and the Inylchek Glacier (p272). Untouched valleys beg exploration but check security if headed to border areas. Tian Shan (p269)

Lake Song-Köl

7 The jewel of central Kyrgyzstan is this high alpine lake (p273), fringed with lush summer pastures and summer-only Kyrgyz yurt camps. You can trek or drive here but the best option is a horse trek, overnighting in yurtstays en route. June to August are the best months to visit Kyrgyzstan's idyllic *jailoo* (summer pastures), when you might even catch a horse games festival or a performance by a Kyrgyz bard or eagle hunter. Bring a sleeping bag. Yurtstay on the *jailoo*

6

7

MARTIN MOOS / GETTY IMAGES ©

ELLEN MACK / GETTY IMAGES ©

Community-Based Tourism

8 This network of homestays, guides, drivers and yurt owners spreads across Kyrgyzstan in an attempt to bring the financial benefits of tourism directly to local communities. For travellers it gives you a contact in every town and opens up a wealth of friendly, affordable homestays and potential excursions to remote sights, lakes and herding communities. Kochkor in Central Kyrgyzstan is the original and best place to start but the idea has also taken firm hold in neighbouring Tajikistan. See p47 for more information. Making a traditional *shyrdak* (carpet)

Fan Mountains

9 The mountains northwest of Dushanbe (p327) rank as Central Asia's premier trekking destination. Dozens of turquoise lakes stud the high mountain valleys. Go on a multiday trek to meet local Tajik shepherds, or drive to the seven lakes (Haft-Kul) of the Marguzor Valley (p333) and do some delightful day hikes from a chain of homestays. You can even visit the ruined old Sogdian city of Penjikent (p331) en route. Check in advance whether the border between Samarkand and Penjikent has reopened. Marguzor Lakes (p333)

Bazaars

10 Central Asia's bazaars have been fuelling Silk Road trade for two millennia. Shopping for melons, carpets and silly hats is perhaps the quintessential Central Asian activity and we'd even say that the local bazaars offer the most direct route to the region's soul. Every town has its own bazaar lined with *chaikhanas* (teahouses), smoking shashlyk, fruit stalls and even animal markets. Our favourite is possibly the Kumtepa bazaar (p167) outside Margilon in the Fergana Valley, though nearby Andijon's Jahon Bazaar (p168) and Osh's Bazaar (p292) are also excellent.

MARTIN MOOS / GETTY IMAGES ©

Konye-Urgench

11 Turkmenistan's premier historical site (p393) is a Unesco World Heritage Site. Once the capital of the Khorezmshahs and a centre of the Muslim world in the 12th century, the city was pulverised by both Chinggis (Genghis) Khan and Timur (Tamerlane). The enigmatic remains include royal mausolea, Sufi shrines and a 59m-tall, 14th-century minaret. It's a short hop across the Uzbekistan border. Gutlug Timur Minaret (p395)

Almaty

12 Central Asia's most cosmopolitan and hedonistic city (p56) is a leafy mix of Russian and Central Asian styles. In a couple of days you can visit the tsarist-era Zenkov Cathedral, view a replica of the famous Scythian-era Golden Man suit, soak in the Arasan Bathhouse and enjoy the region's best cafes, clubs and shops, all fuelled by the country's petrodollar boom. The city is also a gateway to mountain treks and winter sports just south of town and a springboard to Silk Road bus and train routes into China. Interior of a Russian orthodox cathedral

High Roads to China

13 The mountain border crossings of the Torugart and Irkeshtam passes (p310) are without doubt the most exciting and scenic ways to enter or leave Central Asia. The high valleys of the Tian Shan are splendid and there's a satisfying continuity in crossing from ex-Soviet Central Asia into Chinese Turkestan via the storied Uyghur city of Kashgar. The Irkeshtam Pass is logistically easier but the Torugart Pass offers the chance to stop overnight at the atmospheric Tash Rabat Caravanserai. Tash Rabat Caravanserai (p284)

Pamir Highway

14 From the deep, rugged mountain valleys of beautiful Badakhshan the Soviet-built Pamir Highway (p351) climbs up on to the treeless Pamir plateau to the 'wild east' town of Murgab and on past the dramatic azure lake of Karakol into Kyrgyzstan's stunning Alai valley. En route you'll pass ancient tombs, hot springs, remote Kyrgyz yurt camps and some of the most spectacular mountain scenery in Asia. It's one of the world's great mountain road trips. Tackle it in a rented Soviet 4WD or as a challenging bicycle ride. Towards Murgab (p353)

Turkistan

15 The turquoise dome and ornate tilework of the Timurid-era Yasaui Mausoleum is easily Kazakhstan's most beautiful building, and a rare architectural gem in a land ruled by restless nomads. It's also one of the best places to get a sense of Central Asian Sufism and meet local pilgrims as they pray, picnic and tie wishes to trees surrounding the holy shrine. Yasaui Mausoleum (p88)

14

15

Need to Know

For more information, see Survival Guide (p461)

Visas

A major preoccupation. Visa-free in Kyrgyzstan, easy for Kazakhstan, fairly easy for Tajikistan and Uzbekistan, and tricky for Turkmenistan. For full visa information, see p31.

Money

Bring a combination of cash (perhaps around two-thirds of your funds) in US dollars or euros, and a credit card for ATMs in the cities.

Mobile Phones

If you have an 'unlocked' GSM-900 phone, buy a local SIM card and top that up with local scratch cards or at top-up booths. US phone owners might find it cheaper to buy a mobile phone on arrival.

Time

Central Asia time zone (GMT/UTC plus five hours), except giant Kazakhstan which straddles GMT/UTC (plus five and plus six hours).

When to Go

High Season
(Apr–Jun, Sep–Oct)

➡ Comfortable temperatures in the lowlands.

➡ Bazaars overflow with fruit in September.

Shoulder
(Jul & Aug)

➡ Sizzlingly hot in the lowlands, especially in Uzbekistan, Turkmenistan and western Tajikistan.

➡ The best time to visit mountainous Kyrgyzstan, Tajikistan and southeastern Kazakhstan, and for trekking (Jul–Sep).

Low Season
(Nov–Mar)

➡ Cold in Uzbekistan, frozen in sub-Siberian Kazakhstan and snow in the mountains.

➡ Many tourist hotels and B&Bs close in Uzbekistan.

➡ March is a good time weather-wise for Turkmenistan.

Websites

Lonely Planet (www.lonelyplanet.com) The Central Asia branch of the Thorn Tree forum is the place for news on visas, border crossings and more.

Caravanistan (www.caravanistan.com) Peerless online travel guide to the region.

Oriental Express Central Asia (www.orexca.com) Virtual travel guide from a local travel agency.

EurasiaNet (www.eurasianet.org) News and cultural articles, with resource pages for each country.

Pamirs.org (www.pamirs.org) Definitive travel and historical guide to the Pamir region in Tajikistan from Robert Middleton.

Discovery Central Asia (www.centralasia.travel) Interesting articles and cultural details from across Central Asia.

Important Numbers

Police ☎02

Ambulance ☎03

Opening Hours

Banks and offices 9am–noon and 1–5pm Monday to Friday, possibly 9am–noon Saturday. Exchange offices keep longer hours, including weekends.

Museums Generally closed Monday.

Restaurants 11am–9pm; longer opening hours in major cities.

Daily Costs

Budget US$15--5

- US$25–45 in Kazakhstan
- Homestay: US$10–20 per person with two meals
- Chaikhana meal: US$3–5
- Horse hire in Kyrgyzstan: US$15

Midrange US$25–80

- B&B in Bukhara or Samarkand: US$20–40
- Double room in a midrange hotel: US$30–80 (US$50–130 in Kazakhstan)

Top End More than US$80

- Double room in a four-star hotel: US$100
- Tour in Turkmenistan: US$100–150 per person per day in small group.

Don't Forget

- A sun hat, sunglasses and suncream for strong desert and mountain sun.
- The latest government travel warnings (p475), and a small pinch of salt.
- Sleeping bag and water purification if headed into the mountains of Kyrgyzstan and Tajikistan.
- A Russian phrasebook and a paperback novel (hard to find in Central Asia).
- Mementos from home (eg postcards and photos) to break the ice in homestays.
- Floss – to get the mutton out from between your teeth.

Travelling Safely

- Watch for pickpockets in crowded bazaars or bus stations.
- Avoid police and security officials whenever possible (especially in Uzbekistan).
- Make sure your documents and permits are watertight at all times.
- At night don't get into a taxi with more than one person in it.

For more information on safe travel, see p474.

Getting Around

Transport in Central Asia is relatively convenient and abundant in the plains but much patchier in the mountains.

Train High-speed modern trains run to Samarkand and Bukhara in Uzbekistan and between Almaty and Astana in Kazakhstan. Long-distance rail services are less comfortable but a common way to get around huge Kazakhstan.

Bus Fairly reliable and comfortable coaches run between major cities but comfort, reliability and frequency plummet rapidly in rural areas.

Shared taxi The best way to get around Kyrgyzstan, Tajikistan and Uzbekistan. Pay by the seat or buy all four of them for cheap car hire on set routes.

Hired car Useful for the Pamirs and mountain areas of Kyrgyzstan and generally priced per kilometre.

For much more on **getting around**, see p485.

If You Like...

Silk Road Architecture

Nothing connects Central Asia to its storied past quite like its mosques, minarets and medressas. Uzbekistan is the place for some of the world's greatest Islamic architecture.

The Registan, Samarkand A jaw-dropping ensemble of not one but three medressas. Climb the corkscrew minarets for views over Timur's showcase city. (p171)

Kalon Minaret, Bukhara This towering minaret is so impressive that it stopped Chinggis (Genghis) Khan in his tracks 800 years ago. (p192)

Shah-i-Zinda, Samarkand Central Asia's head-spinning turquoise-blue Timurid tilework doesn't get any better than this sublime street of royal tombs. (p173)

Ichon-Qala, Khiva An entire walled city of royal palaces, blue-tiled tombs and mud-baked city walls, frozen in time in the Khorezm oasis. (p205)

Tash Rabat Caravanserai Singularly romantic refuge for caravans and traders, hidden in a high mountain valley near the Chinese border. (p284)

Community-Based Tourism

CBT, Kyrgyzstan Pioneering countrywide network of homestays and service providers that can arrange everything from felt-making to horse trekking. (p247)

Eastern Pamirs Yurtstays are the only way to really see the herding communities, mountain lakes and archaeological sites of the high Pamir mountain range. (p338)

Jizeu (Geisev) Valley, western Pamirs This network of homestays allows hikers to trek to a scenic chain of mountain lakes without the need for bulky camping equipment or food. (p342)

Aksu-Zhabagyly Nature Reserve Kazakhstan's best ecotourism project is great for wildlife-watching and hiking. (p85)

Nuratau Mountains Uzbekistan's only community-tourism effort offers homestays, hiking and horse riding south of Lake Aidarkul. (p186)

Trekking

Central Asia's best-kept secrets are its remote Tian Shan and Pamir ranges, hiding some of Asia's most sublime mountain trails.

Fan Mountains, Tajikistan Jewel-like azure blue lakes, rugged peaks and homestays make this the region's most popular trekking spot. (p326)

Tian Shan, Kyrgyzstan Behind Karakol lies a network of lush forested alpine valleys, hidden lakes and snowcapped peaks, linked by treks of two to seven days. (p272)

Khan Tengri & Inylchek Glaciers Central Asia's most beautiful peak is set in a high amphitheatre of glacier and rock, making it a serious mountain adventure. (p77)

Zailiysky Alatau, Kazakhstan Hiking trails and short trek routes lead from the Almaty city limits through Ile-Alatau National Park to picturesque Ozero Bolshoe Almatinskoe lake. (p74)

IF YOU LIKE... ROAD TRIPS

Tajikistan's Pamir Highway (p351) offers one of the world's great mountain drives, especially if you continue over the mountains into the deserts around Kashgar in China.

(Top) Woman drinking tea, Urgut bazaar (p181), Uzbekistan

(Bottom) Dome of Tilla-Kari Medressa (p171), Samarkand, Uzbekistan

Arslanbob Hike through walnut forests and past waterfalls to the Köl Mazar lakes (four days) or Kyzyl Ünkür (seven days). Book guides and horses through CBT. (p288)

Bazaars

Haggling for carpets, camels or car parts is perhaps the quintessential Central Asian activity.

Osh, Kyrgyzstan The riverside Osh Bazaar bustles every day, but goes mad on Sunday, and is a great place to pick up a white Kyrgyz *ak-kalpak* (traditional felt hat). (p292)

Kumtepa Bazaar, Uzbekistan Sunday offers the best selection of local *khanatlas* (tie-dyed silks) and Uzbek white-beards at this rollicking market 5km outside Margilon. (p167)

Samarkand, Uzbekistan The Siob Bazaar is the city's most photogenic place to stock up on fruit and hot bread, in the shadows of the epic ruined Bibi-Khanym Mosque. (p179)

Carpet-shopping Bukhara (p198), Khiva (p209) and Ashgabat (p382) are the best places to invest in this quintessential Silk Road souvenir, and don't forget Kyrgyz felt *shyrdaks* (p277) in Kochkor.

Urgut, Uzbekistan Sunday and Wednesday mornings are the best times to day-trip from Samarkand to this village bazaar, strong on jewellery and *suzani* textiles. (p181)

Andijon The Jahon Bazaar is the biggest in the Uzbek Fergana Valley, especially on Sunday and Thursday. (p168)

The Nomadic Life

Yurts Stay overnight in an authentic yurt in the high eastern Pamirs or the pastures of Kyrgyzstan, and visit the world's only three-storey yurt in Osh. (p304)

Manaschi There's something other-worldly about listening to a white-bearded bard reciting the Kyrgyz national epic, *Manas*. It's a direct link to the Kyrgyz nomadic past. (p302)

Horse games Summer brings the good life to the *jailoos* (summer pastures), along with horse races, horseback wrestling and Kyrgyz-style kiss-chasy. (p306)

Eagle-hunting Real hunts (with eagles, not *for* eagles) take place in winter but several spots in Kyrgyzstan offer summertime displays from authentic *berkutchi* (eagle hunters). (p272)

Horse trek to Song-Köl The best way to visit this lovely mountain lake is on a horse trek, stopping in herders' yurts en route. Allow four days. (p273)

The Weird & the Downright Odd

Central Asia supplies a daily dose of the unexpected, but for the really odd stuff head for Turkmenistan and remoter Kazakhstan.

Baykonur Cosmodrome, Kazakhstan Book a tour months in advance and you can watch a rocket blast off from Soviet cosmonaut Yuri Gagarin's former launch site. (p90)

Aral Sea The beached fishing boats at Moynaq (p215) in Uzbekistan or Aralsk (p91) in Kazakhstan are a fine place to ponder the nature of environmental folly.

Astana Lie on a beach beside palm trees inside the world's largest tent, Khan Shatyr (p98), then head to the Presidential Cultural Centre (p103) to gawp at 2000-year-old horse innards.

Darvaza Gas Craters At night this burning pit in the Karakum desert resembles nothing less than the fiery gates of Hell. It's weird, even for Turkmenistan. (p384)

Ashgabat A mix between Las Vegas and Pyongyang, oddball highlights here include the Ministry of Fairness, the world's largest handwoven rug and the 12m golden statue of former dictator Turkmenbashi. (p374)

Cultural Immersion

Banyas Sweat the day away or indulge your inner kink with a birch branch flogging at Almaty's Arasan Baths. (p60)

Chaikhana culture Nothing beats the experience of joining the local *aksakals* (white beards) over a pot of green tea, a round of kebabs and a fresh watermelon. (p469)

Russian Orthodox cathedrals Babushkas, incense and sacred liturgies offer a different aspect of Central Asian religious life, best at Tashkent's Assumption Cathedral. (p146)

Visit a Sufi shrine Make a weekend visit to the Yasaui Mausoleum in Turkistan and you'll see families praying, feasting and making wishes by tying rags to sacred trees. (p88)

Opera for a song Shell out a couple of bucks for a classy performance of *Aida* or *Swan Lake* at Tashkent's restored Alisher Navoi (p153) or Almaty's Abay State Opera & Ballet Theatre. (p66)

Off the Beaten Track

Central Asia's remoter gems take some getting to but offer some of the region's most memorable experiences.

Karakalpakstan Tick off the 'Stan within a Stan' with a visit to the Savitsky Museum in Nukus, home to some of the greatest avant-garde Soviet art of the 1930s. (p214)

Mangistau Underground mosques, necropoli and the enigmatically named 'Valley of Balls' await exploration in the deserts around Aktau in western Kazakhstan. (p96)

Desert Castles of Khorezm Hire a car and track down the dozen or more two-millennia-old fortresses known as Elliq-Qala that rise from the Karakum desert like giant sandcastles. (p202)

IF YOU LIKE... DARK SOVIET-ERA HISTORY

Malinovka's ALZhIR museum outside Astana (p71) offers an introduction to the horrors of Soviet labour camps and you can even visit a former KarLag camp outside Karaganda (p111). Tours of the Soviet-era atomic testing site at Semey (p118) are also possible: bring your own Geiger counter.

Ak Orda (Presidential Palace) and parliament buildings, Astana (p98), Kazakhstan

Altay Gorgeous mountain valleys, snowcapped peaks and the myths of Shambhala are the drawcards here, if you can get around the red tape. (p111)

Western Pamirs The wild and remote valleys around Khorog, especially the Bartang Valley, boast incredible scenery, homestays and tough treks, making it a great place for mountain exploration. (p342)

Archaeological Sites

Come equipped with a history book and your imagination, for the following ruins rank as some of the most pivotal historical sites in Asia.

Afrosiab Stand in the footprints of Alexander and view Sogdian-era murals at the melted remains of this 2500-year-old city. (p174)

Penjikent Wander the alleyways and climb the eroded citadel at this once cosmopolitan Sogdian city. (p331)

Merv The 'Queen of the World' boasts eight overlapping cities, including the capital of the Seljuq Turks. (p388)

Otrar This dusty hill changed the course of Central Asian history when Chinggis Khan's emissaries were murdered here, plus it's where Timur (Tamerlane) died. (p87)

Gonur Depe This active archaeological site in the Margiana Oasis dates back to the Bronze Age and may have been the birthplace of Zoroastrianism. (p391)

Termiz Visit Buddhist monasteries, Bactrian temples and Islamic shrines at Termiz, on the border with Afghanistan. (p183)

Month by Month

TOP EVENTS

Navrus, March

Independence Day Celebrations, various months

Asrlar Sadosi Festival, May

Roof of the World Festival, July

At Chabysh Horse Festival, August

March

Perfect weather in the deserts of Turkmenistan, southern Tajikistan and Uzbekistan (towards the end of the month). The Karakum desert blooms like a Jackson Pollock canvas.

Navrus

Central Asia's biggest festival is held round the equinox (21 March in most republics and 22 March in Kazakhstan) and marks the beginning of spring and the Persian new year with games of *buzkashi* (traditional pololike game played with a headless goat), family feasts and funfairs.

April

Spring is kicking in, as blooms start to appear in mountain foothills. Another excellent month to visit lowland areas.

Horse Day

Turkmenistan's Horse Day (the last Sunday in April) offers a chance for horse-lovers to see the country's famous Akhal-Teke horses in action at hippodromes across the country.

May

It's starting to get hot in the lowlands but can still be chilly in the highlands. High season in Uzbekistan means you should make advanced hotel bookings.

Watching Wildlife in Kazakhstan

April and May are the best months to spot Kazakhstan's 36 species of tulip, while May and June are the time to spot hundreds of migratory bird species, especially at Korgalzhyn Nature Reserve (p107).

Asrlar Sadosi Festival

The two-day Arslar Sadosi (Echo of Centuries) festival is held over two days in different locations in Uzbekistan (see www.asrlarsadosi.com). Folk music, a handicrafts bazaar, food, fashion and displays of *kuresh* wrestling and *kopkari (buzkashi)* are the draws.

Silk & Spices Festival

Four-day cultural festival in Bukhara, featuring music and dance, folk art, fashion, handicrafts, exhibitions and maybe even the odd tightrope walker. It can be in June.

July

High summer is the time to visit the mountains of Kyrgyzstan, Tajikistan and southeast Kazakhstan. Rich pastures bring herders to their summer camps.

Astana Day

This festival on 6 July (which just happens to be President Nazarbaev's birthday) sees concerts, fireworks, fairs and parades in Kazakhstan's capital city.

Roof of the World Festival

Badakhshani music, dance, film and handicrafts from across the region make this the mountain cultural festival of the year, with a stunning backdrop at Khorog in the Tajikistan Pamirs.

National Horse Games Festival

Kyzyl-Oi village in Kyrgyzstan's Suusamyr Valley celebrates the summer pastures with games of *ulak-tartysh* (*buzkashi*), horseback races, wrestling, traditional music and food. It's generally the third Saturday of July.

August

Summer continues to sizzle in the lowlands as the mercury hits 40°C. The good life is up in the mountains, with August a great month for trekking at higher altitudes.

Sharq Taronalari Music Festival

The 'Melodies of the Orient' Festival in Samarkand, Uzbekistand, hosts a collection of 50 concerts by Central Asian and world musicians, with fantastic locations such as the Registan as a backdrop. It's held every other year (next one 2015).

At Chabysh Horse Festival

This lively festival of horse games in Murgab, in Tajikistan's eastern Pamirs, happens on the second weekend in August. Count on horse races, equestrian games, handicrafts and *Manas* (Kyrgyz epic) recitals.

Birds of Prey Festival

Visit Bokonbayevo, on the southern shores of Issyk Kul lake, to see hunting displays with golden eagles, folklore music and traditional ceremonies. Great for photos. Third Saturday of August. (p272)

FourE Festival

This alternative lifestyle festival (www.ecofest.kz) brings together three days of yoga, art, workshops and ethnic and spiritual music in a different location outside Almaty each year.

Independence Day, Kyrgyzstan

August 31 brings parades, music concerts and traditional horseback games to Bishkek's hippodrome, to celebrate the anniversary of Kyrgyzstan's independence from the USSR in 1991.

September

A great month to visit almost anywhere. Temperatures are still pleasant in the highlands but the worst of the summer heat is over in the oases. Markets burst with fruit.

Independence Days, Uzbekistan & Tajikistan

September 1 sees nationwide celebrations in the capital of each region of Uzbekistan, with the largest event in Tashkent's Mustaqillik maydoni (Independence Sq; p146). September 9 brings similar festivities to Tajikistan.

October

Another great month in lowland areas, with cool air and sunny skies, though the mercury is starting to drop in the mountains and northern Kazakhstan.

Independence Day, Turkmenistan

October 27 and 28 bring a two-day public holiday to the desert republic, marked by military parades and much pageantry, with the biggest displays in Ashgabat.

December

As Central Asia shivers in sub-zero temperatures, the winter sports season kicks in at ski resorts, notably Chimbulak in Kazakhstan.

Independence Day, Kazakhstan

Concerts, parades, conferences and exhibitions mark the last of the year's Independence Day celebrations on 16 December.

Itineraries

Silk Road Cities

This loop route through Uzbekistan takes in almost all of Central Asia's greatest historical and architectural sites. Fly into **Tashkent** (p139) and get a feel for the big city before taking a domestic flight to Urgench and then a short bus or taxi ride to **Khiva** (p203), comfortably seen in a day. Then take a taxi for an overnight trip to one or two of the crumbing **desert cities** of ancient Khorezm, around **Urgench** (p200).

From Urgench take the long bus or taxi ride down to **Bukhara** (p187), which deserves the most time of all the Silk Road cities. Try to budget a minimum of three days to take in the sights and explore the backstreets.

From here take the golden (actually tarmac) road to **Samarkand** (p169) for a day or two. Soak in the glories of the Registan and Shah-i-Zinda and, if you have time, add on a day trip to **Shakhrisabz** (p181), the birthplace of Timur (Tamerlane).

A potential add-on to this route is to tack on a few days to visit Turkmenistan, visiting **Konye-Urgench** (p393) from Khiva before crossing the desert to **Ashgabat** (p374) and then travelling to Bukhara via the Mausoleum of Sultan Sanjar at **Merv** (p388).

Central Asia Overland: The Silk Road

Much of this itinerary follows ancient Silk Road paths and modern travellers will likely make the same route decisions as early traders, based on cost, ease of transport and the time of year.

Western roads into Central Asia lead from Mashhad in Iran to Ashgabat in Turkmenistan, or from Baku in Azerbaijan (by boat) to Turkmenbashi, also in Turkmenistan. If you only have a transit visa for Turkmenistan you can travel from Mashhad to Mary (to visit the Unesco World Heritage–listed ruins of Merv) in one long day via the crossing at Saraghs, giving you more time at Merv and bypassing Ashgabat.

From **Ashgabat** (p374) the overland route leads to **Merv** (p388) and the Silk Road cities of **Bukhara** (p187), **Samarkand** (p169) and **Tashkent** (p139). Figure on at least three full days in Bukhara and two full days each in Samarkand and Tashkent, preferably more. In Tashkent take a ride on the grand metro, shop Chorsu Bazaar and visit the History Museum and Fine Arts Museum of Uzbekistan, two of Central Asia's best.

From Tashkent head into the Fergana Valley and swing north along the mountain road to relaxed **Bishkek** (p232). From Bishkek cross the border into Kazakhstan to cosmopolitan **Almaty** (p56), visit the sights, attend the opera and make some excursions from the city before taking the train (or bus) to Ürümqi in China.

An alternative from Bishkek is to arrange transport through an agency to take you over the dramatic **Torugart Pass** (p310), visiting the summer pastures around **Kochkor** (p276) and Song-Köl and the photogenic caravanserai at **Tash Rabat** (p284), before crossing the pass to Kashgar. You can then continue along the northern or southern Silk Roads into China proper.

A third alternative if you are in a hurry is to travel from **Tashkent** (p139) to **Andijon** (p168) in the Fergana Valley, cross the border to the bustling bazaar town of **Osh** (p289) and then take a bus, or a combination of bus and taxi, into the high and scenic Alay Valley and over the remote **Irkeshtam Pass** (p310) to Kashgar.

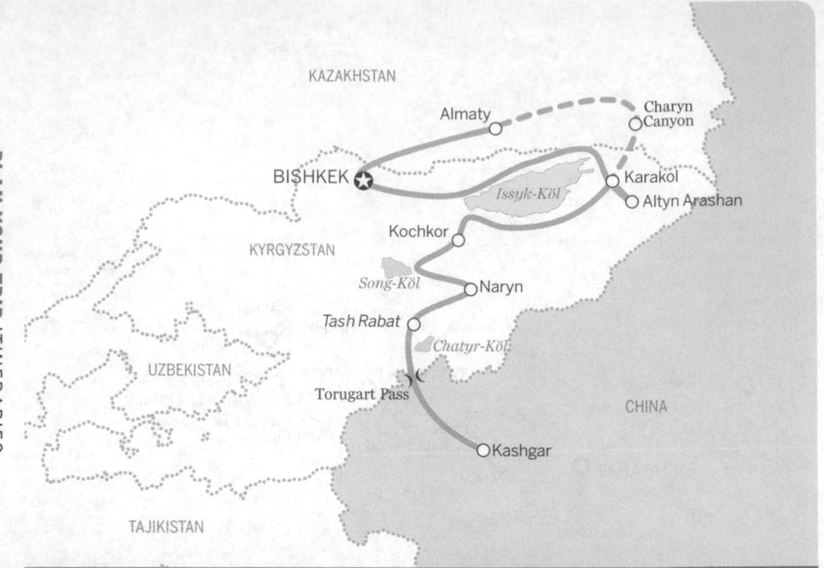

Over the Torugart: Lakes, Herders & Caravanserais

This trip takes in fabulous mountain scenery, a taste of traditional life in the pastures and the roller-coaster ride over the Torugart Pass to Kashgar. There are lots of opportunities for trekking or horse riding on this route.

Kick off with a couple of days in cosmopolitan **Almaty** (p56), with visits to Panfilov Park, the Central State Museum and a soak in the Arasan Baths. From here it's an easy four-hour drive to Kyrgyzstan's capital **Bishkek** (p232), from where you can head east to the blue waters and sandy beaches of Issyk-Köl, the world's second-largest alpine lake.

For an adventurous alternative between Almaty and Issyk-Köl, hire transport to take you to the colourful, eroded **Charyn Canyon** (p77) and on to the Kyrgyz border through the immense, silent Karkara Valley to Karakol.

Take in a couple of days' trekking or visiting the alpine valleys around **Karakol** (p258). The idyllic valley of **Altyn Arashan** (p265) offers great scope for horse riding or the short trek to alpine Ala-Köl and the glorious Karakol Valley. If you have time you can explore the little-visited southern shore, visiting an eagle-hunter en route to Kochkor. If you are low on time head straight to Kochkor from Bishkek.

In small and sleepy **Kochkor** (p276) take advantage of the community-based tourism (CBT) program and spend some time in a yurt- or homestay on the surrounding *jailoos* (summer pastures). This is one of the best ways to glimpse traditional life in Kyrgyzstan. Try to allow three days to link a couple of yurtstays by horse, although most can be visited in an overnight trip. The most popular trip is to the herders' camps around the peaceful lake **Song-Köl** (p273), either by car or on a two-day horseback trip. The pastures are popular with herders and their animals between June and August.

From here head to **Naryn** (p280) and then the Silk Road caravanserai of **Tash Rabat** (p284), where you can stay overnight in yurts and even take an adventurous horse trip to a pass overlooking Chatyr-Köl. From Tash Rabat it's up over the **Torugart Pass** (p310) and into China to wonderful Kashgar for it's epic Sunday Market.

KAZAKHSTAN
KYRGYZSTAN
UZBEKISTAN
Osh
Oybek
Khojand
Istaravshan
Sary Tash
Sary Mogol
Kashgar
Irkeshtam Pass
Samarkand
Penjikent
Iskander-Kul
Kara-Kul
CHINA
DUSHANBE
TAJIKISTAN
Murgab
Khorog
Langar
Wakhan Valley
AFGHANISTAN
PAKISTAN

To Osh via the Pamir Highway

This wild three-week jaunt ranks as one of the world's most beautiful and remote mountain road trips and is not one to rush. Hire a vehicle for at least part of the way and do the drives in daylight.

There are several options to get to **Penjikent** (p331). If the border crossing between Samarkand and Penjikent has reopened, this is your best option. Otherwise, fly from Dushanbe, or cross into Tajikistan from Uzbekistan at Bekabad, transit through **Khojand** (p335) and continue through **Istaravshan** (p334) by shared taxi over the Shakhristan Pass.

In Penjikent you can check out the Sogdian-era archaeological site and then either hire a car for a day trip up to the Marguzor Lakes or arrange a taxi through the mountains to scenic lake **Iskander-Kul** (p326).

Continue the taxi ride through stunning vertical scenery to Tajikistan's mellow capital **Dushanbe** (p316), where you should budget a couple of days to arrange the flight, shared 4WD or hired car for the long but impressive trip along the Afghan border to **Khorog** (p343) in Gorno-Badakhshan.

You can drive from Khorog to Murgab in a day, but there are lots of interesting detours here, especially the beautiful **Wakhan Valley** (p348) and its storybook Yamchun and Abrashim forts. With hired transport, you can cut from **Langar** (p350) to the Pamir Highway and continue to Murgab.

There are loads of side trips to be made from **Murgab** (p353), so try to budget a few days here to visit a local yurt camp in the surrounding high pastures. Headed north, **Kara-Kul** (p356) is a scenic highlight and worth at least a lunch stop or picnic. Once over the border in Kyrgyzstan, at **Sary Tash** (p296), it's worth detouring 40km to **Sary Mogol** (p296) for its fine views of towering Peak Lenin (Ibn Sina).

From here you can continue over the mountains to the Silk Road bazaar town of **Osh** (p289) or better still exit Central Asia via the **Irkeshtam Pass** (p310) to Kashgar, China.

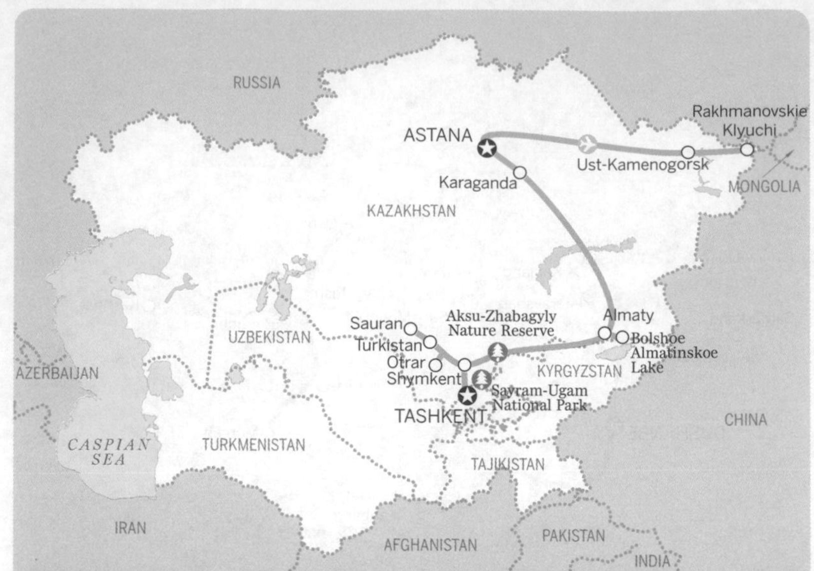

Kazakhstan: South to North

This Kazakh taster takes you from Central Asia into sub-Siberian northern Kazakhstan. From **Tashkent** (p139) it's a half-day trip across the border to vibrant **Shymkent** (p81), with its Central Asian–style bazaars and chaikhanas (teahouses).

From here detour west to **Turkistan** (p87) to soak up Kazakhstan's only architectural masterpiece, the blue-domed 14th-century Timurid tomb of Kozha Akhmed Yasaui. Keep the historical vibe going with a side trip to the nearby ruined Silk Road city of **Sauran** (p89) and a visit south to **Otrar** (p87), the spot where Chinggis (Genghis) Khan's troops first attacked Central Asia and where Timur breathed his last.

Back in Shymkent stock up on some supplies before heading out for some rural hiking, horse riding and tulip-spotting at **Aksu-Zhabagyly Nature Reserve** (p85) or **Sayram-Ugam National Park** (p86), both of which have homestays and ecotourism programs.

An overnight 'Silk Road by rail' train trip will drop you in Almaty, Kazakhstan's largest city. There is plenty to do here, including visiting the iconic Scythian-era Golden Man, before hitting Central Asia's most active club scene. Walk off the next day's hang-over on a hike to **Bolshoe Almatinskoe Lake** (p73), set in the lovely spurs of the Tian Shan.

From Almaty take the high-speed overnight train to the gritty coal city of **Karaganda** (p108). Touch Soviet-era rocket parts at the excellent Ecological Museum and then take a sobering day trip to visit the former gulags at Dolinka and Spassk.

Just a few hours away across the steppe is the modern capital of **Astana** (p98). After oggling the bizarre mix of architecture you can visit the Oceanarium and guess how far you are from the nearest sea (1700km).

Plenty of international flights serve Astana but to continue exploring take a flight to **Ust-Kamenogorsk** (p112) and then a long drive to **Rakhmanovskie Klyuchi** (p111) to start some fabulous hikes or horse treks through the valleys of the Altay, with views of mystical Mt Belukha. You'll need to arrange a tour a month or more in advance to get the required permits.

Plan Your Trip
Visas & Permits

Visas and permits can be the single biggest headache associated with travel in ex-Soviet Central Asia. Collecting visas for a multi-country trip through Central Asia can take months and cost hundreds of US dollars. Visa regulations are getting easier every year but our best advice remains 'start early and do your research'.

Visas

The good news is that the visa situation in Central Asia is much easier than just a couple of years ago. Single-entry tourist visas of up to 30 days for all countries except Turkmenistan are now a relative formality for most nationalities, with no need for the once notoriously pesky letter of invitation (LOI). Kyrgyzstan offers visa-free travel for most nationalities and Kazakhstan and Tajikistan might follow suit. It's even possible to get a visa on arrival at most airports, as long as you have arranged this in advance with a travel agency. Only Turkmenistan requires you to jump through some serious logistical hoops, including booking a guided tour.

The steps to obtain a visa and the attention it gets after you arrive differ for each republic, but their outlines are similar.

Applying for a Visa

Visa applications can be made in person or via post at most of the republics' overseas embassies or consulates. If your country doesn't have Central Asian representation you'll have to courier your passport to the nearest embassy, arrange a visa on arrival, or arrange your itinerary to get the visa in another Central Asian republic or elsewhere en route.

Embassies will want the following documents:

Visas at a Glance

Kazakhstan

No Letter of Invitation (LOI) needed for 30- or 60-day tourist visas for most nationalities; visas are date-specific; no extensions possible; registration required if entering the country overland. (p131)

Uzbekistan

No LOI needed for US citizens and most European nationalities for visas up to 30 days; visas are date-specific; extensions difficult but possible through a travel agency. (p225)

Kyrgyzstan

The easiest: visa-free for most nationalities for stays of up to 60 days for both air and land entry; extensions possible, or simply leave and re-enter the country; no registration for tourists. (p309)

Tajikistan

No LOI needed for tourist visas; visas are date-specific; extensions possible but tricky; visa-free program planned; no registration needed for tourist visas under 45 days; registration for private visas required and expensive. (p367)

Turkmenistan

The hardest: tourist visas only possible with expensive pre-booked tour; three- to five-day transit visas possible with fixed dates and entry/exit points. (p405)

➡ a photocopy of the validity and personal information pages of your passport (some Uzbekistan embassies require a copy of *all* passport pages!)

➡ anywhere between one and three passport-size photos

➡ a completed application form, which you can generally download from the embassy website.

In addition to these, you will also need:

➡ at least six months validity in your passport and two clean pages

➡ proof of onward transport (for a transit visa)

With the exception of Turkmenistan, visas do not list the towns to be visited. The tourist-visa application for Turkmenistan requires you to list the name of every town you want to visit, and most of these places, excluding the capital, will be printed on your visa.

Bear in mind that most visas have either fixed-entry dates or fixed-validity dates, so you will have to carefully plan the dates of your itinerary in advance. If you are weaving in and out of republics, eg from Uzbekistan to Tajikistan's Pamir Highway, Kyrgyzstan and then back to Uzbekistan, you'll need to ensure that the first visa is still valid when you return to that republic (and that it's a double- or multiple-entry visa).

Even the most helpful Central Asian embassies in the West normally take a week to issue a visa. Many embassies will speed the process up for an express fee (often double the normal fee). Central Asian embassies within the Commonwealth of Independent States (CIS) seem to be quicker.

Visa payment sometimes has to be in a neighbouring bank, not the embassy itself, and you'll need to bring back the receipt as proof of payment.

Visas can be quite expensive, especially for US citizens who routinely pay much more for their visas than other nationalities (retaliation for the fees the US government charges Central Asian visa applicants). Budget a couple of hundred dollars for a multi-'stan trip.

Try to allow time for delays and screw-ups. Errors do happen – check the dates and other information on your visa carefully before you hit the road, and try to find out what the Cyrillic or other writing says.

Letters of Invitation

The key to getting a tourist visa for Turkmenistan or a business, longer-duration or multiple-entry visa or a visa on arrival for other republics is 'visa support',

GETTING CURRENT INFORMATION

Online

Central Asia visa rules change all the time. The following websites are a good option for up-to-date visa information:

Caravanistan (www.caravanistan.com)

Thorn Tree (www.lonelyplanet.com/thorntree)

Stantours (www.stantours.com)

Embassies

Central Asian embassies abroad offer comprehensive information on visas:

Kazakhstan www.kazakhembus.com; www.kazconsulny.org; www.kazembassy.org.uk; also www.mfa.gov.kz/en

Kyrgyzstan www.kgembassy.org; www.kyrgyz-embassy.org.uk; www.botschaft-kirgisien.de

Tajikistan www.tjus.org; www.tajikembassy.be; www.tajembassy.org.uk; www.botschaft-tadschikistan.de

Turkmenistan www.turkmenistanembassy.org; www.turkmenembassy.org.uk

Uzbekistan www.uzbekconsulny.org; www.uzbekistan.org; www.uzbekistan.de; www.uzbekembassy.org; www.ouzbekistan.fr (in French)

which means a Letter of Invitation (LOI), approved by the Ministries of Foreign Affairs and/or Interior, from a private individual, company or state organisation in the country you want to visit. After obtaining ministry approval, your sponsor (normally a travel agent) sends the invitation to you, and when you apply at a consular office for your visa it is matched with a copy sent directly to them from the Ministry of Foreign Affairs.

The cheapest way to get a visa invitation is directly through a Central Asian travel agency, many of whom will sell you a letter of visa support for between US$30 and US$100. Stantours (www.stantours.com) is one agency that is frequently recommended. A few Western travel agencies can arrange visa invitations but charge up to five times the local fee.

Try to apply for letters of invitation a month, or preferably two months, in advance. Individual sponsors may need months to get their invitations approved before they can even be sent to you.

Visas on Arrival

If there's no convenient embassy in your country, you can get a visa on arrival at Astana and Almaty (in Kazakhstan), Dushanbe (Tajikistan) and Ashgabat (Turkmenistan) airports, but normally only if you have a LOI and have arranged this in advance with your agency. Some reports suggest that you can now get a visa on arrival in Dushanbe without an LOI, though this not recommended. A visa on arrival at Tashkent (Uzbekistan) is possible (with an LOI) but only if you come from a country without an Uzbekistan embassy. Visa-free entry at Bishkek and Osh airports in Kyrgyzstan make these the easiest fly-in options.

Responsible sponsors and agencies send representatives to meet their invitees at the airport and smooth their way through immigration. Even so, consular officials at the airport can be notoriously hard to find, especially if your flight arrives in the middle of the night, and they may not be able to find your records scribbled in their big black book.

You may also need to persuade the airline that you are guaranteed a visa as many are keen to avoid the costs and fines associated with bringing you back if your papers aren't in order. Try to get a visa in advance if possible.

Getting Central Asian Visas in Central Asia

If you are on a long overland trip it's possible to get your Central Asia visas en route in Central Asia, as long as you don't mind hanging around the Central Asian capitals for a few days (or even weeks) and spending a lot of time in visa queues. Bishkek (Kyrgyzstan) is a good place to load up on Central Asian visas.

However, it's generally best to get a visa in your home country when possible.

Transit & Multiple-Entry Visas

Even if you are just passing through a republic (eg flying into Almaty and transferring overland to Bishkek) you will need a transit visa.

You might also need transit visas for some trips even if you're not stopping in the country. For example, you will need a Kazakh transit visa to take the bus or train from Tashkent in Uzbekistan to Bishkek in Kyrgyzstan, or to take the train from Moscow to Tashkent, as both routes pass through Kazakhstan.

You may also need a re-entry visa (or multiple-entry visa) to get back into the first country if your bus or train dips temporarily into a neighbouring republic (most likely in remote parts of the Fergana Valley).

Train trips can be particularly tricky. New routings mean that you no longer need a Turkmen transit visa to take the Uzbek train between Tashkent and Urgench. Less convenient connections such as Tashkent to the Fergana Valley by train (which requires a Tajik transit visa and a double-entry Uzbek visa) are worth avoiding.

Visa Extensions

Extending an ordinary tourist visa after you arrive is relatively easy in Kyrgyzstan, a bureaucratic tussle in Tajikistan and Uzbekistan and almost impossible in Kazakhstan and Turkmenistan. Travel agencies can normally help

CHINESE VISAS IN CENTRAL ASIA

Chinese visas are a real pain to organise in Central Asia, with most Chinese embassies now demanding a LOI, a letter from your employers and even bank statements. The Chinese embassies in Almaty (Kazakhstan) and Dushanbe (Tajikistan) do not issue visas to non-residents. Bishkek (Kyrgyzstan) and Tashkent (Uzbekistan) are better places to try. The best advice is to get a Chinese visa before you set off, though remember that you must normally enter China within 90 days of your visa being issued.

and are your best bet but will charge a fee. You may find it easier to travel to a neighbouring republic and arrange another tourist visa.

Travel Permits

Visiting some border or strategic areas requires additional permits, some easy to obtain, others of which will require travel agency support and several weeks of planning. The most common destinations requiring permits include:

- Areas in Kazakhstan near the Chinese border, including the Altay mountains in the northeast and areas close to Mt Khan Tengri in the southeast, require special permits that can take up to 45 days to procure.
- Baykonur Cosmodrome in Kazakhstan can only be visited on tours organised through agencies. You need to start the paperwork process at least one month before your visit.
- Visits to the Semipalatinsk Polygon nuclear-testing site and its command town Kurchatov (both in Kazakhstan) need to be organised through tour agencies or Kazakhstan's National Nuclear Centre.
- In Kyrgyzstan any place within 50km of the Chinese border and not an open border crossing (such as the Inylchek Glacier, Alay Valley and Peak Lenin) requires a military border permit that is fairly easy to obtain through a trekking agency.
- The Gorno-Badakhshan (GBAO) region of Tajikistan needs a separate permit, which you can get at most embassies abroad (Bishkek is a good choice) or in Dushanbe in a day.

Turkmenistan presents a more complicated picture, as much of the country outside the main cities (restricted border regions) has to be listed on your visa for you to be able to visit it. You'll need a travel agency to get the visa in the first place, so your visa acts as your permit.

Plan Your Trip

Border Crossings

Whether kicking back on a Silk Road train trip between Kazakhstan and China or opting for an adventurous mountain crossing to Kashgar, the good news is that some of Central Asia's border crossings rank as regional highlights. Others, unfortunately, can be a chaotic, tiresome nightmare. Avoid the pitfalls with some pre-planning and the following advice.

Border Crossings to/from Central Asia

Central Asia is like a giant colander, pierced by a huge range of border crossings, from snowy mountain passes to desert crossings, ferries across the Caspian Sea to bridges over the Oxus River.

When crossing international borders to or from Central Asia, you essentially have the choice of using international through transport or using separate local transport on either side of the border. Through services such as the train or bus service between Almaty (Kazakhstan) and Ürümqi (China) are convenient. The main downside is that you often have to wait for hours at the border as a whole bus or train load of passengers go through immigration and customs. Most passengers are local traders and so have giant bags that customs officers root around in until they find a bribe.

At most other borders you'll arrange a bus, taxi or shared taxi to the border, go through border formalities on both sides, and then arrange onward transport on the other side. It's only tricky if there's a gap of no-man's land that you have to cross, such as at the Irkeshtam Pass in Kyrgyzstan.

Note that there are dozens of crossings between Russia and Kazakhstan; see p134 for an overview of these.

Most Scenic Border Crossings

Ishkashim, Wakhan Valley (p367) (Afghanistan–Tajikistan)

Torugart Pass (p310) (Kyrgyzstan–China)

Irkeshtam Pass (p310) (Kyrgyzstan–China)

Most Remote Border

Temirbaba (p133) (Turkmenistan–Kazakhstan)

Biggest Border Headache

Torugart Pass (p310) (Kyrgyzstan–China)

Newest Border Crossing

Qolma (Kulma) Pass (p367) (Tajikistan–China), so new that it's not actually open yet, though it is planned.

Currently Closed

Penjikent (p368) (Uzbekistan–Tajikistan)

Karamyk/Jirgital (p368) (Kyrgyzstan–Tajikistan)

Border Crossings Within Central Asia

Central Asian republics share some extremely convoluted borders. During the Soviet era most of these existed on paper only but in recent years they have solidified into full international crossings so make sure you have the necessary visas.

Except for a few transborder connections between Kazakhstan and Kyrgyzstan, there's little through transport between republics these days, so at most crossings you'll have to take a bus, taxi or shared taxi to/from the border, walk across the border and arrange onward transport on the other side. Shared taxis run to and from most borders from the nearest town. Transport is generally only a problem at the most remote crossings.

Borders between the Central Asia republics are subject to political tensions and can close suddenly in the event of demonstrations or violence. The Uzbekistan–Tajikistan border is particularly susceptible to closure so check before hand.

General Tips

➡ You'll likely have to change money at the borders. Most don't have formal exchange booths so you may have to change with moneychangers. Check rates at banks in the nearest towns before making a crossing.

➡ Bring small bills to change money at the border and if you are unsure of the rate only change as much as you need to get you to the nearest town, as rates are often lower at the border.

➡ It's a good idea to isolate the $50 bill you want to change before arriving at the border, so you don't have to go digging around your money belt on the border and watch all your hundred dollar bills spill out onto the floor.

➡ Make sure you go through customs and get a customs form on arrival. This is especially important when entering Uzbekistan, where you should declare all your money and fill out two customs forms to avoid trouble later.

➡ Some borders are open 24 hours, others close at dusk. Aim to cross before mid-afternoon to ensure onward transport.

➡ If crossing to China, avoid crossing on the public holidays of either country (or even Russia for the Torugart).

➡ Chinese national holidays fall on 1 January, 8 March, 1 July, 1 August, the spring festival (some time in February) and the weeks following the major holidays of 1 May and 1 October.

➡ Russian national holidays fall on 1 and 7 January, 8 March, 1 and 9 May, 12 June and 7 November.

➡ Beware that some international border crossings are closed at the weekend.

➡ If crossing a border on a train, bus or, especially, boat bring enough food and water for potential delays at the border.

➡ In general always be patient, friendly and calm at borders.

MAJOR BORDER CROSSINGS INTO CENTRAL ASIA

BORDER	CROSSING	MEANS OF TRANSPORT	COMMENTS
1 Iran–Turkmenistan	Gaudan/Bajgiran (p405)	car	From Mashhad to Ashgabat; change transport at the border.
2 Iran–Turkmenistan	Saraghs (p405)	car/rail	The best bet if you want to head straight for Mary/Merv.
3 Azerbaijan–Turkmenistan	Turkmenbashi (p385)	boat	12 to 18 hours on an unreliable cargo boat. Try to upgrade to a cabin when on board.
4 China–Tajikistan	Qolma (Kulma) Pass (p367)	taxi	Technically opened in 2013 but travellers currently not allowed to cross. Check in advance.
5 China–Kazakhstan	Khorgos (p132)	bus	Direct sleeper buses run from Yining (12 hours) and Ürümqi (24 hours) to Almaty, or take the new train to the border and then a bus on to Yining in China.
6 China–Kazakhstan	Dostyk/Alashankou (p132)	rail	Twice-weekly direct trains between Almaty and Ürümqi take 31 hours and cost US$125.
7 China–Kazakhstan	Maykapshagay/Jeminay (Jimunai) (p132)	bus	Little-used crossing but direct buses between Ürümqi and Ust-Kamenogorsk.
8 China–Kyrgyzstan	Torugart Pass (p310)	car	Tricky to arrange and relatively expensive as you must hire your own transport in advance on both sides. Closed weekends.
9 China–Kyrgyzstan	Irkeshtam Pass (p310)	taxi/bus	Twice-weekly bus between Kashgar and Osh (US$85) or take a taxi. Closed weekends.
10 Uzbekistan–Afghanistan	Friendship Bridge Termiz/Hayratan (p226)	taxi	Security is a concern on the Afghan side. One hour from Mazar-e-Sharif.
11 Tajikistan–Afghanistan	Ishkashim (p367)	taxi	Incredibly scenic; for access to Afghanistan's Wakhan Valley. Time a crossing with the Saturday trans-border market.
12 Azerbaijan–Kazakhstan	Aktau (p133)	boat	Passenger-carrying cargo boat with no fixed schedule goes roughly once a week in summer, once every two weeks in winter; takes 18 hours or more.

Border Crossings

CHERNYAEVKA

(Uzbekistan–Kazakhstan) No through transport, onward shared taxi or marshrutka transport to Shymkent and Tashkent. (pp 133, 226)

OYBEK

(Uzbekistan–Tajikistan) The best option for northern Tajikistan. The nearby Bekabad crossing is not open to foreigners. (p226)

TAZHEN

(Kazakhstan–Uzbekistan) Remote desert road and rail crossing between Beyneu and Kungrad, used by trains from Russia to Tashkent. (p133)

SHAVAT/DASHOGUS

(Turkmenistan–Uzbekistan) The best option between Khiva and Dashogus/Konye-Urgench. From Nukus take the less-used alternative further west via Hojeli. (p406)

TEMIRBABA/GARABOGAZ

(Turkmenistan–Kazakhstan) Extremely remote, partially dirt track between Zhanaozen and Turkmenbashi, with 4WDs (and maybe soon trains) making the 10-hour trip. (pp 133, 406)

FARAB/ALAT

(Turkmenistan–Uzbekistan) Turkmenabat to Bukhara, requires a 10-minute walk across no-man's land. US$12–14 entry tax into Turkmenistan must be paid in US dollars. (p406)

PENJIKENT

(Uzbekistan–Tajikistan) Currently closed due to political tensions. Check in advance.

DENAU/TURSANZADE

(Uzbekistan–Tajikistan) Useful crossing if headed from southern Uzbekistan to Dushanbe. (pp 227, 368)

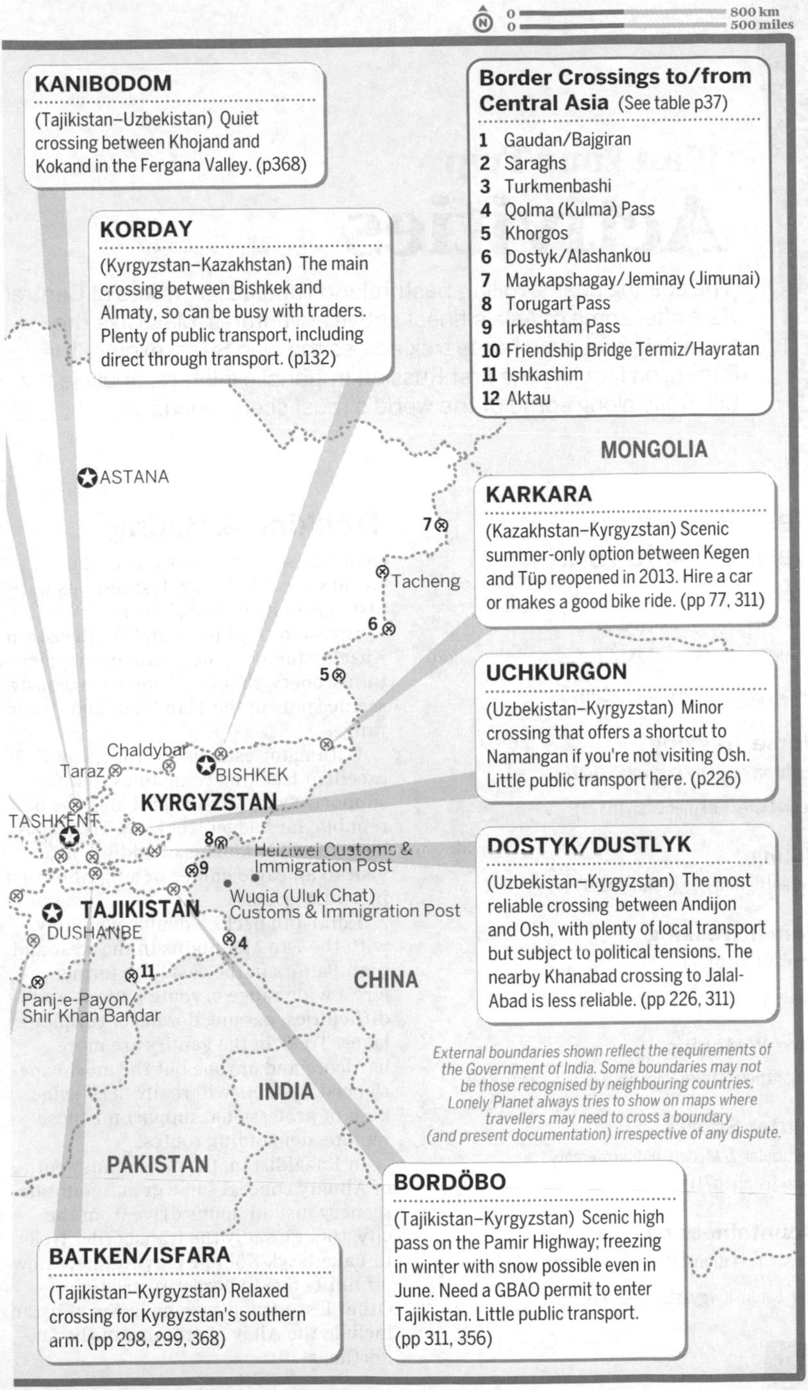

0 — 800 km
0 — 500 miles

Border Crossings to/from Central Asia (See table p37)

1 Gaudan/Bajgiran
2 Saraghs
3 Turkmenbashi
4 Qolma (Kulma) Pass
5 Khorgos
6 Dostyk/Alashankou
7 Maykapshagay/Jeminay (Jimunai)
8 Torugart Pass
9 Irkeshtam Pass
10 Friendship Bridge Termiz/Hayratan
11 Ishkashim
12 Aktau

KANIBODOM

(Tajikistan–Uzbekistan) Quiet crossing between Khojand and Kokand in the Fergana Valley. (p368)

KORDAY

(Kyrgyzstan–Kazakhstan) The main crossing between Bishkek and Almaty, so can be busy with traders. Plenty of public transport, including direct through transport. (p132)

KARKARA

(Kazakhstan–Kyrgyzstan) Scenic summer-only option between Kegen and Tüp reopened in 2013. Hire a car or makes a good bike ride. (pp 77, 311)

UCHKURGON

(Uzbekistan–Kyrgyzstan) Minor crossing that offers a shortcut to Namangan if you're not visiting Osh. Little public transport here. (p226)

DOSTYK/DUSTLYK

(Uzbekistan–Kyrgyzstan) The most reliable crossing between Andijon and Osh, with plenty of local transport but subject to political tensions. The nearby Khanabad crossing to Jalal-Abad is less reliable. (pp 226, 311)

BATKEN/ISFARA

(Tajikistan–Kyrgyzstan) Relaxed crossing for Kyrgyzstan's southern arm. (pp 298, 299, 368)

BORDÖBO

(Tajikistan–Kyrgyzstan) Scenic high pass on the Pamir Highway; freezing in winter with snow possible even in June. Need a GBAO permit to enter Tajikistan. Little public transport. (pp 311, 356)

MONGOLIA
ASTANA
Tacheng
Chaldybar
Taraz
BISHKEK
KYRGYZSTAN
TASHKENT
Heiziwei Customs & Immigration Post
Wuqia (Uluk Chat) Customs & Immigration Post
TAJIKISTAN
DUSHANBE
Panj-e-Payon/ Shir Khan Bandar
CHINA
INDIA
PAKISTAN

External boundaries shown reflect the requirements of the Government of India. Some boundaries may not be those recognised by neighbouring countries. Lonely Planet always tries to show on maps where travellers may need to cross a boundary (and present documentation) irrespective of any dispute.

Plan Your Trip

Activities

The soaring peaks, rolling pasturelands and desert tracts of Central Asia offer some of Asia's finest active adventures. Make like the Kazakh hordes on a horse trek across the Tian Shan, explore the Pamirs on foot like the first Russian Imperial explorers, or cycle the Silk Road along some of the world's most scenic roads.

Best Places in Central Asia for...

Trekking

Tian Shan, Kyrgyzstan (p272)

Pamirs, Tajikistan (p338)

Fan Mountains, Tajikistan (p326)

Horse Trekking

Kochkor, central Kyrgyzstan (p276)

Geok-Dere, Turkmenistan (p377)

Biking

Pamir Highway, Tajikistan (p351)

Camel Trekking

Uzbekistan (p137)

Eastern Pamirs, Tajikistan (p338)

Bird Watching

Korgalzhyn Nature Reserve, Kazakhstan (p107)

Winter Sports

Chimbulak & Medeu, outside Almaty, Kazakhstan (p71)

Mountaineering

Ala-Archa National Park, Kyrgyzstan (p250)

Peak Lenin, Kyrgyzstan (p297)

Trekking & Hiking

Central Asia is not only one of the world's great trekking destinations but also one of its best-kept secrets. Kyrgyzstan, Tajikistan and southeastern Kazakhstan hold the cream of the mountain scenery, thanks to the outrageously scenic spurs of the Tian Shan and Pamir ranges.

With many established routes and excellent trekking companies to offer support, Kyrgyzstan is probably the best republic for budget trekking. Treks here have the added bonus of adding on a visit to an eagle hunter or a night or two in a yurt en route.

Tajikistan packs a double whammy, with the Fan Mountains in the west and high Pamirs in the east. The former offers a wide range of route options and difficulties, passing dozens of turquoise lakes. Treks in the Pamirs are more hardcore and anyone but the most experienced trekkers will really need some kind of professional support for these remote, demanding routes.

In Kazakhstan, the mountains south of Almaty conceal some great mountain scenery just an hour's drive from the city, though sadly the transborder treks to Lake Issyk-Köl in Kyrgyzstan are now off limits due to border restrictions. Other less-visited regions in Kazakhstan include the Altay Mountains in the far northeast.

For more off-the-beaten-track treks in Kyrgyzstan, try the three-day trek from Sokuluk Canyon to Suusamyr Valley; from the Shamsy Valley south of Tokmok to yurtstays at Sarala-Saz; or from Kyzyl-Oi to Köl-Tör lake. Another option is the trek from Chong-Kemin Valley to Grigorievka or to Jasy-Köl and back; arrange horses in Kaindy.

In Tajikistan there are several interesting short trekking routes in the western Pamirs that combine trekking with rural homestays, including at Bodomdara and Rivak.

What Kind of Trek?

Self-supported trekking is possible but not always easy in Central Asia. There are no trekking lodges and few porters, so you will have to carry all your own food for the trek. Public transport to the trailheads can be patchy, slow and uncomfortable so it's generally worth shelling out the extra money for a taxi. Some trekking areas are at the junction of several republics, requiring you to carry multiple simultaneous visas and a fistful of different currencies. It's possible to hire donkeys at many trailheads (eg in the Fan Mountains) and hire horses in Kyrgyzstan (for around US$10 per day) and the Tajikistan Pamirs (US$20 per day). Organisations like CBT in Kyrgyzstan, and META and PECTA in Tajikistan can often offer logistical support.

There is some outdoor gear for sale in Bishkek and Almaty. You can also hire simple tents, sleeping bags and stoves from Karakol, Arslanbob and Bishkek in Kyrgyzstan and in Penjikent and Khorog in Tajikistan, but in general you are always much better off bringing your own gear. A multifuel (petrol) stove is most useful, though you will need to clean the burners regularly as local fuel is of extremely poor quality. Camping gas canisters are generally available in Karakol.

Karakol is the main centre of trekking. The tourist information centre here sells 1:100,000 topo maps and has a folder detailing trekking routes. Several companies here offer a range of logistical support.

Trustworthy local knowledge, and preferably a local guide, are essential for trekking in Central Asia. The various branches of CBT in Kyrgyzstan can put you in touch with a general guide, though for someone with a guaranteed knowledge of mountain routes you are better off arranging this with a trekking agency. Trekking and horse guides are available for around US$20 to US$35 through community-tourism programs in the Fan Mountains.

There are lots of competent trekking agencies in Central Asia that can arrange a full service trek. See the various entries in the main republic chapters for details. Treks organised through local trekking agencies cost from US$50 per person per day, far cheaper than international companies.

When to Go

The best walking season is June to September, but be ready for bad weather at any time. Most high-altitude treks or climbs take place in July or August; lower areas can be scorching hot during these months.

Trekking Permits & Problems

Permits are needed for some border areas of Kazakhstan, including the central Tian Shan and the Altay region. These take up to 45 days to procure so

USEFUL WEBSITES

www.trekkinginthepamirs.com Trekking in the Pamirs and Zerafshan regions.

www.pamirs.org/trekking.htm Great trekking section on this excellent website, with other sections on cycling and rafting.

www.kac.centralasia.kg Kyrgyz Alpine Club for climbing and expeditions.

www.pamirs.wordpress.com Bit dated but still useful blog on kayaking Tajikistan's rivers.

www.kayakussr.com Information and support on paddling rivers in the Pamirs and Tian Shan.

apply ahead of time if you plan to trek in these regions.

In Kyrgyzstan any place within 50km of the Chinese border (such as the Inylchek Glacier, the Alay Valley, the Turkestan range or Peak Lenin) requires a military border permit which is fairly easy to obtain through a trekking agency.

While most commonly used trekking routes are quite safe, mountain routes on the borders of southeastern Kyrgyzstan and Tajikistan are best avoided. Some border areas around here are mined. Discuss your route with a trekking agency before you wander off into these hills, and take a local guide.

Maps

The major trekking/climbing maps for Central Asia are published and available abroad:

Central Tian Shan (EWP; www.ewpnet.com) 1:150,000; Inylchek Glacier and surroundings.

Fan Mountains (EWP; www.ewpnet.com) 1:100,000; Fan Mountains in Tajikistan.

Pamir Trans Alai Mountains (EWP; www.ewpnet.com) 1:200,000; Peak Lenin and the Fedchenko Glacier.

Lenin Peak (Gecko Maps; www.geckomaps.com) 1:100,000; topographical map of the mountain.

Khan Tengri, Tian Shan and **Inylchek** (Alpenvereinskarte) 1:100,000; two detailed climbing maps of the central Tian Shan.

GeoID (p244), TUK (p245) and Novinomad (p245) in Bishkek sell useful maps of major trekking regions. You can buy 1:100,000 topographical maps of the trek routes around southeast Lake Issyk-Köl at the tourist information centre at Karakol. For more on maps in Kyrgystan see p307.

Note that on Russian maps, passes marked Unclassified (N/K) or 1A are simple, with slopes no steeper than 30°; glaciers, where they exist, are flat and without open crevasses. Grade 1B passes may have ice patches or glaciers with hidden crevasses and may require ropes. Passes of grade 2A and above may require special equipment and technical climbing skills.

Hiking

Day hiking is a major outdoor pursuit for Almaty residents and there are fine hikes from Chimbulak, among others. The Sayram-Ugam National Park and Aksu-Zhabagyly Nature Reserve are two beautiful areas of hiking country on the fringes of the Tian Shan between the southern Kazakhstan cities of Shymkent and Taraz. Rakhmanovskie Klyuchi, in far east Kazakhstan, is the starting point for hikes up the sublimely beautiful Altay valleys that fall off the slopes of Mt Belukha. Zapadno-Altaysky (Western Altay) Nature Reserve near Ust-Kamenogorsk is also good for hiking.

You can make nice day hikes from bases in Ala-Archa National Park, near Bishkek, and Altyn Arashan, near Karakol, both in Kyrgyzstan. The Wakhan and Pshart valleys in the Pamirs of Tajikistan offer superb valley walks, as does the Jizeu (Geisev) Valley, where you can leave the tent behind and overnight in village homestays.

Local hiking clubs are an excellent way to get out of the cities for the weekend, get some mountain air and meet up with local expats.

TOP TREKKING AREAS

- **Fan Mountains** (p326), Tajikistan – routes from three days to two weeks.
- Alpine-like valleys of the **Tian Shan** (p272), around Karakol, Kyrgyzstan.
- Walnut forests and waterfalls around **Arslanbob** (p286), Kyrgyzstan.
- **Khan Tengri** and **Inylchek Glacier** (p77) – from Kyrgyzstan or Kazakhstan.
- Around **Almaty**, Kazakhstan – either from Ozero Bolshoe Almatinskoe (p73) or Chimbulak (p71) or further away in the Kolsay Lakes region (p76).
- **Ala-Archa National Park** (p250), Kyrgyzstan – just two hours from the capital.

If you're in Dushanbe for the weekend in summer tag along with one of the day hikes led by Hike Tajikistan (p317). The twice-monthly excursions of the Tashkent Hiking Club (p155) are also a good bet.

Horse Trekking

Kyrgyzstan is the perfect place to saddle up and explore the high pastures. CBT and Shepherd's Life coordinators throughout the country arrange overnight horse treks to *jailoos* (summer pastures) around central Kyrgyzstan, or longer expeditions on horseback lasting up to two weeks. Horse hire costs the equivalent of around US$15 per day, or around US$50 per person per day with a guide, yurtstay and food.

Horseback is the perfect way to arrive at Song-Köl. Trips can depart from either Jangy Talap, Chayek, Jumgal or Chekildek and take around three days, staying in yurts en route. The six-day horse trek from Song-Köl to Tash Rabat via the Mazar Valley is an adventurous choice.

There are also good horse treks from Karakol (Altyn Arashan offers some lovely day trips) and Tamga (on the southern shores of Lake Issyk-Köl), as well as Naryn, Arslanbob, Kazarman and Ak-Terek north of Özgön. Kegeti Canyon, east of Bishkek, is another popular place for horse riding.

For organised trips in Kyrgyzstan, **Asiarando** (www.asiarando.com), Pegasus Horse Trekking (p257) and Shepherds Way (p270) have all been recommended.

The Pamirs of Tajikistan and Kyrgyzstan are also sublime places for a horse trek. The **Pamir Trek Association** (www.pamirtrek.com) is an association of horse guides from the Tajikistan Pamirs and Kyrgyzstan Pamir Alai valley that offers horse treks in these regions.

For a classy ride, you can't do better than astride a thoroughbred Akhal-Teke in Turkmenistan. The Alaja Farm (p377) stables at Geok-Dere, outside Ashgabat, offer half-day rides, and some travel agencies can arrange multiday horse treks. **DN Tours** (www.dntours.com) offers an 11-day desert ride on Akhal-Tekes, with camping and the opportunity to stay in local villages. **Stantours** (www.stantours.com) offers a week-long horse-riding trip through the Kopet Dag Mountains.

Kan Tengri (p68) offers horse treks through the desert landscapes of Altyn-Emel National Park and also in the central Tian Shan. There are further horseback options in the ecotourism centres of Aksu-Zhabagyly Nature Reserve and Sayram-Ugam National Park (ride between them in three days), at the Kolsay Lakes in southeast Kazakhstan and at Zapadno-Altaysky (Western Altay) Nature Reserve near Ust-Kamenogorsk. These are generally more expensive than in neighbouring Kyrgyzstan, with horse hire starting at US$25 per day.

The German company Kasachstan Reisen (p126) offers interesting horse-riding, 4WD and trekking trips in Kazakhstan, in partnership with local Kazakh agencies.

Camel Trekking

If you've got Silk Road fever and imagine a multiday caravan across the wastes of Central Asia, you could be in for a disappointment. Bukhara travel agencies arrange camel treks north of Nurata around Lake Aidarkul and there are also possibilities at Ayaz-Qala in northwest Uzbekistan but these are mostly short jaunts from comfortable tourist yurts (with electricity, plumbing and three-course meals). The best time for low-altitude desert camel trekking is from March to May, when the spring rains turn the floor of the Kyzylkum Desert into a Jackson Pollock canvas.

For the full-on 'Marco Polo' experience, META in Tajikistan can give information on one- to three-day treks on Bactrian camels in the high-altitude Rang-Kul region of the eastern Pamirs.

Mountain Biking & Cycling

Several tour companies offer supported biking trips over the Torugart Pass, although die-hard do-it-yourselfers will find the Irkeshtam crossing logistically easier. The Kegeti Canyon and pass in northern Kyrgyzstan is another biking location favoured by adventure-travel companies.

In Kyrgyzstan the Karkara Valley offers quiet country back roads. From here you can cycle around the southern shore of Lake Issyk-Köl and then up into central Kyrgyzstan. Karakol's IGPA (p263) is a cooperative of guides that can take you on five-day mountain bike trips from Karakol if you bring your own bike. Mountain bikes can be rented in Karakol and Arslanbob for local rides, though most travellers on multi-day trips bring their own bikes.

A growing number of die-hards organise their own long-distance mountain-bike trips across Central Asia. The most popular route is probably the Pamir Highway in Tajikistan, which is a spectacular but hard trip. Cyclists who have done the route recommend transporting your bike to Khorog and starting from there. The highway is paved but winds can make pedalling hard work. Several cyclists have reported being harassed and extorted in border areas, including by border guards. Still, it's one of the world's great bike trips. For tips and bike travelogues around Central Asia see the following websites:

- www.carryoncycling.com
- www.trans-tadji.info
- www.cyclingabout.com
- www.timbarnes.ndo.co.uk
- www.crazyguyonabike.com/doc/standiet

You can rent mountain bikes for local trips in Karakol, Arslanbob and Murgab. You can get repairs and some bike parts in Bishkek.

Muztoo (☎055-582 4435, 245 503; http://muztoo.ch) in Osh, Kyrgyzstan, arranges motorbike tours of Central Asia and rents trial bikes.

Rafting

Intrepid rafters and kayakers have started to explore Central Asia's remote white water but commercial operations are still limited.

Hamsafar Travel in Tajikistan can help with information on kayaking and rafting in Tajikistan.

Tashkent operators run fairly tame rafting trips in September and October on the Syr-Darya river. There's plenty of exciting white water nearby on the Ugam, Chatkal and Pskem Rivers: talk to **Asia Raft** (www.asiaraft.uz) in Tashkent.

Mountaineering & Rock Climbing

Central Asian 'alpinism' was very popular during the Soviet era, when climbers dragged their crampons from all over the communist bloc to tackle the region's five impressive 'Snow Leopards' (peaks over 7000m).

Top of the line for altitude junkies are Khan Tengri, Pik Pobedy and other peaks of the central Tian Shan in eastern Kyrgyzstan and southeast Kazakhstan. Khan Tengri is a stunningly beautiful peak. Massive Pobedy is the world's most northern 7000m-plus peak and the hardest of Central Asia's 7000m-plus summits.

Several Almaty and Bishkek tour agents can arrange trips to this region, including helicopter flights to the base camps during the climbing season from the end of July to early September. Even if you aren't a climber, these are fine treks that lead into a breathtaking mountain amphitheatre. You will need a border zone permit for either side and a mountaineering permit (US$105) on the Kyrgyz side to climb here.

The other prime high-altitude playground is the Pamir in southern Kyrgyzstan and eastern Tajikistan, especially Peak Lenin (Ibn Sina), accessed from the north side at Achik Tash base camp. Lenin is a non-technical climb and is considered one of the easiest 7000m summits, yet it has claimed the most lives. The season is July and August. Bishkek-based companies like Ak-Sai, Tien Shan Travel and Asia Mountains operate commercial expeditions from base camps at Achik Tash.

The most accessible climbing is in Ala-Archa National Park, just outside

Bishkek, where popular routes from the Ak-Say glacier require just a couple of days. Mt Korona, Mt Uchityel and Mt Free Korea are the most popular peaks here. The website of the **Alpine Fund** (www.alpinefund.org) in Bishkek is a good resource for this region.

Other 4000m-plus peaks include Pik Sayram in the Aksu-Zhabagyly Nature Reserve and Mt Belukha in east Kazakhstan's northern Altay Mountains. Experienced climbers will find that plenty of unclimbed summits await, especially in the Kokshal-Tau range near the border with China.

Kyrgyzstan: A Climber's Map & Guide, by Garth Willis and Martin Gamache, and published by the American Alpine Club, is a map and mini-guide that covers Ala-Archa, the western Kokshal-Tau and Karavshin regions.

Two of the most exciting and least known rock climbing destinations in Asia are Ak-Suu peak in southwestern Kyrgyzstan (known as 'Central Asia's Patagonia') and the Zamin-Karkor tower at Margeb in northern Tajikistan. For something a lot less technical try the four-day ascent of Babashata from Arslanbob in southern Kyrgyzstan.

Mountaineering and climbing equipment is hard to find in the region so you should bring your own gear.

Winter Sports

Central Asia's ski season is approximately November to April, with local variations. The region's best-known and best-equipped downhill area is **Chimbulak** (Shymbulak; www.shimbulak.kz), a day-trip from Almaty. The new Ak-Bulak and **Tabagan** (www.tabagan.kz) resorts near Talgar, 90 minutes from Almaty, both have good facilities. Figure on about US$60 per day for lift pass and equipment hire.

Skiing is still in its infancy in Kyrgyzstan, but there are several options in the Kyrgyz Alatau valleys (especially Ala-Archa), south of Bishkek and at Karakol. It's possible to rent skis and boards in Bishkek through TUK (p245), as well as in Karakol. The relatively modern Karakol Ski Base (p267) in Karakol has chair lifts, accommodation and rental equipment between November and March.

Nearly every sports-related agency in Central Asia offers heli-skiing, in which old Aeroflot MI-8 helicopters drop you off on remote high peaks and you ski down. Most guarantee from 3000 to 4000 vertical metres per day for descents of up to 5km but require a group of 12 to 15 people. The Kyrgyz Alatau range behind Bishkek is one of the cheapest places to try out heli-skiing, or try the Chimgan and Chatkal ranges behind Tashkent (book through Asia Adventures, p155).

Kazakhstan's pristine Altay Mountains are renowned for cross-country skiing; the best place to do this is Rakhmanovskie Klyuchi. Arslanbob in Kyrgyzstan is also surprisingly well set up for cross-country skiing and you can rent a limited number of skis and boots here. A few travel firms in Kazakhstan and Kyrgyzstan offer ski-mountaineering trips in the central Tian Shan in July and August, and in the Zailiysky Alatau and Küngey Alatau ranges from February to April.

The Medeu ice rink just outside Almaty is one of the largest speed-skating rinks in the world (larger than a football pitch). It's open to the public daily from November to April.

Four-Wheel Drive Trips

The back roads of Kyrgyzstan, and particularly Tajikistan's Badakhshan region, offer great scope for adventure travel in an indestructible Russian UAZ 4WD. Four-wheel drives can be hired from around US$0.50 per kilometre in both countries.

In Kyrgyzstan one possible 4WD itinerary leads from Talas over the Kara Bura Pass into the Chatkal river valley and then around to Lake Sary-Chelek. Other tracks lead from Naryn to Barskoön, and Barskoön to Inylchek, through the high Tian Shan.

It's well worth hiring a 4WD from Murgab in the eastern Pamirs for trips out to such gorgeously remote places as Shaimak, Jalang and Zor-Kul.

More 4WD fun, of a slightly sandier nature, is possible in Turkmenistan.

One exciting itinerary is the trip from Yangykala Canyon across the Karakum desert to the Darvaza Gas Craters. Expect plenty of dune bashing, sleeping under starry skies and stops for tea in remote Turkmen villages.

Other Activities

Several companies organise caving trips, especially around Osh, in Kyrgyzstan, and Chimgan, north of Tashkent in Uzbekistan. Spelunkers will get a kick from exploring the miles of twisting tunnels that make up the Karlyuk Caves (Central Asia's largest), deep underneath Turkmenistan's Kugitang Nature Reserve. It's even possible to scuba dive in Lake Issyk-Köl, though some of the equipment used looks like props from a 1960s Jacques Cousteau documentary.

There are some fine opportunities for nature spotting. The wetlands of Kazakhstan's Korgalzhyn Nature Reserve lie at the crossroads of two major bird migration routes, attracting 300 species including the world's most northerly flamingo habitat (April to September). The tulips of Aksu-Zhabagyly Nature Reserve are world famous and several local and foreign companies run tours to this area in spring. The following tour operator websites are a great resource for birdwatching in Kazakhstan:

- www.kazakhstanbirdtours.com
- www.naturetrek.co.uk
- www.wingsbirds.com

Odyssey Travel (www.odysseytravel.com.au), in Australia, operates archaeological tours to the Khorezm region of Uzbekistan, during which you'll spend two weeks on an archaeological dig, followed by a short general tour of the country.

Sport fishing is an option in the Ili delta in Kazakhstan.

Plan Your Trip

Community-Based Tourism

Central Asia's community-based tourism organisations offer some of the region's best and most exciting experiences, at fantastic value. Connect with these organisations for an incredible grassroots experience and sleep better in your yurtstay at night knowing that your money is going directly to the family you are staying with, rather than a middleman in Bishkek or abroad.

The Idea

At the end of the 1990s, with few economic options left to Kyrgyzstan, development organisations started to look to new sources of income to support remote communities, starting with tourism. The idea was to help connect intrepid tourists to a series of local service providers, from drivers to herders, in a fair and mutually beneficial way, while supporting local craft production and sustainable tourism practices.

The phenomenon started in central Kyrgyzstan with Swiss help (Helvetas) and has since rapidly spread throughout the region. Today these organisations offer everything from homestays and vehicle hire to horse treks and adventures across the country. They are your keys to an authentic budget adventure on the cheap.

In addition to gung-ho adventures, most community-tourism organisations offer a range of cultural activities. CBT in Kyrgyzstan can organise displays of felt-making or eagle-hunting. EIRC in Kazakhstan arranges fun workshops making *kumys* (fermented mare's milk) and concerts of traditional Kazakh music.

Program coordinators sustain themselves through a 15% commission or a small coordinator's fee. A few teething problems remain to be addressed,

Community-Tourism Contacts

Kazakhstan

Ecotourism Information Resource Centre (p68; EIRC; www.eco-tourism.kz)

Wild Nature (p86; www.wildnature-kz.narod.ru)

Uzbekistan

Nuratau-Kyzylkum Biosphere Reserve (p186; www.nuratau.com)

Kyrgyzstan

Community Based Tourism (p247; www.cbtkyrgyzstan.kg)

CBT plus Eco (p277; www.cbtpluseco.kg)

Tajikistan

Pamir Eco-Cultural Tourism Association (p346; PECTA; www.pecta.tj)

Zerafshan Tourism Development Association (p333; ZTDA; www.ztda-tourism.tj/en)

Murgab Ecotourism Association (p354; META; www.meta.tj)

including issues with nepotism, reliability and the tendency for service providers to break away and found their own rival businesses, and most of the organisations are not yet financially self-supporting. Remember also that these are not professional tourism companies, so be sure to pack a sense of humour and expect some delays and schedule changes during your trip.

Country Programs

Community Based Tourism in Kyrgyzstan is the region's leader, with a network of a dozen locations across the country, sometimes overlapping with original organisation Shepherd's Life. Most towns in Kyrgyzstan have CBT-inspired homestays and the organisation now offers everything from homestays and horse treks to folk music concerts and horse-racing festivals.

In Tajikistan, Murgab Ecotourism Association (META) can put you in touch with remote yurtstays, fixed-price 4WD hire and English-speaking guides in a region devoid of any formal tourist infrastructure. Mountain Societies Development & Support Project (MSDSP) in Khorog has helped establish homestays in the western Pamirs, including the popular homestay and hiking program in the Jizeu (Geisev) Valley. For information on these and local drivers and guides visit the nonprofit Pamirs Eco-Cultural Tourism Association (PECTA) office in Khorog.

Further east in Penjikent, the Zerafshan Tourism Development Association is the key to linking together homestays to make a 4WD trip in the remote Haft-Kul, Zerafshan and Yagnob valleys, or hiring guides, donkeys and equipment for a trek in the dramatic Fan Mountains.

The hub for ecotourism in Kazakhstan is the Ecotourism Information Resource Centre, which offers similar grassroots adventures and homestays, from flamingo-watching at Korgalzhyn Nature Reserve to horse riding in Sayram-Ugam National Park, though at higher prices than elsewhere in the region. Wild Nature also offers homestays, horse treks and nature-watching trips. The best destinations are probably Aksu-Zhabagyly Nature Reserve and nearby Sayram-Ugam National Park (www.ugam.kz).

The idea is starting to make its way into Uzbekistan through a Unesco-supported program in the Nuratau-Kyzylkum Biosphere Reserve.

Central Asia's community-based tourism projects are a fantastic resource for independent travellers and deserve your support. Our advice is to try to pack some flexibility and extra time into your trip to take advantage of what a particular branch offers. You can expect the experience to rank among the highlights of your travels.

TOP COMMUNITY-BASED ADVENTURES

The following adventurous trips can be arranged by community-tourism programs in Kyrgyzstan and Tajikistan and offer exciting ways to get off the beaten track without blowing your budget.

- Two- or three-day horse trip across the *jailoo* (summer pasture) from Kyzart, Jumgal or Kurtka (Jangy Talap) to Song-Köl, Kyrgyzstan. (p273)
- Four-day trek from Arslanbob to the holy lakes of the Köl-Mazar and on to Kyzyl Ünkur, Kyrgyzstan. (p287)
- Three-day trip from Kochkor to Köl-Ükök lake, Kyrgyzstan. (p278)
- Horse trek from Kyzyl-Oi to Balik Köl (two or three days), Kyrgyzstan. (p279)
- Six-day horse trek from Eki-Naryn to Bokonbayevo, Kyrgyzstan. (p282)
- Hunting with eagles in Bokonbayevo, Kyrgyzstan. (p272)
- Camel trekking for three days on the 'Roof of the World' at Rang-Kul. (p355)
- Excursion to Chatyr-Köl from Tash Rabat – day hike/horse trip or overnight at the lake, Kyrgyzstan. (p285)

Countries at a Glance

Kazakhstan is one of the last great blanks on the travel map, with interesting and quirky sites separated by vast amounts of nothing.

Tops for cultural travellers is Uzbekistan, home to historic Silk Road cities, epic architecture and the region's most stylish private guesthouses. Don't miss it.

Further south the vowel-challenged mountain republic of Kyrgyzstan is the place for outdoorsy types to find a grassroots adventure on the cheap. Plus it'll give you a gazillion points at Scrabble.

Tajikistan offers the region's most outlandish high-altitude scenery and its most stunning road trips. Fabulous trekking and the region's most humbling hospitality make this the cutting edge of adventure travel.

Turkmenistan is the 'North Korea of Central Asia' – hard to get into and a real curiosity once you are there.

Kazakhstan

Scenery
Steppe
Surreal

Scenery

Kazakhstan has an impressive range of scenery: for mountains, hike the Tian Shan valleys around Almaty; for valleys, try the ecotourism project at Aksu-Zhabagyly Nature Reserve; and for remote splendour, visit the Altay.

Steppe

The centre and north are the Kazakh heartland where Eurasian steppe meets Russian sub-Siberia. Labour camps, nature reserves, ecotourism and literary icons are the attractions.

Surreal

For moments of weird, nothing beats Kazakhstan; our favourites are the Aral Sea at Aralsk and the underground mosques in the deserts of Mangistau. For cutting-edge architecture in the middle of nowhere Astana is unrivalled.

p52

Uzbekistan

Architecture
Culture
History

Architecture

Uzbekistan boasts some of the Islamic world's greatest architecture. Samarkand, Bukhara and Khiva are the unmissable standouts, all offering epic ensembles and backstreet gems.

Chaikhana

Uzbekistan is the shashlyk-scented heartland of Central Asia. After a visit to photogenic bazaars in Andijon and Samarkand, join white-bearded *aksakals* (revered elders) for a pot of tea at the region's most atmospheric teahouses.

Empires

The centre of the Silk Road is the heartland of Timur, from his birthplace in Shakhrisabsz to his mausoleum in Samarkand; a land of despotic emirs, desert castles and the footprints of Alexander the Great and Chinggis (Genghis) Khan.

p137

Kyrgyzstan

Activities
Culture
Road Trips

Alpine Splendour

Forested valleys and summer pastures beg to be explored, either on foot or horseback. The Tian Shan mountains are the literal high point, dotted with gorgeous lakes.

Nomadic Life

Community-based homestays and yurts offer the keys to unlock the country. Use them as a base to learn how to make a *shyrdak* (felt carpet), hear a performance of the epic *Manas,* take in some traditional horse games or watch an eagle hunter in action.

Silk Routes

Ancient trading routes criss-cross Kyrgyzstan. From the 2000-year-old bazaar town of Osh take the high roads to the pitch-perfect caravanserai of Tash Rabat, before crossing the high passes to Kashgar.

p228

Tajikistan

Scenery
Road Trips
Culture

The Pamirs

Mountains are the big draw here, from the Fan Mountains in the west to the huge Pamir peaks in the east and the views of the Hindu Kush from the Wakhan Valley. Trek, drive, ride or climb; the landscapes are stunning.

Road Trips

Central Asia's most spectacular drive is from Khorog to Osh along the Pamir Highway, but the taxi rides from Penjikent to Dushanbe and around Khorog are also stunning. Hire a vehicle for a multiday adventure.

Homestays

The many homestays in the spectacular valleys of the western Pamirs or Fan Mountains offer humbling hospitality. Alternatively, experience the semi-nomadic life at a herder's yurt in the eastern Pamirs.

p312

Turkmenistan

History
Offbeat Travel
Desert

Lost Empires

The deserts are littered with the bones of the past. Five different cities make up Merv, once one of Asia's great cities, while the ruins of the Khorezmshah empire lie among the mausolea and minarets of Konye-Urgench.

Weird & Wonderful

Ashgabat is full of oddly grandiose buildings and surreal monuments to the cult of personality. From underground lakes to dinosaur footprints, almost everything in Turkmenistan is unexpected.

Desert

Cross the Karakum desert on the overland routes to Uzbekistan, stopping off at the burning crater pit at Darvaza. Come early in March for cooler temperatures and desert blooms.

p370

On the Road

Kazakhstan
p52
Kyrgyzstan
p228
Uzbekistan
p137
Turkmenistan
p370
Tajikistan
p312

Kazakhstan Казахстан

Includes ➡

Best Parks & Reserves

- Aksu-Zhabagyly (p85)
- Sayram-Ugam (p86)
- Korgalzhyn (p106)
- Ile-Alatau (p73)
- Altyn-Emel (p78)
- Kolsay Lakes (p76)

Best Architecture

- Yasaui Mausoleum (p88)
- Khan Shatyr (p98)
- Palace of Peace & Accord (p99)

Why Go?

The world's ninth-biggest country is the most economically advanced of the 'stans', thanks to its abundant reserves of oil and most other valuable minerals. This means generally better standards of accommodation, restaurants and transport than elsewhere in Central Asia. The biggest city, Almaty, is almost reminiscent of Europe with its leafy avenues, chic cafes, glossy shopping centres and hedonistic nightlife. The capital Astana, on the windswept northern steppe, has been transformed into a 21st-century showpiece with a profusion of bold futuristic architecture. But it's beyond the cities that you'll find the greatest travel adventures, whether hiking in the high mountains and green valleys of the Tian Shan, searching for wildlife on the lake-dotted steppe, enjoying home-spun hospitality in village guesthouses, or jolting across the western deserts to remote underground mosques.

When to Go

Almaty

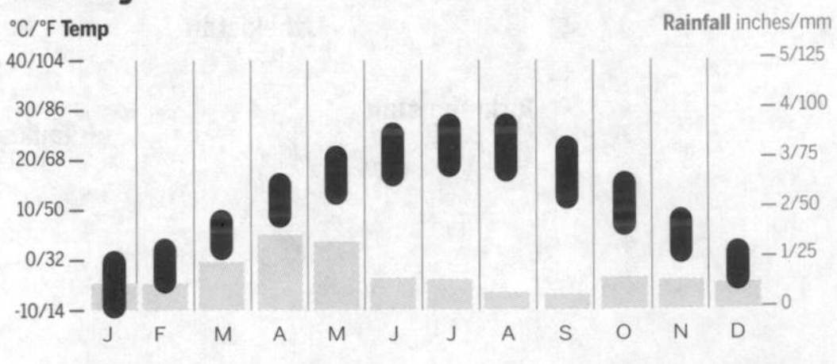

Mid-Apr–early Jun The steppe and hills blossom and migrating birds flock in.

May–Sep The weather is perfect and from July it's hiking season.

Nov–Apr It's cold, but skiers enjoy Central Asia's best facilities at Chimbulak.

Visas & Permits

Citizens of EU states, Australia, Canada, Israel, Japan, New Zealand, Norway, South Korea, Switzerland, the USA and some other countries can normally obtain tourist visas without a letter of invitation (LOI) at Kazakhstan consulates or embassies.

For most other visas you must obtain a LOI before applying, available through most travel agencies in Kazakhstan and Central Asia travel specialists in other countries, normally for US$50 to US$100. See p131 for further visas information. Registration is required if you are staying in Kazakhstan more than five days - see p127.

Special permits are needed to visit areas close to the Chinese border and are only available through tour firms taking you to these areas. Processing can take up to 45 days. See p129.

COSTS

Relative Cost

Slightly more expensive than Uzbekistan, cheaper than Turkmenistan.

Daily Expenses

- Hostel dorm (Almaty or Astana) 2000–2500T
- Comfortable hotel double 10,000T+
- Street snack 50–150T, good restaurant meal 2500T+
- Train from Almaty to Astana (1230km) *platskartny* (hard-sleeper train)/*kupeyny* (soft-sleeper train) 4030/6380T, plane 21,500T

Price Ranges

- **Sleeping** (per two people): $ <8000T, $$ 8000–20,000T, $$$ >20,000T
- **Eating** (main course): $ <1000T, $$ 1000–2000T, $$$ >2000T

Itineraries

- **Three days** Explore Almaty and make a trip into the mountains south of the city. If you're travelling on to Kyrgyzstan in summer, use the Karkara Valley crossing.
- **One week** Extend the three-day itinerary with time in southern Kazakhstan – Shymkent, lovely Aksu-Zhabagyly Nature Reserve and the splendour of Turkistan – or head for Astana, Kazakhstan's spectacular new capital.
- **One month** You can get round the whole country, taking in more adventurous and remote destinations such as the Aral Sea, the dramatic deserts outside Aktau, or the pristine, beautiful Altay Mountains in the northeast.

TOP TIP

Make the effort to get beyond Kazakhstan's cities to the beautiful mountain, steppe or desert country, and the hospitality of rural homestays and guesthouses. Side trips to Aksu-Zhabagyly Nature Reserve or Sayram-Ugam National Park are easy.

Fast Facts

- **Area** 2.7 million sq km
- **Capital** Astana
- **Country code** ☎7
- **Languages** Kazakh, Russian
- **Population** 17 million
- **Famous for** oil, steppe, Borat

Exchange Rates

COUNTRY	UNIT	TENGE
Australia	A$1	140T
Canada	C$1	148T
China	Y1	25T
Euro zone	€1	203T
Japan	Y100	160T
NZ	NZ$1	123T
Russia	R10	46T
UK	UK£1	237T
USA	US$1	153T

Resources

- www.visitkazakhstan.kz
- www.kazakhembus.com
- www.en.tengrinews.kz
- www.timeout.kz
- www.afisha.kz
- www.voxpopuli.kz

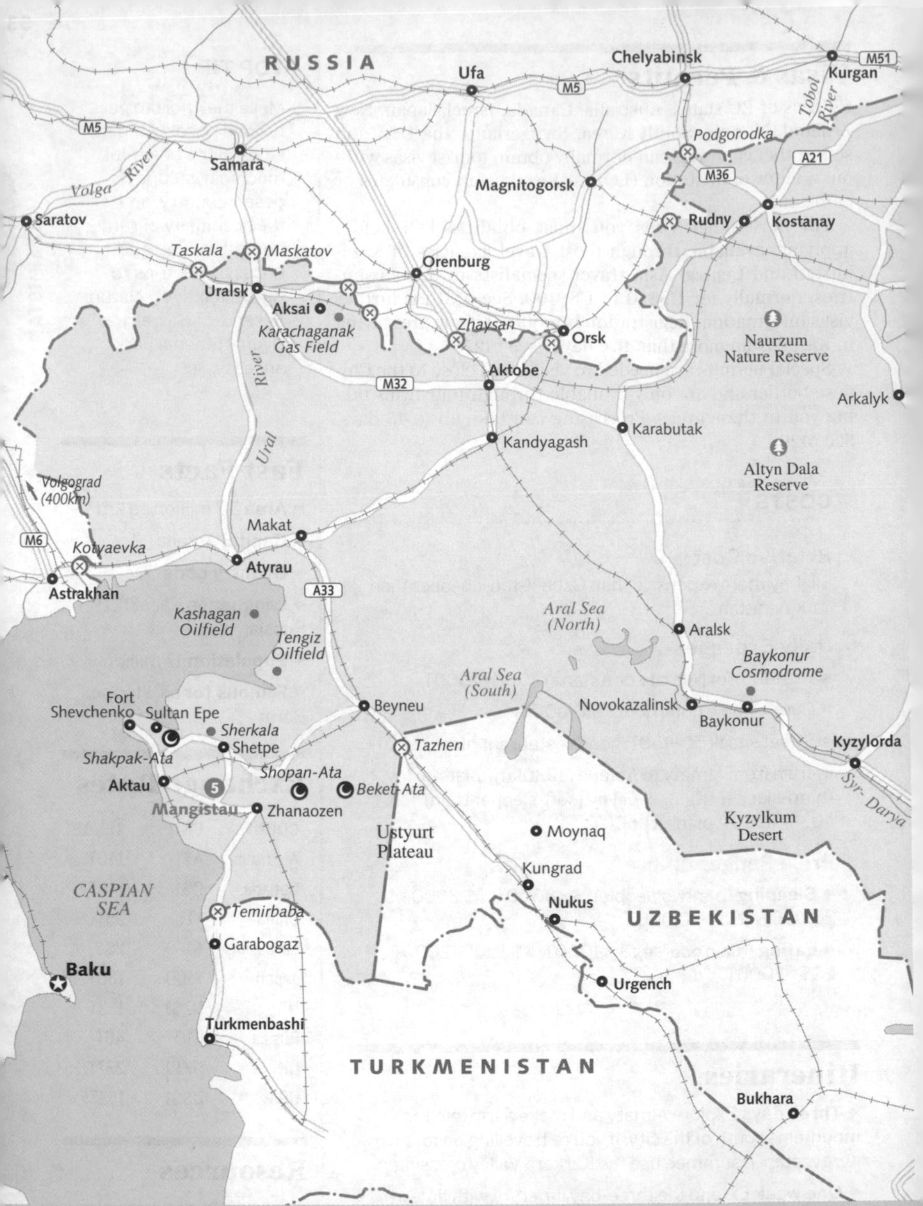

Kazakhstan Highlights

1. Explore **Almaty** (p56), the leafy, sophisticated metropolis with spectacular mountains on its doorstep.

2. Hike, homestay and horse ride amid gorgeous mountain scenery in **Aksu-Zhabagyly Nature Reserve** (p85).

3. Be awed by 21st-century fantasy architecture in the brand-new capital of **Astana** (p98).

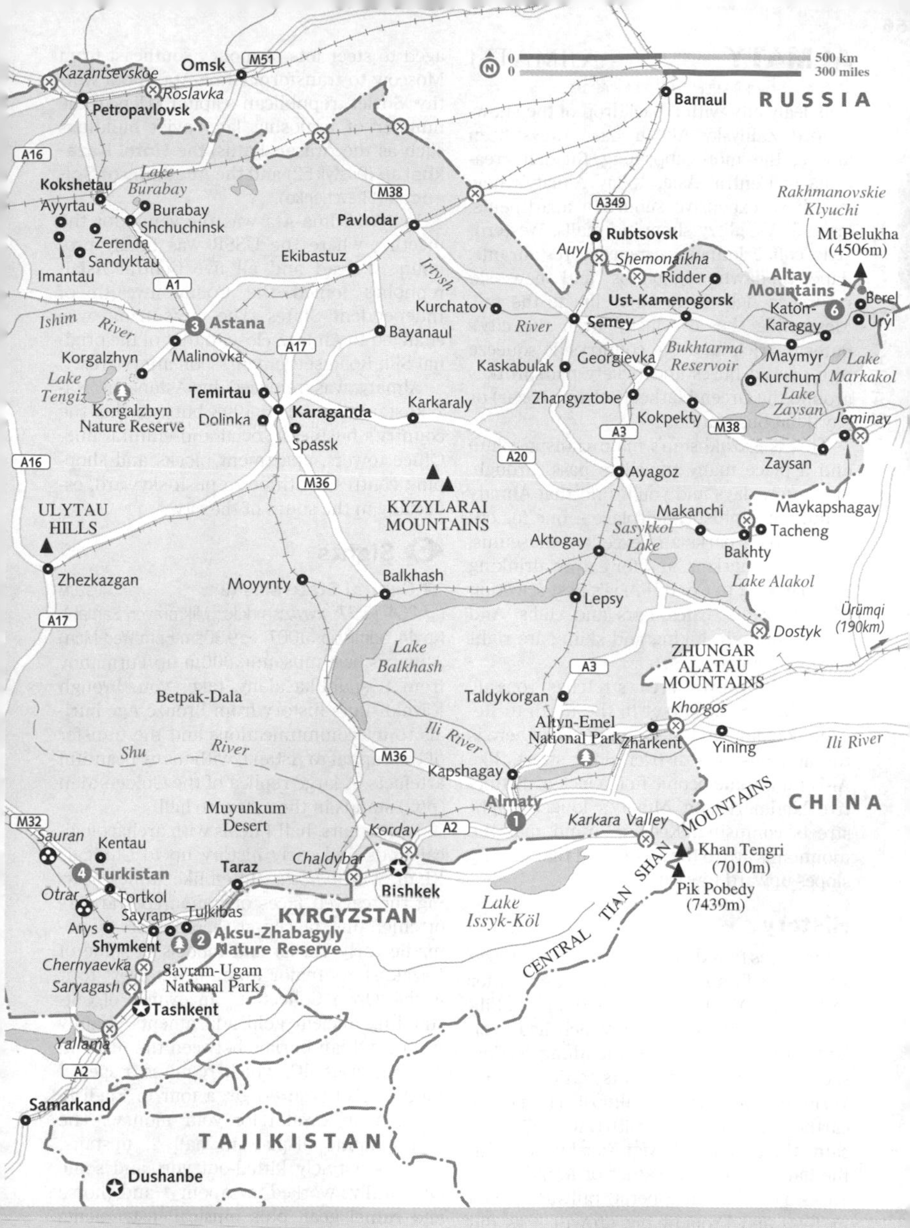

4 Visit the beautiful Timurid architecture at the country's holiest site at **Turkistan** (p87).

5 Explore remote desert country, honeycombed with canyons, underground mosques and ancient necropolises at **Mangistau** (p96).

6 Visit the **Altay Mountains** (p111), a pristine, green, eastern region of mountains and lakes, with great trekking and touring – but plan ahead for the required border-zone permit.

ALMATY АЛМАТЫ

☎727 / POP 1.4 MILLION / ELEV 850M

This leafy city with a backdrop of the snow-capped Zailiysky Alatau has always been among the more appealing Russian creations in Central Asia. Today Almaty's new rich have expensive suburban apartments, large SUVs, glitzy shopping malls, Western-style coffee lounges, expensive restaurants, dance-till-dawn nightclubs and new ski resorts to help them enjoy life to the full. Meanwhile the less lucky from the city's outer districts and the countryside squeeze into packed buses and rickety marshrutkas around the Green Market (Zelyony Bazar) or Sayakhat bus station.

This is Kazakhstan's main transport hub and a place many travellers pass through. Stay a few days and you'll find that Almaty is quite a sophisticated place – one for enjoying green parks and excellent museums, shops and markets, and for eating, drinking and partying in Central Asia's best selection of restaurants, cafes, bars and clubs. And great mountain hiking and skiing are right on the doorstep.

The downtown area stretches roughly from the Green Market in the north to Respublika alany in the south. South of here is the new business district along streets like Al-Farabi. Some people find a lack of distinctive landmarks on Almaty's long, straight streets confusing. Keep in mind that the mountains are to the south, and that the city slopes upward towards them.

History

Almaty was founded in 1854, when the Kazakhs were still nomads, as a Russian frontier fort named Verny, on the site of an old Silk Road oasis called Almatu, which had been laid waste long before by the Mongols. Cossacks and Siberian peasants settled around Verny, but the town was almost flattened by earthquakes in 1887 and 1911. In 1927, it became the capital of Soviet Kazakhstan, with the name Alma-Ata (Father of Apples). The Turksib (Turkestan–Siberia) railway arrived in 1930 and brought big growth – as did WWII, when factories were relocated here from Nazi-threatened western USSR and many Slavs came to work in them. Numbers of ethnic Koreans, forcibly resettled from the Russian Far East, arrived too.

In the 1970s and '80s Kazakhstan's leader Dinmukhamed Kunaev, the only Central Asian member of the Soviet Politburo, managed to steer lots of money southeast from Moscow to transform Alma-Ata into a worthy Soviet republican capital. Hence the number of imposing late-Soviet buildings such as the Arasan Baths, the **Hotel Kazakhstan** (Dostyk 52) and the **Academy of Sciences** (Shevchenko).

In 1991 Alma-Ata was the venue for the meeting where the USSR was finally pronounced dead and all five Central Asian republics joined the Commonwealth of Independent States. The city's name was changed to Almaty, close to that of the original Silk Road settlement, soon afterwards.

Almaty was replaced by Astana as Kazakhstan's capital in 1998 but remains the country's business, social and cultural hub. Office towers, apartment blocks and shopping centres continue to push skyward, especially in the south of the city.

Sights

★Central State Museum MUSEUM

(☎264 55 77; www.csmrk.kz; Mikrorayon Samal-1, No 44; admission 100T; ⏲9.30am-6pm Wed-Mon) Almaty's best museum, 300m up Furmanov from Respublika alany, takes you through Kazakhstan's history from Bronze Age burials to telecommunications and the transfer of the capital to Astana, with many beautiful artefacts. A large replica of the Golden Man (p62) stands in the entrance hall.

Downstairs, hall 1 deals with archaeological finds and early history up to Chinggis Khan, with *balbals* (totemlike stones bearing the carved faces of honoured warriors or chieftains, placed at sacred spots by nomadic early Turks) and models of some of Kazakhstan's major monuments. Next to it is the 'Open Collection', an exhibit of outstanding ancient gold adornments, mainly from Scythian burials between the 6th and 3rd centuries BC, which requires a special 1300T ticket (you do get a tour in English, Russian or Kazakh for your money). The ethnographic display in hall 2, upstairs, features a finely kitted-out yurt and some beautifully worked weaponry and horse and camel gear, plus musical instruments and exotic costumes going back to the 18th century. Halls 3 and 4 on floor 4 deal with the 20th and 21st centuries, including exhibits on some of Kazakhstan's many ethnic groups. It's just a pity that the museum's signage in nonlocal languages is limited to 'Don't touch, please!' Get there by bus 2, 63, 73 or 86 up Furmanov.

★Kok-Tobe HILL

(Green Hill; http://kok-tobe.kz) This 1100m hill on the city's southeast edge is crowned by a 372m-high TV tower visible from far and wide, and affords great views over the city and the mountains, plus an assortment of attractions at the top. The easy way up is by the smooth **cable car** (one-way/return 1000/2000T; ⏰every 15min 11am-midnight Mon, Wed & Thu, 6pm-midnight Tue, 11am-1am Fri-Sun), which glides up in six minutes from beside the **Palace of the Republic** (☎291 35 61; Dostyk 56).

At the top you'll find assorted cafes and restaurants, craft shops, a roller-coaster, a minizoo, a children's playground – and life-sized bronze statues of the four Beatles, placed here on the initiative of local fans in 2007. The work of Almaty sculptor Eduard Kazaryan, this is claimed to be the world's only monument showing all the Fab Four together. You can sit beside a guitar-strumming John on the bench.

The cable car and other facilities may close early, or not open at all, in poor weather. The cheaper way up Kok-Tobe is by bus 95 (opposite Ramstor on Furmanov) or 99 (south up Abylay Khan, east on Abay, south on Dostyk) to their terminus on Omarova, where a **shuttle minibus** (one-way/return 300/500T, every few minutes from 10am to 1am), runs the final 1.25km up the hill.

Panfilov Park PARK

(btwn Gogol & Qazybek Bi) This large and attractive rectangle of greenery is one of central Almaty's most popular strolling and hangout places for all ages. At its heart stands the candy-coloured **Zenkov Cathedral**, Kazakhstan's nearest (albeit distant) relative to St Basil's Cathedral and one of Almaty's few surviving tsarist-era buildings. Designed by AP Zenkov in 1904, the cathedral is built entirely of wood (including the nails).

Used as a museum and concert hall in Soviet times, it was returned to the Russian Orthodox Church in 1995 and has been restored with colourful icons and murals. Services are held at 8am and 5pm.

The park is named for the Panfilov Heroes, 28 soldiers of an Almaty infantry unit who died fighting off Nazi tanks in a village outside Moscow in 1941. They are commemorated at the fearsome **war memorial** east of the cathedral, which depicts soldiers from all 15 Soviet republics bursting out of a map of the USSR. An eternal flame honouring the fallen of 1917–20 (the Civil War) and 1941–45 (WWII) flickers in front of the giant black monument.

Kazakh Museum of Folk Musical Instruments MUSEUM

(☎291 69 17; Zenkov 24; ⏰9am-5pm Tue-Sun) In a striking 1908 wooden building (another work of cathedral architect Zenkov) at the east end of Panfilov Park, the city's most original museum reopened in mid-2013 after a full revamp. As well as seeing and hearing its fine collection of traditional Kazakh instruments – wooden harps and horns, bagpipes, the lutelike two-stringed *dombra* and the violalike *kobyz* – there is now the chance to take classes in playing some of them.

Kazakhstan Museum of Arts MUSEUM

(☎394 57 18; www.gmirk.kz; Mikrorayon Koktem-3, No 22/1; admission 100T; ⏰10am-6pm Tue-Sun) This is the best art collection in the country, with Kazakh, Russian and some Western European art and a room of top-class modern Kazakh handicrafts, with much explanatory

CITY & STREET NAMES

Kazakh names replaced the Soviet-era Russian names of most Kazakhstan cities in the 1990s (Almaty for Alma-Ata, Taraz for Dzhambul, Semey for Semipalatinsk, Aktau for Shevchenko). In a few cases, mostly in the heavily ethnic-Russian north, the old names are still more commonly used: more people talk of Uralsk rather than Oral, and of Ust-Kamenogorsk than Oskemen.

Many street names too were changed after independence, but two decades later many locals are still more familiar with the old Soviet names. In central Almaty, the main north–south streets are Dostyk (formerly Lenina), Konaev (Karla Marxa), Furmanov, Abylay Khan (Kommunistichesky), Zheltoksan (Mira) and Seyfullin. The key east–west streets are Zhibek Zholy (Gorkogo), Gogol, Tole Bi (Komsomolskaya), Abay and Satpaev. When telling taxi drivers where you want to go, it's often easiest to give the nearest street corner (*ugol* in Russian), and you'll sound less like an Almaty novice if you use the Soviet street names (eg *'ugol Lenina i Komosomolskaya'*).

Almaty

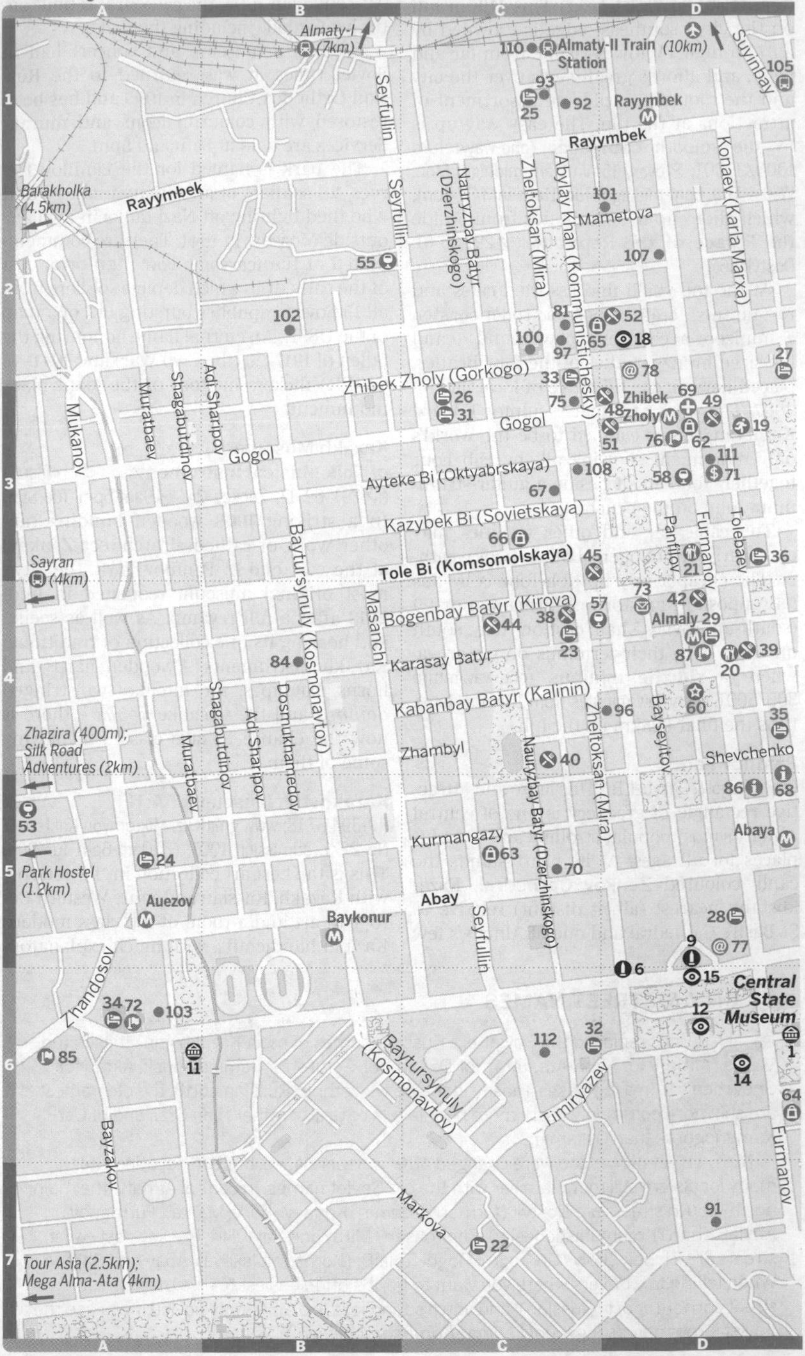

Almaty-I (7km)
110 Almaty-II Train Station
(10km)
Suyinbay
105
93
25
92
Rayymbek
Rayymbek
Seyfullin
Barakholka (4.5km)
Rayymbek
Nauryzbay Batyr (Dzerzhinskogo)
Zheltoksan (Mira)
Abylay Khan (Kommunistichesky)
Konaev (Karla Marxa)
101
Mametova
107
55
102
81
52
65
18
100
97
27
78
33
Zhibek Zholy (Gorkogo)
26
31
75
Zhibek Zholy
69
49
48
19
76
62
51
Gogol
Mukanov
Muratbaev
Shagabutdinov
Adi Sharipov
Gogol
111
108
58
71
Ayteke Bi (Oktyabrskaya)
67
Kazybek Bi (Sovietskaya)
66
Panfilov
Furmanov
Tolebaev
Sayran (4km)
Tole Bi (Komsomolskaya)
45
21
36
Baytursynuly (Kosmonavtov)
Masanchi
73
Bogenbay Batyr (Kirova)
57
42
38
44
Almaly 29
23
87
39
20
84
Karasay Batyr
Kabanbay Batyr (Kalinin)
96
Bayseyitov
60
Shagabutdinov
Adi Sharipov
Dosmukhamedov
Muratbaev
Zheltoksan (Mira)
35
Zhazira (400m); Silk Road Adventures (2km)
Zhambyl
Nauryzbay Batyr (Dzerzhinskogo)
40
Shevchenko
86
68
53
Abaya
Kurmangazy
63
70
24
Park Hostel (1.2km)
Auezov
Abay
Baykonur
Seyfullin
28
9
77
6
15
Central State Museum
12
Zhandosov
34
72
103
112
32
1
85
11
Baytursynuly (Kosmonavtov)
14
Timiryazev
64
Bayzakov
Furmanov
Markova
91
22
Tour Asia (2.5km); Mega Alma-Ata (4km)

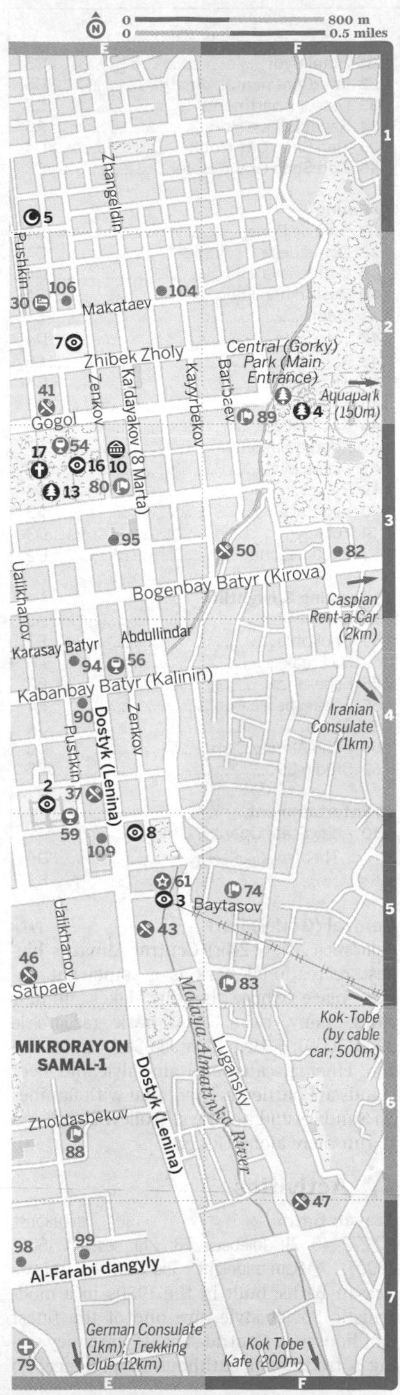

material in English. Particularly interesting are the room on Russia's Mir Iskusstva movement and the large collection of paintings by Kazakh Abylkhan Kasteev (1904–73).

Kasteev's clear portraits, landscapes and scenes of Soviet progress (railways, collective farming) obviously toed the party line but his technique is fabulous. Bus 95 west along Satpaev from Furmanov gets you here.

Green Market MARKET

(Zelyony Bazar, Kok Bazar; ☎273 89 61; Zhibek Zholy 53; ⏰8am-6pm Tue-Sun) This large, two-level market has a true flavour of Central Asia, and is worth putting on your itinerary even if you're not really food shopping. Stalls are piled with nuts, fresh and dried fruit, smoked fish, spices, ready-made Korean salads, vegetables, medicinal herbs, cheeses, sausages and enormous hunks of fresh meat.

You can get *kymyz* (fermented horse milk), *shubat* (fermented camel's milk) and freshly squeezed pomegranate juice here too – and cafes dotted around the place will serve a bowl of *laghman* (long, stout noodles) or *plov* (fried rice with vegetables and sometimes meat) with tea and bread for less than 600T.

Respublika Alany PLAZA

This broad, Soviet-created ceremonial square provides a panoramic view of the snowcapped mountains on a clear morning. Its focus is the tall **Independence Monument**. The stone column is surmounted with a replica Golden Man standing on a winged snow leopard. Around its base are statues of a Kazakh family; behind is a semicircular wall of low-relief bronze sculptures depicting scenes from Kazakhstan's history, from Golden Man times at the left end to Nazarbaev at the right.

Overlooking the square from the south is the neoclassical-style **Maslikhat** (City Council) building. Southeast of here, opposite the Central State Museum, is a large official **Presidential Residence** (Furmanov 205). At the top of Zheltoksan, the striking **Dawn of Freedom Monument** honours those killed and injured on Respublika alany on 17 December 1986 during the Zheltoksan (December) protests, the first unrest unleashed in Central Asia by the Gorbachev era of glasnost. Possibly as many as 250 people were killed when police opened fire on rioters protesting against the appointment of a Russian, Gennady Kol-

Almaty

Top Sights

1	Central State Museum	D6

Sights

2	Academy of Sciences	E4
3	Cable Car	E5
4	Central (Gorky) Park	F2
5	Central Mosque	E1
6	Dawn of Freedom Monument	D6
7	Green Market	E2
8	Hotel Kazakhstan	E5
9	Independence Monument	D5
10	Kazakh Museum of Folk Musical Instruments	E3
11	Kazakhstan Museum of Arts	A6
12	Maslikhat	D6
13	Panfilov Park	E3
14	Presidential Residence	D6
15	Respublika Alany	D6
16	War Memorial	E3
17	Zenkov Cathedral	E3
18	Zhibek Zholy	D2

Activities, Courses & Tours

19	Arasan Baths	D3
20	Fischer	D4
21	Snowshop	D3

Sleeping

22	Almaty Backpackers	C7
23	Ambassador Hotel	C4
24	Apple Hostel	A5
25	Hotel Astra	C1
26	Hotel Kazzhol	C3
27	Hotel Otrar	D2
28	Hotel Saulet	D5
29	Hotel Saya	D4
30	Hotel Turkistan	E2
31	Hotel Uyut	C3
32	InterContinental Almaty	C6
33	Lessor Apartments	C2
34	Rahat Palace Hotel	A6
35	Tien Shan City Hotel	D4
36	Tien Shan Grand Hotel	D3

Eating

37	Café de Paris	E4
38	Coffeedelia	C4
39	Coffeedelia	D4
40	Dastarkhan Food	C4
41	Eldoro	E2
42	Entrecôte	D4
43	Kaganat	E5
44	Kaganat	C4
45	Kaganat	C3
46	Kaganat	E5
47	Khodja Nasreddin	F7
48	Mama Mia	D3
49	Restoran Printsessa	D3
50	Venetsia	F3
51	Yubileyny	D3
52	Zheti Kazyna	D2

Drinking & Nightlife

53	Bar Pivnitsa	A5
54	Chukotka	E3
	Da Freak	(see 54)
55	Esperanza	B2
56	Shakespeare Pub	E4
57	Shtab	C4
58	Soho Almaty Club	D3
59	Studio 69	E5

Entertainment

60	Abay State Opera & Ballet Theatre	D4

bin, as head of the Kazakhstan Communist Party. You can reach Respublika alany on bus 2, 63, 73 or 86 up Furmanov to the corner of Satpaev.

Zhibek Zholy STREET

(Arbat) The pedestrianised stretch of this street in the lower, northern, part of the centre is Almaty's (sort of) version of Moscow's Arbat. It's dotted with inexpensive cafes, a few buskers and kitsch art stands.

Central Mosque MOSQUE

(Pushkin 16) Almaty's multitowered, gold-domed, white-marble central mosque, built in 1999, is one of the largest in the country, with space for 3000 worshippers in the finely decorated main prayer hall. It's open for visits daily except Friday; women must cover their heads, arms and legs.

Central (Gorky) Park PARK

(admission 70T; 24hr) Central Almaty's biggest recreational park is a somewhat untidy place whose boating lakes, funfair rides, pony rides, **Aquapark** (adult/child 3900/3000T; 11am-10pm Jun-Sep), rather sad zoo, cinema, cafes and shashlyk and beer stands are particularly popular with families on Sundays and holidays. Trolleybuses 1 and 12 run there along Gogol.

Activities

Arasan Baths BATHHOUSE

(272 46 71; Tolebaev 78; 2hr session 1600-2900T; 8am-midnight Tue-Sun) Almaty's Arasan Baths, built in the 1980s in a modernistic Soviet style, are one of the finest bathhouses in Central Asia. If you fancy trying a traditional bathhouse experience, go

61 Palace of the Republic E5

Shopping

62 Akademkniga D3
Amanulla Shafii .... (see 28)
Central State Museum .... (see 1)
63 Limpopo C5
64 Ramstor D6
65 Robinzon C2
66 Silk Way City C3

Information

67 A13 .... C3
68 Almaty Info Centre D5
Altyn-Emel National Park Office .... (see 81)
69 Apteka No 2 .... D3
70 Arnai Tours C5
71 ATF Bank D3
72 British Embassy Office A6
73 Central Post Office D4
74 Chinese Consulate F5
75 DHL C3
Ecotourism Information Resource Centre .... (see 68)
76 French Consulate D3
77 Gosu D5
78 Gosu D2
79 Interteach E7
80 Japanese Embassy Office E3
81 Jibek Joly C2
82 Kan Tengri F3
Kazakhstan Tourism Association .... (see 68)
83 Kyrgyz Consulate F5
84 Migration Police B4
85 Russian Consulate A6
86 Tourist Information Center D5
87 Turkmen Consulate D4
88 US Consulate E6
89 Uzbek Embassy F2
Web Club .... (see 64)

Transport

90 Air Arabia E4
91 Air Astana D7
Asiana Airlines .... (see 8)
92 Atameken C1
93 Bakhytty Zhol C1
94 British Airways E4
95 China Southern Airlines E3
96 Czech Airlines D4
97 Dixie Travel C2
98 Etihad Airways E7
99 Europcar E7
100 Gorodskoy Aerovokzal C2
101 Hainan Airlines D2
International Airport Almaty (agency) .... (see 100)
102 KLM B2
103 Lufthansa A6
104 Rent A Car Ivan E2
S7 .... (see 56)
105 Sayakhat Bus Station D1
106 Somon Air E2
Tajik Air .... (see 106)
107 Transaero D2
108 Transavia C3
109 Transavia E5
110 Turan Express kiosk C1
111 Turkish Airlines D3
Turkmenistan Airlines .... (see 100)
112 Ukraine International Airlines C6

with a friend or two and you'll find it's an enjoyable and relaxing experience, and the routine is easy to pick up. You can choose from Russian-Finnish or oriental baths, each with men's and women's sections.

Private rooms for four to six people (6000T to 10,000T) are also available. Stalls in the lobby sell soap, towels, flip-flops and *veniki* (bunches of oak and birch leaves for lashing yourself to stimulate the circulation). All sorts of massages are on offer too.

Tours

Alma Team CITY TOUR

(☎705-146 3963; almateam@lenta.ru; 3hr tour 4000T) Recommended city tours with English- and/or German-speaking students or ex-students of Almaty's German-Kazakh University, who have guide training and present their city and country from a fresh, personal viewpoint. Itineraries are geared to customers' interests.

Festivals & Events

As well as regular annual events, frequent one-off festivals of music, food, cinema and more brighten up Almaty's calendar – check www.afisha.kz or www.timeout.kz.

Nauryz CULTURAL FESTIVAL

(Navrus) The big spring festival on 22 March and celebrated throughout Central Asia, sees colourful parades in the city, and horse racing and often *kokpar* (*buzkashi;* the traditional Central Asian polo-like sport played with a headless goat carcass) at the **Hippodrome** (☎294 86 00; Zhansugirov) several kilometres north of the centre.

THE GOLDEN MAN – OR WOMAN?

The Golden Man (Altyn Adam in Kazakh) is a warrior's costume from about the 5th century BC that was found in 1969 in a Saka tomb near Yesik (Issik), about 60km east of Almaty. It is made of more than 4000 separate gold pieces, many of them finely worked with animal motifs, and has a 70cm-high headdress bearing skyward-pointing arrows, a pair of snarling snow leopards and a two-headed winged mythical beast. The Golden Man has become modern Kazakhstan's favourite national symbol.

The conventional wisdom is that the skeleton found inside the costume was that of a young Saka prince killed in battle. But there is a strong countercurrent of thought that the Golden Man was in fact a Golden Woman, and that Kazakhstan's nation-makers have deliberately misrepresented the gender to suit Kazakh stereotypes. Archaeologist Jeannine Davis-Kimball argues in *Warrior Women* (2002) that the body was too badly damaged for its gender to be determined, and that other goods in the tomb suggest it was a woman. One intriguing school of thought identifies the Golden Woman with Tomiris, a queen of the Massagetes tribe who defeated the invading forces of Persian emperor Cyrus the Great.

The original Golden Man is apparently kept safe in the National Bank building in Almaty, but replicas adorn museums all over the country.

International Jazz Festival MUSIC FESTIVAL
(www.jazz.kz) International artists jam it up in various venues over several days in April.

FourEFestival ALTERNATIVE FESTIVAL
(www.ecofest.kz) This 'eco-ethno-emotional-evolution festival' brings together three days of yoga, art, workshops and ethnic and spiritual music in a different natural location outside Almaty each August. No alcohol or tobacco!

Eurasia International Film Festival FILM FESTIVAL
Free screenings of dozens of films, mostly from CIS countries but some from Western Europe, over several days, plus occasional fly-ins by Hollywood celebs. Held in September.

Almaty Day CITY FESTIVAL
The annual city festival on 16 Spetember sees numerous indoor and outdoor musical events and exhibitions (usually with one dedicated to locally grown apples), and fireworks.

Sleeping

Except for a handful of travellers' hostels, accommodation in Almaty is expensive for what you get. There's very little at normal midrange prices, though international apartment-rental site **airbnb** (www.airbnb.com) has a good range of apartments from around 8000T. There's no shortage of classy 35,000T-plus hotels for those who are probably not paying their own bills.

Apple Hostel HOSTEL $
(☎701-220 2275; www.apple-hostel.kz; Kvartira 95, 2nd fl, Blok B, Zhiloy Kompleks Zhastar-1, Kurmangazy 145; dm 2800T;) The Apple has a friendly atmosphere and welcoming English-speaking owner, and is reasonably well located one block north of Auezov metro station. It offers male and female dorms, one twin room (same price), a decent kitchen, a pleasant carpeted sitting/eating room, two bathrooms, and a free washing machine.

The entrance is from the yard behind the building: dial 95 on the keypad if you find the right door – or phone them to come out and meet you. Airport transfers available for 2500T.

Almaty Backpackers HOSTEL $
(Silk Road Backpackers; ☎778-951 1711; almatybackpackers@gmail.com; Markov 46A; dm 1900-2900T, s/d 3400/6600T;) Though still being built at research time, this hostel was already open and shaping up to be one of the best in town. It's certainly the most spacious, with large rooms and a good outdoor area where a sociable atmosphere can develop. All rooms, including the dorms (three to six bunks), have their own bathrooms, there's a good kitchen and the washing machine is free.

You can get there by bus 79 from the airport. Get off at the corner of Timiryazev and Markov and walk 200m south: the hostel is a two-storey building behind Markov 46.

Park Hostel HOSTEL $
(☎707-470 8005; www.hostel-almaty.kz; Shevchenko 190; dm 2000T; 📶) Though west of the central area (a 700m walk north from Alatau metro station), the Park is cosy, well-equipped, clean and friendly, with male, female and mixed dorms (three to six people) and a good kitchen. Washing machine, coffee, tea and drinking water are free.

The entrance is at the back of the building, towards the east end, with a small sign outside when we visited.

Lessor Apartments APARTMENT $
(☎279 50 74; www.lessor.kz; office Zheltoksan 74; apt US$49-80; ⊙office 10am-9pm; ❄📶) Lessor rents out ordinary city-centre apartments for two to four people with kitchen and bathroom, most within a five-minute walk of its office. They have normal local home furnishings, so you get some sense of what local living is like. If you book ahead then call on arrival in Almaty, staff will explain how to reach your apartment and will meet you there. The office entrance is on Zhibek Zholy.

Hotel Saulet HOTEL $
(☎263 47 10; www.hotel-saulet.kz; Furmanov 187; dm 3000T, d 8000-18,000T, all incl breakfast; ❄📶) The Saulet's bare, clean, non-AC, five-person dorms – with single beds or bunks, toilet, basin and shared showers – are an acceptable budget option. The more expensive rooms are reasonably pleasant if you're looking for a midrange private room. The sign above the door just says 'Hotel Konak Uy Gostinitsa' ('hotel' in three languages).

Hotel Turkistan HOTEL $
(☎266 41 36; www.turkistan-hotel.kz; Makataev 49; s with shared shower 3000T, r with private bathroom 6500-8000T; 🚭❄📶) This hotel opposite the Green Market, used by many regional traders, is reasonable value but security is not the tightest. Standard rooms are in reasonable condition and have carpets, small bathtub and (if facing the street) balconies.

Hotel Astra HOTEL $$
(☎246 86 88; www.astra-hotel.kz; Zheltoksan 12; s 13,800T, d 16,800-18,000T, incl breakfast; 🚭❄📶🏊) A short walk from Almaty-II train station, this is a relatively good-value place with professional, English-speaking reception and pleasant, clean, carpeted rooms. The restaurant serves all meals and the bar never closes.

Hotel Saya HOTEL $$
(☎272 32 65; www.saya-hotel.kz; Furmanov 135; r incl breakfast 15,600-20,700T; P❄📶) Helpful, Russian-speaking staff and just 15 unexciting if well-equipped rooms. The breakfast is spartan but this is as near a sensible price as you'll get for a midrange-quality hotel in Almaty.

★ **Hotel Kazzhol** HOTEL $$$
(☎250 50 16; www.hotelkazzhol.kz; Gogol 127/1; s 13,000-38,000T, d 24,000-42,500T, incl breakfast; P🚭❄@📶🏊) The cheaper rooms in this efficient, sparkling-clean hotel on a quiet lane off Zhibek Zholy are the best value at this price level. Desk staff speak English, and the smart rooms all have writing desks and international satellite TV. Breakfast is a good buffet and the fitness centre has a 20m pool. Airport and station transfers available.

Ambassador Hotel HOTEL $$$
(☎250 89 89; www.ambassadorhotel.kz; Zheltoksan 121; s/d incl breakfast 33,600/44,800T; P❄@📶) A very good medium-sized hotel in the heart of the city, in a modernised 1930s building with classical decor and a good Turkish/European restaurant. Free airport pickups are offered, and there are 30% discounts on Saturday, Sunday and other days if rooms are available. Wi-fi is US$14 per day.

InterContinental Almaty HOTEL $$$
(☎250 50 00; www.intercontinental.com; Zheltoksan 181; r incl breakfast from 53,600T; P🚭❄@📶🏊) This glitzy high-rise is the lodging of choice for many foreign businessfolk. It has plenty of five-star amenities, including four restaurants, a classy fitness centre (with pool) and spa, tennis courts and a beer garden. Rooms are very comfy. Rates are generally lower from Friday to Sunday nights.

Tien Shan Grand Hotel HOTEL $$$
(☎244 96 99; www.tienshanhotels.com; Bogenbay Batyr 115; s/d incl breakfast from 33,000/37,000T; P🚭❄@📶🏊) An elegant hotel in the handsome former Geology Ministry building, with attractive, good-sized rooms and friendly staff. Rates include an excellent spa with saunas and a good pool.

Hotel Uyut HOTEL $$$
(☎279 55 11; www.hotel-uyut.kz; Gogol 127/1; s 13,000-37,500T, d 23,500-42,000T, incl breakfast; P🚭❄@📶) The Uyut has a traditionally

ornate decor, and is a welcoming and, as its name translates, cosy place to hang your head.

Tien Shan City Hotel HOTEL $$$
(393 05 99; www.tienshanhotels.com; Konaev 151; s/d incl breakfast 21,000/25,000T;) This hotel has excellent, huge, carpeted and well-equipped rooms with balcony, and a friendly, English-speaking reception.

Rahat Palace Hotel HOTEL $$$
(250 12 34; www.rahatpalace.com; Satpaev 29/6; s/d incl breakfast from 44,800/51,520T;) A classy business-oriented hotel with more reasonable rates than most competitors, the Rahat boasts two good restaurants, a spa as well as a fitness centre with pool, and a summer beer garden. Glass lifts glide up and down its glass-domed lobby, and the good-size rooms have big, comfy beds and, on the upper floors at the front, panoramic views.

Hotel Otrar HOTEL $$$
(250 68 69; www.group.kz; Gogol 73; s/d incl breakfast from 22,000/24,000T;) Well situated facing Panfilov Park, the Otrar is a modernised Soviet establishment whose well-kept rooms are equipped with comfy beds, red carpets, polished wood furniture, balconies and bathtubs. Enjoy the good buffet breakfast in a fancy dining room.

Eating

You won't find a better range of good restaurants anywhere else in Central Asia. A large range of international cuisines is represented and there's also plenty of variety at the budget end.

There are plenty of large, well-stocked supermarkets with both local and imported goods on their shelves. **Yubileyny** (250 75 50; cnr Gogol & Abylay Khan; 24hr) is one of the biggest central supermarkets, with a huge wine section, among other temptations. There are several quick-eat and take-away food options out front, too, with inexpensive *bliny* (pancakes), *manty* (steamed dumplings), *samsa* (pastry pies), *khachapuri* (Georgian cheese bread), *baursaki* (fried dough balls or triangles) and more. For fresh produce, don't miss the Green Market (p59).

Kok Tobe Kafe CENTRAL ASIAN $
(cnr Omarova & Tattimbet; shashlyk 400-800T; noon-10pm approx Apr-Sep) For terrific tender shashlyk, grilled to a turn, at good prices, it's hard to beat this semi-open-air summer cafe known by expats as 'The Pit' (for its toilet, but don't let that put you off). The 14 varieties on offer run from pork to liver to duck but the good old *baranina* (lamb) is tops. They do good salads, *dolma* (stuffed vine leaves) and *khachapuri*, and plenty of well-priced beer, too.

An added attraction is that it overlooks the Malaya Almatinka riverside path, a favourite with fashionable walkers, joggers and bikers (and a nice way to get to the cafe!).

Dastarkhan Food CAFETERIA $
(267 37 37; www.dastarkhan-food.kz; Nauryzbay Batyr 122/124; mains 350-1000T; 24hr;) This superior cafeteria with attractive decor and spacious layout serves up a big choice of well-prepared dishes from salads, soups and *bliny* to *laghman, plov,* Korean *kuksi* (noodle, meat and vegetable soup) and assorted fish and meat mains. Draught beer too. Long lunchtime queues Monday to Friday.

Zhazira CENTRAL ASIAN $
(375 40 46; Zhambyl 175; mains 500-1100T; 10am-10pm;) There's very good Dungan (Chinese Muslim) food at this clean and efficient spot. You can't go wrong with the *guyru* or *suyru laghman* (both with strips of meat – the *suyru* has larger strips of meat). Four people could share the spicy chicken-and-potato dish *dapan-dzhi* (2400T; large platter of spiced chicken and potatoes).

Kaganat CAFETERIA $
(mains 300-800T; 8am-10pm;) This popular cafeteria chain will feed you satisfactorily and cheaply all day. Soups, salads, breads, assorted hot mains and desserts are on offer. There are branches at: **Abylay Khan** (261 75 22; Abylay Khan 105); **Bogenbay Batyr** (267 60 96; Bogenbay Batyr 148); **Dostyk** (264 02 46; Dostyk 108); and **Satpaev** (255 86 82; Satpaev 7A).

★ **Coffeedelia** CAFE $$
(sandwiches, pasta & pizzas 1200-2400T, coffee, tea, & cakes 300-900T; 8am-midnight Mon-Fri, 9am-midnight Sat & Sun;) This fashionable coffee house with a relaxed atmosphere, fabulous cakes and pastries, and good coffees, teas, juices and breakfasts is an evergreen chart-topper on the big Almaty cafe scene. The **Kabanbay Batyr** (272 64 09; Kabanbay Batyr 79) branch is busy and has a great pavement terrace; the **Zheltoksan** (261 26 80; Zheltoksan 117) site is a bit mellower.

Venetsia CENTRAL ASIAN $$
(cnr Kayyrbekov & Tole Bi; mains 1000-1800T; ⊙11am-midnight) Hugely popular Venetsia sits beside the little Malaya Almatinka River and its outdoor terrace is a great place to eat on a summer evening. There's a huge choice of Central Asian and Caucasian dishes, including Kazakh *beshbarmak* (flat noodles with meat cooked in a vegetable broth which is eaten separately), and the many varieties of shashlyk are among the best choices.

For accompaniment order the *zakuska kavkazskaya,* a huge plate of fresh greens. A singer and keyboardist play inside from 8pm and things often get lively with a bit of dancing.

Khodja Nasreddin UZBEK $$
(Lugansky 54; mains 1100-2500T; ⊙noon-midnight) This is one of Almaty's best Uzbek restaurants and especially nice in summer when you can sit around the courtyard. Go for the *plov prazdnichny* (festival *plov*), *kazan kebab* (lamb ribs and fried potatoes) or a good old shashlyk with spicy *adzhuka* sauce. The *pichini* (potato and cheese pies) make a good side dish.

Restoran Printsessa CHINESE $$
(Princess; ☎261 06 27; Tolebaev 53; dishes 1000-4500T; ⊙noon-midnight;) Come to this large, bustling restaurant for a filling, good-value Chinese meal. The menu offers a big choice including an excellent chicken, chilli and peanut dish.

Eldoro INTERNATIONAL $$
(Pushkin 44; mains 850-2250T; ⊙24hr;) This informal place near Panfilov Park has such a long, varied menu that you can't imagine they'd do it all justice – but the crowds day and night testify that they pretty much do. Go for breakfast, a burger, shashlyk, a steak, lasagne, salads, drinks – or the good-value set lunch served from 11.30am to 2.30pm Monday to Friday.

Mama Mia ITALIAN $$
(☎273 38 73; Gogol 87; dishes 1300-2300T; ⊙11am-midnight;) A bright, relaxed, little pizza/pasta/salad house, with efficient service and a good choice of tasty food.

Zheti Kazyna CENTRAL ASIAN $$$
(☎273 25 87; Abylay Khan 58A; mains 1000-10,000T; ⊙noon-midnight;) This exotically decorated, Central Asian–themed restaurant is a place to come for quality regional cooking. Old favourites such as *manty, laghman,* shashlyk, *plov* and spicy Dungan noodles are styled for the Western palate, and it's a good place to try Kazakh specialities including *beshbarmak* and horse steaks.

You can have a two-course meal with a couple of drinks for 4000T to 5000T. The entrance is actually on Makataev.

Café de Paris FRENCH $$$
(Shevchenko 18; mains 1300-3500T; ⊙11am-midnight;) This is an excellent French cafe/restaurant where you can eat light on a croque monsieur or creative salad, or tuck into a steak haché, beef entrecôte or veal ragout. The dining room has white tablecloths and old-Paris prints, or you can sit under streetside trees on the outdoor terrace.

Entrecôte EUROPEAN $$$
(Bogenbay Batyr 132; mains 1950-4500T; ⊙noon-midnight;) Come to this cellar-style restaurant with dark-wood tables and panelling for a meaty feast. Regulars vouch for the pepper steak as the best in the city, and there are fine salads too. Don't be alarmed by the karaoke sign outside – it's in a separate room.

Drinking & Nightlife

Finding a drink for any budget isn't difficult in Almaty, as the distinction between cafes, restaurants and bars is blurred, to say the least. Beer gardens under sunshades sprout around the city in summer.

The nouveau-riche crowd and Almaty's students and 20-somethings have spawned a hedonistic nocturnal scene. There are lots of special events and parties: www.timeout.kz, www.afisha.kz and www.night.kz all have good listings (in Russian).

★**Chukotka** BAR, CLUB
(www.chukotka.kz; Gogol 40; ⊙noon-3am Fri & Sat;) Good rock bands from around 9pm and DJs spinning house, soul, hip-hop and disco after midnight make sure the dance floor is never still at this hippest of Almaty nightspots, inside Panfilov Park. The crowd is open-minded, student-to-30s and gay-friendly. The free admission helps, as do the relatively reasonable drink prices.

The upstairs section, called Dacha, has DJs only and a slightly more sedate atmosphere, and opens every night except Monday (but can be dead midweek). You can eat in both sections.

Shakespeare Pub PUB
(www.shakespeare.kz; Dostyk 40; noon-1am Sun-Thu, noon-2am Fri & Sat;) Almaty's premier expat drinking hole is a large pub-like space always with a lively atmosphere (especially Friday and Saturday nights), a big drinks selection, and soccer on the (not too obtrusive) screens. Locals also like it, and the Shakespeare does pretty good pub food too, including some of the best pizzas in town.

Soho Almaty Club BAR
(267 03 67; www.soho.kz; Kazybek Bi 65; after 7pm Fri & Sat admission 1000T; 10am-1am Sun-Thu, 10am-5am Fri & Sat) Expats and locals pack Soho for tankards of beer, international food and crowded dancing to the good resident rock/jazz/blues band from 10pm. It's got a sort of urban-global theme, with assorted American and Beatles photos mixed in with flags for every nationality.

Da Freak CLUB
(273 13 37; Gogol 40; admission 1000-2000T; midnight-7am Fri & Sat nights) The best electronic club in town, Freak has two dance floors, two bars, top local DJs and sometimes guests from Moscow or Western Europe. The clientele is a cool, studenty crowd into house, techno, trance and indie. It's in Panfilov Park, right next to another nocturnal favourite, Chukotka.

Shtab BAR
(272 24 40; Zheltoksan 132; beer 0.5L 280-1000T; 9am-midnight) A quaint little beer bar opposite Hotel Ambassador, with a dozen indoor and outdoor tables and a big choice of local and foreign draught beers.

Bar Pivnitsa BAR
(Zhambyl 174; beer 0.5L 280-600T; noon-midnight) No 'pub' decor, no expat prices, no loud music – this beer bar is a place where you can just sit and chat over a variety of local and foreign brews, and that's just what the predominantly local clientele enjoy doing.

Esperanza CLUB
(299 66 99; www.esperanza.kz; Seyfullin 481; admission men 1000-2000T, women free-1000T, Mon free; 10pm-6am Sun-Thu, 10pm-8am Fri & Sat) With two nightclubs and four restaurants, cafes and bars all in one building, Turkish-owned 'Esperanza City' attracts a wide-ranging crowd and is among the few places still alive after 2am early in the week. One club plays R&B and house; the other, '80s and '90s retro (the admission price covers both). On Friday and Saturday they get jam-packed and can be a lot of fun.

Gay & Lesbian Venues

There is a gay scene in Almaty but bars and clubs often open, close and change location quickly. The gay community tends to make contact and find out what's happening through websites such as www.gay.kz and www.qguys.kz.

Studio 69 GAY
(Kurmangazy 125; 9pm-6am) The nearest thing to a typical gay bar in the West, Studio 69 primarily welcomes gay men and has a fairly relaxed atmosphere and a not specially good drag show. It's entered through another nightclub, Barvikha.

☆ Entertainment

Almaty has a good theatre and musical scene. Check www.timeout.kz, www.afisha.kz and www.night.kz for listings, and keep an eye open for concerts by Kazakh folk-music ensembles such as **Sazgen Sazy** (www.sazgen-sazy.kz) or Otrar Sazy.

Abay State Opera & Ballet Theatre OPERA, BALLET
(272 79 34; www.gatob.kz; Kabanbay Batyr 110; admission 600-4000T; ticket office 10am-2pm & 3-6pm) Almaty's top cultural venue stages three or four performances a week at 5pm or 6.30pm. Some get sold out a week or more ahead. Popular favourites such as *Swan Lake, La Bohème, Aida* and *Carmen* are among the regular shows. Also look out for Kazakh operas such as *Abay* and *Abylay Khan*.

Shopping

Almaty's middle class shops at modern supermarkets and malls are stocked with expensive, often imported, goods, and there are international brand stores dotted all around the city centre. The main malls include **Silk Way City** (267 74 70; Tole Bi 71; 24hr), **Ramstor** (258 75 75; Furmanov 226; 10am-10pm) and the biggest, **Mega Alma-Ata** (232 25 01; Rozybakiev 247A; 10am-10pm). For sports gear head to **Limpopo** (Seyfullin 534; 10am-7.30pm Mon-Sat, 10am-6pm Sun), with mountain bikes and winter sports equipment, or **Robinzon** (Abylay Khan 60; 10am-7pm Mon-Fri, 10am-6pm Sat), which has everything for hikers, campers, rafters, fishers and hunters.

The Rahat Palace (p64), InterContinental Almaty (p63) and Otrar (p64) hotels have bookshops or stalls with titles in English, including some on Kazakhstan.

Kok-Tobe SOUVENIRS
(11am-10pm) Souvenir stalls atop Kok-Tobe hill sell some of the city's best selections of kitsch Kazakh souvenirs – fur and felt hats, traditional jewellery, ornamental swords, and miniature yurts, camels and Golden Men.

Central State Museum HANDICRAFTS
(Mikrorayon Samal-1, No 44; 9.30am-6pm Wed-Mon) The ground-floor shop here has a good but pricey selection of Kazakh carpets (60,000T to 80,000T for a 2m-by-3m one) and other Kazakh souvenirs. The museum also hosts excellent Central Asian craft fairs, often on the first weekend of March, June, September and December.

Barakholka MARKET
(8am-5pm Tue-Sun) This huge, crowded madhouse is on the ring road in the north-western outskirts. Uzbeks, Chinese, Uyghurs and others converge here to sell everything from animals and fridges to cars and fur hats, at very good prices. Chinese goods predominate. Weekends, especially early Sunday morning, are the busiest times.

Watch out for pickpockets, and the police, who may demand to see conspicuous Westerners' passports. To get there, take any 'Barakholka' bus westbound on Rayymbek.

Amanulla Shafii HANDICRAFTS
(Hotel Saulet, Furmanov 187; 10am-6pm Mon-Fri) Amanulla's little shop has a decent range of reasonably priced Kazakh carpets and dearer ones from Turkmenistan and Afghanistan.

Akademkniga MAPS
(Furmanov 91; 10am-8pm Mon-Fri, 10am-7pm Sat & Sun) Best place in Kazakhstan for hiking, road and city maps; also has dictionaries and phrasebooks.

Information

Almost all foreign embassies are in Astana, but there are plenty of consulates in Almaty.

DANGERS & ANNOYANCES

Almaty is a pretty safe town, but you should still exercise normal precautions. The most common emergencies for Westerners here concern late-night activities – people robbed in taxis after emerging inebriated from bars and nightclubs, and the like.

Scams

Watch out for the 'Wallet Full of Dollars': someone finds a wallet on the ground as you pass, and discovers a lot of money inside. They offer to share the loot with you and if you get involved, another person appears, claiming the wallet is theirs and that it originally contained much more money. They then demand compensation or threaten to take you to the police. So ignore anyone who 'finds' or 'loses' a wallet, and keep walking without hesitation.

INTERNET ACCESS

Gosu (www.gosuclub.kz; per hr 300T; 24hr) Though often busy with excited young men playing computer games, this internet cafe has a couple of convenient locations, on Respublika alany (Respublika alany 13) and on Zhibek Zholy (cnr Zhibek Zholy & Bayseyitov).

Web Club (Ramstor; Furmanov 226; per hr 350T; 9am-11pm) Fairly peaceful shopping-mall facility.

LEFT LUGGAGE

Left luggage offices in the airport (ground floor) and Almaty-II station are open 24 hours, charging 750T and 400T respectively, per item for 24 hours.

MEDICAL SERVICES

Apteka No 2 (cnr Furmanov & Gogol; 7am-1am) Pharmacies (Kazakh: *darikhana;* Russian: *apteka*) all over Almaty sell both Western and medical products. No 2 is the biggest and best stocked.

Interteach (320 02 00; www.interteach.kz; Furmanov 275D; 9am-10pm Mon-Fri, 9am-6pm Sat & Sun) International clinic with some English-speaking family doctors, dentists and specialists; 1st consultation 4500T to 7000T, one-week membership including ambulance service and in-patient treatment available.

MONEY

There are exchange kiosks at the transport terminals and on most main streets. An ATM is never far away: the airport, all shopping malls, most banks and some supermarkets and shops have them.

ATF Bank (Furmanov 100; 9am-1pm & 2-6pm Mon-Fri) This may be the only bank in Almaty that exchanges travellers cheques (US dollar American Express cheques are definitely acceptable; others may be).

POST

Central Post Office (Bogenbay Batyr 134; 8am-7pm Mon-Fri, 8.30am-5.30pm Sat, 9am-2pm Sun)

DHL (258 85 88; www.dhl.kz; Gogol 99; 10.30am-7pm Mon-Fri)

REGISTRATION

Migration Police (☎261 19 22; Karasay Batyr 109A; ⊙9am-1pm & 3-6pm Mon-Fri, 9am-1pm Sat) If you need to register with the migration police and you choose to do it in person, this is where you must come. The entrance is actually from Baytursynuly: the building is set back between Baytursynuly 61 and 63. At the time of writing processing is free and normally takes 15 to 30 minutes, but you should arrive close to morning opening time in case of any delays.

See p127 for information on what documents to take. A notary's office outside the entrance can help you fill in the application form for 100T, and makes photocopies.

TOURIST INFORMATION

Almaty Info Centre (☎272 39 60; www.almaty-info.net; Tolebaev 174; ⊙9am-1pm & 2-6pm Mon-Fri) Run by the Kazakhstan Tourism Association (☎272 40 30; www.kaztour-association.com), this centre and its website offer masses of information about Almaty and Kazakhstan, some of it useful to expats and businesses as well as tourists. Sharing the premises is the Ecotourism Information Resource Centre (p68).

Tourist Information Center (☎390 88 86; www.visitalmaty.kz) Run by the Almaty City Tourism Department, these centres have a map and a booklet to give out and are very willing to help and answer questions. The airport (⊙24hr) booth, on the arrivals level, is good on city transport and other practical details. There is also a branch in the city (Kurmangazy 33; ⊙9am-6pm Mon-Fri).

TRAVEL, TOUR & ADVENTURE AGENCIES

There are a number of general travel agencies useful for travel tickets, hotel bookings, visa support, outings from the city and longer tours. Stantours is particularly well geared up for independent travellers.

Kan Tengri, Tour Asia, Trekking Club and Karlygash Makatova specialise in active trips.

A13 (☎333 52 13; www.a13.travel; Zheltoksan 87; ⊙10am-7pm Mon-Fri, 10am-2pm Sat) This agency can arrange treks, rafting and other active trips in southeast Kazakhstan at reasonable prices. Give them at least a week to make arrangements.

Arnai Tours (☎267 40 77; www.arnaitours.kz; Abay 59; ⊙10am-6pm Mon-Fri) This experienced, English- and German-speaking agency offers varied group and individual trips including Baykonur Cosmodrome launch trips and national park and nature reserve tours.

Ecotourism Information Resource Centre (EIRC; ☎272 53 63; www.eco-tourism.kz; Tolebaev 174; ⊙9am-1pm & 2-6pm Mon-Fri) The helpful, English-speaking information centre for community ecotourism programs can help with bookings and travel arrangements to ecotourism villages – but note that some destinations listed on its website were no longer available at research time. Also offers car excursions with English-speaking guides (around 25,000T per day), weekend bus trips with Russian-speaking guides to places of interest around southeast Kazakhstan (one-day trips cost 2800T to 4000T per person), and rafting on the Chilik or Ili rivers (8000T to 9000T per person).

Jibek Joly (☎250 04 45; www.jibekjoly.kz; Room 131, Hotel Zhetisu, Abylay Khan 55; ⊙9am-6pm Mon-Fri) This efficient agency runs cottage accommodation at Kolsay Lakes and elsewhere in southeast Kazakhstan, offers tours to Altyn-Emel National Park, Aksu-Zhabagyly Nature Reserve and other southern destinations, provides visa support and can help with border-zone permits.

Kan Tengri (☎291 02 00; www.kantengri.kz; Kasteev 10; ⊙office 9am-6pm Mon-Fri) Kazakhstan's top adventure-travel company, highly respected in mountain tourism, Kan Tengri focuses on climbs, trekking and mountain biking in the central Tian Shan (including Mt Khan Tengri) and Zailiysky Alatau. Also offers horse treks, bird-watching and botanical tours. Most trips last between one and three weeks: a two-week trek typically costs around €2000 per person.

Minimum group size is usually six. The company's director is Kazbek Valiev, the first Kazakh to scale Mt Everest.

Karlygash (Karla) Makatova (☎701-755 2086; kmakatova@yahoo.com) Independent one-woman operator who has long organised trips for the expat community and travellers – day hikes, treks, climbs, drives, kayaking, helicopter flights and more. Her trips are spirited, not too expensive, and a good way to meet locals and expats.

Silk Road Adventures (☎268 27 43; www.silkroadadventures.info; Anosov 133-30; ⊙9am-6pm Mon-Fri, 9am-2pm Sat) Long-established, highly experienced operator offering all kinds of long and short, individual and group trips throughout Kazakhstan and Central Asia, including hiking in the mountains near Almaty and the Altay, Mangistau 4WD tours, and Baykonur Cosmodrome visits.

Stantours (☎247 61 29, 705-118 4619; www.stantours.com) Expert operation with excellent personal service, and is a specialist in visas for all Central Asia. Also provides air and train tickets, and can book accommodation and tours throughout Central Asia, including Turkmenistan tours and active tours to offbeat locations. Prices are reasonable. Contact Stantours by email or phone.

Tour Asia (☎376 57 13; www.tourasia.kz; Baikadamov 30-1) Long-established company offering trekking and mountaineering in the central Tian Shan, the mountains south of Almaty and the Pamirs, plus bird watching, other nature tours and more.

Trekking Club (☎226 82 28; www.trekkingclub.kz; Svezhest 217) Expert agency offering hikes, treks and climbs in the mountains south of Almaty and treks in and around the Turgen Gorge east of the city, where they have a well-equipped tent camp. The office is on the road towards Ozero Bolshoe Almatinskoe, about 15km southwest of the city centre.

Valentina Guesthouse (☎777-668 6399, 360 30 92; http://valentina-gh.narod.ru; Zhabaev 62A, Akzhar) Valentina's is a guesthouse out in the southwest suburbs, 14km from the centre, that also functions as a travel agency, providing ticketing, accommodation bookings, inexpensive tours and visa support for guests and nonguests alike. Arrangements can be made by email. English-speaking manager Marat is a former mountain rescuer and knows the Almaty region like the back of his hand.

Trips out of Almaty are typically around US$150 to US$200 per day, plus US$10 per person on day trips and US$50 per person per day on longer trips (including accommodation).

Getting There & Away

Almaty is Kazakhstan's main air hub and is linked to most major Kazakhstan cities by daily trains. Minibuses and shared taxis run to many places in the southeast of the country. Longer hauls are generally more comfortable by train. For information on transport to the borders with Kyrgyzstan, Russia and Uzbekistan, see p132.

AIR

The **airport** (www.almatyairport.com; Maylin 2) is 13km north of the centre; its website gives schedules and daily flight information.

Within Kazakhstan, Air Astana flies around nine times daily to Astana (21,540T) and once or more daily to cities including Aktau (28,800T), Aktobe (28,470T), Atyrau (38,190T), Karaganda (21,785T), Kyzylorda (17,340T), Shymkent (18,050T) and Ust-Kamenogorsk (20,760T). SCAT flies daily to Astana and Semey (both from 15,500T) and a few days each week to Aktau (from 27,000T), Atyrau (from 27,500T), Karaganda (from 15,500T), Petropavlovsk (from 25,000T), Shymkent (from 16,500T), Taraz (from 17,500T) and Ust-Kamenogorsk (from 19,500T). Bek Air has a daily flight to Astana (from 15,000T) and three weekly to Uralsk (from 29,000T).

Airlines

You can buy air tickets at many travel agencies and *aviakassy* (air-ticket offices) including several in the Gorodskoy Aerovokzal (p70), where the agency **International Airport Almaty** (☎279 52 72; Gorodskoy Aerovokzal, Zhibek Zholy 111; ⏲24hr) opens round the clock. **Transavia** (www.transavia-travel.kz), with branches found at the **Airport** (☎270 33 01; ⏲24hr), **Dostyk** (☎261 04 14; Dostyk 85; ⏲9am-9pm) and **Zheltoksan** (☎258 33 06; Zheltoksan 104, entrance on Ayteke Bi; ⏲9am-9pm) is useful for tickets on most airlines including some lacking their own sales offices such as SCAT, Hainan Airlines, Uzbekistan Airways and Rossiya.

Air Arabia (☎328 04 04; www.airarabia.com; Keremet Travel, Kabanbay Batyr 49/76; ⏲9am-7pm Mon-Fri, 10am-3pm Sun) To/from Sharjah.

Air Astana (☎call centre 244 44 77; www.airastana.com; Hall 2B, Nurly Tau Business Centre, Al-Farabi 19; ⏲call centre 24hr) Many domestic and international destinations.

Asiana Airlines (☎356 32 35; www.flyasiana.com; Aksunkar Hotel, Airport) To/from Seoul.

Bek Air (☎270 32 32; www.bekair.com; Airport) To/from Astana and Uralsk.

British Airways (☎272 40 40; Pushkin 63/30; ⏲9am-6pm Mon-Fri) To/from London.

China Southern Airlines (☎250 13 68; www.cs-air.com; Tole Bi 23A; ⏲9.30am-1pm & 2.30-4.30pm Mon-Fri) To/from Ürümqi.

Czech Airlines (☎261 12 56; www.czechairlines.com; Zheltoksan 144; ⏲10am-6pm Mon-Fri) To/from Prague.

Etihad Airways (☎330 30 00; www.etihad.com; CDC1 Business Centre, Furmanov 240G; ⏲9am-5.30pm Mon-Fri, 1-6pm Sat) To/from Abu Dhabi.

Hainan Airlines (☎321 85 85; http://hnair.com; Mametova 29; ⏲9am-6pm) To/from Beijing.

KLM (☎250 77 47; www.klm.com; Makataev 127/9; ⏲9am-6pm Mon-Fri, 10am-2pm Sat) To/from Amsterdam.

Lufthansa (☎333 50 25; www.lufthansa.com; Rahat Palace Hotel, Satpaev 29/6; ⏲10am-6.30pm Mon-Fri) To/from Frankfurt.

Mahan Air (www.mahan.aero) To/from Tehran.

Pegasus Airlines (☎273 17 17; www.flypgs.com) To/from İstanbul.

Rossiya (www.rossiya-airlines.com) To/from St Petersburg.

S7 (☎315 33 66; www.s7.ru; Dostyk 40) To/from Novosibirsk.

SCAT (☎228 65 01; www.scat.kz) Several domestic destinations.

Somon Air (☎397 63 48; www.somonair.com; Office 207, Makataev 47; ⏲9am-6pm) To/from Dushanbe.

Tajik Air (☎397 63 48; www.tajikair.tj; Office 207, Makataev 47; ⏲9am-6pm) To/from Dushanbe.

Transaero (☎250 20 02; www.transaero.ru; Furmanov 53; ⏲9am-9pm) To/from Moscow.

Turkish Airlines (☎333 38 49; www.turkishairlines.com; Furmanov 100; ⏰9am-1pm & 2-6pm Mon-Fri) To/from İstanbul.

Turkmenistan Airlines (☎250 21 07; www.turkmenairlines.com; Office 36, Gorodskoy Aerovokzal, Zhibek Zholy 111) To/from Ashgabat.

Ukraine International Airlines (☎315 04 14, 24hr call centre 800 333 30 50; www.flyuia.com; Keremet 5) To/from Kiev.

For information on international connections, see p131 and p478.

BUS, MINIBUS & TAXI

Long-distance buses use **Sayran bus station** (☎276 26 86, 396 70 63; cnr Tole Bi & Utegen Batyr), 5km west of the centre. Destinations (schedules subject to change) include Astana (6500T, 19 hours, 2pm and 10.30pm), Karaganda (5570T, 16 hours, three daily), Shymkent (2600T, 11 hours, three overnight buses), Taraz (2200T, eight hours, three overnight buses), Turkistan (3000T, 14 hours, 6pm and 10pm) and Ust-Kamenogorsk (4500T, 22 hours, two daily). Quicker minibuses and shared taxis to some of the nearer destinations wait at the front of the bus station building or on Utegen Batyr at the side. To Taraz it's 2500T (eight hours) by minibus and 5000T (seven hours) by shared taxi.

Most nearby destinations are served by the ramshackle **Sayakhat bus station** (☎380 74 44; Rayymbek), on the northern edge of the city centre. A minibus to Kegen (1000T, five to six hours) leaves between 7am and 9am (when it fills with passengers); a small bus to Zhalanash (1500T, six hours) and Saty (2000T, eight hours) goes from the street outside the station's east side between 6am and 7am. You may also be able to find shared taxis to these destinations – ask around Sayakhat a day or two ahead.

For international destinations to/from Sayran bus station, see p132.

CAR & MOTORCYCLE

If you're planning to do much travelling outside Almaty, self-drive rental is an option provided you are prepared for possible encounters with the traffic police. Self-drive rates for one or two days start around 7500T per day. Check all the small print very carefully, including daily kilometre limits and restrictions on where you can take the car.

Motorcyclists in need of help or advice should head to Eldoro (p65) restaurant, where owner Yeldos Ametbay is a nexus of the local motorbike community and a willing source of assistance.

Dixie Travel (www.dixie.kz; Zheltoksan 59; ⏰9am-6pm Mon-Fri) This firm allows its rental cars to be driven anywhere in Kazakhstan.

Europcar (www.europcar.com) The only major international rental firm represented here has branches at the airport (☎270 30 72; ⏰9am-1pm & 2.30-6.30pm) and in the city (☎263 59 37; Office 3, Mikrorayon Samal-2, No 30; ⏰9am-1pm & 2.30-6.30pm Mon-Fri).

Rent A Car Ivan (www.rentacarivan.kz; Baisheva 3)

TRAIN

Most long-distance trains stop at both **Almaty-I station** (☎296 33 92), 8km north of the centre at the end of Seyfullin, and the more central **Almaty-II station** (☎296 15 44), at the north end of Abylay Khan, though a few trains only go to one or the other. There are several train ticket offices in the centre, including in the **Gorodskoy Aerovokzal** (City Air Terminal; Zhibek Zholy 111; ⏰ticket offices 9am-7pm). Ticket offices in the stations, and **Atameken** (Abylay Khan; ⏰24hr) and **Bakhytty Zhol** (Abylay Khan; ⏰24hr) near Almaty-II, are open 24 hours. You need to show your passport when buying tickets.

Destinations served at least daily (in some cases several times daily) from Almaty-II, with typical *kupeyny* (2nd-class) fares, include Aktau (Mangyshlak; 10,690T, 72 hours), Aktobe (8320T, 42 hours), Aralsk (Aralskoe More; 6480T, 30 to 37 hours), Astana (6380T, 13 to 20 hours), Karaganda (5580T, 10 to 16 hours), Shymkent (3480T, 11 to 17 hours), Taraz (2890T, 7½ to 12 hours), Turkistan (4140T, 17 to 22 hours) and Ust-Kamenogorsk (Zashchita; 4130T, 24 hours). Trains for Semey (4480T, 19 to 22 hours) and Novosibirsk (21,480T, 37 to 39 hours) go daily from Almaty-I, every two days from Almaty-II.

Some services to Karaganda and Astana are sleek, fast, Spanish-built Talgo trains (with lovely clean bathrooms). Train 1, a Talgo, departs Almaty-II at 7.54pm, reaching Astana at 8.25am (tourist/business class 10,230/16,900T).

For international destinations to/from Almaty-II train station, see p132.

ℹ Getting Around

TO/FROM THE AIRPORT

Bus 79 immediately outside the arrivals hall runs about every 10 minutes from about 6am to 9pm to the city centre (a 30- to 40-minute ride), where it travels south along Furmanov, west on Abay, south on Baytursynuly then west on Timiryazev (and the same in reverse going back to the airport). Bus fares are 80T. Further buses go from a bus stop 400m along the street outside the airport parking-area exit:

Bus 86 Sayakhat bus station, south on Furmanov passing Central State Museum and Ramstor, southwest on Al-Farabi.

Bus 92 Sayakhat bus station, west on Rayymbek, south on Nauryzbay Batyr, west on Abay (returning to the airport, it heads north on Zheltoksan instead of Nauryzbay Batyr).

The regular taxi fare between the airport and the centre is 2000T, although drivers at the airport will try for much more. One reliable taxi firm that you can call to book a cab is **Almaty Taxi** (☎ 255 53 33, 158; http://almatytaxi.kz; ⏰ 24hr). Freelance cabs charge around 1000T: you can usually find them about 50m along the street outside the airport car-park exit.

BUS, TRAM & TROLLEYBUS

Buses, trolleybuses and trams (all 80T) run from 6 or 7am to 10 or 11pm. They can get very crowded, so if you have much baggage or are short of time, it's easier to take a taxi. All services mentioned here follow the same routes in both directions unless stated.

To/From Sayran Bus Station

Buses 16, 37 and 126 run east along Tole Bi to the centre. The 16 and 126 eventually turn north on Konaev then east on Gogol, passing Panfilov Park. The 37 turns north on Zheltoksan then east on Rayymbek to Sayakhat bus station; going out to Sayran it heads south on Nauryzbay Batyr instead of Zheltoksan. Bus 65 heads into the centre along Abay, then goes north down Dostyk. Bus 45 heads to Respublika alany and Ramstor on Furmanov.

To/From the Train Stations

From Almaty-II, trolleybuses 5 and 6 head south on Abylay Khan, then west on Abay.

From Almaty-I, buses 2 and 73 run to the centre, travelling south on Furmanov to the Central State Museum and beyond.

Other Useful Routes

In the central area, Furmanov is the main artery for north–south routes, along with Nauryzbay Batyr (southbound) and Zheltoksan (northbound). Gogol and Abay are the principal east–west arteries.

Bus 29 Sayakhat bus station, Zhangeldin, Kaldayakov, Bogenbay Batyr (Kabanbay Batyr northbound), Dostyk, Butakovka.

Bus 66 Gogol (north side of Panfilov Park), Kaldayakov, Tole Bi (Kazybek Bi northbound), Dostyk, Abay, Zhandosov.

Bus 105 Furmanov, Abay, Baytursynuly, Timiryazev.

Trolleybus 1 Gorky Park, Gogol, Auezov to Timiryazev.

Trolleybus 12 Gorky Park, Gogol, Auezov, Zhandosov.

METRO

Almaty's shiny new metro, opened in 2011, runs from Rayymbek station, near Almaty-II train station, about 3km south beneath Furmanov as far as Abay, then 4km west beneath Abay to Alatau station. There are five intermediate stations en route. It's useful for some cross-city trips. Rides cost 80T and trains run about every 10 minutes, 6.30am to 11.30pm. Carry your passport (not just a photocopy), as police at stations love checking ID documents and may not be satisfied with copies.

TAXI

There are some official taxis – marked with chequerboard logos or other obvious signs – but many private cars also act as freelance taxis. Stand at the roadside with your arm slightly raised and you'll rarely have to wait more than six or eight cars before one stops. Just say where you're going and how much you're offering. If you can't agree a price, let the car go and wait for another. A ride in the centre of Almaty should cost 200T to 400T depending on distance (sometimes a bit more at night).

Around Almaty

There are some great outings to be made right on Almaty's doorstep, notably into the Zailiysky Alatau range, a beautiful spur of the Tian Shan to the south of the city. The main access routes into the Zailiysky Alatau are the Malaya (Little) Almatinka valley, where the winter sports centres Medeu and Chimbulak are found, and the Bolshaya (Big) Almatinka valley, leading up to Ozero Bolshoe Almatinskoe (Big Almaty Lake). Note that foreigners are not allowed to walk into Kyrgyzstan through these mountains, and permits are officially required on some routes approaching the border.

Good Russian-language hiking maps covering the area are sold at Akademkniga (p67).

Medeu & Chimbulak

Медеу & Чимбулак

These are Almaty's winter-sports playgrounds in the Malaya Almatinka valley. The facilities were comprehensively upgraded for Almaty's hosting of the 2011 Asian Winter Games. Medeu, about 15km southeast of central Almaty, at an altitude of 1700m, is a scattering of buildings around the huge Medeu ice rink. Chimbulak, further up the valley at 2200m, is Central Asia's top skiing centre. The two are connected by road and a cable car installed in 2011. Medeu is always several degrees cooler than Almaty, and Chimbulak is cooler still. Except in summer, rain in Almaty means snow and zero visibility at the higher elevations.

The 10,500-sq-metre **Medeu ice rink** (☎ 727-386 95 33; www.medey.kz; adult/child 1800/400T; ⏰ 10am-4pm & 6-11pm Thu-Sun approx

Around Almaty

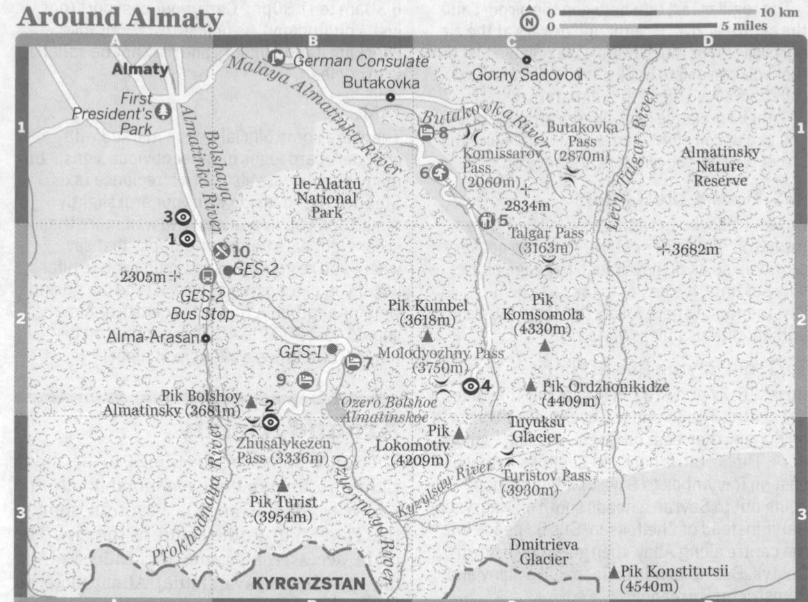

Nov-Apr), built in 1972, is made for speed skating and many champion skaters have trained here, though you certainly don't need to be an expert to skate here. For a less crowded experience come on a Thursday or Friday. Ice-skate rental is 1000T per two hours (bring your passport as you may need to deposit it as security). Outside the ice-skating season plenty of people still come to Medeu for a stroll, hike, picnic or mountain biking in the surrounding valleys and hills.

What looks like a dam in the main valley above the ice rink is actually there to stop avalanches and mudslides. The road climbs a further 4.5km from this barrier to the **Chimbulak ski resort** (Shymbulak; ☎727-330 85 00; www.shymbulak.com; 1-day skier's lift pass 5500-7000T, child 3000-4000T; ⏱ski lifts in ski season 10am-5pm Mon-Fri, 9am-5pm Sat-Sun), which has runs for all levels and a total drop of 900m. The ski season lasts from approximately November to mid-April. Skis and snowboards rent for 3500T to 15,000T per day depending on condition (bring your passport): it can be cheaper to rent in Almaty at shops such as **Snowshop** (http://snowshop.kz; Furmanov 117; per day snowboard & boots 2500T, mountain bike 2000T; ⏱10am-8pm) or **Fischer** (Furmanov 124; per day set ski gear 3000T, snowboard & boots 5000T, mountain bike 2500T; ⏱10am-8pm) if you can manage to get the gear up to Chimbulak. These places rent mountain bikes in summer too.

Non-skiers can take a return trip on the Kombi 1 and Kombi 2 ski lifts (a mixture of open chairlifts and small cabins) from Chimbulak up to the Talgar Pass for 2500T. The lifts also operate some days outside the ski season – normally 10am to 5pm, Friday to Sunday, from June to some time in September (weather permitting).

Sleeping & Eating

Hotel Chimbulak HOTEL $$$
(☎727-390 93 93; www.shymbulakhotel.kz; r incl breakfast 20,000-55,000T; P ⊖ ⊜) The large lodge at Chimbulak has a great location at the foot of the ski lifts, but the rooms, though they have balconies, are bland and well used. Rates are about 40% lower outside the skiing season.

Samal Resort & Spa LUXURY HOTEL $$$
(☎727-330 23 11; http://tienshan-hotels.com; Gornaya 548; s/d incl breakfast from 35,000/38,000T; P ❄ @ ⊜ ≋) The luxury stay in the foothills, Samal Resort sits 3km north of Medeu. Designed in a successful Silk Road–style with arches and tilework, it's both super-comfortable and peaceful, and has a top-class spa.

Around Almaty

Sights

Activities, Courses & Tours

Sleeping

Eating

Assorti INTERNATIONAL **$$$**
(www.assorti.kz; Chimbulak; mains 1400-4500T; 10am-9pm Mon-Fri, 10am-11pm Sat & Sun;) Chimbulak's rustic shashlyk stalls disappeared with the Asian Games, replaced by a small collection of medium-to-expensive small-chain eateries. Assorti, offering everything from pizza to *plov* to steaks in a large, semi-lounge-like space, is a reliable bet.

Trader Vic's Island Bar & Grill INTERNATIONAL **$$$**
(Medeu; mains 1500-6000T; noon midnight) Medeu has a few snack stalls but for anything more substantial head into this tropical-island-themed spot in the bottom of the ice-rink building, where you can get anything from a spinach salad to fish tacos to a fillet steak, and plenty of tropical cocktails.

Getting There & Around

Bus 6 runs to Medeu (80T, 30 minutes) every 30 to 45 minutes (6.30am to 8pm) from Dostyk, opposite the Hotel Kazakhstan, in Almaty. If you're heading straight on up to Chimbulak in the cable car, get off at the cable car station, 1km before Medeu ice rink. The last bus back down leaves Medeu at 8.40pm

Medeu-Chimbulak Cable Car (round-trip adult/child 2500/1500T, combined roundtrip ticket with Chimbulak Kombi 1 & Kombi 2 ski lifts 3500/2000T; ski season 9.30am-6pm Mon-Wed & Fri, 9.30am-midnight Thu, 8.30am-midnight Sat, 8.30am-6pm Sun, other months noon-8pm Mon-Thu, 10am-10pm Fri-Sun) The cable car lifts you smoothly and panoramically from Medeu to Chimbulak in 25 minutes. It may close for maintenance for a couple of weeks just after and before the ski season, which runs from approximately early November to mid-April, depending on snowfall.

Ozero Bolshoe Almatinskoe Area Окрестности Большого Алматинского озера

West of and parallel to the Malaya Almatinka valley lies its 'big sister', the Bolshaya Almatinka valley. The paved road south up this valley starts beside the colonnaded entrance to the First President's Park on Al-Farabi on the southern edge of Almaty. After 7km you reach the entrance to the **Ile-Alatau National Park** (admission per person 373T). Immediately before the park gate is the **Sunkar Falcon Centre** (727-269 12 35; admission 200T; 10am-last client). Sunkar also keeps hunting dogs and caged wolves and is worth a look any time, but the real attraction is the entertaining display of trained raptors in flight (1000T) at 5pm daily except Monday.

About 1km past the park gate is the restaurant complex **Tau Dastarkhan** (727-275 91 40; www.tau-dastarkhan.kz), with half a dozen midrange and top-end restaurants in a pretty woodland water-garden setting. The road forks 250m past here, at a spot known as GES-2 after a small hydroelectric station nearby. The right branch heads to the settlement of Alma-Arasan (4km). The left branch follows the Bolshaya Almatinka River upstream, passing another small hydroelectric station, GES-1, after 8km, and reaching **Ozero Bolshoe Almatinskoe** (Big Almaty Lake) after a further 7km. The picturesque turquoise lake, 1.6km long, rests in a rocky bowl at 2500m altitude and is a good birdwatching spot, especially during the May migration. Border guards are often present around the lake so it's not advisable to walk along its east side (this path eventually leads to the Kyrgyzstan border), though a ramble on the west side is usually acceptable.

Two kilometres up the track to the west from the lake, at 2750m, is the outlandish **Tian Shan Astronomical Observatory**, sometimes still referred to by its Soviet-era acronym, GAISh. This has the second-biggest telescope in the former USSR, with magnification of around 600 times. It only operates at part-capacity now due to shortage of funds, but when the astronomer is in residence he'll give tours (in Russian) of

HIKING & TREKKING AROUND ALMATY

The higher reaches of the Zailiysky Alatau are beautiful and spectacular, with many peaks over 4000m, deep river valleys, many glaciers, and Tian Shan firs on the steep valley sides. The Kazakhstan–Kyrgyzstan 'green border' – foot trails through the mountains – is closed for foreigners, with border guards patrolling the access routes, so it's no longer possible to trek all the way across the mountains to Lake Issyk-Köl in Kyrgyzstan. Some routes that approach the border without crossing it also tend to fall foul of the border guards, but it is still possible to take a hike of one or a few days in the Zailiysky Alatau. To avoid problems with the border guards, go with a knowledgeable guide, or at least get the most reliable information possible from Almaty sources (such as trekking agencies) beforehand.

Agencies such as Trekking Club (p69), Silk Road Adventures (p68), Kan Tengri (p68), Tour Asia (p68), Valentina Guesthouse (p69), A13 (p68) and Karlygash Makatova (p68) in Almaty can provide guides and organisational support for mountain treks. Rates for small-group treks of more than one day with English-speaking guides start at 30,000T to 40,000T per day, including car transfers.

On any mountain hike or trek, you *must* be equipped for bad conditions. The trekking season lasts from about mid-May to mid-September; July and August have the most reliable weather, but at any time it can rain or snow in the mountains, even when it's warm in Almaty. If you're caught unprepared by a sudden storm, it could be fatal. There is also year-round avalanche danger wherever you see snow. Altitude sickness can affect anyone who ascends rapidly above 2500m, so spending a night to acclimatise on the way up is advisable.

Medeu to Butakovka

This is a relatively leisurely hike of three to four hours, through wooded hills in the middle section, with buses at both ends. Start by heading east up the paved side-road 100m downhill from the Medeu ice rink. After about 1.5km take the track up to the left between two large properties with high stone perimeter walls. About 800m up here, take the path heading left up through the trees for 500m to the Komissarov Pass (2060m). Cross straight over the little pass and descend the valley path about 1.5km to the paved road at Berezovaya Roshka. You then have a 5km road walk down the valley to Butakovka village, passing a couple of picnic spots and shashlyk joints and some enormous high-walled mansions. From Butakovka bus 29R heads back to Almaty (Dostyk) once or twice an hour.

the working sections for 1000T. At the head of the Zhusalykezen Pass (3336m), 6km up to the southwest from the observatory (the road continues paved all the way), is **Kosmostantsia**, a group of mostly wrecked buildings belonging to scientific research institutes.

Sleeping & Eating

Tian Shan Astronomical Observatory OBSERVATORY **$$**
(☎701-798 9830, 777-247 5537; r per person 4500T; P) The ramshackle observatory above Ozero Bolshoe Almatinskoe has a few basic but perfectly adequate rooms with hot showers and soft mattresses. There's a kitchen where you can cook – or organise for the staff to cook for you. This unique lodging certainly has prime lake and mountain views and it's open all year.

Call ahead to ensure you'll get past the border guards around the lake and to ensure a room at busy times, especially May to September. The phone numbers will get you through to the manager, Aydar, who speaks some English. Staff here can help you clear any possible bureaucratic hurdles about access to the Zhusalykezen Pass.

Alpiyskaya Roza HOTEL **$$**
(Alpine Rose; ☎727-747 43 58; www.alpina.kz; r with shared bathroom 10,000T, with private bathroom 15,000-35,000T, incl breakfast; P) Rooms at this pink chalet-style hotel are very plain for the price, but its location just 4km down the road from Ozero Bolshoe Almatinskoe makes it a potentially handy base for hikers. It's open all year and has a restaurant/bar with a warming fireplace.

Day Walks from Chimbulak

In summer, it's a 3km hike (or ride on the ski lift!) from Chimbulak up to the Talgar Pass at 3163m, where you can see glacier-flanked Pik Komsomola (4330m) rising 3km to the south. Or you can head on up the valley road from Chimbulak. It continues upward for 8km, with some steepish sections, to end at about 3500m beneath the glaciers ringing the top of the valley. If you are going up to these high elevations it's advisable to spend a night acclimatising first.

Ozero Bolshoe Almatinskoe & Zhusalykezen Pass

The road up to the Zhusalykezen Pass is now paved all the way, but if you prefer to do this traditionally popular route (or just part of it) on foot, it's still a fine walk – about 22km all the way from the **GES-2 bus stop** to the pass, with an ascent of nearly 1900m. For acclimatisation reasons it's A good idea to give it two days, with a night en route.

You can start walking where bus 28 terminates at GES-2, or save 8km by taking a taxi to GES-1 (around 5000T from central Almaty). Here, climb the metal steps beside the broad water pipe rising sharply up the valley, then walk up beside the pipe for the most direct route to Ozero Bolshoe Almatinskoe (two to three hours). From the lake, follow the road uphill to the right to the observatory (40 minutes). From the observatory it's about 2½ hours up the road to Kosmostantsia at the Zhusalykezen Pass (3336m). From here you can continue 2km north to Pik Bolshoe Almatinsky (3681m), which affords great views back down to Almaty (smog permitting); or 2km south to Pik Turist (3954m), which is easier walking though higher. Unfortunately it's no longer possible to return to Almaty by descending westward to the Prokhodnaya valley, as the route through Alma-Arasan has been blocked.

Chimbulak to Alpiyskaya Roza Hotel

This two-day route doesn't stray too close to the Kyrgyzstan border or Ozero Bolshoe Almatinskoe so is unlikely to fall foul of border guards. From Chimbulak, hike up the valley road to the **Tuyuksu meteorological station** (where it's possible to sleep) then ascend westward and cross the Molodyozhny Pass (3750m). Descend the scree on the west side of the pass, cross the Kumbel River (in the morning, before it rises with melt water), cross the next ridge west and follow the Chukur (Shukyr) river down to the Alpiyskaya Roza.

Avlabar GEORGIAN **$$**
(☎727-270 56 46; Tau Dastarkhan; mains 1000-4000T; ⏰10am-midnight) One of the best options in Tau Dastarkhan, Avlabar serves savoury Georgian specialties from *khachapuri* to *chanakhi* (a lamb, potato, eggplant and tomato dish), plus good Georgian wine of course. It has both indoor and outdoor sections – if it's chilly outside, staff come round with tiger-stripe rugs to keep you warm.

ℹ Getting There & Away

From central Almaty, bus 63 runs south on Furmanov and along Al-Farabi to the First President's Park. Here you can switch to bus 28, heading up the valley about every 30 minutes from 7am to 7pm, as far as the GES-2 fork. To walk from GES-2 to the lake takes four or five hours, with a rise of nearly 1100m.

A taxi from the city centre costs around 6000T one-way to the lake and around 10,000T to Kosmostantsia, plus around 2000T per hour for any waiting time. Almost any Almaty travel agency can organise a day trip to the lake (prices start around 30,000T per carload).

SOUTHEAST KAZAKHSTAN

The region from Almaty to Lake Balkhash is known as Zhetisu (Russian: Semirechie), meaning Land of Seven Rivers. There are actually more than 800 rivers, many fed by glaciers in the mountains along the Kyrgyz and Chinese borders. This is one of Kazakhstan's most varied regions, with plenty to see and do using Almaty as a base.

Kolsay Lakes

ОЗЁРА КОЛЬСАЙ

These three pretty lakes lie amid the steep, forested foothills of the Küngey Alatau, 110km southeast of Almaty as the crow flies, but almost 300km by road, via Chilik (Shelek) and Zhalanash. They are strung along the Kolsay River, about 1800m to 2800m high, southwest of the village of Saty.

From Saty it's about 12km by road to the 1km-long Nizhny (Lower) Kolsay lake at 1800m. On the way you pay a national park admission fee of 700T per person per day. The Sredny (Middle) Kolsay lake at 2250m is the biggest and most beautiful, 5km up from the lower lake via a hike of about three hours. From the middle lake to the smaller Verkhny (Upper) Kolsay lake at 2800m, where the forests give way to alpine grasslands, is about 4km and three hours' walking.

Stay away from Kolsay in May and June when ticks are present, raising a risk of tick-borne encephalitis.

Sleeping & Eating

Saty Homestays HOMESTAY $
(per person incl 3 meals 3500-4000T) The Ecotourism Information Resource Centre (p68) in Almaty can help you book into six homestays in Saty. The families can provide cars or horses to the lower lake, and horses from there to the middle lake, at around 1000T for a car and 3000T to 5000T per day for a horse.

Jibek Joly Cottages LODGE $
(Nizhny Kolsay Lake; r per person with shared bathroom 2250-3250T Sun-Thu, 4500-6500T Fri & Sat, with private bathroom 4250T Sun-Thu, 8500T Fri & Sat; P) Jibek Joly has three quite comfy wooden cottages, with two- and four-person bedrooms, on a hillside above Nizhny Kolsay lake. You will receive

Southeast Kazakhstan

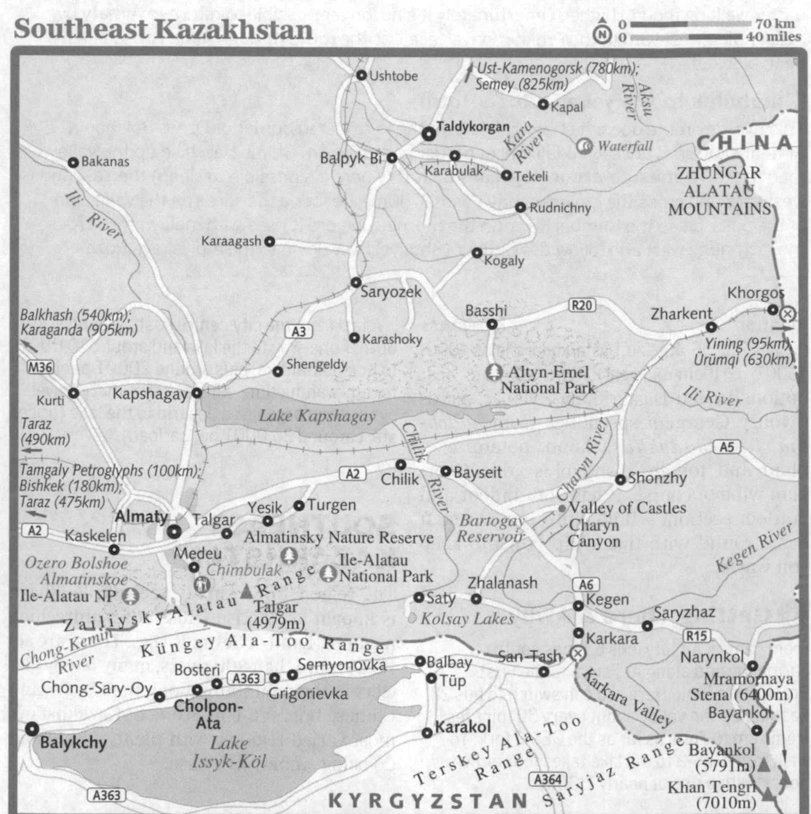

three meals a day for 2000T, or you can cook yourself in the well-equipped kitchen. If you prefer to camp, they'll rent you a two-person tent for 5000T per day including sleeping bag and mat.

ℹ Getting There & Away

A small bus to Saty (2000T, eight hours) normally leaves Almaty's Sayakhat bus station between 6am and 7am. Alternatively, take a taxi to Saty for around 12,000T from Sayakhat, or find a shared taxi to Zhalanash (2000T; ask at Sayakhat a day or two before you plan to go), then take a taxi to Saty (25km) or the first lake. Taxis from Saty to the first lake cost 1000T.

Many people visit the lakes on two-night tours: Jibek Joly (p68) does trips leaving Almaty on Friday evening and returning on Sunday evening, for 15,000T to 21,000T per person including most meals and a hike to the middle lake.

Charyn Canyon
ЧАРЫНСКИЙ КАНЬОН

The swift Charyn (Sharyn) River has carved a 150m- to 300m-deep canyon into the otherwise flat steppe some 200km east of Almaty, and time has weathered this into some weird and colourful rock formations, especially in the branch canyon known as the Valley of Castles (Dolina Zamkov). This is no Grand Canyon, but it's worth a trip. You can take a long day trip from Almaty for around 40,000T per carload through the less expensive agencies, or 4000T per person on weekend bus trips through the Ecotourism Information Resource Centre (p68). April, May, June, September and October are the best months to come: it's too hot in summer. There's a 600T-per-person national park fee to enter the canyon area, which is not always enforced.

Getting here by public transport is possible, but you may not be able to get back the same day. Take the morning minibus from Almaty's Sayakhat bus station heading to Kegen, and get off at the signposted turn-off to the canyon about 190km from Almaty, just before the road starts descending into the Charyn valley. From here it's 10km east along a fairly flat dirt road to a parking area and then 3km (about one hour) down through the Valley of Castles to the river. If you're lucky you might get a taxi or a lift to the parking area; if not, it's a walk!

Don't try to swim in the river, which is deceptively fast.

Karkara Valley
КАРКАРАНСКАЯ ДОЛИНА

The beautiful, broad valley of the Karkara River is an age-old summer pasture for herds from both sides of what's now the Kazakhstan–Kyrgyzstan border.

From Kegen, 250km by road east of Almaty, a scenic road heads south up a valley to Karkara village, and then to the border post about 28km from Kegen. The border reopened from June to October 2013 after being closed for several years, and it is likely that it will open again for a similar period in future years. From the border the road veers west towards Tüp and Lake Issyk-Köl in Kyrgyzstan. No public transport reaches the border from either side, but a minibus leaves Almaty's Sayakhat bus station between 7am and 9am daily for Kegen (1000T, five to six hours). From Kegen you can get up the valley to the border by hitching or by taxi. You may also be able to find shared taxis to Kegen from Sayakhat.

At San-Tash, 19km into Kyrgyzstan, you can find a bus or shared jeep to Tüp or Karakol, but the easier way onward is to organise a car pick-up at the border to take you to Karakol (US$60) through CBT Karakol (p263).

From late June to late August, mountain-tourism company Kan Tengri (p68) maintains a summer **base camp** (Karkara Valley; per person full board €50) at 2200m on the Kazakh side of the international border. Primarily a staging post for treks and climbing expeditions to the central Tian Shan, the camp offers tent accommodation to all comers, with hot showers, a cafe and a bar. A three-day trip from Almaty, including a helicopter flight to Mt Khan Tengri, costs about €300 per person; contact the company at least one week in advance.

Central Tian Shan
ЦЕНТРАЛЬНЫЙ ТЯНЬ ШАНЬ

Kazakhstan's highest and most magnificent mountains rise in the country's far southeastern corner where it meets Kyrgyzstan and China. Mt Khan Tengri (7010m) on the Kyrgyz border is widely considered the most beautiful and demanding peak in the Tian Shan, and there are many more 5000m-plus peaks around it, including Mramornaya

Stena (Marble Wall, 6400m) on the Kazakh-Chinese border.

Khan Tengri is flanked by two long, west-running glaciers, the North Inylchek Glacier on its Kazakh side and the South Inylchek glacier on its Kyrgyz side.

Mountain-tourism firm Kan Tengri (p68) offers a variety of exciting one- to three-week trek trips and full-scale mountaineering expeditions in this area in July and August, using base camps on the Inylchek glaciers at altitudes of around 4000m. Access is often by helicopter, using the Karkara Valley base camp as a staging post.

A typical two-week trekking trip costs around €2000. Many trips include helicopter flights around the main peaks and glacier hikes to the foot of Khan Tengri and/or Pik Pobedy on the Kyrgyzstan/China border. The major peak accessible to trekkers is Karly Tau (5450m), a three-day expedition out of the North Inylchek base camp.

Tamgaly Petroglyphs
ПЕТРОГЛИФЫ ТАМГАЛЫ

The World Heritage–listed Tamgaly petroglyphs are the most impressive of many petroglyph groups in southeastern Kazakhstan. Set in a lushly vegetated canyon in an otherwise arid region near Karabastau village, 170km northwest of Almaty, they number more than 4000 separate carvings from the Bronze Age and later, in several groups. The varied images include sun-headed idols, women in childbirth, hunting scenes and a big variety of animals, and are best seen in the afternoon when most sunlight reaches them.

The canyon was a ritual site for nomadic peoples from at least 3000 years ago. Don't confuse Tamgaly with Tamgaly Tas, which is a smaller and more recent petroglyph site on the Ili River. Many Almaty agencies can organise day trips: 30,000T to 35,000T per carload is a fair price with an English-speaking guide.

Altyn-Emel National Park
НАЦИОНАЛЬНЫЙ ПАРК АЛТЫН-ЭМЕЛЬ

Though expensive to visit, this large, 4600-sq-km national park stretching northeast from Lake Kapshagay is worth it if you like beautiful desolation and unusual natural and archaeological attractions. It's famous for the **Singing Dune**, which hums like an aircraft engine when the weather is suitably windy and dry, but archaeology fans will be absorbed by the **Terekty petroglyphs** and the 31 **Besshatyr burial mounds**, which are one of the biggest groups of Scythian tombs known anywhere. In spring and early autumn you can hope to see rare goitred gazelles (zheyran), argali sheep and wild ass *(kulan)*.

You need to be in a vehicle to visit the park and visitors must stick to three linear routes of between 80km and 160km (one-way) each. The western route (No 2), accessed through Shengeldy village, is the easiest reached from Almaty and includes the Terekty petroglyphs and Besshatyr mounds. The central (No 1) and eastern (No 3) routes are both accessed through Basshi village inside the park's northern edge: No 1 reaches the Singing Dune, while No 3 gets into some of the park's most remote territory, in the Katutau and Aktau mountains. It's difficult to cover more than one route in one day.

The park runs five simple **hotels** (per person 2500-5000T, breakfast/lunch/dinner 500/1500/1000T) – best is **Hotel Altyn-Emel** (Basshi; per person 5000T); three others are on route No 2, and one on route No 1. You can camp for free at one location on each route.

The park's **Almaty office** (☎727-250 04 51; altynemel.almaty.office@mail.ru; Room 244, Hotel Zhetisu, Abylay Khan 55; ⏲9am-noon & 2-6pm Mon-Fri, 9am-1pm Sat) provides information, takes hotel bookings and can issue the necessary permits for all three routes. The **head office** (☎705-610 2511; altynemel.kadr@mail.ru; Askarbeka 73, Basshi) issues permits for routes 1 and 3 only. Obligatory daily fees are 974T per person for park entry, 200T ecological charge per vehicle, and 600T per group for a park guide.

Organising an independent visit can be complicated and uncertain: overall the best bet is to arrange everything through an Almaty agency. Typical prices from Jibek Joly (p68) for a two-day jaunt range from 50,000T to 100,000T for transport (up to four people) plus around 10,000T per person for accommodation, food and park fees (less if you camp). Jibek Joly is also hoping to introduce fixed-date tours, which would be cheaper.

SOUTHERN KAZAKHSTAN

This is the most Kazakh part of Kazakhstan: Kazakhs are generally the great majority in the population, having been settled here in large numbers during Soviet collectivisation. It is also the only region of Kazakhstan that was within the sphere of the Silk Road and the settled civilisations of Transoxiana in medieval times.

Chief among its varied attractions are the pristine mountain country of Aksu-Zhabagyly Nature Reserve and the Yasaui Mausoleum at Turkistan, Kazakhstan's most sacred Muslim shrine and a fine piece of Timurid architecture. Shymkent is the region's main city.

Taraz ТАРАЗ

7262 / POP 317,000

Situated on the route from Tashkent and Shymkent to Bishkek and Almaty, Taraz is one of Kazakhstan's oldest cities. In the 11th and 12th centuries it was a wealthy Silk Road stop and capital of the Turkic Karakhanid state, but it was comprehensively levelled by Chinggis Khan and effectively disappeared until the existing town was founded in the 19th century, as a northern frontier town of the Kokand khanate. Today it's a mostly Soviet-built place with leafy boulevards, which has staged a commerce-based comeback since the bleak 1990s. Ironically the search for Taraz's lustrous past has killed off its most interesting modern feature, the Green Market, which had a true Silk Road bazaar feel but has been closed to allow archaeologists to excavate the heart of medieval Taraz beneath its site.

In Soviet times Taraz was called Dzhambul, after the locally born Kazakh bard Zhambyl Zhabaev. The centre of town is Dostyk alany, a large ceremonial square surrounded by off-pink governmental buildings.

Sights

Regional Museum MUSEUM
(43 25 85; Tole Bi 55; admission 150T; 9am-6pm Tue-Fri, 10am-7pm Sat & Sun) The pride and joy of what is one of Kazakhstan's best local museums is the domed rear building housing an unusually impressive collection of *balbals*. Also in the rear courtyard is a room dedicated to medieval Taraz, displaying chiefly paintings and pottery. The main building holds a respectable array of stuffed wildlife, battle paintings, chunky Kazakh jewellery and a yurt lavishly decked out in the style of a century ago.

Taraz

Sights
1 Dauitbek Mausoleum D2
2 Karakhan Mausoleum D2
3 Reconstructed Medieval Mosque.......D2
4 Regional Museum C1

Sleeping
5 Hotel Gazovik C1

Eating
6 Kafe Real A2
7 Stambul Kafesi.................................C1
8 Traktir Medved.................................B1

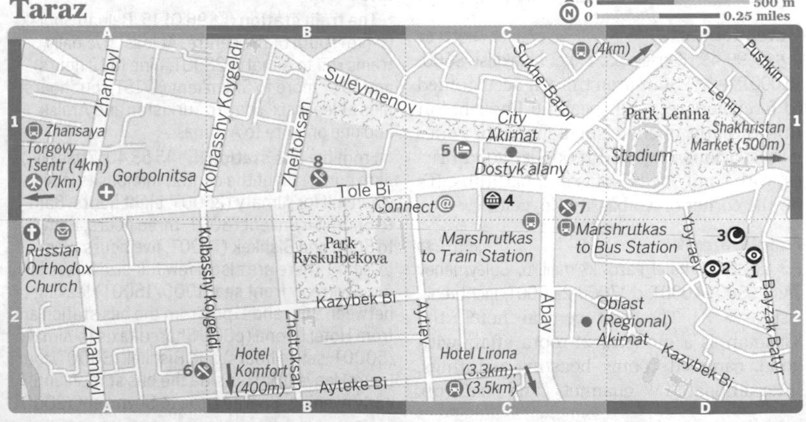

Shakhristan Market MARKET
(Tole Bi; ⏲7am-7pm) For a taste of the bazaar atmosphere for which Taraz used to be celebrated, have a wander round busy Shakhristan market, across the road from the now boarded-up Green Market. Cheap Chinese clothes and shoes predominate but there's a small food section towards the east end, and a couple of inexpensive cafes.

Mausoleums
A wooded park on Ybyraev, 700m east of Dostyk alany, contains reconstructions of two small but important medieval mausoleums. Both house cloth-covered sarcophagi and are Islamic holy sites; leave shoes outside. The **Karakhan Mausoleum** (⏲9am-6pm), originally built in the 12th century, contains the tomb of a revered Karakhanid potentate known as Karakhan or Aulie-Ata (Holy Father). The **Dauitbek Mausoleum** (⏲9am-6pm), for a 13th-century Mongol viceroy, is said to have been built lopsided in revenge for the man's infamous cruelty. Behind it is a modern reconstruction of the 9th- to 12th-century **mosque** in which Aulie-Ata is believed to have prayed, but you may find it locked up.

Sleeping

Hotel Lirona HOTEL $
(☎50 01 67; tarazlirona@mail.ru; Bayzak Batyr 194; r without breakfast 3000-5000T, incl breakfast 5000-8000T; P❄📶) Just 200m straight ahead outside the train station, but inconvenient for everything else, the Lirona has good rooms for its prices. They're clean and comfy and the most expensive are very big, though the three cheapest are windowless and share bathrooms. There's a guest kitchen. Reservations (500T) are worthwhile.

Hotel Komfort HOTEL $$
(☎45 99 49; Konaev 63; r incl breakfast 8000-15,000T; P📶) Staff aren't much accustomed to foreigners yet, and speak no English, but this recently opened small hotel provides very spacious, carpeted rooms at good prices, with comfy beds, sofas and bathtubs. It's on the corner of Kolbasshy Koygeldi.

Hotel Gazovik HOTEL $$
(☎43 32 33; hotel_gazovik@mail.ru; Suleymenov 7A; s 9500-14,000T, d 17,000-22,000T, incl breakfast; P❄📶) The best central hotel, the 'Gasman' is a modern, 21-room affair with good, carpeted rooms boasting paintings, international TV channels and bathtub. The half-*lux* rooms are considerably larger than the boxlike standard singles. Reception staff speak some English and there's a Russian/European restaurant (dishes 1000T to 2000T) downstairs.

Eating

Stambul Kafesi TURKISH $
(Cafe Istanbul; ☎45 39 79; Abay 117A; mains 700-1100T; ⏲11am-11pm) Step into this clean, efficient Turkish cafe for pizza-like *pide*, shashlyk and excellent doner kebabs.

Traktir Medved RUSSIAN $$
(Tole Bi 56; mains 800-2100T; ⏲11am-1am; 📋) Russian-tavern-style Medved (Bear), with a warm atmosphere and efficient service, prepares pretty good meat dishes, soups and salads. The numerous shashlyk varieties include several vegetarian options.

Kafe Real CENTRAL ASIAN $$
(Kolbasshy Koygeldi 208; mains 900-1600T; ⏲noon-midnight) Dedicated, oddly enough, to Real Madrid football (soccer) team, this pleasant garden restaurant offers a good range of meat dishes including plenty of shashlyk varieties. There's draft beer, filtered or unfiltered, to go with your food.

Information

Connect (Tole Bi 59; internet per hr 130T; ⏲10am-midnight) Internet cafe with helpful young staff.

Getting There & Away

Taraz' **Aulie-Ata airport** (☎31 61 37), 8km from the centre off the Shymkent road (1000T by taxi), has four SCAT flights a week each to Almaty (from 18,000T) and Astana (from 27,000T).

The **train station** (☎96 01 15; Baluan Sholak) is 4km south of the centre. At least five daily trains run to Almaty (2890T, nine to 12 hours) and 10 or more to Shymkent (1715T, four hours), plus at least six a day to Turkistan and Aralsk, and one or more to Astana.

From the **bus station** (☎45 53 40; Zhambyl), 4km northeast of the centre, minibuses leave when full for Almaty (2500T, eight hours, 8am to 6pm), Shymkent (800T, three hours, 8am to 8pm) and Bishkek (1200T, five hours, 8am to 8pm). There are also a few full-size buses to Almaty (rear/front seat 1000/1500T) leaving between 9pm and 11pm from the bus station and from Hotel Lirona (p80). Shared taxis to Almaty (5000T, seven hours) and Bishkek (3000T, four hours) leave from outside the bus station until early evening. Shared taxis to Shymkent (2000T,

OFF THE BEATEN TRACK

AKYRTAS

Lovers of mysterious, remote ruins should venture out to Akyrtas, on the steppe 6km south of Aksholak (Akchulak), a village and train station 35km east of Taraz on the Almaty road. What you'll find here is a rectangular precinct about 180m long and 150m wide with the low remains of massively thick perimeter walls built from 1.5m-long sandstone blocks, the bases of equally massive columns, jumbles of stones from around 100 rooms around a central open space, and evidence of an ingenious water supply system. It's a place for the imagination, with no certainty about when it was built or even whether it was completed. The weight of opinion is that it was built as a summer residence for a local Arab or Karluk Turk ruler between the 8th and 11th centuries.

Merke (Merki)-bound minibuses from Taraz bus station, leaving between 6am and 6pm, will drop you at Aksholak for 300T, then you'll need a taxi from there.

2½ hours) go until about 10pm from **Zhansaya Torgovy Tsentr** (Tauke Khan), a small shopping centre 5km west of the centre.

Getting Around

From the (westbound) bus stop across the road from the bus station, marshrutkas 1 and 46 run to Abay just south of Tole Bi in the centre; No 1 continues to the train station. From the stop immediately to the right outside the train station, marshrutkas 47 and 57 run to Abay just south of Tole Bi, and marshrutka 40 and bus 40 head through the centre on Kazybek Bi (westbound), Kolbasshy Koygeldi (northbound) and Tole Bi (westbound) and on out west to Zhansaya Torgovy Tsentr. Fares are 45T to 55T.

Around Taraz

Aysha-Bibi & Babazha-Khatun Mausoleums

In Aysha-Bibi village, 16km west of Taraz on the Shymkent road, are the tombs of two 11th- or 12th-century women, legendary protagonists of a local *Romeo and Juliet* tale. The Aysha-Bibi mausoleum, though heavily restored in 2000–2002, is probably the only authentically old building around Taraz. Made of delicate terracotta bricks in more than 50 different motifs forming lovely patterns, the building looks almost weightless. The story goes that Aysha, daughter of a famed scholar, fell in love with Karakhan, lord of Taraz, but Aysha's father forbade them to marry. The lovers swore a secret pact and Aysha eventually set off for Taraz with her companion Babazha-Khatun. Aysha collapsed from exhaustion/sickness/snake bite; Babazha-Khatun rushed to Karakhan, who raced to his beloved just in time to marry her before she expired. Karakhan had her tomb built on the spot, later adding Babazha-Khatun's mausoleum, with its unusual pointed, fluted roof (this building was totally rebuilt in 2000–2002).

The mausoleums are about 300m (signposted) south off the main road in the village, where Shymkent-bound minibuses from Taraz will drop you.

Shymkent ШЫМКЕНТ

7252 / POP 650,000 / ELEV 510M

Southern Kazakhstan's most vibrant city, with bustling bazaars and a lively downtown, Shymkent (Russian: Chimkent) has more of a Central Asian buzz on its leafy streets than anywhere else in the country. The Mongols razed a minor Silk Road stop here; the Kokand khanate built a frontier fort in the 19th century; Russia took it in 1864; and the whole place was rebuilt in Soviet times. Little more than 100km from Uzbekistan's capital Tashkent, today Shymkent is a thriving trade centre and also produces cement, cigarettes and phosphates and refines oil – and brews two of Kazakhstan's best beers, Shymkentskoe Pivo and the Bavarian-style microbrew Sigma. Its population is about 65% Kazakh and about 14% Uzbek. Mosquitoes can be an irritant from June to August.

Sights

Central or Upper Bazaar MARKET
(Ortalyk bazar, Verkhny rynok; Tashenov; 8am-8pm Tue-Sun) The central bazaar is now somewhat diminished after the conversion of its outlying sprawl into parks and the removal of many traders to markets on the city's outskirts, but it still bustles and is a reminder of Shymkent's long trading history.

Shymkent

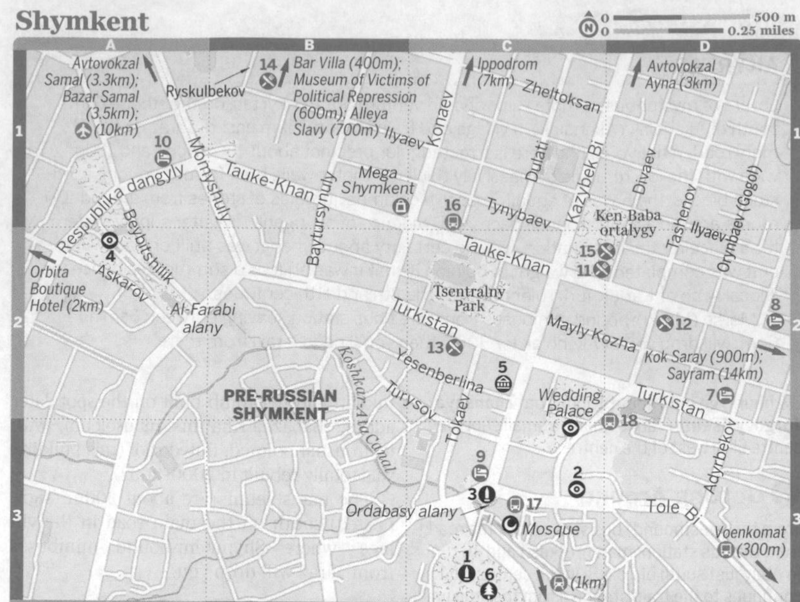

Shymkent

Sights

1 Altyn Shanyrak C3
2 Central or Upper Bazaar C3
3 Independence Monument C3
4 Kiyal alemi A2
5 Regional Museum C2
6 Tauelsizdik sayabagy C3

Sleeping

7 Hotel Dostyk D2
8 Hotel Nurotau D2
9 Hotel Ordabasy C3
10 Motel Bayterek-Sapar A1

Eating

11 Bar Karavan C2
12 Eldoro D2
13 Ladushki C2
14 Madlen B1
15 Madlen D2

Transport

16 Buses to Airport C1
17 Buses to Train Station C3
18 Marshrutkas & Taxis to Dikankol, Kaskasu & Tonkeris D2

Regional Museum MUSEUM
(☎53 02 19; Kazybek Bi 13; admission 200T; ⏲10am-7pm Tue-Sun) The main museum has reasonable exhibits in Kazakh and/or Russian on Shymkent's caravan-town history, plus material on old Otrar, and displays upstairs on the Russian, Soviet and post-independence eras. Spot the photos of Shymkent's best-known daughter – gymnast Nellie Kim, winner of five Olympic golds in 1976 and 1980.

Museum of Victims of Political Repression MUSEUM
(Sayasi kugyn-surgin kurbandary muzeyi; ☎21 05 25; Ryskulbekov; admission 100T; ⏲9am-6pm Mon-Sat) In this small museum photos and documents on Soviet oppression in Kazakhstan and its most celebrated victims surround a central sculpture showing freedom-striving figures restrained by a Soviet banner. A 200T booklet with some English text (if available) helps in understanding what's here.

Equally sobering is **Alleya Slavy** (Alley of Glory) in the park across the street, lined with plaques bearing the names of the more than 140,000 people from the south Kazakhstan region who lost their lives during WWII.

Bazar Samal MARKET
(Ryskulov; ⏲8am-8pm Tue-Sun) Of several new markets around the city fringes, Bazar Samal, next to Samal bus station, is the biggest

and most interesting, with a particularly colourful array of rugs and textiles, as well as food and millions of items of clothing.

Parks & Squares

Central Shymkent's several parks are popular hangouts, especially on summer evenings. Most popular are Ken Baba ortalygy, with its many cafes, restaurants and children's rides, and the amusement park **Kiyal alemi** (Respublika dangyly; ⏲10am-midnight, shorter hr in winter). Southeast of Kiyal alemi, across the small Koshkar-Ata canal, you'll find the few remaining streets of **pre-Russian Shymkent** – a quiet, villagelike area of wooden houses.

Tauelsizdik Sayabagy PARK

(Independence Park) Tauelsizdik sayabagy, accessed by footbridge from the tall, Mother Earth–topped **Independence Monument** (Ordabasy alany), was inaugurated in 2011 for the 20th anniversary of Kazakhstan's independence. It focuses on Ramizder alany (Symbols Sq) which contains assorted national and ethnic-Kazakh symbols designed to inspire feelings of national unity, dominated by the tall **Altyn Shanyrak** (Golden Shanyrak) monument, representing the central roof opening of a yurt.

Festivals & Events

Shymkent's **Nauryz** celebrations, on 22 March, are among the biggest in the country. *Kokpar,* horse races, *audaryspak* (horseback wrestling) and *kyz kuu* (a boy-girl horseback chase) all happen at the Ippodrom (Hippodrome) on the northern edge of the city.

Sleeping

Hotel Nurotau HOTEL $

(☎53 61 34; Tauke-Khan 67; s 4000T, d 5000-7000T, tr 9000T; ❄📶) Much better than it looks from outside, the Nurotau has friendly staff and clean, comfy, carpeted rooms with glassed in showers. No breakfast, but they'll fill the teapot in your room with free tea or coffee.

Hotel Ordabasy HOTEL $

(☎53 64 21; Kazybek Bi 1; r incl breakfast 6000-10,500T; ❄) The Ordabasy has survived from Soviet times with renovated rooms sporting varnished-parquet floors, where everything works OK even if there are already a few cracks in the plasterwork.

Motel Bayterek-Sapar HOTEL $

(☎33 75 55; www.saparhotels.com; Respublika dangyly 4; s 3900-4900T, d 4900-5900T, incl breakfast; 🚭❄) Clean, air-conditioned rooms of varied sizes, inside the Sapar shopping mall. Bathrooms are shared (with squat toilets and hot showers) but are spotless. Reception staff speak a little English and rates include an hour in the sauna.

Hotel Dostyk HOTEL $$

(☎54 84 98; www.hoteldostyk.kz; Adyrbekov 17; s 9000-11,900T, d 17,000-18,500T; P❄@📶) The rooms aren't as spiffy as the lobby but they're modern and comfortable, with apricot paint and touches like tea, coffee, kettle and dressing gowns. Receptionists are amiable and English-speaking and breakfast is a decent buffet affair.

★**Orbita Boutique Hotel** BOUTIQUE HOTEL $$$

(☎40 72 71; http://orbitahotel.kz; Abay dangyly 27; s 15,000-25,000T, d 22,000-27,000T, all incl breakfast; P🚭❄📶) This little gem 2km west of the centre has just a handful of rooms, all individually and pleasingly designed with features like half-timbering and exposed brick – one even has an African theme – and equipped with tea/coffee makers and well-stocked minibars. Attentive, English-fluent receptionists inhabit the conservatory-like upstairs lobby.

There's a restaurant downstairs and several others along the leafy street. It offers free airport pickups too.

Eating

Eldoro INTERNATIONAL $

(Tauke-Khan 80; dishes 220-1600T; ⏲7am-5am; 📋) Large, bright and informal, with efficient service, Eldoro is good for anything from pizza or salads to steaks, shashlyk or breakfast pancakes. It does good fresh-squeezed juices (440T) and reasonably priced beer too – and there's no obligatory service charge.

Bar Karavan CENTRAL ASIAN $

(☎54 52 83; Ken Baba ortalygy; mains 600-1000T; ⏲11am-1am) Karavan offers Uzbek *plov,* Kazakh *beshbarmak,* and Russian *bifstroganof,* but those in the know come for the very tasty Uyghur *burro-laghman* (fried *laghman*). In warm weather you can sit outside in small platform pavilions.

Madlen CAFE $

(☎21 06 91; Ilyaev 17; dishes 400-900T; ⏲10am-midnight) Good cafe with tasty cakes, croissants and desserts, and a leafy pavement terrace too. Has another **branch** (10am-1am) in Ken Baba ortalygy.

Ladushki CAFETERIA $
(Turkistan 12; items 45-200T; 8am-9pm) With decor like a kids' restaurant, Ladushki is actually a very popular and good-value cafeteria where you can get a serve of *manty* or *bliny,* or two pastries and a coffee, for under 300T.

★**Kok Saray** UZBEK $$
(43 22 30; Tauke-Khan 121; mains 700-1500T; 10am-1am) Atmospheric multi-roomed Kok Saray, with carved-wood pillars, murals and an airy front terrace, serves the best Uzbek food in town (and in Kazakhstan, claim aficionados). Don't miss the perfect *plov* (*tashkentsky* with white rice, *andizhansky* with black) or the superb *samsas,* which include a delicious pumpkin *(s tykvoe)* variety. You can't miss its bright lights after dark.

Bar Villa INTERNATIONAL $$$
(Zheltoksan 9/2; mains 1700-3300T; noon-midnight) Overlooking the park behind Kinoteatr Kakakhstan, Bar Villa's two levels of mostly sofa seating have big windows to enjoy the leafy view, and there's a three-level garden terrace for summer. The well-prepared fare focuses on pasta, salads and grills including several sausage varieties, and an excellent picture menu makes up for the lack of an English-language version.

Drinking & Nightlife

The cafes and restaurants in and around Ken Baba ortalygy are the most popular and fun place for evening drinks, and there's live music for dancing nightly from 8pm to midnight at Bar Karavan (p83).

Getting There & Away

AIR

From the **airport** (45 50 31), 10km northwest of the centre, there are two or three daily flights with Air Astana or SCAT to Almaty (from 16,500T) and one or two to Astana (from 23,290T), plus two or three weekly with SCAT to Aktau (33,400T) and three weekly Moscow flights with Transaero.

BUS, MINIBUS & TAXI

The several bus stations are scattered around the city fringes, the most important being **Avtovokzal Samal** (45 12 41; Ryskulov), 4km north of the centre, and **Avtovokzal Ayna** (cnr Zhibek Zholy & Aymautov), 3km northeast of the centre. For Almaty (2000T to 3000T, 11 hours), about 10 air-conditioned buses leave from Ayna between 7pm and 7.30pm, four from a yard outside the train station at 7pm, and others every half-hour from 6pm to 8.30pm from Samal. You can go and book seats for all of these earlier in the day.

For Taraz, minibuses (800T, three hours) depart Samal from 8am to 7pm, and shared taxis (2000T) go from just outside Samal's entrance. For Turkistan minibuses (1000T, 2½ hours) or buses (500T, three hours) go about hourly, 9am to 6pm, from Samal.

For Chernyaevka on the Uzbek border, minibuses (800T, two hours) leave Samal when full between 9am and 6pm – less frequent in the afternoon. For Bishkek there's a bus (2000T, eight hours) at 6.30pm from Samal.

TRAIN

From the **train station** (95 21 20; Kabanbay Batyr), 1.5km southeast of Ordabasy alany, at least seven trains a day go to Almaty (3480T, 13 to 17 hours), Turkistan (1590T to 3020T, three to 4½ hours) and Kyzylorda (2560T, seven to 12 hours); 10 go to Taraz (1715T, four hours) and five to Aralsk (3820T to 6950T, 16 to 22 hours). A convenient overnight service to Almaty is train 12 at 6.30pm. There are also trains to Astana, Mangyshlak (Aktau) and Aktobe daily, and Tashkent three or four times weekly.

Getting Around

Taxis to the centre cost 1000T to 1200T from the airport and 400T to 500T from Samal or Ayna bus stations. In the city, almost any taxi will take you anywhere for 300T to 400T.

Some useful buses (fare 50T; all running both directions along their routes):

5 Train station, Ordabasy alany, Tashenov, Tauke-Khan, Respublika dangyly

12 Airport, Tauke-Khan, Kazybek Bi, Ordabasy alany, train station

19 Ordabasy alany, Avtovokzal Ayna

69 Ordabasy alany, Kazybek Bi, Tauke-Khan, Baytursynuly, Avtovokzal Samal

Around Shymkent

Sayram Сайрам

POP 36,000

About 14km east of Shymkent, the busy little town of Sayram was a Silk Road stop long before Shymkent existed and dates back possibly 3000 years. Kozha Akhmed Yasaui (p87) was born here and Sayram is a stop for many pilgrims en route to his mausoleum at Turkistan. Sayram's population today is almost entirely Uzbek.

Most of the main monuments can be seen in a walk of about one and a half hours starting from Sayram's central traffic lights. Take the eastern (slightly uphill) street, Amir Temur, and then the first (narrow) street on the right after 300m. About 120m along, in a fenced field on your right, is the circular, brick-built **Kydyra Minaret** (Khyzyr Munarasy), about 15m high and possibly dating from the 10th century. You can climb up inside to view the Aksu-Zhabagyly Mountains away to the east. Return to the central crossroads and continue straight ahead, passing the bazaar on your left. Just after the bazaar, on the right, is the 13th-century **Karashash-Ana Mausoleum**, where Akhmed Yasaui's mother lies beneath the central tombstone. Continue 250m, passing the modern **Friday Mosque** on your right, to the large **Mirali Bobo Mausoleum**, where a leading 10th-century Islamic scholar lies buried.

Now turn back towards the central crossroads but turn into the first street on the left, marked Botbay Ata Kesenesi. The high bank on your right along here is part of the old **city walls**. Fork right after 180m, and the street ends at a larger street, Yusuf Sayrami. To your right is a **double-arched gate** erected in 1999 for Sayram's official 3000th birthday. Head left along the street and in 90m you'll reach a **green and yellow sign** marking the spot where, according to legend, Kozha Akhmed Yasaui's mentor Aristan Bab handed him a sacred persimmon stone received by Aristan Bab from the Prophet Mohammed (notwithstanding the five-century gap between the lives of the Prophet Mohammed and Akhmed Yasaui). About 250m past this spot, turn left into a cemetery to the three-domed **Abdul-Aziz Baba Mausoleum**, whose occupant is believed to have been a leader of the Arabic forces that brought Islam to the Sayram area in AD 766. Pilgrims come here for help in averting the 'evil eye'. From here return to the central crossroads.

Several central chaikhanas (teahouses) serve inexpensive shashlyk, tea, *lavash* bread, soups and *plov*. Absurdly overcrowded marshrutkas to Sayram (80T, 40 minutes) leave Shymkent's Ayna bus station about every 15 minutes until around 7pm.

Aksu-Zhabagyly Nature Reserve

This beautiful 1319-sq-km patch of green valleys, rushing rivers, snowcapped peaks and high-level glaciers, abutting the Kyrgyz and Uzbek borders, is the oldest (1926) and one of the most enjoyable and easiest visited of Kazakhstan's nature reserves. Sitting at the west end of the Talassky Alatau (the most northwesterly spur of the Tian Shan), it stretches from the edge of the steppe at about 1200m up to 4239m at Pik Sayram. The main access point is the village of Zhabagyly, 70km east of Shymkent as the crow flies.

The diversity of life in this area where mountains meet steppe is great for botanists, birders and nature lovers in general. Some of Kazakhstan's best nature guides are based locally, making this also a good base for visiting other regional attractions including the Karatau mountains (rich in endemic plants), steppe lakes, deserts and historical/cultural sites like Turkistan and Otrar.

The famous, bright-red Greig's tulip is one of over 1300 flowering plants in the reserve. It dots the alpine meadows, and is quite common even in villages, from mid-April to early May. Wildlife you may see includes ibex, argali sheep, red marmots, paradise flycatchers, golden eagles and Tien Shan brown bears (about 90 inhabit the reserve; chances of sightings are best in spring). About eight snow leopards are also thought to be here. You can visit at any time, but the best weather is from April to September. For birders and botanists, April and May are favourite.

Sights & Activities

From Zhabagyly village it's 6km southeast to the nearest reserve entrance, then 6km (about 1½ hours' walk) to **Kshi-Kaindy**, a mountain refuge near a waterfall at 1700m, then a further 6km to **Ulken-Kaindy**, a second refuge. From Ulken-Kaindy it's 10km to a group of some 2000 stones with **petroglyphs** up to 900 years old, below a glacier descending from the 3800m peak Kaskabulak. A good way to visit these sites is by horse, spending two nights at Ulken-Kaindy. More demanding treks will take you over 3500m passes with nights spent in caves. Another great spot is the 300m-deep **Aksu Canyon** at the reserve's western extremity, a 25km drive from Zhabagyly village.

Obligatory daily fees for entering the reserve are 2000T per person, plus 2000T per group for an accompanying ranger. The excellent local accommodation options will deal with these for you and offer a range of well-run trips in the reserve and further afield – their websites are great information sources. Typical local trip prices include: English-speaking guide 7000T to 9000T per day; horse 5000T to 6000T per day; three-passenger 4WD vehicle to Aksu Canyon and back 17,000T; camping in the reserve including meals 7500T per person.

Sleeping & Eating

It's best to contact these places in advance to give them time to make plans for your visit.

Misha Norets HOMESTAY $
(☎701-693 1547; norets_1969@mail.ru; Satpaeva 25-2, Tulkibas; per person with 3 meals 5000T; P ⊜ ᯤ) In Tulkibas, 18km west of Zhabagyly village, amiable, English-speaking Misha offers homestay accommodation with good meals in his simple family home with an indoor hot-water bathroom. He can also accommodate guests in a comfortable modern home in Maityube (Michurin) village 3km away. Misha is one of the area's best guides (with a reasonable fee of 5000T per day) and can take you anywhere in the region including the highest parts of Aksu-Zhabagyly reserve.

★**Wild Nature** HOMESTAY $$
(Dikaya Priroda; ☎775-793 2246; www.wildnature-kz.narod.ru; Taldybulak 14, Zhabagyly; per person with 2/3 meals 6700/8000T, 'couchsurfing' per person 2000T) This NGO runs one of Kazakhstan's longest-running community tourism programs, with comfortable homestays in houses with hot showers and good local meals. Wild Nature director Svetlana Baskakova also offers a 'couchsurfing' option in her own home for budget travellers.

Svetlana is a highly knowledgeable biologist and great guide who speaks excellent English, and offers a variety of short local trips and longer nature-focused trips. The latter include exciting one-week brown-bear-spotting trips (€2250 per person) and 10-day snow-leopard-tracking trips (€3000) in the reserve, and south Kazakhstan birding tours.

Tourbaza Ruslan GUESTHOUSE, CAMPING $$
(☎72538-555 85, 702-528 4627; www.zhabagly.com; Abay 24, Zhabagyly; tent 1000T, s/d 5000/8000T, 3 meals per person 4000T; ᯤ) Run by a Kazakh-Dutch family, Ruslan has six good rooms at their main house in the village, and four twin-bed rooms in a lovely country property on the edge of the nature reserve, 7km from the village (800T per car, or two to three hours' walk). You can also camp there in rented tents or (June to September) sleep in a yurt.

Meals are available at both places but it also has good guest kitchens. The village house has wi-fi too.

Zhenja & Lyuda's Boarding House GUESTHOUSE $$
(Dom Zheni i Lyudy; ☎72538-5 55 84, 701-717 5851; www.aksuinn.com; Abay 36, Zhabagyly; per person with 3 meals 8000T; P ⊜ ᯤ) This cosy guesthouse-cum-small-hotel on Zhabagyly's main street has rooms with two comfy single beds and private bathroom, and vegetarian meals can be arranged. Owner Yevgeny Belousov, a highly knowledgeable biologist, speaks English, has been in the guesthouse and tour business over 20 years, and knows the area extremely well.

A wide range of trips in the reserve and further afield are available. There's even a hide for photographing birds in the garden.

Getting There & Away

Marshrutkas to Zhabagyly village (400T, two hours) leave Shymkent's Ayna bus station around 11am and sometimes 2pm. Alternatively, there are marshrutkas about every half-hour, 7.30am to 3pm, from Ayna to Turar-Ryskulov (also called Turarkent or Vanovka; 350T, 1½ hours) on the Taraz highway, where you can get a taxi from the market for the 20km trip to Zhabagyly (200/800T shared/whole). Transport to Tulkibas is also available at Turar-Ryskulov.

From Almaty or Taraz you can take a train to Tulkibas and arrange to be picked up there (usual cost to Zhabagyly: 2200T). Train 33, departing Almaty-II station about 8pm daily, reaches Tulkibas (3220T) at about 8am. Or come by bus or taxi and get out at Akbiik, 7km east of Turar-Ryskulov, then take a taxi (around 500T) for the 12km trip to Zhabagyly.

Accommodation options also offer car transfers from various pickup points – from Shymkent or Taraz costs 7000T to 9000T.

Sayram-Ugam National Park

This mountainous park abutting the Uzbek border immediately southwest of the Aksu-Zhabagyly reserve is less well known than its neighbour, but offers similar attractions and is generally cheaper to visit. A community-tourism program provides homestays in the villages of Kaskasu, Dikankol and Tonkeris, in beautiful foothill country where grasslands meet wooded foothills, and in the main access town Lenger.

Good outings include horse or 4WD trips to the western end of the spectacular **Aksu Canyon** from Tonkeris, foot or horse day-trips into **Kaskasu Canyon** from pretty Kaskasu village, and the highlight two-to-three-day camping trip by foot or horse to beautiful **Susingen Lake** from Kaskasu or Dikankol. This high-mountain lake empties at the end of June when the ice blocking its outlet melts, and does not fill again until the winter freeze. Horse trips cost around 15,000/25,000T per day for one/two people including meals and guide.

It's best to make contact in advance with the community tourism organisation **Ugam Public Association** (director 701-222 0328, director's English-speaking son Askar 701-111 8192, office 75247-6 29 92; www.ugam.kz; Tole Bi, Lenger; office normally 9am-6pm Mon-Fri), directed by ex-airforce pilot Alikhan Abdeshev. The office, down a lane beside the Ostanovka Voenkomat bus stop in Lenger, is about 15 minutes' walk from Lenger bus station. Community-tourism prices are 3000T to 5000T per day for a guide, 15,000T per day for an English translator, 3000T to 5000T per day per horse, and 5000T per person for homestays including three meals. The park entrance fee is 450T per person per day. The homestays have comfortable beds in clean rooms, and traditional *banyas* (bathhouses), and serve good local food. Except at Lenger, toilets are outside. At Kaskasu and Lenger you can sleep in yurts.

Lenger is 27km southeast of Shymkent; Dikankol is 47km, Kaskasu is 57km and Tonkeris is 70km. Ugam Public Association offers car transfers for 60T per kilometre. Marshrutkas (150T to 200T, 45 minutes), shared taxis (200T) and much slower buses to Lenger leave frequently (about 7am to 6pm) from the Voenkomat bus stop on Tole Bi in Shymkent. For Dikankol, Kaskasu and Tonkeris marshrutkas (400T to 600T, one to 1½ hours, every two to three hours), buses (around 300T, 1½ to two hours, three or four times daily) and occasional shared taxis go from Tashenov near Shymkent's Central Bazaar. Shared taxis run to Kaskasu from Lenger's market.

Otrar

About 150km northwest of Shymkent lie the ruins of the town that brought Chinggis Khan to Central Asia. Much of the rest of Asia and Europe might have been spared Mongol carnage if Otrar's Khorezmshah governor had not had Chinggis Khan's merchant-envoys murdered here in 1218. In reprisal for the envoy outrage, the following year Chinggis' forces merciessly trashed Otrar, which until then had been one of the most important Silk Road towns in the fertile Syr-Darya valley. It was rebuilt afterwards but eventually abandoned around 1700 after being trashed again by the Zhungars (Oyrats). Today it's just a large dusty mound, known as **Otyrar-Tobe** (approx 8am-dusk) FREE, 11km north of the small town of Shauildir, but archaeologists have exposed some interesting sections: a now partly reconstructed bastion and piece of city wall, the pillar stumps of the main mosque, low walls of the 14th-century Palace of Berdibek (where that other great pillager, Timur, died, en route to conquer China, in 1405), a few residential areas and a bathhouse. In its heyday Otrar spread over nearly 10 times the area of the mound itself.

En route from Shymkent, stop at the good **Otrar Museum** (72544-2 11 50; Zhibek Zholy 1) in Shauildir (closed for renovations at research time but expected to reopen by 2014).

Three kilometres west of Otyrar-Tobe is the **Aristan-Bab Mausoleum**, the tomb of an early mentor of Kozha Akhmed Yasaui. The existing domed, brick building here dates from 1907 and is a stop for pilgrims heading to Turkistan.

Minibuses (700T, 2½ hours) to Shauildir leave about hourly, 7am to 6pm, from Shymkent's Samal bus station. Shared taxis from Samal cost 1000T. A taxi from Shauildir to Otyrar-Tobe, Aristan-Bab and back shouldn't cost more than 2000T. There's no direct public transport between Shauildir and Turkistan, but a one-way taxi costs about 3500T including an hour's stop at Otyrar-Tobe.

Turkistan ТУРКИСТАН

At Turkistan, 165km northwest of Shymkent (an easy day-trip), stands Kazakhstan's greatest architectural monument and most important pilgrimage site. The mausoleum of the first great Turkic Muslim holy man, Kozha Akhmed Yasaui, was built by Timur in the late 14th century on a grand scale comparable with his magnificent creations

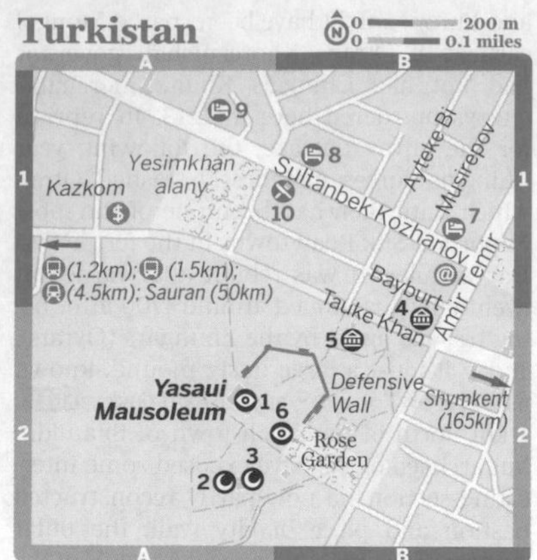

Turkistan

Top Sights
1 Yasaui Mausoleum A2

Sights
2 Friday Mosque A2
3 Hilvet Semi-Underground Mosque A2
4 Historical-Cultural-Ethnographic Centre B2
5 History Museum B2
6 Mausoleum of Rabigha-Sultan Begum B2

Sleeping
7 Hotel Edem B1
8 Hotel Sabina B1
9 Hotel Turkistan A1

Eating
Edem Restaurant .... (see 7)
10 Kafe Aspan B1

in Samarkand, and has no rivals in Kazakhstan for man-made beauty.

Turkistan was already an important trade and religious centre (under the name Yasy) when the revered Sufi teacher and mystical poet Kozha Akhmed Yasaui came to live here in the 12th century. Yasaui was born at Sayram, probably in 1103, underwent ascetic Sufi training in Bukhara, then lived much of the rest of his life in Turkistan, dying here about 1166. He founded the Yasauia Sufi order and had the gift of communicating his understanding to ordinary people through poems and sermons in a Turkic vernacular, a major reason for his enduring popularity.

Yasaui's original small tomb was already a place of pilgrimage before Timur ordered a far grander mausoleum built here in the 1390s. Timur died before it was completed and the main facade was left unfinished – today it remains bare of the beautiful tilework that adorns the rest of the building, with scaffolding poles still protruding. From the 16th to 18th centuries Turkistan was the capital of the Kazakh khans.

Coming by road from Shymkent, you can disembark your minibus when the mausoleum looms into view on your left as you enter Turkistan.

Sights

The Yasaui Mausoleum sits amid pretty grounds which contain several lesser monuments.

★Yasaui Mausoleum MAUSOLEUM
(7am-9pm approx May-Sep, 9am-1pm & 2-6pm rest of year) FREE The main chamber is capped with an 18m-wide dome, above a vast, 2000kg, metal *kazan* (cauldron) for holy water, given by Timur. Around this central hall are 34 smaller rooms on two floors. Yasaui's tomb lies behind an ornate wooden door at the end of the main chamber: you can view it through grilles from corridors on either side. The right-hand corridor contains the tomb of Abylay Khan, leader of Kazakh resistance to the Zhungars in the 18th century.

Off the main chamber's far left corner is the mausoleum's carpeted mosque, with a beautifully tiled *mihrab* (Mecca-facing niche). Except in the mosque, visitors to the mausoleum don't usually remove shoes though women normally wear headscarves (available at the entrance).

The glorious blue, turquoise and white tiling on the outside of the building merits close inspection. Note the particularly lovely fluted rear dome, above Yasaui's tomb chamber.

Historical-Cultural-Ethnographic Centre MUSEUM
(Tarikhi-Madeni-Etnografiyalyk Ortalyk; Tauke Khan; admission 200T; 9am-7pm) This big, proud new museum has three floors of colourful exhibits on regional history, from prehistoric petroglyphs to the obligatory Nazarbaev homage on the top floor. Much of the material is paintings, maps and dioramas, since the collection of actual artefacts is sparse before the 19th century. Explanatory information is in Kazakh only, but free tours in English are available.

History Museum MUSEUM
(⏲9am-1pm & 3-6pm) FREE The History Museum, in the Yasaui Mausoleum grounds, focuses mostly on Kozha Akhmed Yasaui, Sufism and Islamic learning. There are models of the Yasaui Mausoleum, the Aristan Bab Mausoleum and the Hilvet semi-underground mosque. There is some English-language labelling.

Mausoleum of Rabigha-Sultan Begum MAUSOLEUM
This small building is actually a replica of the 15th-century original (which was torn down in 1898). Rabiga-Sultan Begum was a great-granddaughter of Timur whose husband Abylkayyr Khan, a 15th-century leader of the then-nomadic Uzbeks, put the finishing touches to the structure of the Yasaui mausoleum's facade.

Hilvet Semi-Underground Mosque MOSQUE
On a small hill within the Yasaui Mausoleum grounds stands the 12th- to 15th-century Hilvet semi-underground mosque, with the cell to which Kozha Akhmed Yasaui is said to have withdrawn towards the end of his life. Next to it stands the wood-pillared, 19th century **Friday Mosque** (Zhuma meshiti).

Sleeping & Eating

Hotel Edem HOTEL $
(☎3 35 71; edem_kz@mail.ru; Sultanbek Kozhanov 6A; r incl breakfast 5000-9500T;) Overall the best sleeping option, the Edem has pleasant rooms with wood-and-wrought-iron beds and cane furnishings. Thoughtful touches like lamps reachable from your bed balance out the occasional absent toilet seat. Also here is the town's best **restaurant** (mains 800-2400T; ⏲8am-midnight), with a courtyard garden that is a fine place to down good shashlyk, salads and beer.

The garden also turns into Turkistan's most popular nightspot in summer, so ask for a back room if you aim to slumber before midnight.

Hotel Sabina HOTEL $
(☎3 14 05; Sultanbek Kozhanov 16; r 3000-4000T;) Turkistan's budget option is a well kept, friendly place with eight smallish but clean and decent rooms, sharing bathrooms. Those upstairs are bigger and brighter, with TVs and a better bathroom.

Hotel Turkistan HOTEL $
(☎4 14 26; gturkiestan@mail.ru; Sultanbek Kozhanov; r 5000T, lux 13,000T; P) The Turkistan has a grand domed lobby, oil paintings, thick red carpets and sizeable, well-looked-after rooms, but a rather dour atmosphere. Breakfast costs 500T to 1000T.

Kafe Aspan CENTRAL ASIAN $
(Sultanbek Kozhanov; dishes 200-550T; ⏲10am-11pm) A neat and tranquil spot on the main street, with good salads, soups and meat dishes.

Information

Internet (Sultanbek Kozhanov 1; internet per hr 150T; ⏲10am-9pm)

Kazkom (Tauke Khan 371; ⏲9am-noon & 2-6pm Mon-Fri) This bank does currency exchange and has 24-hour ATMs.

Getting There & Around

Three bus/minibus terminals are strung close together along Tauke Khan 2km west of the Yasaui Mausoleum. Vehicles to Shymkent leave when full and are most frequent before 10am to 11am. **Merey Avtobeketi**, first up on the left, has

OFF THE BEATEN TRACK

SAURAN САУРАН

Northwest of Turkistan stand the best preserved and most atmospheric ruins of all the many ruined Silk Road cities in the Syr-Darya valley. Sauran was capital of the Mongol White Horde in the 14th century, and 16th-century writers described it as a 'pleasant' and 'cheerful' city with two high minarets and a sophisticated water-supply system. Its circuit of limestone walls, plus remains of some bastions and gates, still stand despite conquerors and the elements. Sauran is visible as a long, low mound about 2.5km southwest from the Turkistan–Kyzylorda highway, some 50km out of Turkistan and about 13km past the village of Sauran. Closer up, the ruins loom like something out of *The Lord of the Rings* (but remember: this is Sauran, not Sauron). They are normally unsupervised. A taxi from Turkistan should cost around 5000T round trip: ask for Krepost (Fortress) Sauran to distinguish it from Sauran village.

minibuses to Shymkent (500T, 2½ hours) and some services to Taraz and Almaty. **Altyn Orda Avtobeketi**, almost opposite, has more comfortable Shymkent vans (800T), a bus to Bishkek (2500T, 11 hours) at 6pm, and further Taraz and Almaty services. The main **Avtovokzal**, 250m further along on the left, has 800T Shymkent vans till late afternoon, plus minibuses to Kyzylorda (1000T, four hours) until about 7pm.

The **train station**, at the far end of Tauke Khan, 3km past the bus stations, has nine daily trains northwest to Kyzylorda (1770T to 3480T, four to eight hours), four or more to Aralsk (3215T to 5920T, 13 to 19 hours) and Aktobe (5480T to 8990T, 23 to 29 hours), eight or more daily southeast to Shymkent (1590T to 3020T, three to 4½ hours), five or more to Almaty (4140T, 17 to 22 hours), at least two trains most days to Tashkent (5450T to 11,125T, eight to nine hours), and one most days to Bishkek (9640T to 9950T, 17 hours).

Marshrutkas 2 and 10 (40T) run between Sultanbek Kozhanov and the bus and train stations.

Kyzylorda КЫЗЫЛОРДА

7242 / POP 199,000

On the Syr-Darya 290km northwest of Turkistan, Kyzylorda became capital of Soviet Kazakhstan in 1925 but was replaced by cooler Almaty when the Turksib railway reached there in 1929. Oil and gas operations in the South Turgay Basin, mainly Chinese-owned, underpin its economy today. Kyzylorda's chief role for most travellers is as a staging post for Aralsk or Baykonur. Carry your passport in town: police can be very zealous with document checks.

The **Regional Museum** (27 62 74; Auezov 20; foreigner/Kazakhstani 500/200T; 9am-1pm & 3-7pm Tue-Sun) spreads over 11 rooms, ranging from abandoned Silk Road cities and the Aral Sea to renowned local musicians, mostly labelled in Kazakh only. Your enjoyment may be diluted by the museum's security guards, who gave us a thorough body scan then followed us round room by room.

Sleeping & Eating

Hotel Kayr HOTEL **$**

(27 67 97; Aytbaeva 29; s/d with shared bathroom 7000/7500T, with private bathroom 9500/12,000T, incl breakfast;) The Kayr, 1km southeast of the train station, is at the cheap end of the price scale by Kyzylorda standards and has well-kept, comfy rooms. Shared bathrooms are good and clean, though the rooms that go with them are smallish.

WORTH A TRIP

BAYKONUR COSMODROME

The Baykonur Cosmodrome, a 6717-sq-km area of semidesert about 250km northwest of Kyzylorda, has been the launch site for all Soviet- and Russian-manned space flights since Yury Gagarin, the first human in space, was lobbed up here in 1961. In fact the cosmodrome is 300km southwest of the original town of Baykonur, but the USSR told the International Aeronautical Federation that Gagarin's launch point was Baykonur, and that name also stuck to the real site. The military town built to guard and service the cosmodrome, formerly called Leninsk, has now acquired the name Baykonur too. The Kyzylorda–Aralsk road and railway pass between the town and the cosmodrome, some of whose installations are visible (the whole site stretches about 75km north). The town's train station is called Toretam (Russian: Tyuratam).

Since the collapse of the USSR, Kazakhstan has leased the cosmodrome and town to Russia until 2050. Baykonur today has nine launch complexes and sends up astronauts from many countries, including space tourists, as well as unmanned spacecraft. Following the end of the USA's space shuttle program in 2010, it's the world's only launch centre for human space flight apart from China's Jiuquan.

Visitors to the cosmodrome and Baykonur town require advance permission from the Russian space agency, **Roscosmos** (www.roscosmos.ru), and the only practicable way in is through a well-connected travel agency. Among the few agencies offering visits on a regular basis are Almaty-based Silk Road Adventures (p68) and Arnai Tours (p68), and Karaganda-based Nomadic Travel Kazakhstan (p110). Three-day trips planned to coincide with launches, including return flights from Almaty to Kyzylorda, cost from around €900 to €1400 per person. You can cut costs by starting the tour at Toretam station. Launch dates are known three to six months ahead and you need to start the paperwork at least one month in advance, but better two months.

Hotel Selena Star HOTEL $$
(☎27 56 26; Begim-Ana 30; s/d incl breakfast 9600/11,600T; P ❄ @) A well-run option 900m southeast of the train station. Rooms are comfy and well-sized, and there's an enormous billiards room if you're in the mood for a frame.

Tagam CAFETERIA $
(cnr Korkyt Ata & Baytursynuly; mains 500-900T; 24hr;) This large, very clean, self-service restaurant does a range of well-priced and decently presented fare from *manty* and grilled chicken to salads and *shubat* (fermented camel's milk).

Getting There & Around

Air Astana flies daily to Almaty (from 17,340T) and Astana (from 20,250T); SCAT flies to Aktau and Karaganda. The **train station** (Auelbekov), on the northern edge of the centre, has at least eight daily departures to Aralsk (2220T to 4790T, seven to 10 hours), Turkistan (1770T to 3480T, four to eight hours) and Shymkent (2560T; seven to 12 hours). A bus to Aralsk (1200T, nine hours) leaves at 10pm from about June to September only, from the southeast corner of the square in front of the train station. Three daily buses to Turkistan (800T, five hours) and Shymkent (1300T, eight hours) and two to Almaty (3800T, 20 hours), plus marshrutkas to Turkistan (1000T) and Shymkent (1500T), go from the shabby **Avtovokzal Saltanat** (Bokeykhan 64), 3.5km south of the centre. Bus 1 (50T) travels slowly between the train station and Avtovokzal Saltanat via the city centre.

Aralsk (Aral) АРАЛЬСК (АРАЛ)

☎72433 / POP 30,000

Four decades ago Aralsk, 450km northwest of Kyzylorda, was an important fishing port on the shores of the Aral Sea, with a population twice its current size. A large mosaic in its train station depicts how in 1921 Aralsk's comrades provided fish for people starving in Russia. Today most of the Aral Sea is gone, victim of Soviet irrigation schemes that took water from its lifelines, the Syr-Darya and Amu-Darya rivers, and pushed the shoreline 60km out from Aralsk. If you want to witness the Aral Sea environmental disaster firsthand, Aralsk is easier to visit than similarly defunct ports in Uzbekistan – and less gloomy, as efforts to save the northern part of the Aral Sea are succeeding and its fishing industry is growing again.

There are two central **internet cafes** (Abilkayyr Khan; internet per hr 300T; 24hr) on the main street, and several ATMs on the main square, just north of Abilkayyr Khan.

Sights & Activities

Aral Tenizi TOUR
(☎2 22 56, 701-662 7163, 705-449 3732; www.aralsea.net; Makataev 10-13; office 9am-6pm Mon-Fri) The NGO Aral Tenizi, which works to revive the Aral fishing industry, can arrange 4WDs and drivers to visit the sites. Ask for English-speaking Serik Dyusenbaev. A half-day trip to the Zhalanash ship cemetery (p91) and the sea costs 15,000T for up to four people. A day trip to the Kok-Aral Dam, 220km from Aralsk (about 3½ hours each way), is 35,000T.

A day trip to Zhalanash and on to tiny Tastubek, 25km further and the nearest village to the seashore (4km), is 20,000T: you can swim in the sea from an earth beach near Tastubek, and short outings (up to an hour) in fishers' boats can be arranged for around 5000T.

Aral Tenizi charges all clients a 3000T membership fee per group. Try to make contact ahead, to allow time to make your arrangements.

Ship Cemetery SHIP CEMETERY
Near Zhalanash (Zhambyl), a former fishing village 55km west of Aralsk and now some 10km from the seashore, you can still see a ship cemetery, where three abandoned hulks rust in the sand, providing shelter for those other ships of the desert, the area's wandering camels. A few years ago there were more ships, but several have been spirited away by scrap-metal scavengers.

Fishermen's Museum MUSEUM
(Makataev; admission 200T; 9am-noon & 3-7pm Mon-Sat) Four fishing boats stand on pedestals beside Aralsk's former harbour, near the town centre, as a tribute to fallen heroes. The biggest of the four now forms part of the recently established Fishermen's Museum, which has fishing gear, paintings, photos and maps from Soviet times, and a 10-minute video. The boat's interior has been partly refurbished and you can climb up on deck.

History Museum MUSEUM
(Yesetov; admission 250T, photos 100T each; 9am-noon & 3-7pm Mon-Sat) Aralsk's small history museum has a few desiccation

photos, some imaginative oil paintings and around 15 jars preserving different Aral Sea fish species – all now again present in the North Aral except for the sturgeon. There's also a large diorama depicting a battle between Bolshevik and White forces near Aralsk in 1919.

Sleeping & Eating

Homestays HOMESTAY $
(per person incl breakfast/3 meals 3000/4500T) Aral Tenizi (p91) offers clean and comfortable host-family accommodation in two Aralsk homes with hot showers. It can also arrange more basic homestays (outside toilets, no showers) in Tastubek and other villages for around 3000T per person including meals, but note that there's an extra 10,000T driver's fee on any overnight trips.

Aral Hotel HOTEL $
(☎2 14 79; Makataev 14; r 4000-7000T; ❄) Aralsk's only hotel stands between the former harbour and the Aral Tenizi NGO office. It's basic and a bit dilapidated, but the two 7000T rooms do have hot showers (the others have no showers at all, just a toilet and cold-water washbasin).

Chin-Son KAZAKH, KOREAN $
(Makataev; mains 500-1000T; ⏱11am-midnight) Chin-Son, opposite the Aral Tenizi NGO office, is the best eating option, with Kazakh, Russian and spicy Korean dishes.

Getting There & Around

Aralsk's **train station** (☎9 50 72), called Aralskoe More, is 1km northeast of the central square. There are at least four daily departures northwest to Aktobe (2890T to 5700T, 10 to 11½ hours) and southeast to Kyzylorda (2390T to 4790T, seven to 10 hours), Turkistan (3215T to 5920T, 13 to 19 hours), Shymkent (3820T to 6950T, 16 to 22 hours) and Almaty (5960T to 6480T, 30 to 37 hours), plus trains to Tashkent (11,890T to 23,670T, 21 to 24 hours) and Bishkek (17,000T to 17,910T, 30 hours) five or six days a week.

In July and August tickets often sell out a week ahead: buy your onward or return tickets in advance.

THE ARAL SEA: ON ITS WAY BACK TO ARALSK

Four decades after they last saw the Aral Sea in their harbour, the people of Aralsk have real hope that it will be back soon.

Helped by international aid and lending agencies, Kazakhstan has revived the northern Aral by building the 14km-long Kok-Aral Dam, completed in 2005, across the last channel connecting the northern and southern parts of the sea. With no outlet to the south, the North Aral has risen again with water from the Syr-Darya. Rehabilitated waterworks along the river have helped by increasing the water flow into the sea, and by 2012 the North Aral had crept back to within 18km of Aralsk.

Now, a second dyke, 4m higher than the Kok-Aral Dam, is to be built across the mouth of Saryshyganak Bay, the sea's northeastern arm which used to reach Aralsk. At the same time a new channel will be cut from the Syr-Darya to feed water into Saryshyganak Bay. It's hoped the new dyke will be ready by 2016, and that the waters will reach Aralsk in 2017.

In the 1990s the fishing catch in the North Aral was limited to flounder, the only species able to survive the sea's extreme salinity then. Since 2005, at least 15 types of freshwater fish have returned to the North Aral via the Syr-Darya. Fishers travel from their villages, often now 25km or 30km from the shore, to take out small boats from which they catch carp, catfish, pike and the valuable pike-perch, which is exported to Russia and Poland. The total annual catch is up to around 4800 tonnes (about a quarter of what the Aral provided in its heyday). Four fish-processing plants are operating again around the North Aral, with more expected to open.

Locals also hope that revival of the North Aral and Saryshyganak Bay will help reduce the noxious sandy, salty windstorms that plague communities such as Aralsk.

The Kok-Aral Dam has condemned the supersaline, fishless remnants of the South Aral to accelerated evaporation, but most experts consider that already a lost cause, with no hope of more water from its main source, the Amu-Darya, which flows through Turkmenistan and Uzbekistan.

A bus to Kyzylorda (1200T, nine hours) leaves the train station at 10pm from about June to September only. No public transport runs along the good 600km road to Aktobe. Aral Tenizi can provide taxis to or from Kyzylorda for 35,000T to 40,000T (six to seven hours).

WESTERN KAZAKHSTAN

Western Kazakhstan – so far west that the part beyond the Ural River is in Europe – is a gateway to Central Asia from the Caucasus and the Volga and Ural regions of Russia. Kazakhstan's biggest oil and gas fields – Tengiz (oil), Karachaganak (gas) and the offshore oil of Kashagan beneath the Caspian Sea – and a glut of other mineral resources have brought boom times to the west's main cities, but elsewhere the human population is sparse and the landscape is chiefly desert and steppe.

For those with a taste for adventurous exploring, the deserts outside the Caspian-side city of Aktau, dotted with underground mosques, ancient necropolises, wandering camels and spectacular rock formations, are just the ticket. The other main cities – Atyrau, Aktobe and Uralsk – have limited interest for travellers except as overland transit points. The region is one hour behind Astana time (which is used by the rest of the country), but train timetables often still use Astana time.

Aktau — АКТАУ

7292 / POP 180,000

An entry point into Central Asia by air from the Caucasus and İstanbul, and by an irregular ferry from Baku (Azerbaijan), Aktau perches on Kazakhstan's Caspian shore. With some sandy beaches, low-key summer tourism and a temperate climate (several degrees above zero in January), it's a pleasant enough town for a day or two – but the area's main interest, other than transport connections, is the natural and man-made wonders of the surrounding region, Mangistau.

Local uranium and oil finds were the reason Soviet architects began to lay out a model town of wide, straight streets in this remote location in 1958. The uranium, from an open-cast mine 30km northeast, fed Aktau's nuclear fast breeder reactor, which generated the town's electricity, powered its desalination plant and produced uranium concentrate for military purposes. Uranium mining, nuclear power and associated industries were wound down in the 1990s, but Aktau has since gained a new lease of life as a centre for oil and gas operations, both onshore and offshore.

The only significant street with a name is Kazakhstan Respublikasy Prezidentininy dangyly (you can understand why many people still call it Lenina). Aktau addresses are based on *mikrorayon* (microdistrict) building numbers: 4-17-29 means Microdistrict 4, Building 17, Apartment 29.

Sights & Activities

From the **MiG fighter plane memorial** you can descend steps to the breezy **seafront**, a mixture of low cliffs, rocks and thin sandy strips, with assorted cafes and bars that are lively in summer (when some of them double as open-air discos). A narrow street followed by a pedestrian promenade parallel the coast for 1km south from here. The wider, more popular **Dostar Beach** (admission 100T) is about 4km further southeast.

Regional Museum — MUSEUM
(Dom 23A, Mikrorayon 9; foreigner/Kazakhstani 400/200T, 9am-1pm & 2-6pm Tue-Fri, 10am-5pm Sat & Sun) Recently renovated, the Regional Museum has moderately interesting exhibits ranging from Caspian fish to the early Mangistau oil industry.

Briz-Aktau — SAILING
(701-913 4077, 52 30 50; www.marin.kz; Dom 1, Mikrorayon 5; per hr 25,000-40,000T; office 9am-6pm Mon-Fri) Take a sail on the blue Caspian waters in a beautiful 12m French-built sail/motor catamaran. Briz's professionally skippered boats, for up to 10 passengers, can go for any period from an hour upward (including overnight). All boats have four two-person cabins, plus a galley area.

It is conveniently berthed at **Yakht-Klub Briz** (Mikrorayon 1). You can contact the firm by phone outside office hours.

Sleeping

Hotel Keremet — HOTEL $
(50 15 69; Dom 20, Mikrorayon 3; dm 1500T, s/d 2000/3500T, r half lux/lux 4000/5000T;) Rooms at this budget option are worn and mosquito-prone, and the cheapest have shared bathrooms, but all have air-con. There's a cafe adjoining and staff cheer up if you can manage some words of Russian for them.

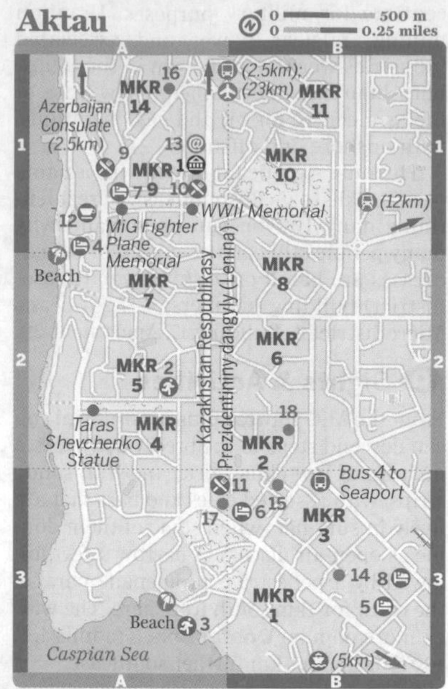

Aktau

Sights

1 Regional Museum A1

Activities, Courses & Tours

2 Briz-Aktau A2
3 Yakht-Klub Briz A3

Sleeping

4 Hotel Kaspiysky Bereg A1
5 Hotel Keremet B3
6 Hotel Shams B3
7 Renaissance Aktau Hotel A1
8 Silk Way Hotel B3

Eating

9 Bakkara A1
10 Costa's Cafe A1
11 Guns & Roses A3

Drinking & Nightlife

12 Lido A1

Information

13 Matrix Internet A1
14 Migration Police B3
15 Partner Tour B3

Transport

16 Alban Avia A1
17 Dilizhans Aktau A3
18 Paromnaya Kassa B2

Silk Way Hotel HOTEL $$
(☎50 59 09; www.silkwayaktau.com; Dom 25A, Mikrorayon 3; s/d incl breakfast from 10,000/12,000T; P ❄ 📶) Silk Way has a friendly, English-speaking reception and spacious, impeccable, well-equipped, if bland, rooms. There's also an international restaurant.

Hotel Kaspiysky Bereg HOTEL $$
(Caspian Shore Hotel; ☎51 17 18; kaspii-mangistau@mail.ru; Mikrorayon 7; s 7000-12,000T, d 14,000T, s/d with shared bathroom 3000/6000T, all incl breakfast; ❄ 📶) This homey small hotel near the seashore has good-sized, carpeted rooms. The most expensive boast attractive Chinese silk 'paintings' and have glassed-in terraces facing the sea (through trees). The eight small shared bathrooms downstairs are decent deals if you can get one.

Hotel Shams HOTEL $$
(☎50 07 36; Dom 70, Mikrorayon 2; r incl breakfast 7000-12,000T; ❄) Little Shams offers a friendly welcome and eight reasonable rooms with pine furnishings and international TV channels, despite an unpromising entrance through a metal door at the back of the Shams Kafe building (the sign just says Konak Uy).

★**Renaissance Aktau Hotel** HOTEL $$$
(☎30 06 00; www.marriott.com; Mikrorayon 9; r incl breakfast Sun-Thu from 61,600T, Fri & Sat 35,840T; P ⊖ ❄ @ 📶 ≋) The favourite of Western businessfolk, the Renaissance provides very comfy, brightly decorated, well-equipped rooms, plus a great sea-view terrace, good outdoor pool, health club with heated pool, and a host of other facilities.

Eating

Several seafront cafes below the MiG monument serve up fried chicken, *manty* and meat/fish/vegetable shashlyk (500T to 1700T), and have outdoor tables in summer.

Costa's Cafe INTERNATIONAL $$
(Torgovy Tsentr Ardager, Mikrorayon 9; dishes 700-3500T; ⏲9am-2am; 📶 🗐) Bright, clean and pleasant, with an outdoor terrace, Costa's is a sound bet for anything from English breakfast to pancakes, pasta, salads or cakes.

★**Bakkara** CENTRAL ASIAN $$$
(Mikrorayon 14; mains 1100-2800T; ⏲noon-1am; 📶) The best shashlyk in town – tender lamb, pork or sturgeon – are grilled up at this place with no sign but recognisable by the trees lining its perimeter. The shashlyk go down a treat with chips, a salad and a

mug of beer, especially in the shady garden in warm weather.

Guns & Roses PUB $$$
(52 49 41; Kazakhstan Respublikasy Prezidentininy dangyly, Dom 66, Mikrorayon 2; mains 1500-4500T; 11am-2am Sun-Thu, 11am-4am Fri & Sat;) The best of Aktau's handful of British-style pubs, Guns & Roses serves generous burgers, steaks and pizzas, shows sport on TV and hosts a live rock/jazz/pop band from 10pm Thursday to Saturday.

Drinking & Nightlife

Lido CAFE
(Mikrorayon 7; 4pm-3am) Lido's two open-air decks are packed for summer night drinks.

Information

There's an Azerbaijan consulate (p125) in Aktau.

Matrix Internet (Dom 22, Mikrorayon 9; internet per hr 200T; 24hr) In the building with a huge painting of Abylay Khan on its street end.

Migration Police (47 48 89; Dom 123, Mikrorayon 3; 9am-noon Mon-Thu & Sat) Come here if you need to register your visa.

Partner Tour (52 60 88; www.partner-tur.ru; Office 5, Dom 12, Mikrorayon 2; 10am-6pm Mon-Fri) This well-organised agency can set up guided trips from one to seven days around the sights of Mangistau. Contact them at least a couple of days ahead. English- and German-speaking guides are available.

WORTH A TRIP

THE PILGRIMAGE TO BEKET-ATA

Beket-Ata, 285km east of Aktau, is an underground mosque to which the clairvoyant and teacher Beket-Ata (1750–1813) retreated in the later part of his life, ultimately dying and being buried here. A Mangistau native, Beket-Ata studied in Khiva (Uzbekistan) and on his return he is believed to have set up four mosques, including this one where he founded a Sufi school. Every day dozens of pilgrims – and hundreds on holidays – make the bumpy journey across the deserts to pray and receive Beket-Ata's inspiration. The underground mosque (three caves) is set in a rocky outcrop overlooking a desert canyon.

Aktau tour companies run two-day 4WD trips to Beket-Ata costing around 80,000T to 100,000T for up to four people. Private drivers will do it for much less – ask at your hotel and check the Beket-Ata ads in *Tumba* newspaper, where you'll find Toyota Land Cruisers that may cost 25,000T to 30,000T round-trip and minibuses charging as little as 4000T per person. Alternatively, take an early public minibus or shared taxi from Aktau bus station to the dusty oil town of **Zhanaozen**, 150km east by paved road. Zhanaozen saw serious unrest in 2011, when an oil workers' strike ended with security forces shooting dead at least 14 unarmed demonstrators, but there have been no reported violent outbreaks since then. From Zhanaozen bazaar, 4WDs (3500/14,000T per person/vehicle round-trip) and more uncomfortable minibuses (3000T per person) leave in the morning for Beket-Ata. You'll spend most of the five- or six-hour, 135km trip lurching and bumping along steppe and desert tracks. En route, vehicles stop at **Shopan-Ata**, an underground mosque and large necropolis dating back to at least the 10th century, where Shopan-Ata, a disciple of Kozha Akhmed Yasaui, dwelt. Most groups sleep (free) in the pilgrim hostel–cum-mosque-cum–dining hall at Beket-Ata, before leaving early next morning. Zhanaozen has hotels in the street along the east end of the bazaar, including **Hotel Lyuks** (72934-3 32 64; Rakhmet Otesinov; r incl breakfast 6000-16,000T;), with large rooms in reasonable condition, and the more dilapidated but quite friendly **Hotel Zhansaya** (72934-3 49 29; Rakhmet Otesinov; s 2000-3500T, d 4000-7000T;). Best in town is **Hotel Temirkazyk** (72934-5 25 47; www.temirkazykhotel.kz; ulitsa 2, Mikrorayon Aray 1; s/d incl breakfast from 11,000/13,000;), with good, big, comfy rooms and a decent cafe/restaurant.

On arrival at Shopan-Ata and Beket-Ata all visitors are expected to purify themselves by using the squat toilets. If you're travelling with pilgrims, be ready to join in prayers, ritual walks around sacred trees and communal meals of the Kazakh national dish *beshbarmak*.

Getting There & Away

The airport (p132), 23km north of the centre, has an always-open **air-ticket office** (☎60 97 54; ⏲24hr). A useful train-ticket agency is **Dilizhans Aktau** (☎50 83 38; South Wing, Hotel Aktau, Mikrorayon 2; ⏲9am-8pm).

AIR

Air Astana flies daily to Almaty (from 28,800T), Atyrau (from 12,800T), Astana (from 27,650T) and to İstanbul (from 43,200T) twice weekly. SCAT goes daily to Atyrau (from 11,200T), four or five times weekly to Astana (from 26,700T), Aktobe (from 19,700T) and Uralsk (from 21,700T), and once or twice weekly to Kyzylorda (from 26,700T), Shymkent (from 34,500T), Kiev (from 39,600T), Baku (from 26,400T), Tbilisi (from 25,600T), Yerevan (from 23,600T) and Astrakhan (from 25,800T) and other southern Russian cities. Azerbaijan Airlines flies to Baku (from 25,000T) daily – tickets from, among others, **Alban Avia** (☎42 74 00; Dom 59, Mikrorayon 14; ⏲9am-7pm). Transaero operates three weekly flights to Moscow (from 36,000T).

BOAT

A ferry to Baku (Azerbaijan) leaves irregularly from the seaport in the southeast of town.

See p133 for more details.

MINIBUS & SHARED TAXI

From the bus station, in the north of town, minibuses leave when full, until 7pm, to Shetpe (580T, 2½ hours) and Zhanaozen (590T, 2½ hours). Shared taxis to Shetpe (1500T, two hours) go from the street immediately north of the bus station; shared taxis to Zhanaozen (1500T, two hours) go from the street to the south.

TRAIN

Aktau's train station, called Mangyshlak or Mangistau, is 12km east of the centre. It lies near the end of a branch line off the Atyrau–Uzbekistan line, so journeys to anywhere are l-o-n-g. Trains leave daily for Aktobe (4430T, 29 hours), Atyrau (3520T, 21 hours), Almaty (10,690T, 70 hours) and Kungrad (Uzbekistan; *platskartny* 6350T, 25 hours), and every two days for Astana (8990T, 44 hours) and Moscow (*platskartny* 26,250, 71 hours). A newly-built line crossing the Kazakhstan–Turkmenistan border may make it possible to take a train to Ashgabat.

Getting Around

City buses cost 35T. The frequent bus 3 runs north up Kazakhstan Respublikasy Prezidentininy dangyly then east to the bus station (the second stop after the big gold-domed mosque), and vice-versa. Bus 4 runs about every half-hour (7am to 8pm) from the seaport to the centre; going out to the port you can catch it on the north side of Mikrorayon 3.

Taxis within town cost 200T to 300T. For the train station expect to pay 1000T, for the airport 2000T, and the seaport 500T.

Around Aktau

The stony deserts of the **Mangistau** region stretch 400km east from Aktau to the Uzbekistan border. This labyrinth of dramatic canyons, weirdly eroded, multicoloured rock outcrops, mysterious underground mosques and ancient necropolises is only beginning to be explored, even by archaeologists. A minor branch of the Silk Road once ran across these wastes, and sacred sites, some with strong Sufic associations, are located where people buried their dead or where holy men dwelt. The underground mosques may have originated as cave hermitages for ascetics who retreated to the deserts.

A few sites can be reached by public transport of various sorts, but for most places you need a knowledgeable driver with a 4WD vehicle. Getting to these places across the otherworldly deserscapes, with only the occasional herd of camels or sheep for company, is part of the fun. Partner Tour (p95), in Aktau, and Almaty-based Stantours (p68) and Silk Road Adventures (p68), are experienced operators offering trips. Day trips

MANGISTAU NECROPOLISES

All of Kazakhstan is dotted with picturesque cemeteries or necropolises set outside villages and towns, and Mangistau has a notable concentration of them: locals boast the figure 362. Many of these date back to nomadic times, when tribes would bury their dead at special sites. Fascinating carvings adorn many of the older stone monuments – the commonest forms are the *kulpytas*, a carved stone column; the *koitas*, a stylised ram; the *koshkar-tas*, a more realistic ram; and the sarcophaguslike *sandyk-tas*. One of the most interesting necropolises is **Koshkar Ata**, at Akshukur, beside the main road 15km north of Aktau. Its skyline of miniature domes and towers resembles some fairytale city, and just inside the entrance is a fine old *koshkar-tas*.

from Aktau in a 4WD for up to four passengers generally cost 40,000T to 60,000T; itineraries of several days, camping most nights, are also available.

Shakpak-Ata & Sultan Epe

Shakpak-Ata is perhaps the most intriguing of all Mangistau's underground mosques – a cross-shaped affair with three entrances and four chambers, cut into a cliff close to the Caspian coast. It's 133km north of Aktau and 37km northwest of the village of Taushik – the final 11km, north from the Taushik–Fort Shevchenko road, is down a stony, bumpy track. Shakpak-Ata probably dates back to the 10th century, and its walls are adorned with deeply incised Arabic inscriptions, sculpted columns, weirdly weathered niches and drawings of horses and hands. The cliff is peppered with burial niches, and there's a necropolis of similar age below it, with more than 2000 tombs.

The signposted turning to **Sultan Epe**, another underground mosque and necropolis pairing, is 7km past the Shakpak-Ata turning on the Taushik–Fort Shevchenko road. You first reach the **Kenty-Baba Necropolis**, 7km from the road, with two towerlike mausoleums and other carved monuments. Sultan Epe is about 1km beyond, on the edge of a deep canyon. The necropolis – tomb of holy man Sultan Epe, considered the protector of sailors – is rich in carvings, while the underground mosque, of similar age to Shakpak-Ata, comprises several small rooms and low passages.

Around Shetpe

The small town of Shetpe is 150km northeast of Aktau by paved road (two and a half hours by minibus from Aktau bus station). About 35km towards Shetpe from the crossroads where the Shetpe and Taushik roads divide, a signposted 4km side-road leads up to **Otpan Tau**, Mangistau's highest hill (532m), where a modern 'historical-cultural complex', affording great panoramas, includes three gold-domed towers, a she-wolf monument (by legend the first Kazakhs were born from a wolf), and a symbolic torch commemorating the legendary use of this site for warning beacons.

The awesome 332m-high, 1km-long chalk outcrop **Sherkala** (Lion Rock) rises mysteriously from the desert about 22km northwest from Shetpe by paved road. A three-hour taxi round-trip from Shetpe bazaar should cost 4000T, including a couple of other interesting spots nearby. Shortly before you reach the track turn-off to Sherkala, a 'Kyzylkala Kalashygy' sign indicates a 1km track to the remnants of the small Silk Road settlement of **Kyzylkala**, beside a small green oasis with trees. Over to your right as you approach Sherkala from the road is the abandoned, little-known **Temir Abdal Ata cave-shrine**, with the carved stones of an abandoned necropolis scattered in front of it.

In a 4WD it's possible to combine this area with Shakpak-Ata and Sultan Epe in one longish day trip.

NORTHERN KAZAKHSTAN

This is the most Russified part of Kazakhstan but it's also the location of the eye-catching new capital, Astana, chief showpiece of President Nazarbaev's vision of the prosperous, cosmopolitan Kazakhstan of the future.

The northern steppes also harbour surprising areas of natural beauty: the flamingo-filled lakes of Korgalzhyn; the hills, forests and lakes around Burabay; and the picturesque Kyzylarai mountains southeast of Karaganda.

Until the 19th century, this region was largely untouched except by Kazakh nomads and their herds. As Russia's hand stretched southwards, Russian and Ukrainian settlers came to farm the steppe – a million or more by 1900. In Soviet times, the Kazakhs were forced into collective farms, and industrial cities such as Karaganda and Kostanay sprouted to exploit coal, iron ore and other minerals, while over a million political prisoners suffered in the huge KarLag labour camp complex around Karaganda. In the 1950s vast areas of steppe were turned over to wheat in Nikita Khrushchev's Virgin Lands scheme, bringing in yet more settlers.

In the 1950s most of the labour camps were closed, but a lot of survivors stayed. After the Soviet collapse many ethnic Germans, Russian and Ukrainians emigrated, but Kazakhs still number less than one-third in several areas.

The climate is sharply continental and the most pleasant months to travel are May to September. In January and February *average* temperatures in Astana range between -11°C and -22°C, and bitter steppe winds can make it feel colder still.

Astana АСТАНА

☎7172 / POP 776,000 / ELEV 350M

The country's new capital has risen fast from the northern steppe and is already a showpiece for 21st-century Kazakhstan. It is scheduled to go on rising and spreading into a city of more than one million people by 2030. Its skyline grows more fantastical by the year as landmark buildings, many of them by leading international architects, sprout in a variety of Asian, Western, Soviet and wacky futuristic styles. Several spectacular structures are open to visitors and it's hard not be impressed by the very concept of the place.

Astana was just a medium-sized provincial city known for its bitter winters when President Nazarbaev named it out of the blue in 1994 as Kazakhstan's future capital. It formally took over from Almaty in 1997. The old centre north of the Ishim (Yesil) River, known as the *'pravy bereg'*, right bank, lives on as a commercial and services centre. South of the river (the *'levy bereg'*, left bank), governmental and business buildings are going up, and also cultural, sports, leisure and shopping centres, hotels, a university and eye-catching residential developments. Some have dubbed Astana the 'Dubai of the steppe'.

The city began life in 1830 as a Russian fortress called Akmola (Kazakh for 'white tomb'). In the 1950s Akmola became the headquarters of the Virgin Lands scheme and in 1961 it was renamed Tselinograd (Virgin Lands City). After the USSR collapsed, Akmola got back its old name. In 1998 it was renamed again, as Astana – Kazakh for 'capital'. Reasons cited by Nazarbaev for the change were Astana's more central and less earthquake-prone location than Almaty, and better transport links with Russia. He may also have wanted to head off secessionist sentiments among northern Kazakhstan's large ethnic Russian population.

Some find Astana an impersonal place, but Kazakhstan's ambitious and talented are increasingly drawn here. It's easy to question the spending of billions on prestige architecture, but many citizens are clearly proud of their new capital.

Sights & Activities

New City

★Khan Shatyr NOTABLE BUILDING

(www.khanshatyr.com; Turan dangyly 37; ⏰10am-10pm; 👪) Astana's most extraordinary building (so far), the Khan Shatyr is a 150m-high, translucent, tent-like structure made of ethylene tetrafluoroethylene (ETFE), a heat-absorbing material that produces summer temperatures inside even when it's -30°C outside. Touted as a 'lifestyle centre with world-class shopping', from outside it resembles nothing so much as a drunkenly leaning circus tent, while the multilevel interior contains yet another shopping mall and food court but also several other attractions for children and adults.

These include a drop tower, flume ride and 500m-long monorail (admission for all three: 1500T) and, on the top level, the **Sky Beach Club** (Khan shatyr, Turan 37; adult/child Mon-Fri 6000/3500T, Sat-Sun 8000/3500T, tour 1500T; ⏰10am-10pm) with a big swimming pool, sandy beach, palm trees and water slide, where those who can afford it can imagine they're on a tropical coast in the middle of the Eurasian steppe. Opened in 2010, the Khan Shatyr was designed by celebrated British architect Norman Foster and marks, for the moment, the western end of the main axis of new Astana. To its east, across a park, stands the grand headquarters of the state energy company, **KazMunayGaz** (Kabanbay Batyr), with Nurzhol bulvar beginning beyond it.

City Park PARK

The large, somewhat untidy city park abuts the south side of the Ishim River. On its southern edge you'll find the **Atameken** (☎22 16 36; admission 400T, English-language tour 500T; ⏰9am-9pm), a 200m-long, walk-around country map with models of major buildings, and **Duman** (☎24 22 22; www.duman.kz; oceanarium adult/child 1500/700T; ⏰10am-10pm), an amusement centre most worth visiting for its oceanarium, which has over 2000 creatures from the world's oceans and a 70m shark tunnel.

Nurzhol Bulvar

This central showpiece boulevard of Kazakhstan's new governmental and monumental zone is a 2km line of gardens and plazas leading east from the KazMunayGaz building to the presidential palace and flanked by a sequence of large and imaginative buildings. Bus 21 runs here from the train station via Zhenis, Abay, Saryarka, Turan and Kabanbay Batyr, stopping on Konaev near the Bayterek Monument. Returning, catch it heading west on Konaev.

★Bayterek Monument MONUMENT

(☎24 08 35; adult/child 500/150T; ⏰10am-9pm) Nurzhol bulvar's centrepiece is the 97m-high Bayterek monument, a white latticed tower crowned by a large glass orb. This embodies a Kazakh legend in which the mythical bird Samruk lays a golden egg containing the secrets of human desires and happiness in a tall poplar tree, beyond human reach. A lift glides visitors up inside the egg, where you can ponder the symbolism, enjoy expansive views and place your hand in a print of President Nazarbaev's palm while gazing eastward towards his palace. The egg-domed **National Archive** stands just west of the Bayeterek.

Ploshchad Poyushchykh Fontanov PLAZA

(Singing Fountains Square) The eastern half of the Nurzhol bulvar starts with this plaza which springs to life with music-and-water shows at 9pm on summer evenings. Further east stand twin golden-green, conical business centres: the southern one contains the headquarters of **Samryk-Kazyna**, Kazakhstan's sovereign wealth fund. Curving away left and right from these towers are the two **wings** of the **House of Ministries**, and straight ahead, behind pretty flower gardens, stands the white-pillared presidential palace, the **Ak Orda**.

The two towers of parliament, the **Senate** and **Mazhilis**, rise behind the northern ministerial building. At the south end of the space before the Ak Orda is the turquoise-tiled **Central Concert Hall** (architects: Manfredi and Luca Nicoletti, Italy), whose design is intended to evoke the petals of a flower.

Nur Astana Mosque MOSQUE

(Kabanbay Batyr 36) A block south of the western part of Nurzhol bulvar stands the beautiful four-minaret Nur Astana mosque, opened in 2005. Its prayer hall (for men only – women use the upper gallery) is an exquisite multidomed space with inscriptions and geometrical patterning in blue, white, gold and red.

Northern Lights ARCHITECTURE

These three light-green apartment towers with wavy sides are a prominent feature of the western part of the boulevard. Opposite stand the **Emerald Towers**, office blocks whose tops splay outward like the pages of opening books, and further west looms the tall **Transport & Communications Ministry**, dubbed the 'Lighter' for its form by irreverent locals.

East of Nurzhol Bulvar

The new city's axis continues east across the Ishim River behind the Ak Orda. From Nurzhol bulvar, you can hop on bus 40, eastbound along Dostyk, to Baytursynuly just north of the Palace of Peace & Accord, or bus 21 eastbound on Konaev to Tauelsizdik just south of the same palace.

★Palace of Peace & Accord ARCHITECTURE

(Dvorets Mira i Soglasya; ☎74 47 44; Tauelsizdik; tours adult/child 500/300T; ⏰tours every 30min, 10am-7.30pm, to 6.30pm Oct-Apr) This beautiful, glass-and-steel pyramid was opened in 2006 as the home for the triennial Congress of World and Traditional Religions, hosted by Kazakhstan (next in 2015). The half-hour tour (English-speaking guides available) shows you a 1350-seat opera hall, the 3rd-floor atrium where the religions congress is held, and the apex conference room with windows filled with stained-glass doves (by British artist Brian Clarke). Full of symmetry and symbolism, the pyramid is beautifully illuminated and a highlight of the city.

Designed by Norman Foster, it's conceived as Astana's symbolic centre, and by 2030 (when the city is planned to have spread well beyond its current extents) it should be near the geographical centre too.

Palace of Independence PALACE

(Dvorets Nezavisimosti; ☎70 03 89; Tauelsizdik; tours 400T; ⏰10am-1pm & 2-5pm Tue-Sun) The Palace of Independence is well worth a visit especially for its huge scale model of how Astana is planned to look in 2030. It also holds an interesting ethnographic hall with exhibits similar to those at the Presidential Cultural Centre (p103). English-language tours are available. In front of the palace, the 91m-high **Kazak Yeli Monument** (Kazakh Country Monument) is intended to symbolise the historic destiny of Kazakhstan's people: it's topped by a

Astana

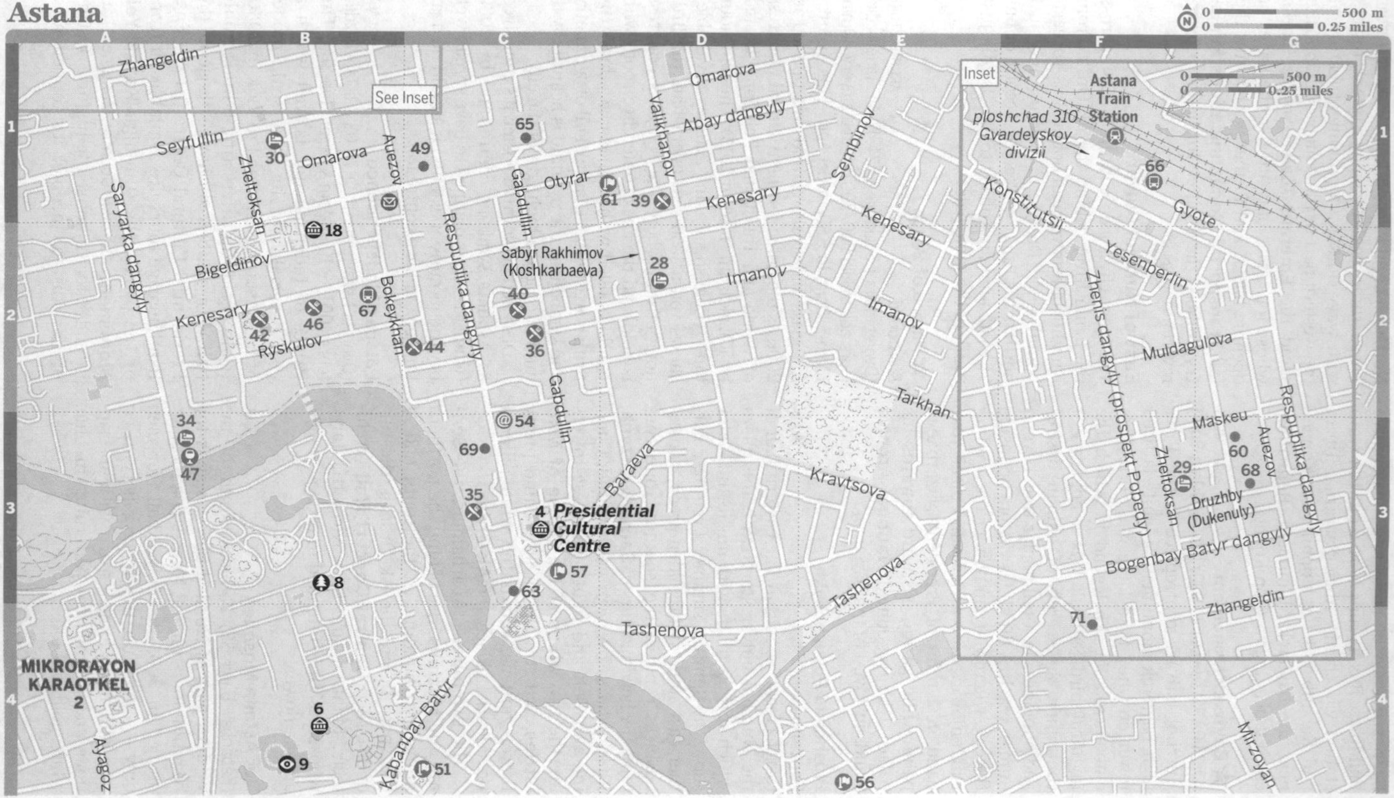

0 — 500 m
0 — 0.25 miles

A B C D E F G
1 2 3 4

Zhangeldin
See Inset
Omarova
Abay dangyly
Seyfullin
30
Omarova
Auezov
49
65
Gabdullin
Otyrar
61
39
Valikhanov
Kenesary
Sembinov
Kenesary
Saryarka dangyly
Zheltoksan
18
Respublika dangyly
Bigeldinov
Sabyr Rakhimov (Koshkarbaeva)
28
Imanov
Imanov
Kenesary
42
46
67
Bokeykhan
40
36
44
Ryskulov
Gabdullin
Tarkhan
34
47
54
69
Baraeva
Kravtsova
35
4 **Presidential Cultural Centre**
57
8
63
Tashenova
Tashenova
MIKRORAYON KARAOTKEL
2
6
9
Ayagoz
Kabanbay Batyr
51
56
Mirzoyan

Inset
0 — 500 m
0 — 0.25 miles
Astana Train Station
ploshchad 310 Gvardeyskoy divizii
66
Konstitutsii
Gyote
Yesenberlin
Zhenis dangyly (prospekt Pobedy)
Muldagulova
Maskeu
60
Auezov
68
29
Zheltoksan
Druzhby (Dukenuly)
Respublika dangyly
Bogenbay Batyr dangyly
Zhangeldin
71

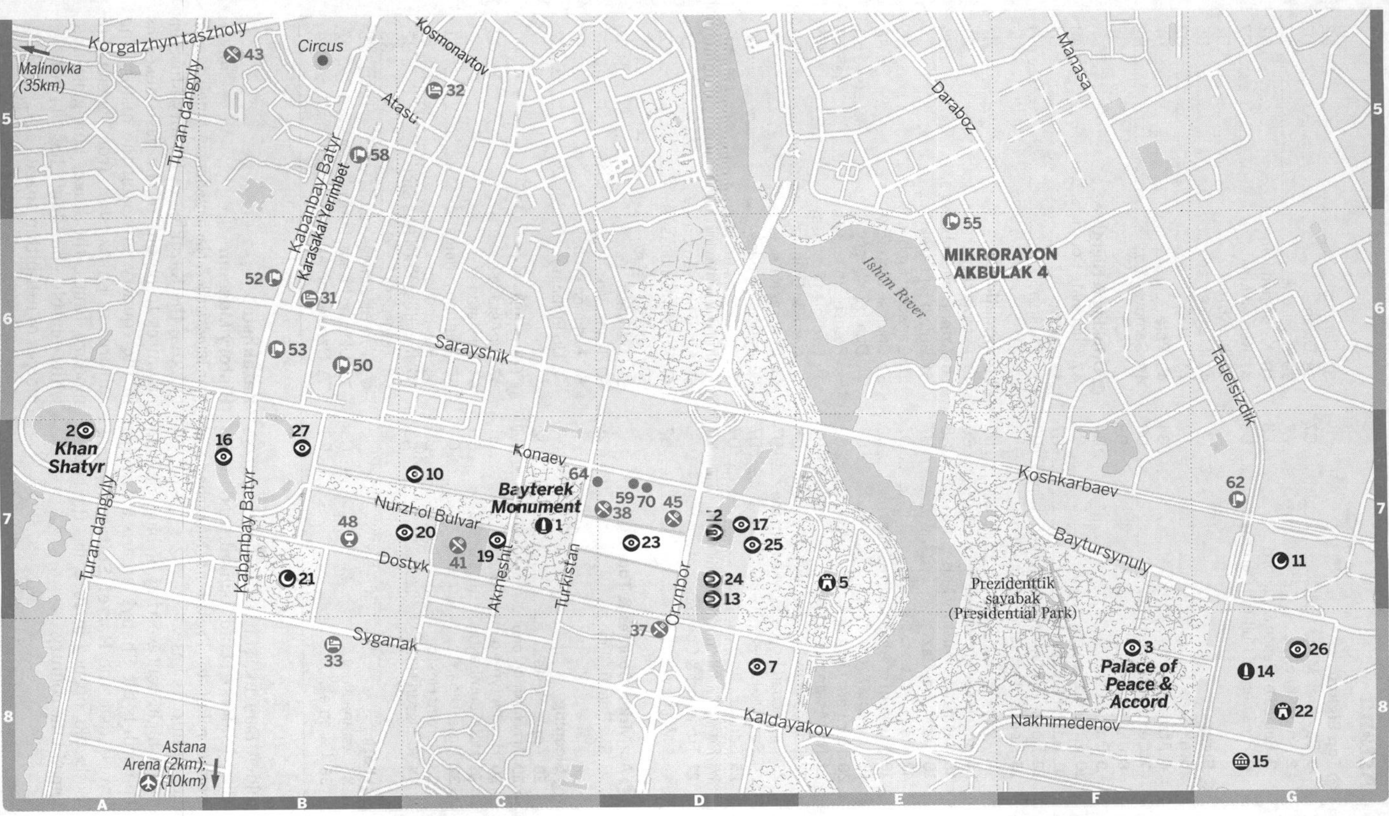
Korgalzhyn taszholy
Malinovka (35km)
Circus
43
Kosmonavtov
32
Atasu
Turan dangyly
58
Kabanbay Batyr
Karasakal Yerimbet
52
31
53
50
Sarayshik
Manasa
Daraboz
55
MIKRORAYON AKBULAK 4
Ishim River
Tauelsizdik
2
Khan Shatyr
16
27
10
Konaev
64
59
70
45
38
Bayterek Monument
1
Nurzhol Bulvar
48
20
41
19
Akmeshit
Turkistan
23
Orynbor
2
17
25
24
13
5
Dostyk
21
Kabanbay Batyr
Turan dangyly
37
Syganak
33
7
Kaldayakov
Koshkarbaev
62
Baytursynuly
11
Prezidenttik sayabak (Presidential Park)
3
Palace of Peace & Accord
Nakhimedenov
26
14
22
15
Astana Arena (2km); (10km)
A
B
C
D
E
F
G
5
6
7
8

Astana

Top Sights
1 Bayterek Monument ... C7
2 Khan Shatyr ... A7
3 Palace of Peace & Accord ... F8
4 Presidential Cultural Centre ... C3

Sights
5 Ak Orda ... E7
6 Atameken ... B4
7 Central Concert Hall ... D8
8 City Park ... B3
9 Duman ... B4
10 Emerald Towers ... C7
11 Hazret Sultan Mosque ... G7
12 House of Ministries (Northern Wing) ... D7
13 House of Ministries (Southern Wing) ... D7
14 Kazak Yeli Monument ... G8
15 Kazakhstan History Museum ... G8
16 KazMunayGaz ... B7
17 Mazhilis ... D7
18 Museum of the First President ... B2
19 National Archive ... C7
20 Northern Lights ... C7
21 Nur Astana Mosque ... B7
22 Palace of Independence ... G8
23 Ploshchad Poyushchykh Fontanov ... D7
24 Samryk-Kazyna ... D7
25 Senate ... D7
26 Shabyt ... G8
27 Transport & Communications Ministry ... B7

Activities, Courses & Tours
Sky Beach Club ... (see 2)

Sleeping
28 Apple Hostel ... D2
29 Art Hotel Astana ... F3
30 Hotel Altyn-Adam ... B1
31 Hotel Jumbaktas ... B6
32 Hotel Ulpan ... C5
33 Nomad Hostel ... B8
34 Radisson Hotel ... A3

Eating
35 Astana Nury ... C3
36 Caramel ... C2
37 Caramel ... D8
38 Divan ... D7
39 Eagilik ... D1
40 Kafe Shymkent ... C2
41 Keruen Mall ... C7
42 Line Brew ... B2
43 Mega Astana ... B5
44 Rafè ... C2
45 Rafè ... D7
46 Samovar ... B2

Drinking & Nightlife
47 Chocolate Room ... A3
48 Insomnia ... B7
Pivnitsa ... (see 47)

Information
49 Akmolaturist ... C1
50 Azerbaijan Embassy ... B6
51 British Embassy ... C4
52 Canadian Embassy ... B6
53 Chinese Embassy ... B6
Dutch Embassy ... (see 51)
French Embassy ... (see 51)
Georgian Embassy ... (see 50)
German Embassy ... (see 51)
54 Internet Kafe Best ... C3
55 Iranian Embassy ... E6
Japanese Embassy ... (see 51)
Kyrgyz Embassy ... (see 50)
56 Mongolian Embassy ... E4
57 Russian Embassy ... C3
58 Tajik Embassy ... B5
59 Transavia ... D7
60 Transavia ... G3
61 Turkmen Embassy ... D1
62 US Embassy ... G7

Transport
63 Air Astana ... C3
64 Air Astana ... C7
65 Austrian Airlines ... C1
66 Bus Station ... F1
67 Kongress Kholl Bus Stop ... B2
68 Transaero ... G3
69 Turkish Airlines ... C3
70 Ukraine International Airways ... D7
71 Uzbekistan Airways ... F4

golden Samruk, statues of heroic *batyrs* (clan leaders) stand behind, and a 5m bronze relief of President Nazarbaev is tucked into its base.

The high, concave ring of blue glass to the north is the **Shabyt**, an arts university. Beyond that, the **Hazret Sultan Mosque** (Tauelsizdik), opened in 2012, has the largest dome in the country.

Kazakhstan History Museum MUSEUM
(cnr Tauelsizdik & Nakhimedenov) Due to open by 2014, the Kazakhstan History Museum promises to be one of the best museums in the country. Covering the history and culture of Kazakhstan from ancient to modern times, the huge, blue-glass-and-white-marble building has 14,000 sq metres of exhibition space.

Old City

The right bank is a mix of Soviet and post-independence architecture, plus a few now historic-looking tsarist-era houses.

★Presidential Cultural Centre MUSEUM

(☎22 33 19; Respublika dangyly 2; English-language tour 2000T; ⏰10am-5pm Tue-Sun) FREE The yurt-shaped Presidential Cultural Centre houses an excellent museum whose highlight is the 2nd floor, with outstanding collections of Kazakh jewellery and 'gold and gold-makings'. These include gold jewellery and replicas from the Scythian burial mounds at Berel (p111) and the Issyk burial mound (where the Golden Man was found), replicas of the Golden Man and the 'second Golden Man' from western Kazakhstan (p135), a bejewelled replica of a horse from the Berel tomb, and real 4th-century-BC horse innards pickled in formaldehyde!

The ground floor holds models of Astana buildings and a room of traditional Kazakh items: a brightly decked yurt, colourful carpets, crafts and costumes, elaborate horse tackle. The 3rd floor covers Kazakhstan from the 15th to 20th centuries.

Museum of the First President MUSEUM

(☎75 12 92; Beibitshilik 11; ⏰10am-1pm & 2-5pm Tue-Sun) FREE Housed in the former presidential palace, this museum is an intriguing peep into the pomp and circumstance surrounding the country's leader. A succession of lavish galleries and halls, including the old presidential office itself, is decked with beautiful gifts to President Nazarbaev from foreign governments and suitably grateful citizens. Staff will lend you an English-language booklet to help you understand what's what. The entrance is on Abay dangyly.

Tours

Astana Bus Tours BUS TOUR

(☎24 27 47; http://kochevnik.com.kz; adult/child 2400/1200T; ⏰9am-9pm Mar-Nov) This hop-on-hop-off tourist bus service in open-top double-deckers – the first of its kind in Central Asia – started rolling in 2013 and provides an easy option for getting round Astana's sights. Buses go every 40 minutes, with 30 stops along a route that starts and ends outside the train station and includes Respublika dangyly, the Khan Shatyr, Bayterek Monument, Palace of Peace & Accord and Astana Arena (the national stadium).

Tickets are valid for 24 hours and you can pay when you first board.

Festivals & Events

Astana Day (www.astanaday.kz) on 6 July is celebrated in a big way, with the square behind the Palace of Peace & Accord usually being the focus for concerts, a fairground and fireworks, and other events happening around the city. The date (also a national holiday) coincides with President Nazarbaev's birthday.

Sleeping

Hotel prices are high, but a couple of hostels provide relief for backpackers.

Apple Hostel HOSTEL $

(☎707-847 3836; www.apple-hostel.kz; Sabyr Rakhimov (Koshkarbaeva) 22; dm 2500T; ❄📶) This friendly, well-kept little hostel in the old city is unsigned and hard to find, so it's a good idea to contact them ahead of arrival. It offers spacious four- and six-person dorms, a well-equipped kitchen, two bathrooms, and free tea, coffee and drinking water. The entrance is up a small staircase next to Akku dry-cleaners, just inside the southernmost archway into the courtyard of Sabyr Rakhimov 22 (a huge apartment block).

Bus 48 eastward on Gyote from the train and bus stations stops nearby at the corner of Ualikhanov and Imanov. The hostel will pick you up from either station for 1000T.

Nomad Hostel HOSTEL $

(☎707-557 0756; www.facebook.com/nomadhostel; Kvartira 112, 5th fl, podezd 3, Zhiloy Kompleks Nomad, Syganak 10; dm 2500T; ⊖@📶) Though rather chaotically run by management who are often absent, Nomad occupies a modern, clean apartment with a good kitchen and sitting area, six-person bunk dorms, and one bathroom. Bus 21 from the train station stops just along the street. Contact them ahead to make sure someone will be there to help you get in (there are no signs).

Art Hotel Astana HOTEL $$

(☎30 20 20; artastana@gmail.com; Zheltoksan 42; s/d incl breakfast 8000/15,000T; P📶) The location halfway between the train station and old centre is not very convenient for anything, but the Art Hotel is near bus routes, and with its friendly, relaxed young staff and successfully modernist decor – flower-shaped washbasins, artfully scattered mirrors – is a pleasant place to stay. The lounge-style **Chill-out Cafe** (mains 800-2700T; 24hr;) is another big plus.

Hotel Ulpan HOTEL $$
(57 16 83; http://ulpan.ucoz.ru; Khalel Dosmukhammeduly 11; s 8000T, d 9000-10,000T;) As much guesthouse as hotel, this small family-run establishment on a quiet street is as close as you'll get to the left-bank attractions at midrange prices. The bright rooms have shiny bedspreads and little flower prints. Breakfast is available in your room for 800T to 1000T. One family member speaks some English.

Hotel Altyn-Adam HOTEL $$
(32 77 24; altyn.adam@mail.ru; Seyfullin 26; s 9000-15,000T, d 15,000-17,000T, incl breakfast; P) Rooms at the 'Golden Man' are nothing fancy but cosy, well sized and perfectly comfortable. It has a good little cafe/restaurant. Staff speak no English but are welcoming enough.

Hotel Jumbaktas HOTEL $$$
(57 97 77; www.jumbaktas.kz; Karasakal Yerimbet 65; s/d incl breakfast from 22,000/28,500T; P) The building is a modern, 10-storey, glass cylinder but the inside has an elegant air with chandeliers and patterned marble floor in the lobby, and good-sized, attractively comfy rooms in golds and russets. Reception is welcoming and English-speaking, and by Astana standards it's good value for a hotel of this quality close to Nurzhol bulvar.

★ **Radisson Hotel** HOTEL $$$
(99 00 00; www.radissonblu.com/hotel-astana; Saryarka dangyly 4; s/d incl breakfast from US$442/498; P @) The abode of choice for many Western business and official visitors, the three-towered Radisson provides the expected comfort and professional service. Standard rooms feature heated bathroom floors and the larger business-class rooms have their own espresso machines. The huge gleaming lobby encompasses lounge areas, shops, a bar and an excellent Mediterranean restaurant.

Eating

Samovar RUSSIAN $
(32 43 16; Kenesary 24; mains 450-1400T; 8am-6am;) A cheerful restaurant/cafe where helpful, red-silk-shirted or -skirted staff serve a good range of fare from breakfasts and *bliny* to soups, *manty, laghman* and meat and fish mains.

Eagilik CAFE $
(Books & Coffee; Kenesary 61/1; items 250-400T; 1-9pm Tue-Fri, 10am-7pm Sat, 2-7pm Sun;) The relaxed cafe at this friendly English bookshop, a bit of an expat hangout, does a very welcome range of home-made quiches, pies, cakes and cinnamon rolls. The coffee's fine too. The shop (open from 10am Monday to Friday) sells a good range of English-language books on Central Asia.

Divan TURKISH $$
(Nurzhol bulvar 12; mains 1500-2400T; 9am-11pm) The menu at this friendly Turkish eatery is little more than a series of lamb/chicken/beef kebabs and shashlyk, and salads, but it's all good – as are the views of the Bayterek monument and dancing fountains from the window tables. No alcohol.

Caramel CAFE $$
(29 33 00; Zhiloy Kompleks Nursaya 2, Dostyk 13; coffees, cakes & pastries 500-1000T, breakfast 600-1500T; 11am-2am;) A tasteful, spacious and relaxed coffee house that's great to drop into for a late breakfast (including English and continental) or a caffeine-and-strudel pick-me-up. The **original branch** (22 25 41; Imanov 10A; 9am-midnight;) in the old city is just as good.

Kafe Shymkent CENTRAL ASIAN $$
(Imanov 3; mains 700-1700T; 7am-11.30pm) Shymkent is a spacious, clean and efficient local restaurant doing dependable local staples from eggs and *bliny* to *plov*, shashlyk, *manty* and beefsteak with mushrooms. It's on a rear corner of the Kazyna shopping centre.

★ **Astana Nury** CENTRAL ASIAN $$$
(43 93 39; Respublika dangyly 3/2; mains 1900-5500T; 10am-midnight;) This top-class Azerbaijani restaurant has excellent service and two lovely decks overlooking the river as well as an inside dining room with beautiful Azeri decor. The many varieties of shashlyk and Azeri *pilaw (plov)* dishes are among the best on the menu and at its cheaper end.

Line Brew INTERNATIONAL $$$
(23 74 44; Kenesary 20; mains 2300-5400T, 0.5L beer 500-1400T; noon-2am;) You can't miss Line Brew's large, red-brick castle building, and the interior is, well, like a tavern inside a castle. The excellent food runs from Greek salad to Angus and horse steaks and grilled

seabass. A shashlyk grill flames in the middle, and a nice pop/rock/jazz band plays nightly except Sunday. There are plenty of Belgian and other beers, including unfiltered varieties.

Rafè EUROPEAN $$$
(Bokeykhan 16; mains 1300-3500T; ⏲8am-midnight Mon-Fri, 10am-midnight Sat & Sun;) This cosy, relaxed cafe/restaurant is great for coffee and delectable cakes/desserts but also good for mostly Italian main dishes, from risotto or pizza to duck with tagliatelle and cherry tomatoes. Salads are overpriced. It also has a **branch** (⏲8am-midnight Mon-Fri, 10am-midnight Sat-Sun;) on Nurzhol bulvar.

Food Courts

Mega Astana (Korgalzhin taszholy 1; ⏲food court 10am-midnight), **Keruen Mall** (Dostyk 9; ⏲food court 10am-midnight) and the Khan Shatyr (p98) all have convenient **food courts** (dishes 400-1800T), good cafes and branches of **Assorti** (mains 900-3500T; ⏲noon-midnight), which does good pizzas and grills in a relaxed ambience.

Drinking & Nightlife

Face control and dress codes are the norm at the better clubs, and don't go before midnight.

Insomnia CLUB
(Dostyk 3; ⏲10pm-4am Tue-Sat) Insomnia pulls in a more progressive, free-thinking crowd than the general hipsterish run of Astana clubs, and focuses less on stylish decor than on a big dance floor and top sound system – a place to dance to house, pop and rave. 'Expats welcome,' says management, and admission is a reasonable 1000T.

Pivnitsa BAR
(Saryarka dangyly 2; ⏲noon-2am;) This Czech cellar-bar – stone walls, wooden booths and long wood tables – is a convivial place for mugs of the unfiltered house beer, Kelly (700T for 0.5L), and sausages, steaks and other meaty fare (dishes 1400T to 4000T) to soak it up. It's entered from the riverside just below the Radisson Hotel.

Chocolate Room CLUB
(Shokolad; ☎701-550 0017; Saryarka dangyly 2; ⏲11pm-5am Fri & Sat;) Once past the face control (look your smart-casual very best) you'll have a wild time dancing to hip-hop, dance and '80s DJs with Astana's beautiful 20-somethings at the coolest club in town. Admission is free but you'll have to get a place at the bar unless you can pay 75,000T for a table (with food). It's entered from the riverside below the Radisson Hotel.

Information

Astana is home to nearly all foreign embassies in Kazakhstan; see p124 for more information.

Internet Kafe Best (☎21 11 67; Respublika dangyly 8; internet per hr 200T; ⏲9am-2am) A well-equipped place with scanning, fax, photocopying and Skype.

Main Post Office (Auezov 71; ⏲8am-7pm Mon-Fri, 9am-6pm Sat, 10am-3pm Sun)

Getting There & Away

Astana is well connected with the rest of the country and the rest of the world. The train and bus stations are side by side, 3km north of centre. Astana International Airport (p132) is 14km south.

EXPO 2017 ASTANA

Astana expects to gain its biggest profile boost yet when it stages the Expo 2017 world's fair. Perhaps surprisingly in a country whose economy relies heavily on oil, gas and other minerals, the theme of Expo 2017 Astana (www.expo2017astana.com) will be 'Future Energy' – alternative energy and energy-saving technology. Kazakhstan officialdom has been at pains to argue that the country is ultimately committed to a green economy. The Expo site, in the southeast of the city, is planned to be self-sufficient in energy, with solar cells and its own wind farm.

With something over two million visitors expected during the three months of the fair, it will certainly be a big boost for Astana's development. Kazakhstan hopes to attract €1 billion in foreign investment for Expo on top of €250 million from the government. A new motorway and a new high-speed railway from Almaty are planned to be ready for the fair, cutting the driving time from around 12 to eight hours, and the train journey to five hours. A futuristic new station is to be constructed near the Expo site.

AIR

There are at least eight daily flights to Almaty by Air Astana (from 21,540T) and one or two each by SCAT (from 15,915T) and Bek Air (from 15,000T). Other domestic destinations served direct by Air Astana include Aktau (from 27,650T), Aktobe (from 21,740T), Atyrau (from 25,545T), Ust-Kamenogorsk (from 17,360T) and Shymkent (from 23,290T). SCAT also flies at least five times weekly to Atyrau (from 23,915T), Aktau (from 25,915T), Semey (from 20,000T), Taraz (from 27,100T) and Shymkent (from 23,150T). The airport website has full schedules.

Transavia is a useful air-ticket agency located on the Right Bank (☎58 05 06; Beibitshilik 44) and the Left Bank. (☎50 82 74; Konaev 14/1)

See p131 for information on international flights.

Airlines

Air Astana (☎44 44 77) Branches at Right Bank (Office 9, 2nd fl, Ramstor, Dom 11, Mikrorayon Samal; ⏲9am-6pm Mon-Fri); Left Bank (Office 26, 1st fl, Konaev 14B; ⏲9am-9pm); airport (☎44 44 77; ⏲24hr)

Austrian Airlines (☎59 58 888) Branches at city (Hotel Ramada Plaza, Abay 47; ⏲10am-7pm Mon-Fri); airport (⏲midnight-2am Mon-Wed & Fri-Sat, 9-10.30pm Mon-Wed & Sat)

Bek Air (☎28 65 39; Airport) Tickets sold by Transavia (p106).

Lufthansa (☎28 64 82; Airport; ⏲9-11pm Mon-Wed & Sat, 1-2.30am Mon, Wed & Fri)

SCAT (☎28 65 01) Tickets sold by Transavia (p106).

Transaero (☎call centre 91 14 00; ⏲24hr) Branches at city (☎31 83 50; Druzhby 7; ⏲9am-9pm); airport (☎77 72 66)

Turkish Airlines Branches at city (☎57 08 49; Respublika dangyly 5; ⏲9am-6pm Mon-Fri); airport (☎43 33 22; ⏲midnight-5am Mon, Wed & Fri)

Ukraine International Airways (☎800 333 3050; ⏲24hr) Office in city (☎50 82 74; Konaev 14).

Uzbekistan Airways (☎32 82 44; Office 17, Saryarka dangyly 31)

BUS, MINIBUS & TAXI

From the **bus station** (☎38 11 35; www.saparzhai.kz; Gyote 5) buses and minibuses travel slowly to many destinations including Almaty (6500T, 19 hours, two daily), Karaganda (1200T, 4½ hours, every 30 minutes, 7am to 9pm), Petropavlovsk (3000T, 10 hours, seven daily), Semey (4700T, 15 hours, four daily) and Ust-Kamenogorsk (6000T, 19 hours, two daily). There's also daily service to Omsk in Russia. A bus to Bayan-Ölgii (Ulgiy; 12,000T, 37 hours) in Mongolia, via Barnaul and Gorno-Altaysk in Russia, normally goes twice a month, with dates known at the start of each month.

Private minibuses and taxis to Karaganda (minibus/shared taxi 1500/2500T, three hours) and Burabay wait outside the bus station.

TRAIN

From the **train station** (☎38 07 07; Gyote 7), the speedy, comfortable Talgo (train 2) to Karaganda (tourist/business class 2970/4920T, 2½ hours) and Almaty (10,230/16,900T, 12½ hours) leaves at 7.15pm, but can get booked up days ahead. Other trains go to Karaganda (1715T to 1910T, three to five hours) at least 13 times daily, and to Almaty (5040T to 6380T, 19 to 21 hours) at least three times daily. There are also daily trains to Petropavlovsk, Shymkent, Aktobe, Yekaterinburg and Moscow, and trains to Semey at least every two days. Service to Ürümqi, China, has been an on-off affair, but at the time of writing train 54 with carriages to Ürümqi (20,000T, 38 hours) leaves at 5.30pm on Saturday.

Getting Around

Astana has an excellent city bus (60T) network; check www.astana.kz for route maps in English. Buses start between 6am and 7am and finish between 10pm and 11pm.

Bus 10 runs about every 15 minutes from the bus station to the airport (a one-hour trip), via Zhenis, Moldagulova, Beibitshilik, Seyfullin, Respublika, Konaev (westbound) and Kabanbay Batyr (and vice-versa). A taxi between the airport and centre is usually 2500T. Buses 25 and 31 run from the train station along Zhenis and Kenesary to the **Kongress Kholl** (Congress Hall) stop in the old city centre, then on to the south end of Respublika dangyly.

Taxi drivers ask 500T to 700T for rides of 2km to 3km. You can usually flag down a passing car for less.

Around Astana

During the Stalin years **Malinovka** (also called Akmol), 35km west of Astana, housed ALZhIR, a notorious camp for wives and children of men who were interned elsewhere as 'betrayers of the motherland'. The **ALZhIR Museum-Memorial Complex** (http://alzhir-eng.ucoz.ru; admission 200T; ⏲10am-6pm Tue-Sun) poignantly evokes the camp's horrors, displaying a transportation wagon, a replica guard post and photos and possessions of the prisoners, as well as explanatory material in English on the Gulag system in Kazakhstan.

About 100km further west past Malinovka is the Unesco World Heritage–listed **Korgalzhyn Nature Reserve**. With over 200 steppe lakes in and around the reserve, the area is a vital stop on major bird migration routes from Africa, the Middle East and India to summer breeding grounds in Siberia. From June to September salty Lake Tengiz supports the world's most northerly flamingo colony, several thousand strong. Some 4000 of the world's 10,000 critically endangered sociable lapwings spend their summers in the area too. Bird watchers from around the world flock in during May and June for the northward migration.

A good **visitors centre** (☎71637-2 10 13; Madin Rakhimzhan 20, Korgalzhyn; admission 300T; ⊙10am 1pm & 2-5pm Wed-Sat) in Korgalzhyn village near the reserve, has exhibits on birds, migration and the local area, and houses the **reserve office** (☎director 71637-2 16 50; Madin Rakhimzhan 20, Korgalzhyn; ⊙Mon-Fri). The village has several simple but clean **guesthouses** (Gostevye doma; per person incl 3 meals 6000T) whose owners will organise trips into the reserve and to other nearer, also bird-rich, lakes outside the reserve. A day-trip to Lake Tengiz, requiring a 4WD vehicle, costs around 10,000T for around four people plus 3000T for an official reserve guide; a car day-trip to Lake Birtaban, 11km from the village, is only around 3000T.

The guesthouse of **Bibinur & Marat Alimzhanov** (☎71637-2 18 00, 702-453 6128; pana-07@inbox.ru; Abay 10/2, Korgalzhyn; P ☏ ♿) is particularly recommended. They have a nice four-room wooden house specially for guests, make excellent food, have vehicles for excursions and Astana transfers (8000T one-way per car), and can organise folk dance/music events for guests (Marat leads a local group). Other options include **Gostevoy Dom U Nadezhdy** (☎71637-21159, 702-923 9248; Chokan Ualikhanov 12/2, Korgalzhyn), run by the friendly Shabarshovs, and the house of **Timur Iskakov** (☎71637-2 10 64, 701-622 4800; timur_iskak@mail.ru; Gorky 9, Korgalzhyn; ☏), who speaks a little English.

Astana-based **Akmolaturist** (☎7172-33 02 04, 7172-33 02 07; www.akmolatourist.kz; Office 22, Hotel Abay, Respublika dangyly 33, Astana; ⊙10am-6pm Mon-Fri) has two **cabins** (Karazhar; d/q cabin 3000/4000T; ⊙May-Sep; P) beside Sultankeldy Lake inside the reserve, and will be able to sort out permits and guides.

Minibuses to Malinovka (350T, one hour) and Korgalzhyn (1400T, three hours) leave Astana bus station eight times daily. Shared taxis to Korgalzhyn (1500T, two hours) go from outside the bus station. The first minibus, at 10am, is often full so you should buy your ticket at least an hour ahead; the next one is at 11.50am. Coming back from Malinovka you can get a shared taxi (300T) behind the blue Sauda Uyi building 600m along the street from the museum entrance.

Lake Burabay ОЗЕРО БУРАБАЙ

☎71630

Lake Burabay (formerly Borovoe), 240km north of Astana, is the focus of Burabay National Nature Park (www.gnpp.kz), a picturesque 835-sq-km area of lakes, hills, pine forests and strange rock formations that has given birth to several Kazakh legends. Accommodation and other facilities here are continually improving, but schemes for a massive lakeside resort have not yet come to fruition.

The small town of Burabay stretches about 2.5km along the lake's northeast shore. On the main road here, the park's **Visitor Centre & Nature Museum** (Vizit-Tsentr & Tabigat Murazhayy; Kenesary; admission 500T; ⊙10am-7pm Tue-Sun) contains a diverse display of stuffed wildlife from Kazakhstan's national parks, two ATMs, and souvenir shops selling a park map for 300T. Included in the museum ticket is an adjoining outdoor zoo with two Przewalski's horses, several deer (including three maral) and various eagles, bears, wolves, argali sheep and yaks in small enclosures.

A well-made **walking path** parallels the road for 9km from the lake's southeast to northwest corners via Burabay town. Heading west from the town it's 4km to picturesque **Goluboy Zaliv** (Blue Bay). The most celebrated Burabay legend links **Zhumbaktas**, the Sphinx-like rock sticking out of the lake here, with **Okzhetpes**, the striking 380m-tall rock pile rising on the shore behind it. While Abylay Khan's army was fighting the Zhungars back in the 18th century, the story goes, a beautiful princess was captured and brought to Burabay, where many Kazakh warriors wanted her as a wife. The princess agreed to marry the first warrior who could shoot an arrow to the top of Okzhetpes. All failed, hence the name Okzhetpes, which means 'Unreachable by Arrows'. The distraught princess then drowned herself in the lake, thus creating Zhumbaktas (Mysterious Stone).

You can rent a **rowing boat** (per 30/60 min 1000/2000T) at Goluboy Zaliv to paddle out to Zhumbaktas. Continue 1.75km further round the lake to reach **Polyana Abylay Khana** (Abylay Khan's Clearing), where the warrior hero reputedly once assembled his forces during his Zhungar campaigns. A tall, eagle-topped monument, with good old Ab astride a snow leopard, stands in the clearing. A path from the back of the clearing leads up 947m **Mt Kokshetau**, the highest peak in the park (about 1½ hours to the top).

A shorter, gentler climb, with good views of both Lake Burabay and Lake Bolshoe Chebachie to its north, is **Mt Bolektau**. This takes about half an hour by the track heading up to the right just before the Km 4 post heading west from Burabay town.

Local agencies offer a variety of group trips in the park with Russian-speaking guides. Gentle gradients make for good **cycling**: to rent a bike look for '*Prokat Velosipedov*' signs along the main road in Burabay.

Sleeping

The choice of hotels in and near Burabay town is wide and good. It's also fairly easy to rent rooms, cabins, apartments or even yurts for 1000T to 2500T per person: look for signs saying '*sdam komnati/domiki/kvartiry/yurty*' along the main street, Kenesary.

Baza Otdykha Akmolaturist No 1 TURBAZA $
(☎7 15 11; www.akmolatourist.kz/borovoe; Kenesary 55, Burabay; per person 2250-2750T) By the roundabout at the entrance to Burabay from Shchuchinsk, this little place provides cosy rooms for two to six people, with a shared kitchen and clean shared bathrooms. You can book through Akmolaturist (p107) in Astana.

Kokshebel Lake Resort HOTEL $$
(☎7 11 97; sales-kokshebel@mail.ru; Kenesary 2A; cabins 15,000-20,000T, r 25,000-35,000T, incl breakfast; P ⊜ ❄ ☰ ≋) Kokshebel is a well-built, well-run hotel with attractive pine-wooded grounds stretching down to the lakeshore (with private beach) at the west end of town. The rooms are comfortable and well equipped. The cosy wooden cabins, holding up to four people, are under the pines close to the lake. Guests can amuse themselves with billiards, darts, table tennis or a sauna.

Hotel Nursat HOTEL $$
(☎7 13 01; www.bereke-burabai.com; Kenesary 26, Burabay; r incl breakfast 7000-16,000T; P ☰) This red-brick hotel, one of a few almost opposite the Nature Museum, has large, bright and comfy if plain rooms.

Eating

Kafe Taranchi CENTRAL ASIAN $$
(Kenesary; mains 800-1200T; ⊙10am-2am Jun-Aug) The Taranchi has an unmissable pink, castlelike exterior, a short walk west of the main bus stop in Burabay. Good Uyghur *laghman*, *plov* and *tosh-kan* (a spicy meat, onion and noodles dish), and some Russian dishes, are served in an interior that conjures up an old caravanserai.

Kafe Alina CENTRAL ASIAN $$
(☎7 20 20; Kenesary 21; dishes 250-2400T; ⊙9am-5am; ⊜) Just east of the Burabay bus stop, Alina is done out in pinks and purples and turns out respectable versions of everything from *bliny* to *kuksi* (Korean noodle, meat and vegetable soup) to shashlyk to salmon with red caviar. It has a nice summer terrace.

Getting There & Around

Minibuses (1500T to 1800T, three hours) and shared taxis (2500T) to Burabay leave from outside Astana's bus station when full. Daytime departures are plentiful in summer and at weekends. More plentiful transport (at least 19 buses or minibuses) runs from Astana to Shchuchinsk, on the Astana–Kokshetau road 15km south of the lake. From Shchuchinsk small white buses (150T, 30 minutes) run every 40 minutes (7am to 7pm) to Burabay, or there are shared/charter taxis for 250/1000T. In Burabay the bus and taxi stop is just off the main street, Kenesary, towards the west end of town.

Karaganda (Karagandy) КАРАГАНДА (ҚАРАҒАНДЫ)

☎7212 / POP 459,000 / ELEV 550M

Smack in the steppe heartland, 220km southeast of Astana, Karaganda is most famous for two things: coal and labour camps. The two are intimately connected, as the vast 'KarLag' network of Stalin-era camps around Karaganda was set up to provide food and labour for the mines. Prison labour also built much of Karaganda itself.

During the depressed 1990s many of Karaganda's ethnic-German residents (descendants of Stalin-era deportees) emigrated to Germany. But Karaganda has bounced back and today the central areas of the city are a pleasant surprise, with a lively buzz and plenty of parks and broad tree-lined streets, all prettily illuminated after dark. Bukhar Zhyrau dangyly, the main street, heads north through the centre from the train and bus stations.

Sights

★Karaganda Ecological Museum MUSEUM

(☎41 33 44; http://ecomuseum.kz; Bukhar Zhyrau dangyly 47; admission per person without tour 120T, with tour 150-250T; ⌚9am-7pm Mon-Fri, by arrangement Sat & Sun) The Karaganda Ecological Museum, run by a dedicated, campaigning environmental NGO, has to be the most imaginative museum in the country. Everything can be touched, and this includes large rocket parts that have fallen on the steppe after Baykonur space launches, and debris collected from the Semipalatinsk Polygon. Other display topics include the saiga antelope and chemical safety in Kazakhstan. The guided tours, available in English, are well worth it and are best requested in advance. The entrance is beneath an 'Ortalykkazzherkoynauy' sign at the side of the Bank RBK building.

Karaganda Oblast Museum MUSEUM

(☎56 48 62; Yerubaev 38; admission 150T; ⌚9am-6pm) The recently modernised regional museum has ample displays on local history, including a section on KarLag. Guided tours (150T), available in English, add significantly to the interest.

Central Park PARK

The leafy Central Park stretches over 2km from north to south, with a large lake at its heart. Its main entrance is off the west side of mid-Bukhar Zhyrau.

Karaganda

Top Sights
1 Karaganda Ecological Museum ... A3

Sights
2 Central Park ... A3
3 Karaganda Oblast Museum ... B2

Sleeping
4 Hotel Ar-Nuvo ... A2
5 Hotel Edem ... B4
6 Hotel Gratsia ... B4

Eating
7 Assorti ... B4
8 Pivovaroff ... A2
Rational ... (see 11)

Entertainment
9 Elvis ... B3
10 Svintsovy Dirizhabl ... A1

Transport
11 Bus Station ... B5

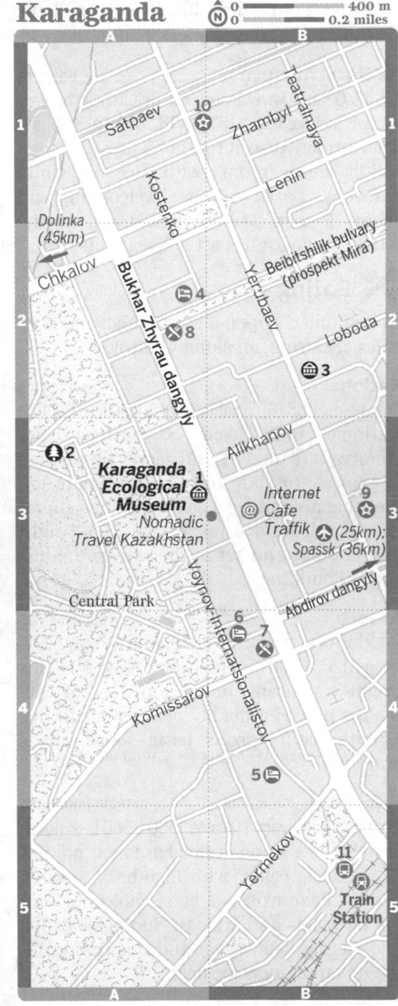

Sleeping

Hotel Gratsia HOTEL $
(☎41 24 59; hotel-gracia@mail.ru; Voynov-Internatsionalistov; s/d with shared shower 3500/5000T, r with bathroom 6000-8000T) A decent-value budget place, the Gratsia has well-used but well-kept and clean rooms. It's painted salmon pink and its sign just says 'Gostinitsa'.

Hotel Edem HOTEL $$
(☎91 08 94; edem_karaganda@mail.ru; Yermekov 29/4; s 7000-8000T, d 8000-16,000T; P ᯤ) The Edem offers plain but neat, clean rooms with carpets, good wooden furniture and thick wallpaper. It's not exactly accustomed to foreigners but one or two receptionists speak a bit of English. Breakfast is available for 800T.

★ **Hotel Ar-Nuvo** HOTEL $$
(☎42 02 84; www.arnuvo.kz; Beibitshilik bulvary 4A; s/d incl breakfast 16,500/18,500T; P ❄ @ ᯤ) This attractive, well-run hotel provides cosy, solidly comfy rooms with nice big white bathtubs. Desk staff are welcoming and there's a good 24-hour restaurant. As the name implies, it has art nouveau touches.

Eating

In summer, open-air shashlyk-and-beer cafes are strung all along Abdirov.

Rational CAFETERIA $
(Yermekov 58/6; mains 400-1000T; ⏲24hr) Rational bills itself a 'business-class *stolovaya* (canteen)' and serves up a range of typical Russian and Central Asian staples that are indeed a cut above the general run of self-service restaurants. It's bright and popular and set in the side of the bus station building.

Assorti EUROPEAN $$
(☎91 17 07; City Mall, Bukhar Zhyrau dangyly 59/2; mains 1200-3100T; ⏲noon-2am; ⊖ ᯤ ▤) This bright restaurant on the top floor of City Mall is part of a quality national chain. It's a fine place for pizzas, pasta, soups, salads and grills.

Pivovaroff INTERNATIONAL $$$
(Beibitshilik bulvary 1; mains 1500-3500T; ⏲noon-2am) Set in a stone-walled basement not unlike a castle cellar, with high-back wooden booths, Pivovaroff is a good choice for dining on salads and grills (including shashlyk and German sausages) and quaffing unfiltered Staronemetskoe beer.

Entertainment

Svintsovy Dirizhabl LIVE MUSIC
(http://vk.com/krglsd; Yerubaev 4A) Karaganda is a Kazakh rock music hot spot and 'Lead Zeppelin' is the top club for live bands. Gigs typically run from about 7pm to 11pm, on Friday, Saturday or Sunday. Name bands from Russia appear every couple of weeks or so. Check the website or karaganda.night.kz for schedules and prices.

Elvis LIVE MUSIC
(☎31 97 40; www.music-club.kz; Yerubaev 50A; ⏲7pm-3am) Elvis is a fun place to listen to live rock and roll, jazz or blues (nightly from 10pm), drink some beer and eat good food – especially in the open air in summer.

Information

Internet Cafe Traffik (Bukhar Zhyrau dangyly 46; internet per hr 240T; ⏲9am-9pm) Efficient place along a lane beside the Abzal shopping centre.

Nomadic Travel Kazakhstan (☎99 61 65; www.nomadic.kz; Office 209, Bukhar Zhyrau dangyly 49; ⏲9am-6pm Mon-Fri) If you want to explore the steppe heartland, climb its hills, photograph saiga or birds, visit remote archaeological and historic sites and experience vast panoramas, with English-speaking guides, this dynamic group of young travel enthusiasts is just the ticket. The office is a good place for regional tourist information, and it has an excellent city and regional tourist map available.

Trips last from one to 10 days. Transport can be by bicycle or minibus, with accommodation in hotels, village homestays, tents or herders' huts. Most trips are arranged to order but they do advertise a few open trips on their website or Facebook. Typical prices for the longer trips are 20,000T to 30,000T per day per person, varying with group size. One- or two-day trips can be anywhere from 10,000T to over 80,000T per day per person.

Perhaps the most original trip is the six-day 'Back in the USSR' offering, which includes the Semipalatinsk nuclear polygon, Gulag camps and Russian civil war sites. Baykonur Cosmodrome visits are also offered. Other destinations:

Kyzylarai mountains Around 300km southeast of Karaganda, with walks, horse rides, 3000-year-old stone necropolises, the steppe's highest mountain (1565m Aksoran) and homestays in the felt-making village of Shabanbay Bi.

Ulytau hills North of Zhezkazgan, with Bronze Age petroglyphs and the mausoleums of Chinggis Khan's eldest son, Jochi, and Alasha-Khan, who is considered the founding father of the Kazakh people.

ℹ Getting There & Around

Karaganda's **airport** (☎42 85 42; http://kgf.aero), 24km southeast of the centre (3000T by taxi), has Air Astana flights to Almaty (from 23,340T) daily, and SCAT flights to Almaty (from 16,000T), Ust-Kamenogorsk (from 14,000T) and Kyzylorda (from 14,000T) three or four times weekly. Transaero flies to Moscow, and Rossiya to St Petersburg.

The **train station** (☎43 36 36; Yermekov; 📶) has at least 15 daily trains to Astana (1030T to 2970T, 2½ to 5½ hours) and six to Almaty (4430T to 10,225T, 10 to 16 hours). There are also daily trains to Petropavlovsk and Shymkent, and departures to Semey, Moscow and various Siberian cities several days a week. Book ahead as Karaganda is a midroute station.

Destinations from the **bus station** (☎43 18 18; www.avokzal.kz; Yermekova 58/6) include Almaty (5570T, 16 to 19 hours, three daily), Astana (1200T, 4½ hours, every half-hour, 6.30am to 8pm), Semey (3900T to 3975T, 16 to 19 hours, one or two daily) and Ust-Kamenogorsk (5000T, 20 to 23 hours, one daily). Other daily buses head as far as Petropavlovsk, Bishkek and Barnaul (Russia). Minivans (1500T) and shared taxis (2500T) outside the bus station will whisk you to Astana in three hours.

Bus 1 (50T) from the train station runs north along Bukhar Zhyrau dangyly then east along Beibitshilik.

Around Karaganda

Dolinka village, about 45km southwest of Karaganda, was the administrative centre for the whole KarLag system, whose territory extended over 1200 sq km. The excellent 14-room **KarLag Museum** (Museum of the Victims of Political Repressions; ☎72156-5 82 22; Shkolnaya 39, Dolinka; admission 420T; ⏰9am-6pm Mon-Sat) here, housed in the old KarLag headquarters building, gives a

OFF THE BEATEN TRACK

ALTAY MOUNTAINS — АЛТАЙ

In the far eastern corner of Kazakhstan the magnificent Altay Mountains spread across the borders to Russia, China and, 50km away, Mongolia. To visit this area you need to plan well ahead and go with a good travel firm such as Altai Expeditions (p115) or Imperia Turizma (p115), who can obtain the border-zone permit that is required beyond the village of Uryl (Orel).

The hassle of getting to this sparsely populated region is certainly well worth it. Rolling meadows, snow-covered peaks, forested hillsides, glaciers, pristine lakes and rivers, archaeological sites, and rustic villages with Kazakh horsemen riding by make for scenery of epic proportions. Twin-headed Mt Belukha (4506m), on the Kazakh–Russian border, has many mystical associations and Asian legends refer to it as the location of the paradisal realm of Shambhala.

The season of easiest movement and decent weather is short in the Altay – mid-June to the end of September. Imperia Turizma offers 12-day trips from Ust-Kamenogorsk, with a week's trekking in the Belukha foothills, for 75,000T per person in groups of around 10 (bring your own tent and sleeping gear). Altai Expeditions offers a trip to the foot of Belukha with packhorses, English-speaking guide, cook, tents and sleeping mats included, and some nights in guesthouses or hotels, for €2430/1890/1440 per person in two-/four-/six-person groups. It also does a 13-day 'Altai Lakes' trip, with eight days on horseback, for €3200/2550 per person in two-/four-person groups.

Near **Berel** you can visit the excavations of a famous group of Scythian burial mounds, where in 1997 archaeologists discovered the amazingly preserved body of a 4th-century BC prince, buried with several horses and carriages.

The health resort of **Rakhmanovskie Klyuchi** (Rakhmanov's Springs; ☎7232-26 37 44; www.altaytravel.ru; office Protozanov 25/1, Ust-Kamenogorsk; d/q with shared bathroom 14,000/20,000T, cottage for 4 17,250T, full board per person 3125-4250T; ⏰office 9am-6pm Mon-Fri) nestles in a mountain valley, 30km up a track from Berel village, and offers the Altay's cosiest accommodation. You'll find wooden cottages, some with kitchen, linked by boardwalks through pine forests; and mountain bikes and trips to lakes and waterfalls in the area are offered to guests. You can see Mt Belukha from the Radostny Pass, a one-hour walk up from the resort.

vivid idea of the conditions and suffering of the victims through recreations of cells and other rooms, dioramas and paintings, as well as memorabilia such as photos, letters and furnishings. KarLag death rates reached 30% a year at times. There is much explanatory material in English but the English-language tour (600T per group) is well worthwhile – call ahead to book one. Also in the village are other KarLag relics including a hospital, a clinic, the officers' club and the Mamochkino children's cemetery. Get to Dolinka by Shakhtinsk-bound bus 121, leaving Karaganda bus station every 10 to 20 minutes. Get off at the Vtoroy Shakht stop after about one hour (120T), walk or take a shared taxi into Dolinka (1.5km) and ask for the *muzey* (museum).

Spassk, 35km south of Karaganda on the Almaty highway, was the site of a KarLag camp where foreign prisoners of war were kept after WWII. Beside the highway is the mass grave of some 5000 prisoners, with eerie groups of crosses scattered around the site, and monuments installed by several countries whose nationals died here. A round-trip taxi to Spassk should cost about 2500T from Karaganda.

Nomadic Travel Kazakhstan (p110) takes trips to both these sites for 23,000T per group of up to five.

EASTERN KAZAKHSTAN

Ust-Kamenogorsk, a relatively prosperous regional capital, is the gateway to a large region of mountains, lakes and villages with good hiking, horse riding, biking, rafting and other activities. The Altay Mountains, at its eastern extremity, are one of the most beautiful corners of Kazakhstan but you must plan well ahead to get a border-zone permit to visit them. The region's other main city, Semey, is best known for the infamous Polygon nuclear-testing zone nearby, but is one of Kazakhstan's most culturally and historically interesting cities.

Ust-Kamenogorsk (Oskemen) УСТЬ-КАМЕНОГОРСК (ӨСКЕМЕН)

☎7232 / POP 298,000 / ELEV 280M

Ust-Kamenogorsk is a lively city with generally low-key Soviet architecture, at the confluence of the Irtysh and Ulba Rivers. Founded as a Russian fort in 1720, 'Ust' has grown from a small town since the 1940s, when Russians and Ukrainians began arriving to mine and process the area's copper, lead, silver and zinc. These industries still keep Ust out of the economic doldrums, but are bad news for air quality.

Ust-Kamenogorsk (Oskemen)

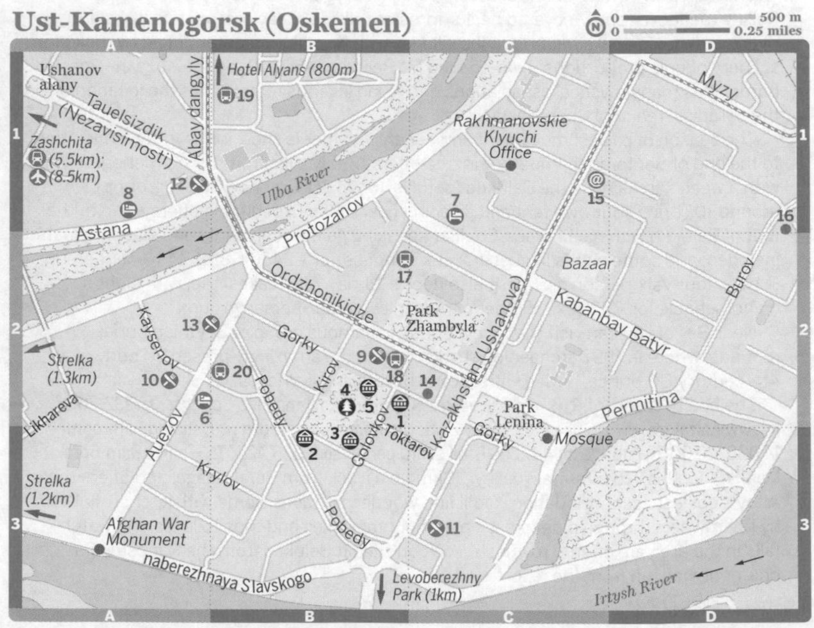

Sights

★Levoberezhny Park PARK
(Left-Bank Park; adult/child 300/100T; 10am-7pm) This large new park on the south bank of the Irtysh contains several interesting exhibits and is well worth a couple of hours of your time. Moving west from the entrance through still-growing botanical gardens you reach the Ethnographical Exhibition which comprises houses in the traditional styles of over a dozen of Kazakhstan's ethnic groups, from Chechens and Tatars to Koreans and Uyghurs.

Returning eastward along the northern side of the park, you encounter pavilions with exhibits on WWII heroes, the Afghan War and the Chernobyl 'Liquidators' – those involved in the 'clean-up' opeation after the 1986 Chernobyl nuclear disaster in Ukraine. Returning towards the entrance past a long alley of Soviet weaponry, you'll find a collection of Soviet-era statues – multiple Lenins but also artistic figures like Mayakovsky, Gorky and even Tolstoy – assembled against a backdrop of the shiny blue domes of Ust's newest mosque. You can reach the park by bus 60 eastbound on Ordzhonikidze, to the first stop after the river (60T).

Park Zhastar PARK
(daylight) The pretty, beautifully maintained central park makes for a pleasant stroll, and several of Ust-Kamenogorsk's oldest buildings and some worthwhile museums are clustered around it. In the park itself is a replica **Russian pioneer village** (admission 200T; varies) of log cabins, furnished and decorated in period style.

History Museum MUSEUM
(25 54 60; Kaysenov 40; Kazakhstani/foreigner 250/500T; 9am-5pm Wed-Mon) The good History Museum has a natural-history section with stuffed regional wildlife, including a snow leopard and a giant maral deer, and human history exhibits that reveal the huge number of ancient burial mounds in the region.

Ethnography Museum MUSEUM
(26 46 61; admission per branch 200T; 9am-5pm) The Ethnography Museum is in two buildings facing opposite corners of Park Zhastar. **Korpus No 1** (Gorky 59) exhibits the traditional culture of the Kazakhs of east Kazakhstan region; **Korpus No 2** (Kaysenov 67) is devoted to the many other ethnic groups in the region.

Strelka VIEWPOINT
It's nice to take a walk to the Strelka (Arrow), the point of land where the Irtysh and Ulba meet, marked by a large Heroes of the Soviet Union memorial.

Sleeping

Hotel Alyans HOTEL $
(22 29 45; Abay dangyly 20; dm 2500T, s/d 4000/5000T;) This fairly friendly budget option, 1km north of the bus station (two tram stops), sits on the top floor of a seven-storey green building bearing the word 'Nursat'. Rooms are clean and hold either two or four; bathrooms are shared.

Hotel Irtysh HOTEL $$
(25 09 85; irtysh-hotel@mail.ru; Auezov 22; s/d incl breakfast from 8500/11,000T; P) This

Ust-Kamenogorsk (Oskemen)

Sights
1 Ethnography Museum Korpus No 1 ..... B2
2 Ethnography Museum Korpus No 2..... B3
3 History Museum B3
4 Park Zhastar B2
5 Russian pioneer Village B2

Sleeping
6 Hotel Irtysh A2
7 Hotel Ust-Kamenogorsk C1
8 Shiny River Hotel A1

Eating
BarBQ ..... (see 13)
9 Kofe Blyuz B2
10 Maslenitsa A2
11 Pitstsa Blyuz C3
12 Pitstsa Blyuz A1
Pitstsa Blyuz ..... (see 9)
13 Teplitsa B2

Information
14 Altai Expeditions C2
15 American Corner C1
16 Imperia Turizma D1

Transport
17 Bus 12 to Airport B2
18 Bus 60 to Levoberezhny Park B2
19 Bus Station B1
20 Buses 2 & 39 to Airport B2

Soviet-era establishment is a bit cosier and more accustomed to foreigners than comparable hotels, though reception staff seem to suffer from deep depression. Rooms are all renovated, and fitted out in shades of brown.

Hotel Ust-Kamenogorsk HOTEL **$$**
(☎26 18 01; www.hotel-oskemen.kz; Kabanbay Batyr 158; s 4000-20,000T, d 6000-22,000T, all incl breakfast; ❄📶) A large Soviet-era hotel with renovated rooms in decent condition. All have bathrooms, carpets and thick leopard-spot or tiger-stripe blankets. The wi-fi signal is erratic.

Shiny River Hotel HOTEL **$$$**
(☎76 65 25; www.shinyriverhotel.kz; Astana 8/1; s 12,000-31,000T, d 15,000-35,000T, all incl breakfast; P❄@📶) This excellent modern hotel overlooking the Ulba has sober but tasteful and very comfy rooms, with shiny silk cushions and bedspreads, plus two bars, two classy restaurants and an in-house travel agency.

Eating

★Pitstsa Blyuz PIZZERIA, RUSSIAN **$**
(Pizza Blues; pizzas 500-620T; ⏲9am-11pm) Highly popular local chain in several locations including **Gorky** (☎24 81 67; Gorky 56; 📶), **Tauelsizdik** (☎76 51 01; Tauelsizdik 1) and **Kazakhstan** (☎25 23 66; Kazakhstan 64) serving pretty good pizzas and salads, and great ice cream and *bliny,* in clean, bright surroundings. Also at the Gorky location is the slightly more expensive **Kofe Blyuz** (Coffee Blues; ☎26 47 04; dishes 340-1440T; ⏲9am-11pm; 📶), with great coffee and desserts, burgers, burritos, breakfasts, fresh juices and cocktails.

Teplitsa CAFETERIA **$**
(☎20 89 59; Auezov 43; mains 350-800T; ⏲9am-11pm) Teplitsa (Greenhouse) is a stylish update on the old *stolovaya* (cafeteria) concept. There's plenty of freshly prepared food to choose from, and it's hard to beat the tasty sausages grilled to order in front of

WORTH A TRIP

OUT & ABOUT FROM UST-KAMENOGORSK

Even if you have left it too late to get the border-zone permit needed to visit the Altay Mountains proper or other areas near the Chinese border, there's still plenty of good country within reach of Ust-Kamenogorsk that's good for hiking, horse or bike riding, rafting or just exploring. Public transport around the region is limited; it's easier if you organise trips through a good Ust-Kamenogorsk agency such as Altai Expeditions (p115) or Imperia Turizma (p115).

The mining town of **Ridder** (formerly Leninogorsk), 110km northeast of Ust-Kamenogorsk, is the gateway to beautiful mountain country abutting the Russian border, including the **Zapadno-Altaysky (Western Altay) Nature Reserve**. There are several campgrounds with cabins along the road heading east through the nature reserve from Ridder to the border, and good, not-too-demanding hiking and trekking in the **Ivanovsky Khrebet** hills south of the road. (Note: foreigners are not allowed to cross into Russia by this road.) Altai Expeditions charges around €75 per person per day for Ivanovsky Khrebet trips with English-speaking guides. Imperia Turizma offers two/three-day treks in the Ridder area for 9000/13,000T per person including transport and meals, or a day's rafting for 20,000T per person not including transport or meals. Eleven buses a day run to Ridder (900T, three hours) from Ust-Kamenogorsk bus station.

Within easy day-trip distance south of Ust-Kamenogorsk is the intriguing **Akbaur** Bronze Age astronomical and petroglyph complex (Altai Expeditions charges 7000T per car for a half-day trip), and the ruined medieval Buddhist monastery **Ablainskit**.

About 200km east of Ust-Kamenogorsk, **Maymyr** village is a good base for hikes and rides around the broad Naryn valley and the high mountains to the south. Altai Expeditions offers comfy cottage or yurtstays here, and good horse riding. Further south and southeast the highly varied terrain ranges from deserts and dramatic rock formations on the north side of Lake Zaysan to the pristine, 35km-long, 1400m-high **Lake Markakol**, accessible in summer by a hairy mountain-pass 4WD track from Katon-Karagay, the 'Austrian Road'. Altai Expeditions' wide-ranging 10-day 'Nomad' 4WD tour (around €1900/1500 per person for two-/four-person groups) encompasses this area. You do need a border-zone permit for Markakol, however.

you. The 600T set lunch (Monday to Friday) is good value.

Maslenitsa RUSSIAN **$**
(25 09 00; Kaysenov 117a; mains 320-850T; 9am-11pm;) The house speciality, ham-and-cheese-stuffed *bliny*, are unique in this neck of the woods. It's an informal two-level place, decorated in pine from the counter to the rafters, and does a big choice of good *bliny*, soups, salads, cakes and main dishes. Order at the counter.

BarBQ EUROPEAN, RUSSIAN **$$**
(20 89 60; Auezov 43; mains 1000-2300T; 11am-midnight;) Relatively upscale but still with a relaxed feel, BarBQ occupies spacious but discreetly arranged upstairs premises with expansive views, and is excellent for steaks, sausages, kebabs and other grills.

Information

Staff at the **American Corner** (Room 28a, Pushkin Library, Kazakhstan 102; internet per hr 220T; 9am-6pm Tue-Sun), a US cultural centre, let visitors use the web free for the first 30 minutes.

Altai Expeditions (www.altaiexpeditions.kz; Office 122, Gorky 46, Ust-Kamenogorsk; 10am-7pm Mon-Fri) Run by experienced, enthusiastic Andrey Yurchenkov, highly-recommended Altai Expeditions offers a big range of active trips and nature tours with English-speaking guides. Trips run in the Kazakh, Russian, Mongolian and Chinese Altay and areas nearer to Ust-Kamenogorsk, from day trips to serious foot or horse treks or 4WD tours with hotel or guesthouse accommodation.

Imperia Turizma (7232-26 11 08; www.imper-tour.kz; Burov 20, Ust-Kamenogorsk; 9am-6pm Mon-Fri) Offers activities in the Ridder area north of Ust, 10-day treks to the foot of Mt Belukha (75,000T per person), and more. Office staff speak some English.

Getting There & Away

AIR

From the airport Air Astana flies daily to Almaty (from 20,760T) and Astana (from 17,360T); SCAT flies to Almaty (from 16,380T), Astana (from 17,380T), Karaganda (from 14,000T), Zaysan (6000T) and Moscow (from 50,830T) two to four times weekly. S7 Airlines flies to Moscow three times weekly. A useful ticket agency is El Tur Vostok.

BUS

From the main bus station buses run six times daily to Semey (1300T, four hours), once or twice each day to Almaty (4500T, 22 hours), Astana (5000T, 17 hours), Karaganda (4000T to 5000T, 21 hours), and Barnaul (3350T to 4200T, 12 hours) and Novosibirsk (6000T, 17 hours) in Russia. Shared taxis to Semey from the bus station cost 2500T – you're most likely to find one earlyish in the morning.

Buses to Ürümqi, China (9000T, 28 hours), also go from the bus station at 6.15pm Tuesday, Thursday and Sunday, via the border at Maykapshagay.

TRAIN

Ust-Kamenogorsk's main train station is Zashchita, off Tauelsizdik 7km northwest of the centre. One daily train heads south to Almaty (4130T, 24 hours). Other trains from Zashchita head initially north into Russia to meet the Semey–Novosibirsk line: at the time of writing foreigners are not allowed to take these trains (although they can cross the same border, north of Shemonaykha, by bus or car!). For other trains heading south, get a taxi (shared/charter 2000/8000T, 2½ hours) or occasional bus (530T, three hours) from Ust-Kamenogorsk bus station to Zhangyztobe, 150km southwest, where at least three daily trains head to Almaty (3520T to 3810T, 16 to 18 hours). You can buy tickets for trains from Zashchita or Zhangyztobe at El Tur Vostok.

Getting Around

Buses 2 and 39 (80T) run to the airport from Auezov in the centre, and bus 12 from Kirov. A taxi costs around 2000T.

From Abay dangyly outside the bus station, trams 1, 2, 3 and 4 (55T) run to Ordzhonikidze and Kazakhstan on the east side of the Ulba; bus 6 (60T) will take you to Auezov for the Hotel Irtysh. Bus 1 and tram 3 link Zashchita train station with the city centre.

Semey (Semipalatinsk) СЕМЕЙ (СЕМИПАЛАТИНСК)

7222 / POP 304,000 / ELEV 200M

Though sadly best known to the world for the Soviet nuclear-testing ground nearby, the Polygon, Semey (formerly Semipalatinsk), has an unusually rich cultural heritage that makes it one of Kazakhstan's most interesting provincial cities. Founded in 1718 as a Russian fortification against the Zhungars, it stands 200km down the Irtysh from Ust-Kamenogorsk, in the heartland of the Kazakh Middle Horde, noted for their eloquence and intellect. The area has produced several major Kazakh writers and teachers, notably the national poet Abay Kunanbaev (1845–1904), and Semey was a home in exile to the great Russian writer Fyodor Dostoevsky.

Between 1949 and 1989 the Soviet military exploded some 460 nuclear bombs in the Semipalatinsk Polygon, an area of steppe west of the city. Not even villagers living close by were given protection or warning of the dangers. An unprecedented wave of popular protest, the Nevada-Semipalatinsk Movement, was largely instrumental in halting the tests in 1989, and President Nazarbaev closed the site in 1991. But the tragic effects linger: genetic mutations, cancers, weakened immune systems and mental illness continue to destroy lives and occupy hospitals and clinics in and around Semey. The UN Development Programme has calculated that more than 1.3 million people have been adversely affected by the tests.

Sights

Dostoevsky Museum MUSEUM
(52 19 42; Dostoevskogo 118; admission 150T; 9am-6pm Mon-Sat) The well laid-out Dostoevsky Museum incorporates the wooden house where the exiled writer lived from 1857 to 1859 with his wife and baby. The displays range over Dostoevsky's life and works, including his five years in jail at Oms and five years of enforced military service at Semey. His rooms have been maintained in the style of his day. Tours, in English, Russian or Kazakh, cost 300T.

It was in Semey that Dostoevsky made friends with the extraordinary Shokan Ualikhanov (Chokan Valikhanov), a prince of the Kazakh Middle Horde, explorer, intellectual and spy in the Russian army. A statue of both men stands outside the museum.

Abay Museum MUSEUM
(52 24 22; Lenin 12; 10am-1pm & 2-6pm Tue-Sat) FREE The large Abay Museum

Semey

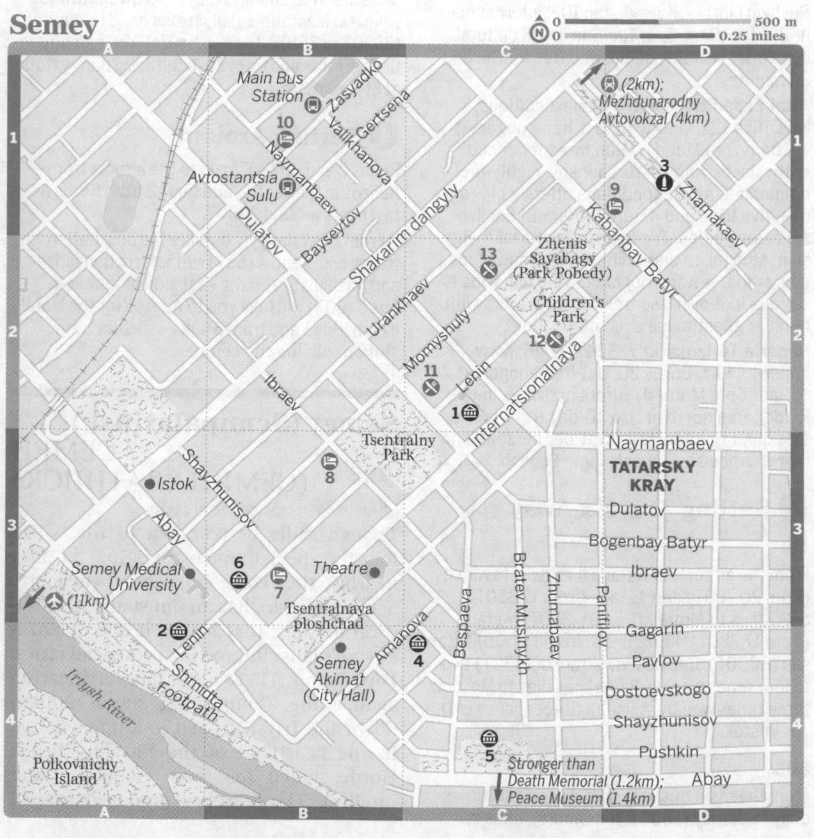

is dedicated to the 19th-century humanist poet Abay Kunanbaev (see boxed text p120). Along with displays about Abay's life and work, the museum has many 19th-century artefacts, and sections on the Kazakh nomadic tradition and Abay's literary successors, including Mukhtar Auezov (1897–1961), author of the epic novel *Abay Zholy* (The Path of Abay). Guided tours are free and English-speaking guides may be available.

History & Local Studies Museum MUSEUM
(☎52 07 32; www.semeymusey.kz; Abay 90; admission 150T; ⏰9am-5pm Mon-Sat) This museum has plenty of material on regional history including some rare archaeological pieces, and a collection of traditional Kazakh artefacts. Founded in 1883, it claims to be the oldest museum in Kazakhstan. Tours are 300T.

Fine Arts Museum MUSEUM
(☎52 31 84; www.muzey-nev.semstar.com; Pushkin 108; foreigner/Kazakhstani 600/300T; ⏰10am-6pm Tue-Sat) The collection here, one of the country's best, covers Kazakh, Russian and Western European art from the 16th century onwards, including a not-to-be-missed Rembrandt etching and work by top 19th-century Russians such as Levitan and Kramskoy.

Anatomical Museum MUSEUM
(Lenin 1; ⏰8.30am-4pm) FREE In an unmarked building that's part of Semey Medical University, this one-room museum exhibits the usual pickled organs you might expect medical students to look at – but also a gruesome collection of babies and embryos with appalling deformities caused by nuclear radiation from Polygon. Not for the squeamish. It's in room 28, upstairs. Ask nicely for the key in room 22.

Polkovnichy Island ISLAND
Rural Polkovnichy Island is across a long bridge over the Irtysh. On the left, 600m past the end of the bridge, is the sombre and impressive **Stronger than Death memorial**, erected in 2001 for victims of the nuclear tests. Above the marble centrepiece of a mother covering her child billows a Polygon mushroom cloud etched into a 30m-high black tombstone. Due to open nearby by 2014 is a new **Peace Museum**, in a 24m-diameter glass sphere resting on a pair of giant stone hands.

Communist Statues MONUMENT
A curious collection of 15 communist busts and statues, mostly Lenins, stands in a small park behind Hotel Semey, as if no one quite wanted do away with them entirely.

Sleeping

Hotel Semey HOTEL $
(☎50 30 04; www.semey.semstar.com; Kabanbay Batyr 26; s 4500-7000T, d 7000-15,000T, incl breakfast; P ⊖ ❄ @ ☎) Hotel Semey has that unmistakable Soviet aura but staff are reasonably helpful and the rooms have been modernised. Dinner is included with some 7000T rooms and all of the more expensive ones.

Hotel Tengri HOTEL $
(☎56 60 35; Zasyadko 73; r 3000T) This cheapie near the main bus station has utterly ordinary but acceptable rooms with bathroom, off its ground-floor cafe or upstairs.

Hotel Binar HOTEL $$
(☎52 36 39; binarkz@yandex.ru; Lenin 6; s/d incl breakfast from 8600/11,900T; P ❄ ☎) A low-key place in an attractive two-storey, century-old building, the Binar is great value for its standard of accommodation. The very spacious rooms are cosy and carpeted, and the Jacuzzi-style showers will spray you from any angle you choose.

Hotel Nomad HOTEL $$
(☎52 04 44; www.hotelnomad.kz; Ibraev 149; s/d incl breakfast 12,000/18,000T; P ❄ @ ☎) The best hotel in town, new in 2007, overlooks the central park. For a place of this quality

Semey

Sights
1 Abay Museum ... C2
2 Anatomical Museum ... A4
3 Communist Statues ... D1
4 Dostoevsky Museum ... C4
5 Fine Arts Museum ... C4
6 History & Local Studies Museum ... B3

Sleeping
7 Hotel Binar ... B3
8 Hotel Nomad ... B3
9 Hotel Semey ... D1
10 Hotel Tengri ... B1

Eating
11 Abat ... C2
12 Kofeman ... C2
13 Pepperoni ... C2

the prices are excellent. Rooms are unfussy but tasteful and well equipped, desk staff speak English, and room rates include a proper breakfast.

Eating

Abat RUSSIAN **$**
(☎56 85 33; Dulatov; terrace mains 600-1200T, cafeteria dishes 150-500T; ⏰terrace 11am-1am, cafeteria 9am-10pm) The outdoor terrace cafe here has a fun atmosphere in summer and serves reasonable shashlyk, other meat dishes, salads and desserts. The indoor cafeteria is inexpensive and run-of-the-mill, with offerings such as *plov*, pizza, *manty* and fried chicken.

Pepperoni ITALIAN **$$**
(Momyshuly 35; mains 800-2000T; ⏰11am-midnight; 📋) If there's such a thing as a pizza lounge, this is it, with sink-into chairs and elegant but relaxed ambience. The pizzas have thin crusts and successful topping combos. There are risottos and pasta too, plus good salads with surprising ingredients: the 'Guinea pumpkins' turn out to be aubergines.

Kofeman INTERNATIONAL **$$**
(☎56 55 38; Internatsionalnaya 43; dishes 200-1600T; ⏰10am-1am; 📶) Semey's fashionable coffee lounge, also doing American and Mexican breakfasts, pasta, burgers, steaks, cheesecake and alcoholic drinks. The latte is such a work of art it's a shame to drink it!

Information

Istok (☎52 48 99; vcistok@yandex.ru; Office 241, Abay 102; ⏰9am-6pm Mon-Fri) Environmental NGO Istok can take you on one-day tours to Kurchatov or the Shyngystau hills south of Semey, homeland of Abay Kunanbaev and other noted Kazakh writers. Prices are reasonable and English-speakers may be available.

Getting There & Away

From the **airport** (☎60 00 01), 11km south of the centre, SCAT flies daily to Almaty (27,100T) and five times weekly to Astana (20,000T).

From the **main bus station** (☎52 08 15; Valikhanova 167), next to the busy bazaar, eight daily buses run to Ust-Kamenogorsk (1300T, four hours), three to Astana (3400T, 14 hours) and two to Karaganda (3300T,19 hours). Shared taxis to Ust-Kamenogorsk (2500T, 2½ hours) gather here too. Two daily buses to Barnaul, Russia (3600T, 11 hours), and three a week to Ürümqi, China (9100T, 32 hours), go from the **Mezhdunarodny Avtovokzal** (International Bus Station; ☎51 47 97; Karzhaubayuly 249) in the north of the city.

The **train station** (☎38 12 32; Privokzalnaya 1), just off the north end of Shakarim dangyly, has two or more daily departures to Almaty (4130T to 4480T, 19 to 21 hours), one every two days to Astana (3520T, 17 hours), and one or more daily north to Barnaul (10,250T, 11½ hours) and Novosibirsk (13,530T, 17½ hours).

Getting Around

Buses 11 and 13 (45T) run from the train station to the centre along Shakarim dangyly. Bus 33 heads from the train station to the main bazaar (near the main bus station) then along Kabanbay Batyr and Internatsionalnaya to Tsentralnaya ploshchad, then eventually to the airport. Buses 35 and 41 also run between Tsentralnaya ploshchad and the bazaar. Taxis cost 2000T to or from the airport.

Around Semey

Kurchatov & the Polygon

The town of Kurchatov, 120km west of Semey, was the command centre for the Semipalatinsk Polygon. The nuclear testing zone itself stretched some 100km to 120km south and west from Kurchatov. Today, the rather desolate town is home to Kazakhstan's **National Nuclear Centre** (Natsionalny Yaderny Tsentr; ☎72251-2 33 33, tel/fax 72251-2 38 58; www.nnc.kz; Zdanie (Bldg) 054b, Krasnoarmeyskaya 2, Kurchatov), which, among other things, works on the development of nuclear power in Kazakhstan. You can travel freely to the town and have a walk around – the central square is dominated by the large, Stalinist-neoclassical town hall (formerly the Polygon's headquarters), and a rather manic-looking statue of Igor Kurchatov himself, the director of the Soviet atomic bomb program. But you won't get into any of the museums or institutes unless you organise a trip through an agency such as Istok (p118) in Semey (which charges US$100 per car plus US$10 per hour waiting time), or try obtaining permission yourself by email or fax (in English is OK) a week or more ahead to the Director at the National Nuclear Centre.

The **museum** (☎72251-2 34 13; ⏰9am-6pm Mon-Fri) FREE in the Radiation Safety & Ecology Institute includes a model of the first test site (where aircraft, buildings and live animals were placed close to the explosion to test its effects), along with pickled animal parts, models of other blast sites, and a lump of granite turned to something more like pumice by a nuclear blast.

Four buses a day run to Kurchatov (820T, three hours) from Semey's **Avtostantsia Sulu** (Naymanbaev). A taxi round-trip from Semey with an hour or two in Kurchatov costs around 10,000T.

Though some parts of the Polygon itself can be visited safely, it would be lunacy to wander in without an expert guide. Two professional travel agencies that can arrange trips with proper safety equipment and precautions are Karaganda-based Nomadic Travel Kazakhstan (p110) and Ust-Kamenogorsk's Altai Expeditions (p115). Give them at least two weeks to make arrangements. You can expect to see sites such as the Opytnoe Pole (location of the first nuclear test), the 'Atomic Lake' (a water-filled bomb crater created as an experiment in 'peaceful' landscape change) and the Degelen mountains, where bombs were exploded in tunnels cut into hillsides.

UNDERSTAND KAZAKHSTAN

Kazakhstan Today

President Nursultan Nazarbaev was elected to another seven-year presidential term in 2011. Born into a rural peasant family in 1940, Nazarbaev has ruled Kazakhstan since late Soviet times, and still garners Soviet-style percentages of the vote – 95.5% in 2011, an election criticised by international observers (like every other post-Soviet election here) for its irregularities. Nazarbaev has fostered a strong personality cult – his picture and words of wisdom greet you on billboards everywhere you go – and there is nothing to stop him staying at the top for as long as his health holds. In 2010 parliament named him 'Leader of the Nation', enabling him to exert a strong influence over government if he ceases to be president.

Nazarbaev doesn't hide his belief that the economy comes first and democracy second. He has certainly delivered on the economy, using international investment to help develop Kazakhstan's vast resources of oil, gas and almost every other known valuable mineral. Economic growth averaged a very strong 8% a year in the decade up to 2012. By 2013 Kazakhstan was the world's 17th biggest oil producer, pumping 1.6 million barrels per day, and the Kashagan field in the Caspian Sea – the world's biggest oilfield outside the Middle East – was expected to come on stream by 2014, eventually adding another million barrels to the total.

Nazarbaev certainly does not welcome political opposition, but he has managed to forge a largely peaceful and increasingly prosperous country, which keeps him popular enough among the population at large. In the main cities it's easy to see – from the ostentatious imported motors, the expensive restaurants and the nightclubs where some locals will happily plonk down the equivalent of hundreds of dollars to reserve a table – that Kazakhstan's new rich are quite numerous. And there's a sizeable middle-class developing. Yet those who are excluded from the networks of the new wealthy have begun to get disgruntled about corruption and poor health and education services as well as poverty. This was brutally highlighted in 2011 when a strike by government oil workers in the western town of Zhanaozen ended with security forces shooting dead at least 14 demonstrators – the first time independent Kazakhstan had seen social unrest and violence on such a scale.

There is no apparent strategy in place for a transition to multiparty democracy, nor – despite Nazarbaev's age and rumours of health problems – any obvious heir apparent, which fuels a lot of gossip and shadowy manoeuvrings behind the scenes. Nazarbaev's extremely rich and powerful son-in-law Timur Kulibaev is one possible candidate.

Critics of Nazarbaev continue to be put out of action. Prominent human-rights activist Yevgeny Zhovtis received a four-year manslaughter sentence in 2009 after a driving accident, and in the wake of the Zhanaozen events, opposition politician Vladimir Kozlov got a seven and-a-half year sentence for attempting to overthrow the government by encouraging strikes. Both trials were condemned as unfair by human-rights groups. The media rights body Reporters Without Borders ranked Kazakhstan 160th out of 179 countries in its 2013 press freedom index.

Kazakhstan's Soviet state-run economy was dismantled in the 1990s, but corruption remains a barrier to a true free-market economy: Kazakhstan ranked 133rd out of 174 countries in the 2012 Corruption Perceptions Index of Transparency International.

History

Kazakhstan as a single entity with defined boundaries was an invention of the Soviet regime in the 1920s. Before that, the great bulk of this territory was part of the domain of nomadic horseback animal herders that stretched right across the Eurasian steppe. At times some of its various peoples fell under the sway of regional or continental potentates; at other times they were left to sort themselves out. From around the 9th century AD the far south came within the ambit of the settled Silk Road civilisations of Transoxiana (the area between the Amu-Darya and Syr-Darya rivers). A people who can be identified as Kazakhs first emerged in southeastern Kazakhstan in the 15th century. Over time they came to cover a territory roughly approximating modern Kazakhstan, though some of this continued to be governed periodically from elsewhere and/or occupied by other peoples. The borders of Soviet Kazakhstan excluded some Kazakh-populated areas and included some areas with non-Kazakh populations.

Early Peoples

Kazakhstan's early history is a shadowy procession of nomadic peoples, most of whom moved in from the east and left few records. By around 500 BC southern Kazakhstan was inhabited by the Saka, part of the vast network of nomadic Scythian cultures that stretched across the steppes from the Altay to Ukraine. The Saka left many burial mounds, in some of which fabulous hoards of gold jewellery, often with animal motifs, have been found (many examples can be seen in Kazakhstan's museums). Most splendid of all is the 'Golden Man', a warrior's costume that has become a Kazakhstan national symbol (p62).

From 200 BC the Huns, followed by various Turkic peoples, arrived from what are now Mongolia and northern China. The early Turks left totemlike carved stones known as *balbals,* bearing the images of honoured chiefs, at sacred and burial sites, and these too can be seen in many Kazakhstan museums. From about AD 550 to 750 the southern half of Kazakhstan was the western extremity of the Manchuria-based Kök (Blue) Turk empire.

The far south was within the sphere of the Bukhara-based Samanid dynasty from the mid-9th century, and here cities such as Otrar and Yasy (Turkistan) developed on the back of agriculture and Silk Road trade. The Karakhanid Turks from the southern Kazakh steppe ousted the Samanids in the late 10th century, taking up the Samanids' settled ways (and Islam) and constructing some of Kazakhstan's earliest surviving buildings (in and around Taraz).

Chinggis (Genghis) Khan

Around 1130 AD the Karakhanids were displaced by the Khitans, a Buddhist people driven out of Mongolia and northern China. The Khitan state, known as the Karakitay empire, stretched from Xinjiang to Transoxiana, but in the early 13th century it became prey to rising powers at both extremities. To the west, based in Khorezm, south of the Aral Sea, was the Khorezmshah empire, which took Transoxiana in 1210. To the east was Chinggis Khan, who sent an army to crush the Karakitay in 1218, then turned to the Khorezmshah empire,

ABAY, CULTURAL ICON

Writer, translator and educator Abay (Ibrahim) Kunanbaev (1845–1904) was born in the Shyngystau hills south of Semey. Son of a prosperous Kazakh noble, he studied at both a medressa and a Russian school in Semey. His later translations of Russian and other foreign literature into Kazakh, and his public readings of them, as well as his own work such as the philosophical *Forty-One Black Words,* were the beginning of Kazakh as a literary language and helped to broaden Kazakhs' horizons.

Abay valued Kazakh traditions but was also pro-Russian. 'Study Russian culture and art – it is the key to life,' he wrote. In Soviet times Abay's reputation had Moscow's stamp of approval, and his Russophile writings were enshrined. Today he remains the number one Kazakh cultural icon.

which had misguidedly murdered 450 of his merchants at Otrar. The biggest-ever Mongol army (200,000 or so) sacked the Khorezmian cities of Otrar, Bukhara and Samarkand, then swept on towards Europe and the Middle East. Central Asia became part of the Mongol empire.

On Chinggis Khan's death in 1227, his enormous empire was divided between his sons. The lands farthest from the Mongol heartland – north and west of the Aral Sea – went to the descendants of his eldest son Jochi and became known as the Golden Horde. Southeastern Kazakhstan was part of the Chaghatai khanate, the lands that went to Chinggis' second son Chaghatai. In the late 14th century far southern Kazakhstan was conquered by Timur from Samarkand, who constructed Kazakhstan's one great surviving Silk Road building, the Yasaui Mausoleum at Turkistan.

The Kazakhs

The story of the Kazakhs starts with the Uzbeks, a group of Islamised Mongols named after leader Özbeg (Uzbek), who were left in control of most of the Kazakh steppe as the Golden Horde disintegrated in the 15th century.

In 1468 an internal feud split the Uzbeks into two groups. Those who ended up south of the Syr-Darya ruled from Bukhara as the Shaybanid dynasty and ultimately gave their name to modern Uzbekistan. Those who stayed north remained nomadic and became the Kazakhs, taking their name from a Turkic word meaning free rider or adventurer. The Kazakh khanate that resulted was a confederation of nomadic peoples that by the 18th century stretched over most of southern, western and central Kazakhstan, descendants of the Mongols and earlier Turkic inhabitants.

The Kazakhs grouped into three 'hordes' *(zhuz),* with which Kazakhs today still identify: the Great Horde in the south, the Middle Horde in the centre, north and east, and the Little Horde in the west. Each was ruled by a khan and comprised a number of clans whose leaders held the title *axial, bi* or *batyr*.

The Zhungars (Oyrats), a warlike Mongol clan, subjugated eastern Kazakhstan between 1690 and 1720 in what Kazakhs call the Great Disaster. Abylay Khan, a Middle Horde leader who tried to unify Kazakh resistance to the Zhungars after 1720, was eventually elected khan of all three hordes in 1771, but by that time they were well on the way to becoming Russian vassals.

The Russians Arrive

Russia's expansion across Siberia ran up against the Zhungars, against whom they built a line of forts along the Kazakhs' northern border. The Kazakhs sought tsarist protection from the Zhungars, and the khans of all three hordes swore loyalty to the Russian crown between 1731 and 1742. Russia gradually extended its 'protection' of the khanates to their annexation and abolition, despite repeated Kazakh uprisings. By some estimates one million of the four million Kazakhs died in revolts and famines before 1870. Meanwhile, the abolition of serfdom in Russia and Ukraine in 1861 stimulated peasant settlers to move into Kazakhstan.

Communist Takeover & 'Development'

In the chaos following the Russian Revolution of 1917, a Kazakh nationalist party, Alash Orda, tried to establish an independent government, based in Semey. As the Russian Civil War raged across Kazakhstan, Alash Orda eventually sided with the Bolsheviks, who emerged victorious in 1920 – only for Alash members soon to be purged from the Communist Party of Kazakhstan (CPK). Meanwhile several hundred thousand Kazakhs fled to China and elsewhere.

The next disaster to befall the Kazakhs was denomadisation, between 1929 and 1933. Under Soviet government, the world's biggest group of seminomadic people was pushed one step up the Marxist evolutionary ladder to become settled farmers in new collectives. Unused to agriculture, they died in their hundreds of thousands from famine and disease.

In the 1930s and '40s more and more people from other parts of the USSR – prisoners and others – were sent to work in labour camps and new industrial towns in Kazakhstan. They included entire peoples deported en masse from western areas of the USSR around the time of WWII. A further 800,000 migrants arrived in the 1950s when Nikita Khrushchev decided to plough up 250,000 sq km of north Kazakhstan steppe to grow wheat in the Virgin Lands scheme.

The labour camps were wound down in the mid-1950s, but many survivors stayed on, and yet more Russians, Ukrainians and other Soviet nationalities arrived to mine and process Kazakhstan's coal, iron and oil. The proportion of Kazakhs in Kazakhstan's population fell below 30%.

During the Cold War the USSR decided Kazakhstan was 'empty' and 'remote' enough to use for its chief nuclear bomb testing ground (the Semipalatinsk Polygon). In 1989 Kazakhstan produced the first great popular protest movement the USSR had seen: the Nevada-Semey (Semipalatinsk) Movement, which forced an end to nuclear tests in Kazakhstan.

Independent Kazakhstan

Nursultan Nazarbaev began to rise up the CPK ranks in the 1970s. He became the party's first secretary in 1989 and has ruled Kazakhstan ever since. In 1991 Nazarbaev did not welcome the breakup of the USSR, and Kazakhstan was the last Soviet republic to declare independence. Multiparty elections in 1994 returned a parliament that obstructed Nazarbaev's free-market economic reforms, and he dissolved it in 1995, with new elections returning an assembly favourable to him. Soon afterwards an overwhelming referendum majority extended his presidential term until 2000.

In 1997 Nazarbaev moved Kazakhstan's capital from Almaty to Astana, then a medium-sized northern city, citing Astana's more central and less earthquake-prone location, and greater proximity to Russia. Astana has been transformed into a capital for the 21st century with some spectacular new buildings and is a key symbol of Nazarbaev's vision of Kazakhstan as a Eurasian economic and political hub.

Nazarbaev's economic program was based on developing Kazakhstan's vast mineral resources. Western companies paid huge amounts to get a slice of Kazakhstan's large oil and gas reserves, and by the dawn of the 21st century the country was posting 9% to 10% economic growth year after year, which kept Nazarbaev popular enough and helped maintain ethnic harmony too.

In 1999 Nazarbaev was assured of victory in new presidential elections after the main opposition leader, Akezhan Kazhegeldin, was barred from standing. Nazarbaev won new seven-year presidential terms in 2005, and then in 2011, both with over 90% of the vote. His political rivals and critics were frequently sacked, jailed or even, in two cases in 2005 and 2006, found shot dead. The government denied any involvement in the deaths.

People

Although Kazakhs form the majority of Kazakhstan's population, this is a multiethnic country where the government encourages everyone to think of themselves as Kazakhstanis as well as ethnic Kazakhs, Russians, Ukrainians etc. Of the 17 million population, 63% are Kazakhs – a big upswing since Soviet times. Since independence in 1991, over three million Russians, Germans and Ukrainians have left Kazakhstan and over 800,000 *oralman* (ethnic Kazakhs repatriating from other countries) have arrived. Other ethnic groups are Russians (24%), Uzbeks (3%), Ukrainians (2%), Germans, Tatars and Uyghurs (1% to 1.5% each), and more than 100 others. Southern areas of Kazakhstan today are about 90% Kazakh, while in some northern towns the majority population is ethnic Russian.

Kazakh culture, rooted in oral tradition, survives strongest in the countryside, although urban Kazakhs are also showing a growing interest in their roots. City-dwellers often still decorate their homes with colourful, yurt-style carpets and tapestries.

Family, respect for elders and traditions of hospitality remain very important to Kazakhs. Ancestry determines a person's *zhuz* (horde) and clan. The best ancestor of all is Chinggis Khan, and right up to the 20th century the Kazakh nobility consisted of those who could trace their lineage back to him.

Kazakh tradition is most on display during the spring festival Nauryz (Navrus; 22 March), when families gather, don traditional dress, eat special food, and enjoy traditional music and games rooted in their equestrian traditions, such as *kokpar (bukzashi)* and *kyz kuu* (a boy–girl horse chase – if he wins he gets to kiss her; if she wins she beats him with her riding whip). Falconry (hunting with birds of prey) is another still-beloved Kazakh tradition. Also lingering from the past is the practice of bride stealing (with or without the bride's consent), which can still happen in some rural areas and the more Kazakh-dominated towns in the south.

Religion

Islam, Kazakhs' predominant faith, is at its strongest in the deep south and has a strong Sufic strain. Pilgrimages to the mausoleum of Kozha Akhmed Yasaui at Turkistan and the desert shrine of Beket-Ata, east of Aktau, are important ways for Kazakh Muslims to affirm their faith. Christianity (mainly Russian Orthodox) claims about a quarter of the population. The government stresses Kazakhstan's tradition of religious tolerance.

Arts

Music

Kazakh traditional music is popular and you may well hear it in taxis or minibuses as well as at organised concerts. The music is largely folk tunes: short on pounding excitement, it captures the soulful rhythms of nomadic life on the steppe. The national instrument is the *dombra,* a small two-stringed lute with an oval box shape. Other instruments include the *kobyz* (a two-stringed fiddle), whose sound is said to have brought Chinggis Khan to tears, and the *sybyzgy* (two flutes strapped together like abbreviated pan pipes). Keep an eye open for shows by the colourfully garbed Sazgen Sazy and Otrar Sazy folk orchestras. Roksonaki and Ulytau are groups that provide an interesting crossover between indigenous sounds and imported rhythms like rock, pop and jazz.

The most skilled singers or bards are called *akyns,* and undoubtedly the most important form of Kazakh traditional art is the *aitys,* a duel between two *dombra* players who challenge each other in poetic lyrics. You might catch one of these live during Nauryz or other holidays.

Crafts

In pre-Soviet times the Kazakhs developed high skills in the crafts associated with nomadic life – brightly woven carpets, wall hangings and ornate wooden chests for yurts, chunky jewellery, elaborate horse tackle and weaponry and splendid costumes for special occasions. You can admire these in almost any museum in Kazakhstan.

Environment

The Land

Except for mountain chains along its southeastern and eastern borders, Kazakhstan is pretty flat. At 2.7 million sq km, it's about the size of Western Europe. Southeast Kazakhstan lies along the northern edge of the Tian Shan, where Mt Khan Tengri (7010m) pegs the China–Kazakhstan–Kyrgyzstan border. In the northeast, some peaks in the Altay top 4000m.

The north of the country is mostly treeless steppe, with much of its original grassland now turned over to wheat or other agriculture. A surprising number of lakes and scattered ranges of hills break up the steppe. Further south and west it is increasingly arid, becoming desert or semidesert.

The most important rivers are the Syr-Darya, flowing across the south of Kazakhstan to the Aral Sea; the Ili, flowing out of China into Lake Balkhash; and the Irtysh, which flows across northeast Kazakhstan into Siberia. Lake Balkhash in the central east is now (following the demise of the Aral Sea) the largest lake in Central Asia (17,000 sq km), though nowhere more than 26m deep.

Wildlife

Kazakhstan's mountains are rich in wildlife, including bear, lynx, argali sheep, ibex, wolves, wild boar, deer, and the elusive snow leopard, of which an estimated 200 roam mountainous border areas from the Altay to Aksu-Zhabagyly Nature Reserve. Two types of antelope – the saiga and the goitred gazelle (zheyran) – roam the steppe in much smaller numbers than they used to. The saiga's numbers fell from over a million in the early 1990s to about 40,000 by 2002, largely due to uncontrolled hunting for meat and horn after the Soviet collapse. It's staging a bit of a comeback with the help of a combined government–NGO program to conserve steppe habitats in central Kazakhstan. In Altyn-Emel National Park, Przewalski's horses, extinct in Kazakhstan since 1940, have been reintroduced from zoos in Europe. For some encouraging wildlife conservation news check out the **Association for the Conservation of Biodiversity in Kazakhstan** (http://acbk.kz) and, on the saiga specifically, www.saiga-conservation.com.

The golden eagle on Kazakhstan's flag is a good omen for ornithologists. Hundreds of bird species are to be seen, from the paradise flycatchers of Aksu-Zhabagyly and the flamingos and sociable lapwings of Korgalzhyn to the relict gulls of Lake Alakol.

Environmental Issues

Kazakhstan is still grappling with the fearful legacy of Soviet exploitation and mismanagement. The Aral Sea catastrophe (see box p92 and also p459) is well known, and the country also continues to suffer from the fallout, literal and metaphorical, of Soviet nuclear tests, conducted mainly near Semey. Industrial air pollution continues at high rates in most of the Soviet industrial centres including Ust-Kamenogorsk, Karaganda, Ekibastuz and Kostanay.

The development of Kazakhstan's oil reserves in and near the Caspian Sea is adding to concerns for the world's largest lake. Nearly 1500 oil wells lie within reach of Caspian storm surge floods, and there have already been leaks from wells submerged by the sea's 3m rise since the 1970s (the Caspian's level oscillates periodically, as a result, it's thought, of climatic factors). There are fears that the giant offshore Kashagan field, due to start pumping by 2014, could put paid to the last natural breeding ground of the beluga (white) sturgeon, source of the world's best caviar, and threaten the breeding grounds of the endangered Caspian seal, one of the world's smallest seals.

SURVIVAL GUIDE

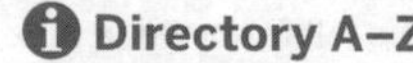

Directory A–Z

ACCOMMODATION

All Kazakhstan cities have a broad range of hotels, from basic (but usually clean) to comfortable modern establishments. Prices are high for Central Asia: you'll rarely get a double with private bathroom for under 5000T (US$33), or much comfort or style for less than 10,000T (and double that in Almaty or Astana). But backpacker hostels with dorm beds for 2000T to 2500T have made a welcome appearance in Almaty and Astana.

In some areas near national parks or nature reserves, there are good homestay or guesthouse options at around 4000T to 6000T per person with meals included.

Many hotels offer discounts of up to 50% if you occupy the room for no more than 12 hours, a period known as a *pol-sutki*. But bizarrely, some hotels charge you for making an advance reservation. Most of the time you can get a room in any accommodation place you want, but a reservation will at least give you peace of mind when arriving in a strange town. Some midrange and top-end places may fill up if there's is a congress or similar event in town.

Another economical, often free, option, and a great way to meet locals, is accommodation in private homes through networks such as **Couchsurfing** (www.couchsurfing.org), which is well represented in Kazakhstan.

ACTIVITIES

The mountain regions abutting the Kyrgyz, Chinese and Russian borders offer the greatest outdoor excitement. In the south and southeast there's good hiking, mountain biking and horse riding in the Zailiysky Alatau near Almaty, and at Kolsay Lakes, Aksu-Zhabagyly Nature Reserve and Sayram-Ugam National Park. Ust-Kamenogorsk is the gateway to a mountainous northeastern area full of adventurous possibilities, culminating in the beautiful Altay Mountains. Exciting biking, hiking and riding among Kazakhstan's central steppes and hills are offered by Karaganda-based Nomadic Travel Kazakhstan (p110).

Ascents of Mt Belukha in the Altay, and Khan Tengri and other peaks in the central Tian Shan, are superb challenges for climbers in July and August. In winter skiers and snowboarders enjoy Central Asia's best facilities at the modern Chimbulak resort near Almaty.

Rafters can tackle the Chilik or Ili rivers out of Almaty and several rivers out of Ust-Kamenogorsk.

Kazakhstan is an emerging bird-watching destination, lying on early-summer migration routes from Africa, India and the Middle East to Siberia, with hundreds of species to be seen. The mountains south of Almaty and the deserts northwest of the city are good areas, as are the Aksu-Zhabagyly and Korgalzhyn nature reserves.

CUSTOM REGULATIONS

Customs declaration forms don't need to be filled on entering the country unless you're carrying goods above normal duty-free limits. Up to US$3000 cash in any currency can be taken in or out of the country without a written declaration.

EMBASSIES & CONSULATES

Kazakhstan Embassies in Central Asia

Kazakhstan has embassies in Tashkent, Uzbekistan (p222); Bishkek, Kyrgyzstan (p307); Ashgabat, Turkmenistan (p401); and Dushanbe, Tajikistan (p364).

Kazakhstan Embassies & Consulates in Other Countries

See www.mfa.kz for details of Kazakhstan's embassies and consulates.

Kazakhstan Embassy, Azerbaijan (012-465 6247; www.kazembassy.az; H Aliyeva proezd 15, dom 8, Baku; visa applications 9.30-11.30am Tue-Fri)

Kazakhstan Embassy, Canada (613-695 8055; www.kazembassy.ca; Suite 603, 150 Metcalfe St, Ottawa, K2P 1P1)

Kazakhstan Embassies & Consulates, China Beijing (consular section 010-6532 4779; www.kazembchina.org; 9 Dong 6 Jie, San Li Tun, 100600; visa applications 9am-1pm Mon & Wed-Fri); Hong Kong Consulate (2548 3841; www.consul-kazakhstan.org.hk; Unit 3106, 31 fl, West Tower, Shun Tak Centre, 200 Connaught Rd Central, Sheung-Wan; visa applications 10am-1pm Mon-Fri); Shanghai Consulate (021-6275 2838; shanghai@mfa.kz; Room 1003-1005, Orient International Plaza, 85 Loushanguan Rd, 200336; visa applications 9.30am-12.30pm Mon, Tue, Thu & Fri); Visa & Passport office in Ürümqi (0991-381 5796; pvs_mid@yahoo.cn; Kunming Lu 31; 9am-1pm Mon-Fri)

Kazakhstan Embassy, France (1-4561 5201; www.amb-kazakhstan.fr; 59 rue Pierre Charron, 75008 Paris)

Kazakhstan Embassy, Georgia (32-2997684; tbilisi@mfa.kz; Shatberashvili 23, Tbilisi 0179; visa applications 11am-1pm Mon, Wed & Thu)

Kazakhstan Embassy, Germany (030-4700 7110; www.botschaft-kaz.de; Nordendstrasse 14-17, 13156 Berlin) Consulates in Bonn, Frankfurt, Hanover and Munich.

Kazakhstan Embassy, Iran (021-2256 5933; iran@mfa.kz; 4 North Hedayat St, cnr Masjed Alley, Darrus, Tehran)

Kazakhstan Embassy, Japan (03-3589 1821; www.embkazjp.org; 1-8-14 Azabudai, Minato-ku, Tokyo 106-0041)

Kazakhstan Embassy, Mongolia (011-34 54 08; info@kazembassy.mn; Zaisan 31/6, Khan-Uul district, 'Twin' city, Ulaanbaatar)

Kazakhstan Embassies & Consulates, Russia (9.30am-12.30pm Mon, Tue, Thu & Fri) Moscow (495-627 17 01; www.kazembassy.ru; Chistoprudny bulvar 3a); Astrakhan Consulate (8512-25 18 85; http://astra-consul.ru; Akvarelnaya 2B); Omsk Consulate (3812-32 52 13; www.kz-omsk.ru; Valikhanova 9); St Petersburg Consulate (812-335 25 46; http://kazconsulate.spb.ru; Vilensky pereulok 15)

Kazakhstan Embassy, UK (020-7925 1757; www.kazembassy.org.uk; 125 Pall Mall, London, SW1Y 5EA)

Kazakhstan Embassy, US (202-232 5488; www.kazakhembus.com; 1401 16th St NW, Washington, DC 20036)

Embassies & Consulates in Kazakhstan

Most embassies are in Astana, although a few remain in Almaty.

Azerbaijan Embassy Astana (7172-24 15 81; www.azembassy.kz; Diplomatichesky Gorodok B-6); Aktau Consulate (7292-42 23 00; http://azconsulateaktau.kz; Dom 30, Mikrorayon 15; 10am-1pm Mon-Fri) To find the Aktau consulate, take bus 2 north on Aktau's boulevard to its last stop, walk 250m further, then go 200m up the street beside Dom 38. Take your passport on all visits as the police box outside the consulate may ask you to register with them before entering.

Canadian Embassy (7172-47 55 77; www.kazakhstan.gc.ca; Kabanbay Batyr 13/1, Astana)

Chinese Embassies & Consulates Astana (7172-79 35 83; http://kz.china-embassy.org; Block 5, Kabanbay Batyr 28; visa applications 9am-noon Mon, Wed & Fri); Almaty Consulate (727-270 02 21; consulate_alm@mfa.gov.cn; Baytasov 12)

Dutch Embassy (7172-55 54 50; http://kazakhstan.nlembassy.org; Kosmonavtov 62, Astana)

French Embassies & Consulates Astana (7172-79 51 00; www.ambafrance-kz.org;

CARRYING YOUR PASSPORT

Officially, foreigners are supposed to carry their passport and migration card with them at all times in Kazakhstan. Police may ask to see it at any time. In theory, a certified copy of your passport, from your country's embassy or consulate, is also acceptable; embassies and consulates generally charge around US$50 for these.

In practice, police may often be satisfied with photocopies of your passport's ID and visa pages and your migration card. Equally, at other times they may not accept even an embassy-certified copy and may insist on seeing the original passport.

On balance, it's best to carry both your original passport and migration card (and take very good care of them) *and* photocopies – and produce the latter initially to any police.

Kosmonavtov 62); Almaty Consulate (☎727-396 98 00; www.ambafrance-kz.org; Furmanov 99)

Georgian Embassy (☎7172-24 32 58; astana.emb.@mfa.gov.ge; Diplomatichesky Gorodok C-4, Astana)

German Embassies & Consulates Astana (☎7172-79 12 00; www.kasachstan.diplo.de; Kosmonavtov 62); Almaty Consulate (☎727-262 83 41/6; www.kasachstan.diplo.de; Ivanilova 2, Mikrorayon Gorny Gigant)

Iranian Embassies & Consulates Astana (☎7172-79 23 25; http:astana.mfa.ir; Daraboz 21, Mikrorayon Akbulak 4); Almaty Consulate (☎727-396 62 27; Radlova 5a)

Japanese Embassies & Consulates Astana (☎7172-97 78 43; www.kz.emb-japan.go.jp; 5th fl, Kosmonavtov 62); Almaty office (☎727-298 06 00; www.kz.emb-japan.go.jp; 3rd fl, Kazybek Bi 41)

Kyrgyz Embassies & Consulates Astana (☎7172-24 20 40; kr@mail.online.kz; Diplomatichesky Gorodok B-5); Almaty Consulate (☎727-226 21 22; consul.agencykg@mail.kz; Lugansky 30a; ⊙visa applications 9am-12.30pm Mon-Fri)

Mongolian Embassies & Consulates Astana (☎7172-96 51 55; www.monembassy.gov.mn; Daraboz 35, Mikrorayon Akbulak 2); Almaty Consulate (☎727-265 35 70; almaty@mfat.gov.mn; Musabaev 1)

Russian Embassies & Consulates Astana (☎7172-44 08 06, consular section 7172-44 07 83; www.rfembassy.kz; Baraeva 4; ⊙visa applications 9.30am-12.30pm Tue & Thu); Uralsk Consulate (☎7112-51 16 26; www.uralsk.mid.ru; Mukhita 78); Almaty Consulate (☎727-274 71 72, 727-275 64 16; www.almaata.mid.ru; Zhandosov 4; ⊙visa applications 9.30am-12.30pm Tue)

Tajik Embassies & Consulates Astana (☎7172-24 09 29; tajemb-astana@mail.ru; Karasakal Yerimbet (Marsovaya) 15); Almaty office (☎727-269 70 59; tgenconsulate_almaty@mail.ru; Sanatornaya 16, Mikrorayon Baganashyl; ⊙visa applications 9am-noon Mon-Fri, visa issuance 2-5pm Mon-Fri) For the Almaty office, take bus 63 south from Furmanov as far as the Pediatria Instituty stop on Al-Farabi. Walk 100m further and continue straight over where Al-Farabi bends right at traffic lights. The consular section entrance is on the left, 200m up this road, Syrgabekov.

Turkmen Embassies & Consulates Astana (☎7172-31 27 67; www.turkmenembassy.kz; Otyrar 8/1; ⊙10am-1pm Mon-Thu); Almaty Consulate (☎727-272 69 44; Furmanov 137; ⊙visa applications 10am-1pm Mon-Thu)

UK Embassies & Consulates Astana (☎7172-55 62 00; http://gov.uk/world/kazakhstan; 6th fl, Kosmonavtov 62); Almaty office (☎727-250 61 91; http://gov.uk/world/kazakhstan; 7th fl, Rahat Palace Hotel Business Centre, Satpaev 29/6)

USA Embassies & Consulates Astana (☎7172-70 21 00; http://kazakhstan.usembassy.gov; Koshkarbaev 3); Almaty Consulate (☎727-250 76 12; http://kazakhstan.usembassy.gov; Zholdasbekov 97, Mikrorayon Samal-2)

Uzbek Embassy (☎727-291 78 86, consular section 727-291 02 35; www.uzembassy.kz; Baribaev 36, Almaty; ⊙visa applications 2-6pm Mon, Tue, Thu & Fri)

FESTIVALS & EVENTS

The biggest festivities around the country are for Nauryz, the Muslim spring festival on 22 March, with traditional sports, music festivals and family get-togethers. Shymkent is a particularly good place to be for Nauryz. Major religious festivals – the Muslim Qurban Ait and Eid al-Fitr, and Russian Orthodox Christmas (7 January) – are widely celebrated though they're not official holidays.

WILDLIFE & NATURE TOURS

The **Association for the Conservation of Biodiversity in Kazakhstan** (http://acbk.kz) offers a fascinating 10-day tour (€1850 per person) visiting three key central wildlife areas – the bird-rich Korgalzhyn wetlands, the recently designated Altyn Dala reserve (a key saiga habitat), and the rarely-visited Naurzum Nature Reserve.

Svetlana Baskakova of Wild Nature (p86), based at Aksu-Zhabagyly Nature Reserve, is an expert biologist and great guide for almost any nature-focused trip you like, including exciting brown-bear-spotting and snow-leopard-tracking trips in Aksu-Zhabagyly itself.

Kasachstan Reisen (☎in Germany 030-4285 2005, in Kazakhstan 701-407 9611; www.kasachstanreisen.de) offers good ornithological, entomological, botanical (especially wild tulips in spring) and a variety of other tours, normally led by multilingual Kazakhstan expert Dagmar Schreiber.

Rubythroat Birding Tours (http://rubythroatbirding.com) is recommended for bird watchers and has expert guides.

FOOD & DRINK

The food culture of Kazakhstan is rooted in the Kazakhs' nomadic past, where the most readily available food was usually horses and sheep. The Kazakh national dish is *beshbarmak*, chunks of long-boiled mutton, beef, or perhaps horsemeat, served in a huge bowl atop flat squares of pasta with onions and sometimes potatoes. The broth from the meat is drunk separately.

In bazaars and some restaurants you'll come across horsemeat in various forms. Menus may offer a plate of cold horsemeats as a starter, and horse steak as a main dish. *Kazy, shuzhuk/shuzhak* and *karta* are all types of horsemeat sausage, in horse-intestine casing. *Kuurdak* (or *kuyrdak*) is a fatty stew of potatoes, meat and offal from a horse, sheep or cow, boiled in a pot for two to three hours.

Across the country you'll also find ubiquitous Central Asian dishes such as shashlyk, *laghman* (long, stout noodles), *manty* (steamed dumplings), *plov* (pilaf) and *samsa*. Kazakhs make a sweet *plov* with dried apricots, raisins and prunes. In summer open-air beer and shashlyk bars, with glowing (or flaming) grills out front, spring up in every town.

A favourite local snack is *baursaki*, fried dough balls or triangles, not unlike heavy doughnuts. Kazakhstan is reckoned to be the original source of apples and wild apple trees still grow in parts of the southeast.

The cuisines of some non-Kazakh groups – Russian, Korean, Uyghur, Dungan – are also prominent. A sign in Arabic script usually indicates a Uyghur restaurant and good *laghman* to be had inside. The major cities have their share of international restaurants too.

Kymyz (fermented mare's milk) is a popular drink. It's mildly alcoholic with a sour, slightly fizzy taste. You can buy it, as well as *shubat* (fermented camel's milk), in many supermarkets as well as in markets and the countryside.

For more information on regional food and drink see p465.

Dining Out

Most midrange and top-end restaurants add 10% to 15% service charge to the bill, which doesn't go to those who provide the service, so you should provide a tip as well – around 300T to 500T is standard. The 'business lunch' *(biznes lanch, kompleksny obed)* offered by many restaurants is usually a good-value set meal, typically comprising soup or salad, main course, dessert and drink.

INTERNET ACCESS

Public internet facilities are fairly abundant, generally charging 200T to 300T per hour. Nearly all backpacker hostels, and midrange and top-end hotels, and some cafes and restaurants, have wi-fi (usually free).

> **KAZAKHSTAN EMERGENCY NUMBERS**
>
> **Ambulance** (☎103)
> **Emergency (general)** (☎112)
> **Police** (☎102)

MONEY

- Prices are usually quoted in the national currency, tenge (T), but occasionally US dollars or euros.
- ATMs abound at banks, shopping centres, supermarkets, hotels, some train stations and elsewhere. Look for 'Bankomat' signs. Most accept at least Maestro, Cirrus, Visa and MasterCard.
- You can make purchases with credit cards (Visa and MasterCard preferred) at a fair number of shops, restaurants, hotels and travel agencies. There is often a surcharge for doing so.
- Exchange offices (marked 'Obmen Valyuty') are common on city streets.

PUBLIC HOLIDAYS

New Year 1 and 2 January
International Women's Day 8 March
Nauryz 21–23 March
Kazakhstan Peoples Unity Day 1 May
Victory Day 9 May
Astana Day 6 July
Constitution Day 30 August
Independence Day 16 December

REGISTRATION

For citizens of the 28 EU states, Australia, Canada, Israel, Japan, New Zealand, Norway, South Korea, Switzerland the USA and a few other countries, registration is occasionally carried out when visas are issued at a Kazakhstan embassy or consulate, indicated by a large round stamp on a migration card that is supplied together with the visa. If it doesn't happen there, it normally happens automatically when you arrive at the country's international airports. Two entry stamps (one is not enough) on your migration card are the indication that registration has taken place and is valid until you leave the country.

Travellers entering by land or sea, or who for any reason don't get registered on airport arrival, have to register with the migration police (Migratsionnaya Politsia, Koshi-Kon Politsiyasi, OVIR) no later than the fifth day of their stay in the country if they are staying in Kazakhstan beyond that day (counting the arrival date as the first day). If you leave the country before day five is finished, registration is not necessary.

Many hotels and travel agencies can handle your registration for a fee of around 3000T to 5000T, or you can spend time going to the migration police in Almaty, Astana or one of Kazakhstan's 14 regional capitals. Registration is supposed to be free, and usually is, though it's possible some offices might request 'administrative charges' of up to 1000T or so. Migration police offices are generally open for limited hours, often in the morning only, and some close completely on certain weekdays as well as weekends. They also close on public holidays and often on Mondays following public holidays that fall on a weekend. Take your migration card and passport, photocopies of the migration card and the passport's personal-details and Kazakhstan-visa pages, and the address of your hotel (don't give a private address). You may have to fill in a form in Russian, available at the migration-police office and often also at nearby photocopy shops (which can often help you fill it in). You'll be told when to come back and collect your documents, which could be any time from 15 minutes to two working days later. The official fine for registering late is US$100.

Note that if you have a double-entry or triple-entry visa, you must be registered again each time you re-enter Kazakhstan (unless you are leaving again within five days).

The registration rules change from time to time and may be interpreted differently in different places: check the situation when you get your visa and again when you reach Kazakhstan. Immigration police outside Almaty, even in Astana, will often only register you for five to 10 days, meaning that you will have to re-register elsewhere if you stay in the country longer.

If your visa was obtained with a letter of invitation (LOI) and you are registering at a migration police office, they may want to see not just the LOI itself but also extra paperwork from the LOI issuer. If you can't obtain this (for example if the issuer is in Almaty and you are on the other side of the country), provincial migration police will often only register you for five days or even refuse to register you at all – check with your LOI provider in advance if this is a possibility.

SAFE TRAVEL

Kazakhstan is a safe country to travel in, provided you follow normal safety precautions. Since 2011 there have been a few scattered violent attacks, blamed by the government on Islamist terrorism, and that year security forces shot dead at least 14 demonstrators in the western town of Zhanaozen – but you would have to be very unlucky to be in the wrong place at the wrong time.

For more information on safe travel, as well as tips for dealing with police and other officials, see p474.

TELEPHONE

You can make phone calls for cash from some internet cafes and (less common) shops and kiosks with phones for public use.

International Calling Cards

You can cut costs for international calls from landlines or mobile phones by using pre-paid cards such as the Nursat i-Card+, sold at mobile-phone shops, petrol stations, kiosks and some supermarkets. You scratch off a PIN then dial a local access number given on the card. Calling instructions are then available in English. Calls cost around 12T per minute to the USA, Canada or China; 20T per minute to Uzbekistan or Russia; 35T to 95T per minute to other Central Asian countries, Britain, Germany, Italy and France.

Mobile (Cell) Phones

Almost everyone in Kazakhstan has a mobile phone and it's easy to get a local SIM card for your phone if you have an unlocked GSM-900 frequency phone (this includes most European mobiles but not most North American ones). Shops and kiosks selling SIM cards with call credit for a few hundred tenge are everywhere. Take your passport when you go

HOW TO DIAL FROM KAZAKHSTAN PHONES

FROM	TO	DIAL
Any phone	Mobile in Kazakhstan or Russia	☎8 + mobile number *or* ☎7 + mobile number
Landline	Other countries except Russia	☎8 + 10 + country code + area code + local number
Landline	Landline in other Kazakh city or Russia	☎8 + area code + local number
Landline	Landline in same city	local number only
Mobile	Landline in Kazakhstan or Russia	☎8 + area code + local number *or* ☎7 + area code + local number
Mobile	Other countries except Russia	country code + area code + local number

to buy. The same outlets often sell inexpensive phones too, and will top up your credit for cash or with PIN cards.

- KCell and Beeline are the best networks for nationwide coverage.
- Typically 1000T credit gives you one to two hours of talking to a combination of mobile and landline numbers.

Telephone Numbers

- Mobile numbers have 10 digits.
- Landlines have a three-, four- or five-digit area code followed by a local number: the area code plus the local number always totals 10 digits.
- The Kazakhstan country code is ☎7.

TRAVEL PERMITS

A special border-zone permit is needed for travel to areas near the Chinese border, notably the Altay Mountains and Mt Khan Tengri. The only way to obtain these is through tour firms taking you to these areas, who will normally include the permit charge (about 7000T) in their trip cost. Processing can take up to 45 days, so plan well ahead.

A permit is also officially required for areas near the Kyrgyz border in the mountains south of Almaty. Local guides in Almaty know the score.

Baykonur Cosmodrome and the Semipalatinsk Polygon can only be visited on tours organised through agencies. You need to start the paperwork one to two months ahead for Baykonur and about two weeks ahead for the Polygon.

Entry to nature reserves usually requires a permit, normally arranged quickly through the local reserve office, for anything up to 2000T.

VISAS FOR ONWARD TRAVEL

Visa practices change all the time. See p32 for some useful sources on recent changes, and p125 for embassy contact details.

Azerbaijan

The best option is a 30-day tourist e-visa organised through an agency, costing US$100 for all nationalities through **Azerbaijan24** (www.azerbaijan24.com) or Stantours (p68). You receive the visa by email (currently within three weeks), and there is no need to bother with any consulate. But you do have to show confirmed hotel bookings for all or most of your visit – automated online confirmations direct from hotels are acceptable.

Paper 30-day tourist visas are also available within five working days from the Azerbaijan Astana embassy (p125) or the Aktau consulate (p125) if you have a LOI. LOIs currently cost US$60 from Azerbaijan24 and Stantours, but the price can fluctuate wildly. Fees for the visa itself depend on your passport (US$118 for UK citizens, €60 for most other Europeans, US$160 for Americans). Five-day transit visas are available without a LOI for US$20; processing takes up to five working days. At the Aktau consulate you must supply one photo with a white background, and photocopies of your passport data page and your last Azerbaijan visa (if you had one). You pay the fee at a bank about 1.5km away on the day you collect the visa, before going to the consulate.

China

Getting a Chinese visa in Kazakhstan is difficult-to-impossible. Policy and practice change frequently; at the time of writing, visas were not being issued at the Chinese Almaty consulate (p125) for non-residents, and only a few people succeeded in getting tourist visas (in five to seven days) in Astana (p125), showing proof of sufficient funds (for example bank statements), flight bookings in and out of China, hotel bookings and an itinerary for their whole stay, and proof of employment. No LOI needed but don't say you are going to Xinjiang. The price is around 4300/6400T for single/double entry (30 days per entry).

It's much better to get your Chinese visa before you leave home (bearing in mind you have to enter China within three months), or in Hong Kong, where procedures are easy and inexpensive.

Kyrgyzstan

For those who still need visas, the Kyrgyzstan Almaty consulate's (p126) 'normal' processing time is 10 working days, with most visas costing US$55 to US$80; but same-day express processing is usually available for US$100 to US$150. Take your passport, a photocopy and one photo. Some nationalities also have to provide a LOI (see p309). You have to make three visits to the consulate: one to put in the application, one to come back with the bank receipt for payment, and one to pick up the visa.

Russia

The Russian Almaty consulate (p126) and Astana embassy (p126) are practically impossible for anything but transit visas. Travellers have obtained transit visas in one or two days without LOIs for around 14,000T. You may have to show an onward ticket out of Russia and a visa for the onward country. Visa duration is up to 10 days depending on the duration of your transit in Russia; you may have to enter Russia within three days of the visa being issued. Opening hours for applications are just one or two mornings a week: no one speaks English but if you can manage to call ahead for an appointment it should help. Application forms are available online (only), at http://visa.kdmid.ru. Astana is generally less unfriendly than Almaty.

Tajikistan

Tourist visas are issued in Tajikistan's Almaty embassy office (p126) without LOIs. For a one-month tourist visa (US$100 for same-day processing), provide photocopies of your passport and Kazakh visa and a written request to the ambassador. This office has also issued the GBAO permit for travel in the Pamirs, though this may change.

Turkmenistan

To get a Turkmen visa you either need to book a tour through a travel agency, or have visas for the bordering countries from which you will enter Turkmenistan and leave Turkmenistan (these can include Azerbaijan), enabling you to get a transit visa. Transit visas are also available if you fly in or fly out (but not normally both). You have to go in person with your passport to the Turkmen embassy (p126) or consulate (get there before opening time). Transit visas cost US$55 for most nationalities and processing takes five to 10 working days: it's sometimes possible to apply in one city and pick up your visa in another, as you don't have to hand over your original passport with the application.

Uzbekistan

Citizens of some, mostly Western, countries (see p225 for a list) can obtain visas without a LOI but processing for these at the Uzbek Almaty embassy (p126) takes much longer – typically four or five working days, against on-the-spot processing if you have a LOI. Some Almaty travel agents can provide Uzbek LOIs hassle-free if given enough time (US$40 for about two weeks' processing at Stantours (p68)). Go to the embassy at least 30 minutes before opening time, put your name on a list and you'll probably get in before the door closes.

In the peak summer travel season you may need to get there in the morning. All applicants should take their passport, a photocopy of it, their Kazakh visa and registration, one photo, a LOI and a completed application form (normally supplied with an LOI or available at http://evisa.mfa.uz). Tourist visas cost US$55/65/75 for seven/15/30 days, US$95 for three months: for more than one entry, add US$10 per entry. US citizens pay US$160 for any visa. Payments must normally be in US dollars.

VISAS FOR KAZAKHSTAN

Kazakhstan visa rules and practices change quite frequently; information on recent changes is available from recommended travel agents and the websites of Kazakhstan embassies and consulates.

No visa at all is needed for visits up to 14 days for Hong Kong citizens, 30 days for Turkish citizens, or 90 days for CIS or Georgian citizens. For citizens of 40-odd other countries that Kazakhstan officially considers 'economically developed and politically stable' – including the 28 EU states, Australia, Canada, Israel, Japan, New Zealand, Norway, South Korea, Switzerland and the USA – Kazakh consulates or embassies will normally issue one-month, single-entry tourist or business visas, or two-month double-entry tourist visas, *without* a letter of invitation (LOI). Required documentation normally includes your passport and a photocopy of it, a letter from you explaining the purpose of your visit, one or two photos and an application form, which is sometimes available on embassy websites. (Some Kazakh consulates, however, mainly in non-Western countries, insist on evidence of hotel bookings for non-LOI visas, or won't issue double-entry tourist visas without a LOI.)

For other visas, or if you are not from one of the visa-free or 'economically developed' states, you must obtain 'visa support' in the form of a LOI. This is available, usually by email, through most travel agencies in Kazakhstan, Central Asia travel specialists in other countries, or Kazakh businesses. You'll need to submit a copy of the LOI in your visa application to the embassy or consulate. Agents' fees for providing LOIs normally range from around US$50 to US$100 depending on the visa required: LOIs must be applied for at least two weeks before you enter Kazakhstan, and you should allow one to two weeks to obtain the LOI before you apply for the visa itself (but note that LOIs cannot normally be issued more than two months before your arrival in Kazakhstan).

The maximum length of a tourist visa is 90 days (triple-entry with three visits of a maximum 30 days each); for uninterrupted stays you can get a 90-day single-entry business visa.

Fees for the visa itself depend on the type of visa and your nationality. A single-entry, one-month tourist visa is normally US$40 to US$50 (but US$160 for US citizens). Some

VOLUNTEERING

United Nations Volunteers (www.unv.org) is active in Kazakhstan in health, poverty and environmental fields and in coordinating local volunteer projects.

Getting There & Away

ENTERING KAZAKHSTAN

As long as you have your visa organised you should have no problems getting into Kazakhstan. Keep the migration card you receive in your passport: you have to hand it in when you leave the country. What you must pay special attention to is registration (p127).

AIR

Kazakhstan has good international air connections through numerous carriers including the good national airline, **Air Astana** (www.airastana.com). The best fares from Western Europe are often via İstanbul with Turkish Airlines or Pegasus, or via Kiev with Ukraine International Airways.

In addition to flights to/from Almaty, Astana and Aktau airports, Atyrau has direct flights to/from Amsterdam and İstanbul. Several cities around the country have direct Moscow flights.

See p478 for further information on international flights into Central Asia, and the Almaty (p69) and Astana (p106) Getting There & Away sections in this chapter for details of airline offices.

Almaty Airport

Almaty International Airport (p69) is the country's busiest. There are several direct flights each week to/from Amsterdam (KLM), Frankfurt (Lufthansa), İstanbul (Turkish and Pegasus Airlines), London (British Airways) and Prague (Czech Airlines). Air Astana also serves these destinations.

Air Astana and Transaero have daily flights to/from Moscow; Air Astana and Rossiya fly to/from St Petersburg; and S7 flies to/from Novosibirsk (all from US$230 one way).

Air Astana and Ukraine International connect Almaty with Kiev, and Air Astana provides Baku and Tbilisi flights (all from US$240 one-way).

Within Central Asia, Air Astana makes a few weekly flights to/from Bishkek, Kyrgyzstan (from US$80); Air Astana and/or Uzbekistan

consulates will deal with visa applications by mail; others, including most in Asia, require you to apply for and collect your visa in person. Processing time at consulates in the West is normally at least five working days.

Single-entry, one-month, tourist or business visas (US$45 to US$100) may also be available on arrival at Almaty or Astana airports with a LOI specifying where you are arriving, but this is only an option for citizens or residents of countries without a Kazakh consulate. If you request a LOI from a travel agency for this purpose, tell them why: not all agencies can provide LOIs suitable for visas on arrival. Also check with the agency about any other paperwork you must provide on arrival and about currently acceptable means of payment: you may be required to pay in cash US dollars or tenge.

If you are in a country without a Kazakh embassy or consulate (such as Australia, Ireland, New Zealand or Sweden), you can apply to Kazakh missions in other countries – those in Brussels and Vienna are among the more efficient and less expensive in Europe. Visa agents will do the legwork for fees of around US$50 to US$90 per visa, plus courier charges.

Getting visas in countries en route to Kazakhstan is quite feasible. Processing at Kazakhstan consulates in the Caucasus countries, Turkey and Central Asia normally takes four or five working days (occasionally less). Applying at Kazakh missions in China is sometimes more difficult: additional documentation might be requested, and processing sometimes takes longer than five working days. The visa office at Ürümqi has a habit of changing its location and opening hours frequently. The consulate in Hong Kong may insist on a LOI or hotel bookings for your whole stay, plus a bunch of other documents. When applying anywhere outside your own country it helps to have a photocopy of your visa and/or passport entry stamp for the country where you're applying, as well as the other necessary documents.

Extensions

Extending a Kazakh visa is generally only possible with a medical certificate stating you are unable to travel.

Airways go daily to/from Tashkent in Uzbekistan (from US$145); Tajikistan's Dushanbe is served daily by Air Astana, Tajik Air or Somon Air (from US$150); and Turkmenistan Airlines flies twice weekly to/from Ashgabat (US$240).

Elsewhere within Asia, Air Astana flies to/from Bangkok (from US$550 one-way), Beijing (also served by Hainan Airlines; US$490), Delhi (US$340), Hong Kong (US$380), Kuala Lumpur (US$600), Seoul (also served by Asiana; US$660) and Ürümqi (also served by China Southern; US$245).

Astana Airport

Astana International Airport (☎70 29 99; www.astanaairport.kz) has a range of international flights, with Lufthansa and Air Astana flying from Frankfurt; Austrian Airlines from Vienna; and Turkish Airlines and Air Astana from İstanbul. Air Astana also flies from Baku (from US$240 one way), Beijing (US$675), Bishkek (US$130), Kiev (along with Ukraine International; US$225), Moscow (with Transaero; US$245), Novosibirsk (US$225), St Petersburg (with Rossiya; US$270), Tashkent (with Uzbekistan Airways; US$160), Ürümqi (with China Southern; US$175) and Yekaterinburg (US$205).

Aktau Airport

Aktau Airport (☎60 97 55; www.aktau-airport.kz) in the far west is a hub for trans-Caspian flights, with direct services to/from Baku, (from US$165 one-way), Tbilisi (US$170), Yerevan (US$155), İstanbul (US$280), Astrakhan (US$170) and several other cities in southern Russia, and Kiev (US$265). Most flights are with the Kazakhstani airline SCAT.

LAND

To/From China

Buses run daily to Ürümqi (24 hours) and twice weekly to Yining (12 hours) from Almaty's Sayran bus station (p70), via the border at Khorgos. Sleeper buses leave for Ürümqi at 7am (8900T) and 7pm (7600T) daily: you can book three days ahead but tickets are usually available on departure day: be ready to show your Chinese visa. Sleeper buses to Yining (4700T, 12 hours), about 100km beyond Khorgos, depart at 7am Wednesday and Saturday. An alternative is to take a bus (1500T, five daily) or shared taxi (3000T) to Zharkent, 40km before Khorgos, then a taxi (about 800T) or minibus to the border, and a bus or taxi on from there. The crossing is often crammed with Kazakh and Uyghur families and traders with vast amounts of baggage.

From Ürümqi to Almaty, at least two buses depart at 7pm daily (Beijing time) from **Nianzigan bus station international section** (☎0991-587 8637; 51 Heilongjiang Rd, Saybagh district, Ürümqi). From Yining bus station there are buses daily at 7am Beijing time.

The Zhibek Zholy (Silk Road) train departs Almaty-II station (p70) for Ürümqi at 1am on Sunday and Tuesday, taking a scheduled 31 hours and crossing the border at Dostyk (Druzhba). *Kupeyny* (2nd-class couchette) tickets cost 19,500T. Tickets are sold in the main ticket hall at Almaty-II and are usually still available in the last few days before departure: press 'Mezhdunarodnaya Kassa' on the machine next to the information bureau to get a number for the ticket queue. Be ready to show your Chinese visa. The trains have restaurant cars but the food is poor and overpriced. At Dostyk, you have to wait several hours while the train bogies are changed and customs checks take place. The train toilets are locked during this time except for the 20-minute dash between the Kazakhstan and China border posts: get in line early for this! The return train departs Ürümqi at 00.20am (Beijing time) on the same days: the **ticket office** (☎0991-778 0576; Yaou Jiuvdian Hotel, Ürümqi; ⏲10am-1pm & 3.30-6pm Mon, Wed, Thu & Sat) is in the Yaou Jiuvdian Hotel next to the station – best to book two or three days ahead.

Another train option, which takes you to the border at Khorgos, is train No 393, operated by private train company **Turan Express** (www.turanexpress.kz). This leaves Almaty-I station at 11.20pm on odd dates, taking eight hours to Altynkol, a few kilometres short of the border. A 15-minute bus transfer to the Khorgos border is included in the fare of 2500T *(platskartny)*. From the border you will need a bus or taxi for the 100km on to Yining, from which there are three daily trains to Ürümqi. In Almaty tickets are sold at the **Turan Express kiosk** (☎771-789 1473; Kassa No 16; ⏲9am-9pm) in the main booking hall at Almaty-II station, as well as at Almaty-I. The return train No 394 departs Altynkol at 8.45pm on even dates.

A weekly train departs Astana for Ürümqi on Saturday afternoon, with the return train leaving Ürümqi late Monday night or very early Tuesday. Ürümqi also has bus connections with Ust-Kamenogorsk and Semey.

To/From Kyrgyzstan

Official Kazakh–Kyrgyz border crossings are largely hassle free, but the 'green border' – trails through the mountains, without border posts – has been closed for several years.

From Almaty's Sayran bus station (p70), there are plenty of minibuses (1300T, three to four hours, hourly 6am to 11pm) and shared taxis (3000T) to Bishkek in Kyrgyzstan, crossing the border at Korday. Minibuses and shared taxis also run from Taraz to Bishkek, and there are also buses from Shymkent and Turkistan to Bishkek – all crossing the border at Chaldybar.

The scenic Karkara Valley crossing, south of Kegen, reopened from June to October 2013 after being closed for several years and it is expected it will reopen for similar periods in future summers. No public transport makes this crossing but you can get through by a combination of hitching, taxi or pre-arranged vehicle transfers. See p77 for further information.

To/From Mongolia

Kazakhstan has no border with Mongolia but there is an approximately twice-monthly bus service from Karaganda and Astana to Bayan-Ölgii in western Mongolia, via Barnaul and Gorno-Altaysk in Russia.

To/From Russia

All main Kazakhstan cities have train service to/from Moscow via other Russian cities, daily or every two days. 'Fast' train No 7/8 takes 80 hours between Moscow's Paveletsky station and Almaty-II train station (p70, about US$350 in *kupeyny*), running every two days (on odd dates) via Saratov, Uralsk, Aktobe and Shymkent.

See Overland from Russia (p135) for information on road and bus routes between Russia and Kazakhstan.

Many Kazakh cities also have trains to/from Siberian cities. Daily trains along the 'Turksib' line take 37 to 39 hours between Novosibirsk and Almaty (US$140), via Semey. Daily trains from Moscow's Kazansky station to Astana take around 57 hours for US$345.

To/From Turkmenistan

The remote Temirbaba border point is 165km south of Zhanaozen, which is 150km east of Aktau. Turkmen 4WDs from Zhanaozen bus station take around 10 hours, including two to three hours at the border, for the trip to Turkmenbashi (5000/20,000T per person/vehicle). You're most likely to find a shared vehicle early in the morning. The road is unpaved for about the last 45km to the border and 30km south of it.

A new railway has been built from Zhanaozen (called Uzen on some timetables) to Bereket in western Turkmenistan. If and when passenger services start running, it should be possible to take a train from Aktau to Ashgabat.

To/From Uzbekistan

The main road border between Shymkent and Tashkent, at Chernyaevka (Zhibek Zholy/Gisht Koprik), is connected with Shymkent's Avtovokzal Samal (p84) bus station by fairly frequent marshrutkas (800T, two hours) – more frequent in the morning. Queues of four to six hours are not uncommon for crossing into Kazakhstan, due to the numbers of Uzbeks heading north in search of work; waits are generally shorter going southbound. For the short ride between the border and central Tashkent you need a taxi.

Crossing the border by train is a way to avoid queues. The railway border at Saryagash, a few kilometres north of Tashkent, is crossed by about a dozen trains each way per week, the majority heading to/from Moscow or the Urals via Turkistan, Kyzylorda and Aktobe, but two or three heading to/from Shymkent and Almaty. From Almaty, train 369 (23,250T, 24 hours) departs every four days from Almaty-I (p70); train 321 (12,250T, 26 hours) leaves on Sundays from Almaty-II (p70) and continues to Samarkand.

A new high-speed train service between Almaty and Tashkent, due to be introduced in 2014, is expected to cut journey times between the two cities by one-third or more.

For travellers with their own vehicles, the Yallama crossing, about 60km southwest of Tashkent, is a quicker option than Chernyaevka.

A remote desert road and rail crossing exists at Tazhen (also called Oazis) between Beyneu, western Kazakhstan, and Kungrad, Uzbekistan. Trains from Russia to Tashkent via Samarkand (four weekly) use this route, coming into Kazakhstan via Atyrau, and there is daily service between Aktau and Kungrad. The little-used road is paved on the Uzbek side but unpaved (and terrible) between the border and Beyneu.

SEA

A very irregular ferry sails between Aktau and Baku (in Azerbaijan). It's a cargo ship that carries some passengers and a small number of vehicles and leaves when its hold fills, and there can be anything from two days to two weeks between sailings (on average it's about once a week in summer). Tickets (18,000T for a bunk in a windowless four-person cabin) go on sale at the **Paromnaya Kassa** (Ferry Ticket Office; ☎50 03 46, after 6pm 44 51 25; Office 1, Dom 33, Mikrorayon 2, Aktau; ⊙9am-1pm & 2-6pm) when the ship leaves Baku for the scheduled 18-hour crossing – in theory that's about 24 hours before it departs Aktau. 'In theory' because the ship sometimes waits a long time outside Aktau – three days is not unknown (and the same can happen arriving at Baku). Leave a photocopy of your passport and a contact number at the Paromnaya Kassa and they'll call you when tickets become available. Take food for the voyage: the food on board is expensive and poor. Note that immigration officials may require all travellers leaving Aktau on the ferry to have registered their Kazakhstan visas, even if they are leaving within the normal five-day registration-free period.

In Baku, tickets are only sold on the day of departure: you must check with the ticket office near the Turkmenistan ferry dock every morning to find out if there's a sailing. The ferry actually leaves from the port about 7km further east.

OVERLAND FROM RUSSIA

Kazakhstan's 6846km border with Russia has 18 'multilateral' road crossings (open to all nationalities), and around 15 rail crossings.

Western Europe–Western China Highway

The new 'Western Europe–Western China' highway, a massive project to boost trans-Asia commerce, will provide the best driving option from European Russia into Kazakhstan when it is completed. It runs from St Petersburg to Moscow, Kazan and Orenburg, then across Kazakhstan via Aktobe, Kyzylorda, Shymkent, Taraz and Almaty, into China at Khorgos then across China via Ürümqi to the seaport Lianyungang. Long sections of new four- and two-lane highway are open across Kazakhstan, and the completion of the Kazan-Orenburg-Aktobe section (due 2015) will make this the best road approach to Kazakhstan.

Road Crossings

The main multilateral road crossings (listed from west to east):

- Kotyaevka (between Astrakhan and Atyrau) The westernmost entry point, but some roads on the Kazakh side are very poor, notably the appalling 230km Makat-Bayganin stretch between Atyrau and Aktobe.
- Taskala (between Saratov and Uralsk)
- Mashtakov (between Samara and Uralsk)
- Zhaysan (between Orenburg and Aktobe)
- Podgorodka (Kayrak; between Chelyabinsk and Kostanay)
- Kazantsevskoe (between Kurgan and Petropavlovsk)
- Roslavka (Karakoga; between Omsk and Petropavlovsk)
- Auyl (between Rubtsovsk and Semey)
- Shemonaikha (between Rubtsovsk and Ust-Kamenogorsk)

Bus & Shared Taxi

Bus services, and in some cases shared taxis, connect cities within striking distance of the border. Daily bus services include Astrakhan-Atyrau (2800T, eight hours), Samara-Uralsk (2450T, six hours), Orenburg-Aktobe (2500T, six hours), Tyumen-Petropavlovsk (3700T, 10 hours), Barnaul-Semey (3600T, 11 hours) and Novosibirsk-Ust-Kamenogorsk (6000T, 17 hours).

By Train

The major rail routes:

- Moscow–Saratov–Uralsk–Aktobe–Kyzylorda–Almaty
- Moscow–Samara–Orenburg–Aktobe–Kyzylorda–Tashkent/Bishkek
- Moscow–Volgograd–Atyrau–Beyneu–Uzbekistan (Kungrad, Samarkand, Tashkent)
- Moscow–Chelyabinsk–Petropavlovsk/Kostanay–Astana
- Novosibirsk–Barnaul–Semey–Almaty: the 'Turksib'
- Vladivostok–Irkutsk–Novosibirsk–Omsk–Petropavlovsk: from the east

Atyrau — АТЫРАУ

Atyrau (population 170,000), 30km up the Ural River from the Caspian Sea, straddles the Europe/Asia boundary. The cheapest sleep is the **Komnaty Otdykha** (☎7122-95 56 05; dm 2000T, s/d 3400/6000T), entered from the train station platform. It's basic and short on security, but clean, and half-price for less than 12 hours. The central **Ak Zhaik Hotel** (☎7122-32 78 81; www.akzhaikhotel.com; Abay 4; s/d incl breakfast 16,060/25,580T; P ❄ @) has comfy rooms and a slew of facilities including a British-style pub.

Atyrau lies on the Moscow–Volgograd–Uzbekistan rail route. Within Kazakhstan, trains go daily to Aktau (Mangyshlak; 3520T, 21 hours), Aktobe (2830T, 16 hours) and Almaty (9660T to 30,250T, 36 to 50 hours); for Uzbekistan there are trains to Nukus, Samarkand and Tashkent (29,390T, 45 to 50 hours) four times weekly; for Russia, trains head to Astrakhan (7900T, 13 hours), Volgograd and Moscow (28,960T, 41 hours) several times weekly. Buses (2800T, nine hours), minibuses (4500T, five hours) and shared taxis (7000T, five hours) leave for Uralsk from the bus station until early evening.

Uralsk (Oral)

УРАЛЬСК (ОРАЛ)

Beautiful traditional Russian architecture adorns the leafy centre of Uralsk (population 203,000), which sits on the European bank of the Ural River. The cheaper rooms in **Hotel Oral** (Hotel Uralsk; ☎7112-50 79 32; Kurmangazy 80; s/d with shared bathroom 3500/3800T, with private bathroom 6000/7000T; P ❄) are an acceptable, basic, central budget option; the nicest sleep is the **Pushkin Hotel** (☎7112-51 35 60; www.pushkinhotel.com; Dostyk 148b; s/d incl breakfast from 16,000/20,000T; P ❄ ᯤ).

There are trains to Aktobe (2560T, 10 to 13 hours, two daily), Almaty (10,328T, 51 to 58 hours, one daily) and Moscow (25,122T, 27 hours, every two days). Note that trains to or from Aktobe (including those to/from Almaty) duck into Russia en route: reports are that you can travel on them with a single-entry Kazakhstan visa and do not require a Russian visa for that stretch, but do confirm this before travelling. Minibuses to Atyrau (4500T, five hours) and shared taxis to Aktobe (8000T, five hours) leave from the train station. The road to Aktobe stays inside Kazakhstani territory.

Aktobe

АҚТӨБЕ

This city of 370,000 has experienced an influx of oil and gas companies and an accompanying facelift.

Hotel Ilek (☎7132-96 01 01; www.ilek.kz; Ayteke-bi 44; s/d from 4800/6000T; ⊖ ❄ ᯤ), two blocks from the train station, has a range of accommodation starting with small but neat and clean 'standard' rooms with private bathroom. Top digs are at the modern, well-run **Hotel Dastan** (☎7132-90 10 00; www.dastanhotel.kz; Bogenbay Batyr 2; s/d incl breakfast from 21,000/24,360T; P ⊖ ❄ @ ᯤ).

Trains run daily to Aralsk (2680T to 5610T, 10 to 12 hours), Almaty (8320T, 41 to 48 hours) and Moscow (33,680T, 34 to 36 hours); and several times weekly to Tashkent (22,620T to 28,860T, 31 to 36 hours) and Bishkek (23,250T, 40 hours).

There's no public road transport south to Aralsk and Kyzylorda. The local motorbike club, **Asar Motor Aktobe** (☎701-339 7714, 7132-22 83 53; zobenko1969@mail.ru; Aviagorodok 124), near the airport, offers a helpful free checkover of travellers' motorbikes, cars or 4WDs, space to work on vehicles, and information on road conditions. Ask for Gennady Zobenko.

Petropavlovsk (Petropavl)

ПЕТРОПАВЛОВСК (ПЕТРОПАВЛ)

The most attractive city near the northern stretch of Kazakhstan's border with Russia, Petropavlovsk was founded in the 1750s and is older and architecturally more diverse than many cities in Kazakhstan.

Hotel Kochevnik (☎7152-46 01 31; Amangeldy 163; s/d from 3500/4000T), basic but clean and in a quiet but central location, is a good budget bet. Well-run **Hotel Skif** (☎7152-46 88 07; www.hotelskif.kz; Parkovaya 118; s/d incl breakfast from 8500/12,000T; P ᯤ ✕), with large, contemporary rooms and an excellent 24-hour restaurant, is a fine midrange choice.

The fast, comfortable Talgo train No 152 to Astana (tourist/business class 4590/7600T, six hours) and Almaty (16,215/23,750T, 19 hours) runs every two days. At least two other trains head daily to Astana (2560T, eight to 11 hours), and daily trains head to many Russian cities including Moscow (47,800T, 39 to 45 hours) and Omsk (7350T to 11,108T, 4½ hours). Rail timetables here use Moscow time.

Getting Around

AIR

A good network of domestic flights links cities all around Kazakhstan and fares are reasonable. The main airlines are the international-standard **Air Astana** (KC; www.airastana.com), and **SCAT** (DV; www.scat.kz), which like all other Kazakhstani airlines except Air Astana, has been banned from flying to EU countries because it does not meet internationally accepted safety requirements.

Airlines offer various fares on each route and we have quoted the lowest ones commonly available within about a month before departure, typically 15,000T (US$100) to 30,000T. Closer to departure, you might pay up to double.

Tickets are sold by abundant travel agencies and *aviakassy* (air-ticket offices) in cities. Air Astana and SCAT also issue e-tickets online, payable with international credit cards – though the SCAT website is in Russian only.

BUS, MINIBUS & MARSHRUTKA

With a few exceptions such as the busy Shymkent–Almaty and Astana–Karaganda routes, intercity bus services are poor and getting worse, with less frequent departures in increasingly aged buses from ramshackle bus stations. Nevertheless buses are an option for trips of up to five or six hours – generally a bit faster than trains and with fares similar to *platskartny* (3rd-class) on trains – typically around 500T per 100km. For longer trips trains are generally more comfortable.

Many short and medium-length routes (up to three or four hours) are now covered more frequently by modern, relatively comfortable minibuses (and a few marshrutkas – less comfortable, Russian-built, combi-type vehicles). These generally cost about 50% more than buses and go quicker.

CAR & MOTORCYCLE

Traffic police and poor roads (in that order) are the main hazards of driving in Kazakhstan. Main intercity roads may have bad, potholed stretches but are mostly in decent condition. Huge infrastructure projects are massively improving some major trunk routes.

Traffic police may stop motorists just to check their papers, and have a reputation for finding irregularities that they may then overlook if bribed. Go very slowly past any parked police vehicle or police observation post. The blood-alcohol limit is zero. Don't run red lights and do stick to speed limits (usually 50km/hr in cities and 90km/hr outside them).

You should carry an International Driving Permit as well as your home-country licence.

For many trips it is easier, and no more expensive, to take a taxi or tour than to rent a self-drive car, but there are self-drive options if that suits your needs best. **Europcar** (www.europcar.com) has rental offices in Almaty and Astana. You can also rent through local agencies or travel agencies. Short-term self-drive rates start at around 7500T (US$50) per day. Renters must normally be aged 25 or older and have held their licence at least one year (three years with some firms). Check the small print very carefully: some companies, for example, don't allow vehicles to be taken out of the local *oblast* (region).

TAXI

For many intercity, trips taxis offer a much faster alternative to buses and minibuses. They're generally found waiting outside bus and train stations and you can either rent the whole cab or share it with three other passengers at a quarter of the price (about double the corresponding bus fare). Sharing may involve some time waiting around for other passengers to materialise.

TRAIN

Trains serve all cities and many smaller places. They're a good way to experience Kazakhstan's terrain, vast size and people. Except for small local trains, tickets are best bought in advance. Station ticket queues can be slow, but all cities also have downtown train-booking offices, called *Zheleznodorozhnaya Kassa* (Russian) or *Temir Zhol Kassasy* (Kazakh), where you can buy tickets more conveniently at a small commission. Always take your passport when buying tickets.

Trains are generally slower than road travel but for longer intercity trips are the only option other than flying. Fares in *platskartny* (3rd-class open-bunk carriages) are similar to bus fares. *Kupeyny* (2nd-class four-person couchettes) costs about 50% more – typically 300T to 400T per hour of travel. We have quoted *kupeyny* fares, unless stated otherwise.

Timetable information is available in English at www.poezda.net (with fares in Russian roubles) and in Russian and Kazakh at temirzholy.kz and epay.railways.kz. This last company has an online booking facility that accepts international credit cards but is still only in Russian and Kazakh (users collect tickets from machines or ticket counters at stations).

Uzbekistan

Includes ➡

Best Places to Eat

- City Grill (p151)
- National Food (p150)
- Platan (p178)
- Minzifa (p197)
- Ogahiy Fish Restaurant (p209)

Best Places to Stay

- Jahongir B&B (p176)
- Amulet (p196)
- Hovli Poyon B&B (p196)
- Komil Hotel (p196)
- Meros B&B (p207)

Why Go?

The region's cradle of culture for more than two millennia, Uzbekistan is the proud home to a spellbinding arsenal of architecture and ancient cities, all deeply infused with the bloody, fascinating history of the Silk Road. In terms of sights alone, Uzbekistan is Central Asia's biggest draw and most impressive showstopper.

Samarkand, Bukhara and Khiva never fail to impress visitors with their fabulous mosques, medressas and mausoleums, while its more eccentric attractions, such as the fast disappearing Aral Sea, the fortresses of desperately remote Karakalpakstan, its boom town capital Tashkent and the ecotourism opportunities of the Nuratau Mountains, mean that even the most diverse tastes can be catered for.

Despite being a harshly governed police state, Uzbekistan remains an extremely friendly country where hospitality remains an essential element of daily life and you'll be made to feel genuinely welcome by the people you meet.

When to Go

Tashkent

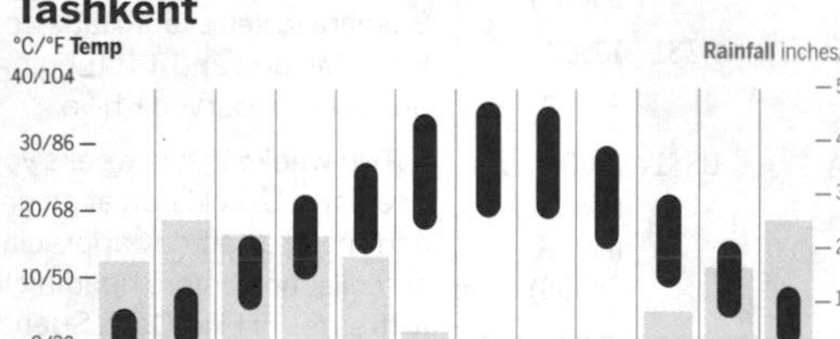

Apr–Jun Clear skies, sunshine and cool air combine to create perfect travel conditions.

Jul The extreme heat of the summer means bargains can be had at many hotels.

Sep–Oct Days remain warm despite the summer having passed, and it's yet to get cold.

TOP TIP

Uzbekistan has some charming accommodation, but it's important to book in advance during high season, especially in Bukhara, Khiva and Samarkand, where the best places will normally be full. Lesser options are unfortunately still a big step down in comfort and atmosphere.

Fast Facts

- **Area** 447,400 sq km
- **Capital** Tashkent
- **Country code** ☎ 998
- **Languages** Uzbek, Russian, Tajik, Karakalpak
- **Population** 29.3 million
- **Famous for** *plov*, carpets, cotton, pomegranates, Timur (Tamerlane)

Exchange Rates

COUNTRY	UNIT	SOM (OFFICIAL RATE)
Australia	A$1	1900S
Canada	C$1	2000S
Euro zone	€1	2830S (black market 3500S)
NZ	NZ$1	1650S
UK	£1	3300S
USA	US$1	2100S (black market 2800S)

Resources

- www.advantour.com
- www.arostr.uz
- www.caravanistan.com
- www.stantours.com
- www.uznews.net

Visas & Permits

Uzbek visas are needed by almost all nationalities. They are relatively painless to obtain, and some nationalities no longer require a Letter of Invitation (Canadians, New Zealanders and Australians are exempt). Once in Uzbekistan, it's important to register at a hotel and to continue to do so at least every three nights (ideally for every night of your stay). The registration slips will be inspected when you leave the country, so it's important to retain them. For more information on visas see p225.

COSTS

Relative Cost

Cheaper than Kazakhstan, more expensive than Tajikistan.

Daily Expenses

- Basic hotel double US$25
- Comfortable hotel double US$40
- Street snack 3000S, good restaurant meal 20,000S
- Bullet train to Bukhara economy/business 37,000/57,000S, bus 30,000S, flight US$50

Price Ranges

- **Sleeping** (per two people) $ < US$40, $$ US$40–80, $$$ > US$80
- **Eating** (main course) $ < 6000S, $$ 6000–15,000S, $$$ >15,000S

Itineraries

- **One week** In one week you can cover 'the big three' in a trans-steppe dash. Start in impressive Samarkand to explore the pearls of Timurid-era architecture, zip to enchanting Bukhara to see Lyabi-Hauz, tour the Ark, and gape at the 47m Kalon Minaret and its stunning medressa before continuing to perfectly preserved Khiva.
- **Two weeks** In two weeks you can do the five major places of interest in Uzbekistan at an unhurried pace. Fly west to Nukus and spend a half-day appreciating Central Asia's greatest art collection before heading to Khiva via the ancient ruined fortresses of Elliq-Qala. Spend a few days in both Bukhara and Samarkand before ending up in Tashkent for some museum hopping, good food and a night or two on the town.
- **One month** All of the above sights can be seen in a month at a more relaxed pace. You can also visit both Termiz and the Fergana Valley and devote more time to exploring Uzbekistan's natural wonders, including hiking, rafting or skiing in Ugam-Chatkal National Park, and community-based tourism in the Nuratau Mountains.

TASHKENT (TOSHKENT)

71 / POP 2.2 MILLION

Sprawling Tashkent is Central Asia's hub and the place where everything in Uzbekistan happens. It's one part newly built national capital, thick with the institutions of power, one part leafy Soviet city, and yet another part sleepy Uzbek town, where traditionally clad farmers cart their wares through a maze of mud-walled houses to the grinding crowds of the bazaar. Tashkent is a fascinating jumble of contradictions that's well worth exploring over several days.

Like most places that travellers use mainly to get somewhere else, Tashkent doesn't always immediately charm visitors, but it's a surprisingly fun and interesting place, with the best restaurants, museums and nightlife in the country. There's also plenty of opportunity to escape the metropolis for great hiking, rafting and skiing in Ugam-Chatkal National Park, just a 1½-hour drive away.

History

Tashkent's earliest incarnation might have been as the settlement of Ming-Uruk (Thousand Apricot Trees) in the 2nd or 1st century BC. By the time the Arabs took it in AD 751 it was a major caravan crossroads. It was given the name Toshkent (Tashkent, 'City of Stone' in Turkic) in about the 11th century.

The Khorezmshahs, one of the ruling dynasties of Central Asia and Persia from the late 11th to the early 13th centuries, and Chinggis Khan stubbed out Tashkent in the early 13th century, although it slowly recovered under the Mongols and then under Timur and grew more prosperous under the Shaybanids, the founding dynasty of what effectively became modern Uzbekistan, ruling from the mid-15th until the start of the 17th century.

The khan of Kokand annexed Tashkent in 1809. In 1865, as the Emir of Bukhara was preparing to snatch it away, the Russians under General Mikhail Grigorevich Chernyaev beat him to it, against the orders of the tsar and despite being outnumbered 15 to one. They found a proud town, enclosed by a 25km-long wall with 11 gates (of which not a trace remains today).

The newly installed Governor General Konstantin Kaufman gradually widened the imperial net around the other Central Asian khanates. Tashkent also became the tsarists' (and later the Soviets') main centre for espionage in Asia, during the protracted imperial rivalry with Britain known as the Great Game.

Tashkent became the capital of the Turkestan Autonomous SSR, declared in 1918. When this was further split, the capital of the new Uzbek Autonomous SSR became Samarkand. In 1930 this status was restored to Tashkent.

Physically, Tashkent was changed forever on 25 April 1966, when a massive earthquake levelled vast areas of the town and left 300,000 people homeless. The city's current look dates from rebuilding efforts in the late '60s and '70s, though a slew of post-Independence structures to house the new institutions of state have also graced the city.

Security in the city, particularly in the metro stations, has been high since February 1999, when six car bombs killed 16 and injured more than 120. The blasts were attributed by the government to Islamic extremists, but it will probably never be known who was responsible.

Sights

Modern Tashkent is a big, sprawling city that's best appreciated for its whole rather than its parts. If you're short on time, pick your spots and hone in on them by car. At minimum check out Khast Imom, Chorsu Bazaar and a few museums. If you have a few more days cover as much as you can on foot – you'll catch random glimpses of city life that are often more rewarding than the sights themselves. Old Town makes for the best wandering.

Sheikhantaur Mausoleum Complex MAUSOLEUM

(Navoi ko'chasi; M Alisher Navoi) Across Navoi from the Navoi Literary Museum are three 15th-century mausoleums. The biggest, on the grounds of the Tashkent Islamic University, bears the name of **Yunus Khan**, grandfather of the Mughal emperor and Andijon native Babur. The mausoleum itself sits locked and idle, but you can check out its attractive Timurid-style *pishtak* (entrance portal). Access is from Abdulla Kodiri. Two smaller mausoleums are east of the university grounds, accessible via a small side street running north from Navoi – the pointy-roofed **Kaldirgochbiy** and the twin-domed **Shaykh Hovendi Tahur**. Next to the latter is a mosque with beautifully carved wooden doors and attractive tilework.

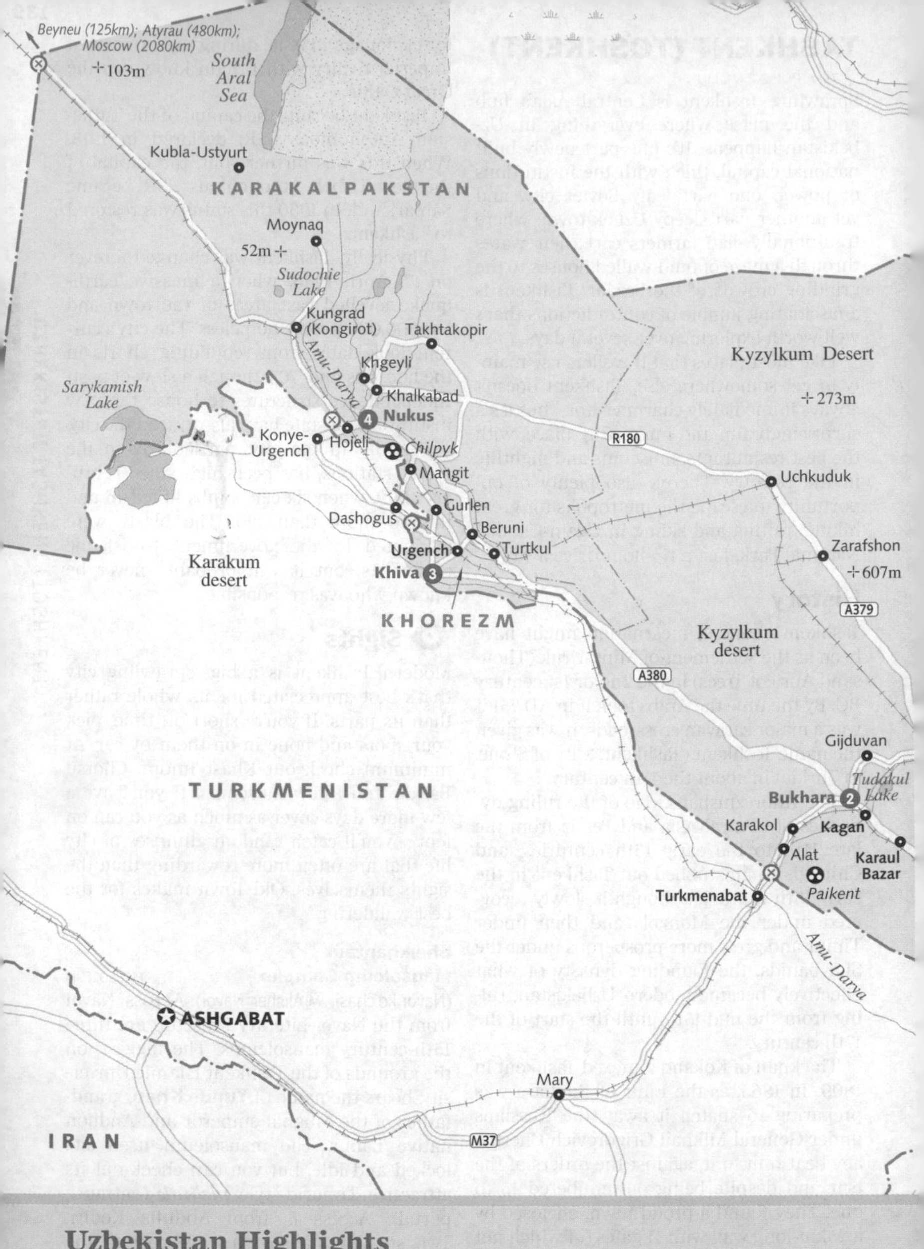

Uzbekistan Highlights

1. Visit the breathtaking **Registan** (p171) in Samarkand which leads to a formidable cast of larger-than-life Timurid architectural gems.

2. Explore the exquisitely preserved holy city of **Bukhara** (p187) boasting stunning 15th-century medressas, awesome B&Bs and a fascinating history.

3. Travel to the last independent Central Asian khanate, **Khiva** (p203), frozen in time behind mud walls in the middle of the Kyzylkum desert.

❹ See Central Asia's greatest art collection, the unmissable **Savitsky Collection** (p211) in Nukus.

❺ Buy silk in **Margilon** (p167), ceramics in **Rishton** (p168) and beautiful handmade carpets just about everywhere in Uzbekistan.

Tashkent

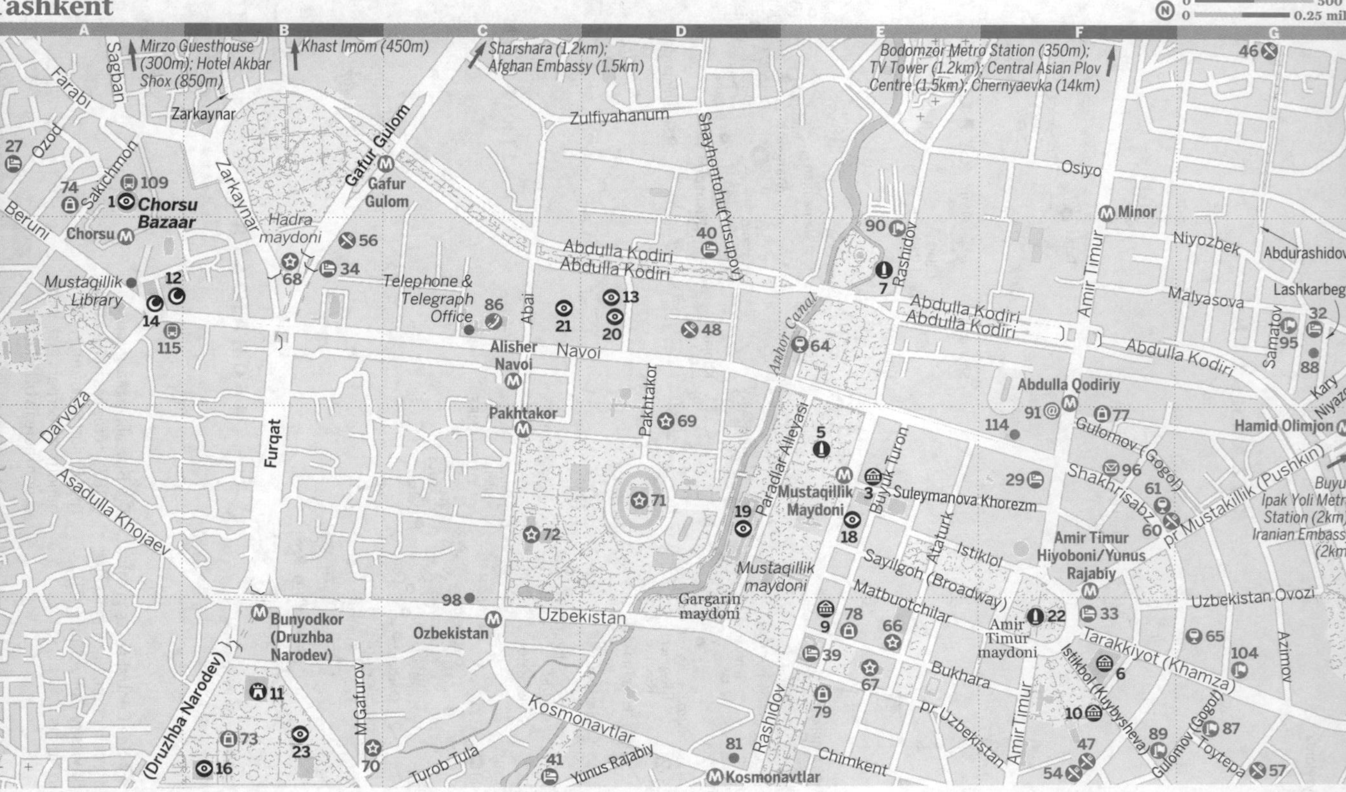
0 500 m
0 0.25 miles
Mirzo Guesthouse (300m); Hotel Akbar Shox (850m)
Khast Imom (450m)
Sharshara (1.2km); Afghan Embassy (1.5km)
Bodomzor Metro Station (350m); TV Tower (1.2km); Central Asian Plov Centre (1.5km); Chernyaevka (14km)
Buyuk Ipak Yoli Metro Station (2km); Iranian Embassy (2km)
Farabi
Sagban
Zarkaynar
Ozod
Sakichmon
Chorsu Bazaar
Chorsu
Beruni
Mustaqillik Library
Hadra maydoni
Gafur Gulom
Zulfiyahanum
Shayhontohur(Yusupov)
Abdulla Kodiri
Telephone & Telegraph Office
Abai
Alisher Navoi
Navoi
Pakhtakor
Darvoza
Furqat
Asadulla Khojaev
Anhor Canal
Paradlar Alleyasi
Mustaqillik Maydoni
Mustaqillik maydoni
Gargarin maydoni
Uzbekistan
Ozbekistan
Bunyodkor (Druzhba Narodev)
(Druzhba Narodev)
M Gafurov
Kosmonavtlar
Turob Tula
Yunus Rajabiy
Rashidov
Chimkent
Osiyo
Minor
Amir Timur
Niyozbek
Abdurashidov
Malyasova
Lashkarbegi
Samatov
Kary Niyazov
Abdulla Qodiriy
Hamid Olimjon
Gulomov (Gogol)
Shakhrisabz
pr Mustakillik (Pushkin)
Buyuk Turon
Suleymanova Khorezm
Ataturk
Istiklol
Sayilgoh (Broadway)
Matbuotchilar
Amir Timur Hiyoboni/Yunus Rajabiy
Amir Timur maydoni
Uzbekistan Ovozi
Tarakkiyot (Khamza)
Istikbol (Kuybysheva)
Bukhara
pr Uzbekistan
Azimov
Toytepa

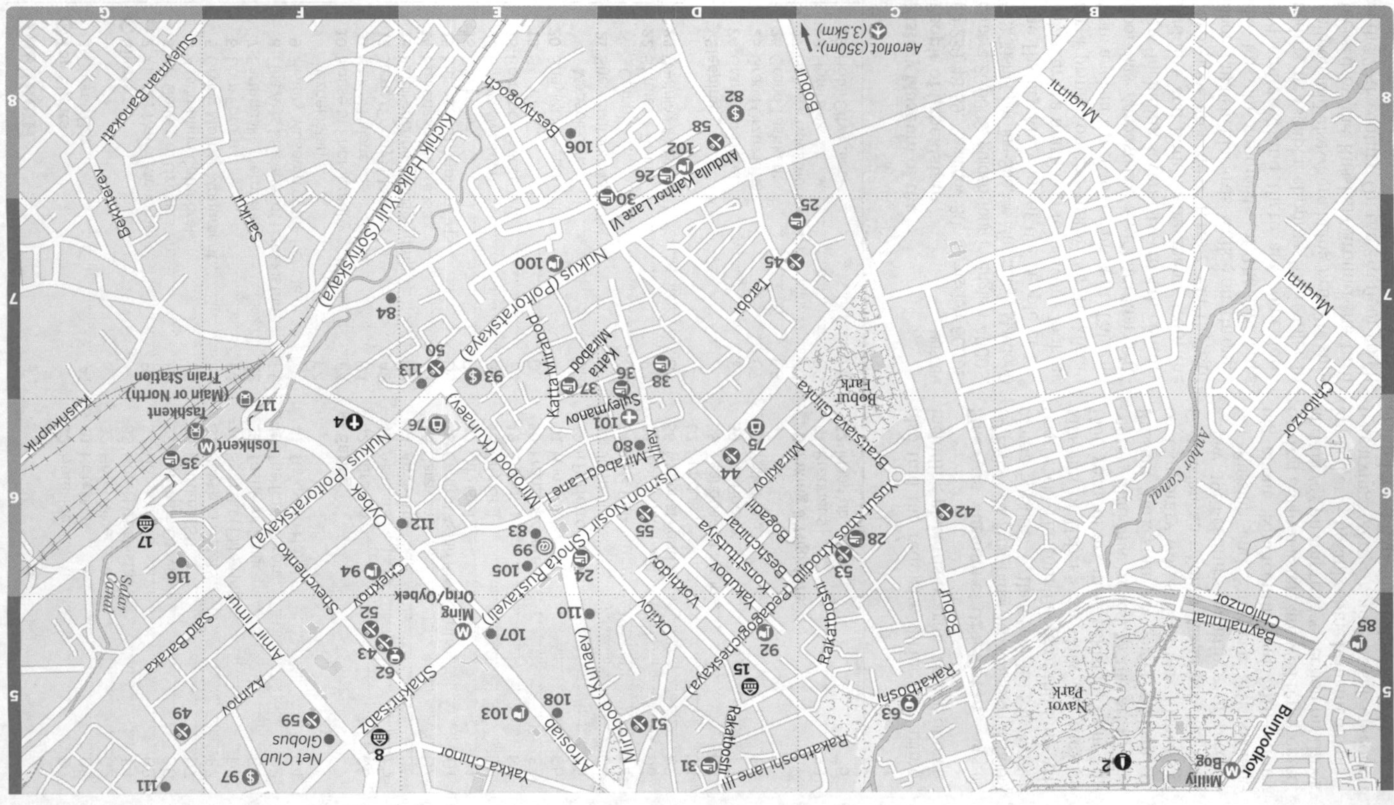
Suleyman Banokat
Bekhterev
Sarikul
Kichik Halka Yuli (Sofiyskaya)
Beshyogoch
Abdulla Kahhor Lane VI
Bobur
Aeroflot (350m); (3.5km)
Mugimi
Kushkuprik
Tashkent (Main or North) Train Station
Toshkent
Nukus (Poltoratskaya)
Katta Mirabod
Katta Mirabod
Suleymanov
Tarobi
Ivliev
Mirabod Lane I
Mirobod (Kunaev)
Usmon Nosir
Bobur Park
Bratislava Glinka
Mirakilov
Yusuf Khos Khodjib (Pedagogicheskaya)
Bogadil
Beshchinar
Konstitutsiya
Yakubov
Vokhidov
Okilov
Oybek
Shota Rustaveli
Ming Oriq/Oybek
Chekhov
Shevchenko
Amir Timur
Said Baraka
Salar Canal
Azimov
Shakhrisabz
Net Club Globus
Yakka Chinor
Afrosiab
Rakatboshi
Rakatboshi lane III
Navoi Park
Milliy Bog
Bunyodkor
Baynalmilal Chilonzor
Anhor Canal
Chilonzor

Tashkent

Top Sights

1 Chorsu Bazaar A1

Sights

2 Alisher Navoi Monument B5
3 Art Gallery of Uzbekistan E3
4 Assumption Cathedral F6
5 Crying Mother Monument E3
6 Dom Forum F4
7 Earthquake Memorial E2
8 Fine Arts Museum of Uzbekistan F5
9 History Museum of the People of Uzbekistan E4
10 House of Photography F4
11 Istiklol Palace B4
12 Juma (Friday) Mosque A2
13 Kaldirgochbiy Mausoleum D2
14 Kulkedash Medressa A2
15 Museum of Applied Arts D5
16 Oliy Majlis B4
17 Railway Museum G6
18 Romanov Palace E3
19 Senate D3
20 Shaykh Hovendi Tahur Mausoleum D2
21 Sheikhantaur Mausoleum Complex C2
22 Statue of Timur F4
23 Wedding Palace B4

Sleeping

24 Grand Mir Hotel E6
25 Grand Orzu Hotel C7
26 Grand Tashkent D8
27 Gulnara Guesthouse A1
28 Hotel Bek C6
29 Hotel City Palace F3
30 Hotel Ideal D7
31 Hotel Nur D5
32 Hotel Silver G2
33 Hotel Uzbekistan F4
34 Hotel Xadra B2
35 Komnata Otdykha G6
36 Raddus JSS D7
37 Rovshan Hotel E7
38 Sam Buh Elite Hotel D7
39 Tashkent Palace E4
40 The Park Turon D2
41 Turkiston Hotel C4

Eating

42 Affresco C6
43 Afsona F5
44 Amaretto D6
45 Caravan D7
46 Central Asian Plov Centre G1
47 City Grill F4
48 City Grill D2
49 Efendi G5
50 Franz Bäckerei E7
51 Han Kuk Kwan D5
52 Il Perfetto F5
53 Jumanji C6
54 Kafe Kafe F4
55 Manas Art Cafe D6
56 National Food B2
57 Sunduk G4
58 Teahouse Shafran D8
59 The Rooms F5
60 Yolki Palki F3

Drinking & Nightlife

61 Brauhaus F3
62 Irish Pub F5

History Museum of the People of Uzbekistan MUSEUM

(☎239 48 39; Rashidov 30; admission 6000S, camera 20,000S, guided tour in English 4000S; ⏰9.30am-6pm Tue-Sun; Ⓜ Mustaqillik Maydoni) The History Museum of the People of Uzbekistan is a must-stop for anyone looking for a primer on the history of Turkestan from ancient times to the present. The 2nd floor has Zoroastrian and Buddhist artefacts, including several 1st- to 4th-century Buddhas and Buddha fragments from the Fayoz-Tepe area near Termiz. On the 3rd floor English placards walk you through the Russian conquests of the khanates and emirates, and there are some foreboding newspaper clippings of revolts in Andijon and elsewhere being brutally suppressed by the Russians around the turn of the 20th century. On the 3rd floor you'll also find the requisite shrine to Karimov, including placards bearing choice quotes.

Fine Arts Museum of Uzbekistan MUSEUM

(☎236 47 73; Amir Timur 16; admission 10,000S, camera 50,000S; ⏰11am-5pm Tue-Sat; Ⓜ Ming Oriq/Oybek) The four floors of the Fine Arts Museum of Uzbekistan walk you through 1500 years of art in Uzbekistan, from 7th-century Buddhist relics, to the art of pre-Russian Turkestan, to Soviet realism, to contemporary works. There are displays of East Asian and South Asian art and even a few 19th-century paintings of second-tier Russian and European artists hanging about. Nineteenth- and 20th-century Central Asian masters are well represented, and there's an impressive section on Uzbek applied art – notably some brilliant old plaster carvings *(ghanch)* and the silk-on-cotton embroidered hangings called *suzani*.

63 K.T. Komba C5
64 Traktir Sam Prishyol E2
65 VM G4

Entertainment
66 Academic Russian Drama Theatre E4
67 Alisher Navoi Opera & Ballet Theatre E4
68 Circus B2
69 Ilkhom Theatre D3
70 Muqimi Musical Theatre B4
71 Pakhtakor Stadium D3
72 Tashkent State Conservatory C3

Shopping
73 Abulkasim Medressa B4
74 Chorsu Antiques A1
75 Human House D6
Knizhny Mir .... (see 111)
76 Mirobod Bazaar E6
77 Oloy Bazaar F3
78 Sharq Ziyokori E4
79 Toshkent Univermagi E4

Information
80 Advantour D6
81 Arostr Tourism D4
82 Asaka Bank D8
83 Asia Adventures E6
84 Asian Special Tourism F7
85 Azerbaijan Embassy A5
86 Central Telephone & Telegraph Office C2
87 Chinese Embassy G4
88 Culture Ministry Antiques Certification Office G2
89 French Embassy F4
90 German Embassy E2
91 Internet F3
92 Italian Embassy D5
93 Kapital Bank E7
94 Kazakhstan Embassy F6
95 Kyrgyz Embassy G2
96 Main Post Office F3
97 National Bank of Uzbekistan F5
98 OVIR Central Office C4
99 Prime Time E6
100 Russian Embassy E7
101 Safo Tibbiyot Clinic D6
102 Tajikistan Embassy D8
103 Turkmenistan Embassy E5
104 UK Embassy G4

Transport
105 AC Kyrgyzstan E6
106 Air Baltic E8
107 Asiana Airlines E5
108 China Southern E5
109 Chorsu Bazaar Bus Stop A1
110 Czech Airlines E5
Grand Mir Bus Stop .... (see 24)
111 Iran Air G5
112 Korean Air E6
113 Transaero E7
TsUM Bus Stop .... (see 79)
114 Turkish Airlines F3
115 Turkuaz/GUM Bus Stop A2
116 Uzbekistan Airways G6
117 Vokzal Bus Stop F6

Museum of Applied Arts MUSEUM
(☎256 39 43; Rakatboshi 15; admission 6500S, tour 8500S; ⊙9am-6pm; Ⓜ Kosmonavtlar) The Museum of Applied Arts occupies an exquisite house full of bright *ghanch* and carved wood. It was built in the 1930s, at the height of the Soviet period, but nonetheless serves as a sneak preview of the older architectural highlights lurking in Bukhara and Samarkand. The ceramic and textile exhibits here, with English descriptions, are a fine way to bone up on the regional decorative styles of Uzbekistan, and there's a pricey gift shop to trap impulse buyers.

Art Gallery of Uzbekistan MUSEUM
(Buyuk Turon 2; admission 3000S, guided tour 6000S; ⊙11am-5pm Tue-Sat; Ⓜ Mustaqillik Maydoni) One of the more recent additions to Tashkent's museum scene is this impressive building, within the vast halls of which rotating exhibits of Uzbekistan's top contemporary artists are rolled out. With both temporary exhibits and a permanent collection, it's an interesting survey of the national psyche, as well as being one that (of course) has been given the official stamp of approval.

House of Photography MUSEUM
(Istikbol 4; admission 3000S; ⊙10am-4pm Mon-Sat; Ⓜ Amir Timur Hiyoboni/Yunus Rajabiy) The House of Photography hosts rotating exhibits of Uzbekistan's top contemporary photographers as well as shows by international names in the field and is one of Tashkent's artier, edgier spots.

Railway Museum MUSEUM
(☎299 70 40; Amir Timur 1; admission 3000S, guide (Russian only) 5000S; ⊙9am-6pm; Ⓜ Toshkent) The magnificent collection of 1930s to 1950s

Soviet locomotives at the open-air Railway Museum will thrill train buffs and is worth visiting even if you aren't one. You have license to clamber all over any train with an open door. Guided tours are in Russian only, but kids will love the mini railway (2100S per ride).

Amir Timur Maydoni

Tashkent's main streets radiate from Amir Timur maydoni, desecrated by Karimov without warning in 2010 as part of his grand plan to 'beautify' the city. The dozens of century-old chinar (plane) trees that provided shade for the legions of chess players and strollers who once populated the park were all cut down. With the chess players now gone, the **statue of Timur** on horseback in the middle of the square cuts a lonely figure. A glance under the statue reveals that the stallion has been divested of a certain reproductive appendage. Just who stole it is one of Tashkent's great mysteries. Fortunately the horse's formidable family jewels remain intact.

Nobody is quite sure why Karimov cut down the chinar trees but conventional wisdom holds that he wanted to allow unobstructed views of the new, preposterously large **Dom Forum**. It's usually closed but occasionally hosts state-sponsored events for honoured guests. You may recognise the tigers on the facade from the Sher Dor Medressa at the Registan in Samarkand.

Further west, good-luck pelicans guard the gates to **Mustaqillik maydoni** (Independence Square), where crowds gather to watch parades on Independence day and whenever else Karimov wants to stir up a bit of nationalistic spirit. The shiny white edifice on the west side of the square is the relatively new **Senate building** (Paradlar Alleyasi). East of the square across Rashidov, the animal-festooned facade of the tsarist-era **Romanov Palace** (Buyuk Turon; Ⓜ Mustaqillik maydoni) faces the Art Gallery of Uzbekistan, and is now closed to the public.

North of Mustaqillik maydoni is the **Crying Mother Monument**. Fronted by an eternal flame, it was constructed in 1999 to honour the 400,000 Uzbek soldiers who died in WWII. The niches along its two corridors house their names.

The New Soviet men and women who rebuilt Tashkent after the 1966 earthquake are remembered in stone at the **Earthquake Memorial**. Soviet propagandists made much of the battalions of these 'fraternal peoples' and eager urban planners who came from around the Soviet Union to help with reconstruction. But when Moscow later announced it would give 20% of the newly built apartments to these (mainly Russian) volunteers and invite them to stay, local resentment boiled over in street brawls between Uzbeks and Russians in the so-called Pakhtakor Incident of May 1969.

It's worth taking the metro to reach some of these sites, if only to visit some of the lavishly decorated stations. A must is the Kosmonavtlar station, with its unearthly images of Amir Timur's astronomer grandson, Ulugbek, and Soviet cosmonaut Yuri Gagarin, among others.

TV Tower TOWER

(☎150 90 24; Amir Timur 109; admission 5000S; ⏲10am-8pm, restaurant 10am-11pm Tue-Sun; Ⓜ Bodomzor) The TV Tower, a 375m three-legged monster, the epitome of Soviet design, stands north of the city centre but can be seen from all over town. The price of admission gets you up to the 100m viewing platform and you'll need your passport to buy a ticket. To go up to the next level (about 220m) you'll have to grease the guard's palm – 10,000S should do the trick. At 110m there's a revolving restaurant that serves a decidedly mediocre set Russian meal.

Assumption Cathedral CHURCH

(Uspensky Sobor; Nukus ko'chasi) It's impossible to miss the handsome gold onion domes and the 50m belltower of the impressive Assumption Cathedral. Built in 1958 and renovated in the 1990s, this is the biggest of the four Orthodox churches in Tashkent.

Old Town

The Old Town (Uzbek: *eski shahar,* Russian: *stary gorod*) starts beside the Chorsu Bazaar. A maze of narrow dirt streets is lined with low mudbrick houses and dotted with mosques and old medressas.

Taxi drivers get lost easily here. On foot, you could easily get lost too, but that's part of the fun. Wandering around you may be invited into someone's home, where you'll discover that the blank outer walls of traditional homes conceal cool, peaceful garden courtyards.

★**Chorsu Bazaar** MARKET

(9am-6pm; Ⓜ Chorsu) Tashkent's most famous farmers market, topped by a giant green dome, is a delightful slice of city life spilling into the streets off Old Town's southern edge. If it grows and it's edible, it's here. There are acres of spices arranged in brightly coloured mountains; Volkswagen-sized sacks of grain; entire sheds dedicated to candy, dairy products and bread; interminable rows of freshly slaughtered livestock; and – of course – scores of pomegranates, melons, persimmons, huge mutant tomatoes and whatever fruits are in season. Souvenir hunters will find *kurpacha* (colourful sitting mattresses), skull caps, *chapan* (traditional cloaks) and knives here.

Kulkedash Medressa MEDRESSA

(Beruni ko'chasi; admission 4000S; ⌚10am-6pm) The grand Kulkedash medressa sits beside Tashkent's principal **Juma (Friday) Mosque** on a hill overlooking Chorsu Bazaar. The mosque was built in the 1990s on the site of a 16th-century mosque destroyed by the Soviets. On warm Friday mornings the plaza in front overflows with worshippers.

Khast Imom

The official religious centre of the republic, located 2km north of the Circus, is also definitely one of the best places to see 'old Tashkent'. A big renovation in recent years has left the complex looking better than ever. The Leviathan **Hazroti Imom Friday mosque** (Karasaray; Ⓜ Gofur Gulom), flanked by two 54m minarets, is a recent construction, having been ordered by President Karimov in 2007. Behind it is the sprawling **Khast Imom Square**. The Muslim Board of Uzbekistan, whose grand mufti is roughly the Islamic equivalent of an archbishop, occupies a new building to the north of the mosque.

Moyie Mubarek Library Museum LIBRARY

(admission 10,000S; ⌚9am-noon & 2-5pm Mon-Fri, 10am-3pm Sat; Ⓜ Gofur Gulom) The primary attraction of the Khast Imom square is this library museum, which houses the 7th-century Osman Quran (Uthman Quran), said to be the world's oldest. This enormous deerskin tome was brought to Samarkand by Timur, then taken to Moscow by the Russians in 1868 before being returned to Tashkent by Lenin in 1924 as an act of goodwill towards Turkestan's Muslims. It is Tashkent's most impressive and important sight. The museum also contains 30 or 40 rare 13th-century books among its collection. The library is next to the spartan 1856 **Telyashayakh Mosque**.

Barak Khan Medressa MEDRESSA

(Ⓜ Gofur Gulom) Souvenir shops occupy the student rooms of this 16th-century medressa located on the west side of Khast Imom square.

Mausoleum of Abu Bakr Kaffal Shoshi MAUSOLEUM

(Ⓜ Gofur Gulom) This little 16th-century mausoleum of Abu Bakr Kaffal Shoshi, an Islamic scholar and poet of the Shaybanid period, is located northwest of Khast Imom square. The front room contains his large tomb and five smaller ones. Larger tombs of three more sheikhs are at the back.

Navoi Park

Downtown Tashkent's largest park will appeal to anyone with a taste for eccentricity. Soviet architects had a field day here, erecting a pod of spectacularly hideous concrete monstrosities, such as the **Istiklol Palace** (Navoi Park; Ⓜ Bunyodkur or Milliy Bog), formerly the People's Friendship Palace, which appears like a moon-landing station from a 1950s film set, and the chunky **Wedding Palace** (Ⓜ Bunyodkur or Milliy Bog).

The tightly guarded building southwest of Istiklol Palace is the **Oliy Majlis** (Parliament; Ⓜ Bunyodkur or Milliy Bog), the lower house of parliament. It currently functions as a giant rubber stamp in its infrequent sessions. Nearby are a vast promenade and a post-Soviet **Alisher Navoi monument** (Ⓜ Bunyodkur or Milliy Bog).

Sleeping

Tashkent's accommodation scene is slowly improving and becoming more competitive, but it's still underwhelming, so book ahead during the peak months to ensure you can stay where you want. The foreign operators of several of Tashkent's fancier hotels pulled out of Uzbekistan in the wake of the 2005 Andijon incident (p215), turning management over to the state, meaning that there are no truly international standard business hotels at present. Nearly all hotels in Tashkent use the official rate when calculating their prices, so rooms are up to a third cheaper if you change your dollars or euro on the black market. This doesn't work with backpacker haunts, however. Also be aware that registration is taken far more seriously here than elsewhere in the country. You're likely not to be accepted as a guest in many places if you don't have all your registration stamps ready for inspection, so be sure your paperwork is in order!

★ **Gulnara Guesthouse** GUESTHOUSE $
(☎+998-712 406 336, +998-983 600 774; gulnarahotel@gmail.com; Ozod 40; dm US$15, s without/with bathroom US$20/30, d US$35/45; ❄ 📶; Ⓜ Chorsu) Gulnara's is the pick of the budget bunch in Tashkent. There's a friendly family atmosphere in the lovely courtyard and the addition of four new rooms and fresh coats of paint on everything inspire confidence. The shared bathrooms are very clean and extras such as a laundry service, book exchange and hearty breakfasts make this an understandably popular choice. The location in the Old Town is also good, with the metro a short walk away. English is spoken.

Mirzo Guesthouse GUESTHOUSE $
(☎+998 933 934 333, +998 933 796 668; www.turkturizm.uz; Sagban 95; r without/with bathroom per person US$15/20; ❄ 📶; Ⓜ Chorsu) After a recent renovation, Mirzo Guesthouse has come out in very good shape, with redone bathrooms, new mattresses and constant hot water. The historic building features gorgeous carved wooden ceilings, a courtyard full of roses and there's tonnes of ethnographic knick-knacks on display to boot. Loquacious owner Mirzo, an eccentric historian, likes to play the *dutar* (two-stringed guitar) and his son speaks excellent English.

Komnata Otdykha HOSTEL $
(Olish Xonasi; ☎ inside train station 299 72 29, outside train station 299 76 49; inside train station s/d US$30/36, outside train station dm/d US$14/32; Ⓜ Toshkent) There are two accommodation options at Tashkent's main train station, one inside the station itself (meaning you'll need to pass through security each time you enter) and one that is accessible from the street outside. The property outside the station has six-bed dorms, as well as a double 'lux' room. Inside the station all rooms are 'lux', meaning they have their own bathrooms. Not a bad budget option – the rooms are clean and bright and staff are vaguely friendly. Note that tenancy in all rooms runs from 8am to 8am and that breakfast is not included.

Hotel Xadra BUDGET HOTEL $
(☎244 27 13; Gafur Gulom 53A; s/d with bathroom US$15/39, s/d shared bathroom US$10/25; Ⓜ Gafor Galom) Once the darkest hole in all of Central Asia, these budget digs border on the liveable these days, although they still draw plenty of shady characters. Rooms with bathrooms also have TV and air con, while the cheapest rooms have no such luxuries. Reception (such as it is) is on the 2nd floor. Breakfast not included.

Hotel Ideal HOTEL $$
(☎254 70 77, 254 17 29; hotel-ideal@mail.ru; Beshyogosh 96; s/d US$46/58; ❄ 📶; Ⓜ Toshkent) This welcome addition to Tashkent's sleeping scene is a little out of the way, but offers clean, cosy and pleasant rooms and has friendly English-speaking staff. Add on an extra US$15 per room for breakfast and wi-fi to be included. The cheapest standards are attic rooms with sloping ceilings, while the pricier ones are very spacious.

Turkiston Hotel HOTEL $$
(☎239 18 21; www.turkistonhotel.uz; Yunus Rajabiy 64; s US$40-50; d US$50-60; ❄ 📶 🏊; Ⓜ Kosmonavtlar) Nestled in a sleepy and leafy residential area of central Tashkent, this musty old classic offers good value. Rooms are rather on the small side, and bathrooms are showing their age, but it's pleasant enough.

Grand Tashkent HOTEL $$
(☎255 05 99; www.grand-tashkent.com; Abdulla Kahhor Lane VI; s/d/tw/tr US$48/53/58/65; ✈ ❄ 📶; Ⓜ Toshkent) The name may be a total misnomer, but this midrange place offers decent value. Its standard rooms are fine, if rather small, while its improved rooms (around US$10 extra) all come equipped with bath tubs, fridges, wooden ceilings and plenty of daylight.

Grand Orzu Hotel HOTEL $$
(☎120 88 77; info@grandorzu.com; Tarobi 27; s/d from US$50/60; P ❄ 📶 🏊; Ⓜ Toshkent) This self-contained place within a pleasantly green residential neighbourhood boasts a pool and pleasant restaurant out the back. Rooms are very forgettable, but reasonably priced for what they offer.

Sam Buh Elite Hotel HOTEL $$
(☎120 88 21, 120 88 26; sambuh.hotel@gmail.com; Ivliev 14; s/d US$47/72; ❄ @; Ⓜ Oybek) The name is something of a misnomer for these rather sordid-feeling quarters off a residential backstreet. Foreign guests are assigned the 'improved' rooms, and they are fine, with fridges and ok bathrooms, although some came with rather strange smells when we visited.

Raddus JSS HOTEL $$

(☎120 77 48; raddus-jss@list.ru; Suleymanov 39/41; s/d US$51/73; ; M Oybek) A much-needed renovation brought this place up to the standards of its midrange brethren in the Mirobodsky District. The cover over the courtyard out back is a questionable call, but the rooms look brand new and some have king-sized beds for couples.

Rovshan Hotel HOTEL $$

(☎120 77 47; www.rovshanhotel.com; Katta Mirobod 118; s/d US$54/62; ; M Oybek) Not thrilling and rather characterless, but nonetheless a solid midrange option in the quiet Mirobodsky District. The twin beds are more comfy than in other hotels of this ilk, and a lux with king-sized bed is just a small step up in price.

Hotel Silver HOTEL $$

(☎+998 514 400 078; Niyobek Yuli 54; s/d US$33/43; ; M Hamid Olimjon) Called both the Hotel Silver and the Hotel Silver Dew, this 12-room place is rather obscurely located (off Karay Niyazov kochasi), but not too far from the metro and a decent deal in a pleasantly residential neighbourhood. There's hot water in the otherwise fairly poor bathrooms, and rooms are clean, each with a TV.

Hotel Akbar Shox HOTEL $$

(☎246 06 02; Sagban 5; per person US$35; ; M Chorsu) Rather inconveniently located, this is still a decent enough fall-back option, with slightly musty but spacious rooms and admittedly fairly cramped bathrooms. It's 750m north of the Chorsu metro station.

★Hotel Nur BOUTIQUE HOTEL $$$

(☎140 08 21, 140 08 20; Rakatboshi 3A; r from US$80; ; M Kosmonovtlar) This fantastic new place is just what Tashkent needs – a well-located, upmarket but affordable hotel that has style, security and good service. It has a big pool and garden (perfect for breakfast in the sun), spacious and well-decorated rooms and staff who fall over themselves to be helpful.

★Hotel Bek BOUTIQUE HOTEL $$$

(☎215 58 88; www.bek-hotel.uz; Yusuf Khos Khodjib 64A; s/d from US$90/100; ; M Kosmonovtlar) With friendly and professional English-speaking staff, spotless rooms, stylish touches and a small but very welcome courtyard pool, this hotel is a great choice for business travellers or those looking for some comfort. King-size beds, reliable wi-fi and a relaxed and friendly atmosphere are this place's hallmarks, and about the only complaint is that you're a good 15-minute walk from the nearest metro station.

Tashkent Palace HOTEL $$$

(☎120 58 00; reservations@tashkent-palace.com; Buyuk Turon 56; s/d from US$160/180; ; M Kosmonovtlar) This grand Soviet-era place has a superbly central location, though its age was beginning to show when we last visited. A floor-by-floor renovation was scheduled for 2014, so things may soon change. Rooms are a good size, many with balconies and fridges. Use of the pool, sauna and gym is free for guests, while in-room internet costs US$15 per day, though it's free in the lobby.

Hotel City Palace HOTEL $$$

(☎238 30 00; citypalace.marketing@gmail.com; Amir Timur 15; s/d from US$160/180; ; M Abdulla Qodiriy) Despite a fairly tasteless and characterless lobby, the upper floors of this hotel are well decorated and rooms have good furnishings, including inviting king-sized beds with fine linens, writing desks and some impressive city views.

Hotel Uzbekistan HOTEL $$$

(☎113 10 12, 113 11 11; www.hoteluzbekistan.uz; Tarakkiyot 45; s/d from US$100/130; ; M Amir Timur Hiyoboni) This old dinosaur towering over central Amir Timur maydoni has reinvented itself as Tashkent's best-value top-end hotel. Where there were once scowling *babushkas* there are now more helpful receptionists, although don't expect to feel totally welcome. Rooms are now rather sleek and modern with flat-screen TVs, cushy white comforters and shiny bathrooms.

The Park Turon HOTEL $$$

(☎140 60 00; www.theparkturon.com; Abdulla Kodiri 1; s/d US$140/150; ; M Alisher Navoi) Once the Leningrad Hotel, the totally refurbished Park Turon now has Indian-Uzbek management, as its incense-infused lobby, Indian restaurant and popularity with Indian businesspeople demonstrates. However, while the renovation has been very thorough, the rooms' low ceilings and rather cramped layout remains unchanged. Flat-screen TVs, the fluffiest towels in Tashkent, a gym and a sauna sweeten the deal somewhat.

Eating

You'll eat better in Tashkent than anywhere else in Uzbekistan and perhaps even than most of Central Asia as a whole. This is no great reason to get excited though, but after a long journey through the region, arriving in Tashkent is something of a culinary event.

Tashkent's burgeoning middle class loves to drink good coffee and eat cakes, is crazy for sushi and particularly Italian food, and also enjoys more traditionally popular cuisines such as Russian, Caucasian and Central Asian. The large Korean population in Tashkent means that there's plenty of authentic Korean food to be had, while street food from shashlyk to *laghman* (noodles, also a noodle soup) can be tried almost anywhere.

Western-style supermarkets and minimarkets are now abundant, but for fresh produce you are much better off at a farmers market. Most restaurants add on a 15% to 20% service charge.

Kafe Kafe CAFE $
(Shakhrisabz; 8am-10pm; M Oybek) A slice of Bohemia in the centre of decidedly unbohemian Tashkent, this hip outfit has eclectic, comfortable furniture, writing all over the walls, and fun and friendly staff, not to mention the best coffee and cake in town. Smoothies and a breakfast menu featuring such Central Asian rarities as eggs benedict (10,000S) are also available.

Franz Bäckerei BAKERY $
(Nukus ko'chasi; cakes from 5000S; 8am-8pm Mon-Sat; M Toshkent) This Austrian-run bakery has brought a much-needed combination of baked goods and real coffee to Tashkent's deprived expats. You can drop in to pick up the city's best fresh bread, or stop by for a coffee and pastry at the airy and bright cafe.

★ **Jumanji** INTERNATIONAL $$
(www.jumanji.uz; Yusuf Khos Khodjib 62/2; mains 5,000-15,000S; noon-11pm Mon-Sat, 5-11pm Sun; ; M Kosmonavtlar) A charming, laidback and family-friendly environment reigns here. There's a varied and interesting menu that runs from Georgian specialties to Asian dishes and traditional Uzbek soups, while the coolly efficient staff ensure that this is one of Tashkent's most perenially enjoyable eating experiences.

★ **National Food** UZBEK $$
(Milliy Taomlar; Gafur Gulom 1; dishes 5000-15,000S; 6am-10pm; M Gafur Gulom) You'll be hard pressed to find a restaurant with more local colour than this bustling eatery opposite the Circus. Walk through the entrance, overhung with goat parts, and be greeted by giant *kazan* (cauldrons) filled with various national specialities. In addition to the requisite *plov,* and *laghman,* you can sample *beshbarmak, dimlama* (braised meat, potatoes, onions and vegetables), *halim* (meat porridge) and *naryn* (horsemeat sausage served with cold noodles), the

PLOV GLORIOUS PLOV

Few things excite the Uzbek palate like *plov,* that delicious conglomeration of rice, vegetables and meat bits swimming in lamb fat and oil. This Central Asian staple has been elevated to the status of religion in Uzbekistan, the country with which it's most closely associated. Each province has its own style, which locals loudly and proudly proclaim is the best in Uzbekistan – and by default the world. That *plov* is an aphrodisiac goes without saying. Uzbeks joke that the word for 'foreplay' in Uzbek is '*plov*'. Men put the best cuts of meat in the *plov* on Thursday; not coincidentally, Thursday is when most Uzbek babies are conceived. Drinking the oil at the bottom of the *kazan* (large *plov* cauldron) is said to add particular spark to a man's libido.

To sample the city's best *plov* – and drink the oil if you dare – head to the celebration of *plov* that is the **Central Asian Plov Centre** (cnr Abdurashidov & Ergashev; plov 5000S; lunch). Walk past the mob of people crowding around steaming *kazans* and take a seat inside, where a waitress will eventually come and serve you. Your group's order will arrive Uzbek-style on a single plate from which everybody will eat. The best day to come? Why Thursday, of course! Other worthy *plov* options include a lunch-time restaurant just north of the Chorsu Bazaar atrium, and National Food opposite the Circus on Gafur Gulom.

latter prepared in the main dining room by an animated assembly line of middle-aged women.

Sunduk FRENCH $$

(Azimov 63; mains 8000-20,000S; 9.30am-midnight Mon-Sat; ; Amir Timur Hiyoboni) The comfort food at this diminutive eatery, kitted out like a French country kitchen, is as perfect as the handwriting on the menus – on homemade paper, no less. The good-value business lunch is popular with the diplomatic set, many of whom work nearby.

Efendi TURKISH $$

(233 15 02; Azimov 79A; mains 9000-16,000S; 9am-midnight; ; Oybek) This sprawling, non-alcoholic Turkish place has a menu, but don't bother – just saunter inside and pick out a kebab and a mouth-watering salad from the refrigerated display case, and retire to the shaded outdoor seating to enjoy it as Tashkent's traffic roars on by.

Manas Art Cafe KYRGYZ $$

(712 523 811; Yakubov 12; mains 9000-25,000S; 11am-11pm; ; Oybek) To dine in a yurt without schlepping over the desert on a camel, head here. There are a few yurts decorated in traditional style, with chill-out tunes and *shisha* (hookah) smoke wafting through the air. It specialises in Kyrgyz cuisine such as *beshbarmak*. Reservations recommended.

Yolki Palki RUSSIAN $$

(Shakhrisabz 5; mains 5000-15,000S; 11am-11pm; ; Amir Timur Hiyoboni) Sprawling Russian chain famous for all-you-can-eat hot and cold salad bars with every Ukrainian and Russian speciality imaginable. No service charge.

★City Grill INTERNATIONAL $$$

(www.citygrill.uz; Shakhrisabz 23; mains 15,000-50,000S; noon-midnight; ; Amir Timur Hiyoboni, Mustaqillik Maydoni) The brand new and very central flagship for the City Grill is a great spot for a sophisticated and good-value business lunch (18,500S) or a blow-out dinner. Specialising in steak and pasta, the menu here is varied and uses delicious fresh produce. There's also a fantastic selection of salads, soups and other meat grills. Service is discreet and efficient, and the original **location** (Shayhontohur 1;) is also still working and offers similarly excellent fare.

★Han Kuk Kwan KOREAN $$$

(Yusuf Khos Khodjib 1; mains 18,000-30,000S; noon-10pm; ; Kosmonavtlar) Tashkent's large population of ethnic Koreans is what drives demand for all those Korean restaurants around town. Popular Han Kuk Kwan is one of the best. It fries up absolutely delicious dishes such as *bi-bim-bab* (rice, egg, vegetables and chopped meat fried together in a stone bowl) right at your table and service is charming.

Caravan UZBEK $$$

(150 66 06; www.caravan.uz; Abdulla Kahhor 22; mains 20,000-60,000S; 11am-11pm;) Tashkent's quintessential theme restaurant is tarted up like a made-for-Hollywood Uzbek home. The original menu is heavy on arcane but well-prepared Uzbek dishes. The walls are festooned with purchasable paintings by local artists, and the attached store, filled with high-quality crafts from all over the country, is open late, making Caravan a great place for a last-minute gift-buying spree.

Teahouse Shafran ARAB $$$

(www.caravangroup.uz; 69 Abdulla Kahhor Lane VI; mains 20,000-35,000S; noon-midnight;) There's a gorgeous, stylish feel to this charming teahouse aimed at foreigners and well-off locals. It's part of the ubiquitous Caravan group, and its menu runs from shish kebabs and salads to delicious curries such as lamb and chicken biriyani.

Il Perfetto ITALIAN $$$

(Shevchenko 30; 15,000-30,000S; 10am-11pm; ; Ming Oriq/Oybek) Its air-conditioned interior lives up to the name on a hot Tashkent day, although you can eat al fresco in the shade on the street outside as well. This new location for a popular Italian place boasts an open-plan kitchen, friendly staff and a menu covering classic Italian dishes from pasta and salad to risotto. Takeaway is available.

The Rooms INTERNATIONAL $$$

(Amir Timur 33; mains 30,000-40,000S; 6pm-midnight; ; Oybek) There are many rooms at this swanky place, and you can choose your 'environment' as much as your cuisine – so you can sit in the boudoir and eat Japanese food, or enjoy European dishes with a shisha in the Moroccan themed room.

Amaretto ITALIAN $$$

(215 55 57; Shota Rustaveli ko'chasi; mains 15,000-40,000S; ; Oybek) The mouth-watering

Italian food, professional English-speaking service and subdued, candlelit ambience combine to make this the obvious choice for a romantic dinner. We prefer the shady terrace to the rather garish dining rooms inside, but wherever you eat, the excellent Italian food and large wine list are winners.

Afsona UZBEK $$$
(Shevchenko 30; mains 15,000-30,000S; ⌚ noon-11pm; Ⓜ Ming Oriq/Oybek) This smart new restaurant aims to deliver Uzbek cuisine with a contemporary touch, by revivifying old favourites such as *plov* and *laghman,* cooking with a wider range of flavours and – thank god – by not employing the ethnographic museum approach to décor. A good place for imaginative takes on Uzbek food without the Silk Road theme park treatment.

Affresco ITALIAN $$$
(www.caravangroup.uz; Bobur 14; 20,000-50,000S; ⌚ noon-11pm) Pricey and somewhat kitschy, Affresco remains riotously popular with locals and travellers. Its full Italian menu is well-realised and there's a large wine list to boot.

Drinking & Nightlife

Tashkent has a lively and rapidly changing nightlife, although it's aimed largely at the Landcruiser classes and you may well feel conspicuous arriving at some clubs' velvet ropes without designer threads, sunglasses worn at midnight and a bevvie of models by your side. Reservations are a good idea to ensure entrance. The website www.afisha.uz (Russian only) is an invaluable and regularly updated guide to what's on.

Irish Pub PUB
(Shevchenko 30; beer from 5000S; ⌚ 11am-11pm; Ⓜ Oybek) There's Irish homebrew here, along with overpriced food and usually at least a smattering of expats who gather here for Happy Hour on Fridays.

VM BAR
(Shakhrisabz 33a; ⌚ 7pm-late; Ⓜ Amir Timur Hiyoboni) For flat-out debauchery, it's hard to beat this hipsterish student venue. Ostensibly a warm-up (or warm-down) bar for club-goers, its small dance floor often takes on a life of its own, obviating the need to go elsewhere.

Traktir Sam Prishyol PUB
(Navoi 2; mains 18,000-40,000S; ⌚ 11am-midnight; Ⓜ Mustaqillik Maydoni) Occupying a prime, shady nook right on the Ankhor Canal, this microbrewery has some of the best (and best-priced) homebrew in town. Their recipe was supposedly invented by German monks in 1514. Tuck into a large menu of grilled meats, fresh fish and pizza in one of the shaded eaves, or just knock back several cold beers or cocktails.

Brauhaus PUB
(Shakhrisabz 5; beer from 5000S; ⌚ 11am-midnight; 📶; Ⓜ Toshkent) Sports fans flock here to watch big football matches on one of several screens in the cavernous basement. Upstairs features live music, German sausages and other beer-hall classics, which you can wash down with any of 12 varieties of homebrew, including a *weissbier* (wheat beer).

K.T. Komba NIGHTCLUB
(Catacoomba; Rakatboshi 23; admission from 15,000S; ⌚ Fri & Sat; Ⓜ Kosmonavtlar) This is the premier weekend playground for the young, smart local set. It gets going after midnight and the party goes on until dawn. Music is kept interesting by guest DJs and live acts.

☆ Entertainment

Opera, theatre and ballet options are readily available, most performing from traditional repertoires with the exception of the Ilkhom Theatre, which is arguably Central Asia's most progressive theatre. There are lots of cinemas in Tashkent, but they show films exclusively dubbed into Russian, so they're unlikely to be of interest to most visitors. For listings, check out www.tashkent-events.info for expatriate-oriented events news, and www.afisha.uz (in Russian) for general entertainment listings.

★ Ilkhom Theatre THEATRE
(Inspiration Theatre; ☎ 241 22 41; www.ilkhom.com; Pakhtakor 5; tickets 8000-15,000S; ⌚ box office 11am-6.30pm, shows 6.30pm Tue-Sun; Ⓜ Pakhtakor) Tashkent's main cultural highlight is this progressive theatre, which stages productions in Russian but often with English subtitles. Known for bucking trends, its productions often touch on gay themes and racial subjects, putting off more conservative elements of Uzbek society. The Ilkhom's director, Mark Weil, who founded the theatre in 1976, was tragically stabbed to death in 2007, allegedly for blaspheming the Prophet Mohammed in his Pushkin-inspired play *Imitations of the Koran.* But the theatre continues to thrive and produce

cutting-edge plays as well as occasional jazz concerts and art exhibitions in its lobby. *Imitations of the Koran* remains in the repertoire today.

Pakhtakor Stadium FOOTBALL
(Cotton Picker stadium; M Pakhtakor) Soccer matches are held at the Pakhtakor Stadium, in the central park between Uzbekistan and Navoi. Tickets (local matches 2000S to 8000S, international matches 5000S to 15,000S) can be bought directly from the stadium box office.

Alisher Navoi Opera & Ballet Theatre THEATRE
(☎233 90 81; Ataturk 28; M Kosmonavtlar) Tashkent's main opera and ballet theatre was undergoing a total renovation at the time of research. Once it reopens, it will no doubt be well worth visiting, as much to see the impressive interiors as to see the repertoire of classical opera and ballet normally performed here.

Circus CIRCUS
(☎244 37 31; Gafur Gulom 1; tickets 2000-7000S; 3pm Sat, noon & 3pm Sun, closed Jun-Aug; M Gafur Gulom) This popular kiddie diversion sells out quickly.

Academic Russian Drama Theatre THEATRE
(☎238 81 65; www.ardt.uz; Ataturk 24; tickets 4000-7000S; shows 6.30pm Wed-Fri, 5pm Sat & Sun; M Amir Timur Hiyoboni) Classical Russian and Western drama as well as some more modern pieces, all performed in Russian.

Muqimi Musical Theatre THEATRE
(☎245 16 33; M Gafurov 187; tickets from 3000S; shows 6pm; M Bunyodkor) Best bet for traditional Uzbek folk singing, dancing and operettas.

Tashkent State Conservatory CONCERT HALL
(☎241 29 91; Abai 1; M Ozbekistan) Chamber concerts, Uzbek and Western vocal and instrumental recitals in an impressive new edifice. Entrance is around the back.

Shopping

Ask around about private sellers who peddle high-quality Turkmen carpets and *suzani* from their apartments at reasonable prices. It's recommended that you certify antique purchases with the vendor or with the **Culture Ministry Antiques Certification Office** (☎237 07 38; Lashkarbegi 19; 9am-5pm Mon-Fri; M Hamid Olimjon), which is roughly opposite the Latvian embassy.

The multiple sister restaurants of Caravan double as art galleries and have on-site handicraft shops. The prices are competitive with shops across the country, making them reasonable places to stock up on items you might have missed while travelling. The ceramics of Rustam Usmanov and other Rishton masters are also sold here.

Tashkent has at least 16 open-air farmers markets or bazaars (Uzbek: dekhon bozori, Russian: kolkhozny rynok or bazar). Chorsu, Mirobod and Oloy bazaars are the most interesting to visit.

★ **Abulkasim Medressa** HANDICRAFTS
(Navoi Park; 9am-6pm; M Milliy Bog) Close to the Oliy Majlis in Navoi Park, this medressa has been turned into an artisans' school and workshop where local wood carvers, lacquerware makers, metal workers and miniature painters ply and teach their craft. It's a great place to buy the fruits of their labour, plus souvenirs such as *suzani, rospic* (lacquer boxes) and ceramics.

Chorsu Antiques ANTIQUES
(Sakichmon; 10am-5pm; M Chorsu) It's not one but rather several antique shops nestled amid a row of hardware and trinket shops behind Chorsu Bazaar. There are some *suzani* of exceptional quality here, but you'll want to haggle hard.

Human House CLOTHING
(☎255 44 11; www.humanhuman.net; Usmon Nosir 30/9; 10am-7pm Mon-Sat; M Oybek) This shop not only has carpets, skull caps, *suzani* and textiles from various Uzbek provinces, but it also doubles as one of Tashkent's most fashionable boutiques, featuring modern clothing infused with Uzbek styles and designs. Tours of the factory are available by appointment.

Knizhny Mir BOOKS
(Book World; Toytepa 1; 9am-7pm Mon-Sat; M Amir Timur Hiyoboni) This bookshop has a decent map selection along with a smattering of English-language classics.

Sharq Ziyokori MAPS
(Bukhara 26; 9am-6pm Mon-Sat; M Kosmonavtlar) Has maps of Tashkent, Uzbekistan and most provincial centres, plus excellent 1:450,000 maps of most provinces published by Ozbekiston Viloyatlari.

Tezykovka Bazaar FLEA MARKET
(Tolarik 1; ⌚Sun) The local, vast flea market of Tezykovka Bazaar is also known as Yangiobod Market. This sombre sea of junk – 'everything from hedgehogs to jackets' as one resident put it – is located in the Khamza District, and reached by bus 30 from the Mustaqillik Maydoni metro. Keep a close watch on your purse or wallet in this or any bazaar.

Mirobod Bazaar FARMERS MARKET
(Gospitalny Bazaar; Mirabod ko'chasi; ⌚8am-6pm; Ⓜ Toshkent) A fiesta of fruit bathing in the teal-green glow of its giant, octagonal flying saucer of a roof.

Oloy Bazaar FARMERS MARKET
(Alaysky Bazaar; Amir Timur ko'chasi; ⌚7am-7pm; Ⓜ Abdulla Qodiriy) Lacks the character of Chorsu, but locals say it has the best, if priciest, produce.

Toshkent Univermagi DEPARTMENT STORE
(TsUM; cnr Uzbekistan & Rashidov; ⌚9am-7pm Mon-Sat; Ⓜ Kosmonavtlar) It doesn't have the atmosphere of the bazaars, but for the best prices and a surprisingly good selection of silk by the metre, try this old Soviet-style department store.

ℹ Information

DANGERS & ANNOYANCES

Tashkent is generally a safe place. Unlike in years gone by, the legions of *militsia* (police) around won't bother you too much. However, metro station entrances are the one place you'll continue to meet police officers, most of whom will let you continue on your way once they've looked inside your bag. Have your passport and valid registration slips on you when riding the metro, and don't even think of taking photos down there.

Tashkent's airport is a generally annoying place. Lines at both immigration and customs are long and disorganised and the whole process can last two or three hours. If you are offered 'help' with your forms or luggage when going through customs, you should politely decline unless you're happy to pay a premium for this service. Ask for two customs forms in English and fill them out on your own.

EMERGENCY

Ambulance (☎03)
Fire Service (☎01)
Police (☎02)

INTERNET ACCESS

With nearly all hotels and many restaurants offering wireless, it's unlikely that you'll need to use internet cafes. We've listed a few central options here, but you'll find them all over the city. The best wireless hotspot, convenient to the hotels in Mirobodsky District, is in the lobby of the four-star **Grand Mir Hotel** (☎140 20 00; Mirobod 2). Ordering a coffee earns you free wi-fi for the day.

Internet (Amir Timur 4; per hr 1800S; ⌚9am-11pm) No gamers here.

Net Club Globus (Shakhrisabz; 2000S per hour; ⌚9am-11pm; Ⓜ Oybek) Underneath the Centre Lavash fast food outlet.

Prime Time (Mirobod12; per hr 2000S; ⌚24hr; Ⓜ Oybek) Fast connection, and hot dogs are sold at the kiosk out front.

MEDICAL SERVICES

In the case of a medical emergency contact your embassy, which can assist with evacuation. Local hospitals are a lot less expensive than Safo Tibbiyot Clinic and Tashkent International Medical Clinic, but are often less than sanitary.

Safo Tibbiyot Clinic (☎255 31 36; www.safouz.com; Ivliev 21; consultation US$10; ⌚9am-6pm; Ⓜ Oybek) Has English-speaking Uzbek doctors. In Mirobodsky District off Usmon Nosir.

Tashkent International Medical Clinic (TIMC; ☎120 1120, 291 07 26, 291 01 42; www.tashclinic.org; Sarikul 38; consultation US$65, after hr US$150; ⌚8am-5pm Mon-Fri) Has state-of-the-art medical and dental facilities and is run by Western and Western-trained doctors who speak English. It's difficult to find; call for directions.

MONEY

Nearly all travellers exchange money on the black market and pay for everything in som, making Tashkent far more affordable than it looks on paper. All open-air farmers markets are teeming with black-market money changers able to change dollars (and usually euro) until early evening.

The ATMs in town are often cashless, and divide into those of **Asaka Bank** (Abdulla Kahhor 73; ⌚9am-5pm Mon-Fri), which offers US dollars to MasterCard holders at 0% commission, and those that operate with Visa cards and give out either US dollars or Uzbek som. Asaka ATMs can be found at the Park Turon and Grand Mir hotels. More prevalent, but rarely functional, are the Visa-card ATMs located in most four-star hotels, including the Tashkent Palace and the Park Turon.

National Bank of Uzbekistan (NBU; Gulomov 95; ⌚8.30am-4pm Mon-Fri; Ⓜ Amir Timur Hiyoboni) Cashes travellers cheques in room

213. For Visa cash advances (3.5%), head to room 212, where English is spoken.

Kapital Bank (Nukus ko'chasi; ⏲9am-5pm Mon-Fri; Ⓜ Toshkent) Charges 2% for cash advances against Visa cards. The office is on the ground floor to the right as you enter the building.

POST

In addition to the **main post office** (pochta bulimi; Shakhrisabz 7; ⏲9am-8pm; Ⓜ Abdulla Qodiriy), there are smaller post offices scattered around town, including a branch near Chorsu Bazaar.

REGISTRATION

OVIR Central Office (☎132 65 70, 231 45 40; Uzbekistan 49A; ⏲9am-5pm Mon-Fri; Ⓜ Ozbekistan)

TELEPHONE

Central Telephone & Telegraph Office (Navoi 28; ⏲9am-6pm; Ⓜ Alisher Navoi) Great connection and a plethora of other telecom services available.

TRAVEL & TOUR AGENCIES

Independent travellers will be happy to know that it's actually easy to go it alone in Uzbekistan. Still, even if you're organising your trip alone, travel agencies can still be useful for planning hassle-free excursions, prearranging domestic air tickets and securing qualified guides for outdoor activities such as trekking, rafting and heli-skiing. Also, if you need a letter of invitation to apply for a visa (see p225) then the assistance of a travel agency is usually essential.

Advantour (☎150 30 20; www.advantour.com; Mirobod lane I 47A; ⏲9am-6pm Mon-Fri; Ⓜ Oybek) Advantour draws rave reviews for its service and can customise tours for both groups and individuals in Uzbekistan and across Central Asia. The personable and knowledgeable owners speak perfect English, and all the major services, from visa support to hotel booking, tours and transportation can be arranged.

Arostr Tourism (☎+998 901 868 648, 256 40 67; www.arostr.uz; Afrosiab 13, office 66; ⏲9am-6pm Mon-Fri; Ⓜ Kosmonavtlar) Arostr is a solid choice for individual travellers as it arranges obligation-free visas, can book hotels, guides and transport and its comprehensive website is a good source of general travel advice.

Asia Adventures (☎252 72 87, 150 62 80; www.centralasia-adventures.com; Kunaev 27/10, office 23; ⏲9am-6pm Mon-Fri; Ⓜ Oybek) This adventure-travel specialist offers a range of exciting mountaineering, camel safari and heli-skiing tours throughout the country, as well as more traditional guided tours of Khiva, Bukhara and Samarkand.

Asian Special Tourism (AST; ☎281 58 60; www.ast.uz; Mironshoh tupik III 18; ⏲9am-6pm Mon-Fri; Ⓜ Toshkent) Few people know the local mountains like agency lead guide Boris Karpov, who also leads the twice-per-month excursions of the Tashkent Hiking Club. This company also runs one- to three-day easy rafting trips on the Syr-Darya around Bekobod, plus the full gamut of standard tours.

Stantours (www.stantours.com) Based in Kazakhstan, David Berghof's superb Stantours arranges obligation-free Uzbek visas and doles out up-to-the-minute advice on securing Central Asian visas in Tashkent, as well as other services such as hotel and flight booking.

VISA EXTENSIONS

One-week visa extensions (US$40) are relatively easy to obtain at the airport – bring plenty of patience, though.

Getting There & Away

AIR

The main international gateways to Tashkent are Moscow, İstanbul, Paris, Frankfurt, Riga and Dubai. Low cost airline Air Baltic's flights from Riga are usually the cheapest route from Europe and North America. Sample one-way fares to/from Tashkent include: Urumqi US$555, Astana US$225, İstanbul US$490, Moscow US$280.

Domestic flights leave from the new domestic terminal (called Terminal 3), about 5km from the international terminal, which is 6km south of the centre.

From Tashkent, Uzbekistan Airways flies to Andijon (US$37, two weekly), Bukhara (US$50, at least daily), Fergana (US$42, daily except Sunday), Nukus (US$68, two daily), Termiz (US$67, three daily), Samarkand (US$21, at least daily) and Urgench (US$85, multiple daily).

Airline Offices

AC Kyrgyzstan (☎252 16 45; Mirobod 27; ⏲9am-6pm Mon-Fri; Ⓜ Oybek) Flies to Bishkek.

Aeroflot (☎120 05 55; Bobur 73; ⏲9am-6pm Mon-Sat) Daily flights to Moscow and connections on to the rest of the world.

Air Baltic (☎120 90 12; Beshyogoch 104A, 2nd fl; ⏲9am-6pm Mon-Sat) Cheap connections to all over Europe via Riga.

Asiana Airlines (☎140 09 01, 140 09 00; Afrosiab 16, Angel's Food Bldg, 2nd fl; ⏲9am-6pm Mon-Sat; Ⓜ Oybek) Flies to Seoul.

China Southern (☎252 16 04; Afrosiab 2, Dalston Business Centre, 2nd fl; ⏰9am-6pm Mon-Fri; Ⓜ Oybek) Flies to Ürümqi and Beijing.

Czech Airlines (☎120 89 89; Air Travel Systems, Mirobod 12/19; ⏰9am-6pm Mon-Fri; Ⓜ Kosmonavtlar) Two flights per week to Prague.

Iran Air (☎233 81 63; Toytepa 1; ⏰9am-6pm Sun-Thu; Ⓜ Amir Timur Hiyoboni) Flies once a week to Tehran.

Korean Air (☎129 20 01; Oybek 28/14; ⏰9am-6pm Mon-Fri; Ⓜ Oybek) Flies to Seoul.

Transaero (☎129 75 55; Nukus kochasi; ⏰9am-6pm Mon-Fri; Ⓜ Toshkent) Flights to Moscow.

Turkish Airlines (☎236 79 89; Navoi 11A; ⏰9am-6pm Mon-Fri; Ⓜ Abdulla Qodiriy) Frequent flights to İstanbul and connections around the world.

Uzbekistan Airways (☎140 02 00; Amur Timur 51; ⏰8am-8pm; Ⓜ Toshkent) Flies to Almaty, Baku, Bangkok, Beijing, Bishkek, Delhi, Dubai, Frankfurt, İstanbul, London, Moscow, Paris, Rome, Seoul and Tel-Aviv, as well as operating domestic flights around the country.

Buying Tickets

International tickets can be bought at any of the ubiquitous *aviakassa* (private travel agents) around town. Domestic tickets can only be bought at the Uzbekistan Airways office in the centre of town, or either the domestic or international terminals of the airport. These must be purchased in cash (US dollars) by foreigners.

BUS & SHARED TAXI

Private buses, marshrutkas and shared taxis to Samarkand, Bukhara (Buxoro) and Urgench leave from two locations: from the Sobir Rahimov private bus station (not to be confused with the public bus station) on prospekt Bunyodkor (Druzhba Narodov), about 7km southwest of Navoi Park, near Sobir Rahimov metro; and from the huge private bus yard behind the Ippodrom Bazaar, 3km beyond Sobir Rahimov metro on pr Bunyodkor. Rides to Termiz, Denau and Karshi leave exclusively from the latter.

The **public bus station** (Tashkent Avtovokzal; ☎279 3929; pr Bunyodkor), across the street from Sobir Rahimov metro, has a smattering of scheduled trips to most major cities.

The main departure point for shared taxis and marshrutkas to the Fergana Valley is near Kuyluk Bazaar, about 20 minutes east of the centre on the Fergana Hwy. Take bus 68 eastbound along Navoi from the Turkuaz stop, or tram 9 from Usmon Nosir ko'chasi or the train station. Alternatively, it's a 7000S taxi ride from the centre.

TRAIN

The most comfortable, if not the most flexible, way to travel westward from Tashkent is via train out of Tashkent's **train station** (zheleznodorozhny vokzal; ☎299 72 16, 299 76 40), next to the Tashkent metro station.

The brand new, super fast 'Afrosoiyob' bullet train to Samarkand departs daily at 8am (economy/business 51,000/68,000S, 2½ hours), while the far cheaper but still very fast 'Sharq' train departs Tashkent at 8.30am daily to Samarkand (economy/business 27,000/41,000S, 3 hrs 40 mins) and continues to Bukhara (economy/business 37,000/57,000S, 6½ hrs).

Slower Soviet-era passenger trains trundle to those and other cities. The following prices are for *platskartny/kupe* (3rd class/2nd class sleeper) carriages: Bukhara (38,000/55,000S, 11 hours, nightly), Nukus (65,000/95,000S, 22 hours, six weekly), Samarkand (29,000/42,000S, 6½ hours, frequent), Termiz (48,000/72,000S, 14 hours, even dates) and Urgench (60,000/88,000S, 22 hours, four weekly).

BUS, SHARED TAXI & MARSHRUTKA

There aren't any schedules, but there are dozens of vehicles heading to all of the following destinations throughout the day. As long as you don't arrive too late in the afternoon, you'll have no problem finding a ride and should be on your way within an hour.

DESTINATION	SHARED TAXI (COST/DURATION)	MARSHRUTKA (COST/DURATION)	BUS (COST/DURATION)
Andijon	40,000S/5hr	25,000S/7hr	-
Bukhara	80,000S/6½hr	50,000S/8hr	30,000S/10hr
Fergana	30,000S/4hr	15,000S/5½hr	-
Kokand	20,000S/3hr	10,000S/4hr	-
Samarkand	25,000S/3½hr	20,000S/4½hr	16,000S/6hr
Termiz	65,000S/9hr	40,000S/12hr	24,000S/13hr
Urgench/Khiva	100,000/12hr	70,000S/13hr	50,000S/20hr

Tashkent Metro

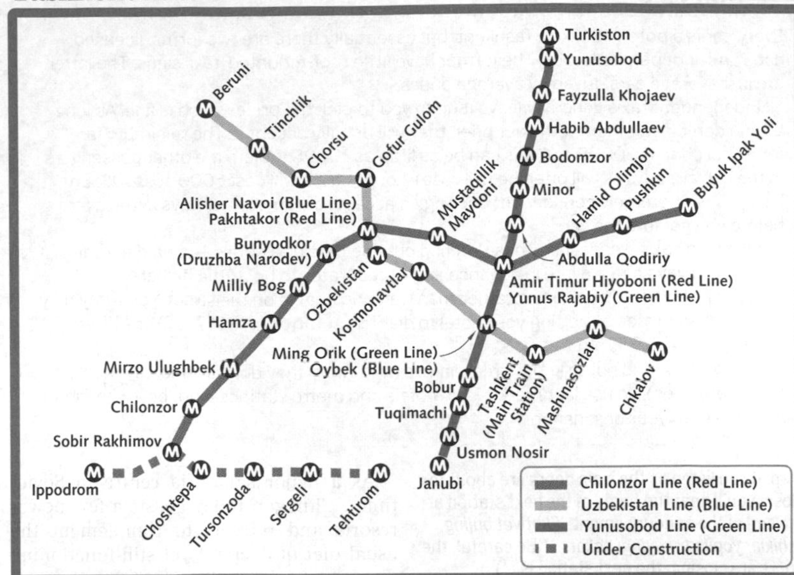

Buying Tickets

The main ticket booth is to the right as you enter the train station; the ticket booth for slow local (*prigorodny*, or 'suburban') trains is on the left. As there are always long lines, many travellers get travel agencies to book tickets for them, or use the 'Hall of Luxury for Rail Passengers', which can be found in the right-hand side of the ticket office. For a very reasonable 3000S per ticket commission, you'll avoid the long lines. You'll need your passport to purchase train tickets (a photocopy won't do).

Getting Around

TO/FROM THE AIRPORT

Buses are the cheapest way to/from the airport. Coming from the airport, they're also an alternative to the taxi drivers who routinely try to rip off out-of-towners. Unfortunately they stop running at 10.30pm despite the fact that many flights arrive in the middle of the night.

Bus 67 travels from the airport to the Intercon via Usmon Nosir, Shakhrisabz and Amir Timur, a 35-minute journey. Marshrutka 62 follows the same route. Buses 11 and 76 go from the airport to Chorsu Bazaar via Bobur and Furqat streets. Bus 11 also connects the international terminal (terminal 2) and the domestic terminal (terminal 3).

The 7km, 20-minute taxi ride to/from the centre of Tashkent should cost no more than 5000S, but you'll need to bargain very hard to get that price at the airport. To elude the airport taxis, simply walk out to the main road to hail a car on the street, or take any bus heading roughly towards the centre and flag down a cheaper taxi there.

If you do end up taking an airport taxi, make sure to agree on a firm price beforehand.

CAR

Any hotel or travel agency can arrange a comfortable private car and driver from about US$10 per hour. You'll pay less – US$5 to US$8 per hour, depending on your negotiating skills – on the street, but you'll usually need some basic Russian for this.

METRO

Tashkent's **metro** (per trip 600S; ⏲ 5am-midnight) is the easiest way to get around. During the day you'll never wait more than five minutes for a train, and the stations are clean and safe, though the security is tight. You'll be required to have your bags inspected twice on the way in to any station, though normally the police are not interested in shake downs, but be sure you always have your passport and registration slips with you. You'll need to buy a *zheton* (token) for each trip. Be aware that photography is strictly forbidden inside the stations.

Despite the use of Uzbek for signs and announcements, the system is easy to use, and well enough signposted that you hardly need a

TAXI TIPS

Every car is a potential taxi in Tashkent, but essentially there are two forms: licensed cabs and 'independent' cabs. The former have little roof-mounted 'taxi' signs. The latter are just average cars driven by average dudes.

Independent taxis generally leave it up to you to pick the price, which is fine. As long as you don't insult them with your offer, they will usually accept it. The minimum fare for a short hop is 3000S, but this can be as little as 1000S if there are other passengers in the cab already (as will often be the case). Longer trips will cost 5000-10,000S: unless you're supremely confident of offering an acceptable amount, always agree a fare before you get into the car.

Licensed cabs – especially those waiting outside bars and hotels – are a different beast, so always agree a fare in advance and expect rates to be a little higher.

If you just want to book a taxi rather than wait and haggle on the street, you'll pay only slightly higher rates by getting your hotel to dial **Taksi Lider** (☎244 77 77) or **Millennium Taxi** (☎129 55 55).

Cab drivers tend not to know street names (and when they do, it's generally the Soviet-era ones), so use landmarks – big hotels and metro stations work best – to direct your driver to your destination.

map. If you listen as the train doors are about to close, you'll hear the name of the next station at the end of the announcement: '*Ekhtiyot buling, eshiklar yopiladi; keyingi bekat...*' ('Be careful, the doors are closing; the next station is...').

PUBLIC TRANSPORT

Buses, trolleybuses and trams cost 600S, payable on board to the conductor or driver. Most of them are marked in Latinised Uzbek and given a number (though some older buses are still marked in Cyrillic).

The destination of public buses, trams, trolleybuses and marshrutkas is written clearly in the window. Useful stops for tourists include: the **Chorsu Bazaar** and **Turkuaz/GUM stops**, on opposite sides of Navoi near Hotel Chorsu; the **train station ('Vokzal') stop** on Shevchenko opposite the train station; the **Grand Mir** (Rossiya) Hotel on Shuta Rustaveli; and **TsUM** (Toshkent Univermagi).

Around Tashkent

Chimgan & Around

Just over an hour northeast of Tashkent by car lies **Ugam-Chatkal National Park**, an outdoor haven loaded with hiking and adventure-sport opportunities as well as more relaxing pursuits. The mountains here are not quite as extreme or scenic as the higher peaks around Almaty and Bishkek, but certain activities (heli-skiing, trekking and rafting come to mind) are more accessible and at least as challenging.

As a major sanatoria centre in Soviet times, Chimgan today boasts a few newer resorts and retreats to complement the usual diet of decrepit yet still-functioning concrete Soviet hulks. And the Chorvok Reservoir offers more mellow outdoor pursuits such as fishing, swimming and canoeing – ask about these at the Chorvok Oromgohi hotel.

This entire area is known locally as Chimgan, a reference to both its biggest town and its central peak, Bolshoy Chimgan (3309m).

Activities

Trekking

Ugam-Chatkal National Park covers the mountainous area west and southwest of the Kyrgyzstan border, from the city of Angren in the south all the way up to the Pskem Mountains in the fingerlike, glacier-infested wedge of land jutting into Kyrgyzstan, northeast of Chimgan town. The Pskem top out at 4319m but are off limits to all but well-heeled heli-skiers because of their location in a sensitive border zone. Should the situation change, this will become prime virgin trekking territory.

For now, all of the national park's accessible terrain lies in the Chatkal Mountains, which stretch into Kyrgyzstan. Lacking the stratospheric height of the big Kyrgyz and Tajik peaks, the appeal of the Chatkals is their accessibility. Escaping civilisation involves walking just a short way out of the Chimgan or Beldersoy ski areas.

Hook up with the Tashkent Hiking Club or talk to Boris at Asian Special Tourism to get the scoop on day and overnight hiking possibilities around here.

A guide is highly recommended for all hikes as the routes are not marked and topographical maps are about as common as Caspian Tigers (which died out from these parts in the 1970s). Guides are mandatory for multiday hikes to secure the necessary border-zone permits and ensure that you don't inadvertently walk into Kyrgyzstan (highly possible given the jigsaw borders).

Skiing & Heli-skiing

In the winter months, downhill skiing is possible at the Beldersoy and Chimgan ski areas. They encompass both the best and the worst of Soviet-style ski resorts. The best: limited grooming, excellent free-riding, some unexpectedly steep terrain, rock-bottom prices and plenty of hot wine and shashlyk. The worst: crummy lifts, limited total acreage and no snow-making to speak of.

The best terrain is way up above the tree line at Beldersoy, accessible by a lone T-bar. From the base, a long, slow double chairlift leads up to the T-bar. With just one chairlift and two trails, Chimgan is more for beginners, but also has challenging free-riding off-piste. A full-day lift pass at either 'resort' costs 25,000S, or you can pay by the ride (T-bar/chairlift 2000/5000S). Beldersoy has surprisingly passable equipment available for hire.

While the resorts are not worth a special trip to Uzbekistan, the helicopter skiing most definitely is, as the Chatkal and Pskem Mountains are reputed to get some of the driest, fluffiest powder you'll find anywhere. Figure on paying US$500 per day for heli-skiing – a bargain by international standards. Book through Asia Adventures.

Rafting

In the warmer months, white-water rafting trips are possible on the raging gazpacho of the Pskem, Ugam and Chatkal rivers. Talk to **Asia Raft** (☎71 267 09 18; www.asiaraft.uz; Mavlono Riezi 77) in Tashkent.

Sleeping

Hotel Chimgan SANATORIUM $

(☎90 105 50 02; Chimgan; r per person incl full board US$15) Here's your chance to experience one of those (barely) still-standing Soviet relics. With a mix of threadbare but clean doubles and quads, it's *the* place to stay for skiers and hikers on a budget.

Around Tashkent

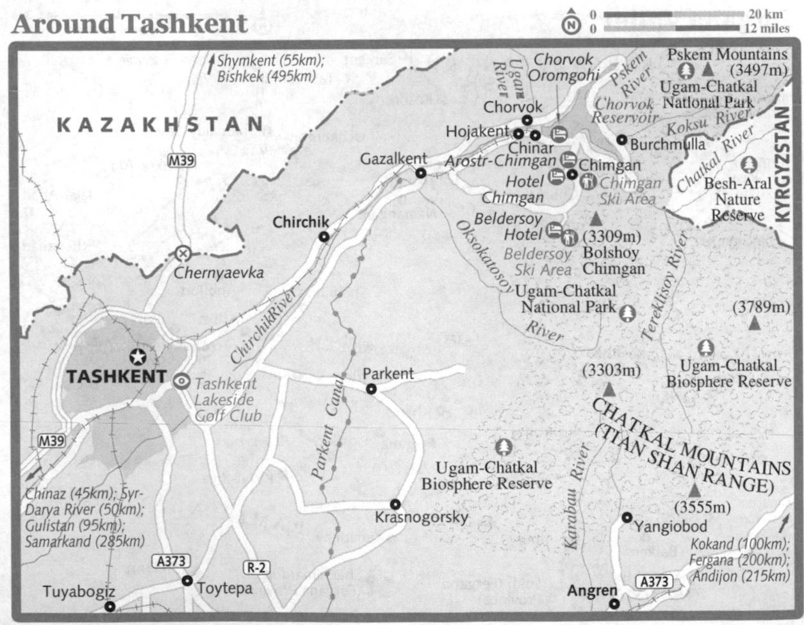

Chorvok Oromgohi HOTEL **$$**
(☎90 188 05 53; Posyolok Bokachul; s/d from US$35/45) This huge pyramid on the shore of the Chorvok Reservoir will certainly catch your eye, for better or for worse. Standard rooms are pretty basic fare; you're paying for the balconies with mountain or lake views.

Beldersoy Hotel HOTEL **$$$**
(☎90 176 38 26; r from US$100; ❄🏊) This swanky four-season mountain lodge belonging to Beldersoy ski area is just outside Chimgan and is the best bet for well-heeled skiers and hikers.

ℹ Getting There & Away

To get to Chimgan from Tashkent, take a marshrutka (3000S) or shared taxi (6000S) from Buyuk Ipak Yoli metro to Gazalkent (50 minutes) and transfer to a shared taxi to Chimgan (10,000S, 40 minutes). A private taxi direct to Chimgan from Tashkent from the metro costs about 80,000S.

FERGANA VALLEY

The first thought many visitors have on arrival in the Fergana Valley is, 'Where's the valley?' From this broad (22,000 sq km), flat bowl, the surrounding mountain ranges (Tian Shan to the north and the Pamir Alay to the south) seem to stand back at enormous distances – when you can see them, that is. More often these spectacular peaks are shrouded in a layer of smog, produced by what is both Uzbekistan's most populous and its most industrial region. The drive here from Tashkent is fairly spectacular, however, passing a huge reservoir and crossing a high mountain pass before descending towards Kokand.

Fergana is also the country's fruit and cotton basket. Drained by the upper Syr-Darya, the Fergana Valley is one big oasis, with some of the finest soil and climate in Central Asia. Already by the 2nd century BC the Greeks, Persians and Chinese found a prosperous kingdom based on farming, with some 70 towns and villages. The Russians were quick to realise the valley's fecundity, and Soviet rulers enslaved it to an obsessive raw-cotton monoculture that still exists today. It is also the centre of Central Asian silk production.

The valley's eight million people are thoroughly Uzbek – 90% overall and higher in the smaller towns. The province has always wielded a large share of Uzbekistan's political, economic and religious influence. Fergana was at the centre of numerous revolts against the tsar and later the Bolsheviks. In

Fergana Valley

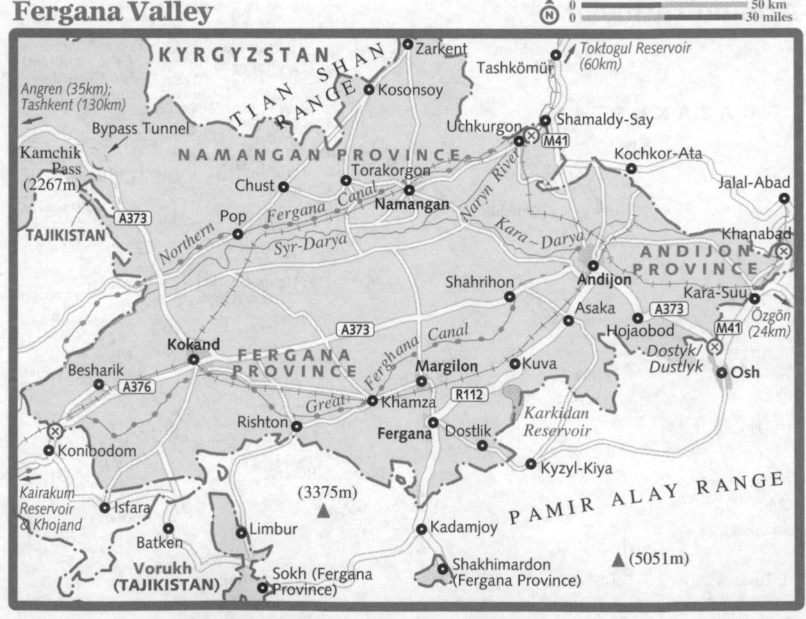

the 1990s the valley gave birth to Islamic extremism in Central Asia. President Karimov's brutal crackdown on alleged extremists eventually came to a head in the form of the Andijon Massacre in 2005, the memory of which still haunts the region today.

The post-Andijon crackdown has increased the police presence in the valley, but it's not something that's likely to affect most tourists as long as they keep a low profile. The valley's people remain among the most hospitable and friendly in the country. Other attractions are exceptional crafts and several kaleidoscopic bazaars.

Dangers & Annoyances

Standards of dress are a potential source of misunderstanding in the valley. Except perhaps in the centre of Russified Fergana town, too much tourist flesh will be frowned upon, so dress modestly (ie no shorts or tight-fitting clothes). Women travellers have reported being harassed when walking alone in cities such as Andijon, especially at night.

Security is tight compared with other parts of the country and all foreigners entering the Fergana Valley must register at a major roadblock west of the tunnels separating the valley from Tashkent. The police are friendly enough, just keep your passport at the ready, be agreeable when being questioned, and be sure to get a registration slip for each night you're in the valley.

Getting There & Around

There is no public bus service between Tashkent and the Fergana Valley – buses aren't allowed on the scenic, winding road through the mountains, which is best negotiated by shared taxi as opposed to wobbly looking Daewoo Damas marshrutkas.

The few slow trains that lumber between Tashkent and the Fergana Valley go through Tajikistan. Do not board these without a Tajik transit visa and a double-entry Uzbek visa.

Within the valley, slow local trains link Kokand and Andijon, but most travel is by shared taxi, marshrutka or bus.

Kokand (Qo'qon)

☎73 / POP 200,000

As the valley's first significant town on the road from Tashkent, Kokand is a gateway to the region and stopping point for many travellers. With a historically interesting palace and several medressas and mosques, it makes for a worthwhile half-day visit.

This was the capital of the Kokand khanate in the 18th and 19th centuries and the valley's true 'hotbed' in those days – second only to Bukhara as a religious centre in Central Asia, with at least 35 medressas and hundreds of mosques. But if you walk the streets today, you will find only a polite, subdued Uzbek town, its old centre hedged by colonial avenues, bearing little resemblance to Bukhara.

Nationalists fed up with empty revolutionary promises met here in January 1918 and declared a rival administration, the 'Muslim Provincial Government of Autonomous Turkestan' led by Mustafa Chokaev. The Tashkent Soviet immediately had the town sacked, most of its holy buildings desecrated or destroyed and 14,000 Kokandis slaughtered.

Traditionally conservative Kokand is changing fast. The central squares, streets and parks have been given massive makeovers in recent years, giving this ancient town a surprisingly modern feel that you can escape from in the backstreets.

Sights

Khan's Palace PALACE

(☎553 60 46; http:museum.dinosoft.uz; Istiklol 2; admission 3000S, guided tours 60000S; ⏰9am-5pm) The Khan's Palace, with seven courtyards and 114 rooms, was built in 1873, though its dazzling tiled exterior makes it look so perfect that you'd be forgiven for thinking it was as new as the modern park that surrounds it. Just three years after its completion, the tsar's troops arrived, blew up its fortifications and abolished the khan's job.

The Khan in question was Khudayar Khan, a cruel ruler who had previously been chummy with the Russians. Just two years after completing the palace, Khudayar was forced into exile by his own subjects, winding up under Russian protection in Orenburg. As his heirs quarrelled for the throne, the Russians moved in and snuffed out the khanate, in the process breaking a promise to eventually return Khudayar to the throne. The homesick khan later fled Orenburg and embarked on an epic odyssey through Central and South Asia before dying of disease near Herat.

Roughly half of the palace used to be taken up by the harem, which the Russians demolished in 1919. Khudayar's 43 concubines would wait to be chosen as wife for

Kokand

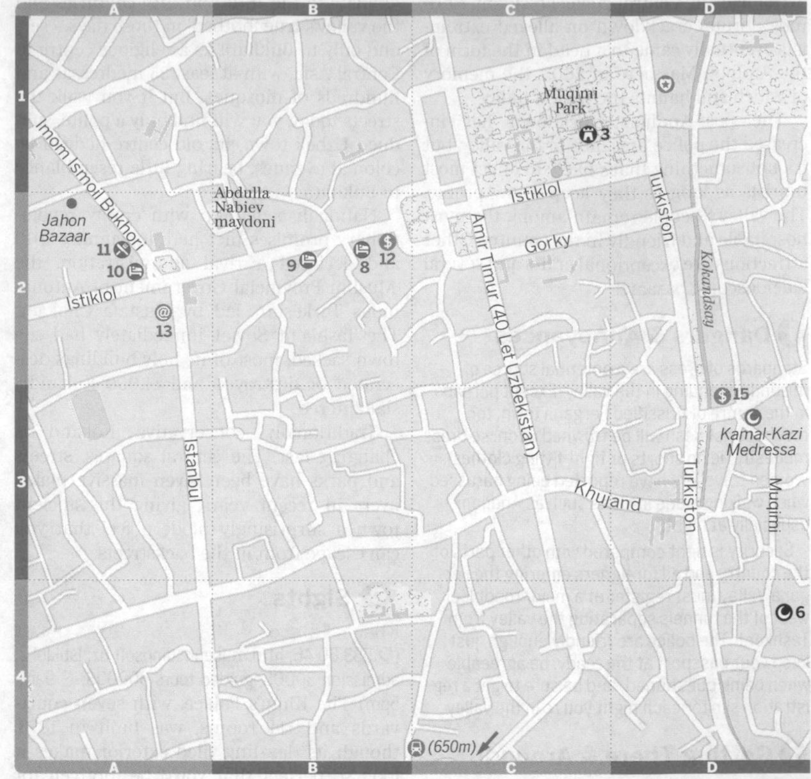

the night – Islam allows only four wives so the khan kept a mullah at hand for a quick marriage ceremony (the marriage set up to last just one night).

Six courtyards remain and their 27 rooms collectively house the Kokand Regional Studies Museum, with displays of varying degrees of interest, and rudimentary signage in English.

Narbutabey Mosque & Medressa MOSQUE

(Akbar Islamov) FREE The Bolsheviks closed the 1799 Narbutabey Medressa, but it opened after independence only to have Karimov shut it down again in 2008. It's now open again and tourists are welcome to visit the medressa (now named the Mir Medressa) and adjacent mosque, which Stalin reopened to win wartime support from Muslim subjects.

Dakhma-i-Shokhon MAUSOLEUM

(Grave of Kings) Entering the graveyard's north gate from the street, proceed straight to the 1830s Dakhma-i-Shokhon (the tomb of Umar Khan and other family members) which has an elegant wooden portal carved with the poetry of Umar's wife, Nodira.

Modari Khan Mausoleum MAUSOLEUM

To the west of the Dakhma-i-Shokhon tomb, the unrestored Modari Khan Mausoleum, built in 1825 for Umar's mother, lies under a bright, sky-blue cupola.

Stone Tablet of Nodira MAUSOLEUM

Originally buried behind Modari Khan, Nodira was adopted by the Soviets as a model Uzbek woman and moved to a prominent place beneath a white stone tablet, beyond Dakhma-i-Shokhon near the graveyard's south gate.

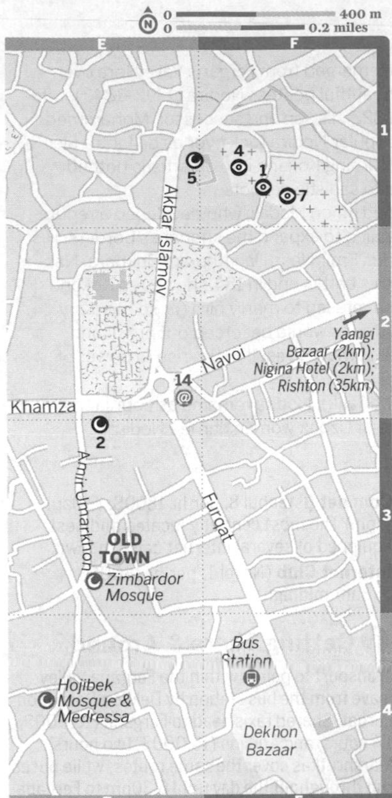

Kokand

Sights

1 Dakhma-i-Shokhon ... F1
2 Jami Mosque Museum ... E3
3 Khan's Palace ... C1
4 Modari Khan Mausoleum ... F1
5 Narbutabey Mosque & Medressa ... E1
6 Sahib Mian Hazrat Medressa ... D4
7 Stone Tablet of Nodira ... F1

Sleeping

8 Hotel Istiqlol ... B2
9 Hotel Khudayarkhan ... B2
10 Hotel Kokand ... A2

Eating

Capriz ... (see 10)
11 Rohatbahsh Chaikhana ... A2

Information

12 Asaka Bank ... B2
13 Com.net ... A2
14 Internet Club ... E2
15 National Bank of Uzbekistan ... D3

Sahib Mian Hazrat Medressa MEDRESSA
(Murqimi; museum admission 2000S; ⏲9am-6pm) Walk five minutes down Muqimi ko'chasi from Khamza ko'chasi to the truncated remnants of the large 19th-century Sahib Mian Hazrat Medressa, where the great Uzbek poet and 'democrat' Mohammedamin Muqimi (1850–1903) lived and studied for the last 33 years of his life. There is a small **museum** in Muqimi's old room, which contains a few of his personal belongings, plus Arabic calligraphy by Muqimi himself.

Jami Mosque Museum MOSQUE
(Khamza 5; admission US$1; ⏲9am-5pm) Kokand's most impressive mosque, built by Umar Khan in 1812, is centred on a 22m minaret and includes a colourful 100m-long *aivan* (portico) supported by 98 red-wood columns brought from India. The entire complex has reverted to its former Soviet guise as a museum, with one room housing a collection of *suzani* and ceramics from the region. The large wall separating the courtyard from the street was being torn down when we visited, heralding a possible new look for the complex.

Sleeping & Eating

For budget accommodation you are better off continuing on to Fergana. At the time of writing a midrange option, **Hotel Istiqlol** (☎+998 916 999 007, +998 916 876 544; off Istiqlol; s/d US$30/50), was newly opened, but hadn't yet received a license to accommodate foreigners. This should change in the near future.

Hotel Kokand HOTEL $
(☎+998 954 004 081, 552 64 03; Imom Ismoil Bukhori 1; s/d/tr US$20/36/54; ❄📶) Following a decent renovation that has seen the implementation of daring colour schemes yet has failed to do much about the dismal bathrooms, the Kokand is a perfectly decent choice and is very popular with locals. All rooms have sofas and TV. Wi-fi is in the lobby only.

Nigina Hotel HOTEL $
(☎552 85 33; Usta Bozor; s/d US$21/36; ❄) Its location out by Yaangi Bazaar is a minus, but it's clean and less expensive than anything in the centre. If you're travelling solo and nobody else turns up, you'll have the shared double to yourself.

NODIRA

Of the pastiche of colourful characters to have emerged from Fergana Valley lore over the years, perhaps the most beloved was the beautiful poetess Nodira (1792–1842), wife of Umar Khan of Kokand. When Umar died in 1822, his son and successor, Mohammed Ali (Madali Khan), was only 12 years old. The popular Nodira took over as de facto ruler of the khanate for the better part of a decade, turning Kokand into an artistic hotbed and oasis of liberalism in a region accustomed to sadistic despots.

Unfortunately, little of this liberal spirit rubbed off on Madali, who developed a reputation for ruthlessness during a successful campaign to expand the khanate's borders. His territorial ambitions drew the ire of the notorious Emir Nasrullah Khan of Bukhara. Nasrullah would eventually get the upper hand in this battle, and in 1842 he seized Kokand and executed Madali, his brother and, when she refused to marry him (or so the story goes), Nodira. Within three months the Emir's troops would be forced out of Kokand, touching off a battle for succession that would ultimately result in the rise to power of Khudayar Khan, a distant cousin of Madali.

Best known for her poetry (in both Uzbek and Tajik), Nodira remains as popular as ever today, as evidenced by the preponderance of Uzbek women named Nodira.

Hotel Khudayarkhan HOTEL **$$**
(☎553 77 47, 552 22 44; www.khan.uz; Istiklol 31; s/d US$33/59; ❄📶) By far the best option in town, the family-run Khudayarkhan (sometimes simply called Hotel Khan) exhibits an unusual amount of panache for Uzbekistan. Little extras such as felt slippers, free bottled water and flat-screen TVs make all the difference. Rooms are modern, stylishly furnished and have good bathrooms with high water pressure. Request a quieter room away from the main road.

Rohatbahsh Chaikhana TEAHOUSE **$**
(Imom Ismoil Bukhori 1; shashlyk 2000S; ⌚8am-8pm) This popular chaikhana (teahouse), also known as Jahon Chaikhana, tends to close earlier than advertised, but during daylight hours it's the best option in town.

Capriz CAFE **$$**
(Imom Ismoil Bukhori 1; mains 5000-11,000S; ⌚8am-10pm) Clean premises and a menu of Russian and Uzbek staples makes this Kokand's best all-around eating option. We can heartily recommend the *prazhskaya kotleta* (Prague cutlet: fried beef with eggs and cheese).

Information

Black market money changers hang out at Dekhon Bazaar (the main farmers market), near the bus station. OVIR's Kokand office does not handle foreigner registrations; register in Fergana if you're not staying in a hotel here.

Asaka Bank (Istiklol ko'chasi; ⌚9am-5pm Mon-Fri) Advances cash on MasterCard.

Com.net (İstanbul 8; per hr 1800S; ⌚9am-11pm) The most centrally located and best equipped of several internet cafes in town.

Internet Club (Navoi 1; per hr 1600S; ⌚8am-midnight)

Getting There & Around

Transport to points within the Fergana Valley leave from the bus station by Dekhon Bazaar on Furqat. Shared taxis head to Fergana (10,000S, 1¼ hours) and Andijon (15,000S, two hours). Marshrutkas cover the same routes, while buses run throughout the day until 6.30pm to Fergana (5000S, two hours) and Andijon (10,000S, four hours). Regular buses to Rishton (2500S, 45 minutes), leave from the Yaangi Bazaar, 2km east of the main bus station.

Shared taxis to Tashkent congregate at what's known to locals as 'Pitak Tashkent' about 5km north of town (20,000S, four hours). A taxi to here from the centre of Kokand will cost you 3000S.

From the **train station** (Amir Timur 40), there is a 5am train to Andijon via Namangan, and a 2.30pm train to Andijon via Margilon (both 3000S, five hours).

Useful public transport options include marshrutka 2 or 4 from Dekhon Bazaar to the Hotel Kokand area, and marshrutka 15, 28 or 40 north from the bazaar to the Jami Mosque.

Fergana (Farg'ona)

☎73 / POP 216,000

Tree-lined avenues and pastel-plastered tsarist buildings give Fergana the feel of a mini-Tashkent. Throw in the best services and accommodation in the region, plus a central location, and you have the most obvious base from which to explore the rest of the valley.

Fergana is the valley's least ancient and least Uzbek city. It began in 1877 as Novy Margelan (New Margilon), a colonial annexe to nearby Margilon. It became Fergana in the 1920s. It's a nice enough place to hang out, and somewhat cosmopolitan with its relatively high proportion of Russian and Korean inhabitants.

Sights

Bazaar MARKET

Fergana's most appealing attraction is the bazaar, filled with good-natured Uzbek traders, leavened with Korean and Russian vendors selling homemade specialities. It sprawls over several blocks north of the centre, and is a pleasant place to explore and to soak up local colour.

Museum of Regional Studies MUSEUM

(224 31 91; Murabbiylar 26; admission 4000S; 9am-5pm Wed-Sun, to 1pm Mon) The sparse Museum of Regional Studies covers the Fergana region, including Kokand and Margilon. Visitors can inspect satellite photos of a green, lush Fergana Valley nestled amid snow-capped peaks.

Sleeping

Asia Hotel and Club Hotel 777 accept som converted at official rates; the rest convert at black-market rates.

Valentina's Guesthouse HOMESTAY $

(224 89 05; daniol26@yandex.ru; Al-Farghoni 11, apt 10; r per person US$15;) This very Russian homestay has six big, comfortable rooms with king-sized beds in two neighbouring Soviet apartments. The hulking apartment block, topped by a huge antenna, sticks out like a sore thumb; take the left-hand entrance and walk to the fourth floor (the lift is unreliable). Valentina speaks Russian and is exceptionally friendly.

Golden Valley Homestay APARTMENTS $

(215 07 33; ijod@inbox.ru; Shakirovoy 10; r per person US$15;) Golden Valley has three well-maintained apartments for you to stay in. Walk east from Hotel Ziyorat for 1km on Kurbunjon Dodhoh, go left on Shakirovoy, and immediately turn right. Or call for a pick-up.

★ **Taj Mahal Hotel** HOTEL $$

(224 45 25; Marifat ko'chasi 38; s/d/lux US$38/49/57-68;) This brand new place has no link to India – the owners told us they simply liked the name – but it's nevertheless the best choice in town, with a very central location, sparkling rooms with comfortable furnishings and friendly staff.

Club Hotel 777 RESORT $$

(224 37 77; Pushkin 7A; s/d from US$50/70;) With a few bungalows and a festive poolside bar, this sprawling number just south of the centre is about as close as you're likely to come to Club Med in double-landlocked Uzbekistan. The tour-group oriented 'Three Sevens' excels in all facets save the location.

Asia Hotel HOTEL $$$

(224 52 21; www.asiahotels.uz; Navoi 26; s/d from US$55/83;) A comfortable, if pricey option used by the Marco Polo travel agency, but also open to individual travellers.

Hotel Ziyorat HOTEL

(224 77 42; Dekhon 2A) This hotel was undergoing a total refit when we visited. Expect a step up in price and quality from its former cheap, unrenovated, unabashedly Soviet self.

Eating & Drinking

Shashlyk stands occupy Al-Farghoni Park in the warm months; a cluster of them are along pedestrian Mustaqillik near the TsUM department store.

★ **Bravo** INTERNATIONAL $$

(Khojand 12; mains 8000-12,000S; 9am-11pm;) Nowhere is Fergana's liberal bent more evident than in this bohemian little cafe. The shabby-chic interior is plastered with the products of local artists and awash with the strains of live jazz. In the warmer months the action moves outside to the patio where there are *tapchan* (teabeds) in the sunshine.

Traktir Ostrov Sokrovish INTERNATIONAL $$

(Treasure Island Tavern; Marifat 45; mains 5000-25,000S; 10am-midnight;) This centrally located place hums with locals at all times of the day, and when it's warm outside the summer terrace is the place to be. The food is nothing special, but there is the luxury (rare in Uzbekistan) of choice, with pizza, sushi and salads to supplement the usual offerings of shashky and soup.

Fergana

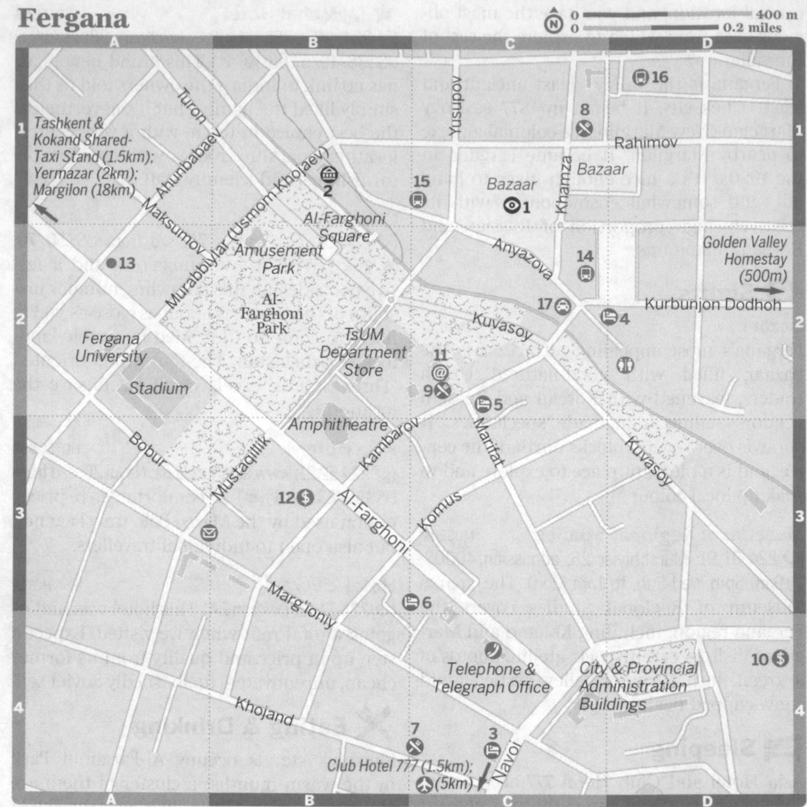

Chimyan CHAIKHANA
(cnr Rahimov & Khamza; mains 4000S) Near the bazaar you'll find several chaikhanas, including Chimyan.

Information

Black-market money changers can be found at the bazaar. The Asia Hotel has a 24-hour official currency exchange.

Asaka Bank (cnr Navoi & Kuvasoy; ⏲9am-5pm Mon-Fri) You can get cash out on your MasterCard here.

Lion Net (Kambarov 47; per hr 1200S; ⏲24hr) Internet access.

National Bank of Uzbekistan (Al-Farghoni 35; ⏲9am-5pm Mon-Fri) A cash-advance office for Visa cardholders is on the 3rd floor.

OVIR (Office of Visas & Registration; Ahunbabaev 36; ⏲9am-5pm Mon-Fri)

Post Office (Mustaqillik 35; ⏲7am-7pm)

Getting There & Away

AIR

Uzbekistan Airways has flights to/from Tashkent (US$42, daily except Sunday).

BUS & SHARED TAXI

Shared taxis depart from a lot opposite the Hotel Ziyorat in the centre of town to Kokand (10,000S, one hour) and Andijon (10,0000S, 1¼ hours) throughout the day, as soon as they're full.

More shared taxis, marshrutkas and buses depart to Andijon throughout the day from the **old long-distance bus station**, north of the bazaar (marshrutka/taxi per seat 10,000S, 1¼ hours; bus 5000S, two hours). This is also a good spot to find rides to Margilon (marshrutka/taxi per seat 1500/2500S, 20 minutes). Change in Margilon for Namangan.

Buses to Rishton (4000S, 50 minutes) and Kokand (6500S, two hours) use the **new local bus station** southeast of the bazaar. Marshrutkas to Rishton and Margilon depart from a stop

Fergana

Sights

1 Bazaar C1
2 Museum of Regional Studies B1

Sleeping

3 Asia Hotel C4
4 Hotel Ziyorat D2
5 Taj Mahal Hotel C2
6 Valentina's Guesthouse C3

Eating

7 Bravo C4
8 Chimyan C1
9 Traktir Ostrov Sokrovish C2

Information

10 Asaka Bank D4
11 Lion Net C2
12 National Bank of Uzbekistan B3
13 OVIR A2

Transport

14 New Local Bus Station C2
15 New Long-Distance Bus Station C1
16 Old Long-Distance Bus Station D1
17 Taxis to Kokand C2

near yet another bus station, the **new long-distance bus station**.

Shared taxis to Tashkent (30,000S, five hours), as well as more to Kokand, leave from a stop on the road to Margilon near Yermazar Bazaar, 2km northwest of the centre.

Getting Around

The airport is a 25-minute trip on marshrutka 6 to/from the new local bus station. Going to the airport you can flag it down in front of Asia Hotel, but check with the driver to make sure he's going all the way to the *aeroport*.

Around Fergana

Margilon (Marg'ilan)

73 / POP 197,000

If you've been travelling along the Silk Road seeking answers to where, in fact, this highly touted fabric comes from, Margilon and its Yodgorlik Silk Factory will be your answer. Uzbekistan is the world's third-largest silk producer, and Margilon is the traditional centre of the industry.

Although there is little to show for it, Margilon has been around for a long time, probably since the 1st century BC. For centuries its merchant clans, key players in Central Asia's commerce and silk trade, were said to be a law unto themselves; even in the closing decades of Soviet rule, this was the heart of Uzbekistan's black-market economy. Margilon is also one of the country's most devoutly Islamic cities.

Sights

A good tour guide should be able to get keen silk connoisseurs into the private homes of weavers whose silk is for sale at Kumtepa Bazaar. They should also be able to organise tours to one of Margilon's larger commercial silk factories.

There's no need to spend the night here, but if you decide to, your choices are the modern **Hotel Atlas** (279 00 75; hoteladras@gmail.com; B Margiloni 32; s/d US$30/50;), which has an impressive lobby but rather ordinary rooms with hard mattresses, or you can get the Yodgorlik Silk Factory to arrange a homestay.

Yodgorlik Silk Factory FACTORY

(233 88 24; silk@mail.ru; Imam Zakhriddin; admission 10,000S; 8am-5pm Mon-Sat Apr-Oct, Mon-Fri Nov-Mar) Margilon's main attraction is this fascinating factory, which can be explored on a tour where you'll witness traditional methods of silk production from steaming and unravelling the cocoons to the weaving of the dazzling *khanatlas* (hand-woven silk, patterned on one side) fabrics for which Margilon is famous. After the tour (available in English, French, Russian or German), you can buy silk by the metre and offset your purchases against your entry fee. There is also premade clothing, carpets and embroidered items for sale.

Kumtepa Bazaar BAZAAR

(Thu & Sun) A much less sanitised experience than the Silk Factory is Margilon's fantastic Kumtepa Bazaar, 5km west of the centre. It's a time capsule full of weathered Uzbek men in traditional clothing exchanging solemn greetings and gossiping over endless pots of tea, with hardly a Russian or a tourist in sight. Margilon's conservative streak, extreme even by Fergana Valley standards, is in full view here, with Uzbek matrons dressed almost exclusively in the locally produced *khanatlas* dresses and head scarves and men in skull caps and *chapan*. Rows of handmade *khanatlas* and *adras* silk, available for just 4000S to 5000S per metre, are both the shopping highlight and the visual highlight – have your camera ready. It's probably the most interesting bazaar in the country. The main day for the bazaar is Sunday, but it also works on Thursdays.

Take a taxi (5000S) or 'Bozor' mashrutka to get here.

Getting There & Away

Marshrutkas and taxis drop you off near the town's main intersection, kitty-corner from the central bazaar.

Rishton

73 / POP 22,000

This town just north of the Kyrgyzstan border is famous for the ubiquitous cobalt and green pottery fashioned from its fine clay. About 90% of the ceramics you see in souvenir stores across Uzbekistan originates here – most of it handmade.

Some one thousand potters make a living from the legendary local loam, which is so pure that it requires no additives (besides water) before being chucked on the wheel.

Of those thousand potters only a handful are considered true masters who still use traditional techniques. Among them is Rustam Usmanov, erstwhile art director of the defunct local collectivised ceramics factory. He runs the **Rishton Ceramic Museum** (271 18 65, 452 15 85; Ar-Roshidony 230; 9am-6pm) out of his home 1km west of the centre on the main road to Kokand. Usmanov gives free tours of his workshop as well as lunch (20,000S) and vodka shots to travellers who call ahead.

Rishton is best visited as a stop between Fergana and Kokand. It's about a 45-minute shared taxi ride from either (4000S), or take a slower bus (2500S).

Andijon

74 / POP 580,000

Andijon – the Fergana Valley's largest city and its spiritual mecca – will forever be linked with the bloodshed of 13 May 2005 (see p219). The very word 'Andijon' is a hot potato in Uzbekistan; just mentioning it is enough to stop any conversation in its tracks. That's a shame because both culturally and linguistically Andijon is probably the country's purest Uzbek city, and the best place to observe Uzbeks in their element.

Sights

Jahon Bazaar BAZAAR

(9am-6pm) Andijon's Jahon Bazaar is the biggest bazaar on the Uzbek side of the Fergana Valley. Sunday and Thursday are its busiest days, and there are also silk stalls here, in case you miss Kumtepa Bazaar in Margilon. From Kolkhoz Bazaar, it's 4km northeast on marshrutka 6, 10 or anything saying Жахон бозор/Jahon Bozor.

Jome Mosque & Medressa MOSQUE

(admission 4000S; 9am-4pm Tue-Sun) Across from Eski Bazaar (on Oltinkul) is the handsome 19th-century Jome Mosque & Medressa, said to be the only building to survive the 1902 earthquake. It reopened as a working medressa in the 1990s but was turned into a museum of local ethnography after a police crackdown on suspected Islamic militants. The museum's highlight is its collection of folk instruments.

Babur Literary Museum MUSEUM

(Bazernaya 21; admission 2500S; 9am-6pm Tue-Sat) This museum occupies the site of the royal apartments where Zahiruddin Babur lived and studied as a boy within Ark-Ichy, the town's long-gone citadel. Born in 1483 in Andijon to Fergana's ruler, Umar Sheikh Mirzo (a descendant of Timur), Babur inherited his father's kingdom before he was even a teenager. The young king took Samarkand at the tender age of 14, but subsequently lost both Samarkand and Fergana and was driven into Afghanistan by the Uzbek Shaybanids before ultimately going on to found the Mughal Empire in India. However, this museum focuses on Babur's literary exploits, specifically his Baburnama, a vast memoir of Babur's fascinating and tumultuous life.

Sleeping & Eating

There are several modern hotels in town, and a large choice of chaikhanas around the bazaars and just about everywhere else.

Hotel Andijon HOTEL $

(226 23 88; Fitrat 241; r without/with bathroom US$12/18, half-lux US$28) This no-frills Soviet-style hotel across from Navoi Sq sports a typical mix of tatty unrenovated rooms and somewhat renovated half-*lux* rooms. The shared bathroom is appalling – opt for a private one.

Hamkor Hotel HOTEL $$
(☎150 30 20; Babur 53; s/d US$50/70; ❄📶) Well located in the centre of the city, this modern hotel boasts spacious rooms, English-speaking staff and an abnormal understanding of the needs of travellers.

Bosco RUSSIAN $$
(Istiklol 8; mains 8000-15,000S; ⏰9am-9pm) For something fancier than *plov*, try Bosco, which serves up good soups and a standard menu of Russian classics.

ℹ Information

Black market money changers can be found outside Eski Bazaar. Head to **Asaka Bank** (Furkat 2A) for MasterCard cash advances, while the **National Bank of Uzbekistan** (Navoi 42) takes care of Visa cash advances.

ℹ Getting There & Around

Uzbekistan Airways (wwww.uzairways.com; airport) has four weekly flights to/from Tashkent (US$37, twice weekly). The airport is 3km southwest of the train station.

All public transport and shared taxis leave from in and around the bus station. There are plenty of rides to Fergana (marshrutka/taxi per seat 10,000S, 1¼ hours; bus 5000S, two hours) and Tashkent (shared taxi 30,000S, five hours).

Marshrutka 33 travels from Eski Bazaar in the old town past Navoi Sq, Villa Elegant Hotel and Hotel Oltyn Vody before passing near the airport. Any marshrutka signboarded 'Ески Шахар' ('Eski Shahar' or Old Town) goes to Eski Bazaar.

CENTRAL UZBEKISTAN

Samarkand (Samarqand)

☎66 / POP 596,300 / ELEV 710M

We travel not for trafficking alone,

By hotter winds our fiery hearts are fanned.

For lust of knowing what should not be known

We take the Golden Road to Samarkand.

These final lines of James Elroy Flecker's 1913 poem *The Golden Journey to Samarkand* evoke the romance of Uzbekistan's most glorious city. No name is so evocative of the Silk Road as Samarkand. For most people it has the mythical resonance of Atlantis, fixed in the Western popular imagination by poets and playwrights of bygone eras, few of whom saw the city in the flesh.

On the ground the sublime, larger-than-life monuments of Timur, the technicolour bazaar and the city's long, rich history indeed work some kind of magic. Surrounding these islands of majesty, modern Samarkand sprawls across acres of Soviet-built buildings, parks and broad avenues used by buzzing Daewoo taxis.

You can visit most of Samarkand's high-profile attractions in two or three days. If you're short on time, at least see the Registan, Gur-e-Amir, Bibi-Khanym Mosque and Shah-i-Zinda.

Away from the main attractions Samarkand is a modern, well-groomed city, which has smartened itself up enormously in the past decade. This process has involved building walls around some of the less sightly parts of the old town, which many consider to have made the old city rather sterile, blocking off streets that have been linking quarters for centuries. While this 'disneyfication' of this once chaotic place is undeniable, it's also true to say that Samarkand remains a breathtaking place to visit.

History

Samarkand (Marakanda to the Greeks), one of Central Asia's oldest settlements, was probably founded in the 5th century BC. It was already the cosmopolitan, walled capital of the Sogdian empire when it was taken in 329 BC by Alexander the Great, who said, 'Everything I have heard about Marakanda is true, except that it's more beautiful than I ever imagined.'

A key Silk Road city, it sat on the crossroads leading to China, India and Persia, bringing in trade and artisans. From the 6th to the 13th century it grew into a city more populous than it is today, changing hands every couple of centuries – Western Turks, Arabs, Persian Samanids, Karakhanids, Seljuq Turks, Mongolian Karakitay and Khorezmshah have all ruled here – before being obliterated by Chinggis Khan in 1220.

This might have been the end of the story, but in 1370 Timur decided to make Samarkand his capital, and over the next 35 years forged a new, almost-mythical city –

Samarkand

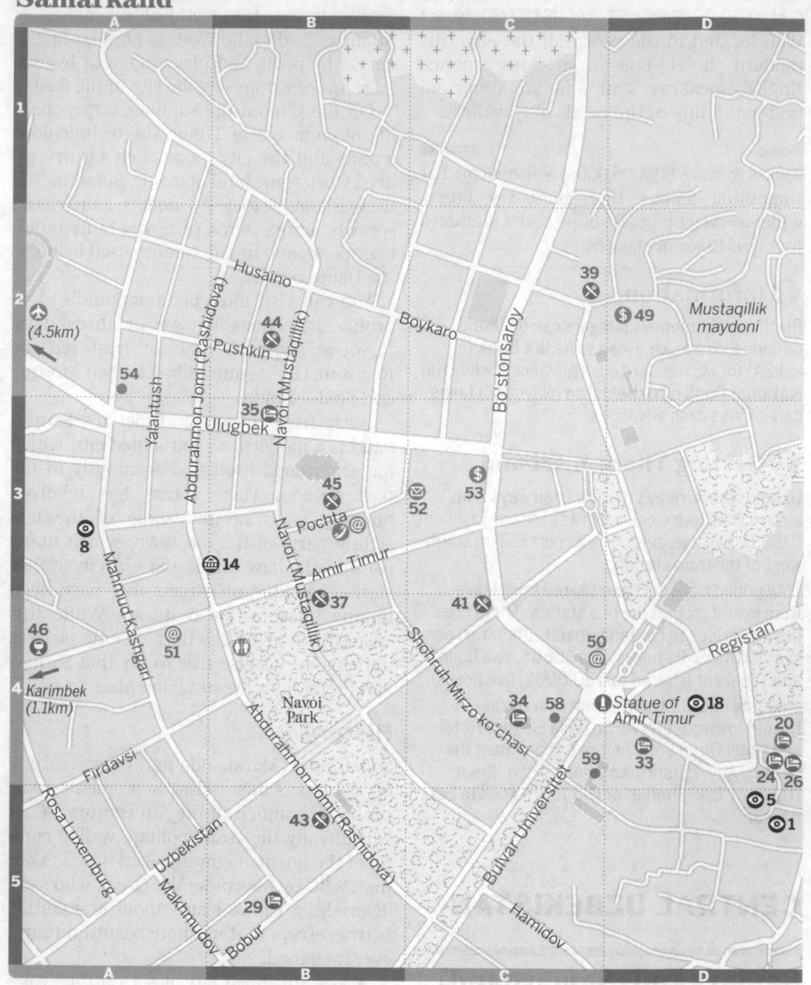

Central Asia's economic and cultural epicentre. His grandson Ulugbek ruled until 1449 and made it an intellectual centre as well.

When the Uzbek Shaybanids came in the 16th century and moved their capital to Bukhara, Samarkand went into decline. For several decades in the 18th century, after a series of earthquakes, it was essentially uninhabited. The emir of Bukhara forcibly repopulated the town towards the end of the century, but it was only truly resuscitated by the Russians, who forced its surrender in May 1868 and linked it to the Russian Empire by the Trans-Caspian railway 20 years later.

Sights

You can enter the courtyards of some of the main sights outside working hours for free or by 'tipping' the guard on duty; the Registan and Bibi-Khanym are spectacular in the early morning light; Gur-e-Amir is sublime by night.

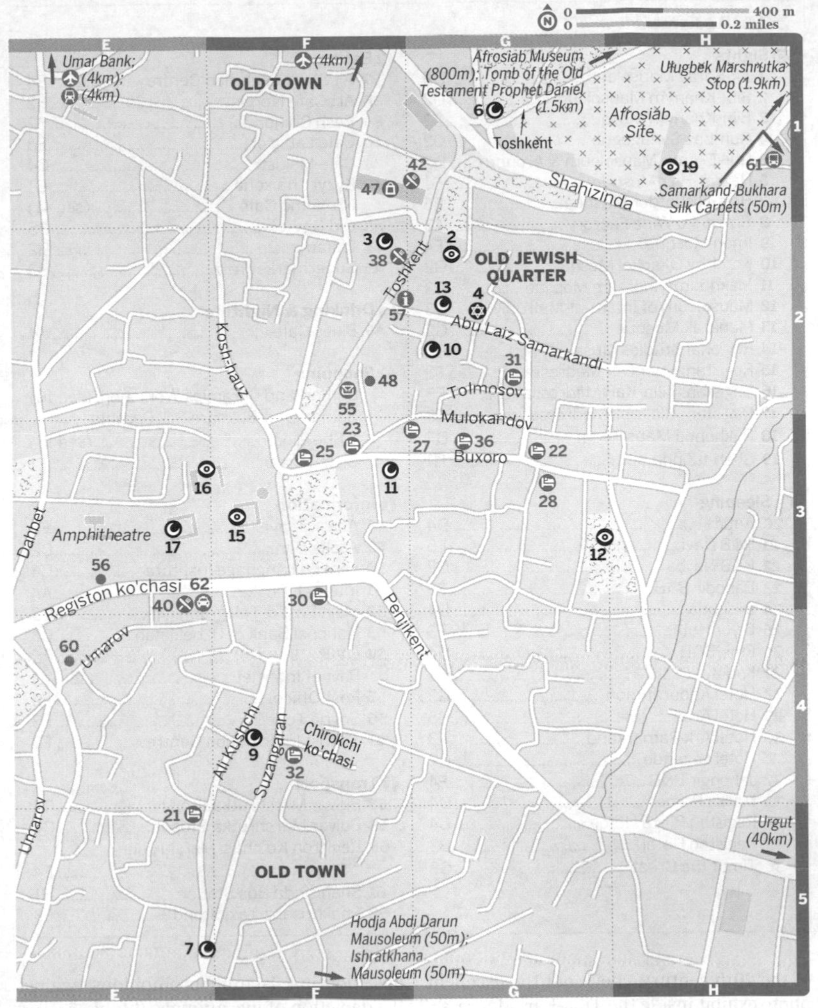

Old Town

The Registan PLAZA

(cnr Registan & Toshkent; admission 14,400S; 9am-8pm Apr-Oct, 9am-5pm Nov-Mar) This ensemble of majestic, tilting medressas – a near-overload of majolica, azure mosaics and vast, well-proportioned spaces – is the centrepiece of the city, and arguably the most awesome single sight in Central Asia. The Registan, which translates to 'Sandy Place' in Tajik, was medieval Samarkand's commercial centre and the plaza was probably a wall-to-wall bazaar.

The three grand edifices here are among the world's oldest preserved medressas, anything older having been destroyed by Chinggis Khan. They have taken their knocks over the years courtesy of the frequent earthquakes that buffet the region; that they are still standing is a testament to the incredible craftsmanship of their builders. The Soviets, to their credit, worked feverishly to restore these beleaguered treasures, but they also took some questionable liberties, such as the capricious addition of a blue outer dome to the Tilla-Kari Medressa. For an idea of just how ruined the medressas were at the start

Samarkand

Sights

1 Ak-Saray Mausoleum ... D5
2 Bibi-Khanym Mausoleum ... G2
3 Bibi-Khanym Mosque ... F2
4 Gumbaz Synagogue ... G2
5 Gur-E-Amir Mausoleum & Around ... D5
6 Hazrat-Hizr Mosque ... G1
7 Hoja-Nisbatdor Mosque ... E5
8 Hovrenko Wine Factory ... A3
9 Imon Mosque ... F4
10 Koroboy Oksokol Mosque ... G2
11 Makhdumi Khorezm Mosque ... F3
12 Mausoleum of Imam-al-Matrudiy ... G3
13 Mubarak Mosque ... G2
14 Regional Studies Museum ... B3
15 Registan: Sher Dor Medressa ... F3
16 Registan: Tilla-Kari Medressa ... E3
17 Registan: Ulugbek Medressa ... E3
18 Rukhobod Mausoleum ... D4
19 Shah-i-Zinda ... H1

Sleeping

20 Antica ... D4
21 B&B Davr ... E5
22 B&B Najiba ... G3
23 Bahodir B&B ... F3
24 Dilshoda ... D4
25 Diyor Hotel ... F3
26 Emir B&B ... D4
27 Furkat ... G3
28 Hotel Abdurahmon ... G3
29 Hotel Arba ... B5
30 Hotel Ark Samarkand ... F3
31 Hotel Légende ... G2
32 Jahongir B&B ... F4
33 Malika Prime ... D4
34 Registan Plaza Hotel ... C4
35 Registon Hotel ... B3
36 Timur the Great ... G3

Eating

37 Alt Stadt Laghman Centre ... B4
38 Art Cafe Norgis ... F2
39 Besh Chinor ... C2
40 Cafe Labig'or ... E3
41 Cafe Magistr ... C4
42 Kyzyl Chaixona ... G1
No Name Café ... (see 41)
43 Old City ... B5
44 Platan ... B2
45 Supermarket Aziz ... B3

Drinking & Nightlife

46 Blues Cafe ... A4

Shopping

Samarkand Ceramics Workshop . (see 16)
Samarkand-Bukhara Silk Carpets Showroom ... (see 15)
47 Siob Bazaar ... F1

Information

48 Abask Travel ... F2
49 Asaka Bank ... D2
50 Foreign Language Institute ... C4
51 Internet Tim ... A4
52 Main Post & Telegraph Office ... C3
53 National Bank of Uzbekistan ... C3
54 OVIR ... A2
Paynet Internet ... (see 41)
55 Post Office ... F2
56 Sogda Tour ... E3
57 Tourist Information Centre ... F2

Transport

58 Bulvar Marshrutka Stop I ... C4
59 Bulvar Marshrutka Stop II ... C4
60 Registon Ko'chasi Marshrutka Stop ... E4
61 Shahizinda Bus Station ... H1
62 Shakhrisabz Taxi Stand ... E3

of the 20th century, check out the excellent photo exhibit inside the Tilla-Kari Medressa.

Ulugbek Medressa, on the west side, is the original medressa, finished in 1420 under Ulugbek (who is said to have taught mathematics here; other subjects taught here included theology, astronomy and philosophy). Beneath the little corner domes were lecture halls, and at the rear a large mosque with a beautiful interior and an austere teaching room to one side.

The other buildings are rough imitations by the Shaybanid Emir Yalangtush. The entrance portal of the **Sher Dor (Lion) Medressa**, opposite Ulugbek's and finished in 1636, is decorated with roaring felines that look like tigers but are meant to be lions, flouting Islamic prohibitions against the depiction of live animals. It took 17 years to build but hasn't held up as well as the Ulugbek Medressa, built in just three years.

In between them is the **Tilla-Kari (Gold-Covered) Medressa**, completed in 1660, with a pleasant, gardenlike courtyard. The highlight here is the mosque, which is on the left-hand side of the courtyard and is intricately decorated with gold to symbolise Samarkand's wealth at the time it was built. The mosque's delicate ceiling, oozing gold leaf, is flat but its tapered design makes it look domed from the inside. Inside the mosque is a magnificent picture gallery featuring blown-up black-and-white photos of old Samarkand.

Another interesting picture gallery is the Ulugbek Medressa's mosque. Many of the medressas' former dormitory rooms are now art and souvenir shops. In the high season mock weddings are put on for tourists in the Sher Dor courtyard, while tacky sound-and-light shows take place in the square.

From dawn until opening time police guards offer to clandestinely escort visitors to the top of a minaret for 10,000S or more, but this is negotiable. If you come during the day, note that your ticket is valid all day, allowing you to come back and photograph the complex at the various times of day needed for the sunlight to be coming from the right direction. However, tell the complex security guards if you'd like to do this, otherwise they will tear your ticket and you won't be able to reuse it.

Bibi-Khanym Mosque MOSQUE

(Toshkent yo'li; admission 9000S; ⏲8am-7pm Apr-Oct, 9am-5pm Nov-Mar) The enormous congregational Bibi-Khanym Mosque, northeast of the Registan, was finished shortly before Timur's death and must have been the jewel of his empire. Once one of the Islamic world's biggest mosques (the cupola of the main mosque is 41m high and the *pishtak* 38m), it pushed contemporary construction techniques to the limit.

Slowly crumbling over the years, the mosque partially collapsed in an earthquake in 1897 before being rebuilt in the 1970s. Today it's badly in need of further restoration work, especially on its façade, while the mosque itself looks as though it may fall in on itself at any moment, although the souvenir sellers inside continue to ply their trade without an apparent worry in the world.

Legend says that Bibi-Khanym, Timur's Chinese wife, ordered the mosque built as a surprise while he was away. The architect fell madly in love with her and refused to finish the job unless he could give her a kiss. The smooch left a mark and Timur, on seeing it, executed the architect and decreed that women should henceforth wear veils so as not to tempt other men.

The interior courtyard contains an enormous marble Quran stand that lends some scale to the place. Local lore has it that any woman who crawls under the stand will have lots of children. The courtyard also contains two smaller mosques. The one on the left as you enter through the enormous main gate has an impressive unrestored interior festooned with Arabic calligraphy.

Bibi-Khanym Mausoleum MAUSOLEUM

(Toshkent yo'li; admission 7000S; ⏲8am-6pm) Across Toshkent yo'li is Bibi-Khanym's own compact 14th-century mausoleum, brightly restored in 2007. It's rather overpriced for what it is, given the impressive mosque across the road only costs slightly more.

Shah-i-Zinda CEMETERY

(Avenue of Mausoleums; Shahizinda; admission 6000S; ⏲7am-8pm Apr-Oct, 9am-5pm Nov-Mar) Samarkand's most moving and beloved site is this stunning avenue of mausoleums, which contains some of the richest tilework in the Muslim world. The name, which means 'Tomb of the Living King', refers to its original, innermost and holiest shrine – a complex of cool, quiet rooms around what is probably the grave of Qusam ibn-Abbas, a cousin of the Prophet Mohammed who is said to have brought Islam to this area in the 7th century.

A shrine to Qusam existed here on the edge of Afrosiab long before the Mongols ransacked it in the 13th century. Shah-i-Zinda began to assume its current form in the 14th century as Timur and later Ulugbek buried their family and favourites near the Living King.

After remarkably surviving more than seven centuries with only minor touch-up work, many of the tombs were aggressively and controversially restored in 2005. As a result, much of the brilliant mosaic, majolica and terracotta work you see today is not original.

The most beautiful tomb is the Shodi Mulk Oko Mausoleum (1372), resting place of a sister and niece of Timur, second on the left after the entry stairs. The exquisite majolica and terracotta work here – notice the minuscule amount of space between the tiles – was of such exceptional quality that it merited almost no restoration.

Shah-i-Zinda is an important place of pilgrimage, so enter with respect and dress conservatively. At the end of the pathway between the mausoleums, the complex opens up into Samarkand's main cemetery, which is a fascinating place to walk.

Russian Town

Gur-E-Amir Mausoleum & Around MAUSOLEUM

(Bo'stonsaroy ko'chasi; admission 9000S; ⏲8am-7pm Apr-Oct, 9am-5pm Nov-Mar) Timur, along with two sons and two grandsons (including Ulugbek), lies beneath the surprisingly modest Gur-e-Amir Mausoleum and its trademark fluted azure dome.

Timur had built a simple crypt for himself at Shakhrisabz, and had this one built in 1404 for his grandson and proposed heir, Mohammed Sultan, who had died the previous year. But the story goes that when Timur died unexpectedly of pneumonia in Kazakhstan (in the course of planning an expedition against the Chinese) in the winter of 1405, the passes back to Shakhrisabz were snowed in and he was interred here instead.

As with other Muslim mausoleums, the stones are just markers; the actual crypts are in a chamber beneath. In the centre is Timur's stone, once a single block of dark-green jade. In 1740 the warlord Nadir Shah carried it off to Persia, where it was accidentally broken in two – from which time Nadir Shah is said to have had a run of very bad luck, including the near death of his son. At the urging of his religious advisers he returned the stone to Samarkand and, of course, his son recovered.

The plain marble marker to the left of Timur's is that of Ulugbek; to the right is that of Mersaid Baraka, one of Timur's teachers. In front lies Mohammed Sultan. The stones behind Timur's mark the graves of his sons Shah Rukh (the father of Ulugbek) and Miran Shah. Behind these lies Sheikh Seyid Umar, the most revered of Timur's teachers, said to be a descendent of the Prophet Mohammed. Timur ordered Gur-e-Amir built around Umar's tomb.

Soviet anthropologist Mikhail Gerasimov opened the crypts in 1941 and among other things confirmed that Timur was tall for the era (1.7m) and lame in his right leg and arm (from injuries suffered when he was 25) – and that Ulugbek died from being beheaded. According to every tour guide's favourite anecdote, he found on Timur's grave an inscription to the effect that 'whoever opens this will be defeated by an enemy more fearsome than I'. The next day, 22 June, Hitler attacked the Soviet Union.

Ak-Saray Mausoleum MAUSOLEUM

(Shohruh Mirzo ko'chasi; admission 3000S; ⏲9am-6pm) Behind the ugly new wall surrounding Gur-e-Amir is the little Ak-Saray Mausoleum, with some bright frescoes and majolica tilework inside. The frescoes were barely visible before being restored in 2008.

Rukhobod Mausoleum MAUSOLEUM

(Registan; ⏲9am-6pm) Rukhobod Mausoleum, dated 1380 and possibly the city's oldest surviving monument, now serves as a souvenir and craft shop.

Ancient Samarkand (Afrosiab)

At a 2.2-sq-km site called Afrosiab, northeast of Siob Bazaar, excavations of Marakanda (early Samarkand) lie more or less abandoned to the elements.

If it's not too hot, the best way to reach Afrosiab is on foot. Cross the intersection north of Bibi-Khanym and follow Toshkent yo'li for about 1km to the Afrosiab Museum. Ulugbek's Observatory is 1.5km beyond that. Alternatively, take bus 70 to the Ulugbek marshrutka stop from Usto Umar ko'chasi opposite Shah-i-Zinda, or any bus signposted Bulungur or Jambay from the new Shahizinda bus station, 200m east of Shah-i-Zinda.

Afrosiab Museum MUSEUM

(Toshkent yo'li; admission 9000S; ⏲9am-5pm) The Afrosiab Museum was built around one of Samarkand's more important archaeological finds, a chipped 7th-century fresco of the Sogdian King Varkhouman receiving ranks of foreign dignitaries astride ranks of elephants, camels and horses. You'll see reproductions of this iconic fresco throughout the country. It was only discovered in 1965 during the construction of Toshkent yo'li. The 2nd floor of the museum leads the visitor on a chronological tour of the 11 layers of civilisation that is Afrosiab. There's passable signage in English upstairs, but the fresco itself is only signed in French, so a guided tour can be useful.

Tomb of the Old Testament Prophet Daniel MAUSOLEUM

(admission 5000S; ⏲9am-8.30pm Apr-Oct, to 5pm Nov-Mar) The restored Tomb of the Old Testament Prophet Daniel lies on the banks of the Siob River (turn left off Toshkent yo'li 400m northeast of the Afrosiab Museum). The building is a long, low structure topped with five domes, containing an 18m sarcophagus – legend has it that Daniel's body grows by half an inch a year and thus the sarcophagus has to be enlarged. His remains, which date to at least the 5th century BC, were brought here for good luck by Timur from Susa, Iran (suspiciously, an alleged tomb of Daniel can also be found in Susa).

Ulugbek's Observatory OBSERVATORY
(Toshkent yo'li; admission 9000S; ⌚8am-7pm Apr-Oct, 9am-5pm Nov-Mar) The remains of Ulugbek's Observatory is one of the great archaeological finds of the 20th century. Ulugbek was probably more famous as an astronomer than as a ruler. His 30m astrolab, designed to observe star positions, was part of a three-storey observatory he built in the 1420s. All that remains now is the instrument's curved track, unearthed in 1908. The small on-site museum has some miniatures depicting Ulugbek and a few old ceramics and other artefacts unearthed in Afrosiab.

Navoi Ko'chasi & Park

Samarkand's Russified downtown area tends to escape tourists' radars, which is unfortunate because it's quite un-Sovietised and charming.

Regional Studies Museum MUSEUM
(Abdurahmon Jomi 51; admission 9000S; ⌚9am-5pm) The Regional Studies Museum occupies an old Jewish merchant's house, and has a lavish wing devoted to Jewish history, with old photos of Samarkand's once-prominent population of both European and Bukhara Jews. The rest of the museum contains the standard line-up of old ceramics, stuffed animals and historical displays.

Hazrat-Hizr Mosque MOSQUE
(Toshkent yo'li; admission 7000S; ⌚8am-6pm) Across the intersection from the Siob Bazaar, the Hazrat-Hizr Mosque occupies a hill on the fringes of Afrosiab. The 8th-century mosque that once stood here was burnt to the ground by Chinggis Khan in the 13th century and was not rebuilt until 1854. In the 1990s it was lovingly restored by a wealthy Bukharan and today it's Samarkand's most beautiful mosque, with a fine domed interior and views of Bibi-Khanym, Shah-i-Zinda and Afrosiab from the minaret. The ribbed *aivan* ceiling drips colour.

Ishratkhana Mausoleum MAUSOLEUM
(Sadriddin Ayni) If you prefer your ruins really ruined, it's worth the slog out to the *Tomb Raider*-style, 15th-century Ishratkhana Mausoleum, newly topped by a tin roof.

WHERE'S THE OLD TOWN?

In recent years, city planners have completely redesigned Samarkand to seal off older sections of town from tourists' view. Roads have been rerouted, and statues of Navoi, Gorky, Gagarin and others have disappeared or been relocated. Hideous walls have been erected around Gur-e-Amir and behind the Registan, and virtually all access points between the old town and touristy Tashkent and Registan streets have been closed off.

Plucky travellers who do manage to find their way into the old town will be rewarded with an authentic slice of *mahalla* (neighbourhood) life. The most interesting neighbourhood is the old Jewish Quarter, accessible by a gate off Toshkent yo'li, next to the Tourist Information Centre. From the gate, walk east along the main lane, Abu Laiz Samarkandi, and find the gloriously faded **Koroboy Oksokol Mosque** down an alley on your right. Continuing along Abu Laiz Samarkandi, pass the diminutive **Mubarak Mosque** on your left and proceed to the neighbourhood *hammomi* (public baths), which are sadly no longer working. Take a left on unmarked Denau ko'chasi, opposite the *hammomi*, and look for the working 19th-century **Gumbaz Synagogue** (☎+998 91 552 72 68) a few houses down on the left. You're welcome to visit the synagogue, which was built for the Bukharan Jews of Samarkand in 1891, but call ahead to be sure that there will be someone there. There are approximately 50 Jews remaining in Samarkand, with numbers decreasing all the time, according to Rabbi Yusuf Fakar.

Wander through the lanes south of the *hammomi* until you locate the tidy new **Mausoleum of Imam-al-Matrudiy** (Buxoro). Just west of here is the more interesting **Makhdumi Khorezm Mosque** (Buxoro), with a colourful ceiling under its *aivan* and some fine interior tilework. Other neighbourhoods worth wandering are west-southwest of Bibi-Khanym and behind Gur-e-Amir.

With a preponderance of pigeons and an eerie crypt in the basement, this is the place to film your horror movie. It's an easy walk from the Old Town – follow Suzangaran ko'chasi from the Registan and then at the very end turn left onto Andijon ko'chasi.

Hodja Abdi Darun Mausoleum MAUSOLEUM
(Sadriddin Ayni) Across the street from Ishratkhana Mausoleum is the Hodja Abdi Darun Mausoleum, which shares a tranquil, shady courtyard with a mosque and a *hauz* (artificial stone pool).

Imon Mosque MOSQUE
(⌚dawn-dusk) This small, 19th-century Imon Mosque has an open porch, tall carved columns and a brightly restored ceiling. The mosque is located between two streets, Air Kushchi and Suzangaran. Respectfully dressed visitors are always welcome.

Hoja-Nisbatdor Mosque MOSQUE
The lovely Hoja-Nisbatdor Mosque, on Suzangaran near Andijon ko'chasi, has a large *aivan* embraced by walls inlaid with beautifully restored *ghanch* (carved alabaster).

Hovrenko Wine Factory MUSEM
(☎+998 915 347 745; Mahmud Kashgari; tasting 16,000S per person, museum admission free; ⌚9am-6pm Apr-Oct) Wine tasting tours that take in a range of 10 locally produced wines, *balzams* and cognacs are possible at the Hovrenko Wine Factory, in a converted 19th-century Jewish industrialist's house. The small attached museum has no signage in English, but you're welcome to look around even if you're not doing a tasting. Call ahead to ensure there's availability.

Tours

The going rate for trained guides is US$35 per day, or US$5 per hour. Your hotel will almost certainly be able to hook you up with someone trusted and experienced, but the following are recommended:

Farruh Bahronov GUIDE
(☎+998 93 348 0102, 235 00 98; faruhb@yahoo.com) Farruh offers tours in English and French, as well as running his own travel agency, Abask Travel, that can organise everything from accommodation and visas to transport services, and cultural and eco tours.

Valentina Belova GUIDE
(☎241 88 07) The grand dame of Samarkand's guides. Speaks English.

Daulet Negmadjanov GUIDE
(☎+998 90 276 1791, 237 34 76; daulat63@mail.ru) A charming and knowledgeable English-speaking driver and guide to Samarkand and the surrounding area. He has his own car, and provides reliable and affordable services.

Denis Vikulov GUIDE
(☎+998 915 502 772; denis-guide@rambler.ru) Offers tours in English and Russian, and offers transfers and tours to other cities with his car.

Festivals & Events

During Samarkand's **Navrus Festival** you'll find dancing, live music and other performances, and fireworks in Navoi Park. Ask travel agencies or tour guides about the annual Navrus *kupkari* (Tajik: *buzkashi;* traditional polo-like game played with a headless goat carcass) match in Urgut or Koshrabot.

The city is also home to the **Sharq Taronalari** (en.sharqtaronalari.uz) classical Oriental music festival, held every other year (next in August 2015 and 2017) on the Registan.

Sleeping

Samarkand's B&Bs aren't quite up to Bukhara's lofty standards but are preferable to the tour group–laden hotels.

★Jahongir B&B B&B $
(☎+998 915 550 808, 235 78 99; www.jahongirbandb.com; Chirokchi 4; s/d/tr/q US$35/45/65/75 s/d with shared bathroom US$28/38; wifi) This charming place in an old town neighbourhood unaltered by Samarkand's relentless modernisation has two courtyards sprinkled with vines and flowers and a selection of comfortable and inviting rooms. Each is equipped with a fridge and some have a TV, while bathrooms are modern. Highly recommended.

B&B Davr B&B $
(☎+998 91 521 67 48, 235 47 48; davrhotel@mail.ru; Ali Kushchi 43; s/d/tr US$20/40/60; wifi) Tucked away in an unchanged old town neighbourhood, the Davr gets great feedback and it's easy to see why. Staff are helpful, the rooms are clean and have surprisingly elaborate ceilings, and dinners in the 19th-century house next door are highly recommended. Rooms are fan-cooled.

Hotel Abdurahmon B&B $
(☎235 43 05, 235 47 59; Buxoro 1/7; s/d US$15/25; ❄) A well-signposted Old Town guesthouse, this good-value place is just off Buxoro. The two-floor courtyard property has simple, clean rooms with basic bathrooms that have hot water. Some English is spoken.

Timur the Great B&B $
(☎235 03 38, 235 19 80; timurthegreat@mail.ru; Buhoro 84; s/d/tr US$15/30/40; ❄📶) Following a renovation, the four simple but pleasant rooms here surround an awning-covered courtyard. It's good value and well located on the edge of the old town.

B&B Najiba B&B $
(☎+998 91 534 2242, 235 36 26; Mubarak 83; s/d US$25/35) This small family-run guesthouse has been operating for 12 years, and it's a good place to get the flavour and atmosphere of life in Samarkand's old town. All four rooms boast private bathrooms with hot running water, ceiling fans and access to the pleasant courtyard.

Bahodir B&B B&B $
(☎235 43 05, 235 47 59; Mulokandov 132; dm from US$10, s/d US$15/25; ❄📶) Just moments from the Registan, this rather dank guesthouse is cheap but passable, and the notebook filled with backpacker advice is useful, even if the steamy common bathroom and the dilapidated en suite rooms leave a lot to be desired. Ask to see several rooms, as standards vary.

★**Antica** GUESTHOUSE $$
(☎+998 93 336 17 92, 235 20 92; anticasamarkand@hotmail.com; Iskandarov 58; s/d without bathroom US$30/40, s/d/tr with bathroom from US$35/50/65; ❄📶) A gorgeous garden courtyard shaded by pomegranate, persimmon and fig trees make this busy family home a joy to stay at. Breakfast is a feast, though some rooms are rather cramped and bathrooms can be tiny – the newer rooms have more space and better decor. Fittings in the older ones include hand-carved walnut-wood doors and ribbed, brightly painted ceilings. A great cultural experience.

★**Hotel Arba** BOUTIQUE HOTEL $$
(☎233 6067; www.hotel-arba.com; Mahmud Koshgari 92; s/d/tr US$25/47/65; ❄📶) This new addition to the hotel scene is the closest thing Samarkand has to a boutique hotel. It's stylishly decked out, with exposed brickwork, scattered antiques, flat screen TVs and big, comfortable beds. It's a way from the Registan in the Russian part of town, but it's well worth the walk for prices this reasonable. Staff are also remarkably friendly – book ahead.

Furkat B&B $$
(☎235 32 61, 235 62 99; hotelfurkat@mail.ru; Mulokandov 105; s/d/tr US$35/50/60, s with shared bathroom US$15; ❄) Peacocks roam the yard at Samarkand's original B&B. There's a dizzying variety of rooms in a sprawling three-storey, old-town edifice. Top-floor rooms have splendid views of the Registan and the snowcapped mountains surrounding Samarkand, while the four single rooms with a shared bathroom are great bargains. Breakfast and evening drinks are served on the fantastic rooftop terrace, while there are a few extra rooms in the annexe across the street should the main hotel be full.

Emir B&B B&B $$
(☎235 07 35, 235 74 61; muhandis2005@mail.ru; Oksaroy 142; s/d/tr US$30/40/60; ❄📶) The eight rooms here are clean and cosy, and have heated floors in their bathrooms, which is great in winter. There's a large and very pleasant communal area that's traditionally furnished with some lovely carpets. English is spoken by the owner's son.

Diyor Hotel HOTEL $$
(☎+998 902 120 743, 235 75 71; Toshkent 43; r/ste US$50/60; ❄) Right on the main tourist thoroughfare and moments from the Registan, the Diyor is a tiny place with just five big and bright rooms. The largest of which, the *'lux'* has a large balcony and even more space than the others. Wi-fi was about to be installed in mid 2013.

Hotel Légende HISTORIC HOTEL $$
(☎233 74 81; www.legendm7.com; Tolmosov 60; s/d US$35/45; ❄) For atmosphere alone, this 175-year-old house deep in the Jewish Quarter can't be beaten: rooms surround a lush courtyard, have gorgeous ceilings and are awash in old carpets and textiles. However, in other ways the Légende is rather down at heel and in need of a management rethink, with poorly maintained rooms, very basic bathrooms and no internet. Even if you're not staying here, it's worth considering arranging a *plov* dinner here for the impressive setting.

Dilshoda GUESTHOUSE $$
(231 03 18, 235 03 87; dil_servis@mail.ru; Oksaroy 150; s/d/tr US$26/49/56;) Set in the shadow of Gur-e-Amir, this B&B serves up warm, if basic, rooms with narrow beds and tiny bathrooms. However, there's a tantalising view from the first floor balcony and the chipper host family serves up mouth-watering three-course dinners (US$8.50) on request. There's a second, far more modern property around the corner should this one be full.

Malika Prime HOTEL $$$
(233 01 97, 233 43 49; www.malika-samarkand.com; Bo'stonsaroy; s/d US$60/80;) The best of the Malika chain's two Samarkand hotels is well situated between the old and new towns. The highlight is the roof-deck terrace overlooking the Gur-e-Amir next door. While the 22 rooms themselves are nothing special, being somewhat dark and anonymous compared to the property's promising exterior, they do have impressive ceilings and are comfortable and spacious. The hotel is very popular with tour groups.

Registon Hotel HOTEL $$$
(233 5590; Ulugbek 16; s/d US$65/85;) The Registon looks good with spacious rooms that have fridges and decent bathrooms, although they can hardly be said to be bursting with character. There's wi-fi downstairs in the lobby, and you're in the Russian town, a fair walk from the sights, but better located for shopping and dining options.

Registan Plaza Hotel HOTEL $$$
(233 40 86, 233 24 75; www.uzhotelpresident.com; Shohruh 53; s/d US$100/150/190;) The rebranded former Hotel President is currently the smartest property in town, although several total refurbishments of other hotels will probably change this soon enough. The vast lobby here is impressive, if somewhat sterile, and the 165 rooms are large, comfortable but characterless, though they have good bathrooms, minibars and cable TV and the location is excellent.

Hotel Ark Samarkand HOTEL $$$
(235 69 41; www.ark-samarkand.uz; Penjikent 9; d/tr/q US$45/85/90;) With its fantastic location near the Registan and renovated, comfy rooms, this place is a good choice, though it's on the pricey side for what it offers, and bathrooms can be rather small. There's a second location with similar standards and prices further down the road if the main hotel is full.

Eating & Drinking

Most restaurants are in the newer Russian part of town, far removed from the touristy Registan area, where there's a dearth of choice. Samarkand is distinctly quiet at night, but there are a few places that stay busy after sundown.

Supermarket Aziz (Pochta 6; 8am-8pm) is Samarkand's best-stocked supermarket.

Cafe Labig'or UZBEK $
(Registan; mains 3000-6000S; 8am-11pm) The best of the numerous choices across from the Registan, this two-floor restaurant has a pleasant and breezy upstairs terrace that's often as busy with locals and the squawks of peacocks as it is with travellers. The menu is oral only (the young staff speak some English), but focuses on the usual Uzbek standards. The *lulya kebab* (minced lamb and herb kebab) was excellent when we visited.

Kyzyl Chaixona CHAIKHANA $
(Siob Bazaar; 2500-5000S; 7am-7pm) The clean 'red teahouse' within the confines of Samarkand's main market has a pleasant outdoor area and low, low prices. Expect *somsa* (samosa), shashlyk and soups amid the chaotic atmosphere of the market traders.

★ **Platan** INTERNATIONAL $$
(Pushkin 2; mains 7000-11,000S; 10am-11pm;) Possibly the best restaurant in Samarkand, Platan has a gorgeous summer terrace for shady al fresco dining in the summer months, while inside there's a choice of two dining rooms, one of which is on the noisy side and favoured by tour groups while the other has white tablecloths and a rather classier feel. The menu, which includes Arabian-, Thai- and Egyptian-style meat dishes, is no less charismatic, and the salad menu is extraordinary in its variety: try the excellent *lobio*, a Georgian bean, walnut, garlic, lemon and parsley salad, or the equally tasty coleslaw and apple-based 'Diet Salad'.

Old City INTERNATIONAL $$
(Abdurahmon Jomi 100/1; mains 8,000-20,000; 10am-11pm) This charming place in the centre of the Russian part of town is highly recommended for its long and interesting menu that takes in everything from local dishes to Russian and Italian cuisine.

Service is friendly and assured, and while it caters largely to tourists, it's certainly no trap.

Karimbek UZBEK $$
(Gagarin 194; mains 8000-20,000S; ⏲8am-11pm; ▣) This Uzbek theme restaurant remains one of the most popular places for groups and independent travellers alike. The national- and Russian-influenced cuisine can be enjoyed in a variety of settings, from private country hut to airy streetside patio. A nightly belly-dancing show jiggles to life around 8pm. It's a 3000S cab ride from the centre of town.

Cafe Magistr CAFE $$
(Bo'stonsaroy 30/45; mains 4000-8000S; ⏲7.30am-11pm; ☰▣) Right in the heart of the city, this bright, two-room cafe aimed at students does the job just fine: you can have everything from real coffee to a full breakfast menu (3500-6000S) as well as enjoy salads, burgers and pizza. There's paid wi-fi.

Art Cafe Norgis UZBEK $$
(Toshkent yo'li; mains 5000-8000S; ⏲9am-10pm; ☰▣) A handy place for lunch between the Registan and the Bibi Khanym Mosque (and with stellar views of the latter from the popular terrace), this 'art cafe' is purely the haunt of tour groups, but as the food is decent and there's nothing else around, we've included it here. The menu is made up of unexciting Uzbek standards, but a pleasant yoghurt and spice side dish and piping hot fresh bread are highlights.

Besh Chinor UZBEK $$
(Temerchilar; mains 7000-25,000S; ⏲9am-10pm) Following a recent refit, this low-key and traditional place is a great spot for *plov*, *manty* (steamed dumplings) or kebabs. It's clean and friendly, though Russian is barely spoken, let alone English.

No Name Café INTERNATIONAL $$
(Cnr Mustakillik & Bo'stonsaroy ko'chasi; mains 6000-10,000S; ⏲9am-11pm; ☰▣) This new place may have a lurid green interior and a TV blaring out Uzbek pop music, but its menu makes for a pleasant change from the normal fare on offer, and even includes sushi (10,000-20,000S per set). There's also a full breakfast menu and wi-fi available through access cards you can purchase.

Alt Stadt Laghman Centre UYGHUR $$
(Navoi 49; laghman 10,000-30,000S; ⏲11am-11pm) Wash down traditional *laghman* and other Uyghur specialities with affordable unfiltered homebrew on a pleasant people-watching terrace behind Cinema Samarkand. Avoid the rather dark and dank interior.

Blues Cafe BAR
(Amir Timur 66; mains 10,000-20,000; ⏲1-11pm) A surprisingly tasteful and low-lit bar deep in the Russian old town, Blue Cafe no longer has live music, but that may change (a forlorn piano stands in memory of a happier time). Instead there's an '80s soundtrack, real coffee, a full menu and cocktails to be had.

Shopping

There are souvenir shops and craft workshops of varying quality at all the big sights, in particular at the Rukhobod Mausoleum and the Registan. There are also several noteworthy antique shops in Tilla-Kari Medressa and one in Sher Dor Medressa, but textile and *suzani* buffs are better off going to Urgut. Multilingual Bobir has a traditional musical instrument shop in Sher Dor Medressa, and gives spontaneous concerts, while accomplished miniaturist Mansur Nurillaev, who makes miniatures of buildings of Samarkand, is worth a visit at the Rukhobod Mausoleum.

Samarkand Ceramics Workshop CERAMICS
(Tilla-Kari Medressa; ⏲9am-6pm) At the Registan look out for the Samarkand Ceramics Workshop, one of the few places still practising the Samarkand school of ceramic-making.

Samarkand-Bukhara Silk Carpets Showroom CARPETS
(Sher Dor Medressa; ⏲8am-7pm) Samarkand-Bukhara Silk Carpets has a Registan-based showroom with its trademark high-quality woven silk tapestries and *suzani* carpets on display.

Siob Bazaar MARKET
(⏲7am-7pm) Around and behind Bibi-Khanym, the frenetic, colourful main market Siob Bazaar is a great place for vegetarians and photographers, and may reward silk and souvenir hunters as well. You can also change money here, on the far side of the market near Rudaiky, the main road.

Information

INTERNET ACCESS

Wi-fi can be found at most hotels and for free at Platan restaurant, while it's available for a fee at Cafe Magistr and No Name Cafe.

Foreign Language Institute (Bo'stonsaroy 23; per hr 1200S; 8am-8pm Mon-Sat) Inside the institute itself, go through the security gate on Buston Saroy.

Paynet Internet (Bo'stonsaroy 30/45; per hour 1500S; 8am-10pm) Wedged between Cafe Magistr and No Name Cafe, Paynet's access is fast.

International Telephone Office (Pochta 9; per hr 1200S; 8am-10pm) The best internet place in town, housed in cool, bright and spacious premises with booths for privacy and no gamers.

Internet Tim (Amir Timur 31; per hour 1200S; 8am-11pm) Another decent option.

MONEY

Black-market moneychangers hang out around Siob Bazaar, although you'll find it easier to get a better rate at the Kryty Rynok in the new town, where you'll be less mobbed as well. Hotel Registon Plaza has an exchange office that changes money at the official rate, and an ATM, which is rarely in use.

Asaka Bank (Mustaqillik maydoni; 9am-5pm Mon-Fri) Advances cash on MasterCard.

National Bank of Uzbekistan (cnr Bo'stonsaroy & Ulugbek; 9am-5pm Mon-Fri) Cashes travellers cheques and handles Visa card cash advances.

POST & COMMUNICATIONS

International Telephone Office (Pochta 9; 24hr) International calls, and also access to skype via the internet cafe.

Main Post & Telegraph Office (Pochta 5; 8am-5pm)

REGISTRATION

OVIR (233 69 34; cnr Mahmud Kashgari & Ulugbek; 9am-6pm Mon-Fri) Look for large metal gate.

TRAVEL & TOUR AGENCIES

Most B&Bs double as travel agencies and/or can organise cars, guides, camel trekking and yurtstays around Lake Aidarkul, and homestays in the Nuratau-Kyzylkum Biosphere Reserve. Antica and Hotel Légende are particularly resourceful. A new, privately run **Tourist Information Centre** (+998 993 722 6656; Cnr Toshkent & Abu Laiz Samarkandi; 8am-7pm), between the Registan and the Bibi-Khanym Mosque, offers a full range of services, including arranging train tickets, tours and booking hotels. Staff speak English and there are good maps of the city on sale as well.

Tour guides Denis Vikulov and Farruh Bahronov are also good fixers. Denis has a car and will travel, and is fixing up a 19th-century Jewish Quarter building to serve meals to tourists. Farruh runs **Abask Travel** (+998 93 348 0102; Toshkent 41; 9am-6pm Mon-Fri) out of his souvenir store – look for the store with the woodworking workshop inside. **Sogda Tour** (235 29 85, 235 36 09; www.sogda-tour.com; Registan 38; 9am-6pm Mon-Fri), located behind Mojiza restaurant, has refreshing ideas for touring the region, including excursions to the caves and mountains around Darbent and Boysun. Daulet Negmadjanov (p176) is an English-speaking driver and guide to Samarkand and the surrounding area. He has his own car, and provides reliable and affordable services.

Getting There & Away

AIR

Uzbekistan Airways (812 13 17; www.uzairways.com; Airport) flies between Samarkand and Tashkent once or twice daily except on Mondays and Fridays for US$21. You can only buy domestic tickets at the airport office in US dollars. A taxi from the centre of town will cost you 5000S. There are also direct flights to Moscow.

LAND

The main departure point to Tashkent for private buses and shared taxis is the Ulugbek marshrutka stop, about 200m east of the observatory (bus/shared taxi per seat 16,000/25,000S, six/3½ hours), although there are approximately nine buses per day from the **Shahizinda bus station**, leaving on the hour from 6am.

Shared taxis to Termiz (40,000S, five hours) gather at 'Grebnoy Kanal' on the city's outskirts about 6km east of the Ulugbek stop.

Buses to Bukhara originate in Tashkent and pass by the highway opposite the Ulugbek stop (20,000S, 4½ hours). Buses pass at least every hour, and traffic is heaviest in the late afternoon. Departures peter out around 5pm because of the nationally imposed 10pm curfew on bus traffic. There is one daily bus to Urgench (40,000S, 12 hours) every day at 8.50am, which continues to Nukus (45,000S, 13½ hours).

Shared taxis to Bukhara involve a transfer in Navoi. The main departure point to Navoi (20,000S, two hours) is the Povorot marshrutka stop about 2.5km west of the Crying Mother monument on Ulugbek ko'chasi. Take any marshrutkas signposted 'Поворот'. Shared taxis from Navoi to Bukhara take an hour and cost a further 20,000S.

For **Shakhrisabz**, shared taxis (25,000S, 1½ hours) congregate at the end of Suzangaran, just off Registan.

TRAIN

The brand new, super fast 'Afrosoiyob' bullet train to Tashkent departs daily during the week at 5pm (economy/business 51,000/68,000S, 2½ hours) and at 6pm on Saturday and Sunday. Meanwhile the far cheaper 'Sharq' train leaves Samarkand at 11.20am daily (economy/business 27,000/41,000S, 3hrs 40 mins).

If you're heading to Bukhara (economy/business 25,000/40,000S, 3hrs), the 'Sharq' train originating in Tashkent rolls through Samarkand's station daily and departs at 11:55am. There's also a cheaper but far slower and less convenient overnight train to Bukhara (*platskartny/kupeyny* 12,000/20,000S) leaving at 2.11am each day, and arriving in Bukhara at 7.15am.

The trains from Tashkent to Urgench, Termiz and Kungrad via Nukus go via Samarkand.

The **train station** (☎ 229 15 32; Rudaki) is 5km northwest of Navoi Park. Take any bus or marshrutka that says 'Вокзал', such as bus 22 or marshrutkas 3, 27, 35 or 72, from the **Registan** or **Bulvar stops**. You can buy train tickets for a small commission at the Tourist Information Centre (p180) on Toshkent.

Getting Around

TO/FROM THE AIRPORT

Marshrutka 56 goes from the airport to the Registan marshrutka stop, while marshrutkas 10 and 60 and bus 45 go to the **Bulvar (Бульвар) stop** near Hotel Samarkand. A taxi from the airport to the Registan will cost about 5000S, or walk 500m out to the main road and pay 3000S.

PUBLIC TRANSPORT

Marshrutkas (600S) and buses (400S) run from about 6am until 8pm or 9pm. To get between the Registan stop and Navoi in the heart of the downtown area take any vehicle marked ГУМ (GUM), such as bus 3, 22 or 32, or marshrutka 6 or 35. A taxi between the old town and new town should cost 3000S, the minimum charge for cabs in Samarkand.

Around Samarkand

Urgut

This town's **bazaar** is one of the best places in the country to buy jewellery, *suzani* and antique clothing. Prices are lower and the quality is on par with anything sold in Samarkand and Bukhara, but you'll have to negotiate hard. It overflows with tourists in the high season – go in the low season when tourists are scarce and prices drop even further. Arrive at the crack of dawn for the best selection.

While the bazaar is open every day, the textile and jewellery section, located at the back of the main bazaar, only happens on Sunday and Wednesday, and to a lesser extent on Saturday too. To get here from Samarkand, take a shared taxi (5000S) or marshrutka (3000S) from the Registan stop (45 minutes).

Shakhrisabz (Shahrisabz)

☎75 / POP 75,000

Shakhrisabz is a small, un-Russified town south of Samarkand, across the hills in the Kashkadarya province, and is a lovely drive from Samarkand with some spectacular views. The town is a pleasant Uzbek backwater and seems to be nothing special – until you start bumping into the ruins dotted around its backstreets, and the megalomaniac ghosts of a wholly different place materialise. This is Timur's hometown, and once upon a time it probably put Samarkand itself in the shade. It's an interesting day trip from Samarkand, and a good base for hiking in the mountains.

Timur was born on 9 April 1336 into the Barlas clan of local aristocrats, at the village of Hoja Ilghar, 13km to the south. Ancient even then, Shakhrisabz (called Kesh at the time) was a kind of family seat. As he rose to power, Timur gave it its present name (Tajik for 'Green Town') and turned it into an extended family monument. Most of its current attractions were built here by Timur (including a tomb intended for himself) or his grandson Ulugbek.

Sights

Ak-Saray Palace RUIN

(White Palace; admission free, access to staircase 3000S; ⏲9am-6pm) Just north of the centre, Timur's summer palace has as much grandeur per square centimetre as anything in Samarkand. There's actually nothing left of it except bits of the gigantic, 38m-high *pishtak,* covered with gorgeous, unrestored filigree-like mosaics. This crumbling relic, blending seamlessly with everyday life, will thrill critics of Samarkand's zealous restoration efforts: indeed, coming here will give you some idea of how Samarkand would have looked a century ago.

Ak-Saray was probably Timur's most ambitious project – work began in 1380 and

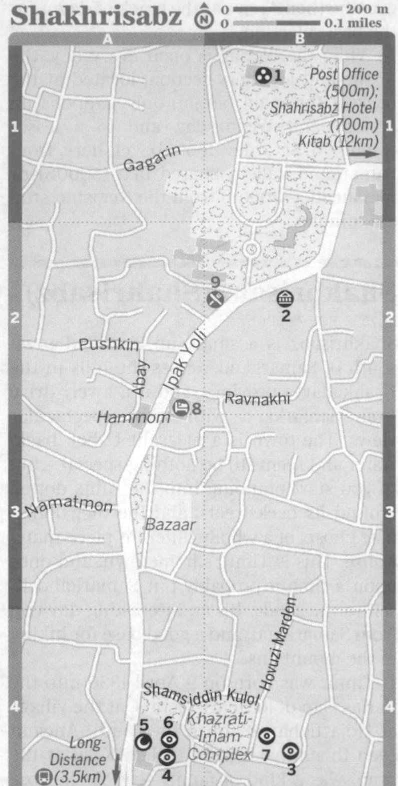

Shakhrisabz

Sights

1 Ak-Saray Palace B1
2 Amir Timur Museum B2
3 Crypt of Timur B4
4 Dorut Tilyovat A4
Gumbazi Seyidan .... (see 4)
5 Kok-Gumbaz Mosque A4
6 Mausoleum of Sheikh Shamseddin Kulyal A4
7 Tomb of Jehangir B4

Sleeping

8 Fayzullah Ravnakhi B&B A2

Eating

9 Aquarium B2

took some 24 years to complete. Its creation followed a successful campaign in Khorezm and the 'import' of many of its finest artisans. It's well worth climbing to the top of the *pishtak* to truly appreciate its height and imagine what the rest of the palace was like, in size and glory. The arch was a staggering 22.5m wide, and collapsed 200 years ago.

A new statue of Amir Timur stands in what was the palace centre. It's not uncommon to see 10 weddings at a time posing here for photos at weekends, creating quite a mob scene. Ak-Saray has been a Unesco World Heritage Site since 2000.

Kok-Gumbaz Mosque MOSQUE

(Ipak Yoli; 8.30am-6pm) FREE This large Friday mosque was completed by Ulugbek in 1437 in honour of his father Shah Rukh (who was Timur's son). The name, appropriately, means 'blue dome'. The palm trees painted on the interior walls are calling cards of its original Indian and Iranian designers.

Dorut Tilyovat MAUSOLEUM

(House of Meditation) Behind Kok-Gumbaz is Dorut Tilyovat, the original burial complex of Timur's forebears. Under the dome on the left is the **Mausoleum of Sheikh Shamseddin Kulyal**, spiritual tutor to Timur and his father, Amir Taragay (who might also be buried here). The mausoleum was completed by Timur in 1374.

On the right is the ornate **Gumbazi Seyidan** (Dome of the Seyyids), which Ulugbek finished in 1438 as a mausoleum for his own descendants (although it's not clear whether any are buried in it).

Khazrati-Imam Complex MAUSOLEUM

(Hovuzi Mardon) A walkway leads east from Kok-Gumbaz to a few melancholy remnants of a 3500-sq-metre mausoleum complex called Dorussiadat or Dorussaodat (Seat of Power and Might), which Timur finished in 1392 and which may have overshadowed even the Ak-Saray Palace. The main survivor is the tall, crumbling **Tomb of Jehangir**, Timur's eldest and favourite son, who died at 22. It's also the resting place for another son, Umar Sheikh (Timur's other sons are with him at Gur-e-Amir in Samarkand).

In an alley behind the mausoleum (and within the perimeter of the long-gone Dorussiadat) is a bunker with a wooden door leading to an underground room, the **Crypt of Timur**. The room, plain except for Quranic quotations on the arches, is nearly filled by a single stone casket. On the casket are biographical inscriptions about Timur, from which it was inferred (when the room was discovered in 1963) that this crypt was intended for him. Inside are two unidentified corpses.

Amir Timur Museum MUSEUM
(Ipak Yoli; admission 4000S; ⏲9am-4.30pm Mon-Fri, until 2pm Sat & Sun) Housed inside the renovated Chubin Medressa is this simple museum. Its highlight is a model depicting Timur's entire kingdom, from Egypt to Kashgar. Beyond the boundaries of the kingdom, a yellow line illustrates his 'protectorates', including Kiev and Moscow. If that doesn't interest you, the museum is probably not worth the price of admission, although there are some old Buddhist and Zoroastrian artefacts here that predate Timur by many centuries.

Sleeping & Eating

The main hotel in town, the Orient Star, was being totally renovated when we visited. If it's still closed when you visit, there are a couple of other accommodation options if you want to stay the night. Food is not a highlight here: along Ipak Yoli there is a strip of chaikhanas whose fortunes ebb and flow like the surrounding desert sands.

Fayzullah Ravnakhi B&B B&B $
(☎+998 91 320 7318, 521 02 77; Ravnakhi 55; r per person incl half board US$20) This homey spot has two unique quads and one cosy double. The quads are basically open spaces with patchwork carpeting, two basic beds and not much else. Staff will throw a couple of *kurpacha* on the floor to accommodate bigger groups. The friendly owner, Lutfullokhon Asamov, who speaks English and also works as a guide to the nearby Hissar Mountains, can arrange hiking trips with notice.

Shahrisabz Hotel HOTEL $$
(Ipak Yoli 2; s/d/ste US$50/70/100; ❄📶🏊) This new hotel is the only midrange accommodation in town and it has clean and comfy rooms with fridges, safes and cable TV. There's an on-site restaurant and a sauna (30,000S per hour).

Aquarium UZBEK $
(Ipak Yoli 22; mains 2500-5000S; ⏲8am-9pm) This bustling cafe is in view of Ak-Saray and serves up the usual shashlyk, *shulpa*, *laghman* and vodka shots.

Information

Most Samarkand guides can arrange day trips to Shakhrisabz, including a driver and a tour of all the main sights. Change money for blackmarket rates at the bazaar.

Getting There & Around

Shakhrisabz is about 90km from Samarkand, over the 1788m Takhtakaracha (Amankutan) Pass, a glorious drive that is one of the highlights of a trip here. The pass is occasionally closed by snow from January to March, forcing a three-hour detour around the mountains.

Buses and shared taxis to a handful of other destinations leave from the long-distance bus station, south of town. To Tashkent's Ippodrom station there are about six daily buses (20,000S, eight hours) and regular shared taxis (30,000S, five hours). To get to Bukhara take a shared taxi to Karshi (6000S, 1½ hours) and change there.

Termiz

☎76 / POP 140,000 / ELEV 380M

The last stop in Uzbekistan on the way to Afghanistan, Termiz is a colourful border-town with an edgy, Wild West feel. While the present day city bears few traces of its colourful cosmopolitan history, the surrounding area is full of archaeological finds, many of which come together in Termiz's excellent museum.

Sights

The highlight of any trip to Termiz is its excellent archaeological museum. There are also several other sights around Termiz that can be visited in a half-day. Figure on paying a driver US$5 per hour, or about US$15 for a half-day tour.

The main sights lurk northwest of the city on the road to Karshi. Driving out here you'll notice various piles of rubble in the cotton fields of what used to be Termiz (and is now known as Old Termiz). These are Buddhist ruins, levelled by Chinggis Khan along with the rest of Old Termiz in 1220.

Termiz's other main sights are clustered northeast of town off the airport road.

Termiz Archaeological Museum MUSEUM
(Al-Termizi 29; admission 10,000S; ⏲9am-5.30pm) The Termiz Archaeological Museum is reason enough to visit Termiz. Unveiled in 2001, the museum is a treasure trove of artefacts collected from the many ravaged civilisations that pepper the Surkhandarya province of which Termiz is the main city. The highlight would have to be the collection of 3rd- to 4th-century Buddhist artefacts. The museum also has an excellent model of Surkhandarya that depicts the area's most important archaeological sights. Serious archaeological buffs

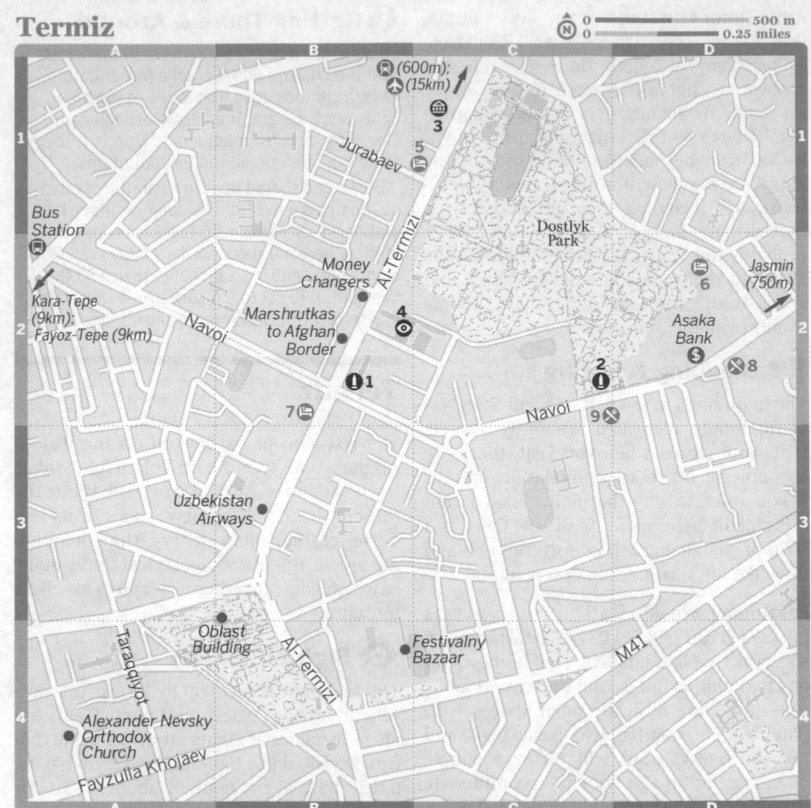

can use this map to plot their course to a wealth of caves, petroglyphs and excavations in the north of Surkhandarya province.

Fayoz-Tepe RUIN

Today archaeologists are busy trying to reverse some of the damage at Fayoz-Tepe, a 3rd-century-AD Buddhist monastery complex 9km west of the bus station. Discovered only in 1968, in recent years it has been restored and a teapot dome put over the monastery's original stupa, visible through a glass window.

Kara-Tepe RUIN

Looking southwest from Fayoz-Tepe, the remains of Kara-Tepe, a Buddhist cave monastery, are visible on the banks of the Amu-Darya, opposite the Afghan border. You need special permission to visit Kara-Tepe – ask at the Archaeological Museum.

Mausoleum of Al-Hakim al-Termizi MAUSOLEUM

Closer to town is a slightly younger but still quite sacred edifice, the Mausoleum of Al-Hakim al-Termizi. Its namesake was a 9th-century Sufi philosopher, known locally as Al-Hakim, the city's patron saint. In a triumph for preservationists, the interior's cheap plaster *ghanch*-work, spuriously installed as part of the government's general monument beautification drive, has been removed to expose the original 15th-century brick.

The mausoleum gets packed to the gills on Wednesday, when the faithful are served lunch. The Amu-Darya and Afghanistan are once again in sight here; photographing the border is forbidden. To get out here catch marshrutka 15 heading north on Al-Termizi from **Yubileyny Bazaar** (600S, 20 minutes), just north of the **clock tower**.

Termiz

Sights
1 Clock Tower B2
2 Navoi Statue C2
3 Termiz Archaeological Museum C1
4 Yubileyny Bazaar B2

Sleeping
5 Asson Hotel C1
6 Hotel Meridian D2
7 Surhan Atlantic B2

Eating
8 Azizbek D2
9 Restoran Farhod C2

Sultan Saodat Ensemble MAUSOLEUM
The restored Timurid-style Sultan Saodat Ensemble of mausoleums probably won't impress you if you've been to Samarkand. Buried here are members of the Sayyid dynasty, which ruled Termiz from the 11th to 15th centuries.

Kyr Kyz RUIN
Murky legend has it that 40 young women lived here in the mud-walled Kyr Kyz ('Forty Girls') fortress in the 11th century, successfully fighting off sex-crazed nomads after their nobleman-husband was slain, although the story changes depending on whom you hear it from.

Tours

Rayhon GUIDE
(☎+998 915 808 189) Rayhon speaks English and can arrange tours of the city and further afield in Surkhandarya province.

Sleeping

Termiz has some great-value accommodation. Breakfast is not included at the majority of places.

Surhan Atlantic HOTEL $
(☎222 75 99; cnr Al-Termizi & Navoi; s/d from US$15/16; ❄) The smartly renovated Soviet rooms here are an incredible deal, with big, clean bathrooms, balconies and white cotton bedspreads. The manager doesn't speak English, but he's very friendly. Add US$3.50 per room for a TV. There's a pleasant garden too, as well as a small cafe.

Asson Hotel HOTEL $$
(☎227 58 76; cnr Al-Termizi & Jurabaev; s/d US$45/70 ste US$80-120; ❄) Refurbished in pleasant pale green tones, the Asson is perfectly located for the archaeological museum and well situated in the thick of things. Rooms are clean and bright, though bathrooms are still rather aged.

Hotel Meridian HOTEL $$
(☎227 48 51; Alpomysh 23; s/d incl breakfast US$55/75, ♣) This modern high rise place has nothing to do with the Meridien group, but it does boast large, smart and clean rooms in pastel colours and a decent restaurant (that's open well into the evening), as well as a sauna.

Eating & Drinking

Azizbek UZBEK $$
(Navoi ko'chasi; mains 5000-30,000S; ⏰9am-11pm) This friendly place is worth the detour from the centre of town; its staff are charmingly friendly, the bread is some of the best in the country and the menu of grilled meat, salads and beer makes for a perfect meal when served on the shady outdoor patio. Upstairs a smokey disco gets busy with locals in the evenings.

Restoran Farhod UZBEK $$
(Navoi ko'chasi; mains 8000-28,000S; ⏰8am-11pm) Opposite the **Navoi statue** some way from the bustle of Al-Termizi is this unassuming looking place. Go inside though, and you'll find a permanently bustling local favourite where Uzbek national dishes and a range of delicious kebabs are served up. There are also private booths available, should you fancy some peace and quiet.

Information

Asaka Bank (Navoi 45; ⏰9am-5pm Mon-Fri) Currency exchange and cash advances on MasterCards.

Getting There & Around

Uzbekistan Airways (☎222 85 77; Al-Termizi 11) has three flights a day to/from Tashkent (US$67). You can buy tickets in town, or at the airport, which is 15km north of town. To get to the airport take marshrutka 264, which runs up Al-Termizi (1000S). A taxi costs 8000S.

On arrival in Termiz, you'll need to register your arrival with the police, as you're entering a sensitive border zone. On seeing your foreign passport, you'll be directed to the relevant office at the airport terminal, and the process is very straightforward.

Shared taxi is the way to go to Samarkand (40,000S, five hours) and Karshi (20,000S, 3½ hours). Transfer in Karshi for Bukhara. There's also a 6am bus to Samarkand (18,000S, 8½ hours). There are a couple of morning buses to Tashkent (24,000S, 13 hours), or take a shared taxi (65,000S, nine hours).

All of the above leave from the **bus station**, a straight shot west on either Jurabaev (marshrutkas 18 and 20) or Navoi (marshrutkas 6, 7 and 8).

Trains to Termiz from Tashkent/Samarkand no longer go through Turkmenistan thanks to a brand-new track opened in 2009 that links Guzor and Termiz via Boysun and Jarkurgan. There's a train to Tashkent on all odd dates of the month (*platskartny/kupeyny* 48,000/72,000S, 14 hours) with stops in Boysun, Karshi and Samarkand. The return trip departs Tashkent on even days at 9.20pm.

Local trains depart several times daily to Denau (2700S; three hours), and continue another hour to Sariosiyo at the Tajik border.

Nurata

436 / POP 30,000

To the north of the featureless Samarkand-Bukhara 'Royal Road', the Pamir-Alay Mountains produce one final blip on the map before fading unceremoniously into desertified insignificance. The Nuratau Mountains, which top out at 2169m, have in recent years become the centre of Uzbekistan's growing ecotourism movement. Modest Nurata town makes a logical base for jumping off to the mountains or to one of several nearby yurt camps.

Nurata itself is most famous for its old, circle-patterned *suzani*, which can sell for thousands of dollars at international auctions, but it also has a few quirky tourist attractions, most notably an old **fortress of Alexander the Great**. Behind the fortress, a path leads 4km to the **Zukarnay Petroglyphs**, which date to the Bronze Age. Ask the curator at the museum how to find the trail. If it's too hot to walk, there are sometimes guys with motorcycles hanging out near the museum who will whisk you out there for a couple of thousand som.

Beneath Alexander's fortress you'll encounter the anomaly of several hundred trout occupying a pool and well next to a 16th-century mosque and a 9th-century mausoleum. This is the **Chashma Spring** (admission US$1), formed, it is said, where the Prophet Mohammed's son-in-law Hazrat Ali drove his staff into the ground. The 'holy' fish live off the mineral-laden waters of the spring and canals that feed it.

Accommodation in Nurata itself is pretty grim. Your best bet is the dilapidated **Hotel Nur** (323 00 16; s/d without bathroom US$7/12), 500m from Chashma Spring on the road to the centre, which is the only hotel in town and has a ground-floor restaurant. Close to the centre, Mr Nemat runs a pleasant **homestay** (523 18 74) with a *hammoni* (bath), and can prepare meals and organise excursions.

Activities

After briefly taking in Nurata's sights, you'll want to hightail it to the yurt camps to the north of Nurata. There are four within shooting distance. Two are about 60km due north of Nurata in Yangikazgan; two others are further east in Dungalok near the shores of manmade Lake Aidarkul, formed from the diverted waters of the Syr-Darya in 1969.

GOING LOCAL IN THE NURATAU MOUNTAINS

South of Lake Aidarkul, there is great hiking and bird watching in the mountains of the **Nuratau-Kyzylkum Biosphere Reserve**, which is also the site of a wonderful community-based tourism project (www.nuratau.com). Families in several villages have converted their homes into rustic guesthouses where they welcome guests with overwhelming hospitality. The area is ideal for hiking and horse-riding. You can also enjoy the fresh mountain air and sleep on a *tapchan* (tea bed) under the stars. In winter you can even observe authentic *kupkari* matches (a traditional polo-like game played with a headless goat carcass). This is a great opportunity to experience the traditional life of a Tajik-speaking mountain farmer family in their element – and a great way to ward off architecture burnout if you've seen one too many medressas.

For further information, check the website or contact the **office** (72 452 1200, +998 902 650 680; travelresponsible@gmail.com) in Yangiqishloq, a small town 70km west of Jizzakh. Registration can be done in the guesthouses or in the office. Alternatively, you can arrange a trip to the mountains with a homestay through most tour companies or through the Antica B&B in Samarkand.

All yurt camps include short **camel trekking** rides in their rates; the ones in Dungalok offer fishing. Longer treks, including multiple-day excursions, are also possible for an extra charge.

The comfortable camel-hair yurts, most of them tastefully decorated with carpets and *suzani,* sleep six to eight people. Prices vary from camp to camp according to the level of comfort. Rates include three meals a day, as there's no option but to eat in camp. Camps close from November to mid-March, and sometimes during July and August. Showing up unannounced isn't a good idea; you're far better off calling ahead and arranging a deal via the office of a travel agency, that way your transfers will be taken care of, and you can tailor your package to your needs where possible.

Sputnik Camel Camp YURTSTAY
(☎223 8081; sputnik-navoi@yandex.ru; Yangikazgan; per person US$50) The first and probably the fanciest of the lot, run by the mischievous, tough-as-nails Radik. Has attractive dining yurt and lots of creature comforts.

Yangikazgan Yurt Camp YURTSTAY
(☎225 1419; Yangikazgan; per person US$45) There's welcome electricity and creature comforts here, but the dining room is in a cement building that rather detracts from the otherwise traditional vibe. It's quite close to Sputnik, in the middle of the desert, 6km north of Yangikazgan.

Aidar Yurt Camp YURTCAMP
(☎222 5618, 223 9546; Dungalok; per person US$45) The closest camp to the lake, just 10km away, Aidar has 11 charmingly decorated yurts, as well as electricity and hot water.

Safari Camp YURTCAMP
(☎+998 79 225 5417, +998 79 2238081; sputnik-navoi@yandex.com; Dungalok; per person US$40) With ten colourfully decorated, Kazakh-style yurts, this place is popular with groups and has electricity, hot showers and plenty of creature comforts.

ℹ Getting There & Away

To get to Nurata, make your way from Bukhara or Samarkand to Navoi, then take a shared taxi (10,000S, one hour) or marshrutka (6000S). In Nurata sporadic marshrutkas run to Dungalok and Yangikazgan, but you'll likely have to hire a private car, or arrange a transfer with your yurt camp. Negotiations start at 50,000S one-way to the yurt camps.

Bukhara (Buxoro)

☎65 / POP 263,000

Central Asia's holiest city, Bukhara has buildings spanning a thousand years of history, and a thoroughly lived-in old centre that hasn't changed too much in two centuries. It is one of the best places in Central Asia for a glimpse of pre-Russian Turkestan.

Most of the centre is an architectural preserve, full of medressas, minarets, a massive royal fortress and the remnants of a once-vast market complex. Government restoration efforts have been more subtle and less indiscriminate than in flashier Samarkand, and the city's accommodation options are by far the best and most atmospheric in the country.

Until a century ago Bukhara was watered by a network of canals and some 200 stone pools where people gathered and gossiped, drank and washed. As the water wasn't changed often, Bukhara was famous for plagues; the average 19th-century Bukharan is said to have died by the age of 32. The Bolsheviks modernised the system and drained the pools, although it's most famous, Lyabi Hauz, remains a cool, mulberry-tree shaded oasis at the heart of the city.

You'll need at least two days to look around. Try to allow time to lose yourself in the old town; it's easy to overdose on the 140-odd protected buildings and miss the whole for its many parts.

History

It was as capital of the Samanid state in the 9th and 10th centuries that Bukhara – Bukhoro-i-sharif (Noble Bukhara), the 'Pillar of Islam' – blossomed as Central Asia's religious and cultural heart. Among those nurtured here were the philosopher-scientist Ibn Sina and the poets Firdausi and Rudaki – figures of a similar stature in the Persian Islamic world as, for example, Newton or Shakespeare in the West.

After two centuries under the smaller Karakhanid and Karakitay dynasties, Bukhara succumbed in 1220 to Chinggis Khan, and in 1370 fell under the shadow of Timur's Samarkand.

A second lease of life came in the 16th century when the Uzbek Shaybanids made it the capital of what came to be known as the Bukhara khanate. The centre of Shaybanid Bukhara was a vast marketplace with dozens of specialist bazaars and caravanserais,

Bukhara

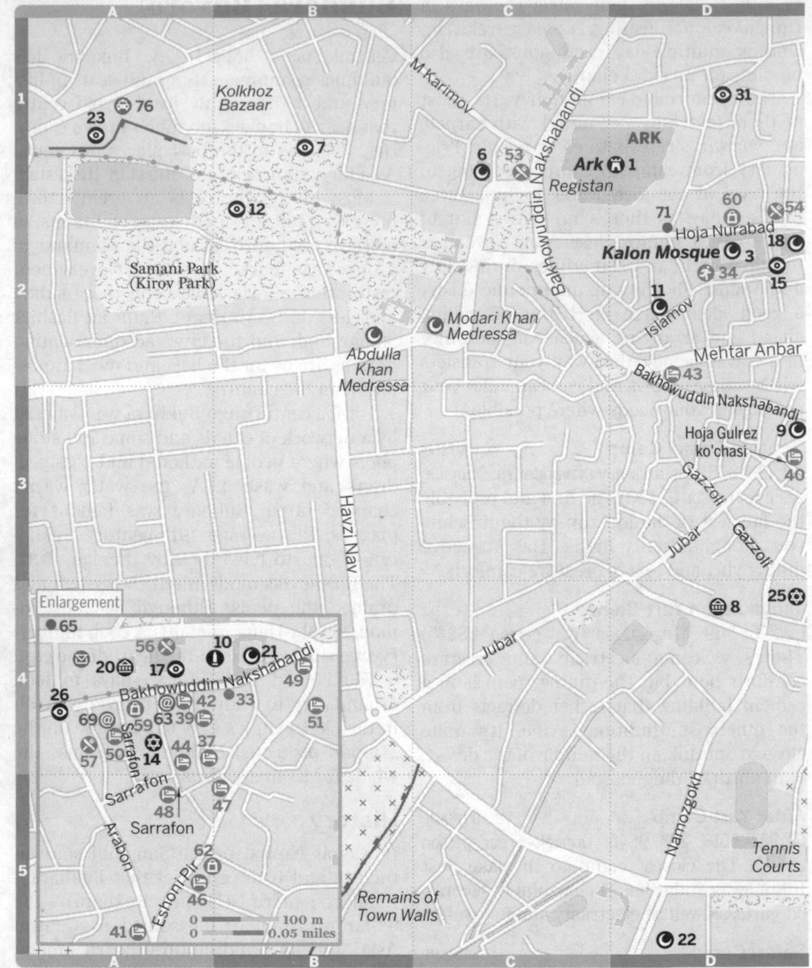

more than 100 medressas (with 10,000 students) and more than 300 mosques.

In 1753 Mohammed Rahim, the local deputy of a Persian ruler, proclaimed himself emir, founding the Mangit dynasty that was to rule until the Bolsheviks came. Several depraved rulers filled Rahim's shoes; the worst was probably Nasrullah Khan (also called 'the Butcher' behind his back), who ascended the throne in 1826 by killing off his brothers and 28 other relatives. He made himself a household name in Victorian England after he executed two British officers.

In 1868, Russian troops under General Kaufman occupied Samarkand (which at the time was within Emir Muzaffar Khan's domains). Soon afterward Bukhara surrendered, and was made a protectorate of the tsar, with the emirs still nominally in charge.

In 1918 a party of emissaries arrived from Tashkent (by then under Bolshevik control) to persuade Emir Alim Khan to surrender peacefully. The wily despot stalled long enough to allow his agents to stir up an anti-Russian mob that slaughtered nearly the whole delegation, and the emir's own army

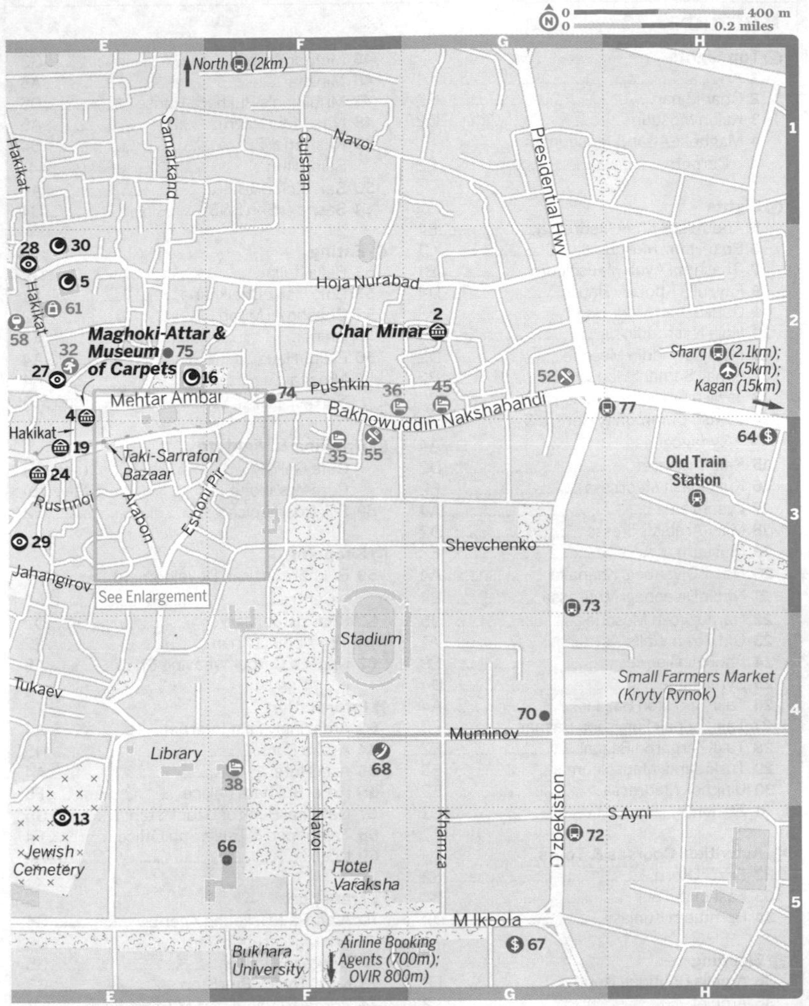

sent a larger Russian detachment packing, back towards Tashkent.

But the humiliated Bolsheviks had their revenge. Following an orchestrated 'uprising' in Charjou (now Turkmenabat in Turkmenistan) by local revolutionaries calling themselves the Young Bukharans, and an equally premeditated request for help, Red Army troops from Khiva and Tashkent under General Mikhail Frunze stormed the Ark (citadel) and captured Bukhara.

Bukhara won a short 'independence' as the Bukhara People's Republic, but after showing rather too much interest in Pan-Turkism it was absorbed in 1924 into the newly created Uzbek SSR.

Sights

Lyabi-Hauz & Around

Lyabi-Hauz PLAZA

Lyabi-Hauz, a plaza built around a pool in 1620 (the name is Tajik for 'around the pool'), is the most peaceful and interesting spot in town – shaded by mulberry trees as old as the pool. The old tea-sipping, chess-board-clutching Uzbek men who once

Bukhara

Top Sights
1 Ark ... D1
2 Char Minar ... G2
3 Kalon Mosque ... D2
4 Maghoki-Attar & Museum of Carpets ... E2

Sights
5 Abdul Aziz Khan Medressa ... E2
6 Bolo-Hauz Mosque ... C1
7 Chashma Ayub Mausoleum ... B1
8 Fayzulla Khojaev House ... D4
9 Gaukushan Medressa ... D3
10 Hoja Nasruddin ... B4
11 Hoja Zayniddin Mosque ... D2
12 Ismail Samani Mausoleum ... B2
13 Jewish Cemetery ... E5
14 Jewish Community Centre & Synagogue ... A4
15 Kalon Minaret ... D2
16 Kukeldash Medressa ... E2
17 Lyabi-Hauz ... A4
18 Mir-i-Arab Medressa ... D2
19 Museum of Art ... E3
20 Nadir Divanbegi Khanaka ... A4
21 Nadir Divanbegi Medressa ... B4
22 Namozgokh Mosque ... D5
23 Old Town Walls ... A1
24 Photo Gallery ... E3
25 Synagogue ... D4
26 Taki-Sarrafon Bazaar ... A4
27 Taki-Telpak Furushon Bazaar ... E2
28 Taki-Zargaron Bazaar ... E2
29 Turki Jandi Mausoleum ... E3
30 Ulugbek Medressa ... E2
31 Zindon ... D1

Activities, Courses & Tours
32 Bozori Kord ... E2
33 East Line Tour ... B4
34 Hammom Kunjak ... D2

Sleeping
35 Amelia Boutique Hotel ... F3
36 Amulet ... F2
37 Emir B&B ... A4
38 Grand Bukhara Hotel ... F4
39 Hotel Sultan ... A4
40 Hovli Poyon B&B ... D3
41 Komil Hotel ... A5
42 Lyabi House Hotel ... A4
43 Madina & Ilyos ... D2
44 Malikjon B&B House ... A4
45 Mehtar Ambar ... G2
46 Minzifa ... A5
47 Mubinjon's Bukhara House ... B5
48 Nasriddin Navruz ... A5
49 Rustam & Zuxro ... B4
Salom Inn ... (see 44)
50 Sarrafon B&B ... A4
51 Sasha & Son B&B ... B4

Eating
52 Bella Italia ... G2
53 Bolo Hauz Chaikhana ... C1
54 Chashmai Mirob ... D2
55 Chinar ... F3
56 Lyabi-Hauz ... A4
57 Minzifa ... A4
Saroy ... (see 59)

Drinking & Nightlife
Cafe Gallery ... (see 42)
Cafe Wishbone ... (see 58)
58 Silk Road Spices ... E2

Shopping
59 Bukhara Artisan Development Centre ... A4
60 Shahriston Market ... D2
61 Tim Abdulla Khan ... E2
62 Unesco Carpet Weaving Shop ... A5

Information
63 Amazingly Fast Internet ... A4
64 Asaka Bank ... H3
65 Asia Hotel ... A4
66 Hotel Bukhara Palace ... F5
67 National Bank of Uzbekistan ... G5
68 Telephone & Telegraph Office ... F4
69 Ucell ... A4

Transport
70 Air & Rail Ticketing Agents ... G4
71 Ark Marshrutka Stop ... D2
72 Gorgaz Bus Stop ... G5
73 Kryty Rynok Bus Stop ... G3
74 Primary Lyabi-Hauz Marshrutka Stop ... F2
75 Secondary Lyabi-Hauz Marshrutka Stop ... E2
76 Shared taxis to Karakol & Olot (Turkmen border) ... A1
77 Vokzal Bus Stop ... H2

inhabited this corner of town have been moved on by local entrepreneurs bent on cashing in on the tourist trade. Still, the plaza maintains its old-world style and has managed to fend off the glitz to which Samarkand's Registan has succumbed, although loud music of an evening is to be expected. It's still a gorgeous place to sit throughout the day.

Hoja Nasruddin MONUMENT

On the east side of Lyabi-Hauz is a statue of Hoja Nasruddin, a semi-mythical 'wise fool' who appears in Sufi teaching-tales around the world.

Nadir Divanbegi Medressa MEDRESSA

(Lyabi-Hauz; admission 1000S, valid 3 days; 8am-6pm; P) The Nadir Divanbegi Medressa was built as a caravanserai, but the khan thought it was a medressa and it dutifully became one in 1622. It's notable for its stunning exterior tilework, which depicts a pair of peacocks holding lambs either side of a sun with a human face, in direct contravention of the Islamic prohibition against depicting living creatures. Inside you'll find a few craft and carpet stalls.

Nadir Divanbegi Khanaka HISTORIC BUILDING

(Lyabi-Hauz; 9am-6pm) FREE On the west side of the square, and built at the same time, is the Nadir Divanbegi Khanaka, a sufi cloister used for religious ceremonies, debates and instruction. Both this and the medressa opposite are named for Abdul Aziz Khan's treasury minister, who financed them in the 17th century. It's the poor relation to the Nadir Divanbegi Medressa it faces across Lyabi-Hauz, but inside there's a worthwhile display of old photos, paintings and a model of Bukhara.

Kukeldash Medressa MEDRESSA

(Bakhowuddin Nakshabandi ko'chasi) The Kukeldash Medressa, built in 1569 by Abdullah II, was at the time the biggest Islamic school in Central Asia. It now hosts an evening puppet, wrestling and, disappointingly, a cock fight show, that's aimed at tourists.

Taki-Sarrafon & Taki-Telpak Furushon Area

Covered Bazaars MARKET

(Hakikat; 7am-8pm) From Shaybanid times, the area west and north from Lyabi-Hauz was a vast warren of market lanes, arcades and crossroad minibazaars whose multi-domed roofs were designed to draw in cool air. Three remaining domed bazaars, heavily renovated in Soviet times, were among dozens of specialised bazaars in the town – **Taki-Sarrafon** (moneychangers), **Taki-Telpak Furushon** (cap makers) and **Taki-Zargaron** (jewellers). They remain only loosely faithful to those designations today.

★ **Maghoki-Attar & Museum of Carpets** MUSEUM

(Pit of the herbalists; Arabon; admission 2300S; museum 9am-5pm) Between the two covered bazaars, in what was the old herb-and-spice bazaar, is Central Asia's oldest surviving mosque, the Maghoki-Attar, a lovely mishmash of 9th-century facade and 16th-century reconstruction.

This is probably also the town's holiest spot: under it in the 1930s archaeologists found bits of a 5th-century Zoroastrian temple ruined by the Arabs and an earlier Buddhist temple. According to legend, the mosque survived the Mongols by being buried by locals in sand. Indeed, only the top of the mosque was visible when the digging began in the 1930s; the present plaza surrounding it is the 12th-century level of the town.

A section of the excavations has been left deliberately exposed inside. The building today ostensibly functions as a **museum** exhibiting Bukhara carpets and prayer mats. Climb the stairs inside the mosque for a view of the Zoroastrian remains.

The charming staff will tell you that until the 16th century, Bukhara's Jews are said to have used the mosque in the evenings as a synagogue – a wonderful image of the cosmopolitan tolerance that was once such a part of Bukhara's identity.

Taki-Zargaron Area

Ulugbek Medressa MEDRESSA

(Hoja Nurabad ko'chasi; medressa admission (for both Ulugbek & Abdul Aziz Khan) 2000S, valid three days; museum admission 1000S; museum 9am-4.30pm) Built in 1417, this is Central Asia's oldest medressa, and may well be familiar to you as it became a model for many others. The blue-tiled medressa, one of three built by Ulugbek (the others are at Gijduvan, 45km away on the road to Samarkand, and in Samarkand's Registan complex), is unrestored and much in need of conservation work – the central alcove in the courtyard recently collapsed and work is needed almost everywhere.

There are no stalls here, just some empty cells and a small **museum** with some great old photos, including one of the Kalon Minaret looking the worse for wear after the Soviets bombed it in the 1920s.

Abdul Aziz Khan Medressa MEDRESSA
(museum of wood carvings admission 1000S; ⏲ 9am-5pm) FREE The student rooms at the 16th-century Abdul Aziz Khan Medressa are occupied, rather typically, by souvenir shops. This is an unrestored gem, built by its namesake to outdo the Ulugbek Medressa, across the street. The highlight is the prayer room, now a **museum of wood carvings**, with jaw-dropping *ghanch* stalactites dripping from the ceiling. It is said that Abdul Aziz had the image of his face covertly embedded in the prayer room's mihrab (Mecca-facing niche) to get around the Sunni Muslim prohibition against depicting living beings (Abdul Aziz Khan was a Shiite). The only other medressa in town that depicts living beings is the Nadir Divanbegi Medressa.

Kalon Minaret & Around

Kalon Minaret MINARET
When it was built by the Karakhanid ruler Arslan Khan in 1127, the Kalon Minaret was probably the tallest building in Central Asia – *kalon* means 'great' in Tajik. It's an incredible piece of work, 47m tall with 10m-deep foundations (including reeds stacked underneath in an early form of earthquake-proofing), and has stood for almost nine centuries. Chinggis Khan was so dumbfounded by it that he ordered it spared.

Its 14 ornamental bands, all different, include the first use of the glazed blue tiles that were to saturate Central Asia under Timur. Up and down the south and east sides are faintly lighter patches, marking the restoration of damage caused by Frunze's artillery in 1920. Its 105 inner stairs, accessible from the Kalon Mosque, have been closed off to tourists for several years but may reopen.

A legend says that Arslan Khan killed an imam after a quarrel. That night in a dream the imam told him, 'You have killed me; now oblige me by laying my head on a spot where nobody can tread', and the tower was built over his grave.

★ **Kalon Mosque** MOSQUE
(Hoja Nurabad; admission 2000S; ⏲ 8am-8pm) At the foot of the minaret, on the site of an earlier mosque destroyed by Chinggis Khan, is the 16th-century congregational Kalon Mosque, big enough for 10,000 people. Its courtyard has some spectacular tile work. Used in Soviet times as a warehouse, it was reopened as a place of worship in 1991.

Mir-i-Arab Medressa MEDRESSA
Opposite the Kalon mosque, its luminous blue domes in sharp contrast to the surrounding brown, is the working Mir-i-Arab Medressa. Especially at sunset, it's among

STODDART & CONOLLY

On 24 June 1842 Colonel Charles Stoddart and Captain Arthur Conolly were marched out from a dungeon cell before a huge crowd in front of the Ark, the emir's fortified citadel, made to dig their own graves and, to the sound of drums and reed pipes from atop the fortress walls, were beheaded.

Colonel Stoddart had arrived three years earlier on a mission to reassure Emir Nasrullah Khan about Britain's invasion of Afghanistan. But his superiors, underestimating the emir's vanity and megalomania, had sent him with no gifts, and with a letter not from Queen Victoria (whom Nasrullah regarded as an equal sovereign), but from the governor-general of India. To compound matters Stoddart violated local protocol by riding, rather than walking, up to the Ark. The piqued Nasrullah had him thrown into jail, where he was to spend much of his time at the bottom of the so-called 'bug pit', in the company of assorted rodents and scaly creatures.

Captain Conolly arrived in 1841 to try to secure Stoddart's release. But the emir, believing him to be part of a British plot with the khans of Khiva and Kokand, tossed Conolly in jail too. After the disastrous British retreat from Kabul, the emir, convinced that Britain was a second-rate power and having received no reply to an earlier letter to Queen Victoria, had both men executed.

Despite public outrage back in England, the British government chose to let the matter drop. Furious friends and relatives raised enough money to send their own emissary, an oddball clergyman named Joseph Wolff, to Bukhara to verify the news. According to Peter Hopkirk in *The Great Game*, Wolff himself only escaped death because the emir thought him hilarious, dressed up in his full clerical regalia.

Uzbekistan's most striking medressas. Mir-i-Arab was a 16th-century Naqshbandi sheikh from Yemen who had a strong influence on the Shaybanid ruler Ubaidullah Khan. Tourists can technically only go as far as the foyer. However, if you ask permission you may be allowed to view the tombs of Mir-i-Arab and Ubaidullah Khan in a room under the northern dome. From there you get a decent view of the courtyard, where you might see students playing ping-pong.

The Ark & Around

★Ark FORTRESS

(☎224 38 53; Registan Sq; admission 4500S, admission with guide 7500S; ⏰9am-5pm) The spectacular-looking Ark, a royal town-within-a-town, is Bukhara's oldest structure, occupied from the 5th century right up until 1920, when it was bombed by the Red Army. It's about 80% ruins inside now, except for some remaining royal quarters, now housing several **museums**.

At the top of the entrance ramp is the 17th-century **Juma (Friday) Mosque**. Turn right into a corridor with courtyards off both sides. First on the left are the former living quarters of the emir's *kushbegi* (prime minister), now housing an archaeological museum and a nature museum where you can see what healthy cotton looks like (in contrast to the forlorn, stunted variety you'll see growing in central Uzbekistan).

Second on the left is the oldest surviving part of the Ark, the vast **Reception & Coronation Court**, whose roof fell in during the 1920 bombardment. The last coronation to take place here was Alim Khan's in 1910. The submerged chamber on the right wall was the treasury, and behind this room was the harem.

To the right of the corridor were the open-air royal stables and the *noghorahona* (a room for drums and musical instruments used during public spectacles in the square below).

Around the Salamhona (Protocol Court) at the end of the corridor are what remain of the royal apartments. These apparently fell into such disrepair that the last two emirs preferred full-time residence at the summer palace. Now there are several museums here, the most interesting of which covers Bukhara's history from the Shaybanids to the tsars. Displays include items imported to Bukhara, including an enormous *samovar* made in Tula, Russia. Another room contains the emir's throne as well as portraits of the ill-fated British officers Stoddart and Conolly, who were eventually executed in front of the fortress on medieval Bukhara's main square, the **Registan**.

Behind the Ark is the **Zindon** (admission 2300S; ⏰9am-5pm Wed-Mon), the jail, now euphemistically called the **Museum of Law & Legislation**. Cheerful attractions include a torture chamber complete with shackles used on prisoners and several dungeons, including the gruesome fourth cell, the 6.5m deep *kanakhona* (bug pit), where Stoddart and Conolly languished in a dark chamber filled with lice, scorpions and vermin. There are also some fascinating early 20th century photographs of pre-Soviet Bukhara taken by Russian photographer Sergey Prokudin-Gorsky.

Beside a pool opposite the Ark's gate is the **Bolo-Hauz Mosque**, the emirs' official place of worship, built in 1718. Beside it is a now-disused 33m **water tower**, built by the Russians in 1927.

Ismail Samani Mausoleum & Around

Ismail Samani Mausoleum MAUSOLEUM

(Samani Park) This mausoleum in Samani Park, completed in 905, is the town's oldest Muslim monument and probably its sturdiest architecturally. Built for Ismail Samani (the Samanid dynasty's founder), his father and grandson, its intricate baked terracotta brickwork – which gradually changes 'personality' through the day as the shadows shift – disguises walls almost 2m thick, helping it survive without restoration (except of the spiked dome) for 11 centuries. Behind the park is one of the few remaining, eroded sections (a total of 2km out of an original 12km) of the Shaybanid **town walls**; another big section is about 500m west of the **Namozgokh Mosque**.

Chashma Ayub Mausoleum MAUSOLEUM

(Samani Park; admission 2000S; ⏰9am-5pm Tue-Sun) The peculiar Chashma Ayub mausoleum was built from the 12th to 16th centuries over a spring. The name means 'Spring of Job'; legend has it the spring appeared after Job struck his staff on the ground here. Inside is a small water museum where you can drink from the spring. Next door is a glistening glass-walled memorial to Imam Ismail al-Bukhari.

Fayzulla Khojaev House & Around

Fayzulla Khojaev House MUSEUM
(☎224 41 88; Tukaev; admission 3500S, camera 2300S; ⊙9am-5pm) The Fayzulla Khojaev House was once home to one of Bukhara's many infamous personalities, the man who plotted with the Bolsheviks to dump Emir Alim Khan. Fayzulla Khojaev was rewarded with the presidency of the Bukhara People's Republic, chairmanship of the Council of People's Commissars of the Uzbek SSR, and finally liquidation by Stalin.

The house was built in 1891 by his father, Ubaidullah, a wealthy merchant. Fayzulla lived here until 1925, when the Soviets converted it into a school. Meticulous restoration of the elegant frescoes, *ghanch*, latticework and Bukhara-style ceiling beams (carved, unpainted elm) has returned it to its former glory. If there's a tour group present you may be treated to a fashion show, but it's well worth visiting for the gorgeous interiors.

Turki Jandi Mausoleum MAUSOLEUM
(Namozgokh ko'chasi; ⊙7am-7pm) Deep in the old town is the tiny, decrepit Turki Jandi mausoleum, favoured for getting one's prayers answered. Its importance is signalled by the hundreds of other graves around it – allegedly in stacks 30m deep! Turki Jandi's tomb is accessed through the mosque under the taller, second cupola. A well inside the mosque contains holy water that locals drink from a cooler near the complex entrance. Have the chatty mullah show you the sections of original 10th-century Arabic script on the mosque's doors, allegedly inscribed by Turki Jandi himself.

★**Char Minar** HISTORIC BUILDING
Photogenic little Char Minar, in a maze of alleys between Pushkin and Hoja Nurabad, bears more relation to Indian styles than to anything Bukharan. This was the gatehouse of a long-gone medressa built in 1807. The name means 'Four Minarets' in Tajik, although they aren't strictly speaking minarets but rather decorative towers.

Gaukushan Medressa MEDRESSA
At the intersection of Jubar and Bakhowuddin Nakshabandi ko'chasi is the interesting 16th-century Gaukushan Medressa, with chipped majolica on its unrestored facade.

Museum of Art MUSEUM
(Bakhowuddin Nakshabandi ko'chasi; admission 1200S; ⊙9am-5pm Wed-Mon) The Museum of Art has a worthy collection of mostly 20th-century paintings by Bukharan artists. It's in the former headquarters of the Russian Central Asian Bank (1912). Look out for works by Zelim Saidjuddin, the Bukharan artist featured in Colin Thubron's *Lost Heart of Asia* and *Shadow of the Silk Road*.

BUKHARA'S JEWS

South of Lyabi-Hauz is what's left of the old town's unique **Jewish Quarter**. There have been Jews in Bukhara (Buxoro) since perhaps the 12th or 13th century. They developed their own unique culture with its own language – Bukhori, which is related to Persian but uses the Hebrew alphabet. Bukhara's Jews still speak it, as do about 10,000 Bukhara Jews who now live elsewhere, mainly in Israel.

The Bukhara Jews managed to become major players in Bukharan commerce, in spite of deep-rooted, institutionalised discrimination. Bukhara Jews made up 7% of Bukhara's population at the time of the Soviet Union's collapse, but today only a few hundred remain.

The **Jewish community centre & synagogue** (☎510 18 33, 224 23 80; Sarrafon 20), roughly across from Salom Inn, holds regular services and also sponsors a functioning Jewish school just around the corner. A century ago there were at least seven synagogues here, reduced after 1920 to two. The second **synagogue** is located south of Kukluk Bazaar – from the ruined mosque on Namozgokh, take a left onto Gulzor ko'chasi, then turn right at the red garage door (number 3) and you'll find the synagogue on the right a little further down the street.

The **Jewish Cemetery** (Muminov; ⊙8am-6pm), just south of the Old Town, is perhaps the most impressive evidence of the previous size of the local Jewish community. It's a very well maintained and huge space, with centuries of tombs on display.

Photo Gallery GALLERY
(admission free; ⏲9am-7.30pm) The Museum of Art is a Photo Gallery containing mesmerising photos of Bukhara Jews, gypsies and city life shot by Bukhara Iranian photographer Shavkat Boltaev.

Hoja Zayniddin Mosque MOSQUE
(⏲7am-7pm) In Bukhara's backstreets between Hoja Nurabad and Islamov, across from the Ark on Hoja Nurabad, the interior of the 16th-century Hoja Zayniddin Mosque has a tremendous *aivan* and some of the best original mosaic and *ghanch*-work you're going to see anywhere.

Activities

★Bozori Kord BATHHOUSE
(Hakikat ko'chasi; admission 60,000S; ⏲6am-midnight Wed-Mon, noon-midnight Tue) Bozori Kord is an age-old Bukharan bathhouse where little has changed for centuries. It's now solidly oriented to tourists (hence the hefty entry fee), but otherwise totally authentic and a fantastic experience. You'll be put through an hour-long process that involves working up a sweat in the hammam, being washed down, massaged and stretched and then rubbed all over with ginger and left to sweat it out again. The baths are open to men only until noon; afterwards it's open to all.

Hammom Kunjak BATHHOUSE
(Ibodov 4; admission 70,000S; ⏲9am-4pm) This ancient Bukharan bathhouse, in the shadow of the Kalon Minaret, is for women only. It's traditionally where women bring their newborn babies at 40 days of age for a first ritual wash, and is also available for private group rental after-hours.

Tours

Most hotels and B&Bs can arrange guides. We also recommend the following, all of whom speak English.

Gulya Khamidova (☎+998 907 185 889)

Noila Kazidzanova (☎+998 907 182 012, 228 20 12; barocco@yandex.ru)

Zinnat Ashurova (☎190 71 27)

Festivals

The four-day **Silk & Spices Festival** in May or June is a celebration of local folk art as well as silk and spices, with lots of music and dancing in the streets. Contact East Line Tour (p199) or one of the B&Bs to establish when the festival is on.

Sleeping

Bukhara's wonderful, largely traditional-style B&Bs set the standard for accommodation in Central Asia. They tend to be surprisingly large courtyard houses tucked away in the backstreets of the old town with rooms awash with traditional *ghanch* and pieces of antique furniture. Several of their traditional dining rooms in Bukhara are even considered to be part of the city's Unesco World Heritage status. It's essential to book ahead during busy times of the year, as the very best hotels can be booked for weeks ahead of time.

Mubinjon's Bukhara House B&B $
(☎224 20 05; Eshoni Pir; dm US$8) Bukhara's pioneer B&B is housed in a home dating from 1766. Traditional *kurpacha* are spread on the floor of the four rooms here and the bathrooms are basic (with no hot water) but sanitary. The legendary Mubinjon – a true Bukharan eccentric – doesn't speak much English but makes himself understood. Check out the wonderful light blue antique Volga while you're here – cultural experiences don't come much better than this! Breakfast is not included.

Sarrafon B&B B&B $
(☎+998 91 402 0641, 223 64 63; www.sarrafon-travel.uz; Sarrafon 4; dm US$15, s/d US$20/30; ❄📶) Expanding from four to seven rooms in 2013, Sarrafon has forged a reputation for being great value due to its ideal location, friendly host family and quality breakfasts. It may be rather low on traditional charms, but it has some nice touches such as local carpets on the floors and walls, and you won't get a much better deal than this just off Lyabi-Hauz.

Rustam & Zuxro B&B $
(☎+998 90 511 0550, +998 65 224 3080; hotelr@mail.ru; Bakhowuddin Nakshabandi 116; dm/s/d US$10/25/35; ❄📶) A good budget option just a stone's throw from Lyabi-Hauz, the large carpeted rooms have flat screen TVs, fridges and decent bathrooms. A recent expansion has brought eight new rooms and there are more on the way.

Madina & Ilyos B&B $
(☎+998 905 125 820, 224 61 62; madina-ilyos.blogspot.de; Mehtar Ambar 18; r without bathroom US$8-10, d with bathroom per person US$15-20) This perennial backpacker fave is famous for being great value and for being hard to find. Walk past No 18, hang a left and look

for a blue wooden door, also marked No 18. Madina now has an annexe with 10 rooms at Mehtar Ambar 15. Call for free pick up from the airport, bus or train station.

★**Amulet** HISTORIC HOTEL **$$**
(☎224 53 42; www.amulet-hotel.com; Bakhowuddin Nakshabandi 73; s/d/tr US$50/70/90; ❄📶) Housed inside the converted 1861 Said Kamol Medressa, this charming 8-room place has all the comforts you need without sacrificing an inch of its traditional flavour. Out back is a fabulous, decaying 18th-century mosque that the hotel plans to convert into a restaurant, while the traditional *sandal* (sitting area), complete with heated floor, makes for a cosy place to relax in the winter months. Book way ahead if you plan to stay here.

★**Amelia Boutique Hotel** BOUTIQUE HOTEL **$$**
(☎224 12 63; www.hotelamelia.com; Bozor Hoja 1; s/d from US$50/65; ❄📶) It's the proactive and passionate management here that really puts this boutique hotel on the map. Unlike so many hotels, the owners seem to have really thought long and hard about how best to make people enjoy their stay. Housed in the former house of a Jewish merchant, the hotel's ten individually named rooms are all very different, including a mud-walled suite and a recreation of the famous Sogdian fresco from the Afrosiab Museum in Samarkand. Bathrooms are modern and in great condition, with free goodies, while the stunning 18th-century breakfast room is reason enough to stay here alone.

★**Komil Hotel** BOUTIQUE HOTEL **$$**
(☎223 87 80; www.komiltravel.com; Barakyon 40; s/d/tr/ste from US$45/60/75/80; ❄@📶) This friendly 18-room hotel has stunning *ghanch*-work and a young, laid-back proprietor who speaks fluent English. The rooms are gorgeous, and the 19th-century dining room is a pure pleasure to breakfast in. Even some of the recently built rooms are decorated in a very traditional style, while the interiors of the older ones are all original. This is also a great place to eat (real coffee is even on offer!) and a popular choice for vegetarians, for whom Komil is a lifeline.

★**Hovli Poyon B&B** B&B **$$**
(☎224 18 65; hovli-poyon@mail.ru; Hoja Gulrez 13; s/d US$45/60; ❄📶) Few Bukhara B&Bs are more memorable than this one, set in a 19th-century house dripping with both character and history. It was a gift for Emir Ahad Khan, and both the grand *aivan* and huge vine-strewn and ethnography-filled courtyard festooned with fruit trees are emir-worthy. The rooms, of various sizes, have all been recently renovated and feel a bit too modern to be truly traditional – the rooms at the front of the house are the most authentic.

★**Lyabi House Hotel** B&B **$$**
(☎224 24 84; www.lyabihouse.com; Husainov 7; s/d/tr US$50/70/90; ❄📶) No place in town better combines authentic old-Bukhara design with modern amenities. Highlights are the eclectic range of rooms and the dignified and vast *aivan* with carved wooden columns, where breakfast is served – worth stopping by to see even if you're not staying here. Request a room away from the noisy reception area.

Salom Inn B&B **$$**
(☎224 37 33; www.salomtravel.com; Sarrafon 3; s/d/tr US$50/75/90; ❄📶) Housed in the courtyard of an old mansion in the Jewish Quarter, this charming place has lively and enthusiastic management who have created smart rooms stuffed full of handicrafts that boast traditionally carved wooden ceilings and handmade local sheets. The vine-clad courtyard is also a great place to relax. Highly recommended.

Mehtar Ambar HISTORIC HOTEL **$$**
(☎+998 65 750 77 99, 224 41 68; mekhtarambar@inbox.ru; Bakhowuddin Nakshabandi 91; s/d/tr US$43/53/65; ❄📶) Mehtar Ambar is more austere in all senses than the next door Amulet; it's a more authentic medressa experience, but it's also rather less friendly. The 2nd-floor rooms are brighter than the ground-floor rooms, while the breakfast room is a *ghanch*-laden gem.

Emir B&B BOUTIQUE HOTEL **$$**
(☎224 49 65; www.emirtravel.com; Husainov 17; s/d/tr US$35/50/65; ❄@) This place consists of two old Jewish Quarter houses set around twin courtyards and run by the friendly and knowledgeable Milla. One has traditional-style rooms filled with antiques, *ghanch* and trinket-laden niches, the other is all new and shiny – both have comfy beds and good bathrooms.

Sasha & Son B&B B&B **$$**
(☎224 49 66; www.sashasonhotels.com; Eshoni Pir 3; s/d US$60/68; ❄📶) Behind a beautifully

carved wooden front door is a maze connecting several small buildings with new rooms elaborately done up in old style. All rooms have satellite TV and snazzy bathrooms with fine tilework. The location is excellent, just moments from Lyabi-Hauz.

Malikjon B&B House B&B **$$**
(☎224 50 50; malikjon_house@bk.ru; Sarrafon 9; s/d/tr US$30/40/50; ❄📶) This pleasant 11 room courtyard hotel may not be the most atmospheric of the lot, but it has simple, clean rooms with attractively painted ceilings and a terrace under traditional beams.

Nasriddin Navruz B&B **$$**
(☎224 34 57; www.nasriddinhotel.com; Babahanov 37; s/d US$25/40; ❄) This friendly, family-run place is not a particularly traditional option despite being found in the middle of the old town. The rooms surround a small yard, and it's a comfortable option for those on a tight budget.

Minzifa BOUTIQUE HOTEL **$$$**
(☎224 56 28; www.minzifa.com; Eshoni Pir 63; s/d US$70/85; ❄📶) The ubiquitous local style is faithfully on display at this superb courtyard hotel, although the decor is toned down by softer than usual colour schemes. It has some of the friendliest service in town, ultra-comfy oversized twin beds and 12 uniquely decorated rooms with bamboo roofs and dripping with *ghanch*. Bathrooms are large (with tubs) and other comforts include TVs and fridges.

Hotel Sultan HOTEL **$$$**
(☎224 2435; www.bukhara-sultanhotel.com; Bakhowuddin Nakshabandi 100; s/d US$80/108; ❄📶) You're paying for the prime location here, directly in front of Lyabi-Hauz, and this is definitely the best place in town to get old town location combined with modern comforts. Rooms are modern and not particularly large, but each has a small balcony, and many of them open onto a traditional Bukharan courtyard.

Grand Bukhara Hotel HOTEL **$$$**
(☎223 13 26; info@bukharatourist.com; Muminov 8; s/d from US$59/106; P❄📶) If you've had enough of the local flavour and are looking for Western-style luxury, this high-rise in the new part of town has been transformed from dusty monstrosity into a pillar of poshness, with slick white duvet covers and a bevy of amenities.

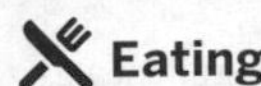

Eating

You don't go to Bukhara for the food, that's for sure, though things have improved in recent years. Many courtyard hotels offer meals, and most offer these to non-guests, so it's worth enquiring if you'd like to avoid the tourist-heavy fare around Lyabi-Hauz.

For self-caterers there are farmers markets, including Kolkhoz Bazaar and the morning-only Kukluk Bazaar, buried deep in the Jewish Quarter.

★ **Minzifa** INTERNATIONAL **$$**
(☎224 61 75; Bakhowuddin Nakshabandi; mains 9000-20,000S; ⏲11am-11pm; 🖉📋) Still Bukhara's most charming restaurant is this perennially popular place with a fantastic roof terrace on which to dine al fresco in the summer months. There's also a cosy and traditional dining room where live piano music can often be heard. The menu takes in Uzbek classics and also a range of European dishes and is good for vegetarians. The service is friendly and professional; reserve at least a day or two ahead during high season.

★ **Saroy** INTERNATIONAL **$$**
(Sarrafon; mains 8000-15,000S; ⏲12.30-11.30pm; 🖉📋) A very welcome new addition to the eating scene, this restaurant fronting Lyabi-Hauz is housed in a beautifully appointed two-storey building with both traditional and modern touches. The large menu has plenty of vegetarian choices among its tasty mains and the well-trained, English-speaking staff are helpful and friendly. We can heartily recommend the unfortunately named Beef Jiz (fried beef with vegetables).

Lyabi-Hauz UZBEK **$$**
(Lyabi-Hauz; mains from 7000-20,000S; ⏲9am-11pm) Dining al fresco around the venerable pool with grey-beards, local families and (increasingly) plenty of other tourists is the quintessential Bukhara experience. There are two chaikhanas here, both serving shashlyk, *plov, kovurma laghman* (with meat and tomato sauce) and cold beer. There's also live music most evenings, making this a pleasant spot for an evening drink.

Chashmai Mirob UZBEK **$$**
(Hoja Nurabad ko'chasi; mains 6000-7000S; ⏲10am-10pm, closed Nov-Mar; 📋) It's known more for its fabulous view of Mir-i-Arab

than for its food, but you can still eat passably here, though you may be swamped by tour groups if you're unlucky. The menu is heavy on Russian classics and you can preorder *plov*.

Chinar UZBEK **$$**
(Bakhowuddin Nakshabandi; mains 5000-10,000S; 8am-11pm;) Occupying a large, newly built property just a short stroll from Lyabi-Hauz, this self-styled chaikhana is actually a full restaurant rather than just a teahouse. Choose between the upstairs roof terrace (and check out those majestic heron statues) or sit downstairs in the main dining room. The food focuses on Uzbek classics, with a few Russian and Caucasian dishes.

Bella Italia ITALIAN **$$**
(Bakhowuddin Nakshabandi; mains 8000-18,000S; 11am-11pm;) There is surprisingly decent Italian food at this pleasant space inside a shopping centre. As you'd expect, there's pizza and pasta and it's a godsend for vegetarians.

Bolo Hauz Chaikhana UZBEK **$$**
(Afrosiab; mains 5000-8000S; 9am-8pm) This large chaikhana in the park opposite the Ark is an ideal place for a cheap and simple meal of Uzbek salads, soups, *plov* or beef noodles.

Drinking & Nightlife

For anything rowdier than puppets and coffee you must head southeast of the centre into the newer part of town, but the nightclubs here are decidedly provincial (read: mostly male). The exception is the busy nightclub in the basement of the Hotel Asia, a short walk from Lyabi-Hauz.

★Silk Road Spices CHAIKHANA
(Halim Ibodov 5; set tea & sweets 12,000S per person; 9am-7pm) This boutique teahouse offers a delightful diversion from all that sightseeing. It has six spicy varieties of tea and coffee, served with rich local sweets such as halva and *nabat* (crystal sugar) in a cosy, traditional atmosphere.

Cafe Gallery CAFE
(Bakhowuddin Nakshabandi; 9am-11pm) This pioneering, family-run cafe has good coffee available and well-intended, if rather slow service. There's a selection of sweet items available too, and its central location makes it the best place for a caffeine injection in town.

Cafe Wishbone CAFE
(Hakikat 1A; 9am-8pm) A new German-Uzbek coffee shop where you can get real coffee and choose from a selection of cakes, but given its German management, the interior design leaves quite a lot to be desired and where's the wi-fi? Still, a cappuccino on the terrace is very welcome.

Shopping

With many tourist sights overflowing with vendors, it's not hard to find a souvenir in Bukhara. They are, of course, of varying quality.

Tim Abdulla Khan CARPETS
(Hakikat ko'chasi; 9am-6pm) For carpets, you couldn't ask for a better shopping atmosphere than at the silk-weaving centre in this late-16th-century building, located near Taki-Telpak Furushon Bazaar (a *tim* was a general market). Vendors are not pushy and will openly inform you on what's handmade and what's machine-made. You can watch silk-clothing makers in action here.

Unesco Carpet Weaving Shop CARPETS
(Eshoni Pir 57; 9am-5pm Mon-Sat) This no longer has anything to do with Unesco (which helped them launch in 2001), but you can still observe weavers here hand making pricey silk carpets and *suzani* with unique Bukhara designs.

Bukhara Artisan Development Centre HANDICRAFTS
(Bakhowuddin Nakshabandi ko'chasi; 9am-6pm Mon-Sat) Here you can watch artisans at work on a variety of handicrafts including *suzani*, miniature paintings, jewellery boxes and chess sets.

Shahriston Market MARKET
(Hoja Nurabad; 7am-6pm) The virtually tourist-free Shahriston Market is in a large courtyard, where locals trade jewellery, carpets, clothing and other handicrafts among themselves and relative bargains can be had compared to things on sale down the street in the traveller-oriented covered markets.

Information

INTERNET ACCESS

Wi-fi can now be found in almost all but the most basic hotels, though it's often not working (always check with your own phone or laptop before you check in if it's important to you), and is often restricted to the lobby area. There are plenty of internet cafes, however.

Ucell (Bakhowuddin Nakshabandi 88; per hr 2000S; ⌚9am-11pm) Right on Lyabi-Hauz, this place offers the cheapest access in the centre.

Amazingly Fast Internet (Bakhowuddin Nakshabandi; per hour 3000S; ⌚8am-midnight) Great name, although it might not always be the case.

MONEY

Most vendors around Taki-Sarrafon (Bakhowuddin Nakshabandi) and elsewhere exchange money at fair black-market rates. You can also change money at the bus station and with some hotel owners (others will have a money changer who can drop by if they call them). Official exchange booths are at Taki-Sarrafon and **Asia Hotel** (Mehtar Ambar). The latter also advances cash for Visa cardholders, as does **Hotel Bukhara Palace** (☎223 50 04; Navoi 8) and the **National Bank of Uzbekistan** (M Ikbola 3; ⌚9am-5pm Mon-Fri). **Asaka Bank** (Bakhautdin Naqshband 168; ⌚9am-5pm Mon-Fri) does MasterCard cash advances.

REGISTRATION

OVIR (☎223 88 68; Murtazaev 10/3; ⌚9am-5pm Mon-Fri) Some way south of the center of the new town, register here if you are not staying in an official hotel.

TELEPHONE & FAX

Telephone & Telegraph Office (Muminov 8; ⌚24hr) International calls for standard Uztelekom rates.

TOURIST INFORMATION

For a place as geared towards tourism as Bukhara, it's incredible that the once-excellent tourist information centre has closed, and B&Bs have had to step in to fill the void. Most B&Bs can sort you out with just about anything you need from drivers and train tickets to guides and maps.

TRAVEL & TOUR AGENCIES

Several B&Bs have attached travel agencies. The best are Emir, Komil, Salom and Sarrafon. Besides yurtstays near Nurata and homestays near Yangikishlok (which just about any hotel can arrange), area attractions include endangered Persian gazelles north of Karaul Bazaar, swimming in Tudakul Lake and the excavated remains of the pre-Islamic era city of Paikent, 60km southwest of Bukhara.

East Line Tour (☎224 22 69; www.eastlinetour.com; Bakhautdin Naqshband 98) runs the full gamut of tours, but specialises in bird-watching tours around Tudakul Lake and further afield. It's also the only agency that rents bikes (US$15 per day, leave your passport as a deposit). They'll also buy train tickets for you (with a 12,000S commission per ticket) and can organise guides, hotels and entertainment shows.

Getting There & Away

AIR

Uzbekistan Airways (☎225 39 46; Airport) has flights from Bukhara to Tashkent (US$50, at least daily), plus a weekly flight to Urgench (US$57, Sunday) in the high season. You can only book domestic flights at the airport (and must pay in US dollars), while international flights can be bought at any of the numerous 'aviakassa' in the new town.

LAND

All eastbound transport leaves from the North Bus Station, about 3km north of the centre. A cab here will cost you 5000S. Here you'll find plenty of private buses (Navoi 5000S, 2½ hours; Samarkand 20,000S, 4½ hours; Tashkent 30,000S, eight to 10 hours) and shared taxis (Navoi 20,000S, one hour; Tashkent 80,000S, 6½ hours), plus a few marshrutkas. Shared taxis to Samarkand (40,000S, three hours) involve a change of car in Navoi.

About 1.5km north of here is Karvon Bazaar, departure point for Urgench and Khiva-bound transport. Shared taxis congregate in a lot on the less-crowded south end of the market. The going rate is 70,000S per seat for Urgench (4½ hours). Drivers demand a little extra for Khiva; you're better off transferring in Urgench. For buses to Urgench (20,000S, eight hours), you have to wait out on the main road in front of the taxi stand and flag buses originating in Tashkent, which come through sporadically in the morning – start early if you want to take the bus.

To get to the North Bus Station and Karvon Bazaar take marshrutka 61 from the **secondary Lyabi-Hauz marshrutka stop** (near Asia Hotel).

The 'Sharq' bus station east of the centre no longer functions as such, but it's still a shared taxis departure point. Find transport to Karshi (30,000S, two hours), Shakhrisabz (60,000S, four hours), and Denau on the Tajik border (70,000S, 5½ hours). Change in Karshi for Termiz (from Karshi 35,000S, 3½ hours).

TRAIN

The **train station** (☎524 65 93; Kagan) is 9km southeast of Bukhara in Kagan. The 'Sharq' express train zips from Bukhara to Tashkent every morning at 8:05am (37,000S, seven hours) via Samarkand (25,000S, three hours). There are also far cheaper trains to both Tashkent and Samarkand that use old Soviet-era rolling stock – a good option for saving on ticket prices and hotel costs.

Otherwise, Bukhara is a bit of a backwater for trains – the main national services from

Tashkent to Nukus, Kungrad, Urgench and Russia go via Navoi, not Bukhara.

To get to Kagan take marshrutka 68 from the Lyabi-Hauz stop (800S, 25 minutes). There are several **air and rail ticketing agents** on Mustaqillik around the Kryty Rynok farmers' market.

Getting Around

TO/FROM THE AIRPORT

The airport is 6km east of town. Figure on around 6000S for the 10-minute taxi trip between the centre and the airport. Marshrutka 100 or bus 10 to/from the Vokzal, **Kryty Rynok** or **Gorgaz** stops takes 15 to 20 minutes.

BICYCLE RENTAL

In a town that's perfect for exploring by bike, East Line Tour (p199) is the only agency that rents quality ones (per day US$15, bring your passport as deposit).

PUBLIC TRANSPORT & TAXI

From the **primary Lyabi-Hauz marshrutka stop**, marshrutka 52 goes to the new part of town via Mustaqillik, while both 52 and 68 pass by the useful **Vokzal stop**, where you can pick up transport going just about anywhere. Useful destinations are Kolkhoz (Dekhon) Bazaar, the **Ark stop** and Karvon Bazaar.

You should be able to get anywhere in the centre of town in a taxi for about 3000S, so long as you avoid the taxi drivers who hang out around Lyabi Hauz. From the centre a one-way taxi should cost about 10,000S to Kagan; less to Emir's Summer Palace.

Around Bukhara

Emir's Summer Palace

For a look at the kitsch lifestyle of the last emir, Alim Khan, go out to his summer palace, Sitorai Mohi Hosa (Star-and-Moon Garden), now a **museum** (228 50 47; admission 12,000S; 9am-7pm Apr-Oct, to 5pm Nov-Mar), 6km north of Bukhara.

The three-building compound was a joint effort for Alim Khan by Russian architects (outside) and local artisans (inside), and no punches were pulled in showing off both the finest and the gaudiest aspects of both styles. A 50-watt Russian generator provided the first electricity the emirate had ever seen. In front of the harem is a pool where the women frolicked, overlooked by a wooden pavilion from which – says every tour guide – the emir tossed an apple to his chosen bedmate.

To get here from Bukhara take bus 7 or marshrutka 70 from the Vokzal stop. The palace is at the end of the line.

KHOREZM (XORAZM)

Urgench (Urganch)

62 / POP 140,000

Urgench, the capital of Khorezm province, is a standard-issue Soviet grid of broad streets and empty squares, 450km northwest of Bukhara across the desolation of the Kyzylkum desert. When the Amu-Darya changed course in the 16th century, the people of Konye-Urgench (then called Urgench), 150km downriver in present-day Turkmenistan, were left without water and started a new town here. Today travellers use Urgench mainly as a transport hub for Khiva, 35km southwest. It's also the jumping-off point for the 'Golden Ring' of ancient fortresses in southern Karakalpakstan. It's not the kind of place you're likely to want to hang around in, but it can be useful as a stop over.

Sleeping & Eating

Shashlyk stands are located along pedestrian Uzbekistan ko'chasi. Go one short block north from the Hotel Urgench and take a left.

Hotel Urgench HOTEL $$
(226 20 24; Al-Khorezmi 35/1; d/lux US$23/36;) This previously notorious hotel has been renovated and now displays perfectly acceptable, clean, Soviet-style rooms. It's worth trying bargaining. To get here, head up the main avenue from the station, cross the bridge and take the first right a block after the main square. Breakfast is not included.

Khorezm Palace LUXURY HOTEL $$$
(224 99 99; www.khorezmpalace.uz; Al-Beruni 2; s/d/ste US$60/110/140;) Urgench's fancier sleeping option has all the amenities you would expect at these prices, all tucked away neatly behind a glass façade. It's also a short distance from the main square where Al-Beruni and Al-Khorezmi meet. If you approach the square from the station, take a right off the square and the hotel will be on your right-hand side.

Khorezm

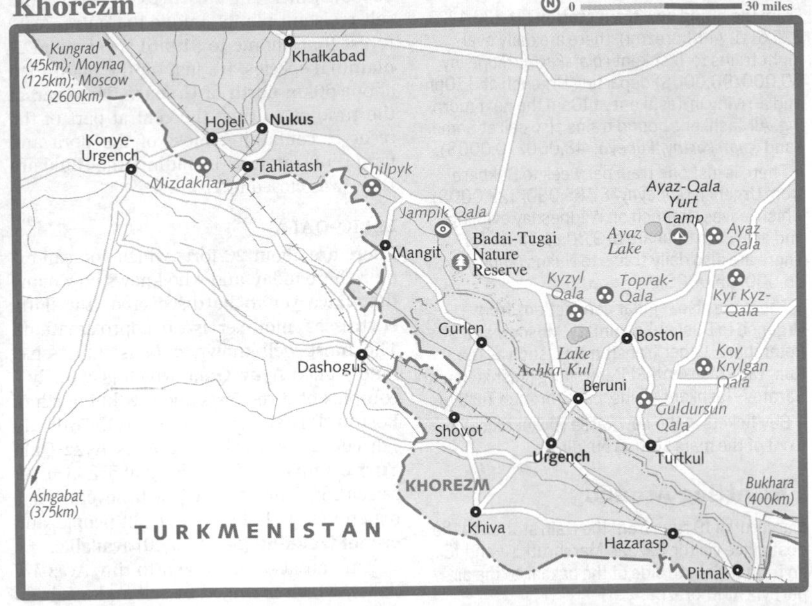

Chaikhana Urgench CHAIKHANA $
(Al-Khorezmi 35/1; mains 3000-5000S; ⌚8am-10pm) Located right next to the Hotel Urgench is this cafe serving shashlyk, *laghman* and *plov*.

Information

Bahadir & Bakhtiyar Rakhamov (☎512 12 41, Bahadir 352 41 06, Bakhtiyar 517 51 33) English-speaking father-and-son driving team, offering excursions to the *qalas* (fortresses; US$70 per carload, including unlimited stops).

Delia Madrashimova (☎290 96 36; per day US$35) This English-speaking guide is your best bet for excursions to the *qalas* or Khiva.

Internet Cafe (Al-Khorezmi 1; per hr 1000S; ⌚9am-9pm)

Post, Telephone & Telegraph Office (Al-Khorezmi 1; ⌚24hr)

Getting There & Away

AIR

Uzbekistan Airways (☎226 88 60; Al-Khorezmi 1; ⌚8am-7pm) has one to four flights daily to Tashkent (US$85) and four weekly flights to St Petersburg and Moscow. Several Tashkent-bound flights per week stop in Bukhara in the high season.

LAND

Shared taxi is the favoured way across the Kyzylkum desert to Bukhara and beyond. Regular shared taxis leave from a stand near the bus station to Bukhara (70,000S, 4½ hours) and to Tashkent (100,000S, 12 hours). You can always break up the journey to Tashkent or Samarkand in Bukhara – you'll need to do this to get to Samarkand as you won't find direct taxis here.

The new **bus station** (Al-Khorezmi), just outside of the train station, was being built at the time of research. There's a midday bus to Bukhara (20,000S, eight hours), two daily buses to Samarkand (30,000S, 12 hours) and a few buses to Tashkent (50,000S, 20 hours) via Bukhara and Samarkand.

Shared taxis (20,000S, 1½ hours) to Nukus congregate at Olympic (Olympiysky) Stadium, about 2km north of the centre. Traffic is heaviest in the morning. If nothing's going to Nukus, go to Beruni and change there. There's also a 10am bus to Nukus that departs from Raytsentr Bazaar (11,000S, three hours).

The trolleybus to Khiva (1000S, 1½ hours) waits on Al-Beruni one block west of the post office. The stand for shared taxis to Khiva (3000S, 20 minutes) is south of the bazaar on Al-Beruni, about 250m west of the trolleybus stop. Shared taxis to Beruni and Boston hang out roughly opposite the Khiva taxi stand on Al-Beruni.

TRAIN

From the brand new **train station** (☎220 4223, 225 6111; Al-Khorezmi), there are daily overnight trains to Tashkent (*platskartny/kupeyny* 60,000/90,000S) departing Urgench at 3.10pm and arriving in Tashkent at 10am the next morning. All Tashkent-bound trains also call at Samarkand (*platskartny/kupeyny* 48,000/70,000S).

There is just one train per week to Bukhara from Urgench (*kupeyny/SV* 65,000/123,000S), which leaves Urgench on Wednesday evening and arrives in Bukhara at 9.30am Thursday. There are also daily trains to Nukus (*kupeyny/SV* 36,000/65,000S).

There are also regular connections from Urgench to Dushanbe, Almaty, Moscow and St Petersburg. Other transit trains, such as the Kungrad–Tashkent, St Petersburg–Tashkent and Saratov–Tashkent trains, pass through Turtkul.

Buy tickets in the new *kassa* (ticket office) in front of the main station building.

Getting Around

Marshrutka 19 runs from the train station to the post office via the bazaar. Marshrutka 3 and 13 go from the south side of the bazaar to the airport via Al-Khorezmi.

Around Urgench

Ancient Khorezm

The Amu-Darya delta, stretching from southeast of Urgench to the Aral Sea, has been inhabited for millennia and was an important oasis long before Urgench or even Khiva were important. The historical name of the delta area, which includes parts of modern-day northern Turkmenistan, was Khorezm.

The ruins of many Khorezmian towns and forts, some well over 2000 years old, still stand east and north of Urgench in southern Karakalpakstan. With help from Unesco, local tourism officials have dubbed this area the 'Golden Ring of Ancient Khorezm'. The area's traditional name is Elliq-Qala (Fifty Fortresses).

For fans of old castles in the sand, this is an area not to be missed. Outdoor and nature enthusiasts will also find plenty to do here, from scrambling among the *qala* ruins, to camel trekking near Ayaz-Qala. There is also the possibility of hiking in the **Badai-Tugai Biosphere Reserve** (admission per person US$25, camping charge per person US$35), which is a *tugai* (trees, shrubs and salt-resistant plants unique to Central Asia) forest that's home to 91 bird species and 21 mammal species. It's just off the main road about 60km north of Urgench. However, at the time of writing, the central part of the reserve, containing most of the flora and fauna of interest including the Bukhara Deer, was closed to visitors.

ELLIQ-QALA

There are about 20 forts which you can explore here today, and who knows how many that have yet to be discovered (the 'Fifty Fortresses' moniker is an approximation). The most well-known *qala* is impressive, mud-walled **Ayaz-Qala**, which is actually a complex of three forts about 23km north of Boston (Bustan). Its heyday was the 6th and 7th centuries. In its shadow is **Ayaz-Qala Yurt Camp** (☎8361-350 5909, 61-532 43 61; per person US$25, meals US$10), with several yurts big enough to hold five to eight people, and **camel trekking** (per hr US$10) available.

You can also hike down to tiny Ayaz *kol* (lake), which is ringed by salt and has been drained. Check whether you need to bring your own food supplies before you head here and bring a torch. Call ahead to reserve yurts and camels, and to discuss transport options. Tour groups often book out Ayaz-Qala, especially for lunch. At other times you're practically at one with the desert.

The oldest, most unique, and most difficult-to-pronounce fort is circular **Koy Krylgan Qala**, which archaeologists believe doubled as a pagan temple and an observatory complex. It was in use as early as the 4th century BC. Drivers will be reluctant to take you here via the poor road from Beruni; instead, drive south towards Turtkul and turn north on a paved road towards the mammoth **Guldursun Qala**, built as early as the 1st century but in use until the Middle Ages. Koy Krylgan Qala is 18km east of Guldursun Qala.

Two other not-to-be-missed *qalas* are **Toprak Qala** and **Kyzyl Qala**, on opposite sides of the road about 10km west of Boston. The former was the main temple complex of Khorezm kings who ruled this area in the 3rd and 4th centuries. Near the latter you'll see local middle and high-school children and university students working the cotton fields in the autumn.

Getting There & Away

The only way to explore Elliq-Qala is with private transport. Make absolutely sure your driver knows this area well and negotiate hard. Most drivers in Urgench and Khiva charge US$50 to US$80 for an all-day excursion with unlimited stops, or slightly less for an abbreviated tour of two or three forts. Nukus drivers charge more. The best strategy is to visit Guldursun Qala first and go anticlockwise, but you may have to insist on this! You can save money by travelling to Beruni or Boston by public transport and hiring a taxi there. A one-way taxi from Boston to Ayaz-Qala costs approximately 15,000S.

Khiva (Xiva)

62 / POP 50,000

Khiva's name, redolent of slave caravans, barbaric cruelty, terrible desert journeys and steppes infested with wild tribesmen, struck fear into all but the boldest 19th-century hearts. Nowadays it's a friendly and welcoming Silk Road old town that's very well set up for tourism, and a mere 35km southwest of the major transport hub of Urgench.

The historic heart of Khiva has been so well preserved that it's often criticised as lifeless – a 'museum city'. Even if you subscribe to that theory, you'll have to admit that it's one helluva museum. To walk through the walls and catch that first glimpse of the fabled Ichon-Qala (inner walled city) in all its monotoned, mud-walled glory is like stepping into another era.

You can see it all in a daytrip from Urgench, but you'll absorb it better by staying longer. Khiva is at its best at dawn, sunset and by night, when the moonlit silhouettes of the tilting columns and medressas, viewed from twisting alleyways, work their magic.

History

Legend has it that Khiva was founded when Shem, son of Noah, discovered a well here; his people called it Kheivak, from which the name Khiva is said to be derived. The **original well** is in the courtyard of an 18th-century house in the northwest of the old town (look for a small white door in a mud wall).

Khiva certainly existed by the 8th century as a minor fort and trading post on a side branch of the Silk Road, but while Khorezm prospered on and off from the 10th to the 14th centuries, its capital was at Old Urgench (present-day Konye-Urgench in Turkmenistan), and Khiva remained a bit player.

It wasn't until well after Konye-Urgench had been finished off by Timur that Khiva's time came. When the Uzbek Shaybanids moved into the decaying Timurid empire in the early 16th century, one branch founded a state in Khorezm and made Khiva their capital in 1592.

The town ran a busy slave market that was to shape the destiny of the Khivan khanate for more than three centuries. Most slaves were brought by Turkmen tribesmen from the Karakum desert or Kazakh tribes of the steppes, who raided those unlucky enough to live or travel nearby.

Russian Interest Awakens

In the early 18th century, Khiva had offered to submit to Peter the Great of Russia in return for help against marauding tribes. In a belated response, a force of about 4000, led by Prince Alexandr Bekovich, arrived in Khiva in 1717.

Unfortunately for them, the khan at the time, Shergazi Khan, had lost interest in being a vassal of the tsar. He came out to meet them, suggesting they disperse to outlying villages where they could be more comfortably accommodated. This done, the Khivans annihilated the invaders, leaving just a handful to make their way back with the news. Shergazi Khan sent Bekovich's head to his Central Asian rival, the Emir of Bukhara, and kept the rest of him on display.

In 1740, Khiva was wrecked by a less gullible invader, Nadir Shah of Persia, and Khorezm became for awhile a northern outpost of the Persian empire. By the end of the 18th century it was rebuilt and began taking a small share in the growing trade between Russia and the Bukhara and Kokand khanates. Its slave market, the biggest in Central Asia, continued unabated, augmented by Russians captured as they pushed their borders southwards and eastwards.

Russian Conquest

When the Russians finally sent a properly organised expedition against Khiva, it was no contest. In 1873 General Konstantin Kaufman's 13,000-strong forces advanced on Khiva from the north, west and east. After some initial guerrilla resistance, mainly by Yomud Turkmen tribesmen, Mohammed Rakhim II Khan surrendered unconditionally. Kaufman then indulged in a massacre of the Yomud. The khan became a vassal of the tsar and his silver throne was packed off to Russia.

Khiva

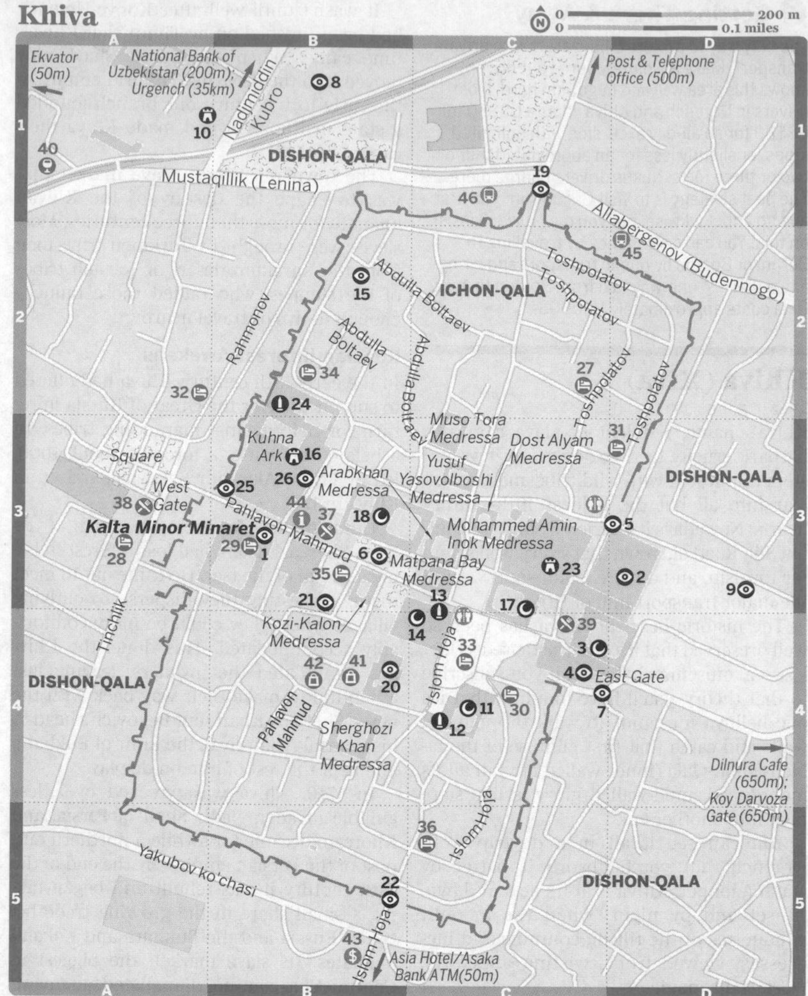

The enfeebled khanate of Khiva struggled on until 1920 when the Bolshevik general Mikhail Frunze installed the Khorezm People's Republic in its place. This, like the similar republic in Bukhara, was theoretically independent of the USSR. But its leaders swung away from socialism towards Pan-Turkism, and in 1924 their republic was absorbed into the new Uzbek SSR.

Sights

Note that access to nearly all sights in Khiva's old town is possible only through one good-value ticket that can be bought at the West Gate of the city. The ticket is valid for two consecutive days, and includes all but a handful of smaller museums and the occasional minaret. Keen photographers and anyone with a taste for beauty should head out in the late afternoon for spectacular views of Khiva's mostly west-facing facades bathed in the orange glow of the setting sun. The top of the West wall, the watchtower at the Kuhna Ark, and the **Ferris wheel** outside the Ichon-Qala's North Gate offer the best viewpoints.

Khiva

Top Sights
1 Kalta Minor Minaret B3

Sights
2 Allakuli Khan Bazaar & Caravanserai D3
3 Allakuli Khan Medressa C4
4 Anusha Khan Baths C4
5 Bazaar Entrance D3
6 Camel Pen B3
7 East Gate C4
8 Ferris Wheel B1
9 Ichon-Qala Gates & Walls D3
10 Isfandiyar Palace A1
11 Islom-Hoja Medressa C4
12 Islom-Hoja Minaret C4
13 Juma Minaret C3
14 Juma Mosque C4
15 Kheivak Well B2
16 Kuhna Ark B3
17 Kutlimurodinok Medressa C3
18 Mohammed Rakhim Khan Medressa B3
19 North Gate C1
20 Pahlavon Mahmud Mausoleum B4
21 Sayid Alauddin Mausoleum B3
22 South Gate B5
23 Tosh-Hovli Palace C3
24 Watchtower B2
25 West Gate B3
26 Zindon B3

Sleeping
27 Annexe C2
28 Hotel Isakhoja A3
29 Hotel Orient Star B3
30 Hotel Xiva Atabek C4
31 Islambek D3
32 Lali-Opa A2
33 Malika Kheivak C4
34 Meros B&B B2
35 Mirzoboshi B3
36 Shaherezada Khiva C5

Eating
37 Bir Gumbaz B3
38 Chaixana Rustamboi A3
Kheivak Restaurant .... (see 33)
39 Khorezm Art Restaurant C4

Drinking & Nightlife
40 Ekvator A1

Entertainment
Fashion & Traditional Dance Show .... (see 3)

Shopping
41 Khiva Silk Carpet Workshop B4
42 Khiva Suzani Centre B4

Information
43 Asia Hotel B5
44 Tourist Information Office B3

Transport
45 Morning Bus to Turkmen Border D2
Shared Taxis to Urgench .... (see 46)
46 Trolleybus Stop for Urgench C1

Ichon-Qala Gates & Walls HISTORIC SITE

(2-day adult/student 25,000S/18,000S, camera 6500S; ticket booth & sights 9am-6pm) You are free to walk around the Ichon-Qala without a ticket, you just won't be able to access (or, technically, to photograph) any sights. The **North**, **East** and **South Gates** are known as, respectively, the Bogcha-Darvoza (Garden Gate), Polvon-Darvoza (Strongman's Gate) and Tosh-Darvoza (Stone Gate), but the main ticket office can be found in the twin-turreted **West Gate** (Ota-Darvoza, literally 'Father Gate', a 1970s reconstruction – the original was wrecked in 1920), the main entrance to the old city. One highlight for which no ticket is needed is the walk along the northwestern section of the wall. The stairs – such as they are – can be found at the North Gate. The 2.5km-long mud walls date from the 18th century, and were rebuilt after being destroyed by the Persians.

Kuhna Ark FORT

(watchtower admission 3000S; 9am-6pm) To your left after you enter the West Gate stands the Kuhna Ark – the Khiva rulers' own fortress and residence, first built in the 12th century by one Ok Shihbobo, then expanded by the khans in the 17th century. The khans' harem, mint, stables, arsenal, barracks, mosque and jail were all here.

The small, low-slung building to the left of the entrance outside the main fortress, on the east side of the building, is the **Zindon** (Khans' Jail), with a simple display of chains, manacles and weapons, suggesting how poor an idea falling foul of the Khan would have been.

Once inside the Ark, the first passage to the right takes you into the 19th-century **Summer Mosque** – open-air and spectacularly ornate with superb blue-and-white plant-motif tiling and a red, orange and gold roof. Beside it is the old **mint**, now a museum that exhibits bank notes and coins that were minted here, including money printed on silk. Unfortunately labeling is only in Uzbek.

Straight ahead from the Ark entrance is the restored, open-air **throne room**, where khans dispensed judgement. The circular area on the ground was for the royal yurt, which the no-longer-nomadic khans still liked to use.

At the back right corner of the throne room, a door in the wall leads to a flight of steps up to the **watchtower**, the original part of the Kuhna Ark, set right against the Ichon-Qala's massive west wall. It's well worth paying the fee to climb up here – the city views are extraordinary.

Mohammed Rakhim Khan Medressa — MEDRESSA

(⏲9am-6pm) East of the Kuhna Ark, across an open space that was once a busy palace square (and place of execution), the 19th-century Mohammed Rakhim Khan Medressa is named after the khan who surrendered to Russia in 1873 (although he had, at least, kept Khiva independent a few years longer than Bukhara).

A hotchpotch of a museum within is partly dedicated to this khan and his son, Isfandiyar. Mohammed Rakhim Khan was also a poet under the pen name Feruz.

Khiva's token **camel**, Katya, waits for tourists to pose with her outside the medressa's south wall.

★Kalta Minor Minaret — MINARET

Just south of the Kuhna Ark stands the fat, turquoise-tiled Kalta Minor Minaret. This unfinished minaret was begun in 1851 by Mohammed Amin Khan, who according to legend wanted to build a minaret so high he could see all the way to Bukhara.

Unfortunately, the khan dropped dead in 1855 and it was never finished, leaving the beautifully tiled structure looking distinctly unusual and rather stumpy. It's currently not possible to climb the structure.

East of the minaret, beside the medressa, is the small, plain **Sayid Alauddin Mausoleum**, dating to 1310 when Khiva was under the Golden Horde of the Mongol empire. You might find people praying in front of the 19th-century tiled sarcophagus.

Juma Mosque — MOSQUE

(Pahlavon Mahmud ko'chasi; Minaret admission 3000S; ⏲9am-6pm) Continuing east from the Sayid Alauddin Mausoleum, the large Juma Mosque is interesting for the 218 wooden columns supporting its roof – a concept thought to be derived from ancient Arabian mosques. Six or seven of the columns date from the original 10th-century mosque (see if you can spot them), though the present building dates from the 18th century. From inside, you can climb the very dark stairway (clambering rather awkwardly past the young Uzbek couples who use the staircase for trysts) up to the pigeon-poop-splattered gallery of the 47m **Juma Minaret**.

Allakuli Khan Medressa — MEDRESSA

Just east of the Juma Mosque, a lane leading north from Pahlavon Mahmud ko'chasi contains some of Khiva's most interesting buildings, most of them created by Allakuli Khan – known as the 'builder khan' – in the 1830s and '40s. First there's the tall Allakuli Khan Medressa and the earlier **Kutlimurodinok Medressa** (1804–12), facing each other across the street, with nearly matching facades. The latter now houses an art museum.

North of the Allakuli Khan Medressa are the **Allakuli Khan Bazaar & Caravanserai**. The **entrance** to both is through tall wooden gates beside the medressa. The bazaar is a domed market arcade, still catering to traders, which opens onto Khiva's modern **Dekhon Bazaar** at its east end. Both bazaars and the caravanserai were closed for extensive renovations when we visited.

Opposite the Allakuli Khan Medressa to the south are the 1855 **Abdulla Khan Medressa**, which holds a tiny nature museum, and little **Ak Mosque** (1657). The latter contains the **Anusha Khan Baths** (Anushahon Hammomi) – closed at the time of our last visit – and a carpet shop.

The **East Gate**, a long, vaulted 19th-century passage with several sets of immense carved doors, bridges the baths and the bazaar area. The slave market was held here, and niches in the passage walls once held slaves for sale. Just outside the gate is a working mosque that overflows with wizened old men on Fridays.

Tosh-hovli Palace — PALACE

(⏲9am-6pm) This palace, which means 'Stone House', contains Khiva's most sumptuous interior decoration, including ceramic tiles, carved stone and wood, and *ghanch*. Built by Allakuli Khan between 1832 and 1841 as a more splendid alternative to the Kuhna Ark, it's said to have more than 150 rooms off nine courtyards, with high ceilings designed to catch any breeze. Allakuli was a man in a hurry – the Tosh-Hovli's first architect was executed for failing to complete the job in two years.

Two separate entrances take you into two separate wings of the palace. Don't miss the harder-to-spot south wing, where the throne room and a sumptuous *aivan* are located.

Islom-Hoja Medressa MEDRESSA
(Islom Hoja; minaret admission 3000S; ⏲9am-6pm) Walk south from the Abdulla Khan Medressa to the Islom-Hoja Medressa and minaret – Khiva's newest Islamic monuments, both built in 1910. You can climb the **minaret**. With bands of turquoise and red tiling, it looks rather like an uncommonly lovely lighthouse. At 57m tall, it's Uzbekistan's highest.

The medressa holds Khiva's best museum, the **Museum of Applied Arts**. It exhibits Khorezm handicrafts through the ages – fine woodcarving; metalwork; Uzbek and Turkmen carpets; stone carved with Arabic script (which was in use in Khorezm from the 8th to the 20th centuries); and large pots called *hum* for storing food underground.

Islom Hoja himself was an early-20th-century grand vizier and a liberal (by Khivan standards): he founded a European-style school, brought long-distance telegraph to the city and built a hospital. For his popularity, the khan and clergy had him assassinated.

Pahlavon Mahmud Mausoleum MAUSOLEUM
(Islom Hoja; admission 4000S; ⏲9am-6pm) This revered mausoleum, with its sublime courtyard and stately tilework, is one of the town's most beautiful spots. Pahlavon Mahmud was a poet, philosopher and legendary wrestler who became Khiva's patron saint. His 1326 tomb was rebuilt in the 19th century and then requisitioned in 1913 by the khan of the day as the family mausoleum.

The beautiful Persian-style chamber under the turquoise dome at the north end of the courtyard holds the tomb of Mohammed Rakhim Khan. Pahlavon Mahmud's tomb, to the left off the first chamber, has some of Khiva's loveliest tiling on the sarcophagus and the walls. Tombs of other khans stand unmarked east and west of the main building, outside the courtyard.

Isfandiyar Palace PALACE
(Mustaqillik; ⏲9am-6pm) The Isfandiyar Palace (also called the Palace of Narallabay) was built between 1906 and 1912, and like the Emir's Summer Palace in Bukhara displays some fascinatingly overdone decorations in a messy collision of East and West. Despite being located just outside the walls of the Ichon-Qala, admission here is included on the two-day ticket. The rooms are largely bare, allowing one to fully appreciate the gold-embroidered ceilings and lavish touches such as 4m-high mirrors and a 50kg chandelier. The harem, in case you're wondering, was behind the huge wall to the west of the palace and while it has been undergoing renovation for years, there was no suggestion of its imminent reopening when we passed by.

Tours

The following guides offer tailored tours to Khiva and the area nearby. They all speak English, with the exception of Amon who speaks French.

Ali Madaminov (☎+998 912 792 829)

Amon (☎719 80 50, +998 907 131 383)

Anush Boltaeva (☎+998 914 315 799)

Jonibek Roziev (☎+998 909 544 382, +998 912 780 306; joni.uz@gmail.com)

Muhammad Yunusov (☎+998 919 166 632; muhammad-987@inbox.ru)

Temur Madaminov (☎+998 914 315 799)

Sleeping

Negotiating often bears fruit at Khiva hotels. You'll save money paying in som at the Orient Star and Malika hotels; at most others, it won't matter. Only the Malika hotels, Asia Hotel and a few others stay open from December to February. In high season (April-June & Sept-Oct), it's a good idea to book ahead, or you won't be able to stay in the better options here, many of which are booked up weeks ahead.

★ **Meros B&B** B&B **$**
(☎+998 943 153 700, 375 76 42; www.meroskhiva.com; Abdulla Boltaev 57; s/d/tr US$20/30/40; ❄📶) Staying at this gorgeous, family-run place is an absolute treat: of the six simple rooms, four have charming balconies

while all six have traditional-style ceilings. The rooms share a lovely sitting room and access to a superb roof terrace with great Ichon Qala views. The breakfast is excellent and real coffee is available too. Don't miss the beautiful dining room, with an *aivan*-style painted ceiling installed by the owner, a restoration master. Reservations are usually essential.

★Hotel Xiva Atabek B&B $
(+998 919 984 242, 375 61 77; barnush@mail.ru; Islom Hoja 68; s/d US$15/20;) The full renovation of this one-time homestay has been a great success, and the brand new rooms are sparkling clean and bright. It's superbly located in the middle of the Ichon Qala and comes with a friendly family on hand to look after you. Barno speaks very good English and breakfast even comes with espresso – true luxury in Khiva!

Lali-Opa B&B $
(375 44 49; www.laliopa.com; Rahmonov 11A; dm/s/d US$11/20/30;) This friendly little guesthouse, located just a few steps outside the West Gate, boasts the cheapest en suite rooms in town. The dorms share facilities, however, and rooms are fairly charmless, but what it lacks in character it makes up for in friendly service.

Hotel Isakhoja B&B $
(+998 622 977 726, 375 92 83; isaqjan02@mail.ru; Tinchlik ko'chasi; s/d US$25/35;) A solid-value option located just outside the West Gate. Rooms lack character, the wall-to-wall carpeting is ageing and the bathrooms are definitely a weak spot, but you could swing a camel in what are certainly Khiva's largest rooms. There are great views from the roof terrace.

Mirzoboshi B&B $
(512 27 53, 375 27 53; mirzaboshi@inbox.ru; Pahlavon Mahmud 1; dm/s/d US$15/20/30) This mud- and brick-walled B&B is located right in the heart of the Ichon-Qala across from Katya the camel's lair; the entrance is around the back. You essentially move in with the family by occupying one of the two dorm rooms (a double and a quad). For more privacy and comfort but less traditional charm, opt for their clean and modern **annexe** (375 91 88; Toshpolatov 24; s/d US$15/30; @).

Islambek HOTEL $
(375 23 46, 375 30 23; www.islambekhotel.nm.ru; Toshpolatov 60; s/d/lux US$20/30/40;) This 21-room place is a relative giant in the tiny Ichon Qala, and while it's certainly lacking the traditional charm of many of Khiva's B&Bs, it's a good deal and well-situated. The wallpapered rooms may make little attempt to recreate the khanate, but they do have traditionally carved wooden doors. Don't miss taking tea on the roof, where the views are fantastic.

Hotel Orient Star HISTORIC HOTEL $$
(+998 943 152 600, 375 68 59; doniyoraa@rambler.ru; Pahlavon Mahmud 1; s/d US$60/80;) This unique hotel offers you the fabulous chance of staying inside the 19th-century Mohammed Amin Khan Medressa. Accommodation in the 78 converted *hujra* (study cells) is somewhat austere, but with cable TVs, domed roofs and fancy stone bathrooms in place you need not live a completely hermit-like existence. Definitely Khiva's most atmospheric hotel in the upper price ranges: room 42 has the best views.

Shaherezada Khiva BOUTIQUE HOTEL $$
(375 95 65; www.khivashaherezada.uz; Islom Hoja 35; s/d/tr US$45/70/80;) Very popular with tour groups and tirelessly cleaned by a seemingly never-ending stream of daughters, the Shaherezada is nevertheless something of a let down on other fronts: unreliable hot water supply, poor wi-fi signal and a generous if rather weird breakfast spread mean that it's rather overpriced for what it is. On the plus side, there's lots of beautiful wood carvings, including the memorable front door, which was hand-carved in the workshop of the owner.

Malika Kheivak HOTEL $$$
(375 76 10, 375 77 87; www.malikahotels.com; Islom Hoja; s/d US$60/90;) This 22-room hotel in the heart of the Ichon Qala is by far the most modern, amenity-laden choice within the city walls, but it's pricey and popular with tour groups. The pleasant courtyard will look better when it's finally planted, while all the furnishing and fittings in the rooms are modern and stylish, with wooden floorboards, good bathrooms and flat screen TVs. The Malika chain has two additional upmarket offerings just outside the North and West gates.

Eating & Drinking

Despite its ever-growing tourism industry, Khiva has a poor selection of restaurants to choose from. The chaikhanas in the Ichon-

Qala are OK but gouge you on food and especially beer. Leave the Ichon-Qala and prices suddenly halve.

Ichon-Qala

★Khorezm Art Restaurant UZBEK $$
(Allakuli Khan Medressa; mains 5000-7000S; 9am-10pm;) Charmingly located in a low-lit and cosy stone building with a bamboo roof, local handicrafts and photography on the walls, the Khorezm Art Restaurant is definitely one of the best choices in town. Yes, the service can be erratic (if always well-intentioned) and yes, it's a popular spot for tour groups, but dinner on the terrace can't be beaten and the menu, which includes fried dumplings, a delicious carrot salad and an excellent pumpkin soup, is very enticing indeed.

Bir Gumbaz UZBEK $$
(Pahlavon Mahmud; mains 7000-15,000S; 9am-10pm) Rather overpriced (you're paying for the premium location, with superb Kalta Minor minaret views from the terrace), this place serves up tasty Uzbek standards and offers hookahs and even real coffee. There's an inside dining room if you're in Khiva during the colder months.

Kheivak Restaurant UZBEK $$
(Islom Hoja; mains 6000-8000S; 9am-11pm;) The Malika Kheivak hotel has a pleasant sun-dappled courtyard covered with traditional *tapchan* and tables. It's a very handy spot for lunch in the Ichon Qala, even though the food is nothing special and service can be frustratingly relaxed.

Dishon-Qala

Dilnura Cafe UZBEK $
(opposite Koy-Darvoza; mains 5000S; 10am-11pm) Well worth the short walk out of the east gate to enjoy unique Khivan specialities such as *fityi* (small meat pies with Uzbek spices), *turkhum barak* (pasta with eggs), *shurva* (meat soup) and *shivit oshi* (meat over noodles embedded with dill). Walking out of the city's East Gate, it's on your left after you pass a small mosque on your right.

Chaixana Rustamboi CHAIKHANA $$
(Tinchlik; mains 6000-10,000S; 9am-10pm) Opposite Khiva's West Gate and yet remarkably almost tourist free, this unpretentious place packs in the locals for drinks and simple, filling meals. Choose from dishes such as chicken tabaka, *plov* and beef *laghman*, but be prepared for some communications difficulties – no English is spoken and barely any Russian for that matter!

★Ogahiy Fish Restaurant FISH $$$
(carp per kg 22,000S; 9am-10pm) This charming place is wrapped around a couple of ponds, among vineyards in a bucolic spot 3.5km northwest of Isfandiyar Palace. Take marshrutka 2 from the trolleybus stop and get off at the large blue sign saying Ogahiy Bogi, from where it's a 500m walk down a sideroad to the restaurant. A taxi from the Ichon Qala will cost around 4000S one way. Once there the friendly staff will fry up some fresh carp for you, keep the cold beer coming and make you feel right at home.

Ekvator NIGHTCLUB
(Mustaqillik; noon-midnight) This bar-cum-club would have the builders of the 1912 Nurullaboy Medressa that it occupies rolling in their graves. It has a cavernous interior and a dance floor that occasionally comes to life on weekends.

☆ Entertainment

Fashion & Traditional Dance Show TRADITIONAL DANCE
(admission 15,000S; first show 4pm) The Fashion & Traditional Dance Show takes place in the Allakuli Khan Medressa four times nightly in the high season, every hour from 4pm. Book tickets through the tourist information office or at the gate, and be sure to ask for a discount, which is often granted to individual tourists.

Shopping

Souvenir and craft shops line the streets of the Ichon-Qala and are wedged into many attractions. The best quality is to be found in the Kutlimurodinok Medressa, which contains several handicraft workshops as well.

Khiva Silk Carpet Workshop CARPETS
(www.khiva.info/khivasilk; Pahlavon Mahmud; 9am-6pm Mon-Fri) Apprentice carpet makers hand-weave silk rugs patterned after Khiva-style majolica tiles, doors and miniature paintings. There's lots of natural-dyed silk hanging around and you can watch women work the looms. During the high season, there's usually an English-speaking guide on hand to give you an introduction to the processes used.

Khiva Suzani Centre CARPETS
(Pahlavon Mahmud; ⌚9am-7pm) The British Council and Operation Mercy helped this centre get its wings in 2004. The now-independent centre churns out marvellous handmade silk and *adras* creations.

ℹ Information

While most hotels have wi-fi, it tends to be highly unreliable, so if this is important to you, check it's working before checking in. Otherwise the Malika Kheivak hotel's restaurant was the only wi-fi hotspot when we visited. There are plenty of black-market money changers around; ask at the Tourist Information Office or just head to the Dekhon Bazaar. Bring plenty of cash to Khiva – if the MasterCard ATM in the Asia Hotel isn't working, then the nearest place to get a cash advance is the National Bank of Uzbekistan in Urgench.

Asia Hotel (☎375 81 98; Yakubov) Has an infrequently working Asaka Bank ATM machine that accepts MasterCard.

Post & Telephone Office (Amir Timur 23; ⌚9am-7pm Mon-Sat) Located 650m north of the North Gate.

Tourist Information Office (☎375 69 28; www.khivamuseum.uz; Pahlavon Mahmoud; ⌚9am-7pm) Offers internet access (3000S per hour), changes money, organises tours and guides for both Khiva itself and to the fortresses of Khorezm (US$7 per hour or US$30 per day) and sells maps and information booklets. English is spoken and staff seem genuinely interested in helping. An additional useful service for non-Russian speakers is the organisation of taxis to Bukhara and Nukus, as well as the purchase of train tickets.

ℹ Getting There & Away

You can travel between Urgench and Khiva by **shared taxi** (3000S, 20 minutes), leaving from the stand by the trolleybus stop, just outside the North Gate. The interminable **trolleybus** (600S, 1½ hours) is another option.

If you're heading east to Bukhara, your best bet is a shared taxi from Urgench. The Tourist Information Office may be able to match you with other travellers for this trip, and alternatively can arrange taxi services to Bukhara direct from Khiva (70,000/280,000S per place/taxi). A taxi to Nukus can be picked up in Urgench (20,000S per place, 1½ hours), or the Tourist Information Office can order you a pricey one (195,000S for up to four people, 2 hours) direct from your Khiva hotel. It's worth asking your guesthouse if they can arrange a cheaper one.

A couple of late-morning and early-afternoon private buses per day depart when full to Tashkent (50,000S, 21 hours) via Samarkand and Bukhara from the Koy-Darvoza Gate, east of the Ichon-Qala.

There's no train station or airport in Khiva itself, but nearby Urgench has both. See the Urgench section for details of connections from there. Note that it's not currently possible to buy tickets for flights from Urgench in Khiva.

KARAKALPAKSTAN

If you're attracted to desolation, you'll love the Republic of Karakalpakstan. The Karakalpaks, who today number only about 400,000 of the republic's 1.2 million population (there are almost as many Kazakhs), are a formerly nomadic and fishing people who are struggling to recapture a sense of national identity after being collectivised or urbanised in Soviet times. Karakalpak, the official language of the republic, is Turkic, close to Kazakh and less so to Uzbek.

The destruction of the Aral Sea has rendered Karakalpakstan one of Uzbekistan's most depressed regions. The capital, Nukus, feels half deserted, and a drive into outlying areas reveals a region of dying towns and blighted landscapes. In a cruel irony, Karakalpaks have been forced to embrace the devil in the sense that cotton – the very crop that devastated the Aral Sea in the first place – is now one of the region's main industries. The long-running government practice of forcing state workers and school children into the cotton fields is alive and well here, as any autumn jaunt into the Karakalpak countryside will prove.

For all the indignities it has suffered, the Aral has been generous in defeat, yielding vast oil and gas reserves in its dried-up seabed. Unfortunately, the spoils so far have been divided between Chinese investors and their Tashkent-based patrons, with little trickling down to the people of Karakalpakstan.

Nukus (No'kis)

☎61 / POP 260,000

The isolated, Soviet creation of Nukus is definitely one of Uzbekistan's least appealing cities and gets few visitors relative to its attractive Silk Road cousins. However, as the gateway to the fast-disappearing Aral Sea and home to the remarkable Savitsky Museum – one of the best collections of Soviet art in the world – there is actually a reason to

Nukus

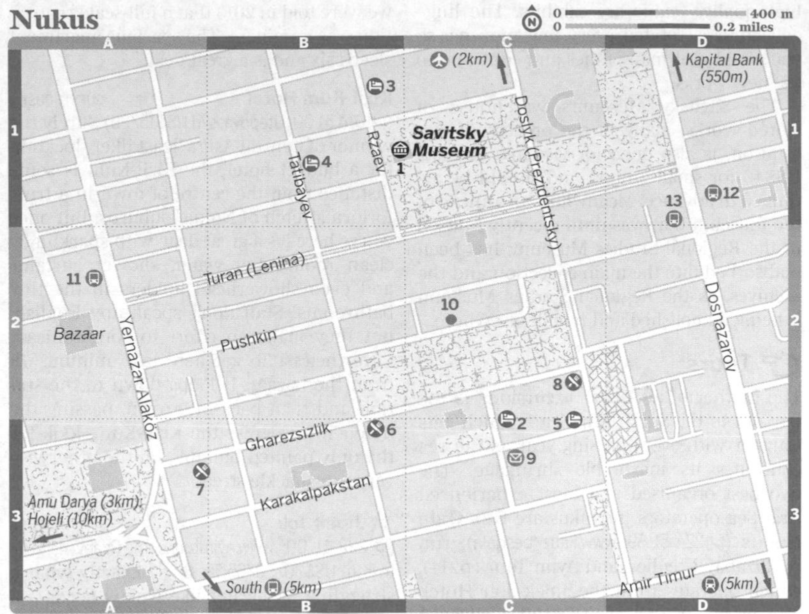

come here, other than taking in the general sense of hopelessness and desolation.

Sights

★Savitsky Museum MUSEUM

(☎222 25 56; www.savitskycollection.org; Rzaev 127; adult/student 15,000S/10,000S, camera 75,000S, guide 10,000S; ⏲9am-1pm & 2-5pm Mon-Fri, 10am-4pm Sat & Sun) The Savitsky Museum houses one of the most remarkable art collections in the former Soviet Union. The museum owns some 90,000 artefacts and pieces of art – including more than 15,000 paintings – only a fraction of which are actually on display. About half of the paintings were brought here in Soviet times by renegade artist and ethnographer Igor Savitsky, who managed to work within the system to preserve an entire generation of avant-garde work that was proscribed and destroyed elsewhere in the country for not conforming to the socialist realism of the times. The paintings found protection in these isolated backwaters (Nukus, after all, being literally the last place you'd look for anything) and it's interesting to hear how this nonconformist museum survived during the Soviet era. An English-language guided tour can really help to contextualise the collection and acts

Nukus

Top Sights

1 Savitsky Museum B1

Sleeping

2 Hotel Nukus C3
3 Jipek Joli B1
4 Jipek Joli Annexe B1
5 Rahnamo Hotel C3

Eating

6 Bes Qala B3
7 Mona Lisa A3
8 Sheraton Cafe C2

Information

Ayim Tour .... (see 3)
9 Post & Telephone Office C3
Savitsky Museum .... (see 1)
Troya Internet .... (see 2)

Transport

10 Airline Booking Office C2
11 Bazaar Marshrutka Stop A2
12 Buses to Airport D1
13 Buses to Train Station D1

as an introduction to the fascinating stories behind many of the paintings.

The museum has impressive archaeological, ethnographic and folk art collections to match its collection of paintings, as well as high-quality temporary exhibits. The huge collection is rotated every few months, so you could visit many times and continue to see new works.

The Savitsky Museum's warehouse of stored works, many in the process of restoration, is also open for viewing. It costs US$40 for small groups, and should be arranged in advance. Meanwhile, an annexe of the museum that was until recently housed in the Regional Studies Museum, has been reabsorbed into the main collection and the archives, as the Regional Studies Museum is being demolished and rebuilt elsewhere.

Tours

The mother of all Uzbek excursions is the trip out to the South Aral Sea – which gets tougher with every passing year as the sea continues its inexorable shrinkage. The two best organised and most experienced Aral Sea operators in Nukus are **Bes Qala Nukus** (☎224 51 69; www.kr.uz/besqala), run by Tazabay Uteuliev, and Ayim Tour (p214), which operates from the Jipek Joli Hotel. The overnight trips cost US$420 to US$450 for a car (more for a Landcruiser than a UAZ), plus US$35 per person for food and a bit more for extras like sleeping bags and tents. Others doing similar tours are **Omirbay Sarsenbayev** (☎+998 945 796 115; omish_87@mail.ru), **Ayap Ismayilov** (☎505 07 75) and **Oktyabr Dospanov** (☎222 67 57, 351 13 65; oktyabrd@gmail.com). All guides speak English except Ayap.

Festivals & Events

The annual **Pakhta-Bairam** festival takes place on the first Sunday after Karakalpakstan meets its cotton-picking quota, usually in late November or early December. Competitions are held in traditional sports such as wrestling, ram-fighting and cock-fighting.

Sleeping

Tazabay Utiliev of Bes Qala Nukus (p212) arranges apartment rentals with registration.

Hotel Nukus HOTEL $
(☎222 89 41; Lumumba 4; d/tr from US$30/40, apt US$100; ❄) Conveniently located in the heart of town, this old hotel has been spruced up nicely and the staff can even be quite friendly once you've warmed them up. The rooms show their age, however, with torn wallpaper and poor bathrooms, though we were told in 2013 that a full-scale renovation was imminent. The spacious apartment sleeps six and is a great deal.

Kizil-Kum Hotel GUESTHOUSE $
(☎614 51 00; Utepova; s/d US$15/25) Surely the winner of Central Asia's 'least likely location for a budget hotel', the Kizil-Kum is some distance from the centre of town in a truly forlorn stretch of Nukus' suburbs. But once you're here it's a great deal, with sparklingly clean rooms, hot water, shower curtains and even showerhead holders in the tiny bathrooms! Staff don't speak any English, but they make an effort to communicate nevertheless. To get here take minibus 78 from the bazaar. It loops down to the station and then back into town, passing the hotel. To recognise the Kizil-Kum, look for the only painted building on the otherwise very ramshackle street.

★ **Jipek Joli** HOTEL $$
(☎222 11 00; www.ayimtour.com; Rzaev 4; s/d/tr from US$30/50/65; ❄@📶) Exactly what a struggling backwater like Nukus needs – a well-run hotel with enthusiastic and responsive English-speaking staff to help you make onward plans. This extremely comfortable, 18-room place is well furnished and spacious, with luxuries such as fridges, TV and good wireless reception even in the rooms. Hot water can be unreliable, but otherwise this is by far the best place in town. There's a second even more modern **annexe** (☎224 25 25; www.ayimtour.com; Tatibayev 50; s/d/tr US$30/50/65; ❄📶) just a block and a half away, should the main building be full.

Rahnamo Hotel HOTEL $$$
(☎222 47 43; www.hotel.rahnamo.uz; Karakalpakstan; s/d US$75/90; ❄📶) This study in beige offers 13 rooms, all of which are very comfortable and spacious, though drearily lacking in atmosphere. It's very well located, however, and staff are polite and English-speaking.

Eating

Eating is still a fairly dreary experience in Nukus. You'll find cheap and cheerful restaurants and street food places along Gharezsizlik, while there are a couple of other better, pricier places nearby too.

Sheraton Cafe RUSSIAN $$
(Gharezsizlik 53; mains 10,000-30,000S; ⏲10am-11pm; 📋) With its red-and-cream upholstered dining room, this chintzy place may

not live up to its hotel namesake, but Russian pop music and friendly staff at least keep it down-to-earth. There's a menu dominated by Russian 'classics' and there's even a form of espresso available.

Mona Lisa CAUCASIAN **$$**
(Gharezsizlik 107; 4500-12,000S; 11am-11pm) While Mona Lisa may be quite low on atmosphere, its menu is far more interesting than the standard dishes offered by the nearby Uzbek cafes, and includes Caucasian specialities such as *fidzhin* (Ossetian meat pies) and Georgian stews. Don't come to eat in a hurry though, but do check out the 'fine for crashed things' section of the menu while you wait.

Bes Qala UZBEK **$$**
(Gharezsizlik; mains 8000-20,000S; 11am-11pm) A welcome addition to the eating scene in Nukus, this echoey place is divided into two large, wood-upholstered dining halls, and is often in use for the celebration of local weddings. When it's not, it's a good place to try a large selection of Uzbek, Karakalpak and Russian dishes.

Information

There are plenty of black-market money changers near the entrance to the bazaar. Two good

A VISIT TO THE ARAL SEA

Catching a glimpse of the notorious Aral Sea's new southern shoreline holds no small amount of appeal for adventurous travellers. The favoured route these days is straight north from Moynaq. It's essential to go with an experienced driver with intimate knowledge of the tracks heading north from Moynaq and Kungrad.

We drove west for awhile along the sea's former shoreline and then set out across the dried-up sea bed, where oil refineries belched fire and black smoke in an eerie scene reminiscent of a *Mad Max* movie. After half-an-hour we left the smokestacks behind and entered the heart of the Aral Sea bed. The part we were traversing had been dry for so long that already a forest of sage brush had sprouted. Then the foliage petered out, and we entered a land of interminable salt flats receding into mirages in every direction.

In front of us loomed the Ustyurt Plateau, stretching into Kazakhstan to the north and all the way to the Caspian Sea to the west. We had a picnic lunch in the shadow of cliffs that once abutted the western border of the Aral Sea, before ascending to the top of the plateau. There wasn't much up there, although it's said to be prime grounds for hunting boar, fowl and rare Saiga antelope. Our drivers picked out their route then sped across the top of the plateau, often at breakneck speeds. After about 45 minutes an intensely blue slick appeared on the horizon. It was our first sighting of the Aral Sea. Against the barren backdrop of the dried-up sea bed and the rocky Ustyurt Plateau it looked profoundly beautiful, all the more so for what it represented – the futility of man's attempts to subjugate nature.

An hour later we drew level with the water's edge. Here, recently exposed bits of sea bed were rendered in various shades of grey. The bits closest to the water were the darkest. They still glistened, like mudflats exposed by low tide, only in this case the low tide was eternal. The mud would soon dry up and crack. In a few years it might sprout sage brush and draw oil prospectors. Thus was the future of the South Aral Sea.

Watching the Aral Sea recede before our eyes was moving and depressing. We rode in silence for another 45 minutes before descending to our campsite near the water's edge. It had taken us about five hours to get out here from Moynaq (including many stops), and it was already getting chilly. Only two of us remained committed to swimming. To do so required wading through 50 metres of knee-deep muck before the water became deep enough to submerge. It proved worth the slog. The water was salty enough to suspend a brick. We lay flat on our backs without moving a muscle, buoyant as corks.

That night we were treated to a stunning harvest-moonrise over the Aral. Conversation, vodka, a huge meal, and a cold, restless night of sleep in a camouflaged tent followed. The next morning I departed about as satisfied as one could be with an organised tour, armed with the following painfully obvious advice: see it while you still can.

Greg Bloom, Lonely Planet author

websites about the region are www.karakalpakstan.org or www.karakalpak.com. There are no ATMs in Nukus, but over-the-counter withdrawals can be made at Kapital Bank (Visa) and Asaka Bank (MasterCard).

Asaka Bank (Turtkul Bazare 1A; ⏲9am-5pm Mon-Fri) MasterCard cash advances. It's out past the train station.

Kapital Bank (Aimurzaev; ⏲9am-5pm Mon-Fri) Gives cash advances on Visa cards, with a 2% commission. To get here walk north up Dosnazarov from the centre until you get to Aimurzaev ko'chasi, turn right into Aimurzaev and the bank is on your left.

Troya Internet (Lumumba 4; per hr 1200S; ⏲9am-11pm) Located in the basement of Hotel Nukus.

Post & Telephone Office (Karakalpakstan 7; ⏲post 7am-7pm, telephone 24hr)

Savitsky Museum (☎222 25 56; www.savitskycollection.org; Rzaev 127; ⏲9am-1pm & 2-5pm Mon-Fri, 10am-4pm Sat & Sun) The best art museum in Central Asia doubles as Nukus' de facto tourist information centre. The multilingual staff know the region well and can organise homestays and tours to Mizdakhan, Moynaq and the Elliq-Qala region.

Ayim Tour (☎222 11 00; www.ayimtour.com; Jipek Joli Hotel, Rzaev; ⏲9am-5pm Mon-Sat) The only officially licensed travel agency in Nukus, this friendly company is a godsend to independent travellers looking to make the most of their time in Karakalpakstan. They offer everything from Aral Sea expeditions and tours of Khorezm's fortresses to local homestays and interpreters.

Getting There & Away

AIR

Uzbekistan Airways has flights to Tashkent (US$68, two daily) and Moscow (US$310, three weekly). Book tickets at the **airline booking office** (☎222 79 95; Pushkin 43; ⏲9am-7pm).

LAND

Shared taxis to Urgench (20,000S, 1½ hours), Tashkent (120,000S, 14 hours), Samarkand (120,000S, eight hours), Bukhara (100,000S, five hours), Khiva (25,000, two hours), Beruni (25,000S, one hour) and Boston (25,000S, one hour) depart from the **South (New) Bus Station** (☎223 22 93; Yuzhny Avtovokzal), 6km south of town. To get here take marshrutka 34 from the **bazaar** or the train station.

Buses from the South Bus Station lumber to Urgench (11,000S, three hours, 3pm daily), Samarkand (43,000S, 13 hours, 11am daily) via Bukhara (29,000S), Tashkent (60,000S, 20 hours, noon daily) and Boston (7300S, 1½ hours, 1pm daily).

TRAIN

Nukus' **train station** (☎223 29 58) is 5.5km south of the town centre. Take marshrutka 1, 3, 4 or 48 from the bazaar to get here. There are trains most days to Tashkent (*platskartny/kupeyny* 63,000/95,000S, 22 hours) that call in Samarkand (*platskartny/kupeyny* 57,000/77,000, 14 hours). Nukus is a stop on the Moscow-Dushanbe train line and services to Dushanbe (calling at Tashkent) pass through on Tuesdays, Thursdays and Saturdays. There's also a Tuesday train to Almaty that calls at Tashkent.

Getting Around

Bus 15 goes between the airport and train station along Dosnazarov; a handy **stop** is at the corner of Pushkin. A taxi from the airport, train or bus station to the centre costs about 5000S.

Around Nukus

Mizdakhan

On a hill 13km west of Nukus, near Hojeli, are the remains of ancient Mizdakhan, once the second-largest city in Khorezm. Inhabited from the 4th century BC until the 14th century AD, Mizdakhan remained a sacred place even after Timur destroyed it; tombs and mosques continued to be built here right up to the 20th century.

Today the main attraction is a hill littered with those mosques and mausoleums – some ruined, some intact. The most impressive is the restored **Mausoleum of Mazlum Khan Slu**, dating from the 12th to 14th centuries.

On the neighbouring hill towards the Turkmen border are the remains of a 4th- to 3rd-century BC fortress called **Gyaur-Qala**, which is worth checking out if you missed the forts of Elliq-Qala.

To get here from Nukus, take a shared taxi from the Nukus bazaar to Hojeli (5000S, 20 minutes), then get in a shared taxi bound for the Turkmen border and get off after 3km in Mizdakhan. A private taxi from Nukus will cost around 50,000S return with wait time.

Moynaq (Mo'ynoq)

☎61 / POP 12,000

Moynaq, 210km north of Nukus, encapsulates more visibly than anywhere else the absurd tragedy of the Aral Sea. Once one of the sea's two major fishing ports, it now stands almost 200km from the water. What remains of Moynaq's fishing fleet lies rusting on the sand in the former seabed.

The mostly Kazakh residents have moved away in droves, and today Moynaq is a virtual ghost town populated by livestock herders and the elderly looking after grandchildren whose parents have left to find work elsewhere. The few who remain suffer the full force of the Aral Sea disaster, with hotter summers, colder winters, debilitating sand-salt-dust storms, and a gamut of health problems.

Moynaq used to be on an isthmus connecting the Ush Say (Tiger's Tail) peninsula to the shore. You can appreciate this on the approach to the town, where the road is raised above the surrounding land. The town itself consists of one seemingly endless main street linking the bus station at its southeast end with the Oybek Hotel and the ships graveyard to the northwest.

Sights

Poignant reminders of Moynaq's tragedy are everywhere: the sign at the entrance to the town has a fish on it; a fishing boat stands as a kind of monument on a makeshift pedestal near Government House.

From the Aral Sea memorial you can spot a lake southeast of town, created in an attempt to restore the formerly mild local climate. It didn't quite work, but it's at least given the locals a source of recreation.

Museum MUSEUM
(Main Rd; admission 5000S, camera 5000S; 9am-6pm Tue-Sun) The local museum in the city hall has some interesting photos and paintings of the area prospering before the disaster.

Beached Ships SHIP CEMETERY
The beached ships are a five-minute walk from the Oybek Hotel, across the main road and beyond the collection of homes. Once difficult to find, most ships have now been moved to a centralised location beneath the Aral Sea memorial, which occupies a bluff that was once the Aral Sea's bank.

Sleeping

Don't spend the night in Moynaq unless you have to. The town's only hotel, the Oybek, was being reconstructed in 2013, so things may get better soon, but until then you're limited to homestays. Bring your own food, or arrange in advance to be fed, as you'll find almost nothing for sale.

Koshkarbai Artikov HOMESTAY $
(+998 937 165 386; Nasirov 146; per person incl breakfast US$10) Koshkarbai's big house sleeps up to 9 people, and his daughter speaks English, although it may be easier to get your hotel in Nukus to arrange a stay here. Facilities are basic, there's an outdoor toilet but there is hot water. Lunch and dinner can be provided at extra cost and with notice.

Makhmudjan Aitzhanov HOMESTAY $
(+998 934 893 090, +998 939 200 155; Amir Timur 2; per person incl full board US$20) Makhmudjan Aitzhanov's homestay is an easy walk from the bus station and his family cooks filling *plov* dinners. There's no central plumbing but there's a tap and shower outside. If you've brought your own food, a B&B only deal is US$15 per person.

Getting There & Away

Several buses make the trip from Nukus (10,000S, four hours) via Kungrad (Kongirot) and depart from Nukus' bazaar. Most return buses from Moynaq depart in the morning. All buses to Moynaq are standing-room-only; board early if you want a seat.

It's swifter and far more comfortable to take a shared taxi or marshrutka to Kungrad from a stop opposite the train station, and transfer at Kungrad's train station to a marshrutka or another shared taxi. This will cost about 30,000S in total and save you two hours of driving time. Arrive in Kungrad by mid-afternoon to ensure an onward ride.

A day trip from Nukus in an ordinary taxi should cost around 200,000S, depending on your negotiating skills.

UNDERSTAND UZBEKISTAN

Uzbekistan Today

Any account of contemporary Uzbekistan has to begin with the chilling events of 13 May 2005 in the eastern city of Andijon, which rocked the country and went on to shock the world. The 'Andijon Massacre', as it was later dubbed, was touched off when two dozen powerful local businessmen were jailed for being members of Akramiya, an allegedly extremist Islamic movement banned by the Uzbek government. A group of their allies stormed the prison where they were being held, touching off a massive but largely peaceful demonstration in Andijon's main square. The authorities responded; over the next few hours, somewhere between 155 and 1000 civilians were killed by government troops.

International condemnation of Andijon was swift in coming. When Uzbekistan refused to allow an independent international investigation, the US withdrew most of its aid and the EU enforced sanctions and an arms embargo. Karimov evicted American forces from the strategically important Karshi-Khanabad (K2) airbase near Karshi (the less-critical Germans remained at their base in Termiz). The US Peace Corps and high-profile NGOs such as Freedom House, the Open Society Institute and UNHCR were forced to leave in the face of registration problems or similar technicalities.

Domestically, Karimov used the Andijon events to launch what Human Rights Watch called an 'unprecedented' crackdown against opposition political activists and independent journalists. International journalists were not immune, with most news agencies being forced out of the country in the years following the massacre, although there has been a gradual return in recent years. Today it remains extremely difficult for a Western journalist to get a visa to Uzbekistan.

Yet it appears that time heals old wounds, and relations with the West have gradually improved. The EU eased its sanctions in 2008 and lifted the arms embargo in 2009.

The US has taken a more cautious approach, but all signs point to a *rapprochement*. In 2009 Uzbekistan granted the US permission to use Uzbek territory to transport supplies to Afghanistan. A string of high-profile diplomatic visits followed, leading some to speculate that the US may once again be granted fully-fledged use of the K2 airbase.

Meanwhile, despite a constitutional two-term limit, Karimov quietly won a third successive term in 2007, running practically unopposed; he is expected to win his fourth term in December 2014. Despite being in his mid-70s and rumoured to be in very poor health, the Uzbek president shows few signs of relinquishing his grip on power any time soon. His glamorous pop-singer, businesswoman and diplomat daughter, Gulnara Karimova, has been hotly tipped to be his successor for years. However, her position appeared to have weakened in late 2013, when she became the focus of several corruption investigations in what has been interpreted as a wing-clipping exercise by her rivals for power, most notably Rustam Inoyatov, the head of Uzbekistan's National Security Service.

Many locals worry that after 25 years of rule, with no other nationally prominent politician being allowed to develop a significant power base, the country could be

COTTON PICKIN' MAD

For better or for worse, the Uzbek economy hums to the tune of the 'White Gold'. Truth be told, cotton is – and always was – a poor match for much of Uzbekistan; it's a thirsty crop in a parched land. Decades of monoculture and the drying up of the Aral Sea, which has saturated the land with salt, has done little to help the fecundity of the soil. Poor yields and low government-controlled prices leave farmers too poor to pay for machinery or labour. Yet the government won't let them rotate their crops or convert to fruit. It's all cotton, all the time.

The whole system would collapse entirely but for the country's policy of sending school children, students and adults into the fields every autumn to harvest cotton. The practice has drawn international condemnation and boycotts of products made with Uzbek cotton by Wal-Mart and other juggernauts of the Western apparel industry.

The Uzbek government, which has always denied all accusations, finally passed a law in 2009 banning the forced labour of kids under 16 (it paid little attention to forced adult labour, but then again neither do the critics). Did it curb the practice? Not one bit, according to the Environmental Justice Foundation and Anti-Slavery International, which found evidence of continued widespread 'slave labour' in 2012, when several workers even died during the harvest.

destabilised by the power vacuum left by Karimov's death. Despite the fact that few view Karimov with much fondness, Uzbeks are well aware that it's often a case of 'better the devil you know' in Central Asian politics.

History

The land along the upper Amu-Darya (Oxus River), Syr-Darya (Jaxartes River) and their tributaries has always been different from the rest of Central Asia – more settled than nomadic, with patterns of land use and communality that has changed little from the time of the Achaemenids (6th century BC) to the present day. An attitude of permanence and proprietorship still sets the people of this region apart.

Ancient Empires

The region was part of some very old Persian states, including Bactria, Khorezm and Sogdiana. In the 4th century BC Alexander the Great entered Cyrus the Great's Achaemenid empire. He stopped near Marakanda (Samarkand) and then, having conquered the Sogdians in their homeland mountains, married Roxana, the daughter of a local chieftain.

Out of the northern steppes in the 6th century AD came the Western Turks – the western branch of the empire of the so-called Kök (Blue) Turks. They soon grew attached to life here and abandoned their wandering ways, eventually taking on a significant role in maintaining the existence of the Silk Road. The Arabs brought Islam and a written alphabet to Central Asia in the 8th century but found the region too big and restless to govern.

A return to the Persian fold came with the Samanid dynasty in the 9th and 10th centuries. Its capital, Bukhara, became the centre of an intellectual, religious and commercial renaissance. In the 11th century the Ghaznavids moved into the southern regions. For some time the Turkic Khorezmshahs dominated Central Asia from present-day Konye-Urgench in Turkmenistan, but their reign was cut short by Chinggis Khan in the early 13th century.

Central Asia again became truly 'central' with the rise of Timur (also known as Tamerlane), the ruthless warrior and patron of the arts who fashioned a glittering Islamic capital at Samarkand.

The Uzbeks

Little is known of early Uzbek history. At the time the Golden Horde was founded, Shibaqan (Shayban), a grandson of Chinggis Khan, inherited what is today northern Kazakhstan and adjacent parts of Russia. The greatest khan of these Mongol Shaybani tribes (and probably the one under whom they swapped paganism for Islam) was Özbeg (Uzbek, ruled 1313–40). By the end of the 14th century these tribes had begun to name themselves after him.

The Uzbeks began to move southeast, mixing with sedentary Turkic tribes and adopting the Turkic language; they reached the Syr-Darya in the mid-15th century. Following an internal schism (which gave birth to the proto-Kazakhs), the Uzbeks rallied under Mohammed Shaybani and thundered down upon the remnants of Timur's empire. By the early 1500s, all of Transoxiana ('the land beyond the Oxus') from the Amu-Darya to the Syr-Darya belonged to the Uzbeks, as it has since.

The greatest (and indeed last) of the Shaybanid khans, responsible for some of Bukhara's finest architecture, was Abdullah II, who ruled from 1538 until his death in 1598. After this, as the Silk Road fell into disuse, the empire unravelled under the Shaybanids' distant cousins, the Astrakhanids. By the start of the 19th century the entire region was dominated by three weak, feuding Uzbek city-states – Khiva, Bukhara and Kokand.

The Russians Arrive

In the early 18th century the khan of Khiva made an offer to Peter the Great of Russia (to become his vassal in return for help against marauding Turkmen and Kazakh tribes), stirring the first Russian interest in Central Asia. But by the time the Russians got around to marching on Khiva in 1717, the khan no longer wanted Russian protection, and after a show of hospitality he had almost the entire 4000-strong force slaughtered.

The slave market in Bukhara and Khiva was an excuse for further Russian visits to free a few Russian settlers and travellers. In 1801 the mentally unstable Tsar Paul sent 22,000 Cossacks on a madcap mission to drive the British out of India, along with orders to free the slaves en route. Fortunately for all but the slaves, the tsar was assassinated and the army recalled while struggling across the Kazakh steppes.

The next attempt, by Tsar Nicholas I in 1839, was really a bid to pre-empt expansion into Central Asia by Britain, which had just taken Afghanistan, although Khiva's Russian slaves were the pretext on which General Perovsky's 5200 men and 10,000 camels set out from Orenburg. In January 1840, a British officer, Captain James Abbott, arrived in Khiva (having travelled from Herat in Afghan disguise) offering to negotiate the slaves' release on the khan's behalf, thus nullifying the Russians' excuse for coming.

Unknown to the khan, the Russian force had already turned back, in the face of a devastating winter on the steppes. He agreed to send Abbott to the tsar with an offer to release the slaves in return for an end to Russian military expeditions against Khiva. Incredibly, Abbott made it to St Petersburg.

In search of news of Abbott, Lieutenant Richmond Shakespear reached Khiva the following June and convinced the khan to unilaterally release all Russian slaves in Khiva and even give them an armed escort to the nearest Russian outpost, located on the eastern Caspian Sea. Russian gratitude was doubtlessly mingled with fury over one of the Great Game's boldest propaganda coups.

When the Russians finally rallied 25 years later, the khanates' towns fell like dominoes – Tashkent in 1865 to General Mikhail Chernyaev, Samarkand and Bukhara in 1868, Khiva in 1873, and Kokand in 1875 to General Konstantin Kaufman.

Soviet Daze

Even into the 20th century, most Central Asians identified themselves ethnically as Turks or Persians. The connection between 'Uzbek' and 'Uzbekistan' is very much a Soviet matter. Following the outbreak of the Russian Revolution in 1917 and the infamous sacking of Kokand in 1918, the Bolsheviks proclaimed the Autonomous Soviet Socialist Republic of Turkestan. Temporarily forced out by counter-revolutionary troops and *basmachi* (Muslim guerrilla fighters), they returned two years later and the Khiva and Bukhara khanates were forcibly replaced with 'People's Republics'.

Then in October 1924 the whole map was redrawn on ethnic grounds, and the Uzbeks suddenly had a 'homeland', an official identity and a literary language. The Uzbek Soviet Socialist Republic (SSR) changed shape and composition over the years as it suited Moscow, losing Tajikistan in 1929, acquiring Karakalpakstan from Russia in 1936, taking parts of the steppe from Kazakhstan in 1956 and 1963, then losing some in 1971.

For rural Uzbeks, the main impacts of Soviet rule were the forced and often bloody collectivisation of the republic's mainstay (agriculture) and the massive shift to cotton cultivation. The Uzbek intelligentsia and much of the republic's political leadership was decimated by Stalin's purges. This and the traditional Central Asian respect for authority meant that by the 1980s *glasnost* (openness) and *perestroika* (restructuring) would hardly trickle down here and few significant reforms took place.

Independence

Uzbekistan's first serious noncommunist popular movement, Birlik (Unity), was formed by Tashkent intellectuals in 1989 over issues that included having Uzbek as an official language and the effects of the cotton monoculture. Despite popular support, it was barred from contesting the election in February 1990 for the Uzbek Supreme Soviet (legislature) by the Communist Party. The resulting communist-dominated body elected Islam Karimov, the first secretary of the Communist Party of Uzbekistan (CPUz), to the new post of executive president.

Following the abortive coup in Moscow in August 1991, Karimov declared Uzbekistan independent. Soon afterward the CPUz reinvented itself as the People's Democratic Party of Uzbekistan, inheriting all of its predecessor's property and control apparatus, most of its ideology, and its leader, Karimov.

In December 1991, Uzbekistan held its first direct presidential elections, which Karimov won with 86% of the vote. His only rival was a poet named Muhammad Solih, running for the small, figurehead opposition party Erk (Will or Freedom), who got 12% and was soon driven into exile (where he remains to this day). The real opposition groups, Birlik and the Islamic Renaissance Party (IRP), and all other parties with a religious platform, had been forbidden to take part.

A new constitution unveiled in 1992 declared Uzbekistan 'a secular, democratic presidential republic'. Under Karimov, Uzbekistan would remain secular almost to a fault. But it would remain far from democratic.

Onward to Andijon

The years after independence saw Karimov consolidate his grip on power. Dissent shrivelled thanks to control of the media, police harassment and imprisonment of activists. Through it all, the economy stagnated and the devastating cotton monoculture continued.

A new threat emerged in February 1999 when a series of bomb attacks hit Tashkent. This led to a crackdown on radical Islamic fundamentalists – *wahabis* in the local parlance – that extended to a broad spectrum of opponents. Hundreds of alleged Islamic extremists were arrested. The IRP, with support in the Fergana Valley, was forced underground and Erk was declared illegal.

After extending his first term by referendum, Karimov won a second term as president in January 2000, garnering 92% of the votes. Foreign observers deemed the election a farce and international condemnation was widespread. But the 9/11 attacks on the United States gave Karimov a reprieve. The Uzbek president opened up bases in Termiz and Karshi to the US and NATO for use in the war in Afghanistan, then sat back and watched the US aid money – US$500 million in 2002 alone – start flowing in.

As an added bonus for Karimov, solidarity with the US in the 'War on Terror' effectively gave him a licence to ratchet up his campaign against the *wahabis*. According to human rights groups, Karimov used this license to brand anyone he wanted to silence a 'terrorist'. Another rigged election in 2004, this one parliamentary, drew only modest international criticism.

Such was the situation on 13 May 2005 when events in the eastern city of Andijon rocked the country and instantly demolished Uzbekistan's cosy relationship with the United States.

People

Centuries of tradition as settled people left the Uzbeks in a better position than their nomadic neighbours to fend off Soviet attempts to modify their culture. Traditions of the Silk Road still linger as Uzbeks consider themselves good traders, hospitable hosts and tied to the land.

While Uzbek men toil to make ends meet, women struggle for equality. Considered second-class citizens in the workplace and in the home, women are not given the same rights as their Western counterparts, or even their Kyrgyz and Kazakh neighbours for that matter. Although the Soviets did much to bring women into the mainstream of society, no amount of propaganda could entirely defeat sexist attitudes. There are some signs of change – dress codes continue to liberalise, for example, but old habits die hard and women in conservative families are expected to be subservient to their husbands. Marriages in Uzbek society are traditionally arranged.

Population

By far the most populous country in Central Asia, Uzbekistan boasts almost 30 million people, creating an ethnically and linguistically diverse jigsaw puzzle. Uzbeks make up around 80% of the population, while Tajiks make up 5%, as do ethnic Russians. Kazakhs, Koreans, Tatars, Karakalpaks and Ukrainians make up the other major ethnic minorities. There is still a minuscule Jewish population in Bukhara and an even smaller one in Samarkand.

Tashkent is Uzbekistan's biggest city and the Fergana Valley is home to Uzbekistan's largest concentration of people, a quarter of the population. About three-quarters of the population are ethnic Uzbek. Samarkand, the second city, is Tajik-speaking, as are many of the communities surrounding it, including Bukhara and Karshi. The further west you travel the more sparsely populated the land becomes. Karakalpakstan – home to Kazakhs, Karakalpaks and Khorezmians – has seen its population dwindle as a result of the Aral Sea disaster.

Religion

Close to 90% of Uzbeks claim to be Muslim, although the vast majority are not practising. Most are the moderate Hanafi Sunni variety, with Sufism also popular. About 9% of the population is Christian (mostly Eastern Orthodox), according to the CIA Factbook. The Fergana Valley maintains the greatest Islamic conservative base. Since the 1999 bomb attacks in Tashkent, mosques have been banned from broadcasting the *azan* (call to prayer), and mullahs have been pressured to praise the government in their sermons. Attendance at mosques, already on the decline, fell drastically in the wake of the 2005 Andijon incident.

Arts

Traditional art, music and architecture – evolving over centuries – were placed in a neat little box for preservation following the Soviet creation of the Uzbek SSR. But somehow, in the years to follow, two major centres of progressive art were still allowed to develop: Igor Savitsky's collection of lost art from the 1930s, stashed away in Nukus' Savitsky Museum, and the life stories told inside the late Mark Weil's legendary Ilkhom Theatre in Tashkent.

Contemporary art is, like the media, tightly controlled by the state. Renegade artists who push buttons, such as Weil and photographer Umida Ahmedova, find themselves in trouble. Ahmedova, whose work captures the lives and traditions of ordinary Uzbeks, drew international attention in 2009 when she was arrested and convicted of 'slandering the Uzbek nation' for a series that eventually ran on the BBC website.

While Karimov pardoned her, a glance at the seemingly harmless photos reveals much about the president's artistic ideal: Uzbekistan should be portrayed as clean, orderly, prosperous and modern. This ideal has also had an impact on urban planning – witness the makeover of Samarkand, where planners have cordoned off the old town from tourists' view, and the demolition of Amir Timur maydoni in Tashkent.

Similar laws were invoked in 2013, when five totally unthreatening pop acts were banned from giving live performances in Uzbekistan for the crime of failing to 'praise the motherland, our people and their happiness' in their musical output. Indeed, Uzbeks love Turkish pop, and their own music reflects that. The country's most famous singer is actually President Karimov's politician/socialite/business mogul/Harvard alumni/pop star daughter Gulnara, better known to some by her stage name, Googoosha. Check out her wonderfully awful duet with Gérard Depardieu on YouTube.

Environment

Uzbekistan spans several ecosystems, and topographic and geographic shifts. Its eastern fringes tilt upwards in a knot of rugged mountains – Tashkent's Chatkal and Pskem Mountains run into the western Tian Shan range, and Samarkand's Zarafshon Mountains and a mass of ranges in the southeast flow into the Pamir Alay range. This isolated, rocky and forested terrain makes up an important habitat for the bear, lynx, bustard, mountain goat and even the elusive snow leopard.

To the west of the well-watered mountains are vast plains of desert or steppe. The Amu-Darya (Oxus river) drops out of Tajikistan and winds its way westward along the Turkmen border for more than 2000km before petering out short of Moynaq, cleaving the landscape into two halves: the Karakum (White Sands) desert and the Ustyurt Plateau to the west; and the Kyzylkum (Red Sands) desert to the east. Despite its bleakness, this land is far from dead; the desert is home to the gazelle, various raptors and other critters you'd expect to find – monitors, scorpions and venomous snakes.

There are some 15 nature reserves in Uzbekistan, the largest of which is the Hissar Nature Reserve (750 sq km), due east of Shakhrisabz.

Much of this protected territory is threatened by Uzbekistan's lacklustre environmental protection laws and the deterioration of its national park system, which lacks the funds to prevent illegal logging and poaching. The faltering of the reserves, however, pales in comparison to the Aral Sea disaster, which has been dubbed by some experts as the 'greatest man-made environmental disaster in history'.

Food & Drink

Plov, a Central Asian pilaf consisting of rice and fried vegetables, is the national staple and every region prepares its own distinct version. Every region also has its own variation of *non* bread, commonly known by its Russian name, *lepyoshka;* the raised rim of Kokand's speciality makes it a particularly fine shashlyk plate. Samarkand's *non* resembles a giant bagel without the hole.

Regional staples such as *laghman* (long, flat noodles), *beshbarmak* (noodles with horse meat and broth), *halim* (porridge of boiled meat and wheat) and *naryn* (horse meat sausage with cold noodles) are all popular. *Moshkichiri* and *moshhurda* are meat and mung-bean gruels, respectively. *Dimlama* (also called *bosma*) is meat, potatoes, onions and vegetables braised slowly in a little fat and their own juices; the meatless version is *sabzavotli dimlama. Buglama kovok* (steamed pumpkin) is a light treat.

Uzbeks love their ubiquitous *kurut* (small balls of tart, dried yoghurt) and their *noz* (finely crushed chewing tobacco). *Somsa* (puff pastry stuffed with lamb meat and onion) are also ubiquitous and a great snack when you're out and about at lunch time.

Besides green tea, nonalcoholic drinks include *katyk,* a thin yoghurt that comes plain but can be sweetened if you have some sugar or jam handy. Despite the country's Muslim veneer, it's easy to find beer, and to a lesser extent wine and spirits, anywhere in Uzbekistan and there is no taboo about drinking it.

SURVIVAL GUIDE

Directory A–Z

ACCOMMODATION

The B&B scene in Uzbekistan has taken off more than in any other Central Asian republic. By far the best options are in Bukhara, with Samarkand and Khiva gradually catching up.

Uzbekistan's first community-based tourism program (p186) is going strong in the Nuratau Mountains. Yurtstays are possible too.

Accommodation rates are usually for rooms with private bathroom and include breakfast unless otherwise stated.

Homestayers and especially campers face a range of potential problems related to registration (see p222). It's just about possible to spend a night or two in an unregistered homestay or wild camping, but you'll need to register at a hotel at least every third night, as the law requires every tourist to do so at least once every three days.

ACTIVITIES

Camel trekking, usually combined with a yurtstay, is the most intriguing activity, though most trips are relatively short jaunts around one of the main yurt camps.

East Line Tour (p199) in Bukhara is the authority on **bird watching**, of which Uzbekistan is meant to offer the best in Central Asia.

Other popular outdoor activities are **rafting**, **skiing** and **trekking**, all remarkably accessible from Tashkent. Other good places for a walk include the Nuratau Mountains and the mountains around Boysun and Shakhrisabz in southern Uzbekistan.

DANGERS & ANNOYANCES

As in many totalitarian states, the main danger is the overzealous police. That said, the *militsia* (police) have become much less of a nuisance in recent years. Worried about Uzbekistan's international image and keen to encourage tourism, President Karimov has curbed the police habit of shaking down travellers for bribes at roadside checkpoints in the provinces. Indeed, taxi drivers now *prefer* having tourists in the car, as foreigners supposedly provide 'protection' against spurious roadside checks.

You may still be stopped, particularly on Tashkent's metro, in the sensitive Fergana Valley and in border towns like Termiz. With all of those police around, petty crime and armed robbery are relatively rare.

The main annoyances in Uzbekistan are the need to obsessively collect flimsy and utterly pointless registration slips, and the need to carry around huge piles of cash due to the worthlessness of the som.

EMBASSIES & CONSULATES

Uzbek Embassies in Central Asia

Uzbekistan has embassies in Afghanistan, Kazakhstan (p126), Kyrgyzstan (p307), Tajikistan (p365) and Turkmenistan (p401).

Uzbek Embassies & Consulates

For more Uzbek missions abroad see the website of the **Ministry of Foreign Affairs** (www.mfa.uz).

Uzbek Embassy, China (☎86-10-6532 2551, 86-10-6532 6305; www.uzbekistan.cn; Sanlitun, Beixiao gie 11, Beijing 100600)

Uzbek Embassy, France (☎331-5330 0353; www.ouzbekistan.fr; rue d'Aguesseau, 75008, Paris)

Uzbek Embassy, Germany (☎49-30-394 09 80; www.uzbekistan.de; Perleberger Strasse 62, Berlin 10559) Consulate in Frankfurt.

Uzbek Consulate, Russia (☎7-499-230 00 54; www.uzembassy.ru; 2 Kazachy pereulok II, Moscow, 119017)

Uzbek Embassy, UK (☎44-020-7229 7679; www.uzbekembassy.org; Consular Section, 41 Holland Park , W11 3RP, London)

> **PRACTICALITIES**
>
> Any independent media dealing with Uzbekistan is online and offshore. The government blocks politically sensitive Uzbek-language websites, but you can access most English-language sites, including Facebook and Twitter, from within the country.
>
> Cable and satellite TV are common in all but the cheapest hotels. Satellites receive thousands of channels but usually only a few in English – the BBC, CNN, that's about it.

Uzbek Embassy, USA (1-202-887 5300; www.uzbekistan.org; 1746 Massachusetts Ave NW, Washington DC 20036); Consulate-General in New York (www.uzbekconsulny.org).

Embassies & Consulates in Uzbekistan

Most embassies and consulates are located in Tashkent. For additional embassy listings see www.goldenpages.uz. Hours of operation listed are for visa applications only.

Afghan Embassy (226 73 81, 226 73 80; Batumskaya 1, Shaihan Tahur, Tashkent; 9am-noon & 1.30-4pm Mon-Fri, 9-11.30am drop off, 3-4pm pick up)

Azerbaijan Embassy (273 61 67; Shark Tongi 25, Tashkent; 10am-noon & 3-4pm Mon-Fri)

Chinese Embassy (233 80 88; Gulomov 79, Tashkent; 9am-noon Mon, Wed & Fri)

French Embassy (233 51 57, 233 53 82; www.ambafrance-uz.org; Istikbol 25, Tashkent)

German Embassy (120 84 40, 24hr emergency line 181 54 06; www.taschkent.diplo.de; Rashidov 15, Tashkent)

Iranian Embassy (268 38 77; Parkent 20, Tashkent; 9am-noon Mon-Thu)

Italian Embassy (252 11 19; www.ambtashkent.esteri.it; Yusuf Khos Khodjib 40, Tashkent)

Kazakhstan Embassy (252 16 54; Chekhov 23, Tashkent; drop off 9am-noon, pick-up 4-5pm Mon, Tue, Thu & Fri)

Kyrgyz Embassy (237 47 94; Samatov 30, Tashkent; 10-11.30am & 2.30-4pm Mon-Fri, closed Tue morning & Thu)

Pakistani Embassy (248 21 73; Kichik Halqa Yoli 15, Olmzor, Tashkent)

Russian Embassy (120 35 04; www.russia.uz; Nukus 83, Russia, Tashkent; drop off 10am-12.30pm, pick up 3-4pm Mon-Fri)

Tajikistan Embassy (254 99 66; Abdulla Kahhor Lane VI 61, Tashkent; 8am-11.30am Mon-Fri)

Turkmenistan Embassy (256 94 01; Afrosiab 19, Tashkent; 10am-noon Mon-Thu)

UK Embassy (120 15 00; www.gov.uk/government/world/uzbekistan; Gulomov 67, Tashkent)

US Embassy (120 54 50; uzbekistan.usembassy.gov; Moyqorghon 3, Block V, Tashkent; 9am-6pm Mon-Fri) Take bus 51 from Amir Timur ko'chasi.

FESTIVALS & EVENTS

There are colourful celebrations throughout the country during the vernal equinox festival of **Navrus** (celebrated on 21 March). Festivities typically involve parades, fairs, music, dancing in the streets, plenty of food and, in some places, a rogue game of *kupkari* (traditional polo-like game played with a headless goat carcass). Samarkand has a good one, although the best place to enjoy Navrus is in the countryside.

INTERNET ACCESS

Internet cafes are found in most places travellers go, although access is annoyingly slow outside a handful of spots in Tashkent. Unreliable and slow wi-fi is common in most hotels in bigger cities and other places tourists commonly go (Bukhara and Khiva, for example), but remains practically nonexistent elsewhere.

MONEY

Money is a complicated issue in Uzbekistan, due to the black market. The official rate of the Uzbek som is kept artificially high, and so everyone uses the black market, where your dollars get you approximately 30% more som. And it's easy to feel rich in Uzbekistan – the highest Uzbek note (1000S) is worth less than US$0.50 on the black market. One US$100 bill turns into a plastic bag full of ragged bills, usually tied together with a rubber band.

Bring US dollars with you to Uzbekistan. Euros can also be changed, but it's not as easy. Outside a few larger banks in Tashkent other currencies are totally useless.

A select few ATMs can be found in Tashkent, but you can't rely on them having cash in them. In the provinces, cash advances are usually possible at Asaka Bank for MasterCard holders and at the National Bank of Uzbekistan for Visa cardholders. Commission is 1% to 2% on MasterCard advances and 1% to 4% on Visa card advances. The NBU is also usually the best bet for cashing travellers cheques.

PUBLIC HOLIDAYS

January 1 New Year's Day

January 14 Day of Defenders of the Motherland

March 8 International Women's Day

March 21 Navrus

May 9 Day of Memory and Honour (formerly Victory Day)

September 1 Independence Day

October 1 Teachers' Day

December 8 Constitution Day

REGISTRATION

Registration rules are stricter in Uzbekistan than in most former Soviet countries. The law states clearly that you must register somewhere within three days of arriving in Uzbekistan.

Beyond that, the rules get hazy. Officially you don't need to register if you are staying in a given town for less than three nights. But like everything else in Uzbekistan, this rule is open to interpretation. If the authorities decide you need to be registered for shorter stays, well then you need to be registered. Failure to comply with the 'law' can result in anything from a small bribe being demanded, to a fine of up to a couple of thousand US dollars and deportation.

Such harsh fines are unlikely, but if you go several consecutive days without registering you are asking for trouble – even if technically you have not stayed in any one place for more than two nights. Bottom line: the authorities like to see at least some registration slips in your passport. The more you have, the better, and the only way to be completely safe is to ensure that every night of your stay is accounted for by a registration slip or overnight train ticket. Tashkent hotels in particular can be a real pain in the backside about this – two hotels told us that they would not register someone without a registration slip for every night of their stay, so have your paperwork in order!

Checking into a hotel licensed to take foreigners means automatic registration. If you spend a night in a private home you are supposed to register with the local Office of Visas & Registration (OVIR), but this can create more problems than it solves for you and your hosts. Asking the next hotel you stay at to supply missing registration slips is a possibility, but they may demand a fee for this service or refuse your request outright.

When you leave the country, border officials may thoroughly scrutinise your registration slips or they may not look at them at all. However, the main thing is to be able to produce a convincing bundle when asked. Authorities may also check your registration slips when you are in the country, so carry them with you alongside your passport at all times.

This system creates obvious problems for campers and (less problematically) for homestayers. If you plan to camp your way around Uzbekistan, resign yourself to staying in hotels at least every third night to accumulate some registration slips. If you are missing only a few

THE BLACK MARKET

The disparity between the black-market rate and the National Bank of Uzbekistan official rate was about 30% at the time we visited. This means that travellers will generally achieve 30% savings by paying for everything – including items priced in dollars – with Uzbek som bought on the black market, rather than with US dollars or by credit card. Two main exceptions to this rule are hotels where the black market rate is used, which are particularly common in the big tourist centres of Samarkand, Bukhara and Khiva, and for all internal flights in Uzbekistan, which must be paid for in cash US dollars by foreigners.

There is little to no risk in exchanging money on the black market. However, this could always change so check the situation on the ground to make sure there hasn't been a police crackdown on the technically illegal black-currency trade. Also be aware that a small minority of the black-market moneychangers will trick you: it's perfectly reasonable to count out the vast piles of cash before parting with your dollars. One trick to be on the look out for is money changers putting 500S notes in the middle of the wads of cash, rather than the 1000S notes that should be all the way through.

The defacto black-market money-exchange headquarters in any given city is the central bazaar, but almost anybody and everybody – including hoteliers, restaurateurs, and taxi drivers – are eager to exchange dollars at black-market rates. Ask a neutral person what the going rate for black-market dollar exchange is before agreeing to anything: of course, moneychangers will try to give you a lower rate than you might be entitled to, so shop around and haggle.

Hotels & Travel Agencies

Generally, local convention is to list the prices of hotels and travel-agency services in dollars. However, the following caveats apply:

- Hotels in Tashkent, the Fergana Valley and state-owned hotels outside of Tashkent list prices in dollars, but convert their room prices to som *at the official exchange rate*. This means that travellers will save 30% (at the time of research) by paying with som instead of with dollars or a credit card, if they buy their som on the black market – a great way to save money.
- Most travel agencies and private hotels outside of Tashkent – such as the B&Bs of Bukhara, Samarkand and Khiva – also list prices in dollars. However, they convert their room prices to som *at the black-market rate.* At these places you will not save anything by paying in som.

registration slips upon departure from the country, you should be in the clear – in theory. In practice, police often hassle departing tourists over just one or two missing registration slips. If this happens, stand your ground and argue forcefully that you were in some towns for less than three nights, and were not required to register for those nights.

TELEPHONE

There are two national Uzbek mobile phone providers: Ucell and Beeline. However, in 2013, only residents of Uzbekistan were able to purchase SIM cards, though this may change. Call charges are minuscule and coverage for internet is generally fast and cheap too, so if you're in the country for any amount of time, it's well worth investing in one: try asking a local or at your hotel if an Uzbek citizen will buy a SIM card on your behalf.

Uzbekistan's antiquated fixed-line system is creaky but functional. Local calls cost almost nothing and domestic long-distance calls are cheap. Post offices and minimarts sell a range of cards good for discounted long-distance calls out of Uzbekistan, but it's far cheaper and easier to use Skype in any internet cafe.

To place a call to a mobile phone, dial ☎83 (from a land line) or ☎+998 (from another mobile phone), followed by the two-digit code and the seven-digit number.

To place a call to a land line, dial ☎83 (from either a land line or a mobile phone) followed by the two-digit city code and the seven-digit number. If the city code is three digits, drop the 3 and just dial 8.

If dialling from any Tashkent number (mobile or fixed) to any other Tashkent number, regardless of carrier, just dial the seven-digit number (no code).

To place an international call from a land line, dial ☎8, wait for a tone, then dial ☎10.

We have given mobile phone numbers their full international codes for consistency – even from a local mobile phone, you can still call them by using this number.

TRAVEL PERMITS

Border permits are required for all mountain areas near the Tajik and Kyrgyz borders, including most of Ugam-Chatkal National Park, the Zarafshon and Hissar Mountains, and Zaamin National Park. Secure these with the help of any travel agency that arranges tours in these regions.

VISAS FOR ONWARD TRAVEL

Contact David at Stantours (p155) for updated information and honest advice. If you can avoid purchasing letter of invitation (LOI) support, Stantours will tell you. Most embassies require you to show an onward ticket if you are applying for a transit visa.

Afghanistan

In 2013 the Afghan embassy in Tashkent (p222) ceased issuing tourist visas to non-residents of Uzbekistan. The only exceptions seem to be business travellers and tourists with a letter of recommendation from their own embassies in Tashkent, something that most consulates are unlikely to give. Until this changes, you're better off getting your Afghan visa at home or in another Central Asian country.

Azerbaijan

A 30-day tourist visa from the Azerbaijan embassy (p222) costs US$40 to US$60 depending on your nationality (though fees were in the process of being adjusted when we visited). Two passport photos, a copy of your passport and a LOI are needed. Five-day transit visas (US$25) are also available.

China

The Chinese embassy (p222) issues three-month single-entry visas for US$40 (five day wait) or US$80 for same day pick up. You'll need a copy of your passport and Uzbek visa on a single page, plus copies of hotel and airline bookings into and out of China. Proof of employment (a letter from your company should do) is also sometimes required.

Iran

First you must apply for an authorisation through an Iranian agent. This costs around US$50 and takes one to two weeks to arrive, after which you can apply for a 30-day tourist visa (valid for entry within three months) at the Iranian embassy you elected for collection. Assuming that was Tashkent (p222), the visa processing costs varies from US$50 to US$100.

Kazakhstan

A 30-day tourist visa (US$30) takes five days to process at the Kazakhstan embassy (p222), as does a 60-day double-entry tourist visa (US$60). An LOI is not needed for either, but you need to bring a passport photo and a copy of your passport's photo page. Transit visas cost US$20 for five-day processing and do not require an LOI, but they do require an onward ticket or visa to a third country.

Kyrgyzstan

Visa-free travel to Kyrgyzstan for most nationalities (see p309) means one less piece of Central Asian bureaucracy to worry about.

Pakistan

The Pakistani embassy (p222) in Tashkent only issues tourist visas to residents of Uzbekistan.

Russia

Begin by filling out a visa application form online (visa.kdmid.ru). You'll need to bring your original passport and a copy of its photo page, a passport photo, a tourist voucher and booking confirmation to apply for a single- or double-entry 30-day tourist visa at the Russian embassy (p222). Prices vary enormously depending on nationality and the type of visa and processing you want.

Tajikistan

The consulate is actually across the road from the embassy proper (p222). No invitation is needed, just bring a copy of your passport, one photo and fill out an application form. However, it's a 14-day processing period with no rush option, which makes this a terrible place to get a Tajik visa. Prices vary enormously too, to the point that the consul himself was unable to give us even a ballpark figure for a one-month tourist visa. Transit visas require two passport photos, and a copy of your passport. No onward tickets are needed, but processing time varies from three to 14 days.

Turkmenistan

The entrance to the visa section is behind the main embassy (p222) to the left. Come early (two hours before opening time is not a bad idea) and add your name to the waiting list (you can then go for breakfast and return at 10am when the gates open). Be friendly to the Uzbek guards who police entry to the embassy and they'll ensure you get in; being annoyed about the ridiculous system won't help. Three to five-day transit visas are issued without an LOI for US$50. Allow five to 10 days for transit-visa authorisation, plus another two days for visa processing. Ask about possible urgent rush processing. Tourist visas require expensive tour arrangements through a specialised agent and cost US$30 to US$115, but once you have the required invitation, processing takes just one to three days.

Getting There & Away

ENTERING UZBEKISTAN

As long as your papers are in order, entering Uzbekistan should be relatively easy, long lines at the airport notwithstanding. You will be asked to fill out two identical customs declarations forms, one to turn in and one to keep (which must be

VISAS FOR UZBEKISTAN

Uzbek visa rules depend entirely on the state of Uzbekistan's relations with your country's government. At the time of writing, citizens of the following countries were exempt from Letters of Invitation (LOI): Austria, Belgium, France, Germany, Italy, Japan, Spain, Switzerland, the UK and the US. Everybody else needs an LOI, as do (sometimes) citizens of the above countries who are applying for visas outside their country of citizenship.

If there is no Uzbek embassy in your country, you should be eligible for 'visa-on-arrival' at Tashkent International Airport if you arrange special LOI support for this several weeks in advance through a travel agency or inviting business.

Any Uzbek travel agency can arrange LOI support, but most demand that you also purchase a minimum level of services – usually hotel bookings for at least three nights. A few agencies still provide LOI support with no strings attached, including Arostr Tourism (p155) and Stantours (p155). They charge US$35 for a LOI for a single-entry 30-day tourist visa. Tack on US$10 per entry for multiple-entry visas, and another US$10 per entry for visa-on-arrival support. Allow five to 10 business days for LOI processing, or pay double for four- to five-day 'rush' processing.

The standard tourist visa is a 30-day, single-entry visa. They cost US$70 to US$100 for most nationalities, and at least US$131 for US citizens. Additional entries cost US$10 per entry. Single-entry tourist visas lasting more than 30 days are difficult to obtain. Three-day transit visas (US$30) are possible without an LOI.

Most embassies can issue same-day visas when you present an LOI. Visa processing without an LOI usually takes three to 10 days, depending on the embassy. Be aware that when you apply for your visa in person at an Uzbek embassy, you must have filled in your application form and uploaded a photograph digitally beforehand – this can not be done at the Uzbek embassy in person. Application forms are available online at evisa.mfa.uz.

Visa Extensions

A one-week 'exit visa' (essentially an extension) costing about US$40 is available from an OVIR booth at Tashkent International Airport (p226). Longer extensions are time-consuming, expensive and involve much red tape. Many frustrated travellers give up and go to neighbouring Kazakhstan or Kyrgyzstan to buy a new visa.

handed in upon departure). The customs form is necessary for changing travellers cheques and will smooth your departure, so don't lose it. Declare every cent of every type of money you bring in on your customs form, or face possible penalties.

AIR

If arriving by air, your grand entrance into Uzbekistan will most likely occur at **Tashkent International Airport** (☎71-140 28 04, 71-140 28 01). A few flights from Russia arrive in regional hubs such as Samarkand, Bukhara and Urgench.

The numerous *aviakassa* (private ticket kiosks) scattered around major cities can help book international tickets on national carrier **Uzbekistan Airways** (www.uzairways.com) and other airlines.

Uzbekistan Airways has convenient booking offices in Tashkent, but frustratingly in most cities you'll need to buy domestic flights in the airports themselves, as they were not available online or through *aviakassa* at the time of writing. Pay for airline tickets in US dollars only.

LAND

To/From Afghanistan

The Friendship Bridge linking Termiz with northern Afghanistan has been opened to tourist traffic since 2005. While Afghan officials seem happy with this arrangement, the Uzbeks have been known to close their side of the border for security reasons or other concerns. Contact a reliable travel agency in Tashkent to make sure it's open before setting out.

To get to the *tamozhnya* (border, or 'customs house') from Termiz, take marshrutka 21 from opposite Yubileyny Bazaar (800S, 20 minutes). The bridge is 10km south of town. There's a fair bit of walking involved to get between the various checkpoints on the Uzbek side, and then across the bridge. From the Afghan side you're looking at about a 30-minute, US$10 taxi ride to Mazar-e-Sharif.

To/From Kazakhstan

Despite their very long common border there are just two main places to cross from Uzbekistan into Kazakhstan: Chernyaevka between Tashkent and Shymkent, and the remote Kungrad–Beyneu crossing from Karakalpakstan into Kazakhstan's far west. There's also the secondary Yallama crossing, 60km southwest of Tashkent and the railway crossing at Saryagsh just to the north of Tashkent.

Crossing at Chernyaevka is the easiest from the point of view of public transport, but it can sometimes involve long lines, and waits of up to six hours in extreme cases – go early and be patient. To get to Chernyaevka from Tashkent is a 30,000S taxi ride, or you can take a shared taxi (5000S, 20 minutes) or marshrutka from Yunusobod Bazaar.

If you have your own vehicle, Yallama is where you should cross, as private cars cannot cross at Chernyaevka. To get to Yallama, you can take one of the frequent local trains from Tashkent to Syrdarya, Gulistan and Havast, all of which stop in Chinaz, or take a shared taxi from Sobir Rahimov metro (10,000S, 50 minutes).

The other crossing is by train or road between Karakalpakstan and Beyneu in western Kazakhstan. Train 917 departs daily at 9.20am from Kungrad, about 225km southeast of the border, to Beyneu (10 hours). Other trains crossing this border include Tashkent–St Petersburg (weekly), Tashkent–Saratov (twice weekly) and Moscow–Dushanbe (three weekly).

A new high-speed train service between Almaty and Tashkent, due to be introduced in 2014, is expected to cut journey times between the two cities by one-third or more.

To/From Kyrgyzstan

The only border crossings into Kyrgyzstan that are open to foreigners are at Uchkurgon/Shamaldy-Say (northeast of Namangan) and Dostyk (Dustlyk), between Andijon and Osh. They are generally hassle-free, although long lines do occur.

Most travellers use the Osh crossing. In Andijon, frequent shared taxis to the *tamozhnya* at Dustlyk depart from a stop on Babur St about 400m southeast of the train station (8000S, 40 minutes). Walk across the border and pick up public transport on the other side for the short trip to Osh.

Limited public transport and taxis are available at the Uchkurgon crossing.

To/From Tajikistan

There are two main border crossings between Uzbekistan and Tajikistan: Oybek between Tashkent and Dushanbe and the Denau–Tursanzade crossing in southern Uzbekistan. The very handy Samarkand/Penjikent crossing has been shut for some years now, and showed no sign of reopening at the time of writing.

Those heading from Tashkent to Dushanbe normally drive to Khojand via the pain-free Oybek border crossing and then take a shared taxi from Khojand to Dushanbe (US$20). To get to this border from Tashkent take a marshrutka or shared taxi from Kuyluk Bazaar to Bekobod and get off at Oybek (marshrutka/taxi per seat 20,000/10,000S, 1½ hours), about 35km shy of Bekobod, near Chanak village. An ordinary taxi between Tashkent and Oybek costs about US$30. Once across the border take a taxi to Khojand (US$15), or a taxi to nearby Bostan (US$1) and then a minibus to Khojand.

The fairly remote Denau–Tursanzade crossing can see long lines, and other hassles are reportedly common on the Uzbek side (though other reports suggest that foreigners are often invited to skip the line and enjoy a relatively hassle-free passage). Denau is a 1½-hour drive from Termiz or a five-hour drive from Samarkand. You can get shared taxis to the border from either city, and there are also a few morning marshrutkas. From Termiz, regular shared taxis and marshrutkas head to Denau from the bus station, and there are also three daily local trains directly to the border town of Sariosiyo (4500S, four hours), 15km north of Denau. From Denau, take the train or a marshrutka to Sariosiyo, cross the border and proceed by taxi from Tursanzade to Dushanbe (US$10, 45 minutes).

To/From Turkmenistan

The three border crossings between Uzbekistan and Turkmenistan are reached from Bukhara, Khiva and Nukus. Each crossing requires a potentially sweltering walk of 10 to 20 minutes across no-man's-land due to the absurdly designed border posts. Shared taxis or buses are sometimes available to ferry travellers across, but don't count on them.

From Bukhara a taxi should cost around 80,000S to the border. **Shared taxis** (8000S, 40 minutes) make the trip from Kolkhoz Bazaar to Karakol (or Olot), about 10km short of the border. From Karakol a taxi to the border costs 10,000S. You can also take a slow local train to Olot from Kagan (3000S, two hours, two daily). Once over the border, take a shared taxi to Turkmenabat (8000S, 40 minutes).

From Khiva or Urgench it costs about 30,000S to hire a car to the border, from where it's a short, US$3 taxi ride to Dashogus. Alternatively, you can take a bus to the border from Khiva (2000S, one hour). There's an early morning departure from a **lot outside the North Gate**, and two later departures from Dekhon Bazaar.

From Nukus it's about a 30,000S, 20km ride to the Konye-Urgench *tamozhnya*. Alternatively, take public transport to Hojeli and take a shared taxi from Hojeli to the border (3000S). Once you've walked across the border you can pick up a shared taxi to Konye-Urgench (US$2).

ℹ Getting Around

AIR

Air transport is dirt cheap in Uzbekistan, and is a great way to cover the large distances between big cities. Flights do get booked up though, so try to book at least several days in advance during high season. You can only book domestic flights directly with the airline, which usually means going to the airport in any given city. Online booking, or the booking of domestic flights through travel agencies, was not possible at the time we visited.

BUS & MARSHRUTKA

Clapped-out state buses are fast disappearing from Uzbek roads, undercut by a boom in private buses that do not keep schedules and leave when full. They are newer and more comfortable, but can be slow as drivers and touts are preoccupied with overselling seats and transporting cargo and contraband.

Marshrutkas usually take the form of 11- to 14-seat Russian-made 'Gazelle' vans, or seven-seat Daewoo Damas minivans.

CAR

Hiring your own car (with driver) is possible, provided you have insurance from your home country and a valid international driving licence. Be prepared for the same kind of hassles you'll experience anywhere in the former Soviet Union: lots of random stops and traffic cops fishing for bribes. There are no car-rental agencies, so you'll need to hire a taxi, which is generally affordable even for several days on end; budget around US$60 per day (excluding petrol). Driving is on the right.

SHARED & ORDINARY TAXI

Shared taxis save tons of time but are, of course, more costly than buses. They ply all the main intercity routes and also congregate at most border points. They leave when full from set locations – usually from near bus stations – and run all day and often through the night. Prices fluctuate throughout the day/week/month/year, increasing towards the evening, on weekends and on holidays. You can buy all four seats in a shared taxi if you're in a hurry or just prefer to travel in comfort – this is the standard way most travellers with a midrange budget get around in Uzbekistan as prices remain low.

TRAIN

Trains are perhaps the most comfortable and safest method of intercity transport. The express (*skorostnoy*, or 'high-speed') trains between Tashkent, Samarkand and Bukhara, with airplane-style seating, are faster than a shared taxi and a *lot* more comfortable. Book a couple of days in advance – they're popular. These have 2nd-class, 1st-class and deluxe 'SV' class (private compartment) seating. First class is not noticeably more comfortable than 2nd class.

Other long-haul trains are of the slow but comfortable Soviet variety, with *platskartny* (hard sleeper) and *kupeyny* (soft sleeper) compartments available. Slow, dirt-cheap local *prigorodny* trains, with bench-style seating, cover middle-distance routes such as Samarkand–Bukhara.

Kyrgyzstan Кыргызстан

Includes ➡

Best Community Tourism Outfits

- CBT Karakol (p263)
- CBT Naryn (p281)
- Jailoo Kochkor (p277)
- CBT Arslanbob (p288)

Best Yurtstays

- Song-Köl (p273)
- Kilemche (p275)
- Tash Rabat (p285)
- Ecotour (p246)

Why Go?

Kyrgyzstan is a nation defined by its topography: joyously unspoilt mountainscapes, stark craggy ridges, and rolling summer pastures (*jailoos*) are brought to life by semi-nomadic, yurt-dwelling shepherd cultures. Add to this natural beauty a well-developed network of homestays and the recent introduction of visa-free travel, and it's easy to see why Kyrgyzstan is rapidly becoming the gateway of choice for Western travellers in Central Asia. As can be expected in a country where the vast majority of attractions are rural and high altitude, the timing of your visit is crucial. Summer is ideal with hikes and roads generally accessible. Midsummer also sees Kazakh and Russian tourists converge on the beaches of never-freezing Lake Issyk-Köl. From October to May, much rural accommodation closes down and the yurts that add such character to the alpine vistas are stashed away. So think twice about a winter visit unless you've come to ski.

When to Go

Bishkek

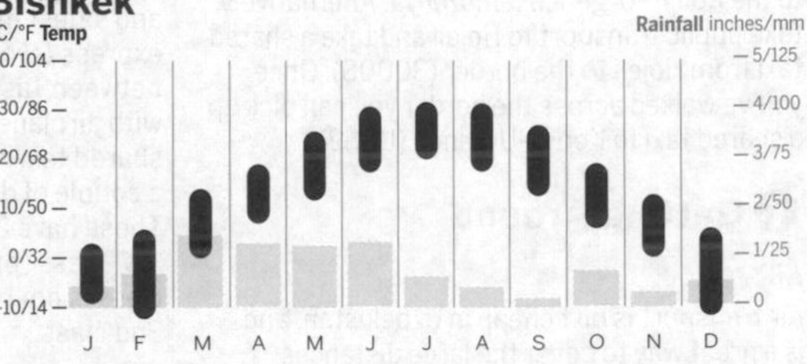

May–Jun Flowers bloom and tourist numbers are low; higher mountains may be snow-bound.

mid-Jul–early Sep Ideal for treks; accommodation heavily booked; cities stifling hot.

Mar Rural accommodation closed; trekking areas inaccessible; good for skiing.

Visas & Permits

At least 60 nationalities can visit Kyrgyzstan without visas, including citizens of Korea, Japan, most major Western countries and former Soviet countries. Many visitors who do need a visa can arrange for one on arrival through an agency. Border-zone permits are required for visiting some border zones but this generally only affects mountaineers climbing in the highest mountain areas. For more information on visas, see p309.

COSTS

Relative Cost

Marginally the cheapest state in Central Asia.

Daily Expenses

- Hostel dorm (Bishkek) 400–900som, midrange hotel US$30–80
- Street snack 15–40som, basic self-service cafeteria meal 60–100som
- Good restaurant meal in Bishkek 400som
- 1L of petrol 42som

Price Ranges

- **Sleeping** (for two people) $ <2000som, $$ 2000–5000som, $$$ >5000som
- **Eating** (main course) $ <100som, $$ 100–300som, $$$ >300som

Itineraries

- **One week** Head for Lake Issyk-Köl where Karakol makes an ideal base for a few days skiing or hiking in the alpine valleys, depending on the season.
- **Two weeks** If you're heading to Uzbekistan from Kyrgyzstan, apply for your Uzbek visa in Bishkek. While it's being processed visit Issyk-Köl and Song-Köl, then return to Bishkek to collect your visa. From Bishkek, head to the Fergana Valley via Osh, stopping in pretty Arslanbob en route.
- **One month** With more time, you can add a two-week pre-arranged horse-trek, mountaineering or trekking expedition to the two-week itinerary.

TOP TIP

Kyrgyzstan's towns aren't attractions in themselves, only bases for exploring the countryside, and our suggestions are just initial pointers. The best way to explore is to simply head out into *jailoos* and hills and find your own way. But remember that everything is seasonal.

Fast Facts

- **Area** 198,500 sq km
- **Capital** Bishkek
- **Country code** ☎996
- **Languages** Kyrgyz, Russian
- **Population** 5.6 million
- **Famous for** Yurts, hats, horsemen

Exchange Rates

COUNTRY	UNIT	SOM
Australia	A$1	45.6som
Canada	C$1	47.5som
China	Y1	8.0som
Euro zone	€1	62.3som
Japan	¥100	49som
NZ	NZ$1	39.6som
Russia	R10	14.9som
UK	UK£1	77.2som
USA	US$1	49.2som

Resources

- www.celestial.com.kg
- www.cbtkyrgyzstan.kg
- www.helvetas.kg
- www.kyrgyzstan.orexca.com
- www.timesca-europe.com

Kyrgyzstan Highlights

❶ Wander the Kyrgyz countryside at its best on a **horse trek** (p304) high into the mountains and across summer pastures.

❷ Star gaze, cloud chase and experience life in a summer herder's yurt at **Lake Song-Köl** (p273), a vast upland lake hemmed by a ribbon of peaks.

❸ Whether passing through Sary Tash en route to China or Tajikistan, heading to the Horse Games at Achik-Tash or scaling Peak Lenin, the snowy peaks of the **Alay Valley** (p296) are unforgettable.

4 Visit the breathtaking yet remarkably accessible alpine scenery of **Ala-Archa** (p250), just an hour from the capital.

5 Enjoy the world's largest walnut forest on a network of blossoming woodland treks at **Arslanbob** (p286).

6 Drive the scenically delightful **Torugart Route** (p310) between Naryn and Kashgar (China) via Torugart.

BISHKEK БИШКЕК

☎0312 / POP 900,000 / ELEV 800M

Green and bustling but short on sights, the location of the country's capital is more of an attraction than its forgettable architecture. Just occasionally, when the air is exceptionally clear, the Kyrgyz Ala-Too materialises as if by magic to create a grand mountain backdrop. For travellers, Bishkek is most useful as a comfortable place to pick up a visa or two while planning their Central Asian adventure.

History

Bishkek town was founded in 1878 on the site of a Russian garrison. Before that, all that was here was the small 1825 Pishpek fortress of the Khan of Kokand. Its name is probably derived from the Sogdian term *peshagakh*, meaning 'place below the mountains'. But as *pishkek/bishkek* is the Kazakh/Kyrgyz term for a plunger-equipped *kymys*-churn there are several far more amusingly crude etymological theories.

From 1926 to 1991, the city's Soviet name was Frunze, honouring locally born Mikhail Frunze, a Russian Civil War commander whose Bolshevik forces seized Khiva and Bukhara in 1920.

Sights

Bishkek's main central attractions are the parks and museums north of Chuy around Ala-Too Square. Don't expect much in the way of architectural thrills. Bigger Soviet buildings are mosty half-hearted concrete lumps but there are a few elegant neo-Classical exceptions such as the State Opera & Ballet Theatre, some spired university buildings and parts of the square around the boxy Philharmonia.

State Historical Museum MUSEUM

(Lenin Museum; Map p234; Ala-Too Square; foreign adult/student 150/75som, local 30/15som; ⏲10am-6pm Tue-Sun Mar-Oct, 9.30am-5pm Tue-Sun Nov-Feb) Thrillingly for Sovietophiles, this 1984 marble-faced cube still retains many splendidly stirring faux-bronze/copper reliefs and bold ceiling murals reflecting the building's former purpose as a state-of-the-art Lenin Museum. Mixed in are a series of photos and mementos from the 2010 revolution (see p301) and portraits of that year's martyrs. The top floor yurt signals a completely disconnected section on ethnology and archaeology. Photos here show items from the museum's rich collection of Scythian gold but the originals are locked away in secured vaults and only shown to VIPs.

Ala-Too Square SQUARE

(Map p234; Chuy 114, Kiev 71) Surveyed by a triumphant statue of Manas, Bishkek's nominal centre is architecturally neo-brutalist in style, but it has a perversely photogenic quality, especially when slowly goose-stepping soldiers change the guard beside the soaring national flagpole. That happens every two hours most of the year, hourly in winter.

In summer, the concrete of the square's northern half is relieved by attractive floral displays and a **musical fountain show** (Map p234; ⏲8pm).

Lenin Statue MONUMENT

(Map p234) Having once dominated Ala-Too Square, Vlad turned his back on the mountains in 2003 and now lurks behind the History Museum. Young skaters and break-dancers practice their daring vaults oblivious to the desperate gesticulations of his pointing arm.

Dubovy (Oak) Park PARK

Where wide, green Erkindik (Freedom Ave) enters this pleasant central park, painters sell a range of locally themed, if typically garish, art. There's a minor sculpture garden amid the oaks behind the park's **statue of Kurmanjan Datka** (Map p234), the 19th-century heroine who also features on Kyrgyzstan's 50som banknote.

State Museum of Fine Arts GALLERY

(Gapar Aitiev Museum of Applied Art; Map p234; ☎66 15 44; Soviet (Abdrakhmanov) 196; adult/student 50/25som; ⏲9am-5pm Tue-Thu & Sat-Sun, 10am-4pm Fri) This gallery's biliously miserable concrete exterior contrasts with the neoclassical grandeur of the Opera opposite but the collections of Kyrgyz embroidery and felt rugs, and the splendid variety of paintings all make a visit worthwhile. Don't miss the amusing reproductions of Egyptian and classical statues.

Frunze House-Museum MUSEUM

(Map p234; Frunze 364; foreigner/local 50/25som; ⏲10am-5pm Tue-Sun) This modest museum forms a concrete shell around the thatched cottage that was allegedly the birthplace of Mikhail Vasilievich Frunze (1885–1925), for whom Bishkek (Pishpek) was renamed shortly after his death. There is little information in English so for many visitors it's enough to simply peep through the windows at the partially visible cottage structure while walking past.

Al Halal Gallery GALLERY

(Map p234; Moskva 49; ⏲11am-6pm Tue-Sat) This small, top-quality modern art gallery is an ideal starting point for an exploration of the vibrant, but often invisible, Bishkek arts scene. If you're keen and lucky, you might be invited to the artists' studios building (Druzhba 3). Some talented local artists including **Andrei Zotov** (www.zotov-art.com.kg) now have their own online galleries.

WWII Monument MONUMENT

(Freedom Sq) Commemorating the 40th anniversary of the end of WWII, this monument is designed to evoke three symbolic yurt struts curving above an eternal flame. It sits within the dauntingly over-sized sunbleached expanse of 'Freedom Sq'.

Activities

Just to the south of the city, you can ski, hike, mountain bike or picnic in the mountains. Tour and trekking agents (p245) can help with logistics; TUK (p245) organises regular small-group excursions, mostly day trips at weekends. To beat the summer heat, Bishkek has numerous swimming pools; for a comprehensive list, check out http:ianbek.kg/?p=13368.

Zhirgal Banya BATHS

(Map p234; Cnr Pravda (Sultan Ibraimov) & Toktogul; adult/child incl locker & towel 250/150som; ⏲noon-11pm Mon-Thu, 7am-11pm Fri-Sun) This large, sex-segregated bathhouse has a twin-cupped facade that looks like a bad architectural joke. However, the low-lit, artistic interior is well maintained and makes a great place to unwind, unless you're uncomfortable with wide-spread nakedness. Manicures (350som) and massages (500som) cost extra, but there's no charge for flogging yourself with *venik* (birch twigs) in traditional Russian style.

Karven Club SWIMMING & FITNESS

(Map p234; ☎68 12 18; Toktogul 77; per hour/day 400/500som; ⏲7am-9.30pm) Outdoor swimming pool with modern fitness centre.

Silk Road Water Centre ADVENTURE SPORTS

(☎051-775 0972, 60 96 19; www.rafting.com.kg) Organises kayaking, fishing and white-water rafting, notably between Tokmok and Balykchy (Class II to IV).

BISHKEK ROAD NAMES

Most city street names have been changed at least once or twice since 1991. Signs and business cards usually indicate the latest Kyrgyz names. However, in speech many locals use the old Soviet-era names. We follow suit, stressing the names most recognisable to taxi drivers. Also note that Russian grammar gives different forms to names according to usage. Thus, for example, major east–west roads Kiev and Moskva will often be pronounced as Moskovskaya and Kievskaya. Be aware that Soviet (aka Sovietskaya) is now officially known as Abdrakhmanov north of the railway line but as Baytik-Baatyr to the south.

Courses

Ease of obtaining student visas, relatively low living expenses and the use of Russian as a virtual *lingua franca* in the city, make Bishkek an appealing destination to study Russian.

London School LANGUAGE COURSE

(Map p240; ☎54 52 62; www.londonschool.kg; Soviet (Abdrakhmanov) 39; per hr 250som, registration basic/intensive 300/1200som) London School's intensive programme offers five 80-minute Russian-language lessons per day starting from the first of each month. The basic programme allows you to do just one or two hours a day for as little as a week, according to teacher availability. Book well ahead for the summer months. Accommodation is available to students in homestays (half board 600som) or above the school in ageing but serviceable self-catering rooms (380som) which pair-share bathrooms and kitchens.

Russian Center of Science and Culture LANGUAGE COURSE

(Map p234; ☎055-500 3976; www.kgz.rs.gov.ru; Erkindik 2/1) Russian courses for a variety of ability levels. Standard courses (US$100 per month) provide three two-hour lessons per week.

Festivals & Events

During **Nooruz** (21 March) and on **Kyrgyz Independence Day** (31 August) traditional Kyrgyz horseback games entice 99% male audiences to the Hippodrome, around 5km

Bishkek

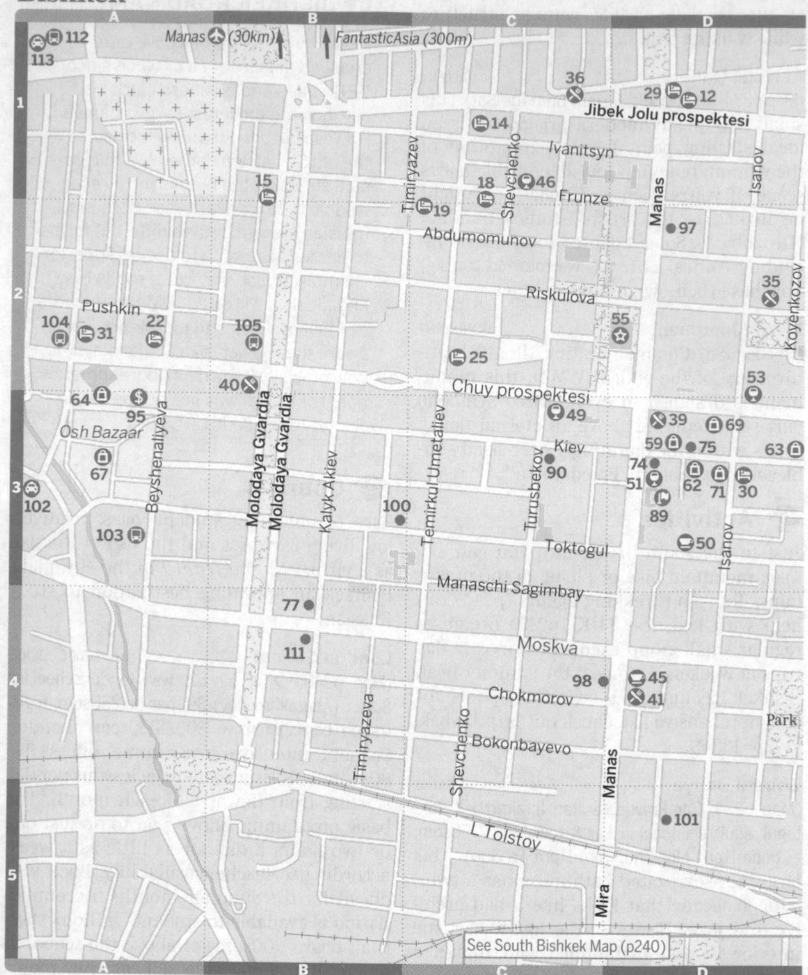

southwest of the centre (an 180som taxi ride). European health-and-safety inspectors would blanch at the over-packed stadium without the hint of a surge barrier.

Sleeping

Backpacker accommodation is based almost entirely around homestay-style hostels. None are very easy to find and calling ahead is always wise as the owners might be away. If you arrive late at night and budget places are full or closed, one option is to try one of the unnamed 'sauna-hotels'. While designed for amorous trysts, many are less seedy than you might expect and between 9pm and 9am they are not only open but might offer 'noch' rates, eg 1500 som for a queen-bed room with decent bathroom at **Manas 117** (Map p234; Just off Jibek Jolu; d per 24hrs/night 3000/1500som).

Rates for midrange hotels generally include breakfast.

City Centre

Sakura Guesthouse HOSTEL **$**

(☎38 02 09, mobile 077-732 4024; http:sakura guesthouse.web.fc2.com/english.html;

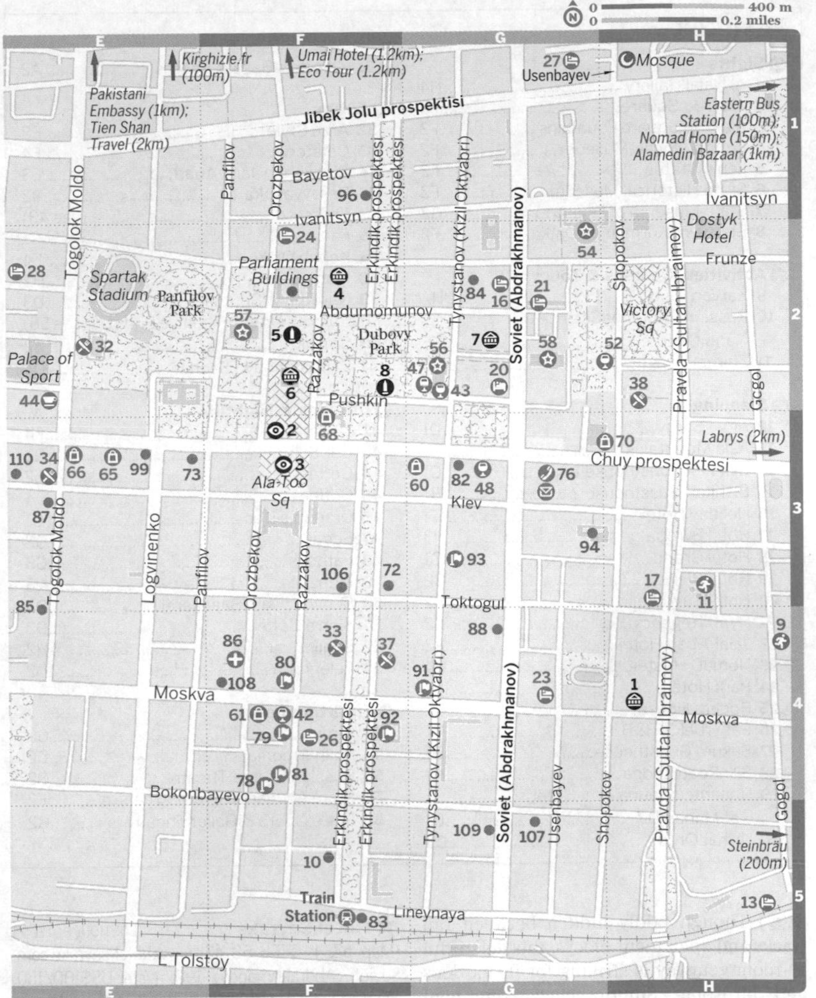

Michurina 38; dm/s/d 400/700/1000som;) If you want to spend under US$10 per person, Sakura is the best-value offering in town. Run by a Kyrgyz-Japanese family, the fresh, neat, if somewhat bland, three-storey accommodation block contains spotlessly clean rooms with shared hot showers. Communal space is limited to a small yard-table and tiny summer kitchen, along with a rooftop that is more for laundry drying than socialising. From the big Gazprom Petrol Station on Jibek Jolu (one block east of Soviet/Abdrakhmanov) walk 200m north up Usenbayev passing the voluble Murtazali Mosque. Take the second unpromising lane left, turning beside Usenbayev 152.

NomaD Hostel HOSTEL $

(Map p234; 97 66 32; http: hostelinkg.com/en/; Usenbayev 44; dm/d US$15/35) Not to be confused with the older, somewhat tired Nomad Home, this neat, brand new Bishkek hostel was amongst the most the popular backpacker choices of summer 2013.

★ **Asia Mountains** HOTEL $$

(Map p234; 690235; www.asiamountains-hotels.com; Lineynaja 1A; s/d US$70/80, ste US$80-100, yurt-spaces s/d/tr/q US$25/35/45/55;

Bishkek

Sights
1 Al Halal Gallery H4
2 Ala-Too Square F3
3 Ala-Too Square Fountains F3
4 Frunze House-Museum F2
5 Lenin Statue F2
6 State Historical Museum F2
7 State Museum of Fine Arts G2
8 Statue of Kurmanjan Datka F2

Activities, Courses & Tours
9 Karven Club H4
10 Russian Center of Science and Culture F5
11 Zhirgal Banya H3

Sleeping
12 Altyn Saray D1
13 Asia Mountains H5
14 Bishkek Guesthouse 1 ..... C1
15 Bishkek Guesthouse 2 ..... B1
16 Holiday Hotel G2
17 Hotel Evropa H3
18 Hotel Grand C1
19 Hotel Rich C2
20 Hotel Sayrake G2
21 Hyatt Regency G2
22 Jalal-Abad Hotel A2
23 NomaD Hostel G4
24 Park Hotel F2
25 Rodem House C2
26 Sabyrbek's B&B F4
27 Sakura Guesthouse G1
28 Silk Road Lodge E2
29 Unnamed Sauna Mini-Hotel at Manas 117 ..... D1
30 Urmat Ordo D3
31 Zamira's Bazaar Rooms A2

Eating
32 Arzu Style E2
33 Cafeteria F4
34 Chaikhana Jalal-Abad E3
35 Derevyashka D2
Espresso ..... (see 43)
36 Faiza C1
37 Kebab Ojak F4
38 Manty Bar H2
39 Narodnyy/Shumkur D3
Russian Drama Theatre Buffet ..... (see 56)
40 Smyak B2
41 Zaporozhnaya Sech D4

Drinking & Nightlife
42 12 Bar F4
43 Bar Suk G2
44 Coffeé E2
45 Coffeé D4
46 Dragon's Den C1
47 Edgar G2
48 Fatboys G3
49 Metro C3
50 Schwarzwald Baeckerei D3
51 Sierra Coffee D3
52 Snail H2
53 Telegraph D2

Entertainment
54 Circus G2
55 Philharmonia D2
56 Russian Drama Theatre G2
57 State Academic Drama Theatre F2
58 State Opera & Ballet Theatre G2

) Though oddly hidden between rail tracks and apartment blocks, this delightful 19-room getaway is striking for its gardens and birdsong. Sun-drenched communal spaces are full of minerals, samovars and artefacts including an open kitchen/sitting room with help-yourself hot drinks and a splendid central fireplace.

Swimming pool and yurt-beds are available May to September. It's unmarked down a tiny lane 100m west of where Gogol dead-ends just beyond the far less inviting King House Hotel.

Plush, spacious rooms at the co-owned, similarly priced **Asia Mountains-2** (Map p240; ☎54 02 06; Gorky 156, (Shoorukov 32); r US$70-80) might be more comfortable, but the hotel doesn't quite have the atmosphere of the original.

★ **Hotel Sayrake** BOUTIQUE HOTEL $$
(Map p234; ☎66 58 43; www.hotel-sayrake.com; Soviet (Abdrakhmanov) 190; r/ste US$100/150;) Superbly central this brand-new, villa-hotel feels like an oligarch's private *pied-a-terre*, ringed by wrought-iron railings and guarded (in the foyer) by a suit of armour. Most of the 13 super-comfortable rooms are oversized with claw-foot baths, modernist Kyrgyz art, large rugs on parquet floors and heavy new wooden fittings. Top (third) floor rooms are timber-clad, some leading off a communal, foliage-decked balcony-veranda. Free cable internet.

★ **Ultimate Adventure B&B** GUESTHOUSE $$
(☎077-911 2211, 67 11 83; www.kirghizie.fr; Kurenkeeva 185; s/d €20/30;) This excellent-

value oasis of a guesthouse has French owners and clean, simple, tasteful bedrooms. Good, hot showers (shared) are set around a vine-terraced garden and a lavish breakfast (included) is served on the summer terrace surveyed by Lenin in a *kalpak*. From the Russian church on Jibek Jolu walk north up Togolok Moldo past the 24-hour Narodny Supermarket, then 200m east. There's no sign. Bicycle hire €20 per day.

Rodem House GUESTHOUSE **$$**
(Map p234; ☎054-322 1433, 93 82 82; cafe.daum.net/Rodem-house; Umetaiev 109; dm/s/d/apt US$22.50/40/60/90; ❄ 📶) An excellent, central, mid-market option in an attractively appointed new villa under Korean management. Laundry, kitchen, garden and a good breakfast are provided along with airport pickup. Oddly, dorm beds are only available when booked ahead online, notably through Hostelworld.com.

Hotel Rich HOTEL **$$**
(Map p234; ☎32 20 38; www.rich.kg; Timiryazev 111; r US$55-80, ste US$100-200; ❄ 📶 🏊) Good value for its genre of nouveau-riche glitz, the rooms are fair sized and not as dazzling as the red-gold of the foyer. A glass-walled gym sits on the large communal upper-floor balcony. Summer dip-pool outside. Limited English spoken.

Altyn Saray HOTEL **$$**
(Map p234; ☎90 91 41; altynsaray.hotel@gmail.ru; Jibek Jolu 541, 3rd fl; s/d/pol-lux/lux 2500/3000/3500/5000; ❄) Above a banquet restaurant (noisy during weddings), the 12 large, new rooms have minibar, desk, wardrobes and neat, plain decor. No breakfast

is served and few services are offered but prices are very fair for rooms of this quality.

Hotel Evropa HOTEL $$$
(Map p234; ☎97 90 70; www.hotelevropa.kg; Pravda (Sultan Ibraimov) 70 ; s/d US$100/130; ❄@📶) This small, new business-boutique hotel with glass elevator uses classic floral-heraldic motifs to add interest to the rooms' stylishly minimal design. Breakfast (included) is served downstairs at Ratatouille, arguably Bishkek's best French restaurant.

Bishkek Boutique Hotel HOTEL $$$
(Map p240; ☎59 33 12; www.bishkek-hotel.com; Kulatov; s/d/lux US$80/120/130; ❄📶) Smart if compact, chocolate-and-cream rooms aimed at business clients on a (relative) budget. Vibrant location.

For budget travellers a rash of new hostels is emerging with several more options likely in the coming years. Until then, at a pinch, you might consider these bleak, longer-running options:

Bishkek Guesthouse 1 (Map p234; ☎34 05 24; Umetaliev 165, cnr Jibek Jolu; dm/s/d/tr 390/890/980/1320som) Cluttered and unlovely with one toilet and shower shared between all guests. Backpacker transport services available.

Bishkek Guesthouse 2 (Map p234; ☎055-215 2207, 64 23 66; www.bishkekhouse.ucoz.com; apt 26, Molodaya Gvardia 72; dm/s/d/tr 390/890/980/1320som; @) Co-owned and every bit as ragged as the original, high in a truly dismal apartment block.

Sabyrbek's B&B (Map p234; ☎055-071 5153, 300710; alymkan@yandex.ru; Razzakov 21; per person dm 400-500som, r 600som; 📶) An intriguing history and great location but utterly dishevelled.

There are many central business hotels in the city centre:

Hyatt Regency (Map p234; ☎66 12 34; www.bishkek.regency.hyatt.com; Soviet (Abdurakhmanov) 191; s/d incl tax US$311/359; ❄@🏊) Smart but overpriced.

Park Hotel (Map p234; ☎66 55 18; www.parkhotel.kg; Orozbekov 87; s/d/lux US$147/167/227-317; ❄@🏊) More characterful than the Hyatt.

Holiday Hotel (Map p234; ☎90 29 00; www.holiday.kg; Soviet (Abdurakhmanov) 204A; r standard/deluxe/ste US$140/180/225; ❄📶🏊) Friendly but functional.

Silk Road Lodge (Map p234; ☎324889; www.silkroadlodge.kg; Abdumomunov 229; s/tw/lux/ste US$130/150/160/170; ❄📶🏊) Partly British-owned.

Hotel Grand (Map p234; ☎340000; www.grandhotel.kg/en/; Frunze 428; d US$85-120, ste US$150-200; ❄📶) Sparkly nouveau-riche.

Urmat Ordo (Map p234; ☎311883; urmatordo.kg; Isanova 85; d/tw/ste US$100/110/130; ❄📶) Super central, if less professional; it's well worth paying $20 extra for the suite.

East of the Centre

Nomad Home HOSTEL $
(☎077-044 0800, 48 21 38; http:nomadshome.googlepages.com; Drevesnaya 10; tent/dm/s/d/yurt 250/350/600/800/900som) This cheap backpacker pad has a small garden but only one toilet and bathroom to service a twin room plus a dim, rather scruffy, dorm packed with 12 bunks. There's a summer kitchen, but no breakfast. It's the fourth house on the left as you walk north of the eastern bus station using the steps opposite the Kassa.

OSH BAZAAR AREA CRASH PADS

If saving money is all that counts you can find a sleeping space for 150 to 200som at half a dozen traders' doss houses across Chuy from Osh Bazaar. Several are on Kuliev with a couple more on Beyshanaliyeva. Don't expect to enjoy the shared squat toilets, low ceilings, prison-style windows and – in many – grubby walls and lights that turn on by connecting live electrical wires. Showers aren't generally available but some places do have a *banya* (Russian-style bathing facility; around 60som extra). Compared to most, **Zamira's** (Map p234; ☎070-063 2000; Kuliev 31; d/tr 500/600som) is relatively clean albeit with no real washing facilities. Scraggy, unadorned box-rooms set around a rough courtyard at the **Jalal-Abad Hotel** (Map p234; ☎077-835 7903; Beyshenaliyeva 50; dm/tr 100/300som) offer about the cheapest 'hotel' beds you'll find in Bishkek, though in fact they're not beds so much as sleeping platforms with mats. The *banya* (50som extra) is reasonably well maintained.

North of the Centre

A handful of options lie close to Leningrad (Bayalinov), which parallels Jibek Jolu around 800m further north. Marshrutka 121 from Soviet via Goin comes this way. Or use 175 (from east bus station) or 167 (from Manas) and walk east from Togolok Moldo.

Amantur Hotel GUESTHOUSE **$**
(37 34 02; www.amantur.312.kg; Leningrad (Bayalinov) 72; tr/q 1500/2000som; ; 121, 175, 167) A possible budget back-up for groups of three or four, these unexpectedly clean, if hardly tasteful, new ensuite rooms are up dodgy-looking stairs above a car-repair works, one block east of Togolok Moldo. No breakfast.

Umai Hotel GUESTHOUSE **$$**
(077-280 2805, 46 08 03; www.umai-hotel-kg.com; Donskoy Pereulok 46A; s/d/tr/ste incl breakfast €30/45/55/60) The eight plain, high-ceilinged, en-suite rooms are very fair value, and are set in a walled garden so peaceful that getting anyone to let you in might require making a phone call. English and German are spoken. The narrow access road heads north from Leningrad (Bayalinov) beside number 53 (between Panfilov and Orozbekov) where marshrutka 121 from Soviet will stop. If you see the Pakistani Embassy, backtrack three very short blocks east.

South of the Centre

InterHouse HOSTEL **$**
(Map p240; 055-587 9777; www.interhouse.kg; Topografic 9; dm/d US$15/30) Those who manage to find it love InterHouse's smartly furnished dorms and the ample communal space – kitchen, dining area and discordant lounge with blush-pink chez-lounge. To get here, head 500m south down Soviet from the Vefa Center, 100m east along Skrabina then dog-leg north/west up the unpaved lane between 41 and 43.

Demi Guesthouse BOUTIQUE HOTEL **$$**
(Map p240; 51 20 12; www.demi.kg; Akhunbaev 10; s/d/ste 2700/3600/5400som;) If you don't mind the slightly remote south-city location, Demi is an excellent midrange choice, with melifluous music in the eclectic lounge-hall and a fountain garden that is pleasant despite regular wafts of traffic noise. The frequent marshrutka 200 from Manas/Mira passes outside.

Hotel Vizit GUESTHOUSE **$$**
(Map p240; 91 31 41; www.visit.kg; Akhunbaev 21A; d/ste 2000/2500som;) The friendly family-run guesthouse has deep brown walls and incongruous stone faux-pillars downstairs, but brighter rooms upstairs (where wi-fi is weak). Road noise can annoy and the location is far from central though very frequent marshrutkas 100 and 200 pass outside. Breakfast served in-room.

Jannat Resort HOTEL **$$$**
(077-799 3423; www.jannat.kg; Alamedin Valley; r US$240-600;) If money is no object and you'd prefer to be close to the mountains, this luxury hotel some 20km south of town makes a great alternative to sleeping in the city. There are no views from the hotel but the Alamedin Valley picnic hikes are just 4km away. Obliging staff speak English and there's an indoor swimming pool with heated mineral spring-water.

Eating

Most restaurants add service charges between 8% and 15%. Some even extort extra for background music.

Samsus (samosas) sold from street stands make a great snack-meal. Ball-shaped versions straight from a tandoor oven cost around 35som while triangular flaky-pastry versions are rarely over 20som.

Several new western-style coffee shops such as Sierra (p242), Coffeé (p242) and **Espresso** (Map p234; www.espresso.kg; 122 Tynystanov; coffee 60-140som, cake/panini 70/120som; 10am-9pm;) are great places to sit, chat and use the free wi-fi.

Narodni 24-hour supermarkets are found all over town. Cheap, if often cheerless, cafeteria-style food is available at many an *askhana/stolovaya* (restaurant/canteen), often hidden away in basements. A few such places have been stylishly tarted up, such as **Smyak** (Map p234; Jash Gvardinya (Molodaya Gvardia), cnr Chuy prospekti; mains 30-70som, chicken 150som, garnish 15som; 24hr).

For the latest reviews consult **Spektator** (www.thespektator.co.uk).

City Centre

Faiza CENTRAL ASIAN **$**
(Map p234; Jibek Jolu; mains 60-160som, service charge per person 10som; 9am-9pm;) High-quality rapid-service local dishes at reasonable prices are brought by waitresses in scarf and tunic to heavy marble-

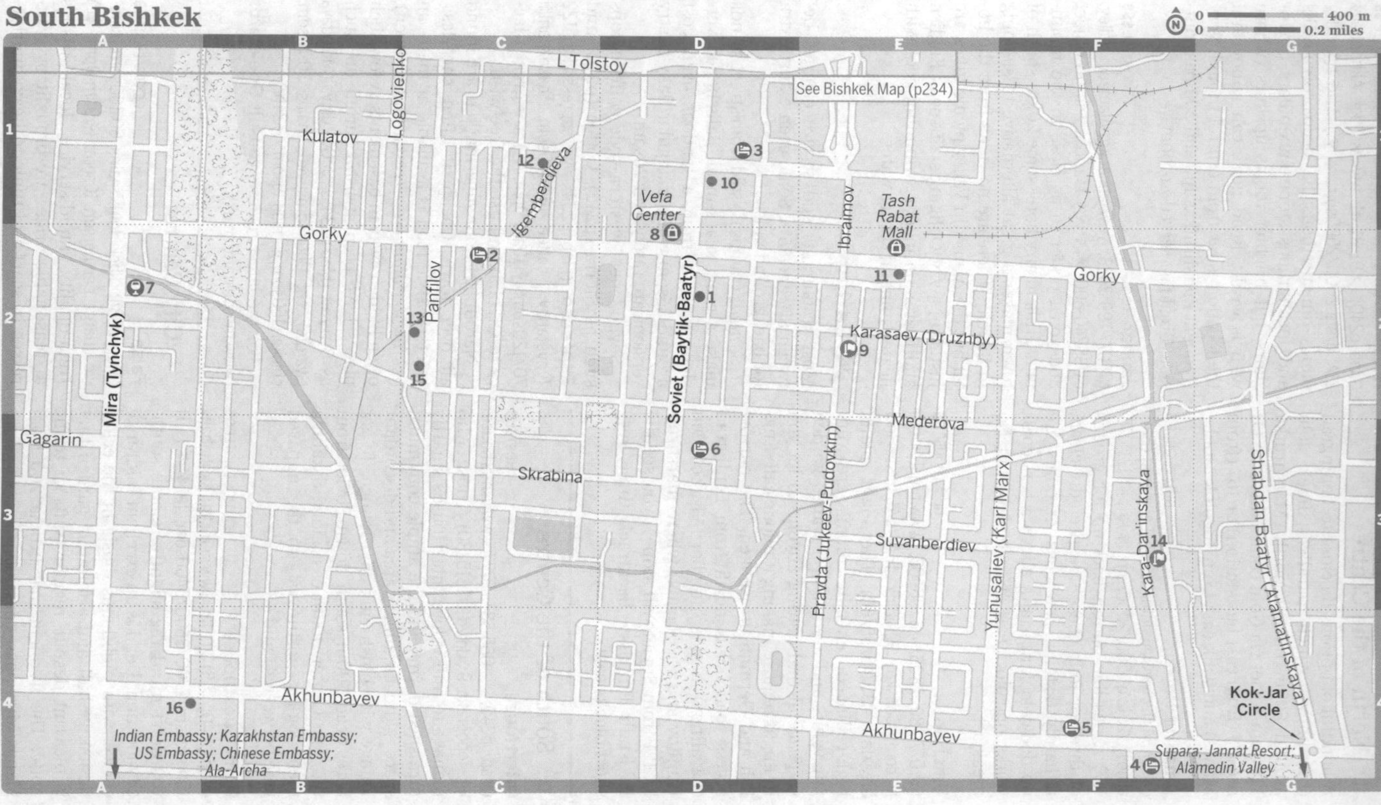
South Bishkek
0 400 m
0 0.2 miles
L Tolstoy
See Bishkek Map (p234)
Logovienko
Kulatov
Igemberdieva
Vefa Center
Tash Rabat Mall
Ibraimov
Gorky
Panfilov
Mira (Tynchyk)
Soviet (Baytik-Baatyr)
Karasaev (Druzhby)
Mederova
Gagarin
Skrabina
Pravda (Jukeev-Pudovkin)
Yunusaliev (Karl Marx)
Suvanberdiev
Kara-Dar'inskaya
Shabdan Baatyr (Alamatinskaya)
Akhunbayev
Kok-Jar Circle
Indian Embassy; Kazakhstan Embassy; US Embassy; Chinese Embassy; Ala-Archa
Supara; Jannat Resort; Alamedin Valley

South Bishkek

Activities, Courses & Tours

1 London School D2

Sleeping

2 Asia Mountains-2 .... C2
3 Bishkek Boutique Hotel D1
4 Demi Guesthouse F4
5 Hotel Vizit F4
6 InterHouse D3

Eating

Vefa Center Food Court .... (see 8)

Drinking & Nightlife

7 Retro Metro A2

Shopping

Red Fox .... (see 10)
8 Vefa Center D2

Information

9 Afghan Embassy E2
10 Ak-Sai D1
11 CBT E2
12 Dostuck Trekking C1
13 Edelweiss C2
14 Tajikistani Embassy F3

Transport

15 Avia Traffic C2
16 Velopro A4

topped tables. Expect queues at lunchtime. Tea costs 30som per pot.

Chaikhana Jalal-Abad CHAIKHANA $
(Map p234; Togolok Moldo 30; mains 80-160som, tea per pot 20som, koumys/bozo/maksim per half-litre 50/30/20som; 8am-midnight;) The faceted facade evokes an archetypal Central Asian teahouse with carved wooden columns, tea beds and octagonal lattice-work pavilions. The main restaurant interior has far less character, but produces a fine selection of well-priced local, Kazakh and southern Kyrgyz dishes.

Kebab Ojak TURKISH $
(Map p234; Erkindik 27; shashlyk meals 110-170som, soup 40som; 10am-9pm;) Tender kebabs served as complete meals with salad, bread and rice are excellent value if you can forgive hopelessly over-lit lavender decor. Halal, no alcohol.

Russian Drama Theatre Buffet RUSSIAN, CENTRAL ASIAN $
(Map p234; Tynystanov, Dubovy Park; mains 60-90som; 8am-8pm) For sheer novelty, seek out this inexpensive cafeteria hidden in the basement of an outwardly drab concrete theatre. The windowless dining room's unique feature is the luridly colourful wallpaper portraying giant 16th- to 17th-century paintings whose gentle debauchery contrasts comically with the squat waitress-*babushkas* in their blue apron-pinnies. The re-heated snacks are forgettable but cheap (albeit 10som more than the labelled prices unless you're a theatre employee). Access is from the theatre's north-side foyer; no ticket required.

Vefa Center Food Court FAST FOOD $
(Map p240; Vefa Mall, 3rd fl, Soviet (Baytik-Baatyr) 100; 10am-10pm) Numerous cuisines from Indian to Japanese to burgers are available in the typical international-style food court on the top floor of this mall overlooking the fountain show in the octagonal atrium.

Narodnyy/Shumkur CAFETERIA $
(Map p234; Chuy 162; mains 60-110som; 24hr) Central all-night supermarket with cheap queue-and-pay cafeteria attached.

Derevyashka RUSSIAN, CENTRAL ASIAN $$
(Map p234; 32 35 74; Riskulova 1; mains 110-280som, beer 60-120som; 24hr) Airy if bare, this pine-and-glass beer hall has large indoor spaces with low couches plus ample outdoor bench tables. Fine pub food includes excellent 'snow chicken' (fried with onions, mushrooms and cheese) and McDonalds-style fries. Big TVs screen pop-vids or sports matches.

Manty Bar CENTRAL ASIAN $$
(Map p234; 055-011 7711, 89 80 27; Shopokova 108b; mains 180-300som, beer/cocktails/wine from 100/180/250som; 11am-11.30pm;) This is a cosy, comfy and very friendly place to compare speciality foods from several Central Asian countries. The signature *manty* (steamed dumplings) have a gourmet brilliance, encased in dreamily light dough as thin as angel wings. The traditional-meets-contemporary decor features warm, tastefully cohesive oranges and browns, and distinctive terracotta tableware. Summer terrace.

Arzu Style KYRGYZ, INTERNATIONAL $$
(Map p234; Togolok Moldo; local mains 130-230som, international 250-500som; 11am-11pm) One of central Bishkek's most convivial upper market eateries has back-lit filigree panels in the more attractive smoking room, but an overload of brand new 'antiques' in the

smoke-free section. Unusually tasty *laghman* (noodles) comes in 16 varieties; for a meat-free option try the misnamed side dish 'Ratatouille', a deliciously light-cooked selection of cubed vegetables.

Zaporozhnaya Sech UKRAINIAN **$$**
(Map p234; Manas 9; blinnies 100-180som, borsch 120som, mains 200-450som, garnish 60-120som, beer 80-150som; ⌚9am-midnight) This new, all-wooden restaurant masquerading as a 19th-century log-cabin cottage serves up typical Ukrainian fare. There's ample shady garden seating behind and you don't have to dine to sit at the bar, which is built around a living tree.

★ **Cafeteria** EUROPEAN **$$$**
(Map p234; ☎62 32 24; Erkindik 30; mains 360-700som, breakfast 160-360som, coffee 100-190som, cocktails 150-290som; ⌚8am-2am, kitchen until midnight) Great for cocktails or coffee, American breakfasts or spicy pitas, vegetarian lasagne or salmon risotto this brilliantly reworked classic building has a semi-circle of columns linking high ceilings with chequerboard floors.

A raised ring of bench-couches accommodates sophisticated *shisha*-smokers while a summer street terrace surveys wooded Erkindik Park.

South of the Centre

Supara KYRGYZ, INTERNATIONAL **$$$**
(☎46 50 51; www.supara.kg; 1a Karagul Akmata, Kok-Jar village; mains 350-800som; ; ; 200, 217) This amusing, professional, though somewhat contrived 'ethno' complex is a caricature of all things traditionally Kyrgyz attracting mainly well-heeled urban locals. Costumed waiters serve a full range of Kyrgyz meals, both authentic and original, in comfortably furnished yurts. 'Treasure House' is a particularly delicious creation, a pastry bowl filled with lean mutton and stir-fried vegetables on a bed of *boorzok*.

Beware that extras are unexpectedly pricey (tea 150som, nan-bread 120som).

There's a decent mountain view from the small dam immediately behind the complex and some days there's a free archery challenge. Supara makes a good stop if you're en route to/from the Alamedin Valley. Marshrutka 217 takes roughly 35 minutes to get here from Vefa Center (last return around 7.30pm).

Drinking & Nightlife

If you're drinking late, for safety's sake it's wise to use one of the taxis that queue outside the pub or club, even if you're only planning to stumble on to the next den of iniquity. Revellers who walk off into the dark streets are occasionally targetted by rascals.

Despite taboos, Bishkek does have LGBT clubs but most are out of the centre and venues change frequently. For the heads-up on the latest gay scene contact **Labrys** (www.labrys.kg; Madina Bazaar).

★ **Sierra Coffee** AMERICAN, COFFEE
(Map p234; ☎31 12 48; www.sierra.kg; 57/1 Manas; coffee from 60som; ⌚7.30am-11pm;) This buzzing, international-style coffeehouse roasts its own beans and gives tobacco-puffers a specially sealed room to protect the lungs of non-smokers. Outside seating in summer, small library of English books.

Coffeé CAFE
(Map p234; Togolok Moldo 40/1; coffee 110-270som, toasted sandwiches 120som, cakes 130som; ⌚9am-midnight;) Excellent if comparatively pricey coffee amid dangling espresso cups, modern vases and 1890s fashion prints – or a medieval city-mural at the **Manas 9 branch** (Map p234; Manas 9;). Veranda seating available.

★ **Bar Suk** NIGHTCLUB
(Map p234; Puskhin 6; beer 170som) Nightclub venues come and go rapidly but Bar Suk is currently THE club for gilded local 20-somethings. It's hip yet unusually welcoming and relaxed despite a bass-amp that's powerful enough to blow-dry your hair. No cover charge, but entry carefully controlled (smart dress, 'no teenagers').

Edgar PUB
(Map p234; Dubovy Park; ⌚noon-midnight) Bishkek's most loveable pub is hidden in a basement beneath the **Russian Drama Theatre** (Map p234; ☎66 20 32; Tynystanov, Dubovy Park), west side, behind Espresso. The surfaces are festooned with old tape-recorders, typewriters, bottles and 20th-century 'antiques' and from around 7pm there's usually a low-key live band playing blues or soft-rock covers. Decent food too. Gets pretty full but there's summer seating outside in the park.

Metro BAR

(Map p234; Chuy 168A; beer from 105som; ⏲10.30am-last customer) Shoehorned into the column-filled foyer of a once-grand Soviet era theatre, this off-beat boozer might feel like post–Vietnam War Bangkok were it not that the clientele (predominantly single, male, Western) are actually glued to the sports blaring on TV.

Steinbräu BEER HALL

(☎43 21 44; Gertse 5; mains 250-750som, sausages 200som, draught beer 65-132som) The setting sun pouring through an upper window illuminates a Kyrgyz yurt-crown draped in hops in this spacious two-level beerhall. The bar is built around a gleaming copper brew-vessel whose excellent micro-brewed beers are the main draw. There's a full menu of German and European meals, or seven types of sausages to snack on. It's hidden amid ageing apartments at the east end of Bokonbayev.

Dragon's Den CAFE-BAR

(Map p234; Frunze 557; beer 70-110som; ⏲9.45am-10pm) Friendly pub-cafe with excellent, inexpensive Svejak beer on tap and a well-considered menu (mains 100som to 350som), including full English breakfasts and a couple of vegetarian choices. The British owner has many a tale to tell. Handy for hotels Grand and Rich.

Promzona LIVE MUSIC, NIGHTCLUB

(☎90 02 44; www.promzona.kg; Cholpon-Atinskaya 16; ⏲8pm-5am) High-quality live bands and dancing without the strict dress codes of the more central clubs. A taxi from town costs around 200som.

Fatboys PUB

(Map p234; Chuy 104; mains 190-300som; ⏲8am-10pm Sun-Thu, 8am-midnight Fri-Sat) With more character than most central pubs, Fatboys' location makes it a good meeting place and there's a local cider on tap.

12 Bar NIGHTCLUB, BAR

(Map p234; Moskva 118, 12th fl; cover varies, Mon free, beer from 200som; ⏲6pm-6am) Atop a downtown high-rise, this self-consciously exclusive bar/nightclub has panoramic views from comfortable sofa-seating where suave guests smoke *shishas* and sip well-mixed cocktails. Upstairs the small outdoor terrace features silver decapitated mannequins and there's a handkerchief of dancefloor (active weekend nights, very late). Smart dress code.

Snail BEER TERRACE

(Map p234; beer 65som; ⏲10am-11pm Apr-Oct weather permitting) Unpretentious open-air pavilions tucked behind the Opera. Good for pints of cheap beer on warm summer evenings, not so good for food.

Retro Metro NIGHTCLUB

(Map p240; www.retro-metro.kg/; Mira 24; cover 300som) Mid-market club with predominantly 1980s music, occasional live bands and a series of curious theme evenings (Addams Family, Theatre Night etc).

Telegraph COCKTAIL BAR

(Map p234; www.telegraph.kg; Chuy 227; beer from 100som, cocktails from 220som, mains 470-860som; ⏲11am-2am, kitchen til midnight; 📶) Long, poised bar-restaurant whose rectilinear, semi-minimalist style seems to have been designed to host a fashion show.

Schwarzwald Baeckerei CAFE

(Map p234; www.schwarzwald-baeckerei.kg; Toktogul 165; coffee/beer 40/53som; ⏲8am-8pm or later) Cheap Senseo coffee and six types of draft beer are served at this sweetly unsophisticated two-table bar-cafe and mini bakery.

☆ Entertainment

State Opera & Ballet Theatre THEATRE

(Map p234; ☎66 15 48; Soviet (Abdrakhmanov) 167) Classical and local productions are staged in this elegant building, usually starting at 5pm Friday to Sunday, autumn to spring. Check the billboards outside for upcoming shows. Same-day tickets are often available.

Philharmonia CONCERT HALL

(Map p234; ☎21 22 35; Chuy 210) Features Western and Kyrgyz orchestral works and the occasional Kyrgyz song-and-dance troupe. The *kassa* (ticket office) is on the west side.

Circus CIRCUS

(Map p234; circus.312.kg; Frunze; tickets 500-800som) Shows, in what looks like a 1950s UFO, can be very impressive.

State Academic Drama Theatre THEATRE

(Map p234; ☎66 58 02; Panfilov 273) On the east side of Panfilov Park, this is the place for popular Kyrgyz-language works, more often than not written by Chinghiz Aitmatov, Kyrgyzstan's premier man of words.

Shopping

Bishkek has the country's best collection of souvenirs and handicrafts, though you might find individual items cheaper at their source (notably *shyrdaks* – felt carpets – in Kochkor).

The city's major markets are Osh Bazaar; **Alamedin Bazaar** (Jibek Jolu prospektesi, at Almatinskaya; daily; trolleybus 7, 8, 9, 11), east of the East Bus Station; and Dordoi, north of town (trolleybus 4), which is full of Chinese goods. None are especially exotic. Shopping centres include the big, glitzy **Bishkek City** (Map p234; Kiev; daily) and **Vefa** (Map p240; Soviet 200; daily) shopping malls and Soviet-era **TsUM** (Map p234; Chuy 155; daily).

Osh Bazaar MARKET
(Map p234; Chuy 202; partly closed on Mondays) Though not visually exotic, Bishkek's most central bazaar has a certain compulsive interest and is an important city landmark. For traditional Kyrgyz clothes, including white imitation-felt *ak kalpak* hats (80som) and colourful shepherds' chests find the **stalls** (Map p234; Osh Bazaar) outside the south tip of the bazaar's Khial building.

Saima SOUVENIRS
(Map p234; Chuy 140; 10am-7pm Mon-Sat) Sells textiles (including silk scarfs) plus postcards, souvenirs, toys and fridge magnets.

Iman SOUVENIRS
(Map p234; Chuy 128; 10am-7pm Mon-Sat) Soviet medals and badges, horse-whips and figurines.

Asia Gallery ARTWORK
(Map p234; 62 45 05; Chuy 108; 10am-1pm & 2-5pm Mon-Sat) The showroom/gallery of the Kyrgyzstan Union of Artists is upstairs, in a faded, once-grand, Stalin-era building which also hides some artists' workshops.

Raritet BOOKSHOP
(Map p234; Pushkin 78, basement, Dom Druzhby) Postcards, basic maps and a mere handful of English-language books plus a museum section and a sweet traditionally styled chaikhana room. Descend the stairs from the west side of the Dom Druzhby building.

Kyrgyz Oyu SOUVENIRS
(Map p234; Chuy 134) Leather, felt and terracotta souvenirs from cute to kitsch. Postcards cost 20som.

Art Salon SOUVENIRS
(Map p234; 31 11 29; Kiev 133; 9am-7pm Mon-Fri, 9am-6pm Sat) Kyrgyz knick-knacks supplemented by Russian matryoshka dolls, barkwork boxes and earthenware figurines.

Atelier CRAFT, SOUVENIRS
(Map p234; www.lamaisonduvoyageur.com; Moskva 122; 10am-7pm Mon-Sat) Crafts, especially fabrics, many labelled with the artist's name and the region they come from.

Tumar Art Salon SOUVENIRS
(Map p234; www.tumar.com; Isanov 80-2) Stylishly presented, high-quality embroidery and pottery, both modern and traditional. Credit cards accepted.

GeoID MAPS
(Map p234; 61 58 32; www.gosreg.kg; Kiev 107, Room 102; 8am-noon & 1-5pm Mon-Fri) Sells Goskartografiya's excellent Bishkek city maps/atlases (110/300som), as well as 1:100,000 trekking maps and 1:200,000 topographicals (200som to 370som). Almost all are in Cyrillic script. Phone two days ahead to ensure your required map is brought up from the storeroom. The entrance is on the building's west side behind pseudo-historical Russian restaurant Pirogoff-Vodkin.

Red Fox OUTDOOR
(Map p240; 59 17 55; www.redfox.ru; Soviet (Bayik-Baatyr) 65, basement; 9am-8pm) Sells camping supplies, mountaineering equipment and brand-name hiking boots.

Information

DANGERS & ANNOYANCES

Bishkek smiles during the day but many streets are unlit after dark and all the normal Central Asian security rules apply: stick to main streets, avoid the parks, and steer clear of the area around the train station.

Crooked plain-clothed 'policemen' are a problem in Bishkek, particularly at Osh Bazaar. Some demand your passport and want to rifle through your bag and wallet with unfortunately predictable results. Legally you are required to carry your passport at all times but it's always worth trying to give them only a copy, at least until you reach a genuine police station. Try not to be cajolled into an unmarked car or other hidden corner.

If you have to leave your passport at an embassy for visa purposes, ask the embassy to stamp an explanation on a photocopy in case you're questioned by 'real' police.

EMERGENCY

Ambulance (☎103)

Police (☎102)

INTERNET ACCESS

Internet cafes are widespread, with several on Soviet around the main post office and many around Osh Bazaar. Wi-fi is increasingly common in hotels and in the new breed of coffee shops. Most connections are free, but a few still charge for minutes and/or megabytes.

LEFT LUGGAGE

Left Luggage (Kamera Khraneniya) (Map p234; Bishkek II train station; small/large bag 25/45som; ⌚2pm-noon) Open 22 hours daily minus a few short breaks, the luggage room is to the right of the main steps as you enter the train station building.

MEDICAL SERVICES

Ubiquitous pharmacies are marked *darykhana* (Kyrgyz) or *apteka* (Russian). Many open 24 hours.

Neomed (Map p234; ☎90 60 90; www.neo med.kg; Orozbekov 46; doctor's consultation 600som) Respected medical centre in classy, central location. Phone for an appointment.

MONEY

Exchange desks and banks offering change are widespread, especially on the central section of Soviet (use the banks to avoid scams). If you have Kazakh Tenge or Chinese Yuan, there are a few **specialist change booths** (Map p234; Kievskaya) near Osh Bazaar with decent buy-sell splits. A few will change Uzbek Sum but at miserly rates.

ATMs are widespread but most accept only Visa. One of very few to accept MasterCard, Maestro, Diners and Amex is hidden beside the reception of hotel Hyatt Regency (p238).

Kazkommertsbank (Map p234; ☎69 03 83; Soviet (Abdrakhmanov) 136; ⌚9am-5pm Mon-Fri) Handles payments for Kazakh visas. Unusually, its ATMs accept MasterCard as well as Visa.

POST & COURIERS

Main Post Office (Postamt; Map p234; Soviet (Abdrakhmanov); ⌚7am-7pm Mon-Sat, 8am-6pm Sun) Postcards can take two months to reach Western Europe.

American Resources International (ARI; Map p234; ☎66 00 77; bishkek@aricargo.com; Erkindik 35; ⌚9am-6pm Mon-Fri) Freight forwarders for those shipping at least 45/100kg from/to Bishkek.

DHL (Map p234; ☎61 11 11; www.dhl.com; Kiev 107; ⌚8am-6pm Mon-Fri, 9am-4pm Sat) International courier.

FedEx (Map p234; ☎65 00 12; K Akiev; ⌚9am-6pm Mon-Fri, 9am-3pm Sat) International courier.

REGISTRATION & VISAS

A couple of different offices handle visa registration and extensions.

Ministry of Foreign Affairs (Consular Section; Map p234; ☎66 32 70; www.dcsmfa.kg; Togolok Moldo 10A; ⌚9.30am-noon Mon-Tue & Thu-Fri) Visa extensions are processed here, but the procedure can be awkward and costly. If you're from a country that's visa exempt it is usually easier to get a Kazakh visa, leave to Almaty then come back again.

Visa Registration (Departament Registratsii Naseleniya; Map p234; ☎66 23 29; Kiev 58; ⌚9.30am-12.30pm & 1.30-5pm Mon-Fri) Most nationals don't need to register but if your nationality is not exempt, ask about the necessary procedure here.

TELEPHONE

Central Telecom Office (Map p234; cnr Soviet (Abdrakhmanov) & Chuy; ⌚7am-10pm) Phones and 20som Skype-computer booths.

TOURIST INFORMATION

There is no tourist office in Bishkek. For activities and meet ups, Bishkek has a reasonably active Couchsurfing group and the TUK excursion programme (p245) might give you ideas for your own adventures. Tour and trekking agencies are often helpful with travel-planning enquiries. NoviNomad (p245) has a traveller noticeboard aimed at Torugart-bound travellers.

TRAVEL & TOUR AGENCIES

Myriad tour operators can whisk you out of the capital and into Kyrgyzstan's glorious hinterlands. Many specialise in trekking and mountaineering. Most will also book flights, arrange transport and help with other travel logistics.

NoviNomad (Map p234; ☎62 23 81; www.novinomad.com; Togolok Moldo 28; ⌚8.30am-noon & 1-4.45pm Mon-Sat) Respected agent for cultural tours, guided biking, Torugart trips, trekking, transport, accommodation bookings and translating services. Sells trekking maps and has a Torugart traveller noticeboard.

TUK (Trekking Union of Kyrgyzstan; Map p234; ☎055-610 1933, 90 91 15; www.tuk.kg; Kiev 168, enter from Turusbekov 51; ⌚9am-5pm Mon-Fri) Bishkek-based association organising walking and hiking trips to a variety of regional beauty spots, mostly one-day excursions at weekends. Joining one of these is a great way to save money on transport but, more importantly, can be a wonderful way to meet a cross-section of expats and locals. TUK members get discounts. Trekking maps and good-value ski rental are available. The office is very helpful with trek planning but sometimes short-staffed. Rafting and skiing trips are also occasionally offered.

CBT (Map p240; ☎077-771 8334, 54 00 69; www.cbtkyrgyzstan.kg; Gorky 58; ⏰9am-6pm Mon-Sat) For rural exploration CBT has a great network of regional offices as well as an extensive network of homestays, guides and transport contacts.

Celestial Mountains/Advantour (Map p234; ☎31 18 14; www.celestial.com.kg; Kiev 131-4) British-born Ian Claytor's agency is almost legendary for its cultural tours, overland trips and Torugart Pass experiences. The websites are encyclopaedic.

Ecotour (☎077-280 2805, 46 08 03; www.ecotour.kg; Donskoy 46A, Umai Hotel) Run by English- and German-speaking sisters Elmira and Zamira. Has seasonal yurt camps at Song-Köl and south of Issyk-Köl, including one in isolated splendor at Temir Kanat (with solar-heated water). Available as short stays for budget travellers or as complete packages. Book ahead.

Kyrgyz Concept (Map p234; ☎90 08 66; www.concept.kg; Tynystanov 231) Kyrgyzstan's biggest tour operator offers cultural tours, visa support, horse treks and homestays, and is flexible with budget demands. It has several offices (including one on Kiev) but this office focuses on tours.

Ak-Sai (Map p240; ☎59 17 59; www.ak-sai.com; Soviet 65) This very active adventure agency operates a series of summer fixed-camps allowing trekkers and mountaineers to travel light in the Karakol, Lenin-Peak, Karavshin/Ak-Suu ('Kyrgyz Patagonia') and Khan Tengri areas. Ak-Sai organises fly-in, fly-out helicopter trips to the latter and a range of packages are available. Many of their camps are also available to independent travellers when availability permits.

Shepherds Way (☎077-251 8315, 66 13 92) If you're planning a horse trek from the south side of Issyk-Köl, it's well worth arranging things in advance in Bishkek with this highly reputable company. Call Ishen (philosophical, great English).

Asia Mountains (Map p234; ☎69 02 35; www.asiamountains.net; Lineynaya 1A; ⏰9am-6pm Mon-Fri, plus Sat in summer) This friendly, well-organised agency offers a gamut of tours and day trips, but their speciality is the ascent of Lenin Peak. Tailor-made climbs, plus four fixed-date departures each summer, depart from their base camp at Achik-Tash (single/double tent US$15/20, breakfast/lunch/dinner US$10/20/15). The office is in the basement of their charming Bishkek hotel.

Ultimate Adventure (☎67 11 83, 077 911 2211; www.kirghizie.fr; Kurenkeeva 185) Bishkek-based French owner Stephane organises tours througout the region, and as far afield as northern Pakistan.

Dostuck Trekking (Map p240; ☎50 30 82, 54 54 55; www.dostuck.com.kg; Igemberdieva 42-1) Long-established agent for treks, mountaineering, yurt-stays and visa help for those nationalities who still require it.

Edelweiss (Map p240; ☎54 20 45; http:edelweisstravel.org; Gastello 19) Offers trekking, mountaineering and skiing – notably heli-skiing – even in summer. Their office is behind red gates three doors southwest along a streamside path between 42 and 40 Panfilov (200m south of Gorky).

AsiaRando (☎517-73 97 78, 313-24 77 11, 313-24 77 10; www.asiarando.com; Padgornaya 67, Rot-Front, Chuy Oblast) French family-owned company offering horse-riding trips from its base in Rotfront, 65km east of Bishkek. Rotfront was originally an ethnic-German Mennonite village and is one of the last places in Central Asia to retain a significant German minority.

CAT (Central Asia Tourism Corporation; Map p234; ☎66 36 64; www.cat.kg; Chuy 124; ⏰9am-6pm Mon-Fri, open Sat for air tickets) Visa support, rental cars, air tickets, accommodation and inclusive tours. Very obliging air-ticketing branch (Central Asia Tourism Corporation; Map p234; ☎89 63 39; www.cat.kg; Manas 57; ⏰9am-6pm Mon-Fri, 9am-5pm Sat) at Manas 57.

Tien Shan Travel (☎46 60 34; www.tien-shan.com; ⏰9am-6pm Mon-Fri) Vladimir Birukov's highly experienced mountaineering and trekking company has a raft of outdoor options and operates base camps on both sides of Khan Tengri, plus at Achik-Tash for Lenin Peak.

FantasticAsia (☎055-530 3025, 45 67 49; www.fantasticasia.net; Ovorodnyi per 8) Multi-faceted travel fixers with a variety of niche websites. Offers tailor-made and off-the-peg tour options, as well as a few fixed-date departures. Business is mostly organised online and run from the home of the obliging Sergei Dubovik, who speaks excellent English.

Top Asia (☎055-595 4239, 66 45 83; www.topasia.kg; Tynystanov 122) Offers a wide range of mountaineering, trekking and tour options in Kyrgyzstan and Central Asia.

ℹ Getting There & Away

AIR

Manas International Airport (☎69 31 09, 69 37 98; www.airport.kg) is 30km north of central Bishkek. For a summary of international flights see p309.

From Manas airport there are between two to five daily connections to Osh (1700som to 4000som), plus several weekly services to

COMMUNITY-BASED TOURISM

One of the great appeals of Kyrgyzstan is the relative ease with which one can organise homestays, yurtstays, local guides and horses thanks to several Kyrgyz grassroots organisations. The most widespread network is CBT (p246) whose most active sub-branches effectively double as tourist offices – notably in Arslanbob, Karakol and Naryn. You can often approach CBT providers independently, but typically this won't get you a discount. That's arguably a good thing as the CBT network is a valuable resource and is worth funding. Nonetheless, several smaller CBT-like outfits do compete in some towns.

Homestay prices vary slightly between regions and according to the 'edelweiss' ranking (the CBT version of a star rating), but the typical range is 450som to 700som per day for bed and breakfast plus 250som per additional meal. Depending on the quality and availability of local restaurants, it is often cheaper to eat out. Horse hire is usually around 700som per day and guides range from 600som to 1400som per day – sometimes you'll need to pay for the guide's food and lodging on top of their daily rate.

The *CBT Guidebook* (200som printed, free to download from www.cbtkyrgyzstan.kg) is a little dated but lists each office's services, a description of local trips and useful, if very schematic, town maps.

Jalal-Abad (from 2500som), Batken (3200som) and Isfana (3500som). Each route crosses high mountains and can be glorious on a clear day. Fierce competition on the Osh routings means that fares can sometimes be discounted as low as 1400som even a day or two before departure.

Airlines

Aeroflot (Map p234; ☎62 00 71; www.aeroflot.ru; Erkindik 64/1) To/from or via Moscow daily.

Air Astana (☎airport desk 90 69 06; www.airastana.com) To (or via) Almaty and Astana. Good-value connections include Tbilisi, Bangkok and various Siberian cities but triple check that your routing doesn't include an internal Astana-Almaty leg unless you have a Kazakhstan visa. Free Bishkek-Cholpan Ata transfers available in summer.

Air Bishkek (Map p234; ☎29 82 13; airbishkek.kg; Manas 95) Flies Bishkek–Osh (daily) and Bishkek–Isfana (Tue, Fri, Sun). Has weekly connections to Ürümqi (China) and Seoul-Incheon (Korea) plus links to half a dozen Russian cities from both Bishkek and Osh.

Air Company Kyrgyzstan (AC Kyrgyzstan; Map p234; ☎31 30 03; www.air.kg; Manas 12a) Twice weekly flights to Tashkent and Ürümqi, several Russian destinations plus domestic hops to Jalal-Abad and Osh.

Avia Traffic (Map p240; ☎54 47 88; www.aero.kg; Panfilov 26) Daily to Osh, thrice weekly to Batken and twice weekly to Dushanbe (Tue, Thu, 7500som), plus connections to various Russian cities including Moscow, Novosibirsk, St Petersburg, Krasnoyarsk and Kazan.

China Southern Airlines (Map p234; ☎66 46 68; www.csair.com/en/; Chuy 128/3) To/from or via Ürümqi, Xinjiang four times weekly.

FlyDubai (Map p234; ☎31 90 00; www.flydubai.com; Kerimbekova 13) Dubai's budget airline.

Pegasus (www.flypgs.com) Big network of budget flights via İstanbul's 'other' airport, SAW.

S7 (Map p234; ☎90 69 06; Bokonbayevo 76/2) Four weekly flights to/via Novosibirsk.

Sky Bishkek (Map p234; ☎62 09 74; www.skybishkek.kg; Moskva 121) One-plane (Saab 340) airline with six weekly hops to Osh and three to Batken.

Tajik Air (www.tajikair.tj) To/from Dushanbe twice weekly.

Turkish Airlines (Map p234; ☎301600; www.turkishairlines.com; Soviet 136) To/from Ulaanbaator (Mongolia), as well as İstanbul daily with global connections.

Ukraine International Airlines (☎24hr call centre +38-044 581 5050; www.flyuia.com) To/from Kiev with good-value European connections.

Ural Airlines (www.uralairlines.ru/en/) Weekly to Yekaterinburg and Moscow.

Uzbekistan Airways (Map p234; ☎61 03 64; www.uzairways.com; Kiev 107) Flies to Tashkent (US$176) four days a week.

BUS & SHARED TAXI

There are two main bus stations. The sprawling **Western Bus Station** (Zapadny Avtovozkal, Avtobeket; Map p234; ☎34 46 96, 65 65 75; Jibek-Jolu prospektesi; 🚌7, 113, 114) handles most long-distance services, notably Karakol and the Issyk-Köl towns, Naryn via Kochkor, Chayek, Talas and Almaty. Hold your breath – this place is thoroughly confusing even for locals. The main Soviet-era building in the middle is almost entirely redundant, except for a few windows pre-selling tickets for night buses and international routes. Then there are three essentially separate minibus areas, each tending to duplicate each other's routings. Minibuses depart from the east and west areas once they're full, while the north area has approximately timetabled services, though departure times rarely seem to fit with those posted. The result is considerable uncertainty making the whole process much more stressful that it needs to be. Out front the same destinations are served by a mass of shared taxis.

The **Eastern Bus Station** (Vastotshny Avtovoksal; ☎48 20 04; Jibek Jolu 263; ⏰6am-7.30pm) is much smaller and better organised. Services are relatively local including Kant, Tokmok (slow/express 40/60som, around one hour, several per hour), Kemin (120som, around two hours, hourly from 10am to 6pm), Kegeti (50som, two hours, 9.30am and 3.30pm) and Issyk-Ata Sanatorium (60som, 2½ hours, 8.30am, 10am, 11.30am, 1.30pm, 5pm, 6pm). However, for the mountain valleys nearest to Bishkek, most marshrutkas start from a variety of points around Osh Bazaar.

There are no minibuses or buses for Osh, Jalal-Abad and Southern Kyrgyzstan. But there are a plethora of shared taxis plus commercial vehicles offering spaces in their cabs or even amongst the cargo. As such, rides can take all day (around 10 hours to Osh is common); it's best to start early and better still to pre-book a place with a driver.

Three places to look for a ride are:

➡ **Osh Bazaar** (Map p234) Drivers typically lurk towards the southern corner, near the canal; there is no organised system, just whispered suggestions of destinations.

➡ **Dordoi Motors** (Deng Xiao Ping 302/1; 🚌148, 199, 220, trolley 14) Official shared taxis to Fergana Valley towns often start in front of the Dordoi Motors company, 3km from Osh Bazaar on the western extension of Chuy. Signs help you find the destinations for which cars are bound. Consider arriving the afternoon before departure to find a driver and phone number rather than waiting around – potentially for hours. And don't confuse Dordoi Motors with Dordoi Bazaar or Dordoi Plaza which are each in entirely different parts of town.

➡ **Western Bus Station dispatchers** (Map p234) If you visit the main bus station, you're unlikely to see any vehicles bound for Osh or the south. Yet tucked away on the outer west side of the main building is a small office from which shared taxis are coordinated. Find a Russian or Kyrgyz speaker and call Majunusov Shermamat (☎077-242 9426) or Tochtonazarov Bilal (☎077-362 3640) to arrange rides to Osh; Aimaktayna Kebekbai (☎077-290 2470) for Jalal-Abad or Kerben.

International Routes

Buses drive right across Kazakhstan to various Russian cities starting mostly from the Western Bus Station, but sometimes from Dordoi Motors.

➡ **Almaty (Kazakhstan)** Use direct minivans (from 400som) or shared taxis from the Western Bus Station, or travel in stages taking marshrutka 285 or 333 (20som, marked **Tamozhna**) to the Kazakh Border via Leninskoe and Lugovoe villages.

➡ **Astana (Kazakhstan)** (1450som, around 20 hours) departs alternate days at 3pm from the Western Bus Station.

➡ **Shymkent (Kazakhstan)** Overnight bus (550som, around 10 hours) departs at 9pm from the Western Bus Station. Handy if you're heading towards Tashkent.

➡ **Kashgar (China)** There's a direct bus to Kashgar at 4pm on Mondays (4020som) from the Eastern Bus Station; however, as it drives via the Torugart Pass, it can currently only be used by Kyrgyz and Chinese citizens.

Sample Domestic Routes

Prices fluctuate with petrol costs and seasonal demand variations. The per seat fares for minibuses/shared taxis include:

➡ Karakol by north route: buses between 7pm and 11pm, 330som (10 hours) via Cholpon-Ata (six hours). Minibuses by day 300som, six hours.

➡ Karakol by south route: bus 8.50pm, 330som

➡ Naryn or Chayek: both 300som, five to six hours, via Kochkor (three hours).

CAR RENTAL

Generally car rental in Central Asia assumes that you engage a vehicle with driver. In Bishkek this is quite easily organised through CBT (p246) (14som to 18som per km) or tour agencies such as NoviNomad (p245) and FantasticAsia (p246), who can find a decent 4WD for around US$0.35 per kilometre. Drivers' meals and overnight expenses usually add US$20 per day, and if you're doing a one-way journey you'll have to pay the return.

Self-drive car rental is in its infancy. The two Bishkek agencies operating to date have only a small selection of vehicles, so although they offer a selection of prices and styles, if you don't book well ahead you might find that choice is limited or non-existent. Plumping for a 4WD vehicle is wise if you're going off the main highways and doesn't necessarily cost more than a city car. Be aware that there is no roadside assistance so if you have a breakdown and are not mechanically adept or fluent in local languages, things can prove awkward. Dealing with occasional police stops will also be a linguistic challenge.

Generally you'll require a passport, driver's licence and security deposit in cash (typically between US$300 and US$1000 according to the vehicle). Insurance is supposedly included but, as ever, you'll need to check the small print carefully.

Kyrgyz Rent-Car (☎077-750 9253; www.carforrent.kg; Elebesova 100) Most cars cost US$80 to US$100 per day but there are a couple at US$40 as well as a minibus at US$100. Ten litres of petrol included. Some English spoken. Drivers must be 21, with two years' driving experience. No mileage limit.

Avtoprokat.kg (☎055-010 8739, 89 99 11; avtoprokat.kg; Chernyshekogo 65, Alamedin) A small selection of mostly 1990s cars start from 1500som per day with discounts of up to 25% for longer rentals. The website shows photos and descriptions of each (in Russian). Maximum mileage 300km per day, within Kyrgyzstan only. You must have a minimum of 18 months' driving experience.

TRAIN

International

A handful of Russia-bound trains from **Bishkek II (main) station** (☎30 02 09) all pass through Kazakhstan so transit visas are required.

- **Moscow** Trains 17 and 27 run each weekday (*platskartny/kupeyny* 9490/14,690som).
- **Yekaterinburg** Train 305 (*platskartny/kupeyny* 5930/8950som) via Astana (3400/4860som).
- **Novosibirsk** Train 358 (*platskartny/kupeyny* 5520/8300som) every four days via Almaty.

Domestic

- **Balykchy** (79som, five hours) This snail-paced, summer-only curiosity departs from Bishkek II (Main) Station at 6.42am, daily in August, weekends only in July. Returns the same afternoon.

Getting Around

TO/FROM THE AIRPORT

Manas airport (p246) is 30km northwest of Bishkek's centre. **Marshrutka 380** (Map p234; Molodaya (Jash) Gvardiya, at 271 Chuy prospektesi; 40som; every 10-20 min) picks up and drops off passengers on Molodaya Gvardiya just 20m north of Chuy. From the airport, the first departure is at 6.30am, the last is at 7.30pm; to the airport, the first departure leaves at 6.40am, with the last at 8pm. At the airport the marshrutka parks just to the right as you exit Arrivals.

Manas Taxi is the only official taxi outfit from the terminal carpark. The fee (450som) should be per car but some drivers will try to wait for extra passengers to double up fares. If you walk through the barrier out of the carpark you'll likely find cheaper cars that don't want to drive back empty, but there can be safety issues with using such random drivers. From town to the airport it can be hard to find a ride for under 600som, especially at the ungodly pre-dawn times that many planes depart.

BICYCLE

Velopro (Map p240; ☎055-599 1137; www.velopro.net; Akhunbayev 128; per day/week US$15/70; 9am-7pm) Bicycle sales, rental and tour possibilities.

Elite Sport (Map p234; ☎31 29 71; www.giant-bicycles.in.kg; Toktogul 170/1; 10am-7pm Mon-Sat, 10am-4pm Sun) Sells and repairs Giant mountain bikes

Velo Leader (Map p234; ☎89 64 04; Moskva 226; 10am-6pm Mon-Fri) Repairs many (but not all) models of bicycle. New bikes available for rental for 300som to 400som per day with a one-week minimum.

BUS, TROLLEYBUS & MARSHRUTKA

Municipal trolleybuses (8som) run a fair network of routes but stops can be a little far apart. Marshrutkas (10som, or 12som after 9pm, pay on entry) are faster and somewhat more frequent but they can be uncomfortably over-full, with claustrophobically low ceilings, and it can be hard to see where you are. There are hundreds of routes. The superb **www.bus.kg** allows you to find the most appropriate service based on your start and end points, and shows each route on a map. However, it's still worth learning major routes and the major signboard shorthand.

Key city centre junctions:

- **ploshad** Ala-Too Square (usually on Kiev)
- **f-nya** philharmonia, ie Manas-Chuy junction
- **tserkov** Jibek Jolu–Togolok Moldo junction
- **goin** Soviet–Jibek Jolu juction
- **mossovet** Soviet–Moskva junction
- **osh r/k** Osh Bazaar
- **yug2 [OR] Vefa** Soviet–Gorky junction

Areas generally indicating out-of-centre directions (working anticlockwise from north):

- **Dordoi R/k** Far north usually via Soviet
- **Maekva** Northwest
- **Pishpek** West, just south of rail tracks at west end of Tolstoy
- **Jal** Inner southwest suburb at west end of Akhunbaev
- **8, 9, 10 M/R** Far south often via Soviet
- **Asanbai [or] M/R12** Southeast via Soviet or Karl Marx
- **Kok Jar** Southeast; could go south via Almatinskaya or east via Akhunbaev
- **Vostok 5** East via Chuy

➡ **Alamedin-1** East beyond Vostok 5; note that this is different from Alamedin r/k, which is the bazaar near the Eastern Bus Station.

Some useful routes:

➡ **Trolleybus 4** All along Moskva, left on Soviet and then north to Dordoi Bazaar.

➡ **Bus 7** Handy for getting from Philarmonia to the Aftovaksal.

➡ **100** Heads west on Akhunaev, up Soviet, loops back south on Alamatin returning to the Kok-Jar roundabout then running westbound the length of Akhunbaev.

➡ **110** From/to Osh Bazaar, along Moskva/Toktogul (east/westbound) then all the way along Soviet to the south.

➡ **113** Eastern Bus Station to Western Bus Station, then circling back via Osh Bazaar and the train station along Mokva then Chuy (east of Pravd) and loops back via Vostok-5 and Alamedin Bazaar.

➡ **114** Essentially the 113 loop in reverse but mostly on Toktogul (westbound) with no diversion to the train station.

➡ **200** Manas/Mira, Akhunbaev, Supara.

➡ **213** Anticlockwise loop around the central area heading westbound on Jibek Jolu, shimmying Isavov, Frunze, Turusbekov, Chuy, Jash Gvardinya (airport bus stop) and Osh Bazaar before returning mostly via Moskva.

➡ **265, 266** Osh Bazaar along Moskva then south down Manas/Mira all the way. 295 does the same southound but returns via Soviet.

➡ **286** Jibek Jolu, Molodozhnaya Gardina (airport bus stand), Chuy and west past Dordoi Motors.

CAR & TAXI

Essentially anyone with a car is a taxi. Official taxis, marked by the checkerboard symbol, are the most reliable. Decent quality taxis include **Super Taxi** (☎152) or **Salam Taxi** (☎188). A short ride in the city costs around 100som, more at night.

There are usually plenty of cars waiting outside nightclubs and popular meeting spots such as **Obama Bar & Grill** (Map p234; www.obama.kg; Toktogul 95).

Around Bishkek

Rolling out of the Kyrgyz Ala-Too range, the Ala-Archa, Alamedin and dozens of parallel streams have created a phalanx of canyons and alpine valleys, good for everything from picnics to trekking and from skiing to mountaineering.

Ala-Archa Canyon

In this grand, accessible Y-shaped valley south of Bishkek, you can sit by a waterfall, hike to a glacier or mountaineer up the region's highest peaks. Around 30km from Bishkek is the *vorota zapovednika*

Around Bishkek

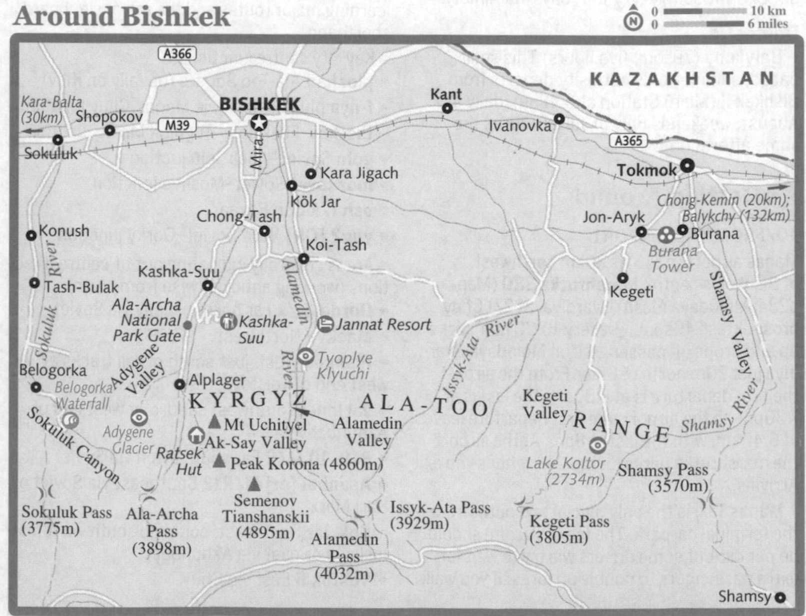

(park gate) where entry fees for the **Ala-Archa state nature park** (foreigner/motorist 80/120som) are payable. Another 12km beyond, the sealed road ends at the main trailhead known as the *alplager*.

GeoID's (p244) 1:50,000 topographic map *Prirodnyy Park Ala-Archa* covers the area should you wish to go off-trail. Alpine Fund has an online **climbing guide** (http:alpinefund.org/Ala-Archa%20guide.html).

ALPLAGER АЛЬПЛАГЕРЬ

ELEV 2100M

Ala-Archa's trailhead is a seasonal gaggle of yurts selling *kymys* (fermented mare's milk), plus a pair of small hotels. The river divides 300m north of here where two idyllic Alpine valleys converge. Relatively well-marked trails lead walkers up both branches – left to the initially steep Ratsek hike, right through the main Ala-Archa Canyon. The area gets relatively busy on summer weekends but can be altogether deserted from October to May.

Recently renovated the small but conspicuous five-level A-frame **Ala-Archa Lodge** (☎055-155 1024; Alplager; d/ste 2500/4000som) has hotel-quality rooms, albeit with already new bathrooms. Of the four 2500som rooms, two are spacious doubles, while the others are rather tight singles. Room 3 is the best deal.

Alp-Lager Hotel (Ala-Archa; d with/without bathroom 2000/500som) has simple, musty old Soviet-era rooms but the beds do have clean sheets. 'Toilet' outside.

RATSEK HIKE

Where the river valley divides 300m north of the *alplager*, the left branch of the trail leads you in four to five glorious hours to a glacier viewpoint. The viewpoint is just 200m up a minor ridge above the isolated 'Ratsek' hut (3370m), which is set in a little handkerchief of meadow surrounded by rocky spires with Patagonian ambitions.

In dry summer conditions it's a strenuous but straight-forward day hike to Ratsek. However, snow can fall in almost any month and wet conditions can leave a few steep sections seriously muddy, and high water can make the two stream crossings virtually impassable. Check conditions with returning hikers. Even if you don't make it all the way to Ratsek hut, there are marvellous alpine views from the 'split-rock' viewpoint just 40 minutes' climb from *alplager* (well before the first stream crossing), and there's a waterfall (frozen November to May) to admire at around the half-way point to Ratsek.

For mountaineers, Ratsek is used as the base camp for a series of acclimatisation peaks, notably Korona (4860m) and Uchityel (4572m). There are also two unmanned first-come, first-served cabins closer to the glaciers. Ornithologists have reported spotting Alpine Accentors (Prunela Colaris) here.

Ratsek Hut, aka **Ak-Say Mountain Lodge** (Ratsek Hut; ☎bookings via Yaroslav 070-179 9931; dm/camping 500/150som; ⏲late-Jun–Sep), has two 14-space bunk rooms (the upper one feels less claustrophobic), and a six-space 'private' room. But don't assume there'll be mattresses or blankets. You'll need your own mat, sleeping bag, food and light as there's no electricity. A caretaker can usually heat up the *banya* (for a whopping 3500som), rent you a saucepan, and sell you firewood, but bring your own food. Left luggage for climbers costs 100som per day.

MAIN CANYON

Forking right where the river valley divides just above the *alplager* offers an initially clear, easy route up the main Ala-Archa Canyon past a couple of yurts. The way is pretty, but the second bridge has now degraded to little more than a single precarious plank that is not for the faint-hearted.

ADYGENE VALLEY

From the *alplager*, backtrack around 300m towards Bishkek and cross a footbridge and you should find yourself heading southwest up the Adygene Valley (you may need to ask for a little help to find the start of the trail). Along this way is a poignant climbers' cemetery in a larch grove. The track continues for about 7km to 3300m, below Adygene Glacier. Where the track divides it's best to keep left – you can return by looping back the other way, but if you fork right, the way is harder to find outbound and involves a scramble across a landslide at one point.

ℹ Getting There & Away

If you're taking a taxi, be sure to clarify that the agreed price is to the *alplager* (typically 500som one way) rather than the Ala-Archa park gate (*vorota zapovednika gate*, 250som). Otherwise you'll need to hitch the last 12km or pay a very considerable supplement. Especially off season, it might be worth arranging a pickup to take you back again. Bargaining might be necessary as some drivers ask a whopping US$40 return, especially when ordered through hotels. You can usually agree on around half that through drivers around Osh Bazaar.

By public transport **marshrutka 265** (Map p234; Beyshenaliyeva; 25som) from ul Beyshenaliyeva usually runs to Kashka-Suu village, terminating 7km short of the park gate. But around five daily services in summer go all the way to the gate (last return around 5pm). On some summer weekends these might even run to the *alplager*, but generally you'll need to walk or hitch the last 12km. Traffic is sparse out of season.

Alamedin Valley
Ущелье Аламедин

This beautiful alpine valley is the most accessible option for those wanting to savour Bishkek's fabulous mountain backdrop with a picnic rather than a serious trek. The valley has a relatively open aspect with curtains of spiky white-tops rising from a partly grassy meadowland valley. Views begin just five minutes' walk from the end of the road, less than 1km beyond the dowdy Soviet-era mineral-water swimming pool, **Tyoplye Klyuchi** (☎33 68 18; per hr 150som; ⏲8am-8pm Tue-Sat, 8am-4pm Sun). Almost as soon as you leave the final little car park there's a choice of routes: you can descend, cross the river and follow the left bank pastures towards a waterfall that's tucked away in the third side valley (around 1½ hour's walk one way); or stay on the right bank for somewhat finer views. However, after around an hour's walk, when you reach a large grassy area, the right-bank path peters out amid thorn bushes and crossing the river there is not recommended unless the water level is very low.

Sokuluk Canyon
Ущелье Сокулук

The 60m **Belogorka Waterfall**, arguably the most impressive in the Bishkek area, is accessed via Sokuluk Canyon. The surrounding valley is dominated by a sharply pointed spike of mountain nicknamed 'Black Finger' towering ahead of what was once the main shepherd's trail to Suusamyr. Following the former track for around an hour, as it winds up hairpin turns out of the valley, takes you past wider, shorter falls and through some very attractive mountainscapes.

The rough access road becomes impassable to cars at a small bridge just before the falls and the nearest public transport, **marshrutka 367** (Map p234; cnr Kuliev & Chuy prospektesi; 25som; ⏲8am-8.30pm) from Bishkek's Osh Bazaar, at best stops 15km short in Belogorka village, with many only going as far as Tash-Bulak or Sokuluk bazaar. Hitching is not likely to be successful except, perhaps, on mid-summer weekends.

TOWARDS ISSYK-KÖL

The new Bishkek–Balykchy highway bypasses Kant, Tokmok and Kemin. Cyclists are advised to take the old road but will still face the heavy traffic and headwinds of the eroded Boom Valley (Boömskoe Ushile, Shoestring Gorge). Hiking away from the main road in the Boom Valley is a series of wind-eroded sandstone towers and pillars sometimes known misleadingly as Clay or Aeolian 'Castles' (see asiamountains.net/en/catalog/excursions/eolian for photos).

Of several other minor attractions that warrant a short detour, the best known is the Burana Tower. Further south are several attractive canyon-valleys notably Kegeti Valley and the 20m Kegey Waterfall, an ice-climb in winter.

Burana Tower
Башня Бурана

Burana is a popular side-trip when driving to Issyk-Köl from Bishkek. In fields east of Kegeti, the Burana Tower is the 24m-high stump of a huge brick minaret, supposedly 11th-century though what you see dates predominantly from a 1950s Soviet restoration. You can climb it from 9am to 5pm (6pm in summer), or admire the slightly leaning structure with its distant mountain backdrop from a grassy mound to the northwest. This is all that's left of the ancient citadel of Balasagun, founded by the Sogdians and later a capital of the Karakhanids, excavated in the 1970s by Russian archaeologists.

Arguably the site's most interesting feature, on the other side of the citadel mound, is a collection of 6th- to 10th-century *balbals* (Turkic totem-like stone markers). There's also a small **museum** (admission 60som, guided tour 10som; ⏲9am-6pm summer, until 5pm in winter) with 11th-century Christian carvings, Buddhist remains and Chinese coins, as well as info on local literary hero Haji Balasagun and his masterwork, the *Kutudhu Bilik*. Next door are the foundations of several mausoleums.

The Shamsy Valley that leads south from Burana has also yielded a rich hoard of Scythian treasure, including a heavy gold burial mask, though the greatest treasures were all either spirited away to St Petersburg or to Bishkek where much is in storage in the bowels of the State Historical Museum (p232).

By public transport take frequent marshrutka 353 to Tokmok (40som, 45 minutes), then a taxi for the last 24km (700som round trip).

Chong-Kemin Valley

Чонг-Кемин Долина

The 80km-long Chong-Kemin Valley, one of Kyrgyzstan's national parks, starts about 140km east of Bishkek and runs along the Kazakh border, providing another great opportunity to roll up your sleeping bag and trek into the hills. A six-day trekking route leads up the valley to Jasy-Köl (Green Lake) and the Ak-Suu Pass (4062m), and then onto Grigoricvka near Cholpan-Ata on the northern shores of Issyk-Köl.

The valley's best accommodation is the **Ashu Guesthouse** (☎031-355 8108, 077-252 4037; www.ashu.kg; Borueva 22, Kalmak-Ashu; d US$50;) in little Kalmak Ashu village. The place has a fresh yet rustic feel, prices include full board and owner Stanbek Toichubaev can organise a range of local activities. Limited wi-fi.

Public transport is limited to a couple of marshrutkas serving Kaindy (110som, 2½ hours) from Bishkek's Eastern Bus Station.

LAKE ISSYK-KÖL

ОЗЕРО ИСЫК-КУЛЬ

More than 170km long and 70km across, Lake Issyk-Köl (Ysyk-Köl, Issyk-Kul) is the world's second-largest alpine lake after Lake Titicaca in South America. The name, meaning 'hot lake', is something of an exaggeration. A combination of extreme depth, thermal activity and mild salinity do indeed ensure the lake never freezes, even in the fierce Central Asian winters, despite lying at an altitude of over 1600m. And the mysteriously temperate waters create an ever-mild microclimate. But the brave summer tourists who swim in the vivid blue waters find views framed not by palms but by the remarkable backdrop of the snow-dappled Ala-Too mountains.

Indeed, while beach 'resorts' attract Kazakh visitors and can make for amusingly discordant photos, the foreshores are often rather mucky with rubbish and the main attraction for Western travellers tends to be the accessible mountain hiking. Parts of the central Tian Shan range accessible from the lake settlements comprise some of the finest trekking territory in Central Asia, with the most popular routes being hops between the valleys south of Karakol.

History

The lake level has periodically risen and fallen over the centuries, inundating ancient shoreline settlements. Artefacts have been recovered from what is now known as the submerged city of Chigu at the lake's eastern end, dating from the 2nd century BC. The Mikhaylovka inlet near Karakol, also reveals the remains of a partly submerged village, though in the last 500 years, geological evidence suggests that water levels have been dropping, albeit only around 2m overall.

Before the Kyrgyz people arrived in the 10th to 15th centuries, this area appears to have been a centre of Saka (Scythian) civilisation. Legend has it that Timur (Tamerlane) later used it as a summer headquarters. There are at least 10 documented settlements currently under the waters of the lake, and treasure hunters have long scoured the lakebed for trinkets, attributing finds to everyone from Christian monks to Chinggis (Genghis) Khan.

In the 1860s and 1870s, after tsarist military officers and explorers had put the lake on Russian maps, immigrants flooded in to found low-rise, laid-back, rough-and-ready towns – the establishment of Karakol in 1869 was followed in the 1870s by Tüp, Teploklyuchenka (now Ak-Suu), Ananyevo, Pokrovka (now Kyzyl-Suu) and a string of others, many of whose Cossack names have stuck. Large numbers of Dungans and Uyghurs arrived in the 1870s and '80s following the suppression of Muslim uprisings in China's Shaanxi, Gansu and Xinjiang provinces. At that time local Kyrgyz and Kazakhs were still mostly nomadic.

In USSR times, health spas were dotted along the lake's shores, but the Issyk-Köl

Lake Issyk-Köl

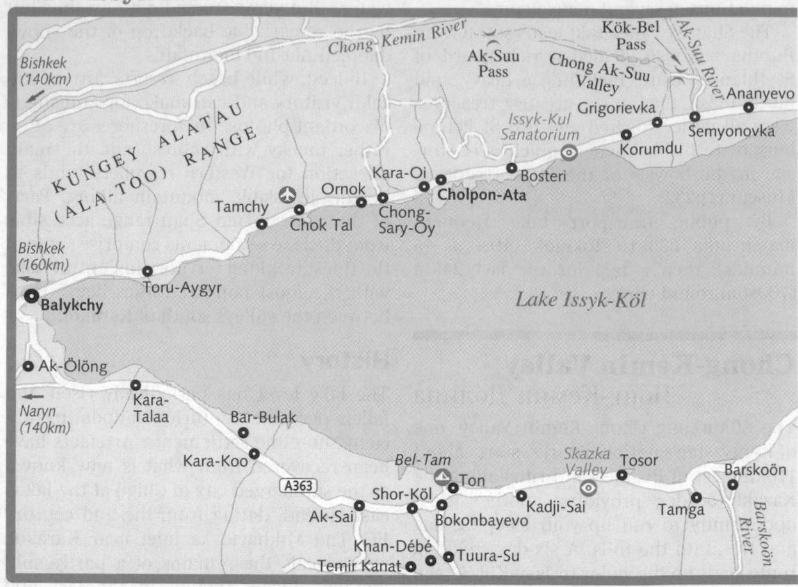

region (along with much of Kyrgyzstan beyond Bishkek) was off limits to foreigners. Locals mention vast, officially sanctioned plantations of opium poppies and cannabis around the lake, though most of these had disappeared under international pressure by the early 1970s. More importantly, Issyk-Köl was used by the Soviet navy to test high-precision torpedoes, far from prying Western eyes. An entire military-research complex grew around Koy-Sary, on the Mikhaylovka inlet near Karakol. After independence in 1991, Russia's new president, Boris Yeltsin, asked that it be continued but Kyrgyz President Askar Akaev shut down the whole thing. These days the most secretive thing in the lake is the mysterious *jekai*, a Kyrgyz version of the Loch Ness monster. Jokes about the 'Kyrgyz navy' refer to a fleet of some 40 ageing naval cutters, now mothballed at Koy-Sary (which remains out-of-bounds to visitors) or decommissioned and hauling goods and tourists up and down the lake. Tourism, which initially crashed along with the Soviet Union, has revived in the last decade thanks to an influx of moneyed Kazakh tourists and Russian athletes, who favour the area's mild climate and high altitude as a winter training zone.

Getting There & Away

The main access routes from Bishkek and Kochkor are from the western corner of the lake via the unexpectedly ugly city of Balykchy, which has at least three central Lenins to spot. Asphalted roads circle the lake, albeit often several kilometres from the waterside. Bishkek–Karakol transport might go either way around the lake, though the north coast road is generally busier, especially in summer.

An alternative route to Kazakhstan leads through the Karkara Valley (summers only) for those with their own transport. There is a rough track that could lead more directly from Almaty's Bolshoe Almatinskoe Lake via the Ozerny and Kok Ayryk Passes to Chong-Sary-Oy near Cholpon-Ata, but there's no immigration post so horse-trekkers or mountain-bikers would need complex special permissions to avoid a serious immigration problem

Northern Issyk-Köl

More than one hundred hotel complexes are dotted along the northern coast of Issyk-Köl, but that doesn't mean the whole area is one long resort. Indeed, hotels are well spread out, most are rather discrete and visitors are often surprised by the extent to which many of the agricultural villages in between seem to have changed little in recent decades. So

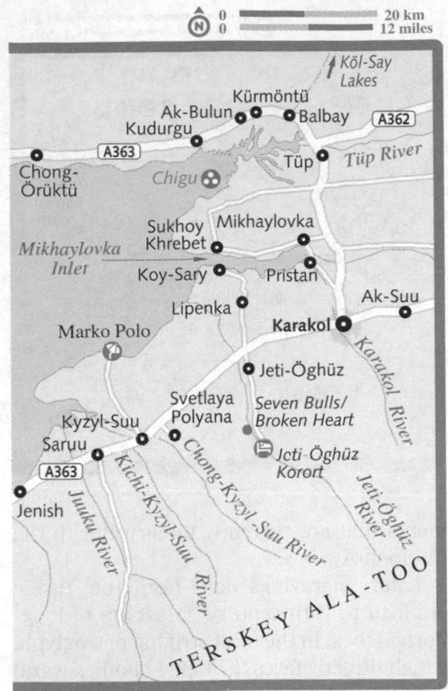

while midsummer weekends see the main road transformed into a veritable tourist conveyor belt, out of season it remains a quiet, mostly charming drive with mountainscapes rising to the north, and like apparitions across the lake away to the south. The main tourist magnet is Cholpan-Ata (and Bosteri). The area further east is particularly rural with occasional roadside *tumuli* (burial mounds) and mud-brick ancient tombs in the fields behind the lines of poplars.

Tamchy Тамчы

3943

This small lakeshore village, 35km west of Cholpon-Ata, has a pretty beach, which had more cows than people on it when we visited. The main curiosity is a comically discordant attempt at building a European chateau-villa amid the beachfront trees. This 'Stary Zamok' is reputedly a hotel of sorts, but was closed at the time of research. There is, however, an easy-to-spot branch of **CBT** (077-335 5611, 212 72; Manas 55) on the main road through town which can help you organise vehicles, horse trips and homestays. Outside the summer season the whole village is virtually dormant.

Around 5km east is the so called Issyk-Köl International Airport, a misleadingly grand name for an airfield without so much as a terminal building. It's generally only used for summer charter flights, mostly from Kazakhstan.

Cholpon-Ata Чолпон-Ата

3943

In midsummer, Cholpon-Ata awakens from its long off-season slumber to become the epicentre of an improbable north Issyk-Köl beach scene: by day there's tanning bods, zipping jet skis and ice-cream licking tots; by night it's open-air cafes, thumping discos and young lovers breaking social mores. Most of the visitors are wealthy Kazakhs and Russians, joined by members of the Bishkek glitterati. That doesn't mean that Cholpon-Ata itself is particularly sophisticated. Most of the swankier resorts are hidden away on exclusive beaches a considerable distance from Cholpon-Ata, with a major cluster 10km east at Bosteri. There, in front of the Dolphin Deluxe Hotel, you'll find a roller coaster and Kyrgyzstan's biggest ferris wheel (150som).

For most westerners the beach scene is of minor interest and travellers generally stop here to glimpse the petroglyphs and to organise short-notice horse treks.

From Thursday to Saturday in summer, virtually all prices – from taxis to hotels – double. But on weekdays outside high season (mid-July to August) you may have the whole place to yourself.

Sights & Activities

As well as the main beach, a smaller but pleasant public beach lies directly north of the yacht club inlet, behind Hotel Ai-Petri.

Ornok forest, north of the petroglyph park, is popular with locals who collect mushrooms here during August. Follow the old logging road on the left side of the valley, keep the river on the right.

Kruiz Yacht Club BOAT RIDES
(055-527 1366, 433 73; boat trip adult/child 200/150som, boat rental per hr 1800-12,000som; boat trips 11am, 3pm & 5pm Jul-Sep) In spring, the setting of moored boats against the snow-capped mountains makes for a very photogenic scene. In summer, several boats offer 90-minute cruises into the middle of the lake, allowing a 15-minute swim stop in the deepest section.

The club also hosts a free, two-cabinet 'museum' and a scuba-diving centre.

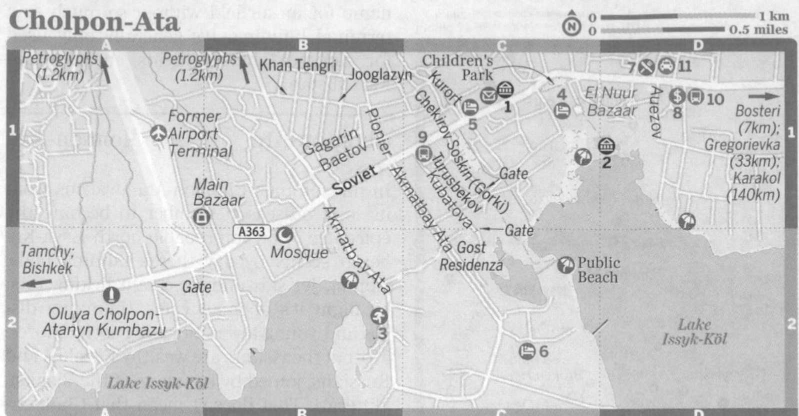

Cholpon-Ata

Sights

1 Regional Museum C1
2 Rukh Ordo D1

Activities, Courses & Tours

3 Kruiz Yacht Club B2
Pegasus Horse Trekking .... (see 5)

Sleeping

4 Gosrezidentsia 2 .... C1
5 Pegasus Guest House C1
6 Tri Korony C2

Eating

Ak-Jol .... (see 9)
7 Green Pub D1

Information

8 Ayyal Bank D1

Transport

9 Avtovokzal C1
10 Karakol Bus Stand D1
11 Taxis D1

Petroglyphs PETROGLYPHS

(Saimaluu Tash; Almakuchkov; foreigner/local 40/10som; ⏲daylight) Directly north of the former airport runway (now a wide road) is an extensive field of glacial boulders, many with pictures scratched or picked into their surfaces. Some of these petroglyphs date from the late Bronze Age (about 1500 BC), but most are Saka-Usun (8th century BC to 1st century AD), predating the arrival of the Kyrgyz in the area. The Saka priests used this sacred site for sacrifices and other rites to the sun god and they lived in the settlements that are currently underwater in the Cholpon-Ata bay.

Later engravings date from the Turkic era (5th to 10th century). Most are of long-horned ibex. In the most striking petroglyph, which directly faces the ticket booth, several ibex are being hunted with tame snow leopards. Many of the other petroglyphs can prove hard to spot or to differentiate from recent graffiti. Real ones have small yellow numbers painted on the rocks. The back side of the welcome board has a map of the site but is not really detailed enough to help much. Late afternoon is a good time to view the stones, most of which face west or south.

From the town centre walk up Akmatbay-Ata to where the asphalt ends then swerve left onto Almakuchkov. The south side of the site is behind black wrought-iron railings but should the gate be closed you can do as shepherds do and enter from the unfenced east side. There's a nice view of Issyk-Köl below. Guided tours of the petroglyphs can be arranged at the regional museum.

Rukh Ordo MUSEUM

(admission 300som; ⏲9am-5pm) This curious museum-cum-theme-park examines Kyrgyz legends, historical characters and the interplay of five religions in a large, somewhat surreal beachfront complex. Attractive setting.

Regional Museum MUSEUM

(Soviet 69; foreigner/local 40/10som, camera 50som; ⏲9am-5pm Mon-Sat, til 6pm summer) This typical, well-presented museum includes copies of locally found Scythian (Saka) gold jewellery and displays on ethnography, Kyrgyz bards, textiles and underwater archaeology plus a 3D model of Issyk-Köl showing visually just how very deep the lake is. Minimal English.

Pegasus Horse Trekking HORSE RIDING
(☎424 50; pegaso@mail.ru; Soviet 81) Pegasus Horse Trekking is run by the same lady who operates the Pegasus Guest House. She organises horse treks to Ornok Valley and along the lakeshore, offers expert instruction for less-confident riders and can arrange multiday excursions to Grigorievka and beyond. With a few days notice she will also organise a display of nomadic equestrian games (20,000som) at the local hippodrome. During July these can be seen for free as part of the horse games.

Sleeping

There are more than 100 hotels, resorts and sanatoria in Cholpan-Ata and neighbouring settlements, and probably as many local homes rent rooms. However, if you come outside of the summer season, almost all will be closed. Contrastingly, at weekends in July and August virtually everything will be full and you might need to rely on elderly ladies who appear at the bus station offering *komnaty* (homestay rooms).

Pegasus Guest House HOMESTAY $
(☎077-245 9901, 424 50; pegaso@mail.ru; Soviet 81; dm without/with breakfast 300/450som) English-speaking Tatiana Kemelevna and her son, Bukit, understand budget backpacker requirements. They offer advice on local activities and their horse-trekking outfit is probably the best organised on this side of the lake. Their traditional Russian cottage is contrastingly basic: two three-bed dorm rooms are each attached to a sitting-area/kitchenette with extra bed, while the toilet is a long drop in the extensive garden. If full, several neighbours rent rooms during the summer.

Tri Korony RESORT HOTEL $$
(s/d/ste Jul-Aug 1800/3500/5600som) Handily central yet away from the main concentration of developments, this 60-room resort has its own stretch of beach and comparatively new facilities. Quoted rates are for full board.

Gosrezidentsia 2 GUESTHOUSE $$$
(☎435 31; www.gosrezidence.kg; Soviet 131; r Jul-Aug 2500-32,320som, off season 1460-21,000som) The site of an old sanatorium was spruced up to host seven heads of state during the 2009 CSTO summit. Mere mortals can stay here when the politicians are away. Every room and suite is different, there's indoor swimming, a covered tennis court and a beach with a jetty.

Eating & Drinking

Most cafes close between October and May. In season there are several appealing choices around Green Pub, and sweet tourist-oriented food windows along the southern end of Chekirov Soskin (Gorky) on the way to the beach.

Ak-Jol CENTRAL ASIAN $
(Turusbekov; mains 70-150som; ⏲8am-6pm Mon-Sat Oct-Jun, 8am-10pm daily Jul-Sep) Behind the bus station, this semi-smart if hardly glorious place serves tasty, rapidly prepared local meals plus more exotic sizzler (*zharovni*) plates.

Green Pub RUSSIAN, BARBECUE $$
(☎429 76; Soviet 11; mains 160-490som; ⏲9am-10pm Oct-Jun, 8.30am-midnight July-Sep) With more atmosphere than most and open year-round, this low-lit, green-decor pub-restaurant with heavy wooden tables and a part-covered summer terrace offers excellent if pricey Russian bar meals including barbecued fish (350som).

Information

The main commercial strip around the **post office** on Soviet has three internet cafes plus several exchange booths and Visa ATMs. The only MasterCard ATM is at **Ayyal Bank** (Soviet) near the Karakol bus stand.

Getting There & Away

Cholpon-Ata, being the premier resort town for nearby and comparatively wealthy Kazakhs, is particularly prone to fluctuating transport costs. During summer, shared-taxi prices double for tourists and locals alike. Prices here are low-season rates.

Westbound transport starts from the **Avtovokzal** (Bus Station) or from the corner of Kubatova at Soviet directly north.

Eastbound transport uses the **Karakol bus stand** (Soviet).

Frequency and price can vary radically with day and season. In season, buses or minibuses run at least hourly to Bishkek (250som, four hours) and nine times daily to Karakol (120som, 2½ hours). Off season the choice will be largely limited to Bishkek–Karakol through transport or shared taxis (300som to Karakol, 600som to Bishkek) which you may have to charter outright from mid-afternoon.

Getting Around

Marshrutka 304 links Cholpan-Ata to Bosteri (15som), but is also the local bus within town, starting in the MPK estate southwest of the petroglyphs then trundling all the way along Soviet (5som per hop).

Local **taxis** gather around the El Nuur Bazaar and rarely charge less than 150som per hop.

Grigorievka Григорьевка

For beautiful grassland-mountains head up the **Chong Ak-Suu Valley** (admission per person 20som, per car 50som), due north of the village of Grigorievka. Cut by a raging river, the valley runs 22km to a trio of small alpine lakes. It's possible to hike the whole way, but you could also hitch a lift or take your own vehicle. In summer there are yurtstays and roadside restaurants along the way, plus another yurtstay at the first lake. Local boys will likely appear to offer horses for rent (300som to 500som per hour), as might falconers charging you for the thrill of holding an eagle on your arm.

Pegasus Horse Trekking (p257) organises horse treks between Grigorievka and Semyonovka gorges, overnighting in either tents or yurts.

The nearby village of Semyonovka offers access to the Kichi (Little) Ak-Suu Valley, which has the Kyrchyn Gorge, a winter-sports centre, and one yurtstay called **Yurta Kubat Sidikov** (☎055-034 2939; bed & breakfast 400som) with two cosy guest yurts, located 2.5km past the ranger gate.

Karakol Каракол

☎3922 / POP 75,000

A dusty grid of treelined streets, Karakol has limited sights but is a good base from which to access some of Central Asia's best skiing and most gloriously accessible alpine treks. The town couldn't really be called beautiful, but a clever photographer might easily make you believe otherwise by selectively counterpointing clear-day backdrops of snowy peaks with the old blue shutters and whitewashed walls of some remnant gingerbread houses. These houses recall the town's Russian-era heydey: founded in 1869 as a support town for the then-new garrison of Teploklyuchenka (Ak-Suu), it housed many merchants, officers and explorers, most famously Nikolai Przewalski in whose honour Karakol was renamed Prezevalsk between 1939 and 1991.

Sights

Dungan Mosque ISLAMIC

(cnr Bektenov & Jusup Abdrakhmanov; foreigners 20som) A tip-tilted triple roof, carved-layered eaves and wooden exterior pillars give this colourful 1910 mosque the look of a Mongolian Buddhist temple. Remarkably it survived the early Bolshevik era, which saw the town's other eight mosques destroyed, though it was closed for worship between 1933 and 1943. It's worth a quick photo stop if you're passing

Animal Market MARKET

(Mal Bazaar, Skotski Bazaar; Udilova; ⏲dawn-10am Sun) Early on Sunday mornings one of Kyrgyzstan's biggest animal markets takes place around 2km north of central Karakol.

OFF THE BEATEN TRACK

KARKARA VALLEY КАРКАРАНСКАЯ ДОЛИНА

Rich pastures fill the immense, silent Karkara (black crane) Valley that straddles the Kyrgyzstan–Kazakhstan border. Attractions include the eponymous migratory birds that stop here in June and again from August to September, as well as a late-August **Shepherds' Festival** with horseback games and eagle hunting held at yurt camps near Char-Kuduk village. San-Tash is famous for its burial mounds, while Karkara helipad, some 20km beyond (near the Kazakhstan border post), is the main access point for summer flights to Inylchek Glacier and the Khan Tengri/Pik Pobedy base camps. For border crossing details (summer only) see p311 and p77.

If you're driving, the turn-off to Karkara from the Issyk-Köl road is beside the Gazprom petrol station 2km northwest of Tüp. The attractive A363 northwest passes Scythian tumuli beside the road at Km 41/175 (west of Ak-Bulun) plus several ancient graveyards, one containing the recently rebuilt mausoleum of Balabai Baatyr.

Typical of such markets, you'll observe scenes at once sad and comical, with locals improbably bundling voluptuous fat-tailed sheep into the back seats of Lada cars. The setting amid semi-derelict flour mills might seem unprepossessing, but on clear days the backdrop of white-topped mountains is more striking from here than from the town centre. Marshrutka 102 drops you amid a melee of vehicles and hay-trucks on Udilova. A series of earthen unloading platforms lead north. Jostle through the chaos to reach a bigger main compound one block north, where you'll find horse sales and vendors of beautiful embossed leather saddlery.

On foot the bazaar is about 25 minutes' walk from Makish Bazaar. Head straight down bumpy Lenina (the clearly signed Bereke Mill is about half way) then cut diagonally across some scrubby wasteland approximately opposite Lenina 279. Alternatively walk up Kydyr Ake, take the second left (beside a cement dealers' store) and follow the traffic.

Holy Trinity Cathedral CHURCH
(Gagarin; ⌚8am-1pm & 2-5pm) Set peacefully amid trees, this hefty wooden structure is topped with green-roofed towers and almost-golden onion domes. The 1872 stone original was destroyed by an 1890 earthquake. Built on the same foundations a new wooden version, finished in 1895, was turned into a club by the Bolsheviks, who removed its five onion-domes in the 1930s. Serious reconstruction began in 1961, but church services only recommenced after 1991. Photos of its various incarnations are displayed in the entry hall. Women need to wear a headscarf to enter.

Colonial Buildings NOTABLE BUILDINGS
The older part of town sprawls southwest from the cathedral with numerous simple but archetypal 'gingerbread' timber houses. A few are comparatively grand former homes of Russian merchants and industrialists, including what's now the Pedagogical College on Gagarin (opposite the cathedral), the **radio and TV office** on Gebze (Kalinina) and another old **merchant's home** at the corner of Koenkӧzova and Lenina.

Regional Museum MUSEUM
(☎218 68; Jamansariev 164; foreigner/local 70/30som, camera 10som; ⌚9am-5pm) Occupying an archetypal 1887 Russian house, this museum has a few Scythian bronze artefacts, local tools and musical instruments, and the recreated interior of a century-old home. Taxidermists' victims share a room with exhibits celebrating the Kumtor Gold Mine (p270). Little is in English except for the section on remarkable Swiss explorer Ella Maillart, who came this way in 1932.

Karakol Zoo ZOO
(N Aytmatova; adult/child 50/30som; ⌚9am-6pm) The small local zoo is a shady spot whose inmates range from farmyard animals to llamas, with a fair selection of locally endangered fauna, including bears, wolves, bobcats and most notably, Przewalski horses.

Pristan

Karakol's port and beach is around 12km north at Pristan, a sad if vaguely curious area of *datchas* (weekend cottages) above which rise a couple of Soviet-era cranes.

Prezhevalski Garden MUSEUM, MONUMENT
(http:kyrgyzstan.orexca.com/rus/museum_prejevalsky.shtml; Pristan; local/foreigner 70/30som, guided tour 30som; ⌚9am-5pm) To overlook the Pristan area (though not the beach) it is worth stopping around 1km before the port and observing the scene from the shrine-like Prezhevalski memorial garden. Other than the minor curiosity of the **view**, the main attraction here is a small, well-presented **museum** dedicated to Nikolai Przewalski, the Russian explorer who died here in 1888 and for whom Karakol was once named. Entered through a neo-Greek portal, there's a giant map of his travels behind a big globe. Note the imaginative rendering of Senegal. Many photos, maps and mementos have English captions but there's no over-arching explanation of his life. The best features are arguably the banknote-style wall murals designed to alter perspective as you walk by. Amid the taxidermy is a stuffed white Przewalski horse, the breed for whose 'discovery' the explorer is best known in the west.

Activities

Karakol's travel and tour agencies (p263) organise a wide range of outdoor activities including trekking, horse riding, skiing, mountaineering and mountain biking.

Sleeping

Between them CBT (p263) and TIC (p263) can suggest around 50 homestays,

Karakol

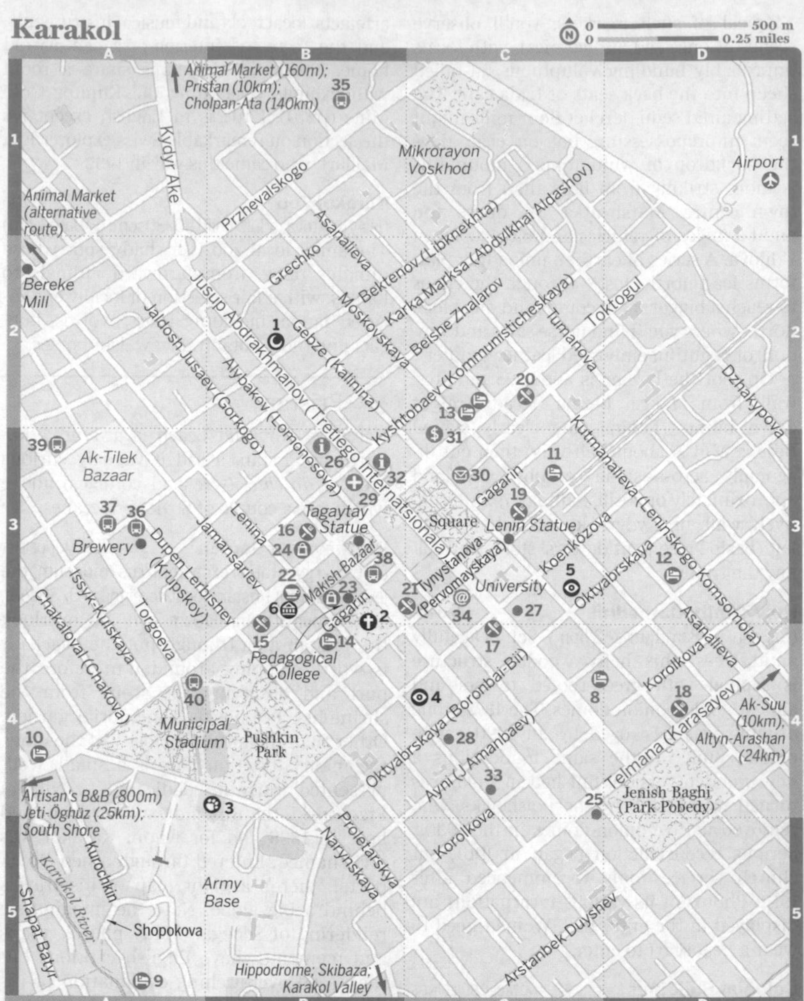

guesthouses and hotels. Most homestays start from 500som per person including breakfast.

★ Teskey Guesthouse GUESTHOUSE, HOMESTAY **$**
(☎077-280 1411, 262 68; www.teskey.webs.com; Asanalieva 44; per person homestay/guesthouse 500/600som; 📶) On a quiet, unpaved backstreet, Teskey's great plus is its knowledgeable, ever-obliging, English-speaking host Talaai. The brand-new guesthouse has super views from the top floor, while across the garden the family home still offers bright, comfortable homestay rooms. Days trips are offered to local sights, notably Jeti-Öghüz. Washing service is available and they rent out two Giant-brand mountain bikes (US$10 per day, no lock).

Yak Tours Hostel HOSTEL **$**
(☎569 01; yaktours@infotel.kg; Gagarin 10; tent 100som, s/d/tr 300/600/900som; Ⓟ) Rooms here are delightful, old-world creations in a genuinely antique house behind heavy wooden gates. Decoration with framed embroidery and painted trunks adds to the joy. The solitary bathroom suffers from an ever-running toilet and a water heater that's rarely turned on, but rooms remain a great

Karakol

Sights
1 Dungan Mosque B2
2 Holy Trinity Cathedral B3
3 Karakol Zoo B4
4 Merchant's Home C4
5 Radio & TV Office C3
6 Regional Museum B3

Sleeping
7 Altamira C2
8 Hotel Amir C4
9 Jamilya's B&B A5
10 Madanor Hotel A4
11 Tagaytay C3
12 Teskey Guesthouse D3
13 Turkestan Yurt Camp C2
14 Yak Tours Hostel B4

Eating
15 Bistro Mustafa B4
16 Fakir Café B3
17 Kalinka C4
18 Kench Café D4
19 Lovely Pizza C3
20 Maximum C2
21 Tou C3

Drinking & Nightlife
22 Karakol Coffee B3

Shopping
23 Kürk Art Gallery B3
24 OVOP B3

Information
25 Alp Tour Issyk Köl C4
26 CBT B3
27 Ecotrek C3
28 IGPA C4
29 Karakol Medical Clinic B3
30 Post & Telephone Office C3
31 RSK Bank C3
32 TIC B3
33 Tour Khan Tengri C4
Turkestan .... (see 13)
34 Vista C3
Yak Tours .... (see 14)

Transport
35 Main Bus Station B1
36 Marshrutka to Ak-Suu A3
37 Marshrutka to Jeti-Öghüz A3
38 Marshrutka to Pristan B3
39 Marshrutka to Tüp area A3
40 Southern Bus Stand A4

deal and this is a good place to meet other travellers, especially when the brilliant old Russian-style dining room downstairs is operative.

Turkestan Yurt Camp YURTSTAY, HOSTEL $
(☎564 89; www.turkestan.biz; Toktogul 273; tent/yurt 100/250som, r 300-400som; ⊙Apr-Nov; P) An attractive Wild-West–style encampment behind the tall wooden climbing wall is home to a yurt camp between May and October. Behind are well-furnished, three-bed dorms in a small house sharing the same decent shower block. Breakfast costs 50som extra (not available April or November).

Artisan's B&B HOMESTAY $
(Gulnara Perizat Guesthouse; ☎055-019 1512, 701 71; madinart1103@gmail.com; Murmansk 114; s/d/tr 500/1000/1500som) Some 2km west of Karakol centre, this wonderfully quirky homestay was built from scratch by its artist/artisan owners. Fanciful carved chairs, '60s-style colour-panel lamps, African masks, framed stamp collections and a stupendous Soviet patchwork banner all add to the fun. Get off marshrutka 112 (from Ak-Tilek Bazaar) at 141 Toktogul then walk north on Harikovskaya. The B&B is on the third left-hand corner where Harikovskaya kinks (facing a school).

Jamilya's B&B HOMESTAY $
(☎054-498 0980, 417 18; kemelov@hotmail.com; Shopokova 34B; per person 700-800som, ensuite 1000som; wifi) The mother-and-son team here both speak excellent English and offer 10 rooms with a hue – lime, lilac, pink, yellow or blue. Spotless bathrooms, hot showers, sit-down toilets, a lounge, dining room, lovely garden and shared balcony looking towards the river. The access road (Kurochkin) is signed from opposite Madanur Hotel. Alternatively marshrutkas 110/111 southbound/northbound pass very near (Shapak Batyr at Iskakov) but you'll need to use the little footbridge.

Altamira GUESTHOUSE $
(☎545 16; www.altamira.kg; Toktogul 227; d/ste 1400/2000som; P wifi) Nine-room new mini-hotel close to the commercial centre.

Madanor Hotel HOTEL $
(☎077-775 7757, 715 38; Toktogul 201; s/d/tr 700/1400/2100som, with breakfast 800/1600/2400; P @ wifi) If you want a new, fully equipped hotel room and are travelling alone, this styleless establishment set

above a small supermarket is good value. But for two people sharing it's worth paying marginally more and chosing the Tagaytay.

Hotel Amir BOUTIQUE HOTEL **$$**
(☎513 15; info@hotelamir.kg; Ayni 78; s/d US$47/65, basement US$45/55; P❄@📶) Karakol's best hotel is brightly painted in raspberry and apricot tones. Cheerful rooms have a 1970s retro vibe and there are brilliant *ala-kiyiz* wall hangings throughout, including a Picasso-like masterpiece behind reception. Downstairs rooms have less light but are discounted. There's a power generator for electricity blackouts.

Tagaytay HOTEL **$$**
(☎521 61; www.tagaytay.org.kg; Tynystanov 29a; s/d/luxe Mar-Nov 1500/2000/2500som, Dec-Feb 2000/3000/4000som; 🚭📶) New, central and sparkling clean, the Tagaytay's finest feature is the ceiling-less communal lounge with attractive artwork, saddle-display and real fire. However, noise from here can reverberate, disturbing light-sleeping guests. Rooms could be a little larger but are still some of the best in Karakol and are brought to life with vivid traditionally patterened duvets. Free wi-fi.

Eating

The Dungan snack-meal *ashlyanfu* (cold, gelatine noodles in a spicy-vinegary sauce) is sold for a few som at the Ak-Tilek Bazaar and at many local dives for 25som a bowl. For free wi-fi and sit-down fast food, try **Tou** (Gorkogo; mains 90som; ⏲9am-midnight; 📶).

Kench Café INTERNATIONAL **$$**
(☎207 07; cnr Telmona & Gebze; meals 150-320som; ⏲11am-11.30pm; 📶📋) Slightly classier than the competition – which doesn't say a lot – Kench has stone-effect walls with playful petroglyphs and stylishly elegant tables that would be better if the chairs fit under them. An English menu has a wide range of usually reliable options including tasty *badanju* (lightly stir-fried chicken with vegetables). Summer terrace has barbecue. Free wi-fi.

Bistro Mustafa HALAL, KYRGYZ **$$**
(Toktokul 108/3; samsa 25som, mains 50-150som; ⏲8am-9pm) Steering just clear of serious tackiness, Mustafa has made more effort than most Karakol eateries to create a sense of style – a mish-mash with Islamic imagery, cases of Soviet badges, mirror walls and faux beam-work. Local delicacies are good value and attractively presented, but service is sweetly incompetent. The all-Cyrillic menu's humorous tone makes it all the harder for foreigners to decipher.

Lovely Pizza PIZZA, SUSHI **$$**
(Tynystanov near Moskovskaya; pizza 200-360som, sushi per piece 35som; ⏲9am-11pm) Karakol's best pan-pizza is served in a slightly scrappy summer yard or in the small, oh-so-pink cocktail bar area with its pearl-effect settee seating. *Kalyan* (water-pipes) to smoke from 250som.

Maximum RESTAURANT **$$**
(126 Toktogul; mains 90-170som; ⏲10am-11.30pm) Cavernous restaurant with a few *shyrdaks* to enliven the walls. Good *azu* (fried beef and onions in sauce on a bed of fries) and *oromo* (plate-sized mostly vegetable-filled giant pasta circles). Sometimes turns disco.

Fakir Café INTERNATIONAL **$$**
(☎510 88; Jaldosh Jusaev (Gorkogo); meals 110-250som; ⏲8am-10pm; 📋) Large and clean, if rather sterile, Fakir makes up for its lack of visual appeal with an inventive, multi-cuisine menu and English-speaking staff.

Kalinka RUSSIAN **$$**
(☎055-558 7870; Jusup Abdrakhmanov 99; blinis 40-70som, meals 125-255som; ⏲10am-10pm; 📋) From the outside, this pretty chocolate-box house looks delightful, but the pop-blasted interior is less appealing and you might wait a long time for the creditable Russian food to arrive... bring some reading material. Menu partly translated.

Drinking & Nightlife

Karakol Coffee COFFEE
(www.facebook.com/karakolcoffee; Toktogul 112a; coffee 70-110som, sandwich 70-150som; ⏲9am-10pm) Karakol's first barista-savvy venue for a well-turned caffeine fix is now a cult traveller hangout. English spoken.

Shopping

★OVOP LOCAL PRODUCTS, CRAFTS
(One Village One Product; ☎543 57; Toktogul; ⏲9am-6pm) Beautifully presented selection of locally sourced products including delicious barberry and apricot juices from Jeti-Öghüz, natural soaps from Tasma, threadless slippers, beeswax candles, silk-felt hybrid products, toys, hats and more.

Kürk Art Gallery SOUVENIRS
(Lenina 152, Makish Bazaar) Many of the most artistically imaginative *shyrdaks* that you see around town are created by this family company, which has several small workshops tucked into the moldering buildings behind the contrastingly spruce shop.

Information

INTERNET ACCESS

Several accommodations and eateries now have free wi-fi. Internet clubs are reasonably common including one at IGPA (p263).

Vista (Tynystanova 23; per hr 30som; 10am-10pm; wi-fi) Friendly, central place near the university.

MEDICAL SERVICES

Karakol Medical Clinic (513 23; Jusup Abdrakhmanov; 8am-5pm) Clinic with a pharmacy on the ground floor.

MONEY

There are several moneychangers along Toktogul, including banks with ATMs accepting Visa cards. However, the nearest ATM for MasterCard or Maestro is in Cholpon-Ata.

RSK Bank (Toktogul; 8.30am-noon & 1-3pm Mon-Fri) Changes US dollars into som and has a Visa ATM.

TOURIST INFORMATION

CBT (550 00, after hr 055-515 0795; cbtkarakol@gmail.com; Jusup Abdrakhmanov 123/20; 9am-noon & 1pm-5pm daily summer, til 4pm Mon-Sat in winter) Genial Azamat is knowlegeable and extremely helpful when answering questions and helping you find the activity, accommodation or trek that suits. As well as homestay options in town, CBT can organise seasonal yurtstays (from mid-June) at Jeti-Öghüz, the Bel-Tam lakeside and Karkara along with excursions, guides, equipment and advice on permits.

TIC (Tourist Information Centre; 523 41; tourinfocentre@gmail.com; Jusup Abdrakhmanov 130; 9am-5pm Mon-Fri, 9am-2pm Sat) Run by student volunteers from the next-door language faculty, this handy office sells 100som city maps, postcards (25som) and has stacks of brochures and information booklets on various accommodation and eating choices.

TRAVEL & TOUR AGENCIES

IGPA (Issyk-Köl Guides & Porters Association; 529 29, Aygula 055-255 2529; www.kyrgyz-tours.info; Lenina 130/1; 9am-9pm) This cooperative of young guides can arrange treks with English, French or German interpreters. Also leads five-day mountain-biking trips to Barskoön via Saruu, Juuku Pass and Ara-Bel Valley (you must bring your own bike). The office is an internet cafe. Aygula speaks English.

Turkestan (054-391 1452, www.turkestan.biz; Toktogul 273) Turkestan specialises in group trekking, has an 'indestructible' Ural 6WD truck-bus and is the local agent for helicopter flights to the Inylchek base camps. Also runs mountaineering trips to Khan

GREAT GAMER

Karakol's Soviet-era name, Prezevalsk, honoured the great explorer Nikolai Przewalski, who died nearby.

Born in Smolensk on 12 April 1839, Przewalski joined the Imperial army but was reputedly unhappy as a young officer. However, he persuaded them that he'd make a better explorer and set off to explore the Ussuri River region in the Russian Far East from 1867 to 1869. Funding proved insufficient but, undeterred, Przewalski managed to cover the costs by raising 12,000 roubles in a poker match. The results of the expedition impressed everyone. The Russian Geographical Society agreed to help finance future trips, and the army gave him the time he needed in return for debriefing him on his return from each trip making him, in effect, an army agent. He never married, going on instead to become a major general and the most honoured of all the tsarist explorers. He focused on Central Asia, launching four major expeditions in 15 years, mainly to Mongolia, Xinjiang and Tibet. On one of his journeys, he discovered the tiny steppe-land horse that now bears his name – Przewalski's horse. You can see a pair of them at Karakol zoo (p259).

During 1888, while preparing for the last of these trips, he unwisely drank the Chuy River water while hunting tigers near Bishkek (then Pishpek). The result was a bout of typhus. He was bundled off to Lake Issyk-Köl for rest and treatment, but realising his imminent demise he wrote to the tsar asking to be buried beside the lake, clothed in full explorer's dress. His grave site at Pristan is now home to a Przewalski museum (p259).

Tengri, heli-skiing, horse treks into the Küngey Ala-Too mountains and visits to eagle hunters. Contact Sergey Pyshnenko.

Yak Tours (☎569 01; yaktours@infotel.kg; Gagarin 10) Backpacker-oriented Altyn-Arashan specialists. English-speaking Valentin Derevyanko ferries masochists to Altyn-Arashan in his 50-year-old 4WD, a mechanical marvel that's in a constant state of running repair. Yak Tours can make on-the-spot arrangements for individual treks and horse trips. Prices are reasonable but be sure to pin down exactly what's included.

Tour Khan Tengri (☎055-047 6606, 525 43; www.tour-khantengri.com; Lenina 114) This experienced outfitter has a well-established trekking and climbing camp located in the Inylchek Valley. Hunting options available mid-August til November.

Alp Tour Issyk-Köl (☎205 48; khanin@infotel.kg; Telmona 154-158) Based in the same building as Karakol's best-equipped (and most visually striking) mountaineering-equipment shop, this professional company offers a range of treks, serious climbs and transfers. Contact Igor.

Getting There & Away

Use the Main Bus Station for Bishkek or Almaty, the Southern Bus Stand for towns along the south side of Issyk-Köl. Marshrutka services from either station run to Balykchy, where passengers for Naryn and Kochkor need to change.

BUSES TO BISHKEK & ALMATY VIA THE NORTHERN SHORE

Buses to Bishkek (300som, eight hours) depart hourly from the **Main Bus Station** (☎229 11; Przhevalskogo; 🚌110, 111) between 7.30am and 1.40pm, and overnight between 7pm and 11pm. Most take the northern route around Issyk-Köl, via Cholpon-Ata (100som). Outside the station, untimetabled minibuses and shared taxis leave when full to Bishkek (minibus/shared taxi 300/600som) and Cholpon-Ata (minibus/shared taxi 120/250som). In summer a daily bus runs to Almaty via Bishkek (not the Karkara Valley).

BUSES TO BALYKCHY VIA THE SOUTHERN SHORE

Buses for Balykchy (200som) via Bokonbayevo (100som) depart from the **Southern Bus Stand** (☎513 53; Toktogul) hourly from 7.50am to 12.50pm, and at 2.50pm. Buses to Bokonbayevo depart at 4.50pm. All pass within 3km of Tamga and Barskoön (80som), but there are direct services to Tamga (80som) at 1pm and 3pm, and to Barskoön at 9.20am, noon and 4pm.

REGIONAL DESTINATIONS

Most local buses leave from one of three points around Ak-Tilek Bazaar. Shared taxis use the same points.

Ak-Suu Marshrutka 350 (20som, several per hour) from the southeast side.

Jeti-Ögüz From the **south corner**, marshrutkas to Jeti-Ögüz village run roughly hourly when full (marshrutka 371, 20som) but rarely before 10am. Marshrutka 355 to Jeti-Ögüz Korort departs once, possibly twice daily, typically late morning and possibly mid-afternoon. Shared taxis cost 30som but sometimes ask 50som.

Tüp area West corner. Rickety buses to San-Tash leave twice daily, around 8am and again around 2pm.

Pristan Buses marked Plazh or Dachy leave roughly hourly from the **corner of Gagarin and Jaldosh Jusaev (Gorkogo)** and pass within 200m of the Przewalski Garden (p259).

Getting Around

MARSHRUTKA

Almost all of the dozen lines pass Ak-Tilek Bazaar on Torgoeva. Useful routes (7som, from 7am to dusk) include:

- **101** Torgoeva–Toktogul–Jaldosh Jusaev (Gorkogo) then southwest on Karasayev and down Fuchika almost to the gates of the national park. Same in reverse.
- **102** Northwest down Gebze, Toktogul, Torgoeva then a one-way loop passing the animal market northbound.
- **111** Loops from Main Bus Station via Ak-Tilek Bazaar, Southern Bus Stand, Madanur Hotel then round the south edge of town then back via Kutmanalieva.
- **110** Route 111 in reverse.

TAXI

For trips within town, taxis including **Narodnoe** (☎403 03) and **Econom** (☎166) charge 50/60som by day/night. Going further afield, be sure to fix the fare and waiting time (100som per hour is normal). It's best to call for a taxi.

There are several taxi stations dotted about town, or wave one down on Toktogul near Makish Bazaar. Ak-Tilek Bazaar tends to be better for longer-distance shared taxis.

BICYCLE

Teskey Guesthouse (p260) and Ecotrek (p269) both have a couple of mountain bikes for rent (US$10 per day).

LOCAL KNOWLEDGE

THE WORLD'S WORST ROAD?

'Russian military jeeps are the best in the world. So we had to make roads dreadful enough to test them.' Thus jokes our weatherbeaten driver Viktor as he squirms his UAZ 4WD through axle-deep mud, crying 'Mamma Mia' at every new tyre-crashing challenge. The vehicle lumbers over football-sized boulders, between stacks of pine-debris, through gushing streams and over treacherously re-frozen snow patches. He reaches for his inhaler as we all join in to crow-bar away half a ton of rock that has fallen across the middle of the roadway. Eventually, despite his endless heroics, the 4WD is finally defeated by an impassable mudhole. But we're barely a kilometre short of the valley lip and wave him farewell as he returns to face the whole odyssey again, this time alone.

Around Karakol

Altyn-Arashan Алтын-Арашан

Probably the most popular destination from Karakol is a spartan hot-spring development called Altyn-Arashan (Golden Spa), set in a postcard-perfect alpine valley at 3000m, with 4260m Pik Palatka looming at its southern end.

Much of the area is a botanical research area called the Arashan State Nature Reserve, which is home to about 20 snow leopards and a handful of bears, although the only animals you're likely to see are the horses and sheep belonging to local families.

During Soviet times it is rumoured that 25 snow leopards were trapped here and shipped to zoos around the world until Moscow cancelled all collecting and hunting permits in 1975.

Altyn-Arashan has several small **hot-spring developments** (admission 200som). Natural hot water flows into a series of concrete pools enclosed by wooden sheds. The pools reek of sulphur but there is a translated certificate pinned to the door extolling the curative properties of these waters and listing, in exhaustive detail, the diseases they will cure.

Each shed is lockable and you can get the key from the house closest to whichever shed you select. It is a great way to relax and it's almost mandatory to run, screaming, into the icy river afterwards.

From the springs it's about a five-hour walk on foot to the snout of the Palatka Glacier, wrapped around Pik Palatka.

Sleeping & Eating

Altyn-Arashan is not a village and its half-dozen houses are not permanently inhabited, though the two lodges (Yak Tours and Arashan) usually have a caretaker in residence and Yak Tours' claims to open year-round. Pitching your tent near one of the lodges usually carries a 100som charge. Lodges serve meals for pre-booked guests and in mid-summer either place might be able to sell non-guests a few food items but it's wise to carry your own food (and water purifying tablets). Either place can organise guides and horses (per hour 100som).

Yak Tours Lodge MOUNTAIN LODGE
(☎039-226 0298; www.altyn-arashan.com; dm/d 250/500som, incl 3 meals 750/1500som) The communal lounge has an atmospheric open fire and tree-trunk support, and the glass-fronted veranda has a single hammock from which to gaze at the view. Rooms are simple and toilets outside are fairly frightening. When the guide, Valentin, stays, the food is excellent. When he's not there things are hit and miss: check whether indeed there will be any food available. The lodge has its own hot-springs bath around 400m upstream (non-guests 100som) and more attractive luke-warm outdoor pools hidden downstream.

Arashan Lodge MOUNTAIN LODGE
(☎039-486 0034; dm incl hot pool usage 500som) The advantage of Arashan Lodge, around 200m beyond Yak Tours', is that there's a hot-pool right on site, but the box-toilets aren't great and the dorm rooms are tightly packed with basic spring camping beds. In mid-summer Arashan's kitchen bakes its own bread but off peak there is not likely to be any food available at all.

Getting There & Away

From Karakol, agencies – notably Yak Tours (p265) – and some independent drivers, including **Viktor Ilin** (☎0555-468255, 704 73, 719 41;

Around Karakol

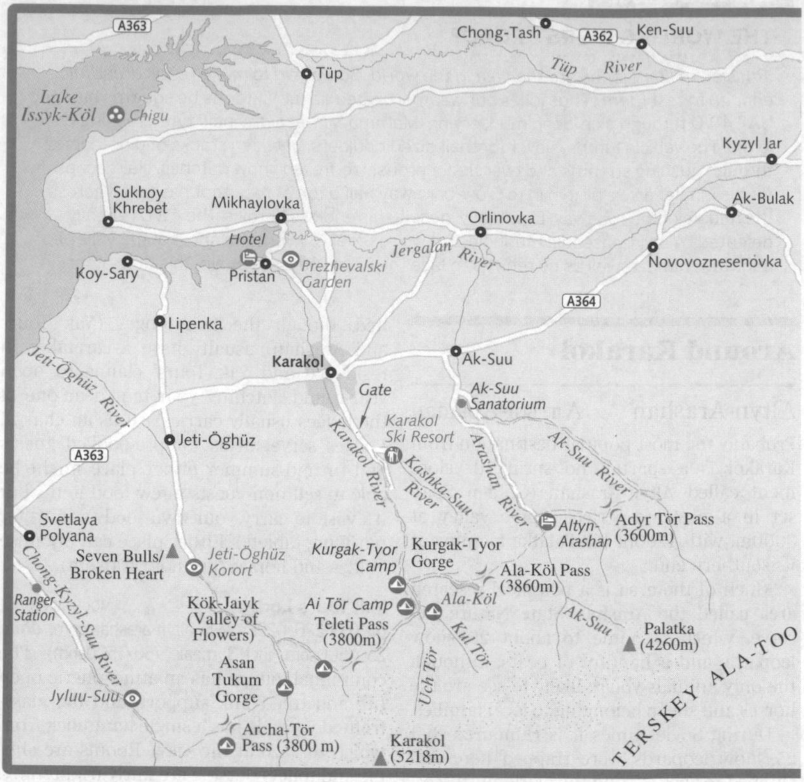

Karakol), offer 4WD transport for 3000som per vehicle (or 300som per person should a pre-arranged vehicle be going anyway). But before booking a transfer, read on.

Around 12km east of central Karakol by good, asphalt road is the Ak-Suu Sanatorium ('*korort*'), terminus of frequent Ak-Suu marshrutka 350 (last return 6pm winter, 8pm summer). From here, Altyn-Arashan is 14km away, using the lane that branches south some 200m before the main sanatorium entrance. This lane degrades into a contender for the world's worst motorable road (p265). When smoothed by winter snows, or when dry and cleared of rocks in mid-summer, you might find that judgement slightly overblown, but in our experience it is simply more pleasant to walk – and the roughly five hours up, 3½ hours back isn't necessarily that much slower than driving. The track is easy to follow. Cross the river after 3km then ignore all further bridges; at 12km from the *kurort* keep left (up, away from the river). There is one small hikers' short cut (where the road does a double hair-pin) but otherwise you'll follow the 4WD tracks all the way. The first half is mostly along the riverside with pine clad slopes towering above. After around 8km there are more views of white-tops, but only a kilometre before the guesthouses do you really see down into the glorious upland valley with towering peaks all around. You can alternatively hike in to Altyn-Arashan as the climax of several possible treks to/from the Karakol Valley (p269), but you'll need to be prepared for potentially treacherous conditions, high altitudes and stretches of path on precarious scree.

Karakol Valley Ущелье Каракол

Due south of Karakol lies the beautiful Karakol Valley, a national park for which a 250som entry fee is collected from foreigners at the gate.

Activities

Trekking

The valley offers some fine hikes, although you really need to invest in a tent, stove and

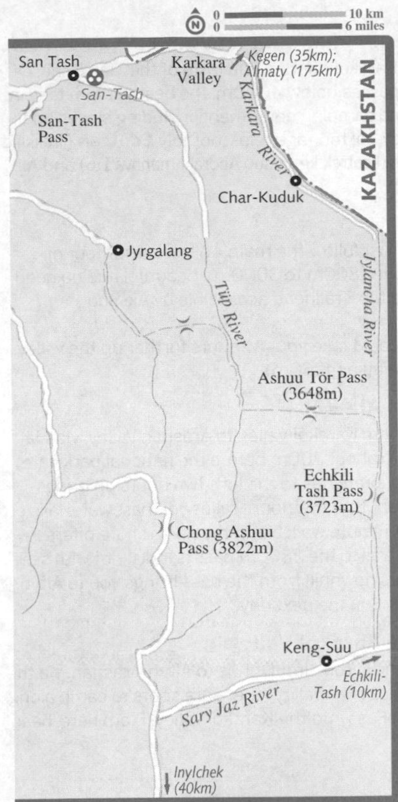

a day's hiking before the valley reveals its charm. Up the main valley, at the junction of several valleys and trekking routes is the Ai Tör camp, run by **Alp Tour Issyk Köl**, with shower, *banya* (US$3), tent sites (100som), mountain rescue, radio service and park permit check.

From May to mid-October you can make a strenuous day hike (or better yet, an overnight camping trip) to a crystal-clear lake called Ala-Köl (3530m). You can also reach this lake in four hours over the ridge from Altyn-Arashan.

Marshrutka 101 from Karakol takes you almost to the park gates.

Skiing

One of Central Asia's top winter-sports playlands has over 20km of pistes and trails, mostly running through coniferous woodlands. The resort has a sledge drag and three decent (second-hand) French chairlifts providing a 740m altitude gain (2300m to 3040m). While obviously weather-dependent, the season usually runs from late November to mid-March. Relatively new rental equipment is available for hire right beside the **lift base** (☎077-253 4081, 514 94; www.karakol-ski.kg; lift pass adult/child 700/500som, ski kit & snowboard rental 400-600som) where there are two similarly priced hotel complexes.

The ski-lift base is about 8km from the southwestern terminus of marshrutka 101. Go through the national park barrier (outside ski season you'll have to pay the 250som park fee), then fork left after 3km beside the isolated **Jaisan Hotel** (☎055-001 4400; Karakol Valley; dm/tr/q 2000/2400/3200som; ⏲variable). A taxi to the lift station costs 500som up, 400som back.

Sleeping

Of the two hotel complexes located at the ski-life base, the better option is **Kapriz** (☎055-190 5175; www.kapriz.kg/kapriz-karakol; d/ste from US$55/110, peak season US$110/160; ⏲Nov-Mar & Jun–mid-Sep). It has unexpectedly stylish rooms in a 21st-century pyramid building accessed through a tunnel beneath the main piste-end. One cheaper guesthouse, **Gostevoy Dom Tumar** (☎055-522 2576; Karakol Ski Resort; tw/tr from 1200/1800som), is around 1km back down towards Karakol at the first hairpin.

Karakol Ski Lodge SKI LODGE **$$**
(Korpus 1 d/ste US$70/100, apt/villa US$100/520; ⏲Nov-Mar & Jun–late-Sep) The ski-lift owners also operate a multi-building lodge with a range of standard rooms plus four-room chalet-style luxury villas tucked into the forest right behind the ski lift. Korpus 2 has a billiard room and restaurant.

Jeti-Ögüz Джети-Огуз

Counterpointing striking red-rock bluffs, pine forests, upland *jailoo* meadows and a soaring alpine backdrop, the Jeti-Öghüz area makes a charming day trip from Karakol or a good starting point for summer-only hikes including taxing multi-day treks to Altyn-Arashan and Ala-Köl (p269).

Sights & Activities

For a quick, easy excursion, come and point your camera at the Seven Bulls for which the whole area is named. To make the experience last a day or two, head up to Kök-Jaiyk by 4WD or on foot.

TREKKING AROUND KARAKOL

The Terskey Ala-Too range that rises behind Karakol offers a fine taste of the Tian Shan. Of the numerous possible routes that climb to passes below 4000m, the best of them take in the alpine lake Ala-Köl. A range of trekking and camping equipment, including stoves and tents, can be rented from CBT (p263) and several tour agencies, notably **Ecotrek** (Trekking Workers Association; ☎070-951 1155, 511 15; www.ecotrek.kg; Jusup Abdrakhmanova 116) and Alp Tour Issyk-Köl (p264).

Ak-Suu Village to Altyn-Arashan

To get from Ak-Suu Village to Altyn-Arashan, just follow the main 4WD track for four or five hours. Easy, despite the great altitude gain (1800m to 3000m), beautiful and no need to carry heavy gear as there are lodges at the top. Trailhead accessible by Ak-Suu marshrutka.

A day-hike extension from Altyn-Arashan could take you 4½ hours further up the valley, branching east and then south for views of Palatka (4260m).

Karakol Valley to Arashan Valley, via Ala-Köl

You'll need a minimum of two nights to hike from Karakol Valley to Arashan Valley, via Ala-Köl. Hike up from the end of the bus 101 route (about 200m before the national park gate) for about six hours to where the Ala-Köl Valley branches to the left. Two hours up brings you to the carved wooden Kurgak Tor camp; another five hours takes you past waterfalls to the high-altitude, barren Ala-Köl lake. A 30-minute walk along the north shore offers camping at the base of the Ala-Köl Pass. The trail to the 3860m pass is indistinct with seriously scary sections on loose scree. Five hours downhill from the pass brings you to Altyn-Arashan, from where you can hike down to Ak-Suu the next day.

Jeti-Öghüz to Altyn-Arashan, via the Karakol Valley

Set aside a minimum of four or five nights to hike from Jeti-Öghüz to Altyn-Arashan, via the Karakol Valley. The trail heads up the Jeti-Öghüz river valley (there are spots to camp along the way), crossing east over the 3800m Teleti Pass into the Karakol Valley. From here, head

Seven Bulls ROCK FORMATION

One of Kyrgyzstan's most photographed natural features, the Seven Bulls (Jeti-Öghüz) is an abrupt serrated ridge of ferric-red sandstone cliffs that have been vertically diced into a series of rounded bluffs. The formation isn't especially big, but it looks particularly striking in late spring when the rock's rosy colours contrast with the surrounding green fields and hills. The ridge rises directly north of the Soviet-era sanatorium, Jeti-Öghüz Korort. For the best view, walk 10 minutes up a ridge-track doubling back behind the pair of shops where the access road's asphalt stops. From this viewpoint you can also look southeast into the deep-cut **Valley of Dragons** (Ushchelie Drakonov), a less colourful feature but photogenic for its heavily wind-sculpted sides.

Seen from the north side, the Seven Bulls ridge appears largely tree-covered with only the deepest crevice of red-rock visible. From this view the ridge goes by the alternative name **Broken Heart** (Razbitoye Sertse) and is associated with many tragic, if romantic, legends.

Kök-Jaiyk LANDSCAPE

(Valley of Flowers) From Jeti-Öghüz Kurort, an unpaved road (impassable with snow from November to March or later) climbs through a dainty pine-dappled valley, crossing and recrossing a gurgling stream on four log bridges. It emerges after around 4km onto a grassy mountainside with joyous Sound-of-Music views. Looking south, Alpine peaks form a splendid horizon across the deep, wide Kök-Jaiyk (Valley of Flowers) that falls away in front of you. If you're walking from (and back to) Jeti-Öghüz in one day, use the limited time to explore the first area of mountain-view pastures. However, with more time, or given a decent 4WD, you could descend steeply into the bigger transverse valley, then head right towards the (hard-to-find) waterfall or left across the up to Ala-Köl, and then over to Altyn-Arashan and Ak-Suu. There are some tough sections; it's not for beginners!

Kyzyl-Suu to Altyn-Arashan, via the Jeti-Öghüz & Karakol Valleys

To hike from Kyzyl-Suu to Altyn-Arashan, via the Jeti-Öghüz and Karakol Valleys, you'll need to set aside at least six to eight nights. From Kyzyl-Suu head up the Chong-Kyzyl-Suu Valley to the Jyluu-Suu hot springs or on to a camp site below the 3800m Archa-Tör Pass. The next day cross the pass, head down the Asan Tukum Gorge into the Jeti-Öghüz Valley. From here it's over the Teleti Pass to the Karakol Valley and to Ala-Köl, Altyn-Arashan and Ak-Suu.

Extending Your Trek

You can combine any number of these parallel valleys to make as long a trek as you like. You can also add on wonderful radial hikes up the valleys, for example from Altyn-Arashan to Pik Palatka or up the Kul Tör Valley at the head of the Karakol Valley for views of Karakol Peak (5218m).

There are also longer, more technical variations of these routes that should not be attempted without a knowledgeable guide and some experience with glacier walking.

When to Go

The trekking season around Karakol normally runs from late June to early October. August is a popular time for picking mushrooms; blackcurrants are in season in September. For Altyn-Arashan only, you could go as early as May or as late as the end of October, but nights drop below freezing then and the surrounding mountain passes are snowed over.

Weather is the region's biggest danger, with unexpected chilling storms, especially in May, June, September and October. Streams are in flood in late May and early June; plan crossings for early morning when levels are lowest.

Maps

The 1:100,000 *South-East Issyk-Köl Lake Coast Trekking Map* is sold by the TIC (p263) in Karakol and GeoID (p244) in Bishkek for 250som.

'Fifth Bridge' continuing several kilometres into the heart of the Valley of Flowers. The name is for a mass of poppies that turn the local *jailoos* red in May.

Sleeping & Eating

From June to early September, a handful of yurt camps appear in Kök Jaiyk, including one at the point where the access lane first emerges onto the upland meadows, and others around the fifth bridge in the valley way below. There's also a small homestay-guesthouse on the southwestern edge of Jeti-Öghüz village. At Jeti-Öghüz Korort, the modest but brand new **Kök Jaiyk House Hotel** (Kachim Kulbayev 9, Jeti-Öghüz Korort) is nearing completion opposite the dreary, but well-located, **Sanatorium** (☎039-469 7711; Jeti-Öghüz Korort; d/tr 784/1176som, lux 1060-1590som), an almost comically stereotypical Soviet affair where dinner is served school-lunch style at 7pm precisely (100som) and various 'treatments' include paraffin-wax compresses, mud-electrocutions, sulphur baths and a kind of blanket mummification procedure (all cost around 100som).

There are two shops, one with a basic cafe, near the sanatorium gates.

Getting There & Away

Public transport is very limited and not timetabled. Marshrutka 355 runs from Jeti-Öghüz Korort to Karakol around 9am, returning around noon (40som, 30km, one hour). It sometimes makes a second trip mid-afternoon.

Marshrutka 371 runs from Jeti-Öghüz village to Karakol several times daily (20som), though the first service rarely travels *from* Karakol before 11am. A shared/private taxi costs 30/200som each way. Be aware that Jeti-Öghüz village, while pleasant and with a fine mountain backdrop, has no sights per se and is 12km north of the Korort, ie 5km south of the Karakol–Tamga main road. Shared taxis between the village and Korort cost 30/120som per person/car. Out of season these only run a few times daily. The village's minibus/

GOLD MINE

Amid eternal snows at a phenomenal 4200m altitude, **Kumtor** (www.kumtor.kg/en) is the world's eighth-largest goldfield and produces an estimated 12% of Kyrgyzstan's GDP. Throughout the summer of 2013 protestors clashed with police while barricading the access road and attempting to cut power supplies to the mine. Local people seemed divided as to which story they believe about the motivations of the protesters. Were they genuinely concerned for better environmental conditions? Was it part of a political move agitating for the mine's nationalisation? Or was this simply an attempt to persuade the mine's owners to spend more money in local communities as retribution for the mine not paying their dues to a major protection racket? Whatever the reality, there are no tours of the mine operations and even getting up onto the higher sections of the access road requires a special invitation to get past the various checkpoints.

shared-taxi stops are easy to spot, within 50m of the new silver-domed mosque.

There's no public transport to Kök-Jaiyk. Walking from the Korort is relatively painless, and in summer a regular taxi can take you the 4km to the main viewpoint saving over an hour's hike. Going further by vehicle usually requires a 4WD due to mud or ice patches. Karakol agencies typically ask 2500som per vehicle for a return 4WD day trip from town, including a guided walk to a hard-to-spot waterfall. Exact costs vary depending on conditions and much of Kök-Jaiyk is likely to be entirely inaccessible before mid-April.

Southern Issyk-Köl

There's much dispute as to whether the northern or southern route around Issyk-Köl is the more scenic. Traditionally Western visitors have tended to err in favour of the less busy southern road, especially in summer when it is spared the heaviest tourist traffic en route to the Cholpan-Ata resorts. However, only relatively limited sections of the route have any real lake view – notably between Tamga and Tosor and between Km102 and Km 95 (east of Ton).

Barskoön & Tamga

Барскаун и Тамга

☎3946

This area makes a good all-round base for visiting the south coast of Issyk-Köl, with excellent horse-trekking and hiking routes in the mountains behind Barskoön, decent beaches at Tosor, and a choice of homestays in attractive Tamga. However, transport is still somewhat fiddly and out of season almost all accommodation will be closed or entirely full with long-term resident Russian athletes on winter training programmes.

The area's most illustrious historical resident was the 11th-century Mahmud al-Kashgari, the author of the first-ever comparative dictionary of Turkic languages, *Divan Lughat at-Turk* (A Glossary of Turkish Dialects), written in Baghdad from 1072 to 1074. Locals insist that there was a city of nearly 100,000 people here before the whole site was razed by a grandson of Chinggis Khan. In the 20th century the area was a military staging point in an era of Soviet–Chinese border skirmishes while Tamga became an exclusive sanatorium town for elite officers of the Red Army.

BARSKOÖN

Architecturally forgettable Barskoön (Barskaun in Russian) isn't a destination in itself but is a useful starting point for South Issyk-Köl's best horse treks. And if you're driving past it's worth the minor detour from the main road into Barskoön town to visit the yurt factory.

A pioneer of eco-tourism long before the concept was so named, **Shepherds Way** (☎66 13 92, Bishkek (Ishen) 077-251 8315; www.kyrgyztrek.com) is a professional local company, run by a former shepherding family, organising horse treks into the mountains behind Barskoön. Ishen speaks excellent English. Female guides and cooks are available on request. Shepherds Way has its own **guesthouse** (☎077-212 4144; Podgornaya 35, Barskoön; B&B 850som, full-board 1300som) tucked away from the main village with a large yard, dining yurt, hot showers, sauna and English-speaking staff. Make arrangements in advance as they are not used to walk-in clients.

The **Ak Örgö Yurt Workshop** (☎077-306 4137, 267 54; mekenbek_1958@mail.ru; Lenin 93) became famous after one of its products won the 'most beautiful yurt' competition at the 1995 'Manas 1000' festival and had its work exhibited in Russia, the UK and US. However, it was almost bankrupted when a luxurious US$50,000 yurt ordered for President Bakiev was never paid for given the president's sudden ousting in the 2010 revolution. If you speak Russian, it's fascinating to hear more of these stories, and see the machines used for felt-cutting and wood-bending, though operation depends greatly on the state of orders. Coming from Karakol, take the first Barskoön turn and the workshop (signed 'Tegirmen') is 2.9km up the main road on the right. Contact Mekenbek Osmonaliev.

BARSKOÖN VALLEY

By far the easiest way to get deep into the appealing alpine landscapes behind southern Issyk-Köl is driving up the wide, well-maintained, unpaved truck road that leads all the way to the controversial Kumtor Gold Mine, turning south off the coast road at Km140/80. If you go too far you'll need permits and invitations, but an uncontroversial compromise is stopping after 21km for the **Barskoön Waterfalls**, 2km beyond a curious **truck-on-a-plinth** monument. The smaller, more accessible waterfall is reached within 15 minutes' walk, close to a small **bust of Yuri Gagarin**. The upper falls are distantly visible through the pine trees nearby, but getting there takes a couple of hours' scramble.

In summer, *kymys* is sold from yurts in this area. A return taxi from Tamga costs around 1000som to the waterfall area, 2500/5000som in summer/winter to the 3619m Barskoön Pass. Be aware that on 'transport days', the road becomes a conveyer belt of trucks bringing deliveries to/from the gold mine and the resultant dust clouds undermine any pleasure of a visit, so check locally before arranging a trip.

TAMGA

With a scattering of Russian-style 'gingerbread' cottages, quiet little Tamga is a little more attractive than most of the region's villages. On the hill at the back of town there's a fascinating local **cemetery**. Yurt-shaped grave-frames make photogenic foregrounds for sunset views with Lake Issyk-Köl in the middle-distance.

In the valleys behind Tamga it's possible to trek around 6km to a Tibetan 'Om' inscription on a rock known as **Tamga Tash** but you'll need local help to find it. The Tamga Guesthouse arranges one- to three-day treks or horse trips up to the Tamga Gorges or Ochincheck Lake, or a four-day trip to Chakury Köl at a lofty 3800m.

Tamga is around 2km off the main lakeside road using a road that's marked by a Soviet-era **plane on a plinth** above Km135.6/84.4. Several homestays are on Ozyornaya, the first street to the right once you come into the urban area. About 300m beyond, beside a handful of shops, Issyk-Kulskaya also leads right, forming a de-facto main street with a vaguely Wild-West feel; it reaches a dead end at the sanatorium complex. Though today it's rather down-market, locals are proud of the fact that the world's first cosmonaut, **Yuri Gagarin**, once holidayed here.

Run by a friendly Russian couple, popular **Tamga Guesthouse** (☎253 33; tamgahouse@gmail.com; Ozyornaya 3, Tamga; per person incl breakfast 750som; ⊙May-Oct) sits behind daunting green gates hiding a lovely rear garden. Dinner (250som) is less impressive.

Behind red gates with a green door, **Flora Guesthouse** (☎053-470 0179; Issykkulskaya 19; per person/full-board 250/800som) is a traditional house with an orchard garden in which four simple new guest rooms have been built. Unheated but open from April. Beside the post office shack.

Kuznetsova Homestay (☎253 86; Ozyornaya 12; dm 550-700som, full board 1250som), a relatively new family home, has heating, showers and sit-down toilets, and is one of the only homestays to stay open year-round, though in winter all 12 beds may be full with training Russian sportsmen.

TOSOR ТОСОР

With a grid of unpaved streets leading 1km down to a wide, slightly fly-blown beach, Tosor (Km125 to Km127) is a relatively uncommercial place to stay close to the waterside. The main village shop is a tragi-comic Soviet throwback.

Altyn Kum (☎077-271 6663; cholponordobaeva@rambler.ru; Tosor Beach; per person incl breakfast/full board 600/1000som) is a seasonal tourist yurt-camp at the eastern end of the village beach.

Behind Asema Koyshebayeva's large green-roofed new house are a new set of guest rooms with sauna under construction. **Asema's Guesthouse** (☎077-762 5800; Urozbakova; dm 400-500som, full board 1200som; @) has a big sitting room, and hot showers are shared by five rooms. The family have two cars available for excursions. It's located well down the easternmost road leading from the A363 to the beach. Open year-round but often full with sportsmen in winter.

SKAZKA **УЩЕЛЬЕ 'СКАЗКА'**

The **Skazka Valley** is an area of bare red earth eroded into photogenic corridors, paws and spires of rosy rock. It's hardly Bryce Canyon but it makes a colourful curiosity when deserted in April. In mid-summer the area can be rather overloaded with picnickers. The site is 2.2km off the A363 at Km120, on a rough but drivable track. If you're walking back from Skazka to Tosor there's a short cut through the valley to the northeast that emerges eventually around Km122, 1km west of the roadside Ton Aimagy monument with its wide lake views. Don't try this walk in reverse without a guide.

Getting There & Away

Karakol–Balykchy and Karakol–Bishkek minibuses pass through Tosor but bypass both Barskoön and Tamga by a couple of kilometres each. You'll often need to walk or hitch that last section. However, direct marshrutkas do leave from Tamga at around 8am and 9am to Karakol, plus at 7am to Bishkek. There are also a few direct services from Barskoön. There are no regular taxis but most homestays can rapidly find you a vehicle to visit local sights.

Bokonbayevo, Kadji-Sai & Around

There are attractive red-rock spires at Km101, counterpointed with the derelict Agat mini-resort across the road on the beach. That's around 3km west of the turnoff to the former uranium-mining town of **Kadji-Sai** (4km south of Km104) where homestay-guesthouses include **Zina's** (☎921 37; Sportivnaya 6), run by eagle hunter Ishenbek. Meeting another eagle hunter, **Talgart** (Berkutchi Talgar; photo/demonstration from 500/3000som), is the main reason most travellers consider stopping in the south coast's biggest town, **Bokonbayevo**, and there's a mid-August **Birds of Prey Festival** (admission 600som) at Bel Tam, a yurt-camp complex near the lakeside 1km north of Ton. Bokonbayevo's **CBT** (☎077-797 0767; Bolot Mambetov; ⏲9am-5pm) can provide details of local treks, homestays and various other yurtstays. Some yurts run by Ecotour (p246) can be found further inland at Temir Kanat

CENTRAL TIAN SHAN **ЦЕНТРАЛЬНЫЙ ТЯНЬ-ШАНЬ**

Tian Shan means 'Celestial Mountains' in Chinese and the range does indeed achieve a most heavenly majesty at Kyrgyzstan's easternmost tip. Here, a knot of immense summits culminate in 7439m Pik Pobedy (Victory Peak), the second-highest peak in the former USSR. But though it's slightly shorter, the gracious pyramidal form of 7010m Khan Tengri (Sky Ruler) makes it possibly the most stunningly beautiful of all the region's peaks. Locals call it 'Blood Mountain' due to a crimson hue it often adopts at sunset.

Though reported by 7th-century Chinese explorer Xuan Zang, Khan Tengri was not climbed until 1931 (by a Ukrainian team). Rumbling westwards from both sides of the mountain is the 60km-long Inylchek (Engilchek) Glacier embracing an entire rampart of giant peaks and tributary glaciers. North of where the two arms meet, iceberg-filled lakes are named after Austrian explorer Gottfried Merzbacher who happened upon the lower one in 1903. What makes the lakes unusual is that most summers in early August, their ice banks burst, sending a flood of icy water exploding down into the Inylchek River below.

The central Tian Shan is Central Asia's premier territory for serious trekking and mountaineering. But beware:

- The area is likely to be inaccessible outside July and August.
- You'll need a border zone permit (issued by tour agencies or through CBT (p263) in Karakol but allow time).
- There is almost zero local population so don't expect homestays or hitch-hiking possibilities.
- Unless you are flying in and out by helicopter, getting anywhere near Khan Tengri will require some glacier walking.
- Build in plenty of extra time for bad weather and landslides.

and Tuura-Su village at the west end of the Kongur Ölön Valley. These well-maintained camps offer solar-heated showers, guided horse treks and cultural activities.

At Km59.7, some 28km west of Bokonbayevo, a very rough track takes surprisingly large numbers of local tourists to **Shor-Köl** (aka Tuz-Köl), a small lake so salty that one floats, Dead Sea–style. An associated mud bath adds to the fun. Some of the more attractive roadside scenery in this area is around appealing **Bar-Bulak**.

CENTRAL KYRGYZSTAN

The mountainous heart of Kyrgyzstan offers travellers unrivalled opportunities to explore *jailoos* on foot, horseback or by 4WD. At every turn you will find a family offering to put you up for the night or a group of herdsmen who will eagerly invite you into their yurt for a cup of tea and a bowl of fresh *kymys*. Hospitality is heartfelt, but don't be annoyed if they then sometimes ask for money – NGOs have been persuading locals that travellers should contribute!

The central gem around which the region's tourism revolves is mesmerising Lake Song-Köl. It's a very special place, but don't overlook the crucial fact that the lake is frozen until late spring. Snow is possible year-round and the signature yurts don't appear until June, so timing is everything.

The main access hub for Song-Köl is Kochkor (plus Jumgal/Kyzart) and, to a lesser extent, Naryn, which is also a key staging point en route to China using the very scenic but bureaucratically awkward Torugart Pass. Continuing from Kochkor or Naryn to Kazarman and Osh is another summer-only adventure with minimal transport on lonely, scenic, but rough roads that close altogether in winter.

The region's craftsfolk are famed for producing Kyrgyzstan's best-quality felt *shyrdaks*.

Lake Song-Köl

Озеро Сонг-Кель

Distantly ringed by a saw-toothed horizon of peaks, the wide open landscapes of Song-Köl create a giant stage for constant performances of symphonic cloudscapes. Almost 20km across, and fronted by lush summer pastures, the lake's water colour

- You need to be properly equipped against the cold, which is severe at night, even in summer.
- Give yourself plenty of time to acclimatise to the altitude.

Getting There & Away

Trekking agencies operating here include Ak-Sai (p246), Dostuck Trekking (p246), and Edelweiss (p246) in Bishkek; Turkestan (p263) and Alp Tour Issyk-Köl (p264) in Karakol; and Kan Tengri (p68) in Almaty.

Ak-Sai organises a helicopter shuttle every three days or so from Karkara, so even those who don't want to walk can fly right into the centre of the topographic grandeur, landing at South Inylchek Base Camp where several companies have summer huts and camps. A return flight costs €350, or you can combine a one-way flight with a hike in or out.

If you do trek there are two main options, both requiring agency support to guide you over the treacherous glacier terrain on the later stages, keep you in supplies and let you stay in its base camps. The longest but most interesting route, typically taking seven or eight wild days to reach the main Inylchek glacier, starts from Jyrgalang, 70km east of Karakol. Chartering a 4WD to the police checkpost at Echkili-Tash (around five hours' drive from Karakol) saves about three days from this route.

Easier, but still hardly a stroll, is driving to At-Jailoo camp at the base of Nansen Peak, which leaves you just 18km short of the Inylchek Glacier. It takes around two days from At-Jailoo to Merzbacher meadow, a day more to the various base camps, though groups often make a trekking ascent of Mt Diky (4832m) or Pesni Abaji (4901m) en route. For those not wanting to carry camping gear, Ak-Sai has a series of pre-erected tents and huts in strategic spots en route.

changes magically from tropical turquoise to brooding indigo in seconds as the sun flashes or the storms scud by in a vast meteorological theatre. It's a sublime place to watch the sun come up or to gaze into a cold, crystal-clear night sky heavy with countless stars. At 3016m it's too cold for permanent habitation but between June and September, herders' yurts dot the shoreside meadows every kilometre or so. Since many are part of the community tourism schemes, the area offers an unparalleled opportunity for yurtstay visits or multi-yurt hikes and horse treks which can generally be organised at very short notice (though things can get busy mid-August).

Unpaved tracks, often little more than tyre-tracks in the turf, loop around the lake linking the main concentrations of summer yurts. Each grouping is typically known by the name of the valley/stream that runs through it.

Beware that weather is highly unpredictable. Snow can fall at any time so plan accordingly and be aware that July to mid-September is essentially the only season. While diminishing, the area does have a population of wolves, so if camping independently you'd be wise to do so relatively near to established yurt camps.

The lake is huge so before heading out, consider which is the most appropriate area for your needs. For travellers arriving by car from Kochkor, the easiest drop-in yurtstays to access are CBT Naryn's (p281) **south-coast yurts** or the 10 yurtstays at **Batai-Aral**. If trekking without a guide, the **Kyzart–Tuz-Ashu** route is the easiest one-day option while the **Klemche–Jamanechki–Batai-Aral** route makes a good two-day alternative. With a guide, starting from Kyzart or Jumgal then looping around via Tuz-Ashu and Uzbek-Ashu makes a fine two-night out-and-back option. Horses can be rented for any of the above hikes but aren't strictly needed if you've left your main luggage in Kochkor or Naryn and are travelling light between yurtstays.

Sights & Activities

Getting to Song-Köl is a large part of the experience, especially if hiking or riding in. But even when driving, the unpaved road between Sary-Bulak and Ak-Tal crosses a spectacular pass on either side of the lake, the southern road being marginally better surfaced at present.

Once there, typical activities are hiking and horse riding (per hour/day 200/700som, for guide/horse-guide 800/1400som per day) which is easiest to arrange at the tourist-centred camps at Batai-Aral and Jamanechki, though possible at most yurts with negotiation if you speak some Russian/Kyrgyz. Birdlife includes vultures, numerous raptors and waterfowl including the Indian mountain goose. Tourist organisations arrange occasional horse games at the lake.

Sleeping

A great part of the delight of visiting Song-Köl and its environs is staying in a yurt. Essentially there are three types of yurt groupings:

Shepherd Yurts

When you see just a single yurt the chances are that it doesn't generally accept tourist stays, though if you say hello you might find yourself invited for tea, *kymys* or sheep's head snacks. Having presents to hand (chocolates, biscuits, sausage etc) is useful for such occasions.

Yurtstays

Groups of yurts, often forming trios, are affiliated with the community tourism agencies and offer a floor space with padded bed mat, blankets and sheets for 500som (including breakfast) and 250som extra for dinner and tea. Such places are usually run by genuine herders, but the guest yurt is often a little fancier than a regular shepherd yurt and is shared with other travellers, not the family. Booking many such places is impossible due to the lack of telephone signal, and typically it's fine to simply turn up and request a bed. When things get very busy in mid-August, those arriving independently might lose out to a guided group. Choosing where to sleep is more often a matter of location, and is determined by how you are travelling rather than the price or quality, which tends to be relatively uniform. Very few people speak even a word of English so two useful phrases to learn in Kyrgyz are: '*** *bozi kaida?*' (where is *** yurt?) and '*men ushul dirge jatsam bolobu?*' (may I stay here tonight?).

Tour Yurt Camps

A few special yurt camps are set up by tourist companies specifically for pre-booked tour groups. These, like the NoviNomad camp (p245) at Jamanechki, might include a sit-down toilet shack rather than a long-drop and could offer 'private' yurt facilities.

Batai-Aral

The biggest concentration of yurtstays is at Batai-Aral, very close to the water's edge starting around 5km off the Sary-Bulak–Ak-Tal road. Turn off at Ak-Tash Jailoo, km47/43 and cross the muddy ford. The first cluster of yurts is Shepherds' Life affiliated, then come two trios working with Plus Eco, then a kilometre further seven families each with three or four yurts comprise the relatively tight-packed CBT-Kochkor group. At the third-to-last of these, Mirlan Kasmali yev's wife, Cholpon, speaks some English.

Jamanechki

Three hours dawdling anticlockwise along the lakeside from Batai-Aral you'll spy a lonely **stone tomb-tower** across a meandering stream. Following that stream for around a kilometre up into the Jamanechki valley you'll discover many yurts. The first is CBT affiliated. It's just across an ankle-deep ford on the west side of the stream, and belongs to Birdbek Karayev, whose daughter Kanikey speaks some English. On the east side of the stream, just beyond, is the eight-yurt NoviNomad (p245) camp.

Tuz-Ashu

There are five guest yurts around half an hour's walk clockwise around the lakeside from the point at which the Tuz-Ashu 4WD-road descends to the lake. Further west there are reportedly yurts in the Kyzyl-Kyya and Uzbek-Ashu valleys that will accept passing guests.

Kilemche

Steep-sided green *jailoos* fill the Kilemche (Klemche) Valley, which runs parallel to the north shore of Song-Köl. There are three small family yurtstays well up on the south side of the valley, each about 25 minutes' walk from the 'road' from Kyzart, but up separate side valleys. Each is associated with a different base homestay. West to east there's Tynai Asalbekov with Avaz in Kyzart; Marat Japarov with Stalbek in Jumgal/Dostlugu; and Talai Saralayev with Talgart in Kyzart.

Although not on the lake itself, sleeping or arranging lunch at Kilemche makes an excellent addition to the Song-Köl experience. To walk to the lake from here, take the side valley that leads south around 10 minutes' walk east of Marat's yurts. The path seems to fade at first but becomes clearer up higher as you approach the impressive Jalgis-Karagai pass. The lake is visible from the top. Continue straight ahead into the gulley for Tuz-Ashu, or contour diagonally left on the bigger horse-trail for Jamanechki (around four hours' walk from Kilemche).

To reach Kilemche from Kyzart or Jumgal takes between four and five hours on foot or horseback along a well-worn motor-track, or is an 800som taxi ride. Alternatively from the Kochkor–Chayek road at km46 (around 3km east of the Kyzart Pass), there's a delightful if more strenuous five-hour hiking alternative. Head diagonally following tyre-tracks inexorably upwards towards the obvious zig-zags of the sheep-scuffed 3525m Chaar-Archa pass. The pass is topped by a stone inscribed Chölbay Bulagy. The road and path (better) diverge here but later recombine. Follow the obvious trail down to a small metal bridge, cross that, then contour up and around a high bluff on the far side of which you get views over the splendid Kilemche Valley to Tynai's yurts, but first you'll need to veer slightly eastward to cross the river at the valley bottom by the Tash Saray stable complex. One short section of the descent can turn to mud in heavy rain but otherwise the trek is pretty straightforward and magnificently peaceful.

South Coast

Directly accessible from the Kochkor–Ak-Tal road is the ITMC-Tien Shan camp plus a series of yurts affiliated with CBT-Naryn.

Eating

Some yurtstays can whip up a 200som lunch (*tushku tamak*) for passing hikers if you're not in a hurry. All yurtstays offer dinner (*kechki tamak*) to their guests for a similar price. There are absolutely no shops nor anywhere else to purchase food supplies. When trekking to the lake there are some drinkable streams but few springs, so bring water purifying gear.

Getting There & Away

There is no public transport to Song-Köl, traffic is very thin and access routes are generally impassable from November to early May. Kochkor agencies want around 3000som for a vehicle to Batai-Aral or the south-coast yurts (around three hours), a price that would be the same one way or return. Private drivers might charge less and you'll pay less than half if you wait at the lake for a car that's going back empty. But that can sometimes take a day or two even in mid-summer.

CBT (p281) in Naryn have an interesting deal that drives you to the lake and on to Kochkor for the same price as a return trip and allows you to enjoy both the Ak-Tal and Kalmak–Ashu routes.

The cheapest way to reach the lake is to walk in from the north. A taxi from Kyzart to Kilemche costs around 700som if you want to skip part of the hike.

Lake access is also possible via the unpaved Kara-Keche mining road that branches off the Suusamyr road opposite the copper-roofed new mosque in Dikan (aka Bashkuugandy at Km123/99), 14km east of Chayek. This is currently 4WD only, and is in a ragged state with several bridges washed out, though coal trucks pass by every now and again, and self-sufficient cyclists have managed to pedal this way.

Kochkor Кочкор

3535 / POP 14,000 / ELEV 1800M

Four competing community-tourism outfits make Kochkor (Kochkorka in Russian) an eminently practical base from which to visit Song-Köl and other Kyrgyz *jailoos* nearby. Do be aware that such activities are generally only practicable between June and August. The town is not an attraction in its own right, despite a distant backdrop of mountain peaks. It's at its most interesting on Saturday mornings for the **animal bazaar** (Mal Bazaar; 8am-12.30pm Sat). At other times you could nose around the small **museum** (Sapar Alieva 8; admission 50som; 9am-noon & 1-6pm Mon-Fri), admire busts of **Soviet heroes** or, like virtually everyone else in town, congregate at the **bazaar** (Orozbakova).

Sleeping

There are over two dozen homestays in Kochkor, costing 400som to 650som with breakfast. Each is affiliated with at least one of the four community-tourism agencies so it's worth comparing availability and prices at each. If the agencies are closed, most taxi drivers will know a few B&Bs, many of which are 1km south down Shamen and Shopokova or in a southwestern suburb near the stadium.

Shamen 14 HOMESTAY $
(Lola Kurbanova; 077-360 6117; Ömurov, first alley; B&B/dinner 500/250som) Unusually comfortable family home with freshly decorated rooms, Western-style bathroom and a teabed in the walled yard that is big enough to place one or two tents (150som). It's brilliantly central, albeit down an alley that's off-puttingly dark at night (turn at Ömurov 63). Lola's husband, Jusup, offers good-value transport.

Saadogul Guesthouse HOMESTAY $
(077-315 3143; Ömuraliev 27; B&B/dinner 500/250som) Away from the centre but with mountain views from the top of the road and a dining yurt in the yard, this very friendly family-run place has indoor showers and Saadogul's son speaks English.

Tulekeev B&B HOMESTAY $
(055-927 2788; Soltonkulova 19; bed/breakfast/dinner 350/100/200som) A Jailoo-affiliated guesthouse in a two-storey home with hot shower. Curious upstairs decor includes a wolf pelt and hagiographic memorials to the family patriach.

Hotel ROOMS $
(077-877 3360; Ömurov 30; dm/d/q 150/300/600som) Recently repainted but still ultra basic with long-drop behind the willow tree in yard and no shower whatsoever. Entrance on Kasymov.

Eating & Drinking

BNB Stolovaya CENTRAL ASIAN $
(Orozbakova; mains 25-40som; 8am-7.30pm) Fill up for under US$1 at this popular central canteen with a short menu of prepared local standards.

Café Vizit CENTRAL ASIAN $$
(Orozbakova 131; mains 80-180som, garnish 40som; 9am-9pm Mon-Sat, 9am-6pm Sun) Clean and comfortable, if over-bright and often in a hurry to close early, Vizit is still open later than almost anything else in town and is the only Kochkor eatery with a menu in English. The duck *brazier* (sizzler) is excellent and they prepare one veg-and-potato dish that is actually meat-free.

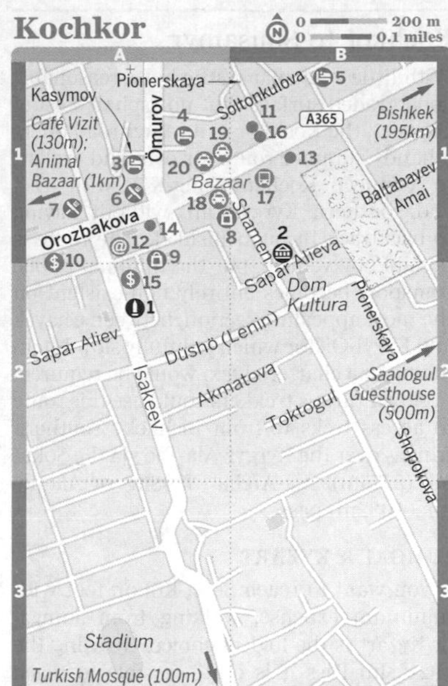

Kochkor

Sights

1 Lenin Statue A2
2 Regional Museum B1

Sleeping

3 Hotel A1
4 Shamen 14 .... A1
5 Tulekeev B&B B1

Eating

6 BNB Stolovaya A1
7 Kafe Azem A1

Shopping

8 Bazaar A1
9 Erkin/Kochkor-Kotu A1

Information

10 Ayylbank A1
11 CBT B1
12 eCenters A1
13 EJT B1
14 Jailoo Tourist Community A1
15 RSK Bank A2
16 Shepherd's Life B1

Transport

17 Marshrutka for Bishkek B1
18 Shared Taxis for Bishkek & Balykchy A1
19 Shared Taxis for Chayek (via Jumgal) A1
20 Shared Taxis to Naryn A1

Kafe Azem CAFE $$
(Isakeev 32; mains 80-140som, garnish 30som; ⏲9am-11pm) Kochkor's grandest venue is primarily a wedding hall but serves a-la-carte when no parties are planned.

Shopping

Kochkor is one of the best places in Kyrgyzstan to buy *shyrdaks*. Both Jailoo (p277) and CBT (p277; Altyn Kol showroom) have selections of naturally dyed felt products

Erkin/Kochkor-Kotu HANDICRAFT
(Women's Cooperative Centre; ☎055-543 5977, Fatima 077-243 5943; Aubakirova 15) Gorgeous collection of local crafts, most for sale, some as 'museum' exhibits inexplicably hidden behind blue gates with red pattern but no sign. Organises culture shows, felt-making displays and has yurts at the back. Theoretically one can sleep in the latter (450som with breakfast) but at present few visitors seem to have taken up the offer.

Information

There's wi-fi access at CBT (p277; per hr 50som) and aging internet computers at **eCenters** (Isakeev 29; per MB 5som; ⏲9am-6pm Mon-Sat) and Jailoo (p277). There are Visa ATMs at **RSK Bank** (Isakaev) and **Ayylbank** (Orozbakova), while on weekends when banks are closed, CBT can change high-vaue US$ and euros at so-so rates.

COMMUNITY-TOURISM OFFICES

What makes Kochkor such an important stop for visitors is that four community-tourism organisations each offer advice, information and a range of services in English. All can arrange homestays both in town and in the surrounding countryside, yurtstays, guides (around 800som), horses (per day 700som), luggage storage and transport. **CBT Kochkor** (☎077-726 5559, 511 14; cbt_kochkor@rambler.ru; Pionerskaya 22A; ⏲9am noon & 1 7pm) is the biggest with the widest network, but **Jailoo** (☎055-549 4203, 077-100 8482; www.jailoo.org; Orozbakova 125/3; ⏲9am-8pm) is often friendlier, slightly cheaper and opens later. Both of these have information offices, giftshops and internet access. Two other outfits, **Shepherds' Life** (p282) and **EJT** (CBT Plus Eco; ☎055-777 0236, 077-251 0628; www.cbtpluseco.kg; Orozbakova) have small box-booths near the bus station, that seem irregularly manned, but once you've found her, Ainoura at Shepherds' Life is helpful and well organised.

Getting There & Away

Many a **marshrutka** passes through Kochkor, mostly Bishkek–Naryn and Bishkek–Chayek services, plus at least one Bishkek–Ming Kush minibus. So it's easy to arrive from Bishkek but, as the majority tend to be full on arrival, it is relatively tough to board here. The only Kochkor-specific services leave the bus station for Bishkek at 9.30am and 3pm, though a 2pm Naryn service is planned for 2014. Buy tickets (150som) one day ahead if possible. Shared taxis leave from various points opposite the bazaar:

- **Bishkek** (250som, 3½ hours)
- **Balykchy** (100som, 40 minutes) For Issyk-Köl
- **Naryn** (250som, three hours)
- **Chayek** (250som, two hours) Mostly late morning.

Jailoo (p277) and **CBT** (p277) can help you organise rides to Song-Köl.

Getting Around

Dial-a-cab rides generally cost 50som within city limits with **Kochkor Taxi** (☎077-231 1511, 077-114 0530) and other firms.

Around Kochkor

Köl-Ükök Кол-Укок

The beautiful 'Treasure Chest' mountain lake above Tes-Tör *jailoo* usually has a couple of yurtstays in July and August (bed/breakfast/dinner 350/100/200som, booked through Jailoo (p277) from which a couple of hours' hike brings you to Köl-Tör glacial lake.

The trip to Köl-Ükök (3042m) is often sold as a horse trek but, if you can handle the 1km gain in altitude, the route is relatively straightforward to follow as an unguided hike. The starting point is Isakaev (formerly Bolshevik) village, turning right after the bridge.

To Isakaev from Kochkor private/shared taxis cost 60/20som; they leave from beside the traffic lights in Kochkor (at the intersection of Ömurov and Orozbakova). If you pay 150som the taxi should continue 5km further to Küpke, the 'winter barns' where the road peters out. Simply continue up the valley along the obvious trail from there.

Allow around six hours for the 17km hike up to the lake, somewhat less for the return.

Kochkor to Suusamyr

With little vehicular traffic but a reasonably good graded surface (but no asphalt west of Chayek), the Kochkor–Suusamyr road offers a handy summer route for overland cyclists to connect Kochkor/Song-Köl with Osh and southern Kyrgyzstan, without having to backtrack through Bishkek. The route is possible by vehicle, but the minimal public transport becomes entirely non-existent on the most appealing section, between Chayek and Kyzyl-Oi, for which painfully slow hitch-hiking or a chartered taxi would be required.

Adventurous trekkers could use this route to access treks to/from Bishkek's southern fringes over the Kyrgyz Ala-Too via the Sokuluk (3775m), Ala-Archa (3898m) or Alamedin (4032m) passes.

JUMGAL & KYZART

If you want to reach Song-Köl on foot with minimum expense, walking from Jumgal or Kyzart is the logical choice. By using the Tuz-Ashu Pass it is quite feasible to reach Song-Köl's north shore in one day. Or you could walk (for four hours or so) to Klemche, stay there in a family yurt and continue the next day to the lake. Both villages have community tourism representatives offering homestays, each of whom can usually (but not always) arrange guides and horses for next day departure should you prefer to be guided or to take one of the less frequented passes (Kara-Kyya, Uzbek-Ashu).

Jumgal (Dostuklu) is a slightly scrappy village but is handily located right on the main Kochkor–Chayek road around Km67 (about 17km west of the attractive pastures of the Kyzart pass). In a faintly signed house, right beside the main road at the western end of the village, is the homestay of Shepherd's Life coordinator **Stalbek Kaparbekov** (☎077-309 8018; Jetigenov Akun 16; homestay 450som, guide per day 600-700som).

Kyzart (Jang-Arykh) is off the main road: turn south on an unpaved road beside the graveyard at Km71.3, then turn east by the mosque and continue 1km to find the homestays of travel-fixers **Avas Tynaibekov** (☎077-730 3059; Kurman-Ata 16, Kyzart) and English-speaking **Talgart Abdyrazakov** (☎077-911 6360; Kurman-Ata 25, Kyzart).

CHAYEK ЧАЕК

As the biggest village in the valley, unremarkable Chayek is the only spot you're likely to find a sit-down lunch between Kochkor

FEELING FELT

Quintessential Kyrgyz felt rugs or decorative pieces called *shyrdak*s are pieced together from cut pieces of sheep's wool after weeks of washing, drying, dyeing and treatment against pests. The appliqué patterns are usually of a *kochkor mujuz* (plant motif), *teke mujuz* (ibex horn motif) or *kyal* (fancy scrollwork) bordered in a style particular to the region of production. Designs became strikingly colourful after synthetic dye became readily available in the 1960s, but natural dyes are making a comeback, notably using pear and raspberry leaves, dahlia and birch root. A handmade *shyrdak* tends to have irregular stitching on the back and tight, even stitching around the panels. More pictorial *ala-kiyiz* (rugs or hangings with 'blurred' coloured panels pressed on) are made by laying out the wool in the desired pattern on a *chiy* (reed) mat, sprinkling hot water, then rolling until the wool strands compact.

There are felt-making cooperatives in Bishkek, Karakol and Kochkor with pieces often sold through CBT and other community tourism offices.

and the Osh–Bishkek highway, courtesy of the modest **Cafe Daan** (Matieva 84; mains 80-110som; 9am-7pm Mon-Sat). Chayek is also the main regional transport terminus with several daily minibuses and an overnight bus service to Bishkek via Kochkor.

Heading west, Kyzyl-Oi is a far nicer place to stay, but there's no public transport (the Ming-Kush marshrutka gets you as far as Aral). If you're stuck awaiting a hitch, Chayek does have a friendly homestay at the western end of town, misleadingly dubbing itself **Hotel of Tourists** (035-362 3879, 070-991 8542; Akal Moldaliev 4; B&B/dinner 450/200som).

KYZYL-OI — КЫЗЫЛ-ОЙ

The name means 'red bowl' though the majestic wide dell it occupies is beautifully burnished in fresh green should you visit in June. Idyllically quiet but for birdsong, sighing poplars and rushing river rapids, access from either direction is through a curtain of steep mountain peaks and ridges along the Kökömeren Valley.

CBT Kyzyl-Oi (031-246 4785, 055-541 7847), beside the main road in the village centre, can suggest horse treks such as the six-hour ride up the **Char Valley** and over the **Kumbel Pass** to **Balik Köl**, where shepherds graze their flocks in summer. Yurtstays might be possible en route. You'll also encounter shepherds at mid-summer *jailoos* in the Sary Kamysh range to the south of town.

There are around a dozen unmarked homestays in Kyzyl-Oi, including the home of helpful CBT coordinator Artyk Kulubaev. About five minutes' walk along the virtually silent main road is **Elvira Mamudbekova's Place** (055-091 1525; Jibek Jolu 7; B&B/dinner 450/200som), backing onto an idyllic stretch of river. Elvira speaks some English and the family is building a new (if still outdoor) bathroom. Next door, **Damira Adurahmanova's Homestay** (055-091 1525; Jibek Jolu 6) is marginally the newest, smartest little house that we visited in town.

Transport is very thin, with shared taxis leaving a few times weekly to Bishkek. Hitching is the only realistic option for the 45km stretch through attractive canyonlands to **Aral** where the road branches off to the dystopian, part-depopulated former uranium mining town of **Ming-Kush**.

KOJOMKUL — КОЖОМКУЛ

Kojomkul village is named after a local hero who stood 2.3m tall and weighed 165kg. Kaba-uulu Kojomkul (1889–1955) remains a legend in these parts. There's a **Kojomkul monument** in the field behind the school, Kojomkul's **mausoleum** sits on the ridge above, and there's a fascinating, if tumbledown, yurt-shaped shrine at the end of town. Built in 1924 it commemmorates one of Kojomkul's friends and the large inscribed stone outside the *gumbaz* was reputedly placed there by Kojomkul single-handedly. Other of the hero's play-stones sit outside a small, new red-roofed **Kojomkul Museum** (admission 50som) on the main road through town.

SUUSAMYR VILLAGE — СУУСАМЫР

Suusamyr village is equidistant (13km by gravel road) from both Kojomkul and the Bishkek–Osh road. Kubanychbek Amankulov (aka Nayaber) has a homestay marked 'tourist info' very close to the main road.

Naryn НАРЫН

3522 / POP 38,000 / ELEV 2030M

Mostly wedged into a striking if slightly foreboding canyon, Naryn is an architecturally unlovely strip town with no real 'sights' beyond a typical local **museum** (Razzakov 4; admission 60som; 9am-noon & 1-5.30pm Mon-Fri) and a 1993 **mosque** with fanciful mosaics, 2.5km west of Naryn's centre. However, it is nonetheless an excellent place to hook up with other summer travellers to rideshare (and thus save money) on crossing the Torugart Pass to China, visiting Tash Rabat Caravanserai or heading across the very rough road to Kazarman (for Osh). Energetic, friendly CBT staff go out of their way to help organise such options and can arrange a series of local treks too. Naryn also makes an alternative launching point from which to reach Song-Köl.

The name Naryn is derived from the Mongolian for 'sunny' – a rare moment of Mongol irony.

Sleeping

CBT (p281) has 15 homestays (B&B per person 600som, meals 250som) in Naryn and Kubat Tour (p281) has half a dozen more (from 400som). Most are in suburban houses and apartment blocks, often in the eastern Moscovskaya suburb. When the community tourism offices are closed for the winter, try **Dushagul** (Razzakov 3, apt 3; B&B 600som) or **Beyshagul** (Razzakov 7, apt 2; B&B 600som), who both have comfortable, fairly standard homestays in apartment blocks near the main bridge. Cheerful driver **Kachkumbek** (077-917 7524; Razzakov 15; B&B 600som) has several apartments nearby.

Beware that occasionally on Thursday and Monday nights in mid-summer accommodation can be overloaded with groups heading to/from Torugart, aiming to arrive for the Sunday market in Kashgar and avoid the border closures on weekends.

Hotel Ala-Too ROOMS $

(521 89; Chanachov 19; s/d/tr/q without bathroom 250/500/750/1000som, with bathroom 450/900/1350/1800som) Naryn's cheapest option, this Soviet-era hulk has a photogenically abandoned restaurant with smashed windows and trees growing out the roof. Repainted bedrooms aren't quite as bad as you might fear, but the beds are lumpy and shared bathrooms are pretty dismal.

Khan Tengri Hotel HOTEL $$

(549 46, Nazgul 055-603 5063; www.khantengrihotel.kg; Jusupova 2; s/d/tr/q incl breakfast 1200/1480/2700/3200som; @) Naryn's newest hotel hides in an unlikely tree-shaded gated yard, and has a stylish feel to its reception area. Rooms are comfortable but much more functional. One internet computer.

Celestial Mountains Guest House GUESTHOUSE $$

(077-993 1125, 504 12; www.cmgh.kg; Razzakov 42; yurt per person 500som, tw/tr without bathroom 1200/1200som, lux d 1500som; @) Neat if unsophisticated rooms mostly share very compact bathrooms with half-sized tubs. Two 'lux' rooms are considerably more comfortable with ensuite facilities. In summer, eight-bedded yurts in the grounds cost 500som per person. Meals available. It's at the end of a small, signed laneway off Razzakov (Moskovskaya).

Eating

Kafe Ademi CENTRAL ASIAN $

(Bazaar Area; mains 70-130som; 8am-7pm) One of several eateries facing the east side of the bazaar, the food here is some of Naryn's best value. The imaginative 'Ademi' dish is a tasty creation, wrapping a meat patty in a lasagne-style pasta sheet and dousing it with cheese and lightly spiced tomato sauce.

Samsakhana BAKERY $

(Lenina 54; snacks/shashlyk 35/130som; 8am-8pm) Main street bakery-window selling fresh tandoor bread, *etnan* (ring-shaped meat-bread) and, with advanced notice, *plov* and *shashlyk*.

Anarkul Apa Café CENTRAL ASIAN $$

(513 17; Orozbak 23; mains 80-170som, garnish 30som, beer 35-60som; 9am-9pm Mon-Fri, 9am-6pm Sat;) Small but relatively upmarket by Naryn standards. Remarkable for having an English-language menu and serving a few meat-free dishes (roast vegetables, cheese spaghetti).

Shopping

Locally produced *shyrdaks* and souvenirs can be purchased from Kubat Tour, CBT or next door at a shop called **Art Gallery** (Lenina 8, apt 59). The 'real' **Art Gallery** (Jakypov 5; admission 50som) itself has a giftshop.

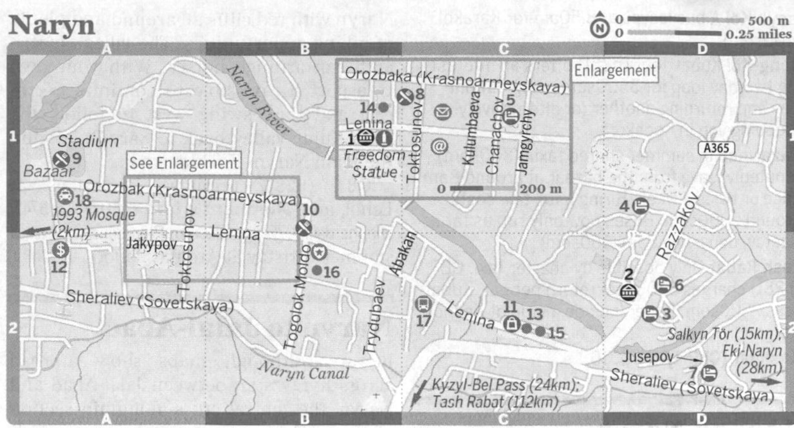

Naryn

Sights
1 Iskusstvo Galeriyasy B1
2 Regional Museum D2

Sleeping
3 Beyshagul's Homestay D2
4 Celestial Mountains Guest House D1
Dushagul's Homestay .... (see 3)
5 Hotel Ala-Too C1
6 Kachkumbek D2
7 Khan Tengri Hotel D2

Eating
8 Anarkul Apa Café C1
9 Kafe Ademi A1
10 Samsakhana B1

Shopping
11 Art Gallery C2

Information
12 Akai Bank A2
13 CBT C2
14 Hakimyat (Municipal Administration Building) B1
15 Kubat Tour C2
16 OVIR B2

Transport
17 Bus Station C2
18 Taxi Stand A1

Information

Naryn is the first/last place to change money after/before the Chinese border. Several banks around the Lenina/Toktosunov junction change clean, unfolded US dollars and euros, and have Visa ATMs. Nowhere takes MasterCard/Maestro.

Akai Bank (Lenina 51; 9am-5pm Mon-Fri) Decent rates for US$ and euro exchange

Telephone Office (Toktosunov; internet per hr 20som; 24hr) Several booths with relatively new computers, and theoretically open 24 hours.

CBT (077-268 9262, 508 65; Lenina 8, apt 2; 9am-6pm or later May-Nov) Youthful Gulira speaks excellent English and is tirelessly keen to help visitors. She can arrange guides, horses, yurtstays, homestays and transport (14som per km). Helpfully the office tries to pair up visitors to save costs on shared rides, and within a day permits and rides can be organised to get you across the Torugart Pass to Kashgar: US$100 per car to the border (including a Tash Rabat excursion) plus US$300/400/500 for two/four/six people to be collected and whisked to Kashgar by their Chinese partners.

Kubat Tour (077-268 9262; www.kubat-tour.from.kg; Lenina 6, apt 51; 9am-6pm May-Oct) Competitive prices on community tourism offerings and Torugart transfers. Some homestay options available.

Getting There & Away

Most longer distance buses, minibuses and shared taxis leave from the **bus station** (Lenina). Those for regional villages leave from the **bazaar**.

Bishkek Minibuses (350som, seven hours) depart between 8am and 11am, with a night bus (270som) at 9pm. Shared taxi drivers linger all day (450som). Any Bishkek service will drop you at Kochkor.

Issyk-Köl A bus leaves at 8.50am for Karakol (400som).

Song-Köl Kubat Tour (p281) offers an interesting two-day loop for 3500som going out one way and returning another (or alternatively dropping you in Kochkor).

Kazarman In summer shared taxis (800som) reputedly leave from the bazaar at around 8am once or twice a week. Hiring a full taxi costs around 5000som. Buses now only run as far as Baetov, departing 8am (150som).

Tash Rabat Only possible by charter taxi. CBT (p281) charges 3400som return per car, Kubat asks 2500som. Either include a stop at Koshoy Korgon.

Kashgar (China) see p310.

Around Naryn

CBT (p281) can give you the low-down on a range of trips around Naryn, including yurtstays in the Ardaktuu Valley, and Tyor Jailoo in the Eki-Naryn Valley. With one day's notice, it can organise multi-day horse treks. Most horse trips start from Kurtka (Jangy Talap) or Eki-Naryn. Ask them about visits to the Tian Shan deer nursery at Irii-Suu (great for kids) and day trips up the Ak-Tam Valley to see petroglyphs.

Possible excursions include:

➡ Eki-Naryn to Bokonbayevo: Six days by horse, via Jiluu Suu.

➡ Kurtka (Jangy Talap) to Song-Köl: Two days by horse, or three days by foot. Starting from Kurtka (Jangy Talap) village, west of Naryn to Song-Köl's southern shore, overnighting in yurts (July and August) or tents.

➡ Naryn State Reserve: 2½ days by horse or 4½ days by foot. Transport by car to the state reserve then you follow the Big Naryn River to Karakalka village, overnighting with the ranger or staying in tents. It is possible to arrange transport or trek independently to Barskoön from Karakalka.

East of Naryn

The scenic Kichi (Little) Naryn Valley stretches to the northeast of Naryn and offers plenty of opportunities for exploration. About 12km along the road is Salkyn Tör, a scenic canyon that makes a great picnic spot and is a popular weekend hang-out for people from Naryn.

About 42km out of Naryn (400som by taxi) is the attractive little town of **Eki-Naryn** with red cliffs all around and plenty of hiking opportunities. The village matriarch can arrange horses. With your own transport it's possible to continue northeast and then swing west to follow the Kara-Kujur Valley back to Sary-Bulak and the main Naryn–Kochkor road.

CBT (p281) arranges homestays at Lehol, and **Shepherd's Life** (☎077-701 3747; shepherdslife076@gmail.com; Pionerskaya) has a summer yurtstay at Ardakty Jailoo.

Naryn to Jalal-Abad

Beware. Although maps show a road across Kyrgyzstan between Jalal-Abad and Naryn, the central cross-mountain section of the road is an unpaved, seasonal affair with barely two vehicles an hour passing through, even in summer. It can become impassable after mudslides and closes altogether from October to late June. Most travellers coming this way break the journey in Kazarman, a service town for the recently re-started Makhmal open-cast gold mine. If you're coming from Song-Köl, there's a very attractive link route across the Moldo Ashuu Pass via 33 switchbacks. A few kilometres after Kurtka (Jangy Talap; homestay available), turn right to find the Kazarman road. You've gone too far if you cross the river bridge (just north of the Naryn–Baetov road west of Ak-Tal).

Kazarman Казарман

☎3738 / POP 15,000 / ELEV 1230M

Don't be put off by Kazarman's grungy concrete centre – a semi-circular fan of dreary four-storey prefabricated apartment blocks ranged round a Soviet-era culture centre (Dom Kulturi). Away from these eyesores, the town's setting is an attractive, wide, mountain-edged valley. Around 20 minutes' walk north of Dom Kulturi, a series of sandy riverside cliffs are best appreciated from the Kara-Suu bridge. For a brilliant overview of the poplar punctuated townscape and soaring backdrop, head in the opposite direction and climb the low, flat cemetery hill at the southern end of Mambetjanov.

The main Naryn–Jalal-Abad through road (Kojaliev) is paralleled a block to the south by Kadyrkulova (with two homestays) and four blocks north by the town's main drag, Jeenaliev (formerly Mira). These are linked by the part road, part footpath Mambetjanov. Just east of where Mambetjanov meets Jeenaliev on the north side of the road is the park office for Sailmaluu Tash, the region's most famous excursion destination. Directly east lie the Dom Kulturi building, Kafe Dostuk and the shared taxi stand. Hidden one block behind that is the pitifully minimal bazaar.

Sleeping

Bakhtygul Chorobaeva Homestay HOMESTAY $
(☎077-768 8803, 077-168 8803; Kadyrkulova 35; B&B/dinner 500/250som) Welcoming and with unusually decent English spoken, Bakhtygul welcomes guests to her traditional home, which is currently undergoing a major rebuild.

Shirinkan Karmyshova Homestay HOMESTAY $
(☎501 01, 077-361 4547; Kadyrkulova 36; B&B/dinner 500/250som) Welcoming family homestay with outdoor shower and toilet, which are a bit of a hike through the extensive orchard garden.

Bujumal Arykmoldoeva's Homestay HOMESTAY $
(☎412 53; Bekten 36; B&B/dinner 500/250som) Low-rise homestead with a rural feel, tea-bed, small parking area and bathroom facilities in the yard. Being the CBT coordinator's house, this is often full while other homestays are quiet.

Eating

Of a trio of cafes on Jeenaliev, our favourite for food quality and variety is **Kafe Dostuk** (Jeenaliev; mains 60-90som; ⌚8am-8pm) beside Dom Kulturi, though **Islam Ashkana** (Jeenaliev; mains 70-100som; ⌚9am-9pm) has a cosier, better-lit decor and sits within one of the town's funkiest buildings.

Information

CBT (☎077-722 4063, 412 53; Bekten 36) Contact coordinator Bujumal Arykmoldoeva at her homestay (p283).

Sailmaluu Tash Park Office (Monpekettik zharalypish parky; ☎502 84; Jeenaliev 64; ⌚9am-1pm & 2-6pm Mon-Fri) Located via the second door in the building directly west of Dom Kulturi. Can organise next-day trips to Saimaluu Tash and collects the entry fee for the park. No English spoken.

Ayyl Bank (Kojaliev 83; ⌚9am-noon & 1-4pm Mon-Fri) The town's main bank has a Visa ATM and changes US$ (but not euros).

Getting There & Away

Remember that all access to the town may be impossible in the winter months when snow blocks the passes from both Jalal-Abad and especially from Naryn. At any time, double check the road situation before setting off.

Road conditions permitting, one or two shared taxis can usually be found for Jalal-Abad (600som, four hours, summer only) departing from Jeenaliev in front of the bazaar between 7am and 11am. Cars for Bishkek (1200som to 1500som, 12 hours) start from across the road. Bishkek cars could drop you in Naryn or Kochkor but the price will still be 1200som to 1500som. Naryn-specific cars (800som, five hours) only leave a couple of times a week. If you're in a hurry it's worth budgeting for the worst-case scenario of having to fork out for all four seats.

Note that if mooted plans gain the necessary funding, a new all-weather road might be built linking Kochkor to Jalal-Abad via Chayek, Aral and Kazarman with a tunnel beneath the Kok-Art pass. But don't hold your breath. The most optimistic estimate for completion is 2017.

Sailmaluu Tash Саймалуу Таш

The several thousand 'embroidered stones' of **Sailmaluu Tash** (foreigner/local 100/50som) are Central Asia's most celebrated collection of petroglyphs. Over the millennia Aryan, Scythian and Turkic peoples have added to the earliest Bronze Age carvings. The carvings are spread over two slopes and depict hunting, shamanistic rites and battle scenes, some dating back more than 1000 years.

The very long day-trip to see the petroglyphs is strenuous and only feasible in July and August, and then only on good weather days. You start with a two-hour 4WD ride, then a steep five to six hour hike in places through shoulder-high grass, in others across a snow/ice field. The park office (p283) in Kazarman, where the admission tickets should be prepurchased, can usually arrange the necessary guide (1000som) and transfer (1000som for up to four people) for next day departure, but there's no spoken English here. At weekends try calling guide **Ataibek Kojoshov** (☎077-917 4677) directly. Kazarman's English-speaking CBT (p283) can arrange things for you, but prices are considerably higher. Bring your own food. And consider renting a horse (500som) and bringing a tent in case you can't get back before dark.

Naryn to Torugart

Be aware that if you plan to cross Torugart to/from China you'll need to arrange things in advance through a tour agency. Remember that the border closes at weekends and on holidays. To explore Chatyr-Köl you'll need a border-zone permit, though this might not be checked if you hike there and back from Tash Rabat. For information on crossing the pass, see p310.

Koshoy Korgon

Worth a brief stop if you're travelling the Naryn–Torugart road, Koshoy Korgan is a 250m square of muddy wall remnants from what is thought to have been a powerful citadel between the 10th and early 13th centuries. One local legend claims that the Kyrgyz epic hero Manas built the citadel and a mausoleum here for his fallen friend Koshoy. Just before the entrance is a 2007 **museum** (☎077-771 2231; admission 50som; ⏰9am-1pm & 2-6pm) which has a striking design and an attractive art collection. The museum's very speculative model suggests how the citadel might once have looked but other exhibits singularly fail to add any further historical context.

The site is 3km off the main road from Km409: head 800m down Köchör, the easternmost street in Kara-Suu village, then left on Abit (at Köchör 44/Abit 33) which curves around to the site.

Tash Rabat — Таш-Рабат

Some 117km from Naryn, Tash Rabat is a small stone caravanserai sunk into the hillside of a photogenic narrow shepherds' valley that's given definition by occasional rocky outcrops. Local sources say it dates from the 15th century, although some sources say the site dates from the 10th century, when it was a Christian monastery. Either

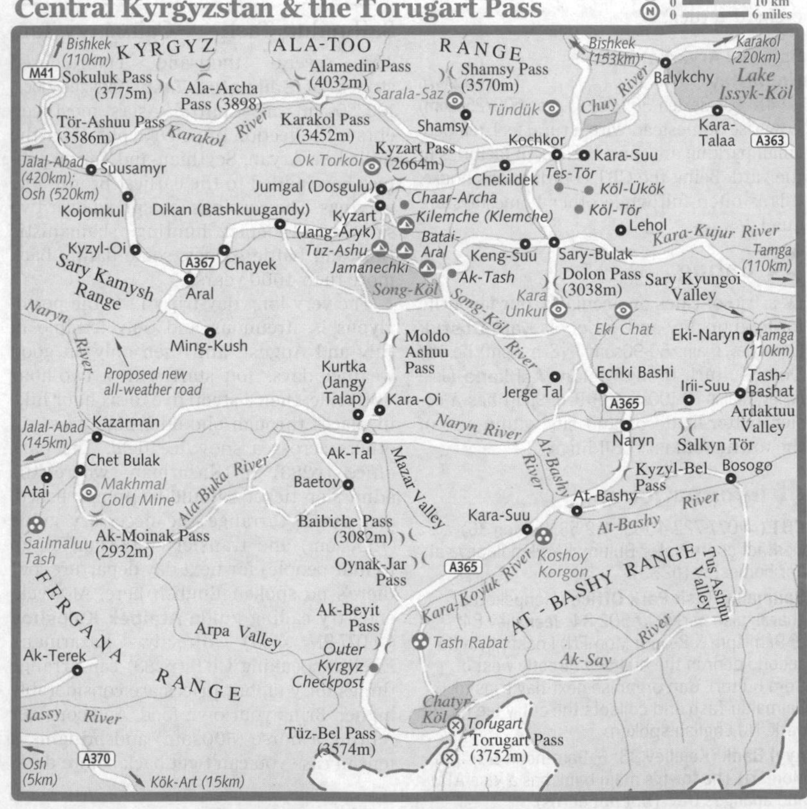

way historians agree that at one time Tash Rabat (Kyrgyz for stone fortress) must have had significant Silk Road political and trade importance to justify the investment in the labour required for its construction.

Its irregular shape and improbable location have fuelled a number of local legends. One relates how a ruling khan devised a test for his two sons to see who was worthy of inheriting his throne. One son, determined to prove that he could provide for his people, pursued the development of education, agriculture and industry. The other son amassed armies and built fortresses. Tash Rabat stands as a silent reminder of a warmongering man who lost a khanate to his philanthropic brother.

Though not very large and almost entirely unadorned within, the domed building has a pleasingly complete look to it thanks to a (somewhat clumsy) Soviet-era restoration. But what makes it especially worth the detour from the main Torugart route is the peaceful valley setting where the only habitation is a series of seasonal yurt camps (mostly for tourists) offering interesting walking or riding options and overnight accommodation.

CHATYR-KÖL ЧАТЫР-КИЛЬ

From Tash Rabat, roughly six hours on foot or by plodding horse should get you to a broad ridge overlooking Chatyr-Köl; if you continue for a couple of hours you can stay the night in a yurt at Chatyr-Köl. The yurt owners at Tash Rabat can arrange horses and guides. You'll need to return the same way unless you have a border-zone permit as these are liable to be checked at a police post on the road route. Better still, consider getting such a permit before heading to the lake at all. Also remember that you are about 3500m high here, so even a short walk could set your head pounding.

Sleeping & Eating

There are four yurt camps in the valleys around Tash Rabat. At the two biggest it's usually possible to drop in without reservations and, anyway, calling is useless except on Sundays when the owners go to At Bashy for the market. Either can organise horse treks to Chatyr-Köl where there are more yurts available.

Omurbek Yurts YURTSTAY $
(☎077-871 3409; Tash Rabat Caravanserai; B&B/dinner/banya 500/250/150som) Comfortable yurts with camp beds right outside the caravanserai. Good food. Omurbek offers a range of horse treks and his daughter Elizat speaks English.

Sabyrbek's Yurts YURTSTAY $
(☎077-222 1252, 077-388 9098; a.tursun23@mail.ru; Tash Rabat Valley; B&B/dinner/banya 500/250/150som; ⏲Jun–mid-Oct) Beautifully set in the valley junction 1.3km before the caravanserai, Sabyrbek's yurts have sturdy wooden-framed beds and there's a small *banya*. Family members speak good English and some French.

Getting There & Away

There's no public transport here. A CBT (p281) taxi (day trip or overnight return) costs 3400som including a side trip to Koshoy Korgon. For US$100 you can continue the next day to Torugart.

OSH & SOUTHERN KYRGYZSTAN

In many ways, Osh and the surrounding areas of the Fergana Valley feel like a different country from the north of Kyrgyzstan. Hotter in terms of climate and of human temperament, the area is the nation's bread basket. Osh and Jalal-Abad, Kyrgyzstan's second- and third-biggest cities, have more in common with the conservative, Islamic Fergana Valley than with industrialised, Russified Bishkek. But the people here are unfailingly hospitable and the region has far more of a classic Central Asian feel than you'll find in the north.

Bishkek to Osh

Visitors linking Bishkek and Kyrgyzstan's second-city, Osh, must choose between a full day's drive crossing two 3000m-plus passes, or a 40-minute flight. Both options have some memorable views when weather obliges. Given the cut-throat competition, flying sometimes costs little more than taking a cramped share taxi. But the Bishkek–Osh drive is worth considering at least in one direction for the sequence of landscape superlatives between Kara-Balta and Toktogul. As usual, townscapes en route offer far less appeal than the scenery, though Özgön near Osh is worth a quick stop. Lengthy en-route detours could take you to regional beauty spots at Arslanbob and Lake Sary-Chelek.

South of **Kara-Balta** the road heads straight towards the wall of the craggy Kyrgyz Ala-Too mountain range, weaving through a crumbling canyon towards the 3586m Tör-Ashuu Pass (toll payable). Before the top, there's a 2.6km-long tunnel through the mountain's upper reaches. This was the scene of a fatal 2001 carbon-monoxide poisoning disaster and cyclists would do better to flag down a truck and drive through.

Beyond the tunnel's southern end is the gravel road to Chayek via Suusamyr and Kyzyl-Oi – a charming rural, but little-trafficked, back-route to Song-Köl and Kochkor. The main Osh road continues across the yawning **Suusamyr Basin**, a classic example of Kyrgyz herding country, with plenty of summer roadside yurts offering fresh *kymys*.

After another 1¼ hours' very attractive rural drive, a large red **horseback Manas Statue** marks the side road to Taraz (Kazakhstan) leading over the bald, bleak Otmek Pass (3330m) and passing through **Talas** (pop 30,000) – fabled as the legendary last resting place of Kyrgyzstan's epic hero, Manas.

Half an hour's drive beyond the Taraz turning, the main Osh road climbs the long, broad **Ala-Bel Pass** (3184m) then descends into a beautiful valley that's part of the **Chychkan State Zoological Reserve**.

Vehicles take over an hour to loop around the vast **Toktogul Reservoir**, named for well-known *akyn* (Kyrgyz bard) Toktogul Satilganov (1884–1933), who was born near what is now forgettable **Toktogul town** (population 16,000). **Kara-Köl** (not Karakol), site of the reservoir's 210m-high dam (essentially invisible to passing traffic), marks a significant change of landscapes as the road navigates the gorge of the lower Naryn River, with its sheer walls and towering pillars of red sandstone.

Scenery becomes less magical on reaching the depressing urban ribbon of coal-mining town **Tashkömür**. The only reason to stop here is if you're gambling on catching the 1.20pm bus to Kara-Jigach for lakes **Sary-Chelek** (biosphere fee foreigner/local 500/50som) and arguably lovelier, less touristed **Kyzyl-Kul/Kara-Suu** (no entry fee). Both are beautiful if you have your own transport or plan a multi-day trek between them – contact **Almambet** (☎374-26 04 17, 770-15 26 35) in Kara-Suu village for homestays, guides and tent-hire. However, the awkward access logistics are disincentives for those on public transport.

In comparison, appealing **Arslanbob** is pretty simple to reach and very well set up for passing visitors. The turnoff is at Sovetskoye (km543/121), north of Bazar-Kurgan. The scenery from here to Osh intersperses patchworks of sunflower and maize fields with dry grassy hills. **Jalal-Abad**, Kyrgyzstan's pleasantly green, unassuming third city isn't worth a special stop unless you're cutting across country to Kazarman on a rough, summer-only mountain road towards Naryn.

An hour further, passingly interesting **Özgön** has a historic minaret and a three-in-one 12th-century brick mausoleum complex.

Arslanbob АРСЛАНБОБ

☎3722 / ELEV 1600M

The Babash-Ata Mountains form an impressive wall of snow-sprinkled crags behind the elevated 'oasis' of Arslanbob. Ethnically Uzbek and religiously conservative, the very large village sprawls almost invisibly along a network of tree-shaded lanes, and is surrounded by a vast tract of blossoming woodland that constitutes the world's largest walnut grove. According to local legend, the grove's seed-nuts were a miraculous gift from the Prophet Mohammad to a modest gardener who he had charged with finding paradise on earth.

A very well-organised branch of CBT (p288) can help organise virtually anything you're likely to need. Their office is 200m uphill from the shop-ringed main square/minibus stand. When the door is locked, phone.

Sights

The real attractions around Arslanbob are hikes, horse treks, cycle rides or ski adventures in the surrounding mountains and forests. But Arslanbob's glorious, garden-homestays are also a great place to unwind.

Waterfalls WATERFALL

If you're just here to relax, it's worth sampling the village's schizophrenic atmosphere at Arslanbob's signature waterfalls. Neither are especially memorable per se but the excitable local tourists buying candy-floss, yoghurt-balls and dodgey ice creams are fun to observe. And just walking there you'll get a better sense of the village's layout, impressive setting and part-timbered older mud-brick architecture. Just beyond the top of the smaller, more accessible **Twin Waterfall** (Vodapad; admission 10som), a footpath leaves behind the melee of souvenir stalls and crosses the stream. It zig-zags up for 15 minutes cutting through a brief taster of the walnut grove then emerging onto an upper bank with glorious views over the Babash-Ata peaks. You can distantly make out the narrow 80m ribbon of the **Long Waterfall** (Bolshoy Vodapad; admission 10som), which is probably more satisfying than the two-hour walk to get there (locals go by 4WD) and 15-minute scree scramble to the base.

Turbaza HOLIDAY CAMP
(☎528 40; Rahim Palvan 83) If you're not tired of people-watching, there's more fun to be had at the *Turbaza*, a decrepit yet still active Soviet-era holiday camp replete with punch-machines, an awfully grimy open-air swimming pool and a ragged disco pavilion where city kids strut to *I'm Sexy and I know it*, watched aghast by heavily veiled local women. Well worth the 20-minute walk, straight up from CBT.

Activities

CBT (p288) can arrange mountaineering, skiing and mountain-biking activities, as well as harvesting walnuts, often at very short notice. They are very professional but do tend to press clients to engage a cook as well as a guide. Such cooks produce lunches every bit as good as CBT claims, but even so, for one-day treks there's no need to be pressured into taking one if you are satisfied with simply carrying a picnic. Tents/mats/sleeping bags (per night 200/150/70som) are available for hire but it's best to bring your own gear in case CBT run short.

For a full day hike, explore the walnut forest en route to the shrine of Ibn Abbas, or the Dashman walnut forest via Gumhana village and Jaradar.

Mountain Biking CYCLING
(bike-rental/guide per day 600/800som) Half a dozen bikes are available from CBT, which suggests three satellite-mapped loop-routes.

Skiing WINTER SPORTS
(ski-rental/sledge-rental/guide/cook per day 300/50/900/700som; ⏲Jan & Feb) In winter CBT organises alpine touring ski trips into various high *jailoos* or even just around the village according to your requirements and skill levels. Limited supplies of skis/snowshoes and boots are available for hire.

Mountaineering CLIMBING
(mountaineering-guide/cook/porter per day plus meals 1200/1000/600som; ⏲summer) Reaching the top of **Babashata** peak (4427m, four days round-trip) is somewhere between trekking and mountaineering, and although you don't need to be an expert climber you should have some mountain experience. CBT organises guides.

Nut Harvest AGRICULTURAL ACTIVITY
(⏲mid-Sep) From mid-September the town undergoes a mass exodus when locals move into the forest and go nuts. Each year 1500 tonnes of walnuts (and 5000 tonnes of apples, pistachios and cherry plums) are harvested in the Arslanbob Valley, and by all accounts gathering nuts is fun. Tradition dictates that during the harvest each family kill a sheep and share the meat with their neighbours. The fire-lit autumn nights are a time to sing songs, retell stories and eat way too much greasy mutton.

Trekking

CBT (p288) can arrange trekking options from a half-day stroll to a 10-day slog to Saimaluu Tash (with pick-up to Kazarman).

A popular three- to four-day horse-trek encompasses the four Köl Mazar 'holy' mountain lakes. Instead of retracing your steps you can continue over the Kerets Pass and east along the Kerets Valley, with the Nurbuu-Tau Mountains to the north, until you swing south down the **Kyzyl Ünkür** (Red Cavern) Valley southeast of Arslanbob. That valley offers its own network of hiking and fishing routes. You could drive as far as tiny Kön-Köl, then hike northeast over the Kymysh Bel Pass (3754m) to the fish-stocked Kara-Suu Lake. From here you can head down the Kara-Suu Valley to join the main Bishkek–Osh road at Kök Bel, between Kara-Köl and Toktogul, or return on a loop back to Kyzyl Ünkür via Kön-Köl Pass, either way making an intrepid week of trekking.

Sleeping

There are 18 **CBT-affiliated homestays** (☎077-745 0266, 077-334 2476; arslanbob_2003@rambler.ru; per night incl breakfast 350-400som, lunch/dinner 100som) scattered very widely around the village. These are hard to find without help and some are as much as 5km from the central square/bazaar. The best tactic is generally to visit CBT, which numbers each guesthouse and displays basic descriptions and photos on the wall. They'll find out which places have space and call someone to show you the way. Our favourites are Bunyad Mirzamaksudov's for the fabulous views, and Zinaida for its quiet central location and flower-filled courtyard garden.

Zinaida Homestay HOMESTAY **$**
(B&B No 11; ☎070-966 7080, 077-329 2434; Aral 11; dm 350som) Quiet, central and blessed with a gorgeous flower-filled garden. Fatima speaks English. From the main square walk west, take the first turn left (south) opposite Torgovaya Tochka shop, then make an S-shaped route for 150m or so to find the pale blue gates above which is a window displaying a red triangular Kyrgyzstan Hospitality logo.

Bunyad Mirzamaksudaov HOMESTAY **$**
(B&B No 12; ☎077-341 5068; A Bazarov 34; dm 400som) Relatively new house with super valley views from the *topchan* (dining pavilion). It's down a small dead-end lane to the right of the road leading from the bazaar towards the Twin Waterfall. The turn is about 150m after that road swings north.

Eating

There are six simple cafe-chaikhanas (meals 80som) in the main square/bazaar area, of which three are perched over the river (none with great views) and one attractively shaded beneath an ancient Chinor (plane) tree. There are even less sophisticated drink-stands and *shashlyk* burners at the Twin Waterfall and beside the *turbaza*. By arrangement any homestay offers a choice of dinner (180som) but all guests should agree to take the same option.

Chaikhana Chinor CHAIKHANA
(meals 80som; ⏲8am-7.30pm) Specialises in *samsa* and fresh bread (baked til 7pm), but also serves *plov* and *manti* beneath a majestic ancient plane tree.

Information

There is no internet cafe but mobile phone access is good. There are no formal money-exchange offices so bring ample stocks of som.

CBT (☎077-834 2476, 077-334 2476; arslanbob_2003@rambler.ru; Rahim Palvan 6; ⏲call if closed) Very well-organised CBT can help with everything from homestays and transport to horse treks, skiing and mountain-bike rental. Hayat speaks English well.

Getting There & Away

Arslanbob is 3½ hours' drive from Osh. By marshrutka you'll need to change in both Jalal-Abad and Bazar Kurgan. Although the latter is 3km west of the Osh–Bishkek highway, Jalal-Abad–Masy and Jalal-Abad–Kockor Ata minibuses divert here (30som, 40 minutes from Jalal-Abad). Bazar–Kurgan–Arslanbob marshrutkas marked Arstanbap run roughly twice an hour til 6pm or later (50som, one hour). If arriving from the north, jump off at Sovetskoye (Km543/121) where there's a well-signed junction. Passing Arslanbob marshrutkas can usually squeeze in extra passengers here. Direct shared taxis leave from Arslanbob to Bishkek most mornings (1000som to 1500som). CBT can book a space if you ask the day before.

Getting Around

In summer, shared bench-seat pick-ups with stripey canopies gather in the main square to shuttle visitors to the *turbaza* (per person 20som) or Twin Waterfall (per person 20som). To the access path for the Long Waterfall, 4WDs ask 500som per vehicle.

Jalal-Abad ДЖАЛАЛ-АБАД

☎3722 / POP 74,000

If you're transiting between Osh and Kazarman or Arslanbob, you'll probably need to change vehicles in the leafy, laid-back spa town of Jalal-Abad. Although it's Kyrgyzstan's third-largest city there are no real sights and almost everything of use to travellers is within 10 minutes' walk of the central bazaar, though you'll need a taxi to reach the town's best hotel, **Roza Park** (☎730 90; www.facebook.com/rozaparkhotel; Baltagula 183; s/d/tw 2000/2500/3000; P❄@📶). Two blocks southeast of the bazaar, the glitzier **Hotel Tian Shan** (Lenina; s/d/ste US$60/65/80) is easier to find. Three blocks northwest at the central square, the turquoise Soviet-era **Hotel Mölmöl** (☎550 59; Lenina 17; s/d with cold shower 335/636som, d with hot shower 840som, ste 1500som) has typically decrepit standard rooms but the newly rebuilt suites are as kitchily well-restored as the new foyer. From here walk a block northwest past the park then 50m northeast to find the once-pleasant **Hotel Kainar** (☎204 55; J Bakiev 20; s/d/tr/ste 500/700/1500/1500som), whose rooms are now very poorly maintained and distinctly drain-scented. A few homestays are available through **CBT** (☎219 62, Ruhsora 077-237 6602; cbt_ja@rambler.ru; Toktogul 20; B&B with outdoor/indoor bathroom 550/700som; ⏲9am-5pm Mon-Fri).

Across Lenina from the southeast corner of the bazaar, tree-shaded **Kafe Elnura** (Lenina; tea/kebabs from 10/45som, mains 90-250som; ⏲24hr) is a great summer chaikhana. Opposite Hotel Mölmöl, **Shirin Foods** (Lenina 19; burger/pide/pizza 60/90/200som; ⏲9am-10pm; 📶) offers an air-conditioned 'fast' food experience that's almost unique for the region, though the fresh-baked pide (Turkish pizzas) are far better than their microwaved burgers.

ℹ Getting There & Around

AIR

AC Kyrgyzstan flies six times a week to/from Bishkek (2500som to 3500som). Buy tickets at the airport or **Sputnik Agency** (☎507 06; Lenina 17). Marshrutkas 1 and 5 from the centre go to the airport via the bus station. A taxi to the airport costs 50som to 80som.

BUS & SHARED TAXI

Minibuses use the main bus station 3km west (by marshrutka 110). Shared taxis departing from various points around the bazaar charge around double.

Osh (120som, 1¾ hours) Twice hourly minibus until 6pm via **Özgön** (Uzgen, 60som, 50 minutes) where you might consider a half-hour stop to explore the appealing bazaar and to see a trio of conjoined 12th-century brick mausolea just off the main drag.

Bazaar Korgon (30som, 40 minutes) For Arslanbob. Take Maci- or Kochkor Ata–bound minibuses (three per hour).

Kazarman In summer, when the road is open, cars to Kazarman congregate in the northeastern corner of the yard behind the Manas Avtobeket. To find it from the bazaar, walk up Chekhov one block, right on Babkina then right again through the covered toll gateway. The Kazarman cars lurk immediately to the left but hidden behind a pile of wrecked old kiosks.

Bishkek Shared taxis (typically 1100som, nine hours) depart regularly from the bus station.

Minibus 110 runs along Lenina from the bazaar to the bus station and beyond (8som).

Özgön Өзгөн

☎3233 / POP 49,000

While its sights don't add up to much, Özgön (Uzgen) makes a good brief stop if you're driving the main road to/from Osh. The busy bazaar has an earthy, untouristed charm and is fronted by a pair of majolica-pattern tiled towers which might be mid-20th-century but still dream Silk Road dreams. Citadels on this raised riverbank site reputedly date back 2000 years and the town was a Karakhanid capital a millennium ago. However, the only genuinely historic buildings today are an 11th-century brick minaret and a neighbouring three-in-one 12th-century mausoleum-complex in shades of red-brown clay. The monuments, 600m east of the bazaar, aren't likely to hold your attention for long, but coming here can be a good way to meet local students wanting to practice their English. Stories about their families' experience of Özgön's murderous 1990 inter-ethnic violence can be shocking.

Osh–Jalal-Abad marshrutkas pick up/drop off passengers near the bazaar. For Özgön-specific services there's a minibus station tucked away one block further east, then north.

Osh ОШ

☎3222 / POP 300,000

With a remarkable five-headed crag leaping out of the very town centre, Kyrgyzstan's second city certainly has a highly distinctive visual focus. While there's little of architectural merit to show for 3000 years of history, Osh's sprawling bazaar and hospitable citizens provide an atmosphere that is far more archetypically Central Asian than you will find in Bishkek.

For most travellers Osh is predominantly a launch or arrival point for buses to/from China, for transiting from Uzbekistan's Fergana Valley, or for accessing Tajikistan's memorable Pamir Highway. Inexpensive international flights (via Turkey and Dubai) can also make it a savvy gateway to Central Asia.

History

Locals maintain that 'Osh is older than Rome'. Legends credit all sorts of people with its founding, from King Solomon (Suleyman) to Alexander the Great. Certainly it must have been a major hub on the Silk Road from its earliest days. The Mongols smashed it in the 13th century, but in the following centuries it bounced back, more prosperous than ever. In 1496, Babur, later the founder of the Mughal-Indian dynasty, passed through as a teenager from his native Fergana and commissioned the modest prayer-room on top of Suleiman Too. Osh was absorbed into the Kokand Khanate in 1762 and later fell to Russian forces.

Osh

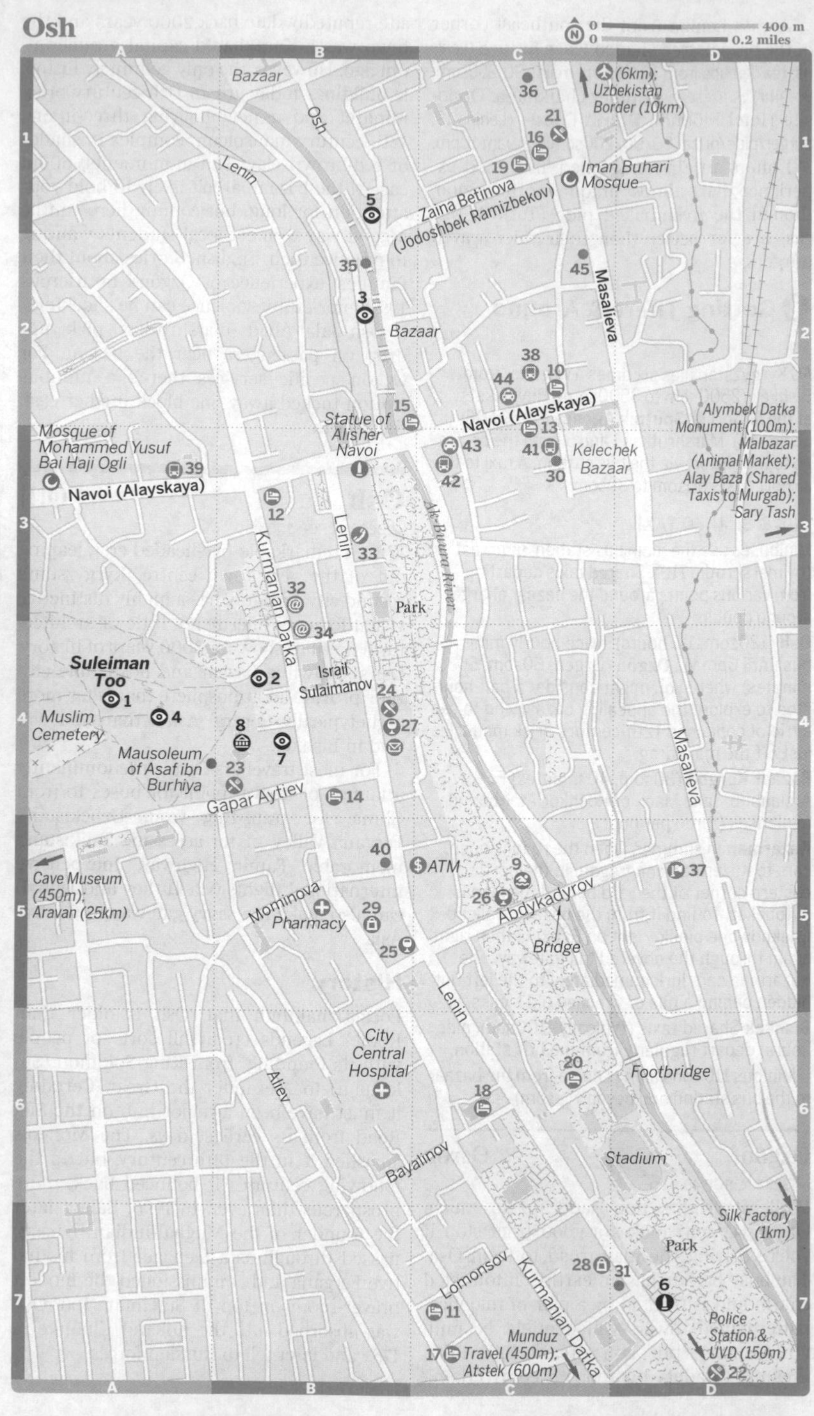
0 400 m
0 0.2 miles
Bazaar
Osh
Lenin
(6km);
Uzbekistan
Border (10km)
Iman Buhari
Mosque
Zaina Betinova
(Jodoshbek Ramizbekov)
Masalieva
Bazaar
Navoi (Alayskaya)
Statue of
Alisher
Navoi
Alymbek Datka
Monument (100m);
Malbazar
(Animal Market);
Alay Baza (Shared
Taxis to Murgab);
Sary Tash
Kelechek
Bazaar
Mosque of
Mohammed Yusuf
Bai Haji Ogli
Navoi (Alayskaya)
Kurmanjan Datka
Lenin
Ak-Buura River
Park
Suleiman
Too
Israil
Sulaimanov
Muslim
Cemetery
Mausoleum
of Asaf ibn
Burhiya
Gapar Aytiev
Masalieva
Cave Museum
(450m);
Aravan (25km)
ATM
Mominova
Pharmacy
Abdykadyrov
Bridge
Lenin
City
Central
Hospital
Footbridge
Aliev
Stadium
Bayalinov
Silk Factory
(1km)
Park
Lomonsov
Kurmanjan Datka
Police
Station &
UVD (150m)
Munduz
Travel (450m);
Atstek (600m)

Osh

Top Sights
1 Suleiman Too A4

Sights
2 Alien Fairy Cake B4
3 Bazaar B2
4 Dom Babura A4
5 Jayma Bazaar B1
6 Lenin Statue D7
7 Three-Storey Yurt B4
8 UTAMK B4

Activities, Courses & Tours
9 Bolshoe Riba C5

Sleeping
10 Deluxe Hotel C2
11 Eco House C7
12 Hotel Alay B3
13 Hotel Pekin C2
14 Hotel Sanabar B4
15 Kristal Hotel B2
16 Mira Homestay C1
17 New hotel complex C7
18 Osh-Nuru C6
19 Taj Mahal C1
20 TES Guesthouse C6

Eating
21 Ala-Too C1
22 Izyum D7
23 Osh Ordo B4
24 Tsarskii Dvor B4

Drinking & Nightlife
25 Bridge B5
26 Feel City C5
27 Parliament B4

Shopping
28 Kyrgyz Konyagy C7
29 Saimalu Tash B5

Information
CBT Alay .... (see 12)
30 Eastern Visa C3
31 Fotosalon 12 .... D7
32 Internet Cafes B3
Kazkommerts Bank .... (see 19)
33 Main Telecom Office B3
34 Meganet B4
35 Moneychangers B2
MuzToo .... (see 8)
36 Osh Guesthouse C1
37 Russian Consulate Osh D5

Transport
38 Argomak 4WD Stand C2
39 Batken Minibus Stand A3
40 China Southern B5
41 Kashgar Bus C3
42 Minibus Station C3
43 Shared Taxi Stand C3
44 Shared Taxi Stand for Bishkek C2
45 Ural Airlines C2

Osh suffers a kind of demographic schizophrenia, being a major centre of Kyrgyzstan but with a strong (40%) Uzbek population more in tune with Uzbekistan and the rest of the Fergana Valley. The absurd international borders, created by Joseph Stalin's divide-and-rule mentality, still has consequences – ethnic strife rocked the area in 1990 and again in 2010, and while generally invisible to passing travellers, there remains an ominously palpable undercurrent of enmity between elements of the Kyrgyz and Uzbek population.

Sights

★ Suleiman Too CRAGS

(Solomon's Throne; admission 5som; ⏲9am-8pm) This five-peaked rocky crag seems to loom above the city wherever you go. It has been a Muslim place of pilgrimage for centuries, supposedly because the Prophet Mohammed once prayed here. Its slopes are indented with many a cave and crevice each reputed to have different curative or spiritual properties (many detailed on photo-boards in the Cave Museum; p292. One such is fertility mini-cave **Ene-Beshik**, its rocks worn smooth by young ladies slithering in to aid their motherly aspirations. You'll see it right beside the path to the Cave Museum as you descend westward from Suleiman Too's main viewpoint. On that crag lies the one-room **Dom Babura** (Babur's House; Suleiman Too), a 1989 reconstruction of a historic prayer-room whose tradition dates back to 1497, when 14-year-old Zahiruddin Babur of Fergana built himself a little prayer-retreat here. Later famed as progenitor of the Mogul Dynasty, Babur's place of worship later became highly revered but subsequent incarnations have been destroyed notably by both earthquake (1853) and, in the 1960s, by a 'mysterious' explosion.

Allow around 20 minutes' sweaty climb on the hairpin stairway to Dom Babura from Suleiman Too's main entrance, which is beside the strange silver-domed building that looks like an **alien fairy cake**, but actually contains a photography salon. Inside newlyweds can be snapped on honeymoon at the Taj Mahal without actually bothering to leave Osh.

Cave Museum MUSEUM
(foreigner/local 50/20som; ⏲9am-noon & 1-6pm) What appears to be a gigantic Georgian lady's-bonnet protrudes from a southwestern crag of Suleiman Too. This marks the exit hole of a cave within which a museum attempts to illustrate the region's histo-religous development. However, it's most interesting for the glass-sphere lamps and the views as you exit (via steep stairs past mangy stuffed animals). Tri-lingual photo panels explain which crevice on Suleiman Too is appropriate for curing which ailment.

UTAMK MUSEUM
(NHAMC; ☎271 32; foreigner/local 50/20som, photos each 10som, guides 20som; ⏲9am-noon & 1-6pm) Built during the Osh 3000 celebrations, this museum has some imaginative displays like a case of weapons apparently caught up in a mad whirlwind. The great archaeological finds, historical documents and moving photos of the 1916 uprising (p423) could be so much more interesting were there more English explanations.

Three-Storey Yurt NOTABLE BUILDING
(foreigner/local 50/20som; ⏲8am-9pm) Outside UTAMK is a giant yurt built in three vertical sections. Although interesting for its mere existence, its colourful interior is little more than a gift shop with costumes in which to pose for photos (extra fee). There's also a cursory exhibition about 19th-century heroes Alymbek and Kurmanjan Datka.

Bazaar MARKET
Osh Bazaar is one of Central Asia's biggest markets, dealing in everything from traditional hats and knives to seasonal fruit to horseshoes forged at the smithies in the bazaar. Many stalls are crafted from old container boxes and banal warehouse architecture but there's a fascinating bustle nonetheless, stretching for about 1km astride the river. Most dynamic on Sunday mornings, partly closed on Monday.

Marshrutka signs 'bazaar' usually imply the eastern entrance, also known as **Jayma Bazaar**.

Lenin Statue MONUMENT
(Lenin Sq; 🚌2) One of the most impressive Lenin statues still standing in all of Central Asia appears to be beseeching the authorities to pull down the massive Kyrgyz flag flapping in front of him.

Animal Market MARKET
(Malbazaar; M41 road, km4; ⏲6am-1pm Sun) If you're in Osh on a Sunday morning, it's worth hopping on marshrutka 105 or bus 5 to the routes' eastern terminus where hundreds of sheep, donkeys, horses and cattle go on sale.

Activities

Locals swim in the **Ak-Buura River** during summer or head to the **Bolshoe Riba** (Big Fish Pool; big pool/small pool 60/100som; ⏲9am-10pm) swimming pool, under the Abdykadyrov Bridge. The smaller pool is cleaner.

Sleeping

Biy Ordo HOSTEL, GUESTHOUSE $
(www.biyordo.com; Saliyeva 39; 6-/3-bed dm 300/700som, s/d/semi-lux 1000/1800/2000; P ⊖ ❄ @ ≈; 🚌122) New Biy Ordo is worth the 10-minute marshrutka ride (122 from Kelechek Bazaar) for the three great-value dorms. The six-bed bunk-room has lockers and all rooms come with new AC and ensuite bathrooms. Youthful owner, Munar, speaks fluent English and understands backpacker needs. From the airport a booked pick-up costs 200som or get off marshrutka 107 outside BTA Bank on Razakova, then walk one block west to Saliyeva street.

Mira Homestay GUESTHOUSE $
(☎055-884 5520; Zaina Betinova 18a; per person 300som) Friendly Mira speaks English and has three well-maintained ensuite guest rooms for rent at astonishingly reasonable prices. You'll need to call her to arrange arrival as reaching the unmarked apartment requires getting through two locked doors, but the location is handily central – around 30m north of Kazkommerts Bank.

Hotel Sanabar GUESTHOUSE $
(☎299 72; Gapar Aytiev 7; d 700som) On the upper floor of a house that seems simultaneously both half-built and half-crumbling, there are just three rooms. Each has a basic bathroom, and although one is tiny, it's still relatively good value. Close to the Suleiman Too entrance.

Hotel Alay HOTEL $
(☎577 33; Kurmanjan Datka 280, enter from Navoi; s/d/q from 200/400/500som, 3rd-fl tw 600-1000som, d with bathroom 1300som) The cheapest

rooms on the tatty fourth floor are depressingly decrepit. Those on the third floor are simple but altogether more acceptable, though the ones with ensuite bathrooms are already starting to look unsightly. Stick to the 600som twins as the shared bathrooms are relatively decent on this floor. No top sheet.

Osh-Nuru HOTEL $
(055-170 0450, 756 14; www.osh-nuru.kg; Bayalinov 1; economy s/d/lux 700/800/1350som, renovated incl breakfast 1000/1300/3500som; ; 142) Unlike most of Kyrgyzstan's big, concrete former-Soviet hotels, there are no foreigner supplements here, the receptionist speaks some English and the renovated rooms have been rebuilt to a very decent standard. The unexciting 'economy' rooms, however, have simply been re-wallpapered and don't include breakfast so are a false saving. Free wi-fi in lobby.

Eco House GUESTHOUSE $$
(032-222 0945; guesthouse_osh@mail.ru; Lomonsov 25; s/tw/tr 1700/2000/2500som; ; 2) Popular with short-term business visitors, this cosy, super-clean guesthouse has a small veranda–breakfast room and garden. The eight guestrooms are unusually well appointed with great hot showers, satellite TV, free wi-fi, and some modest attempts to add decorative touches (artificial flowers, leaf-paintings, wall hangings).

Kristal Hotel HOTEL $$
(054-397 6837, 783 61; Navoi 50a; s/d/ste 1800/2500/3500;) Extremely handy for both the bazaar and minibus station, the well-kept rooms feel clean and fresh, albeit in typical sickly pastel hues and with chiffon curtains. Abstract flower carpets, geyser, fridge.

Deluxe Hotel HOTEL $$
(782 61; Navoi 35; d with shared/private bathroom 1000/2800som;) Pleasant, functional newish hotel facing Kerechek Bazaar. The three cheaper rooms share two toilets and a shower.

TES Guesthouse GUESTHOUSE $$
(573 43, 215 48; guesthouse@tes-centre.org; Say Boyu 5; yurt-bed 500som, s/d without bathroom 1000/1800som, with bathroom 2000/3400som; P) TES is notable for its peaceful garden setting where there are two-bedded yurts rented out dorm-style (no lockers) in summer. Rooms are faultlessly clean, if staid and the public areas have oddments of locally produced art. Help yourself to coffee or tea in the pine-floored lounge where breakfast is included. Laundry costs 150som per load. AC in ensuite rooms. Camping (per person 400som) includes breakfast, shower and internet. English spoken.

If all of our recommendations are full, there are plenty of other options:

Taj Mahal (396 52, 055-573 9047; Zaina Betinova; dm 300som, d 800-1000som) is a half-hearted budget option close to Mira Homestay (p292).

Osh Guesthouse (Bahadir 055-861 9333, Daniyar 077-237 2311, Farhad 055-009 3390; oshguesthouse.ucoz.com; Masalieva 8/48, 3rd stairway, top fl, apt 48; dm/s/d 290/690/840som; @), also nearby Mira is a helpful, but preposterously cramped, down-market option whose main appeal is the owners' ability to organise fair-value transport.

Hotel Pekin (055-217 8090, 782 73; Navoi 11a; s/d/tr/lux 1400/1800/2400/3200som) Chinese speakers will feel at home at this recently repainted midrange option.

A **new hotel complex** – a big, six-storey hotel – is under construction directly south of Eco House.

Eating & Drinking

Izyum INTERNATIONAL, BAR $$
(055-111 9119; Lenin 214; breakfast dishes 50-220som, small/large pizza from 180/230som, mains 100-300som, beer/cocktails from 80/120som; 8am-midnight, kitchen til 11pm;) Osh's most complete drinking/dining experience is a hit in summer for its riverside and woodland tea/dining platforms, but it also has a stylishly angular cafe with amply piled cushions on wide sofa seats. Slightly spongy pizza supplements sushi, steaks and local food choices. Separated enough not to disturb diners, the bar is stacked with back-lit bottles. Dancing is possible as the evening wears on.

Tsarskii Dvor INTERNATIONAL, PUB $$
(Lenin; mains 180-350som, steak 500som, beer 70-90som, cocktails 100-250som; 11am-midnight, kitchen til 11pm) This big ski-lodge–style log chalet has heavy wooden throne seats, a rear beer terrace and a range of barbecues, fish dishes and sausages. There's a 20som cover when musicians play (soft sax). Nightclub behind.

Ala-Too CENTRAL ASIAN $
(Masaliev 16A; mains 50-150som, shashlyk 50som; 8am-11pm) Cavernous, old-fashioned

OFF THE BEATEN TRACK

KOJO-KELEN

The mild agricultural undulations around Osh aren't Kyrgyzstan's most photogenic vistas and many daytrips suggested by well-meaning locals (Özgön's mausolea, Aravan's horse petroglyphs) can feel like little more than time-passers. However, the city's southern horizon is distantly pierced with dramatic mountains. You could see these peaks much closer by heading for Kojo-Kelen. That's 110km from Osh, 75km off the Batken road via the Papan Reservoir. Around the little red-earth village you'll find two impressive canyons, a 50m waterfall, cliffs, a pilgrim grotto and one of Kyrgyzstan's most picturesque areas of wind-eroded stone formations. There are various hiking options including a two-day guided trek to Sary-Mogol (tents required) that crosses the 4185m Jiptik Pass with phenomenal panoramas of the Alay Mountains.

chaikhana-restaurant with curtained-off family booths and excellent home-made *laghman* noodles. There are several other chaikhanas along the same strip.

Osh Ordo CENTRAL ASIAN $$
(Gapar Aytiev 11; tea 10som, mains 170-250som; 9am-10pm) Above the over-glitzy main restaurant is a summer rooftop with great views of Suleiman Too from stylish new tea pavilions, some set on rocker-wheels.

Atstek INTERNATIONAL $$
(Aztec; 055-750 0100; Kurmanjan Datka 203/2; coffee 30-70som, mains 190-390som, steak & fish 500-600som; 10.30am-11pm;) Smart restaurant with inverted Aztec pyramid lamps and a wide-ranging menu including Mexican dishes. The cafe section serves top-notch espressos at remarkably inexpensive prices.

Bridge PUB
(Lenin 301; 24hrs) Large, mood-lit basement pub with leather and tartan seats around a fireplace licking electric flames. Extensive cocktail and beer list plus a selection of 'world' food including tasty chicken fajitas.

Parliament NIGHTCLUB
(Lenin; cover men/women 100/50som, beer 60-150som; 6pm-3am summer) Dance away the summer nights in this breezy, partly open-air disco tucked into the parkland between Tsarskii Dvor and Koreana Korean restaurants.

Feel City NIGHTCLUB
(077-777 7850; Glavni Most; 7pm-2am) Beneath the big Abdykadyrov bridge, there's a lounge-bar/karaoke, restaurant section and disco that favours '80s and '90s Russian hits on weekend nights.

Shopping

The southwest entrance to the main bazaar has several stalls selling cheap *ak kalpak* hats (from 80som), embroidered gowns, satin tunics and musical instruments.

Kyrgyz Konyagy BRANDY
(www.cognac.kg; Lenin 233/9; 11am-9pm) Sells a full range of Kyrgyz brandies from 200som to 7000som per half-litre according to quality and aging (various sizes of bottles available). Flavoured brandies make great gifts (80som for 100ml of the delicious cedar-nut version) and there are also herb-honey liqueurs infused with barberry, walnut, buckthorn or pomegranate (185som). A stand-bar allows you to taste your purchases – once you've paid.

Saimalu Tash ART, SOUVENIRS
(Kurmanjan Datka 244; 10am-7pm Mon-Sat) Small but attractive art and textiles shop.

Information

INTERNET ACCESS

There is a good crop of **internet clubs** around the university buildings on Kurmanjan Datka. The square outside UTAMK has free public-access internet courtesy of US tax payers.

Meganet (Kurmanjan Datka; per hr 35som; 9.30am-7pm) Reliable internet connection.

MONEY

For banks with good dollar, euro and rouble exchange rates look on Lenin, south of the post office, and along Navoi. A few **moneychangers' kiosks** hidden deep within the bazaar will change Uzbek som, Tajik somoni and Chinese RMB at miserly rates. Visa ATMs are widespread, there are multi-card ATMs at the airport and a MasterCard/Maestro ATM beneath Taj Mahal Hotel at **Kazkomerts Bank** (Kazcom; Zaina Betinova 13; 9am-1pm & 2-6pm Mon-Fri).

POST & TELEPHONE

Main Post Office (Lenin 320; ⌚8am-5pm Mon-Fri)

Main Telecom Office (Lenin 422; ⌚24hr)

TOURIST INFORMATION

CBT Alay (☎055-507 7621; www.cbtalayblog.blogspot.com; Kurmanjan Datka 280, Hotel Alay, 2nd fl, room 3; ⌚9am-6pm Mon-Fri, 9am-2pm Sat) Has a handful of Osh homestays and organises a range of tours, notably from Sary-Mogol.

TRAVEL & TOUR AGENCIES

Munduz Travel (☎077-234 5000, 055-585 9000, 555 00, 266 55; www.munduz.kg; Kurmanjan Datka 124, entry from Asrankulov; ⌚8.30am-6pm Mon-Sat & some Sun) This reliable, long-standing commercial agency can arrange transport to Irkeshtam (US$200 per vehicle) and Murgab (Tajikistan; US$450 4WD), get Peak Lenin permits relatively rapidly (US$35 in three working days), GBAO permits for Tajikistan (US$85/50 same day/two working days) and much more.

Osh Guesthouse (☎Daniyar 077-237 2311; oshguesthouse.ucoz.com; Masaliev 8/48, 3rd stairway, top fl, apt 48; dm/s/d 290/690/840som) Osh's unlikely traveller hub can't be recommended for its claustrophobically cramped accommodation but helpful, English-speaking, travel fixer–owners use their big whiteboard to match travellers seeking to share rides.

Competitive prices for charter cars include Murgab, Tajikistan US$255; Irkeshtam Pass US$158; and Bishkek via Arslanbob US$180 (in two days). Tajikistan GBAO permits can also be arranged (three/one working days US$45/61).

The guesthouse is ludicrously hard to find. Walk north from Imam Buhari Mosque, take the kiosk-lined alley left between 10 and 14 Masaliev, turn swiftly right at the rubbish bin area then left after the second building. Call at the unmarked door at the top of the third dodgy-looking stairwell.

MuzToo (☎055-582 4435, 245 503; http:muztoo.ch; UTAMK Museum) Swiss-run agent for motorbike tours and rentals. Yamaha-XT 600 trail bikes cost around US$145/900 per day/week.

Group trips can include support vehicle but you'll need to do your own upkeep and basic mechanical repairs.

VISAS

Fotosalon 12 (Lenin 235; 8 photos for 120som; ⌚9am-5pm Mon-Sat) Cheap passport snaps for your visa application taken at the far end of an otherwise derelict building.

ℹ Getting There & Away

AIR

Up to five flights daily link with Bishkek on a variety of carriers (discount/standard/business 1300/1900/4000som). International connections include Dubai twice weekly on FlyDubai and İstanbul thrice weekly on Turkish. During summer 2013, London–Osh return flights were up to £200 cheaper than London–Bishkek returns.

There's one weekly flight to Ürümqi (Xinjiang, China) on both Air Company Kyrgyzstan and **China Southern** (Lenin 305). There are also direct flights to nearly a dozen Russian cities. Numerous air-ticket agents lie directly south of **Ural Airlines** (www.uralairlines.ru; Masalieva 28).

'International' Osh airport's facilities are comically minimal without even a baggage carousel. A bright, unadorned and very basic cafe in the basement opens 24 hours and there's a trio of ATMs, but minimal shopping facilities.

BUS & CAR

To Elsewhere in Kyrgyzstan

Minibuses to the following destinations leave from the **main minibus station** (Stary Avtovokzal; Navoi):

Jalal-Abad (120som, 1¾hr) Every 35 minutes, via **Özgön** (60som, 50mins).

Sary-Chelek (370som, five hours) 7.15am

Sary Tash (300som, four hours) 2pm. In winter check road conditions with drivers (on ☎0552-092 22 70, ☎055-036 8400 or ☎077-283 2220) before setting off. Typically continues via Sary-Mogol (400som) to Daroot-Korgon (450som). Shared taxis/informal minibuses charge similar fares and depart from the rear area of the Agromak 4WD stand.

Toktogul (420som, five hours) 7.15am

From other starting points:

Bishkek There are no buses. Shared-taxi fares fluctuate (800som to 1400som) according to demand and vehicle type but 1200som is common. Typically takes 10 hours. Cars lurk in a **parking area** hidden away just off Navoi, accessed by the footpath beside children's shop Detskiy Mir. Ideally organise the ride one day in advance, best of all having your host phone for you to be picked up from your guesthouse.

Batken (for Khojand, Tajikistan) Minibus 537 (290som, 4½hrs) leaves from the **Batken minibus stand** (Navoi 70) at 7.15am, 8.30am, 10am and noon.

To Tajikistan & China

Murgab (Tajikistan) Tajik 4WDs charge 1500som per person in a crushed-full 4WD (typically six people in four seats) taking around 12 hours. You might find such a 4WD at the **Argomak** but more likely you'll need to head out to the **Murgab-Baza** (off M41; 105), some 4km east of the Masalieva junction. Take marshrutka 105, get off 300m before the Animal Market (Malbazaar) turning and walk three minutes up the dead-end lane directly east of Aida timber shop. Departures could be any time but are most typically around 3am. If so it usually makes sense to sleep the night before at the Murgab-Baza's very rough-and-ready **crash-pad** (077-804 4755, Almakhan 077-804 4735; Murgab-Baza; dm 150som).

To see the scenic route more comfortably (and by day) consider sharing a charter vehicle. Note that such 4WDs will need special drivers' papers for the border zone and preferrably an oversized fuel tank. Osh Guesthouse (p295) can often find vehicles at short notice (US$255) and can sort out GBAO permits (essential) should you have forgotten to get one with your Tajik visa.

Kashgar (Xinjiang, China) Direct **buses** (055-265 1252, 077-265 1252; Pekin Complex, Navoi; 570 Chinese Yuan; bus 6pm Wed & Sun) depart between 6pm and midnight on Wednesdays and Sundays from the Pekin Trade Centre. Tickets are sold from a small office (the second door on the right as you walk the dead-end alley along west side of the Kerechek Bazaar). If you can't find it ask at the nearby Pekin Hotel or ask next door at Eastern Visa. Making the trip in hops via Sary Tash is more complicated but cheaper and generally more interesting.

Getting Around

Marshrutka 107 takes 25 minutes from Jayma Bazaar to the airport (9som) via Masalieva, but beware some 107 buses go instead to Dostuk/Druzhba, the Uzbekistan border post so check the destination panel. Routes 142, 137, 138 and 116 also head to the border post for the same cost as any city service (bus/marshrutka 5/8som).

Bus 2 and numerous marshrutka routes drive along Navoi, past the minibus station, then head southbound on Kurmanjan Datka, returning northbound on Lenin (at least north of Lomonsov).

Marshrutka 105 comes up Temur, turns east on Gapar Aytiev near the Suleiman Too Mosque, uses Lenin/Kurmanjan Datka north/south to Navoi, then sidesteps heading east to the Animal Market on Furkat.

A taxi costs from 50som within the centre, 200som to the airport. If you arrive at the airport after 8pm, taxis will rarely accept less than 400som to take you into town, though Biy Ordo hostel (p292) will collect guests for 200som.

Alay Valley
АЛАЙСКАЯ ДОЛИНА

Platoons of vast, ever-snowy mountains march along the southern flank of the Alay Valley whose considerable width (up to 30km) makes the scene especially memorable – at least when the haze and cloud clear.

Visitors en route to China via Irkeshtam or to Tajikistan via Bordöbo can get a taste of the scenery from Sary Tash. Both routes cross high-altitude passes but while the Irkeshtam route is fairly easy to do in DIY hops, hitching the road to Murgab (via Bordöbo) can be frustratingly slow with no regular transport: bring a tent in case you're stranded in the (potentially frigid) wilderness.

An excellent new road follows the Alay Valley southwest from Sary Tash to Garm (Tajikistan), but for now the Tajik–Kyrgyz border at Karamyk is inexplicably closed to foreigners. Even so, it might still be worth continuing part way (30km) to dusty **Sary-Mogol** for the best view of 7134m **Peak Lenin**.

Sary Tash — Сары-Таш

3243

Conveniently situated at the convergence of the roads to Osh, Murgab (Tajikistan) and Kashgar (China) via Irkeshtam, Sary Tash is a small triangle of a village with superb mid-distance views over a southern horizon of dazzling mountains. There are minimal facilities (two small shops, no regular taxis), but three homestays are well-signed close to the main junction/petrol stand. There's a good value truckers' cafe at the north edge of town.

In summer, the Daroot-Korgon–Osh minibus passes through Sary Tash at around 8am (300som, four hours) returning around 4pm. Shared taxis to Osh cost 350som.

Hitching a ride the well-paved 74km to the Irkeshtam border (one hour) is fairly easy from around 7am (expect to pay around 300som per person) or leave the evening before and sleep in one of several basic cafe-wagons at the Kyrgyz border post to ensure an early start for Kashgar.

Sary-Mogol — Сары-Могол

3243

The dusty village of Sary-Mogol, 30km west of Sary Tash, offers the valley's best views of Peak Lenin. **CBT** (Umar Tashbekov 077-261 1096) has a homestay near the village administration office *(ail okmotu)* that can arrange guides/horse treks including a seven-hour hike across the valley towards the mountains ending up at a yurtstay near **Lake Tolpur**. Near here there are views across the river to Achik-Tash, the Peak Lenin base camp, but as long as you stay on the Lake Tolpur side, CBT claims you don't need the border-zone pass.

The 2pm marshrutka from Osh to Daroot-Korgon drives past Sary-Mogol and through Kashka-Suu. A 4WD to Achik-Tash costs US$27 from CBT in Sary-Mogol, but you might get a cheaper ride from Kashka-Suu. The 4WD track is painfully degraded.

Peak Lenin & Achik-Tash

The highest summit of the Pamir Alay, 7134m **Peak Lenin** straddles the border between Kyrgyzstan (where it's officially called Koh-i-Garmo) and Tajikistan (which renamed it Mt Abuali Ibn Sino). For climbers, access is almost always from the Kyrgyz side where the lack of any peak fees and the unusually straightforward approach makes Peak Lenin one of the world's most popular and accessible 7000ers. But although the snow-covered ridges and slopes are not technically difficult for most experienced mountaineers, the altitude and infamously changeable weather can be. And the mountain holds the sad record for the world's worst mountaineering disaster when, in 1991, an earthquake-triggered avalanche obliterated Camp II on the Razdelnaya approach, killing 43 climbers in the process.

Base camp at **Achik-Tash** meadows (3600m), 30km south of Sary-Mogol, is unusually comfortable for a mountain of this height, with a series of agencies operating a veritable tent city in summer. Non-climbers can visit the camp on the first weekend of August, when CBT organises a festival of horse games here. Permit restrictions are lifted for those days, but at other times you'll need a **border area permit** (US$20 to US$30) organised through a trekking agency. Some agents take a month to get this, but Munduz Travel (p295) and CBT (p295) can usually organise things in a few days.

Southwestern Kyrgyzstan

Cradling the Fergana Valley, Kyrgyzstan's southwestern cartographic 'claw' is eccentrically sewn with enclaves of Uzbek and Tajik territory. At the claw's southern edge, Kyrgyzstan meets Tajikistan at the mind-bogglingly steep Turkestan Ridge, a dizzying wall of jagged mountains often dubbed 'Kyrgyzstan's Patagonia'.

The beautiful pyramid-shaped **Ak-Suu peak** (5359m), with its sheer 2km-high wall, is one of the world's extreme rock-climbing destinations. The region is totally lacking in infrastructure, or even roads, so you'll have to trek in from **Ozgorush**, where esteemed local guide Nuruddin runs a small homestay. Another superlative area for climbers is the trio of valleys lined with granite spires that lead south from **Karavshin**. Ak-Sai Travel (p246) operates four fixed-tent **summer camps** (dm/breakfast/lunch/dinner €10/10/20/20) at Ak-Tash Valley, Orto-Chashma Valley, Kara-Suu Gorge (Karavshin) and Ak-Suu Valley (Lyalak). These are open to independent travellers. Several Bishkek mountaineering companies offer treks and climbs in these areas, including Tien Shan Travel (p246), with 21-day climbing tours for groups of at least four experienced mountaineers from €1056 per person (excluding flights). Or you can arrange a tailor-made programme via local specialist Batken Travel Service below. Plan ahead as the higher mountain areas typically require permits.

Batken — Баткен

Spread out, but little more than an oversized village, Batken is the transport hub for southwestern Kyrgyzstan and home to affable travel fixer, Junusbek, whose **Batken Travel Service** (☎077-277 6691, 055-277 6691; www.facebook.com/BatkenTravelService; Engels 7) is based in his hard-to-find central home. Batken town is not an attraction per se, but if you're changing transport between Osh and Khojand (Tajikistan) it would be a travesty not to spend at least a few hours getting closer to the wondrous mountains that lie tantalisingly close behind. For a relatively easy half-day taster, drive through **Kara-Bulak** village and on another eight (very rough) kilometres towards **Suu-Bashi** – a walled spring-pool set in a fabulous *jailoo* valley backed by a wall of rocky ridges and peaks. Quick stops in Kara-Bulak could include a small museum and the gently quaint **Muz-Bulak** (Kara-Bulak; admission 10som; ⏲weather dependent) (literally Ice Spring) just beyond the Soviet-era children's camp. It's a

THE OSH–BATKEN BUS CONUNDRUM

The Osh–Batken highway is being rebuilt. The fast Kadamjay–Batken section opened in 2013 taking an entirely new route avoiding Uzbekistan's exclave of Sokh. While less visually spectacular than the the old Osh–Sokh–Batken route, mountain vistas still appear briefly, notably at Km201, Km207 and after Km217 (asphalt ends abruptly at Km220).

Arguably the most dramatic views are just half an hour's drive out of Osh with snowy alpine peaks rising impressively to the south near the turnoff to Kojo-Kelen (75km via Papan Reservoir).

For foreigners using the Osh–Batken road, there's still a small but potentially annoying bureaucratic niggle – ie the road cuts through a 10km slice of Uzbek territory directly east of Kadamjay. You don't pass through a real border check and there's actually no real way of leaving the road til re-emerging in Kyrgyzstan proper – indeed locals generally drive straight through without even noticing. However, technically foreigners should drive around this section. In your own vehicle it's highly likely that Kyrgyz troops will force you to do just that – it only adds around 7km, albeit annoyingly sandy so rather a pain for motorcycles. By shared taxi you can generally pay an extra 1000som per vehicle and ask the driver to go *'cherez obyezd'*. If you're on the Osh–Batken marshrutka there's a conundrum as the drivers won't divert. Readers and our authors (twice) have simply sat at the back of the minibus and sailed through without incident. But if you want to be strictly legal and avoid any risk, you might consider nipping off the first marshrutka at Kyzyl-Kiya or Kadamjay and taking a diversion-routed taxi between those towns (50km, around 800som).

picnic spot with flowering shrubs, twisted fences and merrily naive sculptures.

Sleeping & Eating

From the bus station walk west past the bazaar, then north to find at least five simple cafes on Nurgazieva.

Altyn-Ordo HOTEL $
(☎ 607 22; Sabyrbekob 14; per bed 300-1000som) Signed only as 'Gostinitsa', Altyn-Ordo is one block north of the bus station facing the park. Cheaper rooms are within the small, Soviet-era two-storey structure which is slightly bedraggled but better than many of the type. A small new annex has far superior en-suite rooms, mostly in three-room suites with *shyrdak*-style rugs.

Soltanat Homestay HOMESTAY $
(per bed 350-450som) Across the road from Altyn-Ordo is the inexpensive, if lacklustre, Soltanat Homestay. Don't be fooled by the attractive house where you enter – most rooms are a block further south across the school yard in an extension to the disused former Univermag store.

★**Altyn-Beshik** HOTEL $$
(☎ 077-227 7668, 516 16; Faygullaeva 76; s/d/lux incl breakfast 1000/1200/1500som; P ❄ wifi) If you don't mind the short taxi ride (or marshrutka 101 hop), Batken's best choice is the Altyn-Beshik, hidden 150m east off the main road, 2km south of the airport. It's clean, fresh and set around a yard full of covered tea-booths and apricot trees. Some rooms have air-conditioning and the breakfast is generous. Don't confuse it with the much more central Altyn-Ordo.

Information

Above **Galaxy Internet** (Nurgazieva 10; per hr 30som; ⏲ 9am-midnight), a block west then north of the bus station, **Eko Islamik Bank** (Nurgazieva 10; ⏲ 9am-noon & 1-4pm Mon-Fri) gives fair rates for US dollars, poorer rates for euros and won't necessarily exchange Tajik somoni at all. **RSK Bank** (Sadykova), a block further north, just east of the central Erkindik statue, has a Visa ATM.

Getting There & Away

The bus station is opposite the bazaar, a block east of Nurgaziev, the main street.

Osh Minibuses, departing at 7.15am, 8.30am, 10am and noon (290som, 5½ hours), steam straight through the Uzbek no-man's-land area after Kadamjay (see box above). Most vehicles stop for tea at Kyzyl-Kiya. Shared taxis to Bishkek (1500som) and Osh (500som to 600som) are prepared to take foreigners via diversion (obyezd) road if paid 1000som extra on top of the total per-car fare.

Isfara, Tajikistan A single mustard yellow minibus (☎077-881 7887) shuttles through the border three times daily each way, stopping very briefly at Batken bus station at 8.30am, 11am and 2pm (40som, 40 minutes) to pick up passengers. Isfara shared taxis (per seat/car 100/300som) leave from Razzakov street around the corner from the main administrative building.

UNDERSTAND KYRGYZSTAN

Kyrgyzstan Today

For years, Kyrgyz politicians have been navigating a geopolitical tightrope between China, Russia and the US over the Manas Air Base. From 2001 it was used by the US to conduct cargo and fuel sorties to Afghanistan; it is now the main gateway from which US troops are being withdrawn from that war. However, true to Almazbek Atambayev's presidential pledge, the base is due to close by July 2014. Meanwhile Russia's air base at Kant, 20km east of Bishkek, will continue to function. Some analysts see this as a major geopolitical victory for Moscow.

Kyrgyzstan maintains good relations with its eastern neighbour and biggest trading partner, China. Seemingly endless trucks bring goods across the Torugart and Irkeshtam Passes but worryingly for the economy, almost all return empty.

Kazakhstan is both the figurative and literal big brother to Kyrgyzstan, with Kazakhstan owning 40% of the nation's banks. Relations with Uzbekistan are contrastingly tense, with an ongoing war of words over water and energy usage exacerbated by ethnic tensions, notably the fallout of the June 2010 Osh riots but also the 2013 skirmishes around the Uzbek enclave of Sokh.

The national economy is disproportionately reliant on the Canadian-owned Kumtor mine (p270). During 2013, there were major disturbances on the south coast of Issyk-Köl as demonstrators cut roads and power supplies to the high-altitude mine, ostensibly to demand reparations for supposed environmental damages. Or perhaps to persuade the company to renegotiate a joint-venture agreement giving the state a substantial stake in the business.

History

Early Civilisations

The earliest recorded residents of what is now Kyrgyzstan were Saka warrior clans (aka Scythians). Rich bronze and gold relics have been recovered from Scythian burial mounds dating between the 6th century BC and the 5th century AD. Thereafter the region came under the control of various Turkic alliances with a sizeable population living on the shores of Lake Issyk-Köl. The Talas Valley was the scene of a pivotal battle in 751, when the Turks, along with their Arab and Tibetan allies, drove a large Tang Chinese army out of Central Asia.

The cultured Turkic Karakhanids ruled from the 10th to 12th centuries, instilling Islam as a generalised creed from multiple city-centres including Balasagun (the site of the now-lonely Burana Tower) and Özgön (Uzgen), at the edge of the Fergana Valley.

Ancestors of today's Kyrgyz people probably lived in Siberia's upper Yenisey Basin until at least the 10th century, when, under the influence of Mongol incursions, they began migrating south into the Tian Shan – more urgently with the rise of Chinggis

SOVIET SECRETS

The town of Chong-Tash, 10km from Kashka-Suu village, holds a dark secret. On one night in 1937, the entire Soviet Kyrgyz government – nearly 140 people in all – were rounded up, brought here and shot dead; their bodies dumped in a disused brick kiln on the site. By the 1980s almost no one alive knew of this, by which time the site had been converted to a ski resort. But a watchman at the time of the murders, sworn to secrecy, told his daughter on his deathbed, and she waited until *perestroika* to tell police.

In 1991 the bodies were moved to a mass grave across the road, with a simple memorial, apparently paid for by the Kyrgyz author Chinghiz Aitmatov (whose father may have been one of the victims). The remains of the kiln are inside a fence nearby.

Minibus 365 runs daily to Chong-Tash from near Osh Bazaar in Bishkek.

(Genghis) Khan in the 13th century. Present-day Kyrgyzstan was part of the inheritance of Chinggis' second son, Chaghatai.

In 1685, the arrival of the ruthless Mongol Oyrats of the Zhungarian (Dzungarian) empire drove vast numbers of Kyrgyz south into the Fergana and Pamir Alay regions, and on into present-day Tajikistan. The Manchu (Qing) defeat of the Oyrats in 1758 left the Kyrgyz as de-facto subjects of the Chinese, who mainly left the locals to their nomadic ways.

The Russian Occupation

As the Russians moved closer during the 19th century, various Kyrgyz clan leaders made their own peace with either Russia or the neighbouring khanate of Kokand. Bishkek – then comprising only the Pishpek fort – fell in 1862 to a combined Russian-Kyrgyz force. The Kyrgyz were gradually eased into the tsar's provinces of Fergana and Semireche while Russian settlers arrived steadily over subsequent decades. In 1916 the Russian Imperial army attempted to 'requisition' Krygyz men for noncombatant labour battalions as part of World War I mobilisation. The result was a revolt that was put down so brutally that over 120,000 died – nearly a sixth of all Kyrgyz in the empire. A similar number fled to China in what became known as the *urkun* (exodus).

After the Russian revolutions, Kyrgyz lands became part of the Turkestan ASSR (within the Russian Federation, 1918), a separate Kara-Kyrgyz Autonomous province (*Oblast*) in 1924, then a Kyrgyz ASSR from February 1926, which became a full Soviet Socialist Republic (SSR) in December 1936, when the region was known as Soviet Kirghizia.

Many nomads were settled in the course of land reforms in the 1920s, and more were forcibly settled during the cruel collectivisation campaign during the 1930s, giving rise to a reinvigorated rebellion by the *basmachi,* Muslim guerrilla fighters. Vast swathes of the new Kyrgyz elite died in the course of Stalin's purges.

Remote Kyrgyzstan was a perfect place for secret Soviet uranium mining (at Mayluu-Suu above the Fergana Valley, Ming-Kush in the interior and Kadji-Sai at Lake Issyk-Köl), and naval weapons development (at the eastern end of Issyk-Köl). Kyrgyzstan is still dealing with the environmental problems created during this time.

Kyrgyz Independence

Elections for the Kyrgyz Supreme Soviet (legislature) were held in traditional Soviet rubber-stamp style in February 1990, with the Kyrgyz Communist Party (KCP) walking away with nearly all of the seats. After multiple ballots a compromise candidate, Askar Akaev, a physicist and president of the Kyrgyz Academy of Sciences, was elected as leader. On 31 August 1991, the Kyrgyz Supreme Soviet reluctantly voted to declare Kyrgyzstan's independence, the first Central Asian republic to do so. Six weeks later Akaev was re-elected as president, running unopposed.

Land and housing were at the root of Central Asia's most infamous 'ethnic' violence, during which at least 300 people were killed in 1990, when violence broke out between Kyrgyz and Uzbeks around Osh and Özgön, a majority-Uzbek area stuck onto Kyrgyzstan in the 1930s.

Akaev initially established himself as a persistent reformer, restructuring the executive apparatus to suit his liberal political and economic attitudes, and instituting reforms considered to be the most radical in the Central Asian republics.

In the late 1990s the country faced a new threat – Islamic radicals and terrorism. In 1999 and 2000, militants from the Islamic Movement of Uzbekistan (IMU; based in Tajikistan) staged a series of brazen kidnappings of foreign workers and climbers in the province of Batken. Kyrgyz security forces largely contained the threat while IMU leadership fell to US bombs in Afghanistan.

The Tulip Revolution

By the early 2000s, Kyrgyzstan's democratic credentials were once again backsliding in the face of growing corruption, nepotism and civil unrest. The 2005 parliamentary elections were plagued by accusations of harassment and government censure. Demonstrators stormed government buildings in Jalal-Abad and civil unrest soon spread to Osh and Bishkek. On 24 March the relatively peaceful Tulip Revolution effectively overthrew the government amid bouts of looting and vandalism. President Akaev fled by helicopter to Kazakhstan and on to Moscow – subsequently resigning and becoming a university lecturer. New presidential elections were held in July 2005; the opposition leader and former prime minister, Kurmanbek Bakiev, swept to victory.

THE KIDNAPPED BRIDE

Kyrgyz men have a way of sweeping a woman off her feet – off her feet and into a waiting car. Distinctively Kyrgyz, *ala kachuu* (bride kidnapping) is a very hands-on way to find a wife. There is some dispute as to how 'traditional' the practice is and it's officially illegal, but it's once again on the upswing, with some villages apparently seeing a majority of marriages starting with an abduction. Many locals say the practice is a reassertion of national identity. Others point to the rising cost of wedding celebrations and the expense of the traditional 'bride price'. If both sides tacitly agree, a well-executed abduction can in fact prove a clever way to dramatically slash wedding costs. But not all *ala kachuu* grabs are quaint money-saving devices. In the case of a genuine kidnap, the woman does still have the right to refuse if she can sustain hours of haranguing by the groom-thief's female family members, who attempt to make her wear a symbolic bridal headscarf. But often she'll succumb, fearing an implied shame or worse if she refuses: according to human rights campaigners **Restless Beings** (www.restlessbeings.org), over 20% of non-consentual abductions result in 'rape and sexual torture'. And the girl's family, once contacted, often pressure her to agree to the marriage.

The issue of *ala kachuu* came to the fore with the 2007 Kyrgyz movie *Boz Salkyn*. In English, there are several enlightening online documentaries notably by **Petr Lom** (www.pbs.org/frontlineworld/stories/kyrgyzstan) and **Thomas Morton** (www.youtube.com/watch?v=DKAusMNTNnk) showing real-life kidnap stories.

The Bakiev Era

Bakiev's first term in office was hardly a bed of tulips. The one-time opposition leader soon faced the same criticisms levelled at his predecessor – corruption and abuse of power. Wide-scale street demonstrations in 2006 and 2007 forced him into concessions that curbed his presidential power. Bakiev's promises of peace and security were also derailed by a spate of high-profile political assassinations – three members of parliament were murdered in the late 2000s.

Bakiev was re-elected in July 2009 amid widespread accusations of ballot rigging and media censure. Voters, unable to unseat Bakiev with the ballot, reverted to a tried and true method of overthrowing Kyrgyz leaders – revolution. On 6 and 7 April 2010, opposition crowds massed in Talas and Bishkek. What was intended to be a demonstration against the government turned into a riot in both cities. Security forces were overwhelmed and the protestors stormed the halls of government. By the end of the day some 88 people had been killed and more than 500 injured in the fighting.

Bakiev fled, first to southern Kyrgyzstan, then Kazakhstan and finally to Belarus. The Kyrgyz opposition set up an interim government with Roza Otombayeva as its new leader. While many in Bishkek saw Bakiev's overthrow as positive in the fight against corruption, his removal caused serious ripples in southern Kyrgyzstan, where local politicians saw the changes as an attempt to weaken their position. When a 'power grab' by Bakiev loyalists in Jalal-Abad was countered by a local militia consisting partly of ethnic Uzbeks, the result was an explosion of politicised riots which culminated in the June 2010 Osh riots. While the exact circumstances remain highly controversial, the result was over 400 deaths (74% of these Uzbeks) and more than 100,000 ethnic Uzbeks fleeing, at least temporarily, to Uzbekistan.

People

Of approximately 80 ethno-linguistic groups in Kyrgyzstan, the main trio are:

- Kyrgyz: 66%
- Uzbek: 14%
- Russian: 10%

Notable minorities include Ukrainians, Uyghurs and Dungans (Hui Muslims originally from China).

Since 1989 there has been a major exodus of Slavs and Germans, but Kyrgyz (along with Kazakhs) remain probably the most Russified Central Asian people. Russian remains the *lingua franca* in Bishkek and northern Kyrgyzstan, but is less commonly spoken in the south. About one fifth of working adults are overseas, sending home remittances, most notably from Russia.

WHO ARE KYRGYZ?

The term Kyrgyz derives from *kyrk* (40) for the 40 Kyrgyz tribes of the Manad epic, each of which is represented by a 'flame' on the sun-circle of the national flag. Confusingly, Russians colonising the region originally used the term Kyrgyz more generally for both Kyrgyz and Kazakhs, the former being initially specified as 'Kara-Kyrgyz' (Black Kyrgyz).

About two-thirds of the population lives in rural areas. Regional clan identities are relatively strong with a north–south cultural division that's a potentially destabilising factor within society, along with the tensions between ethnic Kyrgyz and Uzbek groups. Although generally invisible to visitors, such tensions have occasionally boiled over very violently, notably in 1990 at Özgön, and in June 2010 in Osh and Jalal-Abad.

Religion

The population is overwhelmingly Muslim. Northern Kyrgyz are more Russified and less likely to follow strict Muslim doctrine than their cousins in the south. Nonetheless, Islamic observance is growing rapidly, partially as a reaction against perceived corruption in the secular sphere. Dwindling communities of Russian Orthodox Christians are still visible, particularly in Bishkek and Karakol, both of which have active Orthodox cathedrals.

Arts

Literature

Central Asian literature has traditionally been popularised in the form of songs, poems and stories by itinerant minstrels or bards, called *akyn* in Kyrgyz. Among the better-known 20th-century Kyrgyz *akyns* are Togolok Moldo (aka Bayymbet Abdyrakhmanov), Sayakbay Karalayev and Sagymbay Orozbakov.

Kyrgyzstan's best-known author is Chinghiz Aitmatov (1928–2008), whose works have been translated into English, German and French. Among his novels, which are also revealing looks at Kyrgyz life and culture, are *Djamila* (1967), *The White Steamship* (1970), *Early Cranes* (1975) and *Piebald Dog Running Along the Shore* (1978); the latter was made into a prize-winning Russian film in 1990.

MANAS

The *Manas* epic is a cycle of oral legends, 20 times longer than Homer's *Odyssey*. It tells of the formation of the Kyrgyz people with the original narrative revolving around the exploits of *batyr* (heroic warrior) *Manas* as he carves out a homeland for his people in the face of hostile hordes. Subsequent stories feature his son Semetei, grandson Seitek and widow Kanikey.

The epic was only first written down in the mid-19th century (by Kazakh ethnographer Chokan Valikhanov) and even today it remains very much part of oral tradition. *Akyns* who can recite or improvise from the epics are considered in a class by themselves and are known as *manaschi*. According to tradition, bona fide *manaschi* find their role in life after a long illness or life-changing dream.

Since independence, the *Manas* epic has become a cultural rallying point for the Kyrgyz. Manas statues grace virtually every city. Although there's much dispute as to the age of the epics, Kyrgyzstan celebrated what was purported to be the 1000th anniversary of Manas' birth in 1995. There's also a tomb near Talas touted as being the hero's final resting place, a legend that certainly encourages local pilgrims.

Other Arts

Kyrgyzstan's Aktan Abdykalykov is one of Central Asia's most accomplished filmmakers. His 1998 bittersweet coming-of-age *Beshkempir* (*The Adopted Son*) was released to critical acclaim, and *Maimil* (*The Chimp*) received an honourable mention at Cannes in 2001.

Tengri: Blue Heavens (2008) is a French-made film that follows the romantic pairing of a down-on-his-luck Kazakh fisherman with a Kyrgyz widow, set and shot in Kyrgyzstan.

Kyrgyz traditional music is played on a mixture of two-stringed *komuz* lutes, a vertical violin known as a *kyl kyayk*, flutes, drums, long horns and mouth harps (*temir komuz*, or *jygach ooz* with a string).

Pop and rap music sung in both Russian and Kyrgyz are popular among young urbanites. Look out for CDs by pop singers Aya Sadykova and Sezdbek Iskenaliev, and rapper Tata Ulan, all of whom mix traditional lyrics about their homeland with 21st-century beats.

Environment

Wildlife & Reserves

Kyrgyzstan offers an annual refuge for thousands of migrating birds, including rare cranes and geese. The country is believed to have a population of a few hundred snow leopards with Sarychat-Ertash a closed reserve partially intended to preserve them. Issyk-Köl and Sary-Chelek lakes are Unesco-affiliated biosphere reserves.

Environmental Issues

Fresh water, locked up in the form of glaciers, is one of Kyrgyzstan's greatest natural resources, but the glaciers have been shrinking alarmingly – albeit not perhaps as catastrophically as a 2008 UN report feared.

Despite a well-established seasonal rotation, there are problems with over-grazing of meadows near villages. And contrastingly there's a simultaneous under-grazing of more distant *jailoos* made inaccessible by the increasing costs of transport or lack of infrastructure.

In Soviet days, the Kyrgyz SSR's uranium mining sector earned the sobriquet 'Atomic Fortress of the Tian Shan'. A number of former mine sites still threaten to leak their radioactive contents into rivers and groundwater. Meanwhile there remain major controversies over the ownership and operation of active mines, notably the massive Canadian-run Kumtor Gold Mine. According to the BBC, this operation reportedly produces around 12% of Kyrgyzstan's GDP, but its high mountain location at the source of many river systems makes its environmental credentials particularly sensitive. In 1998 a Kumtor truck carrying almost two tonnes of cyanide and sodium hydrochloride fell into the Barskoön River leading to a widespread evacuation, though the exact number of casualties remains a source of considerable dispute.

Food & Drink

As everywhere in Central Asia, finding local meat-free meals is a tall order. In big cities your best hope will likely be in Chinese or Italian restaurants.

Tea is liquid hospitality and cups should only be half-filled – adding more suggests that one's in a hurry to get away. Bread is holy and should not be thrown away with standard rubbish nor placed upside down on a table.

A great resource on Kyrgyz cuisine is www.tastes.kg.

Typical Kyrgyz dishes include:

- *Laghman*: Mildly spicy, fat noodles generally served in soup, though *bozo laghman* is fried. There are numerous other variants.
- *Beshbarmak*: Literally 'five fingers', since it is traditionally eaten by hand. The usual recipe sees large flat noodles topped with lamb and/or horsemeat cooked in vegetable broth.
- *Kesme*: Thick noodle soup with small bits of potato, vegetable and meat.
- *Mampar*: Tomato-based meat stew with gnocchi-like pasta pieces.
- *Shorpo*: Mutton soup.
- *Jurkop:* Braised meat and vegetable dish with noodles.
- *Hoshan*: Fried and steamed dumplings, similar to *manty* (stuffed dumplings); best right off the fire from markets.
- *Ashlyanfu*: Cold rice-noodles, jelly, vinegar and eggs.
- *Fyntyozi*: Spicy, cold rice noodles.
- *Gyanfan*: Rice with a meat and vegetable sauce.
- *Kymys:* Fermented mare's milk, mostly available in spring and early summer; the national drink.
- *Bozo:* Thick, fizzy drink made from boiled fermented millet or other grains. *Jarma* and *maksym* are fermented barley drinks, made with yeast and yoghurt. 'Shoro' is the best-known brand name with vendors serving from chilled barrels at most street corners in Bishkek and Osh.
- *Boorsok*: Empty ravioli-sized fried dough-parcels to dunk in drinks or cream.
- *Kurut*: Small, very hard balls of tart, dried yoghurt; a favourite snack.

Horsemeat sausages known as *kazy*, *karta* or *chuchuk* are a popular vodka chaser.

Also try the steamed buns made with *jusai*, a mountain grass of the onion family.

In homes, but not restaurants, tea is traditionally made very strong in a pot then diluted when served.

SURVIVAL GUIDE

Directory A–Z

ACCOMMODATION

Homestays are the bedrock of accommodation in rural Kyrgyzstan, with bed and breakfast (B&B) rarely costing more than 700som. There's an approximate rating system of one, two, or three edelweiss, but even some of the best options are likely to have an outside toilet. The lowliest will have a long drop and bucket-water bathing.

Yurtstays – easiest to arrange around Song-Köl and Tash Rabat – work on a homestay basis, with mats on the floor and shared longdrop somewhere nearby. There are also private tourist yurt camps where you might get a bed and some privacy, and even a sit-down (but still outside) toilet. The latter cater mostly to groups on pre-arranged tours but are open to anyone if there's space.

Bishkek and Osh are developing new backpacker-style hostels that are a good notch above the thrown-together apartment-hostels of the last decade. Surviving Soviet-era hotels can often prove horribly decrepit or only half-heartedly reconstructed. Such places are sometimes useful as rock bottom crash-pad options but a few, notably in Bishkek, think themselves 'real' hotels and ask discriminatory foreigner prices, thereby negating any possible logic for suffering the burping old plumbing.

When staying at cheaper local hotels, double check whether a price quoted is per room or per person. If the latter it may mean a random stranger plonking his backpack on the bed beside you, dormitory style.

The main cities (Bishkek, Osh, Jalal-Abad and Karakol) all now boast new midrange hotels. Top-end accommodation is so far limited to Bishkek and a few of the resorts scattered around Issyk-Köl.

ACTIVITIES

Horse Riding

Kyrgyzstan is the best place in Central Asia to saddle up and join the seasonal nomads on the high pastures. CBT offices throughout the country can organise horse hire for around 700som per day. Jumping on a horse without pre-booking is easiest at the yurt camps of Batai-Aral (beside Song-Köl) and in the Grigorievka Valley of northern Issyk-Köl. Several agencies advertise organised horse treks though most simply sub-contract. For a well-organised tour with decent horses it's worth approaching reputable providers directly, including Shepherds Way (p270) and AsiaRando (p246). There's also **Pamirtrek** (☎077-343 8032, 031-230 4640; info@pamirtrek.com), an association of independent Pamir equestrian guides.

Some self-sufficient travellers have occasionally purchased their own horses/donkeys for around US$1000/300 at animal markets in Osh or Özgön (where prices are relatively reasonable) and, after a month or two riding or cajoling them across the mountains, sell them again in Bishkek, conceivably for a modest profit. In reality such an idea requires considerable experience and relies on finding a well-trained animal, not the cheapest one around.

A good source of equestrian insight, notably about the sturdy Kyrgyz breed, is **Kyrgyz Ate** (www.atchabysh.org).

HOME SWEET YURT

Nothing gets the nomadic blood racing through your veins like lying awake in a yurt at night under a heavy pile of blankets wondering if wolves will come and eat your horse.

Yurts (*bosuy* in Kyrgyz, *kiiz-uy* in Kazakh) are the archetypal shepherd shelters – circular homes made of multilayered felt *(kiyiz* or *kiiz)* stretched around a collapsable wooden frame *(kerege)*. The outer felt layer is coated in waterproof sheep fat, the innermost lined with woven grass matting to block the wind. Long woollen strips secure the walls and poles.

The interior is richly decorated with textiles, wall coverings, quilts, cushions, camel and horse bags, and ornately worked chests. Floors are lined with thick felt *(koshma)* and covered with bright carpets *(shyrdaks* or *ala-kiyiz)*, and sometimes yak skin.

Look up: the central wheel-like *tunduk* that supports the roof is none other than the design depicted in the middle of Kyrgyzstan's national flag.

Learn more with Celestial Mountains' online **Yurt Site** (www.yurts.kg).

Mountaineering & Climbing

For those seeking real expeditions, Kyrgyzstan offers the allure of three 7000m+ peaks, notably the majestic Khan Tengri and relatively 'easy' Peak Lenin (partly in Tajikistan but accessed from Kyrgyzstan). The latter is also probably the world's most accessible and inexpensive peak to climb but don't let those relative terms fool you into complacency. It can still be a killer. There are many unclimbed peaks, notably in the Kokshal range bordering China, and a remarkable series of cliffs and ridges in southwestern Kyrgyzstan. The granite walls of the Karavshin area are world class, but their popularity has yet to fully recover from an infamous episode in 2000 when four rash American climbers were kidnapped by IMU militants on the 750m-tall Yellow Wall. The tale, thought by some to be highly over-dramatised, was the subject of Greg Child's 2002 book *Over the Edge*.

For climbers and mountaineers wanting less full-on challenges, there are lots of options in the valleys south of Bishkek. The Kyrgyz Alpine Club's useful website (www.kac.centralasia.kg) is blocked by some servers as a security threat.

Rafting

Silk Road Water Centre (p233) organises rafting on the Kökömeren (Grade IV), Chuy (Grade III), Naryn (Grade IV) and Chong-Kemin (Grades II to III) rivers. The season runs from 25 June until mid-September. Wetsuits are essential in the glacial melt water.

Skiing

Despite the fact that 94% of the country averages over 2700m, skiing in Kyrgyzstan is still in its infancy. Currently the only 'ski fields' are around Bishkek and Karakol. The season runs from mid-November until mid-March. With the advent of heli-skiing, Russian-built MI-8 helicopters are ferrying adrenalin-junkies to altitudes of over 4500m for descents of up to 5km.

Trekking

Covered in mountains and lakes, Kyrgyzstan offers unrivalled opportunities to take to the hills. The areas around Bishkek, Karakol, Kochkor, Naryn, Arslanbob and Sary-Chelek are the major trekking regions, although any CBT office will suggest countless alternatives.

Border area permits are required to access some of the most important mountaineering areas, notably the Central Tian Shan (Khan Tengri), Ak-Suu/Karavshin and Peak Lenin regions. Agencies can organise these as part of a package but many are increasingly reticent to do so for non-guests. The cost is typically around US$30 and agents advise leaving a month for the processing, but some agents can speed things up and have the documents within a couple of days.

CUSTOMS REGULATIONS

Exporting antiques is heavily restricted. If you've bought anything that looks remotely old and didn't get a certificate saying it's not, you can get one from the 1st floor of the Foreign Department of the **Ministry of Education, Science & Culture** (Map p234; ☎62 68 17; Rm 210, cnr Tynystanov & Frunze, Bishkek)

DANGERS & ANNOYANCES

Whatever news reports might imply during the country's very occasional riots and revolutions, Kyrgyzstan is a pretty safe place to travel. For those planning adventure activities in wild, open mountainous spaces, precautions should be obvious: be aware of rapidly changeable weather patterns, extreme mountain terrain and the easily under-estimated effects of altitude sickness before setting off. Always let someone know where you are going and when you expect to be back.

➡ **Driving** If possible before engaging a ride, double check the road readiness of the vehicle and the sobriety of your driver. Reputable tour operators might charge slightly more but have an image to maintain.

➡ **Theft** Kyrgyz cities are generally safe but theft can happen, especially at night in Bishkek and Karakol. Keep valuables locked in your hotel and consider taking taxis if venturing out late.

➡ **Police Trouble** Although generally limited to a few annoying hotspots (Osh Bazaar in Bishkek is one), travellers continue to report shake-downs from corrupt cops wanting an excuse to fine you or simply rifle through your cash and reappropriate some of it. The best approach is generally not to hand over your passport to plain-clothes officers until you have reached an official station, though in reality this isn't always as easy as it sounds, especially as legally you are supposed to carry your passport at all times.

➡ **Flowers** In country areas (including Sokuluk Canyon) don't pick flowers, especially not the pale-blue bell-shaped ones known as Issykulskiy Koren. Though attractive, this is in fact *aconitum soongaricum*, a highly toxic variant of wolfsbane which can cause fatal heart attacks if the sap is ingested.

➡ **Ticks** Recent research suggests that life-threatening strains of tick-borne encephalitis, already present in Kazakhstan, have recently become a potential danger in Kyrgyzstan. The first recorded human fatality was bitten at Ala-Archa in 2009. Tick-repellant and suitable protective clothing are thus recommended if walking and camping, especially during June/July in long grass at around 2000m.

EMBASSIES & CONSULATES

For a full list of embassies see the website of the **Ministry of Foreign Affairs** (www.dcsmfa.kg).

Kyrgyz Embassies in Central Asia

There are Kyrgyz diplomatic missions in Almaty and Astana, Kazakhstan (p126); Ashgabat, Turkmenistan (p401); Dushanbe, Tajikistan (p126); and Tashkent, Uzbekistan (p222).

Kyrgyz Embassies & Consulates

For most Western nationals, tourist visas are no longer required; embassy listings have been reduced to a few regional countries where those who do need visas might apply en route.

Kyrgyz Missions in China (☎010-6468-1297; www.kyrgyzstanembassy.net; Xiaun Road, King's Villas No 18, H 10/11; ⏰applications 9am-11am Mon, Wed & Fri) One month visa costs 1360/745/465 Chinese Yuan processed in one/three/seven days. Chinese citizens will need to get visa approval from Bishkek which adds around US$15 and up to ten days. The Ürümqi Consulate (38 Hetan Beilu; ⏰noon-2pm Mon-Fri) is at the Central Asia Hotel.

Kyrgyz Missions in Iran Mashhad (☎051-818444); Tehran (☎021-229 8323, ☎021-283 0354; krembiri@kanoon.net; Bldg 12, 5th Naranjastan Alley, Pasdaran St).

Kyrgyz Missions in Russia (☎095-237 4571, 095-237 4882, 095-237 4601; fax 237 4452; Bolshaya Ordynka ulitsa 64, Moscow) Also in Ekaterinburg.

Kyrgyz Missions in Turkey Ankara (☎312-446 84 08; kirgiz-o@tr-net.net.tr; Boyabat Sokak 11, Gaziosmanpasa); Istanbul (☎212-235 6767; genkon@tr.net; 7 Lamartin Caddesi, Taksim).

Embassies & Consulates in Kyrgyzstan

For letters of support, try travel agencies such as Kyrgyz Concept (p246) and CAT (p246). The nearest Turkmen embassy is in Almaty (p126).

Afghan Embassy (Map p240; ☎0312-54 38 02; J Pudovkin (Pravda south) 24, Bishkek; ⏰9.30am-4pm Mon-Thu, 9.30am-noon Fri) Visa availability depends on your discussion with the consul and, presumably, your ability to show you understand the security situation where you plan to head. Some travellers report success, with visas issued within a day or two (transit/tourist US$30/60).

Chinese Embassy (☎0312-59 74 85; http:kg.chineseembassy.org/rus/lsqw; Mira 299/7, Bishkek; ⏰9.15am-11.30am Mon, Wed & Fri; 🚌8, 265, 295, 307) The embassy is way down Mira (Tynchtyk). Get off bus 8 or marshrutka 295, 265, or 307 at Rakhat Cafe, follow the pylons west for one block, then walk diagonally across a playing field. The consular entrance is at the far (western) side, but as of late 2013 no longer accepts visa applications from non-resident foreigners.

French Embassy (Map p234; ☎0312-30 07 11; cad.bichkek-amba@diplomatie.gouv.fr; Bokonbayevo 113, Bishkek)

German Embassy (Map p234; ☎0312-90 50 00; www.bischkek.diplo.de; Razzakov 28, Bishkek)

Indian Embassy (☎0312-21 78 06; embassyofindia.kg; 15a Aeroportinskaya St, Bishkek; ⏰10am-12.30pm Mon-Fri) Two blocks west of Mira behind the Ak-Keme Hotel.

Iranian Embassy (Map p234; ☎0312-62 12 81 after dialling press 2 then 0; Razzakov 36, Bishkek; ⏰9.30am-noon Mon-Fri) You'll need an invitation letter (best arranged in advance

HORSING AROUND

Horse sports are very popular in Kyrgyzstan and have seen a revival in recent years. The most unforgettable of these is an all-out mounted brawl over a headless goat whose body must be thrown into a circular 'goal'. Known as *kok boru, ulak-tartysh* or *buzkashi*, the Kyrgyz term meaning 'grey wolf' reveals its origins as a hunting exercise. The form played in Kyrgyzstan is essentially a team sport in contrast to the free-for-all version of Tajikistan, but either way it's a remarkably full-on event at which riders and horses can take an incredible battering. A national competition comes to a climax in Bishkek during Nooruz on 21 March. Games are also often incorporated into Independence Day celebrations and other festivals.

Other classic games include *at chabysh*, a horse race over a distance of 20km to 30km; *jumby atmai*, horseback archery; *tiyin enmei*, where contestants pick up coins off the ground while galloping past; and *udarysh*, horseback wrestling. Then there's *kyz-kumay* (kiss the girl) in which a male rider furiously chases a woman on horseback in an attempt to kiss her. Then in the return leg, the woman gets to chase and whip her pretend 'suitor'. Ah, young love. This allegedly began as a formalised alternative to bride abduction.

Community tourism outfits can often arrange demonstrations upon request if you give several days' notice.

but possible for $10 in around two or three weeks through Persia Agency; p309). Once you have the letter, the visa application takes two days and costs €50 for most nationals, €180 for Brits.

Japanese Embassy (Map p234; ☎0312-32 53 87; www.kg.emb-japan.go.jp; Razzakov 16, Bishkek)

Kazakhstan Embassy (☎0312-69 20 95; www.kaz-emb.kg; Mira (Tynchtyk) 95A, Bishkek; ⏰9am-noon Mon-Tue & Thu-Fri; 🚌8, 265, 266, 295) Bus (not trolleybus) 8 gets you handily close from Jibek Jolu via Shopokova (south of Sakura Guesthouse), Soviet (after Chuy), along Gorky from Vefa then down Mira.

Russian Embassy (Map p234; ☎consular section 0312-61 26 14; www.kyrgyz.mid.ru; Manas 55, Consular entrance on Kiev, Bishkek; ⏰1-3pm Tue & Thu) The consular department is around the back, reached from Kiev St.

Russian Consulate Osh (☎0312-263 04; http: rusconsosh.kg; Bobulova (Lumumba) 77, Bishkek)

Tajikistani Embassy (Map p240; ☎0312-51 16 37; www.tajikemb.kg; Kara-Dar'inskaya 36, Bishkek; single-/double-entry tourist visa US$75/85 plus 100som; ⏰9am-1pm & 2-5pm Mon-Fri) As long as the consul's in town, one-month tourist visas are available in 24 hours, often the same day or even while you wait during quieter periods. The GBAO permit is free if you ask for it. The embassy is two blocks north of Akhunbayev or 500m east of Yunusaliev St (Karl Marx) via Suvanberdiev, which ends outside. Numerous Asanbai-bound marshrutkas can drop you at the Yusunaliev/Suvanberdiev junction (Yusunaliev 85) including routes 212 from Kiev via Vefa Mall, 196 from Moskov, 175 on a long loop including Goin and the east bus station, and 122 from Tsum via Pravda). Trolleybus 17 (12) works too.

Turkish Embassy (Map p234; ☎0312-90 59 00; www.bishkek.emb.mfa.gov.tr/; Moskva 89, Bishkek)

UK Embassy (Map p234; ☎0312-30 36 37; www.gov.uk/world/kyrgyzstan; Erkindik 21, 4th fl, room 404, Bishkek)

US Embassy (☎0312-55 12 41; http:bishkek.usembassy.gov; Mira (Tynchtyk) 171, Bishkek)

Uzbekistan Embassy (Map p234; ☎0312-66 20 65; Tynystanov 104/38, Bishkek; ⏰10am-1pm Tue-Fri, phone for appointment 2pm-4pm Mon-Fri) Far from friendly.

FESTIVALS & EVENTS

Kyrgyzstan offers a number of festivals in summer, though many of them seem to be put on for tourists. The best and most authentic events are the **horse games** at the end of July and August (notably Independence Day, 31 August) at Bishkek, Cholpon-Ata, Karakol and the *jailoos* around Song-Köl and Kochkor.

During **Nooruz** (21 March) celebrations there are numerous sporting events, traditional games and music festivals.

The **Birds of Prey Festival**, held early August in Bokonbayevo, offers an excellent opportunity to see eagle hunters and falconers compete.

INTERNET ACCESS

Internet clubs are fairly common but do double check whether you're being charged a flat rate per hour or if there's a 'traffic' fee on top (ie a per megabyte charge) which can mount up alarmingly fast due to underlying programme updates even if you don't think you're downloading or streaming anything.

Wi-fi is increasingly widespread, and often free in hotels and smarter city cafes, but speeds can be variable. Mobile 3G internet is also variable but increasingly widespread; if you have a laptop it's well worth investing in a dongle to allow you mobile wi-fi almost anywhere there's a phone signal. Dongles (around 1000som plus SIM-card) tend to be company-specific. We found Beeline's to work consistently well, and for 33som per day you can get unlimited internet usage (no refund for unused days).

MAPS

GeoID (p244) in Bishkek is usually the cheapest source of maps by Goskartografiya, the state cartography unit. Their excellent (if mostly Cyrillic script) topographic maps include:

Ala-Archa (1:50,000) In English.

Kyrgyz Range/Kungey Ala-Too 1:100,000 topographical map covering the mountains south of Bishkek on one side, and the trekking area south of Tamga (Issyk-Köl) on the other.

Northern Issyk-Kul 1:100,000 topographical map covering trekking routes between Grigorievka and the Chong-Kemin Valley.

Sokh (1:200,000) Alay Mountains.

South-East Issyk-Kul Lake Coast 1:100,000 map showing trekking routes south of Karakol, including the Jeti-Ögüz, Altyn-Arashan and Ala Köl areas. Backed by a 1:1,300,000 country map showing archaeological sites and historic 'Silk Routes'.

Tsentralniy Tyan-Shan (1:150,000) Schematic map of Inylchek Glacier and around.

Orux (www.oruxmaps.com) is a very powerful map source and viewer for Android smartphones.

Soviet era 1:200,000 topographical maps covering the whole of Kyrgyzstan can be downloaded from mapstor.com for US$35.

MEDIA

The *Times of Central Asia* (www.timesca-europe.com), Bishkek's English-language newspaper, is free from some top hotels.

MONEY

Banks and licensed moneychanger booths (marked *obmen balyot*) exchange US dollars provided the notes are post 2003 and unblemished, in near-mint condition. Trying to get change for a 5000som note will likely be met with a look of horror.

There is no black market for currency transactions and changing money back again is not problematic. We quote prices in the currency that the businesses themselves use. That's normally som, but can be US dollars or euros for some hotels and tour companies.

If you need to wire money, MoneyGram has services at main post offices and Western Union works through many banks.

Travellers cheques are hard to cash but ATMs are increasingly common in all major towns. Most dispense both US dollars and som and work with Visa, but the whole country has under 20 ATMs that accept MasterCard or Maestro, mostly Kazkommertzbank. These are most usefully in Bishkek (10 locations), Osh (3) and Cholpan-Ata (1).

POST

Airmail postcards cost 30som (plus 14% tax!) to any country. Courier agents DHL (p245) and **FedEx** (www.fedex.com) are represented.

PUBLIC HOLIDAYS

Muslim festivals change dates annually (see p469 for more information). The most important, **Orozo Ait** (Eid-al-Fitr, the end of Ramadan) and **Kurban Ait** (Eid-al-Azha, Feast of Sacrifice), are national holidays. Other dates are fixed, but might actually be celebrated on the nearest Monday or Friday:

1 January New Year's Day
7 January Russian Orthodox Christmas
23 February Army Day
8 March International Women's Day
21–23 March Nooruz (Novruz)
1 May International Labour Day
5 May Constitution Day
9 May WWII Victory Day
31 August Independence Day
7 November Anniversary of the October Revolution

REGISTRATION

If you're one of the unlucky nationalities to need a visa you might also need to register within three days of arriving in Kyrgyzstan. Ask your hotel or at OVIR (p245).

SHOPPING

The classic souvenir is a traditional *kalpak* hat, available in a range of qualities from as little as 80som from bazaars, much more from souvenir shops. Classic feltwork including colourful *shyrdaks* make great presents and are available in most towns through community tourist offices and souvenir shops; OVOP (p262) and Tumar (p244) have particularly fine collections. US residents can order imaginative, if pricey, versions back home through **Aizada** (www.kyrgyzfelt.com). Other typical mementos include pottery figurines, miniature yurts, embroidered bags, horse whips, *kymys* shakers, leather boxes, felt slippers, Kyrgyz musical instruments and chess sets featuring Manas and his entourage.

TELEPHONE

Mobile numbers are 10 digits, landlines have five or six digits. SIM cards are very inexpensive and are often given away to arriving passengers at Manas Airport. No registration is required. Calls are only a few som per minute and a mobile phone can prove highly useful when hoteliers aren't home when you arrive.

Central telecom offices usually offer booths with Skype-computers for cheaper international calls.

TRAVEL PERMITS

Many frontier areas and virtually any place within 50km of the Chinese border require military border permits. Peak Lenin base camp and the whole Khan Tengri area fall into such zones. For around US$30, CBT (p246) or trekking agencies can usually get one for you. Applications can take anywhere from two days to a month depending on the agent. If you're travelling to/from an open border crossing with a valid onward visa, you are generally exempt from the permit requirement, but special (easy if pricey) permission is required for the Torugart Pass crossing.

VISAS FOR ONWARD TRAVEL

Some visa applications require a Letter of Invitation (LOI), usually an expensive formality organised through a travel agency or online fixer.

Afghanistan

Visa costs vary by nationality, starting from US$30/60 transit/tourist. Issuance takes only a day or two but seems to depend on your discussion with the consul (p306) and, presumably, your ability to demonstrate you understand the security situation where you're planning to head.

China

Until late 2013 it was possible to get a Chinese visa within around two weeks through agencies including Bishkek's Kyrgyz Concept (p246) or Osh's **Eastern Visa** (☎077-090 8900; df-@live.cn; Pekin Complex; ⊙9am-7pm). However, for now China has ceased issuing visas to any non resident foreigners.

India

Tourist visas cost 2025som from the Indian embassy in Bishkek (p306). Non-Kyrgyz nationals must pay an extra 480som to cover the cost of faxes sent to the Indian embassy in your home country (allow around one week).

Iran

Once you have a visa clearance code from Tehran the visa application takes two days and costs €50 for most nationals, €180 for Brits. Americans can only visit by tour. The sensible way to be sure of getting visa clearance is applying online through a reputable travel agency like www.key2persia.com or www.persianvoyages.com, ideally allowing several weeks for the procedure, which you can start from anywhere – you simply need to know which embassy you plan to collect it from. In principle such clearance can be arranged much more cheaply (US$10) in Bishkek through **Persia Agency** (Map p234; Soviet 166b), but we have not tested the theory ourselves. Some nationalities report getting a five-day transit visa without supporting documents in around one week.

Kazakhstan

One-month tourist visas cost US$30/60/90 for single/double/triple entries from the Kazakhstan embassy (p307) and are usually ready three days later. Single/double transit visas cost US$20/40 and are generally available the next working day.

Fees for your visa need to be paid several kilometres away at Kazkommertsbank (p245). Most travellers arrive at the embassy as it opens then dash to the bank to return with the receipt before 11.30am (return taxi fare 250som), but if you know the right fee, it can prove easier to pre-pay and bring the receipt to start with.

Russia

Applications at the Russian embassy (p307) are only accepted from 1pm to 3pm Tuesday and Thursday. With an original LOI and health insurance certificate some travellers have succeeded in getting a tourist visa issued within three days. But don't make any assumptions.

Tajikistan

Providing that the consul (p307) is in town, 30-day visas (or 45-day visas on request) are painlessly available for US$75/85 single/double entry, plus a 100som processing fee. A full GBAO permit is stamped in on request at no extra cost. One photograph, no need for LOI. The process usually takes one day, but can last only 15 minutes if there's no queue. But if the consul's away there's no visa issuance at all.

Uzbekistan

Call between 2pm and 4pm Monday to Friday to be put on the visitors' list (usually possible for the next working day, but not Mondays). Fill in the online application form at evisa.mfa.uz, then turn up at the appointed hour (usually 10am with everyone else) bringing a 3x4cm photo and a copy of your passport including every page with any kind of stamp. Most nationalities pay US$75/105 to receive the visa in four/seven working days but Americans pay more and things can take considerably longer if the embassy is busy. Fortunately they usually allow you to keep your passport during processing so you can apply then head off to the hills. Alternatively, visas can be issued the same day if you have a pre-arranged agency LOI, but that requires advanced planning and more money.

Getting There & Away

AIR

Bishkek's **Manas airport** (☎ 69 31 09, 69 37 98; www.airport.kg) is the main hub with relatively inexpensive international connections on Turkish and Pegasus (via İstanbul), Flydubai (via Dubai), Ukrainian International (via Kiev) and Aeroflot (via Moscow). Osh

VISAS FOR KYRGYZSTAN

Around 60 nationalities can stay for 60 days or longer without a visa, including citizens of most major Western and former Soviet countries, plus Koreans and Japanese. Israelis, Serbians, Romanians and Bulgarians are not included, but are amongst a list of 21 nationalities (including citizens of several Southeast Asian and South American countries) who can get visas without a LOI, often on the spot for US$110/125 single/double entry. Nationalities not on either list – including Chinese citizens – generally require a visa-support LOI approved by the Ministry of Foreign Affairs (p245) in Bishkek.

If you need a visa and there is no Kyrgyz embassy in your country, going through a Kazakh embassy instead is sometimes possible. Some Bishkek travel agencies including Dostuck Trekking (p246) claim they can organise visas on arrival given suitable preparation.

Visa Extensions

Visa extensions can prove fiddly. It's often easier and far cheaper to simply leave the country and return.

(p295) is also increasingly well linked via İstanbul, Dubai and various Russian cities. Both cities have flights to China via Ürümqi.

For airline listings see p247.

LAND

To/From China

There are two land routes to Kashgar in Xinjiang, China, where the official time zone ('Beijing Time') is GMT+8, though unofficial 'Xinjiang Time' is GMT+6, ie the same as Kyrgyzstan in summer.

Both routes are fiddly and essentially take a very long day so start early and bring food and drink. Both are scenically inspiring (the Torugart route more consistently so) and cross high mountain passes. Beware of intense cold and potential road closures when snow-bound in winter.

Both borders close at weekends and public holidays. Be careful if travelling on Fridays in case there's a delay or road closure (landslide, unexpected holiday) meaning you're stuck until Monday.

On the Chinese side, both routes involve crossing well over 100km between inner and outer frontier posts through a restricted border zone within which bicycles must be put on a vehicle.

Irkeshtam Route

The main route is via Irkeshtam and Sary Tash. A twice weekly Kashgar–Osh sleeper bus costing 580Yuan (around US$90) leaves Kashgar's International Bus Station at 9am Beijing Time on Mondays and Thursdays arriving between 2am and 6am the next morning in Osh (don't worry, you can stay sleeping on the bus til dawn if it's early). The bus returns from outside the Pekin Hotel in central Osh on Sunday and Tuesday nights around midnight. Buy tickets one day ahead.

Doing the trip in sections works out much cheaper – typically under US$35, albeit highly variable depending on how many other travellers cross that day and share the taxi or van cost between Chinese border posts. Crossing independently you get the added bonus of a night in Sary Tash, with its beautiful clear-weather views of Alay Valley mountainscapes, plus the views between there and Osh which the through-bus typically passes at night.

From Sary Tash hitch or share a taxi (per person/car 300/1200som) for 73km to the main Kyrgyz border post. Either leave around 7am to reach the border just after 8am or start the afternoon before and sleep at one of the basic cafe-wagons (bed 100som to 200som) right beside the border compound. Either way walk past the queue of trucks and get your passport stamped, then after that's checked, arrange a ride with the next passing truck for the following 7km. Leave your bags in the truck for the first two passport checks, but say goodbye at the upper Chinese customs station. Here your passport is checked but not stamped while your bags, camera, computer, iPad, books etc are very extensively searched for anything suspicious (films watched, photos checked, files opened).

Once a decent number of travellers have been thus checked, their passports are collected and given to an approved taxi driver who will drive you the whopping 140km to the **main Chinese border station** (Heiziwei; ⌚10.30am-2pm & 4-8pm Beijing Time, which is two hours ahead of Kyrgyz time). This costs 100/160 Chinese Yuan per person in a four-seat taxi/10-seat van, but if you're alone you might have to pay for the whole vehicle. This cost should reduce once the excellent new highway is opened. For now the old road runs tantalisingly alongside the new highway for a gruelling five hours' of seemingly endless bumps.

You get stamped into China at a big, airport-style complex. There's no bank but there is usually a moneychanger lurking just after customs offering a not unreasonable US$1=Y6. A taxi to Wuqia minibus/shared taxi station costs 5 Chinese Yuan. Or walk 3km – down a long grand avenue then right on Yingbin Lu. Minibuses to Kashgar (23 to 30 Yuan) currently take 1¾ hours but this too will reduce once the new highway is officially opened.

You'll be dropped at the Hua Hue Hotel from which the Id Kah Mosque and Pamir Hostel (backpackers' hangout) is 1.5km straight ahead (bus 8). In the opposite direction, minibuses to Wuqia leave from an indoor stand tucked into the south (river-facing) side of the same block as the International Bus Station, beneath a big sign misleadingly suggesting a bowling alley.

Torugart Route

The Torugart Pass to Naryn is used by Bishkek–Kashgar and Bishkek–Artush sleeper buses, but foreigners are not allowed to take those services and can only use this border by using agency transfers on both sides. Your name needs to be on a stamped passenger manifest (Chinese side) and a passport copy must be sent to the Kyrgyz agent. Such bureaucracy makes this route disproportionately expensive – the cheapest offers we found for groups of three/seven people were around US$110/85 per head. Alone you'd be asked nearly US$500. There are several ways to find other travellers or pre-arranged groups to join:

- in Bishkek, consult the notice board at NoviNomad (p245)
- in Naryn, ask CBT (p281) or Kubat Tour (p281)
- in Kashgar, seek out fellow travellers at the **Pamir Hostel** (www.pamirhostel.com; Nuo'er Beixilu, facing Id Kah Mosque, Kashgar) or **Old**

Town Hostel (☎+86-9982-82 32 62; www.kashgaroldcity.hostel.com/; Wusitangboyi Lu 233, Kashgar) and/or ask agencies **Uighur Tours** (☎+86-1339-9773 311; www.uighurtour.com; Qinibagh Hotel, old lobby, Kashgar) or **Old Road Tours** (☎+86-1389-9132 103; http:oldroadtours.com; Seman Hotel) whether they have groups you can join.

Cyclists need to have agency-arranged vehicles organised on the Chinese side and an official letter allowing them to ride under their own steam on the Kyrgyz side: subject to some strict rules about not deviating from the main road before the inner frontier post.

The whole Kashgar–Naryn route (typically nine to 12 hours) is scenically delightful, if weather conditions oblige, though the mesmerising views of high-altitude lake Chatyr-Köl tend to be slightly marred by power lines.

To/From Kazakhstan

Bishkek–Almaty Minibuses/private cars shuttle directly between the capitals (400/450som, 4½ hours) as full. Alternatively, take a Tamozhna marshrutka to the border (p248).

Karkara Closed to foreigners for several years, the back-door route into Kazakhstan via the Karkara Valley has reopened (summers only) since 2013 but there's no cross border public transport. Coming from the Kazakhstan side, take a Kegen-bound marshrutka, then a taxi for the last 28km to the border. Pre-arranged with **CBT Karakol**, a pickup from the border costs US$60 per car to Issyk-Köl. Hitchhiking is possible if you have tents and are prepared to wait a day or two.

To/From Tajikistan

Pamir Highway Bordöbo checkpoint between Murgab and Sary Tash is open for foreign ers whose Tajik visa includes a GBAO permit validated 'Murgab district'.

A vehicle from Osh to Murgab costs anywhere between US$200 to US$300 and this can be split between five people (but it can be difficult to find other travellers willing to share the cost). It takes around eight hours to reach the border from Osh (consider breaking the journey in Sary Tash). The border opens at dawn. This is cold and rugged territory so pack warm clothing. Remind the Kyrgyz border guards to stamp your passport – they sometimes forget.

Karamyk Although the Alay Valley route to Garm opened briefly in late 2012, the Karamyk border is currently closed again for all foreigners. Rumours suggest that it might reopen in 2015 but don't hold your breath.

Batken–Isfara In the Fergana Valley, crossing the border between Batken and Isfara (*not* Isfana) in Tajikistan is quick and painless. Taxis and the odd marshrutka make through trips so there's no need to change vehicles at the border. This route is your only Kyrgyzstan–Tajikistan option if you failed to get a GBAO permit for the Murgab route. Reaching Batken has a minor bureaucratic twist (see p298).

To/From Uzbekistan

There are no direct passenger trains between Kyrgyzstan and Uzbekistan.

Dostyk (Dustlyk) The main Fergana border to Andijon is on the outskirts of Osh reached by very regular marshrutkas (8som). Although there are often long lines, Western travellers are often pushed to the front of the queue. Walk across the border and jump in a frequent shared taxi to Andijon (8000S, 40 minutes). Beware that at times of political tension, this border has been known to close for considerable periods.

Getting Around

Only a handful of routes employ full-size buses, but minibuses, some timetabled, others departing when full, wait for passengers at most bus stations as do shared taxis. If you pay for all four seats the latter will also act as private one-way taxis. Agency or CBT-arranged drivers generally cost around double since they must cover the probability of returning empty, but such options are still worth considering for complex routes with multiple or overnight stops, and you'll often get a better vehicle (not necessarily English speaking drivers, though). Typical rates are between 14som and 18som per kilometre plus an overnight fee between 700som to 1000som to cover the driver's expenses. Self-drive car rental is a new concept but there are two local agencies in Bishkek (p249). Swiss-run MuzToo (p295) in Osh rents Yamaha-600 trail motorbikes but they don't come cheap.

Tajikistan Таджикистан

Includes ➡

Best Places to Meet Travellers

- Pamir Lodge (p344)
- PECTA (p346)
- ZTB (p333)
- Hamsafar (p323)
- TIC (p354)
- Cafe Segafredo (p322)

Best Rural Homestays

- Kholov (Habib) Homestay (p330)
- Jafr Agro-Eco Centre (p325)
- Dasha's Homestay (p342)
- Mubarak Homestay (p342)
- Roma's Homestay (p341)

Why Go?

Where 'Great Game' spies and explorers once ventured, Tajikistan's awesomely dramatic highland landscapes are now testing playgrounds for hardy climbers, trekkers and adventure travellers. Nascent rural homestay programs mean you might stay in timelessly photogenic rural villages hosted by gold-toothed, white-bearded patriarchs in iridescent *joma* robes. The people, predominantly Persian- rather than Turkic-speaking, are enormously hospitable but little English is spoken and rural transport is so irregular that you will probably want to fork out for a rented 4WD.

But the marvels of the Wakhan Valley, the starkly beautiful 'Roof of the World' Pamirs and the breathtaking lakes and pinnacles of the Fan Mountains all contribute to making Tajikistan arguably Central Asia's most exciting destination.

When to Go

Dushanbe

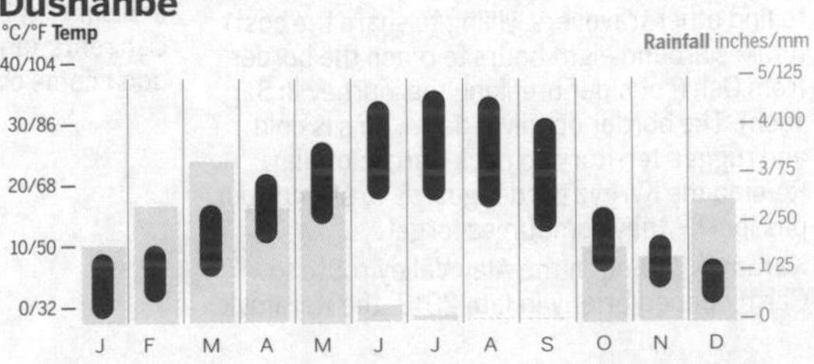

Mid-Jun–Sep The cities sizzle, but this is the only viable time for high Pamir treks.

Apr–May Mild in the lowlands; heavy showers cause landslides blocking mountain roads.

Nov–Feb Temperatures in the Pamirs drop to between -20°C and -45°C.

Visas & Permits

There is much talk about allowing visa-free entry to Tajikistan, but as yet the draft law has not been ratified. Nonetheless, for most Western nationals, getting the visa is relatively fast and painless (p367). If you plan to head to eastern Tajikistan, be sure to request a GBAO permit (p366) at the same time, without which your visa isn't valid in the Badakhshan area of the Pamirs – Tajikistan's single biggest drawcard. Applying for a permit and visa usually takes only one day in Bishkek.

COSTS

Relative Cost

More expensive than Kyrgyzstan, cheaper than Uzbekistan (unless you're renting a 4WD).

Daily Expenses

- Rural homestay half-board US$10–18
- Midrange hotel US$50–120
- Street snack 5–10TJS' good restaurant meal 65TJS
- 1L of petrol 5.50TJS

Prive Ranges

- **Sleeping** (for two people): $ <250TJS, $$ 250–600TJS, $$$ >600TJS
- **Eating** (main course): $ <20TJS, $$ 20–50TJS, $$$ >50TJS

Itineraries

- **One week** Enter Tajikistan via the western route from Osh, Kyrgyzstan, making your way to Dushanbe via Khojand, Istaravshan, Iskander-Kul and Murgab, perhaps making a side trip to Penjikent and a short trek in the Fan Mountains.
- **Two weeks** Ten days is really the minimum amount of time required to travel from Dushanbe to Osh the hard way – via the Pamir Highway – especially if you plan to arrange things as you go. Break up the journey in Rushan for Jizeu and spend as much of the time as you can afford in the Wakhan Valley.
- **Three weeks** Combine the one- and two-week itineraries to make a loop from Osh.

TOP TIP

Don't skimp on 4WD rental. Although pricey, having a car and driver can utterly transform your experience of the Pamirs, where transport is otherwise incredibly limited.

Fast Facts

- **Area** 143,100 sq km
- **Capital** Dushanbe
- **Country code** ☎ 992
- **Languages** Tajik, Russian, Uzbek, half a dozen Pamiri languages, Kyrgyz
- **Population** 7.9 million
- **Famous for** Pamir Highway, mountain hospitality, drug trafficking
- **Time zones** Murgab district is on Kyrgyz Time, the rest of Tajikistan is one hour behind.

Exchange Rates

COUNTRY	UNIT	TJS
Australia	A$1	4.42TJS
Canada	C$1	4.62TJS
China	Y100	77.4TJS
Euro zone	€1	6.34TJS
Japan	¥100	4.79TJS
NZ	NZ$1	3.88TJS
Russia	R100	14.6
UK	UK£1	7.54TJS
USA	US$1	4.77TJS

Resources

- www.asiaplus.tj/en
- www.pamirs.org
- http:tajiktourism.com
- http:tdc.tj
- www.trekkinginthe pamirs.com

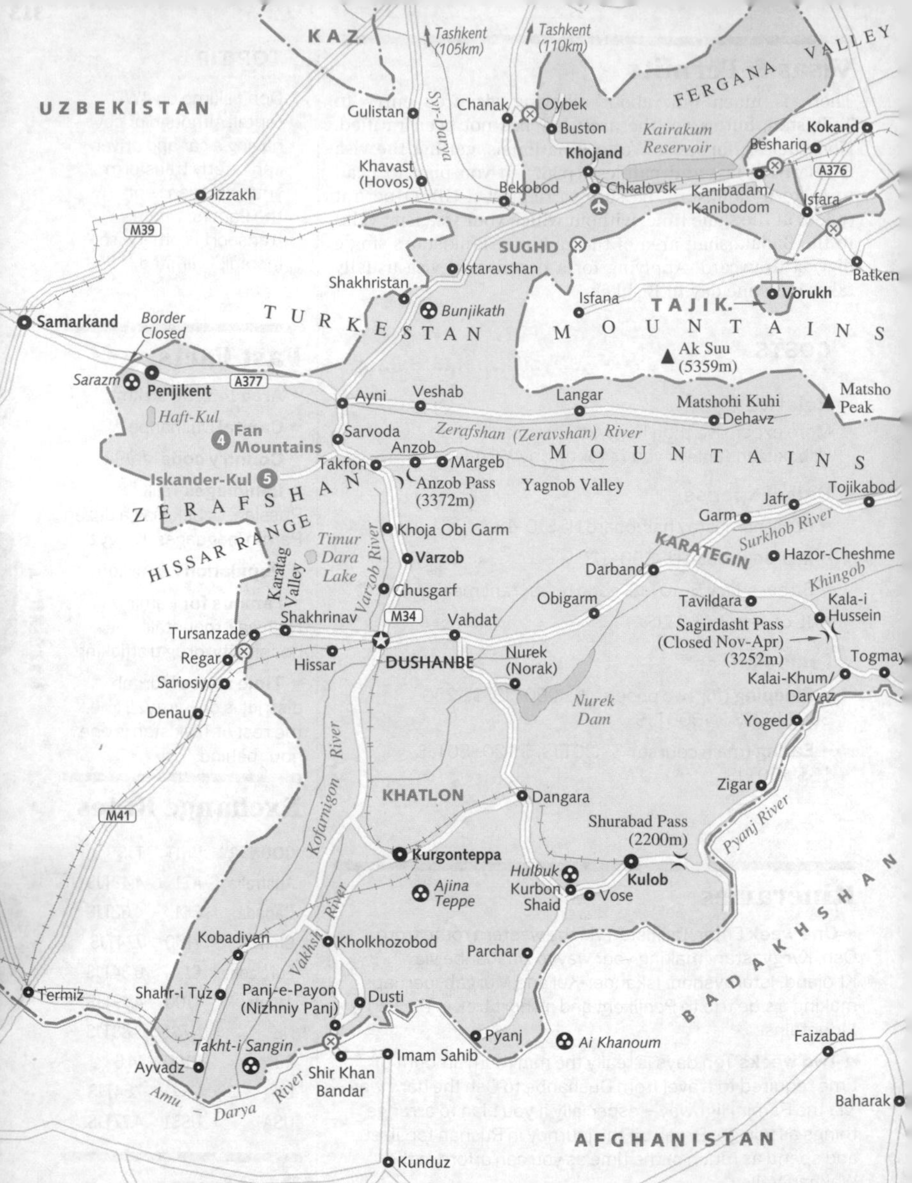

Tajikistan Highlights

1. Visit high-altitude lakes and fine community-based homestays along the **Pamir Highway** (p351), one of the world's great road trips.

2. Explore the remote and beautiful valley bordering Afghanistan, with Silk Road forts and spectacular views of the snowbound Hindu Kush in **Wakhan Valley** (p348).

3. Dangle across a river, hike to one of Central Asia's most idyllic scenes and get up close and personal with Kyrgyz herders, under a spectacular Pamiri sky in **Jizeu Valley** (p342).

4 Trek the austere but beautiful **Fan Mountains** (p326), with its turquoise lakes and Tajik shepherds.

5 Wander the shores, go for a hike or just relax along the eastern end of the Fan Mountains at **Iskander-Kul** (p326).

DUSHANBE ДУШАНБЕ

☎37 / POP 600,000 / ELEV 800M

Backed by a hazy phalanx of mountains, Dushanbe is a city in rapid transition. Its long, tree-lined central avenue still passes a collection of pastel-hued neoclassical buildings from its original Soviet incarnation. But much is threatened with the demolition ball as a whole new gamut of glitzy, oversized newcomers rise in a style that is often an intriguingly discordant blend of Roman triumphalism and budget futurism. The focus for this curious renaissance is a manicured central park dominated by a vast new museum and the world's tallest flag pole. Around the edges, the city has plenty of musty Brezhnev-era apartment-block ghettos. Yet remarkably, especially given the city's dangerous image during the 1990s' civil war, today the atmosphere is one of unthreatening calm... perhaps not unrelated to the fact that so much of the male population are away working in Russia.

History

Although there are hints of settlement here dating from the 5th century BC, modern-day Dushanbe was a small, poor village until the 1920s. So unimportant that its name, meaning Monday, was simply synonymous with the day of its weekly bazaar.

Dushanbe saw a brief flurry of excitement in 1920 when the last emir of Bukhara took refuge here, fleeing from the advancing Bolsheviks. But despite this and a 1922 *basmachi* (muslim guerrilla fighters) takeover, Dushanbe quickly reverted to Bolshevik authority.

Things suddenly changed in 1929 when the railroad arrived and Dushanbe was made the capital of the new Soviet Tajik republic. It was known as Stalinabad until the 1950s, by which stage the population had been greatly swollen, initially with Tajik émigrés from Bukhara and Samarkand, then many more during the 1940s including around 50,000 Germans, both POWs and Soviet-German exiles from Russia (coming directly, or arriving after periods in Siberia). As Tajikistan's cotton and silk industries were heavy-handedly instituted, so Dushanbe developed as a processing, industrial and administrative centre.

As the USSR crumbled, Dushanbe was the epicentre of riots in 1990 and demonstrations in the autumn of 1991. During the civil war, a dusk-to-dawn curfew saw armed gangs controlling the roads in and shoot-outs occurring between rival clans. But random acts of violence had petered out by 2002 and over the last decade the city's image has transitioned into one of calm, and apparently prosperous, confidence with barely a bullet hole to remind visitors of the bad old days.

Sights

National Museum MUSEUM

(Osorkhonai Milli; foreigner/camera 25/10TJS; ⏲10am-4pm Tue-Sat, noon-7pm Sun) Opened in 2013, the impressively airy National Museum is especially strong on archaeological exhibits, both real and recreated. The reconstruction of the Ajina-Tepe Buddhist monastery site is particularly successful in conjuring up the feeling of how the 7th-century original might have appeared. Labels mostly include English translations and though ill-lit, the top floor art gallery has some great works. The building fritters away masses of space in a vast atrium which, from the east, makes it look like the love child of a classical mansion and gigantic cement mixer.

Bayrak (World's Tallest Flagpost) FLAG

Built to commemorate 20 years of independence, the world's tallest flagpolw (165m) is the centrepiece of Dushanbe's growing ensemble of fountain-parks and public buildings including the new **National Library** and the gold-domed **Palace of Nations** government building.

National Museum of Antiquities of Tajikistan MUSEUM

(☎227 13 50; www.afc.ryukoku.ac.jp/tj; Ak Rajabov 7; foreigner/local 20/5TJS; ⏲10am-5pm Tue-Fri, 10am-4pm Sat, 10am-2pm Sun) Though the interior is dowdy and poorly illuminated, the archaeological collection here is excellent. In many cases what you'll see are the originals from which copies were made for the outwardly far grander new National Museum. Notably, the 13m-long sleeping Buddha here is the real one as removed from Ajina Teppe in 1966, when Soviet archaeologists sliced it into 92 pieces. Dating from the Kushan era (around 500 AD), it is the largest known Buddha figure in Central Asia.

Gurminj Museum MUSEUM

(☎573 10 76; www.gurminj.tj; Bokhtar 23; admission 10TJS; ⏲11am-6pm) Hidden within a private family compound behind unmarked green gates is a three-room collection of antique musical instruments from all across Central Asia. What makes the place special is that local musicians often gather here to practise/jam together creating a special musical magic. It's unmarked, diagonally opposite the obvious 'justice' mosaic.

Writers' Union Building NOTABLE BUILDING
(Somoni) Tajikistan's Persian past is invoked in the facade of the Writers' Union Building. It's adorned like a medieval cathedral with saintly, sculpted-stone figures of Sadruddin Ayni, Omar Khayam, Firdausi and other writers from the Persian pantheon.

Statue of Ismoil Somoni STATUE
(Ismail Samani) Dushanbe's most visible monument to nation-building sees the 10th-century founder of the Samanid dynasty emerging through a giant crown-topped theatrical hoop waving a wand. Rising behind him, the **Parchan** is a gold-topped white-marble column reminiscent of a Roman centurion's standard.

Rudaki Statue STATUE
On his pond-fronted garden plinth, beneath an impressive blue mosaic arc full of stars, Rudaki appears to be taking a curtain call after a 10th-century *X-Factor* performance.

Green Bazaar MARKET
(Shah Mansur Bazaar; cnr Lokhuti & Nissor Muhammed) The bustling and colourful Shah Mansur Bazaar is the heartbeat of Dushanbe trade and the best place to stock up on travel snacks from dried fruit to Korean kimchi.

Botanical Gardens PARK
(admission 2TJS; ⌚8am-7pm) The extensive Botanical Gardens are a favourite of canoodling couples. The east-central entrance gateway is designed in ancient Iranian style and dotted between the trees are beautifully carved wooden pavilions.

Victory Park PARK
For the best views over the city, watch the sun set over a draught beer from Victory Park whose impressive WWII monument is also worth a look.

World's Biggest Teahouse ARCHITECTURE
(Somoni) Still under construction, this vast festival of blue semi-traditional tiling is reputed to have cost a mind-bending percentage of the national GDP. It is rising near to Komsomol Park, one of several popular family-friendly relaxation spots.

Activities

Hash House Harriers ACTIVITY
(Facebook: Dushanbe Hash House Harriers) 'Drinkers with a running problem' generally do their thing at 3pm on Saturdays.

Hike Tajikistan HIKING
(www.facebook.com/hike.tajikistan; ⌚Sun) On Sundays when weather permits, groups of expats and locals take hiking or skiing day trips organised through social media. Typical cost around 80TJS.

AquaPark WATERPARK
(www.waterpark.tj; adult/child weekend 75/45TJS, weekday 70/40TJS; ⌚9.30am-6.30pm) A godsend for expats with kids but it's well out in the westernmost suburbs so is a bit of a trek for those without transport.

Sleeping

Dushanbe has no international-style backpacker hostels. The few homestays are hard to track down and other budget options are ageing Soviet-era hotels. Private, modern midrange mansion-hotels often hide in suburban lanes.

★ **Hotel Tajikmatlubot** HOTEL $
(☎224 64 87; Rudaki 137; per person US$30; ❄📶) Brilliant value for Dushanbe, especially for single travellers, each of the 11 rooms is a veritable suite, well-appointed albeit with rather luridly glossy wallpaper. It's in the south wing of the lumpsome blue Ittifoki building with a pretty garden behind.

Makhbuba Mansurova's Homestay HOMESTAY $
(☎856 91 66, 221 20 83; Zekhni first side-lane, 11; dm US$20, breakfast US$3) Makhbuba's house offers clean mattresses and a tea bed in the garden, across which is a hot-water bathroom and Western-style loo. It's wonderfully central but can get hot when packed body-to-body in busy summers. Off season you might get a whole room alone. It's southeast of the obvious TV transmitter.

Adventurer's Inn GUESTHOUSE $
(☎228 00 93; www.hamsafar-travel.com; Pulod Tolis 5/11; dm/tent space/floor space US$18/8/8; 📶) Hamsafar's rather makeshift guesthouse is the nearest Dushanbe comes to a travellers' hangout. Four rooms share two bathrooms plus a kitchen, but in summer backpackers' tents and bed rolls also fill much of the small yard-garden. It's awkward to find by vehicle. On foot, walk west from Vadanosos (Varzob)

Dushanbe

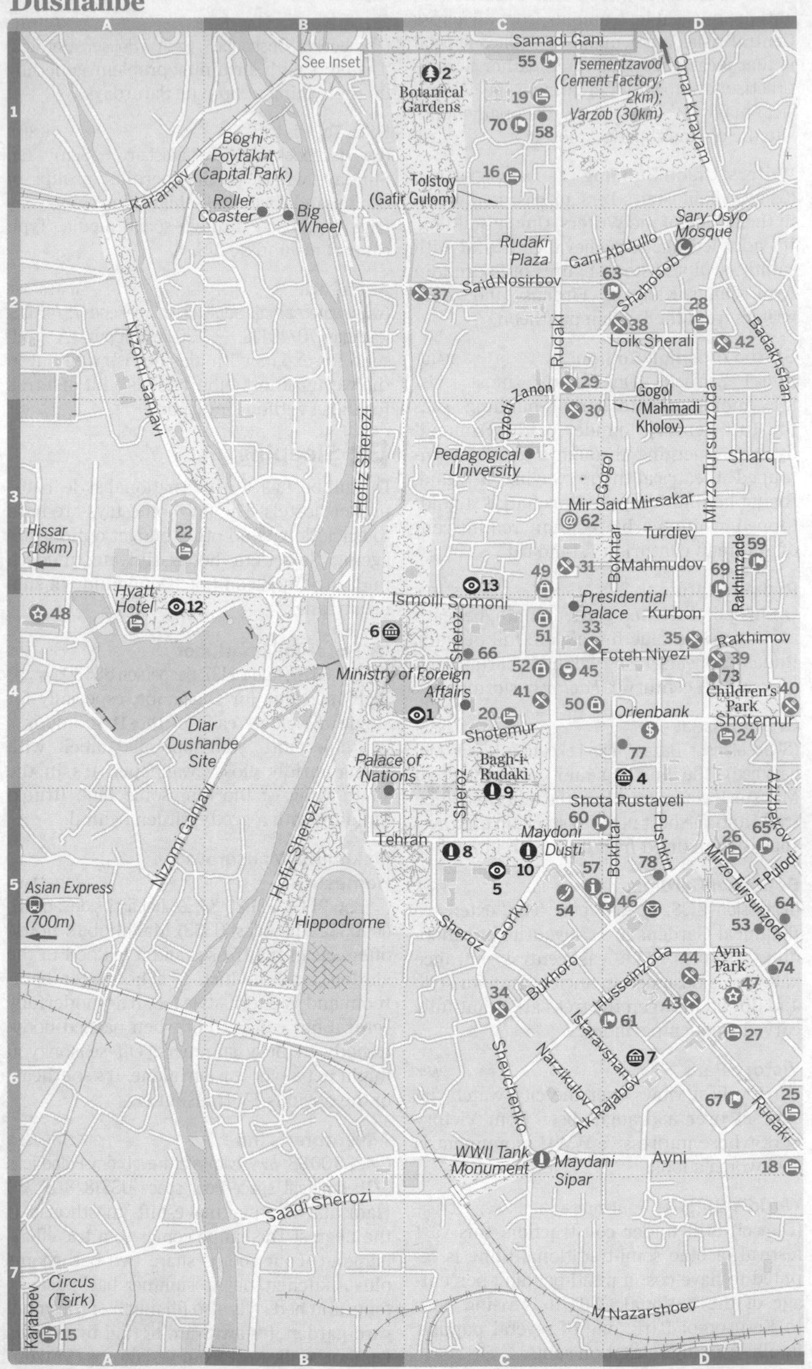
Samadi Gani
See Inset
55
2
Botanical Gardens
Tsementzavod (Cement Factory; 2km); Varzob (30km)
19
70
58
Omar Khayam
Boghi Poytakht (Capital Park)
16
Tolstoy (Gafir Gulom)
Karamov
Roller Coaster
Big Wheel
Sary Osyo Mosque
Rudaki Plaza
Gani Abdullo
Said Nosirbov
37
63
Shahobob
28
38
Loik Sherali
42
Badakhshan
Nizomi Ganjavi
Rudaki
29
Ozodi Zanon
30
Gogol (Mahmadi Kholov)
Mirzo Tursunzoda
Hofiz Sherozi
Pedagogical University
Sharq
Gogol
Mir Said Mirsakar
62
Hissar (18km)
22
Turdiev
59
Rakhimzade
49
31
Bokhtar
Mahmudov
69
13
Hyatt Hotel
12
Presidential Palace
Kurbon
48
Ismoili Somoni
6
Sheroz
51
33
35
Rakhimov
66
Foteh Niyezi
52
45
39
73
Ministry of Foreign Affairs
41
Children's Park
40
1
20
50
Orienbank
Shotemur
24
Shotemur
Diar Dushanbe Site
77
Palace of Nations
Bagh-i-Rudaki
4
9
Azizbekov
Sheroz
Shota Rustaveli
Nizomi Ganjavi
Hofiz Sherozi
60
Maydoni Dusti
26
65
Tehran
8
10
57
78
Pushkin
Mirzo Tursunzoda
T Pulodi
5
Bokhtar
Asian Express (700m)
54
46
64
Hippodrome
Sheroz
Gorky
53
Husseinzoda
44
Ayni Park
74
Bukhoro
47
34
43
Istaravshan
61
27
Narzikulov
7
Shevchenko
Ak Rajabov
67
25
Rudaki
WWII Tank Monument
Maydani Sipar
Ayni
18
Saadi Sherozi
Circus (Tsirk)
Karaboev
15
M Nazarshoev
A
B
C
D
1
2
3
4
5
6
7
TAJIKISTAN DUSHANBE

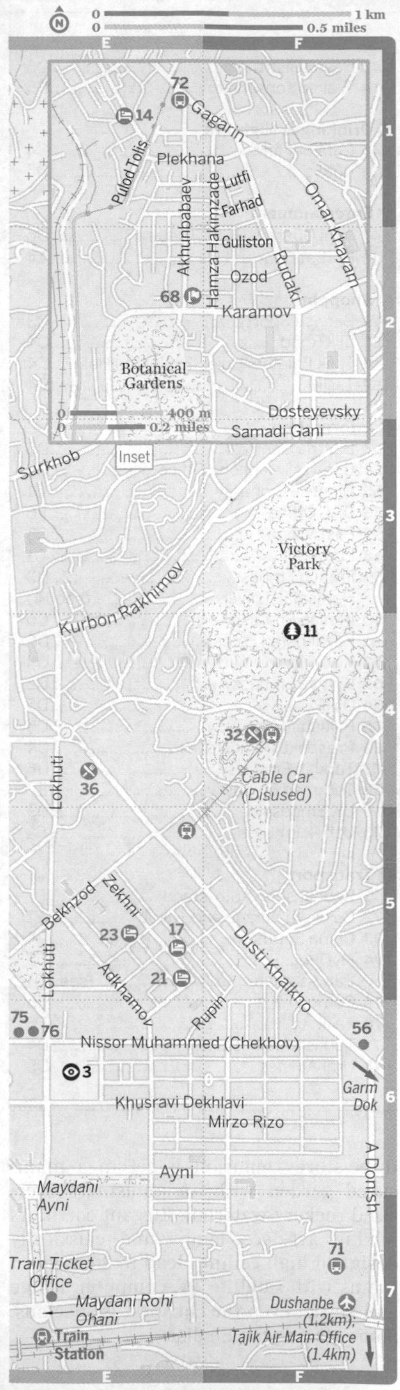

Bazaar and cross the big water pipe using the small footbridge.

Zebo's Homestay HOMESTAY $
(☎224 57 81, Farzona 888 70 96; Mirzo Tursunzoda 178; per person US$15) Simple, very friendly, single-storey private home with three guest beds in two small, stuffy rooms, one with giant teddy. There's access to a hot shower, Western-style loo and modern kitchen with washing machine. If full, guests might get the lounge floor. Farzona speaks English.

Vakhsh Hotel HOTEL $
(☎227 81 88; Rudaki 24; dm/d/tr 75/150/225TJS) This inexpensive yet historic, super-central hotel has barely one working lamp for every eight and the ensuite bathrooms have taken a real battering. However, rooms are survivable and there's a certain melodramatic thrill coming home to the neglected interior of Corinthian columns and intricate mouldings. Some balconies survey the Opera House.

Hotel Poytaht HOTEL $
(☎221 96 55; Rudaki 7; d/tr from 360/390TJS, r without bathroom per person 98TJS; ❄) Large, central and distinctively 1970s Soviet despite some cursory redecoration, rooms are priced per person but individuals might have to share with strangers. The simple *(prastoi)* rooms share acceptable bathrooms but are stiflingly hot in summer. Most ensuite rooms are air-conditioned mini-suites but are as lacking in charm as the fearsome floor ladies who guard the keys.

Hotel Farhang CRASH PAD $
(☎223 31 57; Negmat Karaliev 2; s/d from 60/120TJS) While hardly attractive, rooms are approximately clean with pairs (single plus twin) sharing a sometimes-functioning shower and seatless toilet. Rooms that claim to have air-conditioning cost extra even when the AC doesn't work. It's the pink four-storey building 100m directly south of the UFO-shaped circus (Tsirk). That's 2km west of Meydan Ayni, by marshrutka 2, 25, 33, bus 18, or trolleybus 4.

Hotel Varzish HOSTEL $
(☎400 77 74; Somoni 43, Football Stadium, south stand; dm without/with bathroom 50/70TJS, q 280TJS; 🚌8, 22) Tucked beneath the south stands of the national football stadium (set back, approximately opposite the Hyatt Hotel), rooms aimed primarily for sportsmen have dodgy lighting, peeling wallpaper and are packed with beds. However, for a

Dushanbe

Sights

1 Bayrak (World's Tallest Flagpost) C4
2 Botanical Gardens C1
3 Green Bazaar E6
4 Gurminj Museum D4
5 National Library C5
6 National Museum B4
7 National Museum of Antiquities of Tajikistan D6
8 Parchan C5
9 Rudaki Statue C5
10 Statue of Ismoil Somoni C5
11 Victory Park F4
12 World's Biggest Teahouse A4
13 Writers' Union Building C3

Sleeping

14 Adventurer's Inn E1
15 Hotel Farhang A7
16 Hotel Mercury C1
17 Hotel Meridian E5
18 Hotel Poytaht D6
19 Hotel Tajikmatlubot C1
20 Hotel Tojikiston C4
21 Hotel Twins E5
22 Hotel Varzish A3
23 Makhbuba Mansurova's Homestay E5
24 Marian's Guesthouse D4
25 Serena Hotel D6
26 Taj Palace D5
27 Vakhsh Hotel D6
Vefa Aparthotel .... (see 77)
28 Zebo's Homestay D2

Eating

29 Arirang C2
30 Café Merve C3
31 Chaykhona Rokhat C3
32 Ghalaba F4
33 Izum C4
34 La Grande Dame C6
35 Marco Polo D4
36 Merve Restaurant E4
37 Morning Star Café C2
38 Oshi Abdurahman D2
39 Poitakht Supermarket D4
40 Puppet Kurutob D4
41 Salam Namaste C4
42 Sary Osyo D2
43 Soyuz Bistro D6
44 Traktir Konservator D5

Drinking & Nightlife

45 Café Segafredo C4
46 Public D5

Entertainment

47 Ayni Opera & Ballet Theatre D6
48 Borbat Concert Hall A4

Shopping

49 Barzish Sport C3
50 Silk Road C4
51 Tajik Painters Union Exhibition Hall C4
52 TsUM C4

Information

53 Bactria Centre D5
54 Central Telephone Office C5
55 Chinese Embassy C1
56 DHL Office F6
57 East Vision C5
58 Eurodent C1
59 French Embassy D3
Hamsafar Travel .... (see 14)
60 Iranian Embassy C5
61 Kazakhstan Embassy D6
62 Klub Plazma C3
63 Kyrgyz Embassy D2
64 OVIR D5
65 Pakistani Embassy D5
66 Prospekt Medical Clinic C4
67 Turkish Embassy D6
68 Turkmen Embassy E2
69 UK Embassy D3
70 Uzbek Embassy C1

Transport

71 Badakhshan Auto-stand F7
72 Buses to Varzob and Takob E1
73 China Southern D4
74 FlyDubai D5
Iran Aseman .... (see 20)
75 Somon Air E6
76 Tajik Air E6
77 Turkish Airlines D4
78 Ural Airlines D5

group of three or four travellers on a budget, the ensuite shared quads might be worth considering.

★ **Hotel Mercury** BOUTIQUE HOTEL **$$**
(☎224 44 91; www.hotel-mercury.tj; Tolstoy 9; s/d US$80/100, half-lux US$100/120, lux US$120/140; P ❄ @ 📶) Hidden behind a high wall (with its own ATM) this new, three-storey mansion is set in a manicured garden with an amusingly oversized rockery-waterfall. Elegant corridors mixing art-deco lamps and classically designed high ceilings lead to 20 modern rooms with satellite TV, computer, fridge and kettle: even the cheapest is spacious. Some staff speak English.

Marian's Guesthouse GUESTHOUSE **$$**
(223 01 91; www.mariansguesthouse.com; Shotemur 67/1; r €70-80;) The overwhelming attraction here is the glorious, meticulously tended garden. Rooms are comfortable in a homely, unpretentious style, but are eternally popular with consultants. The building is entirely unmarked down the little alley just after the TV-station building, across from the Children's Park. Breakfast, airport transfer and evening driver service are included. Australian-owned.

Taj Palace HOTEL **$$**
(48-701 71 71; www.taj-palace.tj; Mirzo Tursunzoda 21B; d/tw US$120/140;) Of several similarly priced central business hotels (Asia Palace, Gulistan Tour), the Taj has the edge on quality of fittings, well-lit, wide corridors and ample extras – kettle, fridge, toiletries etc. Staff speak English.

Hotel Meridian BOUTIQUE HOTEL **$$**
(98-881 88 88, 44-620 33 99; www.hotel-meridian.tj; Repina 1st lane, 28; s/d/ste US$80/100/120;) Hidden in a backstreet walled garden with two tea pavilions, this sparkling clean mansion hotel offers great value with fully equipped rooms with computer, fridge and lots of space. The annex has singles for US$75, but there's a significant drop in quality for a mere US$5 discount. Sauna costs extra.

Hotel Twins BOUTIQUE HOTEL **$$**
(90-899 99 98, 221 44 14; www.hoteltwins.tj; Adkhamova 21; d US$100-130;) Probably the only hotel in town with two saunas, Twins takes the design lead from its name dividing the Escher-esque new villa into two distinct wings, one erring more towards the pseudo-classical. Each comfortable room has its own character, and not all are overloaded with nouveau-riche kitsch.

★ **Serena Hotel** HOTEL **$$$**
(48-701 4000; www.serenahotels.com; Rudaki 14; rack/web rates from US$354/230;) Dushanbe's top address gloriously weaves traditional colours, fabrics and woodwork into a light, bright 21st-century tower topped by a small rooftop swimming pool.

Vefa Aparthotel SERVICED APARTMENTS **$$$**
(www.vefacenter.tj; Bokhtar 37/1, 9th-11th fl; apt US$170-240;) If you were considering forking out US$150 for a cramped room at the **Tojikiston** (44-600 99 33; www.hoteltojikiston.com; Shotemur 22; s US$150-320, d US$300-850;), think again. For just US$20 more you can get a spacious, brand-new apartment with kitchen, sitting room and panoramic views. Some apartments come with computer and washing machine.

Eating

For cheap, genuinely local food there are several great if utterly unpretentious places on or near unpromising Loik Sherali: **Sary Osyo** (Tursunzona 129; plov 18TJS; 11am-4pm) for *plov*, Eyyannat for *laghman* and Oshi Abdurahman (p321) for *kurutob*. Better restaurants add a service charge of 10% to 12%. For extensive listings consult www.menu.tj

Chaykhona Rokhat CHAIKHANA **$**
(Rudaki 84; mains 8-17TJS, breakfast 1.40-8TJS; 6am-1am) This unusual combination of Soviet-era institution and grand Persian-style chaikhana is *the* Dushanbe classic – a great place to sip tea (2TJS) or a Simsim beer (11TJS) while people-watching. Food certainly isn't gourmet but it's good value, especially for breakfast. Kitchens work all day even during Ramadan. Some people believe the red tables (front, north) to be better for food than the yellow ones, which has a different kitchen.

Do peep into their remarkable wedding hall section (back, north side) with its magnificently faceted ceilings.

Café Merve TURKISH **$**
(Rudaki 92; mains 15-35TJS, snacks 4-17TJS; 6am-midnight;) Bright and bustling cafeteria churning out Turkish breakfasts, kebabs, pizza, salads, cakes and instant coffee (but no alcohol).

KURUTOB

Tajikistan's contribution to vegetarian cuisine is the *kurutob*, pieces of flat bread replacing meat in a warm yoghurt-based sauce topped with a salad of tomatoes, onions, fresh herbs and perhaps a hot pepper. The best *kurutob* is often found in small, barely marked cafes such as the family yard of **Oshi Abdurahman** (Loik Sherali 25; kurutob/samsa/tea 10/3/3TJS; 10am-7pm). More central is **Puppet Kurutob** (kurutob 10TJS; 6am-8pm), in the side of the mosaic-covered puppet theatre *(kukli teatr)* facing the Children's Park off Shotemur.

Soyuz Bistro CAFETERIA $

(mains 9-15TJS; 24hr) Bright, cheap basement cafeteria with a few Lenin portraits to relieve the stark white walls. Super-central but almost invisible beneath Southern Fried Chicken.

★ **Traktir Konservator** UKRAINIAN $$

(mains 18-55TJS; 11am-10pm;) The brilliantly atmospheric old-Russia decor mixes classic theatre posters, part-plastered wall arches, heavy beams, archaic clocks, flat-irons, antique windows, samovars and stove doors. Even the toilets are packed with humour. The Ukrainian cuisine includes chicken strudel (nuts rolled in chicken breast and doused in lemon sauce), roast quail with grapes, mutton-aubergine stew and various pancakes, as well as expat frighteners such as *sala* and smoked pigs' ears. It's hidden down a side alley behind the obvious Pamir restaurant that faces a park full of other summer cafes amid mature plane trees. Wicked mojitos.

Ghalaba CENTRAL ASIAN $$

(Victory Park; Park Pobedy); mains 20-65TJS; 2pm-1am) For sweeping views over the city it's hard to beat the rustic, vine-draped open-air booths and thatch-covered *tapchans* at Ghalaba. It's right at the upper station of the cable car, which is currently defunct, but reportedly due for renovation in coming years.

La Grande Dame FRENCH, EUROPEAN $$

(227 62 74, 501 00 89; www.lagrandedamecafe.com; cnr Bukhoro & Shevchenko; mains 15-72TJS, pizza 23-37TJS, breakfast items 10-25TJS; 8am-11pm;) Exposed brickwork, classical plaster mouldings, worn parquet and a shady open-air porch create a valiant approximation of an old-world provincial French cafe. Good for blinnies, lunchtime baguettes (12TJS to 15TJS), quiche of the day or just for sipping properly made coffee (12TJS to 17TJS).

Arirang KOREAN $$

(224 43 43; Rudaki 96; mains 30-80TJS, snacks 15-20TJS, rice/beer 4/13TJS; 11.30am-10pm Mon-Sat) Behind a misleadingly dreary facade, Arirang oozes faux-Orient style using ropes, manuscript panelling and bundles of contorted twigs. Savour authentic Korean food at heavy wooden tables or on raised floor mats.

Salam Namaste INDIAN $$

(Rudaki 81; curries 26-45TJS, rice/naan/beer 10/7/13TJS; 11am-11pm;) Genuine Indian food served at a pleasant, unfussy central location.

Merve Restaurant TURKISH $$

(Druzhba Naradov (Dusti Khalkho) 47; mains 18-24TJS; 8am-11pm) This plush branch of Café Merve (p321), beneath a bowling alley, has pleasant covered street-seating.

Izum INTERNATIONAL $$

(98-106 66 66; http://4sq.com/tyrfpl; Foteh Niyezi 44; mains 15-55TJS, beer 13TJS; 10am-11.30pm;) Local fabrics and piled cushions lend a mildly exotic aura to this comfortable restaurant and hubble-bubble bar. It serves excellent salmon steaks plus an unusually extensive series of vegetarian choices including baked pumpkin, lentil burgers and cauliflower cheese.

Marco Polo EUROPEAN, AFGHAN $$$

(Tursunzoda 80; mains 39-150TJS; 11am-11pm;) If it's just too hot outside, retreat to this fake stalactite-filled cavern room with shimmering couch covers and piled colourful cushions. Fun but really pricey.

Self-Catering

Poitakht Supermarket SUPERMARKET

(Tursunzoda 45; 8am-midnight) Well-stocked central supermarket.

Drinking & Nightlife

Dushanbe's outdoor cafe-bars are particularly pleasant on a warm summer evening. Sadly our favourite places in front of the Opera closed in summer 2013 to make way for a big new fountain, but the noisier park behind still has cafes and the ever reliable Chaykhona Rokhat (p321) serves cold, local Simsim draught beer very inexpensively.

★ **Café Segafredo** ITALIAN, CAFE

(Rudaki 70; pasta/mains/coffee/cocktails from 18/35/7/15TJS;) Euro-chic place to recharge on excellent real macchiatos or fresh carrot and apple juice (14TJS). Large street-terrace area, good wi-fi, mostly Italian menu.

Public PUB

(www.facebook.com/irish.publicpub; Bokhtar 2; beer/Guinness/cocktals from 10/38/20TJS; noon-11pm) Convivial Irish pub that's standing room only with expats after work on Friday evenings.

☆ Entertainment

Ayni Opera & Ballet Theatre THEATRE
(☎221 62 91, 221 44 22; Rudaki 28; ⏲Oct-Jun) Built while WWII was raging, the 1942 Opera House was completely refitted in 2009 and its gardens re-landscaped in 2013. Classy interior. Mostly opera and ballet productions.

Borbat Concert Hall PERFORMANCE VENUE
(☎223 51 86; Somoni 26) The Borbat Concert Hall hosts occasional Tajik music concerts.

Shopping

TsUM SOUVENIRS
(Rudaki 83; ⏲9am-6pm Mon-Sat) Amid the shampoo and mobile-phone sellers, is the city's original department store selling water pipes, traditional musical instruments, glazed earthenware, figurines and lovely Iranian boxes. Go upstairs to find ammonites, Soviet-era medals and Tajik robes.

Silk Road SOUVENIRS
(Shotemur 32; ⏲9am-6pm Mon-Fri) Good for mineral trees, stone mosaics, embroidery, scarves and those hard-to-find postcards.

Tajik Painters Union Exhibition Hall ART
(cnr Rudaki & Somoni; ⏲10am-5pm Mon-Fri, to 3pm Sat) Three floors of modern Tajik art, much for sale.

Barzish Sport SPORTS
(Rudaki 91; ⏲8am-6pm Mon-Sat) Sports and outdoors equipment.

ℹ Information

What's On In Dushanbe (WOID) is an expat-oriented email newsletter with a wealth of classifieds, jobs, events, restaurant ads etc. Ask marians@tajnet.tj to put you on the mailing list.

CULTURAL CENTRES

Bactria Centre (☎227 05 54; www.bactria.net; Tursunzoda 12a; ⏲9am-5pm Mon-Fri) Language classes available in Russian and Persian, concerts, art exhibitions and a showroom of Tajikistan artisan crafts. Check their Facebook site for events. The buidling is hidden down a short laneway behind 10 Tursunzoda opposite a new 10-storey apartment building.

INTERNET ACCESS

For good free wi-fi and excellent coffee, linger at Segafredo (p322) or the American **Morning Star Café** (☎228 9464; www.morningstarcafe.net; Said Nosirov 47; sandwiches 9-13TJS, coffee 16-20TJS; ⏲8am-5pm Mon-Sat;). Numerous internet clubs charging 5TJS per hour hide in suburban basements. There's free internet in the gigantic National Library (p316) once you've registered for a 10TJS library card.

Klub Plazma (Rudaki 84; per hr 5TJS; ⏲24hr) City centre.

MEDICAL SERVICES

Prospekt Medical Clinic (☎90-000 55 01, 224 30 92; www.prospektclinic.tj; Niyazi 34; ⏲8am-4.30pm Mon-Fri) Central, expat-favoured medical services.

Eurodent (☎881 10 07, 95-135 65 78; www.eurodent.tj; Rudaki 135A; ⏲8am-7pm) Highly rated dentists.

MONEY

ATMs and licensed moneychangers are widespread across the city, most centrally on Rudaki around the Shotemur junction.

POST

Post Office (Poshtamt; Bukhoro 47; ⏲9am-6pm Mon-Sat)

REGISTRATION & PERMITS

OVIR (☎227 67 11; Mirzo Tursunzoda 5; ⏲8am-noon & 1-5pm Mon-Fri, 8am-noon Sat) GBAO permits are issued in one working day. You'll need to pay the 20TJS fee to Agroinvestbank beside Gulistan Tur Hotel then bring the receipt to this office.

TELEPHONE

Central Telephone Office (Rudaki 55; ⏲24hr) Internet phone service available for cheaper international calls.

TRAVEL & TOUR AGENCIES

Hamsafar Travel (☎501 45 93, 228 00 93; www.hamsafar-travel.com; Pulod Tolis 5/11; ⏲noon-6pm Mon-Sat) Backpacker-orientated agency. As long as he's there, Ruslan can arrange short-notice 4WD, trekking and tailor-made tours. For directions see Adventurer's Inn (p317).

East Vision (☎93-858 55 55; www.traveltajikistan.tj; Rudaki 40a; ⏲9am-6pm Mon-Sat, 10am-5pm Sun) Sells maps, gives travel advice and organises tours, rural homestays and air tickets. Mirzo speaks English well.

Tajikintourservice (☎22 15 55; www.tis.tj; Druzhba Narodov (Dusti Khalkho) 23) Major travel agency offering flight bookings and visa support.

ℹ Getting There & Away

AIR

If you're arriving in Tajikistan via **Dushanbe Airport** (http://airport.tj; Titov 32/2) brace yourself for a long, tedious wait to get through immigration. Things should improve once the new terminal is built.

Agencies along Nissor Muhammed sell international tickets, plus domestic flights to Khojand (several daily, from 340TJS). However, for the 8am flight to Khorog (440TJS), you'll have to go to the **Tajik Air Main Office** (☎48-701 50 42; Titov 32/1; ⏰7am-11am & noon-7pm), one block west of the airport terminal (ideally several days ahead), and put your name and mobile phone number on a waiting list. Even if there appears to be space, you can't be 100% sure you'll go: Khorog flights are grounded at the first sign of bad weather and those with better connections might bump you down the list.

Airline Offices

In addition to those listed below there are several other airlines flying to numerous cities in Russia.

Air Astana (www.airastana.com) Three flights weekly to Almaty (Kazakhstan) and beyond.

China Southern (☎881 31 71; www.flychinasouthern.com; Tursunzoda 45, Paitakht Business Centre; ⏰9am-5pm Mon-Fri) Weekly to Ürümqi, China.

FlyDubai (www.flydubai.com; Bekhzod 1) Wednesdays and Saturdays to/via Dubai (UAE).

Iran Aseman (☎221 97 03; Shotemur 22, Hotel Tojikiston; ⏰8am-5pm Mon-Fri, 8am-2pm Sat) Mondays to Tehran, Thursdays to Mashhad (Iran); both flights cost US$274.

Kam Air (www.kamair.com) Thursdays to Kabul (Afghanistan) from US$230

Somon Air (☎560 00 00, 640 40 50; www.somonair.com; Nissor Muhammed 3; ⏰8am-6pm) Flies to Almaty, Khojand, Dubai, İstanbul (Turkey), Ürümqi (1260TJS), plus six Russian cities.

Tajik Air (☎229 82 06; www.tajikair.tj/en; Nissor Muhammed 5; ⏰8am-6pm) Flies to Bishkek (Kyrgyzstan), Almaty, Delhi (India; US$300), İstanbul, Sharjah (UAE), Tehran, Baku (Azerbaijan; from €250 return), and six Russian destinations.

Turkish Airlines (☎48-701 15 01; kaynak@gsakaynak.tj; Vefa Centre, Bokhtar 37/1; ⏰8.30am-noon & 1-5pm Mon-Fri, to 3pm Sat) The world via İstanbul, twice weekly.

Ural Airlines (☎91-864 49 67; Bukhoro 78, Gulistan Tur Hotel) Various Russian destinations.

MINIBUS & SHARED TAXI

The main bus station has had a very snazzy makeover. It is dominated by **Asian Express** (☎90-710 00 30, 1616; www.asianexpress.tj; Sino 110), whose sleek, modern buses so far serve almost exclusively southwestern Tajikistan including Kurgonteppa (15TJS, two hours, at least hourly), Kulob (Kulyab; 35TJS at 7.30am, 9am and 3pm) and Shahr-i Tuz (25TJS, 8am and 2.30pm). The terminal is 3km west of Dushanbe centre, a two-minute walk north (across rail

THE RASHT VALLEY — РАШТСКАЯ ДОЛИНА

If ongoing discussions succeed in allowing foreigners to cross the Kyrgyz–Tajik border post at Karamyk (hopefully by 2015), the glorious Rasht Valley might begin to gain some of the tourist interest that it deserves. In the 1990s, the area was ravaged then stigmatised for its civil-war role as an opposition centre. But today there's little visible evidence of that era: towns are rebuilt and a mostly excellent asphalt road sweeps through Garm (four hours from Dushanbe) and glides on past magnificent white-topped mountain vistas that are most spectacular beyond Jafr and around Gulistan (4km east of Tojikabod). As infrastructure develops it should become increasingly feasible to arrange treks into the splendid flower-dazzled valleys and get closer to the hidden spikey-topped panoramas that give the area a special magic.

Garm — Гарм

The valley's administrative centre is Garm, where **Caravan Tours** (☎98-899 90 60; www.facebook.com/CaravanToursToRasht) is a nascent local initiative by English-speaking students to entice tourists to explore the area. Their proposed horse treks make a very scenic loop around Hazor Chashme village, 24km by incredibly rough tracks across the river from Garm. Tours encompass some fabulous mountain landscapes from the ridge above Hauz-i-Foluma. Caravan also plans a network of homestays and should be able to help you find transport at fair prices for a modest commission.

Garm's main block is marked predictably enough by a large Somoni statue, with the bazaar across the road largely hidden behind Somoni 48. At the bazaar's southwest corner, **Hotel Vahdat** (☎91-885 83 47; Usman 6; s/d/tr without bathroom 50/70/90TJS, ste 150-300TJS) is unexpectedly neat, if missing numerous light bulbs. The simple, but very clean nine-bed **MSDSP Guesthouse** (Somoni 73; per person US$20, breakfast/dinner US$3/5) hides above the First MicroFinance Bank.

tracks and through a market) from marshrutka route 16, or slightly further, but more obviously, just west of the road running south from the Russian Embassy (marshrutka 25).

Asian Express plans a new bus service to Khojand (75TJS, twice daily). Otherwise shared taxis are the only option for Khojand (six hours) and Istaravshan (five hours) or Penjikent (seven hours) all via Ayni (four hours). Shared taxis depart from the Tsementzavod (Cement Factory; Rudaki; 🚇3) stand in the north of town. Prices range from 100TJS to 120TJS according to vehicle and demand. Bus/trolleybus 3 gets you here along Rudaki.

For Khorog, shared 4WDs/minivans (300/270TJS) take anything from 14 to 20 hours, departing mostly between 6am and 8am from the Badakhshan Auto-stand (Badakshanskaya avtostansiya; M Nazarshoev 149). It's hidden away through a blue gated footpath behind Donish 15 (marshrutka 8 from Green Bazaar) or through the bazaar at Nazarshoev 149 (marshrutka 33 from the train station, route 1 from Maydani Ayni). If you can muster a small group, it's well worth chartering and stopping overnight part way. Kalai-Khum drivers at the same auto-stand charge around 150TJS per person (nine to 12 hours).

Shared vehicles leave for Garm (60TJS to 70TJS, four hours), Tojikabod (five hours) and Jirgatol from Garm Dok (Ayni 82; shared taxi 4, 18), accessible by marshrutka 4 or 18 from Green Bazaar.

Minibuses and shared taxis leave from Zarnisar Bazaar for Hisor.

Varzob (3TJS) and Takob (5TJS) minibuses and cars leave from outside Vadonasos Bazaar.

TRAIN

The train to Moscow (*platskart* 1350TJS) leaves at 3.32am on Mondays, Thursdays and Saturdays routed via Termez, Karshi and Uchkuduk (Uzbekistan), Makat (Kazakhstan) and Volgagrad (1025TJS). **Ticket office** (Rudaki 2; ⌚8am-noon & 1-5pm) is diagonally across the station square.

Getting Around

Trolleybuses/buses cost 0.70/0.80TJS per hop if you have the change, 1TJS if you don't. Undersized marshrutkas want 1/2TJS for a short/long ride.

Useful routes include:

Bus/trolleybus routes 1 and 3 (but not minibus 1) Up and down Rudaki. Officially other public transport isn't allowed on Rudaki but that doesn't stop numerous police-dodging shared taxis (3TJS per seat) furtively popping signs in their windows and taking passengers this way whenever the cops stop watching – especially by night.

Upstairs beside the Megafon office, **Tarabkhonai Paymona** (mains 9-16TJS) is a clean if unspectacular restaurant that opens even during Ramadan.

Shared taxis for Tojikabad (20TJS, 50 minutes) and Jafr (10TJS) start just across the small bridge from the bazaar area, beside Somoni 50. Vehicles for Dushanbe (60TJS to 70TJS, four hours) depart from the western end of town opposite the local bus stand at Somoni 2. There's no regular public transport to Tavildara or Khorog. Charter taxis ask around 250/400 to Tavildara/Khalai-Khum, or you could take a Dushanbe car to Labi-Jar (45TJS, one hour) then attempt to hitch from the police post: reportedly a 10TJS tip to officers there can expedite proceedings. Still, reaching Kalai-Khum from Tavildara might prove difficult.

Jafr

Чафр

The area between Jafr and the Vakhdat Bridge (Km182 to Km194) is one of the Rasht Valley road's most awe-inspiring sections. Jafr itself is a pretty village where botanist, poet and collector Mirzosho Akobirov has spent decades planting seeds and saplings of numerous local and exotic fruit trees in his extensive botanical garden. This is being developed as the **Jafr Agro-Eco Centre** (📞98-804 80 59).

Many trees here have curiously been grafted with several fruit types such that a pistachio tree might simultaneously be producing plums and apricots. A museum and handicraft centre is under construction to better display Mirzosho's private collection of ethnographic and historical knick-knacks and a guesthouse (almost complete) will have one of the best balcony views of any in Tajikistan. No English is spoken, but Mirzosho can organise guides and horses for hiking up the valley over a pass into the bucolic Yasman area.

Trolleybus 12 Runs along Somoni then down Sino past the main bus station.

Marshrutka 8 Zips along Somoni, passing Royal Pub and the giant new teahouse site. It then zig-zags across the centre past the giant flag (westbound only), OVIR, Green Bazaar and the Badakhshan taxi stand before dipping under the railway and doubling back past the airport along Titov.

Marshrutka 16 Much the same as route 8 but at the western end it passes south of the bus station then drives up the western river bank past Diar Dushanbe (a vast new construction site) before joining Somoni east of the Hyatt Hotel.

Marshrutka 25 Southwest from Bekhzod dodging the Opera via Bukhoro then out west via Sherozi past the circus, north up Sino past the bus station, then west at the Russian Embassy.

Most **taxis** charge a flat 20TJS for a ride almost anywhere in town. For short trips the smart white Asian Express cabs are better as they work on the meter system.

Around Dushanbe

A popularly touted tourist offering is **Hissar (Hisor) Fort**, 30km west of Dushanbe (7km by shared taxi beyond Hisor town). Actually, all that survived a 1924 Russian assault was the twin-towered gateway. It's on a massive scale but over-renovation means that it doesn't quite look the 18th-century part. You might prefer to simply unfurl your banknotes and see the scene on a 20TJS note. If you do go, one of a pair of 16th/17th medressas at the site contains a minor museum.

Nurek Reservoir's remarkable opal-blue waters are an attraction for expats who argue over which of the many private houseboats make the best weekend getaway. However, due to the importance of securing Nurek Dam (the world's highest), permits are required, adding an obvious annoyance. The easiest way around this is to use the facilities of **AquaClub** (☎93-732 77 77; http://aquaclub.tj/en; Nurek Reservoir; per person 170-350TJS) with its own new houseboats and various water-based activities.

The **Varzob River** flows beside the main M34 north of Dushanbe, lined by dozens of nouveau-riche villas. There's no one particular place to head for but there are plenty of picturesque locations, including the **Varzob Reservoir** and the 20m **Gusgarf Waterfall**, a 2½-hour walk up a side valley 7km south of Varzob (31km from Dushanbe).

Takob is a ski-resort with summer hiking potential, which is reached via a turnoff 36km north of Dushanbe, just before the President's *dacha* (holiday bungalow).

NORTHERN TAJIKISTAN

Northern Tajikistan's main city, Khojand, sits on a cartographic periscope that pokes up between Kyrgyzstan and Uzbekistan to peer into the mouth of the Fergana Valley.

The M34 road that heads there from Dushanbe, dramatically traverses the Hissar, Zerafshan/Fan and Turkestan mountain ranges. The road is smoothly surfaced with one outrageous exception: the infamous **Anzob Tunnel**. That's a mind-boggling 5km succession of potholes, unlit mid-road hazards and lethally pinging rebar steel spikes. But away from the tunnel nightmare, only a few pylons get between your windows and some truly fabulous geological wizardry.

Beautiful Iskander-Kul lake, dramatic Margeb and the timeless Yagnob and Zerafshan valleys all make great summer excursions. If you have sufficient language competence to organise things independently, the main access points are Sarvoda and Ayni. Otherwise there's excellent English-speaking help in historic Penjikent, further west. Its role as tourist hub has been undermined by Uzbekistan's closure of the border near Samarkand (since 2010) but it's still a key access point for organising trips into the western Fan Mountains.

Fan & Zerafshan Mountains

Iskander-Kul & Sarytag

Искандеркуль и Сарытаг

Between Sarvoda and Ayni the main Dushanbe canyon-road already hints at magnificent glories behind. The easiest way to access them is driving to glorious **Iskander-Kul**, an opal-blue mountain lake that looks almost tropical in strong sunlight. It isn't. At 2195m, don't expect to swim here. But adding greatly to the visual spectacle is the variegated colouration on the superlative mountain backdrop. The scene is especially dramatic around 1.5km before arriving at the lake, but breathtak-

DIY TREKKING IN THE FAN & ZERAFSHAN MOUNTAINS

The splendidly rugged, glaciated Fan Mountains are one of Central Asia's premier trekking destinations, studded with dozens of turquoise lakes and high-mountain vistas. Treks here are for fully equipped, experienced walkers, sometimes requiring stream and ice crossings, and you'll need to deal with both summer heat and potentially serious cold at different altitudes. Stock up with food supplies in Penjikent where ZTDA (p333) and ZTB (p333) sell excellent 1:100,000 guide maps of the Fan Mountains and of Yagnob for those attempting the even more remote Yagnob–Zerafshan treks. EWP also has Fan maps (www.ewpnet.com/fannmap.htm). A superb resource is www.trekkinginthepamirs.com with photos, timings, route notes and some trails GPS-waymarked.

Routes from Artush

Three daily buses from Penjikent run to Artush (homestay available) passing the Rudaki mausoleum at Panjrud.

A two-hour (7km) walk reaches the *alplager* (mountaineers' camp; 2200m), then three more hours' uphill takes you into the Kulikalon bowl, home to a dozen deep-blue lakes. Excellent camping can be found near Dushakha Lake, at the foot of 5489m Chimtarga, the region's highest peak. There are two possible high-pass routes on from here to the beautiful **Alaudin Lakes**.

A three-day trek from the Zitmud village homestay southwest of Artush, crosses the 3810m Dukdon Pass to Sarytag/Iskander-kul.

Routes from Haft Kul

Trails from Haft-Kul (Seven Lakes) between the sixth and seventh lake lead over the Tavasang Pass (3300m) to the Archa Maidan Valley to Zitmud, or cut across the Munora Pass (3520m) to join the Dukdon Pass route to Sarytag and Iskander-Kul.

Yagnob–Zerafshan Treks

A series of trails link the parallel valleys of Yagnob and Zerafshan in around a week, notably the Veshab/Shamtuj-Bedev/Hishortob trail and Langar–Yagnob trail. More easterly routes generally require glacier-crossing sections.

ing views continue as you drive along the 6km of coast road. Higher uplands are accessed by a winding 5km drive up from the president's lakeside *dacha* to **Sarytag village**. Dwarfed by the contorted rocky bulk of Mt Sarytag, the little village (population 300, 38km from Sarvoda) makes a great walking base, whether just strolling to the discordantly ostentatious mansion villa at the village's western limits or for longer Fan Mountain treks.

Sleeping

While sleeping lakeside can be charming, staying in Sarytag provides more hiking options. Assume simplicity, outdoor toilet holes and no spoken English.

LAKESIDE

Remarkably, given the almost total lack of other buildings around Iskander-Kul, there are three waterfront accommodation options.

Asliddin Siroyidinov's Cabin HOMESTAY **$**

Has arguably the best location, but it's small, rather isolated partway round the lake, and only open by arrangement.

Shezok GUESTHOUSE **$**

(s/d 50/100TJS) Close to the barrier where the main access road arrives at the lake, is a relatively new option and the only homestay to have an indoor shower and beds (rather than mats on the floor).

Turbaza Iskanderkul YOUTH COTTAGES **$**

(☎93-504 74 03, 90-500 0227; per person 50-90TJS) A collection of 30 four-room, Soviet-era cabins dotted through a woodland with shared institutional bathroom-blocks that spare no blushes for privacy. It's overpriced compared to homestays but much livelier (at weekends anyway).

SARYTAG

Guesthouse Shahboz HOMESTAY

At the entrance to Sarytag village, this purpose-built little guesthouse is marginally

Fan Mountains

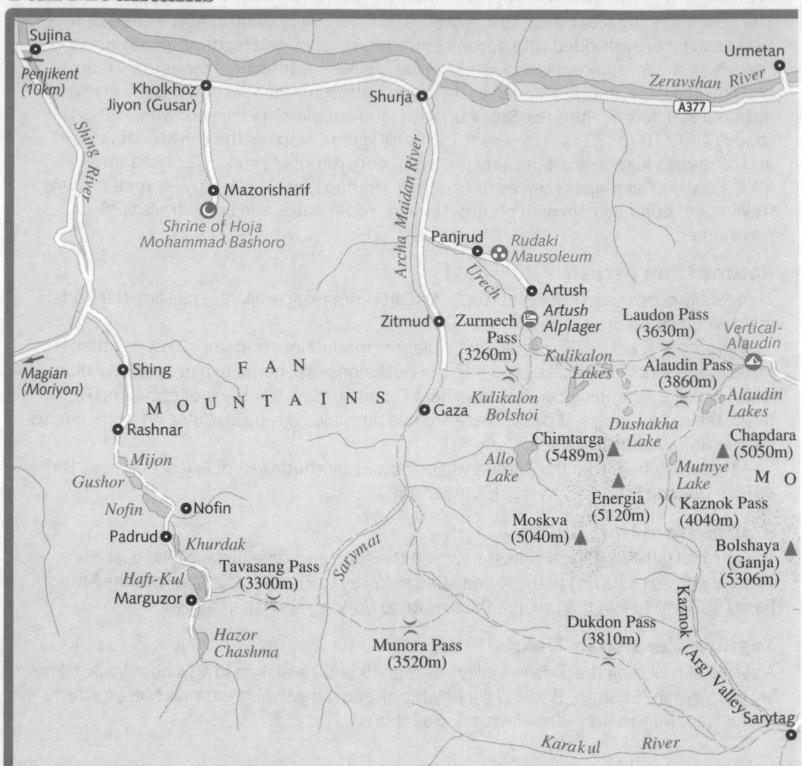

Sarytag's most comfortable option with sit-down (outside) toilet and sweeping views over the village's mountain horizion from their open-sided dining platform.

Dilovar's Homestay HOMESTAY $
(☎92-788 22 35) In the heart of the village, this place wins for its flower garden and may soon be the first place to have a shower (others have *banya*, public bath, for an extra US$5 fee).

Iqbol Homestay HOMESTAY $
(☎92-744 20 30, 92-725 90 81, Israfil 92-790 92 12; B&B US$10, dinner/banya US$5/5) The old building here has the most authentic sleeping room but the worst bathroom, unless you walk to their nearly-complete new building.

Eating

There's one very basic shop (beneath Shezok guesthouse) at the start of the lake. Otherwise you'll be reliant on homestay (or Turbaza) meals and your own supplies.

Getting There & Away

The unpaved road isn't bad but there's no public transport. A taxi from Sarvoda market costs 100TJS to 150TJS. Peak season weekends you might hitch a ride from the M34 junction with Dushanbe partygoers heading to the Turbaza.

Shared taxis for Dushanbe leave Sarytag a few times weekly (from 70TJS), others are organised most days in summer from Shezok guesthouse.

Sarvoda Сарвода

A few drab apartment blocks, factory ruins and a big Soviet silver worker statue hidden in the trees. That's about all there is of Sarvoda. However, its minor roadside bazaar is a handy place to seek rides to Margeb, Iskander-Kul or the Alaudin Lakes. If you're stuck overnight, **Mehmonkhona Yazdon** (☎92-811 13 98; dm 10TJS) has cheap beds and

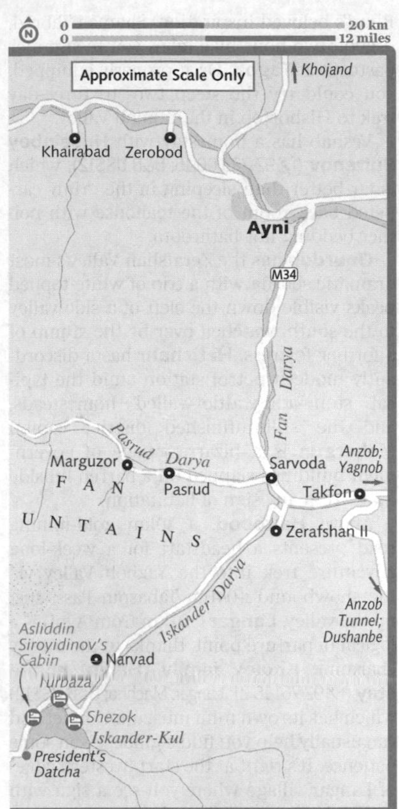

a toilet-hole way down the wooded garden. It's 1km north of the bazaar on the M34, the last house on the left before you cross the river bridge at the Alaudin turning.

Alaudin Lakes

Limpid and dreamily beautiful, the main Alaudin Lake (2780m) is a glorious place for camping, and a possible base for walking into the heart of the Fan Mountains. A popular day hike takes you out to Mutnye ('muddy') Lake (3510m), surrounded by a splendid array of 5000m plus peaks. Alaudin is helpfully accessible, just 3km on foot from a trailhead camp where three valleys meet: taxis ask around 150TJS to drive here from Sarvoda. The western valley eventually takes you across the breathtaking 3630m Laudan Pass to the lovely Kulikalon lakes in around eight hours.

There is a trail of sorts to Iskander-Kul but it crosses the seriously difficult Kaznok Pass (4040m, ice axe and crampons required).

If you're not on a tour, bring all the provisions you'll need from Sarvoda or beyond.

Margeb & the Yagnob Valley

At Km95.5 of the Dushanbe Highway, just east of the small step-layered village of **Takfon**, a dusty, ragged ribbon of former asphalt leads towards the wild Yagnob mountain valley. After 20km you'll pass through **Anzob**, a little market town with some stacked old-stone stables and a curious erosion pillar beside the road. About 2km further you get the first stunning mountain views with **Chumgar** and **Zamin-Karor** rising ahead like massive spiky horns. The latter's towering, near-vertical rock faces have attracted international mountaineering competitions. One grand rock-wall looms almost directly above the upper section of two-centred **Margeb** (Margeb Bolo), a timeless old village whose dramatic location is reason enough to visit even if you've no interest in climbing.

Sayoh Homestay (Safar Rasulov; ☎93-504 02 01; Margeb) is appealingly traditional and delightfully hospitable in the upper village heart. **Zaminkaror Homestay** (Duomahammad Dustov (Klichku Jonik); ☎92-816 27 74; Margeb; dm/breakfast/lunch/dinner US$10/2/5/5) sits five minutes' stroll above, amid photogenic stone stables at the top of the village and is building a new two-room mini-guesthouse in their garden.

Starting 22km past Margeb at **Bedev**, some villages of the upper Yagnob Valley are still home to native speakers of Sogd[ian], a language largely unchanged since the time of Alexander the Great. Some 500 more Sogd-speaking families were forcibly relocated out of the valley to Zafarobad in 1970.

The best starting point to find a ride to Margeb is Sarvoda, where Yagnobi traders stock up at the market. Cars also run most mornings from Margeb to Dushanbe (60TJS per seat). Beware that old maps still show the old road over the Anzob Pass. Sadly that gloriously scenic option has essentially decayed beyond any usability, even for motorcycles.

Ayni Айнӣ

The transport hub for the Mastcho (East Zerafshan) Valley, Ayni has two centres. The main one, on the M34, has moneychanging banks, an ATM, shops and a small area of attractive traditional garden homesteads hidden on alley-footpaths behind what apears to be a stretched silver-domed Dalek. Actually, beneath all the Dalek's battered Plexiglass, there's the heavily eroded 10th-century mud-brick minaret, **Varz-i-Minor**. The mosque beside it has some attractive woodwork.

If you're stuck here overnight, **Varz** (☎92 852 86 86; Rudaki; tr 150TJS) has three new, if somewhat sparse, guestrooms with modern bathrooms and very firm beds. It's upstairs over the modern green-roofed shop-and-wedding hall complex on the main drag.

Some 3km south, just across the M34 bridge, 'krug' is the main taxi stand for Dushanbe (45TJS to 70TJS per seat, 2½ hours) and Sarvoda (20TJS per car). Ayni's second centre is directly east of krug on the Mastcho road, with the 4WD stand for Veshab (15TJS) and the eastern Zerafshan Valley near the hospital, 700m along. In between, the new, soulless **Nuri Rahmon Hotel** (☎92-818 67 67; foreigner dm/s/tw/ste 150/250/460/300TJS, local 80/120/220/180TJS) oddly charges the same for an impressive double-bed suite ('married couple only', 300TJS) as for two beds in a bland four-bed dorm while an austere twin costs 460TJS.

Zerafshan Valley Долина Зеравшан

A bumpily slow road roller-coasters through the Zerafshan Valley that intersperses impressively stark arid rockscapes with splashes of intense irrigated green, though you won't see as much spikey mountain action here as at Margeb or Iskander-Kul, especially if you're driving west on the busier route towards Penjikent.

MASTCHOHI KUHI (UPPER ZERAFSHAN)

Heading east of Ayni into Mastcho, the road is long but gently rewarding with several interesting rural villages and the potential for some strenuous hiking if you're well prepared.

Perhaps the most interesting village is **Veshab**, 47km from Ayni, with a stepped section of old houses at the back of town and a fine perch high above the curling river. In the village centre, opposite the teahouse, **Bobokon Choykhana** (☎91-890 89 28; Veshab; sleeping space 5TJS), a wide footpath descending past the main shop leads in five minutes to a tomb-shrine that looks brand new, but is claimed to be that of Sufi poet Rumi's beloved inspiration, Shams-i Tabrizi. A good two-hour hike takes you to summer pastures at **Tagob**. Or, if properly equipped, you could try the steep two- to three-day trek to Hishortob in the Yagnob Valley.

Veshab has a homestay with **Huseinboy Sultanov** (☎92-723 00 15; B&B US$12), which is far better than sleeping in the grimy carpeted back room of the teahouse with neither bedding nor bathroom.

Oburdon has the Zerafshan Valley's most dramatic setting with a trio of white-topped peaks visible down the cleft of a side valley to the south, watched over by the stump of a former fortress. **Hatishahr** has a discordantly modern petrol station amid the typical stone-and-wattle–walled homesteads, and the still-unfinished district capital **Mehergun** is a bizarre gaggle of government buildings slapped on a barren hillside away from any sign of habitation.

Above **Hairobod**, a 10km gold-mining road presents a headstart for a week-long adventure trek into the Yagnob Valley via the snowbound 4040m Tabaspin Pass. Just up the valley, **Langar** (107km from Ayni) is a logical departure point, thanks to the utterly charming **Kholov family (Habib) homestay** (☎92 761 15 21; Langar, Machho; B&B US$12) which has its own mini museum-cabinet and can usually help you find a guide, given some patience. It's right at the start (western edge) of Langar village where you see a sign with an EU flag logo. No English, summer only.

It's another 90km to **Dehavz**, a shrine village where 5000m peaks start to close in. The 4WD track ends 7km further, a 15km hike short of the Zerafshan Glacier whose loss of 2.5km in 90 years has been cited as a 'proof' of global warming. With equipment and a guide, it should also be possible to trek south across to the Rasht Valley. However, there are no established local systems to help travellers up here so if you don't come with a trekking company, you'll be very much living on your wits and relying on local direction-finding. Not for the uninitiated!

Getting There & Away

A variety of shared 4WDs depart from Ayni's hospital 4WD-stand, mostly in the afternoon, returning the next morning. Once a vehicle is filling up you'll rarely need to pay more than 50TJS per seat but you might wait hours (or days if heading beyond Langar). However, if you become a 4WD's main 'sponsor' you coud be looking at around 800TJS to Langar (five to six hours).

TOWARDS PENJIKENT

Around 40km east of Penjikent, then 9km off the main Ayni road, **Mazor-i-Sharif** has a striking setting, ringed by red-green eroded slopes. It is home to a much-revered 14th-century mausoleum (supposedly marking the older grave of Mohammad Bashoro), most interesting for its ossuary, central pillar and hermit-retreat box-room.

Penjikent Пенжикент

☎3475 / POP 50,000

Famous for its millenium-old archaeological site and as a springboard for Haft-Kul, Penjikent is crossing its fingers that a big new border road and customs post, due for completion by 2015, will encourage Uzbekistan to re-open the frontier and allow a revival in visitor numbers from Samarkand.

Sights

Ancient Penjikent ARCHAEOLOGICAL SITE

(www.orientarch.uni-halle.de/ca/pandzh.htm) On a terrace above the banks of the Zerafshan River, 1.5km southeast of today's Penjikent, are the ruins of a major Sogdian town, which was briefly (5th to 8th centuries) one of the most cosmopolitan cities on the Silk Road. The palace here was originally decorated with ornate hunting scenes and pillars carved in the shape of

Penjikent

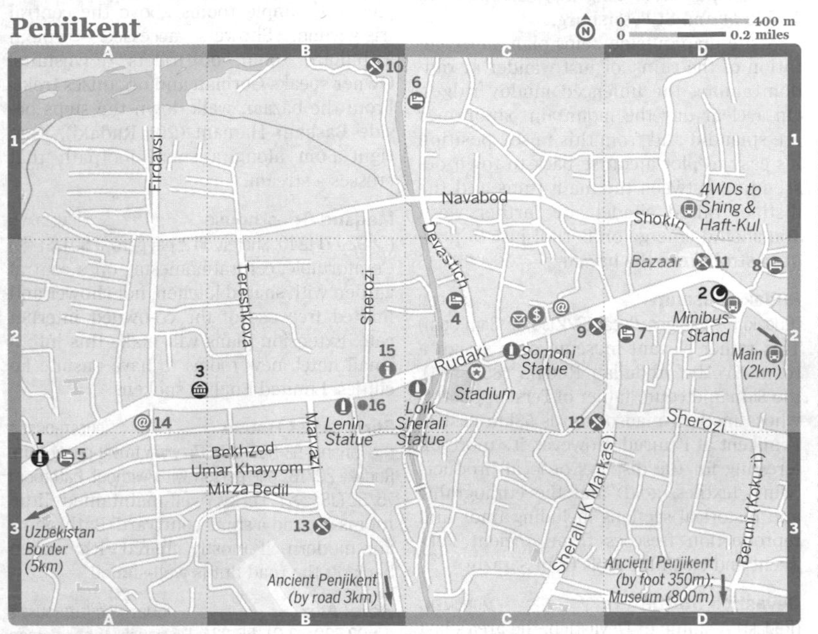

Penjikent

Sights

1 Devastich Statue ... A3
2 Olim Dodkhokh Complex ... D2
3 Rudaki Museum ... A2

Sleeping

4 Dodo Hotel ... C2
5 Elina Guest House ... A3
6 Hotel Aziz ... C1
7 Maqsud Guesthouse ... D2
8 Zurmich Homestay ... D2

Eating

9 Café Safina ... C2
10 Dilkusho ... B1
11 Mukhiddin ... D2
12 Obod ... C2
13 Sayokhat ... B3

Information

14 Internet Tsentr ... A2
Niyazov Niyozkul ... (see 5)
15 Zerafshan Tourism Board ... B2
16 ZTDA Information Centre ... B2

dancing girls. Today the site is just a sunbaked hillside with excavated sunbaked wall-stub ruins. But you can clearly identify the foundations of numerous former buildings in what was the main *shakhristan* (town centre), and seek out hints of an outlying *rabad* (suburb) and necropolis.

Get to the site on marshrutka 5. Ask the driver for Stary Penjikent; from where you're dropped make an obvious four-minute dog-leg walk to the site's southern edge. Here a traditionally styled one-room **museum** (admission 3TJS; ⏰10am-5pm) chronicles the excavations and has painted copies of the best frescoes. The originals, along with most sculptures, pottery and manuscripts, were long ago carted off to Tashkent and St Petersburg.

A site map outside helps plan an exploration of the ruins, or just wander at random among the unfenced muddy ridges. On a clear day the mountain panoramas are splendid and from this raised position it's easy to plot a course back to town descending between the main ruins and the distinct raised citadel site further west. You should emerge on Beruni just 15 minutes' stroll from the bazaar.

Rudaki Museum MUSEUM
(Rudaki 67; foreigner/local 10/2TJS; ⏰8am-5pm) This rather elegant museum does assign a room to Abu Abdullah Rudaki (858–941), the Samanid court 'father of Persian poetry', whose modern mausoleum is 58km east of Penjikent at Panjrud. However, it's more interesting for the displays of local products (wine, textiles, gold) and the ethnograhic and historical sections including finds and reproduction frescoes from Ancient Penjikent and Neolithic tools from Sarazm.

Devastich Statue MONUMENT
(Rudaki) A statue of Devastich, the area's last Sogdian leader, dominates the roundabout at the west end of town.

Olim Dodkhokh Complex MOSQUE
(Rudaki 164) On cold Friday lunchtimes, dozens of older men with flowing white beards, turbans, upturned boots and swishing purple/green irridescent *joma* robes make their way to prayers at this mosque-madrassa complex opposite the bazaar. Though mostly a contemporary rebuild, its origins are 14th century. The best view is from Mafsemi Chaikhana upstairs opposite the Shokhrukh *samsa* (samosa) shop (Rudaki 154).

Sleeping

Beware that from November through April many accommodation options are closed.

Dodo Hotel GUESTHOUSE $
(Hotel_Dodo@mail.ru; Devashtich 34; d/ste 100/120TJS; @ wi-fi) Good value for couples, handily central, with free wi-fi. The suites have large, if plain, sitting rooms with mostly unadorned sick-green walls. Open year-round.

Zurmich Homestay HOMESTAY $
(☎92-759 91 23; zurnach@mail.ru; Bakoli first lane, 24; per person 75TJS; ⏰Apr-Oct) Central, charming homestay with a kitchen, dining room and sitting area shared by three pleasant, simple rooms above the central iris-garden. Showers accessed through a billiard room, box-toilets downstairs. Owner speaks German and organises treks. From the bazaar, walk down the steps beside Bashani Hamam (201 Rudaki), then right 50m along a small footpath that crosses a stream.

Maqsud Guesthouse HOMESTAY $
(☎92-771 12 10; Sheralizod 2; per person 80TJS; @) Comfortable, central homestay off a central garden with shared kitchen, hot shower and limited free use of the co-owned internet cafe. Extension plans will make this into a small hotel, new rooms to have ensuite facilities. Limited English spoken.

Elina Guest House GUESTHOUSE $
(☎Tatiana 93-566 37 37; www.travel-pamir.com; Rudaki 20/16; per person with/without bathroom 75/50TJS; wi-fi) Perky, well-maintained little rooms around a small courtyard. Bathrooms are modern, if mostly shared. It's tucked back off the road but is well-signed.

Hotel Aziz HOMESTAY, GUESTHOUSE $
(☎92-780 33 31, 55 224; Devastich 4; per person US$10) Attached to the home of the Rudaki Museum's English-speaking guide are four ensuite guestrooms and a sizeable billiard room dotted with furniture oddments. Standards aren't luxurious (one bed is held up on a pile of books) but it is the best value in town for single travellers. Call ahead.

Eating

Mukhiddin CHAIKHANA $
(Rudaki 189; samsa 3-5TJS, blini/tea/lagman 1/0.5/12TJS; ⏰6am-4pm) Very popular bazaar chaikhana with fine views and plenty

of breakfast options. Take the door to the direct right of the bazaar's main entrance, beside Megafon.

Obod CENTRAL ASIAN $

(Sherali 42; mains 8-12TJS, kebabs from 4TJS; 8am-10pm Mon-Sat) Behind a vine-fronted facade, eight summer tables loop around a central fountain-pool in a shaded courtyard. Its riverside branch, **Dilkusho** (Obody Poyon; mains 6-20TJS, beer 7TJS; 11am-10pm), is smarter, with traditional pillared colonnade, but on summer evenings the mosquitoes like to dine too.

Café Safina CENTRAL ASIAN $

(Sherali, cnr Rudaki; mains 6-10TJS; 8am-10pm Sun-Fri) Decent indoor place with menus (unlike most chaikhanas) and curtained booth seats for private soirées.

Sayokhat CHAIKHANA $$

(www.panjakent-intour.tj; Marvazi; mains 15-25TJS; 8am-7pm May-Oct) Penjikent's most imaginative eatery, this eccentric new wooden structure is festooned in traditional artefacts and merrily over-endowed with timber stairways.

Information

Internet Tsentr (Rudaki 40; per hr 3TJS; 8am-10pm)

Zerafshan Tourism Board (ZTB; 53 680, Zafar 92-780 77 16; www.zerafshan.info; Rudaki 111-125) This nonprofit union of tourism operators runs a remarkably helpful tourist information office that can help independent budget travellers every bit as well as those seeking tours, transport and guides. Zafar speaks excellent English.

ZTDA Information Centre (56 339; www.ztda-tourism.tj; Rudaki 108; 8am-5pm Mon-Fri summer, 9am-4pm Mon-Fri winter) ZTDA promotes community tourism and organises tours across the region, often revolving around rural homestays, a whole brochure of which they publish complete with photos of each family and their houses (available online). Sells a small selection of handicrafts and its own 1:100,000 Fan Mountains and 1:400,000 Zerafshan Valley maps.

Niyazov Niyozkul (93-588 96 68; niyozkul@mail.ru; Rudaki 20/16) Helpful and trustworthy, Niyozkul is an English-speaking fount of historical and cultural knowledge, familiar with budget traveller needs. He can organise accommodation, trekking support and transport – whether private hires or seats in shared taxis. His unmarked door shares the same gateway with Elina Guesthouse next door.

Getting There & Away

The scenic Penjikent–Ayni road is infuriatingly potholed, but due for reconstruction by 2016. After rain, rockfalls can cause delays but if all is well, shared taxis reach Khojand (120TJS per seat) in six hours, and Dushanbe (100TJS per seat) in five hours from the bus station, 2km east of the central bazaar. Preferably pre-book your ticket and be collected from your accommodation. Three daily buses to Artush via Panjrud currently start opposite the mosque but will eventually relocate to the bus station.

Cars to Istaravshan leave from beside Rudaki 206 opposite the Guliston clothes bazaar. Departures are most plentiful Mondays and Friday mornings before 10am.

To reach Ayni or Sarvoda without paying the full Dushanbe taxi fare, you could take the 10.30am minibus to Umetan (12TJS, around two hours) and switch to the 1.30pm service to Sarvoda (aka Zarafshan 1). However, if you miss the connection there's no formal accommodation in Umetan.

From a building supplies yard, 200m down Shokin from the bazaar, buses run to Shing (2pm, 10TJS) and crammed-full 4WDs (Takhta Bazaar) to the Haft-Kul villages (40TJS) depart around noon, returning the next morning at 6am.

WORTH A TRIP

HAFT-KUL

For a great overnight trip from Penjikent head to Haft-Kul (Seven Lakes; Marguzor Lakes), a 20km-long chain of turquoise pools strung along the western end of the Fan Mountain range. The access road gets very rough but daily shared 4WDs can get you near delightful homestays at Nofin, Padrud and Marguzor. Contact the tourist offices in Penjikent for homestay names and details. The seventh (uppermost) lake is essentially only accessible on foot even if you rent a private 4WD (day return costs around US$80 from Penjikent through Nematov Niyozkul). Beware that beyond Shing the road is prone to mudslides, especially in spring. These can block the route for days. Passport checks are possible at Novichornok.

Getting Around

Minibuses 1 and 4 run along Rudaki from Elina Guest House, past the museum to the bazaar and on to the bus station.

Istaravshan ИСТАРАВШАН

☎3454 / POP 50,000

Called Kir by the Parthians, Cyropol by Alexander the Great and Ura-Tyube by the Russians and Soviets, Istaravshan has a small historical core that is a little better preserved than most in Tajikistan. That isn't saying a great deal, and Bukhara it's certainly not. But then, there aren't any tourists either.

Sights

Mug Teppe FORTRESS

The city's grassy, flat-topped former fortress hill rises northeast of the centre. Stormed by Alexander the Great in 329 BC and Arabs in 772 AD, only minimal mud-wall traces of the original remain. These, however, have been grandly augmented since 2002 by a blue-domed brick entry gateway, built for Istaravshan's 2500th anniversary celebrations. Though quickly becoming dilapidated, it looks great from afar and clear-day views show off the city's mountain horizon to great advantage. Access is from the first traffic lights north of Sadbargi hotel.

Bazaar MARKET

(Lenin; ⏲7am-3pm) The vast, colourful central bazaar is a town unto itself. Don't miss the 12 blacksmith workshops which make top-quality knives using remarkably archaic-looking equipment. They're in the sick-green, low-rise building across from the three-storey, triple arch of the main mustard-yellow bazaar building.

Shahr-e-kuhna OLD TOWN

The old town is a gently intriguing maze of lanes, with interesting houses often tantalisingly hidden from view behind straw-and-wattle plastered walls. Access is via Krupskoe or Tursunzoda streets heading west from 102 or 98 Lenin respectively, either side of the photogenic **Hazrat-i-Shah Mosque** (Lenin 98). Walking along Krupskoe for around 10 minutes you'll spot the 1910 **Hauz-i-Sangin** mosque (Menzhinski 9, at Krupskoe) to the right. Peep in to see its attractively painted ceilings. Backtrack one block, then walk south past a vast unfinished new mosque site, then left on Tursunzoda to find the **Abdullatif Sultan Medressa** (Kök Gumbaz; Tursunzoda), centrepiece of a working Islamic school whose eye-catching Timurid architecture gives it its nickname Blue Dome. Walking another five minutes west brings you to a major road along which marshrutka 3a links between the bazaar and Chor Gumbaz.

Chor Gumbaz ISLAMIC

(Said Nizomaddin Hoja Mazor) In the northwest corner of town is the one-room Mazar-i-Chor Gumbaz whose four tin cupolas conceal some of Tajikistan's most impressive old painted ceilings. If locked, ask at the house behind.

Sary Mazar ISLAMIC

(Yellow Tomb; marshrutka 11, 3a) Old grey-bearded men shaded by even older *chinar* (plane) trees survey a pair of small but ornately stucco-fronted 17th-century tombs beside a mosque and appealingly authentic chaikhana. From the bazaar take marshrutka 3a, get off 300m beyond the cross-sabres gateway, walk straight along Ehsan (15 minutes), then ask!

Sleeping

Sadbargi HOTEL $

(☎91-988 70 48; Lenin 101b; tw 190TJS, s/tw without bathroom 65/90TJS) By far the best option in town. Upstairs above a big modern wedding hall, well-furnished ensuite rooms are ample-sized with comfy beds, kettle, tea, towels and shampoo provided. When not full, single occupancy costs half the twin-room price. Cheaper rooms are neat, simple affairs sharing a semi-clean toilet and shower. During weddings, music rumbles the rafters.

Hotel Jasnovar CRASH PAD $

(☎24 961; r without bathroom 40-50TJS, r with bathroom 80-120TJS) Though once attractive, the simple rooms now range from dishevelled through grubby to objectionable. Only consider this if the Sadbaghi is full. It's 300m south of the Penjikent taxi stand.

Getting There & Around

Dushanbe Shared taxis (100TJS per seat, four hours, 276km) leave from the southern end of the bazaar. A full charter taxi with an overnight in Iskander-Kul starts at around US$150.

Penjikent (80TJS to 100TJS, five hours) Taxis leave from 100m further south, beyond the terminus of marshrutkas 4 and 5, though cheeky freelancers may tell you otherwise hoping to get a full charter.

Khojand Although minibus 314 (8TJS, 90 minutes) should start 3km north of town from the Avtovokzal, some fill up at the same place as the shared taxis (15TJS, 50 minutes), near the blacksmiths workshops opposite the central bazaar.

From the bazaar take marshrutka 6 for the hotel Sadbargi and Avtovokzal, 5A for Mug Teppe and 3A to get close to the old town sights.

Khojand Худжанд

☎3422 / POP 164,500

Khojand (or Khojent/Khujand, formerly Leninabad) is Tajikistan's second-largest city. Although it's a massive sprawl, most hotels and sights are close to Lenin, which snakes north-south-southeast for almost 10km, crossing the Syr-Darya River near the point where Alexander the Great once founded his northernmost Central Asian outpost, Alexandria-Eskhate.

Commanding (and taxing) the entrance to the Fergana Valley, Khojand built palaces, grand mosques and a huge citadel before the Mongols bulldozed the city into oblivion in the early 13th century.

Khojand's population has a strong Uzbek contingent, although it always provided Tajikistan's Soviet elite. When President Nabiev, a Khojand man, was unseated in 1992 and Tajikistan appeared to be becoming an Islamic republic, Khojand (Leninabad) province threatened to secede. Secure behind the Fan Mountains, it managed to escape the ravages of the civil war and remains the wealthiest part of the country. Several sparkling new monuments add to the air of comparative prosperity, the bazaar and mosque complex is impressive, and there are a few historical curiosities to glimpse as you transit between Kyrgyzstan or Uzbekistan and the Fan Mountains.

Sights

Minibus 55 between the Avtostanitsa and Abreshim bus stations passes both of Khojand's two main attractions. For the bazaar and mausoleum get off at the big **WWII Monument** and walk 100m east. For the citadel get off opposite the Hotel/Trade Centre Kheson and walk two blocks west of Lenin down Rajabov.

Panchshanbe Bazaar MARKET

(5am-7pm, 6am-5.30pm winter) The core of the bazaar is an unusually elegant, purpose-built hall (1964) with arched entrance portals and a pink-and-lime-green neoclassical facade – think Stalin meets *1001 Nights*. It's one of the best-stocked markets in Central Asia, especially on Thursday (*panchshanbe* in Tajik).

Sheikh Massal ad-Din complex ISLAMIC

(ploshchad Pobedy) In striking comparison to the bazaar opposite, this religious complex comprises the 1394 brick **mausoleum of Sheikh Massal ad-Din** (1133–1223), covered porticoes with carved wooden pillars, a 20th-century mosque with sensitive, if modern, white-stone frontage and a 21m-high brick minaret dating from 1865. A matching second minaret is nearing completion directly north, attached to a new, traditionally designed brick mosque that looks archetypally Central Asian but for the luridly reflective emerald-green dome.

Citadel FORTRESS

The city's oldest remains are the formless baked-earth walls of the 10th-century citadel, which once boasted seven gates and 6km of fortifications. Earlier this had been the site of Alexander the Great's original settlement. The fort was the scene of pitched battles in 1997 between rebel Uzbek warlords and government troops, during which 300 people were killed. The main section remains occupied by the army but much of the eastern wall has been rebuilt creating an impressive, if one-photo scene, when viewed from the southeast corner. That's where the rebuilt bastion now contains a **museum** (foreigner/local 6/3TJS; 8am-4pm Tue-Fri, 9am-4pm Sat & Sun), lavished with colourful stone mosaics and partly 3D murals though it contains little in the way of historical artefacts. A much more modest one-room **archaeological museum** (Tanbyri 4; foreigner/local 2/0.5TJS; 9am-noon & 1-4pm) inside the central section of the rebuilt wall has a few old plans of the original citadel and allows access to a section of battlements.

Lenin Statue MONUMENT

A 22m-tall statue of Lenin was moved here from Moscow in 1974 when Khojand was called Leninabad. In 2011 Vlad was quietly removed from his central plinth north of the river (replaced by an equally large Somoni) and was re-erected in an obscure retirement

Khojand

spot in the 18th-microrayon suburb. Taxi 20TJS return.

Sleeping

Except for the Sharq and Grand, hotels charge foreigner prices that can be as much as twice what Tajik citizens would pay. Most double rooms at better central hotels have queen (not twin) beds, which you'll find at the overpriced central **Hotel Khujand** (☎659 97; Mavlonbekov 1; lux 220TJS; ❄), next-door **Hotel Vahdat** (☎651 01; Mavlonbekov 3; half lux/lux 220/280TJS; ❄), or the newer, overly colourful **Hotel Heson** (☎648 45; Lenin 3b; d 220-240TJS).

Hotel Leninobod HOTEL $
(☎655 35; Nabiev 51; dm/s/d 70/90/140TJS) Well placed on the corniche with views across the Syr-Darya to northern Khojand's stark rocky backdrop, this patched-up Soviet tower operates only two floors and decor has evolved little since 1990, with dim lighting and a broken lift. Still some rooms have been repainted and the sullen *dezhurnaya* (floor-lady) will fix a pot of tea for 1TJS.

Hotel Sharq HOSTEL $
(Sharq; dm/tw/tr/q 12/30/45/60TJS) Friendly but very basic traders' hostel on the top floor of Panchshanbe Bazaar (entered from half way along the south exterior). There's only one shared toilet and to wash, staff can direct you to a *banya* nearby. Women might feel uncomfortable here.

Hotel Sugd HOTEL $$
(☎411 88; hotel_sugd@mail.ru; Lenin 179a; s/d 180/290TJS, lux 370-400TJS incl breakfast; ❄📶) Khojand's best midrange choice is 150m south of the nasty but more visible Ehson. Neat, carpeted rooms with pale yellow soft furnishings and slightly garish fabric 'art' come with fridge, toiletries and hair dryer. Friendly staff valiantly attempt basic English.

Khojand

Sights

1 Citadel ... A2
2 Historical Museum of Sughd Province ... A2
3 Museum of Archaeology & Fortifications ... A2
4 Panchshanbe Bazaar ... D4
5 Sheikh Massal ad-Din complex ... D4
6 WWII Monument ... D4

Sleeping

7 Grand Hotel Khujand ... A3
8 Hotel Heson ... B2
9 Hotel Khujand ... B3
10 Hotel Leninobod ... A2
11 Hotel Sharq ... D4
12 Hotel Vahdat ... B3

Eating

13 Café Ravshan ... B3
14 Cafe Sharq ... D4

Grand Hotel Khujand BOUTIQUE HOTEL **$$**
(☎605 99; khujand.grand.hotel@mail.ru; Tamburi 20; d 500-600TJS; ❄ 📶) Khojand's best luxury choice, this attractive new place is ideally placed, right opposite the citadel. There are slight art-nouveau touches to the over-glossy wooden furniture and the 16 rooms are indulgently spacious, though some fittings seem more for show than built to last.

Eating

Chaikhanas, *piroshki* sellers and shashlyk grills are plentiful along Rajabov west of Lenin, and around the bazaar where there's a cheap **cafeteria** (Sharq; ⏲4am-10pm) beneath Hotel Sharq.

Café Ravshan CENTRAL ASIAN **$$**
(Rajabov 102; mains 9.50-24TJS, beer 6-10TJS; ⏲6am-10.30pm) This central semi-smart cafe features mirror-facet flowers and chequerboard couch seats. The kitchen barbeques great *okaroshka* (chicken kebabs, 10TJS), but beware of the coffee (2TJS) which is instant and heavily pre-sweetened.

Getting There & Away

There are daily flights to Dushanbe (from 340TJS) and to numerous Russian cities including Novosibirsk (from 820TJS).

There are three main 'bus' stations. Minibuses and shared taxis to Kanibadam/Kanibodom (minibus 328; 8TJS, 1½ hours) for Kokand, Uzbekistan, and to Isfara (minibus 301; 10TJS, two hours, mornings only) for Osh, Kyrgyzstan, leave from the inconspicuous little **Isfara Avtostanitsa** (Lenin), opposite some metal silos 5km southeast of Panchshanbe.

Shared taxis to Penjikent (100TJS, seven hours) and Dushanbe (100TJS to 120TJS per seat, six hours) plus regular minibus 314 to Istaravshan (4TJS, 90 minutes) all leave from the **Yova (Ёва) bus station** (Kamoli Khojandi).

Other Dushanbe shared taxis, plus transport to Oybek (for Tashkent, Uzbekistan) via Buston (10TJS) use the big **Abreshim bus station** out in the distant northeastern suburbs.

Getting Around

Marshrutka 55 (1TJS) links Abreshim bus station to Isfara Avtostanisa; 29 and 33 link the Yova and Abreshim bus stations. The airport, 16km southeast at Chkalovsk, is accessible by minibus 80 (2TJS). All above routes and many more pass along Lenin near the central Rajabov junction. Route 3A links Yova to the Isfara Avtostanisa bus station via Panchshanbe Bazaar.

Isfara Исфара

If you're heading to Kyrgyzstan without an Uzbekistan visa, head first to Isfara, which feels strikingly more prosperous than Batken across the Kyrgyzstan border.

The main east–west street, Markazi, has banks including Amonat Bank and Eskhata Bank (Markezi 31) with Visa/MasterCard ATMs. The latter is beside the new **Ismoil Somoni monument**, opposite the predictably run-down Soviet-era **Hotel Isfara** (Markezi 18; d 20-50TJS). To get there from the bus station take marshrutka 1 or 9 or walk a block north past the bazaar, then 10 minutes crossing the bridge beside the spendid new-but-traditional **Oriyol Teahouse**. Facing the teahouse, **Hotel Vatan** has extremely basic rooms (from 10TJS per bed) and an internet room.

Isfara bus station has direct cars to Dushanbe (130TJS) but they fill slowly. It's often cheaper and rarely much slower to change in Khojand (minibus/shared taxi 10/20TJS) even though you'll need to change bus stations. Batken-bound minibuses (4TJS, 40 minutes) leave at 10am, 1pm and 4pm. The first departure arrives in time (just!) to connect with the last Batken–Osh marshrutka.

THE PAMIRS

Gorno-Badakhshan (eastern Tajikistan) is almost a different country and indeed it has its own special entry requirements (see p366). Officially called Kohistani Badakhshan, though commonly abbreviated to GBAO for its Soviet-era name (Gorno-Badakhshan Autonomous Oblast), the region accounts for 45% of Tajikistan's territory but only 3% of its population. Most of the 212,000 souls who do live here are Pamiris whose irrigated villages lie deep within dramatic rocky valleys above which snow-dusted mountain peaks rise. The eastern region, however, is mostly a stark moonscape plateau, at an altitude of well above 3000m, sparsely populated with Kyrgyz herders whose sheep and yaks eke out an existence in those areas fertile enough for grass to grow.

Locals romantically nickname the region Bam-i-Dunya (the Roof of the World). Westerners talk about 'the Pamirs' often assuming that the term refers to the 5000m plus mountains. You will indeed find three of the four highest peaks of the former Soviet Union here. But the word *pamir* actually translates from ancient Persian as 'rolling pastureland', referring to the valleys between those interconnected mountain ranges.

Sleeping & Eating

Most tourist accommodation in rural Badakhshan is in simple, comfortable homestays, usually typical Pamiri houses with outdoor toilet holes. There are also yurtstays in the eastern Pamir. Formal homestays typically cost around US$15 per person including two meals. If you receive an informal invitation we suggest you still offer around US$10, possibly leaving the money discreetly in an envelope to avoid embarrassment or refusal. PECTA (p346) in Khorog and TIC (p354) in Murgab have extensive homestay lists.

Khorog has cafes and a well-stocked, relatively expensive bazaar. Murgab has very basic diners; its bazaar is very limited and prices are even higher. Few other villages have even a regular shop and unmarked house-stores don't stock much beyond Chinese beer and expired Snickers bars. It's best to eat in homestays. Almost any rural home can provide basic snacks on request. Expect to pay from 3TJS per person (10TJS minimum) for the simplest bread and tea, even if you aren't asked for money.

Getting There & Around

Transport is remarkably sparse. Hitching is slow but possible if you don't mind waiting hours or days. Chances are better on the Pamir Highway between Khorog and Murgab if you learn the Chinese truckers' driving patterns. Hitching Sary Tash to Murgab is virtually impossible unless you meet an unusually merciful tourist vehicle.

Shared 4WDs run at least daily from Khorog to Murgab, Murgab to Osh and from Khorog to local destinations within an hour or two's drive, but frequency is so low that you might wish you'd rented a 4WD with a group of fellow travellers.

For information on travelling around the Wakhan Valley, see p350

4WD HIRE

Hiring a private vehicle with driver gives you a flexibility that you will value greatly in this scenic and fascinating area where transport is otherwise in exceedingly short supply.

Typical per kilometre rates range from US$0.55 to US$0.95, plus US$15 to $20 per day to cover the driver's living expenses on overnight or longer trips. As well as the obvious question of petrol price, the main factors affecting these rates are the type of vehicle you hire, the driver, the route taken (one-way or loop), and where you hire the vehicle.

Type of vehicle While you can typically rent a Niva for around US$0.10/0.20 per km less than a Musso/Pajero, it holds fewer people and is less comfortable. For seriously arduous terrain a UAZ is probably the strongest option but it is very fuel-thirsty and a LandCruiser, which comes a close second for toughness, has better visibility and is far more comfortable... unless you're in the four side-facing back seats.

Driver Ideally meet the driver before departure, give his vehicle the once-over, check that the 4WD is operational and, if crossing to (from) Osh (in Kyrgyzstan), check that the driver has a passport (and GBAO permit). English-language skills have obvious advantages, but in reality a lively, helpful driver is often better than a linguistically capable but sullen or inexperienced one. Drivers under 40 years old are rarely as mechanically capable as old boys.

Return trip You might be travelling one way but the driver needs to get home and you'll generally need to figure those extra kilometres into the price. So making a loop trip has significant cost advantages. However, if you employ a driver who regularly makes a standard route then you need only pay one way (for example, track down a Murgab-based driver in Khorog for a cheaper trip to Murgab).

Finding a ride Most agencies in Murgab and Khorog plus many in Osh, Bishkek and Dushanbe can find you a vehicle. Prices, but also standards, will tend to be higher than arranging in situ. Hamsafar (p323) in Dushanbe, and PECTA (p346) in Khorog, are good at finding cars at reasonably short notice. TIC (p354) in Murgab has a list of local drivers, and all can help pair travellers to cut costs. The other option is to visit the standard taxi stand for the basic route you want to travel, then negotiate with a driver for a full-car hire. Language is the obvious barrier here, especially if you want to make side trips or make long stops.

Petrol Finding petrol can be a problem in the Pamirs. A trip into the more remote corners of the region generally involves at least one dash around town to find a obliging local with a jerry can of diluted fuel and a bucket.

Dushanbe to Khorog

The spectacular Dushanbe–Khorog flight is worth considering if you can somehow get a seat. Otherwise there's a choice from Dushanbe of two main road routes converging at Kalai-Khum, both part asphalt, part bone-cruncher. Most traffic (100% in winter) uses the southern route through harsh heat-baked hills to Kulob (Kulyab), then along a fascinating Afghanistan borderside road.

An alternative Northern Route starts out along the main road to Garm then swerves south at Labi Jar to Tavildara crossing the 3252m Sagirdasht Pass, which is snowbound much of the year and typically closed

KEY TIPS FOR TRAVELLING IN THE PAMIRS

Permits & Maps

- You must have a **GBAO permit** to travel in the Pamirs (see p366). It should list each of the districts: Ishkashim, Murgab, Vanj, Darvaz, Shugnan, Rushan and Roshtqala (most do automatically, but double check). If you extend your visa, you must extend the GBAO permit also to remain in the region.
- **Additional permits** are required for Zor Kul lake, the Tajik National Park or Lake Sarez.
- Buy Marcus Hauser's indispensible 1:500,000 **Pamirs Map**. It's packed with icon-based information including sights and homestays. Sold at Murgab's TIC (p354), Dushanbe's East Vision (p323), Yak Tours (p264) in Karakol, Kyrgyzstan or via www.geckomaps.com. A fundamentally similar **Pamir Tourist Map** costs 60TJS from PECTA (p346).

What to Pack

- Sunglasses and sunscreen
- Torch (flashlight)
- Plenty of cash in both US$ and somani.
- Warm clothing: a fleece and windproof shell should generally suffice in midsummer.
- Sleeping bag and tent are sensible precautions if you're hitch-hiking.
- Mosquito repellant in summer.
- Spare batteries: Khorog, western Pamir and Wakhan villages have mains electricity, but supply is infamously unreliable in Murgab and can't be expected anywhere else in the eastern Pamirs.
- Water purification tablets: bottled water is rarely available outside Khorog; in Murgab it costs a whopping 4TJS per litre.
- gifts: photos of yourself with the Aga Khan (see p361) would be gold-dust!

Money

The only ATMs are in Khorog. None accept Maestro. Banks in Khorog and Murgab can change US$, but not always euros. Homestays accept US$ as well as somani. Kyrgyz som are accepted in Karakul. If you have any somani left over, spend/change them there or in Sary Tash (Kyrgyzstan).

altogether between late October and May. Even when open, broken bridges and difficult fords can be problematic south of Tavildara.

Whichever route you take, an overnight stop en route is highly recommended to break the very long drive and, especially eastbound, not to miss some great views by driving at night. Note that arranging onward transport from small villages can be very tough (especially eastbound), so breaking the journey generally only works if you're prepared to charter a vehicle.

The Pamirs

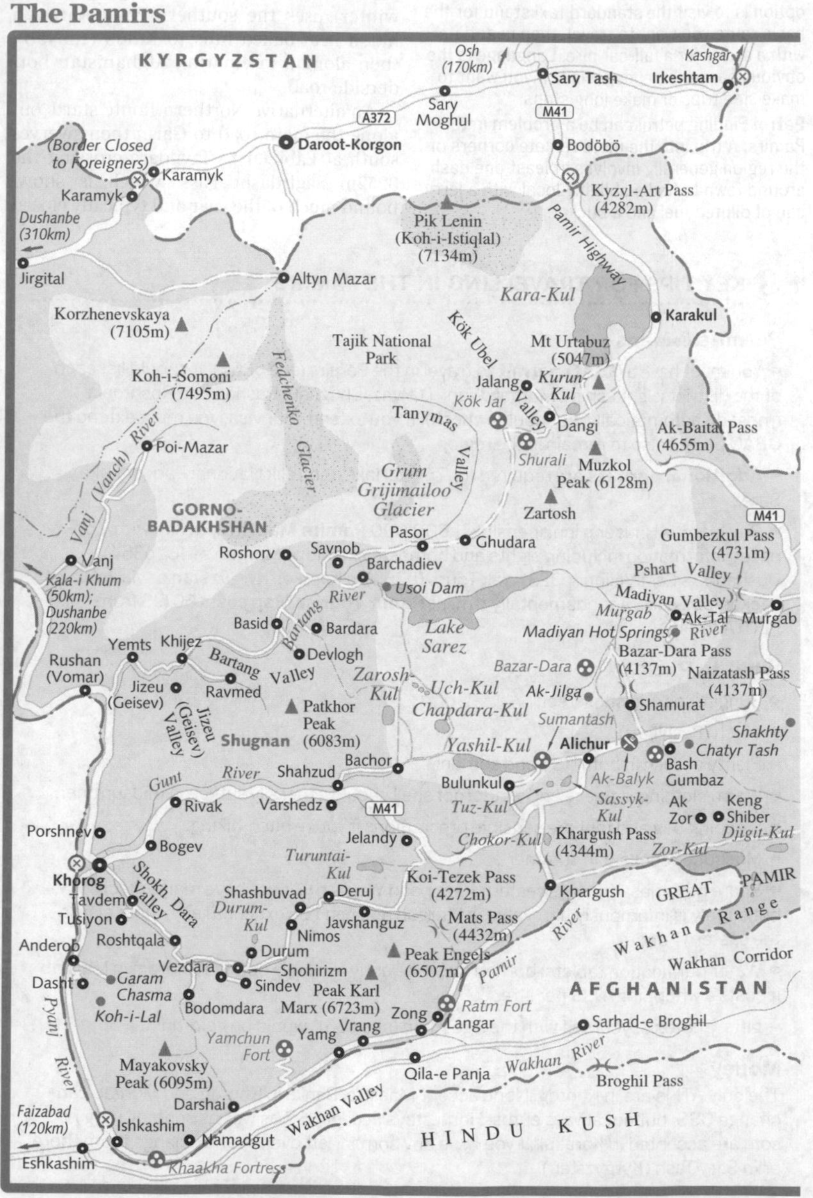

Southern Route

Dushanbe–Khorog can take anywhere between 14 and 20 hours but should become considerably quicker by 2016, once sections of asphalting and many new bridges are finished.

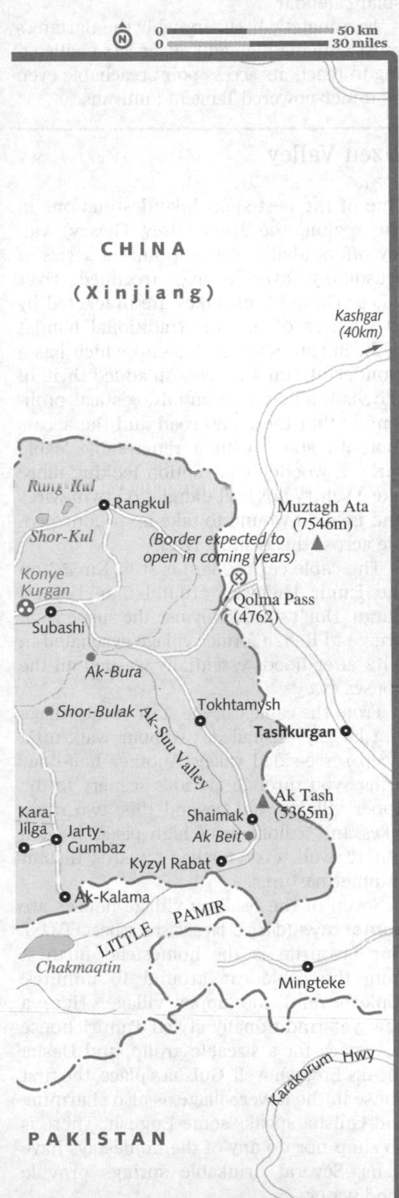

Highlights of the route from Dushanbe include brief views over **Nurek Reservoir** and the startling sight of the 11th-century reconstructed **Hulbuk Fortress-Palace** (☎90-666 7766, 90-800 1708; Kurbon Shahid; local/foreigner 1/5TJS; ⏲9am-1pm & 2-5pm Tue-Sun) at the roadside in Kurbon Shaid. That's 8km west of Vose, with its fanciful new market, and 30km before **Kulob**, Tajikistan's third biggest city. Though otherwise forgettable, Kulob is noted for the much revered shrine of 14th-century polymath **Mir Sayid Ali Hamadani** (Somoni 41, Kulob) – the man credited with taking Islam to Kashmir. Its golden dome and carved woodwork looks brand new but the garden setting is photogenic. Kulob's large bazaar is the last real opportunity to stock up with supplies before the Pamirs. GBAO permits are carefully scrutinised at the top of the modest **Shurabad Pass**, then the road heads down towards a deep rocky valley which becomes seriously awe-inspiring after passing the **first Afghan border bridge**. A narrow, raging river divides the Tajik road from a precarious foot-path-track on the Afghan side, linking hamlets of stone and adobe houses set among splashes of green amid the utterly stark rock faces. Perhaps the most appealing stretch is between **Rogak** and **Khostov** (after the popular **Yakhchi Hisor roadside springs**) where the Afghan-side village has a series of houses perched on rocky riverside outcrops. In the typical valley village of **Yoged**, with its backdrop of wild rock, the appealing little **Hilovat Homestay** (☎98-801 51 60; Yoged Village; per person US$10), by the bridge in an attractive garden signed right beside the main road, is an overnight option, if you don't want to continue the last hour or so to **Kalai-Khum**. The main village of the Darvaz district, Kalai-Khum is sweetly sleepy but is the first place since Kulob to have a few shops. The appealing riverside restaurant **Oriyona** (Kalai-Khum; mains 10-17TJS; ⏲10am-10pm Mon-Sat) is behind the far-from-busy taxi stand junction. A couple of houses down the side lane towards the two-colour converging rivers is the water-serenaded homestay of **Roma Jurayev** (☎93-471 21 17; Kalai-Khum; B&B US$12-15). Around 1km back towards Kulob there's also a simple **MSDSP guesthouse** (dm US$15).

The road south of Kalai-Khum continues to trail the Afghan border with many a picturesque scene. The valley widens at a checkpost at the mouth of the **Vanj**

Valley, which branches east towards the Fedchenko Glacier, one of the world's longest. The glacier nose is a full day out-and-back hike from **Poi-Mazar** where Jafar Kholov has one of the Vanj Valley's two homestays (the other is in Dursher).

Back on the main road, the last 65km into Khorog is decently asphalted from Rushan.

Rushan (Vomar) Рушан (Вомар)

If you're heading into the Pamirs from Dushanbe and want to see Jizeu without first going to Khorog (65km further south), you can hop off at Rushan and organise things there. However, if you're planning to go much further up the Bartang Valley it may be worth heading to Khorog first where there's far more English-language help and a much wider choice of transport.

Though not a special attraction in its own right, Rushan is a pleasant village with shops and mini-restaurants, plus a hotel that's under construction behind the petrol station.

At the far western end of town, tucked behind the big school, **Mubarak Homestay** (☎93-405 23 04; Rushan; per person US$10) is a family home set in shady, flower-filled gardens. There's an indoor shower, sit-down toilet, and a kitchen for guest use. Mubarak speaks some English, and Kurbon (another family member who works in the shop at Rushon's central taxi stand) speaks it even better.

The homestay can help you organise a car to the Jizeu cable car. Shared minivans from central Rushan to Khorog (10TJS to 20TJS) take around one hour on a decent asphalt road, but most depart before 10am. Some mornings there's a Rushan–Dushanbe shared 4WD (300TJS per seat).

Bartang Valley Долина реки Бартанг

Stark and elemental, the Bartang Valley is one of the wildest and most memorable valleys in the western Pamirs. Only the occasional fertile alluvial plain brings a flash of green to the barren rock walls. At times the fragile road inches perilously between the raging river below and sheer cliffs above. Indeed it's not rare for sections to become impossibly rough or require knee-deep fords. Still, strong 4WDs and even some adventurous motorcyclists (carrying enough fuel for 400km) have managed to traverse the whole valley in a few days. If you manage to get beyond Ghudara, it should be possible to continue to Kara-Kul (p356) on the Pamir Highway via Kök Jar and Shurali, where geometric stone symbols are thought to have acted as an ancient Stonehenge-like solar calendar.

Fortunately, Jizeu, arguably the Bartang's most enticing highlight, is far less challenging to reach, its access point reachable even by under-powered Tangem minivans.

Jizeu Valley

POP 105

One of the best short-hike destinations in the region, the Jizeu (Jisev, Geisev) Valley offers idyllic scenes around a series of seasonally over-flowing, treelined river lakes. The prettiest lakes are bracketed by two halves of the tiny traditional hamlet of Jizeu (pronounced Jee-sao) which has a wonderful, timeless feel. An added thrill of the visit, albeit a potential logistical problem, is that there's no road and the access footpath starts with a remarkable 'cable car' – a wooden contraption looking more like a sentry box that dangles on twin wires and is hand-wound to take up to four people across the gushing river.

The cable car is 23km east of Km553 on the Pamir Highway, around 6km beyond Bargu. Don't mistakenly use the suspension bridge to Red, a former village evacuated in 2012 after floods essentially washed all the houses away.

From the cable car, the start of the village is a largely unshaded, two-hour walk up a steep scree-sided valley. Another half-hour brings you through glorious scenery to the upper village. And beyond this, two more lakes and a horizon of high peaks beckon you to walk ever further towards distant summer pastures.

Seven of the 14 Jizeu village houses are **homestays** (dm incl breakfast & dinner 60TJS). Our favourite is the homestead furthest from the cable car, around 10 minutes' walk beyond the upper village. Here a new yet traditionally styled Pamiri house has space for a sizeable group, and Dasha speaks English well. Gulsha's place, the first house in the lower village, is also charming and Gulsha speaks some English. There is no shop nor do any of the homestays have signs. Several drinkable springs provide good water.

LAKE SAREZ: AN ACCIDENT WAITING TO HAPPEN

Geologists warn that Tajikistan faces a potential natural disaster of Biblical proportions in the shape of stark 3239m Lake Sarez, a disarmingly placid-looking body of turquoise water formed in 1911 when an earthquake dislodged an entire mountain side into the path of the Murgab River, obliterating the villages of Usoi and Sarez. A deep lake, now 60km-long and half the size of Lake Geneva, gradually formed behind the 770m-high natural dam of rocks and mud known as the Usoi Dam. This 'dam' is currently considered stable. However, if an earthquake broke or breached it, a huge wall of water could come sweeping down the mountain valleys, wiping away roads and villages as far away as Uzbekistan and beyond. Experts warn that it would be the largest flood ever witnessed by human eyes. Villagers in the Bartang Valley (who would be most affected) have been drilled on escape procedures. These are pretty simple – head for the hills when the doomsday alert arrives.

Visiting Lake Sarez requires advance planning as permits are required from Dushanbe. These can take a month to issue, and even then they are usually only available as part of a tour: ask Khorog agencies. The Sarez trailhead is at Barchadiev which, along with lovely nearby Savnob, has homestays.

Homestay owners can help organise guides if you want to cross over the pass to the Ravmed Valley (two tough days, camping en route). Once across, there are further (unsigned) homestays at Ramved village and at Khijez, 18km downstream, where that valley meets the Basid road again. Ask a local to help you find them.

Getting There & Away

A taxi to the cable car costs around 150TJS from Rushan, curiously not much more than you'd pay from Khorog where vehicles for hire are actually easier to find. Getting back you'll generally need to pre-arrange a pick-up as there is minimal traffic on the Bartang road nor shade in which to wait. Walking back to Rushan (26km) is punishing.

Gulsha at the first Jizeu homestay can often organise a car to Khorog for 200TJS to 250TJS. But it will take time as he'll have to walk to the cable car with you to get mobile phone reception (then only Megafon).

Basid & Bardara Басид & Бардара

The lovely village of Basid, 85km off the Pamir Highway, boasts shrines, scenic forests, good hiking, two homestays and the possibility of joining **PamirLink** (www.pamirlink.org), a three-week live-in-Basid working holiday experience.

There are two more homestays, 9km up a rough side road in Bardara which has two more shrines, a village ice-house (*khalodelnik*) and trails leading up to summer pastures and beyond. Ask a local to point you in the direction of a homestay.

A Khorog–Basid UAZ minibus runs between Basid and Khorog most days (40TJS), leaving Khorog around lunchtime, but there's little other traffic, public or private.

Khorog Хорог

☎3522 / POP 28,000 / ELEV 2100M

Cowering beneath arid, bare-rock peaks, likeable little Khorog is the GBAO's administrative centre and the Pamirs' one real town. It's a fine place to meet fellow travellers and organise exploration into the region's remote mountainscapes and fabulous valleys including the fabled Wakhan. Community tourism organisation PECTA, along with several small tour agencies, make chartering 4WD transport much easier from here than from anywhere else in the region apart, perhaps, from Murgab.

Khorog has one of the best educated populations of any town in Central Asia. English seems much more widely spoken here than in Dushanbe, while the laid-back Ismaili form of Islam means that Muslim strictures are generally less widely observed.

Although at an altitude of over 2000m, Khorog's daytime summer temperatures can sometimes climb into the sweltering 40s. September is the most pleasant time here.

There are few sights per se, though the lovably Soviet-style **regional museum** (Lenin 105; foreigner/local 10/1TJS; ⌚8am-noon & 1-4.30pm Mon-Fri) has some mildly interesting curiosities and the elegantly designed **central park** (⌚6am-midnight) is a

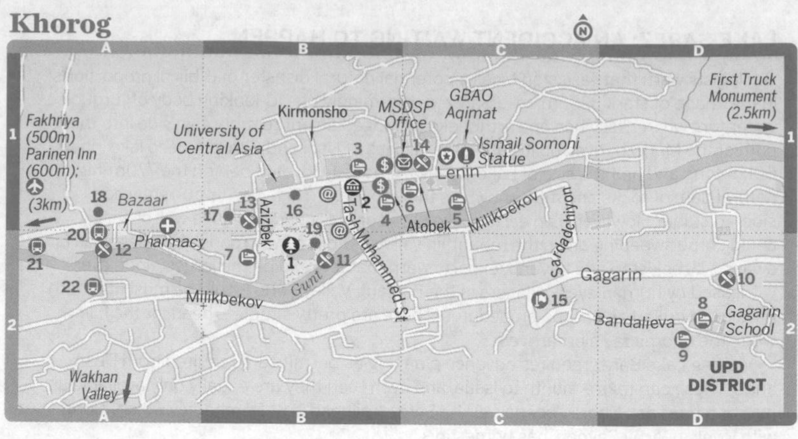

Khorog

Sights
- 1 Central Park B2
- 2 Regional Museum B1

Sleeping
- 3 Bomi Jahon Hotel B1
- 4 Do Nazarbayg Hotel B1
- 5 Hotel Kivekas C1
- 6 Khorog Guest House C1
- 7 Lal Hotel B2
- 8 Lalmo Homestay D2
- 9 Pamir Lodge D2
- Umriniso Homestay .... (see 19)

Eating
- 10 Bar Varka D2
- 11 Chor Bagh B2
- 12 Choykhana Murghob A2
- 13 Delhi Darbar B1
- 14 Shugnon C1

Shopping
- De Pamiri .... (see 19)

Information
- 15 Afghanistan Consulate C2
- 16 OVIR B1
- 17 Pamir Silk Tour B1
- 18 Pamir Tourism A1
- 19 PECTA B2

Transport
- 20 Main Shared Taxi Stand A2
- 21 Shared Vehicles to Dushanbe A2
- 22 Transport to Ishkashim & the Wakhan Area A2

delightfully shady place to stroll. There are attractive views from the **Botanical Gardens** (Botanicheskii Sad; ⏲9am-4pm), 5km east of town.

Meanwhile 5km west of the centre, Saturday mornings bring a colourful **Afghan market** (⏲9am-1pm Sat) as border guards allow folks from both sides of the frontier to trade in a specially penned area.

Sleeping

Khorog has an ever expanding selection of accommodation including numerous homestays (typically US$10 to US$15) at which you should assume shared toilet and bathroom facilities. Ask PECTA (p346) for a list.

Pamir Lodge GUESTHOUSE $
(☎265 45; http://pamirlodge.com; Gagarin (Bandalieva) 46; bed in old/new room US$8/9, terrace sleeping space US$5; Ⓟ) This is the best place in the Pamirs to meet fellow overlanders and independent travellers. Rooms are simple, either mattresses on raised platforms or newer rooms with un-plastered stone walls and fresh-smelling wooden beds but no other furniture. The orchard garden is a pleasant spot overlooked by a wide open-sided balcony-passage where travellers sit for hours swapping tales. Hot shower, outside toilets, breakfast (US$3) by arrangement.

The lodge was established to fund the local *jamoat khana* (Ismaili prayer hall), which is in the grounds. It's a devil to find at night, through gates where the unpaved road makes a slight wiggle west of Gagarin School (School 7).

Umriniso Homestay HOMESTAY $
(☎93-500 69 42; Dubronov 14; B&B US$15) With an incredible location in the central park between PECTA and fast-food cafe Tropikanka, this lovable Pamiri house has the luxury of a sit-down toilet plus a low-powered hot shower and washing machine. Litvia speaks English.

Lalmo Homestay HOMESTAY $
(☎93-508 69 99, 22 69 99; http://pamirhomestay.com; Gagarin (Bandalieva) 2; bed/dinner US$10/5; 📶) With a friendly English-speaking hostess and a beautiful flower garden, it's worth seeking out this homestay up a small stairway facing School 7. It's 200m east of Pamir Lodge.

Bomi Jahon Hotel GUESTHOUSE $
(☎93-553 43 33; bomjahon@inbox.ru; Lenin 64; tw without/with bathroom 144/192TJS; 🚭) Beyond an unprepossessing entrance stairway, rooms are fresh, new and the better ones are spacious with ensuite bathrooms and fridge. Lighting can prove under-powered.

Do Nazarbayg Hotel GUESTHOUSE $
(☎93-410 70 57; nazarbek_ashurov@mail.ru; Atobek 40; s/tw 70/140TJS) Carpets are rucked and wallpaper is bilious green but this new place is as cheap as you'll find for an ensuite private bathroom. Shared kitchen, ony four rooms.

Khorog Guest House HOMESTAY $
(☎93-571 03 20; zubaida.kirgizbekova@gmail.com; Atobek 25; bed US$15, breakfast US$2.50) Attractive timber decor and colourful fabric lampshades give this tiny homestay a design feel. There's a Western-style (shared) loo and warm shower, though water supply is limited to three hours in the morning and three hours in the evening. Two interconnected rooms have pine beds, and there's a traditional Pamiri room with mattresses on the floor. It's unsigned in a side alley.

★**Lal Hotel** BOURTIQUE HOTEL $$
(☎232 30; www.lalhotel.tj; Azizbek 5/1; d incl breakfast US$50-100; ❄📶) You'll find cosy, clean rooms in this guesthouse full of colourful local fabrics, and an apricot tree shading a sitting pavilion in the small flower-filled garden. Laundry (20TJS) and wi-fi (per day 15TJS) cost extra. The pricier rooms have air-conditioning. Just a couple of the cheapest rooms are disappointing.

Hotel Kivekas GUESTHOUSE $$
(☎93-809 19 28, 241 42; kievkas67@mail.ru; Kirov 8a; dm/s/tw/q US$25/60/70/100; ❄) Just four pine-fresh new rooms in a hotel dominated by its oversized sitting/billiard room where loungers face the river. Rooms have fridge, decent air-conditioning and private bathrooms with multi-head showers and a basket of toiletries.

★**Serena Inn** BOUTIQUE HOTEL $$$
(☎93-500 82 24, 232 28; www.serenahotels.com/serenakhorog; s/d/tw/lux US$125/148/148/155; P❄@📶) Khorog's best hotel has just six bedrooms with Western-style bathrooms, mini-fridge and fine linens, around a comfortable lounge-lobby built with Pamiri timbers and design elements. Built for the visits of the Aga Khan, a big attraction is the terraced riverside garden, with lawns, roses and willows framing views across to Afghanistan. It's 5km northwest of Khorog Bazaar.

Eating

Most homestays and guesthouses organise dinner by advance request. There are numerous daytime snack options around the bazaar but only Chor Bagh and Serena Hotel restaurants open on Sundays.

Look out in the bazaar for bottles of locally made sea-buckthorn juice and tart, high-vitamin dog-rose juice *(shipovnik sok)*.

Fakhriya CHAIKHANA $
(Lenin 191; mains 8-14TJS; ⏰10am-8pm Mon-Sat) Deservedly popular for pre-prepared lunches, *manti*, succulent yet lean shashlyk and chilled flagons of *kompot* (fruit cordial), this extensive, easily missed, mid-market chaikhana is female-friendly and pleasantly situated at the riverside within the large gardens of the **Parinen Inn** (☎93-502 37 50, 254 17; parinen_inn@hotmail.com; Lenin 193; s/d/tw US$30/40/50; P🚭).

Choykhana Murghob CENTRAL ASIAN $
(Bazaar; mains/beer/tea 8/7/1TJS; ⏰7am-7pm Mon-Sat) One of many local eateries in the bazaar area, the Murghob has a lacklustre interior but its wide, open balcony overlooks the river beside the main footbridge.

Bar Varka RUSSIAN $
(Gagarin 54; mains 7-14TJS, garnish 2.50-5TJS, beer 8TJS; ⏰11am-10pm Mon-Sat; 📋)

Six-tabled Varka has dim lighting, suffers summer humidity and looks ideal for a petty drug dealer's date, but the salads are good and it's the nearest eatery to Pamir Lodge (p344).

Delhi Darbar INDIAN **$$**
(Azizbek 2; curries 14-25TJS; ⌚11am-10pm Mon-Sat;) It's exciting to find anyone even attempting to offer Indian cuisine in so remote a corner of Central Asia and Delhi Darbar does an unexpectedly good job, especially with some of the vegetarian options. They also have their own small hotel.

Shugnon CENTRAL ASIAN **$$**
(☎214 44; Lenin 42; mains 12-18TJS; ⌚8am-9pm Mon-Sat) The mood-lit, stone-and-brick basement cavern adds fake foliage and dangling musical instruments to create a sense of atmosphere, which is then diminished by constant pop music TV. Staff speak English but the menu is only verbal.

Chor Bagh MULTICUISINE **$$**
(☎290 57; Central Park; mains 16-35TJS; ⌚10am-10pm;) Right in the central park, Chor Bagh is the most attractive restaurant in town with a great open-air pavilion perched above the river for those balmy summer evenings. Sadly, while the food impresses some travellers, we found it to be regularly way below expectations – watery Thai soup, inedible hard-breaded burgers and stodgey cream-chicken on rice. Good for a cold beer, though.

Serena Inn Restaurant RESTAURANT **$$**
(Serena Hotel; mains US$5-8; ⌚noon-3pm & 6-10.30pm) Small, upmarket restaurant with some outdoor seating overlooking the terraced river-garden; good for a beer (21TJS) on the *topchan* (dining pavilion).

Shopping

De Pamiri HANDICRAFTS
(☎248 29; www.depamiri.org; Central Park; ⌚9am-5pm Mon-Fri, 9am-noon Sat) Sharing the PECTA building, this fair-trade craft shop showcases work by dozens of Pamiri artisans with excellent felt rugs and bags, musical instruments, *palas* (woven goat-hair carpets) and embroidered skullcaps.

Information

For information on the Afghan Consulate in Khorog, see p364.

INTERNET ACCESS

There's wi-fi at Lal Hotel (p345, per day 15TJS, and Serena Inn (p345), per minute 0.38TJS. Several small internet cafes are ranged around the post office and a good new one (Lenin, Youth Centre, 2nd fl, room 14; per hr 3TJS; ⌚9am-7pm Mon-Sat) is upstairs in the Youth Centre building. On a Sunday, your best hope is at **Badakhshan Travel** (www.visitbadakhshan.com; Central Park access lane; per hr 3TJS; ⌚7.30am-7pm) beside the currently dormant Chogh Bagh Hotel.

MONEY

Several banks along Lenin change US$ and euros, at least on weekdays. Of six ATMs, none accept Maestro and many have very low maximum withdrawals. The most reliable ATM (Lenin 85) will give up to US$300 on Visa cards.

PERMITS & REGISTRATION

PECTA can organise permits for Zor-Kul (€6 per person per day), the ruby mines south of Anderob (US$5), the Tajik National Park (40TJS per day, theoretically needed if you're headed to Yashil-Kul, for example) and for the gold mines near Rang-Kul (oddly not available from Murgab). Almost all of these require simply a photocopy of your passport and can be instantly issued. Lake Sarez (p343) is different and can take a month or more.

Should you need to register or enquire about visa extensions, **OVIR** (Lenin 117; ⌚8am-noon & 1-5pm Mon-Frit) is beside Amonat Bank.

TOURIST INFORMATION

PECTA (Pamirs Ecotourism Association Information Centre; ☎224 69; www.pecta.tj; Central Park; ⌚8am-8pm May-early Oct) An essential resource for any traveller in the Pamirs, this excellent information office has lists of guides, drivers and homestays, rents simple trekking gear and can help you arrange the right kind of transport for your needs. Zhandiya is a veritable fount of wisdom.

TRAVEL & TOUR AGENCIES

Pamir Silk Tour (☎222 27, 93-505 23 61; www.pamirsilk.travel; Azizbek 1) Very experienced Mullo Abdo Shagarf can arrange mountaineering guides, horse treks and Wakhan adventures.

Pamir Tourism (☎93-500 99 47; www.pamirs-tourism.org; Lenin 105) Ismail Kanunov organises treks, tours, glacier expeditions and homestays throughout the eastern Pamirs.

Tour De Pamir (☎266 61, 93-500 75 57; www.tourdepamir.com) Various tours, competitive rates for taxi-hire. Contact Ergash.

PamirMount (☎91-936 67 72; www.pamirmount-tour.com; Mirsaid Mirshakar 11) Tour and trekking agent specialising in the Bartang Valley.

Getting There & Away

AIR

Depending on your confidence in the pilots of Tajik Air, the Khorog–Dushanbe flight (440TJS) might be one of the most exhilarating or terrifying experiences of your life. For most of the 45-minute flight the aircraft scoots between (not above) mountain valleys, flying with wingtips so close you could swear they kick up swirls of snow. In Soviet days this was the only route on which Aeroflot paid its pilots danger money.

Flights originate in Dushanbe and, in theory, run daily but they are grounded at the first sign of bad weather or if there are insufficient passengers exiting Dushanbe. Even when flights operate, buying tickets is a frustrating game. Budget an extra day or two into your itinerary in case flights are cancelled and be prepared to travel overland if need be.

The **airport ticket office** (Lenin; ⌚8am-noon) is 3km west of town by minivan 1, diagonally across the main road from the airport terminal at the rear of a faux-brick–fronted buiding simply signed Khorogh. Ideally you need to get your name on the list for the day you need to fly, returning one day before with your passport. But the ticket office has a single, absurdly small tunnel window through which to misunderstand the latest news of impending flights and the lack of tickets therefor. If you manage to get on the list, turn up at the airport by 8am the day before you want to leave and see if the plane is actually coming and whether you've been bumped.

SHARED TAXI & 4WD

All departures are 'when full' but prices fluctuate with demand. Be prepared to hang around for hours before finally leaving. Note that very few cars depart on Sundays.

Dushanbe Shared vehicles (300TJS, 14 to 20 hours) leave several times each morning and possibly as late as 1pm from a parking area near Kafe Khatlon.

Murgab Shared 4WDs (150TJS, seven hours) and minivans to Rushan (10JS, 90 minutes), Roshtqala, and Shahzud (for Bachor) depart from the main taxi stand in the bazaar area.

If hitch-hiking to Murgab your best bet is to head to Tank (Km641 of the Pamir Highway, 22km east of Khorog). Here Chinese trucks wait at two 'terminals' (they aren't allowed to transit Khorog by day) with most eastbound trucks leaving around noon (and arriving in Murgab antisocially at around midnight). Drivers generally expect around 30TJS per passenger. Speaking Chinese helps.

Wakhan Valley Vehicles for Ishkashim (50TJS to 120TJS, three hours), Langar (100TJS to 250TJS, seven hours) and other villages park in three closely huddled yards directly across the footbridge from the bazaar. Mid-afternoon you might find that drivers anxious to return home are heavily discounting prices, but you'll risk not finding a ride that day.

Getting Around

Marshrutkas 1 and 3 start beyond the Serena Inn and pass the airport, bazaar and park. Route 1 continues along Lenin out past the **'First Truck' monument** (Khorog GES; 🚌1), while route 3 takes Gagarin past the UPD district to the foot of the Botanical Gardens. Fares are 1/1.5TJS for short/long rides. A taxi from the centre to Pamir Lodge costs 10TJS.

Shokh Dara Valley

Долина Шог Дара

This route's main highlights are occasional glimpses of the distinctive north face of Engels Peak (6507m), and the chance to create a loop-route through some little-visited villages as part of a multiday chartered 4WD-loop.

A kilometre after **Tavdem**'s ancient shrine (now protected within a 1990s octagonal cover-shrine), a 4km 4WD side-track winds up hairpins to **Tusiyon**, whose high pastures are set in a wide rocky amphitheatre with many cleverly designed water-canal innovations.

A dramatically contorted rocky backdrop soars high above the valley's main town, **Roshtqala**, named for the tiny ruined 'red fort' at Km39. At the back of the small bazaar are a couple of very basic eateries, the only restaurants in the Shokh Dara Valley.

It's worth stopping by the signboard for **Shokhirizm village** (Km60) and walking 30 seconds towards a photogenic Grand Canyon–style perch, high above the river gorge into which the road later burrows. Some 11km further at **Sezhd**, a tough, easily missed 4WD track spirals up and over a dusty ridge finally petering out after 6km in the green, very disparate hamlet of **Durum** (population 11). Walk on for 40 minutes from road's end (crossing a tree-trunk bridge almost immediately) to reach a fine viewpoint overlooking the vivid blue-green lake **Durum-Kul**. Driving back, there are some splendidviewsof6000mpeaksonthesouthern horizon.

The views are less inspiring for the next 35km, and the 8th-century **Shashbuvad Fort** looks merely like an unfinished local house. Around Km120 as the road doubles back beside a small mountain stream there are brief but impressive glimpses of peaks **Engels** (6507m) and **Karl Marx** (6723m) peeping above a curiously corrugated intermediate ridge. This area would make for great camping. Alternatively there's a signed homestay if you can get across the river ford at **Javshanguz**, which is less a village than a wide scattering of 65 Pamiri houses spread across several kilometres of valley. A cleft valley frames more views of Marx Peak, but for the next sighting of brilliant knob-topped Engels' glacier ridge, look behind you some 10km beyond Javshanguz as the track degenerates and climbs to the north.

The toughest part of the 4WD road is a river crossing just below the Maisara Pass. This can be mitigated by driving up to a high-altitude shepherd camp halfway to the large lake **Turuntai-Kul**, and crossing the stream at a smaller ford nearby. Rejoin the main track which winds down hairpins to the main Pamir Highway, rejoining it east of Jelandy across a bridge that is only just wide enough for a 4WD.

There are signed homestays at Vezdara, Sindev, Shohirizm and Javshanguz plus at Bodomdara, a very rough 14km off the main road at Bidiz on the trekking route to Darshai.

Getting There & Away

Other than Khorog–Roshtqala minivans (10TJS) there's minimal transport. Adding the Shokh Dara Valley plus Bulunkul to a Wakhan Valley trip, creating a six-day 4WD-loop, should cost around US$600 total for a chartered Land-Cruiser including driver's expenses. Overall, doing the loop clockwise gives the better views.

Wakhan Valley
Ваханская долина

The Wakhan offers up a seemingly endless parade of scenic superlatives. Vivid green villages counterpoint towering valley walls, which open regularly for glimpses of the dazzling white Hindu Kush ('killer of hindus') mountains marking the Afghanistan–Pakistan border. A sprinkling of castle ruins and ibex-horn shrine-walls, even a Buddhist mini *ziggurat*-stupa, add zest. And while you're here you might be tempted to nip into Afghanistan. Beware that without your own wheels, transport is pitifully infrequent. Consider hiring a 4WD in Khorog or Murgab.

Khorog to Ishkashim

The 100km between Khorog and Ishkashim is scenically varied. For the northerly section the border river rages through a narrow valley across which Afghanistan's donkey traffic seems sometimes close enough to touch. Nearer to Ishkashim the river widens, with pretty green meadows that look almost like golf fairways, notably around Sumjin Km92.

Anderob (Km39) is the turn-off for **Garam Chashma** (soak 5TJS; ⏲ men 5am-8am, 3.30pm-4.30pm, women 8am-noon, 1.30pm-3.30pm, 4.30-5.30pm), 6km east. There a natural bowl of mineral deposits forms a hot-spring pool that up close looks less attractive than the brochure photos, and the village is unexpectedly commercialised. Contrastingly few visitors venture 1.7km up hairpins from Anderob's southernmost end to **Dasht Village**. Panoramic views down across Anderob are postcard-perfect. Dasht is home to **Rustom Masain** (☎93-450 06 26; Dasht Village, Anderob), a nationally famous yet seemingly impoverished septugenarian maker of traditional (and sometimes amusingly kitschy) musical instruments.

South of Anderob towards Ishkashim, you'll pass the **Koh-i-Lal ruby mine**. Marco Polo noticed gem mines here in 1274 and Badakhshani rubies remain internationally famed.

Ishkashim Ишкашим

Ishkashim is the Wakhan's regional centre and largest village. It's certainly not an attraction in itself, but if you're here on Saturday morning, don't miss the trans-border market which bustles with Afghan traders in turbans and *pakol* (flat caps). The bazaar is held in three metal-roofed halls 3km west of town on a no-man's-land island (passport but no Afghan visa required). This is also the main **border crossing** (Km 102, Ishkashim-Khorog Highway; ⏲ Mon-Sat) used by most visitors heading for the Afghanistan Wakhan, though it's worth checking the status of the Langar and Shaimak borders. If open, either would prove altogether more useful for reaching the Little Pamir.

Well-marked just west of central Ishkashim, **Hanis Guesthouse** (☎93-582 58 20; vai4hope@gmail.com; Miyona 2, Ishkashim; bed only/half-board/tent-space US$10/18/2; ⏲ Mar-Nov) has the rare luxury of Western toilets and hot showers. It's big, sparse and institutional-looking but popular with travellers sharing Pamir and Afghan travel tips aided by helpful owners (Vali speaks good English). One block east, then south, set amid apricot trees, the new **Hotel Rumi** looks smarter but was closed when we visited.

Ishkashim to Langar

The Tajik Wakhan's greatest appeal lies east of Ishkashim. Poplars, vegetable fields and numerous photogenic oasis villages nestle between soaring arid valley-peaks. Higher snow-whitened pinnacles and glaciers make regular theatrical appearances framed in narrow side valleys across the river on the Afghanistan side. Our favourite roadside viewpoints are at Km131 and between Zong and Langar, but virtually every kilometre has its own delight. The most impressive of several fortress ruins, Yamchun, requires a 6km detour.

NAMADGUT НАМАДГУТ

At Namadgut, some 15km east of Ishkashim, a lumpy, muddy hillock rises right beside the road, topped by a series of mud-wall fragments from the historic **Khaakha Fortress** FREE. The oldest sections are Kushan-era (3rd century BC), but the site has been reused by many other cultures since, and indeed part of the mound was used as a Tajik military watchpost til very recently – the site stares out across the border river directly below. It's worth a 15-minute stop. Gravel pathways and steps make exploration relatively easy.

Amid trees facing the eastern fortress knoll is an Ismaili *mazar* (tomb), one of many places in Central Asia that claims, quite unconvincingly, to be the final resting place of Ali, the Prophet's son-in-law. Next door there's a fairly minimal **museum** (☎93-809 13 36; Namadgut; admission 10TJS; ⌚by arrangement). The most interesting part of a visit is dressing up in a Pamiri *chakman* (judo-style woollen robe) while director Odinmammad Mirzayev plays one of the traditional musical instruments, demonstrates the archaic flint fire-stone or shows you his extensive family tree.

DARSHAI ДАРШАЙ

At Darshai a roaring side river howls out of a narrow canyon and hurtles beneath the road beside which is a *mazor* enclosure including some petroglyphs. But the main attraction is the trek up the **Darshai Gorge**, starting near the bridge and walking around a knoll topped with some minimal fortress ruins, then following a clear path up the east bank of the side river. In under two hours it's easy enough to reach the trail's star attraction, a photogenic *owring,* ie short section of footpath where the trail becomes so perilously narrow that it has been built out on branches and rocks 'sewn' onto the rockface using wire ropes. However, you will need a guide if you want to stay at the yurt camp much further up the valley (five to eight hours' walk), which are used by exclusive hunting groups in winter but are available to walkers in summer. From there it's a very testing day-hike past 6095m **Mayakovsky Peak** and across a snowy 4941m pass to reach the signed homestay at Bodomdara in the Shokh Dara Valley.

In Darshai village you can find guides (per half/full day US$15/25) through local homestays including that of **Gulmammad Matrobov** (☎93-459 42 66; Darshai Village; US$15). His traditionally styled 2001 house is at the end of the first side lane west of the bridge, prominently painted 'VELCOME'. For wildlife photo and hunting 'safaris' visit www.wildlife-tajikistan.org/tourism-in-darshay.

YAMCHUN ЯМЧУН

Two of the Tajik Wakhan's foremost attractions are high above the valley accessed via 6km of hairpins up from Tughoz (look for Chashmai signs, 3km east of central Ptup).

The 12th-century **Yamchun (Zulkhomar) Fort** is the most impressive of the valley's many tumbledown castle ruins, complete with multiple walls and round watchtowers. The site is a 6km switch-backed drive from the main road and sits about 500m above the valley. Climb up the hillside west of the fort for the best views.

About 1km further uphill from the fort are the **Bibi Fatima Springs** (local/foreigner 1/10TJS; ⌚5am-9pm), probably the nicest in the region and named after the Prophet Mohammed's daughter. Women believe they can boost their fertility by visiting the womblike calcite formations. Bring a towel and keep an eye on your valuables as there are no lockers. Men's and women's bath times alternate every half hour.

Vichkut is less a village than a scattering of hillside homesteads, with at least five widely separated homestays strung together by the hairpins that wind up to Yamchun Fort. Our favourite for hospitality, great food and classic Pamiri interiors

WAKHAN VALLEY TRANSPORT

Ishkashim has transport to Khorog (40TJS, three hours) mostly in the mornings. Shared taxis from Langar drive to Khorog on Mondays and Fridays returning the next day except when continuing to Dushanbe (thrice monthly). Especially at weekends locals drive to Bibi Fatema via Yamchun offering some hitching potential though we met several people who'd already been waiting a day for a ride. From Langar to Bulunkul even seasoned hitchhikers sometimes resort to chartering (US$110). Renting a decent 4WD for a multiday Khorog–Murgab trip via the Wakhan costs from around US$400.

is **Charshanbe Sultonasainov's place** (☎93-830 52 39; Vichkut; half-board US$15). It's 2km down the hairpins from the castle entrance, in an unmarked garden with great valley views as you walk to the toilet.

Tucked behind a hut-shack just a three-minute walk west of the castle, **Kurbanasai Homestay** (☎93-876 81 80; per person 50TJS) is simple but has views and a covered *topchan*.

There are four newly built, simple 'hotels' within 300m of the Bibi Fatima Springs of which well-kept **Bomi Johani** (Bibi Fatima; per person 25som) is the most appealing with a good shared kitchen and views from the dining terrace.

YAMG ЯМГ

Some 500m off the main road in Yamg is the reconstructed **house museum** (☎93-456 55 19; Yamg; admission 10TJS; ⏲by request) of Sufi mystic, astronomer and musician Mubarak Kadam Wakhani (1843–1903). One room contains typical ethnographic artefacts, plus books and manuscripts of the master. The other is designed as a classic 19th-century Pamiri home where the caretaker will likely serenade you on a few of the traditional instruments. On the approach lane outside is a 'solar calendar', a stone with a hole focussed on more stones on the ridge to the west across which the sunset aligns on 21 March (Navrus). As you come into town, call first at the house of key-keeper Aydar Malikmamadov (and his English-speaking son, Nozim) who will open the place for you. Aydar's family run two of the village's three homestays.

VRANG ВРАНГ

On an obvious salt-bleached patch of mountainside directly behind Vrang is a five-level stone monument claimed to be an ancient **Buddhist stupa**, though it looks more like a miniature *ziggurat* (stepped pyramid). From the green, unusually big (if feebly stocked) Vakhon shop, walk 200m north then follow the watercourse past an attractive garden. The stupa is directly above but the path does a 15-minute double-back. Far harder to reach are the dozens of hermit caves in the crumbling cliff-face across the chasm from the stupa.

Homestay Rano (☎93-771 12 01; Vrang; per person US$15) is on the main road facing the stupa area, but with a vehicle you might prefer **Jahonbegim Zevarova's place** (☎93-859 22 77; Vrang; per person US$12), 1.5km east with its impressive tree-trunk timbers and tree-lined avenue approach.

ZONG

The ruined Afghan citadel of **Qala-e Panja**, once the largest settlement in the Wakhan, is visible across the river near Zugband, some 10km before Langar. At **Zong**, 5km further east, **Abrashim (Vishim) Qala** (the Silk Fortress) was built to guard this branch of the Silk Road from Chinese and Afghan invaders. The fort offers perhaps the most scenic views of all those in the valley. From **Mauluda Barieva's homestay** (Zong; per person 50som), signed near Zong's western edge, the ruins are a steep one-hour hike straight up (half an hour back).

Langar Лангар

A glorious knot of spiky peaks rise above likeable Langar where the Pamir and Wakhan Rivers join forces to form the Pyanj. The diffuse, green village stretches several kilometres and makes a pleasant exploration base.

By the small main bridge, Langar's *jamoat khana* (prayer house) is easily recognisable by its colourful window frames. Across the road, **Shoh Kambari Oftab Mazar**, a mysteriously evocative Pamiri shrine-garden, is overloaded with ram horns and contorted ancient trees.

Steep rock faces are inscribed with more than 6000 **petroglyphs**, starting around 20 minutes' scramble up the slopes behind Langar school. From the *jamoat khana*, head 400m west then 150m north to find the school. To reach the most accessible set of petroglyphs follow the power lines up from the school, walk east through the cemetery and up the slope at the far end. However, it's hard to tell ancient carvings from copy-cat ibexes amid all the 20th-century grafitti. Seeking them out is mostly appealing for the brilliant mountain panoramas. If you find the trail, it's possible to hike on up (around four hours) to a fine camping spot in Engels Meadows with a jaw-dropping view of Engels Peak.

After a string of hairpins winding up some 5km from Langar, charming **Ratm** is the very last village of the Tajik Wakhan. Perched above the river canyon, atop a three-sided cliff-drop, Ratm's shoulder-high castle ruins stand on a spot that's supposedly been fortified for at least 2300 years. From the roadside sign board it's a lovely if less-than-obvious 20-minute walk through fields and across streams.

With views from the raised Upper Langar garden and solar-heated showers, **Nigina Homestay** (☎03-848 37 20; Upper Langar; half board US$15) is marginally the most appealing if hardest-to-find of three official homestays in Langar. It's the farmstead on the right about eight minutes' walk west of the school, on the lane that parallels the main road on the north side of a low ridge. The other homestays are signposted along the main road, albeit spread out over a considerable distance. There are further options at nearby Hisor.

East of Langar

With no villages, and just two lonely houses along the 70km between Ratm and Khargush military checkpoint, driving the trafficless track east from Langar can feel a little wearing. But driving westbound along the same road is contrastingly exhilarating with serrated fore-ridges and soaring snowy peaks looming ahead of you for at least 30km.

At Khargush checkpoint you'll need prior permission, via PECTA (p346) in Khorog, to take the riverside route via protected **Zor-Kul**, once christened Lake Victoria and considered to be the source of the Oxus River (by the 1842 British expedition of Lieutenant Wood).

Alternativey at Khargush, swing north and head for the M41 near Bulunkul. Once again the route looks better driving in the reverse direction for views south across the snowy Afghan Wakhan. To really appreciate the majesty of the stark mountain scenery, consider the breathless walk up **Panorama Ridge** marked very accurately as a 360-degree viewpoint on Marcus Hauser's **Pamir map**. The steep climb takes 1½ hours (30 minutes back) from a roadside cairn, 7km from Khargush, where the road levels out and the first of two smallish lakes come into view.

Pamir Highway

Памирское шоссе

The Pamir Highway (M41) is the remote high-altitude road from Khorog to Osh whose classic central section crosses Tibetan-style high plateau scenery, occasionally populated by yurts and yaks. It was built by Soviet military engineers between 1931 and 1934 to facilitate troop transport and provisioning.

Blue kilometre posts use two systems. Initially the distances are from Dushanbe (with the distance to the Kyrgyz border marked on the opposite side). This makes central Khorog Km641. At Murgab, Km930, the system changes thereafter showing distances from Khorog/Osh.

Khorog to Murgab

While specific sights are rare, the scenery is truly inspiring virtually every kilometre of the way between Khorog and Murgab. Apart from the painful Jelandy–Bulunkul section, the road is asphalted, albeit rather half-heartedly.

GUNT VALLEY TO KOI-TEZEK PASS

A series of well-watered orchard villages lead out of Khorog and up the Gunt Valley whose rugged valley sides become ever more dramatic as the greenery becomes more sparse. Rocky pinnacles and regular glimpses of white-top peaks are impressive for many miles but especially dramatic after **Dehmyona** (Km685).

Though somewhat awkward to reach without renting a vehicle, **Bachor** makes a great base for adventurous, well-acclimatised, fully-equipped trekkers heading into the high-altitude lakes and glacier-lands of the Tajik National Park (permit fees apply). The village has several homestays (ask around) and locals rent out donkeys/horses. The Bachor turn-off is at **Varshedz**, from which it's 18km. A taxi from Shahzud costs 90TJS, if you can find one.

Back on the highway, the ribbon of turquoise-white river slithers through ever drier upland valleys approaching the functional hot springs outpost of **Jelandy**.

BULUNKUL & YASHIL-KUL БУЛУНКУЛЬ & ЯШИЛЬКУЛЬ

The bumpy 4272m Koi-Tezek Pass leads into lunar-like, high-altitude desert scenery, framed by a series of snowy if relatively unremarkable peaks. After nearly 40km the road starts to descend sharply with sweeping views ahead over stark landscapes and two large salt lakes. As you're descending look for the signed turn-off leading 14km (sign says 16km) to the end-of-the-world settlement of **Bulunkul**. Reportedly the coldest place in Tajikistan, it is a friendly but unaesthetic three-row grid of low-slung, wind-blown houses forming a dusty, functional square. A pretty, if hardly pristine, stream meanders behind, flowing towards mirrorlike lake **Bulun-Kul** (3737m). Viewed in the morning light from the east side (a 4.5km drive from the village), the lake looks magnificent reflecting the mineral swirls of a low, multicoloured ridge opposite, one section looking like a gigantic stylised butterfly.

Much bigger, but arguably less photogenic, **Yashil-Kul** (3734m) means 'green lake' though it's actually bright blue, framed by ochre desert-slopes. From Bulunkul village, the first glimpse is a 4km drive or uphill walk. With patience, hikers can find lukewarm springs on the southern side and stone circles at the mouth of the Bolshoi Marjonai River, but technically you'll need to come prepared with Tajik National Park permits (40TJS per day), obtained in Khorog or Murgab.

BULUNKUL TO MURGAB

Alichur (Km828) is a wide scattering of low, whitewashed hovels, many daubed with the words '*stolovaya*' (canteen) or guesthouse. It's the westernmost limit of Murgab Region's predominantly Kyrgyz community whose occasional yurts dot the mountain-edged plain that stretches over 50km east. Several yurtstays are within 400m of the highway, notably at Km837, Km838.5 and

TO GO OR NOT TO GO? THE AFGHAN WAKHAN

Before leaving home, many travellers imagine Afghanistan to be a perilously dangerous hellhole. Well, that might be true of some areas. But arriving in the GBAO, it comes as a thrilling surprise for many to hear that the Afghan Wakhan is both peaceful and actually open. The Wakhan Corridor is that strange Pinocchio nose of Afghanistan that grew from the machinations of the Great Game, creating a barrier between the Russian and British empires after border treaties in 1895 and 1907. These days you too can gaze upon the area's rugged magnificence that is so gloriously depicted in the photos of **Matthieu Paley** (www.pamirbook.com, http://paleyphoto.com). And if you head up the valley to the Wakhan's incredibly isolated Little Pamir, you can encounter Kyrgyz herders who are some of the most remote, forgotten traditional peoples on the planet. Should you be tempted to go, Afghan visas are usually available within 24 hours in Khorog assuming you have a double-entry Tajik visa. Then from Ishkashim you can just walk in.

But do you really want to? Costs add up fast. The visa charges are US$100 to US$200 depending on your nationality and a taxi for the 6km from the border to Afghan-Eshkashim village costs an unwavering US$20 each way. That's a lot to pay if you're only visiting Eshkashim market for the kudos of a passport stamp.

To continue further you'll need permit letters, which are available in Eshkashim but are hard to arrange without paid help unless you speak local languages. To continue to the Little Pamir, the local taxi union demands an unwavering US$450 per car each way. That's a big chunk of cash to pay considering you'll be bouncing along a track that parallels the smoother Tajik-side road for most of the route, sharing similar views but lacking the network of homestays. If you do make it to the Little Pamir, exiting to Shaimak isn't allowed. The 'highlight' is meeting genuine Kyrgyz nomads but these folks are shockingly poor and the region's sanitation is nonexistent so the experience, while humbling and fascinating, is likely to leave you shell-shocked and possibly unwell. Your insurance company won't necessarily be sympathetic.

Km848, and it's quite possible to see yak herders in the side valleys.

There's a lonely *stolovaya* serving fresh fish beside the tiny, 'holy' pond of the **Ak-Balyk** (White Fish) spring at Km840.

To find the photogenic **Chinese tomb** that features in local tourist literature, turn south at Km858 towards Bash Gumbaz, itself 7km off the main highway. The tomb is 3km outside that village.

A police post at Km928 guards the entrance to Murgab.

Murgab Мургаб/Мурғоб

☎3554 / POP 6500 / ELEV 3576M

Utterly isolated, the wild-east town of Murgab is the logical base from which to explore the eastern Pamirs if you arrive without your own transport. Murgab's box houses and criss-crossing power lines don't create an immediately charming effect, but rocky bone-dry ridges create some interest, as does the ever-white bulk of 7546m Muztagh Ata which, on exceptionally clear days, hangs like a strange cloud upon the eastern horizon. A meandering river valley below the main road level creates the area's nearest approximation to greenery. Murgab's population has significant Tajik and Pamiri contingents, contrasting with surrounding communities which are almost entirely Kyrgyz.

Murgab's layout is confusing, even though there are just two asphalt roads both running south–northeast. The upper one (Somoni) is the main Pamir Highway, bending in front of Pamir Hotel. The lower road is initially called Lenin as it diverges from Somoni 700m south of the hotel. It passes the TIC (directly down partially pedestrianised Ayni from the hotel), the bazaar, petrol stations and very close to META before wiggling around to the 40-Let Pobeda suburb. Beware that addresses usually denote areas not streets.

Festivals

At Chabysh HORSE FESTIVAL

(www.atchabysh.org; ⏲2nd weekend of Aug) FREE Aimed at reviving and strengthening the horsemanship traditions of the Kyrgyz Pamirs, this annual festival features traditional horse sports interspersed with musical turns and poetry recitations. The festival ground is above the main M41, around 5km southwest of central Murgab. Shared taxis shuttle to the site from the bazaar.

Sleeping

There's one hotel and roughly a dozen homestay-guesthouses, most (but not all) with outside toilets. Some are signed but several others make no attempt to advertise themselves. Ask at META (p354), who have a room themselves, and TIC (p354).

Sary Köl Lodge HOMESTAY $

(☎217 89, 93-569 71 01, 93-547 33 91; Sorok Let Pobieda; dm/s/tw 44/58/106TJS, breakfast/dinner 15/20TJS; @) Murgab's most characterful accommodation has several imaginative touches like the goat-horn bathroom pegs. Timber ceilings and whitewashed walls are set off with colourful fabrics. Transformers ensure that the solar power is steady enough to charge your electronic devices though the (outdoor) toilet light is very dim. If you don't have wheels, the location can feel a little inconvenient, 1.5km northeast of the TIC, set back off the lower road in a small, nascent garden.

Erali Guesthouse HOMESTAY $

(☎93-563 75 14, 216 18; dm/B&B/HB US$10/12/16) On the slope northeast of Agroinvest Bank, Erali's has sweeping views across town and as far as Mustagh Ata. It's an older house with aged beams, plenty of traditional Kyrgyz motifs and even a yurt in the yard. Erali speaks English and claims that wi-fi will be installed by 2014.

Suhrob Guesthouse HOMESTAY $

(☎93-848 37 33, 216 53; per person/with dinner/full board US$10/15/18) Suhrob's pluses are the great views from its dining-room terrace and the super-friendly, English-speaking Pamiri welcome. It's the half-wooden house with attached yurt uphill, behind the apartment block at Somoni 33, around 200m northwest of Pamir Hotel.

Tulfabek Guesthouse HOMESTAY $

(☎93-538 91 59; half-board 45TJS or dm 20TJS, shower 10TJS, veg/non-veg meal 8.60/17.60TJS) Opposite Agroinvest Bank on the upper main road, Tulfabek charges separately for showers, beds and each food item, so if you have a modest appetite and don't use the Heath Robinson–esque shower contraption, this homestay is about the cheapest in town. Rooms have real beds, there's an indoor loo and a shared lounge with relatively new sofas.

Pamir Hotel HOTEL $
(☎93-050 58 63, 217 62; dm/s/tw US$10/20/30) This two-floor building at the central bend of the Pamir Highway is the town's only hotel and is a handy landmark. Don't be misled by the new glass frontage: the whole structure is gerry-built with off-line walls and uneven floors. Still, the simple rooms have been very recently repainted and staff regularly clean the communal hot showers and sit-down toilets. Tair speaks English and can fix many traveller problems.

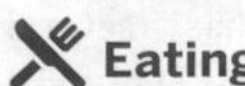

Eating

Most travellers dine at their (or another) homestay-guesthouse. Otherwise **Aida** (mains/samsa 8/5TJS) is marginally the best of five very basic cafes backing the container-box bazaar. Their *samsas* make good snacks but opening times are unpredictable and if other stocks run out sometimes only greasy egg-and-sausage lunches are available.

Pamir Hotel's unmarked bar-restaurant has a range of booze but their meals are rather unimaginative. Beware of the 3TJS extra charge should you decide to have sugar with your tea! Basic groceries are startlingly (if understandably) expensive compared to Dushanbe.

Shopping

Yak House HANDICRAFTS
(☎Salamat 93-410 51 79; Murgab House; ⏲9am-1pm & 2-6pm Mon-Fri or by arrangement) Of the traditional Pamiri and Kyrgyz crafts sold here, the most impressive are pure-woollen shoulder-bags (61TJS) and colourful felt *shyrdak* squares. The shop is within the beautifully designed, circular Murgab House, symbolically incorporating architectural elements from both Kyrgyz yurts and Pamiri houses. It's 1.8km northeast along the M41 from Pamir Hotel. Consider phoning first.

Information

- Murgab district (as far west as Bulunkul) operates on Kyrgyzstan time, ie one hour ahead of Dushanbe and Khorog.
- Electricity supply is irregular, and often pitifully weak. Pamir Hotel seems to get a more regular supply than most, but you'd still be advised to bring a safety plug for any electrical equipment. Sary Köl Lodge has a transformer and stabiliser for its solar-powered plugs.
- T-Cell has the best mobile signal in town, but Megafon also works here and covers the outlying valleys too.

MONEY

Agroinvest Bank (Somoni; ⏲8am-noon & 1-5pm Mon-Fri, 8am-noon Sat) Changes US dollars and euro cash. It's 300m northwest of Pamir Hotel.

TOURIST INFORMATION

TIC (Tourist Information Center Murgab; ☎93-547 56 82; infomurghab@mail.ru; Ayni; ⏲10am-1pm & 3-6pm Mon-Fri, 2-6pm Sat & Sun, closed Dec-Apr) Helpful for free, non-commercial tourist information including contacts for drivers and accommodation throughout the region. Handicrafts are sold here, as are useful Pamir/Murgab maps (97/10TJS). Miserably slow internet costs 12TJS per hour.

META (Murgab Ecotourism Association; ☎Gulnara 93-519 18 02; www.meta.tj; Osh 91; ⏲call ahead) META was the original driving force for community tourism in Murgab and its website remains an ever-evolving treasure trove of resources. Re-organised in 2012, they plan a new information office but til then there's just the front room of valiant volunteer Gulnara's house.

Tajik National Park Officer (☎91-732 16 97, 93-848 37 77) If you are going to Karakul or anywhere else in the Tajik National Park you are supposed to have a ticket (40TJS per day). Call the officer on duty and he should be able to come and sell you one.

TRAVEL & TOUR AGENCIES

Local tour agencies include META spin-offs **Pamir Highway Adventure** (http://pamirhighwayadventure.com), **Pamir Offroad Adventure Guide** (☎934 65 20 05; 2005@gmail.com; opposite TIC) and **Pamir Guides** (www.pamirguides.com; Murgab House). Kyrgyzstan-based **Pamir Trek** (☎996-77-237 60 36, 996-77-343 80 32; www.pamirtrek.com) can also be competitive, especially if you're starting from Osh.

Getting There & Away

From the bazaar, two or three vehicles (4WDs or minivans) leave most mornings to Khorog (120TJS, seven to nine hours, 320km), and one or two head for Osh (150TJS, around 12 hours, 420km). Ideally arrange a place one day ahead. Otherwise expect several hours' wait while they fill up. Frequency reduces in cold months.

Alternatively consider hiring a 4WD between a group of travellers and making a three- or four-day multi-stop trip via the Wakhan Valley. This can be arranged either directly with a driver or through agencies.

For hitching to Khorog, the best bet is with Chinese trucks (offer 30TJS) which stop overnight at a terminal around 2km northeast of central Murgab. These tend to leave en masse around midday for Khorog (stopping 30km short). In the other direction trucks arrive around midnight (hitchhikers report a crash pad with 15TJS sleeping spaces at the terminal), and continue the next day at around 8am for China via the Qolma Pass. Spoken Chinese would often prove helpful.

Shared taxis to Rang-Kul (20TJS) leave in the late afternoon from behind Aida Kafe in the bazaar, returning the next morning.

Murgab can be cut off entirely for a day or two after heavy winter snows or summer flash floods.

Getting Around

Four city-style bicycles are available to rent from **Maribed Saparova** (☎93-703 96 13, 213 38; 70-let Murgab 87; per day US$7), whose unsigned house is a short block east, then two homes south, from Tulfabek Homestay.

Around Murgab

PSHART & MADIYAN VALLEYS ДОЛИНЫ ПШАРТ И МАДИЯН

Two photogenic valleys strike west from either end of Murgab. Pshart, the more northerly, is initially parched and colourful with mineral layers. In contrast the Madiyan Valley's rugged rock walls are set off vividly against lush green riverside pastures and even copses of small trees – an especially lovely sight before sunset around the tiny hamlet of Ak-Tal (Km32), whose tiny whitewashed mosque adds foreground to the cliff-backed scene. From Ak-Tal a very bumpy 4WD track crosses the river and winds up 9km, then down 700m to access some incredibly isolated **hot springs**, which you're likely to have all to yourself, if you dare to cross the river to access them. That requires shimmying along a short, but precarious, 'bridge' missing most of the slats between two steel rails.

It's possible to do a long, strenuous day hike between the Pshart and Madiyan sides, starting up the Gumbezkul side valley from a horse-breeding centre/yurtstay where the Pshart Valley divides. After some steep scrambles and stunning views from 4731m **Gumbezkul Pass**, you pass another yurtstay around 7km before emerging on the Madiyan Valley road around Km18. Agencies can organise a guide plus 4WD drop-off/pick up at either end of the trail for around US$120. Alternatively a minivan taxi to Pshart yurt camp costs 80TJS.

A return 4WD day trip to the Madiyan hot springs runs around US$50 per vehicle.

RANG-KUL РАНГКУЛЬ

For stark, mountain deserts, salt lakes and giant sand dunes you might explore the **Rang-Kul** area. Rang-Kul village has homestays and **ZholKerbez** (☎3554-213 30; Kok-Otok 12, Rang-Kul village) runs yurtstay camel treks (per camel for one/two/three days US$70/90/110, pre-booking essential), but don't underestimate the discomfort of camel-riding.

SHAIMAK ШАЙМАК

To really get off the beaten track, take the road up the Ak-Suu Valley to Shaimak, 126km from Murgab, at the strategic junction of the borders of Tajikistan, Afghanistan, China and Pakistan. This is about as Great Game as it gets! You may need KGB approval to travel past the checkpoint before Tokhtamysh.

After crossing the lovely Subashi plain, the road passes the turn-off to the Qolma Pass, Tajikistan's only border crossing with China (currently closed to foreigners). You may be rewarded with views of Muztagh Ata from here.

At the village of Tokhtamysh you could detour 1km across the river to a damaged bow-shaped geoglyph and the faint ruins of a 19th-century caravanserai. The scenery gets increasingly impressive, passing rolling Pamiri peaks, seasonal lakes and scenic yurts.

Shaimak village (3852m) is located below the impressive 5365m bluff of Ak Tash, and sports a striking whitewashed mosque that looks like it's been borrowed from a Sahara fantasy film set. There are exciting views of the Little Pamir which stretches across into Afghanistan – three days a year in June the border is reportedly opened to cross-border trade with Kyrgyz herders living in extreme isolation on the far side.

On the way back, stop for a quick look at the beehive-shaped tombs at **Konye Kurgan** (Old Tomb), 7km from Murgab.

A return 4WD hire to Shaimak is likely to cost about US$200 (240km trip).

SHAKHTY & ZOR-KUL ШАХТЫ И ЗОРКУЛЬ

The impressive Neolithic cave paintings of **Shakhty** (4200m) are 50km southwest of Murgab, 25km off the Pamir Highway, in the dramatic Kurteskei Valley. Soviet archaeologists apparently took shelter in the cave during a storm one night in 1958, only to awake the next morning open-mouthed in front of the perfectly preserved red-ink paintings of a boar hunt. Check out the strange birdman to the left. Don't get too close to the paintings to avoid damaging them. The cave is a five-minute scramble up the hillside; you'll never find it without a knowledgeable driver/guide.

Agencies suggest a two-day wildlife tour that takes in Shakhty, passes the Shor-Bulak observatory (currently closed to foreigners) and continues south over two minor passes to a seasonal lake rich in birdlife.

In the Istyk River valley is the remote, relatively upmarket Jarty-Gumbaz region hunting camp/guesthouse. In winter it's rented out to hunting groups who pay at least $16,000 to shoot Marco Polo sheep. But in summer it accepts individual travellers (US$40 full board).

Basic accommodation may also be available in yurt camps at **Kara-Jilga**, around 30km further southwest, amid classic Wakhan scenery – epic views over a string of glorious turquoise lakes (Kazan-Kul and Djigit-Kul) to the snowcapped Wakhan range on the Afghan border. Continue west to the end of these lakes and you will be rewarded with rare views of **Zor-Kul** (elevation 4125m) stretching into the distance. Continuing to Khargush and the Wakhan Valley is tough before mid-July due to muddy track conditions and you'll need Zor-Kul permits (issued in by PECTA, p346, in Khorog!) to get past the checkpoints en route.

Karakul & the Road to Kyrgyzstan

North of Murgab, the high-altitude highway follows a fenced area of 'neutral zone' between Tajikistan and China and crosses the 4655m **Ak-Baital (White Horse) Pass**, reputedly one of the easiest places to spot Marco Polo sheep from the road. The region is almost entirely unihabited except for the small, scrappy but intriguing village of **Karakul**, which has an eerie, twilight-zone air about it. It sits at 3914m beside a vast, eponymous lake created by a meteor impact some 10 million years ago. Although salty, lake **Kara-Kul** is frozen and snow-covered til May, but there's a new jetty, plans for regatta (from September 2014) and an ongoing attempt by META (p354) to declare it the world's highest navigable lake, beating Lake Titicaca. Summer boat trips are planned to an island that was once a camp for unfortunate German POWs, who were kept here many years beyond the end of WWII. Landscapes are archetypal Pamir poster-material with long straight stretches of road disappearing into stark yet colourful mineral moonscapes, distantly ringed with white topped mountains in crystal clear air.

Lake Kara-Kul lies within the Unesco-listed Tajik National Park, but park tickets (40TJS per day) aren't needed if you're simply transitting or sleeping overnight in Karakul village (checkpost cops might claim otherwise). Mosquito repellent is useful when the wind drops. Megafone mobile phones have coverage. At least four families offer simple accommodation in very well signed homestays, all walking distance from the shore. Osh-bound shared 4WDs will often stop half an hour for breakfast in Karakul if you ask. However, if you get off here without your own wheels, getting out again might take a day or two. Five families, including **Turgumbay Tuktobekov** (☎090-776 86 55; Karakul), offer 4WD rental (US$0.70 per km, around US$150 to Sary Tash) should there be a vehicle available.

The first Tajik–Kyrgyz border post is 63km north of Karakul, just before the crest of the **Kyzyl-Art Pass** (4282m) from which there are briefly spectacular views of colourful red-brown-green mountain spires. The Kyrgyz post is 20km further at **Bordöbö**, 24km before Sary Tash. Look behind you here for Pamir panoramas. There is no accommodation at either border post so bring a tent if you're attempting the route by highly unreliable hitch-hiking.

UNDERSTAND TAJIKISTAN

Tajikistan Today

In the November 2013 elections President Rakhmonov (who now uses the Tajik spelling 'Rahmon') won a fourth term with a vast majority, officially taking over 83% of the vote. While observers criticised a 'lack of plurality', the elections were peaceful and, judging unscientifically from our numerous conversations with locals, it seems that Rahmon is genuinely popular in much of the country, credited for having ended the 1990s' civil war and for restoring law and order. Photos of his waving figure appear on billboards all over the country. While life remains hard, and reports of massive corruption are apparently corroborated by documents disseminated via Wikileaks, people see steady improvements in infrastructure (re-surfaced roads, mobile telephones, shiny new monuments) and savour the relative stability.

Maintenance of this stability has included heavy-handed military incursions against Islamist insurgents in Garm (2010) and a major battle in Khorog (2012) ostensibly in retribution for the murder of an intelligence officer. The latter saw the whole Gorno-Badakhshan province closed to foreign visitors, completely choking off the latter part of the 2012 tourist season. But tourism is growing. And the national economy has rebounded impressively, at least on paper. Much, however, remains dependant on international aid (over US$60 million a year arrives from the EU alone) and, especially, on remittances from Tajiks working abroad. An estimated million or so Tajiks (mostly men) work abroad, notably in the Russian construction industry, sending back around US$800 million a year. That's around half of Tajikistan's official GDP. While aluminium and cotton together constitute around 80% of Tajikistan's official exports, unofficially, it is estimated that as much as 50% of Tajikistan's economic activity in the last decade was linked to Afghanistan's narcotics trade.

Tajikistan's great natural resource is water, its glacial reserves amounting to 40% of Central Asia's total. Yet despite the huge potential for hydropower, in winter Dushanbe is sometimes without electricity and heating for days. If it's ever finished, the giant Rogun dam, under construction on the Vakhsh River, could change all that. At full power it would supply 80% of Tajikistan's electricity requirements and provide export revenues. But the downstream countries (Uzbekistan and Turkmenistan) remain deeply opposed to the project and engineers have expressed serious doubts about the stability of the dam's design.

Tajikistan is still in the process of formalising the exact delimitation of its borders with Kyrgyzstan and Uzbekistan, while the Chinese border was only settled in 2011

DIGGING UP THE PAST

Visiting Tajikistan's best museums you'll often see finds from and references to a whole series of ancient temple and city sites. Although today most are little more than undulations in the earth, each has a glorious history. Discoveries from these sites are showcased at Dushanbe's National Museum (p316). The website www.afc.ryukoku.ac.jp/tj has more.

Bunjikath The Sogdian site of Bunjikath near Shakhristan was the 8th-century capital of the kingdom of Ushrushana. It is noteworthy for a famous Sogdian mural depicting a wolf suckling twins, a clear echo of the Roman legend of Romulus and Remus that is repeated in statues across the country.

Sarazm Unesco-listed Sarazm is a 5500-year-old site 15km west of Penjikent. One of the oldest city sites in Central Asia, finds here include a fire temple and the grave of a wealthy woman whose lapis beads and seashell bracelets from around the 4th century BC are now at Dushanbe's National Muesum.

Kobadiyan The ancient site of Kobadiyan (7th to 2nd centuries BC) in southern Tajikistan is famed for the nearby discovery in 1877 of the Oxus Treasure, a stunning 2500-year-old Achaemenid treasure-trove unearthed at Takht-i Kobad, which now resides in the British Museum (www.thebritishmuseum.ac.uk/compass, search for 'Oxus Treasure').

Takht-i Sangin A ruined 2300-year-old Graeco-Bactrian temple close to the point where Alexander crossed the Oxus in 329 BC.

Ajina Teppe Southeast of Kurgonteppa is 7th- to 8th-century Ajina Teppe (Witches Hill), where in 1966 archaeologists unearthed a stupa, monastery and Central Asia's largest surviving Buddha statue.

Hulbuk Hulbuk was once the fourth-largest city in Central Asia. Its 9th- to 11th-century citadel and palace have been excavated, and the palace walls are now being dramatically rebuilt. It is at Kurbon Shaid.

after the Tajik government agreed to give Beijing 1142 sq km of territory (around Rang-Kul), much to the dismay of people in Badakhshan who felt that Tajiks had given away their land. But the most sensitive border is with Afghanistan. This has had great geopolitical importance as a logistical supply route during the succession of wars in that country. The withdrawal of US troops by 2014 means a period of uncertainty over the security situation, but Afghanistan is also seen as a potential economic benefit with new road, rail and energy-export links planned, assuming Afghanistan stabilises. If it doesn't, Tajikistan risks being in the firing line of any Taliban spill-over.

History

Tajik Ancestry

Tajik ancestry is a murky area, with roots reaching back to the Bactrians and Sogdians. Tombs from the eastern Pamir show that Saka-Usun tribes were grazing their flocks here from the 5th century BC, when the climate was considerably more lush than today.

In the 1st century BC the Bactrian empire covered most of what is now northern Afghanistan. Their contemporaries, the Sogdians, inhabited the Zerafshan (Zeravshan) Valley in present-day western Tajikistan, where a few traces of this civilisation remain near Penjikent. Alexander the Great battled the Sogdians and besieged Cyropol (Istaravshan), before founding modern-day Khojand. The Sogdians were displaced in the Arab conquest of Central Asia during the 7th century AD. The Sogdian hero Devastich made a last stand against the Arabs at Mt Mug in the Zerafshan Mountains, before he was finally beheaded by the Muslim vanquishers.

Modern Tajikistan traces itself back to the glory days of the Persian Samanid dynasty (819–992 AD), a period of frenzied creative activity that hit its peak during the rule of Ismail Samani (849–907 AD), transliterated in modern Tajik as Ismoil Somoni. Bukhara, the dynastic capital, became the Islamic world's centre of learning, nurturing great talents such as the philosopher-scientist Abu Ali ibn-Sina (known in the West as Avicenna) and the poet Rudaki. Both are now competitively claimed as native sons by Iran, Afghanistan and Tajikistan.

A Blurring of Identity

Under the Samanids, the great towns of Central Asia were Persian, which is one reason Tajikistan still claims Samarkand and Bukhara as its own. However, at the end of the 10th century a succession of Turkic invaders followed up their battlefield successes with cultural conquest. Despite contrasting cultures, the two peoples cohabited peacefully, unified by religion. The Persian-speaking Tajiks adopted Turkic culture and the numerically superior Turks absorbed the Tajik people. Both weathered conquests by the Mongols and, later, Timur (Tamerlane), though most of the territory of modern Tajikistan remained on the fringes of the Timurid empire.

From the 15th century onwards, the Tajiks were subjects of the emirate of Bukhara, who received 50% of Badakhshan's ruby production as a tax. In the mid-18th century the Afghans moved up to engulf all lands south

THE OPIUM HIGHWAY

In modern Central Asia, the Silk Road has become a heroin highway. Worldwide Tajikistan ranks third in seizures of opiates after Iran and Pakistan. But sharing well over 1000km of porous border with the world's largest opium producer (Afghanistan), it's hardly surprising that much more gets through: possibly 200 tonnes of heroin a year. Warlords and criminal gangs control most of the business, although the army, police, Afghan Taliban and border guards are alleged to have fingers in the opium bowl. Drugs have even turned up in Kazakh diplomatic bags and on Russian military flights. In 2005 a homemade aircraft (a parachute with a motor attached) was shot down flying above the border with Tajikistan with 18kg of heroin. In 2009 Russian police seized 80kg of heroin from smugglers on the Dushanbe–Moscow train, a line well known to antinarcotic police as the 'Heroin Express'. Over the years drug money has financed everything in Tajikistan from weapons for the civil war to the poppy palaces that line the Varzob Valley north of Dushanbe.

of the Amu-Darya (Oxus River), along with their resident Tajik population, and later seized parts of Badakhshan including, temporarily, the Rushan and Shughnan regions.

The Great Game & the Basmachi

As part of the Russian Empire's thrust southwards, St Petersburg made the emirate of Bukhara a vassal state in 1868, which gave Russia effective control over what now passes for northern and western Tajikistan. But the Pamirs (today's eastern Tajikistan) remained a no-man's-land, an anomaly that led to a strategic duel between Russia and British India that author Rudyard Kipling was to immortalise as the 'Great Game'. It was in the eastern Pamirs, after visiting Murgab, Alichur and Rang-Kul, that Francis Younghusband was thrown out of the upper Wakhan by his tsarist counterpart, sparking an international crisis. Russia backed up its claims by building a string of forts across the Pamirs, including at Murgab. Border treaties of 1893 and 1895 finally defined Tajikistan's current borders, leaving the Wakhan Corridor as Afghanistan's bizarre cartographical buffer between the two empires.

Following the Russian Revolution of 1917, new provisional governments were established in Central Asia and the Tajiks found themselves first part of the Turkestan (1918–24), then the Uzbekistan (1924–29) Soviet Socialist Republics (SSRs), despite pushing for an autonomous Islamic-oriented republic. The next year Muslim *basmachi* guerrillas (literally 'rebels') under the leadership of Enver Pasha began a campaign to free the region from Bolshevik rule. It took four years for the Bolsheviks to crush this resistance, and in the process entire villages were razed. The surviving guerrillas melted away into Afghanistan, from where they continued to make sporadic raids over the border. Much of the population also fled south during the decade that followed to avoid a series of reprisals, repressions and, later, from forced movements that saw whole villages removed from the mountains (notably around Garm) and moved to the Vakhsh Valley to cultivate cotton plantations.

Soviet Statehood

In 1924, when the Soviet Border Commission set about redefining Central Asia, the Tajiks got their own autonomous republic (ASSR). Although initially only a satellite of Soviet Uzbekistan, this was the first official Tajik state. In 1929 it was upgraded to a full union republic (SSR), although (possibly in reprisal for the *basmachi* revolt) Samarkand and Bukhara – where over 700,000 Tajiks still lived – remained in Uzbekistan. As recently as 1989 the government of Soviet Tajikistan was demanding the 'return' of areas lost in this cultural amputation. Today, tensions with the modern government of Uzbekistan over these cultural centres remain.

The Bolsheviks never fully trusted the Tajikistan SSR and during the 1930s almost all Tajiks in positions of influence within the government were replaced by stooges from Moscow. Some industrialisation of Tajikistan was undertaken following WWII but the republic remained heavily reliant on imports from the rest of the Union for food and standard commodities, as would become painfully apparent after the 1991 collapse of the Soviet trading system.

In the mid-1970s, an underground Islamic Renaissance Party started gathering popular support especially in the south around Kurgan-Tyube (Kurgonteppa). This region had been neglected by Dushanbe's ruling communist elite, who were mainly drawn from the prosperous northern city of Leninabad (now Khojand). Two 1979 events sent serious ripples through Tajik society. In Iran, whose language is essentialy the same as Tajik, the Shah was toppled by an Islamic revolution. And the same year, the Soviets began an invasion of Afghanistan, much of it launched through Tajikistan. The disparity between truth and propaganda became increasingly obvious as massive aid flowed to Afghanistan while Tajikistan suffered with the USSR's worst levels of education, poverty and infant mortality.

From Civil Unrest to Civil War

For years Moscow managed to hold the lid on the pressure cooker of resentment along with the supressed religious sentiments and clan-based tensions that had existed for centuries. But as the Soviet system started unravelling, things exploded. The first serious disturbances were on 12 February 1990 when it was rumoured that Armenian refugees were to be resettled in Dushanbe, a city already short on housing. Riots, deaths and the imposition of a state of emergency followed. Several opposition parties emerged as a result of the crackdown.

On 9 September 1991, following the failed Moscow coup, Tajikistan followed other SSRs by declaring independence. Less than two weeks later Dushanbe's central Lenin statue had been toppled, watched by a large demonstration of rural Muslim folk bussed into the capital by Hezb-e Nahzat-e Islami. Yet in November, elections appeared to favour Rakhmon Nabiev, a former Tajik Communist Party chief (1982–85) who riled the opposition by consolidating an old-guard, Leninabad-oriented power base rather than accommodating the various clan-factions that make up the nation. Sit-in demonstrations on Dushanbe's central square escalated to violent clashes.

In August 1992, antigovernment demonstrators stormed the Presidential Palace and took hostages. A coalition government was formed, but sharing power between regional clans, religious leaders and former communists proved impossible. As a way out of the internecine conflict, Emomali Rakhmonov (now known as Rahmon), the former communist boss of Kulob district, was chosen to front the government. The Kulob fought their way to power with a scorched-earth policy against their Islamic-leaning rivals from the Garm Valley and Kurgan-Tyube.

Frustrated by its marginal position and seeing no future in a collapsing Tajikistan, GBAO (eastern Tajikistan) nominally declared its independence in 1992. Tajikistan was descending into a brutal civil war that would claim over 60,000 lives. Kulyabi forces, led by Sanjak Safarov (who had previously spent 23 years in prison for murder), embarked on a campaign of ethnic cleansing. Anyone found in Dushanbe with a Badakhshan or Khatlon ID card was shot on the spot. November 1992 elections did nothing to resolve the conflict (the opposition in exile refused to take part in the vote) and the Islamic opposition continued the war from bases in the Karategin region and Afghanistan, echoing the *basmachi* campaigns of 70 years earlier. An economic blockade of Badakhshan led to severe famine in the Pamirs, whose people were kept alive by aid from the Aga Khan Foundation.

In late 1994 a second presidential election was held, in which Rakhmonov romped to victory. This surprised no one, as he was the only candidate. Opposition parties had been outlawed.

Precarious Peace

A bad peace is better than a good war.
Khatlon villager

Eventually, pressure from Russia (which then retained forces at some 50 former Soviet military posts along the Afghan border) along with the faltering loyalty of Rakhmonov's own commanders, forced the government to negotiate with the opposition-in-exile. A December 1996 ceasefire was followed up by a peace agreement on 27 June 1997 creating a power-sharing organisation. This guaranteed the United Tajik Opposition (UTO) 30% of the seats in a coalition government in return for an end to the fighting.

The civil war had proven economically as well as physically catastrophic. Always the poorest of the Soviet republics, Tajikistan's GDP per capita had plunged a further 70% since independence. But although some fighting rattled on until 2001, overall peace prevailed and the reconstruction of the country has since been impressively rapid.

People

Tajiks constitute only about 65% of the population. Indeed today there are more Tajiks in Afghanistan than in Tajikistan, while 25% of Tajikistanis are ethnic Uzbeks. 'Tajik' only came to denote a distinct nationality during the 20th century. Although the male skull caps resemble slightly elevated Uzbek ones (black with white arabesques), Tajiks distinguish themselves with their predominantly Persian ancestry and language. Pure-blooded Tajiks tend to have thin, southern European-looking faces, with wide eyes and a Roman nose. In Badakhshan, Pamiris speak related but self-consciously different languages and follow Ismaili Islam (most Tajiks are Sunni). In the Murgab district east of Alichur, most of the people are Kyrgyz. Average family sizes remain high, and over 40% of Tajikistan's population is under the age of 14.

Arts

When Tajikistan was hived off from Uzbekistan in 1929, the new nation-state was forced to leave behind all of its cultural baggage. The new Soviet order set about providing a replacement pantheon of arts, introducing modern drama, opera and ballet, and sending stage-struck Tajik aspirants to study

THE PAMIRI PEOPLE

Language & Faith

The Pamiris of western Gorno-Badakhshan speak several distinct languages, each about as different from lowland Tajik as English is from German. *Khologh* is 'thank you' in Shugnani, the dialect spoken in Khorog and the Gunt Valley (once home to the emirate of Shugnan). Other languages in the mosaic include Wakhi, Ishkashimi and Rushani. What binds these linguistic groups is their shared Ismaili faith. A breakaway sect of Shiite Islam, introduced into Badakhshan in the 11th-century by Nasir Khusraw, Ismailism has no formal clerical structure and no weekly holy day. Instead of mosques they have multipurpose meeting halls called *jamoat khana*. One common manifestation of the religion is the small roadside shrine (*oston* or *mazor*), covered in ibex horns, burnt offerings and round stones, at which passers-by stop to ask for a blessing.

Ismailis revere the Swiss-born Aga Khan, as *Mowlana Hazar Imam*, 49th in a direct line traced back to the prophet. He's far more than just a spiritual leader. It was the Aga Khan's charity foundation that kept almost certain starvation at bay during the civil war and subsequent difficult years. Since then, the foundation has continued helping with projects for the region's agricultural sustainability while providing health care, schools and scholarships to Western universities, fostering an educational ethos that is especially apparent in Khorog.

Homes

From outside, a traditional *huneuni chid* (Pamiri house) looks like a poor, low-slung, mud-stone box. Inside things look very different. Guests are received in the large, five-pillared room with raised areas around four sides. The most distinctive feature is the wooden ceiling built in four concentric squares, each rotated 45 degrees then topped with a skylight which provides most of the illumination. Each ceiling level represents one of the elements: earth, fire, air and water. Carpets line the walls and mattresses take the place of furniture. Amid panels of photographs, pride of place almost inevitably goes to a portrait of the Aga Khan.

The main room's five vertical pillars symbolise Imam Ali, his wife Fatima, the prophet Mohammed (PBUH), and brothers Hassan and Hussein. The place of honour, next to the Hassan pillar (one of two pillars joined together), is reserved for the *khalifa* (village religious leader), so visitors should avoid sitting there.

in Moscow and Leningrad. The policy paid early dividends and the 1940s are considered a golden era of Tajik theatre. A kind of Soviet fame came to some Tajik novelists and poets, such as Mirzo Tursunzade, Loic Sherali and Sadruddin Ayni, the last now remembered more as a deconstructor of national culture because of his campaign to eliminate all Arabic expressions and references to Islam from the Tajik tongue.

Since independence, ancient figures from the region's Persian past have been revived in an attempt to foster a sense of national identity. The most famous of these figures is Ismail Samani (Ismoil Somoni), but also revered is the 10th-century philosopher-scientist Abu Ali ibn-Sina (Avecinna; 980–1037), author of two of the most important books in the history of medicine. He was born in Bukhara when it was the seat of the Persian Samanids. Rudaki (888–941), now celebrated as the father of Persian verse, served as court poet at the same court. Tajiks also venerate Firdausi (940–1020), a poet and composer of the *Shah Nama* (*Book of Kings*), the Persian national epic, and Omar Khayyam (1048–1123), of *Rubaiyat* fame. Both were born in present-day Iran at a time when it was part of an empire that also included the territory now known as Tajikistan. Similar veneration goes out to Kamalddin Bekzod (1455–1535), a brilliant miniaturist painter from Herat.

Pamiris have a particular veneration for Nasir Khusraw (1004–1088), an Ismaili philosopher, poet and preacher who worked in Merv and was exiled to Badakhshan, where he wrote his *Safarname,* the account of his extensive seven-year travels throughout the Muslim world.

Tajik Persian poetry is fused with music by *hafiz* (bard musicians). *Falak* is a popular form of melancholic folk music, often sung *a cappella*. Music and dance are particularly popular among the Pamiri and Kulyabi.

Environment

The Land

Landlocked Tajikistan is Central Asia's smallest republic. Although the western third is lowland plain, more than half of Tajikistan lies above 3000m, whether as the consistantly high Pamir Plateau in the east or a series of deep valleys and towering mountain ranges in the centre and north. At 7495m, Koh-i Somoni (former Pik Kommunizma), is the highest peak in the former Soviet Union and its tributary Fedchenko Glacier, at 72km, is one of the world's longest. However, for pure spectacle, the most beautiful formations are arguably those in the spiky Fan Mountains, along with the distinctive knob-headed Peak Engels (6507m), one of the world's toughest climbs.

Tajikistan's most significant rivers include Pyanj, which forms the Afghanistan border, and the Surkhob/Vakhsh whose potential for hydroelectric power generation holds both promise and danger. The mountainous eastern border with China was redrawn in 2011, ceding around 1% of Tajikistan's territory to its powerful neighbour. To the north, Tajikistan's Stalin-drawn jigsaw of borders with Kyrgyzstan and Uzbekistan include the disconnected Vorukh exclave of Tajik territory stranded completely inside Kyrgyzstan's Fergana Valley holdings.

For administrative purposes the country has three *viloyat* (provinces): Sughd (Khojand), Khatlon (Kurgonteppa) and the 60,000-sq-km autonomous GBAO/Kohistani Badakhshan (Khorog). That leaves much of the central region (including the Garm Valley) ruled directly from Dushanbe.

Wildlife

A 2009 survey in Tajikistan's high Pamir area found around 2400 ibex (*echki* or *kyzyl kyik*) and 23,000 Marco Polo sheep (*arkhar* in Kyrgyz, www.wildlife-tajikistan.org). Curiously in some areas, carefully controlled trophy-hunting of these iconic animals appears to have proven counter-intuitively positive – foreign hunters pay substantial tour fees (typically US$30,000 to US$60,000) which partly funds animal protection program. Indeed when a hunting ban was attempted in 2008, the result was more poaching and rising human consumption of Marco Polo sheep-meat as an alternative to mutton.

The Pamirs also support a tiny number of snow leopards (www.snowleopardconservancy.org). Around the Kayrakkum Reservoir (east of Khojand in northern Tajikistan) there's a critically threatened population of goitered gazelles *(jeyran)*.

Of the country's many attractive bird species, one of the most eye-catching is the bright turquoise European Roller, often seen around Garm. Some unique butterfly species exist around Lake Sarez (see http://dinets.info/parnassius.htm).

Environmental Issues

The 26,000-sq-km Tajik (Pamir) National Park was founded in 1992 as the largest in Central Asia, covering a whopping 18% of Tajikistan. For years this was only really on paper, but things might change somewhat with the park's recognition as a Unesco World Heritage Site in 2013.

The lack of burnable fuel in the eastern Pamir has led to the disappearance of the slow-growing (and fast-burning) *tersken* bush within a radius of 100km from Murgab, adding to desertification in the treeless region. The population of Murgab is considered environmentally unsustainable despite the increasing use of solar and wind power, with wind turbines now providing electricity to run the new mobile phone transmitters.

Tajikistan's glaciers have been retreating, often cited as a possible indicator of global warming, though the latest reports question the extent of this retreat.

Food & Drink

A popular lunch dish is *kurutob:* that's *fatir* bread morsels layered with onion, tomato, parsley and coriander and doused in a yoghurt-based sauce. *Chakka* (known as *yakka* to Tajik speakers around Samarkand and Bukhara) is curd mixed with herbs, typically served with flat bread. Less

RECOMMENDED READING

Essential reading is *Land Beyond the River: The Untold Story of Central Asia* (2003) by former BBC Central Asia correspondent Monica Whitlock, who brilliantly pieces together the 20th-century history of Tajikistan through the life stories of local individuals who witnessed and shaped it. That's usefully supplemented by Paul Bergne's 2007 *The Birth of Tajikistan: National Identity and the Origins of the Republic* (2007), if you can afford a copy.

The weighty *Odyssey Guide to Tajikistan* (2007), by Robert Middleton and Huw Thomas, is a literate and detailed background guide, particularly strong on the history of exploration in the Pamirs. Middleton's far more portable *The Pamirs – History, Archaeology and Culture* is sold at PECTA (p346) in Khorog (60TJS).

commonly available Tajik dishes include *nahud sambusa* (chickpea samosas), *nahud shavla* (chickpea porridge) and *oshi siyo halav,* a unique herb soup. *Tuhum barak* is a tasty egg-filled ravioli coated with sesame-seed oil.

In Badakhshan you might try *borj* – a meat and grain mix that resembles savoury porridge. *Shir chai,* somewhere between milk tea and Tibetan butter tea, makes a popular breakfast in the Pamirs, along with rice pudding (*shir gurch/shir brench* in Kyrgyz/Tajik).

Both Hissar and Dushanbe brew their own beer, though bottled Russian imports like the Baltika range are the most common. Finding gas-free bottled water is challenging outside bigger towns.

SURVIVAL GUIDE

Directory A–Z

ACCOMMODATION

Dushanbe has some respectable midrange business hotels but is particularly short on good, cheap accommodation. In contrast the Pamir, Fan and Zerafshan mountain regions have a good network of homestays but nothing upmarket. Indeed most places have outdoor toilets and few have hot showers. Some, but not all, have signs; community tourism outfits PECTA (p346), META (p354), ZTDA (p333) and tourist information offices have lists of signed-up homestay families.

In places where there's no formal system, it is appropriate to offer around US$10 to US$15 per person if you are hosted. Possibly you'll need to put the money in an envelope to avoid polite refusals. Very few hosts speak English, but most understand Russian.

As with much of Central Asia, accommodation rates are often quoted in US dollars, but payment can be made in either US dollars or somani.

ACTIVITIES

Trekking options are fantastic in Tajikistan, principally in the Fan Mountains and western Pamirs, though these are demanding, remote routes. Trekking guides are available in Khorog for around US$20 to US$40 per day.

Mountaineers will be in heaven and even a few hardcore kayakers are discovering Tajikistan's remote white water. Horse trekking is an option from Bachor and camel trekking is available at Rang-Kul. Rock climbers should head for Margab where Zamin-Karor is a near-vertical 1km rock wall.

Key trekking trailheads are Artush and Alaudin Lakes in the Fan Mountains (p327) and Bachor in the central Pamirs (p351).

DANGERS & ANNOYANCES

Generally Tajikistan is a remarkably safe travel destination.

Landmines and UXO (unexploded ordinance) Left over from the civil war, most have now been mostly cleared, with only 7.5 sq km still considered potentially contaminated (mostly in remote border zones). Most of this land is due to be released by late 2015.

Tap water Not recommended for drinking but many mountain areas have mineral water springs.

Altitude sickness A serious risk especially for hikers attempting anything above 3500m without suitable acclimatisation or for travellers driving the Pamir Highway in a single day from Osh to Karakul or Murgab. Take things very easily when you're first above 3500m and retreat to lower ground if symptoms persist.

Malaria Present in southwestern Tajikistan along the Afghan border and the lower Vakhsh Valley as far north as Kurgonteppa, though travellers rarely visit those areas.

Bed bugs Can be an annoyance in some rural accommodation.

EMBASSIES & CONSULATES

For a full list of embassies see http://mfa.tj

Tajik Embassies in Central Asia

There are Tajik embassies/consulates in Astana and Almaty (Kazakhstan) (p126), Ashgabat (Turkmenistan) (p401), Tashkent (Uzbekistan) (p222) and Bishkek (Kyrgyzstan) (p307).

Tajik Embassies & Consulates in Other Countries

Tajik Embassy, Austria (☎1-409 82 66 11; http://tajikembassy.at; Universitätesstrasse 8/1A, 1090 Vienna) Covering Austria and Switzerland. Single/double tourist visa €20/30 for most citizens.

Tajik Embassy, Azerbaijan (☎012 502 1432; 2-ci Bağlar küç 20, Batamdar, Baku; ⌚3-5pm Tue-Fri; 🚌3) Hard to find but http://katieaune.com/chasing-down-visas-in-baku tells you how.

Tajik Embassy, Belgium (☎02-640 69 33; www.tajikembassy.be; 16 Blvd General Jacques, 1050 Brussels; ⌚9am-noon Wed & Fri) Covers Benelux and France. One-month visa without/with Letter of Invitation €65/25, GBAO permit €20.

Tajik Embassy, China (☎10-6532 2598; www.tajikembassychina.com; LA 01-04 Liangmaqiao Diplomatic Compound, 22 Dongfang Donglu, Chaoyang, Beijing; ⌚9am-noon Mon, Tue & Thu)

Tajik Embassy, Germany (☎030-347 9300; www.botschaft-tadschikistan.de; Perlebergerstr 43, 10559 Berlin; ⌚9am-1pm Mon-Fri)

Tajik Embassy, India (☎11-2615 4282; www.tajikembassy.in; E-12/6, Vasant Vihar, Delhi)

Tajik Embassy, Iran (☎21-229 9584; tajemb.iran@gmail.com; 10, Shahid Zeinali 3rd St, Tehran; ⌚9am-noon Sun, Mon, Wed & Thu)

Tajik Embassy, Japan (☎03-6427-2625; www.tajikistan.jp; Hiroo 3-5-22, Shibuya-ku, Tokyo; ⌚9am-noon Mon-Fri)

Tajik Embassy, Pakistan (☎51-229 3462; www.tajikembassy.pk; House 295, Street 35, F-11/3, Islamabad)

Tajik Embassy Russia, Consular Section (☎95 690-57-36; www.tajembassy.ru; 19 Skaterniy Pereulok, Moscow; ⌚10am-12.30pm Mon, Tue, Thu & Fri; Ⓜ Barrikadnaya) The consular section is separate from the main embassy.

Tajik Embassy, Turkey (☎312-491 1607; www.tajikembassytr.org; Ferit Recai Ertugrul Cad 20, Oran; ⌚9am-4pm Mon, Tue, Thu & Fri) The consulate in İstanbul (Yeni Baglar cad, Billur sok 16) is also good for visas.

Tajik Embassy, UK (☎0208-600 2520; www.tajembassy.org.uk; 26-28 Hammersmith Grove, London, W6 7BA; ⌚10am-noon Mon & Thu) Visa £20 but GBAO permit costs £50 extra.

Tajik Embassy, USA (☎202-223 2666; www.tjus.org; 1005 New Hampshire Ave NW, Washington DC; ⌚9am-noon Mon, Tue, Thu, Fri) Visa/GBAO permit US$25/50;

Embassies & Consulates in Tajikistan

Most embassies are located in Dushanbe.

Afghanistan Consulate (☎93-545 62 48; Gagarin, Khorog; ⌚9am-12.30pm Mon-Fri) A 30-day single-entry tourist visa into Afghanistan is usually issued within 24 hours. You'll need one photo, a self-written letter of purpose (including your planned route), an application form and a photocopy of your passport and Tajik double-entry visa. Costs vary by nationality (most/UK/US US$100/160/200).

Afghanistan Embassy (☎221 67 35; www.afghanembassy.tj; Makhsum, Dushanbe; ⌚9am-noon & 2-4pm Mon-Fri) Quick, relatively painless same-day visas for Afghanistan. Pay fee into nearby bank. It's opposite the German Embassy one block south of Somoni 63.

Chinese Embassy (☎224 21 88; fax 224 41 22; Rudaki 143, Dushanbe; ⌚9am-noon Mon, Wed & Fri) Currently only issues visas for China to locals or those with permanent, resident or one-year visas.

French Embassy (☎221 50 37; http://ambafrance-tj.org; Rakhimzade 17, proezd No 2, Dushanbe)

German Embassy (☎221 21 89; www.duschanbe.diplo.de; Somoni 59/1, Dushanbe; ⌚8.30am-12.30pm Mon-Fri) Represents those EU citizens without an embassy. Despite the official address, it is actually on Makhsum Ave, a block south of Somoni 63.

Iranian Embassy (☎221 00 72; fax 221 04 54; Tehran 18, Dushanbe; ⌚8.30am-12.30pm) Enter on the northeast side, on Bokhtar. You'll need to have pre-arranged an approval code through an agency (eg www.persianvoyages.com) at least two weeks before applying for an Iranian visa, but assuming that worked, the visa should be issued within two days.

Kazakhstan Embassy (☎227 40 08, 221 89 40; www.kazakhembassy.tj; Husseinzoda 31/1, Dushanbe; ⌚9.30am-noon Mon, Tue, Thu & Fri) Upstairs, at the side of a pastel-blue building set behind 11 Husseinzoda. One photo, a copy of your passport and Tajik visa, and insh'Allah the Kazakh visa (US$30) should be ready at 4pm three to five days later.

Kyrgyz Embassy (☎224 26 11; www.kgembassy.tj; Said Nosirov 50, Dushanbe)

Pakistani Embassy (☎223 01 77; www.mofa.gov.pk/tajikistan; Azizbekov 20a, enter from Kurbonov, Dushanbe; ⌚10am-1pm Mon-Fri) Behind the Asia Grand Hotel. Pakistani visas only available to residents of Tajikistan.

Russian Embassy (☎235 98 27; www.rusemb.tj; Sino 29/31, Dushanbe; ⏲10am-12.30pm & 3-5.30pm Mon, 9am-12.30pm & 3-5.30pm Wed-Fri)

Turkish Embassy (☎221 22 08; turemdus@tajik.net; Rudaki 15, Dushanbe)

Turkmen Embassy (☎224 11 62; fax 221 68 84; Akhunbabaev 10, Dushanbe; ⏲application 9.30am-12.30pm Mon-Fri, document collection 3-4pm) Transit visas for Turkmenistan cost US$55, and take around one week with copy of your passport and a visa for the country you are transitting to (ie Iran or Azerbaijan).

UK Embassy (☎224 22 21, emergency 91-770 80 11; http://ukin tajikistan.fco.gov.uk; Mirzo Tursunzoda 65, Dushanbe)

US Embassy (☎229 23 00; http://dushanbe.usembassy.gov; Somoni 109, Dushanbe) Way out in the western suburbs.

Uzbek Embassy (☎224 15 86; www.uz embassy-tadjik.mfa.uz; Sanoi 32, Dushanbe; ⏲9am-noon Mon-Fri) In theory visas for Uzbekistan take a week to process and cost US$75 for most nationals. You'll need to get the form (Anket) filed by the folks at the pale yellow unmarked building, one house east at Sanoi 30 (behind the Mehrob sign). That costs 8TJS and takes 10 minutes but no English is spoken. Several travellers have reported waiting much longer than a week.

FESTIVALS & EVENTS

With its links to a Persian past, Navrus (Nawroz) is the year's biggest festival and you are likely to see song and dance performances. The biggest *buzkashi* (dead-goat polo) matches are generally held around this time, albeit usually in relatively inaccessible locations.

As well as national holidays, Ismaili communities in Badakhshan and beyond celebrate **Imamat Day** (11 July, the anniversary of the current Aga Khan taking over the Ismaili Imamat), **Ruz-i-Nour, the Day of Lights** (25 May, commemmorating the first visit of current Imam to Gorno Badakhshan 1995) and **Ruz-i-Mavlud** (13 December, the Aga Khan's birthday). On all three days you can expect concerts, folklore shows and/or sports events in Khorog City Park, Dushanbe's Ismaili Centre and almost any Ismaili village.

July's **Roof of the World Festival** (www.pamirtours.tj/the_roof_of_the_world_festival) in Khorog features music, singing and dance from across the region.

In early August, Murgab's At Chabysh festival (p353) is aimed at reinvigorating horse traditions among the Pamiri Kyrgyz. Horse games abound but don't expect *buzkashi*.

HOLIDAYS

1 January New Year's Day

8 March International Women's Day

21–23 March Nawroz, or Navrus (Persian New Year), called Ba'at in Badakhshan

1 May International Labour Day

9 May Victory Day (a commemmoration of WWII)

27 June Day of National Unity and Accord (for reconcilliation after the 1990s' civil war)

9 September Independence Day

6 November Constitution Day

Major Islamic hoildays are also celebrated including Idi Kurbon (Eid al-Azha, Feast of Sacrifice) and Idi Fitr (Eid al-Fitr, end of Ramadan). See p469 for dates.

INTERNET ACCESS

Internet cafes are widespread in bigger towns but don't count on getting online in Murgab. Mobile internet coverage is reasonably widespread, allowing connection wherever your chosen server/provider has signal. In reality some rural signals aren't strong enough to do much surfing. Megafon and T-Cell are the best choices though each has its coverage 'holes'. Both offer fast/slow dongles (200/100TJS) for your computer whose free initial traffic-credit may prove sufficient for several week's email usage if you're not streaming or downloading big files.

MAPS

- Marcus Hauser's 1:500,000 maps cover Tajikistan in three very accurate, info-packed sheets, *The Pamirs, Northern Tajikistan* and *Southern Tajikistan*. Each available from www.geckomaps.com.
- A series of detailed maps is downloadable as an offline Android smart-phone app through Oruxmaps.com
- The University of Berne's Centre for Development and Environment has topo and satellite maps of the Pamirs online at http://cdegis.unibe.ch/pamir.

MONEY

The Tajik somani (TJS) is divided into 100 dirham. Somani notes come in one, five, 10, 20, 50 and 100 denominations. Dirham coins are rarely used.

US dollars, euros and Russian roubles are easily changed at city exchange booths and at least one bank in any regional centre. Carrying at least some US-dollar cash makes sense: even in rural areas usually drivers and homestays will accept them should you run out of somani. ATMs are now available in bigger towns (not Murgab) but not all take the cards they claim to and some have preposterously low withdrawal limits. Generally Maestro seems to be harder to use than Visa. There is no black market for currency transactions.

Both Uzbek and Kyrgyz som are accepted in relevant border areas.

Travellers cheques are virtually impossible to cash.

POST

Tajikistan's postal service is ropey. Mail can take a month or more to reach its destination, if it arrives at all, but an international postcard costs only 1.65TJS.

Couriers such as **DHL** (☎ 222 19 99; Druzhba Narodov 62, Dushanbe; ⏰ 9am-6pm Mon-Fri, 9am-noon Sat) are the only reliable way to send important documents.

REGISTRATION

If you have a non-tourist visa, you must register within the first three days of arrival in Tajikistan. Fortunately, however, most nationals holding a tourist visa are spared this annoying formality unless planning to stay for over 30 days. In that case you should visit OVIR before the 30 days are up with a photocopy of your passport, visa and one photo. You'll need to pay two fees (40TJS plus 100/50TJS for non-CIS/CIS citizens) into the appointed bank, and return with the receipts. Khorog and Murgab are relatively painless places to do this as long as the sole accredited official is in town.

There is some confusion over 45-day tourist visas. Some sources claim that such visas always need registration but in our experience (confirmed by OVIR in Murgab and at two border posts) you don't actually need to register if your actual period of stay is less than 30 days.

TELEPHONE

To call internationally (including to other Central Asian republics) dial 10, followed by the country code, the area code (without the 0) and the number. From mobiles no 0 is required, so if calling mobile-to-land-line use the full international format, ☎ 992 plus the zero-less city code.

We found the widest coverage for mobile networks to be on T-Cell (best for Murgab and the only choice for the eastern Wakhan) and Megafon (only carrier in parts of the Zerafshan Valley and Alichur), though **Beeline** (www.beeline.tj) and **Babilon-M** (www.babilon-m.com) also have a few places where they too seem to be the only carrier. As buying a sim card rarely costs more than 5TJS (including 5TJS credit), consider buying a SIM for each carrier.

TRAVEL PERMITS

For travel in the Pamirs you will need a **GBAO permit**. This is quite essential and will be frequently checked. Many embassies abroad will now issue a GBAO permit alongside a visa, which will save you time and hassle in Dushanbe. Some charge around US$50 but a few (notably Bishkek) issue it for free on request. You can alternatively get one in Dushanbe for 20TJS, usually in one working day.

Several specific places including Zor-Kul require permits (p355), but most are easily organised by PECTA (p346) in Khorog.

Lake Sarez (p343) permits are especially awkward to obtain and the lake has been out of bounds to foreign trekkers at times.

VISAS FOR ONWARD TRAVEL

Afghanistan

A 30-day visa (from US$100 depending on nationality) requires a self-penned letter explaining your motivation and route for travel, one photo and a copy of your passport. Usually available the same or next day from either Dushanbe (p364) or Khorog (p364).

China

Only gives visas to long-term residents. Apply elsewhere.

Uzbekistan

Many travellers have reported Dushanbe (p365) a very bad place to apply for Uzbek visas, even those with Letters of Invitation (LOI) being left waiting for a week or two. Better to apply in Bishkek (Kyrgyzstan).

ℹ Getting There & Away

With a limited number of flights and international border crossings, Tajikistan isn't the easiest republic to get to.

ENTERING TAJIKISTAN

Uzbek–Tajik border crossings are hostage to the current state of political relations between the two republics (which are often poor) and sudden unannounced closure by the Uzbeks. The closed Penjikent–Samarkand and Karamyk borders severely reduce Tajikistan's tourism options.

AIR

Tajik Air (www.tajikair.tj) and Somon Air (www.somonair.com) are the main national carriers. The latter has a direct Dushanbe–Frankfurt flight. More popular routes into Tajikistan are on Turkish (www.thy.com) via İstanbul, FlyDubai via Dubai, and Aeroflot via Moscow. There are flights to various Russian cities from Dushanbe, Khojand and Kulob.

Regional connections include four weekly flights from Dushanbe to both Bishkek (Kyrgyzstan) and Almaty (Kazakhstan).

LAND

If you're driving your own vehicle to Tajikistan, beware that entry documents for the car are usually only valid for 14 days creating a bureaucratic headache.

To/From Afghanistan

Kunduz BEWARE. The border at Panj-e-Payon to Kunduz is reportedly open but visiting the Kunduz area is highly discouraged for security reasons.

Wakhan The Afghan Wakhan was peaceful at the time of research. Sadly the ideal crossing point for the Little Pamir region (ie Langar) is not open to foreigners but the Ishkashim border is (from 8am to noon and 1pm to 4pm, Monday to Saturday). You'll need a double-entry Tajik visa (with GBAO permit) since continuing to the rest of Afghanistan would mean transitting the risky route via Faizabad. A taxi to Afghan-Eshkashim village (6km) costs a whopping US$20 from the border bridge. See boxed text p352 before you go.

Khorog A bridge over the Pyanj River at Khorog connects the Afghan and Tajik sides of Badakhshan at the Sheghnan crossing (limited times, closed Sunday), offering 4WD access to remote Lake Shiva but you will need to have transport pre-arranged on the Afghan side. The region is snowbound from October to June and the roads are often washed out in early summer.

To/From China

Qolma Pass DUE TO OPEN. The 4762m Qolma Pass links Murgab to the Karakoram Highway in Xinjiang, north of Tashkurgan, with splendid views of icy Mt Murtagh-Ata ahead of you as you approach from the west on heavily degraded roads. Open to Chinese and Tajiks for years, the border was supposed to open to

VISAS FOR TAJIKISTAN

Technically a Letter of Invitation (LOI) is an official requirement for most visa applications but in reality, Tajik embassies will usually issue a 30-day (sometimes 45-day) tourist visa without one. Annoyingly, there aren't too many Tajik embassies around so you might have to post your passport to an embassy in a neighbouring country and arrange return postage and a method of payment (often in a foreign currency). Allow plenty of time for this.

Bishkek, (p307) in Kyrgyzstan, is a great place to apply for visas that include a GBAO permit (US$75), generally available the same day, as long as the consul is in town. In Tashkent (p222), Uzbekistan, the visa is cheaper (US$37/55 in one week/one day) but they don't give GBAO permits. Vienna, Berlin, Ankara and Delhi are also reportedly ok, while Moscow and Tehran are more difficult. There is a plan to standardise tourist visa prices at all Tajik embassies to US$25 or local equivalent, which has already led to price reductions in London and Washington but those embassies still charge a hefty whack for the GBAO permit.

While we'd advise getting your visa before heading to Tajikistan, tourists from 80 countries (including the EU, USA and Australia) can theoretically obtain a 30-day, single-entry visa on arrival at Dushanbe airport (but not other airports, nor any land border). You'll need a photo, a photocopy of your passport and – annoyingly – an LOI which rather undermines the appeal of the system. GBAO permits are not available at the airport and sometimes the system breaks down, as it did for a week or so in April 2012, leaving visa-less visitors stranded.

If you need a LOI, most Tajik travel agencies can get you one within a few days. Typical costs average US$30 to US$50 with Tajikintourservice (p323), Stantours (p68) or Hamsafar Travel (p323). Although **Tajikistan Visa Company** (www.tajikistanvisa.land.ru) can prove considerably cheaper, several readers have reported problems using them.

In May 2013 the Tajik Lower House passed a law aimed at scrapping visas for tourists of many Western nations but don't get excited yet: the law has not been ratified by the senate and that could take years. Keep a virtual eye on the changing situation through http://sites.google.com/site/tajikistantourism/information.

Visa Extensions

Extending a tourist visa from 30 days to 45 days is usually possible with some perseverance. If you extend your visa, you'll also possibly need to separately extend your GBAO permit and, remember, once over 30 days in the country you'll also need to register with OVIR. Extensions beyond 45 days are unlikely. The extension process can take several days and the exact procedure is likely to change given that the Ministry of Foreign Affairs is still completing the process of moving offices.

CHOOSING YOUR RIDE

The typical choice of chauffeured vehicles in Tajikistan includes:

Ssanyang Muss Very comfortable for three passengers, locals squeeze in seven. All seats face forward. Very popular in Zarafshan Valley.

Tangem Under-powered Chinese minivan. Poor clearance and without 4WD but can manage less challenging roads for around a third of the price of a 4WD.

Landcruiser Tanklike strength and high clearance, comfortable for the front and middle seats but the rear four seats typically face sideways, thus are highly unsuitable for long distances.

UAZ 4WD Brilliantly strong, go-anywhere car but uncomfortable, low-visibility at rear and windows don't always open. High petrol consumption.

UAZ minibus 4WD and remarkably strong, but locals might squash over a dozen people aboard.

Niva Generally the cheapest 4WD option, the Niva breaks easily but mends relatively easily too. Cramped for four passengers.

foreigners in May 2013 but, it seems, nobody told the Chinese border guards. As with the Kyrgyz–Chinese border crossings, it's closed at weekends and you'll have to find a way through the 7km of no-man's-land between customs posts. At times the border has been known to open only 15 days per month so check carefully even once it does open to foreigners.

To/From Kyrgyzstan

Pamir Highway (Osh–Murgab) Over-stuffed shared 4WDs (TJS150 per seat) usually run at least daily leaving before dawn. Northbound you could get off at Sary Tash then continue by marshrutka. Southbound breaking the journey is difficult as all cross-border transport is usually already full. It's unwise to hitch without a tent and warm clothes in case you get stranded overnight: there's no accommodation at the border post. Chartering a vehicle from Murgab to Osh is typically easier and cheaper than doing so in reverse. That's because Murgabis can stock up with provisions and cheaper petrol in Kyrgyzstan but Osh drivers see little advantage in driving to Tajikistan and won't necessarily have the necessary paperwork to do so. So from Osh, seek out a Tajikistan licensed car (p296).

Karamyk (Sary Tash–Garm) CLOSED. The best quality and most direct route from Osh to Dushanbe is oddly closed to foreigners. It briefly opened during the GBAO disturbances of summer 2012 but was firmly closed again to foreigners during 2013. Future opening is possible but by no means assured.

Batken–Isfara (Osh–Khojand) Isfara–Batken taxis and three daily marshrutka drive painlessly across the relaxed, very quiet border. From Batken to Osh there's a new road avoiding the Uzbek enclaves, but one 10km section of road technically does still pass through Uzbekistan near Kadamjai. See boxed text on p298 for tactics.

Isfana–Khojand Officially open but of little practical use to most travellers.

To/From Uzbekistan

Most travellers making a beeline between Tashkent and Dushanbe drive to Khojand and then fly/drive (US$65/TJS100).

Samarkand–Penjikent CLOSED. This crossing used to take under two hours through a combination of minibuses and taxis but the border was closed in 2010. A big new road to the border is under construction and locals hope that traffic will start flowing again by 2015.

Dushanbe–Denau 55km west of Dushanbe, near Tursanzade/Regar. Shared taxis from Dushanbe's Zarnisar Bazaar to the border cost 8TJS per seat (1½ hours). At the border, minibuses run to Denau, where you may find a shared taxi direct to Samarkand.

Khojand–Tashkent The Bekobod border is closed to foreigners but Oybek is (usually) open. Shared taxis run direct from Khojand's Abreshim terminal to Oybek. Once across the border walk a short distance to the main crossroads for a marshrutka to Tashkent. Bekobod-bound buses from Tashkent's Kuyluk Bazaar go via Oybek.

Kokand and the Fergana Valley. From Khojand's Isfara terminal take a minibus to Kanibodom then another 9km to the border. Cross the border by foot and then take a taxi to Kokand or hop via Besh Aryk (Beshariq) by marshrutka.

Getting Around

AIR

Domestic flights are limited to Dushanbe–Khojand and the spectacular but notoriously unreliable Dushanbe–Khorog service (p347).

BUS, MINIBUS & SHARED TAXI

The bus/minibus network is limited, though the new Asia Express bus company plans to expand. For now shared taxis are the only public transport between Dushanbe and Penjikent or Khojand, while shared 4WDs are the main link to Khorog and Murgab.

Travellers commonly organise themselves into groups to rent chauffeured 4WD vehicles in the Pamirs or for chartering a whole shared taxi/vehicle so that they can stop more frequently en route. Several good traveller meeting places are listed (see boxed text opposite), or pre-organise a group through Lonely Planet's Thorn Tree, through Couchsurfing.com or via the forum of www.tajiktourism.com

Turkmenistan

Includes ➡

Best Places to Eat

➡ Çeşme (p380)
➡ Sim Sim (p381)
➡ Köpetdag (p380)
➡ Euphoria (p381)
➡ Chaikhana (p396)

Best Places to Stay

➡ Sofitel Ashgabat Oguzkent Hotel (p379)
➡ Nusay Hotel (p379)
➡ President Hotel (p379)
➡ Hotel Margush (p387)

Why Go?

By far the most mysterious and unexplored of Central Asia's 'stans, Turkmenistan became famous for the truly bizarre dictatorship of President Saparmyrat Niyazov, who ruled as 'Turkmenbashi' ('leader of the Turkmen') until his death in 2006, covering this little-known desert republic with golden statues of himself and grandiose monuments to the achievements of his 'golden age'. But the least-visited of Central Asia's countries is far more than the totalitarian theme park it's often portrayed as being – it is an ancient land of great spirituality, tradition and natural beauty.

The ancient cities of Merv and Konye-Urgench inspire visions of caravans plodding along the ancient Silk Road, while the haunting beauty of the Karakum desert and other quirky natural phenomena are less expected but equally mesmerising sights. The full Turkmen experience is ultimately about mingling with the warm and fascinating Turkmen themselves, whose hospitality is the stuff of legend.

When to Go

Ashgabat

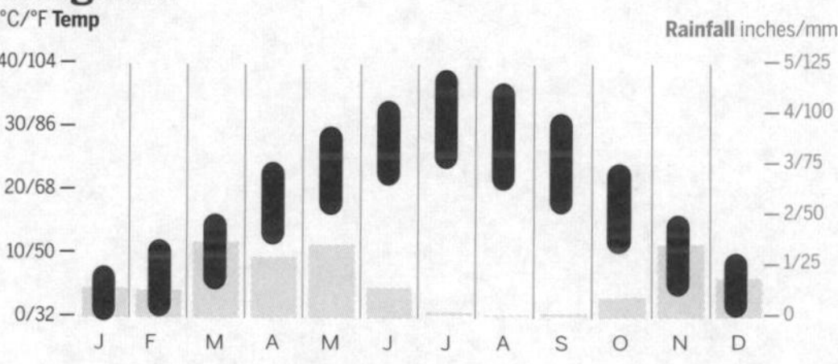

Apr–Jun Bright sunshine and cool temperatures combine to create the best climate for travel.

Sep–Nov The fierce summer heat gradually cools and winter approaches.

Dec Wrap up warm, expect to see snow in the desert and very few other travellers!

Visas & Permits

Everyone requires a visa for Turkmenistan (p405), and unless you're on a transit visa, you will need to be accompanied by a guide for the entire length of your stay in order to obtain one, which makes a trip here quite expensive by regional standards. Permits are required to visit national parks (p403) and visas need to be endorsed to permit travel in various border zones, so it's important to know your itinerary before you begin the visa application process.

COSTS

Relative Cost

The most expensive country in Central Asia.

Daily Expenses

- Basic hotel double US$30; comfortable hotel double US$60
- Street snack 2–10M; good restaurant meal 50M
- Marshrutka from Ashgabat to Konye-Urgench 35M
- Train from Ashgabat to Dashogus 9.58M (*kupe* class), flight 58M (book well in advance)

Price Ranges

- **Sleeping** (per two people): $ <US$25, $$ US$25–70, $$$ >US$70
- **Eating** (main course): $ <20M, $$ 20–50M, $$$ >50M

Itineraries

- **Three days** Arriving on a transit visa, spend a day in fascinatingly weird Ashgabat, cross the Karakum desert and spend the night camping by the Darvaza Gas Craters and then wrap things up with a visit to historic Konye-Urgench.
- **One week** Spend at least three days in and around Ashgabat before heading east to visit the ancient sites of Merv and Gonur. From here, return to Ashgabat and travel north to Konye-Urgench, camping en route at the unforgettable Darvaza Gas Craters.
- **Two weeks** Along with the sights mentioned above, take the time for some activities, such as horseback riding in Geok-Dere, a visit the the Köw Ata underground lake and a trip to the Yangykala Canyon and Turkmenbashi.

TOP TIP

Spending time in Ashgabat means you don't have to be with a guide, and is a good way to cut costs. The other way to avoid travelling with a guide is to get a transit visa (p405), although they tend to only be valid for three to five days, depending on your route across the country.

Fast Facts

- **Area** 488,100 sq km
- **Capital** Ashgabat
- **Country code** ☎ 993
- **Languages** Turkmen, Russian, Uzbek
- **Population** 5.1 million
- **Famous for** multiple personality cults, gas reserves, Akhal-Teke horses, carpets

Exchange Rates

COUNTRY	UNIT	MANAT
Australia	A$1	2.76M
Canada	C$1	2.75M
Euro zone	€1	3.71M
NZ	NZ$1	2.29M
UK	£1	4.36M
USA	US$1	2.85

Resources

- www.chaihana.com
- www.gundogar.org
- www.stantours.com
- www.turkmenistan.gov.tm

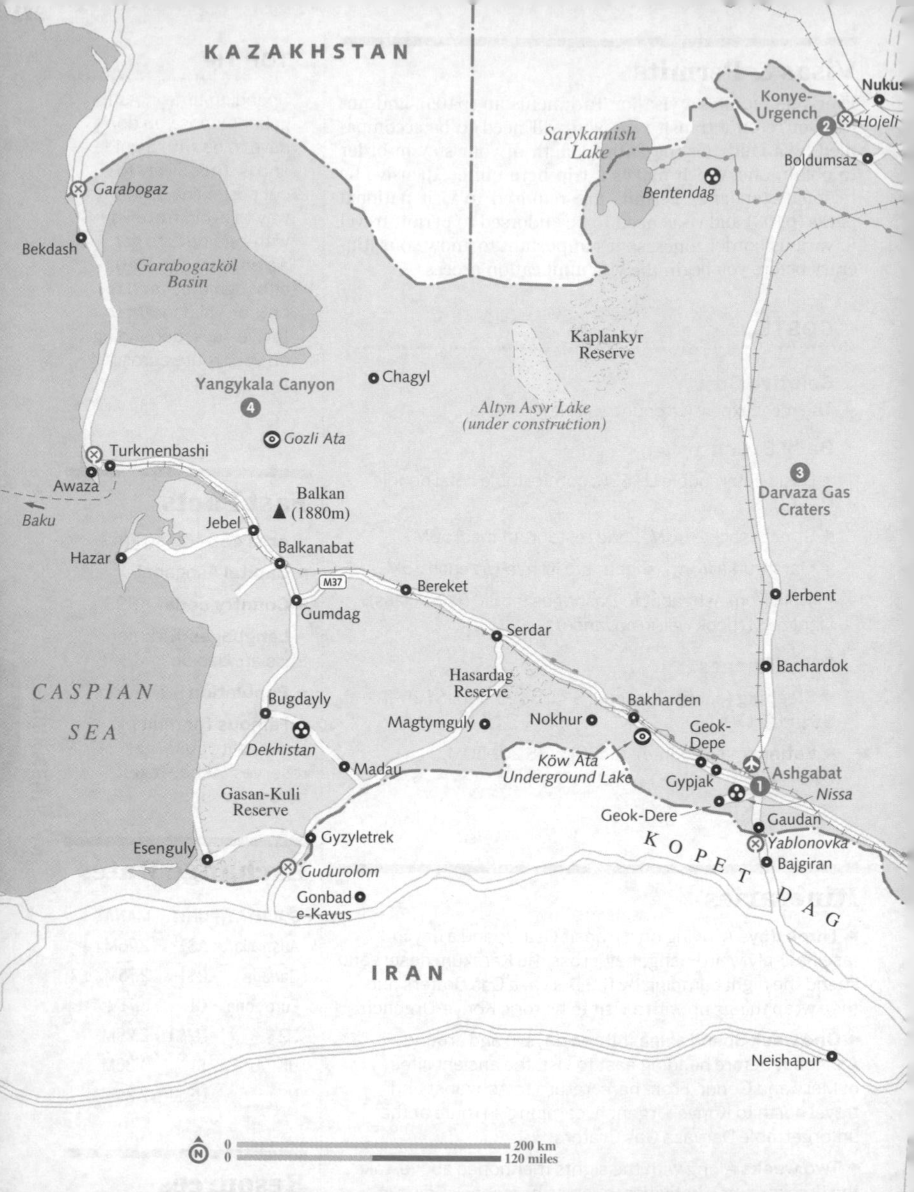

Turkmenistan Highlights

1. Explore the extraordinary, ever-changing Turkmen capital **Ashgabat** (p374), laden with marble palaces, bizarre monuments and more fountains than Las Vegas.

2. Marvel at the minarets and turquoise-tiled mausoleums littering the desert in **Konye-Urgench** (p393), testament to the former glories of the Khorezmshah empire.

3. Visit this bizarre combination of human accident and natural phenomenon at the **Darvaza Gas Craters** (p384) in the lunar landscapes of the Karakum desert.

4 Wander the painted desertscape of **Yangykala Canyon** (p386), which wouldn't look out of place in a John Ford film.

5 Investigate ancient foundations and pottery shards at **Merv** (p388), the most famous archaeological site in Turkmenistan, while nearby the largest archaeological excavation in the Near East **Gonur** (p391) is even more interesting.

ASHGABAT

☎12 / POP 1 MILLION

With its lavish marble palaces, gleaming gold domes and vast expanses of manicured parkland, Ashgabat ('the city of love' in Arabic) has reinvented itself as a showcase city for the newly independent republic and is definitely one of Central Asia's – if not the world's – strangest places. Built almost entirely off the receipts of Turkmenistan's oil and gas revenues, the city's transformation continues at breakneck speed, with whole neighbourhoods facing the wrecking ball in the name of progress, and gleaming white marble monoliths springing up overnight like mushrooms.

Originally developed by the Russians in the late 19th century, Ashgabat became a prosperous, sleepy and largely Russian frontier town on the Trans-Caspian railway. However, at 1am on 6 October 1948, the city vanished in less than a minute, levelled by an earthquake that measured nine on the Richter scale, killing more than 110,000 people (two-thirds of the then population).

Ashgabat was rebuilt in the Soviet style, but its modern incarnation is somewhere between Las Vegas and Pyongyang, with a mixture of Bellagio fountains, Stalinist ministries of state and various monuments and statues designed to help foster a sense of national unity and identity. At its heart it's a surprisingly relaxed city, with a varied dining scene and no shortage of quirky sights, making it a pleasant place to spend a few days absorbing Turkmenistan's bizarre present before heading into the rest of the country to discover its fascinating past.

Sights

Central Ashgabat

Being all but wiped from the earth in 1948, Ashgabat was rebuilt into a ho-hum, low-rise Soviet city of no great beauty. However, since independence the city has again been demolished in vast swathes and is unrecognisable as the Soviet provincial capital of two decades ago.

Independence Square SQUARE
(Map p376) At the centre of Ashgabat is the enormous Independence Square, on which sits the golden-domed **Palace of Turkmenbashi** (the place of work of the former president), the **Ministry of Fairness**, the **Ministry of Defence** and the **Ruhyyet Palace**, all of which were built by the French corporation Bouygues Construction, the one time court builder to Niyazov. Behind this is the **Majlis** (Turkmenistan's parliament building).

Facing what used to be the central Ashgabat location of the Arch of Neutrality, is the **Earthquake Memorial** (Map p376), a bombastic bronze rendering of a bull and child (the baby Niyazov), under which lurks the **Earthquake Museum** (Map p376; ⏲9am-6pm) FREE, which is currently being renovated. Further down this long strip of parkland is the **Soviet war memorial** (Map p376), a pleasingly subtle structure with an eternal flame at its centre. The strip ends with **Magtymguly State University**, the country's leading educational institution.

Statue of Lenin & Around STATUE
(Map p376; off Azadi köçesi) The statue of Lenin in a small park off Azadi köçesi, is a charmingly incongruous assembly of a tiny Lenin on an enormous and very Central Asian plinth surrounded by fountains. Behind Vladimir Illych is the Magtymguly Theatre (p382), where traditional Turkmen performances can be seen. Across the road, Lenin faces an austere concrete building that was once the **Archive of the Communist Party of Turkmenistan**. Its walls feature modernist concrete sculptures made by Ernst Neizvestny, a Russian artist who lived and worked in Ashgabat during the 1970s.

Museum of Fine Arts MUSEUM
(Map p376; ☎39 61 42; Alishera Navoi köçesi 88; admission 33M; ⏲9am-6pm Wed-Mon) The pricey Museum of Fine Arts is located in an impressive building with a big rotunda, two tiers and lots of gold. The collection contains some great Soviet-Turkmen artwork: happy peasant scenes with a backdrop of yurts and smoke-belching factories. There is also a collection of Russian and Western European paintings and a fine selection of Turkmen jewellery and traditional costumes. Guided tours in English are available for a further US$10 per person.

Carpet Museum MUSEUM
(Map p380; ☎44 68 09; Atamurat Nyazov köçesi 158; admission 33M, tour 66M; ⏲9am-6pm Mon-Fri, 9am-2pm Sat) The large, modern Carpet Museum has a vast white-marble facade and high entrance fees, though these are worth

paying if you're interested in this most famous Turkmen handicraft. While there's a limit to the number of rugs the average visitor can stand, the central exhibit, the world's largest handwoven rug, really is something to see (though you can see it hanging from the lobby when you enter – you don't even have to buy a ticket). The 'expert commission' here is the place to have your carpets valued and taxed, and the necessary documentation issued for export.

Azadi Mosque MOSQUE
(Map p380; Shevchenko köçesi) More a statement of foreign-policy leanings than a sign of religious awakening, the Azadi mosque, similar in appearance to the Blue Mosque in İstanbul, stands just south of Magtymguly şayoli, 600m east of the junction with Turkmenbashi.

Mosque of Khezrety Omar MOSQUE
(Map p376) The modern mosque of Khezrety Omar, off Atamurat Niyazov köçesi, is worth visiting for its wonderfully garish painted ceilings.

Iranian Mosque MOSQUE
(Map p376; Tehran köçesi) The angular, futuristic Iranian mosque, illuminated with green neon, is on Görogly köçesi on the western outskirts of the city.

Berzengi

South of Moskovsky şayoli the surreal world of Berzengi begins – an entirely artificial brave new world of white-marble tower blocks, fountains, parks and general emptiness that culminates in the Berzengi Hwy (Archabil şayoli), which is home to a number of hotel complexes, museums and ministries.

Independence Park PARK
(Map p380) The **Altyn Asyr Shopping Centre**, the curious pyramidical shopping centre at the northern end of Independence Park, is reputedly the biggest fountain in the world. Inside it's rather less than impressive – an all but empty two-floor shopping centre, although there's a restaurant on the 6th floor, and it's possible to take the lift up there for great city views.

The **Monument to the Independence of Turkmenistan** known universally to the foreign community as 'the plunger' (for reasons obvious as soon as you see it), is another monument in the same park. This is a popular spot for wedding groups to take photographs with a golden statue of Turkmenbashi. Nearby is a trippy giant copy of Niyazov's once ubiquitous *Ruhnama* ('book of the soul').

Palace of Knowledge NOTABLE BUILDING
(Map p380) Beyond the southern end of Independence Park is the huge, golden-domed Palace of Knowledge, three large buildings that include a library, concert hall and the **Turkmenbashi Museum** (☎48 95 79; Archabil şayoli; admission 28.5M; ⏲9am-6pm Wed-Mon), which, taking a leaf out of Kim Jong-Il's book, houses all the gifts and awards presented to former President Niyazov by various people around the world. Expect to see lots of gold.

National Museum MUSEUM
(Map p380; ☎48 25 90; Archabil şayoli 30; admission per museum 28.5M; ⏲9am-5pm Wed-Sun) Looking like a lost palace in the urban desert, the National Museum occupies a striking position in front of the Kopet Dag (p382). It's actually a collection of three pricey museums – the **History Museum**, the **Nature & Ethnographic Museum** and the **Presidential Museum**. The History Museum is the only one of the three that approaches value for money, so give the others a miss. The lavish Ancient History Hall includes Neolithic tools from western Turkmenistan and relics from the Bronze Age Margiana civilisation, including beautiful amulets, seals, cups and cult paraphernalia. There is also a model of the walled settlement uncovered at Gonur. The Antiquity Hall houses amazing *rhytons*, horn-shaped vessels of intricately carved ivory used for Zoroastrian rituals and official occasions.

Arch of Neutrality MONUMENT
(admission US$10; ⏲9am-8pm) Beyond the National Museum is the President Hotel (p379), some distance behind which you'll see the Arch of Neutrality. Once the centrepiece of Niyazov's Ashgabat, it was erected to celebrate the Turkmen people's unsurprisingly unanimous endorsement of Turkmenbashi's policy of neutrality in 1998. Above the arch itself is the real gem, a 12m-high polished-gold statue of Niyazov, which revolved to follow the sun throughout the day. Now in exile, overlooking his beloved city, Niyazov no longer rotates, but his comedic posture makes it clear why the monument was nicknamed 'batman' by locals.

Ashgabat

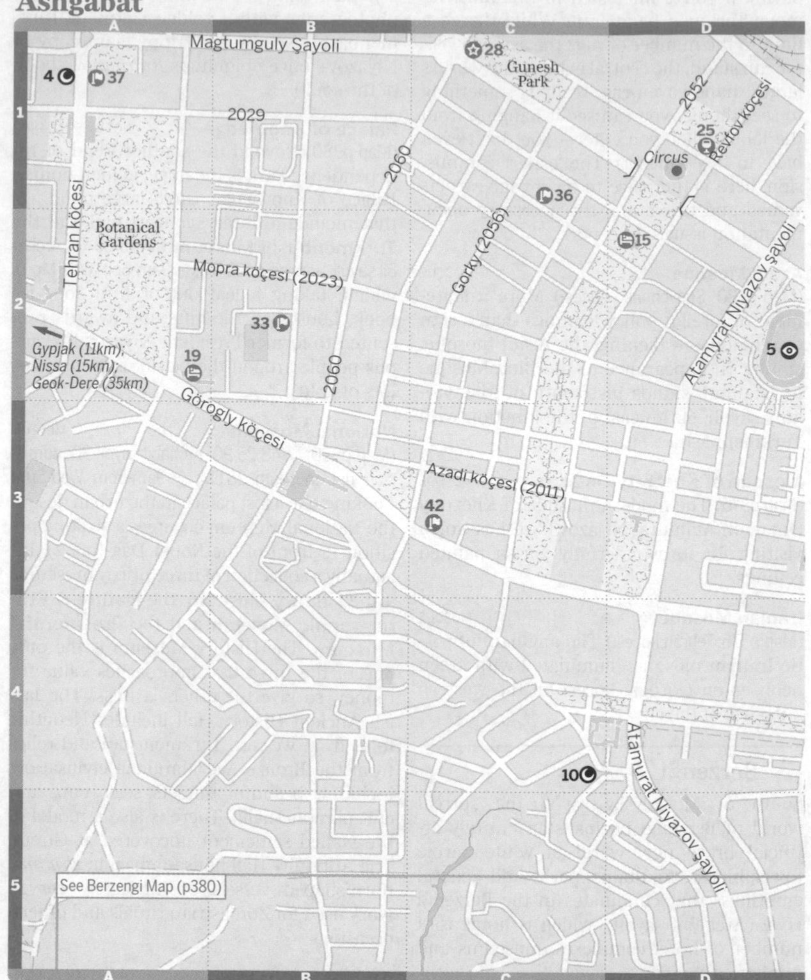

Tolkuchka Bazaar

Once one of Central Asia's most spectacular sights, Ashgabat's legendary Tolkuchka Bazaar is now sadly unregonisable following a government relocation from its time immemorial location in 2010. Now housed in a collection of vast, characterless hangar-style buildings and surrounded by car parks, the new Tolkuchka, or the **Altyn Asyr Market** as it's now officially known, has none of the old market's mercantile soul or chaotic charm. It's a crying shame, although the new premises are no doubt cleaner and offer both vendors and visitors better protection from the fierce desert sun. Few travellers who have experienced markets elsewhere in the region will find the bazaar thrilling, though there are still some good carpets and handicrafts on sale. Remember you'll need to get an export certificate for the carpet before taking it out of the country; these are available at the 'expert commission' at the Carpet Museum (p374).

Tolkuchka is busiest on Thursday, Saturday and Sunday from around 8am to 3pm, but it's open every day. Watch out for pickpockets. The new site is about 10km north

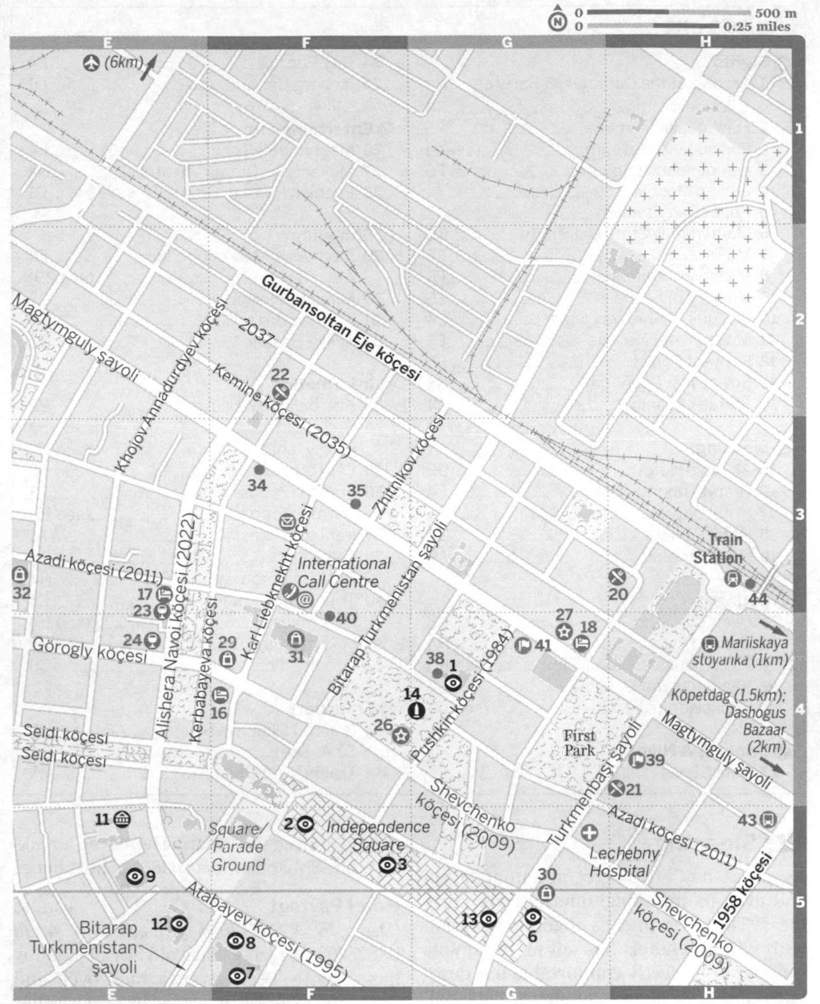

of Ashgabat, approximately 1km past the new city bus station. A taxi should cost around 4M. Buses go there from the corner of Magtymguly şayoli and 1958 köçesi (1958 is a block east of Turkmenbashi şayoli).

Activities

Akhal-Teke horses are Turkmenistan's pride and joy, and many visitors come to Turkmenistan specifically to ride one. Highly recommended is the **Alaja Farm** (☎993 6581 1111, 993 1227 6720; Geok-Dere; per hour 80M), run by Katya Kolestnikova and located in Geok-Dere (also called Nizhny Chuli). This is a professional stable, where the horses are well cared for and well fed (not always the case elsewhere). It's normal to ride for four hours in one day, well worth the price for the beautiful golden stallions and some wonderful riding in the canyons around Geok-Dere. Contact Katya in advance, or just turn up as the farm operates seven days a week. Ask your guide to take you, or hire a taxi. Take the Geok-Depe road out of Ashgabat and turn left at the sign for Geok-Dere. Continue through the village and Alaja is at the end on the right.

Ashgabat

Sights
1 Archive of the Communist Party of Turkmenistan ... G4
2 Earthquake Memorial ... F5
Earthquake Museum ... (see 2)
3 Independence Square ... F5
4 Iranian Mosque ... A1
5 Kopet Dag Stadium ... D2
6 Magtymguly State University ... G5
7 Majlis ... F5
8 Ministry of Defence ... F5
9 Ministry of Fairness ... E5
10 Mosque of Khezrety Omar ... C4
11 Museum of Fine Arts ... E5
12 Ruhyyet Palace ... E5
13 Soviet War Memorial ... G5
14 Statue of Lenin ... G4

Sleeping
15 Ak Altyn Hotel ... D2
16 Grand Turkmen Hotel ... F4
17 Hotel Daýhan ... E3
18 Hotel Paýtagt ... G4
19 Hotel Syýahat ... A2

Eating
20 Çeşme ... H3
21 Coffee House ... H4
Pizza Haus ... (see 18)
22 Seafood Ayna ... F2
Shokoladnitsa ... (see 17)

Drinking & Nightlife
23 Cafe Güneş ... E3
24 City Pub ... E4
25 Iceberg Bar ... D1

Entertainment
26 Magtymguly Theatre ... F4
27 Mollanepes Drama Theatre ... G4
28 Pushkin Russian Drama Theatre ... C1

Shopping
29 Altyn Asyr Marketing Centre ... F4
Altyn Göl ... (see 29)
30 Miras Bookshop ... G5
31 Russian Bazaar ... F4
32 Tekke Bazaar ... E3

Information
33 Azerbaijan Embassy ... B2
34 Brilliant ... F3
Dagsyýahat ... (see 17)
35 DN Tours ... F3
36 French Embassy ... C1
German Embassy ... (see 15)
37 Iranian Embassy ... A1
38 OVIR ... G4
39 Russian Embassy ... H4
40 Tourism-Owadan ... F4
UK Embassy ... (see 15)
41 US Embassy ... G4
42 Uzbek Embassy ... C3

Transport
43 Bus to Tolkuchka Bazaar ... H5
S7 Airlines ... (see 16)
44 Train Ticket Office ... H3

Sleeping

Ashgabat has no budget accommodation and even its midrange offerings are fairly bleak. The government's ongoing obsession with building hotels has left an enormous number of perfectly comfortable but desolate options in the new suburb of Berzengi. Many tour companies suggest that their clients stay in these, although they can be rather isolated and somewhat overpriced.

Hotel Daýhan HOTEL **$$**
(Map p376; ☎93 23 72; Azadi köçesi 69; r US$50; ❄) This tired old Soviet joint downstairs has surprisingly good accommodation upstairs and enjoys a great location. Around half the rooms have been renovated (though prices are the same whether the room has been redone or not!) and have nice paint jobs, decent beds, TV, fridges and hot water, although bathrooms have been tidied up rather than transformed. The 'lux' rooms are two normal rooms joined together and are no newer in design. There's no breakfast, but Shokoladnitsa (p380) is next door.

Hotel Paýtagt HOTEL **$$**
(Map p376; ☎94 02 36; Magtymguly şayoli 74; s/d US$35/50; ❄) Ashgabat's old Soviet standby has recently been given a makeover, and from its exterior it looks like any other modern Ashgabat building. However, the renovations have only made it to selected rooms, and even those that have been redone are small and poorly equipped, with fairly feeble bathrooms (ours didn't have a sink or toilet seat!), and ancient mattresses. That said, rooms are entirely bearable, given the low price and great location. All rooms have balconies, and those designated *lux* are made up of two rooms.

Hotel Syýahat HOTEL **$$**
(Map p376; ☎tel/fax 34 45 08; Görogly köçesi 60a; s/d/lux incl breakfast US$30/50/60; ❄) Rather remotely located, this hulking Soviet-era place isn't a bad deal if you're looking for a

cheap-but-official bed. Rooms come in varying states of decay and each seems to have its own wallpaper pattern. The bathrooms are not a highlight. For an extra US$10 you get a half-*lux* room that comes with TV. Hotel amenities include a bar and sauna. It's located a short taxi ride from downtown, or take bus 4, 10 or 28 to the Hotel Syýahat stop.

Hotel Aziya HOTEL **$$**
(Map p380; ☎48 01 80; Archabil şayoli 31; s/d incl breakfast US$50/60; P ❄) Offering the best value in the city at this price, the Hotel Aziya's rooms are enormous and come complete with flat-screen TV, good Turkmen carpets and eye-wateringly tasteless furniture. Despite the hotel's large size, there are just eight rooms – the rest of the building houses offices. There's a good Chinese restaurant here too, but otherwise you're somewhat out of the city centre on the edge of Berzengi. To get into town, take bus 19 to Görogly köçesi or bus 34 to the station.

★Sofitel Ashgabat
Oguzkent Hotel LUXURY HOTEL **$$$**
(Map p380; ☎44 95 00; www.sofitel.com; Bitarap Turkmenistan şayoli; r from US$230; P ⊖ ❄ ≋) Effortlessly Ashgabat's best hotel, this gleaming palace is perhaps Central Asia's single most impressive place to stay. Combining the local fashion for marble and fountains with the solid management of the French Sofitel hotel chain, this is a full five-star experience with 299 fabulous rooms that include touches such as TVs in the bath, rain showers, fast and free wireless, three pools, a gym, spa, sauna and what is definitely Turkmenistan's best breakfast buffet (even if you're not staying here, treat yourself to the US$20 feast).

Nusay Hotel LUXURY HOTEL **$$$**
(Map p380; ☎22 10 25; nusay-hotel@online.tm; 1995 köçesi 70; s/d US$144/164; ❄ ≋) Following a very fancy transformation, the Nusay is now Ashgabat's best-value luxury option. It's perfectly located between the new and old city, and overlooks the Presidential Palace (which unfortunately gives the area a rather sterile and uptight atmosphere). Rooms are spacious, comfortable and luxuriously appointed. Wireless costs US$5 per 24 hours and works in the lobby only.

Grand Turkmen Hotel HOTEL **$$$**
(Map p376; ☎92 05 55; grandhtl150@gmail.com; Görogly köçesi 50; s/d/ste incl breakfast US$90/106/125; P ❄ @ ≋) Blessed with a fantastic location, the Grand Turkmen is a great choice. The standard rooms are in good shape (if perhaps a little small for the price) and all have balconies. It's a lively downtown place, within easy walking distance of many restaurants and sights, and in-house amenities include a gym and sauna. Wireless is free, but erratic: many guests use the paid premium wireless service (ie one that actually works; US$10 per day).

President Hotel LUXURY HOTEL **$$$**
(Map p380; ☎40 00 00; photelreservation@gmail.com; Archabil şayoli 54; s/d/ste incl breakfast US$165/175/230; P ❄ @ ≋) The lobby at Ashgabat's top hotel says it all – the blur of gold, crystal and marble is enough to make even Donatella Versace exclaim 'too much!' – but if you want to impress and can't quite pay Sofitel prices, this place is for you. Rooms are large and extremely comfortable, and gold-effect fittings predominate throughout. Wireless costs US$5 per 24 hours, but the two pools, gym and sauna are free for guests.

Ak Altyn Hotel HOTEL **$$$**
(Map p376; ☎36 37 00; akaltyn@online.tm; Magtymguly şayoli 141/1; s/d/ste incl breakfast US$75/91/105; P ❄ ≋) The golden-rust facade of this 109-room hotel a short distance to the west of downtown suggests an era of bygone splendour, and that's just what you get here, though the interior is somewhat more impressive than the exterior suggests. The rooms are anonymously styled and comfortable, and there's an outdoor pool, a nightclub and temperamental wireless access in the lobby.

Eating

With the best range of eating options in the country, Ashgabat may not be Paris, but after a long trip through the desert, the hungry traveller will be spoiled for choice.

Erzurum TURKISH **$**
(Map p380; Shevchenko köçesi 53; mains 10-20M; ⏲9am-10.30pm; 🗐) The food is good at this friendly local institution and includes *pide* (Turkish pizza) and delicious kebabs. The service is attentive and swift, although it can get very hot in the summer months due to the wood-fired oven; that's when the outdoor seating comes into its own. There's no alcohol.

Berzengi

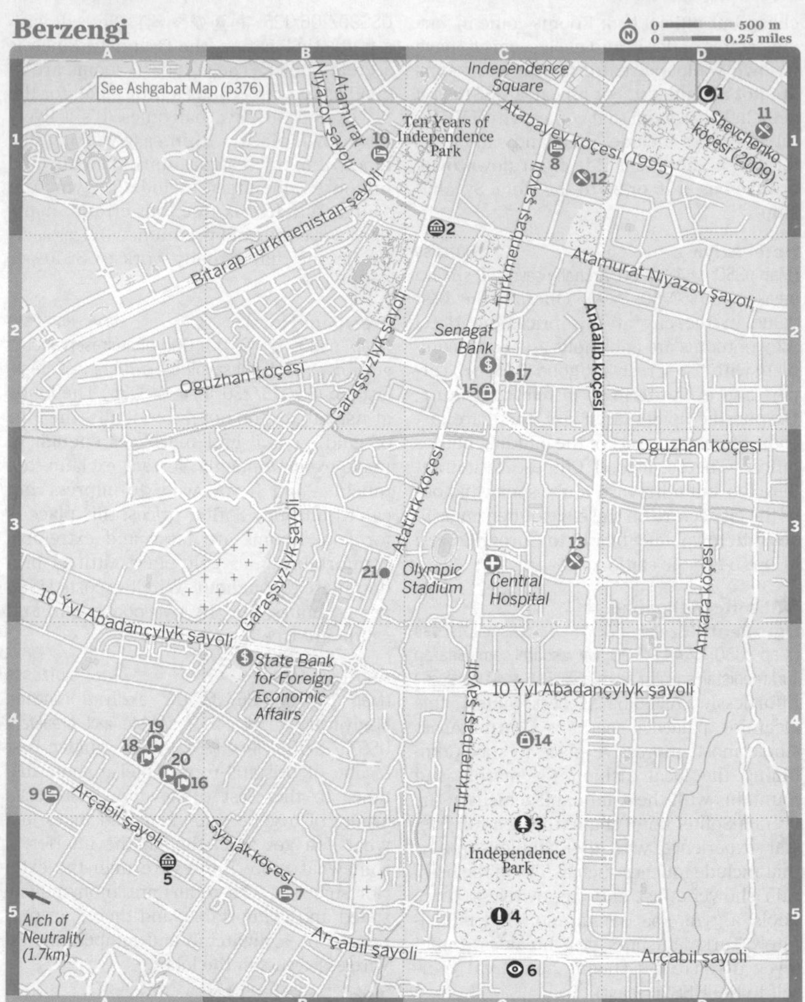

Shokoladnitsa BAKERY $
(Şekerli; Map p376; Azadi köçesi 69; cake from 8M; ⏲9am-10pm) This is a charming spot for a strong Turkish coffee and a sweet cake or pastry.

★ **Çeşme** TURKISH $$
(Map p376; Lakhuti köçesi; per person for kebab & salads 60M; ⏲6-11pm) This charming red-painted cellar in the backstreets between the train station and the Hotel Paýtagt attracts a thoroughly local crowd, but you'll be made to feel very welcome. It's all about the sublime kebabs here and there's no menu, which can make it a bit tricky for non-Russian speakers; but it's hard to go wrong with the selection of meats being grilled and the choice of delicious accompanying sauces and salads (the staff will bring you a selection and you can choose).

Köpetdag INTERNATIONAL $$
(☎27 67 20; Magtymguly şayoli 10; mains 20-40M; ⏲9am-11pm; 🗎) This imaginatively run place set in a charming garden with cabins for private dining, as well as outdoor tables in the shade, is one of Ashgabat's most fashionable restaurants. There's a huge

Berzengi

Sights

1 Azadi Mosque D1
2 Carpet Museum C1
3 Independence Park C5
4 Monument to the Independence of Turkmenistan C5
5 National Museum A5
6 Palace of Knowledge C5
Turkmenbashi Museum .... (see 6)

Sleeping

7 Hotel Aziya B5
8 Nusay Hotel C1
9 President Hotel A4
10 Sofitel Ashgabat Oguzkent Hotel B1

Eating

11 Erzurum D1
12 Euphoria C1
13 Sim Sim C3

Shopping

14 Altyn Asyr Shopping Centre C4
15 Yimpaş C2

Information

16 Afghan Embassy A4
17 Ayan Travel C2
18 Kazakhstan Embassy A4
19 Kyrgyz Embassy A4
20 Tajik Embassy A4
Yimpaş .... (see 15)

Transport

Turkish Airlines .... (see 15)
21 Turkmenistan Airlines B3

menu that takes in cuisines from around the world as well as local standards, and if there are several of you and you really want to have fun, book one of the garish but imaginatively decorated yurts. To get here take buses 4, 10 or 28 from anywhere on Magtymguly.

Euphoria INTERNATIONAL $$
(Map p380; Kulieva köçesi 33; mains 18-45M; 9am-11pm;) Perhaps the most ambitious of Ashgabat's restaurants in design terms, this surprising find tucked away behind the Nusay Hotel also has some great food and delightful staff. The huge menu runs from delicious salads and soups served in bathtub-like bowls, to main courses such as catfish with walnuts in a lemon sauce or lamb brisket in a mustard-and-peppermint sauce.

Seafood Ayna SEAFOOD $$
(Map p376; Kemine köçesi 156a; dishes 30-70M; 10am-10.30pm;) With its fabulously '90s interior and Yeltsin-era feeling of luxury, Seafood Ayna is one of Ashgabat's smarter eating options and one of the few places to get fresh seafood. There's a sushi menu on top of the seafood menu, which includes dishes such as lobster thermidor, octopus salad and baked mussels with Parma ham. The entrance is on the side of the building, not directly on Kemine köçesi.

Coffee House INTERNATIONAL $$
(Güzer; Map p376; 39 60 06; Turkmenbashi şayoli 15A; dishes 24-85M; 9am-11pm;) This place may be a masterwork of kitsch, but its breakfasts are solid and its coffee is decent, making it a prime hangout for the foreign community. Salads, soups and burgers complete the menu.

Pizza Haus PIZZERIA $$
(Map p376; 39 56 30, 39 56 00; Magtymguly şayoli 74; mains 15-50M, pizza 14-17M; 9am-11pm;) This cosy and popular place serves up the best pizza in town, though admittedly that's not a huge culinary achievement. There's a big non-pizza menu too, including a selection of breakfasts and free delivery citywide.

Sim Sim EUROPEAN $$$
(Map p380; 45 33 43; Andaliba köçesi 50/1; 30-200M; 10am-11pm;) Now a decade old, this one-time upstart is something of an establishment favourite. Despite its try-hard-and-fail decor, which is just tacky, the service and food here are top notch. The dishes are international with a strong emphasis on Italian cuisine and include squid salad with pesto sauce, crayfish bisque and even Wagyu steaks. Prices are high, but it's also one of the few places in Turkmenistan to offer a good wine selection. Trying to find the restaurant on your own is hard work; it's unsigned above a supermarket – take a cab, most drivers know it.

Drinking & Nightlife

Nightlife is thin on the ground in Ashgabat and you can hear a pin drop after 11pm, when nearly all the bars and cafes close.

Cafe Güneş BAR
(Map p376; Alishera Navoi köçesi) In a courtyard behind the Hotel Daýhan, this place serves up the cheapest beer in town and does tasty kebabs, with outdoor tables and a friendly atmosphere.

Iceberg Bar BAR
(Map p376; cnr Kemine köçesi & Revfov köçesi; ⏲10am-11pm) This tranquil beer garden, located behind the circus, serves up frothy pints of microbrewed beer and sticks of shashlyk.

City Pub PUB
(Map p376; ☎35 22 88; Alishera Navoi köçesi 54a; mains 15-35M; ⏲9am-10.30pm) Though looking nothing like one, a 'real British pub' has found its way to Central Asia. It's often empty though, with televisions providing the only atmosphere. There's a decent menu here as well, which is best enjoyed in the brighter and generally more pleasant next-door restaurant.

☆ Entertainment

Sport

Ashgabat is a great place for horse-lovers. Every Sunday from the end of March until May, then again from the end of August until mid-November, the **Hippodrome** plays host to dramatic Turkmen horse races. It's 5km east of the city centre – take bus 4 down Magtymguly or a 3M taxi ride.

The local football team is Kopet Dag, which plays at the **Kopet Dag stadium** (Map p376). You should have no trouble picking up a ticket on match days.

Theatres & Concert Halls

Ashgabat offers some excellent venues for watching music and drama productions centred on Turkmen folklore and traditional music. If you'd like to watch Turkmen drama then the **Mollanepes Drama Theatre** (Map p376; ☎35 74 63; Magtymguly şayoli 79; admission 15M) is the place to go. For Turkmen musical performances, visit the **Magtymguly Theatre** (Map p376; ☎35 05 64; Shevchenko köçesi; admission 15M). Russian plays can be seen at the **Pushkin Russian Drama Theatre** (Map p376; ☎36 42 81; Magtymguly şayoli 142; admission 3M) near Gunesh Park.

Shopping

The biggest and best supermarket in town is the **Yimpaş** (Map p380; ☎45 42 66; Turkmenbashi şayoli 54; ⏲7am-11pm), a huge Turkish shopping complex featuring, among other things, the only escalators in Turkmenistan. Here you can buy everything from frozen lobster to Doritos over several floors.

If you want to buy carpets or inexpensive cotton clothing, visit the **Altyn Asyr Marketing Centre** (Map p376), opposite the Grand Turkmen Hotel, which has outlet shops for the carpet and textile industry. The carpets are sold with all the documentation needed to be exported from the country, making it a lot simpler to buy them here. The best selection is available in **Altyn Göl** (Map p376; ☎39 21 56; Görogly köçesi 77; ⏲9am-7.30pm Mon-Fri, to 6pm Sat & Sun).

The best shopping experiences are to be had at one of Ashgabat's many markets. The **Russian Bazaar** (Map p376) is great for food of all kinds, especially fresh fruit and vegetables. The **Tekke Bazaar** (Map p376) is also recommended for foodstuffs and fruit as well as flowers.

Turkmen bookshops are little more than propaganda storefronts to promote national glory, but the best selection of books can be found at **Miras Bookshop** (Map p376; Turkmenbashi şayoli 29; ⏲10am-7pm).

ℹ Information

DANGERS & ANNOYANCES

Take care when photographing public buildings in Ashgabat, you may be shouted at by a police officer. Do not attempt to photograph the Palace of Turkmenbashi or any other ministry; the government quarter in Ashgabat is very off-limits for photography, but there are no signs to this effect.

EMERGENCY

Emergency operators will speak Turkmen or Russian only.

Ambulance (☎03)
Fire Service (☎01)
Police (☎02)

INTERNET ACCESS

There are a few internet cafes in Ashgabat, though for the best connection have a coffee at the Sofitel Ashgabat Oguzkent Hotel (p379) where there's password-free, fast wireless.

Even when hotels have wi-fi, connections are often terrible if they work at all. A far better way to use the internet is to buy a local SIM card for your unlocked smart phone. MTS will sell these to you from its main office in the Russian Bazaar; you'll just need to bring along your passport.

When using internet cafes, bring your passport, know that anything you view or write can be monitored and expect news websites to be blocked.

Internet Café (Map p376; Karl Liebknekht köçesi; per hr 6M; ⏲9am-1pm & 2-9pm) Next to the international call centre, this internet cafe has seven fast terminals.

Yimpaş (Map p380; Turkmenbashi şayoli 54; per hr 6M; ⏲7am-11pm) Internet cafe on the 3rd floor.

LAUNDRY

Floor maids at most hotels will do a load of laundry for around 10M.

Brilliant (Map p376; Magtymguly şayoli 99) Dry-cleaning and normal service washes can be done for reasonable rates here.

Yimpaş (Turkmenbashi şayoli 54; ⏲9am-11pm) Dry-cleaning at this Turkish department store is more expensive than at Brilliant.

MEDICAL SERVICES

Central Hospital (Map p380; ☎45 03 31, 45 03 03; Emre köçesi 1) This large and excellent hospital is the main medical provision in Ashgabat. There's an emergency department and pharmacy, both of which are open 24 hours a day.

Lechebny Hospital (Map p376; ☎39 08 77; Shevchenko köçesi) This Soviet-era hospital in the city centre is less well-equipped than Central Hospital.

MONEY

There are several banks in the city centre, but they're not of much use to travellers as they don't have ATMs or change travellers cheques. Most places change US dollars, and euros too, even though the euro rate is not always displayed. As the exchange rate is fixed, there's no advantage in going to one place over another and there is no longer a black-market rate. There are just two banks that can do credit- and debit-card advances.

Senagat Bank (Map p380; Turkmenbashi şayoli 42; ⏲9am-1pm & 2-6pm Mon-Fri, 9.30am-1pm Sat & Sun) For MasterCard and Maestro advances, go to the Western Union office inside this bank. It's located next to the Yimpaş department store and charges a 3% commission on withdrawals.

State Bank for Foreign Economic Affairs (Türkmenistanyň Daşary Ykdysady Döwlet Banky; Map p380; ☎40 60 40; Garaşsyzlyk şayoli 32; ⏲9.15am-1pm & 2-4pm Mon-Fri, 9.15am-12.30pm Sat) For visa-card advances (with 5% commission), this is the place to come. Go to desks 31 or 32. This is also one of the few banks where you can change currencies other than dollars and euros.

POST

Post Office (Map p376; Mopra köçesi 16; ⏲9am-5pm Mon-Fri, 9am-2pm Sat, 9am-1pm Sun) This main post office is in the city centre.

REGISTRATION

OVIR (State Service for the Registration of Foreign Citizens; Map p376; ☎39 13 37; 2011 köçesi 57; ⏲9am-noon & 2-5pm Mon-Fri, 9am-noon Sat) For tourist registration, in case you're not staying in a hotel.

TELEPHONE & FAX

Most hotels offer international direct dialling (IDD) and fax facilities, although the **International Call Centre** (Map p376; Karl Liebknekht köçesi 33; ⏲8am-7pm) offers better calling and fax rates than hotels.

Getting There & Away

AIR

Flights arrive and depart from **Saparmurat Turkmenbashi Airport** (☎23 38 45, 23 20 34), approximately 6km from the centre of town.

Within Central Asia, the only flights to Ashgabat are from Almaty (Kazakhstan), operated twice a week by Turkmenistan Airlines. Uzbekistan Airways has linked Ashgabat and Tashkent (Uzbekistan) in both directions every Wednesday for years, but the flight was suspended at the time of research.

Domestic Turkmenistan Airlines flights are heavily subsidised, making the ticket prices amazingly low. Consequently, demand is high and flights need to be booked in advance. Every day there are four flights from Ashgabat to Dashogus (58M), Turkmenabat (60M) and Mary (51M), and three daily flights to Turkmenbashi (65M).

Airlines

The following airlines fly to/from Turkmenistan and have offices in Ashgabat.

Lufthansa (☎23 39 47, 23 20 37; www.lufthansa.com; Main Concourse, Saparmurat Turkmenbashi Airport) Five flights per week to Frankfurt via Baku.

S7 Airlines (Map p376; ☎92 30 21; www.s7.ru; Grand Turkmen Hotel, Görogly köçesi 50) Flies between Ashgabat and Moscow three times a week.

Turkish Airlines (Map p380; ☎airport 23 20 59, main office 45 66 48; www.turkishairlines.com; Yimpaş Business Centre, Turkmenbashi şayoli 54) Two daily flights from İstanbul to Ashgabat.

Turkmenistan Airlines (Map p380; ☎39 17 18, 39 17 17; www.turkmenistanairlines.com; Ataturk köçesi 61) Operates good-value flights from Ashgabat to Abu Dhabi, Almaty, Amritsar, Bangkok, Beijing, Birmingham,

Delhi, Dubai, Frankfurt, İstanbul, Kiev, London, Minsk, Moscow and St Petersburg.

Uzbekistan Airways (☎ 23 20 26; Main Concourse, Saparmurat Turkmenbashi Airport) While suspended at present, normally operates a weekly Tashkent to Ashgabat service.

BUS, MARSHRUTKA & SHARED TAXI

Bus stands in Ashgabat are organised by destination, and are used by shared taxis and marshrutki as much as buses. A new bus station is under construction to the north of the city near the new Tolkuchka Bazaar site, but until then public transport leaves from the following three places.

Transport for Mary and Turkmenabat leaves from a makeshift bus station known to locals as the ***Mariiskaya stoyanka*** about 3km east of the centre on the main road out of the city. There are marshrutki to Mary (four hours, 20M) and Turkmenabat (seven hours, 30M). There is also one daily bus to Saraghs from here (five hours, 24M). Taxis from Ashgabat to Mary cost 30M per seat, while taxis to Turkmenabat cost 60M per seat.

Transport for Dashogus and Konye-Urgench leaves from the Dashogus Bazaar (also called Azatlyk Bazaar). A marshrutka to Konye-Urgench costs 35M (seven to eight hours), while a seat in a shared taxi is 40M. Prices to Dashogus are slightly higher: the daily bus takes around nine hours for the trip (25M), while marshrutki (35M) make the trip in six hours. A place in a taxi will cost 40M and the trip takes 5½ hours.

Transport to Turkmenbashi leaves from the Old Airport, to the north of the centre on the road to the current airport. The journey to Turkmenbashi (50M) takes around six hours by marshrutka or taxi.

TRAIN

The modern Ashgabat **train station** (☎ 39 38 04) is at the northern end of Turkmenbashi şayoli, in the heart of 'old' Ashgabat. Though it takes much longer to travel by train than by shared taxi, the fare is cheaper and the journey far more comfortable.

There are daily trains in both directions to Turkmenbashi (15 hours, 10.20M/22.92M), Mary (7½ hours, 7.72M/17.20M), Turkmenabat (12 hours, 11.26M/25.06M) and Dashogus (20 hours, 9.58M). Prices quoted above are for *kupe/SV* (second/first class), except for Dashogus, which has no SV carriage. Very basic third class *(platzkart)* tickets are available for around half the second-class cost, but you'll be in an open carriage in very crowded conditions. Note that tickets are not sold in the main station building, but in the **ticket office** (Map p376) a short distance down the platform.

Getting Around

TO/FROM THE AIRPORT

The easiest way to get into central Ashgabat from Saparmurat Turkmenbashi Airport is to take a taxi. They are both plentiful and cheap, especially if you choose to go with a shared one. You should expect to pay 10M, but agree before getting in, as drivers are likely to try their luck and ask for much more. Buses 1, 18 and 58 leave from outside the airport and go into the centre of Ashgabat (0.2M). However, as many flights to Ashgabat arrive in the middle of the night, the buses may not be running.

PUBLIC TRANSPORT

A fleet of sparkling, modern buses serves Ashgabat along some 70 routes, making getting around the city a doddle. Any ride costs just 0.2M (you just toss the money into the box by the driver as you get on, or give the driver a note if you need change; there are no physical tickets). There is however no single map listing all the routes, so you'll need to improvise and check the nearest bus stop, which will only have information about buses stopping there. It's quite easy to do, as the routes are depicted on a city map, but sadly the print quality is usually so bad that it's hard to be sure which bus goes where, and there are no street names on the map. If in doubt, try asking locals.

As with almost every other city in the former Soviet Union, you can just hold out your arm on the street and a car will soon stop and give you a lift to wherever you need to go. Short hops in the city cost 2M, rising to 3M for longer journeys. Agree on a price before you get in, or hand over the money with supreme confidence when you get out. To order an official taxi call ☎ 35 34 06.

KARAKUM DESERT

The Karakum desert is a sun-scorched expanse of dunes and sparse vegetation in the centre of Turkmenistan. It's Central Asia's hottest desert but manages to support a handful of settlements, including the oasis town of **Jerbent**, 160km north of Ashgabat. A ramshackle collection of homes, battered trucks, yurts and the occasional camel, Jerbent is being slowly consumed by the desert as sands continue to blow off the overgrazed dunes.

While it doesn't look like much, the village does offer a glimpse of rural Turkmen life, and you can watch traditional cooking methods and sit down for tea inside a yurt.

WORTH A TRIP

TURKMENBASHI

Turkmenbashi is Turkmenistan's only major port and the end of the line for travellers heading on to the Caucasus via the ferry to Baku. There's nothing much to keep you here for any length of time, but it's a pleasant and friendly town with a more Russian feel than most Turkmen cities and an enjoyable Caspian Sea location. Budget travellers should overnight at the **Hotel Hazar** (☎2 46 33; fax 2 46 36; Azadi köçesi; s/d 55/85M; ❄), while midrangers should head for the **Hotel Çarlak** (☎2 13 64; fax 2 13 75; Bahri-Hazar köçesi; s/d/ste incl full board 140/200/285M; P❄📶≋), both of which are in the town centre.

From the Turkmenbashi ferry terminal there are frequent untimetabled cargo ships to Baku in Azerbaijan, most of which take passengers (approximately US$100 per person), although there's always the chance that there won't be a departure for several days. Bring all the food you'll need for the 24-hour crossing, and be aware that you may have to wait up to 48 hours or more for a departure, so be prepared to wait (and if your visa is about to run out, you'll need to wait onboard the ferry, having exited Turkmenistan).

The Karakum desert draws visitors for the **Darvaza Gas Craters**, one of Turkmenistan's most unusual sights. The result of Soviet-era gas exploration in the 1950s, the three craters are artificial. One has been set alight and blazes with an incredible strength that's visible from miles away, while the other two contain bubbling mud and water. There have been rumours for years that the burning gas crater will be put out to enable gas exploration in the area, but it was still burning in 2013. Check the latest news with a travel agency in Ashgabat.

Of the three, the fire crater is the most impressive, and it's best seen at night, when the blazing inferno can only be compared to the gates of hell. There is a naturally sheltered camping place behind the small hill, just south of the crater. Getting to the crater is an off-road ride and drivers frequently get lost or get stuck in the dunes. There is no one around to give directions, so make sure you go with somebody who knows the way. If you intend to walk from the road, think twice. While the walk only takes two hours through the dunes, you'll have to spend the night here, as finding your way back to the road without the reference of a huge burning crater is very hard. Even in daylight you may get lost – it's much better to pay for a tour. There are no hotels in the area, but most of the chaikhanas (teahouses) that line the main road just north of the turnoff to the crater offer beds for the night, provide meals and even sell petrol. As there are no signposts for either the turnoff or the chaikhanas, look out for the train line crossing the main road. If coming from Ashgabat, the turnoff for the crater is about 1km before the railway line, and the chaikhanas are a few kilometres afterwards. If you plan to camp at the crater, make sure you sleep a good distance back from its edges, as breathing in the gas all night long can make you very ill.

All buses and marshrutki heading from Ashgabat to both Konye-Urgench and Dashogus go through Jerbent and pass nearby the turnoff for the Darvaza Gas Craters on the main road.

WESTERN TURKMENISTAN

Driving west from Ashgabat, the main road skirts the edges of the Kopet Dag and the Iranian border before opening up into a vast, featureless landscape that is wonderfully Central Asian.

Köw Ata Underground Lake

Like entering Milton's underworld, only with changing rooms and a staircase, a visit to the **Köw Ata Underground Lake** (admission 40M; ⏲dawn-dusk) is a unique experience. You enter a cave at the base of a mountain and walk down a staircase, 65m underground, which takes you into a wonderfully sulphurous subterranean world. At the bottom awaits a superb lake of clear water naturally heated to about 36°C. Underground swimming is one of Central Asia's more unusual activities, and is worth it if you don't mind the steep entry fee – particularly annoying given the facilities here are all in poor condition. The turnoff to the lake is clearly marked along the main Ashgabat–Balkanabat road. By marshrutka or bus from Ashgabat to Balkanabat or Turkmenbashi you could easily ask the driver to stop at the Köw Ata turnoff, although it's a good 90-minute walk from the road. There's a good shashlyk restaurant on site here, making this a great lunch stop.

Gozli Ata & Yangykala Canyon

A respected Sufi teacher in the early 14th century, Gozli Ata had a large following until his untimely death at the hands of Mongol invaders. His **mausoleum** (N 40°20.051', E 54°29.249'), located in a natural depression of rocky desert, is now a popular place of pilgrimage. Gozli Ata's wife is buried in an adjacent mausoleum and, according to custom, visitors must first pray at her last resting place. A cemetery has sprung up nearby; gravestones here contain a notch in the top where water can collect to 'feed' the soul of the deceased. Gozli Ata is 135km north of Balkanabat; an experienced driver is needed to find it.

From the turnoff to Gozli Ata (marked with a 9km sign), another road continues north to **Yangykala Canyon** (N 40°27.656', E 54°42.816'). With bands of pink, red and yellow rock searing across the sides of steep canyon walls, Yangykala is a breathtaking sight and one of the most spectacular natural attractions in Turkmenistan. Just as alluring as the beautiful views is its solitary isolation in the desert; few Turkmen are aware of its existence.

Canyons and cliffs slash for 25km towards the Garabogazköl basin and lie approximately 165km north of Balkanabat and about 160km east of Turkmenbashi, making it easy to slot in a trip to the canyon between the two cities. It's possible to camp on the plateau above the canyon, although it can get windy there. While most tour companies run trips to Yangykala Canyon, not all include it on their standard itineraries, so make enquiries when planning your trip.

EASTERN TURKMENISTAN

Squeezed between the inhospitable Karakum desert and the rugged Afghan frontier, the fertile plains of eastern Turkmenistan have long been an island of prosperity in Central Asia.

The rise of civilisations began in the Bronze Age, reaching their climax with the wondrous city of Merv. In the 13th century invading Mongols put paid to centuries of accumulated wealth, but even today the region continues to outpace the rest of Turkmenistan, thanks mainly to a thriving cotton business.

Mary

☎522 / POP 123,000

The capital of the Mary region is a somewhat spartan Soviet confection of administrative buildings and vast gardens disproportionate to the size of the city. Mary (pronounced MAH-ree) is the centre of the major cotton-growing belt, which gives the city an air of prosperity; the markets bustle on weekends and commerce is surprisingly brisk.

Mary's history dates back to the 1820s when the Tekke Turkmen erected a fortress here, preferring the site to ancient Merv, 30km east. In 1884, a battalion of Russian troops, led by one Lieutenant Alikhanov, convinced the Turkmen to hand over control of the fort before things got bloody. Cotton production quickly picked up and the guarantee of continued wealth came in 1968 when huge natural gas reserves were found 20km west of the city.

Apart from the excellent regional museum there is nothing much of note to see in the town itself, although it makes for a handy base from which to explore the nearby ancient cities of Gonur and Merv.

Sights

Mary Regional Museum MUSEUM
(☎4 50 98; Gowshuthan köçesi; admission 14.15M, entry & guided tour 28.50M; ⏲9am-6pm) Mary's highlight is this excellent museum housed in a sparkling white-marble palace across the river from the centre of town. The enormous premises is home to a collection of taxidermy, temporary exhibits and a gallery of Turkmen art, but the real reason to visit is the superb archaeological collec-

Mary

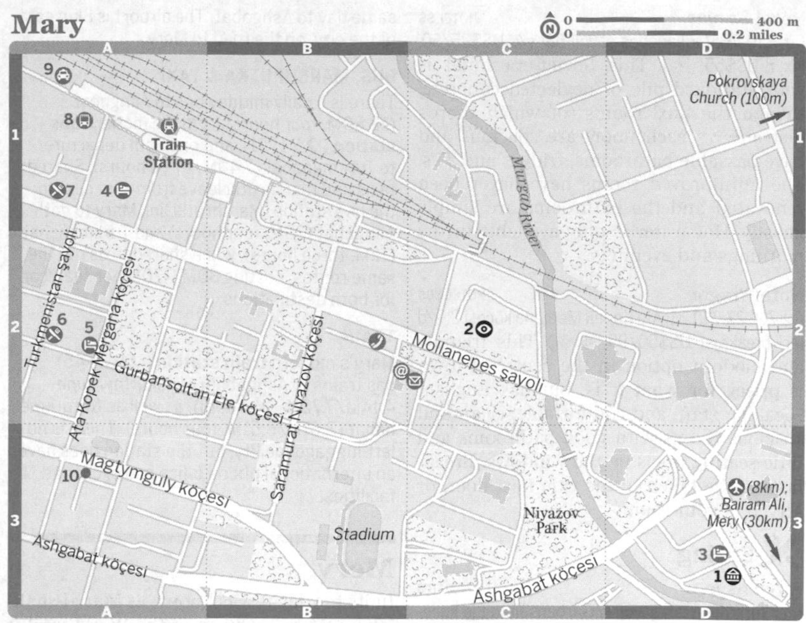

tion on the upper floor, full of discoveries from Margush (Gonur) and Merv, as well as impressively detailed models of both sites. Other highlights include a late third millennium BC tabernacle from Gonur, and lots of impressively preserved porcelain, coins, weapons, jewellery and amphorae. There's also an extensive ethnography section, including a large collection of Turkmen jewellery, carpets, stuffed animals, a fully decorated yurt and pottery from the time of the Mongol occupation. Call ahead to book an English-language guide as English labelling, while consistent, lacks detail.

Pokrovskaya Church CHURCH

(Seydi köçesi) Pokrovskaya Church, a handsome red-brick affair, was built in 1900. The church is surrounded by pleasant parkland and its interior is crammed with religious icons. Cross the river on Mollanepes, then take the left-hand road from the roundabout. The second street you'll get to is Seydi köçesi, turn right into it and the church is at the end.

Zelyony Bazaar MARKET

(Mollanepes şayoli) You can get your fill of local colour as well as your shopping done at the enormous Zelyony Bazaar.

Mary

Sights
1 Mary Regional Museum ... D3
2 Zelyony Bazaar ... C2

Sleeping
3 Hotel Margush ... D3
4 Hotel Sanjar ... A1
5 Hotel Yrsgal ... A2

Eating
6 Altyn Asyr ... A2
7 Çarlak ... A1

Transport
8 Bus Station ... A1
9 Marshrutka & Shared Taxi Stand ... A1
10 Turkmenistan Airlines ... A3

Sleeping

★Hotel Margush HOTEL $$

(☎6 03 86, 6 03 87; Gowshuthan köçesi 20; s/d/ste incl breakfast US$40/60/150; P ❄ ≋) Mary's best accommodation is located near the Murgab River. The 30 comfortable, modern rooms are built around a pleasant lobby, and each contains a TV, fridge and small desk. Other facilities, such as the sauna, fitness centre and pool, are extra.

Hotel Sanjar HOTEL **$$**
(☎7 10 76; Mollanepes şayoli 58; s/d US$25/50, lux r US$55; ❄) This Soviet-era hotel is your standard pile of neglected concrete, though the 'lux' rooms (of which there's just one on each floor) are spacious and have passable bathrooms, fridges and TVs. The unimproved rooms have never been renovated and the bathrooms are simply ghastly. Hot water is only available in the mornings and evenings.

Hotel Yrsgal HOTEL **$$$**
(☎7 21 27, 7 21 31; Ata Kopek Mergana köçesi 2; s/d incl breakfast US$50/95; ❄@) This friendly and modern option in the centre of town is pricey for what it is, but has English-speaking staff, and comfortable, clean and spacious rooms with good bathrooms and little seating areas by the windows. Breakfast can be taken in the cafe next door, or served in your room.

Eating

Altyn Asyr KEBAB **$**
(cnr Turkmenistan şayoli & Gurbansoltan Eje köçesi; mains 8-16M; ⏰9am-10.30pm) This simple kebab spot in the centre of town serves up delicious shashlyk. There's a pleasant patio out by the barbecue. Next door you'll find the similar standard Miras Kafe.

Çarlak KEBAB **$**
(Mollanepes şayoli; mains 3-13M; ⏰9am-11pm) A furiously popular shashlyk place with outside tables, as well as private cabins inside for feasting away from prying eyes.

Information

The central **post office** is 1km east of the Hotel Sanjar off Mollanepes, while the central **telephone office** is 50m northwest of the post office, with the town's **internet cafe** (per hr 6M; ⏰9am-9pm) nearby.

Yevgenia Golubeva (☎cell 993 65 310822, Mary 6 03 05; evgeniagolubeva@yahoo.com) is an experienced, English-speaking tour guide, who used to be the deputy director of the Mary Museum. She can organise highly recommended tours to nearby Merv and Gonur.

Getting There & Away

AIR

Turkmenistan Airlines (☎3 27 77; Magtymguly köçesi 11) has four flights per day to/from Ashgabat (51M). If time is short, you could take a morning flight, visit Merv and return on the same day to Ashgabat. The airport is 8km east of the city, on the road to Merv.

BUS, MARSHRUTKA & TAXI

There is a daily midday bus to Ashgabat (12.60M, four hours) from the modern **bus station** (☎7 11 71), and one 2pm departure to Turkmenabat (7.40M, three hours). Shared taxis and marshrutki leave from a lot next to the bus station. Marshrutki link Mary to both Ashgabat (20M, four hours) and Turkmenabat (12M, three hours), while shared taxis run the same routes, costing 30M/120M per seat/car for both destinations.

TRAIN

Mary's modern **train station** (☎9 22 45) has trains to Ashgabat (*platskartny/kupe* 4.14M/7.72M, 7½ hours), as well as to Turkmenabat (3.61M/6.51M, four hours). There is no left-luggage facility, but the station does have an international phone office and exchange facilities.

Merv

In its heyday it was known as Marv-i-shahjahan, 'Merv – Queen of the World', and it stood alongside Damascus, Baghdad and Cairo as one of the great cities of the Islamic world. A major centre of religious study and a lynchpin on the Silk Road, its importance to the commerce and sophistication of Central Asia cannot be underestimated.

Today, however, almost nothing of the metropolis remains, and you'll need to bring a fair chunk of imagination to get any sense of the place, which makes having a good guide essential, as well as your own transport to cover the large territory of the site.

Merv

Sights

1 Buddhist Stupa D3
2 Ice House B4
3 Ice House B4
4 Ice House C4
5 Koshk B1
6 Kyz Kala A3
7 Little Kyz Kala A3
8 Margush Archaeological Museum A2
9 Mausoleum of Mohammed ibn Zeid A2
10 Mausoleum of Sultan Sanjar B2
11 Mausoleums of Two Askhab B3
12 Mosque & Cistern D2
13 Mosque of Yusuf Hamadani B1

History

Merv was known as Margiana or Margush in Alexander the Great's time. Under the Persian Sassanians, it was considered religiously liberal, with significant populations of Christians, Buddhists and Zoroastrians cohabiting peacefully. As a centre of power, culture and civilisation, Merv reached its greatest heights during the peak of the Silk Road in the 11th and 12th centuries, when the Seljuq Turks made it their capital. Legendary Merv may even have been the inspiration for the tales of Scheherazade's *Thousand and One Nights.*

Merv suffered a number of attacks over the course of its history, but instead of rebuilding on top of the older ruins, Merv slowly spread west. In total, five cities were constructed next to each other, largely because of the shifting rivers. The oldest section was the Erk Kala; in later centuries most people lived in the vast walled city called Sultan Kala.

All of this was completely eradicated in 1221 under the onslaught of the Mongols. In 1218 Chinggis Khan demanded a substantial tithe of grain from Merv, along with the pick of the city's most beautiful young women. The unwise Seljuq response was to slay the tax collectors.

In retribution Tolui, the most brutal of Chinggis Khan's sons, arrived three years later at the head of an army, accepted the peaceful surrender of the terrified citizens, and then proceeded to butcher every last one of them, an estimated 300,000 people.

Sights

On the road towards ancient Merv is a small ticket office for the **Merv complex** (☎6 73 54; admission 11.40M, camera 5.70M, video camera 70M; ⏲8am-7pm) and the **Margush Archaeological Museum** (⏲8am-7pm) FREE.

Merv

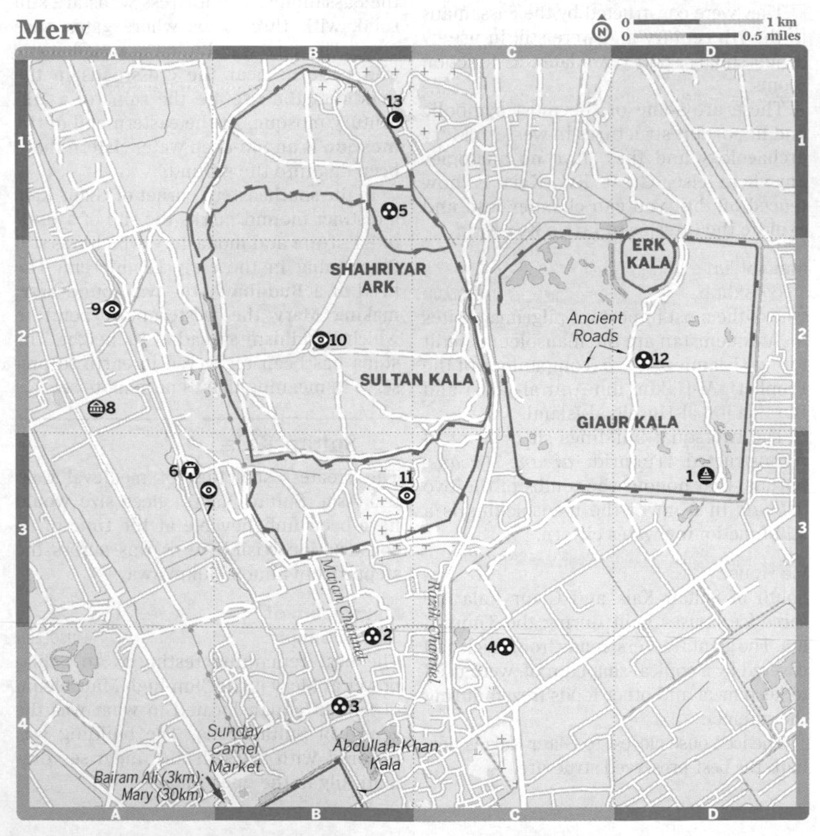

Mausoleum of Mohammed ibn Zeid MAUSOLEUM

From the ticket office, continue east and take your first left (north) to an early-Islamic monument, the 12th-century Mausoleum of Mohammed ibn Zeid. Like the other Sufi shrines (Gozli-Ata and Kubra), this shrine is an important site for Sufi pilgrims.

There's confusion as to who is actually buried under the black marble cenotaph in the centre of the cool, dark shrine. It's definitely not Ibn Zeid, a prominent Shiite teacher who died four centuries before this tomb was built and is known to be buried elsewhere.

Kyz Kala FORTRESS

These two crumbling 7th-century *koshk* (fortresses) outside the walls of Merv are interesting for their 'petrified stockade' walls, as writer Colin Thubron describes them, composed of 'vast clay logs up-ended side by side'.

They were constructed by the Sassanians in the 7th century and were still in use by Seljuq sultans, 600 years later, as function rooms.

These are some of the most symbolic and important structures in western Merv archaeology and they have no analogies anywhere else. Great Kyz Kala is now fenced off, but you can clamber into and explore the interior of **Little Kyz Kala**.

Mausoleums of Two Askhab MAUSOLEUM

One of the most important pilgrimage sites in Turkmenistan are the mausoleums built for two Islamic *askhab* (companions of the Prophet), Al-Hakim ibn Amr al-Jafari and Buraida ibn al-Huseib al-Islami.

The two squat buildings sit in front of reconstructed Timurid *aivans* (*iwans*, portals) that honour the tombs of the two *askhab*. In front of the mausoleums is a still-functioning water cistern.

Ice House RUIN

South of Sultan Kala and Giaur Kala are three ice houses built during the Timurid era. The giant freezers, made from brick and covered by a conical-shaped roof, were used to keep meat and other foods frozen during the summer.

The ice house closest to Giaur Kala is perhaps the best-preserved structure.

Erk Kala

The oldest of the five Merv cities is Erk Kala, an Achaemenid city thought to date from the 6th century BC. Led by Alexander the Great, the Macedonians conquered it and renamed it Alexandria Margiana. Under Parthian control (250 BC to AD 226) Zoroastrianism was the state religion but Erk Kala was also home to Nestorian Christians, Jews and Buddhists.

Today Erk Kala is a big earthen doughnut about 600m across. Deep trenches have been dug into the ramparts by Soviet archaeologists. The ramparts are 50m high, and offer a bird's-eye view of the surrounding savannah-like landscape. On the ramparts it's easy to see small hills that were once towers.

From this vantage point you can see that Erk Kala forms part of the northern section of another fortress – **Giaur Kala**, constructed during the 3rd century BC by the Sassanians. The fortress walls are still solid, with three gaps where gates once were. The city was built on a Hellenistic grid pattern; near the crossroads in the middle of the site are the ruins of a 7th-century mosque. At the eastern end of the **mosque** is an 8m-deep water cistern that's been dug into the ground.

In the southeastern corner of Giaur Kala a distinct mound marks the site of a **Buddhist stupa** and monastery, which was still functioning in the early Islamic era. The head of a Buddha statue was found here, making Merv the westernmost point to which Buddhism spread at its height. The stupa has been recovered in earth to preserve it, meaning there's nothing to see.

Sultan Kala

The greatest structure of medieval Central Asia, Sultan Kala's sheer size would have been unbelievable at the time of its construction, visible as it was across the steppe from almost 30km away.

Mausoleum of Sultan Sanjar MAUSOLEUM

The best remaining testimony to Seljuq power at Merv is the 38m-high Mausoleum of Sultan Sanjar, located in what was the centre of Sultan Kala. The building was restored with Turkish aid and rises dramatically in the open plain.

Sanjar, grandson of Alp-Arslan, died in 1157, reputedly of a broken heart when, after escaping from captivity in Khiva, he came home to find that his beloved Merv had been pillaged by Turkic nomads.

The mausoleum is a simple cube with a barrel-mounted dome on top. Originally it had a magnificent turquoise-tiled outer dome, said to be visible from a day's ride away, but that is long gone. Interior decoration is sparse, though restoration has brought back the blue-and-red frieze in the upper gallery. Inside is Sanjar's simple stone 'tomb' although, fearing grave robbers, he was actually buried elsewhere in an unknown location. The name of the architect, Mohammed Ibn Aziz of Serakhs, is etched into the upper part of the east wall. According to lore, the sultan had his architect executed to prevent him from designing a building to rival this one.

Shahriyar Ark RUIN

The Shahriyar Ark (or Citadel of Sultan Kala) is one of the more interesting parts of Merv. Still visible are its walls, a well-preserved *koshk* (fort) with corrugated walls, and the odd grazing camel.

Mosque of Yusuf Hamadani MOSQUE

North of the Shahriyar Ark, outside the city walls, lies the Mosque of Yusuf Hamadani, built around the tomb of a 12th-century dervish. The complex has been largely rebuilt in the last 10 years and turned into an important pilgrimage site; it is not open to non-Muslims.

Getting There & Away

The only way to see the Merv site without an exhausting walk is by car. From Mary expect to pay 25M for a car and driver for four hours (the minimum amount of time needed to see the main monuments). Buses go between Mary and Bairam Ali every half hour or so; the journey takes about 45 minutes. Guided tours are available from any travel agency and this is the way most people see Merv. Yevgenia Golubeva (p388) in Mary includes Merv on her tour of the area.

Gonur

Long before Merv raised its first tower, Bronze Age villages were assembling along the Murgab River in what is called the Margiana Oasis. The greatest of these ancient settlements, currently being excavated around **Gonur Depe** (Gonur Hill; admission 3M, camera 4M), has stunned the archaeological world for its vast area and complex layout.

The discoveries were first made in 1972 by Russian-Greek archaeologist Viktor Sarianidi, who still works at the site, continually uncovering new findings. Sarianidi considers Gonur to be one of the great civilisations of the ancient world and while this claim may be disputed, it is a fascinating site. What is certain, is that Gonur is one of the oldest fire-worshipping civilisations, parallel to the Bactrian cultures in neighbouring Afghanistan. The first agricultural settlements appeared in the area around 7000 BC, developing a strong agriculture. It is believed the city was slowly abandoned during the Bronze Age as the Murgab River changed course, depriving the city of water. The current excavations have been dated back to 3000 BC.

Sarianidi believes that Gonur was the birthplace of the first monotheistic religion, Zoroastrianism, being at some point the home of the religion's founder, Zoroaster. The adjacent sites have revealed four fire temples, as well as evidence of a cult based around a drug potion prepared from poppy, hemp and ephedra plants. This potent brew is almost certainly the *haoma* (soma elixir) used by the magi whom Zoroaster began preaching against in Zoroastrian texts.

The excavations are ongoing and during your visit you may have a chance to speak with the archaeologists and inspect the most recent findings. There is significant effort being put into conservation, although the work being done (sealing the ruins with mud bricks) is covering up some of the most photogenic portions of the city. The **Royal Palace** and **necropolis** are the most fascinating sites to visit.

Gonur is a two-hour drive from Mary and you'll need at least two hours there. A 4WD is required as the final 20km of road is little more than a rough track in the dirt. You can organise a trip through any travel agency or call Yevgenia Golubeva (p388) in Mary. Expect to pay 120M to hire a driver, and a further 90M for an in-depth guided tour.

There is nowhere in the area to buy food or water, so pack a lunch before setting off.

Turkmenabat

☎422 / POP 254,000

Lying on the banks of the mighty Amu-Darya, between the Karakum desert and the fertile plains of Uzbekistan, sprawling Turkmenabat sits at a crossroads of cultures. The town itself feels as if it's in the geographic centre of nowhere, yet after the mind-numbing drive through the desert, it's something of a surprise to find such a large city appear out of the sand.

The Silk Road city of Amul prospered here until its destruction by the Mongols in 1221, and was reborn under the Russian empire as Charjou, a name you'll still hear used by the remaining Russian-speaking locals. In 2009 a gas pipeline opened here taking Turkmen gas to China, thus ensuring the city's economic prosperity. Despite being the second-largest city in the country, there's nothing much to see or do here, though it's an obvious stopover between Mary and Uzbekistan.

Sights

Turkmenabat has a couple of bustling bazaars. The most convenient is **Zelyony Bazaar**, near the telephone office.

Lebap Regional Museum MUSEUM
(Niyazov şayoli; admission 15M; 9am-6pm Wed-Mon) Turkmenabat's brand new and ridiculously ornate museum could double as Liberace's house (check out those chandeliers!), but it also houses a solid collection of archaeological findings from the Lebap region and a good ethnographic display including a full reconstruction of a Silk Road market. Upstairs there's also a collection of geological findings, including mouldings of the dinosaur footprints from the Kugitang Nature Reserve and a stuffed *zemzen*, a large, fierce and very rarely seen desert lizard.

Russian Orthodox Church CHURCH
(Magtymguly şayoli) A couple of blocks northeast of the Lebap Regional Museum is the Russian Orthodox Church, built to honour St Nicolas in the late 19th century. the church is painted canary yellow and decorated on the interior with a rich collection of icons.

Sleeping

Hotel Gurluşykçy HOTEL $
(☎3 81 85; off Magtymguly şayoli; per person US$18; ❄) This friendly yet unpronounceable hotel is an old Soviet-era place and the cheapest option in town. The rooms

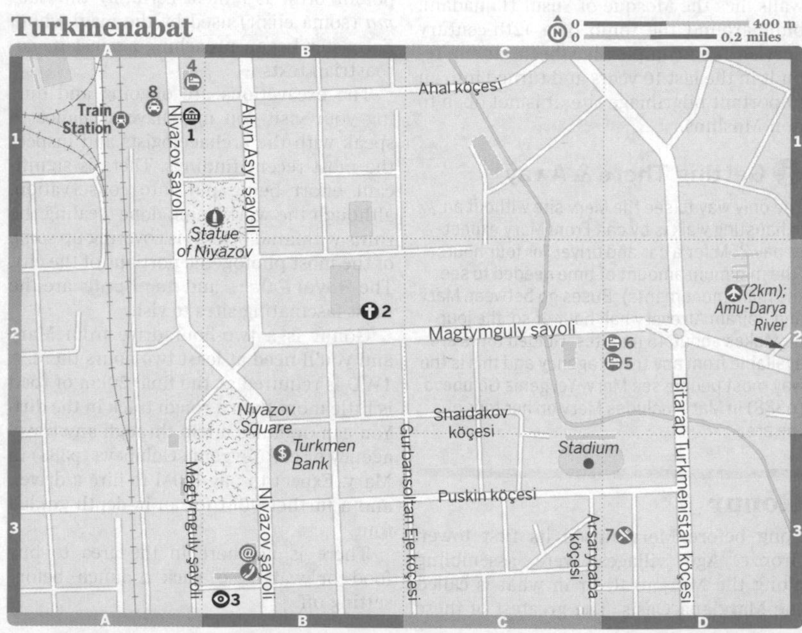

are large apartments with a living room, a couple of bedrooms, and rather awful bathrooms, though there's usually hot water. It is located behind the Hotel Turkmenabat. No English is spoken and air-con is in some rooms only.

Hotel Amu Darya HOTEL **$$**
(☎3 14 30; Niyazov şayoli 14; r US$60; ❄) Despite a recent renovation this place opposite the station has re-emerged looking surprisingly similar to how it did before it went under the knife. Admittedly rooms are nicely painted now, and are as spacious as ever, but there are still no holders for the showerheads.

Hotel Turkmenabat HOTEL **$$**
(☎3 82 92; Magtymguly şayoli; r US$60; ❄) The Turkmenabat offers comfortable rooms, each with high ceilings, a fridge, comfy beds and a tiny TV. There is a pleasant bar and a good restaurant, the Oguzhan.

Eating

You won't be blown away by anything in Turkmenabat, but there are several solid choices.

Oguzhan INTERNATIONAL **$**
(Magtymguly şayoli; mains 6-22M; ⏰9am-10.30pm; ▤) The restaurant at the Hotel Turkmenabat is a good choice – its menu takes in Russian, Central Asian and Caucasian cooking, including Georgian *chakhokhbili* (chicken stew in a spicy tomato sauce). There's a pleasant garden with yurts and a few sun-dappled outdoor tables where you can dine if the dark interior doesn't appeal.

Turkmenabat

Sights
1 Lebap Regional Museum A1
2 Russian Orthodox Church B2
3 Zelyony Bazaar B3

Sleeping
4 Hotel Amu Darya................................. A1
5 Hotel Gurluşykçy D2
6 Hotel Turkmenabat D2

Eating
Oguzhan.. (see 6)
7 Traktir.. D3

Transport
8 Marshrutka & Taxi Stand.................... A1

Traktir RUSSIAN **$$**
(☎3 14 38; off Puskin köçesi; mains 10-30M; ⏰10am-10.30pm; ✍▤) This friendly place has three garish rooms and even in the quietest one you'll still have to compete with the TV to be heard. There's also a bar that's popular with locals. The large menu runs from game to fish, and even includes a miniscule vegetarian section.

Getting There & Away

There are around four dirt-cheap flights a day between Turkmenabat and Ashgabat (60M, one hour). The airport is 2km east of Hotel Turkmenabat. The brand new **train station** (☎3 60 62), in the centre of town, has two daily trains to Ashgabat (11.26M, 12 hours) via Mary (6.51M, four hours). Outside the station you can catch marshrutki or taxis to Mary (30M per seat) and Ashgabat (50M per seat). A ride to the Uzbek border will cost 30M per taxi, but you may need to bargain hard as starting prices can be much higher. The road to Dashogus is in such bad condition that it's not recommended unless you have a 4WD and plenty of time.

NORTHERN TURKMENISTAN

Stalin's modus operandi in Central Asia sought the division of its people, thus resulting in the split of the Khorezm (an ancient kingdom centred around the Amu-Darya delta) oasis – the northern section around Khiva going to Uzbekistan and the southern portion going to Turkmenistan. It remains this way today, with the Amu-Darya river wriggling its way in and out of the Uzbek and Turkmen borders. As part of historic Khorezm, the Turkmen portion still contains a sizeable Uzbek minority and retains a culture apart from the rest of the country. Sadly, the region has not escaped the Aral Sea disaster and suffers from air, soil and water pollution. It's also the poorest part of the country, with little commerce apart from the smuggling of subsidised petrol to Uzbekistan.

Konye-Urgench

☎347 / POP 30,000

The modern town of Konye-Urgench (from Persian 'Old Urgench') is a rural backwater with livestock wandering its chaotic, unpaved roads. Yet centuries ago, this was the centre of the Islamic world, not the end of it.

Khorezm fell to the all-conquering Seljuq Turks, but rose in the 12th century, under a Seljuq dynasty known as the Khorezmshahs, to shape its own far-reaching empire. With its mosques, medressas, libraries and flourishing bazaars, Gurganj (the Persian name for Konye-Urgench) became a centre of the Muslim world, until Khorezmshah Mohammed II moved his capital to Samarkand after capturing that city in 1210.

Chinggis Khan arrived in 1221, seeking revenge for the murder of his envoys in Otrar as ordered by Mohammed II. Old Urgench withstood the siege for six months, and even after the Mongols broke through the city walls the residents fought them in the streets. The Mongols, unused to cities, burnt the houses but the residents still fought from the ruins. In the end, the Mongols diverted the waters of the Amu-Darya and flooded the city, drowning its defenders.

The Mongol generals went in pursuit of Mohammed II who eluded them for months until he finally died of exhaustion in 1221 on an island in the Caspian Sea. The tombs of his father, Tekesh, and grandfather, Il-Arslan, survive and are two of Old Urgench's monuments.

In the following period of peace, Khorezm was ruled as part of the Golden Horde, the huge, wealthy, westernmost of the khanates into which Chinggis Khan's empire was divided after his death. Rebuilt, Urgench was again Khorezm's capital, and grew into what was probably one of Central Asia's most important trading cities – big, beautiful, crowded and with a new generation of monumental buildings.

Then came Timur. Considering Khorezm to be a rival to Samarkand, he comprehensively finished off Old Urgench in 1388. The city was partly rebuilt in the 16th century, but it was abandoned when the Amu-Darya changed its course. (Modern Konye-Urgench dates from the construction of a new canal in the 19th century.)

Today, most of Old Urgench lies underground, but there is enough urban tissue to get an idea of its former glories. Its uniqueness was acknowledged in 2005 when Unesco named it a World Heritage Site. The modern town is somewhat short on tourist facilities and most travellers overnight in Dashogus.

Sights

The ancient city's monuments are dotted like a constellation across a large **site** (admission 11.40M, camera 5.70M; 8am-6pm) straddling the Ashgabat road, 1km south of the main town. One ticket covers all the sights.

Konye-Urgench Museum
MUSEUM

(admission 11.40M; 9am-4pm) The simple Konye-Urgench Museum is housed in the early-20th-century Dash Medressa, just before the main mausoleum complex. It includes some ancient Arabic texts and a few interestingly labelled artefacts from Old Urgench (eg 'blue polished eight-cornered thing'). Note the Christian symbols carved onto some of the stone pieces. Off the medressa courtyard are several rooms containing ethnographic displays of Turkmen culture, including a pottery workshop and carpet looms. To one side of the mosque is the **Matkerim-Ishan Mausoleum**, which is also early 20th century.

Nejameddin Kubra Mausoleum
MAUSOLEUM

The path past the Matkerim-Ishan Mausoleum leads to the Nejameddin Kubra Mausoleum on the left, and the **Sultan Ali Mausoleum** facing it across a shady little courtyard. Nejameddin Kubra (1145–1221) was a famous Khorezm Muslim teacher and poet who founded the Sufic Kubra order, with followers throughout the Islamic world. His tomb is believed to have healing properties and you may find pilgrims praying here. The building has three domes and a tiled portal that appears on the brink of forward collapse. The tombs inside – one for his body and one for his head (which were kindly separated by the Mongols) are extraordinarily colourful with floral-pattern tiles.

Turabeg Khanym Complex
HISTORIC BUILDING

Turabeg Khanym Complex, opposite the ticket office, is still the subject of some debate. Locals and some scholars consider this a mausoleum, though no-one is too sure who is buried here. Some archaeologists contend that it was a throne room built in the 12th century (it appears to have a heating system, which would not have been used in a mausoleum). Whatever its function, this is one of Central Asia's most perfect buildings. Its geometric patterns are in effect a giant calendar signifying humanity's insignificance in the march of time. There are 365 sections on the sparkling mosaic underside of the dome, representing the days of the year; 24 pointed arches immediately beneath the dome representing the hours of the day; 12 bigger arches below representing the months the year; and four big windows representing the weeks of the month. The cupola is unusual in early Islamic architecture and has its equal only in Shiraz, Iran.

Gutlug Timur Minaret MINARET

Crossing the road from Turabeg Khanym Complex to the side of the minaret, the path through a modern cemetery and the 19th-century **Sayid Ahmed Mausoleum** leads to the Gutlug Timur Minaret, built in the 1320s. It's the only surviving part of Old Urgench's main mosque. Decorated with bands of brick and a few turquoise tiles, its 59m-tall minaret is not as tall as it once was, and leans noticeably. It's interesting to note that there is no entrance to the minaret – it was linked to the adjacent mosque by a bridge 7m above the ground. Since that mosque was destroyed, the only way into the minaret is by ladder. There are 144 steps to the top, although you can't climb it now.

Kyrk Molla HILL

The mound of graves called the Kyrk Molla (Forty Mullahs Hill) is a sacred place where Konye-Urgench's inhabitants held their last stand against the Mongols. Here you'll see young women rolling down the hill in a fertility rite – one of Konye-Urgench's more curious attractions.

Sultan Tekesh Mausoleum MAUSOLEUM

Instantly recognisable by its conical turquoise dome, the Sultan Tekesh Mausoleum is one of Konye-Urgench's most beautiful monuments. Tekesh was the 12th-century Khorezmshah who made Khorezm great with conquests as far south as Khorasan (present-day northern Iran and northern Afghanistan). It is believed that he built this mausoleum for himself, along with a big medressa and library (which did not survive) on the same spot. However, some scholars theorise that the building had earlier existed as a Zoroastrian temple. After his death in 1200 Tekesh was apparently buried here, although there is no tomb. There are recent excavations of several early Islamic graves near the entrance to the building.

Il-Arslan Mausoleum MAUSOLEUM

The Il-Arslan Mausoleum is Konye-Urgench's oldest standing monument. The conical dome, with a curious zig-zag brick pattern, is the first of its kind and was exported to Samarkand by Timur. Il-Arslan, who died in 1172, was Tekesh's father. The building is small but well worth a close look. The conical dome with 12 faces is unique, and the collapsing floral terracotta moulding on the facade is also unusual.

Mamun II Minaret MINARET

South of the Il-Arslan Mausoleum lies the base of the Mamun II Minaret, which was built in 1011, reduced to a stump by the Mongols, rebuilt in the 14th century and finally toppled by an earthquake in 1895. Nearby you'll see the so-called portal of an unknown building. The structure is now thought to have been the entrance to the palace of Mohammed Khorezmshah, due to its ornateness and the thickness of its walls.

Sleeping

Ürgenç Hotel HOTEL $

(☎3 44 65; Dashogus köçesi; s/d US$14/28; ❄)
The rooms here are clean, spacious and have bathrooms with hot water – a luxury in a small Turkmen town. There's a small chaikhana here too, offering basic breakfasts and hot meals (order in advance). Staff don't speak English, but are very friendly.

Getting There & Away

The town's makeshift bus station is a scrub of land where taxis, marshrutki and buses pick up passengers. It's opposite the Ürgenç Hotel and a taxi ride from the town centre.

One bus per day goes to Ashgabat (30M, seven to eight hours) and regular marshrutki go to Dashogus (4M, two hours). Taxis leave for Ashgabat (per seat 40M) and Dashogus (per seat 7M) at all times of day.

A taxi to the border with Uzbekistan (20km away) should cost 5M and can be picked up anywhere.

Getting Around

The main sights of Konye-Urgench are spread out so it's best to use a car. There is no public transport as such, but you can flag down a taxi on the main roads or by the market. The trip to the southern monuments and back, with waiting time, should be no more than 10M.

Dashogus

322 / POP 210,000

A creation of the Soviet Union, Dashogus is a sprawling industrial city with a neat, soulless centre and nothing to attract visitors. Even its one semi-sight, some idiosyncratic dinosaur statues, has been removed by the authorities for reasons best known to them. For some local colour, head to the excellent **Bai Bazaar**, where you can buy pretty much anything. There's an **internet cafe** (per hr 6M; 9am-9pm) on the main drag, between the Dashogus and Diyarbekir hotels.

Sleeping

Hotel Dashogus HOTEL $

(5 55 06; Turkmenbashi şayoli 5; r US$18;) This centrally located Soviet dinosaur was largely renovated in 2011, and is run by unbelievably friendly staff. Rooms are now absolutely fine and have balconies and hot water, even though the bathrooms are still very basic. There's no breakfast included, but it's available at the restaurant downstairs.

Hotel Uzboy HOTEL $$

(2 60 15; Turkmenbashi şayoli 19/1; s/d/lux incl breakfast US$30/50/70; P) Dashogus' newest hotel is a white-tile construction on the western side of town. Rooms are rather cramped but have been repainted and have good bathrooms, TVs and fridges. Try to get a room away from the atrium, which can be loud in the evenings.

Eating

★**Chaikhana** TEAHOUSE $

(Zilili 9; set menu 12M; 9am-11pm) This is by far the most atmospheric place in Dashogus to eat – a simple, Uzbek-run chaikhana where you'll eat good home-cooked soups, tasty kebabs and fresh bread. It's a five-minute walk from the Hotel Uzboy: from the hotel head towards the white monument with the flag on it and take the last street on the right before the bridge.

Kafé Marat INTERNATIONAL $

(Turkmenbashi şayoli 15; mains 7-32M; 9am-10.30pm) This festively decorated restaurant is a lively downtown institution, where you can choose from kebabs and pizza to meat and fish dishes. It's on the opposite side of the fountain from the Hotel Dashogus.

Getting There & Away

Dashogus airport is 14km south of the city. Flights from Ashgabat to Dashogus (58M, four daily) take about 50 minutes. Turkmenistan Airlines also flies to Turkmenbashi (69M, four weekly), Turkmenabat (65M, once weekly) and Mary (68M, two weekly).

The bus station is near the Bai Bazaar, in the north of the city. Buses regularly go from here to Konye-Urgench (2M, two hours) and once a day at 6am to Ashgabat (20M, nine hours). Due to the bad state of the road, buses for Turkmenabat were not running at the time of research. Shared taxis go from outside the train station and cost 40M per seat to Ashgabat.

The **train station** (4 68 75) is about 600m east of Gurbansoltan köçesi. One painfully slow train per day goes from here to Konye-Urgench (1.5M, four hours) and one goes to Ashgabat at 12.45pm daily (*platskartny/kupe* 5.08M/9.58M, 20 hours).

UNDERSTAND TURKMENISTAN

Turkmenistan Today

In 2007, following the death of Saparmyrat Niyazov (Turkmenbashi), Turkmenistan's bizarre dictator of more than 20 years, Gurbanguly Berdymukhamedov assumed the presidency. Berdymukhamedov made initial reforms that toned down some of his predecessor's policies: the most egregious initiatives, such as renaming the months of the year and the days of the week after Turkmenbashi's family members, a ban on ballet and the prohibition on listening to music in cars, were all lifted. Yet despite these small signs of reform, no further changes have been forthcoming. While the pathological state paranoia that so thrived under Niyazov has also been toned down, travellers wishing to visit the country continue to go through the same rigorous visa channels and must be accompanied by guides in most cases.

The most recent phase of Turkmenistan's development is dubbed 'the New Era', superseding Niyazov's 'Golden Age', and while the personality cult of Turkmenbashi still survives in the form of monuments and statues throughout the country, there's a mood of moving on in the air, with few people even wanting to talk about the man who dominated every aspect of daily life for the past two decades. And while the new president hasn't exhibited the same lust for adoration as his predecessor, portraits of Berdymukhamedov are ubiquitous and he himself enjoys no meagre personality cult.

Berdymukhamedov won an unsurprising re-election as president in 2012, with some 97% of the vote and unanimous praise from his 'rivals'. However, 2010 wikileaks cable transcripts from the US Embassy in Ashgabat suggested that this high opinion of the president wasn't held by all: '[Berdymukhamedov] does not like people who are smarter than he is. Since he's not a very bright guy ... he is suspicious of a lot of people.'

A new gas pipeline connecting Turkmenistan to China opened in late 2009, ensuring access to the world's fastest growing economy and further economic stability beyond the control of Russia, yet it continues to look unlikely that this economic progress will be matched by political reform and democratisation any time soon.

History

From Conquerors to Communists

Stone Age sites have been identified in the Big Balkan Mountains but the first signs of agricultural settlements appeared in Kopet Dag in the 6th millennium BC. More Bronze Age sites have been located in the Margiana Oasis, where archaeologist Viktor Sarianidi has identified a sophisticated culture that encompassed several villages and an extensive capital. Rivers that shifted over the centuries caused the abandonment of these settlements, but paved the way for a great civilization around Merv. Alexander the Great established a city here on his way to India.

Around the time of Christ, the Parthians, Rome's main rivals for power in the West, set up a capital at Nissa, near present-day Ashgabat. In the 11th century the Seljuq Turks appropriated Merv, Alexander's old city and a Silk Road staging post, as a base from which to expand into Afghanistan.

Two centuries later Chinggis (Genghis) Khan stormed down from the steppes and through Trans-Caspia (the region east of the Caspian Sea) to lay waste to Central Asia. Entire city-states, including Merv and Konye-Urgench, were razed and their populations slaughtered. Unlike Samarkand and Bukhara, the cities to the south failed to recover.

It's not known precisely when the first modern Turkmen appeared, but they are believed to have arrived in modern Turkmenistan in the wake of the Seljuk Turks some time in the 11th century. A collection of displaced nomadic horse-breeding tribes, possibly from the foothills of the Altay Mountains, they found alternative pastures in the oases fringing the Karakum desert and in Persia, Syria and Anatolia (in present-day Turkey). Being nomads, they had no concept of, or interest in, statehood and therefore existed in parallel to the constant dynastic shifts that so totally determined Central Asia's history.

Terrorising the Russians, who had come to 'civilise' the region in the early 19th century, Turkmen captured thousands of the tsar's troops, and sold them into slavery in Khiva and Bukhara. This invited the wrath of the Russian Empire, which finally quelled the wild nomads by massacring thousands of them at Geok-Depe in 1881.

After the Bolshevik revolution in 1917, the communists took Ashgabat in 1919. For a while the region existed as the Turkmen *oblast* (province) of the Turkestan Autonomous Soviet Socialist Republic, before becoming the Turkmen Soviet Socialist Republic (SSR) in 1924.

The Turkmen SSR

Inflamed by Soviet attempts to settle the tribes and collectivise farming, Turkmen resistance continued and a guerrilla war raged until 1936. More than a million Turkmen fled into the Karakum desert or into northern Iran and Afghanistan rather than give up their nomadic ways. The Turkmen also fell foul of a Moscow-directed campaign against religion. Of the 441 mosques in Turkmenistan in 1911, only five remained standing by 1941.

Waves of Russian immigrants brought with them farming technology and blueprints for cotton fields. Turkmenistan's arid climate was hardly conducive to bumper harvests, and to supply the vast quantities of water required the authorities began work in the 1950s on a massive irrigation ditch – the Karakum Canal. The 1100km-long gully runs the length of the republic, bleeding the Amu-Darya (Oxus River) to create a fertile band across the south. Cotton production quadrupled, though the consequences for the Aral Sea have been catastrophic.

In 1985 the relatively unknown Saparmyrat Niyazov was elected General Secretary of the Communist Party of Turkmenistan (CPT) and retained power until the collapse of the Soviet Union. Although totally unprepared for the event, Niyazov was forced to declare independence for Turkmenistan on 27 October 1991.

Independence & the Golden Age

Determined to hold on to power, Niyazov renamed the CPT the Democratic Party of Turkmenistan, before banning all other parties. His cult of personality began to flourish, starting with an order that everyone call him Turkmenbashi, which translates as 'leader of the Turkmen'. The president erected gold statues of himself and plastered buildings with his image. His slogan 'Halk, Watan, Turkmenbaşi' ('People, Nation, Me' – an eerie echo of Hitler's 'Ein Volk, Ein Reich, Ein Führer') was ubiquitous.

Tapping Turkmenistan's vast oil and gas reserves, Niyazov promised a Kuwait-style economy with enormous private wealth. Most of the profits, however, ended up funding ostentatious public-works projects. Public dissent was somewhat placated by large government subsidies for gas, water and electricity.

The free ride was part of Niyazov's much touted 'Turkmen Golden Age' (Altyn Asyr), though its less benevolent side was the Orwellian control of the media that caused Reporters Without Borders to rank Turkmenistan second to last in its press freedom index (just one spot ahead of North Korea).

Despite avoiding an assassin's bullet in 2002, Turkmenbashi proved mortal when he passed away on 21 December 2006, aged 66, the result of a massive heart attack. Having groomed no heir, his death left a power vacuum that for a brief moment opened the door for democratic reform and the return of exiled dissidents. Instead, a surprisingly smooth transfer of power occurred when Deputy Prime Minister Gurbanguly Berdymukhamedov grabbed the reins of power and won backing from Niyazov's inner circle.

He was rubber stamped into office after elections in February 2007 (having won 90% of the popular vote in elections where only the Democratic Party of Turkmenistan fielded candidates, and even Berdymukhamedov's 'rivals' openly supported him). Berdymukhamedov had been Turkmenistan's health minister and rumours that he is the former president's illegitimate son have being doing the rounds for some time. While this is unlikely – Niyazov was only 17 years old when Berdymukhamedov was born – the two men do bear an uncanny resemblance.

RECOMMENDED READING

➡ *Daily Life in Turkmenbashy's Golden Age* (2010) by Sam Tranum. Engaging and perceptive account of two years' work and travel in Turkmenistan from a then Peace Corps volunteer. The best of a crop of volunteer memoirs from Central Asia.

➡ *Unknown Sands: Journeys Around the World's Most Isolated Country* (Dusty Spark, 2006), by John W Kropf. A travel memoir by an American who spent two years living in Ashgabat. Despite living within the confines of the diplomatic community, Kropf manages to sneak away from the capital to give us a perspective of life on the ground for ordinary Turkmen.

➡ *Tribal Nation: The Making of Soviet Turkmenistan* (2006), by Adrienne Lynn Edgar. A scholarly account of the Soviet creation of Turkmenistan, with well-researched details on Soviet nation building of the 1920s and 1930s. The book also provides an understanding of Turkmen language and tribal law.

People

Turkmen remain nomadic at heart, if not still in practice, and carry themselves in a simple yet dignified manner that reflects their rural lifestyle. Nomadic rules, including the treatment of guests, still dominate home life.

Turkmen are guided spiritually by a unique form of Central Asian animism. Holiday breaks are thus used for pilgrimage time. Women in particular use these pilgrimages as an opportunity to take a break from their home life, and you may see caravans of women on buses, headed to shrines around the country where they'll camp, cook and pray.

By the standards of many Muslim societies, women in Turkmenistan enjoy a good amount of freedom and choice. In most cases they tend to be home-makers and mothers, as well as often working in the fields to cultivate crops. Bucking this trend is an urban elite of educated, Westernised women in Ashgabat who work in all fields and enjoy most of the freedoms of their male counterparts. Very few women wear the veil in Turkmenistan, though colourful scarves on the head are ubiquitous.

Population

The population of Turkmenistan is estimated to be just over five million; a census was undertaken in 2012, but its results remained unpublished at the time of writing. Uzbeks, who make up about 5% of the population, live in the border cities of Konye-Urgench, Dashogus and Turkmenabat. Russians have left in huge numbers since independence, as it becomes increasingly hard to work without speaking Turkmen, and dual citizenship was phased out in 2013.

Religion

Turkmen are deeply spiritual people without being particularly religious compared with people in nearby Iran or Afghanistan. Their traditional animist beliefs have been blended over the centuries with Islam, and evidence of this is clear at mosques and mausoleums, which are often decorated with animist features such as snakes and rams' horns. Likewise, pilgrims arrive at these sites bearing tokens such as miniature cribs, indicating a desire for children.

Sunni Islam is the state religion. Despite Turkmenistan's constitutional guarantee of free practice for all faiths, in reality Islam and Orthodox Christianity are the only freely practised religions.

Arts

Turkmen carpets are world famous and can be seen just about everywhere, although the best place to see them is in the bazaar. Silk, embroidery, silver and jewellery are other crafts that have been perfected over the centuries.

The arts have not thrived since the end of Soviet rule. Theatres remain active, albeit with Turkmen-only song-and-dance acts, concerts and drama performances. The most impressive traditional singing, *bakhshi,* deals with folklore, battles and love, and is accompanied by a *dutar* (two-stringed guitar).

Between the Soviets and Niyazov, contemporary Turkmen literature has been all but destroyed. Rahim Esenov was Turkmenistan's best literary hope until he was jailed (in 2004) following the publication of his book *The Crowned Wanderer*. Turkmen are encouraged to read the writings of poet Magtymguly Feraghy (1733–83) and, increasingly, those of President Berdymukhamedov, whose voluminous contributions to literature include a book on wild flowers.

Environment

Effectively a giant desert ringed by oases along the country's borders, Turkmenistan is home to far more varied landscapes than you might expect. To the east are the canyons and lush mountains of the Kugitang Nature Reserve, while to the south the Kopet Dag range rises up in a line towards the Caspian Sea. The territory along the Caspian is particularly unusual – vast mud flats, coloured canyons and the enormous bulk of the Big Balkan massif make this one of the more bleakly beautiful places in the country.

Wildlife

The most famous of Turkmenistan's many interesting species is the Akhal-Teke horse, a beautiful golden creature that is believed to be the ancestor of today's purebred.

Dromedaries (Arabian camels) are everywhere, wandering scenically between villages and towns. Many of the Karakum's nastiest inhabitants are really exciting to see in real life – most importantly the *zemzen*, or *varan*, a large monitor lizard – though these are extremely rare. Despite its large size and particularly painful bite, Turkmen have traditionally welcomed the giant lizard as it devours or scares away snakes (such as cobras), eats mice and eradicates colonies of sandflies. You are also likely to see desert foxes, owls and the very common desert squirrel.

Tarantulas and black widow spiders are both indigenous to Turkmenistan, although you are unlikely to see them. Cobras, vipers and scorpions can all be found in the desert, so tread with caution.

Environmental Issues

Turkmenistan has paid a heavy price for the irrigation of its southern belt, using source water bound for the Aral Sea. While the Aral Sea is in Uzbekistan and Kazakhstan, its disappearance has led to desperate environmental problems in northern Turkmenistan, with the salination of the land taking its toll on the health of local people. Overfishing is another concern, as caviar-bearing sturgeon become rarer in the Caspian Sea. There is very little environmental consciousness in Turkmenistan, where no one bothers to save gas, electricity or water because all are subsidised by the government.

Food & Drink

Similar to other Central Asian countries, shashlyk is the staple dish across Turkmenistan and is considered at its best when cooked over the branches of a saxaul tree. Other favoured snacks include *samsa* (samosa; meat-filled pastries), *plov* (meat, rice and carrots) and a variation on the meat pastry called *fitchi*, which is larger and round in shape.

Dograma, made from bread and pieces of boiled meat and onions, is a traditional Turkmen meal. Other soups include *chorba* (soup of boiled mutton with potato, carrot and turnip, known elsewhere in the region as *shorpa*). *Manty* (steamed dumplings) served with sour cream is another popular dish.

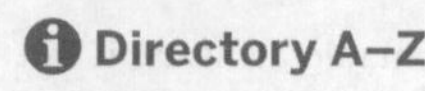

SURVIVAL GUIDE

Directory A–Z

ACCOMMODATION

As a rule hotels throughout the country are easily divided into dilapidated Soviet-era behemoths and newer three- and four-star ventures built since independence. Turkmen citizens can stay at a hotel at a discounted rate, which is usually 60% to 80% less than the price that foreigners are charged. So while you may have to pay for the lodging of your guide, this shouldn't cost more than a few dollars. Do note that foreigners have to pay for hotels in Turkmenistan in cash US dollars, save in the few hotels in the country that accept credit cards.

It's illegal for tourists to sleep in a private home if a licensed hotel exists in the same city; some travellers have got in trouble for staying with a family or in unlicensed guesthouses. This law does not apply for travellers on a transit visa, who do not require registration.

Camping is often the only option in remote places such as the Yangykala Canyon and the Darvaza Gas Craters, and most guides can provide tents and sleeping bags.

ACTIVITIES

Horse-lovers from around the world flock to Turkmenistan to ride the unique Akhal-Teke thoroughbreds. Many travel agencies offer specialist horse-trekking tours with these beautiful creatures.

CUSTOMS REGULATIONS

In Turkmenistan official regulations state that you need permission to export any carpet more than 6 sq m, though trying to export a smaller one without an export licence is also likely to be problematic. In all cases it's best to take your carpet to the Carpet Museum (p374) in Ashgabat, where there is a bureau that will value and tax your purchase, and provide an export licence. This can take up to a few days. There are

PRACTICALITIES

- The main daily newspapers are *Turkmenistan* and the Russian-language *Nevtralny Turkmenistan* (*Neutral Turkmenistan*). All papers glorify the president, as is obvious from the pictures on the front pages. There is no independent or privately owned press.
- The six national TV channels show scenes of Turkmen culture and nature. Satellite TV is widely available in larger cities, and remains the main source of objective news for all Turkmen.

several fees to pay. One certifies that the carpet is not antique, which usually costs US$10 to US$30, while a second is an export fee that costs around US$50 per square metre. As with all government taxes on foreigners, these are paid in US dollars. When you buy a carpet at a state shop, these fees will be included in the price, but double check before handing over your money. Those in a hurry are best advised to buy from one of the many government shops in Ashgabat, where all carpets come complete with an export licence. Despite being more expensive than purchases made at Tolkuchka Bazaar, this still works out as very good value.

DANGERS & ANNOYANCES

Take care when photographing public buildings, especially in Ashgabat. Local police take this seriously and you may have your documents checked even if simply strolling near the Presidential Palace with a camera in your hand. There are no 'no photo' signs anywhere, so you'll need to ask the nearest policeman if it's OK to take a picture.

EMBASSIES & CONSULATES

Turkmen Embassies in Central Asia

Turkmen embassies can be found in Kazakhstan (p126), Uzbekistan (p222) and Tajikistan (p365).

Turkmen Embassies & Consulates in Other Countries

A full list of Turkmen embassies abroad can be found at www.mfa.gov.tm/functions/tmd.html (in Russian).

Turkmen Embassy, Azerbaijan (☎994 12 596 3527; Jalil Mammedguluzade 85/266 14, Baku, Azerbaijan)

Turkmen Embassy, China (☎+86 10 6532 6975; www.turkmenembassy.cn; King's Garden Villas, D-1, Xiaoyunlu 18, 100016, Beijing, China)

Turkmen Embassy, France (☎0153 651 071; 13 rue Picot, 75016, Paris, France)

Turkmen Embassy, Germany (☎030 3010 2451; www.botschaft-turkmenistan.de; Langobardenalle 14, D-14052, Berlin, Germany)

Turkmen Embassy, Iran (☎98 5199 940 584; Kucheye Konsulgari 34, Beydane Shahidan, Mashhad, Iran)

Turkmen Embassy, Russia (☎7 495 691 6636; Filipovsky proyezd 22, Moscow, Russia)

Turkmen Embassy, UK (☎020 7610 5239; www.turkmenembassy.org.uk; 131 Holland Park Ave, London W11 4UT)

Turkmen Embassy, USA (☎202 588 1500; www.turkmenistanembassy.org; 2207 Massachusetts Ave, NW 20008, Washington DC, USA)

Embassies & Consulates in Turkmenistan

Afghan Embassy (Map p380; ☎993 6569 4613, 48 07 57; Garaşsyzlyk şayoli 4/4, Berzengi; ⏰lodging 9am-10.30pm, collection 2-4pm Mon-Fri)

Azerbaijan Embassy (Map p376; ☎391 447, 39 1102; www.azembassyashg.com; Ata Govshundov 112; ⏰9am-1pm lodging, 4.30-6pm collection Mon-Fri)

French Embassy (Map p376; ☎36 35 50, 36 34 68; www.ambafrance-tm.org; 2029 köçesi 38; ⏰9am-1pm & 2-5pm Mon-Fri)

German Embassy (Map p376; ☎36 35 15, 36 35 17; www.auswaertiges-amt.de; Ak Altyn Hotel, Magtymguly şayoli; ⏰9am-noon Mon-Fri)

Iranian Embassy (Map p376; ☎34 14 52; Tehran köçesi 3; ⏰9.30am-11.30am lodging, 11.30am-12.30pm collection Mon-Fri)

Kazakhstan Embassy (Map p380; ☎48 04 69, 48 04 72; Garaşsyzlyk şayoli 11/13, Berzengi; ⏰lodging 9am-noon, collection 5-6pm Tue-Fri)

Kyrgyz Embassy (Map p380; ☎48 22 95; Garaşsyzlyk şayoli 17, Berzengi; ⏰9am-1pm Mon-Fri)

Russian Embassy (Map p376; ☎94 07 41, 94 03 88; www.turkmenistan.mid.ru; Turkmenbashi şayoli 11; ⏰9am-12.30pm Mon, Tue, Thu & Fri)

Tajik Embassy (Map p380; ☎48 18 45; Garaşsyzlyk şayoli 4/2, Berzengi; ⏰9.30am-1pm & 3-6pm Mon-Fri)

UK Embassy (Map p376; ☎36 34 62; 3rd fl, Ak Altyn Hotel, Magtymguly şayoli; ⏰8.30am-12.30pm & 1-4.30pm Mon-Fri)

US Embassy (Map p376; ☎94 00 45; turkmenistan.usembassy.gov; 1984 köçesi 9; ⏰9am-1pm & 2-6pm Mon-Fri)

Uzbek Embassy (Map p376; ☎97 10 62; Görogly köçesi 50A; ⏰10am-1pm & 2-6pm Mon, Wed & Fri)

HOLIDAYS

Turkmenistan has a great number of holidays, though the country largely continues to work as normal during most of them.

1 January New Year

12 January Remembrance Day (Battle of Geok-Depe)

19 February Flag Day (President's Birthday)

8 March Women's Day

21 March Navrus (spring festival); date varies

April (first Sunday) Drop of Water is a Grain of Gold Day

April (last Sunday) Horse Day

9 May Victory Day

18 May Day of Revival & Unity

19 May Magtymguly Poetry Day
May (last Sunday) Carpet Day
August (second Sunday) Melon Holiday
6 October Remembrance Day (1948 Earthquake)
27 & 28 October Independence Day
November (first Saturday) Health Day
November (last Sunday) Harvest Festival
7 December Good Neighbourliness Day
12 December Neutrality Day

INTERNET ACCESS

Internet access, once horrendously slow, expensive and limited to top hotels in Ashgabat, is now available in all big towns through state-run internet cafes. Prices are standardised at 6M per hour, and you'll need to leave your passport with the administrator while you surf. As all internet access is via the state-run www.online.tm, bear in mind that out-going emails may be monitored and many websites (mainly news and politics sites, but also Facebook and Twitter) are blocked, so save any plotting to overthrow the government until you're back home. The only reliable wireless in the country can be found for free at the Sofitel Ashgabat Oguzkent Hotel (p379).

MONEY

The currency in Turkmenistan is the manat (M), which is made up of 100 tenne. There is no longer a black-market currency exchange, which has made everything far more expensive for visitors. All exchange offices change dollars at the fixed rate of 2.85M to the US dollar. Exchange offices are everywhere, take no commission, and will freely exchange US dollars and euros back and forth (you don't need to worry about having official certificates in order to change your money back when you leave the country, for example). US dollars remain the currency of choice for Turkmenistan, and it's best to bring them in various denominations. Notes often need to be in very good condition to be accepted. Euro are also generally easy to change, though less so outside Ashgabat. Don't bring other currencies.

Everything bought in Turkmenistan will be paid for in manats, but travel agencies and hotels still usually require payment in US dollars, so it's best to keep a supply of both currencies with you on the road.

Cash advances on credit cards are only available in Ashgabat at banks and, if you're lucky, at the few functioning ATMs taking international cards (the only reliable one we found was in the Sofitel Ashgabat Oguzkent Hotel (p379), and dispensed only manats). Outside Ashgabat, emergency money can be wired through Western Union only. Credit cards are accepted by a few luxury hotels in Ashgabat but by few other places, and you'd be ill advised to rely on them anywhere. Travellers cheques are not accepted anywhere.

POST

Your post may be read first, but at some stage it should be delivered unless your postcard is truly offensive. Sending a postcard anywhere in the world costs 2M and a 20g letter costs around 2.20M. There are post offices in all towns, usually in the same place as the international phone centre and state-run internet cafe.

REGISTRATION

Anyone entering Turkmenistan on a tourist or business visa must be registered within three working days with the State Service for the Registration of Foreign Citizens (aka OVIR) via the local bureau of the state tourism company. The tour company that invited you will undoubtedly organise this. You will need two passport photos and your entry card, which you'll need to pick up at the airport or the border post where you enter the country. As well as this initial registration, you will automatically be registered by any hotel you stay at in the country for each night you stay with them – this service is included in the room price, and you won't have to do anything. However, travellers on tourist visas are therefore only able to stay in hotels with licences to register foreigners, the only exceptions being when you spend the night in a place without such an establishment, making these the only legal opportunities to stay in a homestay. Transit visa holders do not need to be registered, and can sleep wherever they please.

TELEPHONE

You can call internationally and nationally from most big towns at the main telegraph office, often referred to by its Russian name, *glavny telegraf*.

The major mobile phone provider is MTS (look for the sign MTC – MTS in Cyrillic). Prepaid SIM cards (which allow internet use through a smart phone) are available very cheaply from its offices, though at the time of writing foreigners were only able to purchase them at the main MTS office in the Russian Bazaar (p382) in Ashgabat.

TRAVEL & TOUR AGENCIES

Any traveller not simply in transit through Turkmenistan will usually make contact with one of the following agencies to organise their letter of invitation (LOI). The following companies offer comprehensive services including LOIs, guides, drivers, hotel bookings, city tours and excursions.

Ayan Travel (Map p380; ☎22 16 14, 22 05 03; www.ayan-travel.com; Turkmenbaşy şayoli 81)

Offers comprehensive services including LOIs, guides, drivers, hotel bookings, city tours and other excursions.

Dagsyýahat (Map p376; ☎93 25 59, 93 04 63; tss@online.tm; Hotel Daýhan, Azadi köçesi 69) Offer all services to travellers, including LOIs, guides, drivers and hotel bookings. English-speaking staff at its Ashgabat office are very helpful.

DN Tours (Map p376; ☎27 06 21, 27 04 39; www.dntours.com; Magtymguly şayoli 50) DN Tours offer comprehensive services including LOIs, guides, drivers, hotel bookings, city tours and other excursions.

Stantours (☎+49 3212 103 99 60; www.stantours.com; Almaty) Stantours offer a very high standard of service with their knowledgeable, reliable English-speaking local staff on the ground in Turkmenistan. As well as arranging visa support and tours to every corner of the country and beyond, the Stantours team provide good advice on how to structure trips and are able to tailor itineraries to most budgets and interests. Its main office is in Almaty, Kazakhstan, through which Turkmenistan tours are arranged.

Tourism-Owadan (Map p376; ☎93 04 86; www.owadan.net; Azadi köçesi 65) Offers comprehensive services including LOIs, guides, drivers, hotel bookings, city tours and other excursions throughout the entire country.

TRAVEL PERMITS

Permits are needed to visit the border regions of Turkmenistan. Given that the centre of the country is largely uninhabited desert and the population lies on the periphery, you need permits for some of the most interesting areas. Ashgabat, Mary, Merv, Turkmenabat and Balkanabat are not restricted, but anywhere outside these areas should be listed on your visa, thus giving you permission to go there. Travellers on transit visas can usually transit the border zones along the relevant main road, if they correspond to the country they are supposed to exit to. If you get a tourist or business visa on arrival, you'll automatically have your visa endorsed for all areas of the country.

The following areas are termed 'class one' border zones and entry without documentation is theoretically not possible, though there's actually little chance you'll have your documents checked:

Eastern Turkmenistan Farab, Atamurat (Kerki) plus adjoining areas, Kugitang Nature Reserve, Tagtabazar, Serkhetabat.

Northern Turkmenistan Entire Dashogus region including Konye-Urgench, Dargan-Ata, Gazachak.

Western Turkmenistan Bekdash, Turkmenbashi, Hazar, Dekhistan, Yangykala, Gyzyletrek, Garrygala, Nokhur and surrounding villages.

VISAS FOR ONWARD TRAVEL

Turkmenistan is generally a poor place to pick up visas, with long processing times and embassies that aren't used to independent travellers.

Afghanistan

The Afghan Embassy (p401) can issue one-month tourist visas for US$102. You need to show a letter from your embassy supporting your application, which few embassies will provide, so it's better to get an Afghan visa at home. Transit visas are not issued here.

Azerbaijan

The Azerbaijan Embassy (p401) issues single entry (US$50) and double entry (US$100) tourist visas in five working days. You'll need a copy of your passport, a copy of your birth certificate, two photos and an LOI. Transit visas are not issued.

Iran

Transit visas are processed in 10 days (€30) or 24 hours (€45) at Iran's embassy (p401), as well as 15-day tourist visas in 10 days (€40) or 24 hours (€60). You'll need two passport photos and a copy of the certificate from Saderat Bank at Magtymguly şayoli 181a, showing that you've paid the money into the embassy's account.

Kazakhstan

The Kazakhstan Embassy (p401) issues one-month tourist visas (US$40) and five-day transit visas (US$20); both need five working days to be processed. You'll need a photo, a letter of invitation and a copy of your passport for a tourist visa, and a valid visa for a third country and a plane/train ticket through Kazakhstan to get a transit visa.

Kyrgyzstan

The Kyrgyz Embassy (p401) issues one-month tourist visas (US$50) in seven to 10 working days. However, most travellers no longer require a visa for Kyrgyzstan.

Tajikistan

One-month tourist visas (US$25) are issued at the Tajik Embassy (p401) to anyone with a letter of invititation. You'll need a copy of your passport and the visa will be issued on the same day. Transit visas (US$20) require a third country visa and a plane/train ticket of some kind.

Uzbekistan

The Uzbek Embassy (p401) issues one-month tourist visas (US$75) in three working days. You'll need a copy of your passport, a form filled out online (http://evisa.mfa.uz/evisa_en) and a photo. Transit visas cost US$55 and require a third country visa and a plane/train ticket.

VISAS FOR TURKMENISTAN

All foreigners require a visa to enter Turkmenistan and transit visas are the only visas issued without a letter of invitation (LOI). Prices for visas vary enormously from embassy to embassy.

As a general rule, plan on getting a visa at least six weeks ahead of entry to Turkmenistan, as the process (even for transit visas) is lengthy. Ideally work through a Turkmen travel agent with experience in the field. On entry every visa holder will need to pay an additional US$12 to US$14 fee for an entry card that will list your exit point in Turkmenistan.

Tourist or business visas on arrival are hassle free these days, and are processed quickly at Ashgabat airport (around US$100), as well as being available at the Farab border crossings. For people arriving by boat from Azerbaijan the visa is available on arrival in Turkmenbashi (by arrangement with the consul, who needs to be present), but the Azeri authorities will not let a person without a valid Turkmenistan visa board the ferry in Baku.

For information on registration, see p402; for travel permits, see p403.

Transit Visas

The only visa that allows unaccompanied travel for tourists is the transit visa. Relatively easy to come by, they are normally valid for three days, although sometimes for five days and in rare cases, more. Turkmen embassies in Europe (as opposed to those in Central Asia or Iran) are more likely to grant longer visas. Transit visas can be obtained at any Turkmen consulate, although if you apply without an LOI, the application will need to be forwarded to the Ministry of Foreign Affairs in Ashgabat, meaning a processing time of around 10 to 14 days.

No transit visa is extendable, save in the case of serious illness. The penalty for overstaying a transit visa is US$200, and you may be taken back to Ashgabat and deported on the next available flight at your expense.

Your route will normally not be indicated on the visa, but your entry and exit point (unchangeable) will be, and you may therefore run into trouble going anywhere not obviously between the two points, though document checks on the roads are few and far between these days. Transit visas are usually not valid if you are dealing with a Kazakh routing, a double-entry Uzbekistan visa or even an air ticket out of Ashgabat. Turkmen embassies regularly refuse transit visa applications, so don't count on getting one.

Tourist Visas

Tourist visas are a mixed blessing in Turkmenistan. While they allow the visitor to spend a decent amount of time in the country (up to three weeks as a rule), they require accompaniment by an accredited tour guide, who will meet you at the border and remain with you throughout your trip.

Getting There & Away

ENTERING TURKMENISTAN

Entering the country overland tends to invite more scrutiny than arriving by air. Baggage checks can be very thorough at lonely border posts, while the understaffed airport in Ashgabat seems more interested in processing people quickly rather than pawing through your underwear. You'll need to pay your arrival tax and collect your Entry Travel Pass if you're travelling on a tourist or business visa.

AIR

The only international airport in Turkmenistan is Saparmurat Turkmenbashi Airport (p383) in Ashgabat. For information on flights in and out of Saparmurat Turkmenbashi Airport, see p383.

LAND

Visitors with visas can enter Turkmenistan from all bordering countries, although the borders with Uzbekistan and Iran are the most frequently used. There are no international train or bus services to or from Turkmenistan. All land borders are open from 9am to 6pm daily.

To/From Afghanistan

Serkhetabat (formerly known as Gushgi) is the border town with Afghanistan. Crossing here is now a fairly hassle-free prospect, although be prepared to be thoroughly searched by both Turkmen and Afghan border guards. If you arrive late you'll need to overnight with a local family as there are no hotels in town.

This obviously has cost implications, as you will have to pay your guide a daily rate (usually between US$30 and US$50), as well as pay for their meals and hotels. The latter cost is very small, however, as Turkmen citizens pay a local rate that is at least 60% to 80% less than the foreigner rate. Guides will allow you to roam freely in Ashgabat and the immediate environs unaccompanied, as well as around any other large town – there's no legal requirement for them to be with you throughout the day, but you're not legally allowed to travel in Turkmenistan without them. Most tour companies insist you travel in private transport with the guide.

You can only get a tourist visa by going through a travel agency, as only travel agencies with a licence from the Turkmen government can issue LOIs. Many unaccredited agencies still offer LOI services, however, simply by going through an accredited agency themselves. The LOI will be issued with a list of all restricted border regions you are planning to visit. In turn, these are the places that will be listed on your visa, therefore it's essential you decide what you want to see before applying so that the appropriate restricted regions can be listed. The LOI is approved by the OVIR and takes five days. Anyone working in the media or human rights fields or for political organisations had better not state this on their application, as it's certain to be rejected. Employers are rarely called and asked to verify an applicant's position, but it can happen, so have a good cover story if you work in one of these fields.

Once the LOI is issued (usually emailed to you by your travel agent), you can take it to any Turkmen embassy to get your visa. The original LOI is not needed. The issuing of the visa itself is purely a formality, once the LOI has been issued. Normal processing time is three to seven working days depending on the embassy, but most Turkmen embassies offer an express service for a hefty surcharge, reducing processing time to between 24 hours and three days.

Armed with an LOI there is also the possibility of getting a visa on arrival at Ashgabat airport or the Farab border post by prior arrangement with your travel agent. In the case of Farab, the agent needs to arrange for the consul to be present. In any case the original LOI must be taken to the relevant border and the visa will be issued then and there.

On arrival in Turkmenistan, you must be met by your guide (*geed* in Russian) who will bring you a small green travel document, the Entry Travel Pass (*putyovka* in Russian). You should only exit the country at the point indicated on the travel permit, although if you alter your route there is the possibility of changing this in Ashgabat. To do this you will have to speak to your travel agent or guide and they can see what they can do. It is often possible to extend tourist visas in Ashgabat, again, only with the assistance of your travel agent.

The border post is 3km south of Serkhetabat. Leaving Turkmenistan, there's a 1.5km walk to the first Afghan village of Torghundi and it's a two-hour taxi journey onwards to Herat. If you are coming to Turkmenistan, you'll need to catch a ride from Herat to Torghundi (US$20 in a shared vehicle). Here you need to pay a US$12 to US$14 customs fee at a bank in town (1.5km south of the border), or you might be able to pay an extra 'tip' to the border guard to do this for you.

The Saparmurat border crossing (called Imam Nazar) near Atamurat (also known as Kerki) is used by UN staff, but was not recommended for independent travellers at the time of writing.

To/From Iran

The simplest exit point is Gaudan/Bajgiran, due south of Ashgabat and a corridor between the Kopet Dag into Iran. From Ashgabat, take a taxi (40M to 50M) for the 20km ride to Yablonovka checkpoint. Here you'll have your passport checked, after which you take a marshrutka shuttle to the border. Once through, it's a taxi (US$2.50) across some 20km of no-man's-land to Bajgiran where you can get buses or taxis (US$20, four hours) to Mashhad.

There are also borders with Iran at Saraghs (there is a Mashhad–Saraghs train, but no international trains into Turkmenistan) and Gudurolum (which is reachable by car or taxi only).

To/From Kazakhstan

Shared taxis (120M/480M per seat/car) go from Turkmenbashi, via Garabogaz, across the Kazakh border and on to Zhanaozen (Novy Uzen), where there is further transport to Aktau. From Karabogas to the border the road's a rough dirt track. Delays at the border can occur when caravans of traders appear together. Note that there is absolutely nothing on either side of this remote border – do not try to save money by paying for a taxi to the border post alone, as you'd be extremely lucky to find any onward transport from here.

To/From Uzbekistan

There are three crossings into Turkmenistan from Uzbekistan. Each crossing requires a walk of about 10 to 20 minutes across a ridiculously wide band of no-man's-land. Shared taxis are sometimes available to shuttle travellers across, the cost of which is approximately US$1. Whether they are operating or not when you visit is a matter of luck.

The Farab crossing is closest to Bukhara (Uzbekistan) and Turkmenabat (Turkmenistan). The 45km taxi ride to Farab from Turkmenabat should cost 15M for a taxi or 4M for a seat in a shared taxi. From the border, take a taxi (US$20) to Bukhara, or hire a taxi as far as Uzbek Olot (or Karakol), where you can change to a shared taxi.

The Dashogus crossing is best if you are headed for Khiva or Urgench. A taxi from Dashogus to the Uzbek border is no more than 5M. From the border to Khiva expect to pay around US$10.

Less used is the Hojeli crossing, a 10-minute taxi ride (6M) from Konye-Urgench. Once across the border it's a half-hour drive to Nukus in Karakalpakstan. From the border, take public transport to Hojeli (US$2) or a taxi all the way to Nukus (US$10).

SEA

You can leave and enter Turkmenistan at Turkmenbashi by ferry to/from Baku in Azerbaijan. (p385).

Getting Around

Travellers on tourist visas will have to travel with a guide, and guides usually have their own cars or 4WDs, so getting around Turkmenistan will always be comfortable and straightforward, though not very cheap. It's rare for guides to travel by public transport with you, but it can happen, and will save you some money if it does: try requesting this option in good time with a travel agency, but be aware that it's not normal. Business and transit visa holders will be able to make full use of the public transport options.

ENTRY & DEPARTURE TAX

For entry into Turkmenistan there is a US$12 to US$14 fee per person, depending on your nationality. Bring cash in US dollars for this; change is normally available. International air departure tax is now included in all airline ticket prices. There is no departure tax for domestic travel, nor by land or sea.

AIR

Air transport is super cheap and generally reliable, and well-worth considering if you're in a hurry. Domestic Turkmenistan Airlines flights are heavily subsidised, making the ticket prices amazingly low. Consequently, demand is high and flights need to be booked in advance. Turkmenistan Airlines serves the country's main cities with a fleet of modern Boeing 717s. As the main hub, most flights go in and out of Ashgabat, though there are also flights from Dashogus to Turkmenbashi, Mary and Turkmenabat; from Mary to Turkmenbashi; and from Turkmenbashi to Turkmenabat.

CAR & MOTORCYCLE

Driving through Turkmenistan is perfectly possible, but expensive and full of hassles (road blocks, poor roads) and extra charges. Significantly, there's also a road tax calculated by the kilometre for your route through the country.

MARSHRUTKIS, MINIBUSES & SHARED TAXIS

Marshrutkis and minibuses are the most effective way to get around, though they're cramped for long journeys and you'll often have to wait for some time until they're full for them to depart. Shared taxis are a good alternative to marshrutkas, being faster and more comfortable (and you can even buy the remaining seats in a vehicle if you're in a hurry to get going).

TRAINS

Trains are slow, but comfortable and a great way to see the countryside and meet people.

Understand Central Asia

Central Asia Today

For the people of ex-Soviet Central Asia it's been a turbulent couple of decades since independence in 1991. Each of the republics have grappled with economic collapse, population shifts and resurgent Islam. All have reinvented their past, rehabilitating historical heroes and reinforcing their national languages in an attempt to redefine and shore up what it means to be Central Asian. Despite years of political repression and faltering economies, life is improving slowly, if unevenly, across the region.

Best of Print

The Lost Heart of Asia
(Colin Thubron)
Our favourite travel writer captures the region in beautiful prose. Also try his more recent *Shadow of the Silk Road.*

The Great Game
(Peter Hopkirk)
Fast-paced and immensely readable account of 19th-century Victorian derring-do.

The Land that Disappeared
(Christopher Robbins)
Excellent contemporary account of Kazakhstan.

Best News Websites

Radio Free Europe/Radio Liberty www.rferl.org

New Eurasia www.neweurasia.net

Registan www.registan.net

EurasiaNet www.eurasianet.org

Differing Paths

In addressing their shared post-independence challenges the Central Asian governments are forging quite different paths. Turkmenistan and Kazakhstan are the only republics that seem to have bright economic prospects – sitting pretty on enormous reserves of oil and gas.

Tajikistan is the only one to have experienced the horror of civil war, while the others are all in dread that they will be next to succumb to Islamic fundamentalism and political meltdown. Uzbekistan and (to a lesser extent) Turkmenistan have faced this challenge by sliding into pariah states, where political abductions, torture and trumped-up charges are commonplace.

Only Kyrgyzstan has embraced democracy, with mixed results. The street demonstrations and political violence that unseated Kyrgyz president Bakiev and pushed Kyrgyzstan to the brink of civil war in 2010 have continued with regular street protests.

Political Tensions

The Central Asian republics (particularly Uzbekistan) look south to turbulent Afghanistan in horror, using the perceived threat of Islamic insurgency to justify their increasingly repressive policies. Isolated bombings in Uzbekistan, Turkmenistan and Tajikistan have underscored the threat but it's hard to say whether armed attacks are the cause for repression, or rather a result of it.

Despite claims of Central Asian fraternity, tensions persist. Disputes over water, electricity and gas supplies simmer under the surface and the lack of trust means that regional issues such as the Aral Sea, the drug trade from neighbouring Afghanistan and economic cooperation rarely get the international attention they so desperately need.

Perhaps the greatest challenge to the region's political stability is that none of the autocratic and ageing Central Asian rulers have any obvious political successors. What happens in a post-Karimov Uzbekistan in particular could define the direction of Central Asia in the years to come.

A New Orientation

But it's not all political dictatorship and economic hardship. After the confusion and social turmoil of the 1990s, life has settled for many Central Asians. Economies are growing and standards of living are gradually rising. Grassroots community tourism projects are flourishing in much of the region. International crossings have been retied with China, Afghanistan and Iran, opening up new opportunities for both trade and tourism and reconnecting the region to the rest of the world.

All this reflects the redrawing of Central Asia. Where once Tashkent and Ashgabat looked north to distant Moscow for economic and political direction, modern Central Asians now turn also to China, Turkey, Iran, Europe and the US, all of whom are equally intent on redefining spheres of influence long blocked by the Iron Curtain. The US-led 'War on Terror' raised the stakes in a geopolitical game that envelops everything from transcontinental gas pipelines to US and Russian military bases in the region.

The Future

As Central Asia's new economic and cultural ties strengthen, as oil and gas reserves are discovered and as NATO withdraws its troops through the region from Afghanistan, this little-understood corner will undoubtedly become increasingly important to the security, economy and politics of Russia, Asia and the world beyond.

The challenge for the future governments of Central Asia is to meet the religious, secular and economic desires of its people, while treading the tightrope between authoritarianism and Islamisation. As long as the issues of reform, reconstruction, poverty, development, corruption and succession remain unaddressed, Central Asia will continue to be a potential powder keg.

POPULATION:
65 MILLION

AREA:
4 MILLION SQ KM

HIGHEST MOUNTAIN:
KOH-I SOMONI (7495M)

LOWEST POINT:
KARAGIYE DEPRESSION (-132M)

if Central Asia were 100 people

40 would be Uzbeks
12 would be Tajiks
17 would be Kazakhs
6 would be Kyrgyz
6 would be Turkmen
19 would be Others

belief systems

(% of population)

population per sq km

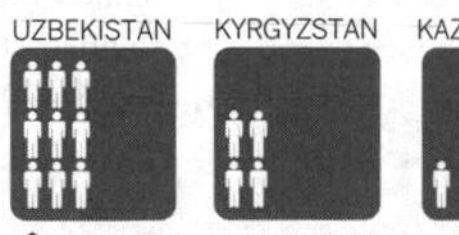

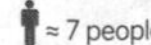

History

Central Asia's epic history is of great continent-spanning empires, of Turkic nomadic invasions and their interactions with settled Persian farmers and traders. Over the centuries peoples, conquerors, cultures, religions and ideas have traversed the region's steppes, deserts and mountain passes, creating a unique and sophisticated culture and swinging the region alternately from the heartland of Asia to the middle of nowhere.

See www.orientarch.uni-halle.de/ca/bud/bud.htm for more on the archaeology of southeastern Central Asia.

Early History

Cultural continuity in Central Asia begins in the late 3rd millennium BC with the Indo-Iranians, speakers of an unrecorded Indo-European dialect related distantly to English. The Indo-Iranians are believed to have passed through Central Asia and Afghanistan on their way from the Indo-European homeland in southern Russia. From Central Asia, groups headed southeast for India and southwest for Iran. These peoples herded cattle, forged iron, invented the wheeled chariot, and buried their dead nobles in burial mounds *(kurgans)*. The Tajik people are linguistic descendants of these ancient migrants. One of these subsequent Indo-European groups was the Sakas (part of a people known as Scythians), who have left *kurgans*, rock carvings and other remains across Central Asia. The most spectacular Saka-era remnant is Kazakhstan's famous 'Golden Man' find, found within a 5th-century *kurgan* outside Almaty.

Central Asia's recorded history begins in the 6th century BC, when the large Achaemenid empire of Persia (modern Iran) created client kingdoms or *satrapies* (provinces) in Central Asia: Sogdiana (Sogdia), Khorezm (later Khiva), Bactria (Afghan Turkestan), Margiana (Merv), Aria (Herat) and Saka (Scythia). Sogdiana was the land between the Amu-Darya and Syr-Darya rivers, called Transoxiana (Beyond the Oxus) by the Romans, where Bukhara and Samarkand would later flourish. Khorezm lay on the lower reaches of the Amu-Darya, south of the Aral Sea, where one day the 19th-century khans of Khiva would rule it from their walled city. Saka, the steppe and desert extending north of the Tian Shan and Syr-Darya, was the home of nomadic warriors until their way of life ended in the early 20th century.

Excavations of Scythian *kurgans* in Kazakhstan have revealed skeletons of female warriors and priestesses, raising connections with classical tales of the Amazons.

TIMELINE

40,000 BC

Remains of Neanderthal man found at Aman-Kutan cave near Samarkand date from 100,000 to 40,000 BC.

3500 BC

The Botai Culture of northern Kazakhstan is one of the first to domesticate horses, as horse-based nomadism becomes the dominant steppe culture.

3000 BC

The Bronze Age site of Gonur-Depe in the Margiana Oasis (Turkmenistan) is considered by some archaeologists to be one of the great cities of the ancient world and an early centre of Zoroastriansim.

Alexander the Great

In 330 BC Alexander the Great, a former pupil of Aristotle, from Macedonia, led his army to a key victory over the last Achaemenid emperor, Darius III, in Mesopotamia. With the defeat of his Persian nemesis, Alexander (356–323 BC) developed a taste for conquest. In 329 BC, aged 28, he reached Bactria, crossed the Oxus (Amu-Darya) on inflated hides and proceeded via Cyropol/Cyropolis (Istaravshan) and Marakanda (Samarkand) towards the Jaxartes (Syr-Darya), which he crossed in order to crush Saka defenders. Perhaps in celebration he founded his ninth city, Alexandria Eskhate (Farthest Alexandria), on the banks of the Jaxartes, where today's Khojand stands.

Alexander met the most stubborn resistance of his career in the Sogdians, who in concert with the Massagetes, a Scythian clan, revolted and under the leadership of Spitamenes held the mountains of Zerafshan until 328 BC. After an 18-month guerrilla war, the rebels' fall was a poignant one: attacked and defeated after Greek troops scaled the cliffs of their last redoubt, the 'Rock of Sogdiana' (its location today

Central Asia is strewn with ancient petroglyphs, some of the best of which can be visited at Saimaluu Tash in Kyrgyzstan and Tamgaly in southeastern Kazakhstan, the latter a Unesco World Heritage Site.

EURASIA'S NOMADIC EMPIRES

The vast steppes of Central Asia and Mongolia were the heartland of one of this planet's most formidable and successful forms of statehood, the nomadic empire. The domestication of the horse in northern Eurasia 5000 years ago, and the subsequent inventions of the saddle and war chariot by the Scythians a millennium later, gave Eurasian nomads an early technological edge. Stirrups in particular allowed them to fire their powerful composite bows in all directions from horseback. The Eurasian grasslands fed horses by the millions, allowing mounted archers to become the unstoppable acme of open-ground warfare for more than 2500 years. It is estimated that Mongol troops had access to half the world's horses during their invasions.

Accounts of nomads by settled communities are notoriously negative, painting them as rampaging barbarians but in fact many nomads lived a comfortable and sophisticated life. Leaders lined their fur cloaks with silk derived from the horse trade with China and made extensive use of richly cast gold jewellery and animal-shaped totems. Kazakhstan's famous Golden Man; see p62 for more information; a high-ranking Saka warrior or priest (and most likely a woman) was buried with more than 4000 gold objects. Some historians even credit Eurasian nomads with the invention of bowed musical instruments through their horsehair-stringed *qobuz*.

It was only the introduction of gunpowder-based weapons in the 15th century that turned the tide back towards the settled fortified cities. It was a technological change that marked the end of Eurasia's great nomadic empires.

2000 BC	329–327 BC	300 BC	138–119 BC
During the second millennium BC, the Amu-Darya (Oxus) river changes flow, draining north into the Aral Sea, instead of west to the Caspian Sea. The resulting Khorezm delta becomes a major centre of development.	Alexander the Great campaigns in Central Asia, founding Khojent (in modern Tajikistan), conquering Marakanda (Samarkand) and marrying the Bactrian princess Roxana.	Parthians rule Iran and southern Central Asia from 300 BC to 200 AD, building their first capital at Nissa in Turkmenistan. Theirs is one of the three greatest empires in the world and rivals Rome.	First Chinese diplomatic mission to Central Asia under Zhang Qian visits the Pamir Alai and Fergana Valley and brings back reports of Central Asia's 'heavenly horses' and a far-off kingdom called Daqin (Rome).

in the Hissar Mountains remains a mystery). Their leader eventually yielded both the fortress and the beautiful Bactrian princess Roxana (Roshanak), whom Alexander married in Balkh in 327 BC.

The brilliant Macedonian generalissimo's three-year sojourn in Central Asia was marked by a growing megalomania. It was at Marakanda (modern Samarkand) that Alexander murdered his right-hand general, Cleitus. He tried to adopt the dress and autocratic court ritual of an Oriental despot, until his Greek and Macedonian followers finally refused to prostrate themselves before him.

When he died in Babylon in 323 BC, Alexander had no named heir (despite fathering a son with Roxana). But his legacy included nothing less than the West's perennial romance with exploration and expansion.

Alexander the Great (Iskander or Sikander) is a popular figure, after whom several lakes and mountains are named. His troops are blamed for the occasional blond-haired, blue-eyed Tajik, though this is more likely the result of Aryan influence.

East Meets West

The aftermath of Alexander's short-lived Macedonian empire in Central Asia saw an explosion of East–West cultural exchange and a chain reaction of nomadic migrations. The Hellenistic successor states of the Seleucid empire in Bactria disseminated the aesthetic values of the classical world deep into Asia. Hellenistic cities and Buddhist monasteries of the 2nd century BC, such as Ai-Khanoum (Alexandria-Oxiana), Takht-i-Sangin and Kobadiyan on the borders of Tajikistan, Uzbekistan and Afghanistan (former Bactria), reveal a fascinating fusion of Greek, Persian and local art forms. Ai-Khanoum boasted not only Greek-style baths, but also a theatre and gymnasium, right on the banks of the Amu-Darya.

Several thousand kilometres east, along the border of Mongolia and China, the expansion of the warlike Xiongnu (Hsiung-nu) confederacy (probably the forebears of the Ephalites, or Huns) uprooted the Yuezhi of western China. The Yuezhi (Yüeh-chih) were sent packing westward along the Ili River into Saka (the borders of Kazakhstan and Kyrgyzstan), whose displaced inhabitants in turn bore down upon the Sogdians to the south.

The Xiongnu were irritating more important powers than the Yuezhi. Although protected behind its expanding Great Wall since about 250 BC, China sought tranquillity on its barbarian frontier. In 138 BC, the Chinese emperor sent a brave volunteer emissary, Zhang Qian, on a secret mission to persuade the Yuezhi king to form an alliance against the Xiongnu.

When he finally got there, 13 years later, Zhang found that the Yuezhi had settled down in Bactria/Tokharistan (southern Tajikistan and northern Afghanistan) to a peaceable life of trade and agriculture, and no longer had an axe to grind with the Xiongnu. But Zhang Qian's mission was still a great success of Chinese diplomacy and exploration, and the stage had been set for the greatest of all East–West contacts: the birth of the Silk Road.

The Sogdians (from modern Tajikistan and Uzbekistan) were the consummate Silk Road traders, so much so that their language became the lingua franca of the Silk Road.

105 BC

Parthia and China exchange embassies and inaugurate official bilateral trade along the caravan route that lies between them. The Silk Road is born.

MATTHIEU PALEY / GETTY IMAGES ©

➡ Silk Road, Kyrgyzstan

AD 78–144

King Kanishka rules the Kushan empire from modern-day Afghanistan. Buddhist monasteries bloom in southern Uzbekistan and Tajikistan as the first human images of Buddha are created.

The Kushans

The peaceable Yuezhi finally came into their own in the 1st century BC when their descendants, the Kushan dynasty, converted to Buddhism. The Kushan empire (250 BC–AD 226) grew to control northern India, Afghanistan and Sogdiana from its base at Kapisa, near modern-day Bagram in Afghanistan. At its height in the first three centuries after Christ, it was one of the world's four superpowers, alongside Rome, China and Parthia.

Vigorous trade on the Silk Road helped fuel and spread Kushan and Buddhist culture. The rich Kushan coinage bears testament to the Silk Road's lively religious ferment, with coins bearing images of Greek, Roman, Buddhist, Persian and Hindu deities.

The art of the empire further fused Persian imperial imagery, Buddhist iconography and Roman realism to create what is now called Gandharan art. The fusion of styles was carried over the mountains to the furthest corners of Transoxiana, Tibet, Kashmir and the Tarim Basin, where it became termed as Serindian art. Indian, Tibetan and Chinese art were permanently affected and the spread of Buddhism changed the face and soul of Asia.

Historical Reads

The Great Game, Peter Hopkirk

The Empire of the Steppes, Renee Grousset

Central Asia, Gavin Hambly

Sassanids, Huns & Sogdians

The Silk Road's first flower faded by about 200 AD, as the Chinese, Roman, Parthian and Kushan empires went into decline. As the climate along the middle section of the Silk Road became drier, Central Asian nomads increasingly sought wealth by plundering, taxing and conquering their settled neighbours. The Persian Sassanids (Sassanians) lost their Inner Asian possessions in the 4th century to the Huns, who ruled a vast area of Central Asia at the same time that Attila was scourging Europe.

The Huns were followed south across the Syr-Darya by the western Turks, who in 559 made an alliance with the Sassanids and ousted the Huns. The western Turks were a branch of the so-called Kök Turks or Blue Turks, whose ancestral homelands were in southern Siberia.

Do a search for 'Central Asia' at www.loc.gov/exhibits/empire for wonderful old photos of Central Asia from the Prokudin-Gorskii collection.

DRAGON HORSES

Central Asia has been famed for its horses for millennia. The earliest Silk Road excursions into the region were designed to bring back the famous 'blood-sweating' (due to parasites or skin infection) horses of Fergana to help Han China fight nomadic tribes harassing its northern frontier. Much of the highly coveted silk that made its way into Central Asia and beyond originally came from the trade of steeds that the Chinese believed were descended from dragons.

440–568

The Hephthalites (White Huns) migrate from the Altai region to occupy Transoxiana, Bactria, Khorasan, and eastern Persia, conquering the Kushans and eventually carving the Buddhas at Bamiyan.

630

Chinese Buddhist pilgrim Xuan Zang travels to India via Issyk-Köl, Tashkent, Samarkand, Balkh and Bamiyan in search of Buddhist texts. En route he visits the summer capital of the Blue Turks at Tokmak, Kyrgyzstan.

642–712

Arab conquest of Central Asia by General Qutaybah ibn Muslim brings Islam to the region. Central Asia is called Mawarannahr in Arabic – the 'Land Beyond the River'.

719

The Sogdians under their ruler Devastich stage a major revolt against Arab rule. Devastich flees to the mountains of northern Tajikistan but the Arabs catch and crucify him three years later.

The mixing of the western Turks' nomadic ruling class with the sedentary Sogdian elite over the next few centuries produced a remarkable ethnic mix and beautiful artwork in Sogdian cities such as Penjikent, Afrosiab (Samarkand) and Varakhsha (near Bukhara), much of which is still visible in museums across the region.

The Arrival of Islam

When the western Turks faded in the late 7th century, an altogether new and formidable power was waiting to fill the void – the army of Islam. Exploding out of Arabia just a few years after the Prophet Mohammed's death, the Muslim armies rolled through Persia in 642 to set up a military base at Merv (modern Turkmenistan) but met stiff resistance from the Turks of Transoxiana. The power struggle to control the lands between the Amu-Darya and Syr-Darya ebbed and flowed but Arab armies under the brilliant General Qutaybah ibn Muslim gradually gained ground, taking Bukhara in 709 and Samarkand three years later.

Before the arrival of Islam, Central Asia sheltered pockets of Zoroastrianism, Manichaeism, Judaism, Nestorian Christianity and Buddhism. In the 8th century there were even Nestorian bishoprics in Herat, Samarkand and Merv.

China, meanwhile, had revived under the Tang dynasty and expanded into Central Asia, murdering the khan of the Tashkent Turks as it flexed its imperial muscles. It was perhaps the most costly incident of skulduggery in Chinese history. The enraged Turks were joined by the opportunistic Arabs and Tibetans; in 751 they squeezed the Chinese forces into the Talas Valley (in present-day Kazakhstan and Kyrgyzstan) and sent them flying back across the Tian Shan, marking the outer limits of the Chinese empire for good.

After the Battle of Talas, the Arab's Central Asian territories receded in the wake of local rebellions. By the 9th century, Transoxiana (now known by the Arabic name Mawarannahr, or the 'Land Beyond the River') had given rise to the peaceful and affluent Samanid dynasty. It generously encouraged development of Persian culture while remaining strictly allied with the Sunni caliph of Baghdad. It was under the Samanids that Bukhara grew into a vanguard of Muslim culture to rival Baghdad, Cairo and Cordoba, garnering it the epithet 'The Pillar of Islam'. Some of the Islamic world's best scholars were nurtured in the city's 113 medressas and the famous library of Bukhara shone as one of the world's great centres of intellectual development.

For more on the Mongols see the excellent book *Storm from the East*, by Robert Marshall.

Samanid Central Asia produced some of history's most important scientists, as well as great writers like court poet Rudaki. Bukharan native and court physician Abu Ali ibn-Sina (Latinised as Avicenna) was the greatest medic in the medieval world, while Al-Biruni, from Khorezm, was the world's foremost astronomer of his age. Confused schoolchildren around the world can thank mathematician Al-Khorezmi (Latinised as Algorismi) for the introduction of algebra (*Al-Jebr* was the title of one of his mathematical works).

747

Chinese army battles Tibetans in the Wakhan Valley of the high Pamirs in an attempt to regain control of the Silk Road.

787–850

Life of Central Asian mathematician Al-Khorezmi (Latinised as Algorismi), who gave his name to the mathematical process called an algorithm. The title of his mathematical work, *Al-Jebr*, reaches Europe as 'algebra'.

819–1005

The heyday of the Samanid dynasty in Bukhara. Its greatest ruler, Ismail Samani, is buried in a beautiful tomb in Bukhara and is celebrated as Tajikistan's founding father.

858–941

Life of Rudaki, court poet of the Samanids, born near modern Penjikent in Tajikistan and considered to be the founder of Tajik/Persian literature.

Karakhanids to Khorezmshahs

By the early 10th century, internal strife at court had weakened the Samanid dynasty and opened the door for two Turkic usurpers to divide up the empire: the Karakhanids held sway from three mighty capitals – Balasagun (Burana in Kyrgyzstan) in the centre of their domain, Talas (Taraz in Kazakhstan) in the west, and Kashgar in the east. It is the Karakhanids who are credited with finally converting the populace of Central Asia to Islam. Further south the Ghaznavids under Mahmoud the Great ruled Samarkand and Bukhara from Ghazni in southern Afghanistan. They in turn are credited with snuffing out Buddhism in the region and introducing Islam to India.

The Karakhanids and Ghaznavids coveted each other's lands. In the mid-11th century, while they were busy invading each other, they were caught off guard by a third Turkic horde, the Seljuqs, who annihilated both after pledging false allegiance to the Ghaznavids. In the Seljuqs' heyday their empire was vast: on the east it bordered the lands of the Buddhist Karakitay, who had swept into Balasagun and Kashgar from China; to the west it extended all the way to the Mediterranean and Red Seas.

An incurable symptom of Inner Asian dynasties through the ages was their near inability to survive the inevitable disputes of succession. The Seljuqs lasted a century before their weakened line succumbed to the Karakitay and to the Seljuqs' own rearguard vassals, the Khorezmshahs. From their capital at Gurganj (present-day Konye-Urgench), the Khorezmshahs burst full-force into the tottering Karakitay. At the end of the 12th century the Khorezmshahs emerged as rulers of all Transoxiana and much of the Muslim world as well.

And so Central Asia might have continued in a perennial state of forgettable wars. As it is, the Khorezmshahs are still remembered primarily as the unlucky stooge left holding the red cape when the angry bull was released.

The Karakitay lent their name to both Cathay (an archaic name for China) and Kitai (the Russian word for China).

One overlooked Silk Road commodity was the trade in slaves. Slaves dominated the global workforce between the 8th and 11th centuries and Turkmen raiders kept the slave markets of Khiva and Bukhara stocked well into the 19th century.

LOST BATTLE, LOST SECRETS

The Chinese lost more than just a fight at the Battle of Talas in 751. To add insult to injury, some of the Chinese rounded up after the battle were experts in the crafts of papermaking and silkmaking. Soon China's best-kept secrets were giving Arab silkmakers in Persia a commercial advantage all over Europe. It was the first mortal blow to the Silk Road. The spread of papermaking to Baghdad and eventually Europe sparked a technological revolution; the impact of this on the development of civilisation cannot be underestimated.

973–1046

Life of scientist Al-Biruni, from Khorezm, the world's foremost astronomer of his time, who knew 500 years before Copernicus that the earth circled the sun and estimated the distance to the moon to within 20km.

980–1037

Life of Abu Ali ibn-Sina (Latinised as Avicenna), from Bukhara, the greatest medic in the medieval world, whose *Canon of Medicine* was the standard textbook for Western doctors until the 17th century.

986

The Russians, in search of a religion, contact Muslim missionaries from Khorezm, but decide not to adopt Islam, opting instead for Orthodox Christianity.

999–1211

The Turkic Karakhanids wrest control of Transoxiana from the Persian Samanids. Dynastic founder Nasr ibn Ali is buried in a mausoleum in Özgön in the Fergana Valley (Kyrgyzstan).

Mongol Terror, Mongol Peace

Chinggis (Genghis) Khan felt he had all the justification in the world to destroy Central Asia. In 1218 a Khorezmian governor in Otrar (modern-day Kazakhstan) received a Mongol delegation to inaugurate trade relations. Scared by distant reports of the new Mongol menace, the governor assassinated them in cold blood. Up until that moment Chinggis had been carefully weighing the alternative strategies for expanding his power: commerce versus conquest. Then came the crude Otrar blunder, and the rest is history.

The Persian historian Juvaini summed up the Mongol invasions succinctly: 'They came, they sapped, they fired, they slew, they looted and they left'.

In early 1219 Chinggis placed himself at the head of an estimated 200,000 men and began to ride west from his stronghold in the Altay. By the next year his armies had sacked Khojand and Otrar (the murderous governor had molten silver poured into his eyes in Chinggis' presence), and Bukhara soon followed.

It was in that brilliant city, as soldiers raped and looted and horses trampled Islamic holy books in the streets, that the unschooled Chinggis ascended to the pulpit in the chief mosque and preached to the terrified congregation. His message: 'I am God's punishment for your sins'. Such shocking psychological warfare is perhaps unrivalled in history. It worked and news eventually filtered back to Europe of the Tartars, an army of 'Devil's Horsemen', sent from the Gates of Hell (Tartarus) to destroy Christendom.

Bukhara was burned to the ground, and the Mongol hordes swept on to conquer and plunder the great cities of Central Asia – Samarkand, Merv, Termiz, Urgench, Herat, Balkh, Bamiyan, Ghazni – and, eventually under Chinggis' generals and heirs, most of Eurasia. No opposing army could match their speed, agility and accuracy with a bow.

NOMADS

From the 9th to 11th centuries the fringes of Central Asia saw a baffling array of shadowy nomadic groups – Oghuz Turks, Pechenegs, Kimaks, Kipchaks, Cumans and Karluks, as well as slave-trading Nogoi Horde – about whom little is known.

Settled civilisation in Central Asia took a serious blow, from which it only began to recover 600 years later under Russian colonisation. Chinggis' descendants controlling Persia favoured Shiite Islam over Sunni Islam, a development which over the centuries isolated Central Asia even more from the currents of the rest of the Sunni Muslim world.

But there was stability, law and order under the Pax Mongolica. In modern terms, the streets were safe and the trains ran on time. The resulting modest flurry of trade on the Silk Road was the background to several famous medieval travellers' journeys, including the most famous of them all, Marco Polo.

On Chinggis Khan's death in 1227, his empire was divided among his sons. The most distant lands, stretching as far as the Ukraine and Moscow and including western and most of northern Kazakhstan, went to Chinggis' grandsons Batu and Orda, and came to be known collectively as the Golden Horde. Chinggis' second son, Chaghatai, got the next most

1077–1220
Khorezmshah empire rises from its capital in Gurganj (Konye-Urgench), shrugging off Seljuq and Karakhitay domination to briefly control most of modern-day Iran, Central Asia and western Afghanistan.

12th century
Merv in Turkmenistan is the largest city in the world, known as the Queen of the World, as the Seljuqs reach the height of their glory. The Seljuq leaders Alp Arslan and Sultan Sanjar are buried here in huge mausolea.

1141
The Shamanic-Buddhist Karakhitay and Khorezmshahs defeat the Muslim Seljuqs at the battle of Qatwan, north of Samarkand. The news filters back to Crusader Europe as the legend of Prester John.

1220–21
Chinggis (Genghis) Khan's army destroys Bukhara, killing 30,000. That city rebels and 160,000 of its inhabitants are killed in a week.

distant portion, including southern Kazakhstan, Uzbekistan, Afghanistan and western Xinjiang; this came to be known as the Chaghatai khanate. The share of the third son, Ogedei, seems to have eventually been divided between the Chaghatai khanate and the Mongol heartland inherited by the youngest son, Tolui. Tolui's portion formed the basis for his son Kublai Khan's Yuan dynasty in China.

Unlike the Golden Horde in Europe and the Yuan court in Beijing, the Chaghatai khans tried to preserve their nomadic lifestyle, complete with the khan's roving tent encampment as 'capital city'. But as the rulers spent more and more time in contact with Muslim collaborators who administered their realm, the Chaghatai line inevitably began to settle down. They even made motions towards conversion to Islam. It was a fight over this issue, in the mid-14th century, that split the khanate in two, with the Muslim Chaghatais holding Transoxiana and the conservative branch retaining the Tian Shan, Kashgar and the vast steppes north and east of the Syr-Darya, an area collectively known as Moghulistan.

At its height the Mongol empire formed the largest contiguous land empire in human history, marking the greatest incursion by steppe nomads into settled society.

Timur & the Timurids

The fracturing of the Mongol empire immediately led to resurgence of the Turkic peoples. From one minor clan near Samarkand arose a tyrant's tyrant, Timur ('the Lame', or Tamerlane). After assembling an army and wresting Transoxiana from Chaghatai rule, Timur went on a spectacular nine-year rampage which ended in 1395 with modern-day Iran, Iraq, Syria, eastern Turkey, the Caucasus and northern India smouldering at his feet.

THE MONGOL KISS OF DEATH

Alongside the exchange of silk, jade, paper and Buddhism, historians rank disease as one of the Silk Road's less salubrious gifts to the world. One school of thought has it that the Black Death plague spread in 1338 from a diseased community of Nestorian Christians at Lake Issyk-Köl in current Kyrgyzstan. Disease-ridden rat fleas then followed merchant caravans along Silk Road trade routes to the Mongol capital of Sarai in the Russian Volga.

By 1343 Mongol Khan Jani Beg of the Golden Horde was famously catapulting the plague-riddled corpses of his dead soldiers over the city walls of Kaffa, in the Crimea peninsula, in one of the world's first examples of biological warfare. The outbreak caused the Genoese population to flee by boat to the Mediterranean coast, spreading the disease deeper into Europe.

In the ensuing six years the Black Death pandemic went on to kill between 30% and 60% of Europe's population and around 100 million people across Asia. It was the Mongols' farewell kiss of death to the world.

1261–64

Nicolo and Matteo Polo (Marco's father and uncle) live in Bukhara for three years before travelling to the court of Khublai Khan. The khan requests they return with 100 priests to argue the merits of Christianity.

YOKO AZIZ / GETTY IMAGES ©

➡ Ulugbek Medressa, Bukhara, Uzbekistan

1336–1405

Timur's (Tamerlane) life, whose campaigns resulted in the deaths of more than one million people. He becomes infamous for building towers or walls made from the cemented heads of a defeated army.

From across his realm, Timur plundered riches and captured artisans and poured them into his capital at Samarkand. The city blossomed, in stark contrast to his conquered lands, into a lavish showcase of treasure and spectacle. Much of the postcard skyline of today's Samarkand dates to Timur's reign. Foreign guests of Timur's, including the Spanish envoy Ruy Gonzales de Clavijo, took home stories of Oriental enchantment and barbarity which fed the West's dreams of a remote and romantic Samarkand.

Timur claimed indirect kinship with Chinggis Khan, but he had little of his forerunner's gift for statecraft. History can be strange: both conquerors savagely slaughtered hundreds of thousands of innocent people, yet one is remembered as a great ruler and the other not. The argument goes that Timur's bloodbaths were insufficiently linked to specific political or military aims. On the other hand, Timur is considered the more cultured and religious of the two men. At any rate, Timur died an old man at Otrar in 1405, having just set out in full force to conquer China.

TIMUR

Timur-i-Leng (Timur the Lame), or Tamerlane, walked with a pronounced limp after a fall from a horse in 1363 left him disabled in his right leg. He also lost two fingers during one battle.

For a scant century after Timur's death his descendants ruled on separately in small kingdoms and duchies. A Timurid renaissance was led by Timur's son Shah Rukh (1377–1447) and his remarkable wife Gowhar Shad, who moved the capital from Samarkand to the cultured city of Herat, populated by artistic luminaries such as the Sufi poets Jami and Alisher Navoi, and the miniaturist painter Behzad, whose work had a huge influence on subsequent Persian and Mughal miniatures.

From 1409 until 1449, Samarkand was governed by the conqueror's mild, scholarly grandson, Ulugbek (Ulugh Bek). Gifted in mathematics and astronomy, he built a large celestial observatory and attracted scientists who gave the city a lustre as a centre of learning for years to come.

In addition to Persian, a Turkic court language came into use called Chaghatai, which survived for centuries as a Central Asian lingua franca.

Uzbeks & Kazakhs

Modern-day Uzbekistan and Kazakhstan, the two principal powers of post-Soviet Central Asia, eye each other warily across the rift dividing their two traditional lifestyles: sedentary agriculture (Uzbeks) and nomadic pastoralism (Kazakhs). Yet these two nations are closely akin and parted ways with a family killing.

The family in question was the dynasty of the Uzbek khans. These rulers, one strand of the modern Uzbek people, had a pedigree reaching back to Chinggis Khan and a homeland in southern Siberia. In the 14th century they converted to Islam, gathered strength, and started moving south. Under Abylkayyr (Abu al-Khayr) Khan they reached the north bank of the Syr-Darya, across which lay the declining Timurid rulers in Transoxiana. But Abylkayyr had enemies within his own family. The

1395

Timur defeats the army of the Golden Horde in southern Russia, fracturing the Mongol empire and allowing the rise of its vassals, the fragmented Russian princes. This marks the predawn of the Russian state.

1468

Uzbek khan Abylkayyr is killed by a family rival, splitting the clan into the Uzbek Shaybanids to the south and the Kazakh khanate to the north.

15th century

The end of the century saw the decline of the overland trade routes, including the Silk Road, due to a new emphasis on trade by sea. Trading cities like Bukhara start a slow decline.

1501–07

The Uzbek Shaybanids capture Samarkand and Bukhara, bringing to an end the Timurid dynasty and forcing Babur to flee south to Kabul and Delhi, eventually to found the Mughal empire in India in 1526.

two factions met in battle in 1468; Abylkayyr was killed and his army defeated.

After this setback, Abylkayyr's grandson Mohammed Shaybani brought the Uzbek khans to power once more and established Uzbek control in Transoxiana, modern-day Uzbekistan. Abylkayyr's rebellious kinsmen became the forefathers of the Kazakh khans.

The Uzbeks gradually adopted the sedentary agricultural life best suited to the fertile river valleys they occupied. Settled life involved cities, which entailed administration, literacy, learning and, wrapped up with all of these, Islam. The Shaybanid dynasty, which ruled until the end of the 16th century, attempted to outdo the Timurids in religious devotion and to carry on their commitment to artistic patronage. But the Silk Road had withered away, usurped by spice ships, and Central Asia's economy had entered full decline. As prosperity fell, so did the region's importance as a centre of the Islamic world.

Babur never returned to his beloved Fergana Valley and his whistful memoirs, the *Baburname* are full of nostalgic laments to the joys of his lost homeland; mostly melons and women, in that order.

The Kazakhs, meanwhile, stayed home on the range, north of the Syr-Darya, and flourished as nomadic herders. Their experience of urban civilisation and organised Islam remained slight compared with their Uzbek cousins. By the 16th century the Kazakhs had solidly filled a power vacuum on the old Scythian steppes between the Ural and Irtysh Rivers and established what was to be the world's last nomadic empire, divided into three hordes: the Great Horde, the Middle Horde and the Little Horde. The Great Horde roamed the steppes of the Zhetisu region (Russian: Semireche), north of the Tian Shan; the Middle Horde occupied the grasslands east of the Aral Sea; and the Little Horde took the lands to the west, as far as the Ural River.

One effect of the Shaybanid expansion was to force Andijon-born ruler Zahiruddin Babur (1483–1530) out of Fergana and Samarkand and into exile in Kabul. In 1526 Babur continued into India, adding his name to the long list of empire builders who have driven armies over the Khyber Pass, where he ultimately founded the magnificent Mughal empire. The word Mughal (a corruption of 'Mongol') is not the only legacy of Babur's rule in India; you don't have to look too hard to see the shape of a Central Asian medressa in the lines of the Taj Mahal.

The Zhungarian Empire

The Oyrats were a western Mongol clan who had been converted to Tibetan Buddhism. Their day in the sun came when they subjugated eastern Kazakhstan, the Tian Shan, Kashgaria and western Mongolia to form the Zhungarian (Dzungarian or Jungarian) empire (1635–1758). Russia's frontier settlers were forced to pay heavy tribute and the Kazakh hordes, with their prize pasturage filling the mountain gap known

For more on the extraordinary life of Timur see *Tamerlane: Sword of Islam, Conqueror of the World* by Justin Marozzi.

1510

Sheybani Khan dies at Merv fighting for the Ottomans against the Safarvids of Iran. The Safarvid general stuffs Sheybani's decapitated head with straw and sends it to the sultan as a gruesome warning.

16th century

The 16th and 17th centuries see the formation of the Turkmen identity, as tribal groupings such as the Tekke, Salor and Yomud emerge from the earlier Oghuz Turks.

1635–1758

Zhungarian (Oyrat) empire terrorises Kazakhstan, Kyrgyzstan and China. When the Oyrats are finally defeated by Manchu China, Kyrgyzstan comes nominally under Chinese rule.

1717

First Russian expedition to Khiva ends in a massacre of 4000 tsarist troops; the decapitated Russian leader's head is sent to the Emir of Bukhara as a gift.

as the Zhungarian Gate, were cruelly and repeatedly pummelled until the Oyrats were liquidated by Manchu China. Stories of this dark period live on in the *Alpamish* and *Manas* epic poems.

The Russians had by this time established a line of fortified outposts on the northern fringe of the Kazakh Steppe. Reeling from the Zhungarian attacks, the Kazakhs (first the Little Horde, then the Middle Horde, then part of the Great Horde) gradually accepted Russian protection over the mid-18th century. It was a clear sign of things to come.

Memory of the Oyrat legacy has been preserved in epic poetry by the Kazakhs and Kyrgyz, who both suffered under the Oyrats' ruthless predations.

The Khanates of Kokand, Khiva & Bukhara

In the fertile oases now called Uzbekistan, the military regime of a Persian interloper named Nadir Shah collapsed in 1747, leaving a political void which was rapidly occupied by a trio of Uzbek khanates.

The three dynasties were the Kungrats, enthroned at Khiva (in the territory of old Khorezm), the Mangits at Bukhara, and the Mins at Kokand; all rivals. The khans of Khiva and Kokand and the emirs of Bukhara seemed able to will the outside world out of existence as they stroked and clawed each other like a box of kittens. Boundaries were impossible to fix as the rivals shuffled their provinces in endless wars.

Unruly nomadic clans produced constant pressure on their periphery. Bukhara and Khiva claimed nominal control over the nomadic Turkmen, who prowled the Karakum desert and provided the khanates with slaves from Persia and the Russian borderlands. Kokand spread into the Tian Shan mountains and the Syr-Darya basin in the early 19th century, while Bukhara further exercised nominal control over northern Afghanistan and much of modern-day Tajikistan.

The khans ruled absolutely as feudal despots. Some of them were capable rulers; some, such as the last emir of Bukhara, were depraved and despised tyrants. In the centuries since Transoxiana had waned as the centre of Islam, levels of education and literacy had plummeted, and superstition and ignorance pervaded even the highest levels of government.

It was no dark age, however – trade was vigorous. This was especially true in Bukhara, where exports of cotton, cloth, silk, karakul fleece and other goods gave it a whopping trade surplus with Russia. Commerce brought in new ideas, with resulting attempts to develop irrigation and even to reform civil administrations. European travellers in the 19th century wrote best-selling travelogues marvelling at the exotic architectural splendour of these distant glimmering capitals.

For more on that quintessential Great Gamester, Francis Younghusband, read Patrick French's excellent biography *Younghusband*.

In many respects, the three khanates closely resembled the feudal city-states of late-medieval Europe. But it is anybody's guess how they and the Kazakh and Kyrgyz nomads might have developed had they been left alone.

1731

Lesser Kazakh Horde places itself under Russian protection, opening up the ensuing annexation of Kazakhstan by tsarist forces and settlers.

1842

Britain suffers disaster in the First Anglo-Afghan War. Later that year British officers Conolly and Stoddart are beheaded in front of the Ark by the Emir of Bukhara, as the Great Game kicks off.

1848

Russia abolishes the Great Horde, ending the last line of rulers directly descended, by both blood and throne, from Chinggis Khan.

1857–1859

Exiled Russian writer Dostoevsky lives in Semey, Kazakhstan, and starts work on one of his most famous novels, *The Brothers Karamazov*.

The Russians Are Coming!

By the turn of the 19th century, Russia's vista to the south was of anachronistic, unstable neighbours, who had a nasty habit of raiding southern settlements, even taking Christian Russians as slaves. Flush with the new currents of imperialism sweeping Europe, the empire found itself embarking willy-nilly upon a century of rapid expansion across the steppe.

The reasons were complex. The main ingredients were the search for a secure, and preferably natural, southern border, combined with nagging fears of British expansion from India and the boldness of individual tsarist officers. And probably, glimmering in the back of every patriotic Russian's mind, there was a vague notion of the 'manifest destiny' of the frontier.

The first people to feel the impact were the Kazakhs. Their agreements in the mid-18th century to accept Russian 'protection' had apparently been understood by St Petersburg as agreements to annexation and a few decades later Tatars and Cossacks were sent to settle and farm the land. Angered, the Kazakhs revolted. As a consequence, the khans of the three hordes were, one by one, stripped of their autonomy, and their lands were made into bona fide Russian colonies, sweet psychological revenge, no doubt, for centuries of invasion by nomadic armies from the east. Kokand was the first of the three Uzbek khanates to be absorbed, followed by Bukhara (1868) and then Khiva (1873).

The last and fiercest people to hold out against the tsarist juggernaut were the Tekke, the largest and most independent of the Turkmen clans. The Russians were trounced in 1879 at a major battle of Teke-Turkmen, but returned with a vengeance in 1881 with a huge force under General Mikhail Dmitrievich Skobelev (who famously rode a white horse and dressed only in white). The siege and capture of Geok-Tepe, the Tekkes' last stronghold, resulted in the death of around 15,000 Tekke and only 268 Russians.

With resistance crushed, the Russians proceeded along the hazily defined Persian frontier area, occupying the Pandjeh Oasis on the Afghan border in 1885 at the southernmost point of their new empire. Throughout the conquest, the government in St Petersburg agonised over every advance. On the ground their hawkish generals took key cities first and asked for permission later.

When it was over, Russia found it had bought a huge new territory – half the size of the USA, geographically and ethnically diverse, and economically rich – fairly cheaply in terms of money and lives, and in just 20 years. It had not gone unnoticed by the world's other great empire further south in British India.

SLAVERY

So many Russian Slavs were captured or sold into slavery by nomadic invaders or slave traders that the word entered the English language as the source of the word 'slave'.

The English word 'horde' comes via French from the Turkic word *ordu*, meaning the yurt or pavilion where a khan held his court.

TIM MAKINS / GETTY IMAGES ©

➡ Dostoevsky Museum, Semey, Kazakhstan

1862–84

Tsarist Russia takes Bishkek (1862), Aulie-Ata (1864), Tashkent (1865), Samarkand (1868), Khiva (1873), Kokand (1877) and Merv (1884), ruled by the Governor-General Konstantin Kaufman in Tashkent.

1877

German geographer Ferdinand von Richthofen coins the term 'Silk Road' to describe the transcontinental network of trade routes between Europe and China.

The Great Game

What do two expanding empires do when their ill-defined frontiers draw near each other? They scramble for control of what's between them, using a mix of secrecy and stealth.

From the Mongol destruction of irrigation canals to the Russian harnessing of water for cotton production and the death of the Aral Sea, the control of water has been central to the region for centuries and will continue to be a source of future contention.

The British called the ensuing struggle for imperial power the 'Great Game'; in Russia it was the 'Tournament of Shadows'. In essence it was the first cold war between East and West. All the ingredients were there: spies and counterspies, demilitarised zones, puppet states and doomsaying governments whipping up smokescreens for their own shady business. All that was lacking was the atom bomb and a Russian leader banging his shoe on the table.

The story of the Great Game would be dull as dishwater except that its centre arena was some of the world's most exotic and remote terrain. The history of Central Asia's international relations from the beginning of the 19th century to the present day can be seen through the prism of the Great Game.

As the Russians spread into Central Asia, the British turned towards their northwestern frontier. The disastrous 1842 First Afghan War took the wind out of the British sails, but only temporarily. By 1848 the British had defeated the Sikhs and taken control of the Punjab and the Peshawar valley. With a grip now on the 'Northern Areas' Britain began a kind of cat-and-mouse game with Russia across the vaguely mapped Pamir and Hindu Kush ranges. Agents posing as scholars, explorers, hunters, merchants – and even Muslim preachers and Buddhist pilgrims – crisscrossed the mountains, mapping the passes, spying on each other and courting local rulers. In 1882 Russia established a consulate in Kashgar and in 1877 a British agency at Gilgit (present day Pakistan) was urgently reopened when the *mir* (hereditary ruler) of Hunza entertained a party of Russians.

The late 19th century witnessed a golden age of Russian exploration in Central Asia. Famous figures such as Semenov, Przewalski and Merzbacher are only today starting to get credit abroad.

Imperial tensions continued with the Russian annexation of Bukhara and Samarkand but it was the Russian occupation of Merv in 1884 that really sent blood pressures through the roof in Britain and India. Merv was a crossroads leading to Herat, an easy gateway to Afghanistan, which in turn offered entry into British India. The British government finally lost its cool the following year when the Russians went south to control Pandjeh.

Then in 1890, Francis Younghusband (later to head a British incursion into Tibet) was sent to do some politicking with Chinese officials in Kashgar. On his way back through the Pamirs he found the range full of Russian troops, and was told to get out or face arrest.

This electrified the British. They raised hell with the Russian government and invaded Hunza the following year; at the same time Russian

1881

Siege of Goek-Tepe in modern Turkmenistan marks the last stand of the Turkmen against Russian annexation. Over 15,000 Tekke are killed.

1885

Britain and Russia go to the brink of war after the Russians annex the Pandjeh Oasis at the height of the Great Game. The British are convinced the Russians have their eyes on Herat and British India beyond.

1888

The Trans-Caspian railway from Krasnovodsk reaches Samarkand. The Orenburg–Tashkent line is completed seven years later, tying Central Asia firmly to the Russian heartland.

1890

Captain Francis Younghusband is thrown out of the Pamirs by his Russian counterpart, much to the outrage of British hawks.

troops skirmished in northeast Afghanistan. After a burst of diplomatic manoeuvring, Anglo-Russian boundary agreements in 1895 and 1907 gave Russia most of the Pamirs and established the Wakhan Corridor, the awkward finger of Afghan territory that divides the two former empires.

The Great Game was over. The Great Lesson for the people of the region was: 'No great power has our interests at heart'. The lesson has powerful implications today.

Colonisation of Turkestan

In 1861, the outbreak of the US Civil War ended Russia's imports of American cotton. To keep the growing textile industry in high gear, the natural place to turn to for cotton was Central Asia. Other sectors of Russian industry were equally interested in the new colonies as sources of cheap raw materials and labour, and as huge markets. Russia's government and captains of industry wisely saw that their own goods could not compete in Europe but in Central Asia they had a captive, virgin market.

In the late 19th century, European immigrants began to flood the tsar's new lands, a million in Kazakhstan alone. The new arrivals were mostly freed Russian and Ukrainian serfs hungry for land of their own. Central Asia also offered a chance for enterprising Russians to climb socially. The first mayor of Pishpek (Bishkek) left Russia as a gunsmith, married well in the provinces, received civil appointments, and ended his life owning a mansion and a sprawling garden estate.

The Russian middle class brought with them straight streets, gas lights, telephones, cinemas, amateur theatre, parks and hotels. All these were contained in enclaves set apart from the original towns. Through their lace curtains the Russians looked out on the Central Asian masses with a fairly indulgent attitude. The Muslim fabric of life was left alone and development, when it came, took the form of small industrial enterprises, irrigation systems and a modest program of primary education.

In culture it was the Kazakhs, as usual, who were the first to be influenced by Russia. A small, Europeanised, educated class began for the first time to think of the Kazakh people as a nation. In part, their ideas came from a new sense of their own illustrious past, which they read about in the works of Russian ethnographers and historians. Their own brilliant but short-lived scholar, Shokan Ualikhanov (Chokan Valikhanov), was a key figure in Kazakh consciousness-raising.

THE GREAT GAME

The phrase 'Great Game' was first coined by British officer Arthur Conolly (later executed in Bukhara) and immortalised by Kipling in his novel *Kim*.

The 1916 Uprising

The outbreak of WWI in 1914 had disastrous consequences in Central Asia. In southeastern Kazakhstan massive herds of Kazakh and Kyrgyz cattle were requisitioned for the war effort, whereas Syr-Darya, Fergana and Samarkand provinces had to provide cotton and food. Then, in 1916,

1898
Rebellion in Andijon in Uzbekistan against the Russians. The insurrection is put down and steps are taken to Russify urban Muslims.

1916
An uprising over forced labour conscription during WWI leads to over 200,000 Kazakhs fleeing to China.

1917
The Bolshevik October Revolution in Russia leads to the creation of the Tashkent Soviet. The Alash Orda movement in Kazakhstan creates an independent state until crushed by the Bolsheviks three years later.

Jul 1919
Anti-Communist allies establish the short-lived independent state of Transcaspia, with help from a small British force from Mashhad. British forces temporarily occupy parts of southern Turkmenistan.

as Russia's hopes in the war plummeted, the tsar demanded men. Local people in the colonies were to be conscripted as noncombatants in labour battalions. To add insult to injury, the action was not called 'mobilisation' but 'requisition', a term usually used for cattle and material.

Exasperated Central Asians just said no. Starting in Tashkent, an uprising swept eastwards over the summer of 1916. It gained in violence, and attracted harsher reprisal, the further east it went. Purposeful attacks on Russian militias and official facilities gave way to massive rioting, raiding and looting. Colonists were massacred, their villages burned, and women and children carried off.

The resulting bloody crackdown is a milestone tragedy in Kyrgyz and Kazakh history. Russian troops and vigilantes gave up all pretence of a 'civilising influence' as whole Kyrgyz and Kazakh villages were brutally slaughtered or set to flight. Manhunts for suspected perpetrators continued all winter, long after an estimated 200,000 Kyrgyz and Kazakh families had fled towards China. The refugees who didn't starve or freeze on the way were shown little mercy in China.

For more on Nazaroff's cat-and-mouse exploits on the run in Central Asia from the Bolsheviks, read his *Hunted Through Central Asia*.

Revolution & Civil War

For a short time after the Russian Revolution of 1917, which toppled the tsar, there was a real feeling of hope in some Central Asian minds. The Central Asian society which the West, out of ignorance and mystification, had labelled backward and inflexible had actually been making preparations for impressive progress. The Young Bukharans and Young Khivans movements agitated for social self-reform, modelling themselves on the Young Turks movement which had begun transforming Turkey in 1908. The Jadidists, adherents of educational reform, had made small gains in modernising Uzbek schools, despite objections from the conservative khanate officials.

In 1917 an independent state was launched in Kokand by young nationalists under the watchful eye of a cabal of Russian cotton barons. This new government intended to put into practice the philosophy of the Jadid movement: to build a strong, autonomous Pan-Turkic polity in Central Asia by modernising the religious establishment and educating the people. Within a year the Kokand government was smashed by the Red Army's newly formed Trans-Caspian front. More than 5000 Kokandis were massacred after the city was captured. Central Asians' illusions about peacefully coexisting with Bolshevik Russia were shattered.

Bolshevik Conquest

Like most Central Asians, Emir Alim Khan of Bukhara hated the godless Bolsheviks. In response to their first ultimatum to submit, he slaughtered the Red emissaries who brought it and declared a holy war. The

1920

Soviet troops seize Khiva and Bukhara, replacing the respective khanate and emirate with People's Soviet Republics.

ELENA LISEYKINA / GETTY IMAGES ©

➡ Khiva, Uzbekistan

1920–26

Basmachi rebel movement in Central Asia reaches a peak, with as many as 16,000 armed men fighting the Soviet army.

emir conspired with White (anti-Bolshevik) Russians and even British political agents, while the Reds concentrated on strengthening party cells within the city.

In December 1918 a counter revolution broke out, apparently organised from within Tashkent jail by a shadowy White Russian agent named Paul Nazaroff. Several districts and cities fell back into the hands of the Whites. The bells of the cathedral church in Tashkent were rung in joy, but it was short-lived. The Bolsheviks defeated the insurrection, snatched back power, and kept it. Nazaroff, freed from jail, was forced to hide and flee across the Tian Shan to Xinjiang, always one step ahead of the dreaded secret police.

The end came swiftly after the arrival in Tashkent of the Red Army commander Mikhail Frunze. Khiva went out with barely a whimper, quietly transforming into the Khorezm People's Republic in February 1920. In September, Mikhail Frunze's fresh, disciplined army captured Bukhara after a four-day siege of the Ark (citadel). The emir fled to Afghanistan, taking with him his company of dancing boys but abandoning his harem to the Bolshevik soldiers.

Mission to Tashkent by FM Bailey recounts the exploits of this British intelligence officer in 1918 Soviet Tashkent. At one stage, under an assumed identity, he was employed as a Bolshevik agent and given the task to track himself down!

The Soviet Era

From the start the Bolsheviks changed the face of Central Asia. Alongside ambitious goals to emancipate women, redistribute land and carry out mass literacy campaigns, the revolutionaries levied grievous requisitions of food, livestock, cotton, land and forced farm labour. Trade and agricultural output in the once-thriving colonies plummeted. The ensuing famines claimed nearly a million lives; some say many more.

Forced Collectivisation

Forced collectivisation was the 'definite stage of development' implicit in time-warping the entire population of Central Asia from feudalism to communism. This occurred during the USSR's grand First Five Year Plan (1928–32). The intent of collectivisation was first to eliminate private property and second, in the case of the nomadic Kazakhs and Kyrgyz, to put an end to their wandering lifestyle.

The effect was disastrous. When the orders arrived, most people simply slaughtered their herds and ate what they could rather than give them up. This led to famine in subsequent years, and widespread disease. Resisters were executed and imprisoned. Evidence exists that during this period Stalin had a personal hand in tinkering with meagre food supplies in order to induce famines. His aims seem to have been to subjugate the people's will and to depopulate Kazakhstan, which was good real estate for Russian expansion.

The collapse of the Soviet Union sent the Central Asian republics into an economic collapse estimated at three times greater than the Great Depression of 1930s America.

1924

The Uzbek SSR (comprising modern Uzbekistan and Tajikistan) and the Turkmen SSR are created out of the Turkestan SSR.

1928–30

Latin script replaces Arabic script in Central Asia, divorcing the region from its Muslim heritage and rendering millions illiterate overnight. Latin is replaced by Cyrillic script in 1939–40.

1929

Tajik SSR created after borders are rejigged and redrawn to create the new republic's requisite minimum one-million population.

1930s

Stalin's genocidal collectivisation programs strike the final blow to nomadic life. Around 20% of Kazakhs leave the country with their flocks and a similar number die in the ensuing famine.

Alexander Cooley's *Great Games, Local Rules* looks at the resurgence of the Great Game in modern Central Asia and its competitive effect on everything from military bases to energy contracts.

Political Repression

Undeveloped Central Asia had no shortage of bright, sincere people willing to work for national liberation and democracy. After the tsar fell they jostled for power in their various parties, movements and factions. Even after they were swallowed into the Soviet state, some members of these groups had high profiles in regional affairs. Such a group was Alash Orda, formed by Kazakhs and Kyrgyz in 1917, which even held the reins of a short-lived autonomous government.

By the late 1920s, the former nationalists and democrats, indeed the entire intelligentsia, were causing Stalin serious problems. From their posts in the communist administration they had front-row seats at the Great Leader's horror show, including collectivisation. Many of them began to reason, and to doubt. Stalin, reading these signs all over the USSR, foresaw that brains could be just as dangerous as guns. Throughout the 1930s he proceeded to have all possible dissenters eliminated. Alash Orda members were among the first to die, in 1927 and 1928.

Thus began the systematic murder, called the Purges, of untold tens of thousands of Central Asians. Arrests were usually made late at night. Confined prisoners were rarely tried; if any charges at all were brought, they ran along the lines of 'having bourgeoisie-nationalist or Pan-Turkic attitudes'. Mass executions and burials were common. Sometimes entire sitting governments were disposed of in this way, as happened in Kyrgyzstan.

Construction of Nationalities

The solution to the 'nationality question' in Central Asia remains the most graphically visible effect of Soviet rule: it drew the lines on the map. Before the Russian Revolution the peoples of Central Asia had no concept of a firm national border. They had plotted their identities by a tangle of criteria: religion, clan, valley or oasis, way of life, even social status. The Soviets, however, believed that such a populace was fertile soil for dangerous Pan-Islamism and Pan-Turkism and that these philosophies were threats to the regime.

'Russia has two faces, an Asiatic face which looks always towards Europe, and a European face which looks always towards Asia.'

Benjamin Disraeli

So, starting in about 1924, nations were invented: Kazakh, Kyrgyz, Tajik, Turkmen, Uzbek. Each was given its own distinct ethnic profile, language, history and territory. Where an existing language or history was not apparent or was not suitably distinct from others, these were supplied and disseminated. Islam was cut away from each national heritage, essentially relegated to the status of an outmoded and oppressive cult, and severely suppressed throughout the Soviet period.

Some say that Stalin personally directed the drawing of the boundary lines. Each of the republics was shaped to contain numerous pockets

1936

Kazakh and Kyrgyz SSRs created. Stalin's 'Great Purge' results in the arrest and execution of political leaders across the Soviet Union.

1937

The entire Kyrgyz Soviet government (140 people) are shot to death and their bodies dumped in a brick kiln at Chong-Tash outside Bishkek, as part of Stalin's purges.

1941–45

More than 22 million Soviet citizens die in WWII, known locally as the Great Patriotic War. Kazakhstan and Uzbekistan each receive over one million refugees.

1948

Ashgabat is destroyed in an earthquake; 110,000, almost two-thirds of the city, perish.

of the different nationalities, and each with long-standing claims to the land. Everyone had to admit that only a strong central government could keep order on such a map. The present face of Central Asia is a product of this 'divide and rule' technique.

Dilip Hiro's *Inside Central Asia* gives perhaps the best general introduction to the recent (and not so recent) political history of the modern Central Asian republics.

World War II

'The Great Patriotic War Against Fascist Germany' galvanised the whole USSR and in the course of the war Central Asia was drawn further into the Soviet fold. Economically the region lost ground from 1941 to 1945 but a sizeable boost came in the form of industrial enterprises arriving ready-to-assemble in train cars: evacuated from the war-threatened parts of the USSR, they were relocated to the remote safety of Central Asia. They remained there after the war and kept on producing.

For many wartime draftees, WWII presented an opportunity to escape the oppressive Stalinist state. One Central Asian scholar claims that more than half of the 1.5 million Central Asians mobilised in the war deserted. Large numbers of them, as well as prisoners of war, actually turned their coats and fought for the Germans against the Soviets.

Agriculture

The tsarist pattern for the Central Asian economy had been overwhelmingly agricultural; so it was with the Soviets. Each republic was 'encouraged' to specialise in a limited range of products, which made their individual economies dependent on the Soviet whole. Tajik SSR built the world's fourth-largest aluminium plant but all the aluminium had to be brought in from outside the region.

The Uzbek SSR soon supplied no less than 64% of Soviet cotton, making the USSR the world's second-largest cotton producer after the USA. Into the cotton bowl poured the diverted waters of the Syr-Darya and Amu-Darya, while downstream the Aral Sea was left to dry up. Over the cotton-scape was spread a whole list of noxious agricultural chemicals, which have wound up polluting waters, blowing around in dust storms, and causing serious health problems for residents of the area.

Another noxious effect of cotton monoculture was what's known as the 'cotton affair' of the Brezhnev years. A huge ring of corrupt officials habitually over-reported cotton production, swindling Moscow out of billions of roubles. When the lid finally blew off in the early 1980s, 2600 participants were arrested and more than 50,000 were kicked out of office, including Brezhnev's own son-in-law.

In 1954 the Soviet leader Nikita Khrushchev launched the Virgin Lands campaign. The purpose was to jolt agricultural production, especially of wheat, to new levels. The method was to put Kazakh SSR's enormous steppes under the plough and resettle huge numbers of Russians

During WWII millions of Koreans, Volga Germans, Poles, Chechens and others whom Stalin suspected might aid the enemy were deported from the borderlands and forcibly relocated en masse. They now form sizeable minorities in all the Central Asian republics.

1954
Virgin Lands campaign in Kazakhstan leads to Slav immigration and, eventually, massive environmental degradation.

1961
Four years after the Sputnik satellite, Yuri Gagarin blasts off from the Baykonur Cosmodrome in Kazakhstan to become the first man in space. The first women in space sets off three years later.

1966
Tashkent is levelled in earthquake, leaving 300,000 homeless. Plans for a new Soviet showcase city are drawn up.

1959–82
Rule of Sharaf Rashidov ushers in an era of corruption and cotton-related scandal in Soviet Uzbekistan, though many locals praise him for promoting Uzbek regional interests and nationalism.

to work the farms. Massive, futuristic irrigation schemes were drawn up to water the formerly arid grassland, with water taken from as far away as the Ob River in Siberia. The initial gains in productivity soon dwindled as the fragile exposed soil of the steppes literally blew away in the wind. The Russians, however, remained.

Benefits of the Soviet Era

In spite of their heavy-handedness, the Soviets made profound improvements in Central Asia. Overall standards of living were raised considerably with the help of health care and a vast new infrastructure. Central Asia was provided with industrial plants, mines, farms, ranches and services employing millions of people. Outside the capitals, the face of the region today is still largely a Soviet one.

Education reached all social levels (previously education was through the limited, men-only network of Islamic schools and medressas), and pure and applied sciences were nurtured. Literacy rates hit 97% and the languages of all nationalities were given standard literary forms. The Kyrgyz language was given an alphabet for the first time.

Soviet women had 'economic equality' and although this meant that they had the chance to study and work alongside men *while* retaining all the responsibilities of homemakers, female literacy approached male levels, maternity leave was introduced and women assumed positions of responsibility in middle-level administration as well as academia.

Artistic expression was encouraged within the confines of communist ideology, and cinemas and theatres were built. The Central Asian republics now boast active communities of professional artists who were trained, sometimes lavishly, by the Soviet state. And through the arts, the republics were allowed to develop their distinctive national traditions and identities (within bounds).

If the Central Asian republics were at all prepared when independence came, they were prepared by the Soviet era.

CHINGGIS KHAN

Genetic testing has revealed that more than 16 million men in Central Asia have the same Y-chromosome as Chinggis (Genghis) Khan.

The Soviet-Afghan War

In 1979 the Soviet army invaded Afghanistan, determined to prop up a crumbling communist regime on their doorstep. In retrospect, someone should have consulted the history books beforehand, for the lessons of history are clear; no one wins a war in Afghanistan.

Of the 50,000 Soviet troops engaged in Afghanistan, up to 20,000 were Central Asians, mainly Tajiks and Uzbeks, drafted into the war to liberate their backward relatives. They faced a poorly equipped but highly motivated guerrilla force, the mujaheddin, united for once in their jihad against the godless invaders.

When the Soviets invaded Afghanistan in December 1979 there were already 8000 Soviet troops and 4000 Soviet advisers in the country.

1979–89

Soviet army invades Afghanistan. The ensuing war with the mujaheddin results in the death of 15,000 Soviets, 1.5 million Afghans, and the exodus of six million refugees.

1989

Nevada Semey Movement forces an end to nuclear tests in Kazakhstan. It is the first great popular protest movement in the USSR. Ethnic violence breaks out in the Fergana Valley.

8 Dec 1991

Collapse of the Soviet Union, as Russia, Ukraine and Belarus found the Commonwealth of Independent States (CIS). Two weeks later the Central Asian ex-Soviet republics join; Gorbachev resigns three days later.

1997

Astana replaces Almaty as the capital of Kazakhstan, shifting focus to the centre of the steppe. An ambitious program of architectural projects is initiated.

Funding for the mujaheddin soon poured in from the USA, determined to bleed the USSR and create a 'Soviet Vietnam'. The biggest covert CIA operation of all time funnelled funds through the Pakistan secret service (Inter-Services Intelligence, or ISI), and the Afghans quickly found themselves in the middle of a proxy Cold War.

In the end, after 10 years of brutal guerrilla war that claimed the lives of 15,000 Soviets and 1.5 million Afghans, the Soviets finally pulled out, limping back over the Amu-Darya to Termiz. They weren't quite massacred to a man as the British before them, but the strains of war indelibly contributed to the cracking of the Soviet empire. Over six million Afghans had fled the country for refugee camps in neighbouring Iran and Pakistan. Afghanistan was shattered and the USSR would never recover.

Presidents Nazarbaev (Kazakhstan; in power since 1989), Karimov (Uzbekistan; 1990) and Rahmon (Tajikistan; 1994) continue to rule without active opposition. President Niyazov of Turkmenistan proclaimed himself 'president for life' in 1999. He died in 2006.

Post-Soviet Central Asia

One Russian humorist has summed up his country's century in two sentences: 'After titanic effort, blood, sweat and tears, the Soviet people brought forth a new system. Unfortunately, it was the wrong one'.

By the spring of 1991 the parliaments of all five Central Asian republics had declared their sovereignty. However, when the failure of the August coup against Gorbachev heralded the end of the USSR, none of the republics were prepared for the reality of independence.

With independence suddenly thrust upon them, the old Soviet guard was essentially the only group with the experience and the means to rule. Most of these men are still in power today. All the Central Asian governments are still authoritarian to some degree, running the gamut from pure *ancien regime*-style autocracy (Turkmenistan), to a tightly controlled mixture of neocommunism and spurious nationalism (Uzbekistan), to a marginally more enlightened 'channelled transition' to democracy and a market economy (Kazakhstan and Kyrgyzstan).

In some ways, not much has changed. In most of the republics the old Communist Party apparatus simply renamed itself using various (unintentionally ironic) combinations of the words 'People', 'Party' and 'Democratic'. Political opposition was completely marginalised (Turkmenistan), banned (Uzbekistan), or tolerated but closely watched (Kazakhstan, Kyrgyzstan and Tajikistan). Kazakhstan suddenly found itself with a space program and nuclear weapons (which it promptly handed back to Russia, making it the only country ever to voluntarily return to nuclear-free status).

All the republics swiftly formed national airlines from whatever Aeroflot planes happened to be parked on their runways on the day after independence.

When a Kazkah shooter won the gold medal at a 2012 international sporting competition in Kuwait, the organisers mistakenly played the theme music to the film *Borat*, instead of the Kazakh national anthem.

13 May 2005

Massacre of between 200 and 1000 unarmed protesters by government troops in Andijon, Uzbekistan. The incident sours relationships between Uzbekistan and the USA and Europe.

2005

Kyrgyzstan's Tulip Revolution sweeps President Akaev from power, forcing curbs on the new president's power.

2006

Turkmenistan's 'President for life' Niyazov (Turkmenbashi) dies, ending one of the modern era's great personality cults.

2010

Violent street demonstrations force Kyrgyz president Bakiev from office, leaving more than 70 dead.

Restless Valley, by Phillip Shishkin, is an excellent collection of reportage, focused on Kyrgyzstan and Uzbekistan and full of tales of revolutions, massacres, organised crime, corruption and the drug trade.

Yet in most ways, everything has changed. The end of the old Soviet subsidies meant a decline in everything from economic subsidies to education levels. The deepest economic trauma was/is felt in the countryside. Most heart-rending were the pensioners, especially the Slavs, whose pensions were made worthless overnight with the devaluation of the rouble.

Throughout the 1990s, one of the most common sights across Central Asia was watery-eyed *babushkas* (old women) sitting quietly on many street corners, surrounded by a few worthless possessions for sale, trying not to look like beggars. Suddenly the Soviet era began to look like a golden age.

PIPE DREAMS – THE NEW GREAT GAME

Central Asia and the Caspian region is a mother lode of energy and raw materials, representing perhaps the most concentrated mass of untapped wealth in the world, a wealth measured in trillions of dollars. It is this fact that quietly drives many countries' Central Asian policies.

All eyes are on Kazakhstan, Central Asia's brightest economy, sitting pretty on what is estimated to be the word's third-largest oil reserves; but don't forget Turkmenistan, which boasts the world's fourth-largest reserves of natural gas. Kazakhstan and Uzbekistan also have major natural gas reserves.

As Western energy firms jockey to strike high-stake deals in a region of interlocking interests, this scramble is taking on a geopolitical significance. Russia's traditional stranglehold on supply routes has been challenged in recent years by new pipelines to Turkey and more pipe dreams are planned through Afghanistan.

China has also become a major player in the scramble for influence. It recently spent billions of dollars to become the main shareholder of PetroKazakhstan and build a 3000km-long pipeline to Ürümqi. There are epic plans to continue this along the former Silk Road to Japan, making China the energy corridor of the east.

Governments are well aware of the dangers of laying major oil pipelines through volatile Central Asia but the strategic need to ensure fuel supplies and the financial rewards are simply too fantastic to walk away from. This superpower competition for oil and gas in the region – dubbed 'round two of the Great Game' – is a rivalry which will have increasing resonance over the ensuing decades.

Jun 2010

At least 200 killed and 400,000 displaced in ethnic clashes between Kyrgyz and Uzbeks in Osh in the Kyrgyz Fergana Valley. Tens of thousands of Uzbek refugees flee to the Uzbekistan–Kyrgyzstan border.

2011

A turbulent year in Kazakhstan sees suicide bombings in Taraz, Atyrau and Aktobe, riots in western Kazakhstan and the reelection of President Nazarbaev with 95% of the vote.

Jul 2012

Singer Jennifer Lopez creates controversy by donning Turkmen national dress and singing 'Happy Birthday' to President Berdymukhamedov, a year after he wins a staged election with 97% of the vote.

2014

US and NATO troops expected to transport 70,000 vehicles and 120,000 shipping containers across Central Asia as part of a withdrawal from Afghanistan, paying hundreds of millions of dollars in transit fees.

The Silk Road

For centuries, the great civilisations of East and West were connected by the Silk Road, a fragile network of shifting intercontinental trade routes that threaded across Asia's highest mountains and bleakest deserts. The heartland of this trade was Central Asia, whose cosmopolitan cities grew fabulously wealthy. Traders, pilgrims, refugees and diplomats all travelled the Silk Road, exchanging ideas, goods and technologies in what has been called history's original 'information superhighway'.

Silk Routes

There was actually no such thing as a single 'Silk Road' – routes changed over the years according to local conditions. Parts of the network might be beset by war, robbers or natural disaster: the northern routes were plagued by nomadic horsemen and a lack of settlements to provide fresh supplies and mounts; the south by fearsome deserts and frozen mountain passes.

Though the road map expanded over the centuries, the network had its main eastern terminus at the Chinese capital Chang'an (modern Xi'an) and extended through the desert and mountains of Central Asia into Iran, the Levant and Constantinople. Major branches headed south over the Karakoram range to India and north via the Zhungarian Gap and across the steppes to Khorezm and the Russian Volga.

Silk Road Seattle (http://depts.washington.edu/silkroad) has articles on Silk Road history, architecture and maps.

Caravans & Trade

Silk was certainly not the only trade on the Silk Road but it epitomised the qualities – light, valuable, exotic and greatly desired – required for such a long-distance trade. China's early need for horses to battle nomads on its northern border was actually the main impetus for the early growth of the Silk Road; the silk was traded to the nomads in exchange for a steady supply of mounts.

Though the balance of trade was heavily stacked in favour of China (as it is today!), traffic ran both ways. China received gold, silver, ivory, lapis, jade, coral, wool, rhino horn, tortoise shell, horses, Mediterranean coloured glass (an industrial mystery as inscrutable to the Chinese as silk was in the West), cucumbers, walnuts, pomegranates, golden peaches from Samarkand, sesame, garlic, grapes and wine, plus – an early Parthian craze – acrobats and ostriches. Goods arriving at the western end included silk, porcelain, paper, tea, ginger, rhubarb, lacquerware, bamboo, Arabian spices and incense, medicinal herbs, gems and perfumes.

And in the middle lay Central Asia, a great clearing house that provided its native beasts – horses and two-humped Bactrian camels – to keep the goods flowing in both directions. There was in fact little 'through traffic' on the Silk Road; caravanners were mostly short- and medium-distance haulers who marketed and took on freight along a given beat. The earliest exchanges were based on barter between steppe nomads and settled towns. Only later did a monetary economy enable long-distance routes to develop.

Silk Road Reading

Silk Road: Monks, Warriors & Merchants, Luce Boulnois

The Ancient Silk Road Map, Jonathan Tucker & Antonia Tozer

The Silk Road in World History, Xinru Liu

The Silk Road

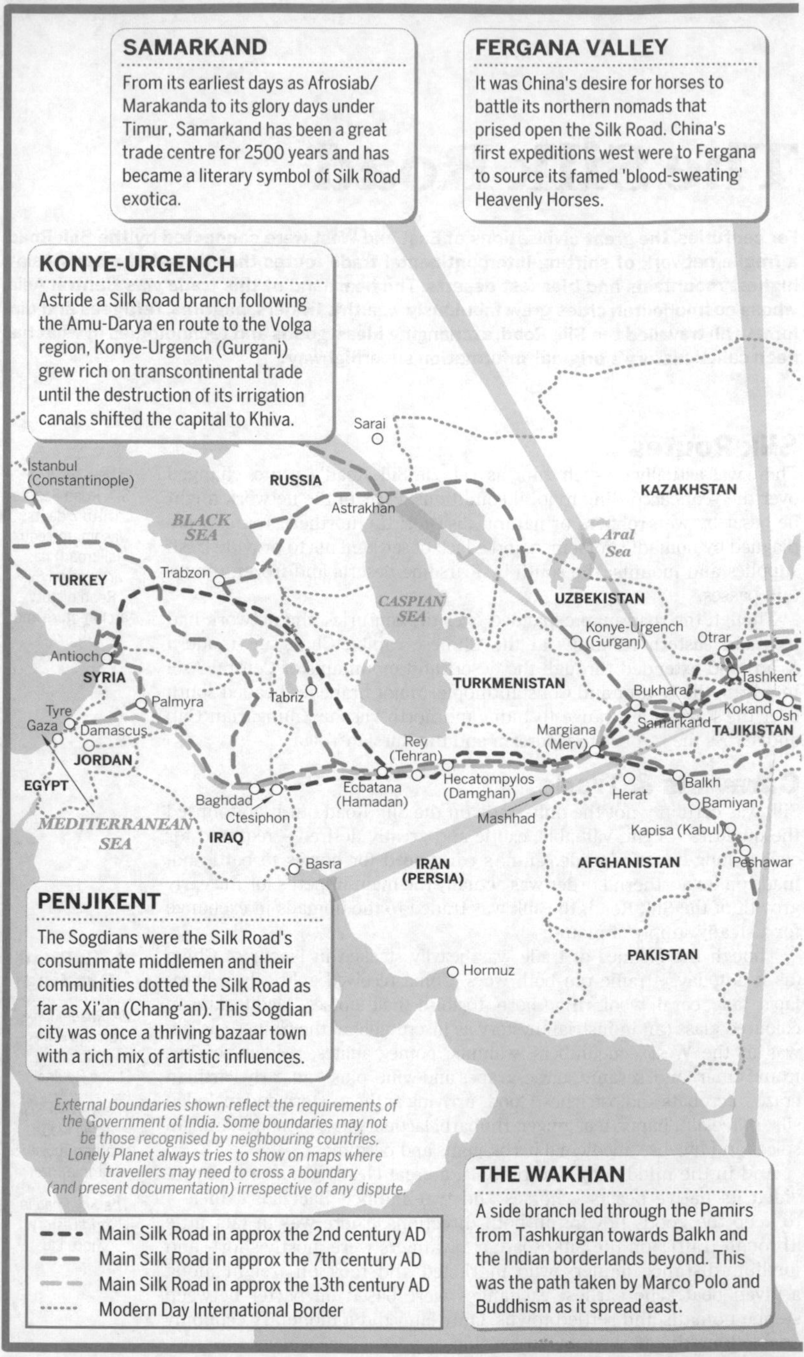

SAMARKAND

From its earliest days as Afrosiab/Marakanda to its glory days under Timur, Samarkand has been a great trade centre for 2500 years and has became a literary symbol of Silk Road exotica.

FERGANA VALLEY

It was China's desire for horses to battle its northern nomads that prised open the Silk Road. China's first expeditions west were to Fergana to source its famed 'blood-sweating' Heavenly Horses.

KONYE-URGENCH

Astride a Silk Road branch following the Amu-Darya en route to the Volga region, Konye-Urgench (Gurganj) grew rich on transcontinental trade until the destruction of its irrigation canals shifted the capital to Khiva.

Sarai
Istanbul (Constantinople)
RUSSIA
KAZAKHSTAN
Astrakhan
BLACK SEA
Aral Sea
TURKEY
Trabzon
CASPIAN SEA
UZBEKISTAN
Konye-Urgench (Gurganj)
Otrar
Tashkent
Antioch
SYRIA
TURKMENISTAN
Bukhara
Kokand
Osh
Palmyra
Tabriz
Samarkand
TAJIKISTAN
Tyre
Gaza
Damascus
Rey (Tehran)
Margiana (Merv)
JORDAN
Herat
Balkh
EGYPT
Baghdad
Ecbatana (Hamadan)
Hecatompylos (Damghan)
Bamiyan
Ctesiphon
Mashhad
Kapisa (Kabul)
MEDITERRANEAN SEA
IRAQ
Peshawar
Basra
IRAN (PERSIA)
AFGHANISTAN
PAKISTAN
Hormuz

PENJIKENT

The Sogdians were the Silk Road's consummate middlemen and their communities dotted the Silk Road as far as Xi'an (Chang'an). This Sogdian city was once a thriving bazaar town with a rich mix of artistic influences.

External boundaries shown reflect the requirements of the Government of India. Some boundaries may not be those recognised by neighbouring countries. Lonely Planet always tries to show on maps where travellers may need to cross a boundary (and present documentation) irrespective of any dispute.

- Main Silk Road in approx the 2nd century AD
- Main Silk Road in approx the 7th century AD
- Main Silk Road in approx the 13th century AD
- Modern Day International Border

THE WAKHAN

A side branch led through the Pamirs from Tashkurgan towards Balkh and the Indian borderlands beyond. This was the path taken by Marco Polo and Buddhism as it spread east.

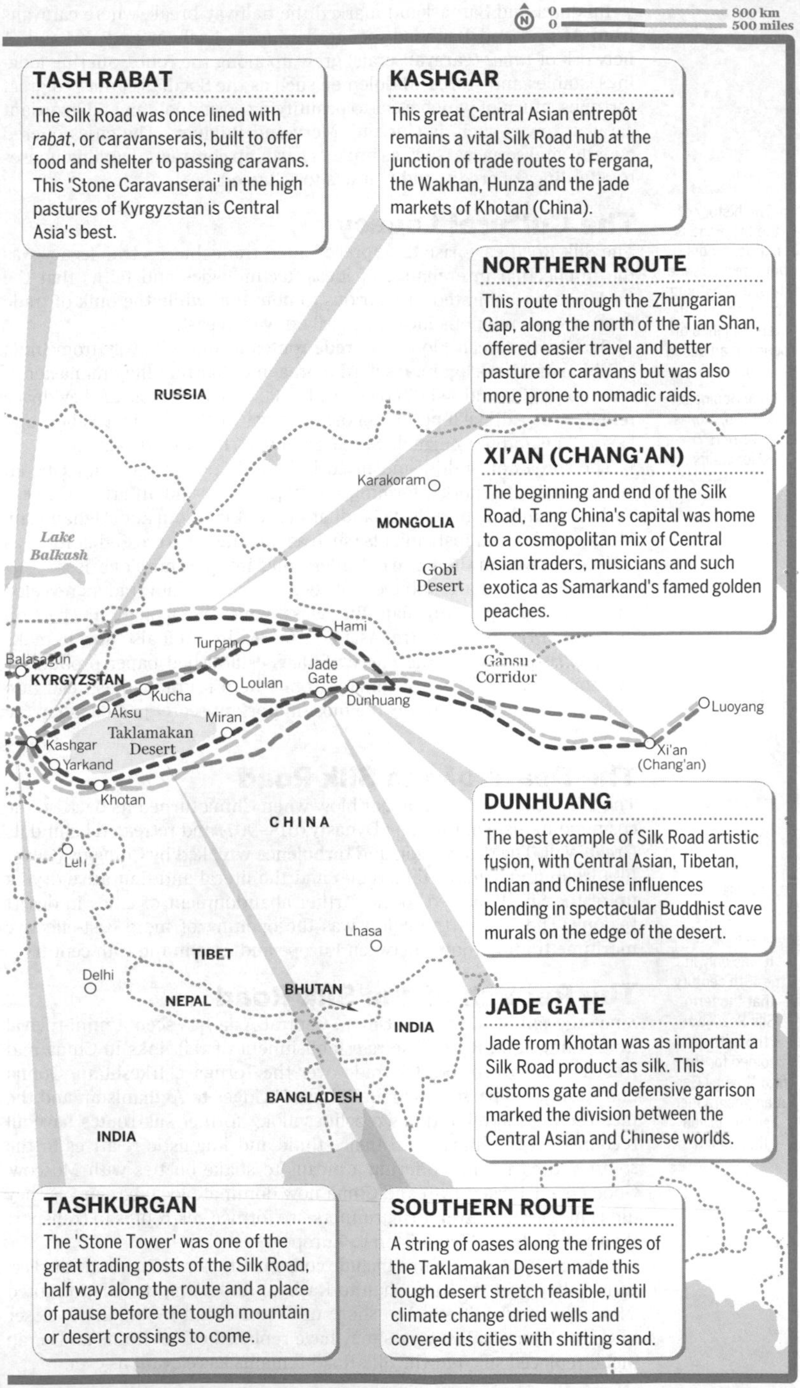

0 800 km
0 500 miles

TASH RABAT

The Silk Road was once lined with *rabat*, or caravanserais, built to offer food and shelter to passing caravans. This 'Stone Caravanserai' in the high pastures of Kyrgyzstan is Central Asia's best.

KASHGAR

This great Central Asian entrepôt remains a vital Silk Road hub at the junction of trade routes to Fergana, the Wakhan, Hunza and the jade markets of Khotan (China).

NORTHERN ROUTE

This route through the Zhungarian Gap, along the north of the Tian Shan, offered easier travel and better pasture for caravans but was also more prone to nomadic raids.

XI'AN (CHANG'AN)

The beginning and end of the Silk Road, Tang China's capital was home to a cosmopolitan mix of Central Asian traders, musicians and such exotica as Samarkand's famed golden peaches.

RUSSIA
Karakoram
MONGOLIA
Lake Balkash
Gobi Desert
Hami
Turpan
Balasagun
KYRGYZSTAN
Jade Gate
Gansu Corridor
Loulan
Kucha
Dunhuang
Luoyang
Aksu
Miran
Taklamakan Desert
Kashgar
Xi'an (Chang'an)
Yarkand
Khotan
CHINA
Leh
Lhasa
TIBET
Delhi
BHUTAN
NEPAL
INDIA
BANGLADESH
INDIA

DUNHUANG

The best example of Silk Road artistic fusion, with Central Asian, Tibetan, Indian and Chinese influences blending in spectacular Buddhist cave murals on the edge of the desert.

JADE GATE

Jade from Khotan was as important a Silk Road product as silk. This customs gate and defensive garrison marked the division between the Central Asian and Chinese worlds.

TASHKURGAN

The 'Stone Tower' was one of the great trading posts of the Silk Road, half way along the route and a place of pause before the tough mountain or desert crossings to come.

SOUTHERN ROUTE

A string of oases along the fringes of the Taklamakan Desert made this tough desert stretch feasible, until climate change dried wells and covered its cities with shifting sand.

Bukhara and Samarkand marked the halfway break, where caravans from Aleppo and Baghdad met traders from Kashgar and Yarkand. A network of *rabat* (caravanserais) grew up along the route, offering lodgings, stables and stores. Middlemen such as the Sogdians amassed great fortunes, much of which went to beautifying cosmopolitan and luxuriant caravan towns such as Gurganj, Merv and Bukhara. The cities offered equally vital services, such as brokers to set up contracts, banking houses to offer lines of credit, and markets to sell goods.

'The history of the Silk Road is neither a poetic nor a picturesque tale; it is nothing more than scattered islands of peace in an ocean of wars.'

Luce Boulnois, *Silk Road: Monks, Warriors & Merchants*

The Cultural Legacy

The Silk Road gave rise to unprecedented trade, but its true legacy was the intellectual interchange of ideas, technologies and faiths that the trade routes facilitated. It's curious to note that while the bulk of trade headed west, religious ideas primarily travelled east.

Buddhism spread along the trade routes to wend its way from India to China and back again. It's hard to imagine that Buddhist monasteries once dotted Central Asia. Today only the faintest archaeological evidence remains; at Adjina-Tepe in Tajikistan, Kuva in the Fergana Valley, and Fayoz-Tepe and the Zurmala Stupa around Termiz in Uzbekistan.

The spread of Buddhism caused Indian, Chinese, Greek and Tibetan artistic styles to merge, forming the exquisite Serindian art of Chinese Turkestan and the Buddhist Gandharan art of Pakistan and Afghanistan. Musical styles and instruments (such as the lute) also crossed borders as artists followed in the wake of traders, pilgrims and missionaries.

To religion and art, add technology transfer. Sogdian traders revealed the skills behind chain mail, fine glass, wine and irrigation. The Chinese not only taught Central Asia how to cast iron but also how to make paper. Prisoners from the Battle of Talas established paper production in Samarkand and then Baghdad, from where it gradually spread into Europe, making it culturally the most important secret passed along the Silk Road.

The Death of the Silk Road

The Silk Road received a major blow when China turned its back on the cosmopolitanism of the Tang Dynasty (618–907) and retreated behind its Great Wall. The destruction and turbulence wreaked by Chinggis (Genghis) Khan and Timur (Tamerlane) and the literal and figurative drying up of the Silk Road led to the further abandonment of cities in desert regions. The nail in the coffin was the opening of more cost-effective maritime trading routes between Europe and Asia in the 16th century

It was only in the 19th century that the term 'Silk Road' was thought up, coined for the first time by German geographer Ferdinand von Richthofen.

The Rebirth of the Silk Road

Since the fall of the Soviet Union, Central Asia has seen a mini-revival in all things Silk Road. The re-establishment of rail links to China and Iran, the growth of border trade over the Torugart, Irkeshtam, Qolma and Khunjerab passes, the rebuilding of bridges to Afghanistan and the increase in vital oil and gas pipelines along former silk routes have all reconnected the 'stans with their ethnic and linguistic relatives to the south and east, while offering a means to shake off ties with Moscow. Goods from Turkey, Iran and China now dominate local bazaars as they did centuries ago. Even drug runners use former silk routes to transport their heroin from Afghanistan to Europe.

Future Silk Road dreams include constructing a rail line from the Fergana Valley over the Tian Shan to Kashgar and using the US-promoted 'New Silk Road Initiative' to shore up Afghanistan by linking it closer to Central Asia. Railway cars may have replaced camel trains and scrap metal replaced silk, but the Silk Road remains as relevant as ever.

People & Culture

From gold-toothed Turkmen in shaggy, dreadlocked hats to high-cheekboned Kyrgyz herders whose eyes still hint at their nomadic past, Central Asia presents a fascinating collection of portraits and peoples. The most noticeable divide (and a largely amicable one) is between the traditionally sedentary peoples, the Uzbeks and Tajiks, and their formerly nomadic neighbours, the Kazakhs, Kyrgyz and Turkmen. In total the population of the former Soviet Central Asia is about 65 million. Few areas of its size are home to such tangled demographics and daunting transitions.

Peoples of the Silk Road

Centuries of migrations and invasions, and a location at the crossroads of Asia have added to Central Asia's ethnic diversity. A trip from Ashgabat, Turkmenistan to Almaty, Kazakhstan reveals an absorbing array of faces from Turkish, Slavic, Chinese and Middle Eastern to downright Mediterranean – surmounted, incidentally, by an equally vast array of hats.

Before the Russian Revolution of 1917, Central Asians usually identified themselves 'ethnically' as either nomad or *sarts* (settled), as Turk or Persian, as simply Muslim, or by their clan. Later, separate nationalities were 'identified' by Soviet scholars as ordered by Stalin. Although it is easy to see the problems this has created, some Kazakhs and Kyrgyz say that they owe their survival as a nation to the Soviet process of nation building.

Each independent republic inherited an ethnic grab bag from the Soviet system. Thus you'll find Uzbek towns in Kyrgyzstan, legions of Tajiks in the cities of Uzbekistan, Kazakhs grazing their cattle in Kyrgyzstan, Turkmen in Uzbekistan – and Russians and Ukrainians everywhere. Given the complicated mix of nationalities across national boundaries, Central Asia's ethnic situation is surprisingly tranquil, for the main part.

Kazakhs in...

Kazakhstan: 10 million

China: 1.4 million

Russia: 600,000

Uzbekistan: 500,000

Mongolia: 140,000

Turkmenistan: 80,000

Kyrgyzstan: 40,000

Kazakhs

The Kazakhs were nomadic horseback pastoralists until the 1920s; indeed the name Kazakh is said to mean 'free warrior' or 'steppe roamer'. Kazakhs trace their roots to the 15th century, when rebellious kinsmen of an Uzbek khan broke away and settled in present-day Kazakhstan. They divide themselves into three main divisions, or *zhuz*, corresponding to the historical Great (southern Kazakhstan), Middle (north and east Kazakhstan) and Little (west Kazakhstan) Hordes. To this day family and ancestry remain crucial to Kazakhs. 'What *zhuz* do you belong to?' is a common opening question.

Most Kazakhs have Mongolian facial features, similar to the Kyrgyz. Most wear Western or Russian clothes, but you may see women – particularly on special occasions – in long dresses with stand-up collars or brightly decorated velvet waistcoats and heavy jewellery. On similar occasions, men may sport baggy shirts and trousers, sleeveless jackets and wool or cotton robes. This outfit may be topped with either a skullcap or a high, tasselled felt hat resembling nothing so much as an elf's hat.

Kazakh literature is based around heroic epics, many of which concern themselves with the 16th-century clashes between the Kazakhs and Kalmucks, and the heroic *batyr* (warriors) of that age. Apart from various equestrian sports, a favourite Kazakh pastime is *aitys,* which involves two people boasting about their own town, region or clan while running down the other's, in verses full of puns and allusions to Kazakh culture. The person who fails to find a witty comeback loses.

Kazakhs adhere rather loosely to Islam. Reasons for this include the Kazakhs' location on the fringe of the Muslim world and their traditionally nomadic lifestyle, which never sat well with central religious authority. Their earliest contacts with the religion, from the 16th century, came courtesy of wandering Sufi dervishes or ascetics. Many were not converted until the 19th century, and shamanism apparently coexisted with Islam even after conversion.

Having a longer history of Russian influence than other Central Asian peoples, and with international influences now flooding in thanks to Kazakhstan's free-market economy and oil wealth, Kazakhs – in the cities at least – are probably Central Asia's most cosmopolitan people. The women appear the most confident and least restricted by tradition in Central Asia – though the custom of bride stealing (with or without her collusion) has not altogether disappeared in rural areas and Kazakhstan's south.

The 10 or so million Kazakhs have only recently become a majority in 'their' country, Kazakhstan.

Kyrgyz in...

Kyrgyzstan: 3 million

Tajikistan: 300,000

Uzbekistan: 180,000

China: 143,000

Afghanistan: 3000

Kyrgyz

As far back as the 2nd century BC, ancestors of the modern Kyrgyz are said to have lived in the upper Yenisey Basin (Ene-Sai, or Yenisey, means 'Mother River' in Kyrgyz) in Siberia. They migrated to the mountains of what is now Kyrgyzstan from the 10th to 15th centuries, some fleeing wars and some arriving in the ranks of Mongol armies.

Many Kyrgyz derive their name from *kyrk kyz,* which means '40 girls', which fits with oral legends of 40 original clan mothers. Today, ties to such clans as the Bugu (the largest clan), Salto (around Bishkek), Adigine (around Osh) and Sary-Bagysh (northern Kyrgyzstan) remain relevant and politicised. Clans are divided into two

BODY LANGUAGE

A heartfelt handshake between Central Asian men is a gesture of great warmth, elegance and beauty. Many Central Asian men also place their right hand on the heart and bow or incline the head slightly, a highly addictive gesture that you may find yourself echoing quite naturally.

Good friends throughout the region shake hands by gently placing their hands, thumbs up, in between another's. There's no grabbing or Western-style firmness, just a light touch. Sometimes a good friend will use his right hand to pat the other's. If you are in a room full of strangers, it's polite to go around the room shaking hands with everyone. Don't be offended if someone offers you his wrist if his hands are dirty. Some say the custom originates from the need to prove that you come unarmed as a friend.

Women don't usually shake hands but touch each others' shoulders with right hands and slightly stroke them. Younger women, in particular, will often kiss an elder woman on the cheek as a sign of respect.

federations, the Otuz Uul (30 Sons) of the north and the Ich Kilik of southern Kyrgyzstan. The southern and northern halves of the country remain culturally, ethnically and politically divided, as demonstrated in the violent political upheaval of 2010.

During special events older Kyrgyz women may wear a large white wimple-like turban (known as an *elechek*) with the number of windings indicating her status. Kyrgyz men wear a white, embroidered, tasselled felt cap called an *ak kalpak*. In winter, older men wear a long sheepskin coat and a round fur-trimmed hat called a *tebbetey*.

Most Kyrgyz now live in towns and villages but herders still do make the annual trek with their yurts up to *jailoos* (summer pastures). Traditions such as the *Manas* epic, horseback sports and eagle-hunting remain important cultural denominators. One lingering nomadic custom is that of wife stealing, whereby a man may simply kidnap a woman he wants to marry (often with some collusion, it must be said), leaving the parents with no option but to negotiate a *kalym* (bride price).

Tajiks in...

Tajikistan: 4.4 million

Afghanistan: 7.7 million

Uzbekistan: 630,000

Kazakhstan: 100,000

China: 33,000

Tajiks

With their Mediterranean features and the occasional green-eyed redhead, the Tajiks are descended from an ancient Indo-European people, the Aryans, making them relatives of present-day Iranians. The term 'Tajik' is a modern invention. Before the 20th century, *taj* was merely a term denoting a Persian speaker (all other Central Asian peoples speak Turkic languages).

Tracing their history back to the Samanids, Bactrians and Sogdians, Tajiks consider themselves to be the oldest ethnic group in Central Asia and one that predates the arrival of the Turkic peoples. Some Tajik nationalists have even demanded that Uzbekistan 'give back' Samarkand and Bukhara, as these cities were long-time centres of Persian culture.

There are in fact many regional Tajik subdivisions and clans (such as the Kulyabis and Khojandis), which is one reason why the country descended into civil war after the fall of the USSR.

Badakhshani or Pamir Tajik (sometimes called mountain Tajiks) are a distinct group, speaking a mix of languages quite distinct from Tajik and following a different branch of Islam. Most Tajiks are Sunni Muslims, but Pamiri Tajiks of the Gorno-Badakhshan region belong to the Ismaili sect of Shiite Islam, and therefore have no formal mosques. Most Badakhshani define themselves primarily according to their valley (Shugni, Rushani, Yazgulami, Wakhi and Ishkashimi), then as Pamiris, and finally as Tajiks.

Traditional Tajik dress for men includes a heavy, quilted coat *(chapan),* tied with a sash that also secures a sheathed dagger, and a black embroidered cap *(tupi),* which is similar to the Uzbek *dopy*. Tajik women could almost be identified in the dark, with their long, psychedelically coloured dresses *(kurta),* matching headscarves *(rumol),* striped trousers worn under the dress *(izor)* and bright slippers.

There are almost eight million Tajiks in Afghanistan (about one quarter of the population) and their language Dari (very similar to Tajik) has served as the language of government for centuries. There are also around 33,000 Sarikol and Wakhi Tajiks in China's Tashkurgan Tajik Autonomous County. Wakhi Tajiks also live in northern Pakistan.

Turkmen in...

Turkmenistan: 3.6 million

Iran: 1 million

Afghanistan: 650,000

Turkmen

Legend has it that all Turkmen are descended from the fabled Oghuz Khan or from the warriors who rallied into clans around his 24

HOLY SMOKE

In markets, stations and parks all over Central Asia you'll see gypsy women and children asking for a few coins to wave their pans of burning herbs around you or the premises. The herb is called *isriq* in Uzbek, and the smoke is said to be good medicine against colds and flu (and the evil eye), and a cheap alternative to scarce medicines. Some people also burn it when they move into a new home.

grandsons. Most historians believe that they were displaced nomadic horse-breeding clans who, in the 10th century, drifted into the oases around the Karakum desert (and into Persia, Syria and Anatolia) from the foothills of the Altay Mountains in the wake of the Seljuq Turks.

Turkmen men are easily recognisable in their huge, shaggy sheepskin hats *(telpek)*, either white (for special occasions) or black with thick ringlets resembling dreadlocks, worn year-round on top of a skullcap, even on the hottest days. As one Turkmen explained it, they'd rather suffer the heat of their own heads than that of the sun. Traditional dress consists of baggy trousers tucked into knee-length boots, and white shirts under the knee-length *khalat*, a cherry-red cotton jacket. Older men wear a long, belted coat.

Turkmen women wear heavy, ankle-length velvet or silk dresses, the favourite colours being wine reds and maroons, with colourful trousers underneath. A woman's hair is always tied back and concealed under a colourful scarf. Older women often wear a *khalat* thrown over their heads as protection from the sun's rays.

The Turkmen shared the nomad's affinity for Sufism, which is strongly represented in Turkmenistan alongside the cult of sheikhs (holy men), amulets, shrines and pilgrimage. The Turkmen language (also called Turkmen) is closest to Azeri. Interestingly, there was a Turkmen literary language as early as the mid-18th century.

Uzbeks in...

Uzbekistan: 18 million

Tajikistan: 1.6 million

Afghanistan: 2.6 million

Kyrgyzstan: 690,000

Kazakhstan: 457,000

Turkmenistan: 396,000

China: 14,700

Uzbeks

The Uzbek khans, Islamised descendants of Chinggis (Genghis) Khan, left their home in southern Siberia in search of conquest, establishing themselves in what is now Uzbekistan by the 15th century, clashing and then mixing with the Timurids. The Uzbek Shaybanid dynasty oversaw the tricky transition from nomad to settler, although the original Mongol clan identities (such as the Kipchak, Mangits and Karluks) remain.

The focal point of Uzbek society is still the network of tight-knit urban *mahalla* (districts) and *kishlak* (rural villages). Advice on all matters is sought from an *aksakal* (revered elder, literally 'white beard'), whose authority is conferred by the community. In general Uzbeks resisted Russification and emerged from Soviet rule with a strong sense of identity and cultural heritage.

Uzbek men traditionally wear long quilted coats tied by a brightly coloured sash. Nearly all wear the *dopy* or *doppilar*, a black, four-sided skullcap embroidered in white. In winter, older men wear a furry *telpek*.

Uzbek women are fond of dresses in sparkly, brightly coloured cloth *(ikat)*, often as a knee-length gown with trousers of the same material underneath. One or two braids worn in the hair indicate that a woman is married; more mean that she is single. Eyebrows that grow together over the bridge of the nose are considered attractive and are often supplemented with pencil for the right effect. Both sexes flash lots of gold teeth.

Slavs

Russians and Ukrainians have settled in Central Asia in several waves, the first in the 19th century with colonisation, and the latest in the 1950s during the Virgin Lands campaign. Numerous villages in remoter parts of Central Asia were founded by the early settlers and are still inhabited by their descendants.

Many Slavs, feeling deeply aggrieved as political and administrative power devolves to 'local' people, have emigrated to Russia and Ukraine. At the height of the migration more than 280,000 Russians left Kazakhstan and 200,000 left Tajikistan in a single year, most of them well-educated professionals. Some have returned, either disillusioned with life in the motherland or reaffirmed in the knowledge that Central Asia is their home, like it or not. Some 3.8 million Russians and 333,000 Ukrainians live in Kazakhstan alone.

Other Peoples

Dungans are Muslim Chinese who first moved across the border in 1882, mainly to Kazakhstan and Kyrgyzstan, to escape persecution after failed Muslim rebellions. Few still speak Chinese, though their cuisine remains distinctive.

More than 500,000 Koreans arrived in Central Asia as deportees in WWII. You'll most likely see them selling their pickled salads in many bazaars.

Five hundred thousand Germans were deported in WWII from their age-old home in the Volga region, or came as settlers (some of them Mennonites) in the late 19th century. Most have since departed to Germany but pockets remain, and you'll come across the occasional village in Central Asia with a German name, such as Rotfront in Kyrgyzstan. Likewise, most Jews, an important part of Bukharan commerce since the 9th century, have moved to Israel (and Queens, New York). The chief rabbi of Central Asia remains in Bukhara, though.

Karakalpaks occupy their own republic in northwest Uzbekistan and have cultural and linguistic ties with Kazakhs, Uzbeks and Kyrgyz.

CUSTOMS

Kazakhs and Kyrgyz share many customs and have similar languages, and in a sense they are simply the steppe (Kazakh) and mountain (Kyrgyz) variants of the same people.

CULTURAL DOS & DON'TS

- Dress codes vary throughout Central Asia. Western-style clothes are acceptable in the capital cities and large towns but avoid wearing singlets, shorts or short skirts in rural areas or the conservative Fergana Valley.
- Working mosques are generally closed to women and often to non-Muslim men, though men will likely be invited in outside of prayer times. In Kazakhstan women can visit many working mosques but may be restricted to a special women's gallery. When visiting a mosque, always take your shoes off at the door. Never walk in front of someone praying to Mecca.
- When you visit someone's home, take your shoes off at the door; you will often find a pair of undersized flip-flops waiting there. Avoid stepping on any carpet if you have your shoes on.
- Try not to blow your nose in public; it's considered rude.
- Central Asian society devotes much respect to its elderly, known as *aksakal* (literally white beards). Always make an effort to shake hands with an elder. Younger men give up their seats to *aksakal*, and foreigners should certainly offer their place in a crowded chaikhana (teahouse). Some Central Asians address elders with a shortened form of the elder's name, adding the suffix 'ke'. Thus Abkhan becomes Abeke, Nursultan becomes Nureke, and so on.

Kurds are another WWII-era addition to the melting pot, with many living in Kazakhstan. Estimates of their numbers in Central Asia range from 150,000 to over a million. Meskhetian Turks have groups in the Fergana (the largest concentration), Chuy and Ili Valleys. It is estimated that there are half a million Uyghurs in the former Soviet Central Asian republics (having moved there from Xinjiang after Chinese persecution in the late 19th century), with about half of these in Kazakhstan.

You may see colourfully dressed South Asian–looking women and children begging or working as fortune tellers. These are Central Asian gypsies called *luli (chuki),* who number around 30,000, speak Tajik and originate from areas around Samarkand, southern Tajikistan and Turkmenistan.

Kazakhs make up 56% of Kazakhstan, Tajiks 65% of Tajikistan, Kyrgyz 66% of Kyrgyzstan, Uzbeks 80% of Uzbekistan and Turkmen 85% of Turkmenistan.

Daily Life

It's been a social rollercoaster in Central Asia since independence: the overall birth rate is down, deaths from all causes are up, life expectancies have dropped and migration (most especially emigration) has reshaped the face of the region. Many older Central Asians lost their social and cultural bearings with the fall of the Soviet Union. Health levels are plummeting, drug addiction is up and alcoholism has acquired the proportions of a national tragedy.

But it's not all bad news. Traditional life is reasserting itself in today's economic vacuum and tourism projects are encouraging traditional crafts, sports and music. Communities remain strong and notions of hospitality remain instinctual despite the economic hardships. After 20 years of uncertainty, most people have found their way in the new order.

BUZKASHI

In a region where many people are descended from hot-blooded nomads, no one would expect badminton to be the national sport. Even so, the regional Central Asian variants of the Afghan game *buzkashi* (literally 'grabbing the dead goat') are wild beyond belief. As close to warfare as a sport can get, *buzkashi* is a bit like rugby on horseback, in which the 'ball' is the headless carcass of a calf, goat or sheep.

The game begins with the carcass in the centre of a circle at one end of a field; at the other end is any number of horsemen who charge toward the carcass when a signal is given. The aim is to gain possession of the carcass and carry it up the field and around a post, with the winning rider being the one who finally drops it back in the circle. All the while there's a frenzied horsebacked tug-of-war going on as each competitor tries to gain possession; smashed noses and wrenched shoulders are all part of the fun.

Not surprisingly, the game is said to date from the days of Chinggis (Genghis) Khan, a time when it enforced the nomadic values necessary for collective survival – courage, adroitness, wit and strength, while propagating a remarkable skill on horseback. The point of the game used to be the honour, and perhaps notoriety, of the victor, but gifts such as silk *chapan* (cloaks), cash or even cars are common these days.

Buzkashi takes place mainly between autumn ploughing and spring planting seasons, in the cooler months of spring and autumn, at weekends, particularly during Navrus or to mark special occasions such as weddings or national days. Look for a game in Kyrgyzstan (where it's known as *ulak-tartysh*), Uzbekistan *(kupkari)* and Kazakhstan *(kokpar)*. Navrus is the best time to find a game on, especially at Hissar (outside Dushanbe) or the hippodrome at Shymkent in Kazakhstan.

Traditional Culture

In Islam, a guest – Muslim or not – has a position of honour not very well understood in the West. If someone visits you and you don't have much to offer, as a Christian you'd be urged to share what you have; as a Muslim you're urged to give it all away. Guests are to be treated with absolute selflessness.

For a visitor to a Muslim country, even one as casual about Islam as Kazakhstan or Kyrgyzstan, this is a constant source of pleasure, temptation and sometimes embarrassment. The majority of Central Asians, especially rural ones, have little to offer but their hospitality, and a casual guest could drain a host's resources and never know it. And yet to refuse such an invitation (or to offer to bring food or to help with the cost) would almost certainly be an insult.

All you can do is enjoy it, honour their customs as best you can, and take yourself courteously out of the picture before you become a burden. If for some reason you do want to decline, couch your refusal in gracious and diplomatic terms, allowing the would-be host to save face. As an example, if you are offered bread, you should at least taste a little piece before taking your leave.

If you are really lucky you might be invited to a *toi* (celebration) such as a *kelin toi* (wedding celebration), a *beshik toi* (nine days after the birth of a child), or a *sunnat toi* (circumcision party). Other celebrations are held to mark the birth, name giving and first haircut of a child.

Out of Steppe: The Lost Peoples of Central Asia follows British author Daniel Metcalfe through five of the 'stans searching for lost communities of Karakalpaks, Bukharan Jews, Germans and Sogdians.

Islam in Central Asia

With the exception of rapidly shrinking communities of Jews and Russian Orthodox Christians, small minorities of Roman Catholics, Baptists and evangelical Lutherans, and a few Buddhists among the Koreans of the Fergana Valley and Kyrgyzstan, nearly everyone from the Caspian Sea to Kashgar is Muslim, at least in principle. The years since independence have seen the resurgence of a faith that is only beginning to recover from 70 years of Soviet-era 'militant atheism'.

The word Islam translates loosely from Arabic as 'the peace that comes from total surrender to God'.

Islam's History & Schisms

In 612 AD, the Prophet Mohammed, then a wealthy Arab of Mecca in present-day Saudi Arabia, began preaching a new religious philosophy, Islam, based on revelations from Allah (Islam's name for God). These revelations were eventually compiled into Islam's holiest book, the Quran.

Islam incorporates elements of Judaism and Christianity (eg heaven and hell, a creation story much like the Garden of Eden, stories similar to Noah's Ark), and shares a reverence for many of the key figures in the Judeo-Christian faith (Abraham/Ibrahim, Moses/Musa, Jesus/Isa), but considers them all to be forerunners of the Prophet Mohammed. While Jews and Christians are respected as People of the Book (ahl al-Kitab), Islam regards itself as the summation of and last word on these faiths.

In 622 the Prophet Mohammed and his followers were forced to flee to Medina due to religious persecution (the Islamic calendar counts its years from this flight, known as Hejira). There he built a political base and an army, taking Mecca in 630 and eventually overrunning Arabia. The militancy of the faith meshed neatly with a latent Arab nationalism and within a century Islam reached from Spain to Central Asia.

Succession disputes after the Prophet's death in 632 soon split the community. When the fourth caliph, the Prophet's son-in-law Ali, was assassinated in 661, his followers and descendants became the founders of the Shiite sect. Others accepted as caliph the governor of Syria, a brother-in-law of the Prophet, and this line has become the modern-day orthodox Sunni sect. In 680 a chance for reconciliation was lost when Ali's surviving son Hussain (Hussein) and most of his male relatives were killed at Kerbala in Iraq by Sunni partisans.

To learn more about Ismailism, try the scholarly *Short History of the Ismailis: Traditions of a Muslim Community*, or *The Isma'ilis: Their History and Doctrines*, both by Farhad Daftary.

About 80% of all Central Asians are Muslim, nearly all of them Sunni (and indeed nearly all of the Hanafi school, one of Sunnism's four main schools of religious law). The main exception is a tightly knit community of Ismailis in the remote western Pamirs of Gorno-Badakhshan in eastern Tajikistan.

A small but increasingly influential community of another Sunni school, the ascetic, fundamentalist Wahhabi, are found mainly in Uzbekistan's Fergana Valley.

Practice

Devout Sunnis pray at prescribed times: before sunrise, just after high noon, in the late afternoon, just after sunset and before retiring. Prayers are preceded if possible by washing, at least of the hands, face and feet. For Ismailis the style of prayer is a personal matter (eg there is no prostration), the mosque is replaced by a community shrine or meditation room and women are less excluded.

Just before fixed prayers a muezzin calls the Sunni and Shiite faithful, traditionally from a minaret, nowadays mostly through a loudspeaker. Islam has no ordained priesthood, but mullahs (scholars, teachers or religious leaders) are trained in theology, respected as interpreters of scripture, and are quite influential in conservative rural areas.

The Quran is considered above criticism: it is the direct word of God as spoken to his Prophet Mohammed. It is supplemented by various traditions such as the Hadith, the collected acts and sayings of the Prophet Mohammed. In its fullest sense Islam is an entire way of life, with guidelines for nearly everything, from preparing and eating food to banking and dress.

The melancholy sounding Arabic *azan* (call to prayer) translates roughly as 'God is most great. There is no god but Allah. Mohammed is God's messenger. Come to prayer, come to security. God is most great'.

Islam in Central Asia

Islam first appeared in Central Asia with Arab invaders in the 7th and 8th centuries, though it was mostly itinerant Sufi missionaries who converted the region over the subsequent centuries.

Islam never was a potent force in the former nomadic societies of the Turkmen, Kazakhs and Kyrgyz, and still isn't. Islam's appeal for nomadic rulers was as much an organisational and political tool as a collection of moral precepts. The nomad's customary law, known as *adat,* has always superceded Islamic sharia law.

There is also a significant blurring between religious and national characteristics, partly because the region was for so long cut of from mainstream Islamic teachings. The majority of Central Asians, although interested in Islam as a common denominator, seem quite happy to toast the Prophet's health with a shot of Russian vodka.

Some archaeologists believe that the Bronze Age site of Gonur-Depe was the birthplace of the world's first monotheist faith, Zoroastrianism, while others believe it to be Balkh just over the border in northern Afghanistan.

The Soviet Era

The Soviet regime long distrusted Islam because of its potential for coherent resistance, both domestically and internationally. Three of the five pillars of Islam (the fast of Ramadan, the *haj* or pilgrimage to Mecca and the *zakat* tax) were outlawed in the 1920s. The banning of polygamy, child marriage, the paying of bride price and the wearing of the paranja (veil) possibly pleased many women but the banning of Arabic script, the holy script of the Quran, was much less popular. Clerical (Christian, Jewish and Buddhist as well as Muslim) land and property were seized. Medressas and other religious schools were closed down. Islam's judicial power was curbed with the dismantling of traditional sharia courts (which were based on Quranic law).

FIVE PILLARS OF ISLAM

Devout Muslims express their faith through the five pillars of Islam.

- The creed that 'There is only one god, Allah, and Mohammed is his prophet'.
- Prayer, five times a day, prostrating towards the holy city of Mecca, in a mosque (for men only) when possible, but at least on Friday, the Muslim holy day.
- Dawn-to-dusk fasting during the holy month of Ramadan.
- Making the *haj* (pilgrimage to Mecca) at least once in one's life.
- Alms giving, in the form of the *zakat*, an obligatory 2.5% tax.

From 1932 to 1936 Stalin mounted a concerted anti-religious campaign in Central Asia, a 'Movement of the Godless', in which mosques were closed and destroyed, and mullahs arrested and executed as saboteurs or spies. Control of the surviving places of worship and teaching was given to the Union of Atheists, which transformed most of them into museums, dance halls, warehouses or factories.

During WWII things improved marginally as Moscow sought domestic and international Muslim support for the war effort. In 1943 four Muslim Religious Boards or 'spiritual directorates', each with a *mufti* (spiritual leader), took over the administration of Soviet Muslims, including one in Tashkent for all of Central Asia (in 1990 another was established for Kazakhstan). Some mosques were reopened and a handful of carefully screened religious leaders were allowed to make the *haj* in 1947.

The percentage of practising Muslims in the ex-Soviet republics ranges from 47% in Kazakhstan to 75% in Kyrgyzstan, 85% in Tajikistan, 88% in Uzbekistan and 89% in Turkmenistan.

But beneath the surface little changed. Any religious activity outside the official mosques was strictly forbidden. By the early 1960s, under Khrushchev's 'back to Lenin' policies, another 1000 mosques were closed. By the beginning of the Gorbachev era, the number of mosques in Central Asia was down to between 150 and 250, and only two medressas were open – Mir-i-Arab in Bukhara and the Imam Ismail al-Bukhari Islamic Institute in Tashkent.

Perhaps the most amazing thing though, after 70 years of concerted Soviet repression, is that so much faith remains intact. Credit for any continuity from pre-Soviet times goes largely to 'underground Islam', in the form of the clandestine Sufi brotherhoods, which preserved some practices and education – and grew in power and influence in Central Asia as a result.

By 1940, after Stalin's attacks on religion, only 1000 of Central Asia's 30,000 mosques remained standing and all 14,500 Islamic schools were closed.

Sufism

The original Sufis were simply purists, unhappy with the worldliness of the early caliphates and seeking knowledge of God through direct personal experience, under the guidance of a teacher or master, variously called a sheikh, *pir, ishan, murshid* or *ustad*. There never was a single Sufi movement; there are manifestations within all branches of Islam. For many adherents music, dance or poetry were routes to a trance-like moment of revelation and direct union with God. Secret recitations, known as *zikr,* and an annual 40-day retreat, known as the *chilla,* remain cornerstones of Sufic practice. This mystical side of Islam parallels similar traditions in other faiths.

Sufis were singularly successful as missionaries, perhaps because of their tolerance of other creeds. It was largely Sufis, not Arab armies, who planted Islam firmly in Central Asia. The personal focus of Sufism was most compatible with the nomadic lifestyle of the Kazakh and Kyrgyz in particular. Although abhorred nowadays in the orthodox Islamic states

PRE-ISLAMIC BELIEFS IN CENTRAL ASIAN ISLAM

The Central Asian brand of Islam is riddled with pre-Islamic influences – just go to any important holy site and notice the kissing, rubbing and circumambulation of venerated objects, women crawling under holy stones to boost their fertility, the shamanic 'wishing trees' tied with bits of coloured rag, the cult of *pirs* (saints) and the Mongol-style poles with horse-hair tassels set over the graves of revered figures.

Candles and flames are often burned at shrines and graves, and both the Tajiks and Turkmen jump over a fire during wedding celebrations or the Qurban (Eid al-Azha) festival, traditions that hark back to fire-worshipping Zoroastrian times. The Turkmen place particular stock in amulets and charms. At Konye-Urgench, Turkmen women even roll en masse down a hillside in an age-old fertility rite.

of Iran and Saudi Arabia, Sufism is in a quiet way dominant in Central Asia. Most shrines you'll see are devoted to one Sufi teacher or another.

When Islam was threatened by invaders (eg the Crusaders), Sufis assumed the role of defenders of the faith, and Sufism became a mass movement of regimented tariqas (brotherhoods), based around certain holy places, often the tombs of the brotherhood's founders. Clandestine, anticommunist tariqas helped Islam weather the Soviet period, and the KGB and its predecessors never seemed able to infiltrate them.

The moderate, non-elitist Naqshbandiya tariqa was the most important in Soviet times, and probably still is. Founded in Bukhara in the 14th century, much of its influence in Central Asia perhaps comes from the high profile of Naqshbandi fighters in two centuries of revolts against the Russians in the Caucasus. A number of well-known 1930s *basmachi* (Muslim guerrilla fighters) leaders were Naqshbandiya.

Another important Sufi sect in Central Asia is the Qadiriya, founded by a teacher from the Caspian region. Others are the Kubra (founded in Khorezm) and Yasauia (founded in the town of Turkistan in Kazakhstan). All these were founded in the 12th century.

Central Asia's most important Sufi shrines are the Bakhautdin Naqshband Mausoleum in Bukhara and the Yasaui Mausoleum at Turkestan in Kazakhstan.

Islam Today

Since independence, Central Asia has seen a resurgence of Islam, and mosques and medressas have sprouted like mushrooms across the region, often financed with Saudi or Iranian money. Even in more religiously conservative Uzbekistan and Tajikistan, these new mosques are as much political as religious statements, and the rise of Islam has as much to do with the search for a Central Asian identity as it does with a rise in religious fervour.

Most Central Asians are torn between the Soviet secularism of the recent past and the region's deeper historical ties to the Muslim world, but few have a very deep knowledge of Islam. Only the Fergana Valley regions of Uzbekistan and southern Kyrgyzstan can be considered strongly Muslim, and only here do women commonly wear the hijab (headscarf).

Jihad: The Rise of Militant Islam in Central Asia by Ahmed Rashid (2002) is an overview of how and why Islamic militant groups rose in the Fergana Valley from the ashes of the Soviet Union.

All the Central Asian governments have taken great care to keep strict tabs on Islam. Only state-approved imams (preacher or religious leader) and state-registered mosques are allowed to operate in most republics. Tajikistan's Islamic Revival Party is the only Islamist party in the region not to be outlawed.

Central Asia has experienced a taste of Islamic extremism, in the form of the Islamic Movement of Uzbekistan (IMU), which launched a series of armed raids and kidnappings in 1999 to 2001 in an attempt to establish an Islamic state in Uzbekistan. The movement has largely disappeared inside Central Asia, but there are fears that extremists may return to Tajikistan and Uzbekistan if they regain a base in Afghanistan.

Under the cloak of the 'war on terror', the Uzbek government has arrested thousands of Muslims as 'extremists', most of them from the Fergana Valley. Some, but not all, are members of the peaceful but radical organisation Hizb-ut-Tahrir (Movement of Liberation), which hopes to establish a global Islamic caliphate and has support across the region.

Turkmenistan also keeps tight controls on Islam. Turkmen mosques have quotations from former President Niyazov's book the *Ruhnama* engraved next to quotations from the Quran. The former chief cleric of Turkmenistan was charged with treason and sentenced to 22 years in prison after refusing to accept the Turkmen president as a messenger of God.

With the old communist ideals discredited, democracy suppressed and economic options stagnating, the fear is that radical Islam will provide an alluring alternative for a Central Asian youth left with few remaining options.

The oldest surviving Quran, the Osman Quran, is kept in Tashkent. It was written just 19 years after the death of the Prophet Mohammed and was later brought to Central Asia by Timur (Tamerlane).

The Arts

Set astride millennia-old trade and migration routes, Central Asia has long blended and fused artistic traditions from Turkic and Persian, Islamic and secular, settled and nomadic worlds, creating in the process an indigenous Central Asian aesthetic.

The Arts and Crafts of Turkestan by Johannes Kalter is a detailed, beautifully illustrated historical guide to the nomadic dwellings, clothing, jewellery and other 'applied art' of Central Asia.

Whether it be the Zoroastrian-inspired sun motif on an Uzbek embroidered *suzani*, the other-worldly performance of a Kyrgyz bard or the visual splendour of a Turkmen carpet, artistic expression lies at the heart of the Central Asian identity.

Folk Art

Central Asian folk art developed in step with a nomadic or semi-nomadic way of life, focusing on transport (horses) and home (yurts). Designs followed the natural beauty of the environment: snow resting on a leaf, the elegance of an ibex horn, the flowers of the steppe. Status and wealth were made apparent by the intricacy of a carved door or a richly adorned horse. Yet art was not merely created for status or pleasure; each item also had a practical function in everyday life. From brightly coloured carpets used for sleeping and woven reed mats designed to block the wind, to leather bottles used for carrying *kumys* (fermented mare's milk); many of today's souvenirs in Kyrgyzstan and Kazakhstan are remnants of a recent nomadic past.

With such emphasis on equestrian culture it is not surprising that horses donned decorative blankets, inlaid wooden saddles, and head and neck adornments. Men hung their wealth on their belts with daggers and sabres in silver sheaths, and embossed leather purses and vessels for drink. Even today the bazaars in Tajikistan and the Fergana Valley are heavy with carved daggers and *pichok* (knives).

Nomads required their wealth to be portable and rich nomadic women wore stupendous jewellery, mostly of silver incorporating semiprecious stones, such as lapis lazuli and cornelian (believed to have magical properties).

To remain portable, furnishings consisted of bright quilts, carpets and *aiyk kap* (woven bags), which were hung on yurt walls for storing plates and clothing. *Kökör* (embossed leather bottles) were used for preparing, transporting and serving *kumys;* these days empty cola bottles suffice.

If you are into carpets, don't miss a visit to Ashgabat's Carpet Museum, which showcases the world's largest hand-tied carpet.

Carpets & Textiles

Most Central Asian peoples have their own traditional rug or carpet styles. The famous 'Bukhara' rugs – so called because they were mostly sold, not made, in Bukhara – are made largely by Turkmen craftsmen in Turkmenistan and northwestern Afghanistan. Deep reds and ochres are the primary palate, with the stylised *gul* (flower) a common motif. The Kyrgyz specialise in *shyrdaks* (felt rugs with appliquéd coloured panels or pressed wool designs called *ala-kiyiz*). Kazakhs specialise in *koshma* (multicoloured felt mats).

Down in the plains, Uzbeks make silk and cotton wall hangings and coverlets such as the beautiful *suzani* (embroidery; *suzan* is Persian for needle). *Suzani* are made in a variety of sizes and used as table covers, cushions and *ruijo* (a bridal bedspread), and thus were a key part of a bride's dowry. Rich with floral or celestial motifs (depictions of people and animals are against Muslim beliefs), an average *suzani* requires about two years to complete. Possibly the most accessible Kazakh textile souvenir is a *tus-kiiz* (*tush-kiyiz* in Kyrgyzstan), a colourful wall hanging made of cotton and silk.

The psychedelic tie-dyed silks known as *ikat* or *khanatlas* are popular throughout the region. Take a close-up tour of how the cloth is made at the Yodgorlik Silk Factory in Margilon (see p167).

For a fictionalised account of the life of Persian poet Omar Khayam, check out Amin Maalouf's imaginative novel *Samarkand*, partially set in Central Asia.

Literature: Bards & Poets

The division into Kazakh literature, Tajik literature, Uzbek literature and so on, is a modern one; formerly there was simply literature in Chaghatai Turkic and literature in Persian. With most pre-20th-century poets, scholars and writers bilingual in Uzbek and Tajik, literature in Central Asia belonged to a shared universality of culture.

Take for example Abu Abdullah Rudaki, a 10th-century Samanid court poet considered the father of Persian literature, who also stars in the national pantheons of Afghanistan, Iran and Tajikistan (he is buried in Penjikent) and is also revered by Uzbeks by dint of being born in the Bukhara emirate. Omar Khayam (1048–1131), famed composer of *rubiayyat* poetry, although a native of what is now northeast Iran, also has strong ties to Balkh and Samarkand, where he spent part of his early life at the court of the Seljuq emir.

Uzbekistan's national poet is Alisher Navoi (1441–1501), who pioneered the use of Turkic in literature. Born in Herat in modern-day Afghanistan, Navoi served the Timurid court of Hussain Baiqara,

Since independence Central Asian art has been closely linked to the search for a new national identity, an identity that had been suppressed for decades during the Soviet era.

TOP PLACES FOR CRAFTS

For those interested in learning about local handicrafts, with an eye to purchasing, consider the following:

- Abulkasim Medressa (p153), Tashkent. Artisan school in a former medressa.
- Ak Örgö Yurt Workshop (p270), Barskoön. If you have plenty of cash and a generous baggage allowance, the ultimate Kyrgyz souvenir is your own personal yurt.
- Bukhara Artisan Development Centre (p198), Bukhara. Watch artisans at work here.
- Caravan (p151), Tashkent. Browse for stylish handicrafts over lunch or a cappuccino.
- De Pamiri (p346), Khorog. Felt carpets, musical instruments and more from the western Pamirs.
- Erkin/Kochkor-Kotu (p277), Kochkor. Some of the country's best *shyrdak*.
- OVOP (p262), Karakol. Good selection of locally sourced products.
- Rishton Ceramic Museum (p168), Rishton, Fergana Valley. The best place to learn about and buy Uzbek ceramics.
- Khiva Silk Carpet Workshop (p209), Khiva. Hand-made Khivan carpets that incorporate local designs with natural dyes.
- Unesco Carpet Weaving Shop (p198), Bukhara. Watch how carpets are made.
- Yak House (p354), Murgab. For Pamiri-style crafts, bags and socks.
- Yodgorlik Silk Factory (p167), Margilon. Silk by the metre, as well as *ikat* dresses, carpets and embroidered items.

commissioning public buildings, advising on policy and writing *divan* (collections) of epic poetry.

Better known to Western audiences is Mawlana Rumi (1207–73), born either in Balkh in Afghanistan or Vakhsh in Tajikistan (both places claim his birth site), and still today said to be the most widely read poet in the United States. Most Tajiks and Uzbeks are well-versed in Iran's national poet Firdausi, whose epic *Shah Nama* (Shahnameh; Book of Kings) tells the popular tale of Rostam and Sohrab, in which the tragic hero Rostam kills his son in a case of mistaken identity.

Art lovers should make the long trip out to the Savitzky Museum in Nukus, Karakalpakstan, for one of the world's great collections of avant-garde Soviet art. For a preview, track down the excellent documentary *The Desert of Forbidden Art* (www.desertofforbiddenart.com).

A strong factor in the universal nature of Central Asian literature was that it was popularised, not in written form but orally by itinerant minstrels, in the form of improvised songs, poems and stories. Known as *bakshi* or *dastanchi* in Turkmen and Uzbek, and *akyn* in Kazakh and Kyrgyz, these storytelling bards earned their living travelling from town to town giving skilled and dramatic recitations of crowd-pleasing verse, tales and epics to audiences gathered in bazaars and chaikhanas (teahouses). With their rhythms, rhymes and improvisation, these performers share much in common with rap artists in the West (but with considerably less bling).

The most famous epic is Kyrgyzstan's *Manas*, said to be the world's longest, and recited by a special category of *akyn* known as *manaschi*, though other peoples have their own epics, including the Uzbek *Alpamish* and Turkmen *Gorkut*. The most popular bards are national heroes, regarded as founders of their national literatures, and memorialised in Soviet-era street names (eg Toktogul, Zhambyl and Abay). Soviet propa-

CENTRAL ASIAN DISCOGRAPHY

The following recordings offer a great introduction to Central Asian music and are our personal favourites.

City of Love (Real World; www.realworld.co.uk) This recording by Ashkabad, a five-piece Turkmen ensemble, has a superb and lilting, Mediterranean feel.

Music of Central Asia Vol 1: Mountain Music of Kyrgyzstan (Smithsonian Folkways; www.folkways.si.edu) Collection of evocative Kyrgyz sounds by Tengir-Too, featuring the *komuz* and Jew's harp, with a section from the *Manas*. Other volumes in the Smithsonian series cover bardic divas, classical *shash maqam*, and music from Badakhshan.

Rough Guide to the Music of Central Asia (World Music Network; www.worldmusic.net) Excellent introduction to the sounds of the Silk Road, from Tajik rap to Kyrgyz folk melodies. Artists include classical singer Munadjat Yulchieva, the Kambarkan Folk Ensemble, Sevara Nazarkhan, Ashkabad, Yulduz Usmanova and Uzbek *tambur* player Turgun Alimatov.

Secret Museum of Mankind, the Central Asia Ethnic Music Classics: 1925–48 (Yazoo; www.shanachie.com) Twenty-six scratchy but wonderfully fresh field recordings of otherwise lost music.

The Selection Album (Blue Flame; www.blueflame.com) Career retrospective from Uzbek pop superstar, one-time politician and exile Yulduz Usmanova.

The Silk Road – A Musical Caravan (Smithsonian Folkways; www.folkways.si.edu) 'Imagine if Marco Polo had a tape recorder' runs the cover note for this academic two-CD collection of traditional recordings by both masters and amateurs, from China to Azerbaijan.

Yol Boisin (Real World; www.realworld.co.uk) This recording by Sevara Nazarkhan, a very accessible Uzbek songstress, has been given a modern production by Hector Zazou. Sevara supported Peter Gabriel on tour in 2007. Her more recent recordings *Sen* (2007) and the more traditional *Tortadur* (2011) are also excellent.

gandists even used *akyns* to praise Lenin or popularise the latest directive from party central. Bardic competitions are still held in some rural areas or during festivals, these days with cash prizes.

It was only with the advent of Bolshevik rule that literacy became widespread. Unfortunately, at the same time, much of the region's classical heritage was suppressed because Moscow feared that it might set a flame to latent nationalist sentiments. Instead writers were encouraged to produce novels and plays in line with official Communist Party themes. While a number of Central Asian poets and novelists found acclaim within the Soviet sphere, such as Tajik Sadruddin Ayni (1878–1954), and Uzbeks Asqad Mukhtar and Abdullah Kodiri, the only native Central Asian author to garner international recognition has been Kyrgyz writer Chinghiz Aitmatov (1928–2008), whose novels such as *Jamilla* and *The Day Lasts More Than A Hundred Years* have been translated into English and other European languages.

One interesting modern work is the exiled Uzbek writer Hamid Ismailov's *The Railway* (2006), a satirical novel that mixes anecdote and fantasy to depict life in the fictional end-of-the-line town of Gilas in Soviet Uzbekistan. The novel was swiftly banned in Uzbekistan.

Music

Although visual arts and literature succumbed to a stifling Soviet-European influence (which they're presently struggling to shrug off), the music of Central Asia remains closely related to the swirling melodies of Anatolia and Persia. The instruments used are similar to those found across Iran, Afghanistan and Chinese Turkestan; the *rabab* (*rubab;* six-stringed mandolin), *dutar* (two-stringed guitar), *tambur* (long-necked lute), *dombra/komuz* (two-stringed Kazakh/Kyrgyz guitar), *kamanche* (Persian violin, played like a cello) and *gijak* (upright spiked fiddle), *ney* (flute), *doira* (tambourine/drum) and *chang* (zither). Most groups add the ubiquitous Russian accordion.

In the past the development of music was closely connected with the art of the bards, but these days the traditions are continued by small folklore ensembles, heavily in demand at weddings and other *toi* (celebrations). In Uzbek and Tajik societies there's a particularly popular form of folk music known as *sozanda*, sung primarily by women accompanied only by percussion instruments such as tablas, bells and castanets. There are also several forms of Central Asian classical music, such as the courtly *shash maqam* (six modes) tradition of Uzbekistan, most of which are taught through the traditional system of *ustad* (master) and *shakirt* (apprentice). Central Asia has a strong tradition of the performer-composer, or *bestekar,* the equivalent of the singer-songwriter, who mixed poetry, humour, current affairs and history into music.

Musical traditions in remote regions like the Pamirs are sometimes preserved in just a few individuals, a situation the Aga Khan Trust for Culture is trying to redress through its music schools scattered throughout Central Asia.

DOSTOEVSKY

Russian writer Fyodor Dostoevsky lived for five years in Semey (then Semipalatinsk), in Kazakhstan, as part of his forced exile from Russia and was married there. His house is now a museum.

Painting

Rendered in a style that foreshadows that of Persian miniature painting, some splendid friezes have been unearthed in the excavations of the Afrosiab palace (6th to 7th centuries), on the outskirts of Samarkand, depicting a colourful caravan led by elephants. You can view copies at Samarkand's Afrosiab Museum. Similar Silk Road–era wall frescoes were discovered at Penjikent and Varakhsha, depicting everything from panthers and griffins to royal banqueting scenes.

The Arab invasion of the 8th century put representational art in Central Asia on hold for the better part of 1300 years. Islam prohibits the depiction of the living, so traditional arts developed in the form of geometric design and calligraphy, combining Islamic script with arabesques, and the carving of doors and screens. Textiles and metalwork took on floral or repetitive, geometric motifs.

The art of the Kyrgyz bards and the classical Tajik-Uzbek music known as *shash maqam* are both included on Unesco's list of 'Masterpieces of the Oral and Intangible Heritage of Humanity'.

Painting and two-dimensional art were only revived under the Soviets, who introduced European aesthetics and set up schools to train local artists in the new fashion. Under Soviet tutelage the pictorial art of Central Asia became a curious hybrid of socialist realism and mock traditionalism – Kyrgyz horsemen riding proudly beside a shiny red tractor, smiling Uzbeks at a chaikhana surrounded by record-breaking cotton harvests. You'll see a good selection of these at most regional museums.

Almaty has Central Asia's most vibrant contemporary arts scene: start your online visual explorations at Ular (www.artular.kz) and Tengri Umai (www.tu.kz).

Architecture

Central Asia's most impressive surviving artistic heritage is its architecture. Some of the world's most audacious and beautiful Islamic buildings grace the cities of Bukhara, Khiva and especially Samarkand (all in Uzbekistan). Few sights symbolise the region more evocatively than the swell of a turquoise dome, a ruined desert citadel or a minaret framed black against a blazing sunset.

Early Influences

Central Asian architecture has its roots in Parthian, Kushan and Graeco-Bactrian desert citadels or fortified palaces, whose structure was defined by the demands of trade, security and water. Iranian, Greek and Indian art blended in the 2000-year-old desert cities of places like Toprak Qala, Nissa and Termiz. Central Asia's position at the border of great empires and astride the transcontinental Silk Road guaranteed a rich flow of artistic influences. Due the destructive urges of Chinggis (Genghis) Khan and other invading empires, only traces have survived from the pre-Islamic era or the first centuries of Arab rule.

For an in-depth look at the Timurid architecture of Samarkand try www.oxuscom.com/timursam.htm.

Environmental constraints naturally defined building construction over the centuries. The lack of local wood and stone forced Central Asian architects to turn to brickwork as the cornerstone of their designs. Tall portals, built to face and catch the prevailing winds, not only looked fabulous but also had a cooling effect in the heat of summer. The influence of a nomadic lifestyle is particularly relevant in Khiva, where you can still see the brick bases built to house the wintertime yurts of the khans.

Several important technological advances spurred the development of architectural arts, principally that of fired brick in the 10th century, coloured tilework in the 12th century and glazed polychrome tilework in the 14th century. Without the seemingly insignificant squinch (the corner bracketing that enables the transition from a square to an eight-, then 16-sided platform), the development of the monumental dome would have stalled. It was this tiny technology that underpinned the breathtaking domes of the Timurid era.

Timurid Architecture

Most of the monumental architecture still standing in Central Asia dates from the time of the Timurids (14th to 15th centuries); rulers who combined barbaric savagery with exquisite artistic sophistication. During his campaigns of terror Timur (Tamerlane) forcibly relocated artisans, from Beijing to Baghdad, to Central Asia, resulting in a splendid fusion of styles in textiles, painting, architecture and metal arts.

The niches in the medressas' front walls were once used as shopkeepers' stalls.

The Timurids' architectural trademark is the beautiful, often ribbed and elongated, azure-blue outer dome. Other signature Timurid traits include the tendency towards ensemble design, the use of a monumental *pishtak* (arched entrance portal) flanked by tapering minarets, and exuberant, multicoloured tilework, all evident in the showiest of showpieces, the Registan in Samarkand.

ARCHITECTURAL HIGHLIGHTS

The following are our picks of the architectural highlights of Central Asia:

Ismail Samani Mausoleum (p193) (900–1000) Mesmerising brickwork, in Bukhara.

Kalon Minaret (p192) (1127) Central Asia's most impressive minaret, at 48m high, in Bukhara.

Mausoleum of Sultan Sanjar (p390) (1157) A huge double-domed Seljuq monument, in Merv.

Shah-i-Zinda (p173) (1300–1400) Features Central Asia's most stunning and varied tilework, in Samarkand.

Bibi-Khanym Mosque (p173) (1399–1404) Timur's intended masterpiece, so colossal that it collapsed as soon as it was finished, in Samarkand.

Gur-e-Amir Mausoleum (p174) (1404) An exquisite ribbed dome, sheltering the tomb of Timur, in Samarkand.

Ak-Saray Palace (p181) (1400–50) Tantalising remains of Timur's once-opulent palace, in Shakhrisabz.

The Registan (p171) (1400–1600) An epic ensemble of medressas, in Samarkand. The Sher Dor (1636) flaunts Islamic tradition by depicting two lions chasing deer, looked down upon by a Mongol-faced sun.

Lyabi-Hauz (p189) (1600) A delightful complex featuring a pool, *khanaka* (pilgrim resthouse) and medressa, in Bukhara.

Char Minar (p194) (1807) A quirky ex-gateway, resembling a chair thrust upside down in the ground, in Bukhara.

Architectural Design

The traditional cities of Bukhara and especially Khiva reveal the most about traditional urban structure. The distinction between *ark* (fortified citadel), *shahristan* (inner city with wealthy residential neighbourhoods, bazaars and city wall) and outlying *rabad* (suburbs) has formed the structure of settlements since the first Central Asian towns appeared 4000 years ago. A second outer city wall surrounded most cities, protecting against desert storms and brigands.

Apart from Islamic religious construction, secular architecture includes palaces (such as the Tosh-Hovli in Khiva), *ark* (forts), *hammom* (multidomed bathhouses), *rabat* (caravanserais), *tim* (shopping arcades), *tok* (or *tak;* covered crossroad bazaars) and the local *hauz* (reservoirs) that supplied the cities with their drinking water.

Unesco World Heritage Sites

- Khiva's Old City, Uzbekistan
- Bukhara, Uzbekistan
- Samarkand, Uzbekistan
- Shakhrisabz, Uzbekistan
- Mausoleum of Kozha Akhmed Yasaui, Kazakhstan
- Konye-Urgench, Turkmenistan
- Ancient Merv, Turkmenistan
- Solomon's Throne, Kyrgyzstan

Mosques

Islam dominates Central Asian architecture. *Masjid* (mosques) trace their earliest design back to the house of the Prophet Mohammed. Common to most is the use of the portal, which leads into a colonnaded space and a covered area for prayer. Some Central Asian mosques, such as the Bolo-Hauz Mosque in Bukhara, have a flat, brightly painted roof, supported by carved wooden columns, while others, such as the Juma Mosque in Khiva, are hypostyle (that is, with a roofed space supported by many pillars).

Whether the place of worship is a *guzar* (local mosque), serving the local community, a *jami masjid* (Friday mosque), built to hold the entire city congregation once a week, or a *namazgokh* (festival mosque), the focal point is always the *mihrab*, a niche that indicates the direction of Mecca. Central Asia's largest modern mosque is the Hazret Sultan Mosque (p102) in Astana, built in 2012.

Medressas

These Islamic colleges, normally two-storeys high, are set around a cloistered central courtyard, punctuated with *aivan* (or *aiwan;* arched portals) on four sides. Rows of little doors in the interior facades lead into *hujra* (cell-like living quarters for students and teachers) or *khanaka* (prayer cells or entire buildings) for the ascetic wandering dervishes who would overnight there.

Most medressas are fronted by monumental portals. On either side of the entrance you will normally find a *darskhana* (lecture room) to the left, and a mosque to the right.

Mausoleums

The *mazar* (mausoleum) has been popular in Central Asia for millennia, either built by rulers to ensure their own immortality or to commemorate holy men. Most *mazars* consist of a *ziaratkhana* (prayer room), set under a domed cupola. The actual tomb may be housed in a central hall, or underground in a side *gurkhana* (tomb). Popular sites offer lodging, washrooms and even kitchens for visiting pilgrims and are centred around the tombs of important Sufi saints. Tombs vary in design from the classic domed cupola style to the pyramid-shaped, tentlike designs of Konye-Urgench, or even whole streets of tombs as found at the glorious Shah-i-Zinda in Samarkand.

Minarets

These tall, tapering towers were designed to summon the faithful during prayer time, so most have internal stairs for the muezzin to climb. They were also used as lookouts to spot invaders, and even, in the case of the Kalon Minaret in Bukhara, as a means of execution. Some minarets (for example at Samarkand's Registan) exist purely for decoration.

COLOURS

Each of Uzbekistan's historic cities has its own distinct colour: greens are most common in Khorezm, khakis in Bukhara and blues in Samarkand.

ARCHITECTURAL GLOSSARY

aivan	covered portico or vaulted portal (also spelt aivan or iwan)
chorsu	market arcade
ghanch	carved and painted alabaster decoration
hammam	bathhouse
hauz	reservoir; artificial pool
jami masjid	Friday mosque
khanaka	pilgrim resthouse; prayer cell or hostel for wandering Sufis
mazar	tomb or mausoleum
medressa	Islamic college or seminary
mihrab	niche in a mosque marking the direction of Mecca
minor	minaret
pishtak	monumental entrance portal
qala	fortress (also *kala*)
rabat	caravanserai
tak	crossroads bazaar (also *tok*)
tim	shopping arcade
ziarat	shrine

Monuments of Central Asia: A Guide to the Archaeology, Art and Architecture of Turkestan by Edgar Knobloch is an excellent overview of the region's architectural heritage.

CENTRAL ASIAN MONUMENTS IN DANGER

The 2012 **World Monuments Fund** (www.wmf.org) list of 'world monuments in danger' includes the necropolis of Mangistau in western Kazakhstan and the Bronze Age archaeological site at Ulug Depe in Turkmenistan. Previous lists have warned about erosion in the desert castles of Khorezm in Uzbekistan, the architecture of Saryarka in Kazakhstan, the ancient ruins of Merv and Nisa in Turkmenistan, and Bukhara's Abdul Aziz Khan Medressa in Uzbekistan.

Decoration

Tilework is the most dramatic form of decoration in Central Asia, instilling a light, graceful air into even the most hulking of Timurid buildings. The deep cobalts and turquoise ('colour of the Turks') of Samarkand's domes have inspired travellers for centuries.

Decoration almost always takes the shape of abstract geometric, floral or calligraphic designs, in keeping with the Islamic prohibition on the representation of living creatures. Geometric and knot *(girikh)* designs were closely linked to the development of Central Asian science – star designs were a favourite with the astronomer king Ulugbek. Calligraphy is common, either in the square, stylised Kufi script favoured by the Timurids or the more scrolling, often foliated thuluth script.

Tiles come in a variety of styles, either stamped, faience (carved onto wet clay and then fired), polychromatic (painted and then fired) or jigsaw-style mosaic.

Patterned brick decoration reached its apex in Central Asia. The Ismail Samani Mausoleum and the Kalon Minaret in Bukhara are two wonderful examples of the use of monochrome brickwork to create a lightness of design.

Take time also to savour the exquisite details of Central Asia's carved *ghanch* (alabaster) and intricately carved and painted wood.

The best surviving caravanserai in Central Asia is the Tash Rabat (stone caravanserai), high in the pastures of central Kyrgyzstan, near the border with China.

Environment

Land-locked Central Asia covers an incredible range of landscapes, from snowcapped peaks to burning deserts, immense inland seas and rolling steppe. It is nothing less than the transition between Europe and Asia. Years of Soviet rule have taken a massive toll on the environment and serious problems remain, fuelled mainly by economic hardship. Despite this, Central Asia still hides some of the wildest and pristine corners on earth.

The Land

A quick spin around the Central Asia of this book would start on the eastern shores of the oil-rich Caspian Sea (actually a salt-water lake). Then dip southeast along the low crest of the Kopet Dag Mountains between Turkmenistan and Iran before heading east along the Turkestan plains, following the Amu-Darya river along the desert border with Uzbekistan and Tajikistan to its headstream, the Pyanj River, and into the high Pamir plateau. Round the eastern nose of the 7000m snow peaks of the Tian Shan range, skip northwestward over the Altay Mountains to float down the massive Irtysh River and then turn west to plod along Kazakhstan's flat, farmed, wooded border with Russia, ending in the basin of the Ural River and the Caspian Sea.

Uzbekistan is one of only two countries in the world defined as double landlocked, ie surrounded by countries which are themselves landlocked.

The sort of blank which is drawn in the minds of many people by the words 'Central Asia' is not entirely unfounded. The overwhelming majority of the territory is flat steppe (arid grassland) and desert. These areas include the Kazakh Steppe, the Betpak Dala (Misfortune) Steppe, the Kyzylkum (Red Sands) desert and the Karakum (Black Sands) desert. The Kyzylkum and Karakum combined make the fourth-largest desert in the world.

Central Asia's mountains are part of the huge chain which swings in a great arc from the Mongolian Altay to the Tibetan Himalaya. Central Asia's high ground is dominated by the Pamirs, a range of rounded, 5000m to 7000m mountains known as the 'Roof of the World', which stretch 500km across Tajikistan. With very broad, flat valleys, which are nearly as high as the lower peaks, the Pamirs might be better described as a plateau (*pamir* roughly means 'pasture' in local dialects). The roof of the Pamir, Tajikistan's 7495m Koh-i Samoni, is the highest point in Central Asia and was the highest in the USSR (when it was known as Kommunizma). The Pamirs is probably the least explored mountain range on earth.

A 600-year-old mausoleum discovered on the dried-out bed of the Aral Sea has indicated that Aral levels might be cyclical to some degree.

Varying from 4000m to more than 7400m, the crests of the Tian Shan form the backbone of eastern Central Asia. Known as the Celestial

EURASIAN KAZAKHSTAN

In Soviet parlance Kazakhstan was considered apart from Central Asia. While it is true that Kazakhstan's enormous territory actually extends westward across the Ural River (the traditional boundary between Europe and Asia), Kazakhstan still shares many geographic, cultural, ethnic and economic similarities and ties with Central Asia 'proper'.

Mountains, the Chinese-named Tian Shan (the local translation is Tengri Tau) extend over 1500km from southwest Kyrgyzstan into China. The summit of the range is Pobedy (7439m) on the Kyrgyzstan–China border. The forested alpine valleys and stunning glacial peaks of the range were favourites among such Russian explorers as Fedchenko, Kostenko, Semenov and Przewalski.

Marco Polo sheep are named after the Italian traveller who wrote of them after visiting the Pamirs: 'There are...wild sheep of great size, whose horns are a good six palms in length.'

These two mountain ranges hold some of the largest glaciers and freshwater supplies on earth (around 17,000 sq km) and are one of the region's most significant natural resources. The 77km-long Fedchenko Glacier is the longest glacier outside the polar regions and allegedly contains more water than the Aral Sea.

The Caspian Sea is called either the world's biggest lake or the world's biggest inland sea. The Caspian Depression, in which it lies, dips to 132m below sea level. Lake Balkhash, a vast, marsh-bordered arc of half-saline water on the Kazakh Steppe, is hardly deeper than a puddle, while mountain-ringed Lake Issyk-Köl in Kyrgyzstan is the fourth-deepest lake in the world. Other glacially fed lakes dot the mountains, including Song-Köl in Kyrgyzstan and stunning Kara-Kul, first described by Marco Polo, in Tajikistan.

Most of Central Asia's rainfall drains internally. What little water flows out of Central Asia goes all the way to the Arctic Ocean, via the Irtysh River. The Ili River waters Lake Balkhash; the Ural makes a short dash across part of Kazakhstan to the Caspian Sea. The region's two mightiest rivers, the Syr-Darya (Jaxartes River) and Amu-Darya (Oxus River), used to replenish the Aral Sea until they were bled dry for cotton. There is evidence that the Amu-Darya once flowed into the Caspian Sea, along the now-dry Uzboy Channel.

Central Asia, as defined by this book, occupies just over 4 million sq km, of which 68% belongs to Kazakhstan.

Geology

The compact, balled-up mass of mountains bordering Tajikistan, Kyrgyzstan, China and Afghanistan is often called the Pamir Knot. It's the hub from which other major ranges extend like radiating ropes: the Himalaya and Karakoram to the southeast, the Hindu Kush to the southwest, the Kunlun to the east and the Tian Shan to the northeast. These young mountains all arose (or more correctly, are arising still) from the shock waves created by the Indian subcontinent smashing into the Asian crustal plate more than 100 million years ago. Amazing as it seems, marine fossils from the original Tethys Sea have been found in the deserts of Central Asia as a testament to the continental collision. The Tian Shan are currently rising at the rate of around 1cm per year.

Central Asia is therefore, unsurprisingly, a major earthquake zone. Ashgabat was 80% destroyed by a massive earthquake in 1948 that killed 110,000 and Tashkent was levelled in 1966. More recently, devastating earthquakes hit the Tajikistan–Afghanistan border in 1997 and 1998.

Since the 1930s Caspian seal numbers have dropped from over a million to 100,000.

Wildlife

Central Asia is home to a unique range of ecosystems and an extraordinary variety of flora and fauna. The ex-Soviet Central Asian republics comprised only 17% of the former USSR's territory, but contained over 50% of its variety in flora and fauna.

The mountains of Kyrgyzstan, Kazakhstan and Tajikistan are the setting for high summer pastures known as *jailoos*. In summertime the wild flowers (including wild irises and edelweiss) are a riot of colour. Marmots and pikas provide food for eagles and lammergeiers, while the elusive snow leopard preys on the ibex, with which it shares a preference for crags and rocky slopes, alongside the Svertsov ram and Marco Polo sheep (argali). Forests of Tian Shan spruce, ash, larch and juniper provide cover for lynxes, wolves, wild boars and brown bears. Lower down in the mountains of southern Kyrgyzstan, Uzbekistan, Tajikistan and Turkmenistan are ancient forests of wild walnut, pistachio, juniper, apricot, cherry and apple. Arslanbob in Kyrgyzstan is home to the world's largest walnut grove.

The steppes (what's left of them after massive Soviet cultivation projects) are covered with grasses and low shrubs such as saxaul. Where they rise to meet foothills, the steppes bear vast fields of wild poppies and several hundred types of tulip, which burst into beautiful bloom in May and June.

The Aral isn't the only body of water drying up. Lake Balkhash in Kazakhstan, which gets its water from the Ili River, has shrunk by 1000 sq km since the 1970s.

Roe deer and saiga, a species of antelope, have their homes on the steppe. The saiga is a slightly ridiculous-looking animal with a huge bulbous nose that once roamed in herds 100,000 strong. The ring-necked pheasant, widely introduced to North America and elsewhere, is native to the Central Asian steppe, as are partridges, black grouse, bustards, and the falcons and hawks that prey on them. Korgalzhyn Nature Reserve in Kazakhstan is home to the world's most northerly colony of pink flamingos.

Rivers and lake shores in the flatlands create a different world, with dense thickets of elm, poplar, reeds and shrubs known as *tugai*, where wild boar, jackal and deer make their homes. Over 90% of *tugai* environment along the Amu-Darya has been lost over the years.

In the barren, stony wastes of the Karakum and Kyzylkum you'll need a sharp eye to catch a glimpse of the goitred gazelle (zheyran). Gophers, sand rats and jerboas are preyed on by various reptiles, including (in Turkmenistan) vipers and cobras.

Turkmenistan's wildlife has a Middle Eastern streak, understandable when you consider that parts of the country are as close to Baghdad as they are to Tashkent. Leopards and porcupines inhabit the parched hills. The *zemzen* or *varan* (desert crocodile) is actually a type of large lizard that can grow up to 1.8m long.

Central Asia has been famed for its horses since Chinese reports of the 'blood-sweating' horses of Fergana, that Han China needed to fight the nomadic tribes harassing its northern frontier. Today's most famous horses are the Akhal-Teke of Turkmenistan, the forefather of the modern Arab thoroughbred. There are only around 2000 thoroughbred Akhal-Teke in the world, of which 1200 are in Turkmenistan.

BIO-DIVERSITY

For more on wildlife protection in Kazakhstan see the Association for the Conservation of Biodiversity of Kazakhstan (www.acbk.kz/en)

Endangered Species

The mountain goose, among other rare species, nests on the shores of Kyrgyzstan's mountain lakes, but the population has shrunk over the years to fewer than 15 pairs worldwide.

The marshlands of the Amu-Darya region of Uzbekistan was once home to the Turan (Caspian) tiger but these became extinct when the last known survivor was shot in 1972. Wild Bactrian camels, once the quintessential Silk Road sight, are now only occasionally seen from the Tajikistan side of the Wakhan Valley.

THE IRBIS

The population of snow leopards in Central Asia and the Russian Altay is estimated at about 1000, out of a global population of around 7000. These magnificent but secretive and solitary animals (known locally as *irbis* or *barys*) are a keystone species, keeping others in balance and check. There are thought to be between 150 and 500 leopards in Kyrgyzstan, with around 200 more each in Kazakhstan and the Pamirs of Tajikistan. Only 5% of these magnificent creatures' habitat is currently protected.

There has been some good news, though: eight Przewalski's horses were recently reintroduced into Kazakhstan's Altyn-Emel National Park after being extinct in the region for 60 years.

Over the last decade Bukhara (Bactrian) deer have also been relocated to reserves in Uzbekistan and Kazakhstan, including Altyn-Emel National Park, raising regional numbers from just 350 to over 1000. You can pat yourself on the back for this; the Altyn-Emel project was partly funded with money generated by ecotourism.

Botanists say that the modern apple has its genetic origins in Kazakhstan; revealingly the largest city, Almaty, translates as 'Father of Apples'.

National Parks

Many of the region's approximately three-dozen *zapovednik* (nature reserves) and *zakazniki* (protected areas) and dozen or so national parks *(gosudarstvenny natsionalny prirodny park)* are accessible for tourists.

The existing system of national parks and protected areas, one of the positive legacies of the USSR, is nevertheless antiquated and inadequate. All suffer from a chronic lack of government funding and are under increasing pressure from grazing, poaching, and firewood gathering. In Kyrgyzstan just 2.5% of the country's area is dedicated to land conservation.

Kazakhstan's new Irgiz-Turgay nature reserve in the northwestern steppes is part of a planned 62,000-sq-km system of protected areas known as the Altyn Dala (Golden Steppe) Conservation Initiative that will eventually see the reintroduction of Przewalski's horses and *onager* (wild Central Asian ass).

The Tajik National Park in the Pamirs of Tajikistan and the Saryarka Steppes and Lakes region of northern Kazakhstan are included in Unesco's list of Natural World Heritage Sites.

NATIONAL PARKS

The easiest protected areas to visit include the following:

Aksu-Zhabagyly Nature Reserve (p85) High biodiversity in southern Kazakhstan, famed for its beautiful tulips. An ecotourism program offers excellent mountain hiking and bird watching.

Ala-Archa National Park (p250) Fine hiking and climbing just outside Bishkek.

Badai-Tugai Biosphere Reserve (p202) Protects a strip of *tugai* riverine forest on the eastern bank of the Amu-Darya in Karakalpakstan. Entry fees pay for food for a Bukhara deer-breeding centre.

Ile-Alatau National Park (p73) Good mountain hiking on Almaty's doorstep, though plans for a 16-lift ski resort at Kok-Zhaylau are controversial.

Karakol Valley (p266) Alpine ecosystem in the Tian Shan, southeast Issyk-Köl, with superb scenery and fine trekking routes.

Kugitang Nature Reserve (p403) The most impressive of Turkmenistan's nature reserves, focused around the country's highest peak and home to the rare markhor mountain goat and several hundred dinosaur footprints.

Sary-Chelek Biosphere Reserve (p286) Remote trekking routes cross this Unesco-sponsored reserve, centred on a large mountain lake.

Sayram-Ugam National Park (p86) Ecotourism programs include hikes and horse treks.

Tajik National Park (p354) Covers most of the eastern Pamirs (18% of the country!) and offers superb mountain trekking and mountain climbing.

Ugam-Chatkal National Park(p158) Unesco-sponsored biosphere reserve, with juniper forests, wild boars, bears and snow leopards, plus some fine hiking and rafting.

Environmental Issues

Central Asia's 'empty' landscapes served as testing grounds for Soviet experiments in taming nature, which resulted in land and water mismanagement and the destruction of natural habitat on an almost unimaginable scale.

Even casual students of the region are familiar with some of the most serious environmental catastrophes: the gradual disappearance of the Aral Sea and the excessive levels of radiation around the Semey (Semipalatinsk) nuclear-testing site. Khrushchev's Virgin Lands scheme, which was planned to boost grain production, resulted in the degradation of hundreds of thousands of square kilometres of Kazakh steppe.

In the economic malaise of the post-Soviet years, the environment has taken a back seat. Whether it is poaching, hunting tours or pollution from gold-mining operations, the lure of hard-currency in an otherwise bleak economic landscape has repeatedly taken priority over nature conservation.

The extreme continental climate of Central Asia is particularly susceptible to global climate change, and glaciers in the Pamirs and Tian Shan are already shrinking by around 15m a year.

Water is, in fact, the only major resource in Tajikistan and Kyrgyzstan and both countries plan a series of giant hydroelectric dams, much to the concern of downstream Uzbekistan and Turkmenistan, for whom water supplies are vital to their cotton-based economies. Central Asia's future is looking increasingly defined by two of nature's greatest gifts: oil and water.

Search the website of the UN Environment Programme (www.grida.no) for reports on the state of Central Asia's environment.

The Aral Sea

The Aral Sea straddles the border between western Uzbekistan and southern Kazakhstan. It's fed by the Syr-Darya and Amu-Darya rivers, flowing down from the Tian Shan and Pamir mountain ranges. Back in the 1950s these rivers brought an average 55 cubic km of water a year to the Aral Sea, which stretched 400km from end to end and 280km from side to side, and covered 66,900 sq km. The sea had, by all accounts, lovely clear water, pristine beaches, enough fish to support a big fishing industry in the ports of Moynaq and Aralsk, and even passenger ferries crossing it from north to south.

Then the USSR's central planners decided to boost cotton production in Uzbekistan, Turkmenistan and Kazakhstan, to feed a leap forward in the Soviet textile industry. But the thirsty new cotton fields, many of them on poorer desert soils and fed by long, unlined canals open to the sun, required much more water per hectare than the old ones. The irrigated area grew by 20% between 1960 and 1980, but the annual water take from the rivers doubled from 45 to 90 cubic km. By the 1980s the annual flow into the Aral Sea was less than a tenth of the 1950s supply.

Production of cotton rose, but the Aral Sea sank. Between 1966 and 1993 its level fell by more than 16m and its eastern and southern shores receded by up to 80km. In 1987 the Aral divided into a smaller northern sea and a larger southern one, each fed, sometimes, by one of the rivers.

The two main fishing ports, Aralsk (Kazakhstan) in the north and Moynaq (Uzbekistan) in the south, were left high and dry when efforts to keep their navigation channels open were abandoned in the early 1980s. Of the 60,000 people who used to live off the Aral fishing industry (harvesting 20,000 tons of fish a year), almost all are gone. These days the rusting hulks of beached fishing boats lie scattered dozens of kilometres from the nearest water. Of the 173 animal species that used to live around the Aral Sea, only 38 survive.

The Aral Sea was once the world's fourth-largest lake. It is now recognised as the world's worst man-made ecological disaster.

The best places to view the Aral disaster are Moynaq in Uzbekistan and Aralsk in Kazakhstan. Aralsk is closer to the actual sea (you can swim!) but Moynaq has more fishing trawlers rusting in the salty desert.

As the sea has shrunk, the climate around the lake has changed: the air is drier, winters are colder and longer, and summers are hotter. Every year 150,000 tons of salt and sand from the exposed bed is blown hundreds of kilometres in big salt-dust sandstorms, which also pick up residues of the chemicals from cultivated land and a former biological weapons testing site. A visit to anywhere near the sea is a ride into a nightmare of blighted towns, land and communities.

Extremes Along the Silk Road, by Nick Middleton, devotes one-third of the book to Kazakhstan, with a trip out to the former biological weapons site at Vozrozhdenie Island in the Aral Sea.

The catalogue of human health problems is awful: salt and dust are blamed for cancers of the throat and oesophagus; poor drinking water has been implicated in high rates of typhoid, paratyphoid, hepatitis and dysentery; and the area has the highest infant mortality rates (over 10%) in the former USSR, as well as high rates of birth deformities.

Long-Term Solutions

Dozens of enquiries, projects and research teams have poked and prodded the Aral problem; locals joke that if every scientist who visited the Aral region had brought a bucket of water the problem would be over by now. The initial outcry over the disaster seems to have largely evaporated, along with the sea, and the focus has shifted from rehabilitating the sea, to stabilising part of the sea and now stabilising the environment around the sea.

In 2005 the little channel still connecting the northern and southern seas was blocked by the Kok-Aral dam, preventing further water loss from the northern sea, but condemning the southern sea to oblivion. The northern sea has risen by 4m since then and should reach a state of equilibrium by about 2025 (see p92). The southern sea, however, is expected to split again and then dry up completely by 2020, though there is a chance that three small lakes could be saved with the construction of small dikes.

Other Environmental Problems

- Cotton is to blame for many of Central Asia's ills. Its cultivation demands high levels of pesticides and fertilisers, which are now found in water, in human and animal milk, and in vegetables and fruit.
- Kazakhstan suffers particularly from industrial pollution. Lake Balkhash has been polluted by copper smelters, and bird and other lake life there is now practically extinct. There are also concerns about oil and other pollution draining into the Caspian Sea.
- Kyrgyzstan has a problem with radioactive seepage from Soviet-era uranium mines. In 1998 almost two tonnes of sodium cyanide destined for the Kumtor gold mine was spilled into the Barskoön River, which made its way into Lake Issyk-Köl.
- A combination of economic hardship, a crisis in funding for wildlife protection and the opening of borders with China (the region's main market for illegal trafficking in animal parts) has seen a huge rise in poaching since the fall of the Soviet Union.
- Tens of thousands of critically endangered saiga antelope are killed every year for their translucent horns, which are sold to Chinese medicine makers. Between 1993 and 2003, saiga numbers declined from more than one million to a shocking 40,000.
- Tens of thousands of musk deer, currently found in Kyrgyzstan, Kazakhstan and Russia, have been killed in the past 20 years for their musk glands.
- In Kazakhstan more than 1000 Saker falcons are poached annually, most of them sold to the Gulf as hunting birds.

ANTELOPE

For more on the plight of the saiga antelope, visit www.saiga-conservation.com

Survival Guide

Directory A–Z

Accommodation

Accommodation options are somewhat uneven across the region. The budget homestays of Kyrgyzstan are excellent and the B&Bs of Uzbekistan offer the most stylish and comfortable midrange options. Kazakhstan has a couple of backpacker hostels, some rural homestays, and good midrange and top-end choices. Tajikistan's Pamir region in particular has an informal network of homes and yurts that offer a fascinating and intimate look at the way local people live.

Budget travellers off the beaten track may still have to use the occasional fossilised Soviet-era hotel but these are generally a last resort.

Oddball accommodation options include sleeping in a **former medressa** (Map p204; ☎998 943 152 600, 375 68 59; doniyoraa@rambler.ru; Pahlavon Mahmud 1; s/d US$60/80; ❄📶) in Khiva or an **astronomical observatory** (Map p72; ☎701-798 9830, 777-247 5537; r per person 4500T; P) outside Almaty.

Budget accommodation can be considered anything under US$25 for a double room in high season.

Midrange hotels and B&Bs range from US$25 to US$70 per night (US$50 to US$100 in capitals like Tashkent, Uzbekistan and much of Kazakhstan). For this you can expect air-con, satellite TV, an internet connection (often patchy wi-fi) and a decent breakfast.

B&Bs

Bukhara, Khiva and Samarkand in Uzbekistan undoubtedly offer the best private accommodation, many of which are stylish boutique-style hotels in historic buildings. Rates tend to be around US$20 per person and include breakfast. Meals are extra but can normally be provided for around US$5 each.

Camping

In the wilds there's normally no problem with you camping, though there is always an inherent security risk with this. Popular trekking routes have established camping areas, frequented by Soviet alpinists during the Soviet era. You can normally camp at a *turbaza* (Soviet-era holiday camp) or yurt camp for a minimal fee.

Homestays

Homestays are happily on the rise. For a bed of blankets on the floor and some type of breakfast you'll probably pay between US$10 and US$15 in rural Tajikistan and Kyrgyzstan, where travel has been revolutionised by networks such as Community-Based Tourism (CBT; www.cbtkyrgyzstan.kg). Kazakhstan also has some rural homestays costing between US$25 and US$35 per person with all meals.

Do not expect hotel-style comforts; rural toilets, for example, can be squatters in the garden. Don't expect anything exotic either – in larger towns you may well end up in a block of flats, in front of a TV all evening. Levels of privacy vary. You might get access to a kitchen, especially if you are in an apartment.

Many local private travel agencies can set you up with a homestay, though prices may be double local rates.

Homestays are priced per person but you generally won't have to share rooms with strangers; however, friends travelling together will be expected to share a room.

LATE-NIGHT TELEPHONE CALLS

Those late-night calls to your room aren't wrong numbers; all hotels with significant numbers of foreigners attract prostitutes, often with the compliance of the front desk. All you can do is work out how to temporarily disable your telephone and don't answer the door.

BOOK YOUR STAY ONLINE

For more accommodation reviews by Lonely Planet authors, check out http://hotels.lonelyplanet.com. You'll find independent reviews, as well as recommendations on the best places to stay. Best of all, you can book online.

Locals you meet on the road may invite you home and ask nothing for it, but remember that most ordinary people have very limited resources, so offer to pay around US$10, with US$5 extra for dinner and breakfast in rural areas.

Couchsurfing (www.couchsurfing.org) is quite well represented in Kazakhstan and Kyrgyzstan.

In Turkmenistan and Uzbekistan, staying with someone who hasn't gone through official channels with the Office of Visas & Registration (OVIR; *Otdel Vis i Registratsii* in Russian) could put them at risk, especially if your own papers aren't in order.

Hotels

Though some are better than others, you often don't get what you pay for in government or Soviet-era tourist hotels, largely because tourists pay higher rates than locals. Windows that don't open or close properly, chronically dim or missing light bulbs and toilets that leak but don't flush are common problems. All beds are single, with pillows the size of suitcases. That said, a lot of Soviet-era hotels have spruced themselves up in recent years and the situation is constantly improving.

Uzbekistan leads the way in midrange private hotels, which are popping up all over the place. There are also a limited number of party or government guesthouses, *dacha* (holiday bungalows) and former government *sanatoria*, which are now open to all. Most cities have a choice of several modern and comfortable private-sector hotels catering mostly to local and international *biznezmen*, where nouveau riche is the dominant style.

Some hotels will take your passport and visa for anywhere from half an hour to your entire stay, to do the required registration paperwork and to keep you from leaving without paying. Don't forget them when you leave – no one is likely to remind you.

We do not mention all of a hotel's price options in our reviews; even the worst hotels often have a few *lux* (deluxe) or half-*lux* (semi-deluxe) suites for about twice the price of a basic room, sometimes with a sofa, bathtub and hot water. Strangely, a room with a large double bed often costs more than two single rooms.

For top-end places you may get a better room rate by booking through a local travel agent or an online booking service, though most hotels offer their own discounts.

Yurtstays

It's easy to arrange a yurtstay in central Kyrgyzstan and the eastern Pamirs region of Tajikistan. Yurts range from comfortable tourist camps with beds, electricity and a nearby toilet, to the real McCoy owned by shepherds who are happy to take in the occasional foreigner for the night. The CBT and Shepherd's Life organisations in Kyrgyzstan, and **Murgab Ecotourism Association** (META; ☎Gulnara 93-519 18 02; www.meta.tj; Osh 91; ⏰call ahead) in Tajikistan offer yurtstays in the mountain pastures of the Tian Shan and Pamirs. Don't expect a great deal of privacy or much in the way of toilet facilities, but it's a fantastic way to get a taste of life on the high pastures (including the freshest yoghurt you've ever tasted!). For upmarket yurtstays try **Ecotour** (☎077-280 2805, 46 08 03; www.ecotour.kg; Donskoy 46A, Umai Hotel) in Kyrgyzstan.

There are also yurts at a half-dozen locations in Kazakhstan, including Aksu-Zhabagyly and Sayram-Ugam national parks, plus Burabay. Uzbekistan has a yurt camp in the Kyzylkum desert near Ayaz-Qala and several yurtstays at Lake Aidarkul.

Children

Children can be a great icebreaker and a good avenue for cultural exchange, but travelling in Central Asia is difficult even for the healthy adult. Long bus and taxi rides over winding mountain passes are a sure route to motion sickness. Central Asian food is difficult to digest no matter what your age, and extreme temperatures – blistering hot in the city, freezing in the mountains – lead to many an uncomfortable moment. Islamic architecture and ruined Karakhanid cities may well leave your children comatose with boredom so make a summer visit to amusement and aqua parks in all the major capitals (except Bishkek).

If you are bringing very young children into Central Asia, nappies are available at department stores, but bring bottles and medicines. Forget about car seats, high chairs, cribs or anything geared for children, though you'll always find a spare lap and helpful hands when boarding buses. It's possible to make a cot out of the blankets supplied in most homestays. *Lux* hotel rooms normally come with an extra connecting room, which can be ideal for children.

FLOOR-LADIES

On every floor of a Soviet-style hotel a *dezhurnaya* (floor-lady) is in charge of handing out keys, getting hot water for washing, or *kipitok* (boiled water) for hot drinks, sometimes for a small fee. Even the most god-awful hotel can be redeemed by a big-hearted floor-lady who can find someone to do your laundry, find a light bulb or stash your bags while you're off on an excursion.

For more advice on travelling with children, pick up Lonely Planet's *Travel with Children*.

We're Riding on a Caravan: An Adventure on the Silk Road by Laurie Krebs is a children's picture book aimed at four- to eight-year-olds that describes a trader's life on the Chinese section of the Silk Road.

Stories from the Silk Road by Cherry Gilchrist is a story book aimed at a similar age group.

Customs Regulations

Barring the occasional greedy official at a remote posting, few Western tourists have major customs problems in Central Asia. When they do, it's usually over the export of 'cultural artefacts'.

Declaring money on entry to a former Soviet republic is an awkward matter. In Uzbekistan you should declare everything (cash and travellers cheques) to the penny; officials at Tashkent airport will likely ask you to pull out your money, and will seize and fine you for the difference between what you have and what you declared. Count up your money privately before you arrive. You won't have a problem unless you are trying to leave with more money than you arrived with, so don't withdraw hundreds of dollars from ATMs in Uzbekistan that you intend to spend elsewhere in Central Asia.

- There are no significant limits on items brought into Central Asia for personal use, except on guns and drugs.
- Heading out, the main prohibitions are 'antiques' and local currency.
- You may well be asked for the customs declaration you filled out when you first entered the country, so save all official-looking documents.
- In Kazakhstan customs forms don't need to be filled in unless you are carrying goods above normal duty-free limits or cash worth more than US$3000.

Exporting Antiques

From the former Soviet republics, you cannot export antiques or anything of 'historical or cultural value' – including art, furnishings, manuscripts, musical instruments, coins, clothing and jewellery – without an export licence and payment of a stiff export duty.

If your purchase looks like it has historical value, you should get a letter saying that it has no such value or that you have permission to take it out anyway. Get this from the vendor, from the Ministry of Culture in the capital, or from a curator at one of the state art museums. Without it, your goods could be seized on departure.

- In Uzbekistan any book or artwork more than 50 years old is considered antique.
- In Turkmenistan 'cultural artefacts' seems to embrace almost all handicrafts and traditional-style clothing, no matter how mundane.
- To export a carpet from Turkmenistan you'll need to get the carpet certified (for a fee) at Ashgabat's Carpet Museum or buy it from one of the state carpet shops. Get a receipt for anything of value that you buy, showing where you got it and how much you paid.

Documents

Besides your passport and visa, there are a number of other documents you may need to keep track of:

- Currency exchange and hard currency purchase receipts – you may need to show these when you sell back local money in a bank (not needed for moneychangers or in Kazakhstan).
- The customs form or entry form that you were given on entering the country.
- Vouchers – if you prepaid accommodation, excursions or transport, these are the only proof that you did so.
- Hotel registration chits – in Uzbekistan you may need to show these little bits of paper (showing when you stayed at each hotel) to OVIR officials.
- Letters of Invitation and any supporting documents/receipts for visa and permit support.
- Student and youth cards are of little use, except as a decoy if someone wants to keep your passport.

It's wise to have at least one photocopy or scan of your passport (front and visa pages) and your travel-insurance policy on your person. It's also a good idea to have a scan of your passport and travel insurance on a flash drive or stored in the cloud.

Electricity

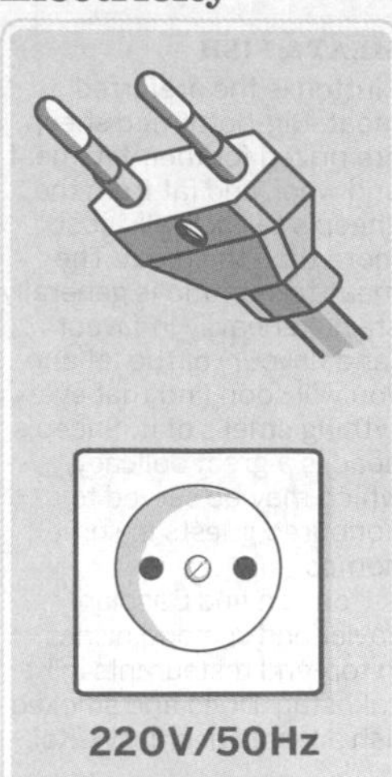

Food

Food should not be the main reason you come to Central Asia. In the first years of independence most restaurants served only standard slop, which somehow seemed to taste (and smell) indelibly of the old USSR. The situation has improved in recent years, particularly in the cities, with a rush of pleasant open-air cafes, fast-food joints and Turkish restaurants. The best way to appreciate regional cuisines, and the region's extraordinary hospitality, is still a meal in a private home.

Central Asian Cuisine

Central Asian food resembles that of the Middle East or the Mediterranean in its use of rice, savoury seasonings, vegetables and legumes, yoghurt and grilled meats. Many dishes may seem familiar from elsewhere – *laghman* (similar to Chinese noodles), *plov* (similar to Persian rice pilafs), nan (flat breads found all over Asia), and *samsa* (the samosa of India) – one more benefit of Silk Road exchange.

The cuisine falls into three overlapping groups:

- The once-nomadic subsistence diet found in large areas of Kazakhstan, Kyrgyzstan and Turkmenistan – mainly meat (including entrails), milk products and bread.
- Diet of the Uzbeks and other settled Turks, which includes pilafs, kebabs, noodles and pasta, stews, elaborate breads and pastries.
- Persian influence, ranging from southern Uzbekistan into Tajikistan, which is distinguished by subtle seasoning, extensive use of vegetables, and fancy sweets.

Staples & Specialities

MENU STANDARDS

The following standards are generally available in every restaurant.

Shashlyk Ubiquitous kebabs of fresh or marinated mutton, beef, minced meat *(farsh* or *lyulya kebab)* or, less commonly, chicken. Usually served with nan bread and vinegary onions. The quality varies from inedible to addictively delicious. Liver kebabs are known in Turkic as *jiger*.

Plov Called *pilau* in Tajikistan, this consists mainly of rice with fried and boiled mutton, onions and carrots, and sometimes raisins, quince, chickpeas or fruit slices, all cooked up in a hemispherical cauldron called a *kazan*. *Plov* is always the *pièce de résistance* when entertaining guests. Uzbekistan is the artery-clogged heart of Central Asian *plov*.

Laghman Noodle dish that includes fried mutton, peppers, tomatoes and onions. Korean, Uyghur and Dungan noodles are generally the best.

Shorpo Soupy stew, also called *shurpa* or *sorpo*, that consists of boiled mutton on the bone with potatoes, carrots and turnips.

Manpar Noodle pieces, meat, vegetables and mild seasoning in broth.

Beshbarmak Popular in Kazakhstan and Kyrgyzstan (*shilpildok* in Uzbek; *myaso po-kazakhsky* in Russian). Large flat noodles with lamb and/or horsemeat are cooked in vegetable broth (the Kazakh version serves the broth separately). It means 'five fingers' since it was traditionally eaten by hand.

Nan (*non* to Uzbeks and Tajiks; *lepyoshka* in Russian) Round bread baked in a *tandyr* (tandoori) oven. Some varieties are prepared with onions, meat or sheep's-tail fat in the dough; others have anise and poppy or sesame seeds placed on top. Nan also serves as an impromptu

NASVAI

Throughout Central Asia you might notice some men chewing and copiously spitting, or talking as if their mouth is full of saliva. *Nasvai* (also known as *nasvar, naswar* or *noz)* is basically finely crushed tobacco, sometimes cut with spices, juniper or lime. As a greenish sludge or as little pellets, it's stuffed under the tongue or inside the cheek, from where the active ingredients leach into the bloodstream, revving up the user's heart rate. Amateurs who fail to clamp it tightly in place, thus allowing the effluent to leak into the throat, might be consumed with nausea.

plate for shashlyk. Homemade breads are often thicker and darker than normal nan. Much better than the boring, square, white-flour Russian loaves known simply as *khleb*.

Salads A refreshing break from heavy main courses, although you'll soon tire of the dreaded *salat tourist* (sliced tomatoes and cucumbers). Parsley, fresh coriander, green onions and dill are served and eaten whole.

Breakfast (*zaftrak* in Russian) Generally consists of tea or instant coffee, bread, jam, some kind of eggs, and maybe yoghurt, cream or semolina.

SNACKS

Variations on the meat-and-dough theme include:

Manty (mantu) Steamed dumplings, a favourite from Mongolia to Turkey.

Chuchvara (*tushbera* in Tajik; *pelmeny* in Russian) A smaller boiled cousin of *manty*, served plain or with vinegar, sour cream or butter, or in soups.

Pirozhki Greasy Russian fried pies filled with potatoes or meat; generally disappointing.

Samsa Meat pie made with flaky pastry and baked in a tandoor oven; best in Kyrgyzstan.

Fruits are eaten fresh, cooked, dried or made into preserves, jams and drinks known as *kompot* or *sok*. In general, May is the best time for apricots, strawberries and cherries, June for peaches and July for grapes and figs. Melons ripen in late summer, but are available as late as January.

Central Asians are fond of dried fruits and nuts, particularly apricots and apricot stones, which when cracked open have a pith that tastes like pistachios. At any time of year you'll find delicious walnuts, peanuts, raisins and almonds, plus great jams (sea-buckthorn jam is a real treat) and wonderful mountain honey.

MEAT & FISH

Mutton is the preferred meat. Big-bottomed sheep are prized for their fat, meat and wool, and fat from the sheep's tail actually costs more than the meat. The meat-to-fat ratio is generally stacked heavily in favour (and flavour) of the fat and you will soon find that everything smells of it. Sheep's head is a great delicacy, which may be served to honoured guests in some homes.

You can find Caspian caviar and seafood dishes in top-end restaurants in Kazakhstan. Dried and smoked fish are sold near Issyk-Köl.

MILK PRODUCTS

Central Asia is known for the richness and delicacy of its fermented dairy products, which use cow, sheep, goat, camel or horse milk. The milk itself is probably unpasteurised, but its cultured

AN INVITATION TO EAT: HOSPITALITY DOS & DON'TS

Being invited home for a meal can be your best introduction to local customs as well as to the best local cuisine. Don't go expecting a quick bite. Your host is likely to take the occasion very seriously. Uzbeks, for example, say *mehmon otanda ulugh*, 'the guest is greater than the father'.

➡ It's important to arrive with a gift. Something for the table (eg some fruit from the market) will do. Better yet would be something for your hosts' children or their parents, preferably brought from your home country (eg postcards, badges, a picture book).

➡ Traditionally, a host will honour an important guest by sacrificing a sheep for them. During these occasions the guest is given the choicest cuts, such as the eyeball, brain or meat from the right cheek of the animal. Try to ensure that your presence doesn't put your host under financial hardship. At least try to leave the choicest morsels for others.

➡ Pulling out your own food or offering to pay someone for their kindness is likely to humiliate them. Some travellers hosted by very poor people have given a small cash gift to the eldest child, saying that it's 'for sweets'.

➡ You will likely be offered water for washing your hands. Dry your hands with the cloth provided; shaking the water off your hands is said to be impolite.

➡ The *dastarkhan* is the central cloth laid on the floor, which acts as the dining table. Never put your foot on or step on this. Try to walk behind, not in front of people when leaving your place and don't step over any part of someone's body. Try not to point the sole of your shoe or foot at anyone as you sit on the floor.

derivatives are safe if kept in hygienic conditions. Many doughs and batters incorporate sour milk products, giving them a tangy flavour.

The fresh yoghurt served up to guests in the mountain pastures of Kyrgyzstan and Tajikistan will be the best you've ever tasted.

Suzma Strained yoghurt creates this tart cottage or cream cheese, used as a garnish or added to soups.

Ayran A salty yoghurt/water mix; the Russian equivalent is called *kefir*.

Katyk A thin, drinkable yoghurt.

Kurut Dried *suzma* rolled into rock-hard marble-size balls that have the half-life of uranium.

Tvorog Russian speciality made from soured milk that is heated to curdle. This is hung in cheesecloth overnight to strain off the whey. Similar to *suzma*.

Kaimak Pure sweet cream, skimmed from fresh milk that has sat overnight. A wickedly tasty breakfast item, that is wonderful with honey.

TURKISH FOOD

Turkish restaurants are popping up everywhere in Central Asia and most are excellent value. Kebabs are popular, while *patlıcan* (aubergine) and *dolma* (stuffed peppers) are the most common vegetable dishes. Desserts include baklava (light pastry covered in syrup) and *sütlaç* (rice pudding).

Pide Similar to a thin-crust pizza.

Lahmacun Cheaper, less substantial version of a pide.

Adana kebab Minced-meat patties.

Iskander kebab Thinly sliced mutton over bread, with yoghurt and a rich tomato sauce – delicious!

Çaçık A light yoghurt, cucumber and mint dip that makes a great snack with *lavash*, a huge bread similar to nan but lighter.

Drinks

Don't drink the tap water. Cheap bottled mineral water is easy to find, but it's normally gassy and very mineral tasting.

Tins of cheap imported instant coffee can be found everywhere; hot water *(kipitok)* is easy to drum up from a hotel floor-lady or homestay.

TEA

Chay (*choy* to Uzbeks and Tajiks; *shay* to Kazakhs) is drunk with reverence.

➡ Green tea (*kok* in Turkic languages; *zelyony* in Russian) is the favourite; locals claim it beats the heat and unblocks you after too much greasy *plov*.

➡ Black tea *(kara* in Turkic languages; *chyorny chay* in Russian) is preferred in Samarkand and Urgench, and by most Russians.

➡ Western Turkmen brew tea with camel's milk and Pamiris use goat's milk.

➡ Wait until you are told where to sit; honoured guests are often seated by Kyrgyz or Kazakh hosts opposite the door (so as not to be disturbed by traffic through it, and because that is the warmest seat in a yurt). Men (and foreign women guests) might eat separately from the women and children of the family.

➡ The meal might begin with a mumbled prayer, followed by tea. The host breaks and distributes bread. After bread, nuts or sweets to 'open the appetite', business or entertainment may begin.

➡ The meal itself is something of a free-for-all. Food is served, and often eaten, from common plates, with hands or big spoons. Pace yourself – eat too slowly and someone may ask if you're ill or unhappy; too eagerly and your plate will be immediately refilled. Praise the cook early and often; your host will worry if you're too quiet.

➡ Devout Muslims consider the left hand unclean, and handling food with it at the table, especially in a private home and with communal dishes, can be off-putting. At a minimum, no one raises food to the lips with the left hand. Try to accept cups and plates of food only with the right hand.

➡ Bread is considered sacred in Central Asia. Don't put it on the ground, turn it upside down or throw it away (leave it on the table or floor cloth). If someone offers you tea in passing and you don't have time for it, they may offer you bread instead. It is polite to break off a piece and eat it, followed by the *amin*. If you arrive with nan at a table, break it up into several pieces for everyone to share.

➡ If alcohol consumption is modest, the meal will end as it began, with tea and a prayer.

➡ Don't eat after the *amin* (p474). This signals thanks for and an end to the meal.

Kazakh tea is taken with milk, salt and butter – the nomadic equivalent of fast food – hot, tasty and high in calories.

VODKA & BEER

The Islamic injunction against alcohol has had little obvious impact in ex-Soviet Central Asia. Most Central Asians enjoy a drink and, like the Russians who introduced them to vodka, take their toasts seriously.

Given the depth of Central Asian hospitality it's impolite to refuse the initial 'bottoms up' (Russian – *vashe zdarovye!*), and/or abstain from at least a symbolic sip at each toast. But there's usually heavy pressure to drain your glass every time – so as not to give offence, it is implied – and the pressure only increases as everybody gets loaded. The Russian phrase *chut chut* may mean 'a little bit', but when applied to a shot of vodka it generally gets translated as 'up to the brim'.

You'll find a wide range of Russian and European beers *(pivo)*. St Petersburg's Baltika is the brew of choice and comes in a wide range of numbers from 0 (nonalcoholic) to 9 (very strong). Baltikas 3 and 6 are the most popular.

Popular local beers on tap include Tian-Shansky, Shimkent (both Kazakh), Sim Sim (Dushanbe) and Siberian Crown (Russian). Kyrgyzstan has a growing range of small microbreweries, including Arpa, Nashe Pivo, Zhivoe, Hoff, Akademia and Venskoye. Draught beer is advertised in Russian as *na razliy, razlivnoe* or *svezhee pivo* (fresh beer).

KUMYS & OTHER ATTRACTIONS

Kumys (properly *kymys* in Kyrgyz; *qymyz* in Kazakh) is fermented mare's milk, a mildly (2% to 3%) alcoholic drink appreciated by most Kazakhs and Kyrgyz. It's available only in spring and summer, when mares are foaling, and takes around three days to ferment. The milk is put into a *chelek* (wooden bucket or barrel) and churned with a wooden plunger called a *bishkek* (from where that city derives its name).

Locals will tell you that *kumys* cures anything from a cold to TB but drinking too much of it may give you diarrhoea. The best *kumys* comes from the herders themselves; the stuff available in the cities is sometimes diluted with cow's milk or water.

Kazakhs and Kyrgyz also like a thick, yeasty, slightly fizzy concoction called *bozo*, made from boiled fermented millet or other grains.

Turkmen, Kazakh and Karakalpak nomads like *shubat* (fermented camel's milk). An early morning glass of breakfast *chal* (camel's milk) in Turkmenistan will wake you up faster than a double espresso.

Where to Eat & Drink

Dining options include streetside stalls and cafes, private restaurants, chaikhanas (teahouses) and, best of all, private homes.

A few midrange and top-end restaurants *(meyramkhana* in Kazakh and Kyrgyz; *oshhona* in Uzbek) in bigger cities offer interesting Central Asian, Turkish, Chinese, Georgian, Korean or European dishes and earnest service. The occasional Siberian salmon or black caviar livens things up.

Beware menu prices in top-end restaurants, as they are often given as per 100g, not per serving (which is more like 250g to 400g). In some restaurants main dishes are just that and you'll have to order garnishes like rice, potatoes or vegetables separately.

What most locals want from a restaurant in the evening is a night out – lots of booze and gale-force techno music or a variety show. Even if there's no music blasting when you come in, the kind staff will most likely turn on (or turn up) the beat, especially for the foreigners.

The canteen *(stolovaya)* is the ordinary citizen's eatery – dreary but cheap, with a limited choice of cutlets or lukewarm *laghman*.

Certain old-town neighbourhoods of Tashkent and Samarkand (both in Uzbekistan) have home restaurants offering genuine home-style cuisine. There is rarely a sign; family members simply solicit customers on the street.

TEAHOUSES

The chaikhana (teahouse; transliterated as *chaykhana* in Turkmen, *chaykana* in Kyrgyz, *choyhona* in Uzbek and Tajik, *shaykhana* in Kazakh) is male Central Asia's essential socio-gastronomic institution, especially in Uzbekistan. Usually shaded, often near a pool or stream, it's as much a men's club as an eatery – although women, including foreigners, are tolerated.

Traditional seating is on a bedlike platform called a *tapchan*, covered with a carpet and topped with a low table. Take your shoes off to sit on the platform, or leave them on and hang your feet over.

SELF-CATERING

Every sizeable town has a colourful bazaar *(rynok* in Russian) or farmers market with hectares of fresh and dried fruit, vegetables, nuts, honey, cheese and bread. Private supermarkets across the region now sell a decent range of European and Russian goods.

Korean and Dungan vendors sell spicy *kimchi* (vegetable salads), a great antidote for mutton overdose. Fresh honey on hot-from-the-oven nan makes a splendid breakfast.

TEA ETIQUETTE

Tea is the drink of hospitality, offered first to every guest, and almost always drunk from a *piala* (small bowl). Bear the following tips in mind.

➡ From a fresh pot, the first cup of tea is often poured away (to clean the *piala*) and then a *piala* of tea is poured out and returned twice into the pot to brew the tea.

➡ A cup filled only a little way up is a compliment, allowing your host to refill it often and keep its contents warm (the offer of a full *piala* of tea is a subtle invitation that it's time to leave).

➡ Pass and accept tea with the right hand; it's extra polite to put the left hand over the heart as you do this.

➡ If your tea is too hot, don't blow on it, but swirl it gently in the cup without spilling any. If it has grown cold, your host will throw it away before refilling the cup.

Vegetarians & Vegans

Central Asia can be difficult for vegetarians; indeed the whole concept of vegetarianism is unfathomable to most locals. Those determined to avoid meat will need to visit plenty of farmers markets.

In restaurants, you'll see lots of tomato and cucumber salads. *Laghman* or soup may be ordered without meat, but the broth is usually meat-based. In private homes there is always bread, jams, salads, whole greens and herbs on the table, and you should be able to put in a word to your host in advance. Even if you specifically ask for vegetarian dishes you'll often discover the odd piece of meat snuck in somewhere – after a while it all seems a bit of a conspiracy.

'Without meat' is *etsiz* in Turkmen; *atsiz* in Kazakh and Kyrgyz; *gushtsiz* in Uzbek; and *biz myasa* in Russian.

Gay & Lesbian Travellers

There is little obvious gay/lesbian community in Central Asia, though there are a couple of gay clubs in Almaty (Kazakhstan). It's not unusual to see young women showing affection towards each other, nor is it uncommon to see men holding hands. However, this is a reflection of Asian culture rather than homosexuality. Whether you're straight or gay, it's best to avoid public displays of affection.

➡ In Uzbekistan, Turkmenistan and Tajikistan, gay male sex is illegal, but lesbian sex does not seem to be illegal (it is seldom spoken about).

➡ Kazakhstan and Kyrgyzstan have lifted the Soviet-era ban on homosexuality.

➡ The website www.gay.kz has information on gay life in Kazakhstan, but in Russian only.

Holidays

Turkmenistan has some particularly wacky holidays, including Melon Day, Horse Day and 'A Drop of Water is a Grain of Gold' Day.

The following Islamic holidays are observed lightly in ex-Soviet Central Asia and are cultural, not public, holidays. Dates are fixed by the Islamic lunar calendar, which is shorter than the Western solar calendar, beginning 10 to 11 days earlier in each solar year. Dates given here are approximate (within a day or two). The holidays normally run from sunset to the next sunset.

Ramadan is observed with little fanfare in most of Central Asia, though you will find some restaurants closed during the day, reopening in the evening as families convene to break the day's fast.

Moulid an-Nabi (13 January 2014, 3 January 2015, 24 December 2016) The birthday of the Prophet Mohammed. A minor celebration in Central Asia, though you might notice mosques are a little fuller.

Ramadan (28 June 2014, 18 June 2015, 7 June 2016) Also known as Ramazan, the month of sunrise-to-sunset fasting. Dates mark the beginning of Ramadan.

Eid al-Fitr (28 July 2014, 18 July 2015, 7 July 2016) Also called Ruza Hayit in Uzbekistan and Orozo Ait in Kyrgyzstan. This involves two or three days of celebrations at the end of Ramadan, with family visits, gifts, a great banquet (known as Iftar) to break the fast and donations to the poor.

Eid al-Azha (4 October 2014, 23/24 September 2015, 13 September 2016) Also called Eid-e Qurban, Kurban Bayram, Qurban Hayit or Kurban Ait in Central Asia. This is the Feast of Sacrifice. Those who can afford it buy and slaughter a goat or sheep, sharing the meat with relatives and with the poor. This is also the season for the *haj* (pilgrimage to Mecca).

NAVRUS

By far the biggest Central Asian holiday is the spring festival of Navrus ('New Days'; also Nauryz in Kazakh, Novruz in Turkmen, Nooruz in Kyrgyz and Nauroz in Dari). Navrus is an adaptation of pre-Islamic vernal equinox or renewal celebrations, celebrated approximately on the spring equinox, though now normally fixed on 21 March (22 March in Kazakhstan). Navrus was being celebrated in Central Asia before Alexander the Great passed through.

In Soviet times this was a private affair, even banned for a time, but it's now an official two-day festival, with traditional games, music and drama festivals, street art and colourful fairs, plus partying, picnics and visiting of family and friends. Families traditionally pay off debts before the start of the holiday.

The traditional Navrus dish, prepared only by women, is *sumalak* – wheat soaked in water for three days until it sprouts, then ground, mixed with oil, flour and sugar, and cooked on a low heat for 24 hours. To add to this, seven items, all beginning with the Arabic sound 'sh', are laid on the dinner table during Navrus – *sharob* (wine), *shir* (milk), *shirinliklar* (sweets), *shakar* (sugar), *sharbat* (sherbet), *sham* (a candle) and *shona* (a new bud). The candles are a throwback to pre-Islamic traditions and the new bud symbolises the renewal of life.

Insurance

Central Asia is an unpredictable place so insurance is a good idea. A minimum of US$1 million medical cover and a 'medevac' clause or policy is essential, as few reliable emergency services are available in the CIS.

Some policies specifically exclude 'dangerous activities', which can include skiing, motorcycling, and even trekking or horse riding. If these are on your agenda, ask about an insurance amendment to permit some of them (at a higher premium).

Few medical services in Central Asia will accept your foreign insurance documents for payment; you'll have to pay on the spot and claim later. Get receipts for everything and save all the paperwork.

Internet Access

Internet access is widely available throughout the region; just look for a roomful of pasty teenagers playing games like *Counterstrike*. The only place where you can't get reliable internet access is Turkmenistan. Most computers in the cities are loaded with Skype and instant messaging software.

Wi-fi is available in many midrange and top-end hotels, especially in Kazakhstan and Uzbekistan (but much less so in Turkmenistan), but connections can be frustrating. You may find it easier to bring a smart phone and get a SIM card with a data package.

You may find your keyboard set to Cyrillic; pressing 'shift' + 'Alt' should change the keyboard language from Cyrillic to English.

Language Courses

The **London School** (Map p240; ☎54 52 62; www.londonschool.kg; Soviet (Abdrakhmanov) 39; per hr 250som, registration basic/intensive 300/1200som) in Bishkek offers intensive Kyrgyz or Russian language tuition for travellers, with both classroom and homestay environments.

The **Russian Center of Science & Cuture** (Map p234; ☎055-500 3976; www.kgz.rs.gov.ru; Erkindik 2/1) in Bishkek also offers month-long language classes in Russian.

In Dushanbe the **Bactria Centre** (Map p318; ☎227 05 54; www.bactria.net; Tursunzoda 12a; ⏲9am-5pm Mon-Fri) runs courses in Russian and Persian.

American Councils (☎202-833-7522; www.americancouncils.org; suite 700, 1776 Massachusetts Ave NW, Washington, DC) organises summer- and year-long academic exchanges and language study programs in Central Asia.

Legal Matters

Visitors are subject to the laws of the country they're visiting. It's unlikely that you will ever actually be arrested, unless there are supportable charges against you.

If you are arrested, authorities in the former Soviet states are obliged to inform your embassy (*pasolstvah* in Russian) immediately and allow you to communicate with a consular official without delay. Most embassies will provide a list of recommended lawyers.

Maps

Buy your general maps of Central Asia before you leave home. For a search of the available maps try www.stanfords.co.uk.

➡ German publisher **Reise Know How** (www.reise-know-how.de) produces good and long-lasting travel maps to Central Asia (*Zentralasien*, 1:700,000) and Kazakhstan (*Kasachstan*).

➡ *Central Asia* (Gizimap, 1999) is a good 1:750,000 general elevation map of the region (plus Kashgar), though it excludes northern Kazakhstan and western Turkmenistan. It usefully marks many trekking routes.

➡ *Central Asia – The Cultural Travel Map along the Silk Road* (Flephanti) is a similar 1:1.5 million Italian map, which concentrates on Uzbekistan and Tajikistan.

➡ Nelles' 1:750,000 *Central Asia* map is also good.

➡ Reliable, locally produced city and regional maps can be found in Kazakhstan and Kyrgyzstan, but are hard to find elsewhere. Especially in Uzbekistan, where many street names have been changed three or four times since independence, any map older than a couple years will drive you crazy.

Money

The 'stans' banking systems have improved greatly in the last few years, with credit-card transactions, wire transfers (particularly Western Union) and regulated foreign exchange available in most towns. In the countryside there are few facilities, so change enough cash to get you back to a main city.

If you plan to travel extensively in the region, it's worth bringing a combination of cash US dollars or euros (the latter particularly in Kazakhstan) and a credit card or two for the cities.

In the convoluted border areas of the Fergana Valley you may need to carry several currencies simultaneously.

Try to avoid large notes in local currency (except to pay your hotel bills), since few people can spare much change.

ATMs

Most cities in ex-Soviet Central Asia have ATMs *(bankomat)* that accept Western credit cards. Turkmenistan has the fewest functioning ATMs.

ATMs in Uzbekistan often give US dollars, which can be useful.

It makes sense to get your cash during working hours, since the last thing you need is to watch your card get eaten alive by an Uzbek ATM.

Some ATMs charge a service fee of around 2%.

Black Market

The existence of licensed moneychangers in every town has done away with the black market in all republics except Uzbekistan, where it is very much alive (p223).

Cash

Cash in US dollars is by far the easiest to exchange, followed by euros. Take a mixture of denominations – larger notes (US$100, US$50) get a better rate, but a cache of small ones (US$10, US$5) is handy for when you're at borders, stuck with a lousy exchange rate or need to pay for services in US dollars. Cash is particularly useful in Uzbekistan, due to the black market. Most hotels in Turkmenistan require payment in cash US dollars.

Make sure notes are in good condition – no worn or torn bills – and that they are dated post-1994. Taxi drivers and market-sellers often fob off their own ragged foreign notes on tourists as change, so of course you should refuse to accept old notes too. US$100 gives you a pile of Uzbek som as thick as an airport paperback.

Credit Cards

It's an excellent idea to bring a credit card, though you shouldn't rely on it completely to finance your trip as there are still only a limited number of places where they can be used. Kazakhstan is the most useful place in

DOLLARS & SOMS

Prices in this book are sometimes given in US dollars or euros, when that is the most reliable price denominator or if that's the currency you'll be quoted on the ground. Even when a price is quoted in dollars you can normally pay in local currency (and technically in Tajikistan and Uzbekistan you actually have to).

You may need cash in US dollars to pay for visas, registration and some services with a private travel agency, though many of the latter now accept credit cards. Although officially you cannot spend foreign currency anywhere in Uzbekistan, private hotels and homestays normally accept US dollars and often give you change in local currency at the market rate. Most other homestays and drivers expect payment in local money.

Central Asia to have a credit or debit card.

Major credit cards can be used for payment at top-end hotels and restaurants, central airline offices, major travel agencies and a few shops throughout the region. Visa is the most widely recognised brand, but others are accepted in most places, as are the Cirrus and Maestro systems.

If you can't find an ATM to accept your card, it's possible to get a cash advance against a Visa card or MasterCard in capitals for commissions of 1% to 3%. You will need your PIN to access the ATMs but not for a cash advance. Asking for the '*terminal*' (the hand-held machine that processes the card transaction) indicates that you want a cash advance. Always get a receipt, in case you are asked for proof of changing money at customs or if there is any discrepancy when you get home.

Remember that by using credit cards in Uzbekistan you fail to make use of the black market.

International Transfers

Money transfers are possible through major banks in all capitals and through **Western Union** (www.westernunion.com), which has partners in banks and post offices everywhere and remains the easiest way to send money. Commissions of 1% to 4% are typical.

Moneychangers

Dealing with licensed moneychangers is the easiest way to change cash in Kyrgyzstan, Kazakhstan and Tajikistan. They are found in small kiosks on nearly every block, and some will give a receipt if you ask them; rates vary by 1% to 2% at most. Licensed changers are completely legal. Moneychangers are marked by signs such as ОБМЕН ВАЛЮТЫ (*obmen valyuty;* currency exchange) and ОБМЕННЫЙ ПУНКТ (*obmenny punkt;* exchange point).

Nearly all tourist hotels have bank-exchange desks, though double check the rates.

EXCHANGE RECEIPTS

Whenever you change money, ask for a receipt (*kvitantsiya* or *spravka* in Russian) showing your name, the date, the amounts in both currencies, the exchange rate and an official signature. Not everyone will give you one, but if you need to resell local currency through the banks (in Uzbekistan or Turkmenistan) you may need enough receipts to cover what you want to resell. You will not need a receipt to sell local currency into US dollars with moneychangers in other countries. Customs officials may want to see exchange receipts at crossings to non-CIS countries but it's unlikely.

Technically you can only sell Uzbek som back at a main city office of the National Bank – not at the airport or the hotels, or the border. The easiest thing, of course, is to spend it before you leave, change it to neighbouring currencies on the black market or swap it with travellers going the other way.

Travellers Cheques

Travellers cheques can be cashed in the major Central Asian capitals (except Dushanbe, Tajikistan) but it is becoming increasingly difficult to do so, particularly in Kazakhstan and Turkmenistan. US-dollar travellers cheques are the best currency to bring. Commissions run between 1% and 3%. It is possible to get your money in dollars instead of local currency, though the commission rate may be a little different.

If visiting Uzbekistan you need to list your travellers cheques on your customs declaration form or you won't be able to cash them.

Security

ATMs and travellers cheques are becoming more common in Central Asia, but you may still end up carrying large wads of cash.

Don't leave money in any form lying around your hotel room. Lock it deep in your luggage or carry it securely zipped in a money belt, with only what you'll need that day accessible in an exterior pocket, wallet or purse.

When paying for anything substantial (eg a hotel bill or an expensive souvenir) or changing money on the street at an exchange kiosk, count out the money beforehand, out of public sight; don't go fumbling in your money belt in full view. There are tales of thieves targeting people coming out of banks with fat cash advances, so keep your eyes open.

Make sure you note the numbers of your cards and travellers cheques and keep the telephone numbers handy to call if they are lost or stolen – and keep all numbers separate from the cards and cheques.

Tipping & Bargaining

Tipping is common in Central Asian cities. Most cafes and restaurants in the capitals add a 10% service charge to the bill, or expect you to round up the total.

➡ Shops have fixed prices but in markets (food, art or souvenirs) bargaining is usually expected.

➡ Always negotiate when arranging transport hire.

➡ In Kyrgyzstan bargaining is usually reserved only for taxi drivers.

➡ In the markets asking prices tend to be in a sane proportion to the expected outcome. Sellers will be genuinely surprised if you reply to their '5000' with '1000'; they're more likely

PRACTICALITIES

- **Video systems** Central Asia has the same video system as Russia, ie Secam, which is incompatible with Australia, most of Europe (apart from France and Greece) and the USA.
- **Electricity** The entire former USSR is nominally 220V at 50 cycles.
- **Newspapers and magazines Steppe Magazine** (www.steppemagazine.com) is a glossy and artsy twice-yearly magazine concentrating on Central Asia. It's for sale sporadically in Central Asia and the UK or by subscription.
- **Weights and measures** Central Asia is metric. When you buy produce in markets make sure you know whether the price is per piece *(shtuk)* or by the kilo.

expecting 3500, 4000 or 4500 in the end.

- The Russian word for 'discount' is *skidka*.

Bribery is a fact of life in Central Asia but try to avoid it where possible – it feeds the already-widespread notion that travellers all just love throwing their money around, and makes it harder for future travellers. In fact a combination of smiles (even if through gritted teeth) and patient persistence can very often work better.

Photography & Video

Equipment

Memory cards for digital cameras are quite prevalent in Central Asia these days. Most internet cafes can burn your photos onto a CD, as long as the burner works. Electricity is quite reliable for charging batteries, except in the remote Pamirs. Good quality batteries are hard to find in rural areas.

Photographing & Filming People

Most Central Asians are happy to have their picture taken, though you should always ask first. You may find people sensitive about you photographing women, especially in rural areas. Women photographers may get away with it if they've established some rapport.

The Russian for 'may I take a photograph?' is *fotografirovat mozhno?* (fa-ta-gruh-*fee*-ra-vut *mozh*-na?). The Dari equivalent is *aks gerefti?*

Post

The postal systems of Central Asia are definitely not for urgent items. A letter or postcard will probably take two weeks or more to get outside the CIS. Kyrgyzstan and Kazakhstan are probably the most reliable places from where to send packages.

Central post offices are the safest places to post things. It can help to write the destination country in Cyrillic too.

If you have something that absolutely must get there, use an international courier company. **DHL** (www.dhl.com) and **FedEx** (www.fedex.com) have offices in major cities.

Express Mail Service (EMS) is a priority mail service offered by post offices that ranks somewhere between normal post and courier post. Prices are considerably cheaper than courier services.

Registration

This relic of the Soviet era allows officials to keep tabs on you once you've arrived.

- In Uzbekistan the hotel or homestay in which you stay the night should register you and give you a chit of paper.
- Kyrgyzstan has ended the need to register.
- In Kazakhstan tourists who fly into the country are generally registered automatically.
- Tourist-visa holders in Tajikistan only need to register if staying for over 30 days.

If you do need to register, the place to go is OVIR. There's one in every town, sometimes in each city district, functioning as the eyes and ears of the Ministry of the Interior's administration for policing foreigners. Though it has a local name in each republic (eg Kushi-Kon Politsiyasi in Kazakhstan, OPVR in Tajikistan, IIB in Uzbekistan, UPVR in Kyrgyzstan), everybody still understands the word OVIR. In some remote areas where there is no OVIR office you may have to register at the *passportny stol* (passport office).

Responsible Travel

Tourism is still relatively new to Central Asia so try to keep your impact as low as possible and create a good precedent for those who follow you.

One of the best ways to ensure your tourist dollars make it to local communities is to support community-based

AMIN

After a meal or prayers, or sometimes when passing a grave site, you might well see both men and women bring their cupped hands together and pass them down their face as if washing. This is the *amin*, a Muslim gesture of thanks, common throughout the region.

tourism projects, and engage local services and guides whenever possible.

The following are a few tips:

- Be respectful of Islamic traditions and don't wear singlets, shorts or short skirts in rural areas or the Fergana Valley.
- Don't hand out sweets or pens to children on the streets, as it encourages begging.
- Buy your snacks, cigarettes, bubble gum etc from the enterprising grannies trying to make ends meet rather than from state-run stores.
- Don't buy items made from endangered species, such as Marco Polo sheep and snow leopards.
- Don't pay to take a photo of someone and don't photograph someone if they don't want you to. If you agree to send someone a photo, make sure you follow through with it.
- Discourage the use of scarce fuels such as firewood and *tersken* (high-altitude bush) in the eastern Pamirs.
- If someone offers to put you up for the night make sure you don't put your host under financial burden. Don't let them sacrifice an animal in your honour (common in the Pamirs) and try to offer money or a gift in return for your host's hospitality.
- Don't let your driver drive too close to archaeological sites and try to stick to existing tracks when driving off road.

Safe Travel

Travel in Central Asia is a delight for those who are ready for it, but a potential nightmare for the unprepared. We get letters from travellers chastising us for overplaying the hassles of travel in Central Asia, and an equal number describing a litany of police hassles, violence and rip-offs. Most people have a problem-free trip but inexperienced travellers should travel with their radar up.

Crime is minimal by Western urban standards, but visitors are tempting, high-profile targets. Central Asian officials and police generally create more problems than they solve. Local and regional transport can be unpredictable, uncomfortable and occasionally unsafe.

If you have an emergency or have your passport stolen, you must immediately contact the nearest embassy (which might be in a neighbouring republic, or even Moscow). It will help if you have a photocopy of your passport to verify who you are. It's a good idea to register with your embassy upon arrival in Central Asia and to carry the telephone numbers of your embassies in the region.

This information, all about the headaches, is not meant to put you off. Rather, it is intended to prepare you for the worst. Here's hoping you don't run into any of these problems.

Alcohol

Whether it's being poured down your throat by a zealous host, or driving others into states of pathological melancholy, brotherly love or violent rage, alcohol can give you a headache in more ways than one. This is especially true in economically depressed areas, where resentment hovers just below the surface and young men may grow abruptly violent.

Crime

If you're the victim of a crime, contact the *militsia* (police), though you may get no help from them at all. Get a report from them if you hope to claim on insurance for anything that was stolen, and contact your closest embassy for a report in English. If your passport is stolen, the police should also provide a letter to OVIR, which is essential for replacing your visa.

Dealing with Officials

The number of corrupt officials on the take has decreased dramatically in the last few years and most travellers make their way through Central Asia without a single run-in with the local *militsia*.

The strongest police presence is in Uzbekistan (particularly in the Tashkent metro), followed by Turkmenistan and Tajikistan, where there are police checkpoints at most municipal and provincial borders. Take a long-distance taxi ride anywhere in the region and you'll likely see your driver paying off traffic cops after being waived down by an orange baton.

It's a near certainty that you'll meet a *gendarme* or two in Uzbekistan, though most only want to see your papers and know where you're going.

If you are approached by the police, there are several rules of thumb to bear in mind:

➡ Your best bet is to be polite, firm and jovial. A forthright, friendly manner – starting right out with an *asalam aleykum* (peace be with you) and a handshake for whomever is in charge – may help to defuse a potential shakedown, whether you are male or female.

➡ If someone refers to a 'regulation', ask to see it in writing. If you are dealing with lower-level officers, ask to see their *nachalnik* (superior).

➡ Ask to see a policeman's ID and, if possible, get a written copy of the ID number. Do not hand over your passport unless you see this ID. Even better, only hand over a photocopy of your passport; claim that your passport is at your hotel or embassy.

➡ Try to avoid being taken somewhere out of the public eye, eg into an office or into the shadows. The objective of most detentions of Westerners is simply to extort money, and by means of intimidation rather than violence. If you're prepared to pull out a paperback and wait them out, most inquisitors on the make will eventually give up.

➡ If you are detained at a police station, insist on calling the duty officer at your embassy or consulate. If your country has no diplomatic representative in the country you're in, call the embassy of a friendly country – for example the UK if you're from Australia or New Zealand.

➡ Make it harder for police on the take by speaking only in your own language.

➡ If officers show signs of force or violence, and provided they are not drunk, do not be afraid to make a scene – dishonest cops will dislike such exposure.

➡ Never sign anything, especially if it's in a language you don't understand. You have the right not to sign anything without consular assistance.

➡ Antinarcotics laws give the police powers to search passengers at bus and train stations. If you are searched, never let the police put their hands in your pockets – take everything out yourself and turn your pockets inside out.

➡ If police officers want to see your money (to check for counterfeit bills) try to take it out only in front of the highest-ranking officer. If any is taken insist on a written receipt for it.

➡ If you have to pay a fine, insist that you do so at a bank and get a receipt for the full amount.

Solo Travellers

There isn't a huge traveller scene in Central Asia but you'll meet other travellers in backpacker guesthouses or hostels in Bishkek and Osh (Kyrgyzstan), Almaty (Kazakhstan), Khorog (Tajikistan) and the main towns in Uzbekistan.

It's generally not too difficult to find travellers to share car-hire costs for the Torugart, Irkeshtam or Pamir Highway trips. Local travel agents and community tourism providers can often help link you up with other travellers or try a post on the **Thorn Tree** (http://thorntree.lonelyplanet.com).

Travelling alone in Turkmenistan can be expensive. Hotel rooms cost almost the same whether you have one or two people in your party and if you are on a tourist visa you'll have to bear the burden of hiring a guide for yourself.

Telephone

International Calls

Private communication centres or (in Tajikistan and Kazakhstan) prepaid internet phone (IP) cards cost a fraction of a conventional international phone call (from around US$0.10 per minute) and the quality is usually as good as through the old Soviet-era landlines.

In smaller towns you place international calls (as well as local and intercity ones) from the central telephone and telegraph offices. You tell a clerk the number and prepay in local currency. After a wait of anything from

GOVERNMENT TRAVEL ADVICE

The following government websites offer travel advisories and information on current hot spots.

➡ **Australian Department of Foreign Affairs** (☎02-6261 3305; www.smartraveller.gov.au) Register online at www.orao.dfat.gov.au.

➡ **British Foreign Office** (☎0845-850 2829; www.gov.uk/foreign-travel-advice)

➡ **Canadian Department of Foreign Affairs** (☎1-800-267 6788; www.travel.gc.ca)

➡ **US State Department** (☎1-888-407 4747; http://travel.state.gov) Register online at https://travelregistration.state.gov.

half a minute to several hours, you're called to a booth. Hotel operators also place calls, but for a hefty surcharge. International calls in the region generally cost between US$0.50 and US$2 per minute.

Calls between CIS countries are now treated as international calls, though they have a different rate. Thus to call Uzbekistan from, say, Kyrgyzstan, you would need to dial Kyrgyzstan's international access code, the Uzbek country code, then the Uzbek city code.

Local Calls

Placing a local or trunk call on Central Asia's telephone systems is usually harder than placing an international one, which is one reason most locals use mobile phones. None of the old Soviet-era token-operated telephones work any more but entrepreneurs often fill the gap in the market by setting up a telephone on a very long extension cable (pay cash to the small Uzbek boy seated by the phone). Some shops have a phone available for calls. Kazakhstan has card-operated phones. Local calls are free from many hotels.

Mobile Phones

Several Central Asian companies have roaming agreements with foreign providers. Local calls and texts with a local SIM card cost pennies. You will probably need a copy of your passport to buy a SIM card and may need a local's help.

SIM cards are easy to get in Kazakhstan, Kyrgyzstan and Tajikistan, hard to get as a foreigner in Uzbekistan and available only from one location in Turkmenistan. Beeline (www.beeline.ru) is a good general choice for most of the region and Bitel is another decent option in Kyrgyzstan.

Note that Central Asian mobile phones work on 900/1800 MHz frequencies. European phones generally share these frequencies but most US mobile phones use 850/1900 frequencies so you will probably need an unlocked quadband American phone if you want to use it in Central Asia. Alternatively just buy a cheap phone on arrival.

Toilets

Public toilets are as scarce as hen's teeth. Those that you can find, eg in parks, and bus and train stations, charge a small fee to use their squatters. Most toilets are awful, the rest are worse. You are always better off sticking to top-end hotels and restaurants or shopping malls.

Carry a small torch for rural restaurant toilets, which rarely have functioning lights, and for trips out to the pit toilet. *Always* carry an emergency stash of toilet paper.

Out in the *jailoos* (pastures) of Kyrgyzstan and Tajikistan there are often no toilets at all. You'll have to go for a hike, find a rock or use the cover of darkness. Always urinate at least 50m from a water source (and downstream!) and dig a hole and burn the paper after defecating.

Toilet paper is sold everywhere, though tissues are a better bet than the industrial strength sandpaper that is ex-Soviet toilet paper. The wastepaper basket in the loo is for used paper and tampons (wrapped in toilet paper).

Before bursting in, check for the signs 'Ж' (Russian: *zhenski*) for women or 'M' *(muzhskoy)* for men.

Tourist Information

Intourist, the old Soviet travel bureau, gave birth to a litter of Central Asian successors, most of which are useless to independent travellers. You are almost always better off with a local community-based tourism project.

That said, there are useful tourist information centres in Almaty in Kazakhstan, at Khorog and Murgab in Tajikistan, in Khiva and Samarkand in Uzbekistan and also at Karakol in Kyrgyzstan. In remote areas local NGOs can often offer advice on accommodation, transport and ecotourism initiatives.

Volunteering

The US Peace Corps has a presence in Tajikistan and Turkmenistan. The UK Voluntary Service Overseas (VSO) operates in Tajikistan.

Volunteers headed to Central Asia should read the following books:

- *Taxi to Tashkent: Two Years with the Peace Corps in Uzbekistan* by Tom Fleming.
- *Chai Budesh? Anyone for Tea?* by Joan Heron, which is subtitled *A Peace Corps Memoir of Turkmenistan.*
- *This Is Not Civilization* by Robert Rosenberg. A novel chronicling the travails of a Peace Corps volunteer that is partly set in Kyrgyzstan.
- *Revolution Baby* by Saffia Farr. An account of three years of expat life raising a baby in Kyrgyzstan.

Volunteer opportunities exist at **Habitat Kyrgyzstan Foundation** (www.habitat.elcat.kg) and the **Sworde-Teppa** (www.sworde-teppa.org.uk) organisation in Kurgonteppa in southern Tajikistan. Some travellers have helped out at community-based tourism projects in Kyrgyzstan.

The American organisation **CDC Development Solutions** (www.cdcdevelopmentsolutions.org) sometimes has a need for volunteers in its Central Asian tourism projects.

Women Travellers

Despite the imposition of Soviet economic 'equality', attitudes in the Central Asian republics remain fairly male-dominated. Many local men cannot understand why women would travel without men, and assume they have ulterior sexual motives. Although harassment is not on the same level as in some Middle Eastern countries, it tends to be more physical. Macho Uzbekistan tops the list, with Kyrgyzstan by far the least sexist.

Both men and women should seek permission before entering a mosque, particularly during prayer times when non-Muslims will feel uncomfortable. Women are generally not allowed in mosques in Tajikistan and the Fergana Valley. Most mosques in cities and the major tourist areas are open to all.

In bigger cities there is no taboo on unaccompanied local women talking to male visitors in public. Local men addressed by a woman in a couple direct their reply to the man, out of a sense of respect. Local women tend not to shake hands or lead in conversations. Because most local women don't drink in public, female visitors may not be offered a shot of the vodka or wine doing the rounds.

Keen sensibilities and a few staunch rules of thumb can make a solo journey rewarding:

- Clothes do matter: a modest dress code is essential (even if local Russian women don't seem to have one).
- Never follow any man – even an official – into a private area. If one insists on seeing your passport, hand over a photocopy; if he pushes you to follow him, walk away into a busy area.
- When riding in shared taxis choose one that already has other female passengers.
- Sit at the front of the bus, preferably between two women, if you can.
- If you feel as though you are being followed or harassed, seek the company of a group of women; most matronly types will automatically take you under their wing.
- Some local men will honestly want to befriend and help you; if you are unsure and have a difficult time shaking them, mention your husband even if he's imaginary.

But it isn't all bad! The opportunities for genuine cross-cultural woman-to-woman interactions can generally be had during homestays, and usually outside the cities. Everyone loves to have their children cooed over and doing so will gain you friends as well as unique experiences. You may well see a side of Central Asia hidden to male travellers.

Work

There aren't many casual work opportunities in the region. What work *is* available is probably limited to English teaching and aid work, both of which are best arranged prior to your arrival in the region.

You may find teaching positions in the region's universities, particularly the following:

American University in Bishkek (www.auca.kg)

Samarkand State Institute of Foreign Languages (www.sifl.50megs.com)

University of Central Asia (www.ucentralasia.org) Planned campuses in Khorog (Tajikistan), Naryn (Kyrgyzstan) and Tekeli (Kazakhstan).

For those with a TEFL or CELTA certificate, the **London School** (www.thelondonschool.org/en) in Bishkek offers teaching posts for a minimum of six months for the academic year, or four months for the summer.

Transport

GETTING THERE & AWAY

Getting to Central Asia is half the fun, whether its part of an overland Silk Road trip or crossing formerly forbidden border posts. Air connections are improving steadily throughout the region, with Tashkent (Uzbekistan) and Almaty (Kazakhstan) the main hubs, though discounted fares can be hard to track down.

The long-distance rail connections are mostly with Mother Russia – from Moscow or the Trans-Siberian Railway to Tashkent, Almaty, Bishkek (Kyrgyzstan) and Astana (Kazakhstan). The only other external rail link is the Silk Road train between Astana/Almaty and Ürümqi in China, with onward rail connections from there.

The other main overland links are three roads from China – one accessible year-round via Ürümqi to Almaty, and two warm-weather routes from Kashgar to Kyrgyzstan, over the Torugart or Irkeshtam passes.

Finally there are the offbeat and somewhat unreliable journeys from Baku (Azerbaijan), across the Caspian Sea by ferry to Turkmenbashi (Turkmenistan) or alternatively to Aktau in Kazakhstan.

This section deals with travel in and out of Central Asia, including advice for getting around the region. For general advice on border crossings see p35, and for specific border crossings see the Getting There & Away section of the relevant country chapte

DEPARTURE TAX

Departure taxes are figured into your air ticket so you won't face any extra charges when you fly out of Central Asia. Turkmenistan is odd as usual, with an arrival tax of around US$14.

Entering Central Asia

Entering Central Asia can be a bit daunting. Many flights arrive in the middle of the night, officials can be unhelpful and you may have to battle a scrum of taxi drivers once you exit the terminal. That said, immigration formalities are increasingly streamlined and you shouldn't face any major issues as long as your documents are in order.

In Uzbekistan its particularly important to make sure you fill out your customs form accurately, claiming all cash and travellers cheques that you are bringing into the country.

Air

The region's main air links to the 'outside' are through the main cities of Almaty (Kazakhstan), Bishkek (Kyrgyzstan), Tashkent (Uzbekistan), Ashgabat (Turkmenistan) and, to a lesser extent, Dushanbe (Tajikistan) and Astana (Kazakhstan). Tiny Osh (Kyrgyzstan) even has a couple of interesting international connections.

A few cities in Kazakhstan have international links to Europe, and cities in all republics have connections to Commonwealth of Independent States (CIS) countries, especially Russia.

Of the many routes in, two handy corridors are via Turkey (thanks to the geopolitics of the future) and via Russia (thanks to the geopolitics of the past). Turkish Airlines has the best connections and in-flight service but is at the higher end of the fare scale, while Russian and Central Asian carriers have the most connections. Turkey also has the advantage of a full house of Central Asian embassies and airline offices. Moscow has four airports and connections can be inconvenient.

Airports

Almaty International Airport (☎727-270 33 33; www.almatyairport.com) A useful gateway to both Kazakhstan and Kyrgyzstan (Bishkek is just three hours by road).

Ashgabat International Airport Less well connected, most reliably by Lufthansa and Turkish Airlines. A new airport is currently under construction, scheduled to open in 2016.

Astana International Airport (☎7172-70 29 99; www.astanaairport.kz) Has a range of international flights.

Bishkek Manas International Airport (www.airport.kg) Kyrgyzstan's main hub with relatively inexpensive international connections

Dushanbe International Airport (☎37-449 44 75; www.airport.tj) The least connected, with most people using Turkish Airlines. The airport is being upgraded and plans are afoot to build a new airport.

Tashkent International Airport (☎71-140 28 01; www.uzairways.com) Possibly the most central airport in Eurasia and the busiest airport in Central Asia. More flights go to Tashkent than to any other city in the region.

Airlines

The following are the main Central Asian airlines, of which Uzbekistan Airways and Air Astana are the best:

Air Astana (www.airastana.com; airline code KC; hub Almaty) Flies Almaty to Abu Dhabi, Amsterdam, Baku, Bishkek, Bangkok, Beijing, Delhi, Dushanbe, Frankfurt, Ho Chi Minh City, Hong Kong, İstanbul, Kiev, Kuala Lumpur, London, Moscow, Novosibirsk, Prague, Seoul, St Petersburg, Tashkent, Tbilisi and Ürümqi; flies Astana to Abu Dhabi, Baku, Beijing, Bishkek, Frankfurt, İstanbul, Kiev, London, Moscow, Novosibirsk, St Petersburg, Tashkent, Ürümqi and Yekaterinburg; flies Atyrau to Amsterdam and İstanbul; flies Kostanay to Hanover; flies Aktau to İstanbul.

Kyrgyzstan Air Company (AC) (www.air.kg; airline code QH; hub Bishkek) Flies to Moscow, Delhi, Dubai, Tashkent, Ürümqi and other Russian destinations.

Somon Air (www.somonair.com; airline code 4J; hub Dushanbe) Flies to Almaty, Dubai, Frankfurt, İstanbul, Moscow, Novosibirsk, St Petersburg, Sochi and Ürümqi.

Tajik Air (www.tajikair.tj; airline code 7J; hub Dushanbe) Flies to Delhi, İstanbul, Kabul, Moscow, Sharjah, Sochi, St Petersburg, Tehran, Ürümqi, Bishkek, Almaty and various Siberian cities.

Turkmenistan Airlines (www.turkmenairlines.com; airline code T5; hub Ashgabat) Flies to Abu Dhabi, Almaty, Amritsar, Bangkok, Beijing, Birmingham, Delhi, Dubai, Frankfurt, İstanbul, Kiev, London, Moscow and St Petersburg.

Uzbekistan Airways (www.uzairways.com; airline code HY; hub Tashkent) Flies to Amritsar, Baku, Bangkok, Beijing, Delhi, Dubai, Frankfurt, Geneva, Islamabad, İstanbul, Kiev, Kuala Lumpur, Lahore, London, Madrid, Milan, Moscow, New York, Paris, Riga, Rome, Seoul, Sharjah, Tel Aviv, Tokyo, Ürümqi and several Russian cities; as well as Astana, Almaty, Ashgabat and Bishkek.

Smaller Central Asian airlines with regional flights include:

Air Bishkek (www.airishkek.kg; airline code KR; hub Bishkek) Flies to Moscow, Seoul and Ürümqi, plus Osh to Moscow.

Avia Traffic Company (www.aero.kg; airline code YK; hub Bishkek) From Bishkek to Dushanbe, Moscow and St Petersburg; From Osh to Moscow, St Petersburg and Ürümqi.

SCAT (www.scat.kz; airline code DV; hubs Almaty, Astana, Shymkent) Kazakh airline flies to Baku, İstanbul, Kiev, Moscow, Tbilisi and Yerevan.

International airlines that fly into Central Asia:

Aeroflot (www.aeroflot.ru; airline code SU; hub Sheremetyevo-2, Moscow) To Tashkent and Bishkek four times weekly.

Air Arabia (www.airarabia.com; airline code G9; hub Sharjah) To Almaty.

AirBaltic (www.airbaltic.com; airline code BT; hub Riga) To Tashkent thrice weekly.

Asiana Airlines (www.flyasiana.com; airline code OZ; hub Kimpo Airport, Seoul) To Tashkent and Almaty.

Austrian Airlines (www.austrian.com; airline code OS; hub Vienna) To Astana.

Azerbaijan Airlines (www.azal.az; airline code AHY; hub Baku) To Aktau.

British Airways (www.britishairways.com; airline code BA; hub London Heathrow) To Almaty thrice weekly.

China Southern (www.csair.com/en, www.flychinasouthern.com; airline code CZ; hub Guangzhou) Ürümqi to Almaty, Ashgabat, Astana, Dushanbe, Tashkent and Bishkek.

Czech Airlines (www.czechairlines.com; airline code OK; hub Prague) To Almaty and Tashkent.

Etihad Airways (www.etihadairways.com; airline code EY; hub Abu Dhabi) Daily to Almaty and four weekly to Astana.

Fly Dubai (www.flydubai.com; airline code FZ; hub Dubai) To Ashgabat, Bishkek, Dushanbe and Osh.

Hainan Airlines (www.hnair.com, www.hainanair.us; airline code HU; hub Beijing) To Almaty.

Iran Air (www.iranair.com; airline code IR; hub Tehran) To Tashkent.

Iran Aseman (www.iaa.ir; airline code EP; hub Tehran) From Tehran and Mashhad to Dushanbe.

Kam Air (www.flykamair.com; airline code RQ; hub Kabul) To Dushanbe.

KLM (www.klm.com; airline code KL; hub Schiphol Airport, Amsterdam) Five weekly to Almaty.

Korean Air (www.koreanair.com; airline code KE; hub Seoul) To Tashkent four times weekly.

Lufthansa (www.lufthansa.com; airline code LH; hub Frankfurt) To Almaty, Astana and Ashgabat (via Baku).

Pegasus Airlines (www.flypgs.com; airline code PC; hub İstanbul Gokcen) Budget Turkish airline flying to Almaty and Bishkek.

Rossiya Russian Airlines (www.rossiya-airlines.com; airline code FV; hub St Petersburg) To Almaty, Astana, Dushanbe, Karaganda, Khojand, Samarkand, Tashkent, Urgench and Bishkek, plus maybe Namangan, Fergana and Osh.

Sibir (S7) Airlines (www.s7.ru; airline code S7; hub Novosibirsk) Novosibirsk to Almaty, Bishkek, Dushanbe, Fergana, Shymkent, Tashkent; flies Moscow to Ashgabat, Khojand, Osh, Pavlodar, Urgench and Ust-Kamenogorsk.

Transaero (www.transaero.ru; airline code UN; hub Domodedovo Airport, Moscow) To Almaty, Astana, Atyrau, Aktau, Karaganda, Kostanay, Shymkent, Uralsk, Tashkent and Bukhara.

Turkish Airlines (www.turkishairlines.com; airline code TK; hub İstanbul) To Tashkent, Ashgabat, Almaty, Astana, Bishkek, Dushanbe and Osh.

Ukraine International Airlines (www.flyuia.com; airline code PS; hub Kiev) To Almaty, Astana and Bishkek.

Tickets

Finding flights to Central Asia isn't always easy, as travel agents are generally unaware of the region and many don't book flights on Russian or Central Asian airlines.

➡ Contact the airlines directly for schedules and contact details of their consolidators, or sales agents, who often sell the airlines' tickets cheaper than the airlines themselves.

➡ Consider paying a little extra for a reliable airline such as KLM or Turkish Airlines, rather than a cash-strapped one such as Tajik Air.

➡ Always check how many stopovers there are, how long these are and what time the flight arrives: many airlines arrive in the dead of night.

➡ Specialist agencies like www.alternativeairlines.com can often book Central Asian airline tickets when others can't.

Visa Checks

You can buy air tickets without a visa but in most places outside Central Asia you will have trouble getting on a plane without one (with the exception of Kyrgyzstan).

Airlines are obliged to fly anyone rejected because of improper papers back home and are fined, so check-in staff tend to act like immigration officers.

If you have made arrangements to get a visa on arrival, have your LOI handy at check-in and check with the airline beforehand.

Airline Safety

Aeroflot, the former Soviet state airline, was decentralised into around 400 splinter airlines and many of these 'baby-flots' now have the worst regional safety record in the world, due to poor maintenance, ageing aircraft and gross overloading.

In general though, the main Central Asian carriers have lifted their services towards international safety standards, at least on international routes.

➡ In 1993 a Tajik Air Yak-40 crashed on take-off from Khorog; it had 81 passengers in its 28 seats.

➡ In 1997 another Tajik Air plane crashed in Sharjah, killing 85 passengers.

➡ In 2004 an Uzbekistan Airways Yak-42 crashed in Termiz killing 37 passengers.

➡ In 2013 21 passengers died when a SCAT Airlines flight from Kokshetau to Almaty crashed during low visibility.

Most Kazakh airlines (except Air Astana) and all Kyrgyz airlines are currently banned from flying into EU airspace. See www.airsafe.com/events/airlines/fsu.htm for

CLIMATE CHANGE & TRAVEL

Every form of transport that relies on carbon-based fuel generates CO_2, the main cause of human-induced climate change. Modern travel is dependent on aeroplaces, which might use less fuel per kilometre per person than most cars but travel much greater distances. The altitude at which aircraft emit gases (including CO_2) and particles also contributes to their climate change impact. Many websites offer 'carbon calculators' that allow people to estimate the carbon emissions generated by their journey and, for those who wish to do so, to offset the impact of the greenhouse gases emitted with contributions to portfolios of climate-friendly initiatives throughout the world. Lonely Planet offsets the carbon footprint of all staff and author travel.

an overview of recent air accidents in the former Soviet Union.

From Asia

From Beijing there are twice weekly flights to Tashkent on Uzbekistan Airways, five weekly to Almaty and Astana on Air Astana and a couple per week to Ashgabat on Turkmenistan Airlines.

Ürümqi in China's Xinjiang province has between two and seven flights a week to/from Almaty, Tashkent, Bishkek, Osh, Dushanbe and Ashgabat. One-way prices are between US$250 and US$350. To Astana it's US$450.

Bangkok, Hong Kong, Delhi and Seoul also have useful connections into Central Asia.

From Australia & New Zealand

Most flights to Central Asia go via Seoul (to pick up Asiana or Korean Air flights to Tashkent and Almaty or Air Astana to Almaty), Kuala Lumpur (for Uzbekistan Airways to Tashkent, Air Astana to Almaty), Bangkok (Uzbekistan Airways to Tashkent, Air Astana to Almaty or Turkmenistan Airlines to Ashgabat) or İstanbul.

Sample routes include Sydney to Tashkent on Malaysia Airlines and Uzbekistan Airways via Kuala Lumpur, and Sydney to Almaty via Seoul on Asiana or Korean Air. China Southern is often among the cheapest options, via Guangzhou and Beijing. Almaty is generally a cheaper option than Tashkent, with fares starting at around A$1500. For Dushanbe and Bishkek you'll probably have to go via İstanbul.

From Continental Europe

The best fares from Europe to Central Asia are with AirBaltic via Riga to Tashkent, though the best range of connections are with Turkish Airlines, via İstanbul. Air Astana offers some of the better fares to Almaty/Astana, from Amsterdam and Frankfurt, or try KLM and Ukraine International (via Kiev).

Somon Air has a direct Frankfurt–Dushanbe flight, costing around €400/640 one way/return.

From Russia

Budget airlines like easyJet and Germanwings fly to Moscow, making it a decent travel option if you are pinching pennies or want to travel overland by train. Remember to figure in the cost of a visa and transfer between airports in Moscow when comparing costs.

There are daily flights from Moscow to most Central Asian cities, including Almaty, Tashkent, Dushanbe, Khojand (weekly), Ashgabat, Bishkek, Osh and many Kazakh cities. One-way fares range from US$220 to US$300. There are slightly fewer connections from St Petersburg. Major Siberian cities such as Novosibirsk also have connections to the Central Asia capitals.

Uzbekistan Airways flies from Moscow to Samarkand, Bukhara, Urgench, Termiz, Andijon and several others several times weekly for around US$230. Aeroflot fly from Moscow to Tashkent and Bishkek.

Transaero (☎495-788 8080; http://transaero.ru/en; 18/1 Sadovaya-Spasskaya, Moscow) is an international-grade airline that flies from Moscow Domodedovo to Astana, Almaty, Tashkent, Bukhara and several other cities in Kazakhstan, and has connections to European destinations.

Note that Moscow has two main international airports: Sheremetyevo (www.svo.aero/en) and Domodedovo (www.domodedovo.ru/en/). Sheremetyevo is itself divided into several terminals: Terminal B (Sheremetyevo-1), the international Terminal F (Sheremetyevo-2), and newly renovated terminals C, D and E.

At the time of research Aeroflot (Terminals D or F) and Air Astana (Terminal E) operated from Sheremetyevo, while Transaero, Tajik Air, Turkmenistan Airways, SCAT, S7, Uzbekistan Airways, Somon Air and Kyrgyzstan Air Company used Domodedovo airport.

You will need to get a Russian transit visa in advance if you have to transfer between airports and you should budget at least four or five hours to negotiate Moscow's crazy traffic.

Travel agencies in Moscow include **Unifest Travel** (☎495-234 6555; http://unifest.ru/en.html; Komsomolsky prospekt 16/2) for rail and air tickets and Central Asia packages, affiliated with the Travellers Guest House.

From Turkey & the Caucasus

Turkish Airlines flies from İstanbul to Almaty (daily), Astana (two to four weekly), Bishkek (daily), Dushanbe (twice weekly), Tashkent (five weekly) and Ashgabat (daily). The various republics' national airlines also fly once or twice a week.

There are also cheap flights from İstanbul's smaller Sabiha Gökçen airport to Bishkek with Turkish budget airline Pegasus.

Alternatively you could fly from İstanbul or Trabzon to Baku, take the ferry to Turkmenbashi and a 12-hour train ride across the desert to Ashgabat.

One-way flights to İstanbul cost around US$400 from most Central Asian capitals.

Air Astana flies from Baku to Almaty and Astana and from Tbilisi to Almaty. There are also flights from Baku, Tbilisi and Yerevan to Aktau two to three times weekly. Uzbekistan Airways makes the connection from Baku to Tashkent.

From the UK

The best return summer fares to Tashkent are around £500 with Uzbekistan Airways (direct), or a bit more with Turkish Airlines or Air Baltic.

The cheapest flights to Bishkek are currently with the budget Turkish airline Pegasus Airlines, which has fares as low £300 return from London Stansted. Be aware that Pegasus have a reputation for losing travellers luggage and that transfers at İstanbul's Sabiha Gökçen can be time-consuming. Check also about cheap flights to Osh with Turkish Airlines.

Fares to Almaty are about £500 return on Turkish Airlines via İstanbul or Transaero via Moscow. KLM and Lufthansa are also good options. British Airways or Air Astana's direct flights from London to Almaty can be good value.

The best flights to Ashgabat are with Lufthansa or Turkish Airlines. A cheaper but harder-to-book option is **Turkmenistan Airlines** (☎Birmingham 0121-558 6363, London 020-8577 2211; fax 8577 9900), which flies two times a week to Ashgabat from London and also four times a week from Birmingham. Most passengers are headed either to/from Amritsar. For cheap fares contact **Amritsar Travel** (www.ashgabatflights.com).

The best way to Dushanbe is on Turkish Airlines via İstanbul but you'll have to be lucky to get a discounted fare.

From USA & Canada

From North America you generally have the choice of routing your trip via İstanbul (Turkish Airlines), Riga (Air Baltic), Moscow (Aeroflot) or a major European city (KLM, British Airways, Lufthansa etc). Stopovers can be lengthy. From the west coast it's possible to fly to Almaty or Tashkent via Seoul on Asiana or Korean Air.

From New York, the best return fares to Central Asia are with Turkish Airlines to Almaty/Tashkent for US$800/1200 return. Fares are a bit more expensive to Ashgabat with Turkish Airlines or Lufthansa. Flights from the west coast are around US$500 more expensive.

Uzbekistan Airways (☎201-489 3954) flies from New York (JFK airport) to Tashkent (via Riga) once a week, an 18-hour flight.

East Site (☎877-800 6287; www.east-site.com) sometimes offer discounted Central Asian fares, including on Uzbekistan Airways.

Bus & Car

To/From China

From China there are one or two sleeper buses a week (Monday and probably Thursday) from Kashgar to Osh (Y580, 21 hours) in Kyrgyzstan via the Irkeshtam Pass. It's also possible to take a series of minibuses and taxis, or hire a car.

Kashgar agencies such as **Kashgar Tours** (www.kashgartours.com), **Old Road Tours** (www.oldroadtours.com) and **Kashgar Guide** (www.kashgarguide.com) can arrange transport to the Torugart and Irkeshtam passes.

Foreigners are still not allowed to take the twice-weekly bus between Kashgar and Bishkek, via Naryn and the Torugart Pass. Mandatory pre-arranged vehicle hire and permits for four people from Kashgar to Naryn costs around US$320 from Kashgar to the border, plus an extra US$120 from the Torugart to Naryn. Thus figure on around US$220/120 per person in a group of two/four from Kashgar to Naryn.

Further north, direct buses also run from Ürümqi (Y440 to Y460, 24 hours, daily) and Yining (Y250, 12 hours, daily) to Almaty. Fares from Almaty cost from US$50/30 to Ürümqi/Yining. You can also take local buses and shared taxis to and from the border at Khorgos.

There are also direct buses from Ust–Kamenogorsk (US$60, 28 hours, twice weekly) and Semey (US$67, 32 hours, three weekly) in Kazakhstan to Ürümqi.

To/From Russia

On completion in 2015, the new 'Western Europe–Western China' highway will offer the easiest driving option from European Russia into Central Asia via Kazakhstan. The route runs from St Petersburg to Moscow, Kazan and Orenburg, then across Kazakhstan to Almaty and into China at Khorgos. For details see p135.

Although driving a car or motorbike is an excellent way to get around Central Asia, bringing your own vehicle is fraught with practical problems. Fuel supply is uneven, though modern petrol stations are springing up throughout the region. Prices per litre swing wildly depending on supply. Petrol comes in four grades – 76, 93, 95 and 98 octane. In the countryside you'll see petrol cowboys selling plastic bottles of fuel from the side of the road, often of very poor quality.

The biggest problem is the traffic police (Russian, GAI). Tajikistan's roads have almost as many checkpoints as potholes. In Uzbekistan and Kazakhstan there are police skulking at every corner, most looking for excuses to wave their orange baton and hit drivers (local or otherwise) with a 'fine' *(straf)*. There are no motoring associations of any kind.

The state insurance offices, splinters of the old Soviet agency Ingosstrakh, have no overseas offices

CLASSES ON RUSSIAN & CENTRAL ASIAN TRAINS

A deluxe sleeping carriage is called *spets-vagon* (SV, Russian for 'special carriage', abbreviated to CB in Cyrillic); some call this *spalny vagon* or 'sleeping carriage', *myagky* (soft) or 1st class. Closed compartments have carpets and upholstered seats, and convert to comfortable sleeping compartments for two.

An ordinary sleeping carriage is called *kupeyny* or *kupe* (which is Russian for compartmentalised), *zhyostky* (hard) or 2nd class. Closed compartments are usually four-person couchettes and are comfortable.

A *platskartny* (reserved-place) or 3rd-class carriage has open-bunk (also known as hard sleeper) accommodation. *Obshchy* (general) or 4th class is unreserved bench-type seating.

With a reservation, your ticket normally shows the numbers of your carriage *(vagon)* and seat *(mesto)*. Class may be shown by what looks like a fraction: eg 1/2 is 1st class two berth, 2/4 is 2nd class four berth.

that we know of, and your own insurance is most unlikely to be valid in Central Asia. You would probably have to arrange insurance anew at each border.

Readers have recommended **Campbell Irvine** (www.cambellirvine.com) as one company in the UK that can often arrange overland vehicle insurance.

Many Kazakh cities have motorbike clubs which will often welcome foreign bikers – and in some cases drivers.

Almaty is easily the best place in Central Asia for getting motorbike repairs done. The website www.horizonsunlimited.com is a good resource for bikers.

If you are thinking of driving out to Central Asia, then consider doing it for charity as part of the **Roof of the World Rally** (http://roofoftheworld.charityrallies.org) or **Tajik Rally** (http://adventure-manufactory.com/en/tajik/tajik-home).

Train

To/From Russia

There are three main rail routes into Central Asia from Russia:

- From Moscow via Samara or Saratov, straight across Kazakhstan via Aktobe and Kyzylorda to Tashkent (3369km), with branch lines to Bishkek and Almaty (4057km).
- From Moscow south of the Aral Sea via Volgograd, Atyrau, Kungrad, Uchquduk, Navoi and Samarkand to Tashkent, with a branch line to Dushanbe.
- Turkestan–Siberian railway or 'Turksib' (see www.turksib.com for timetables) linking the Trans-Siberian Railway at Novosibirsk with Almaty.

Several other lines enter northern Kazakhstan from Russia and meet at Astana, from where a line heads south to Karaganda and Almaty.

Most trains bound for Central Asia depart from Moscow's Kazan (Kazansky) station. Europe dissolves into Asia as you sleep, and morning unveils a vast panorama of the Kazakh steppe.

You will need to check visa requirements carefully. Trains from Moscow to Tashkent demand a Kazakh transit visa and trains between Russia and Kazakhstan might require a multiple-entry Russian visa. Trains to/from Dushanbe are impractical because you will need a Kazakh, multiple-entry Uzbek and possibly even a Turkmen visa.

POPULAR ROUTES

Train connections between Russia and Central Asia have thinned out in recent years but are still a favourite of migrant workers, tourists and drug smugglers. The following are the most popular fast trains from Moscow:

Tashkent (Nos 5/6, three weekly, 66 hours)

Almaty (Nos 7/8, every other day, 80 hours)

Astana (Nos 71/72 and 83/84, daily, 55 hours)

Bishkek (Nos 17/18 and 27/28, five weekly, 76 hours)

Trains out of Moscow have even numbers; those returning have odd numbers.

Other offbeat connections include the St Petersburg–Astana (every four days) and Saratov–Nukus–Tashkent (twice weekly) routes. There are other, slower connections but you could grow old and die on them.

FARES

These days *kupe* fares between Moscow and Central Asia cost about the same as a flight; only *platzkartny* fares are cheaper than flying. Typical fares for a 2nd/3rd-class (*kupeyny/platzkartny*) berth are as follows:

- Moscow–Tashkent US$495/300
- Moscow–Almaty US$330/205

SILK ROAD BY RAIL

Silk Road romantics, train buffs and nervous flyers can cross continents without once having to fasten their seatbelt or turn off their mobile phones. The 'iron Silk Roads' to Central Asia don't have quite the romance or the laid-back feel of the Trans-Siberian Railway, but they allow Eurasia to unfold gradually, as you clank through endless plains, steppe and desert.

From Moscow (or even St Petersburg) you can watch Europe turn to Asia on the three-day, 4000km train trip to Tashkent or Almaty. From here you can add on any number of side trips to Samarkand, Bukhara or even Urgench (for Khiva), the last two of which are on spur lines. Then from Almaty it's possible to continue on the train to Ürümqi in China and even to Kashgar or Hotan.

From Ürümqi you can continue along the Silk Road by train east as far as Beijing, Hong Kong or even Lhasa or Saigon, making for an epic transcontinental ride. It's not always comfortable and it will take some time, so why do it? Because like Everest, it's there.

- Moscow–Astana US$295/180
- Moscow–Bishkek US$320/205

ONLINE RESOURCES

For a useful overview of international trains to/from Central Asia see www.seat61.com/silkroute.htm.

For online timetables and fares, try the following websites:

- www.poezda.net/en
- https://poezda.gdbilet.ru
- http://pass.rzd.ru/main-pass/public/en

PURCHASING TICKETS

To buy tickets from Moscow try **Way to Russia** (www.waytorussia.net), **Real Russia** (www.realrussia.co.uk/trains) or **G&R International** (www.hostels.ru).

To/From China

Completed in 1992, after being delayed almost half a century by Russian–Chinese geopolitics, is a line from China via Ürümqi to Almaty and Astana in Kazakhstan, joining the Turksib for connections on to Siberia.

The 1363km Silk Road train between Ürümqi and Almaty leaves twice a week and takes about 32 hours, which includes several hours at the border for customs checks and to change bogies. Sleeper tickets cost Y804/1225 for hard/soft sleeper in Ürümqi or US$125/195 in Almaty. Soft sleepers are only available on the Kazakh train (departs Almaty on Sunday and Ürümqi on Tuesday). Book trains at least a few days ahead.

There is also a less reliable weekly Astana–Ürümqi service (US$130, 39 hours).

To/From Iran

From the Caspian Sea a rail line crosses Turkmenistan along the Trans-Caspian route. No international trains currently run to or from Turkmenistan, though there are several future possibilities.

A line connects Mashhad in Iran with Ashgabat in Turkmenistan, but no passenger trains run along this line at present.

A new railway between Bereket in western Turkmenistan and Gorgan in northeast Iran is under construction, with a second line from Bereket to Zhanaozen (Uzen) in western Kazakhstan. If and when passenger services start, this could be a wacky option across Turkmenistan between Iran and Kazakhstan.

Sea

The Baku (Azerbaijan) to Turkmenbashi 'ferry' route (US$100, 12 to 18 hours) across the Caspian is a possible way to enter and leave Central Asia.

There are also irregular cargo boats every week or 10 days between Baku and Aktau (US$55 to US$75, 24 hours) in Kazakhstan. One of these ferries sunk in October 2002, killing all 51 people aboard.

- For the Baku–Turkmenbashi boat, once on board you'll likely be offered a cabin by a crewmember, for which you will pay around US$50.
- The best cabins have private bathrooms and are comfortable, although some can be cockroach infested.
- Boats leave around four times a week in both directions, but there is no timetable. You'll simply have to arrive and wait until the ship is full of cargo.
- Leave a couple of days (longer for Aktau) left on your visa in case the boats are delayed, which is common. Some travellers have found themselves waiting for a couple of days to dock in Turkmenbashi, using up valuable time in their fixed-date visa.
- Stock up on food and water beforehand, as there is little or no food available on board. Crossings can end up taking 32 hours or longer.

GETTING AROUND

Flying is the least interesting and arguably the least safe mode of transport in Central Asia, but to some destinations and in some seasons it's the only sensible alternative. Trains are slow, crowded and generally not very convenient outside Kazakhstan. Buses are the most frequent and convenient way to get between towns cheaply, though trips can be cramped and vehicles are prone to breakdowns. The best option in many areas is a car: shared taxis or private drivers are often willing to zip you between cities for little more than a bus fare.

Air

Flying saves time and takes the tedium out of Central Asia's long distances. The Central Asian airlines have some way to go before meeting international safety standards on their domestic routes.

Apart from the national Central Asian airlines, there are a couple of domestic airlines, such as Kazakhstan's **SCAT** (www.scat.kz) and **Bekair** (www.bekair.com); Kyrgyzstan's **Air Bishkek** (www.airbishkek.kg), **Sky Bishkek** (www.skybishkek.kg) and **Avia Traffic** (www.aero.kg); and Tajikistan's **East Air** (www.eastair.tj). Unless you are really counting the pennies all of these except SCAT are generally best avoided.

- Flights are particularly good value in Turkmenistan, where a domestic flight costs around US$20, but you'll have to book them a month or more in advance.
- You generally have to pay for air tickets in local currency (there's often an exchange booth nearby), though you can pay in US dollars in Kyrgyzstan. Some airline offices and travel agencies accept credit cards, especially those in Kazakhstan.
- Domestic and inter-republic services are no-frills; you might get a warm glass of Coke if you are lucky. For long flights consider packing lunch.
- There are no Dushanbe–Tashkent services. Major internal connections still run daily.
- Flights between the biggest cities generally stick to their schedules, but those serving smaller towns are sometimes delayed or cancelled without explanation.
- Routes and individual flights are constantly being cancelled or reintroduced. The only sure way to find out what's flying is to ask at an air booking office.
- Tickets for Central Asian airlines are most easily purchased from private travel agents *(aviakassa)*. You'll often need your passport and visa. Many booking offices have a special window for international flights.

JIGSAW BORDERS

When Stalin drew the borders between the different republics in 1924 no one really expected them to become international boundaries. Areas were portioned off on the map according to the whims and horse-trading of Party leaders, without much regard to the reality on the ground. As these crazy jigsaw borders solidify throughout post-Soviet Central Asia, many towns and enclaves are finding themselves isolated, as the once complex web of regional ties shrinks behind new borderlines.

The Fergana Valley has been particularly affected. Buses no longer run from central Uzbekistan into the Fergana Valley along the natural route via Khojand (in Tajikistan) but rather take the mountain road from Tashkent over the Kamchik Pass (plans are afoot to build a train line along the same route). Travellers (and locals) may find it tricky to get to more remote areas or trekking bases by public transport.

Trains are not immune to these border shenanigans, as many lines cross into neighbouring republics. Trains between Dushanbe and Khojand (both in Tajikistan) route via Uzbekistan (twice) and Turkmenistan, making the line impractical to foreign travellers. Trains running from Aktobe to Uralsk, and Semey to Ust-Kamenogorsk (all in Kazakhstan), pass through Russian territory and foreigners are either not allowed on these trains or may be asked for a Russian visa.

Some problems are short-lived as new transport connections spring up across the region. Uzbekistan has built a railway line to Urgench and Nukus bypassing Turkmenistan and roads have sprung up in Kyrgyz parts of the Fergana Valley to avoid Uzbek border guards. But these are just a few of the thousands of ties that bind the ex-Soviet republics to one another and to Russia, and disentangling them will take decades.

- Air Astana has useful online booking for both international and domestic flights.
- Seating is a bit of a free-for-all (there are often no assigned seats), especially if the flight is overbooked. To minimise the risk of loss or theft, consider carrying everything on board.
- Helicopter flights were once popular in the Tian Shan and Pamir ranges but rising fuel costs have made most services prohibitively expensive (around US$1300 per hour for a chopper). Maintenance is also patchy; avoid them except in summer and go only if the weather is absolutely clear.

Bus

This is the best bet for getting between towns cheaply, if there are no shared taxis. The major transport corridors are served by big long-distance coaches (often reconditioned German or Turkish vehicles), which run on fixed routes and schedules, with fixed stops. They're relatively problem-free and moderately comfortable, with windows that open and sometimes with reclining seats. Luggage is locked safely away below. Journey times depend on road conditions but are somewhat longer than a fast train.

Regional buses are a lot less comfortable and a bit more...interesting. Breakdowns are common. They are also used extensively by small-time traders to shift their goods around the region, and you could gradually become surrounded by boxes, bags, and both live and dead animals.

Private minibuses, generally called *marshrutka* (Russian for fixed-route vehicle), are a bit more expensive, always faster, and usually more hair-raising. They generally have fixed fares and routes but no fixed timetable (or no departure at all if there aren't enough passengers to satisfy the driver), and will stop anywhere along the route. They can be clapped-out heaps or spiffy new Toyota or Chinese-made minivans.

Keep in mind that you're at the mercy of the driver as he picks up cargo here and there, loading it all around the passengers, picks up a few friends, gets petrol, fixes a leaky petrol tank, runs some errands, repairs the engine, loads more crates right up to the ceiling – and then stops every half-hour to fill the radiator with water.

Bus Stations & Tickets

Most cities have a main intercity bus station (*avtovokzal* in Russian, *avtobekat* in Kyrgyz and Uzbek, *avtobeket* in Kazakh, and *istgomush* in Tajik) and may also have regional bus stations (sometimes several) serving local towns.

Try to pick buses originating from where you are, enabling you to buy tickets as much as a day in advance. Tickets for through buses originating in a different city may not be sold until they arrive, amid anxious scrambles. At a pinch you could try paying the driver directly for a place.

Most large bus stations have police who sometimes create headaches for foreigners by demanding documents. Be wary of any policeman who approaches you at a bus station. Long-distance bus stations are, in general, low-life magnets, rarely pleasant after dark. Disregard most bus-station timetables.

Car

Driving a car is an excellent way to get around Central Asia and it needn't be expensive. Main highways between capitals and big cities (eg Almaty–Bishkek–Tashkent–Samarkand–Bukhara) are fast and fairly well maintained. A new motorway between Almaty and Astana is due to be completed by 2017.

Mountain roads (ie most roads in Kyrgyzstan and Tajikistan) can be blocked with snow in winter and plagued by landslides in spring.

Hire

Almaty and Astana have a Europcar franchise and Bishkek has a local car-rental company. Travel agencies can hire you out a Mercedes or 4WD, but you are almost always better off hiring a taxi for the day.

Hiring a car unlocks some of Central Asia's best mountain scenery and is well worth it, despite the cost.

- Community-based tourism organisations and travel agencies hire 4WDs for driving through the more remote areas of Kyrgyzstan, Tajikistan and Kazakhstan.
- Travel agencies have better vehicles but are more expensive.
- CBT in Kyrgyzstan charges between US$0.28 and US$0.38 per km.
- Drivers in Tajikistan's eastern Pamirs charge between US$0.50 and US$0.95 per kilometre for a Russian 4WD.
- Long-distance taxi hire in Turkmenistan works out to around US$0.10 per km.

Taxi

There are two main ways of travelling by car in Central Asia if you don't have your own vehicle: ordinary taxi or shared taxi.

ORDINARY TAXI

One way to travel is to hire an entire taxi for a special route. This is handy for reaching off-the-beaten-track places, where bus connections are hit-and-miss or nonexistent, such as Song-Köl in Kyrgyzstan.

TAXI TIPS

➡ Avoid taxis lurking outside tourist hotels – drivers charge far too much and get uppity when you try to talk them down.

➡ Never get into a taxi with more than one person in it, especially after dark; check the back seat of the car for hidden friends too.

➡ Keep your fare money in a separate pocket to avoid flashing large wads of cash.

➡ Have a map to make it look like you know your route.

➡ If you're staying at a private residence, have the taxi stop at the corner nearest your destination, not the specific address.

➡ Select your driver with care, look over his car (we took one in Kyrgyzstan whose exhaust fumes were funnelled through the back windows) and assess his sobriety before you set off.

➡ You'll have to negotiate a price before you set off. Along routes where there are also shared taxis, ordinary taxis are four times the shared taxi per-person fare.

➡ Make sure everyone is clear which route you will be taking, how long you want the driver to wait at a site and if there are any toll or entry fees to be paid.

➡ You can work out approximate costs by working out the return kilometre distance; assume the average consumption of cars is around 12 litres per 100km and then multiply the number of litres needed by the per litre petrol cost (constantly in flux).

➡ Add to this a daily fee (anything from US$5 up to the cost of the petrol) and a waiting fee of around US$1 per hour.

SHARED TAXI

Shared taxi is the other main form of car travel around Central Asia, whereby a taxi or private car does a regular run between two cities and charges a set rate for each of the four seats in a car.

Cars are quicker and just as comfortable as a bus or train, and are still very affordable.

➡ Cars often wait for passengers outside bus or train stations and some have a sign in the window indicating where they are headed.

➡ Some fares are so cheap that two or three of you can buy all four seats and stretch out. Otherwise smaller cars can be a little cramped.

➡ The most common car is the Russian Zhiguli, fast being replaced by modern Daewoo models such as the Nexia (the most comfortable) and the smaller and cheaper Tico, both made in Central Asia.

➡ The front seat is always the one to aim for; only lemons get the middle back seat.

➡ Shared taxis are particularly useful in Kyrgyzstan along certain major routes such as Bishkek–Almaty, Bishkek–Osh, and Naryn–Bishkek.

➡ Other useful routes are Bukhara–Urgench/Khiva, Samarkand–Termiz, Dushanbe–Khojand and Ashgabat–Mary.

Hitching

In Central Asia there is generally little distinction between hitching and taking a taxi. Anyone with a car will stop if you flag them down (with a low up-and-down wave, not an upturned thumb) and most drivers will expect you to pay for the ride.

➡ When negotiating a reasonable fare it helps to know the equivalent bus or shared-taxi fare.

➡ Hitching to parks and scenic spots is generally much easier on the weekends but you'll lose some of the solitude at these times.

➡ Normal security rules apply when trying to arrange a lift; don't hitch alone, avoid flagging down cars at night and try to size up your driver (and his sobriety) before getting in.

Local Transport

Most sizeable towns have public buses, and sometimes electric trolleybuses. Tashkent and Almaty have a metro system.

➡ Transport is cheap by Western standards, but usually packed; at peak hours it can take several stops for those caught by surprise to even work their way to an exit.

➡ Public transport in smaller towns tends to melt away soon after dark.

Bus, Trolleybus & Tram

Payment methods vary, but the most common method is to pay the driver or conductor cash on exit. Manoeuvre

TRAVEL AGENCIES & ORGANISED TOURS

There are lots of reliable travel agencies inside Central Asia who can help with the logistics of travel in Central Asia – whether it be visas, a few excursions or an entire tailored trip.

The following agencies outside the region can also arrange individual itineraries and/or accommodation, tickets and visa support.

Australia

Passport Travel (☎03-9500 0444; www.travelcentre.com.au; Level 1, 12-14 Glenferrie Rd, Malvern) Silk Road by rail tours.

Russian Gateway Tours (☎02-9745 3333; www.russian-gateway.com.au; 48 The Boulevarde, Strathfield) Airfares to Central Asia, hotel bookings, homestays, visa invitations and airport transfers.

Sundowners Overland (☎03-9672 5300; www.sundownersoverland.com; Level 1, 51 Queen St, Melbourne) Small-group and independent tours into Central Asia.

The UK

Regent Holidays (☎0845-277 3317; www.regent-holidays.co.uk; Froomsgate House, Rupert St, Bristol) Offers tours, and can cobble together an individual itinerary.

Scott's Tours (☎020-7383 5353; www.scottstours.co.uk; 141 Whitfield St, London, W1T 5EW) Hotel bookings, visas and more.

Wild Frontiers (☎020-7736 3968; www.wildfrontierstravel.co.uk) Tailor-made tours with an emphasis on adventure.

The US

Mir Corporation (☎1-800-424-7289; www.mircorp.com) Independent tours, homestays and visa support with accommodation.

Red Star Travel (☎206-522 5995; www.travel2russia.com; Suite 102, 123 Queen Anne Ave N, Seattle) Organises tours, individual itineraries, accommodation, train tickets, visa support with booking.

your way out by asking anyone in the way, *vykhodite?* (getting off?).

Marshrutka

A *marshrutka*, or *marshrutnoe* taxi (marsh-*root*-na-yuh tahk-*see*), is a minibus running along a fixed route. You can get on at fixed stops but can get off anywhere by saying '*zdes pozhaluysta*' (zd-*yes* pa-*zhal*-stuh; here please). Routes are hard to figure out and schedules erratic, and it's usually easier to stick to other transport. Fares are just a little higher than bus fares.

Taxi

There are two kinds of taxis: officially licensed ones and every other car on the road.

- Official taxis are more trustworthy, and sometimes cheaper – if you can find one. They rarely have meters so you'll have to negotiate a fare in advance.
- Let a local friend negotiate a fare for you – they'll do better than you will.
- Unofficial taxis are often private cars driven by people trying to cover their rising petrol costs. Anything with a chequerboard logo in the window is a taxi.
- Stand at the side of the road, extend your arm and wait – as scores of others around you will probably be doing. When someone stops, negotiate a destination and fare. The driver may say '*sadites*' (sit down) or beckon you in, but sort the fare out first. It helps a lot if you can negotiate the price in Russian, even more so in the local language.
- A typical fare across a Central Asian capital is around US$3. Fares go up at night and extra charges are incurred for bookings.

Train

Kazakhstan and to a lesser extent Uzbekistan are probably the only countries where you'll find yourself using the train system much. Travel in the summertime is best done at night.

Connections

➡ Trains are useful to cover the vast distances in Kazakhstan. Certain corridors, such as Almaty–Astana and Almaty–Shymkent are well served by three or four fast trains a day.

➡ The Spanish-built, daily Talgo train between Almaty and Astana takes 12½ hours, against up to 21 hours for other trains, and costs about twice as much (US$80 in tourist class). A new high-speed rail link between the two cities is due to be finished by 2017, reducing the journey time to just five hours.

➡ The high-speed train from Tashkent to Samarkand (2¼ hours) is faster than the buses and features airplane-style seats.

➡ There's also a useful overnight Tashkent–Bukhara run, with a soft sleeper berth for around US$20.

➡ As an indication of journey times, Urgench–Tashkent is 22 hours and Tashkent–Almaty is 25 hours (three weekly).

➡ Turkmenistan has slow but new trains running to most corners of the country. Travel times are long but fares are low. An overnight berth between Ashgabat and the Caspian Sea costs less than US$3.

➡ Elsewhere, connections are drying up as fast as the Aral Sea; few trains run to Dushanbe any more (those that do take a very roundabout route and multiple transit visas) and there are no direct lines, for example, between Ashgabat and any other Central Asian capitals.

➡ Trains to and from Russia can be used for getting around Central Asia and may be faster but any train originating far from where you are is likely to be filthy, crowded and late by the time you board it.

Tickets & Fares

Book at least two days ahead for CIS connections, if you can. You will probably need to show your passport and visa. A few stations have separate windows for advance bookings and for departures within 24 hours; the latter is generally the one with the heaving mob around it (beware of pickpockets). You may also find a city train-ticket office (Russian: *zheleznodorozhnaya kassa* or *Zh D Kassa*) where you can buy train tickets for small or no mark-up, without going to the station. Many tourist hotels have rail-booking desks (including their own mark-up).

➡ If you can't get a ticket for a particular train, it's worth turning up anyway. No matter how full ticket clerks insist a train is, there always seem to be spare *kupeyny* (2nd-class or sleeping carriage) berths. Ask an attendant.

➡ For services in Kazakhstan visit www.railways.kz.

➡ For trains in Uzbekistan see www.uzrailpass.uz.

➡ A few sample *kupeyny* fares (one-way) from Tashkent are US$30 to Urgench and US$20 to Bukhara.

➡ A seat on the daytime fast trains costs US$10/13 from Tashkent to Samarkand/Bukhara (if converting at black-market rates), with a super-fast service to Samarkand/Bukhara costing around US$15/30.

➡ Fares from Almaty include Semey (US$30), Taraz (US$16) and Astana (US$20 or US$92 express).

Health

Stomach and digestive problems are by far the most common health problems faced by visitors to Central Asia. A diet of mutton, bread and *plov* seems to induce diarrhoea and constipation in equal measure!

Since independence, health rates across the region have dropped and many diseases formerly eradicated or controlled in the time of the USSR, such as tuberculosis (TB) and diphtheria, have returned.

Exposure to malaria, rabies and encephalitis is rare and depends largely upon the location and/or months of travel. More common during the searing summer months is heat exhaustion, so make sure you keep cool and hydrated in the 35°C heat. Most short-term travels to the main tourist areas remain problem-free.

BEFORE YOU GO

If you take any regular medication, bring double your needs in case of loss or theft. In most Central Asian countries you can buy many medications over the counter without a doctor's prescription, but it can be difficult to find some of the newer drugs.

Make sure you get your teeth checked before you travel – there are few good dentists in Central Asia as evidenced by the many golden-toothed smiles you'll see. If you wear glasses take a spare pair and your prescription.

Insurance

Even if you are fit and healthy, don't travel without health insurance – accidents do happen. Declare any existing medical conditions you have – the insurance company *will* check if your problem is pre-existing and will not cover you if it is undeclared. You may require extra cover for adventure activities such as rock climbing. If you're uninsured, emergency evacuation is expensive – bills of over US$100,000 are not uncommon.

Make sure you keep all documentation related to any medical expenses you incur.

INTERNET RESOURCES

There is a wealth of travel-health advice on the internet. It's also a good idea to consult your government's travel-health website before departure, if one is available.

Australia (www.dfat.gov.au/travel)

Canada (www.travelhealth.gc.ca)

New Zealand (www.mfat.govt.nz/travel)

UK (www.doh.gov.uk/traveladvice)

USA (www.cdc.gov/travel)

Lonely Planet (www.lonelyplanet.com) Good basic health information.

World Health Organization (WHO; www.who.int/country) A superb book called *International Travel and Health* is revised annually and is available online.

MD Travel Health (www.mdtravelhealth.com) Provides complete travel-health recommendations for every country and is updated daily.

Medical Checklist

Recommended items for a personal medical kit:

- Antibacterial cream (eg mupirocin)
- Antibiotics for diarrhoea (eg norfloxacin, ciprofloxacin or azithromycin for bacterial diarrhoea; tinidazole for giardiasis or amoebic dysentery)
- Antibiotics for skin infections (eg amoxicillin/clavulanate or cephalexin)
- Antifungal cream (eg clotrimazole)
- Antihistamine – there are many options (eg cetirizine for day and promethazine for night)
- Antiseptic (eg Betadine)
- Antispasmodic for stomach cramps (eg Buscopan)
- Decongestant (eg pseudoephedrine)
- DEET-based insect repellent
- Acetazolamide (Diamox) if going to high altitude
- Elastoplasts, bandages, gauze, thermometer (but not mercury), sterile needles and syringes, safety pins and tweezers
- Ibuprofen or another anti-inflammatory
- Laxative
- Oral rehydration solution for diarrhoea (eg Gastrolyte), diarrhoea 'stopper' (eg loperamide) and anti-nausea medication (eg prochlorperazine)
- Paracetamol
- Steroid cream for allergic/itchy rashes (eg 1% to 2% hydrocortisone)
- Thrush (vaginal yeast infection) treatment (eg clotrimazole pessaries or Diflucan tablets)
- Ural or equivalent if prone to urinary tract infections

Recommended Vaccinations

Specialised travel-medicine clinics are your best source of information on which vaccines you should have. Most vaccines don't produce immunity until at least two weeks after they're given, so visit a doctor four to eight weeks before departure.

The only vaccine required by international regulations is yellow fever. Proof of vaccination will be required only if you have visited a country in the yellow-fever zone within the six days prior to entering Kazakhstan.

Uzbekistan, Kazakhstan and Kyrgyzstan all require HIV testing if staying more than three months (two months for Uzbekistan). Foreign tests are accepted under certain conditions, but make sure you check with the embassy of your destination before travelling.

The World Health Organization recommends the following vaccinations for travellers to Central Asia:

Adult Diphtheria & Tetanus Single booster recommended if none in the previous 10 years.

Hepatitis A Provides almost 100% protection for up to a year; a booster after 12 months provides at least another 20 years' protection.

Hepatitis B Now considered routine for most travellers. Given as three shots over six months. A rapid schedule is also available, as is a combined vaccination with hepatitis A. In 95% of people lifetime protection results.

Measles, Mumps & Rubella Two doses required unless you have had the diseases. Occasionally a rash and flulike illness can develop a week after receiving the vaccine. Many young adults require a booster.

Polio Only one booster is required as an adult for lifetime protection.

Typhoid Recommended unless your trip is for less than a week. The vaccine offers around 70% protection, lasts for two to three years and comes as a single shot.

Varicella If you haven't had chickenpox discuss this vaccination with your doctor.

The following immunisations are recommended for long-term travellers (more than one month) or those at special risk:

Meningitis Recommended for long-term backpackers aged under 25.

Rabies Side effects are rare (headache and sore arm).

Tick-Borne Encephalitis (Kyrgyzstan, Kazakhstan, Uzbekistan) Sore arm and headache are the most common side effects.

Further Reading

Lonely Planet's *Healthy Travel – Asia & India* is a handy pocket size and is packed with useful information, including pre-trip planning, emergency first aid, immunisation and disease information, and what to do if you get sick on the road. Other recommended references include *Traveller's Health* by Dr Richard Dawood and *Travelling Well* by Dr Deborah Mills – check out www.travellingwell.com.au.

IN CENTRAL ASIA

Availability of Health Care

Health care throughout Central Asia is basic at best. Any serious problems will require evacuation. Good clinics can provide basic care and may be able to organise evacuation if necessary. In Central Asia a pharmacist is known as an *apoteka* in Russian or *dorikhana* in Turkic. Clinics are widely known as *polikliniks*.

Self-treatment may be appropriate if your problem is minor (eg travellers' diarrhoea), you are carrying the relevant medication and you cannot attend a recommended clinic. It is always better to be assessed by a doctor than to rely on self-treatment.

Buying medication over the counter is not recommended, as poorly stored or out-of-date drugs are common.

To find the nearest reliable medical facility, contact your insurance company, your embassy or a top-end hotel.

Infectious Diseases

Brucellosis

Risk: all countries.

Brucellosis is rare in travellers but common in the local population, and is transmitted via unpasteurised dairy products. Common symptoms include fever, chills, headache, loss of appetite and joint pain.

Hepatitis A

Risk: all countries.

A problem throughout the region, this food- and water-borne virus infects the liver, causing jaundice (yellow skin and eyes), nausea and lethargy. There is no specific treatment for hepatitis A, you just need to allow time for the liver to heal. All travellers to Central Asia should be vaccinated.

Hepatitis B

Risk: all countries.

The only sexually transmitted disease that can be prevented by vaccination, hepatitis B is spread by contact with infected body fluids, including via sexual contact. The long-term consequences can include liver cancer and cirrhosis.

HIV

Risk: all countries.

HIV is transmitted via contaminated body fluids. Avoid unprotected sex, blood transfusions and injections (unless you can see a clean needle being used) in Central Asia.

Leishmaniasis

Risk: Kazakhstan, Turkmenistan, Uzbekistan.

This sandfly-borne parasite is very rare in travellers but common in the local population. There are two forms of leishmaniasis – one which only affects the skin (causing a chronic ulcer) and one affecting the internal organs. Avoid sandfly bites by following insect avoidance guidelines.

Malaria

Risk: southern Tajikistan, southeastern Turkmenistan and far southern Uzbekistan; only present in the warmer summer months (June to October).

Two strategies should be combined to prevent malaria – general mosquito/insect avoidance and antimalaria medications. Before you travel, it is essential you seek medical advice on the right medication and dosage. In general, Chloroquine is recommended for Turkmenistan and southern Uzbekistan. Some resistance to Chloroquine is reported in southern Tajikistan (mainly Khatlon province), so get your doctor's advice on whether to take Chloroquine, Larium (Mefloquine), Doxycycline or Malarone. See the World Malaria Risk Chart (www.iamat.org/pdf/world_malaria_risk_chart.pdf) for detailed information.

To prevent mosquito bites, take the following steps:

- Use a DEET-containing insect repellent on exposed skin. Natural repellents such as citronella can be effective, but must be applied more frequently than products containing DEET.
- Sleep under a mosquito net impregnated with permethrin.
- Choose accommodation with screens and fans (if not air-conditioned).
- Impregnate clothing with permethrin in high-risk areas.
- Wear long sleeves and trousers in light colours.
- Use mosquito coils.
- Spray your room with insect repellent before going out for your evening meal.

Rabies

Risk: all countries.

Still a common problem in most parts of Central Asia, this uniformly fatal disease is spread by the bite or lick of an infected animal – most commonly a dog. Having a pre-travel vaccination (three shots over a one month period) means the postbite treatment is greatly simplified. If an animal bites you, gently wash the wound with soap and water, and apply iodine-based antiseptic. If you are not vaccinated you will need to receive rabies immunoglobulin as soon as possible and seek medical advice.

Tuberculosis (TB)

Risk: all countries.

Medical and aid workers, and long-term travellers who have significant contact with the local population should take precautions against TB. Adults at risk are advised to have pre- and post-travel TB testing. The main symptoms are fever, cough, weight loss, night sweats and tiredness.

Typhoid

Risk: all countries.

This serious bacterial infection is spread via food and water. It results in a high and slowly progressive fever and headache, and may be accompanied by a dry cough and stomach pain. Be aware that vaccination is not 100% effective so you must still be careful what you eat and drink.

Travellers' Diarrhoea

Travellers' diarrhoea is defined as the passage of more than three watery bowel actions within 24 hours, plus at least one other symptom, such as fever, cramps, nausea, vomiting or feeling generally unwell. It is by far the most common problem affecting travellers.

Travellers' diarrhoea is caused by a bacterium and, in most cases, treatment consists of staying well hydrated; rehydration solutions are the best for this. It responds promptly to treatment with antibiotics such as norfloxacin, ciprofloxacin or azithromycin. Loperamide is just a 'stopper' and doesn't get to the cause of the problem. It can be helpful, for example, if you have to go on a long bus ride. Don't take loperamide if you have a fever, or blood in your stools. Seek medical attention quickly if you do not respond to an appropriate antibiotic.

Amoebic Dysentery

Amoebic dysentery is actually rare in travellers but is often misdiagnosed. Symptoms are similar to bacterial diarrhoea, ie fever, bloody diarrhoea and generally feeling unwell. You should always seek reliable medical care if you have blood in your diarrhoea. Treatment involves two drugs: tinidazole or metroniadzole to kill the parasite in your gut, and a second drug to kill the cysts. If left untreated, complications such as liver or gut abscesses can occur.

Giardiasis

Giardia is a parasite that is relatively common in travellers to Central Asia. Symptoms include nausea, bloating, excess gas, fatigue and intermittent diarrhoea. 'Eggy' burps are often attributed solely to giardia. The parasite will eventually go away if left untreated, but this can take months. The treatment of choice is tinidazole; metronidazole is a second option.

Other Diseases

Kazakhstan occasionally reports outbreaks of human plague in the far west. One fatal case of bubonic plague was recorded in Kyrgyzstan in 2013. Outbreaks are often caused by eating diseased meat but are also transmitted by the bites of rodent and marmot fleas.

In 2013 there were outbreaks of anthrax in Kazakhstan.

Crimean-Congo haemorrhagic fever is a severe viral illness characterised by the sudden onset of intense fever, headache, aching limbs, bleeding gums and sometimes a rash of red dots on the skin, a week or two after being bitten by an infected tick. It's a minor risk for trekkers and campers in Central Asia during the summer months. Insect repellent will help keep the blighters off you.

Environmental Hazards

Altitude Sickness

Altitude sickness is a particular problem in high-altitude regions of Kazakhstan, Kyrgyzstan and Tajikistan. With motorable roads (such as the Pamir Highway) climbing passes of over 4000m, it's a problem not just restricted to trekkers.

Altitude sickness may develop in those who ascend rapidly to altitudes greater than 2500m. Being physically fit offers no protection. Risk increases with faster ascents, higher altitudes and greater exertion. Symptoms may include headaches, nausea, vomiting, dizziness, malaise, insomnia and loss of appetite. Severe cases may be complicated by fluid in the lungs or swelling of the brain.

DRINKING WATER

- Never drink tap water, especially in Karakalpakstan, Khorezm, Dushanbe and remoter Kazakhstan.
- Bottled water is generally safe – check the seal is intact at purchase.
- Avoid ice.
- Avoid fresh juices – they may have been watered down.
- Boiling water is the most efficient method of purifying it.
- The best chemical purifier is iodine. It should not be used by pregnant women or those with thyroid problems.
- Water filters should also filter out viruses. Ensure your filter has a chemical barrier such as iodine and a small pore size, eg less than four microns.

To protect yourself against altitude sickness, take 125mg or 250mg of acetazolamide (Diamox) twice or three times daily, starting 24 hours before ascent and continuing for 48 hours after arrival at altitude. Possible side effects include increased urinary volume, numbness, tingling, drowsiness, nausea, myopia and temporary impotence. Acetazolamide should not be given to pregnant women or anyone with a history of sulfa allergy.

When travelling to high altitudes, avoid overexertion, eat light meals, drink lots of fluids and abstain from alcohol. If your symptoms are more than mild or don't resolve promptly, see a doctor.

The **Murgab Ecotourism Association (META)** (META; Gulnara 93-519 18 02; www.meta.tj; Osh 91; call ahead) in Tajikistan's eastern Pamirs has a hyperbaric chamber in case of altitude-related emergencies.

Food

Eating in restaurants is the biggest risk factor for contracting travellers' diarrhoea.

Ways to avoid it include eating only freshly cooked food, avoiding food that has been sitting around in buffets, and eating in busy restaurants with a high turnover of customers. Peel all fruit, cook vegetables and soak salads in iodine water for at least 20 minutes.

Insect Bites

Bedbugs don't carry disease but their bites are very itchy. They live in the cracks of furniture and walls, and then migrate to the bed at night to feed on you. You can treat the itch with an antihistamine.

Ticks (*kleshch* in Russian) are contracted after walking in rural areas. They are commonly found behind the ears, on the belly and in the armpits.

If you have had a tick bite and experience symptoms such as a rash at the site of the bite or elsewhere, fever or muscle aches, you should see a doctor. Doxycycline prevents tick-borne diseases.

Language

In addition to the official languages of the Central Asian countries covered in this book – Kazakh, Kyrgyz, Tajik, Turkmen and Uzbek – the one language most useful for travellers in these countries is still Russian, as you'll find that it's the second language for most adults.

RUSSIAN

Just read the coloured pronunciation guides given next to each Russian phrase in this section as if they were English, and you'll be understood. Note that the symbol kh is pronounced as the 'ch' in the Scottish *loch*, zh as the 's' in 'pleasure', r is rolled and the apostrophe (') indicates a slight y sound. The stressed syllables are indicated with italics.

Basics

Hello.	Здравствуйте.	*zdrast*·vuy·tye
Goodbye.	До свидания.	da svi·*da*·nya
Excuse me.	Простите.	pras·*ti*·tye
Sorry.	Извините.	iz·vi·*ni*·tye
Please.	Пожалуйста.	pa·*zhal*·sta
Thank you.	Спасибо.	spa·*si*·ba
Yes./No.	Да./Нет.	da/nyet

What's your name?
Как вас зовут? — kak vas za·*vut*

My name is ...
Меня зовут ... — mi·*nya* za·vut ...

Do you speak English?
Вы говорите по-английски? — vi ga·va·*ri*·tye pa·an·*gli*·ski

I don't understand.
Я не понимаю. — ya nye pa·ni·*ma*·yu

Accommodation

Do you have a ... room?	У вас есть ...?	u vas yest' ...
single	одноместный номер	ad·na·*myest*·nih *no*·mir
double	номер с двуспальней кроватью	*no*·mir z dvu·*spal'*·nyey kra·va·tyu

How much is it for ...?	Сколько стоит за ...?	*skol'*·ka *sto*·it za ...
a night	ночь	noch'
two people	двоих	dva·*ikh*

Eating & Drinking

I'd like (the menu).
Я бы хотел/хотела (меню). (m/f) — ya bih khat·*yel*/khat·*ye*·la (min·*yu*)

I don't eat ...
Я не ем ... — ya nye yem ...

Please bring the bill.
Принесите, пожалуйста счёт. — pri·ni·*sit*·ye pa·*zhal*·sta shot

Cheers!	За здоровье!	za zda·*rov*·ye
restaurant	ресторан	ris·ta·*ran*

Emergencies

Help!	Помогите!	pa·ma·*gi*·tye
Leave me alone!	Приваливай!	pri·*va*·li·vai

WANT MORE?

For in-depth language information and handy phrases, check out Lonely Planet's *Central Asia Phrasebook*. You'll find it at **shop.lonelyplanet.com**, or you can buy Lonely Planet's iPhone phrasebooks at the Apple App Store.

Numbers – Russian

1	один	a·*din*
2	два	dva
3	три	tri
4	четыре	chi·*ty*·ri
5	пять	pyat'
6	шесть	shest'
7	семь	sem'
8	восемь	*vo*·sim'
9	девять	*de*·vit'
10	десять	*de*·sit'
100	сто	sto
1000	тысяча	*ty*·sya·cha

Call ...!	Вызовите ...!	*vih*·za·vi·tye ...
a doctor	врача	vra·*cha*
the police	милицию	mi·*li*·tsih·yu

I'm lost.
Я заблудился/заблудилась. (m/f) — ya za·blu·*dil*·sa/za·blu·*di*·las'

Where are the toilets?
Где здесь туалет? — gdye zdyes' tu·al·*yet*

Shopping & Services

I need ...
Мне нужно ... — mnye *nuzh*·na ...

How much is it?
Сколько стоит? — *skol'*·ka *sto*·it

That's too expensive.
Это очень дорого. — e·ta o·chen' *do*·ra·ga

bank	банк	bank
market	рынок	*rih*·nak
post office	почта	*poch*·ta

Transport & Directions

a ... ticket	билет ...	bil·*yet* ...
one-way	в один конец	v a·*din* kan·*yets*
return	в оба конца	v *o*·ba kan·*tsa*

Where's (the station)?
Где (станция)? — gdye (*stant*·sih·ya)

When's the next bus/train?
Когда будет следующий автобус/поезд? — kag·*da bu*·dit *slye*·du·yu·shi af·*to*·bus/*po*·ist

Does it stop at ...?
Поезд останавливается в ...? — *po*·yist a·sta·*nav*·li·va·yit·sa v ...

Where is ...?
Где ...? — gdye ...

What's the address?
Какой адрес? — ka·*koy a*·dris

Can you show me (on the map)?
Покажите мне, пожалуйста (на карте). — pa·ka·*zhih*·tye mnye pa·*zhal*·sta (na *kar*·tye)

KAZAKH

Kazakh is a Turkic language. Since 1940 it has been written in a version of the Cyrillic alphabet. It's the state language and is spoken by 64% of the population. Russian has the status of an official language and almost everyone speaks Russian. It is the first language for some urban Kazakhs, as well as the large Russian minority (24% of the population). Street signs are either in Kazakh, Russian or both. In our pronunciation guides, the symbol a is pronounced as in 'man', g as the 'gh' in 'ugh', k as a guttural 'k', n as the 'ng' in 'sing', o as the 'u' in 'fur', u as in 'full' or as the 'oo' in 'fool', h as in 'hat' and i as in 'ill'.

Peace be with you.	assalamu aleykum
And peace with you. (response)	wagaleykum ussalam
Hello.	salamatsyz be
Goodbye.	kosh-sau bolyndar
Thank you.	rakhmet
Yes./No.	ia/zhok
How are you?	khal zhag dayynyz kalay?
I'm well.	zhaksy
Do you speak English?	agylshynsa bilesiz be?
I don't understand.	tusinbeymin

Numbers – Kazakh

1	bir
2	yeki
3	ush
4	tort
5	bes
6	alty
7	etti
8	sakkiz
9	togyz
10	on
100	zhus
1000	myn

Where is...?	... kayda?
How much?	kansha?

airport	auezhay
bus station	avtovokzal/avtobeket
doctor	dariger
friend	dos
hospital	aurukhana
hotel	konak uy/meymankhana
police	politsia
restaurant	meyramkhana
toilet	daretkhana
train station	temir zhol vokzal/beket

bad	zhaman
boiled water	kaynagan su
bread	nan
expensive	kymbat
good	zhaksy
meat	yet
rice	kurish
tea	shay

Monday	duysenbi
Tuesday	seysenbi
Wednesday	sarsenbi
Thursday	beysenbi
Friday	zhuma
Saturday	senbi
Sunday	zheksenbi

KYRGYZ

Kyrgyz is a Turkic language that has been written in a Cyrillic alphabet since the early 1940s. However, Kyrgyzstan is in the process of changing over to a modified Roman alphabet. Russian also has official-language status, but there is a strong push to promote Kyrgyz as the predominant language of government, media and education. In our pronunciation guides, ng is pronounced as in 'sing', ö as the 'u' in 'fur' and ü as the 'ew' in 'few'.

Peace be with you.	asalamu aleykom
And peace with you. (response)	wa aleykum assalam
Hello.	salam
Goodbye.	jakshy kalyngydzar
Thank you.	rakhmat
Yes./No.	ooba/jok
How are you?	jakshysüzbü?

Numbers – Kyrgyz

1	bir
2	eki
3	üch
4	tört
5	besh
6	alty
7	jety
8	segiz
9	toguz
10	on
100	jüz
1000	ming

I'm well.	jakshy
Do you speak English?	siz angliyscha süylöy süzbü?
I don't understand.	men tüshümböy jatamyn
Where is ...?	... kayda?
How much?	kancha?

airport	aeroport
bus station	avtobikel
doctor	doktur
friend	dos
hospital	oruukana
hotel	meymankana
police	militsia
restaurant	restoran
toilet	darakana
train station	temir jol vokzal

bad	jaman
boiled water	kaynatilgan suu
bread	nan
expensive	kymbat
good	jakshy
meat	et
rice	kürüch
tea	chay

Monday	düshömbü
Tuesday	seyshembi
Wednesday	sharshembi
Thursday	beishembi
Friday	juma
Saturday	ishembi
Sunday	jekshembi

TAJIK

The state language of Tajikistan since 1989, Tajik is a Persian language, closely related to Dari (the language of Afghanistan) and Farsi (the language of Iran) – unlike most Central Asian languages, which are Turkic in origin. Tajik was formerly written in a modified Arabic script, then in Roman, but since 1940 a modified Cyrillic script has been used. In our pronunciation guides, gh is pronounced as in 'ugh', ee as in 'fee', q as the 'k' in 'keen', ö as the 'u' in 'fur', kh as the 'h' in 'hat' and j as in 'jig'.

Numbers – Tajik

1	yak
2	du
3	seh
4	chor
5	panj
6	shish
7	khaft
8	khasht
9	nukh
10	dakh
100	sad
1000	khazor

Peace be with you. assalomu aleykum
And peace with you. (response) valeykum assalom
Hello. salom
Goodbye. khayr naboshad
Thank you. rakhmat/teshakkur
Yes./No. kha/ne
How are you? naghzmi shumo?
I'm well. mannaghz
Do you speak English? anglisi meydonet?
I don't understand. man manefakhmam
Where is ...? ... khujo ast?
How much? chand pul?

airport furudgoh
bus station istgoh
doctor duhtur
friend doost
hospital bemorhona/kasalhona
hotel mekhmon'hona
police militsia
restaurant restoran
toilet khojat'hona
train station istgoh rohi ohan

bad ganda
boiled water obi jush
bread non
expensive qimmat
good khub/naghz
meat gusht
rice birinj
tea choy

Monday dushanbe
Tuesday seshanbe
Wednesday chorshanbe
Thursday panjanbe
Friday juma
Saturday shanbe
Sunday yakshanbe

TURKMEN

Turkmen, the state language of Turkmenistan since 1990, belongs to the Turkic language family. It has a significant amount of Russian vocabulary. In Turkmenistan almost everyone speaks Russian or Turkmen. Four different scripts have been used to write Turkmen: first Arabic, then a Turkish-Roman alphabet, from 1940 the Cyrillic alphabet, and since 1996 a modified Roman alphabet.

Peace be with you. salam aleykum
And peace with you. (response) waleykum assalam
Hello. salam
Goodbye. sagh bol
Thank you. tangyr
Yes./No. howa/yok
How are you? siz nahili?

Numbers – Turkmen

1	bir
2	ikeh
3	uch
4	durt
5	besh
6	alty
7	yed
8	sekiz
9	dokuz
10	on
100	yuz
1000	mun

Fine, and you?	onat, a siz?
I don't understand.	men dushenamok
Do you speak English?	siz inglische gepleyarsinizmi?
Where is ...?	... niredeh?
How much?	nyacheh?

airport	aeroport
bus station	durolha
doctor	lukman
friend	dost
hospital	keselkhana
hotel	mikmankhana
police	militsia
restaurant	restoran
toilet	hajat'hana
train station	vokzal

bad	ervet
boiled water	gaina d'lan su
bread	churek
expensive	gummut
good	yakhsheh
meat	et
rice	tui
tea	chay

Monday	dushanbe
Tuesday	seshenbe
Wednesday	charshanbe
Thursday	penshenbe
Friday	anna
Saturday	shenbe
Sunday	yekshanbe

UZBEK

Uzbekistan's major languages are Uzbek, Russian and Tajik. Uzbek, a Turkic language, is official and, with 15 million speakers, the most widely spoken non-Slavic language from the former Soviet states. It was first written in Arabic script, then in Roman letters, and since 1941 in a modified Cyrillic alphabet, but the country has been moving to a Roman alphabet. In our pronunciation guides, gh is pronounced as in 'ugh', k/q as a guttural 'k', u as the 'oo' in 'book' and kh as the 'ch' in 'Bach'.

Peace be with you.	salom alaykhum
And peace with you. (response)	tinch berling
Hello.	salom

Numbers – Uzbek

1	bir
2	ikki
3	uch
4	turt
5	besh
6	olti
7	etti
8	sakkiz
9	tukkiz
10	un
100	yuz
1000	ming

Goodbye.	hayr
Thank you.	rakhmat
Yes./No.	kha/yuk
How are you?	kanday siz?
Do you speak English?	inglizcha bila sizmi?
Where is ...?	... kayerda?
How much?	kancha/nichpul?

airport	tayyorgokh
bus station	avtobeket
doctor	tabib
friend	urmok/doost
hospital	kasalhona
hotel	mehmon'hona
police	militsia
restaurant	restoran
toilet	hojat'hona
train station	temir yul vokzali

bad	yomon
boiled water	kaynatilgan suv
bread	non
expensive	kimmat
good	yakhshi
meat	gusht
rice	guruch
tea	choy

Monday	dushanba
Tuesday	seyshanba
Wednesday	chorshanba
Thursday	payshanba
Friday	juma
Saturday	shanba
Sunday	yakshanba

GLOSSARY

ABBREVIATIONS

A – Arabic
Kaz – Kazakh
Kyr – Kyrgyz
R – Russian
Taj – Tajik
T – general Turkic
Tur – Turkmen
U – Uzbek

-abad (T) – suffix meaning 'town of'
ak (T) – white
ak kalpak (Kyr) – felt hat worn by Kyrgyz men
akimat (T) – regional government office or city hall, also *aqimat*
aksakal (T) – revered elder
akyn (Kyr) – minstrel, bard
ala-kiyiz (Kyr) – felt rug with coloured panels pressed on
alany (Kaz) – square
alplager (R) – mountaineers camp, short for *alpinistskiy lager*
apparatchik (R) – bureaucrat
apteka (R) – pharmacy
arashan (T) – springs
asalam aleykum (A) – traditional Muslim greeting, meaning 'peace be with you'
ASSR – Autonomous Soviet Socialist Republic
askhana (Kaz, Kyr) – local restaurant
aul (T) – yurt or herders' camp
aviakassa (R) – air ticket office
avtobus (R) – bus
avtostantsia (R) – bus stop or bus stand
azan (A) – Muslim call to prayer

babushka (R) – old woman; headscarf worn by Russian peasant women
bagh (Taj, D) – garden
balbal (T) – totemlike stone marker
banya (R) – public bath
basmachi (R) – literally 'bandits'; Muslim guerrilla fighters who resisted the Bolshevik takeover in Central Asia
batyr (Kyr, Kaz) – warrior hero in epics
beg (T) – landlord, gentleman; also spelt *bay* or *bek*
berkutchi (Kyr) – eagle hunter
Bi (Kaz) – honorific Kazakh title given to clan elders
bishkek (Kaz, Kyrg) – see *pishpek*
bosuy (Kyr) – see yurt
bufet (R) – snack bar selling cheap cold meats, boiled eggs, salads, breads, pastries etc
bulvar (R) – boulevard
bulvary (Kyr) – boulevard
buzkashi (T) – traditional polo-like game played with a headless calf, goat or sheep carcass *(buz)*

caravanserai – travellers inn
chabana (Kyr, Kaz) – cowboy
chaikhana (T) – teahouse
chapan (U, Taj) – traditional stripy Uzbek/Tajik cloak
chaykhana (T) – see *chaikhana*
chong (T) – big
choyhona (T) – see *chaikhana*
chuchuk (Kaz) – see *kazy* (in food glossary)
chuchvara (T) – dumplings
CIS – Commonwealth of Independent States; the loose political and economic alliance of most former member republics of the USSR (except the Baltic states and Georgia)
CPK – Communist Party of Kazakhstan

dacha (R) – a holiday bungalow
dangyly (Kaz) – avenue
darikhana (Kaz) – pharmacy
darya (T) – river
dastarkhan (T) – literally 'tablecloth'; feast
depe (Tur) – see *tepe*
dezhurnaya (R) – floor-lady; the female attendant on duty on each floor of a Soviet-style hotel
dom (R) – building
dom otdykha (R) – rest home
doppe (U) – black, four-sided skullcap embroidered in white and worn by men; also *dopi*, *doppa*, *dopy* or *doppilar*
dutar (T) – two-stringed guitar

eshon (A) – Sufi leader, also spelt *ishan*

GAI (R) – traffic police
geoglyph – geometric pattern of stones, often used in astrological observations
gillam (T) – carpet, also *gilim*
glasnost (R) – 'openness' in government that was one aspect of the Gorbachev reforms
gorod (R) – town
Graeco-Bactrian – Hellenistic kingdom and culture centred on northern Afghanistan, southern Uzbekistan and Tajikistan following the conquests of Alexander the Great
Great Game – the geopolitical 'Cold War' of territorial expansion between the Russian and British empires in the 19th and early 20th centuries in Central Asia

Hadith (A) – collected acts and sayings of the Prophet Mohammed
haj (A) – the pilgrimage to Mecca, one of the five pillars of Islam, to be made by devout Muslims at least once during their lifetime
hakimat (T) – see *hakimyat*
hakimyat (Kyr) – municipal administration building
hammam (A) – bathhouse
hammomi (U) – baths
hazrat (A) – honorific title meaning 'majesty' or 'holy'
Hejira (A) – flight of the Prophet Mohammed and his followers to Medina in AD 622
hijab (A) – Muslim woman's veil or headscarf (literally 'modest dress')
hoja (U) – lord, master, gentleman (honorific title)

ikat (U) – tie-dyed silk
IMU – Islamic Movement of Uzbekistan
IRP – Islamic Renaissance Party; grouping of radical

activists dedicated to the formation of Islamic rule in Central Asia
Ismaili (A) – a branch of Shiite Islam

jailoo (Kyr) – summer pasture
jami masjid (A) – Friday mosque
jamoat khana (Taj) – Ismaili prayer hall and meeting hall
juma (U) – Friday, see *jami masjid*

kalon (Taj) – great
kara (T) – black
kassa (R) – cashier or ticket office
kazan (T) – large cauldron (used to cook *plov*)
-kent (T) – suffix meaning 'town of'
khanatlas (U) – see *ikat*
khiyeboni (Taj) – avenue
kino (R) – cinema; also *kinoteatr*
köçesi (Tur) – street
kochasi (U) – street
köchösü (Kyr) – street
koh (Taj) – mountain
kok (T) – blue
kökör (T) – *kumys* storer
kokpar (Kaz) – see *buzkashi*
kolkhoz (R) – collective farm
koshesi (Kaz) – street
koshk (U, Tur) – fortress
koshma (Kaz) – multicoloured felt mats
kozha (Kaz) – see *hoja*
kuchai (Taj) – street
kupeyny (R) – 2nd-class or sleeping carriage on trains; also *kupe*
kupkari (U) – see *buzkashi*
kurgan (T) – burial mound
kurort (R) – thermal-spring complex
kurpacha (U) – colourful sitting mattress for a *tapchan*
kvartal (R) – district
kymyz (Kaz) – see *kumys*
kyz-kumay (Kyr) – traditional game in which a man chases a woman on horseback and tries to kiss her
kyz-kuu (Kaz) – see *kyz-kumay*
kyzyl (T) – red

LOI – Letter of Invitation
lux (R) – deluxe

mahalla (U) – urban neighbourhood
Manas (Kyr) – epic; legendary hero revered by the Kyrgyz
manaschi (Kyr) – type of *akyn* who recites from the Kyrgyz cycle of oral legends
marshrutka (R, T) – short term for *marshrutnoe* and *marshrutny avtobus*
marshrutnoe (R, T) – small bus or van that follows a fixed route but stops on demand to take on or let off passengers, with fares depending on distance travelled
marshrutny avtobus (R, T) – large bus that follows a fixed route but stops on demand to take on or let off passengers, with fares depending on distance travelled
maydoni (U, Taj) – square
mikrorayon (R) – micro region or district
militsia (R, T) – police
MSDSP – Mountain Societies Development Support Project
muezzin (A) – man who calls the Muslim faithful to prayer
mufti (A) – Islamic legal expert or spiritual leader

Naqshband – the most influential of many Sufi secret associations in Central Asia
Navrus (A) – literally 'New Days'; the main Islamic spring festival; has various regional transliterations (Nauroz, Nauryz, Nawruz, Norruz or Novruz)

oblast (R) – province, region
oblys (Kaz) – province, region
OVIR (R) – Otdel Vis i Registratsii; Office of Visas and Registration
Oxus – historic name for the Amu-Darya river

pakhta (T) – cotton
pakhtakor (T) – cotton worker
panjara (T) – trellis of wood, stone or *ghanch* (plaster)
perestroika (R) – literally 'restructuring'; Gorbachev's efforts to revive the economy
piala (T) – bowl
pishpek (Kaz, Kyr) – churn for making *kumys*
platskartny (R) – hard-sleeper train
ploshchad (R) – square
pochta (R) – post office
pol-lux (R) – semideluxe
polyclinic – health centre
propusk (R) – permit
prospekt (R) – avenue

qymyz (Kaz) – see *kumys*

rabab (T) – six-stringed mandolin, also *rubab*
rayon (R) – district

samovar (R) – urn used for heating water for tea, often found on trains
sary (T) – yellow
şayoli (Tur) – street
sharq (Taj, U) – east
shaykhana (T) – see *chaikhana*
Shiite (A) – one of the two main branches of Islam
shyrdak (Kyr) – felt rug with appliqued coloured panels
skibaza (R) – ski base
SSR – Soviet Socialist Republic
stolovaya (R) – canteen, cafeteria
Sufi (A) – mystical tradition in Islam
suzani (U) – bright silk embroidery on cotton cloth

tapchan (Taj) – tea bed
tash (T) – stone
tebbetey (Kyr) – round fur-trimmed hat worn by men
telpek (Tur, U) – sheepskin hat worn by men
toi (T) – celebration
Transoxiana – meaning 'the land beyond the Oxus'; historical term for the region between the Amu-Darya and Syr-Darya rivers
TsUM (R) – *Tsentralny universalny magazin*; central department store
tubiteyka (R) – see *doppe*
tugai – dense forest endemic to Central Asian river valleys and flood plains
turbaza (R) – holiday camp typically with Spartan cabins, plain food, sports, video hall

and bar, usually open only in summer

Turkestan – literally 'the Land of the Turks'; covers Central Asia and Xinjiang (China)

UAZ (R) – Russian 4WD

ulak-tartysh (Kyr) – see *buzkashi*

ulama (A) – class of religious scholars or intellectuals

ulitsa (R) – street

umuvalnik (R) – portable washing basin

univermag (R) – *universalny magazin*; department store

uulu (Kyr) – meaning 'son of'

viloyat (U) – province

vodopad (R) – waterfall

vokzal (R) – train station

ylag oyyny (Karakalpak) – see *buzkashi*

yurt – traditional nomadic 'house', a collapsible cylindrical wood framework covered with felt

zakaznik (R) – protected area

zapovednik (R) – nature reserve

zhyostky (R) – hard carriage on trains

zikr (A) – recitation or contemplation of the names of God; recitation of sacred writings; one part of traditional Sufi practice

FOOD GLOSSARY

abrikos – apricot

agurets – cucumber

amlet – omelette

antrecot – steak

arbuz – watermelon

ayran – salty yoghurt/water mix

barene – jam

befstroganov – beef stroganoff

beshbarmak – flat noodles with lamb, horsemeat or vegetable broth (served separately)

bifshteks – 'beefsteak', glorified hamburger

bitochki – cutlet

bliny - Russian-style pancake

borshch – beetroot and potato soup, often with sour cream

bozo – beverage made from fermented millet

chay – tea

chuisky salat – spicy carrot salad in vinaigrette

chuchvara – dumplings

farel – trout

Frantsuzky salat – beetroot, carrots and French fries

frikadela – fried meatballs

galuptsi – cabbage rolls stuffed with rice and meat

gavyadina – beef

grechka – boiled buckwheat

gribi – mushrooms

gulyash – a dismal miscellany of meat, vegetables and potatoes

jiger – liver

kafe – coffee

kafe s slivkami – coffee with milk

kaimak – sweet cream

kapusty salat – cabbage salad

kartofel fri – French fries, chips

kartofel pure – mashed potato

kartoshka – potato

kasha – porridge

katyk – thin, drinkable yoghurt

kazy – horse-meat sausage

khleb – bread

kolbasa – sausage

kompot – juice

kotleta po-Kievski – chicken Kiev

kumys – fermented mare's milk (also *kymys*)

kuritsa – chicken

kury gril – roast chicken

kuurdak – fatty stew of meat, offal and potato

laghman – noodles

lyulya kebab – beef or mutton meatballs

manpar – noodle bits, meat, vegetables and mild seasoning in broth

manty – small stuffed dumplings

makarony – macaroni, pasta

masla – butter

mastoba – rice soup

mimosa salat – fish and shredded-potato salad

mineralnaya vada – mineral water

morkovi salat – carrot salad

myod/assal – honey

nan – flat bread

okroshka – cold or hot soup made from sour cream, potatoes, eggs and meat

olivye salat – potato, ham, peas and mayonnaise

pelmeni – small dumplings in soup

persik – peach

piva – beer

plov – a rice dish with meat, carrots or other additions (traditionally prepared by men for special celebrations), also known as *pilau*

pomidor – tomato

ragu – beef stew

rassolnik s myasam – soup of marinated cucumber and kidney

ris – rice

sakhar – sugar

salat iz svezhei kapusty – raw cabbage salad

salat tourist – sliced tomatoes and cucumbers

samsa – samosa

shashlyk – meat roasted on skewers over hot coals
shashlyk farshurabanniya – minced-meat (Adana) kebab
shashlyk iz baraniny – mutton kebab
shashlyk iz okorochkov – chicken kebab
shashlyk iz pecheni – liver kebab
shorpo – soup of boiled mutton on the bone with potatoes, carrots and turnips
shubat – fermented camel's milk

sir – cheese
smetana – sour cream
sok – juice/fruit squash
sosiski – frankfurter sausage
stolichny – beef, potatoes, eggs, carrots, mayonnaise and apples
stolovaya vada (biz gaz) – still water (no gas)
sudak zhareny – fried pike or perch
suzma – strained yoghurt, like tart cottage or cream cheese

tvorog – curd with cream and sugar

vinagrad – grapes
vishnya – cherry

yablaka – apple
yitso – egg
yitso barennye – boiled egg
yitso zharennye – fried egg

Behind the Scenes

SEND US YOUR FEEDBACK

We love to hear from travellers – your comments keep us on our toes and help make our books better. Our well-travelled team reads every word on what you loved or loathed about this book. Although we cannot reply individually to postal submissions, we always guarantee that your feedback goes straight to the appropriate authors, in time for the next edition. Each person who sends us information is thanked in the next edition – the most useful submissions are rewarded with a selection of digital PDF chapters.

Visit **lonelyplanet.com/contact** to submit your updates and suggestions or to ask for help. Our award-winning website also features inspirational travel stories, news and discussions.

Note: We may edit, reproduce and incorporate your comments in Lonely Planet products such as guidebooks, websites and digital products, so let us know if you don't want your comments reproduced or your name acknowledged. For a copy of our privacy policy visit lonelyplanet.com/privacy.

OUR READERS

Many thanks to the travellers who used the last edition and wrote to us with helpful hints, useful advice and interesting anecdotes:

A Thomas Allen, Steven Aspland **B** Don Beer, Leon Boelens, Pierre Brouillet, Joe Bryant **C** James Chance, Arthur Clement De Givry, Judy Comont **D** Matthew Dearden, Kieran Drake, Paul-Noël Dumont **F** Sara Frau **G** Bas Geelen, Ask Gudmundsen **H** Margaret Hawthorn, PJ Henry, Miriam Herzfeld, Allan Hubble, Aaron Hurd **J** Martin Jaeckel, Nathan Jones, Martin Jung **K** Wolfgang Keller, David Kerkhoff, Tyler Keys, Hans-Werner Kopp, Martin Král, Aleksandra Krukar **L** Eric-Jan Lens, Fabian Liechti **M** Richard Mallett, Helena Moon, Martijn Munneke **N** Arihe (Eric) Neemann, Pascal Noel **P** Nina Plumbe, Jo Pycroft **R** Jacqueline Ripart, Steve Rogowski, Michal Rudziecki **S** Martina Schroeter, Tanya Semyonova, Roberto Spanghero **T** Frank Techel **V** Marinus Vissers **W** Stefan Wieser, Barry Wilkinson, Kathleen Williams, Sabine Wissel, Barbara Wolfke, Sebastian Wolking, Stephen Wong **Y** Robert Young

AUTHOR THANKS

Bradley Mayhew

Thanks to stalwart co-authors Tom, John, Mark and our anonymous Turkmenistan author. Hard to find a more dedicated and professional bunch of Central Asian travel enthusiasts. Thanks to the much-missed Suzannah Shwer for getting this title up and running one more time.

Mark Elliott

A giant *rakhmat* to Umar Isakov, Anna Keil, Ervin Bartis and family, Janice Setser, Zhandiya Zoolshooeva, Christophe and Nicole, Ed Hewitt, Chris Mathis, Andrew Tucker-Peake, Alick Warburton, Jop Weterings, Phil Riddle, Robin Ord-Smith, Zafar in Penjikent, Will Cooper, Sang Wang, Clement Meynier, Aspia, Flora Renner, the Pamir Lodge crew, Lola, Murat and friends, Aleema Shivji, Taalai and family in Karakol, the memory of Wil Klass. Back home, a million thanks to 'the Kids' for endless support, tea and medals. And to Harriet for waiting and sharing.

Tom Masters

Big thanks to my team of fellow authors: Bradley Mayhew, Mark Elliott, John Noble and Turkmenistan's anonymous author for all their help and intelligence sharing. Thanks also to Janine and the entire in-house team at LPHQ in Melbourne (you shall all be missed!). On the road, a huge debt of gratitude to my intrepid and immensely patient mother, who negotiated the deserts of Uzbekistan with me with hardly a complaint at the complete lack of caffeine and wireless, and who dutifully slogged around towns with me all day visiting various hotels, medressas and museums. Big thanks also to the team at Advantour in Tashkent, particularly Murod and Feruza; to David Berghof at Stantours; to Dowlet and Sasha in Samarkand; Gulnara and Hamid in Bukhara; Hannelore Bendsen in Khiva and the crew at the Jipek Joli in Nukus, especially Era and Aijamal.

John Noble

A project like this is quite impossible without willing help from a whole lot of people. Extra special thanks to Robert and Assely Manson, David Berghof, Svetlana Baskakova, Serik Dyusenbaev, Alikhan and Askar Abdeshev, Vitaly Shuptar, Dagmar Schreiber, Karlygash Makatova, Alexander Petrov, Andrey Yurchenkov, Ali Hudabardy Tash (Kashgar Tourism International, China), Zhamilya Zhukenova, and my fellow authors Bradley, Mark, Tom and the Turkmenistan author.

ACKNOWLEDGMENTS

Climate maps data adapted from Peel MC, Finlayson BL & McMahon TA (2007) 'Updated World Map of the Köppen-Geiger Climate Classification', Hydrology and Earth System Sciences, 11, 1633-44.
Cover photograph: Char Minar, Bukhara, Uzbekistan. Michele Falzone/Corbis ©

THIS BOOK

This 6th edition of Lonely Planet's *Central Asia* guidebook was researched and written by Bradley Mayhew, Mark Elliott, Tom Masters, John Noble and an anonymous author for Turkmenistan. This guidebook was commissioned in Lonely Planet's Melbourne office and produced by the following:

Commissioning Editor Suzannah Shwer

Coordinating Editors Lauren Hunt, Amanda Williamson

Senior Cartographer David Kemp

Book Designer Mazzy Prinsep

Managing Editors Sasha Baskett, Brigitte Ellemor

Senior Editor Karyn Noble

Assisting Editors Paul Harding, Gabrielle Innes, Kate Kiely, Alan Murphy

Assisting Cartographers Julie Dodkins, Mick Garrett, James Leversha

Cover Research Naomi Parker

Language Content Branislava Vladisavljevic

Thanks to Anita Banh, Laura Crawford, Ryan Evans, Errol Hunt, Larissa Frost, Genesys India, Jouve India, Valentina Kremenchutskaya, Anne Mason, Catherine Naghten, Chad Parkhill, Trent Paton. Martine Power, Dianne Schallmeiner, Luna Soo, John Taufa, Angela Tinson

Index

ABBREVIATIONS

Kaz	Kazakhstan
Kyr	Kyrgyzstan
Taj	Tajikistan
Tur	Turkmenistan
Uz	Uzbekistan

Map Pages **000**
Photo Pages **000**

Map Pages **000**
Photo Pages **000**

L

M

Map Pages **000**
Photo Pages **000**

Map Pages **000**
Photo Pages **000**

U

Map Legend

Sights
- Beach
- Bird Sanctuary
- Buddhist
- Castle/Palace
- Christian
- Confucian
- Hindu
- Islamic
- Jain
- Jewish
- Monument
- Museum/Gallery/Historic Building
- Ruin
- Sento Hot Baths/Onsen
- Shinto
- Sikh
- Taoist
- Winery/Vineyard
- Zoo/Wildlife Sanctuary
- Other Sight

Activities, Courses & Tours
- Bodysurfing
- Diving/Snorkelling
- Canoeing/Kayaking
- Course/Tour
- Skiing
- Snorkelling
- Surfing
- Swimming/Pool
- Walking
- Windsurfing
- Other Activity

Sleeping
- Sleeping
- Camping

Eating
- Eating

Drinking & Nightlife
- Drinking & Nightlife
- Cafe

Entertainment
- Entertainment

Shopping
- Shopping

Information
- Bank
- Embassy/Consulate
- Hospital/Medical
- Internet
- Police
- Post Office
- Telephone
- Toilet
- Tourist Information
- Other Information

Geographic
- Beach
- Hut/Shelter
- Lighthouse
- Lookout
- Mountain/Volcano
- Oasis
- Park
- Pass
- Picnic Area
- Waterfall

Population
- Capital (National)
- Capital (State/Province)
- City/Large Town
- Town/Village

Transport
- Airport
- Border crossing
- Bus
- Cable car/Funicular
- Cycling
- Ferry
- Metro station
- Monorail
- Parking
- Petrol station
- Subway station
- Taxi
- Train station/Railway
- Tram
- Underground station
- Other Transport

Note: Not all symbols displayed above appear on the maps in this book

Routes
- Tollway
- Freeway
- Primary
- Secondary
- Tertiary
- Lane
- Unsealed road
- Road under construction
- Plaza/Mall
- Steps
- Tunnel
- Pedestrian overpass
- Walking Tour
- Walking Tour detour
- Path/Walking Trail

Boundaries
- International
- State/Province
- Disputed
- Regional/Suburb
- Marine Park
- Cliff
- Wall

Hydrography
- River, Creek
- Intermittent River
- Canal
- Water
- Dry/Salt/Intermittent Lake
- Reef

Areas
- Airport/Runway
- Beach/Desert
- Cemetery (Christian)
- Cemetery (Other)
- Glacier
- Mudflat
- Park/Forest
- Sight (Building)
- Sportsground
- Swamp/Mangrove

OUR STORY

A beat-up old car, a few dollars in the pocket and a sense of adventure. In 1972 that's all Tony and Maureen Wheeler needed for the trip of a lifetime – across Europe and Asia overland to Australia. It took several months, and at the end – broke but inspired – they sat at their kitchen table writing and stapling together their first travel guide, *Across Asia on the Cheap*. Within a week they'd sold 1500 copies. Lonely Planet was born.

Today, Lonely Planet has offices in Melbourne, London and Oakland, with more than 600 staff and writers. We share Tony's belief that 'a great guidebook should do three things: inform, educate and amuse'.

OUR WRITERS

Bradley Mayhew

Coordinating Author Since first penning the *Odyssey Guide to Uzbekistan* in 1995, Bradley has travelled to almost every corner of Central Asia. This is the fifth time he has coordinated this title. Bradley is the co-author of Lonely Planet guides to Tibet, Nepal and Bhutan, as well as several guides to the Silk Road. He has lectured on Uzbekistan to the Royal Geographical Society and in 2009 travelled from Venice to China in the footsteps of Marco Polo for a five-part Arte/SWR documentary film. An expat Brit, Bradley currently lives in Yellowstone County, Montana. See what Bradley is up to at www.bradleymayhew.blogspot.com.

Mark Elliott

Kyrgyzstan, Tajikistan Back in 1994 Mark Elliott first stumbled into Central Asia with an out-of-date USSR map, a two-day transit visa and the crazy plan of writing a backpacker's guidebook. That guide grew to cover most of the continent, and left Mark with an abiding fascination for the Kyrgyz *jailoos* and a growing tolerance to vodka. He's since driven, hitched, ridden and hiked across most of the region but still feels that the mountain republics, Tajikistan and Kyrgyzstan, are the area's true gems.

Tom Masters

Uzbekistan Tom has been travelling in Central Asia since his student days in Russia, and his fascination with the region grew even further when working at the BBC Central Asian & Caucasus Service after finishing his degree. For this edition of Central Asia, Tom researched Uzbekistan and had a fascinating journey from Tashkent to Moynaq and back again, seeing just how much has changed in the decade since he first visited 'the big three' now that international tourism seems to have arrived for good. Tom lives in Berlin and can be found online at www.tommasters.net.

John Noble

Kazakhstan John, from England, has been visiting and travelling in Kazakhstan since the early post-Soviet years and has witnessed a quantum leap both in the lifestyles of the country's luckier citizens and in facilities and opportunities for travellers – even backpacker hostels now! Top moments of this latest trip: discovering the less-visited western end of Aksu Canyon in Sayram-Ugam National Park and finally getting inside Astana's Khan Shatyr. Wish list: better intercity buses and the reopening of the Kazakhstan–Kyrgyzstan 'green border'.

Turkmenistan We have chosen not to name the author of our Turkmenistan chapter as revealing their identity would put certain people inside Turkmenistan at risk.

Published by Lonely Planet Publications Pty Ltd
ABN 36 005 607 983
6th edition – May 2014
ISBN 978 1 74179 953 8

10 9 8 7 6 5 4 3 2 1
Printed in Singapore